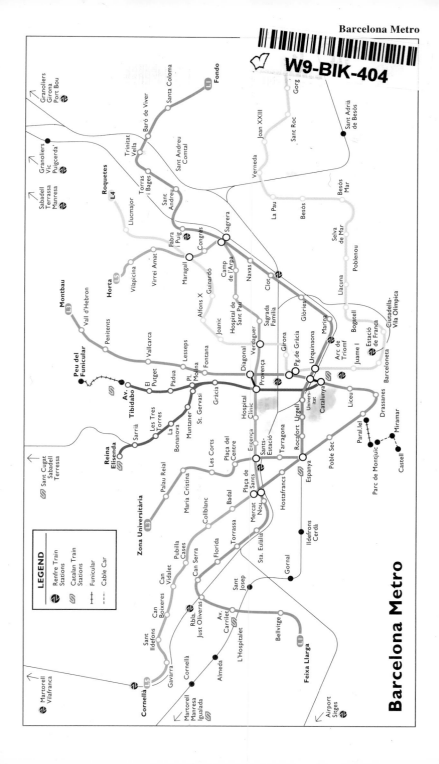

Barcelona Metro

W9-BIK-404

Madrid Metro

LEGEND

⊙ Commuter Stations
⊕ RENFE Train Stations
ℹ Information

Barcelona

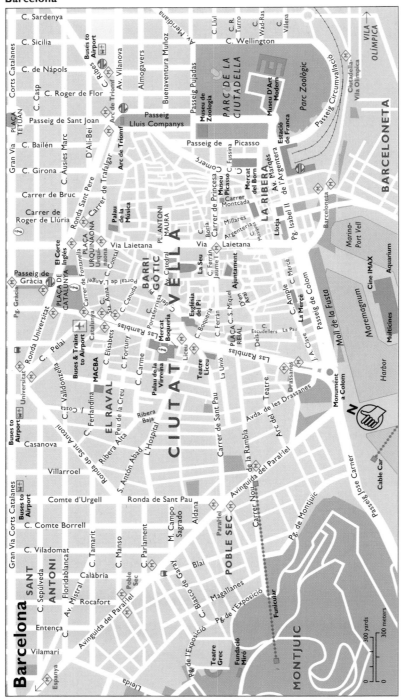

Barcelona

C. Sardenya
C. Sicilia
C. de Nápols
C. Casp
C. Roger de Flor
C. Ausies Marc
C. Bailén
Passeig de Sant Joan
C. Girona
C. Roger de Flor
Carrer de Bruc
Carrer de Roger de Llúria
Passeig de Gràcia
Pg. Gràcia
Ronda Universitat
Gran Via
PLAÇA TETUAN
Gran Via Corts Catalanes
Corts Catalanes

C. Sepúlveda
Comte d'Urgell
Villarroel
Casanova
C. Comte Borrell
C. Viladomat
C. Tamarit
Floridablanca
C. Mistral
Av. Mistral
Entença
Vilamarí
Espanya
Lleida

SANT ANTONI
POBLE SEC
MONTJUIC

Ronda Sant Pere
Carrer de Trafalgar
D'Ali-Bei
Av. Meridiana
Buenaventura Muñoz
Almogavers
Av. Vilanova
Ribes
Arc de Triomf
Passeig Lluís Companys
Passeig de Sant Pere
Palau de la Música
PL. ANTONI MAURA
Via Laietana

C. Llull
C.R. Turro
C. Wellington
Wad-Ras
Villena
Ciutadella Vila Olímpica
VILA OLÍMPICA

PARC DE LA CIUTADELLA
Parc Zoològic
Museu D'Art Modern
Museu de Zoologia
Passeig de Picasso
Passeig Circumval·lació
Estació de Franca
BARCELONETA

EL CORTE INGLÉS
El Corte Inglés
PLAÇA URQUINAONA
Carrer de Fontanella
C. Canuda
C. Comtal
PLAÇA DE CATALUNYA
Ronda Sant Antoni
MACBA
EL RAVAL
CIUTAT VELLA
BARRI GÒTIC
Catalunya
C. Pelai
C. Valldonzella
L. Costa
Ferlandina
S. Antón Abad
L'Hospital
Ribera Alta
Ribera Baja
C. Carme
C. Fortuny
C. Elisabets
Sa. Anna
C. Portaferrissa
Mercat de la Boqueria
Palau de la Virreina
Teatre Liceu
Liceu
La Unió
Portal de l'Àngel
Av. Catedral
La Seu
Església del Pi
C. Boqueria
C. Ferran
C. Ferrán
PLAÇA REIAL
Escudellers
La Pau
C. Borià
Carrer de Montcada
Carrer de Princesa
Museu Picasso
Mercat del Born
LA RIBERA
Via Laietana
Ajuntament
D'en Aroi
C.S. Miquel
Millares
Argenteria
Mosqueta
Llotja
Pg. Isabel II
Av. Marqués de l'Argentera
C. Fussina
Carrer Comerç
C. Ample
C. Mercè
La Merçè
Passeig de Colom
C. Clave
J.A. Clave
Barceloneta
Marina-Port Vell
Moll de la Fusta
Cine IMAX
Aquarium
Maremagnum
Multicines
Harbor
Monument a Colom
Arc del Teatre
Av. de les Drassanes
Carrer de Sant Pau
Aldana
M. Campo Sagrado
Blai
Magallanes
Pg. de l'Exposició
Teatre Grec
Fundació Miró
Funicular
Carrer Nou
Avinguda de la Rambla
Avinguda del Paral·lel
Ronda de Sant Pau
Parallel
Poble Sec
Rocafort
Calàbria
C. Manso
C. Parlament
Pg. de Blasco de Gazel
Pg. Jose Carner
Pg. de Montjuïc
Cable Car
Les Rambles
Les Rambles

300 yards
300 meters
0
0

N

LET'S GO
Spain & Portugal

■ Let's Go writers travel on your budget.

"Guides that penetrate the veneer of the holiday brochures and mine the grit of real life."
—*The Economist*

"The writers seem to have experienced every rooster-packed bus and lunar-surfaced mattress about which they write."
—*The New York Times*

"All the dirt, dirt cheap."
—*People*

■ Great for independent travelers.

"The guides are aimed not only at young budget travelers but at the independent traveler, a sort of streetwise cookbook for traveling alone."
—*The New York Times*

"Flush with candor and irreverence, chock full of budget travel advice."
—*The Des Moines Register*

"An indispensable resource. *Let's Go*'s practical information can be used by every traveler."
—*The Chattanooga Free Press*

■ Let's Go is completely revised each year.

"Only *Let's Go* has the zeal to annually update every title on its list."
—*The Boston Globe*

"Unbeatable: good sight-seeing advice; up-to-date info on restaurants, hotels, and inns; a commitment to money-saving travel; and a wry style that brightens nearly every page."
—*The Washington Post*

■ All the important information you need.

"*Let's Go* authors provide a comedic element while still providing concise information and thorough coverage of the country. Anything you need to know about budget traveling is detailed in this book."
—*The Chicago Sun-Times*

"Value-packed, unbeatable, accurate, and comprehensive."
—*Los Angeles Times*

Let's Go Publications

Let's Go: Alaska & the Pacific Northwest 1999
Let's Go: Australia 1999
Let's Go: Austria & Switzerland 1999
Let's Go: Britain & Ireland 1999
Let's Go: California 1999
Let's Go: Central America 1999
Let's Go: Eastern Europe 1999
Let's Go: Ecuador & the Galápagos Islands 1999
Let's Go: Europe 1999
Let's Go: France 1999
Let's Go: Germany 1999
Let's Go: Greece 1999 **New title!**
Let's Go: India & Nepal 1999
Let's Go: Ireland 1999
Let's Go: Israel & Egypt 1999
Let's Go: Italy 1999
Let's Go: London 1999
Let's Go: Mexico 1999
Let's Go: New York City 1999
Let's Go: New Zealand 1999
Let's Go: Paris 1999
Let's Go: Rome 1999
Let's Go: South Africa 1999 **New title!**
Let's Go: Southeast Asia 1999
Let's Go: Spain & Portugal 1999
Let's Go: Turkey 1999 **New title!**
Let's Go: USA 1999
Let's Go: Washington, D.C. 1999

Let's Go Map Guides

Amsterdam	Madrid
Berlin	New Orleans
Boston	New York City
Chicago	Paris
Florence	Rome
London	San Francisco
Los Angeles	Washington, D.C.

Coming Soon: Prague, Seattle

Let's Go
Publications

Let's Go
Spain &
Portugal
1999

Elena Schneider
Editor

Ethan Thurow
Nicole Anna Barry
Associate Editor

Researcher-Writers:
Marya J. Cohen
Melissa Enriquez
Robin S. Goldstein
Patrick K. Lyons
Massi Osseo-Asare
Natasha M. Sokol

St. Martin's Press ⚬ New York

HELPING LET'S GO

If you want to share your discoveries, suggestions, or corrections, please drop us a line. We read every piece of correspondence, whether a postcard, a 10-page email, or a coconut. Please note that mail received after May 1999 may be too late for the 2000 book, but will be kept for future editions. **Address mail to:**

Let's Go: Spain & Portugal
67 Mount Auburn Street
Cambridge, MA 02138
USA

Visit Let's Go at **http://www.letsgo.com,** or send email to:

feedback@letsgo.com
Subject: "Let's Go: Spain & Portugal"

In addition to the invaluable travel advice our readers share with us, many are kind enough to offer their services as researchers or editors. Unfortunately, our charter enables us to employ only currently enrolled Harvard-Radcliffe students.

Maps by David Lindroth copyright © 1999, 1998, 1997, 1996, 1995, 1994, 1993, 1992, 1991, 1990, 1989, 1988 by St. Martin's Press, Inc.

Distributed outside the USA and Canada by Macmillan.

Let's Go: Spain & Portugal. Copyright © 1999 by Let's Go, Inc. All rights reserved. Printed in the United States of America. No part of this book may be used or reproduced in any manner whatsoever without written permission except in the case of brief quotations embodied in critical articles or reviews. For information, address St. Martin's Press, 175 Fifth Avenue, New York, NY 10010, USA.

ISBN: 0-312-19499-4

First edition
10 9 8 7 6 5 4 3 2 1

Let's Go: Spain & Portugal is written by Let's Go Publications, 67 Mount Auburn Street, Cambridge, MA 02138, USA.

Let's Go® and the thumb logo are trademarks of Let's Go, Inc. Printed in the USA on recycled paper with biodegradable soy ink.

ADVERTISING DISCLAIMER

All advertisements appearing in Let's Go publications are sold by an independent agency not affiliated with the production of the guides. Advertisers are never given preferential treatment, and the guides are researched, written, and published independent of advertising. Advertisements do not imply endorsement of products or services by Let's Go. If you are interested in purchasing advertising space in a Let's Go publication, contact: Let's Go Advertising Sales, 67 Mount Auburn St., Cambridge, MA 02138, USA.

Contents

How to Use This Book

Or, how to digest **SPAM** (**S**pain, **P**ortugal, **A**ndorra, and **M**orocco). In the summer of '98, we sent seven gung-ho researchers to root out the best and the cheapest of what these countries have to offer. All seven survived, lives and bank accounts intact. In your hand lies the precious creation for which they braved loquacious hostel owners and tight-lipped phone booths. Contrary to popular belief, however, this book is not the Bible. Use our findings as a reliable starting point, but remember that stepping off the prescribed path is what makes the adventure your own.

Before heading to the airport, take some time to peruse the **Essentials,** which guides you through preliminary practicalities, from obtaining a passport to surfing the web to choosing a study-abroad program. It addresses **specific concerns,** including those of women travelers; older travelers; gay, lesbian, and bisexual travelers; travelers with disabilities; minority travelers; and vegetarian and kosher travelers. **Getting There** is chock-full of general advice on exactly that, cheaply. The fact-filled **Once There** and **Getting Around** sections describe general resources.

Essentials specific to that country precede each country's coverage. The **Getting There and Around** section explains transportation advice specific to that country, and **Accommodations** gives the scoop on finding a place to crash. Nourish your mind on **Life and Times** and your appetite on **Food and Drink;** dare to learn even more by making use of **Prose to Peruse** and the **Language** and **Literature** sections. At the back of the book is a **Phrasebook** and **Glossary** of oft-used Castilian, Catalan, Galician, Portuguese, Arabic, and French words. **The Appendix** also includes clothing sizes, festivals and holidays, climate info, and conversion charts.

We've organized Spain and Portugal by region, occasionally merging two similar and neighboring regions into one chapter. The chapters on **Spain** are arranged geographically in two clockwise spirals—a tight one around Madrid and a larger one moving from the Castillas northwest to Galicia and around the periphery. **Andorra** gets subsumed within Northeastern Spain, but the petite principality maintains its independence with its very own chapter. **Portugal's** scheme begins in Lisbon, including pleasant towns nearby, jumps down to the sunny Algarve and heads north through Estremadura, along the coast to the northern frontier. **Morocco** begins with Tangier, the European entry point, and the northern and Mediterranean coast, dives inland to the imperial cities in the Middle Atlas, then moves back up north to surge all the way down the Atlantic Coast southwards, and then eventually passes inland to Marrakesh and the southern valleys and deserts.

A regional intro opens each chapter, followed by the regional transport-hub city. Coverage continues clockwise through the region. The **Orientation** and **Practical Information** sections give the dirt on the town's layout and lists valuable services. Under **Accommodations** we rank establishments according to our estimate of their value and quality. The first establishment listed in each section is considered the best, the second the second best and so on. **Food,** with restaurants and markets, is similarly ranked. **Sights** and **Entertainment** give suggestions on what there is to see and do.

So go (don't hurt yourself) and have a blast—these countries rock.

A NOTE TO OUR READERS

The information for this book was gathered by *Let's Go*'s researchers from May through August. Each listing is derived from the assigned researcher's opinion based upon his or her visit at a particular time. The opinions are expressed in a candid and forthright manner. Other travelers might disagree. Those traveling at a different time may have different experiences since prices, dates, hours, and conditions are always subject to change. You are urged to check beforehand to avoid inconvenience and surprises. Travel always involves a certain degree of risk, especially in low-cost areas. When traveling, especially on a budget, always take particular care to ensure your safety.

Change your money with no surprises

Foreign

Exchange

0%

Services

COMMISSION FREE

Offices in Spain

- **Madrid**
  Plaza de las Cortes 2

- **Barcelona**
  Paseo de Gracia 101
  or Ramblas 74

- **Sevilla**
  Plaza Nueva 7

- **Granada**
  Avda. Reyes Católicos 31

- **Palma de Mallorca**
  Avda. Antonio Maura 10

- **Marbella**
  Duque de Ahumada s/n
  Edif. Occidente - Local 3
  Complejo "Marbella 2000"

**Foreign
Exchange**

We are the international experts in Foreign Exchange

List of Maps

Color Maps

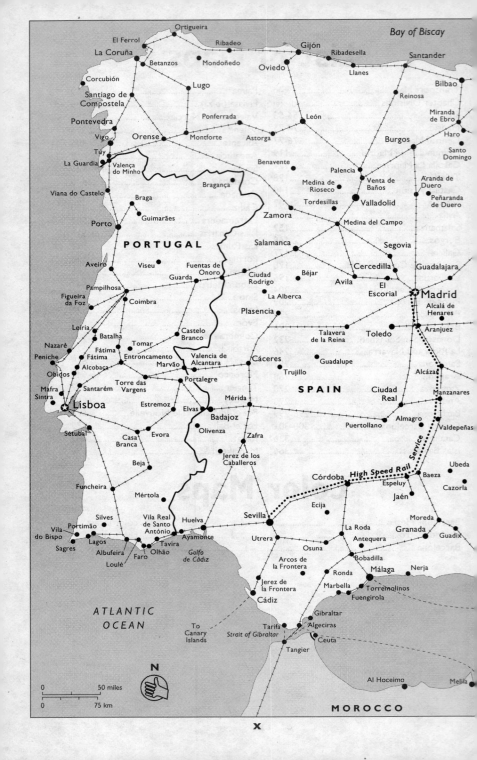

Transport Map

Chapter Divisions

FRANCE

ais Vasco
p. 224-245

Vitoria

NAVARRA
Pamplona

La Rioja
and
Logroño   Navarra
LA   pp. 246-267
OJA

Zaragoza

Aragón
pp. 268-289

Teruel

Cuenca

SPAIN

Valencia

VALENCIA

Alicante

Murcia

MURCIA

Andorra
pp. 290-295

Catalunya
pp. 336-365

Girona

● Barcelona
pp. 296-335

N

0   50 miles

0   75 kilometers

TO
MENORCA →

Mallorca
● Palma

Islas Baleares
pp. 366-391

Ibiza

Formentera

Valencia and
Murcia
pp. 392-417

MEDITERRANEAN SEA

ALGERIA

Let's Go Picks

We've liked, we've disliked, and here's a dose of what we loved. Even to our discerning and discriminating senses, these places won us over. Isn't subjectivity wonderful? How about a Reader's Picks '98? Send us a postcard of your favorite travel haunts. Key: Morocco (M), Portugal (P), and Spain (S). Gibraltar and Andorra? Who needs tax free rocks anyways.

Best beaches: Formentera (S), sprawling, empty, naked (p. 390). **Essaouira (M)**, where Jimi saw castles made of sand (p. 692). **Sagres, Tavira, Sesimbra (P)**, you can't go wrong with these three (p. 575, p. 581, p. 569). **Ses Salines (S)**, oh so fine (p. 390). **Islas Cíes (S)**, idyllic wonderland (p. 187). **O Castro de Baroña (S)**, totally free—even clothing is optional (p. 193). **Tossa de Mar (S),** not one but four white-sand extravaganzas (p. 352).

Best nightlife: Ibiza (S), where fashion is a contest (p. 385). **Madrid (S)**, party from 9 'til 11...that's pm 'til am (p. 108). **Lagos (P)**, more bars per square foot than should be possible (p. 572) **Donostia-San Sebastián (S)**, you mean there's daylife here? (p. 233). **Valencia (S)**, urban dynamite (p. 393). **Marbella (S)**, vogue with the Beautiful People (p. 475). **Barcelona (S)**, ramble on, ramble on (p. 325). **Fez (M)**, oh, wait...nevermind. **Las Palmas, Gran Canaria (S)**, if that's your thing (p. 516).

Best places with no significant sights whatsoever: Viana do Castelo (P), the beach resort of the 21st century (p. 633). **Vejer de la Frontera (S)**, you'll lose yourself in this whitewashed maze (p. 494). **Zafra (S)**, the crème de la crème of the *pueblos blancos* (p. 511). **Formentera (S)**, dunes, mopeds, beach (p. 390). **Camariñas (S)**, cover this place in lace (p. 195). **Ochagavia (S)**, a truly refreshing spot (p. 266).

Best monuments/castles/architecture: Segovia (S), the original Magic Kingdom (p. 141). **Meknès (M)**, its Christian dungeons chill the bones (p. 665). **Granada (S)**, behold the Alhambra and Albaicín (p. 451). **Óbidos (P)**, once a wedding present from a king, this village captures the heart (p. 595). **Barcelona (S)**, *la ciudad de diseño* (p. 296). **Santiago de Compostela (S)**, ahoy pilgrim—you've found your haven (p. 179). **Sant Joan des Abadesses (S)**, Romanesque up the wazoo (p. 358).

Backpacker's best: Picos de Europa (S), our friend Billy couldn't bah enough about them (p. 208). **Alpujarras (S)**, refuge to the Moors, the Bloomsbury group, and new-age Buddhists (p. 462). **High Atlas Mountains (M)**, frolic in the snow—in August (p. 702). **Alto Minho (P)**, the lushest greenery in Portugal (p. 635). **Cercedilla (S)**, skiing, hiking, and more, just 1½ hours from Madrid (p. 120). **Parque Nacional de Ordesa (S)**, an Alps-Rockies combo up along the French border (p. 286). **Menorca (S)**, a sight for sore city eyes (p. 377).

Researcher Faves: Ibiza nighlife, party on (p. 385). **Girona**, beauty in the streets (p. 337). **Marbella**, friendly, people, watch (p. 475). **Marvão**, charm in the 'Tejo (p. 589). **Fez**, all of it (p. 671). **Santiago**, the sights; the artsy bar (p. 179). **Madrid**, platforms going ghetto style (p. 72).

Most sophisticated alcohol consumption: Porto (P). Sip and schmooze (p. 621).
Most amazing spectacle: Marrakech (M), The Assembly of the Dead (p. 697).
Largest hunk of pork: Museo de Jamón, Madrid (S). Babe, we hardly knew ya (p. 91).
Best singers: Santo Domingo de Silos (S), hills alive with chanting monks (p. 173).
Best view from a toilet: El Castillo de Loare (S). Who needs a newspaper? (p. 284).

Essentials

PLANNING YOUR TRIP

■ When to Go

Summer is **high season** for most coastal and interior regions in Spain, Portugal and Morocco (roughly June-Sept.). For ski resorts and the Canary Islands, winter is high season. In many parts of Spain and Portugal, high season extends back to **Semana Santa** (Holy Week, Mar. 29-Apr. 4) and includes festival days (see **Festivals and Holidays**, p. 644). August especially sees slews of tourists, both foreign and domestic; the coastal regions overflow while inland cities empty out, leaving behind closed offices, restaurants, and lodgings.

Traveling in the **off-season** (*temporada baja*) has many advantages, including lighter crowds, lower prices, and greater flexibility. During the winter, university towns burst with vitality, but many smaller (e.g., seaside) towns virtually shut down. Tourist offices and sights cut their hours nearly everywhere. During Morocco's momentous religious event—Ramadan (Dec. 20, 1998-Jan. 19, 1999)—there is little activity outside the sacred realm.

Remember, however, that weather varies tremendously both within and between these countries, and each season offers distinct advantages and disadvantages for the visitor. For more specific weather information, see **Climate**, p. 647.

■ Useful Information

TOURIST OFFICES

Take advantage of the wealth of info tourist offices can provide, be it maps, brochures, or advice.

Tourist Offices of Spain

U.S.: 666 5th Ave., 35th fl., **New York,** NY 10103 (tel. (212) 265 8822; for info packet (888) 657 7246; fax 265 8864; http://www.OKSPAIN.org). 845 North Michigan Ave., **Chicago,** IL 60611 (tel. (312) 642 1992; fax 642 9817). San Vincente Plaza Building, 8383 Wilshire Blvd., Suite 960, **Beverly Hills,** CA 90211 (tel. (213) 658 7188; fax 658 1061). 1221 Brickell Ave., Suite 1850, **Miami,** FL 33131 (tel. (305) 358 1992; fax 358 8223).

Canada: 2 Bloor St. W., 34th fl., **Toronto,** ON M4W 3E2 (tel. (416) 961 3131; fax 961 1992).

U.K.: Manchester Sq., 22-23, **London** W15 5AP (tel. (171) 486 80 77; fax 486 80 34). 24hr. brochure request line (tel. (891) 66 99 20).

Portuguese National Tourist Offices

U.S.: 590 Fifth Ave., 4th fl., **New York,** NY 10036-4704 (tel. (212) 354 4403 or (800) 7678 8425; fax 764-6137; http://www.portugal.org). Portuguese Trade & Tourism Office, 1900 L St. NW, Suite 310, **Washington, D.C.** 20036 (tel. (202) 331 8222; fax 331 8236).

Canada: Portuguese Trade & Tourism Commission, 60 Bloor St. W., Suite 1005, **Toronto,** ON M4W 3B8 (tel. (416) 921 7376; fax 921 1353).

U.K.: Portuguese Trade & Tourism Office, 2nd fl., 22-25A Sackville St., **London** W1X 2LY (tel. (171) 494 14 41; fax 494 18 68).

Ireland: Portuguese Trade & Tourism Board, 54 Dawson St., **Dublin** 2 (tel. (1) 670 91 33 or 670 91 34; fax 670 91 41; email info@icep.ie).

ESSENTIALS

Cheap tickets. Great advice. Nice people.

1-800-2COUNCIL

Great deals on
airfares; hotels; rail passes; study, work and
volunteer programs; travel accessories,
backpacks, and international identity cards.

Council *Travel*

CIEE: Council on International Educational Exchange

United States: Arizona-Tempe; **California**-Berkeley, Davis, Fresno, Fullerton, Isla Vista, La Jolla, Long Beach, Los Angeles (two offices), Northridge, Palo Alto, Pasadena, Sacramento, San Diego (two offices), San Francisco (two offices); **Colorado**-Boulder (two offices), Denver; **Connecticut**-New Haven; **District of Columbia**-Washington D.C.; **Florida**-Miami; **Georgia**-Atlanta; **Illinois**-Chicago, Evanston; **Indiana**-Bloomington; **Iowa**-Ames; **Kansas**- Lawrence; **Louisiana**- New Orleans; **Maryland**-Baltimore, College Park; **Massachussetts**-Amherst, Boston, Cambridge (two offices); **Michigan**-Ann Arbor, East Lansing; **Minnesota**-Minneapolis; **New Jersey**-New Brunswick; **New York**-Ithaca, New York City (three offices); **North Carolina**-Chapel Hill; **Ohio**-Columbus; **Oregon**-Eugene (two offices), Portland; **Pennsylvania**-Lancaster, Philadelphia, Pittsburgh, State College; **Rhode Island**-Providence; **Tennessee**-Knoxville; **Texas**-Austin, Dallas, Houston; **Utah**-Salt Lake City; **Washington**-Seattle (two offices); **Wisconsin**-Madison.

OVERSEAS LOCATIONS: United Kingdom- London; **France**-Paris, Aix-en-Provence, Lyon; **Germany**-Dusseldorf, Koeln, Munich; **Japan**-Tokyo; **Singapore**-Singapore; **Thailand**-Bangkok.

For a complete listing of Council Travel offices, visit us on the web at:

www.counciltravel.com

ESSENTIALS

South Africa: Portuguese Trade and Tourism Office, Embassy of Portugal, 4th fl., Sunnyside Ridge, Sunnyside Drive Parktown, 2193 **Johannesburg** (tel. (11) 484 34 87; fax 484 54 16). Send mail to: P.O. Box 2473, Houghton, 2041 Johannesburg.

Moroccan National Tourist Offices

U.S.: 20 E. 46th St., **New York,** NY 10007 (tel. (212) 557 2521; fax 949 8148).
Canada: Place Montreal Trust, 1800 Avenue McGill Collège, Suite 2450, **Montreal,** Quebec H3A 3J6 (tel. (514) 842 8111; fax 842 5316).
U.K.: 205 Regent St., **London** W1R 7DE (tel. (171) 437 00 73; fax 734 81 72).

TRAVEL ORGANIZATIONS

American Automobile Association (AAA) Travel Related Services, 1000 AAA Dr. (mail stop 100), Heathrow, FL 32746-5063 (tel. (407) 444 7000; fax 444 7380). Provides road maps and travel guides free to members. Offers travel services, and auto insurance. The International Driving Permit (see, p. 10) is available for purchase from local AAA officers. To become a member, call (800) 222 4357.

Council on International Educational Exchange (CIEE), 205 East 42nd St., New York, NY 10017-5706 (tel. (888) 268 6245; fax (212) 822 2699; http://www.ciee.org). Council administers work, volunteer, academic, internship, and professional programs around the world. They also offer identity cards (including the ISIC and the GO25) and a range of publications, among them the useful magazine *Student Travels* (free). Call or write for further information.

Federation of International Youth Travel Organizations (FIYTO), Bredgade 25H, DK-1260 Copenhagen K, Denmark (tel. (45) 33 33 96 00; fax 33 93 96 76; email mailbox@fiyto.org; http://www.fiyto.org). An international organization promoting educational, cultural, and social travel for young people. Member organizations include language schools, educational travel companies, national tourist boards, accommodation centers, and sponsors the GO25 Card (http://www.go25.org).

International Student Travel Confederation (ISTC), Herengracht 479, 1017 BS Amsterdam, The Netherlands (tel. (31) 20 421 2800; fax 20 421 2810; email istcinfo@istc.org; http://www.istc.org). The ISTC is a nonprofit confederation of student travel organizations whose focus is to promote and facilitate travel among young people and students. Member organizations include International Student Surface Travel Association, Student Air Travel Association, IASIS Travel Insurance, the International Association for Educational and Work Exchange Programs, and the International Student Identity Card Association (ISIC).

TRAVEL PUBLICATIONS

Bon Voyage! 2069 W. Bullard Ave., Fresno, CA 93711-1200 (tel. (800) 995 9716 or (209) 447 8441; fax 266 6460; email 70754.3511@compuserve.com). Annual mail order catalogue offers a range of products. Books, travel accessories, luggage, electrical converters, maps, and videos.

The College Connection, Inc. (tel. (619) 551 9770; fax 551 9987; email eurailnow@aol.com; http://www.eurailpass.com). Publishes *The Passport,* a booklet listing hints about every aspect of traveling and studying abroad. This booklet is free to *Let's Go* readers; send your request by email or fax only.

European Festivals Association, 120B, rue de Lausanne, CH-1202 Geneva, Switzerland (tel. (22) 732 28 03; fax 738 40 12; email aef@vtx.ch). Publishes the free booklet *Festivals,* which lists dates and programs of many major European festivals, including music, ballet, and theater events. To receive the booklet, please enclose 5 International Reply Coupons for postage, and address your request to: Dailey-Thorp Travel, Inc., 330 West 58th Street, New York, NY 10019-1817.

Forsyth Travel Library, Inc., 1750 East 131st Street, P.O. Box 480800, Kansas City, MO 64148 (tel. (800) 367 7984; fax (816) 942 6969; email forsyth@avi.net; http://www.forsyth.com). A mail-order service that stocks a wide range of maps and guides for rail and ferry travel in Europe; also sells rail tickets and passes and offers reservation services. Sells the *Thomas Cook European Timetable* for trains, a complete guide to European train departures and arrivals (US$28, with full map of European train routes US$39).

ESSENTIALS

OVERSEAS RENTALS

<u>SECLUDED VILLAS</u> in Europe, Hawaii & Caribbean

<u>CASTLES, COTTAGES & FARMHOUSES</u> in Europe

<u>APARTMENTS & FLATS</u> in European cities

<u>SKI CHALETS</u> in Austria & Switzerland

<u>PRIVATE OCEANFRONT HOMES</u> worldwide

<u>AIR & CAR RENTALS</u>

Cities—5-nights minimum.

Countryside—Saturday to Saturday.

**EUROPA-LET /
TROPICAL INN-LET
I N C.**

(800) 462-4486 · (541) 482-5806 · fax: (541) 482-0660
92 North Main Street, Ashland, Oregon 97520 USA

Discount Airfares to:

- Spain
- Portugal
- Madeira
- Azores
- Pousada & Parador Packages
- Tours • Apartment & Villa Rentals
- Car & Driver • Rental Cars

Call Pinto Basto - 1 (800) 526 - 8539

24 South Main Street New City NY 10956

(914) 639 - 8020 Fax (914) 639 - 8017 email pbtours@aol.com

INTERNET RESOURCES

Nowadays, people can make their own airline, hotel, hostel, or car rental reservations on the internet and connect personally with others abroad. **NetTravel: How Travelers Use the Internet,** by Michael Shapiro, is an informative guide to all aspects of travel planning through the internet (US$25). On the web, **search engines** (services that search for web pages under specific subjects) can significantly aid the search process. **Lycos** (www.a2z.lycos.com), **Alta Vista** (www.altavista.digital.com), and **Excite** (www.excite.com) are among the most popular. **Yahoo!** is a slightly more organized search engine; check out its travel links at www.yahoo.com/Recreation/Travel. Check out **Let's Go's web site** (www.letsgo.com) and find our newsletter, information about our books, an always-current list of region-specific links, and more. *Let's Go* lists web sites specific to certain aspects of travel throughout this chapter.

Arab Net (http://www.arab.net/morocco/morocco_contents.html) has good historical, cultural, and tourist information on Morocco, including a list of links.

The CIA World Factbook (http://www.odci.gov/cia/publications/factbook/index.html) has tons of vital statistics on the country you want to visit.

Foreign Language for Travelers (http://www.travlang.com) can help you brush up on your Spanish, Portuguese, and Arabic.

Sí, Spain (http://www.SiSpain.org), run by the Spanish Ministry of Foreign affairs, offers cultural and historical info, tourist info, and another great set of links.

Spain Online (http://www.spainonline.com) has a vast list of all Spanish websites.

Tourism in Morocco (http://www.tourism-in-Morocco.com) has helpful information on all aspects of traveling to and within Morocco, plus city-specific info.

Turespaña (http://www.tourspain.es) is the official Spanish tourism site. It offers reams of national and city-specific info, an information request service, helpful links on all aspects of travel, and a nifty festival locator.

The United States State Department (http://travel.state.gov) lists current travel advisory warnings, publishes countries' consular fact sheets with information about health, safety, and general travel conditions, and disseminates updates on major terrorism concerns and threats to U.S. tourists.

Welcome to Portugal (http://www.portugal.org) has general info on Portugal plus information of specific interest to the traveler.

Xacobeo 99 (http://www.xacobeo.es) is the Camino de Santiago's official website.

■ Documents And Formalities

All applications should be filed several weeks or months in advance of your planned departure date. Demand for passports is highest between January and August, so try to apply as early as possible. A backlog in processing can spoil your plans.

When you travel, always carry on your person **two or more forms of identification,** including at least one photo ID. A passport combined with a driver's license usually serves as adequate proof of your identity and citizenship. Many establishments, especially banks, require several IDs before cashing traveler's checks. In case of theft or loss, never carry all your forms of ID together. Also carry several extra passport-size photos that you can attach to the sundry IDs or railpasses you may eventually acquire.

EMBASSIES AND CONSULATES

Direct questions concerning visas and passports go to consulates, not embassies (which handle more weighty matters). For info on your home country's embassies and consulates in Spain, Portugal, and Morocco, see p. 41.

Spain

Australia: Embassy: 15 Arkana St., **Yarralumla,** ACT 2600 (tel. (02) 6273 3555). Mailing address: P.O. Box 9076, Deakin, ACT 2600. **Consulates:** Level 24, St. Martins Tower, 31 Market St., **Sydney,** NSW 2000 (tel. (02) 9261 2433 or 9261 2443;

fax 9283 1695). 3rd. fl., 766 Elizabeth St., **Melbourne,** VIC 3000 (tel. (03) 9347 1966 or 9347 1997; fax 9347 7330).

Canada: Embassy: 74 Stanley Ave., **Ottawa,** ON, K1M 1P4 (tel. (613) 747 2252; fax 744 1224). **Consulates:** 1 Westmount Sq., Suite 1456, **Montreal,** PQ H3Z 2P9 (tel. (514) 935 5235; fax 935 4655). Simtoe Place, 200 Front St., Suite 2401, P.O. Box 15, **Toronto,** ON M5V 3K2 (tel. (416) 977 1661; fax 593 4949).

Ireland: Consulate: 17A Merlyn Park, Ballsbridge, **Dublin** 4 (tel. (035) 269 16 40; fax 269 18 54).

New Zealand: Embassy: refer to Embassy in Australia. **Consulates,** Pararekau Island, P.O. Box 71, Papakura, **Auckland** (tel. (9) 298 51 76; fax 299 80 57).

South Africa: Embassy: 169 Pine St., Arcadia, P.O. Box 1633, **Pretoria** 0083 (tel. (012) 344 38 75; fax 343 48 91). 37 Shortmarket St., **Cape Town** 8001 (tel. (012) 22 23 26; fax 22 23 28). **Consulate:** 37 Shortmarket St., **Cape Town** 8001 (tel. (012) 22 24 15; fax 22 23 28.

U.K.: Embassy: 39 Chesham Pl., **London** SW1X 8SB (tel. (171) 235 55 55; fax 259 53 92). **Consulates:** 22-23 Manchester Square, **London** W1M 5AP (tel. (171) 581 59 21; fax 581 78 88). Suite 1A, Brook House, 70, Spring Gardens, **Manchester** M2 2BQ (tel. (161) 236 12 33; fax 228 74 67). 63 N. Castle St., **Edinburgh** EH2 3LJ (tel. (131) 220 18 43, 220 14 39, or 220 14 42; fax 226 45 68).

U.S.: Embassy: 2375 Pennsylvania Ave. NW, **Washington, D.C.** 20037 (tel. (202) 452 0100). **Consulates:** 150 E. 58th St., 30th fl., **New York,** NY 10155 (tel. (212) 355 4080; fax 644 3751). **Others** in Boston, Chicago, Houston, Los Angeles, Miami, New Orleans, Puerto Rico, San Francisco, and Washington, D.C.

Portugal

Australia: Embassy: 23 Culgoa Circuit, **O'Malley,** ACT 2606; mailing address P.O. Box 92, Deakin, ACT 2600 (tel. (02) 6290 1733; fax 6290 1906). **Consulate:** 132 Ocean St., **Edgecliff,** NSW 2027 (tel. (02) 9326 1844; fax 9327 1607). P.O. Box 568, **Sydney,** NSW 2001.

Canada: Embassy: 645 Island Park Dr., **Ottawa,** ON K1Y OB8 (tel. (613) 729 0883; fax 729 4236). **Consulates:** 2020 University, Suite 1725, **Montréal,** QU H3A 2A5 (tel. (514) 499 0621 or 499 0359; fax 499 0366). 121 Richmond St. W., 7th fl., **Toronto,** ON M5H 2K1 (tel. (416) 360 8260 or 360 8261; fax 360 0350). 700 West Pender St., Suite 904, **Vancouver,** BC V6C 1G8 (tel. (604) 688 6515; fax 685 7042). 167 Lombard Ave., Suite 908, **Winnipeg,** MB R3B OV3 (tel./fax (204) 943 8941).

New Zealand: Embassy: refer to Embassy in Australia. **Consulate:** 55 Ford St., **Auckland** 5 (tel. (9) 309 14 54; fax 308 90 61). Deleite touche Tohmatsu, **Wellington** 1 (tel. (4) 72 16 77; fax 472 80 23).

South Africa: Embassy: 599 Leyds Street, Mucklenuk, **Pretoria** (tel. (012) 341 23 40; fax 341 39 75). **Consulates:** 201 Barclay Square, 296 Walker St., Sunnyside, **Pretoria** 0002 (tel. (012) 326 21 41). 902 Nedbank Centre, 63 Strand St., **Cape Town** 8001 (tel. (021) 24 14 54 or 24 14 56; fax 23 57 83). 16th fl., 320 W. St., P.O. Box 315 **Durban** (tel. (031) 305 75 11; fax 304 60 36).

U.K.: Embassy: 11 Belgrave Sq., **London** SW1X 8PP (tel. (171) 235 53 31; fax 245 12 87). **Consulate:** Silver City House, 62 Brompton Rd., **London** SW3 1BJ (tel. (171) 581 87 22).

U.S.: Embassy: 2125 Kalorama Rd. NW, **Washington, D.C.** 20008 (tel. (202) 328 8610; fax 462 3726). **Consulates:** 630 5th Ave., 3rd fl., Suite 310, **New York,** NY 10111 (tel. (212) 246 4580 or 246 4582; fax 459 0190). Others in Boston, Chicago, Coral Gables (FL), the Dominican Republic, Houston, Honolulu, Los Angeles, Newark, New Bedford (MA), New Orleans, Philadelphia, Providence, San Francisco, San Juan (PR), Waterbury (CT), and Washington, D.C.

Morocco

Australia: Embassy: West St., North, **Sydney,** NSW 2060 (tel. (2) 995 767 17; fax 992 310 53).

Canada: Embassy: 38 Range Rd., **Ottawa,** ON. K1N 8J4 (tel. (613) 236 7391 or 236 7392). **Consulate:** 1010 Sherbrooke West St., Suite 1510, **Montreal,** QU H3A 2R7 (tel. (514) 288 8750).

U.K.: Embassy: 40 Queens Gate Gardens, **London** SW7 5NE (tel. (171) 581 50 01; fax 225 38 62).

U.S.: Embassy: 1601 21st St. NW, **Washington, D.C.** 20009 (tel. (202) 462 7979; fax 452 0161). **Consulates:** 10 East 40th. St., 24th fl., **New York,** NY 10016 (tel. (212) 213 9644; fax 758 2625). 1821 Jefferson Place NW, **Washington, D.C.** 20036 (tel. (202) 462 7979; fax 452 0106).

PASSPORTS

Travelers need legal passports and sometimes visas to enter and leave Spain, Portugal, and Morocco. A passport and a return ticket allows **British, Canadian, New Zealand,** and **U.S. citizens** to remain in all three for 90 days. **Australian citizens** may remain in Portugal and Morocco for 90 days with a passport but need a visa to enter Spanish territory. **South African** citizens need a visa to get into all three countries (see **Visas,** p. 8). In all three countries, your passport must be valid for a minimum of six months after your planned end of stay. Returning home with an expired passport is usually illegal. Furthermore, admission as a visitor does not include the right to work, which may be authorized only with a work permit. Entering certain countries to study requires a special visa, and immigration officers may also want to see proof of acceptance from a school and proof that the course of study will take up most of your time in the country, as well as proof that you can support yourself. Some countries require children to carry their own passports. When you enter a country, dress neatly and carry proof of your financial independence and an airplane ticket to depart.

Before you leave, photocopy the page of your passport that contains your photograph, passport number, and other identifying information. Carry one photocopy in a safe place apart from your passport, and leave another copy at home. These measures will help prove your citizenship and facilitate the issuing of a new passport if you lose the original document. If you do lose your passport, immediately notify the local police and the nearest embassy or consulate of your home government.

Australia Citizens must apply for a passport in person at a post office or a passport office. An appointment may be necessary. Passport offices are located in Adelaide, Brisbane, Canberra City, Darwin, Hobart, Melbourne, Newcastle, Perth, and Sydney. Adult passports cost AUS$120 (for a 32 page passport) or AUS$180 (64 page), and a child's costs AUS$60 (32 page) or AUS$90 (64 page). For more info, call toll-free (in Australia) 13 12 32 or visit http://www.austemb.org.

Canada Application forms are available at all passport offices, Canadian missions, and many travel agencies. Passports cost CDN$60, plus a CDN$25 consular fee, are valid for 5 years, and are not renewable. Processing takes approximately 5 business days for applications in-person; allow 3 weeks for mail delivery. For additional info, contact the Canadian Passport Office (tel. (613) 994 3500; http://www.dfait-maeci.gc.ca/passport). There is no charge for re-entering Canada with an expired passport.

Ireland Citizens can apply for a passport by mail to either the Department of Foreign Affairs, Passport Office, Setanta Centre, Molesworth St., Dublin 2 (tel. (01) 671 1633; fax 671 1092), or the Passport Office, Irish Life Building, 1A South Mall, Cork (tel. (021) 272 525; fax 275 770). Obtain an application at a local Garda station or request one from a passport office. The new Passport Express Service, available through post offices, allows citizens to get a passport in 2 weeks for an extra IR£3. Passports cost IR£45 and are valid for 5 years.

New Zealand Application forms for passports are available in New Zealand from travel agents and Department of Internal Affairs Link Centres in the main cities and towns. Applications may also be forwarded to the Passport Office, P.O. Box 10526, Wellington, New Zealand. Standard processing time in New Zealand is 10 working days for correct applications. The fees are adult NZ$80, child under 16 NZ$40, and urgent service an extra NZ$80. Children's names can no longer be endorsed on a parent's passport—they must apply for their own, which are valid for up to 5 years. An adult's passport is valid for up to 10 years. More information is available on the internet at http://www.govt.nz/agency_info/forms.shtml.

South Africa Citizens can apply for a passport at any Home Affairs Office or South African Mission. Tourist passports, valid for 10 years, cost SAR80. If a passport is needed in a hurry, an emergency passport may be issued for SAR50. An application for a permanent passport must accompany the emergency passport application. Time for the completion of an application is normally 3 months or more from the time of submission. Current passports less than 10 years old (counting from date of issuance) may be renewed until December 31, 1999; every citizen whose passport's validity does not extend far beyond this date is urged to renew it as soon as possible, to avoid the expected glut of applications as 2000 approaches. Renewal is free, and turnaround time is usually 2 weeks.

United Kingdom British citizens, British Dependent Territories citizens, British Nationals (overseas), British subjects, and British Overseas citizens may apply for a full passport, valid for 10 years. Application forms are available at passport offices, main post offices, many travel agents, and branches of Lloyds Bank and Artac World Choice. Apply by mail or in person (an additional UK£10) to one of the passport offices, in London, Liverpool, Newport, Peterborough, Glasgow, or Belfast. The fee is UK£31. The London office offers same-day, walk-in rush service; arrive early. The U.K. Passport Agency can be reached by phone at (0990) 21 04 10.

United States Citizens may apply for a passport at any federal or state courthouse or post office authorized to accept passport applications, or at a U.S. Passport Agency, located in Boston, Chicago, Honolulu, Houston, Los Angeles, Miami, New Orleans, New York, Philadelphia, San Francisco, Seattle, Stamford (CT), or Washington, D.C. Refer to the "U.S. Government, State Department" section of the telephone directory or the local post office for addresses. Parents must apply in person for children under age 13. You must apply in person if this passport is your first, if you're under age 18, or if your current passport is more than 12 years old or was issued before your 18th birthday. Passports are valid for 10 years (under 18, 5 years) and cost US$65 (under 18 US$40). Passports may be renewed by mail or in person for US$55. Processing takes 3-4 weeks. Rush service is available for a surcharge of US$30 with proof of departure within 10 working days (e.g., an airplane ticket or itinerary) or for travelers leaving in 2-3 weeks who require visas. Given proof of citizenship, a U.S. embassy or consulate abroad can usually issue a new passport. For more info, call the 24hr. info line for a recorded message (tel. (202) 647 0518).

VISAS

If you wish to stay longer than your passport allows, apply for a visa at a Spanish, Portuguese, or Moroccan embassy or consulate in your own country well before departing (see **Embassies and Consulates,** p. 5). A **visa** is an endorsement that a foreign government stamps into a passport that allows the bearer to stay in that country for a specified purpose and period of time.

For more information, send for *Foreign Entry Requirements* (US$0.50) from the **Consumer Information Center,** Department 363D, Pueblo, CO 81009 (tel. (719) 948n3334; http://www.pueblo.gsa.gov), or contact the **Center for International Business and Travel (CIBT),** 25 West 43rd St., Suite 1420, New York, NY 10036 (tel. (800) 925 2428 or from NYC (212) 575 2811), which secures visas for travel to and from all countries for a variable service charge.

CUSTOMS: INTO SPAIN, PORTUGAL, & MOROCCO

Anything beyond each country's allowance must be **declared** and is charged a **duty.** In **Spain,** for instance, personal belongings, a portable typewriter, one video camera or two still cameras, 10 rolls of film, a portable radio or tape recorder, and one laptop or PC per person are admitted duty-free if they show signs of use. In addition, 200 cigarettes or 50 cigars or 250 grams of loose tobacco, one bottle of wine, and one bottle of liquor per person are admitted duty-free, along with sporting equipment. Any articles exceeding 1,000,000ptas, or the equivalent in another currency, will be charged a duty. The entry requirements for **Portugal** are practically identical. Those coming to **Morocco** can freely import clothes, sporting equipment, "personal effects" (one camera, pair of binoculars, musical instrument, and a radio), one bottle of liquor, 200 cigarettes, and 50 cigars or 250 grams of pipe tobacco. Upon entering a country, you must declare certain items from abroad and must pay a duty on the value of those articles that exceed the allowance established by that country's **customs** service.

> It is illegal to export **Moroccan dirhams,** Morocco's currency. On leaving Morocco, you may convert the *dirhams* in your possession by presenting exchange slips (to prove they were purchased at the official rate) to an authorized bank at your point of departure. Save your receipts as proof each time you change money, and try not to end up with too many extra *dirhams.*

CUSTOMS: GOING HOME

Upon returning home, you must declare all articles you acquired abroad and pay a **duty** on the value of those articles that exceed the allowance established by your country's customs service. Goods and gifts purchased at **duty-free** shops abroad are not exempt from duty or sales tax at your point of return; you must declare these items as well.

Australia Citizens may import AUS$400 (under 18 AUS$200) of goods duty-free, in addition to 1.125L alcohol and 250 cigarettes or 250g tobacco. You must be over 18 to import alcohol or tobacco. All foodstuffs and animal products must be declared on arrival. For information, contact the Regional Director, Australian Customs Service, GPO Box 8, Sydney NSW 2001 (tel. (02) 9213 2000; fax 9213 4000; http://www.customs.gov.au).

Canada Citizens who remain abroad for at least 1 week may bring back up to CDN$500 worth of goods duty-free any time. Citizens or residents who travel for a period between 48 hours and 6 days can bring back up to CDN$200. You are permitted to ship goods except tobacco and alcohol home under the CDN$500 exemption as long as you declare them when you arrive. Goods under the CDN$200 exemption, as well as all alcohol and tobacco, must be in your hand or checked luggage. Citizens of legal age may import in-person up to 200 cigarettes, 50 cigars or cigarillos, 200g loose tobacco, 1.14L wine or alcohol, and 24 355mL cans/bottles of beer; the value of these products is included in the CDN$200 or CDN$500. For more info, phone the 24hr. Automated Customs Information Service at (800) 461 9999, or visit Revenue Canada at http://www.revcan.ca.

Ireland Citizens must declare everything in excess of IR£142 obtained outside the E.U. or duty- and tax-free in the E.U. above the following allowances: 200 cigarettes, 100 cigarillos, 50 cigars, or 250g tobacco; 1L liquor or 2L wine; 2L still wine; 50g perfume; and 250mL toilet water. Goods obtained duty and tax paid in another E.U. country up to a value of IR£460 will not be subject to additional customs duties. Travelers under 17 may not import tobacco or alcohol. For more information, contact The Revenue Commissioners, Dublin Castle (tel. (01) 679 27 77; fax 671 20 21; email taxes@iol.ie; http://www.revenue.ie).

New Zealand Citizens may import up to NZ$700 worth of goods duty-free if they are intended for personal use or are unsolicited gifts. The concession is 200 cigarettes (1 carton) or 250g tobacco or 50 cigars or a combination of all 3 not to exceed 250g. You may also bring in 4.5L of beer or wine and 1.125L of liquor. Only travelers over 17 may import tobacco or alcohol. For more info, contact New Zealand Customs, 50 Anzac Ave., Box 29, Auckland (tel. (09) 377 35 20; fax 309 29 78).

South Africa Citizens may import duty-free: 400 cigarettes, 50 cigars, 250g tobacco, 2L wine, 1L of spirits, 250mL toilet water, and 50mL perfume, and other consumable items up to a value of SAR500. Goods up to a value of SAR10,000 over and above this duty-free allowance are dutiable at 20%; such goods are also exempted from payment of VAT. Items acquired abroad and shipped to the Republic do not qualify for any allowances. For more information, consult the free pamphlet *South African Customs Information,* available in airports or from the Commissioner for Customs and Excise (tel. (12) 314 99 11; fax 328 64 78).

United Kingdom Citizens or visitors arriving in the U.K. from outside the E.U. must declare goods in excess of the following allowances: 200 cigarettes or 100 cigarillos or 50 cigars or 250g tobacco; still table wine (2L); strong liqueurs over 22% volume (1L), or fortified or sparkling wine, other liqueurs (2L); perfume (60 cc/mL); toilet water (250 cc/mL); and UK£145 worth of all other goods including gifts and souvenirs. You must be over 17 to import liquor or tobacco. These allowances also apply to duty-free purchases within the E.U., except for the last category, other goods, which then has an allowance of UK£75. Goods obtained duty and tax paid for personal use within the E.U. do not require any further customs duty. More information is available from Her Majesty's Customs and Excise, Custom House, Nettleton Road, Heathrow Airport, Hounslow, Middlesex TW6 2LA (tel. (0181) 910 3602 or 910 3566; fax 910 3765; http://www.open.gov.uk).

United States Citizens may import US$400 worth of accompanying goods duty-free and must pay a 10% tax on the next US$1000. You must declare all purchases, so have sales slips ready. The US$400 personal exemption covers goods purchased for personal or household use (including gifts) and cannot include more than 100 cigars, 200 cigarettes (1 carton), and 1L of wine or liquor. You must be over 21 to bring liquor into the U.S. If you mail home personal goods of U.S. origin, you can avoid duty charges by marking the package "American goods returned." For more information, consult the brochure *Know Before You Go,* available from the U.S. Customs Service, Box 7407, Washington D.C. 20044 (tel. (202) 927 6724; http://www.customs.ustreas.gov).

YOUTH, STUDENT, & TEACHER IDENTIFICATION

Student identification cards entitle youthful travelers in **Spain, Portugal,** and occasionally **Morocco** to many discounts and some freebies. The **International Student Identity Card (ISIC)** is the most widely accepted form of student identification. It can procure you discounts for sights, theaters, museums, accommodations, meals, train, ferry, bus and airplane transportation, and other services. Present the card wherever you go, and ask about discounts even when none are advertised. It also provides insurance benefits and access to a toll-free 24-hour ISIC helpline (see **Insurance,** p. 23, for more details). For more information, call (800) 626 2427 in the U.S. and Canada; elsewhere call collect (44) 181 666 9025 or 181 666 9025 from the U.K.

Many student travel agencies around the world issue ISICs, including STA Travel in Australia and New Zealand; Travel CUTS and via the web (http://www.isic-canada.org) in Canada; USIT in Ireland and Northern Ireland; SASTS in South Africa; Campus Travel and STA Travel in the U.K.; Council Travel, Let's Go Travel, STA Travel, and via the web (http://www.ciee.org/idcards/index.htm) in the U.S. The card is valid from September to December of the following year and costs US$20. Applicants must be degree-seeking students of a secondary or post-secondary school. Because of the proliferation of phony ISICs, many airlines and some other services require other proof of student identity, such as your school ID card or a signed letter from the registrar attesting to your student status and stamped with the school seal. The **International Teacher Identity Card (ITIC)** offers the same insurance coverage and similar but limited discounts. The fee is US$20. For more information on these cards, consult the organization's web site (http://www.istc.org; email isicinfo@istc.org).

Federation of International Youth Travel Organizations (FIYTO) issues a discount card to travelers who are under 26 but not students. Known as the **GO25 Card,** this one-year card offers many of the same benefits as the ISIC, and most organizations that sell the ISIC also sell the GO25 Card. To apply, you will need a passport, valid driver's license, or copy of a birth certificate; and a passport-sized photo with your name printed on the back. The fee is US$20. Information is available on the web at http://www.ciee.org, or by contacting Travel CUTS in Canada, STA Travel in the U.K., Council Travel in the U.S., or FIYTO headquarters in Denmark (see **Travel Organizations,** p. 3).

DRIVING PERMITS AND CAR INSURANCE

In **Spain** and **Portugal,** travelers often drive with a valid American or Canadian license. The **International Driving Permit (IDP)** is not required by either government nor by most car rental agencies. In **Morocco,** an IDP is officially required. An official IDP is recommended for all three countries: it serves as a credible ID and allows more flexibility in renting a car.

Your IDP, valid for one year, must be issued in your own country before you depart; automobile association affiliates cannot issue IDPs valid in their own country. You must be at least 18 years old to receive an IDP. A valid driver's license from your home country must always accompany the IDP. An application for an IDP usually needs to include one or two photos, a current local license, an additional form of identification, and a fee.

Australians can obtain an IDP (for AUS$15) by contacting their local **Royal Automobile Club,** the **National Royal Motorist Association** if in NSW or the ACT. An application can be obtained at http://www.rac.com.au or by calling (08) 9421 4271. Canadian license holders can obtain an IDP (CDN$10) through any **Canadian Automobile Association** branch office in Canada by contacting CAA, 1145 Hunt Club Rd., Suite 200, K1V 0Y3 (tel. (613) 247 0117, ext. 2025; fax 247 0118; http://www.caa.ca). Citizens of Ireland should drop into their nearest **Automobile Association** office where an IDP can be picked up for IR£4. Phone ((01) 283 3555) or fax (283-3660) for a postal application form. In New Zealand, contact your local **Automobile Association** or their main office at P.O. Box 5, Auckland (tel. (9) 377 4660; fax 302 2037). IDPs cost NZ$8. In South Africa visit your local **Automobile Association of South Africa** (tel. (11) 799 1000; fax 799 1010) office, where IDPs can be picked up for SAR25. In the U.K. IDPs are UK£4 and you can either visit your local **AA Shop** or call (1256) 49 39 32. U.S. license holders can obtain an IDP (US$10) at any **American Automobile Association (AAA)** office or by writing to AAA (see Travel Organizations, p. 3). You do not have to be a member of AAA to receive an IDP.

Most credit cards cover standard **insurance.** If you rent, lease, or borrow a car, you will need a **green card,** or **International Insurance Certificate,** to prove that you have liability insurance. Obtain it through the car rental agency; most include coverage in their prices. Verify whether your auto insurance applies abroad; even if it does, you will still need a green card to certify this fact to foreign officials.

■ Accommodations

For country-specific information on hostels, hotels, and other types of accommodations see the respective country introductions. For **Spain,** see p. 48, for **Portugal,** see p. 482, for **Morocco,** see p. 589.

HOSTELS

Hostels are generally dorm-style accommodations, often in large single-sex rooms with bunk beds, although some hostels do offer private rooms for families and couples. Fees range from US$5 to $25 per night. If you have internet access, check out the **Internet Guide to Hostelling** (http://www.hostels.com), which provides a directory of hostels from around the world in addition to oodles of information about hostelling and backpacking worldwide.

For their various services and lower rates at member hostels, hostelling associations, especially **Hostelling International (HI),** can definitely be worth joining. The over 4500 HI hostels are scattered worldwide and many accept reservations via the International Booking Network (IBN) for a nominal fee. Reservations can be made from any other IBN hostel or via phone. From within the U.S. call (202) 783 6161; outside call your respective national hostelling organization or check http://www.hiayh.org/ushostel/reserva/ibn3.htm for international IBN booking numbers. HI's umbrella organization's web page lists the web addresses and phone numbers of all national associations and can be a great place to begin researching hostelling in a specific region (http://www.iyhf.org). Although you can join HI on the road, it is much easier to do so at home. Here are some of the national associations:

Pack Heavy. Travel Light.

V3 ™

Virtual Backpack·

Access your personal email, addresses, files, bookmarks, weather, news and maps from any computer on the Web.*

exclusively at the
Student Advantage® Network
www.studentadvantage.com

*You can get access to the Web at hostels, airports, libraries and cyber cafés.

An Óige (Irish Youth Hostel Association), 61 Mountjoy St., Dublin 7 (tel. (353 01) 830 4555; fax 1 830 5808; email anoige@iol.ie; http://www.irelandyha.org). One-year membership is IR£7.50, under 18 IR£4, family IR£7.50 for each adult, children under 16 free.

Australian Youth Hostels Association (AYHA), Level 3, 10 Mallett St., Camperdown NSW 2050 (tel. (02) 9565 1699; fax 9565 1325; email YHA@yha.org.au; http://www.yha.org.au). Memberships AUS$44, renewal AUS$27, under 18 AUS$13.

Hostelling International-American Youth Hostels (HI-AYH), 733 15th St. NW, Suite 840, Washington, D.C. 20005 (tel. (202) 783 6161, ext. 136; fax 783 6171; email hiayhserv@hiayh.org; http://www.hiayh.org). Memberships can be purchased at many travel agencies (see **Budget Travel Agencies,** p. 36). One-year membership US$25, under 18 US$10, over 54 US$15, family cards US$35.

Hostelling International-Canada (HI-C) 400-205 Catherine St., Ottawa, Ontario K2P 1C3 (tel. (613) 237 7884; fax 237 7868; email info@hostellingintl.ca; http://www.hostellingintl.ca). Membership packages: One-year CDN$25, CDN$12 under 18; two-year CDN$35; lifetime CDN$175.

Scottish Youth Hostels Association (SYHA), 7 Glebe Crescent, Stirling FK8 2JA (tel. (01786) 89 14 00; fax 89 13 33; email syha@syha.org.uk; http://www.syha.org.uk). Membership UK£6, under 18 UK£2.50.

Youth Hostels Association of England and Wales (YHA), Trevelyan House, 8 St. Stephen's Hill, St. Albans, Hertfordshire AL1 2DY, England (tel. (01727) 85 52 15; fax 84 41 26; email yhacustomerservices@compuserve.com; http://www.yha.org.uk). Enrollment fees are: adults UK£10, under 18 UK£5; family UK£20 for each parent, children under 18 free; single parent UK£10, children under 18 free; lifetime UK£140.

Hostelling International Northern Ireland (HINI), 22-32 Donegall Rd., Belfast BT12 5JN, Northern Ireland (tel. (01232) 32 47 33 or 31 54 35; fax 43 96 99; email info@hini.org.uk; http://www.hini.org.uk). Prices range from UK£8-12. Membership packages: one-year UK£7, under 18 UK£3, family UK£14 for up to 6 children; lifetime UK£50.

Youth Hostels Association of New Zealand (YHANZ), P.O. Box 436, 173 Cashel St., Christchurch 1 (tel. (643) 379 9970; fax 365 4476; email info@yha.org.nz; http://www.yha.org.nz). Annual membership fee NZ$24.

Hostelling International South Africa, P.O. Box 4402, Cape Town 8000 (tel. (021) 24 25 11; fax 24 41 19; email info@hisa.org.za; http://www.hisa.org.za). Membership SAR50, group SAR120, family SAR100, lifetime SAR250.

DORMS

Many **colleges and universities** open their residence halls to travelers when school is not in session—some do so even during term-time. These dorms are often close to student areas, are good sources for information on things to do, places to stay, and possible rides out of town, and are usually very clean. Getting a room may be difficult, but rates tend to be low, and many offer free local calls. The *Campus Lodging Guide* details 609 university and college accommodation options around the world, in addition to more general accommodation information (available in bookstores or online).

HOME EXCHANGE AND RENTALS

Home exchange offers the traveler with various types of homes (houses, apartments, condominiums, villas, even castles in some cases) the opportunity to live like a native. Once you join or contact one of the exchange services listed below, it is then up to you to decide with whom you would like to exchange homes. The website http://www.aitec.edu.au/~bwechner/Documents/Travel/Lists/HomeExchangeClubs.html lists many exchange companies. **Home rentals,** as opposed to exchanges, are much more expensive, and most likely not an option for the budget traveler. But, they can be cheaper than comparably serviced hotels and are suitable for business travelers.

ESSENTIALS

....
KINGSBROOK SINCE *1985*
....

LEARN SPANISH IN BEAUTIFUL BARCELONA
BY THE SEA
Situated in heart of the city

* *12 – 20 HRS PER WEEK*
* *High Quality Teaching At All Levels*
* *Economic Rates*

* *Cultural Activities*
* *Accomodtion Assistance*
* *Airport Pick-Up Service*

Add: Travesera. de Gracia, 60, 1° 3ª
  08006 Barcelona SPAIN
Tel: 34-93-209.37.63
Fax: 34-93-202.15.98 e mail kingsb@ teleline.es

Learn Spanish in Spain

Make your vacation count.
Learn the language and
immerse yourself in Spanish life.
AN EXPERIENCE FOR LIFE !!!

MADRID

SALAMANCA

MÁLAGA

ESCUELA INTERNACIONAL
El Español, experiencia de vivir

Registration Center: C/Talamanca 10
28807 Alcalá de Henares - Madrid (Spain)
Tel: 34 91 883 12 64 - Fax: 34 91 883 13 01
Internet: www.ergos.es/escuelai
E-Mail: escuelai@ergos.es

- **Intensive Language Courses**
- **Learn in Small Groups**
- **Undergraduate Credit**
- **Variety of Housing Options**
- **Activities and Excursions**

ESSENTIALS

Intervac U.S., International & USA Home Exchange, P.O. Box 590504, San Francisco, CA 94159 (tel. (415) 435 3497; fax 435 7440; email IntervacUS@aol.com; http://www.intervac.com). Part of a worldwide home-exchange network. Catalogues list over 10,000 homes in countries worldwide, including Spain and Portugal. Members contact each other directly.

The Invented City: International Home Exchange, 41 Sutter St., Suite 1090, San Francisco, CA 94104 (tel. (800) 788 2489 in the U.S. or (415) 252 1141 elsewhere; fax (415) 252-1171; email invented@aol.com; http://www.invented-city.com). Listing of 1700 homes worldwide in various catalogues.

Hometours International, Inc., P.O. Box 11503, Knoxville, TN 37939 (tel. (800) 367 4668; email hometours@aol.com; http://thor.he.net/Íhometour/), offers various types of lodging in most of Europe, Spain, and Portugal. Brochures of listings are US$6 for each country.

■ Money

This book was researched in the summer of 1998. Since then, prices may have risen by as much as 5-15%. The **exchange rates** (listed in each country's **Essentials** section) were compiled in early September. Since rates fluctuate considerably, check before you go. In Spain the unit of currency is the *peseta* (ptas); in Portugal, the *escudo* ($); in Morocco, the *dirham* (dh).

CURRENCY AND EXCHANGE

If you stay in hostels, eat out at low-price establishments, and see a few sights, expect to spend around US$40 a day in **Spain,** slightly less in **Portugal,** and US$10 in **Morocco.** Intercity transportation and big cities will increase these figures. No matter your budget, you will probably want to carry some surplus cash so you don't get caught without it at night or on a weekend. Personal checks from home will probably not be accepted and even traveler's checks may not be accepted in some locations.

It is cheaper to buy domestic currency than to buy foreign, so as a rule you should convert money after arriving at your destination. However, converting some money before you go lets you avoid the poor exchange rates offered at Iberian airports and train stations. Morocco eases the process somewhat: rates are uniform and banks do not charge commission, so airport exchanges are fine. Still, bring enough foreign currency to last through the first 24 to 72 hours of a trip to avoid getting stuck with no money at night or on a holiday. In Spain and Portugal, banks generally have the best rates, but shop around. Check newspapers for the standard rate.

Banking hours in **Spain** from June through September are Monday through Friday 9am to 2pm; from October to May, banks are also open Saturday 9am to 1pm. Some banks are open in the afternoon as well. Banks charge a minimum commission for currency exchange. Banco Central Hispano often provides good rates, especially on traveller's checks. In **Portugal,** official hours are Monday through Friday 8:30am to 3pm, but play it safe by giving yourself some extra time. In **Morocco,** banking hours are Monday through Friday 8:30 to 11:30am and 2:30 to 4:30pm, during Ramadan from 9:30am to 2pm. In the summer, certain banks close at 1pm and do not re-open in the afternoon. **Exchange offices** often lie near transportation hubs and tend to have longer hours than banks. **Hotels** also often have longer hours but usually charge higher commissions, particularly when cashing traveler's checks. Especially in Morocco, do not try the **black market** for currency exchange—chances are good that you will be swindled.

To minimize losses from commissions, exchange large sums at once, but never more than you can safely carry around or plan to spend. Converting back to your home currency is a waste of money. In Morocco, converting *dirhams* back into dollars is difficult.

TRAVELER'S CHECKS

Traveler's checks are one of the safest and least troublesome means of carrying funds. All checks can be refunded if stolen, and many provide such additional snazzy services as toll-free refund hotlines, emergency message services, and stolen credit card assistance. **American Express** and **Visa** are the most widely recognized, although other major checks are sold, exchanged, cashed, and refunded almost as easily. Regardless of the type, checks are easier to cash in big cities and when denominated in U.S. dollars. Still, across Spain and Portugal there will be at least one place in every town where you can trade your checks for local currency. In Morocco, smaller and more rural establishments may only recognize American Express, if anything at all.

Refunds on lost or stolen checks can be time-consuming. To expedite the process, ask for a list of refund centers when you buy your checks (Bank of America and American Express have over 40,000), leave a list of check numbers with someone at home, store your check receipts in a safe place separate from your checks, and record check numbers when you cash them. Keep a separate supply of cash or traveler's checks for emergencies, never countersign your checks until you are ready to cash them, and always bring your passport with you when you plan to use the checks.

American Express: Call (800) 25 19 02 in Australia; in New Zealand (0800) 44 10 68; in the U.K. (0800) 52 13 13; in the U.S. and Canada (800) 221 7282. Elsewhere, call U.S. collect (801) 964 6665. American Express traveler's checks are now available in 10 currencies: Australian, British, Canadian, Dutch, French, German, Japanese, Saudi Arabian, Swiss, and U.S. They are the most widely recognized worldwide and the easiest to replace if lost or stolen. Checks can be purchased for a small fee (1-4%) at American Express Travel Service Offices and banks. Cardmembers can also buy checks at American Express Dispensers at airport Travel Service Offices, or order them by phone (tel. (800) 673 3782). American Express offices cash their checks commission-free, although they often offer slightly worse rates than banks. You can also buy *Cheques for Two,* which can be signed by either of two people traveling together. Request the American Express booklet *Traveler's Companion,* which lists travel office addresses and stolen check hotlines for each European country. Visit their online travel offices (http://www.aexp.com).

Citicorp: In the U.S. and Canada call (800) 645 6556; in Europe, the Middle East, or Africa (44) 171 508 7007; from elsewhere call U.S. collect (813) 623 1709. Sells both Citicorp and Citicorp Visa traveler's checks in **Spanish pesetas,** U.S., Australian, and Canadian dollars, British pounds, German marks, and Japanese yen. Commission is 1-2% on check purchases. Citicorp's World Courier Service guarantees hand-delivery of traveler's checks when a refund location is not convenient. Open 24hr.

Thomas Cook MasterCard: For 24hr. cashing or refund assistance: from the U.S., Canada, or Caribbean call (800) 223 7373; from the U.K. call (0800) 622 101 free or (1733) 318 950 collect; from anywhere else call (44) 1733 318 950 collect. Offers checks in U.S., Canadian, and Australian dollars, British and Cypriot pounds, French and Swiss francs, German marks, Japanese yen, Dutch guilders, **Spanish pesetas,** South African rand, and Euros. 2% commission for purchases. Thomas Cook offices cash checks commission-free; banks will charge commission.

Visa: Call (800) 227 6811 in the U.S.; in the U.K. (0800) 895 078; from anywhere else in the world call (44) 1733 318 949 and reverse the charges. Any of the above numbers can tell you the location of their nearest office. Any type of Visa traveler's checks can be reported lost at the Visa number.

CREDIT CARDS

In Spain and Portugal, credit cards are sporadically accepted at local establishments, including budget lodgings, restaurants, and supermarkets—more often in big cities. Larger stores, chain stores, and upmarket accomodations almost always accept credit cards. In Morocco, count on credit cards only for airfare, major hotels, and other international organizations. Major credit cards—**MasterCard, Visa, Eurocheque,** and **American Express**—are the most often welcomed and can be used to extract cash advances from associated banks and teller machines throughout Spain, Portugal, and

ESSENTIALS

Morocco. Credit card companies get the wholesale exchange rate, which is generally 5% better than the retail rate used by banks; although some fees usually apply, on the whole credit cards tend to offer a better deal than cash or travellers' checks. All such machines require a **Personal Identification Number (PIN).** If you do not have one, you must ask your credit card company for a PIN before you leave; without it, you will be unable to withdraw cash with your credit card outside the U.S. MasterCard and Visa have different names elsewhere ("EuroCard" or "Access" for MasterCard, "Carte Bleue" or "Barclaycard" for Visa). Don't rely exclusively on one credit card however; teller machines have been known to swallow credit cards whole.

Credit cards are also invaluable in an emergency—an unexpected hospital bill, ticket home, or the loss of traveler's checks—that may leave you temporarily without other resources. Furthermore, credit cards offer an array of other services, from insurance to emergency assistance, that depend completely on the issuer. **American Express** (U.S. tel. (800) 843 2273) has a hefty annual fee (US$55) but offers excellent traveler support services. AmEx cardholders can cash personal checks at AmEx offices outside the U.S. and have mail held for them at over 1700 AmEx offices worldwide. **Visa** (U.S. tel. (800) 336 8472) and **MasterCard** services depend on the issuing organization—call the issuer for more information.

CASH CARDS

Cash cards—popularly called ATM (Automated Teller Machine) cards—are widespread in Spain, Portugal, and, to a lesser extent, Morocco. Depending on the system that your bank at home uses, you can probably access your own personal bank account whenever you need money. Be careful, however, and keep all receipts, even if an ATM won't give you your cash, it may register a withdrawal on your next statement. Happily, ATMs get the same wholesale exchange rate as credit cards. Despite these perks, do some research before relying too heavily on automation. There is often a limit on the amount of money you can withdraw per day, and computer networks sometimes fail. Memorize your PIN code in numeral form since machines outside the U.S. and Canada often don't have letters on their keys. Also, if your PIN is longer than four digits, ask your bank whether the first four digits will work, or whether you need a new number.

The two major international money networks are **Cirrus** (U.S. tel. (800) 424 7787) and **PLUS.** Look for their symbols on ATM displays. For a worldwide ATM unit locator go to http://www.visa.com. Cirrus has cash machines in 80 countries and territories. PLUS covers 115 countries. Carrying one card for each network will provide maximum coverage. There are also helpful websites that allow you to locate Visa and MC ATMs around the world: http://www.visa.com/cgi-bion/vee/pd/atm/main.html and http://www.mastercard.com.atm, respectively.

In larger cities in Spain and Portugal, you may stumble across handy, high-tech **automatic exchange machines.** These ATM-like machines exchange U.S. dollar bills for *pesetas* or *escudos;* unfortunately, they tend to offer inferior exchange rates.

MONEY FROM HOME

Sending money overseas is expensive and often frustrating. Do your best to avoid it by carrying a credit card or a separate stash of emergency travelers' checks. The **American Express** card, in addition to allowing withdrawals at over 100,000 Express Cash ATMs, allows cardholders to draw cash from their checking accounts at any of its major offices (no service charge, no interest). Unless using the AmEx service, avoid cashing checks in foreign currencies.

Money can also be wired abroad through international money transfer services operated by **Western Union** (U.S. tel. (800) 325 6000 for locations and info). The money should be available for pick-up, assuming a local office is open, in 15 minutes.

Some people also choose to send money abroad in cash via **Federal Express** to avoid transmission fees and taxes. FedEx is reasonably reliable; however, this method may be illegal, it involves an element of risk, and it requires that you remain at a legitimate address for a day or two to wait for the money's arrival. In general, it may be safer to swallow the cost of wire transmission and preserve your peace of mind.

In emergencies, U.S. citizens can have money sent via the State Department's **Overseas Citizens Service, American Citizens Services,** Consular Affairs, Room 4811, U.S. Department of State, Washington, D.C. 20520 (tel. (202) 647 5225; nights, Sundays, and holidays 647 4000; email ca@his.com; http://travel.state.gov). For a fee of US$15, the State Department will forward money within hours to the nearest consular office, which will disburse it according to instructions. The office serves only Americans in the direst of straits abroad; non-American travelers should contact their embassies for information on wiring cash. Check with the State Department or the nearest U.S. embassy or consulate for the quickest way to have the money sent.

■ Safety and Security

Emergency phone numbers are **091** and **092** for **Spain** (although in an assertion of regionalism, some provinces are now changing them), **112** in **Portugal,** and **19** and **15** in **Morocco.** On our **maps,** police stations are represented by a exclamation mark (!), hospitals by a cross (+).

PERSONAL SAFETY

Tourists are particularly vulnerable to crime for two reasons: they often carry large amounts of cash and they are not as street savvy as locals. To prevent easy theft, don't keep all of your money or important documents in one place. To avoid unwanted attention, try to **blend in** as much as possible. Respecting local customs may placate would-be hecklers. The gawking camera-toter is a more obvious target than the low-profile traveler. Familiarize yourself with your surroundings before setting out; if you must check a map on the streets, duck into a cafe or shop. Also, carry yourself with confidence. If you look nervous, anxious, or scared, you are more vulnerable.

When exploring a new city, extra vigilance is wise. Find out about unsafe areas from tourist offices, from the manager of your hotel or hostel, or from a local whom you trust. Memorize the emergency number of the city or area you're in at the time. You may want to carry a **whistle** to scare off attackers or attract attention. **Never admit that you're traveling alone,** and if you are, be sure that someone at home knows your itinerary. When walking at night, stick to busy, well-lit streets and don't attempt to cross through deserted areas such as parks and beaches.

Whenever possible, *Let's Go* warns of unsafe neighborhoods and areas, but you should exercise your own judgment and intuition about the safety of your environs. The distribution of people can reveal a great deal about the relative safety of the area; look for children playing, women walking in the open, and other signs of an active community. But don't allow fear of the unknown to turn you into a hermit. Especially in Iberia, explore like there is no tomorrow; just do it with common sense.

Motor vehicle crashes are a leading cause of travel deaths in many parts of the world, so learn local driving signals and practices, and wear a seatbelt. **Sleeping in your car** is one of the most dangerous (and often illegal) ways to get your rest. *Let's Go* does not recommend **hitchhiking** under any circumstances, particularly for women—see **Getting There,** p. 34 for more information.

There is no sure-fire set of precautions that will protect you from all of the situations you might encounter when you travel. A good self-defense course will give you more concrete ways to react to different types of aggression. **Impact, Prepare, and Model Mugging** can refer you to local self-defense courses in the United States (tel. (800) 345 5425), Vancouver, Canada (tel. (604) 878 3838), and Zurich, Switzerland (tel. (411) 261 2423). Workshop and course prices range from US$50-500. Women's and men's courses are offered.

For official travel information and advisories contact: the **Australian Department of Foreign Affairs and Trade** (tel. (2) 6261 9111; http://www.dfat.gov.au); the **Canadian Department of Foreign Affairs and International Trade** (tel. (800) 267 8376;

http://www.dfait-maeci.gc.ca); the **United Kingdom Foreign and Commonwealth Office** (tel. (0171) 238 4503; http://www.fco.gov.uk); or the **United States Department of State** (24hr. tel. (202) 647 5225; http://travel.state.gov).

FINANCIAL SECURITY

Be careful and aware—petty street crime is the plague of tourists. Among the more colorful aspects of large cities are **con artists.** Hustlers often work in groups, and children are among the most effective. Be aware of certain classics: sob stories that require money, rolls of bills "found" on the street, or any distractions to allow them enough time to snatch your bag. Be especially suspicious in unexpected situations. Contact the police if a hustler is particularly insistent or aggressive. Morocco is the worst of the three countries with respect to such shenanigans (see p. 589).

In phonebooths, calling-card numbers can be overheard or seen as you are calling, while city crowds and public transportation are heaven for pickpockets. Don't put a wallet in your back pocket. Never count your money in public and carry as little as feasible. If you carry a purse, buy a sturdy one with a secure clasp, and carry it crosswise on the side away from the street with the clasp against you. Secure packs with small combination padlocks that slip through the two zippers. A **money belt** is the best way to carry cash; you can buy one at most camping supply stores or through the Forsyth Travel Library (see **Travel Publications,** p. 3). As said previously, **photocopy** any important document—bring one with you, leave another at home.

On **buses,** carry your backpack in front of you where you can see it and don't check baggage on **trains.** It's wise to buy a lock to secure your pack to the luggage rack. When traveling in pairs, sleep in alternating shifts. Keep important documents and other valuables on your person and try to sleep on top bunks with your luggage stored above you (if not in bed with you). Never leave your belongings unattended. *Let's Go* lists locker availability in hostels and train stations, but you'll need your own padlock. Lockers are useful, but don't store valuables in them.

Travel Assistance International by Worldwide Assistance Services, Inc. (tel. (800) 821 2828; fax (202) 828 5896; email wassist@aol.com; http://www.worldwide-assistance.com) provides its members with a 24-hour hotline for travel emergencies and referrals in over 200 countries, including Spain, Portugal, and Morocco. The **American Society of Travel Agents** provides extensive informational resources at their website (http://www.astanet.com).

DRUGS AND ALCOHOL

Laws vary from country to country, but, needless to say, **illegal drugs** are best avoided altogether; the average sentence for possession outside the U.S. is about seven years. You are subject to the laws of the country in which you travel, not to those of your home country, and it is your responsibility to familiarize yourself with these laws before leaving. In Spain, Portugal, and Morocco all recreational drugs—including marijuana—are illegal. Buying or selling *any* type of drug may lead to a hefty prison sentence. A meek "I didn't know it was illegal" will not suffice. In Morocco, foreigners with drugs have regularly been arrested and faced severe punishments. Keep in mind that although drugs may seem more prevalent in Morocco, the Moroccan government enforces drug laws more strictly than most governments and frequently uses road-blocks and other measures to search for drug peddlers and users. If you carry **prescription drugs** while you travel, it is vital to have a copy of the prescriptions themselves readily accessible at country borders.

Avoid public drunkenness. It can jeopardize your safety and earn the disdain of locals. In Spain and Portugal, for instance, although consuming alcohol may be a national pastime, flat-out drunkenness is definitely frowned upon.

■ Health

Common sense is the simplest prescription for good health while you travel: eat well, drink and sleep enough, and don't overexert yourself. Travelers complain most often about their feet and their gut, so take precautionary measures. Drinking lots of fluids can often prevent dehydration and constipation, and wearing sturdy shoes and clean socks can help keep your feet dry and comfortable. To minimize the effects of jet lag, "reset" your body's clock by adopting the time of your destination immediately upon arrival. On the whole, Spain and Portugal conform to most Western standards of health, while Morocco—although better than most of Africa—presents more potential health-care hassles. *Let's Go* lists information on how to access 24-hour pharmacies in every major town or city.

BEFORE YOU GO

Although no amount of planning can guarantee an accident-free trip, preparation can help minimize the likelihood of contracting a disease and maximize the chances of receiving effective health-care in the event of an emergency.

For minor health problems, bring a compact **first-aid kit,** including, as a minimum, bandages, aspirin or other pain killer, antibiotic cream, and a Swiss Army knife.

In your passport, write the names of any people you wish to be contacted in case of a medical emergency, and also list any medical conditions of which doctors should be aware. If you wear glasses or contact lenses, carry an extra prescription and pair of glasses. **Allergy** sufferers should find out if their conditions are likely to be aggravated in the regions they plan to visit and obtain a full supply of any necessary medication before the trip, since matching a prescription to a foreign equivalent is not always easy, safe, or possible. Carry up-to-date, legible prescriptions.

Take a look at your **immunization** records before you go; some countries, though not Spain, Portugal, or Morocco, require visitors to carry vaccination certificates. Be sure that the following vaccines are up to date: Measles, Mumps, and Rubella; Diptheria, Tetanus, and Pertussis; Polio; Haemophilus Influenza B; and Hepatitis B. A booster of Tetanus-diptheria (Td) is recommended once every 10 years. Hepatitis A vaccine and/or Immune Globulin (IG) is recommended for travelers to Morocco.

Check that **Morocco** still does not require any health particulars, like a yellow fever vaccination certificate, as do most African countries. Traveling in Africa puts you at a statistically higher risk for typhoid fever, Hepatitis A, parasites, or Hepatitis B (see below). Generally, "tourist" itineraries—meaning visits to modern, densely populated cities and minimal mixing with rural populations—put you at less risk.

For up-to-date information about which vaccinations are recommended for your destination and region-specific health data, try the following resources. The **United States Centers for Disease Control and Prevention** (tel. (888) 232 3299; http://www.cdc.gov) and the **United States State Department** (http://travel.state.gov) compile info on health, entry requirements, and other issues for all countries of the world. For quick information on travel warnings, call **Overseas Citizens' Services** (U.S. tel. (202) 647 5225). Embassies and consulates provide the same data. If you are HIV positive, call in the U.S. (202) 647 1488 for country-specific entry requirements.

Those with medical conditions (e.g., diabetes, allergies to antibiotics, epilepsy, heart conditions) may want to obtain a stainless steel **Medic Alert** (tel. (800) 825 3785) identification tag (US$35), which identifies the disease and gives a 24-hour collect-call information number. Diabetics can contact the **American Diabetes Association** (tel. (800) 232 3472) to receive helpful information and a diabetic ID card, which carries messages in 18 languages explaining the carrier's diabetic status.

If you are concerned about being able to access medical support while traveling, contact one of these two services: **Global Emergency Medical Services** (tel. (800) 860 1111; fax (770) 475 0058) has products called *MedPass* that provide 24-hour international medical assistance and support, and a worldwide network of screened, credentialed English-speaking doctors and hospitals. The **International Association for Medical Assistance to Travelers (IAMAT)** offers a directory of English-speaking doctors around the world among other services. Membership is free. Contact chapters in the **U.S.** (tel. (716) 754 4883; fax (519) 836 3412; email iamat@sentex.net; http://www.sentex.net/~iamat), **Canada** (tel. (416) 652 0137; fax (519) 836 3412), or **New Zealand,** P.O. Box 5049, Christchurch 5.

You don't want to purchase **unnecessary travel coverage,** but if your regular insurance policy does not cover travel abroad, you may wish to purchase additional coverage; check with your insurance carrier to be sure (See **Insurance,** p. 23).

ON-THE-ROAD AILMENTS

You can minimize the chances of contracting a disease while traveling by taking a few precautionary measures. In general, listen to your body—rest when you need to, and don't give a nagging injury the chance to turn into something more serious.

Heat and Cold

Iberia and Morocco can be scorching at times, especially in the summer. Common sense goes a long way toward preventing **heat exhaustion:** relax in hot weather, drink lots of non-alcoholic fluids, and lie down inside if you feel awful. Continuous heat stress can eventually lead to **heatstroke,** characterized by rising body temperature, severe headache, and cessation of sweating. Wear a hat, sunglasses, and a lightweight longsleeve shirt to avoid heatstroke. Victims must be cooled off with wet towels and taken to a doctor as soon as possible.

Always drink enough liquids to keep your urine clear. Alcoholic beverages are dehydrating, as are coffee, strong tea, and caffeinated sodas. If you'll be sweating a lot, be sure to eat enough salty food to prevent electrolyte depletion, which causes severe headaches and worse. Less debilitating, but still dangerous, is **sunburn.** Bring sunscreen with you and apply it liberally.

Extreme cold is just as dangerous as heat—overexposure to cold brings the risk of **hypothermia.** Though not as much of a danger, be careful in the northern regions of Spain and Portugal and at high altitudes. Warning signs are easy to detect. Body temperature drops rapidly, resulting in the failure to produce body heat, and victims may shiver, have poor coordination, feel exhausted, have slurred speech, feel sleepy, hallucinate, or suffer amnesia. *Do not let hypothermia victims fall asleep.* Dress the victims in layers, and watch for **frostbite** when the temperature is below freezing.

Food- and Water-Borne Diseases

In Iberia, **tap water** should be fine, although be more careful in rural areas. In Morocco the water is not as friendly. *Sidi Ali* and *Sidi Harazem* are heavily chlorinated mineral waters, available for about 5dh per 1.5L bottle. To make sure you're not getting tap water, insist on breaking the plastic seal on the bottled water yourself before paying. Also remember that if you can't drink the water, you can't suck the ice. Hikers in all countries should beware of the dreaded parasite giardia (see below).

Food- and water-borne diseases are the number-one cause of illness in North Africa, so watch out. **Food poisoning,** particularly, can spoil your trip. Street vendors, especially in more run-down locales or Morocco, may sell aged or otherwise bad food; avoid unpeeled fruits and vegetables, in particular hard-to-wash greens. To ensure that your food is safe, make sure that everything is cooked properly (deep-fried is good, for once), and be positive the water you drink is clean. Don't order meat "rare," and make sure that eggs are thoroughly cooked, not served sunny-side up. In any case, any food to which you are not accustomed—such as rarer meat in Portugal or the oil- and grease-fest that defines many Spanish dishes—can cause stomach troubles.

Traveler's diarrhea is one dastardly consequence of ignoring the warnings against drinking untreated water. At highest risk are visitors to Morocco and the Canary Islands. Symptoms include diarrhea, nausea, bloating, urgency, and malaise. If the nasties hit you, have quick-energy, non-sugary foods with protein and carbohydrates. Over-the-counter remedies (such as Pepto-Bismol or Immodium A-1) may counteract the problems, but they can complicate serious infections. Avoid anti-diarrheals if you suspect you have been exposed to contaminated food or water, which puts you at risk for other diseases. The most dangerous side effect of diarrhea is dehydration; the simplest and most effective anti-dehydration formula is 8 ounces of (clean) water with some sugar and a bit of salt. If you develop a fever or your symptoms don't go away after four or five days (or if a child develops any symptoms), consult a doctor.

Typhoid Fever is common in villages and rural areas in North Africa. While mostly transmitted through contaminated food and water, it may also be acquired by direct contact with another person. Symptoms include fever, headaches, fatigue, loss of appetite, constipation, and a rash on the abdomen or chest; antibiotics treat typhoid fever. The Center for Disease Control and Prevention recommends vaccinations (70-90% effective) if you will be going outside the "usual tourist itineraries," that is, hiking, camping, and staying in small cities or rural areas.

Parasites (tapeworms, etc.) hide in unsafe water and food. **Giardia** is acquired by drinking untreated water from streams or lakes all over the world, including Western Europe and North Africa. It can stay with you for years. Symptoms of parasitic infections in general include swollen glands or lymph nodes, fever, rashes or itchiness, digestive problems, eye problems, and anemia. Boil your water, wear shoes, avoid bugs, and eat only cooked food.

All travelers are at risk of contracting **Hepatitis A** and **Hepatitis B;** vaccines for both diseases are a good idea regardless of where you are. Hepatitis A is acquired primarily through contaminated food and water (and also unprotected sex). Hepatitis B is transmitted by unprotected sex, sharing needles, or directly touching another person's lesioned skin. If you think you may be sexually active while traveling or if you are working or living in rural areas, you are typically advised to get the vaccination for Hepatitis B. Vaccination should begin six months before traveling. **Hepatitis C** is like Hepatitis B, but transmission occurs primarily through exposure to blood.

Animal- and Insect- Borne Disease

Often animals are not given shots, so that sweet-faced pooch at your feet might very well be disease-ridden. If you are bitten, be concerned about **rabies**—be sure to clean your wound thoroughly and seek medical help immediately.

Many diseases are transmitted by insects—mainly mosquitoes, fleas, ticks, and lice. **Mosquitoes** are most active from dusk to dawn. Wear long pants, long sleeves, and shoes and socks and buy a bednet for camping. Use insect repellents. Calamine lotion or topical cortisones (like Cortaid©) may stop insect bites from itching.

Ticks can be particularly dangerous in rural and forested regions all over Europe. Make sure none have landed on you. **Tick-borne encephalitis** is primarily transmitted during the summer by tick bites. A vaccine is available in Europe, but the risk of contracting the disease is relatively low. Ticks also carry the infamous **Lyme disease,** a bacterial infection marked by a circular bull's-eye rash of 2 in. or more that appears around the bite. Antibiotics are effective if administered early; left untreated, Lyme can cause serious problems in joints. If you do find a tick attached to your skin, grasp the tick's head parts with tweezers as close to your skin as possible and apply slow, steady traction. Removing ticks before they have been attached for more than 24 hours greatly reduces the risk of infection. The risk of both dieseases is greatest when hiking through the forests of Europe.

In Morocco, there is a very limited risk of contracting **malaria.** You do not need to take malaria prevention pills if you stick to a tourist itinerary. Malaria is transmitted by Anopheles mosquitoes that bite during the night. If you plan to hike or stay overnight in more rural, less-populated areas (whether camping or not), you may want to take weekly anti-malarial drugs. Contact your doctor for a prescription.

WOMEN'S HEALTH

Women traveling in unsanitary conditions are vulnerable to urinary tract and bladder infections, common and severely uncomfortable bacterial diseases that cause a burning sensation and painful, and sometimes frequent, urination. To help alleviate symptoms, drink tons of vitamin-C-rich juice (cranberry juice for a urinary tract infection), and plenty of clean water, and urinate frequently, especially right after intercourse. Do not, however, use these methods to *treat* an infection—see a doctor. If left untreated, these infections can be potentially life-threatening. In hot and humid climates, women may also be more susceptible to vaginal thrush and cystitis, two treatable but uncomfortable illnesses. Wearing loosely fitting trousers or a skirt and cotton underwear may help. Tampons (*tampones* in Spanish) and pads *(paños higiénicos)* are sometimes hard to find when traveling, so take some extra supplies along. Refer to the *Handbook for Women Travellers* by Maggie and Gemma Moss or to the women's health guide *Our Bodies, Our Selves* for more extensive info specific to women's health on the road (both available in bookstores or online).

BIRTH CONTROL

Reliable contraceptive devices may be difficult to find while traveling. Women on the pill should bring enough to allow for possible loss or extended stays. Bring a prescription, since forms of the pill vary a good deal. Women who use a diaphragm should have enough contraceptive jelly on hand. Although condoms are increasingly available, you might want to bring extra before you go; availability and quality vary. For info on contraception, condoms, and **abortion** worldwide, contact the **International Planned Parenthood Federation,** European Regional Office, Regent's College Inner Circle, Regent's Park, London NW1 4NS (tel. (0171) 487 7900; fax 487 7950).

STDS, AIDS, AND HIV

Acquired Immune Deficiency Syndrome (AIDS) is a growing problem around the world. The World Health Organization reports that there are 30 million people infected with the HIV virus worldwide. In Spain, 13% of adults newly infected with HIV became infected through heterosexual sex. In Portugal and Morocco, 26% and 89%, respectively, of adults newly infected with HIV become infected through heterosexual sex. Women represent 40% of all new HIV infections worldwide. The easiest mode of HIV transmission is direct blood to blood contact with an HIV+ person, but the most common mode of transmission is sexual intercourse. Health professionals recommend the use of latex condoms. Some countries do screen incoming travelers, primarily those planning extended visits for work or study, and deny entrance to HIV+ people. Contact a relevant consulate for info about this policy.

Sexually transmitted diseases (STDs) such as gonorrhea, chlamydia, genital warts, syphilis, and herpes are a lot easier to catch than HIV. Gonorrhea, chlamydia, and syphilis can be just as serious as HIV if left untreated; fortunately, these diseases are easily treatable if caught in time. There is no cure for herpes or genital warts. Warning signs for STDs include: swelling, sores, bumps, or blisters on sex organs, rectum, or mouth; burning and pain during urination and bowel movements; itching around sex organs; swelling or redness in the throat; and flu-like symptoms with fever, chills, and aches. If these symptoms develop, see a doctor immediately. Condoms may protect you from certain STDs, but oral or even tactile contact can lead to transmission.

■ Insurance

Travel insurance covers four basic areas: medical/ health problems, property loss, trip cancellation/interruption, and emergency evacuation. Beware of buying unnecessary travel coverage—your regular insurance policies may well extend to travel-related medical problems and property loss. Consider purchasing travel insurance if the cost of potential trip cancellation/interruption is greater than you can absorb.

Medical insurance (especially university policies) often covers costs incurred abroad; check with your provider. **Homeowners' insurance** (or your family's coverage) often covers theft during travel. **ISIC** and **ITIC** provide basic insurance benefits, including US$100 per day of in-hospital sickness for a maximum of 60 days, and US$3000 of accident-related medical reimbursement (see **Youth, Student, and Teacher Identification,** p. 10). Cardholders have access to a toll-free 24-hour helpline that provides assistance in medical, legal, and financial emergencies overseas (call in

Bring home more than photos and souvenirs...
Live a Language & Learn a Culture

Español en España

● Salamanca ● Madrid ● Barcelona

Beginner to advanced,
we offer 2, 3, 4, 6, 8, 10 and 12 week
language & culture immersion programs
all year long.
Explore *España* as a local.
Host family and apartment homestays
available

Students of all ages from around the
world study 20-30 hours per week.
Optional excursions, and afternoon
classes in ART, HISTORY or
BUSINESS
Intensive instruction or holiday
experiential learning

Call (800) 648-4809 for prospectus
http://www.eurocentres.com Email: alx-info@eurocentres.com

EUROCENTRES
Language Learning Worldwide

Vacation 'N Learn

LEARN A LANGUAGE WHERE IT IS SPOKEN

Argentina • Austria
Brazil • Canada • Chile
China • Costa Rica
Czechoslovakia • Ecuador
France • Germany

Guatemala • Hungary
Israel • Italy • Japan • Mexico
Portugal • Russia • Spain
Sweden • Switzerland
Taiwan • Venezuela

Intensive Language and Culture Courses

■ Accommodations in selected homestays,
apartments, hotels, dormitories.
■ Programs for all ages, interests and budgets.
■ Short and long term programs.

■ Vacation 'N Learn with us any time of the year!
■ Combine your course with golf, skiing, cooking, or art.
■ Academic credit available.
■ http://www.itctravel.com

Call for a FREE brochure:
LINGUA SERVICE WORLDWIDE℠
211 East 43rd St., Suite 1303, New York, NY 10017 • 212-867-1225 • FAX 212-983-2590

1-800-394-LEARN

the U.S. (713) 267 2525). **Council** (see p. 3) and **Campus** and **STA** (see p. 36) offer a range of plans that can supplement basic insurance coverage.

Remember that insurance companies usually require a copy of the police report for thefts, or evidence of having paid medical expenses (doctor's statements, receipts) before they will honor a claim and may have time limits on filing for reimbursement. Always carry policy numbers and proof of insurance.

The Berkely Group/Carefree Travel Insurance, 100 Garden City Plaza, P.O. Box 9366, Garden City, NY 11530-9366 (tel. (800) 323 3149 or (516) 294 0220; fax 294 1095; info@berkely.com; http://www.berkely.com). Offers comprehensive packages. 24hr. hotline.

Globalcare Travel Insurance, 220 Broadway, Lynnfield, MA 01940 (tel. (800) 821 2488; fax (617) 592 7720); email global@nebc.mv.com; http://www.nebc.mv.com/globalcare. Complete medical, legal, emergency, and travel-related services. On-the-spot payments and special student programs.

Travel Assistance International, by Worldwide Assistance Services, Inc., 1133 15th St. NW, Suite 400, Washington, D.C. 20005-2710 (tel. (800) 821 2828 or (202) 828 5894; fax 828 5896; email wassist@aol.com; http://www.worldwide-assistance.com). Per-Trip and Frequent Traveler plans.

■ Alternatives to Tourism

STUDY ABROAD

For a college experience with spice, look into studying abroad. Foreign study programs vary tremendously in expense, academic quality, living conditions, degree of contact with local students, and exposure to local culture and languages. To immerse yourself in **Spain** in such a way, try U.S. university programs and youth organizations that set students up at Spanish universities and language centers for foreign students. Ask for the names of recent participants in the programs, and get in touch with them. If you are fluent, enroll directly in a Spanish colleges (non-Spanish students have practically taken over Salamanca). Most universities in **Portugal** open their gates to foreign students, and foreigners can enter language and cultural studies programs at most of them. Foreign language schools include **Eurocentres** (tel. (800) 648-4809; fax (703) 684 1495); http://www.eurocentres.com), which offers language programs for all levels in Spain. In Europe contact them at Seestrasse 247, CH-8038 Zurich, Switzerland (tel. (411) 485 50 40; fax 481 61 24).

American Field Service (AFS), 310 SW 4th Avenue, Suite 630, Portland, OR 97204-2608 (tel. (800) 237 4636; fax (503) 241 1653; email afsinfo@afs.org; http//www.afs.org/usa). AFS offers summer, semester, and year-long homestay international exchange programs for high school students and graduating high school seniors. Financial aid available. Exchanges in Portugal and Spain.

American Institute for Foreign Study, College Division, 102 Greenwich Ave., Greenwich, CT 06830 (tel. (800) 727 2437, ext. 6084; http://www.aifs.com). Organizes programs for high school and college study in universities in Spain. Summer, fall, spring, and year-long programs available. Scholarships available.

Education Office of Spain, 150 5th Ave., Suite 918, New York, NY 10011 (tel. (212) 741 5144 or 741 5145); and in the education office of the Spanish Embassy in Washington, D.C. British residents may contact the education Office in the Spanish Embassy in London (see **Embassies and Consulates,** p. 5).

Peterson's, P.O. Box 2123, Princeton, NJ 08543-2123 (tel. (800) 338 3282; fax (609) 243 9150; http://www.petersons.com). Their comprehensive *Study Abroad* annual guide lists programs in countries all over the world and provides essential information on the study abroad experience in general.

Discover
A New World Today!

Learn Spanish in Spain, México, Central and South America

- Classes starting throughout the year
- Small group and private instruction
- Accommodations with host families
- Cultural Activities

- Excursions
- Academic Credit
- Airport Pickup
- Flight Info
- Country Info
- Plus Much More!

Spanish Abroad, Inc.
Toll Free: 888.722.7623
World Wide: 602.947.4652   fax: 602.840.1545
email: info@spanishabroad.com   www.spanishabroad.com
6520 N. 41st St. Paradise Valley, AZ 85253 USA

▼ ▼ ▼ ▼ ▼ Learn Spanish ▼ ▼ ▼ ▼ ▼

Spain • Costa Rica • Guatemala • Honduras
Panamá • El Salvador • Argentina • Chile
Ecuador • Peru • Uruguay • Venezuela • Bolivia
Puerto Rico • Dominican Republic • México

- ▼ Learn Spanish the RIGHT way FAST
- ▼ For all ages and all levels
- ▼ Most programs start on Mondays year round
- ▼ Private tutor or small groups
- ▼ 3-8 hours/day
- ▼ Volunteer and intern options
- ▼ Academic credit available
- ▼ Pre-departure assistance
- ▼ Free travel insurance

AmeriSpan Unlimited
THE BRIDGE BETWEEN CULTURES

Call for free information USA & Canada 1-800-879-6640 • Worldwide 215-751-1100
FAX 215-751-1986 • USA offices: P.O.Box 40007, Philadelphia, PA 19106-0007
Guatemala Office: 6a Avenida Norte #40, Antigua, Guatemala. Tel/Fax 011-502-8-320-164
Email.... info@amerispan.com • WWWeb... http://www.amerispan.com

WORK

There's no better way to submerge yourself in a foreign culture than to become part of its economy. It's easy to find a **temporary job,** but it will rarely be glamorous and may not even pay for your plane fare. Officially, you can hold a job in Iberia and Morocco only with a **work permit.** Your employer must obtain this document—not always the easiest of tasks. Friends in your destination country can help expedite work permits or arrange work-for-accommodations swaps. Many permit-less agricultural workers go untroubled by local authorities. European Union citizens can work in any E.U. country, and if your parents were born in an E.U. country, you may be able to claim dual citizenship or at least the right to a work permit. Students can check with their universities' foreign language departments, which may have connections to job openings abroad. Peterson's (see **Study Abroad,** p. 25) also publishes a Vacation Work series with titles that include *Overseas Summer Jobs 1999, Work Your Way Around the World, Teaching English Abroad,* and *The International Directory of Volunteer Work,* available in bookstores or online.

Childcare International, Ltd. (tel. (0181) 959 36 11 or 906 31 16; fax 906 34 61; email office@childint.demon.co.uk; http://www.childint.demon.co.uk) offers au pair positions in Spain. UK£80 application fee.

InterExchange (tel. (212) 924 0446; fax 924 0575; email interex@earthlink.net; http://www.interexchange.org) offers au pair and teaching opportunities in Spain.

International Schools Services, Educational Staffing Program, P.O. Box 5910, Princeton, NJ 08543 (tel. (609) 452 0990; fax 452 2690; email edustaffing@iss.edu; http://www.iss.edu), recruits qualified teachers and administrators for schools in Africa and Europe. Publishes *The ISS Directory of Overseas Schools.*

Targus-Youth Student Travel (see **Budget Travel Agencies,** p. 36) has *muito* (lots of) info on paid and volunteer work in Portugal.

Surrey Books (tel. (800) 326 4430; fax (312) 751 7330; email SurreyBk@aol.com, http://www.surreybooks.com) publishes *How to Get a Job in Europe: The Insider's Guide* (1995 edition US$18).

Transitions Abroad Publishing, Inc. (tel. (800) 293 0373; fax (413) 256 0373; email trabroad@aol.com; http://www.transabroad.com). Publishes a bi-monthly magazine listing endless opportunities for those seeking to study, work, or travel abroad. They also publish *Work Abroad,* a comprehensive guide to finding and preparing for a job overseas.

VOLUNTEERING

Volunteer jobs are readily available almost everywhere. You may receive room and board in exchange for your labor; the work can be fascinating (or stultifying). You can sometimes avoid the high application fees charged by the organizations that arrange placement by contacting the individual workcamps directly; check with the organizations. Listings in Vacation Work Publications's *International Directory of Voluntary Work* (UK£9) can be helpful (see below).

Council (see **Travel Organizations,** p. 3) has a Voluntary Services Department that offers 2- to 4-week environmental community service, renovation, or archaeological projects in Spain and Morocco. Minimum US$275 placement fee (if you book your airfare through Council); students get 20-50% off.

Experiment in International Living, Summer Programs, Kipling Rd., P.O. Box 676, Brattleboro, VT 05302 (tel. (800) 345 2929; fax (802) 258 3428; email eil@worldlearning.org; http://www.worldlearning.org). It offers educational homestays, community service, ecological adventure, and language training in Europe. Positions as group leaders are available worldwide for qualified college graduates.

Peace Corps, 1990 K St. NW, Washington, D.C. 20526 (tel. (800) 424 8580; fax (202) 606 4469; http://www.peacecorps.gov). Opportunities in Morocco available in agriculture, business, education, the environment, health, and teaching. Volunteers must be U.S. citizens, age 18 and over, and willing to make a 2-year commitment. A bachelor's degree is usually required.

ESSENTIALS

The chance of a lifetime!

Spend a fall or spring semester, or a short-term program in Seville, Spain!

GENERAL INFORMATION
- Beginning, intermediate and advanced Spanish classes
- Home stay/small classes
- Experienced staff—native Spaniards
- Credit transfers by transcript
- Some financial aid available

SEMESTER INFORMATION
- Cost is approximately $7,950
- 16 semester hours credit

SHORT-TERM INFORMATION
- Cost is approximately $2,000
- 4 semester hours credit

SEMESTER DATES
Fall—late-August to mid-December
Spring—late-January to mid-May

SHORT TERM DATES
January, June and/or July—
3½ weeks each

PHONE	**(800) 748-0087**
MAIL	**Trinity Christian College**
	SIS—Dept LGO
	6601 West College Drive
	Palos Heights, IL 60463
WEB	**www.trnty.edu/spain**
EMAIL	**spain@trnty.edu**

Semester in
Spain

A PROGRAM
OF TRINITY CHRISTIAN COLLEGE

Photos courtesy of the Tourist Office of Spain. Additional photos by Lionel Delevingne.

Volunteers for Peace, 43 Tiffany Rd., Belmont, VT 05730 (tel. (802) 259 2759; fax 259 2922; email vfp@vfp.org; http://www.vfp.org). Arranges speedy placement in 2- to 3-week workcamps comprising 10-15 people. Up-to-date listings provided in the annual *International Workcamp Directory* (US$15). Free newsletter.

LONGER STAYS

If looking for a job, it's likely you'll have better luck in cities. Council's work program will help with job-placement and housing (see above). Peterson's (see **Study Abroad,** p. 25) offers a guide to permanent career opportunities overseas called *The Directory of Jobs and Careers Abroad.* In some countries, foreigners cannot own property. Be sure to check out your area of choice for such laws, as well as certain visa, residency, and taxation regulations that could easily thwart your best-laid plans.

■ Specific Concerns

WOMEN TRAVELERS

Women exploring on their own inevitably face additional safety concerns, but it's not hard to be adventurous and safe. In **Spain** men may be freer with unwanted comments and gestures than you are be accustomed to. In **Portugal,** women travelers are treated with respect (blondes, an anomaly among Portuguese, may be the occasional exception).

Trust your instinct when choosing a place to stay. Single rooms that lock from the inside or rooms in organizations that offer rooms for women only can be safer. Some hostels' communal showers are safer than others; check them before settling in. Stick to centrally located accommodations and avoid solitary late-night treks or metro rides. **Hitching** is never safe, even for two women traveling together. Choose train compartments wisely; look for one occupied by other women or couples or ask the conductor to organize one. Always carry extra money in case of emergencies.

In general, **dress** conservatively, especially in rural areas, and avoid looking like a tourist. Shorts and t-shirts in Spain, Portugal, and Morocco scream foreigner. Wearing a wedding band (real or not) may help prevent unwanted overtures. Carry a whistle and look as if you know where you're going (even when you don't).

Still, much is beyond your control. The best answer to verbal harassment is no answer at all. Avoiding eye-contact and feigning deafness can do a world of good that reactions usually don't achieve. If ignoring them doesn't work, don't hesitate to make a scene—most people embarrass or scare easily. Never hesitate to seek out a police officer or a passerby for help. A Model Mugging course can be very helpful preparation (see **Safety and Security,** p. 18).

Although all the above holds, **Morocco** is a special case. Women are often veiled and even secluded in their own homes. Women should never travel alone. Visitors will feel more safe and comfortable (and will avoid offending local sensibilities) by not wearing short skirts, sleeveless tops, shorts, and the like; moreover, females should always wear bras. Women—particularly non-Moroccans—may be gawked at, commented upon, approached by hustlers, followed, and, while in a crowd, have their butts and breasts squeezed. Moroccan women may hiss at "indecently" clad female travelers. Again, the best response to harassment may be silence. Yelling *"shuma"*—meaning shame—will frequently embarrass harassers, especially in the presence of onlookers. If maltreatment persists, protest loudly and often, and look out for a policeman or other respectable figure. Strolling arm in arm with another woman, common in Europe and North Africa, can lessen the risk of harassment or violence; so can wearing a head scarf. Women should not enter local Moroccan **bars;** any other women there are most likely prostitutes. Women in Morocco may also be refused a **room** at vacant hotels and hostels.

For women's **health issues,** see p. 22. For general information, contact the **National Organization for Women (NOW)** (email now@now.org; http://now.org). Main offices include 105 E. 22nd St., Suite 307, New York, NY 10010 (tel. (212) 260 4422); 1000 16th St. NW, Suite 700, Washington, D.C. 20036 (tel. (202) 331 0066); and 3543 18th St., P.O. Box 27, San Francisco, CA 94110 (tel. (415) 861 8960; fax 861 8969).

A Journey of One's Own: Uncommon Advice for the Independent Woman Traveler, by Thalia Zepatos (US$17), The Eighth Mountain Press (tel. (503) 233 3936; fax 233 0774; email soapston@teleport.com), is an interesting book full of good advice, with a bibliography of books and resources. A good annual guide for women (especially lesbian) travelers is **Women's Travel in Your Pocket,** Ferrari Guides (tel. (602) 863 2408; ferrari@q-net.com; http://www.q-net.com). It lists hotels, nightlife, dining, shopping, organizations, group tours, cruises, outdoor adventure, and lesbian events worldwide (US$14, plus shipping).

OLDER TRAVELERS

Senior citizens are eligible for a wide range of discounts on transportation, museums, movies, theaters, concerts, restaurants, and accommodations. If you don't see a senior citizen price listed, ask, and you may be delightfully surprised. Agencies for senior group travel are growing in popularity. Try **ElderTreks,** 597 Markham St., Toronto, Ontario, M6G 2L7, Canada (tel. (800) 741 7956; fax 588 9839; email passages@inforamp.net; http://www.eldertreks.com), or **Walking the World,** P.O. Box 1186, Fort Collins, CO 80522 (tel./fax (970) 498 0500; email walktworld@aol.com).

Elderhostel, 75 Federal St., 3rd Fl., Boston, MA 02110-1941 (tel. (617) 426-7788; email Cadyg@elderhostel.org; http://www.elderhostel.org). For those 55 or over (spouse of any age). 1- to 4-week programs on varied subjects at universities and other learning centers in 70 countries, including Spain, Portugal, and Morocco.

The Globe Piquot Press, P.O. Box 833, Old Saybrook, CT 06475-0833 (tel. (800) 243 0495, fax (800) 820 2329; email info@globe-piquot.com; http://www.globe-piquot.com). Publishes *Europe the European Way* (US$14), which offers general hints for the budget-conscious senior considering a long stay or retiring abroad.

No Problem! Worldwise Tips for Mature Adventurers, by Janice Kenyon. Advice and info on insurance, finances, security, health, packing. Useful appendices. US$16 from Orca Book Publishers, P.O. Box 468, Custer, WA 98240-0468.

Pilot Books (tel. (800) 797 4568; fax (516) 477 0978; email feedback@pilot-books.com; http://www.pilotbooks.com). Publishes a large number of helpful guides for seniors.

BISEXUAL, GAY, AND LESBIAN TRAVELERS

Some consider the gay scene in **Spain** the most open in Europe; in the major cities (Madrid, Barcelona), people are characteristically tolerant. Sitges and Ibiza have particularly vibrant gay communities. Scour bookstores, bars, and kiosks for the bimonthly magazine *Entiendes...?,* with articles in Spanish about gay issues and a comprehensive list of gay services, groups, activities, and, yes, even personal ads.

Portugal is more conservative. Gays and lesbians are generally accepted in Lisbon and, increasingly, in Porto but are invisible elsewhere in the country. No law promotes anti-gay discrimination, but social traditionalism—particularly strident Catholicism—may foster prejudice. Nonetheless, Lisbon staged its first gay rights parade in 1995, manifesting a burgeoning collective gay identity. In **Morocco** civil and Islamic law prohibit homosexuality.

Damron Travel Guides, P.O. Box 422458, San Francisco, CA 94142-2458 (tel. (800) 462 6654; fax (415) 703 9049; email damronco@damron.com; http://www.damron.com). Publishes of multiple helpful guides, including the *Damron Address Book* (US$15) and *The Women's Traveller* (US$13), which list bars, restaurants, guest houses, and services that cater to gay men and lesbians, respectively.

International Gay and Lesbian Travel Association (tel. (800) 448 8550; fax (954) 776 3303; email IGLTA@aol.com; http://www.iglta.org). An organization of over 1350 companies serving gay and lesbian travelers worldwide. Call for lists of travel agents, accommodations, and events.

Spartacus International Gay Guides (US$32.95). Lists bars, restaurants, hotels, and bookstores around the world catering to gays. Also lists hotlines and homosexuality laws for each country. Available in bookstores.

DISABLED TRAVELERS

Wheelchair accessibility varies widely in Iberia but is generally inferior to that in the United States. Access in Morocco is minimal. Guidebooks and brochures may not give accurate accounts on ramps, door widths, and elevator dimensions. Directly asking restaurants, hotels, railways, and airlines about their facilities works best. Those with disabilities should inform airlines and hotels of their disabilities when making arrangements for travel; some time may be needed to prepare special accommodations. In Spain and Portugal, handicapped access is common in modern and big city museums. For those on the internet, check out http://www.geocities.com/Paris/1502 for a good general information website on traveling for the disabled.

For getting around, besides a van rental, rail is usually most convenient. Contact **Rail Europe** (see **By Train,** p. 43) for info on discounted rail travel. Those bringing **guide dogs** must abide by the general procedure for pets. All three countries require veterinarian-issued health and rabies inoculation certificates for pets; well before your departure, send or take these certificates to the nearest consulate to be stamped.

The following groups provide info for disabled travelers or arrange tours or trips:

Facts on File, 11 Penn Plaza, 15th fl., New York, NY 10001 (tel. (212) 967 8800). Publishers of *Resource Directory for the Disabled,* a reference guide for travelers with disabilities (US$45 plus shipping). Available at bookstores or by mail order.

Mobility International USA, P.O. Box 10767, Eugene, OR 97440 (tel. (541) 343 1284 voice and TDD; fax 343 6812; email info@miusa.org; http://www.miusa.org). Sells the 3rd Edition of *A World of Options: A Guide to International Educational Exchange, Community Service, and Travel for Persons with Disabilities* (individuals US$35; organizations US$45).

Moss Rehab Hospital Travel Information Service (tel. (215) 456 9600, TDD (215) 456 9602). A telephone information resource center on international travel accessibility and other travel-related concerns for those with disabilities.

Directions Unlimited, 720 N. Bedford Rd., Bedford Hills, NY 10507 (tel. (800) 533 5343; fax (914) 241 0243). Arranges individual and group vacations, tours, and cruises for the physically disabled. Group tours for blind travelers.

MINORITY TRAVELERS

Spanish people suffer from little interaction with other races. It shows in some expressions, like "Don't be a Moor," meaning mind your manners. Infrequent incidents are never violent or threatening, just a little awkward. They occur out of naivete or ignorance. Don't be struck by a Spaniard's unabashed eagerness when meeting a foreigner who is not caucasian. This reaction is not ethnic insensitivity but rather curiosity, as odd as it may seem. **Portugal** is comfortably anti-racist. Its ethnic composition reflects its rich colonial history (in Africa and the Americas), complementing a healthy indigenous mix (see **Portugal: History and Politics,** p. 484). People of various ethnicities should have little to fear, since post-Salazar Portugal is eager to liberalize. In **Morocco,** nationality invites harassment more than ethnicity. Asian and blond travelers, and those who flaunt their wealth or national identity, are targets.

TRAVELERS WITH CHILDREN

Family vacations can be recipes for disaster unless you slow your pace and plan ahead. Be sure that your child carries some sort of ID in case of an emergency or he or she gets lost. Virtually all museums and tourist attractions and some restaurants, especially chains, have a children's rate. Trains, planes, and buses also often have discounts for kids. Children under two generally fly for 10% of the adult airfare on inter-

national flights (this does not necessarily include a seat). International fares are
usually discounted 25% for children from two to 11.

The following publications offer tips for adults traveling with children:

Backpacking with Babies and Small Children (US$9.95). Published by Wilderness
Press, 2440 Bancroft Way, Berkeley, CA 94704 (tel. (800) 443 7227 or (510) 843
8080; fax 548-1355; email wpress@ix.netcom.com; http://wildernesspress.com).
The third edition was scheduled for release in August 1998.
Take Your Kids to Europe by Cynthia W. Harriman (US$16.95). A budget travel
guide geared toward families. Published by Globe-Pequot Press, 6 Business Park
Rd., Old Saybrook, CT 06475 (tel. (800) 285 4078; fax (860) 395 1418).
How to take Great Trips with Your Kids, by Sanford and Jane Portnoy (US $9.95).
Advice on how to plan trips geared toward the age of your children, packing, and
finding child-friendly accommodations. The Harvard Common Press, 535 Albany
St., Boston, MA 02118 (tel. (888) 657 3755; fax 695 9794).

TRAVELING ALONE

There are many benefits to traveling alone, among them greater independence and
challenge and a greater opportunity to meet locals and fellow travelers alike.

On the other hand, accommodations can be more expensive, as splitting a multi-
person room is often cheaper than a single. Any solo traveler is a more vulnerable tar-
get for harassment and street theft. If questioned, never admit that you are traveling
alone. Maintain regular contact with someone at home who knows your itinerary.
American International Homestays (tel. (800) 876 2048) can provide lodgings with
English-speaking host families all over the world. **A Foxy Old Woman's Guide to
Traveling Alone** offers anecdotes and tips for anyone interested in solitary adventure.
Travel Companion Exchange (tel. (800) 392 1256; email travelpals@erols.com;
http://whytravelalone.com) publishes *Travel Companions*, a monthly newsletter for
those seeking travel partners (subscription US$48).

DIETARY CONCERNS

Vegetarians may find cooking their new pastime after trekking through Spain, Portugal, and Morocco. Fresh and inexpensive produce is available at the many local markets; *Let's Go* lists locations and hours in nearly every town. At restaurants it is often
quite difficult to get a vegetarian meal of any variety. Asking for two first courses
(*primer platos*) may work; the main dish (*segundo plato*) invariably contains meat.
Let's Go lists some exceptions, especially vegetarian-inclined restaurants in larger cities and tourist resorts. For more info contact the **Vegetarian Society of the U.K.** (tel.
(0161) 928 0793; fax 926 9182; email veg@minxnet.co.uk; http://www.vegsoc.org),
publisher of *The European Vegetarian Guide to Hotels and Restaurants*. **The Vegetarian Traveler,** P.O. Box 410205, Cambridge, MA 02141, U.S.A., sells a packet of
16 cards in 16 languages to be presented in restaurants, explaining your diet restrictions. The packet includes Arabic, English, French, Portuguese, and Spanish. When
ordering, you can specify vegan (no meat, dairy, or eggs), lacto (no meat or eggs), or
ovo-lacto (no meat; eggs and dairy allowed) cards. (US$9.95 plus $1 shipping.)

If it's **kosher,** chances are it's not in Spain, Portugal, or Morocco. Nevertheless, *The
Jewish Travel Guide* lists synagogues, kosher restaurants, and Jewish institutions in
over 80 countries, including Iberia and Morocco. (Available in the U.K. from Vallan-
tine Mitchell Publishers; tel. (0181) 599 88 66; fax 599 09 84. Available in the U.S.
from Sepher-Hermon Press; tel. (718) 972-9010. If you are strict in your observance,
preparing your own food may often be necessary.

For a description of typical cuisine in Spain, Portugal, and Morocco, refer to the
Food section preceding each country segment. Health-related concerns, such as diabetes, are dealt with in **Health,** p. 20.

■ Packing

Before you leave, pack your bag, strap it on, and imagine yourself walking uphill on hot asphalt for the next three hours; this exercise should give you a sense of how important it is to pack lightly. A good rule is to lay out only what you absolutely need, then take half the clothes and twice the money. The less you have, the less you have to lose (or store, or carry on your back).

LUGGAGE

Backpack: If you plan to cover most of your itinerary by foot, a sturdy backpack is unbeatable. Get a pack with a strong, padded hip belt to transfer weight from your shoulders to your hips. Good packs cost from US$150 to US$420.

Suitcase or trunk: Fine if you plan to live in one or two cities and explore from there, but a bad idea if you are going to move around a lot. Make sure it has wheels.

Daypack, rucksack, or courier bag: Bringing a smaller bag in addition to your pack or suitcase allows you to leave your big bag behind while you go sight-seeing.

Moneybelt or neck pouch: Guard your money, passport, railpass, and other important articles in either one of these items, available at any good camping store. The moneybelt should tuck inside the waist of your pants or skirt.

CLOTHING AND FOOTWEAR

In Spain and Portugal, **shorts,** deemed unfashionable, are relatively uncommon. In Morocco, especially for women, they are virtually unacceptable. Beyond this fact, standard Western wear works in Iberia. Morocco has different, slightly stricter standards. Dressing conservatively is the best bet for safety and sanity. Avoid short skirts, sleeveless tops, and shorts. For more details, see **Specific Concerns: Women Travelers,** p. 29.

You may anticipate situations that require more than the jeans and t-shirt uniform. In Spain and Portugal, people dress, and they dress well. In general, style veers toward a slightly cleaner and tighter cut than in England or the United States. At any nightclub, another pair of shoes and unwrinkled clothes are the absolute minimum required to avoid feeling out of place. The appendix has a useful **clothing size** and **conversion chart,** see p. 648.

Clothing: When choosing your travel wardrobe, aim for versatility and comfort, and avoid fabrics that wrinkle easily. Always bring a jacket or wool sweater.

Walking shoes: Well-cushioned **sneakers** are good for walking, although you may want to consider a good water-proofed pair of **hiking boots.** A double pair of socks will cushion feet, keep them dry, and help prevent blisters. Bring a pair of flip-flops for the shower. Talcum powder can prevent sores, and moleskin is great for blisters. Break in your shoes before you leave.

Rain gear: A waterproof jacket and a backpack cover will take care of you and your stuff. Gore-Tex is a miracle fabric that's both waterproof and breathable; it's mandatory if you plan on hiking. Avoid cotton as outerwear if you will be outdoors a lot.

MISCELLANEOUS

Stores across Europe and Morocco stock most **toiletries.** In **Morocco,** toilet paper is scarce at hostels, but is sold at grocery stores, many newsstands, and tobacco shops.

Check our **Orientation and Practical Information** listings of each town to find out whether and where English language books are sold.

Sleepsacks: If you plan to stay in **hostels,** there may be a linen charge; you can make the requisite sleepsack yourself. Fold a full-size sheet in half, then sew it closed along the open long side and one of the short sides. Or, buy it at HI outlet stores.

Contact lenses: Machines that heat-disinfect contact lenses will require a converter so consider switching temporarily to a chemical disinfection system—check with your lens dispenser to see if it is safe to switch. Contact lens supplies are sometimes rare or expensive. Bring enough saline and cleaner for your entire vacation. In any case, bring a backup pair of glasses.

Washing clothes: *Let's Go* provides information on laundromats in larger cities, but sometimes it may be easier to use a sink. Bring a small bar or tube of detergent soap and string for a clothes line.

Electric current: In Spain, Portugal, and Morocco, electricity is 220 volts AC, enough to fry any 110V North American appliance. 220V electrical appliances don't like 110V current, either. Visit a hardware store for an adapter (which changes the shape of the plug) and a converter (that changes the voltage). Don't make the mistake of using only an adapter (unless appliance instructions explicitly state otherwise), or you'll melt your gadgetry.

Film: It's expensive just about everywhere. Bring film from home and, if you will be seriously upset if the pictures are ruined, develop it at home. If you are not a serious photographer, you may want to consider bringing a **disposable camera** or two rather than an expensive permanent one. Despite disclaimers, airport security X-rays *can* fog film, so either buy a lead-lined pouch, sold at camera stores, or ask the security to hand inspect it. Always pack it in your carry-on luggage, since higher-intensity X-rays are used on checked luggage.

Other useful items: pocketknife; first-aid kit; sealable plastic bags; alarm clock; needle and thread; safety pins; sunglasses; a Walkman; plastic water bottle; string (makeshift clothesline and lashing material); towel; padlock; whistle; rubber bands; toilet paper; flashlight; earplugs; insect repellant; electrical tape (for patching tears); clothespins; maps and phrasebooks; tweezers; sunscreen; vitamins. Some items not always readily available or affordable on the road: deodorant; razors; condoms; tampons.

GETTING THERE

■ By Plane

The price you pay for airfare varies widely depending on from whom you purchase your ticket and how flexible your travel plans are. Understanding the airline industry's byzantine pricing system is the best way of finding a cheap fare. Very generally, courier fares (if you can deal with restrictions) are the cheapest, followed by tickets bought from consolidators and stand-by seating. Last minute specials, airfare wars, and charter flights, however, can often beat these fares. Always get quotes from different sources; an hour or two of research can save you hundreds of dollars. Call every toll-free number and don't be afraid to ask about discounts, as it's unlikely they'll be volunteered. Knowledgeable **travel agents,** particularly those specializing in and around Iberia and Morocco, can provide excellent guidance. An agent whose clients fly mostly to Nassau or Miami will not be the best person to hunt down a bargain flight to Barcelona. Travel agents may not want to spend time finding the cheapest fares (for which they receive the lowest commissions), but if you travel often you should definitely find an agent who will cater to you and your needs and track down deals in exchange for your frequent business.

Students and others under 26 should never need to pay full price for a ticket. Seniors can also get great deals; many airlines offer senior traveler clubs or airline passes with few restrictions and discounts for their companions as well. Sunday newspapers often have travel sections that list bargain fares from the local airport. Special deals to countries in Asia and Africa may also be advertised in publications targeted at immigrants from that country, or among agents who cater to specific ethnic communities. Outsmart airline reps with the phone-book-sized *Official Airline Guide* (check your local library—at US$359 per year, the tome costs as much as some flights), a monthly guide listing nearly every scheduled flight in the world and toll-free phone numbers for all airlines that allow you to call in reservations directly. More accessible is Michael McColl's *The Worldwide Guide to Cheap Airfare* (US$15).

There is also a wealth of travel information to be found on the internet. The **Air Traveler's Handbook** (http://www.cs.cmu.edu/afs/cs.cmu.edu/user/mkant/Public/Travel/airfare.html) is an excellent source of general information on air travel. **TravelHUB** (http://www.travelhub.com) provides a directory of travel agents that includes a searchable database of fares from over 500 consolidators (see **Ticket Consolidators,** below). Edward Hasbrouck maintains a **Consolidators FAQ** (http://www.travel-library.com/air-travel/consolidators.html) that provides great background on finding cheap international flights. Groups such as the **Air Courier Association** (http://www.aircourier.org) offer information about traveling as a courier and provide up-to-date listings of last minute opportunities. **Travelocity** (http://www.travelocity.com) operates a searchable online database of published airfares, which you can reserve online.

Most airfares peak between mid-June and early September. Midweek (Monday through Thursday mornings) round-trip flights run about US$40-50 cheaper than on weekends; weekend flights, however, are generally less crowded. Traveling from hub to hub will guarantee you more competitive fares. Ironically, Madrid and Lisbon are small cities by airline standards; consider a less direct but likely cheaper flight across the Atlantic to London, Amsterdam, Brussels, or Luxembourg. Return-date flexibility is usually not an option for the budget traveler; traveling with an "open return" ticket can be pricier than fixing a return date and paying to change it. Whenever flying internationally, pick up your ticket well in advance of the departure date, have the flight confirmed within 72 hours of departure, and arrive at the airport at least three hours before your flight.

COMMERCIAL AIRLINES

The airlines' published airfares should be just the beginning of your search. If you pay an airline's lowest published fare, you may waste hundreds of dollars. For the adventurous or the bargain-hungry, there are other, perhaps more inconvenient or time-consuming options. Before shopping around it is a good idea to find out the average commercial price in order to measure how great a "bargain" you are being offered.

The commercial airlines' lowest regular offer is the **Advance Purchase Excursion Fare (APEX);** specials advertised in newspapers may be cheaper but have more restrictions and fewer available seats. APEX fares provide you with confirmed reservations and allow "open-jaw" tickets (landing in and returning from different cities). Generally, reservations must be made seven to 21 days in advance, with seven- to 14-day minimum and up to 90-day maximum stay limits, and hefty cancellation and change penalties (fees rise in summer). Book APEX fares early during peak season; by May you will have a hard time getting the departure date you want.

Major U.S. and European airlines serve Spain, Portugal and Morocco. **Iberia** flies between Spain and all major international cities. **Aviaco,** a subsidiary of Iberia, covers only domestic routes. **Air Europa** flies out of New York City and most European cities to Spain. **SpanAir** offers international and domestic flights out of Spain at comparable rates. For more info on Spanish airlines, see **Getting There and Around,** p. 46. **TAP Air Portugal** serves Lisbon and other Portuguese cities from major international cities; **Portugália** is a smaller Portuguese carrier. For more info, see **Getting There and Around,** p. 481. **Royal Air Maroc** flies from Morocco to the U.S. and most major cities in Europe, including Madrid and Lisbon. For more info, see **Getting There and Around,** p. 587.

Days of the Week

While round-trip tickets may be cheaper during the week than on weekends, they also mean crowded flights, which in turn means competition for frequent-flier upgrades. Scheduling weekend flights is more expensive, but less crowded, and proves the best bet for using frequent-flier upgrades. Most business travelers travel on Thursdays, which makes stiff competition for upgrade hunters. Saturdays and Sundays present the best opportunities for frequent fliers.

BUDGET TRAVEL AGENCIES

Students and people under 26 ("youth") with proper ID qualify for enticing reduced airfares. These fares are rarely available from airlines or travel agents but instead from student travel agencies that negotiate special reduced-rate bulk purchase with the airlines and then resell them to the youth market. Return-date change fees also tend to be lower (around US$35 per segment through Council or Let's Go Travel). Most flights are on major airlines, although in peak season some agencies may sell seats on less-reliable chartered aircraft. Student travel agencies can also help non-students and people over 26 but probably won't be able to get the same low fares.

Campus Travel, 52 Grosvenor Gardens, London SW1W 0AG (http://www.campus-travel.co.uk). 46 branches in the U.K. Student and youth fares on plane, train, boat, and bus travel. Skytrekker flexible airline tickets. Discount and ID cards for students and youths, travel insurance for students and those under 35, and maps and guides. Publishes travel suggestion booklets. Telephone booking service: in Manchester call (0161) 273 17 21; in Scotland call (0131) 668 33 03; in Europe call (0171) 730 34 02; in North America call (0171) 730 21 01; worldwide call (0171) 730 81 11.

Council Charter, 205 E. 42nd St., New York, NY 10017 (tel. (212) 661 0311; fax 972 0194). Offers a combination of inexpensive charter and scheduled airfares from a variety of U.S. gateways to most major European destinations. One-way fares and open jaws (fly into one city and out of another) are available.

Council Travel (http://www.ciee.org/travel/index.htm), the travel division of Council, is a full-service travel agency specializing in youth and budget travel. They offer discount airfares on scheduled airlines, railpasses, hosteling cards, low-cost accommodations, guidebooks, budget tours, travel gear, and international student (ISIC), youth (GO25), and teacher (ITIC) identity cards. U.S. offices include: Emory Village, 1561 N. Decatur Rd., **Atlanta,** GA 30307 (tel. (404) 377 9997); 2000 Guadalupe, **Austin,** TX 78705 (tel. (512) 472 4931); 273 Newbury St., **Boston,** MA 02116 (tel. (617) 266 1926); 1138 13th St., **Boulder,** CO 80302 (tel. (303) 447 8101); 1153 N. Dearborn, **Chicago,** IL 60610 (tel. (312) 951 0585); 10904 Lindbrook Dr., **Los Angeles,** CA 90024 (tel. (310) 208 3551); 1501 University Ave. SE, Suite 300, **Minneapolis,** MN 55414 (tel. (612) 379 2323); 205 E. 42nd St., **New York,** NY 10017 (tel. (212) 822 2700); 953 Garnet Ave., **San Diego,** CA 92109 (tel. (619) 270 6401); 530 Bush St., **San Francisco,** CA 94108 (tel. (415) 421 3473); 1314 NE 43rd St., Suite 210, **Seattle,** WA 98105 (tel. (206) 632 2448); 3300 M St. NW, **Washington, D.C.** 20007 (tel. (202) 337 6464). **For U.S. cities not listed,** call 800 226 8624. Offices also in 28A Poland St. (Oxford Circus), **London,** W1V 3DB (tel. (0171) 287 3337); **Paris** (tel. 0146 55 55 65); and **Munich** (tel. (089) 39 50 22).

CTS Travel, 220 Kensington High St., W8 (tel. (0171) 937 33 66 for travel in Europe, 937 33 88 for travel worldwide; fax 937 90 27). Tube: High St. Kensington. Also at 44 Goodge St., W1. Tube: Goodge St. Specializes in student/youth travel and discount flights.

Educational Travel Centre (ETC), 438 North Frances St., Madison, WI 53703 (tel. (800) 747 5551; fax (608) 256 2042; email edtrav@execpc.com; http://www.edtrav.com). Flight information, HI-AYH cards, Eurail, and regional rail passes. Write for their free pamphlet *Taking Off.* Student and budget airfares.

Eurolines, 52 Grosvenor Gardens, Victoria, London SW1W 0AU (tel. (0158) 240 45 11 main office, or (0171) 730 82 35 in London). Specializes in coach travel throughout Western and Eastern Europe.

Students Flights Inc., 5010 East Shea Blvd., Suite A104, Scottsdale, AZ 85254 (tel. (800) 255 8000 or (602) 951 1177; fax 951 1216; email jost@isecard.com; http://isecard.com). Also sells Eurail and Europasses, and international student exchange identity cards.

Let's Go Travel, Harvard Student Agencies, 17 Holyoke St., Cambridge, MA 02138 (tel. (617) 495 9649; fax 495 7956; email travel@hsa.net; http://hsa.net/travel). Railpasses, HI-AYH memberships, ISICs, ITICs, FIYTO cards, guidebooks, maps, bargain flights, and a complete line of budget travel gear. All items available by mail; call or write for a catalogue.

Rail Europe Inc., 226 Westchester Ave., White Plains, NY 10604 (tel. (800) 438 7245; fax 432 1329; http://www.raileurope.com). Sells all Eurail products and passes, national railpasses including Brit Rail and German Rail passes, and point-to-point tickets. Up-to-date information on all rail travel in Europe.

STA Travel, 6560 Scottsdale Rd., Suite F100, Scottsdale, AZ 85253 (tel. (800) 777 0112 nationwide; fax (602) 922 0793; http://sta-travel.com). A student and youth travel organization with over 150 offices worldwide offering discount airfares for young travelers, railpasses, accommodations, tours, insurance, and ISICs. 16 offices in the U.S. include: 297 Newbury St., **Boston,** MA 02115 (tel. (617) 266 6014); 429 S. Dearborn St., **Chicago,** IL 60605 (tel. (312) 786 9050); 7202 Melrose Ave., **Los Angeles,** CA 90046 (tel. (213) 934 8722); 10 Downing St., Suite G, **New York,** NY 10003 (tel. (212) 627 3111); 4341 University Way NE, **Seattle,** WA 98105 (tel. (206) 633 5000); 2401 Pennsylvania Ave., **Washington, D.C.** 20037 (tel. (202) 887 0912); 51 Grant Ave., **San Francisco,** CA 94108 (tel. (415) 391 8407); University of Miami, 1000 Whitten University Ctr., 1306 Stanford Dr., **Coral Gables,** FL 33146 (tel. (305) 284 1044). In the U.K., 6 Wrights Ln., **London** W8 6TA (tel. (0171) 938 47 11 for North American travel). In New Zealand, 10 High St., **Auckland** (tel. (09) 309 97 23). In Australia, 222 Faraday St., **Melbourne** VIC 3050 (tel. (03) 349 69 11).

Tagus-Youth Travel, R. Camilo Castelo Branco, **Lisbon** 20 1150 (tel. (1) 352 59 86). Portugal's youth travel agency. Geared mainly toward Portuguese youth, but great for booking student airline tickets. Info on discount transportation, HI and student ID cards, student residences, camping, and study visits in Portugal. English, Spanish, and French spoken.

Travel CUTS (Canadian Universities Travel Services Limited), 187 College St., Toronto, Ontario M5T 1P7 (tel. (416) 979 2406; fax 979 8167; email mail@travelcuts). Canada's national student travel bureau and equivalent of Council, with 40 offices across Canada. Also in the U.K., 295-A Regent St., **London** W1R 7YA (tel. (0171) 637 31 61). Discounted domestic and international airfares open to all; special student fares to all destinations with valid ISIC. Issues ISIC, FIYTO, GO25, and HI hostel cards, as well as railpasses. Offers free *Student Traveller* magazine, and information on the Student Work Abroad Program (SWAP).

Travel Management International (TMI), 1129 East Wayzata, Wayzata, MN 55391 (tel. (612) 404 7164 or (800) 245 3672). Diligent, prompt, and very helpful travel service offering student fares and discounts.

Unitravel, 117 North Warson Rd., St. Louis, MO 63132 (tel. (800) 325 2222; fax (314) 569 2503). Offers discounted airfares on major scheduled airlines from the U.S. to Europe, Africa, and Asia.

Usit Youth and Student Travel, 19-21 Aston Quay, O'Connell Bridge, Dublin 2 (tel. (01) 677 8117; fax 679 8833). In the U.S.: New York Student Center, 895 Amsterdam Ave., New York, NY 10025 (tel. (212) 663 5435; email usitny@aol.com). Additional offices in Cork, Galway, Limerick, Waterford, Maynooth, Coleraine, Derry, Athlone, Jordanstown, and Belfast. Specializes in youth and student travel. Offers low-cost tickets and flexible travel arrangements all over the world. Supplies ISIC and FIYTO-GO 25 cards in Ireland only.

Viajes TIVE, C. José Ortega y Gasset, 71, **Madrid** 28006 (tel. (1) 347 77 78; fax 401 81 60). Spain's national chain of student travel agencies, with offices almost everywhere. They peddle discount travel tickets, ISICs, and HI memberships, and dispense transportation info.

Wasteels, 7041 Grand National Dr., Suite 207, Orlando, FL 32819 (tel. (407) 351 2537; in **London** (0171) 834 70 66). A huge chain in Europe, with 200,000 locations. Information in English can be requested from the London office (tel. (0171) 834 70 66; fax 630 76 28). Sells the Wasteels BIJ tickets, which are discounted (30-45% off regular fare) 2nd-class international point-to-point train tickets with unlimited stopovers (must be under 26 on the first day of travel); sold *only* in Europe.

TICKET CONSOLIDATORS

Most airlines in the world are heavily regulated, which means that their published fares may be significantly more expensive than the market price available from a **ticket consolidator.** Ticket consolidators resell unsold tickets on commercial and charter airlines at unpublished fares; a 30-40% price reduction is not uncommon.

Consolidator tickets provide the greatest discounts over published fares when you are traveling: on short notice (you bypass advance purchase requirements, since you aren't tangled in airline bureaucracy); on a high-priced trip; to an offbeat destination; or in the peak season, when published fares are jacked way up. There are rarely age constraints or stay limitations, but unlike tickets bought through an airline, you won't be able to use your tickets on another flight if you miss yours, and you will have to go back to the consolidator rather than the airline for a refund. These tickets are often for coach seats on connecting (not direct) flights on foreign airlines, and that frequent-flyer miles may not be credited. Decide what you can and can't live with before shopping.

Not all consolidators deal with the general public; many sell tickets only through travel agents. **Bucket shops** are retail agencies that specialize in getting cheap tickets. Although ticket prices are marked up slightly, bucket shops generally have access to a larger market than would be available to the public and can also get tickets from wholesale consolidators. Generally, a dealer **specializing** in travel to the country of your destination will provide more options and cheaper tickets. The **Association of Special Fares Agents (ASFA)** maintains a database of specialized dealers for particular regions (http://www.ntsltd.com/asfa). For travel in Spain, check **Viajes Colon Travel** (http://www.arrakis.es/balearik/vctravel.htm). For Portugal, try **Astrolabio** (http://www.astrolabio.pt). Also ask about accommodations and car rental discounts; some consolidators have fingers in many pies.

Look for bucket shops' tiny ads in the travel section of weekend papers. In the U.S., try the *Sunday New York Times;* in Australia, use the *Sydney Times;* in London, a call to the Air Travel Advisory Bureau (tel. (0171) 636 50 00) can provide names of reliable consolidators and discount flight specialists. Kelly Monaghan's *Consolidators: Air Travel's Bargain Basement* is an invaluable source for more information and lists of consolidators by location and destination (US$8 from bookstores or online).

When using a ticket consolidator, be a smart shopper and check out the competition. Among the many reputable and trustworthy companies are, unfortunately, some shady wheeler-dealers. Contact the local Better Business Bureau to find out how long the company has been in business and its track record. Although not necessary, it is preferable to deal with consolidators close to home so you can visit in person if necessary. Ask to receive your tickets as quickly as possible so you have time to fix any problems. Get the company's policy in writing: insist on a **receipt** that gives full details about the tickets, refunds, and restrictions, and record who you talked to and when. It may be worth paying with a credit card (despite the 2-5% fee) so you can stop payment if you never receive your tickets. Beware the "bait and switch" gag: shyster firms will advertise a super-low fare and then tell a caller that it has been sold. Although this excuse is viable, if they can't offer you a price near the advertised fare on *any* date, it is a scam to lure in customers—report them to the Better Business Bureau.

Always try to contact specialists in your region. Several consolidators sell tickets to Spain, Portugal, and Morocco. Among these are: **AESU** (tel. (800) 638 7640; http://www.aesu.com); **Air Travel Discounts, Inc.** (tel. (800) 888 2621) services Spain and Portugal, but not Morocco; **Campus Travel** (tel. (800) 328 3359); **Central Holidays** (tel. (800) 935 5000; http://www.centralholidays.com); **4th Dimension Tours** (tel. (800) 343 0020); **Picasso Travel** (tel. (800) 742 2776); and **Plus Ultra** (tel. (800) 367 7724); http://www.spaintours.com).

For destinations **worldwide,** try **Airfare Busters** (tel. (800) 232 8783); **Pennsylvania Travel** (tel. (800) 331 0947); **Cheap Tickets** (tel. (800) 377 1000); and **Travac** (tel. (800) 872 8800; fax (212) 714 9063; email mail@travac.com; http://www.travac.com). **NOW Voyager,** 74 Varick St., Suite 307, New York, NY 10013 (tel. (212) 431 1616; fax 334 5243); email info@nowvoyagertravel.com; http://www.nowvoyagertravel.com) acts as a consolidator and books discounted international flights, mostly from New York, as well as courier flights (annual fee US$50). For a processing fee, depending on the number of travelers and the itinerary, **Travel Avenue** (tel. (800) 333 3335; fax (312) 876 1254; http://www.travelavenue.com) will search for the lowest international airfare available, including consolidated prices, and even provide a 5% rebate on fares over US$350. To **Europe,** try **Rebel** (tel. (800) 227 3235; fax (805) 294 0981; email travel@rebeltours.com; http://www.rebeltours.com).

COURIER COMPANIES

Those who travel light should consider flying internationally as a **courier,** where ridiculously low fares often come at the price of heavy restrictions. The company hiring you will use your checked luggage space for freight; you're usually allowed to bring only carry-ons, although some firms allow you to check luggage, depending on the trip. You are responsible for the safe delivery of the baggage claim slips (given to you by a courier company representative) to the representative waiting for you when you arrive—don't screw up or you will be blacklisted as a courier. You will probably never see the cargo you are transporting—the company handles it all—and airport officials know that couriers are not responsible for the baggage checked for them. Restrictions to watch for: you must be over 21 (18 in some cases), have a valid passport, and procure your own visa (if necessary); most flights are round-trip only with short fixed-length stays (usually one week); only single tickets are issued (but a companion may be able to get a next-day flight); and most flights out of the US are from New York. Round-trip fares to Western Europe from the U.S. range from US$100-400 (during the off-season) to US$200-550 (in summer). Keep in mind that last-minute deals for all courier flights can get you significantly cheaper or even free flights. Becoming a member of the **Air Courier Association** (tel. (800) 282 1202; http://www.aircourier.org) is a good way to start; they give you a listing of all reputable courier brokers and the flights they are offering, along with a hefty courier manual and a bimonthly newsletter of updated opportunities ($30 one-time fee plus $28 annual dues). For an annual fee of $45, the **International Association of Air Travel Couriers** (tel. (561) 582 8320; email iaatc@courier.org; http://www.courier.org) informs travelers (via computer, fax, and mailings) of courier opportunities worldwide. **NOW Voyager** acts as an agent for many courier flights worldwide and offers special last-minute deals to European cities for as little as US$200 round-trip plus a US$50 registration fee. They also act as a consolidator (see **Ticket Consolidators,** p. 37, for all contact information). Another agent to try is **Halbart Express** (tel. (718) 656 5000; fax 917 0708).

You can also go directly through courier companies in New York or check a bookstore, library, or online for handbooks such as *Air Courier Bargains* (US$15). The *Courier Air Travel Handbook* (US$10) explains how to travel as an air courier and contains names, phone numbers, and contact points of courier companies.

Better Safe than Sorry

Everyone who flies should be concerned with airline safety. The type and age of the aircraft often indicate the airline's safety level—aircraft not produced by Boeing, Airbus, McDonnell Douglas, or Fokker sometimes fall below acceptable standards, and aircraft over 20 years old require increased levels of maintenance. If you're flying a foreign airline, especially to developing countries, consult one of the following organizations. Travel agencies can tell you the type and age of aircraft on a particular route, as can the *Official Airline Guide* (http://www.oag.com), which can be especially useful in Eastern Europe where less-reliable equipment is often used for inter-city travel. The **International Airline Passengers Association** (tel. (972) 404 9980) provides region-specific safety information. The **Federal Aviation Administration** (http://www.faa.gov) reviews the airline authorities for countries whose airlines enter the U.S. and divides the countries into three categories; stick with carriers in category 1. Call the **U.S. State Department** (tel. (202) 647 5225; http://travel.state.gov/travel_warnings.html) to check for posted travel advisories that sometimes involve foreign carriers.

STAND-BY FLIGHTS

Airhitch, 2641 Broadway, 3rd fl., New York, NY 10025 (tel. (800) 326 2009 or (212) 864 2000, fax 864 5489) and Los Angeles, CA (tel. (310) 726 5000), will add a certain thrill to the prospects of when you will leave and where exactly you will end up. Complete flexibility in the dates and cities of arrival and departure is necessary. Flights to Europe cost US$159 each way when departing from the Northeast, $239 from the West Coast or Northwest, $209 from the Midwest, and $189 from the Southeast. Travel within the USA and Europe is also possible, with rates ranging from $79 to $139. The snag is that you buy not a ticket but the promise that you will get to a destination near where you're intending to go within a window of time (usually 5 days) from a location in a region you've specified. You call in before your date-range to hear all of your flight options for the next seven days and your probability of boarding. You then decide which flights you want to try to make and present a voucher at the airport that grants you the right to board a flight on a space-available basis. This procedure must be followed again for the return trip. Be aware that you may receive a monetary refund only if all available flights that departed within your date-range from the specified region are full, but future travel credit is always available. There are several offices in Europe, so you can wait to register for your return; the main one is in Paris (tel. (01) 47 00 16 30).

AirTech.Com, 588 Broadway, Suite 204, New York, NY 10012 (tel. (212) 219 7000; fax 219 0066; email fly@airtech.com; http://www.airtech.com), offers a very similar service. Their travel window is one to four days. Rates to and from Europe (continually updated; call and verify) are: Northeast US$169; West Coast US$229; and Midwest/Southeast US$199. Upon registration and payment, AirTech.Com sends you a FlightPass with a contact date falling soon before your travel window, when you are to call them for flight instructions. Note that the service is one-way—you must go through the same procedure to return—and that no refunds are granted unless the company fails to get you a seat before your travel window expires. AirTech.Com also arranges courier flights and regular confirmed-reserved flights at discount rates.

Be sure to read all the fine print in your agreements with either company—a call to The Better Business Bureau of New York City may be worthwhile. Be warned that it is difficult to receive refunds, and that clients' vouchers will not be honored when an airline fails to receive payment in time.

CHARTER FLIGHTS

Charters are flights a tour operator contracts with an airline (usually one specializing in charters) to fly extra loads of passengers to peak-season destinations. Charters are often cheaper than flights on scheduled airlines, especially during peak seasons, although fare wars, consolidator tickets, and small airlines can often beat charter prices. Some charters operate nonstop, and restrictions on minimum advance-purchase and minimum stay are more lenient. Charter flights fly less frequently than major airlines, however, making refunds particularly difficult, and are also almost always fully booked. Schedules and itineraries may change or be cancelled at the last moment (as late as 48 hours before the trip and without a full refund), and check-in, boarding, and baggage claim are often much slower. As always, pay with a credit card if you can; consider traveler's insurance against trip interruption.

Many consolidators such as **Travac** and **Travel Avenue** (see **Ticket Consolidators,** p. 37) also offer charter options. Don't be afraid to call every number and hunt for the best deal. Eleventh-hour **discount clubs** and **fare brokers** offer members savings on travel, including charter flights and tour packages. Research your options carefully. **Travelers Advantage,** Stamford, CT (tel. (800) 548 1116; http://www.travelersadvantage.com; US$49 annual fee), specializes in European travel and tour packages. Study these organizations' contracts closely; you don't want to end up with an unwanted overnight layover.

■ By Boat

For when you really have travel time to spare, **Ford's Travel Guides,** 19448 Londelius St., Northridge, CA 91324 (tel. (818) 701 7414; fax 701 7415), lists **freighter companies** that will take passengers worldwide. Ask for their *Freighter Travel Guide and Waterways of the World* (US$16, plus $2.50 postage if mailed outside the US).

ONCE THERE

■ Tourist Offices

Spain

Most towns have a centrally located **Oficina de Turismo** (called **Turismos**) that distributes info on sights, lodgings, and events and occasionally a free map. Bigger cities may have more than one, and there is often a regional office. Different branches' services and brochures don't always overlap. Although they do not book accommodations, many will show you the way to local lodgings. In smaller towns the staff may not speak English, and maps and brochures may remain untranslated.

Portugal

The national tourist board is the **Direção Geral do Turismo (DGT).** Their offices are in virtually every city; look for the **"Turismo"** sign. Services offered are similar to those in Spain, and in the bigger offices, finding an English or French speaker is usually no problem.

Morocco

Most cities have a centrally located **Office Nationale Marocaine de Tourisme (ONMT).** They may offer a free map and information on sights, markets, accommodations, and official guides. Some even store luggage and change money when banks are closed. Many cities also have a **Syndicat d'Initiative,** a city tourist office, with the same services. Neither office is particularly well geared for the budget traveler.

■ Embassies and Consulates

Foreign embassies are in Madrid, Lisbon, and Rabat; consulates are usually in other major cities. In Spain and Portugal, embassies and consulates are usually open Monday through Friday, mornings and evenings, with siestas in-between—call for specific hours. In Morocco, most embassies and consulates are open Monday through Friday from around 8am to noon with some reopening after lunch until 6pm. In both Iberia and Morocco, early morning is the easiest time to contact all the embassies and consulates listed. Consulates give legal advice, and medical referrals and can readily contact relatives back home. In extreme cases, they may offer emergency financial assistance. For the embassies and consulates of Spain, Portugal, and Morocco in your home country, see **Embassies and Consulates,** p. 5.

Spain

Australian Embassy: Santa Engracia, 120, **Madrid** 28003 (tel. 91 579 04 28; fax 91 442 53 62; email information@embaustralia.es; http://www.embaustralia.es). **Consulates:** Gran Vía Carlos III, 98, 3rd fl., **Barcelona** 08028 (tel. 93 330 94 96; fax 93 411 09 04). Federico Rubio, 14, **Sevilla** 41004 (tel. 95 422 09 71; fax 95 421 11 45). **British Embassy:** C. Fernando el Santo, 16, **Madrid** 28010 (tel. 91 319 02 00; fax 91 308 10 33). **Consulates:** Centro Colón, Marqués de la Ensenada, 16, 2nd fl., **Madrid** 28004 (tel. 91 308 52 01; fax 91 308 08 82). **Consulate-General:** Edificio Torre de Barcelona, Av. Diagonal, 477, 13th fl., **Barcelona** 08036 (tel. 93 419 90 44; fax 93 405 24 11; email brconbcn@alba.mssl.es). Pl. Nueva, 8B, **Sevilla** 41001 (tel. 95 422 88 75; fax 95 421 03 23). Alameda de Urquijo, 2, 8th fl., **Bilbao** 48008 (tel. 94 415

76 00; fax 94 415 77 11). Pl. Mayor, 3D, **Palma de Mallorca** 07002 (tel. 971 71 24 45; fax 971 71 75 20). Av. Isidor Macabich, 45, 1st. fl., Apartavo 307, **Ibiza** 07800, Balearic Islands (tel. 971 30 18 18; fax 971 30 19 72). Pl. Calvo Sotelo, 1/2, **Alicante** 03001 (tel. 96 521 60 22; fax 96 514 05 28). Po. de Pereda, 27, **Santander** 39004 (tel. 942 22 00 00; fax 942 22 29 41). Edificio Duquesa, Duquesa de Parcent, 8, **Málaga** 29001 (tel. 95 221 75 71; fax 95 222 11 30); Edificio Cataluna C. Luis Morote, 6, 3rd fl., **Las Palmas** 35007 (tel. 928 26 25 08; fax 928 26 77 74).

Canadian Embassies: C. Núñez de Balboa, 35, **Madrid** 28001 (tel. 91 431 43 00; fax 91 435 74 88; http://info.ic.gc.ca/Tourism). **Consulates:** Passeig de Gràcia, 77, 3rd fl., **Barcelona** 08008 (tel. 93 215 07 04; fax 93 487 91 17). Edificio Horizonte, Pl. Malagueta, 2, 1st fl., **Málaga** 29016 (tel. 95 222 33 46; fax 95 222 40 23; email concon@microcad.es).

Irish Embassy: Po. Castellana, 46, **Madrid** 28046 (tel. 91 576 35 00; 91 435 16 77).

New Zealand Embassy: Pl. de La Lealtad, 2, **Madrid** 28014 (tel. 91 523 02 26; fax 91 523 01 71). **Consulate:** Travesera de Gracia, 64, 4th fl., **Barcelona** 08006 (tel. 93 209 03 99; fax 93 202 08 90).

South African Embassy: Claudio Coello, 91, 6th fl., **Madrid** 28006 (tel. 91 436 37 80; fax 91 577 74 14). **Consulates:** Teodora Lamadrid, 7-11, **Barcelona** 08022 (tel. 93 418 64 45; fax 93 418 05 38; email sudafrica@ceisei.es). Las Mercedes, 31-4, Las Arenas, **Bilbao** (Vizcaya) 48930 (tel./fax 94 464 11 24). Franchy y Roca, 5, 6th fl., **Las Palmas de Gran Canaria** 35007 (tel. 928 22 60 04; fax 928 22 60 15).

U.S. Embassies: C. Serrano, 75, **Madrid** 28006 (tel. 91 587 22 00; fax 91 587 23 03). **Consulate General:** Passeig Reina Elisenda, 23, **Barcelona** 08034 (tel. 93 280 22 27; fax 93 205 52 06). **Consular Agencies:** Po. Delicias, 7, **Sevilla** 41012 (tel. 95 423 18 85; fax 95 423 20 40). Edificio Arca, C. Los Martínez Escobar, 3, Oficina 7, **Las Palmas** 35007 (tel. 928 27 12 59; fax 928 22 58 63). Centro Comercial "Las Rampas," Fase 2, Planta 1, Locales 12G7 & 12G8, **Fuengirola (Málaga)** 29640 (tel. 95 247 48 91; fax 95 246 51 89); C. Paz 6, Local 5, **Valencia** 46003 (tel. 96 351 69 73; fax 96 352 95 65). Cantón Grande, 6-8 E, **La Coruña** 15003 (tel. 981 21 32 33; fax 981 22 88 08). Av. Jaume III, 26, **Palma de Mallorca** 07012 (tel. 971 72 50 51).

Portugal

Australian Embassy: Refer to the Australian Embassy in Paris: 4, rue Jean Rey, 15th arrondisement Paris 75724 France (tel. (01) 40 59 33 00; fax (01) 40 59 33 10).

British Embassy: R. São Bernardo, 33, 1200 **Lisbon** (tel. (1) 392 40 00; fax 392 41 86; Britembassy@mail.telepac.pt). **Consulates:** Av. da Boavista, 3072, 4100 **Porto** (tel. (2) 618 47 89; fax 610 04 38). Largo Francisco A. Mauricio, 71st fl., 8500 **Portimão** (tel. (8) 241 78 04; fax 241 78 06).

Canadian Embassy: Av. Liberdade, 144, 4th fl., 1250 **Lisbon** (tel. (1) 347 48 92; fax 347 64 66).

Irish Embassy: R. da Imprensa à Estrela, 4th fl., Suite 1, 1200 **Lisbon** (tel. (1) 392 94 90; fax 397 73 63).

New Zealand Embassy: Refer to the British Embassy in Lisbon or the New Zealand Embassy in Italy at Via Zara, 28, **Rome** 00198 (tel. 06 440 29 28/29/30; fax 06 440 29 84; nzemb.rom@agora.stm.it).

South African Embassy: Av. Luis Bivar, 10, 1097 **Lisbon** (tel. (1) 353 50 41; fax 353 57 13; email SAfrican@mail.EUnet.pt).

U.S. Embassy: Av. Forças Armadas, 1600 **Lisbon** (tel. (1) 727 33 00; fax 727 23 54).

Morocco

Algerian, 159 bd. Moulay Idriss (tel. 80 41 75).

British Embassy: 17 bd. de la Tour Hassan, B.P. 45, **Rabat** (tel. (7) 72 09 05 or 72 09 06; fax 70 45 31). **Consulates:** 43 bd. d'Anfa, B.P. 13, #762, **Casablanca** 01 (tel. (2) 22 17 41 or 29 58 96; fax 26 57 79). 41 bd. Mohammed V, B.P. 2122, **Tangiers** (tel. (9) 94 15 57; fax 94 22 84).

Canadian Embassy: 13 Bis, Jaafar Assadik, B.P. 709, Agdal, **Rabat** (tel. (7) 67 28 80; fax 67 21 87). **Consulate:** For visas only 31 Rue Hanza, B.P. 709, Agdal, **Rabat** (tel. (7) 67 23 75 or 67 23 77; fax 67 24 31).

Irish Embassy: Refer to the Irish Embassy in Lisbon (above). In case of emergency, contact any Commonwealth embassy.

Australian Embassy: Refer to the Canadian Embassy in Cairo (above). In case of emergency, contact any Commonwealth embassy.

New Zealand Embassy: Refer to the New Zealand Embassy in Spain (above). In case of emergency, contact any Commonwealth embassy.

Tunisian, 36A bd. d'Anfa, Casablanca (tel. 22 19 20 or 27 49 67).

U.S. Embassy: 2 Av. de Marrakesh, **Rabat** (tel. (7) 76 22 65; fax 76 56 61). 24hr. emergency phone (tel. (7) 76 96 39). **Consulate:** 8 bd. Moulay Youssef, **Casablanca** (tel. (2) 26 45 50; fax 20 41 27).

■ Getting Around

For country-specific information on traveling, traveling organizations, and travel discounts, see the respective **Getting There and Around** sections in each country's introduction. For **Spain,** see p. 46; for **Portugal,** check out p. 481; and for **Morocco,** try p. 587.

BY TRAIN

To this day trains remain the budget travelers' preferred mode of travel through Europe. Bring food and water with you on trips; the on-board cafes can be pricey, and train water can be undrinkable. Trains are far from theft-proof, so lock your compartment door if you can, and always keep valuables on your person.

Many train stations have different counters for domestic and international tickets, seat reservations, and information. Even with a railpass, you are not guaranteed a seat on a train unless you make a reservations (US$3-10). Reservations are often required on major, high-speed lines (such as France's TGV or Spain's AVE), and it may be necessary to purchase a supplement (around $US10 for AVE). For overnight travel, a tight, open bunk called a *couchette* is an affordable luxury (about US$20; reserve ahead).

Railpasses

Ideally conceived, a railpass allows you to jump on any train in Europe, go wherever you want whenever you want, and change your plans at will. With your railpass you will receive a timetable for major routes and a map with details on possible ferry, steamer, bus, car rental, and hotel discounts. In practice, it's not so simple. You still must stand in line to pay for supplements, seat reservations, and *couchette* reservations, as well as to have your pass validated when you first use it. Importantly, railpasses don't always pay off. You may find it tough to make your railpass pay for itself in Spain, Portugal, or Morocco, in addition to other countries where train fares are reasonable, distances short, or buses preferable. If, however, the total cost of your trips nears the price of the pass, the convenience of avoiding ticket lines may be worth the difference. For ballpark estimates, consult a travel agent (see **Budget Travel Agencies,** p. 36), the **DERTravel** railpass brochure, or **RailEurope's** brochure or voice system for prices of point-to-point tickets (see below). Add them up and compare with railpass prices.

A **Eurailpass** remains perhaps the best option for non-E.U. travelers. Eurailpasses offer unlimited travel during their duration and are valid in all major European countries (including Spain and Portugal, but not Morocco). Eurailpasses (and Europass, see below) are designed by the E.U. itself and are purchasable only by non-Europeans almost exclusively from non-European distributors. These passes must be sold at uniform prices determined by the E.U., so no one travel agent is better than another as far as the pass itself is concerned. Some agents, however, tack on a $10 handling fee and others offer different perks with purchase of a railpass, so shop around.

The first class **Eurailpass** rarely pays off; it is offered for 15 days (US$538), 21 days (US$698), one month (US$864), two months (US$1224), or three months (US$1512). Those traveling in a group of two to five might prefer the **Eurail Saverpass,** which allows unlimited first-class travel for 15 days (US$458 per person), 21 days (US$594), one month (US$734), two months (US$1040), or three months (US$1286). Travelers ages 12 to 25 can buy a **Eurail Youthpass,** good for 15 days (US$376), 21 days (US $489), one month (US$605), two months (US$857), or three months (US $1059) of second-class travel. **Eurail Flexipasses** allow limited first-class travel within a two-month period: 10 days of travel US$634, 15 days US$836. These prices drop to US$540 and US$710, respectively, when traveling in a group of two to five. **Youth Flexipasses,** for those under 26 who wish to travel second-class, are available for US$444 or US$585, respectively. Children ages four to 11 pay half price, and children under four travel free.

The **Europass** combines France, Germany, Italy, Spain, and Switzerland in one plan. With a Europass you can travel in any of these five countires from five to 15 days within a window of two months. First-class adult prices begin at US$326 and increase incrementally by US$42 for each extra day of travel. With purchase of a first-class ticket you can buy an identical ticket for your traveling partner for 40% off. Second-class youth tickets begin at US$216 and increase incrementally by $29 for each extra day of travel. Children between the ages of four to 11 travel for half the price of a first-class ticket. You can add associate countries (including Portugal) for a fee: $60 for one associated country, less for subsequent countries. The Europass introduces planning complications; you must plan your routes so that they make use only of countries you've "purchased." They're serious about this restriction: if you cut through a country you haven't purchased you will be fined. You should plan your itinerary before buying a Europass. It will save you money if your travels are confined to between three and five adjacent Western European countries or if you know that you want to go only to large cities. Europasses are not appropriate if you like to take lots of side trips—you'll waste rail days. If you're tempted to add lots of rail days and associate countries, consider the Eurailpass.

It is best to buy your Eurail or Europass before leaving. Once you are in Europe, you will probably have to use a credit card to buy over the phone from a railpass agent in a non-E.U. country, who can send the pass to you by express mail. Contact Let's Go Travel (see **Budget Travel Agencies,** p. 36) or almost any travel agent handling European travel. Eurailpasses are not refundable once validated; if your pass is completely unused and unvalidated and you have the original purchase documents, you can get an 85% refund from the place of purchase. You can get a replacement for a lost pass only if you have purchased insurance on it under the Pass Protection Plan (US$10). All Eurailpasses can be purchased from a travel agent or from **Rail Europe Group,** 500 Mamaroneck Ave., Harrison, NY 10528 (in U.S. tel. (800) 438 7245; fax (800) 432 1329; in Canada tel. (800) 361 7245; fax (905) 602 4198; http://www.raileurope.com), which also sells point-to-point tickets. They offer special rates for groups of 10 or more traveling together.

For E.U. citizens, there are **InterRail Passes,** for which six months' residence in Europe makes you eligible. There are 8 InterRail zones: A (Republic of Ireland, Great Britain, Northern Ireland), B (Norway, Sweden, Finland), C (Germany, Austria, Denmark, and Switzerland), D (Croatia, Czech Republic, Hungary, Poland, Slovakia), E (France, Belgium, Netherlands, Luxembourg), F (Spain, Portugal, Morocco), G (Italy, Greece, Slovenia, Turkey), and H (Bulgaria, Romania, Yugoslavia, Macedonia). You can buy a pass good for 22 days in one zone (under 26 UK£169, over 26 £229) or one month in two (£209, £279), three (£229, £309), or all eight (£259, £349) zones. Tickets are available at main train stations and travel agents throughout Spain and Portugal.

If your travels will be limited to Spain and or Portugal consider a regional or national railpass or a national rail-and-drive pass. See the respective national **Getting There and Around** sections for more details (for Spain, p. 46; for Portugal, p. 481). Check with a railpass agent before leaving for purchasing details.

Rail tickets

For travelers under 26, **BIJ** tickets (Billets Internationals de Jeunesse) are a great alternative to railpasses. Available for international trips within Europe, they knock 20-40% off regular second-class fares. Tickets are good for 60 days after purchase and allow a number of stopovers along the normal direct route of the train journey. Issued for a specific international route between two points, they must be used in the direction and order of the designated route (side- or back-tracking must be done at your expense) and must be bought in Europe. They are available from European travel agents. Contact **Wasteels** (in England tel. (0171) 834 70 66; fax 630 76 28) for info.

Useful Resources

The ultimate reference for planning rail trips is the **Thomas Cook European Timetable** (US$28; with a map of Europe that includes train and ferry routes US$39; postage US$5). This timetable, updated monthly, covers all major and most minor train routes in Europe. In North America, order it from **Forsyth Travel Library** (see **Travel Publications,** p. 3). In Europe find it at any **Thomas Cook Money Exchange Center.** In the rest of the world, call 1733 503 571, or write Thomas Cook Publishing, P.O. Box 227, Thorpe Wood, Peterborough, PE3 6PU, U.K. Also available from Forsyth Travel library, or in bookstores, is **Traveling Europe's Trains** (US$15) by Jay Brunhouse, which includes maps and sightseeing suggestions. The annual railpass special edition of the free Rick Steves' **Europe Through the Back Door** travel newsletter and catalogue (tel. (425) 771 8303; fax 771 0833; email rick@ricksteves.com; http://www.ricksteves.com), available by mail or on the web, provides comparative analysis of European railpasses with national or regional passes and point-to-point tickets.

BY BUS

In Portugal and Morocco, the bus system is more extensive and efficient than rail options. In Spain, trains are perhaps preferable for longer journeys, but buses have much more extensive coverage of the country. In all three countries, bus travel is often more confusing, with scores of different stations and companies in many cities.

    Eurolines, 4 Cardiff Rd., Luton LU1 1PP, U.K. (tel. (01582) 40 45 11; fax (01582) 40 06 94; in London (0171) 730 82 35; email welcome@eurolines.uk.com; http://www.eurolines.co.uk), offers the Eurolines Pass with unlimited 30-day (UK£199; under 26 and over 60 UK£159) or 60-day (UK£249; under 26 and over 60 UK£199) travel between 30 major tourist destinations, including Madrid and Barcelona. They also offer great connections between Spain, Portugal, and Morocco. The Barcelona office (tel. 93 490 40 00; http://www.travelcom.es/juliavia) at Estación de Autobuses de SANTS, C. Viriato, s/n, has more info. **Eurobus UK Ltd.,** Coldborough House, Market Street, Bracknell, Berkshire RG121JA, U.K. (tel. (01344) 30 03 01; fax 86 07 80; email info@eurobus.uk.com; http://www.eurobus.uk.com), offers cheap bus trips to 25 major cities in 10 major European countries, including Spain and Portugal, for those between ages 18 and 38. The buses, with English speaking guides and drivers, stop door-to-door at one hostel or budget hotel per city and let you hop on and off. Tickets are sold by zone; for any one zone US$195, for any two zones US$299, for all three zones US$319. Travelers under 26 are eligible for discounts on all tickets. For purchase in the U.S., contact Commonwealth Express (tel. (800) 387 6287); in Canada contact Travel CUTS (see **Budget Travel Agencies,** p. 39).

BY CAR

Cars offer speed, freedom, access to the countryside, and an escape from the town-to-town mentality of trains. Unfortunately, they also insulate you from the *esprit de corps* of rail traveling. Although a single traveler won't save by renting a car, four usually will. If you don't want to travel exclusively by car, both rail-and-drive packages and fly-and-drive packages are available for both Spain and Portugal. Contact Rail Europe (see **By Train,** above) or other major travel agents.

    You can **rent** a car from a U.S.-based firm (Alamo, Avis, Budget, or Hertz), a European-wide company (Europcar), a local company, or from a tour operator, which will arrange a rental for you from a European company at its own rates. Multinationals offer greater flexibility, but tour operators often strike better deals. Local companies, especially in Morocco, can be unreliable. Expect to pay US$150 to 450 per week for

ESSENTIALS

a small car from an international firm. Reserve well before leaving for Europe (it's cheaper anyway) and pay in advance if at all possible. Always check if prices quoted include tax and collision insurance; some credit card companies will cover this automatically. Check the terms of insurance, particularly the size of the deductible. Ask your airline about special fly-and-drive packages; you may get up to one week of free or discounted rental. Minimum age is 21 in Iberia and Morocco. For more rules, restrictions, and tips, see the **Getting Around: By Car** sections of each country. For Spain see, p. 47; for Portugal, see p. 482; for Morocco, see p. 587.

Try **Auto Europe,** 39 Commercial St., P.O. Box 7006, Portland, ME 04101 (tel. (800) 223 5555; fax (800) 235 6321; email webmaster@autoeurope.com; http://www.autoeurope.com); **Avis Rent a Car** (tel. (800) 331 1084; http://www.avis.com), with locations throughout western and eastern Europe; **Budget Rent a Car** (tel. (800) 472 3325; http://www.budgetrentacar.com); **Europe by Car,** One Rockefeller Plaza, New York, NY 10020 (tel. (800) 223 1516 or (212) 581 3040; fax (212) 246 1458; http://www.europebycar.com); **National Car Rental** (tel. in U.S. (800) 227-3876; in Canada (800) 227 7368; in France (01) 45 00 08 06); **Hertz Rent a Car** (tel. (800) 654-3001; http://www.hertz.com), throughout Europe; or **Kemwel Holiday Autos** (tel. (800) 678 0678; email kha@kemwel.com; http://www.kemwel.com).

For longer than 17 days, **leasing** can be cheaper than renting; it is often the only option for those ages 18 to 21. The cheapest leases are agreements to buy the car and then sell it back to the manufacturer at a prearranged price. As far as you're concerned, though, it's a lease and doesn't entail enormous financial transactions. Leases generally include insurance and are not taxed. Expect to pay at least US$1200 for 60 days. Contact **Auto Europe, Europe by Car,** or **Kemwel Holiday Autos.** You will need to make arrangements in advance.

If you're brave and know what you're doing, **buying** a used car or van in Europe and selling it just before you leave can provide the cheapest wheels for longer trips. David Shore and Patty Campbell's **Europe by Van and Motorhome** (US$14) guides you through the entire process of renting, leasing, buying, and selling vehicles in Europe. To order, call or email Shore/Campbell Publications (tel./fax (800) 659 5222 or (760) 723 6184; email shorecam@aol.com; http://members.aol.com/europevan).

Before setting off, know the laws of the countries in which you'll be driving. The **Association for Safe International Road Travel (ASIRT)** can provide more specific information about road conditions. They are located at 11769 Gainsborough Rd., Potomac, MD 20854 (tel. (301) 983 5252; fax 983 3663; email asirt@erols.com; http://www.asirt.org). More general info is available from your local automobile association (see **Driving Permits and Car Insurance,** p. 10).

FLYING AROUND

Flying across Europe on regularly scheduled flights can devour your budget. **Alitalia** (in U.S. tel. (800) 223 5730; http://www.alitalia.it) sells "Europlus," a set of cheap flight coupons, in conjunction with a transatlantic flight on Alitalia. To non-Europe residents, **Lufthansa** (tel. (800) 399 5838; fax (800) 522 2329; http://www.lufthansa.com) offers "Discover Europe," a package of coupons that varies in cost, depending on country of origin. For U.S. residents, tickets cost US$125 to 200.

United States citizens can purchase **Eurair** (tel. (888) 387 2479 fax (512) 404 1291; http://www.eurair.com) passes (US$90 each, airport taxes not included) to travel between 50 European cities. In general, always consult budget travel agents, student travel agents, and local newspapers for discounts. The **Air Travel Advisory Bureau** in London (tel. (0171) 636 50 00; http://www.atab.co.uk) can also point the way to discount flights. In addition, many European airlines give intercontinental passengers discounts on flights within Europe after arrival. Check with a travel agent for details.

BY BOAT

Travel by boat is an enchanting alternative much favored by Europeans but overlooked by most foreigners. The majority of European ferries are comfortable and well equipped. Check in at least two hours early for a prime spot. Avoid the astronomically priced cafeterias by bringing your own food. Ask for discounts; ISIC holders can often get student fares, and Eurail passholders get many reductions and free trips. You'll occasionally have to pay a small port tax (under US$10). Advance planning and reserved ticket purchases through a travel agency can spare you days of waiting in dreary ports for the next boat to embark.

Mediterranean ferries may be the most glamorous, but they can also be the most rocky. Reservations are recommended, especially in July and August, when ships are insufferably crowded and expensive. Bring toilet paper—there is occasionally a dearth on board. Ferries run on erratic schedules, with varying prices, so shop around for the best deal. Beware of dinky, unreliable companies that often do not take reservations.

Trasmediterránea offers high quality service around the edges of Spain, Portugal, and Morocco, including service between the Balearic Islands and Canary Islands (Spanish national 24hr. reservation and info tel. 902 45 46 45). For more info on transportation to the Balearics and Canaries, see p. 333 and p. 468, respectively. Frequent ferries also shuttle back and forth between Spain and Morocco. For more info see **Getting There and Around,** p. 587. Smaller companies operate regionally. Check your desired destination's write-up for more transportation details.

BY BICYCLE

Today, biking is one of the key elements of the classic budget Eurovoyage. With the proliferation of mountain bikes, you can do some serious natural sight-seeing.

Touring involves pedaling both yourself and everything you own in **panniers** (bags that strap to your bike). Prepare before you leave: have your bike tuned up, learn how to fix it, and train. Once there, wear visible clothing, drink plenty of water (even if you're not thirsty), and ride on the same side as the traffic. A bike helmet is essential (US$30-150), as is a lock. U-shaped **Citadel** or **Kryptonite** (US$30) are insured against theft of your bike for one to two years. **Bike Nashbar** (tel. (800) 627 4227; fax (800) 456-1223; http://www.nashbar.com) has excellent prices and cheerfully beats advertised competitors' offers by US$50. They ship anywhere in the U.S. or Canada.

In **Spain,** cycling is an old passion and you will see and meet many other serious cyclists on weekends, especially near big cities. The Camino de Santiago in the north is a popular touring route. In **Portugal,** biking is less common and hence a bit less safe. In **Morocco,** bicycling is considerably more dangerous, but not impossible. A **mountain bike** adds the off-road riding option and is sturdier, but slower, than a road bike. Mountain bikes are especially useful in Morocco, where it is often safer to ride on the dirt shoulder than on the road.

Renting a bike beats bringing your own only if you are touring casually or for a short time, as it is hard to rent a good bike. Many airlines will count your bike as your second free piece of luggage, a few charge. The additional fee can run US$60-110 each trip. Bikes must be packed in a cardboard box with the pedals and front wheel detached. Get a box from your local bike shop or buy a plastic one—your bike will thank you. Most ferries let you take your bike for free or a nominal fee. On trains the cost varies from small to substantial.

For info about touring routes, consult national tourist offices. Road maps are key; **Michelin road maps** are clear and detailed. If you are nervous about striking out on your own, **Blue Marble Travel** (in U.S. tel. (800) 258 8689; in Canada (519) 624 2494; in Paris 01 42 36 02 34; http://www.blumarbl.com) offers bike tours designed for adults aged 20 to 50. Pedal with or without your 10 to 15 companions through Spain, Portugal, the Alps, Austria, France, Germany, Italy, and Scandinavia.

ESSENTIALS

BY MOPED AND MOTORCYCLE

Motorized bikes offer an enjoyable, relatively cheap way to tour coastal areas and countryside, particularly where there are few cars. They don't use much gas, can be put on trains and ferries, and are a compromise between the high cost of car travel and the limited range of bicycles. Yet, they're uncomfortable for long distances, dangerous in the rain, and unpredictable on rough roads and gravel. Always wear a helmet, and never ride with a backpack. If you've never been on a moped before, a twisting mountain road is not the place to start. Expect to spend about US$20-35 per day; try auto repair shops, and bargain. Motorcycles normally require a license. Before renting, ask if the quoted price includes tax and insurance, or you may be hit with an unexpected additional fee. Avoid handing your passport over as a deposit; if you have an accident or mechanical failure you may not get it back until you cover all repairs. Pay ahead of time instead.

In **Spain,** mopeders are thick on the coast and not uncommon on highways. Most cities have rental agencies (US$30 per day, less in coastal areas where tourist rentals are more common). Portugal, too, is revving up its engines. Although two-wheeling is less popular here than in the rest of Europe, rental places have opened up in most cities and in many tourist centers. Ask at the local tourist office for details.

BY THUMB

Let's Go strongly urges you to consider seriously the risks before you choose to hitch. We do not recommend hitching as a safe means of transportation, and none of the information presented here is intended to do so.

No one should hitch without careful consideration of the risks involved. Not everyone can be an airplane pilot, but any bozo can drive a car. Hitching means entrusting your life to a random person who happens to stop beside you on the road and risking theft, assault, sexual harassment, and unsafe driving. In spite of these dangers, there are gains to hitching. Favorable hitching experiences allow you to meet local people and get where you're going, especially where public transportation is sketchy. The choice, however, remains yours.

A **woman traveling alone should not hitch.** A man and a woman are a safer combination, while two men will have a harder time. In **Iberia,** hitching is neither the quickest nor the most reliable or safest means of transportation. In **Morocco,** one should not hitch.

Where one stands is vital. Experienced hitchers pick a spot outside of built-up areas, where drivers can stop, return to the road without causing an accident, and have time to look over potential passengers as they approach. Hitching (or even standing) on super-highways is usually illegal: one may thumb only at rest stops or at the entrance ramps to highways. In the Practical Information section of many cities, we list the tram or bus lines that take travelers to strategic points for hitching out.

Finally, success will depend on what one looks like. Successful hitchers travel light and stack their belongings in a compact but visible cluster. Most Europeans signal with an open hand rather than a thumb; many write their destination on a sign in large, bold letters and draw a smiley-face under it. Drivers prefer hitchers who are neat and wholesome. No one stops for anyone wearing sunglasses.

Safety issues are always imperative, even for those who are not hitching alone. Safety-minded hitchers avoid getting in the back of a two-door car, and they never let go of their backpacks. They will not get into a car that they can't get out of again in a hurry. If they ever feel threatened, they insist on being let off, regardless of where they are. Acting as if they are going to open the car door or vomit on the upholstery will usually get a driver to stop. Hitchhiking at night can be particularly dangerous; experienced hitchers stand in well-lit places and expect drivers to be leery of nocturnal thumbers (or open-handers).

Look for ride services (listed in the Practical Information for major cities), a cross between hitchhiking and the ride boards, which pair drivers with riders; the fee varies according to destination. Riders and drivers can enter their names on the internet through the **Taxistop** website (http://www/taxistop.be). Foreign exchange schools, universities, and foreign language schools often have ride bulletin boards.

In **Spain,** hitchers report that Castilla and Andalucía offer little more than a long, hot wait, and that hitchhiking out of Madrid—in any direction—is virtually impossible. The Mediterranean Coast and the islands rate as more promising. Approaching people for rides at gas stations near highways and rest stops reportedly gets results.

In **Portugal,** hitchers are a rare commodity. Beach-bound locals occasionally hitch in summer but otherwise stick to the inexpensive bus system; most of the thumbers you'll see are tourists. Rides are easiest to come by between smaller towns. Again, best results are reputedly at gas stations near highways and rest stops.

Almost no one in **Morocco** hitches, although flagging down buses and trains may feel similar. Transportation is dirt cheap by European and North American standards. If Moroccans do pick up a foreigner, they will most likely expect payment for the ride. Hitching is more frequent in the south and in the mountains.

BY FOOT

Europe's grandest scenery can often be seen only by foot. *Let's Go* describes many daytrips for those who want to hoof it, but native inhabitants, hostel proprietors, and fellow travelers are the best source of tips. Many European countries have hiking and mountaineering organizations, some of which provide inexpensive, simple accommodations in splendid settings. Check your local bookstore for popular trails.

KEEPING IN TOUCH

▓ Mailing from Home

Sending airmail to Spain from the U.S. requires between 4 and 7 days. To Portugal, allow 7 to 10 days. Airmail to Morocco usually requires around two weeks, but it could either go more quickly or much, much more slowly. Mailing from European locations to any of these countries is a few days faster; from Australia, New Zealand, or South Africa, a couple days slower. Mail sent to smaller towns will take longer. For faster service, there are more expensive options available from private companies and your national postal office. **Federal Express** (in U.S. tel. for international operator (800) 247 4747) is available to and from these countries, in Morocco by contract with World Express. Whether private or public, express services can provide delivery in one to three days.

For information on **mailing home** from Spain, Portugal, and Morocco, see the respective **Keeping in Touch** sections in each country intro. For Spain, turn to p. 49, for Portugal, flip to p. 483, and for Morocco, try p. 589.

Mail can be sent internationally through **Poste Restante, Posta Restante,** or **Lista de Correos** in Spain (all equivalent to General Delivery) to any city or town. Mark the envelope "HOLD" and address it with the last name capitalized and underlined. The postal code listed should be that for General Delivery, not for the city center. If you are not sure, leave the postal code out altogether—the mail should arrive anyway.

Spain: mail should be addressed as follows: <u>ROUX</u>, Allison; Lista de Correos; City Name; Postal Code; SPAIN; AIR MAIL.

Portugal: general delivery mail is *Posta Restante.* Mail should be addressed as follows: <u>THUROW</u>, Torben; Posta Restante; Post Office Street Address; City Name; Postal Code; PORTUGAL; AIR MAIL. Be warned—the system is far from efficient.

Morocco: general delivery mail is *Poste Restante,* but it may not get there. Send mail to a major hotel or AmEx office instead. If you want to try, mail should be addressed as follows: <u>O'GRADY</u>, Padraig; Poste Restante; Post Office Address; City Name; MOROCCO; AIR MAIL. The mail will go to a special desk in the central post office, unless you specify a post office by street address or postal code. As mail is sometimes misfiled, request your mail under both first and last names (in Morocco also try "M" for "Mr." or "Ms."). Bring a passport or international student ID card for identification. If you must leave town while expecting mail, you can have that mail forwarded to another general delivery address.

American Express travel offices throughout Iberia and Morocco will act as a mail service for cardholders if you contact them in advance. Under this free **"Client Letter Service,"** they will hold mail for no more than 30 days, forward upon request, and accept telegrams. Just like *Poste Restante,* the last name of the person to whom the mail is addressed should be capitalized and underlined. Some offices will offer these services to non-cardholders (especially those who have purchased AmEx Travelers' Cheques), but you must call ahead to make sure. *Let's Go* lists AmEx office locations for most large cities in the **Practical Information** section. A complete list is available free from AmEx (in U.S. tel. (800) 528 4800, in UK 171 930 4411; http://www.americanexpress.com).

■ Calling the Region

Let's Go lists the city **telephone code** under **Practical Information** in Portugal and Morocco. The bracketed 0 for Portugal and Morocco codes is necessary **only if you are calling from a different area code within the same country.** If you are calling from another country, you will not need to dial the parenthesized number. For example, we have listed the telephone code for Lisbon as (0)1. To reach Lisbon from elsewhere in Portugal, dial 01, then the number. To reach Lisbon from another country, dial 1, then the number. Spain no longer has city or area codes. **In this Essentials section, Let's Go has included city codes but omitted such parenthesized long-distance code numbers.** For example, we have not included the 1 necessary to dial long-distance within the United States.

To place a direct international call, dial the international access code (011 from the U.S. and Canada, 0011 from Australia, 00 from the U.K. and Northern Ireland, 09 from Ireland) + country code + city code + local number. You can call the operator beforehand to get an idea of how much your call will cost. Other **international access codes,** in addition to **country codes,** are listed on the inside back cover. Remember time differences when you call; there is a list in the **Appendix** (see p. 648).

■ Telephones

For **country-specific information on calling** within and from Spain, Portugal, and Morocco, see each country's **Keeping in Touch** section (for Spain, see p. 49, for Portugal, see p. 483, for Morocco, see p. 589). Wherever possible, use a calling card (see **calling cards** below) for international phone calls, as the long distance rates for national phone services in all three countries are unpredictable and steep. For all types of calls, phone rates tend to be highest in the morning, lower in the evening, and lowest on Sunday and late at night.

You can make international calls directly from **pay phones,** but you will need to drop your coins as quickly as your words. Phone cash cards in various denominations are available in all three countries and are much more convenient. Be wary of more expensive, private pay phones and flee from the insidious in-room hotel phone call. Although incredibly convenient, these calls invariably include an arbitrary and sky-high surcharge. Using a calling card or a call-back service from the hotel phone usually, but not always, circumvents such charges.

English-speaking operators are available for both local and international assistance. In most countries, these operators will place **collect calls** for you. American operators can be reached by dialing the MCI or AT&T access number specific for the country from which you are calling.

Calling cards are a much better deal. For more information, call **AT&T** about its **USADirect** and **World Connect** services (tel. (888) 288 4685; from abroad (810) 262 6644 collect); **Sprint** (tel. (800) 877 4646; from abroad (913) 624 5335 collect); or **MCI WorldPhone** and **World Reach** (tel. (800) 444 4141; from abroad dial the country's MCI access number). In Canada, contact Bell Canada **Canada Direct** (tel. (800) 561 8868); in the U.K., British Telecom **BT Direct** (tel. (800) 34 51 44); in Ireland, Telecom Éireann **Ireland Direct** (tel. (800) 250 250); in Australia, Telstra **Australia Direct** (tel. 13 22 00); in New Zealand, **Telecom New Zealand** (tel. 123); and in South Africa, **Telkom South Africa** (tel. 09 03).The **calling card codes** to access each service are listed on the inside back cover. Ask about their other travel services. Many of these and other long distance carriers provide legal and medical advice, exchange rate information, and translation services.

Callback phone services, especially when calling the U.S., are often the cheapest way to call. Under these plans, you call a specified number, ring once, and hang up. The company's computer calls back and gives you a U.S. dial tone. You can then make as many calls as you want, at rates about 20-60% lower than you'd pay using credit cards or pay phones. This option is most economical for loquacious travelers, as services may include a minimum billing per month. For more info or to sign up, call **America Tele-Fone** (tel. (800) 321 5817) or **Telegroup** (tel. (800) 338 0225).

■ Electronic Mail (email)

The wave of the future, email is an attractive communication option and increasingly easy to access in Spain, Portugal, and Morocco. In Spain, a cyber cafe is listed in the Practical Information section of most cities. You will usually pay around 500-1000ptas per hour in Spain. In Portugal and Morocco, cyber cafes are fewer and farther between but exist for major cities. Portuguese cyber cafes usually run about 600-1100$ per hour. Keep your eyes open—new cyber cafes are springing up everywhere.

With a minimum of computer knowledge and a little planning, email lets you beam messages anywhere and instantly for no per-message charges. One option is to befriend college students as you go and ask if you can use their email accounts. If you're not the finagling type, **Traveltales.com** (http://traveltales.com) provides free, web-based email for travelers and maintains a list of over 500 cybercafes throughout the world (they also sell a book of cyber cafes on their website, for those so inclined), travel links, and a travelers' chat room. Other free, web-based email providers include **Hotmail** (http://www.hotmail.com), **Yahoo! Mail** (http://mail.yahoo.com), and **US-ANET** (http://www.usa.net). Many free email providers are funded by advertising, and some require subscribers to fill out a questionnaire. For information on internet accessibility world-wide, contact http://www.nsrc.org, which has a host of connections to sites supplying further internet information on any country.

If you're already hooked up to the infobahn at home, you should be able to find access numbers for your destination country; check with your internet provider before leaving. If you're not connected, one comparatively cheap, easy-to-use provider is **America Online**, 8615 Westwood Center Drive, Vienna, VA 22070 (tel. (800) 827 6364; http://www.aol.com), with connecting websites for Australia, Canada, France, Germany, Japan, Sweden, and U.K). The interactive computer service now offers **"GLOBALnet,"** making it possible for American net-junkies to access the internet, sexy chat rooms, and of course email through their home accounts while traveling in 70 countries. The hurdles for budget travelers are the US$6-12 per hour surcharge and the fact that GLOBALnet only works on computers with AOL software already installed. In other words, to use the service you must travel with your own portable computer or install the software on computers as you go and log on as a guest.

■ Other Communication Options

For more country specific information on other communication options, especially faxes, see the respective **Keeping in Touch** sections. For **Spain,** see p. 49, for **Portugal,** hit p. 483, for **Morocco,** hop to p. 589. Faxes can be sent and received to all three countries via public and private companies.

Between May 2 and Octoberfest, **EurAide,** P.O. Box 2375, Naperville, IL 60567 (tel. (630) 420 2343; fax 420 2369; http://www.cube.net/kmu/euraide.html), offers **Overseas Access,** a service useful to travelers without a set itinerary. The cost is US$15 per week or US$40 per month plus a US$15 registration fee. To reach you, people call, fax, or use the internet to leave a message; you receive it by calling Munich whenever you wish, which is cheaper than calling overseas. You may also leave messages for callers to pick up by phone. The web-site also provides Eurail time-table information, and order forms for railpasses as well as making reservations on European trains.

SPAIN

US $1 = 148.53 pesetas (ptas)	100ptas = US $0.67
CDN $1 = 96.58ptas	100ptas = CDN $1.04
UK £1 = 247.74ptas	100ptas = UK £0.40
IR £1 = 212.41ptas	100ptas = IR £0.47
AUS $1 = 86.66ptas	100ptas = AUS $1.15
NZ $1 = 74.55ptas	100ptas = NZ $1.34
SAR 1 = 23.80ptas	100ptas = SAR 4.20
POR 1$ = 0.8285ptas	100ptas = POR 120.70$
MOR 1 dh = 15.56ptas	100ptas = MOR 6.42dh
EURO = 167.51ptas	100ptas = EURO 0.60

ESSENTIALS

■ Getting There and Around

Transportation to and within Spain is uniformly good, with a few rural exceptions. The easiest, quickest, and perhaps cheapest method of entering Spain is by plane, although Barcelona is well-connected to the European rail system. Buses have the most extensive coverage and are probably the best option for short trips. Trains are best for longer journeys within Spain, as domestic flights usually cost significantly more. Spain's few islands are accessible by both plane and ferry. See p. 27 for general information about traveling to Europe, p. 36 for general information about traveling around Europe, whether by plane, train, bus, car, or foot.

BY PLANE

All major international airlines offer service to Madrid and Barcelona, most serve the Balearic and Canary Islands, and many serve Spain's smaller cities. **Iberia** (for reservations and info tel.: in U.S. and Canada (800) 772-4642; in U.K. (171) 8 30 00 11; in Spain 902 400 500; in South Africa (11) 884 92 55; in Ireland (1) 407 30 17; http://www.iberia.com) serves all domestic locations and all major international cities, including the U.S. **Aviaco,** a subsidiary of Iberia, covers only domestic routes. Ask about youth and other discounts—Iberia usually offers a range of ticket types with different restrictions and prices. Some Iberian fares purchased in the U.S. require a 21-day minimum advance purchase, and children under age 12 may be eligible for 25% off Iberian fares with a 21-day advanced purchase.

Iberia's two less-established domestic competitors often offer cheaper fares and are worth seriously investigating. **Air Europa** (in U.S. tel. (888) 238-7672 or (718) 244-6016; in Spain tel. (902) 30 06 00; easyspain@g-air-europa.es; http://www.g-aireuropa.es) flies out of New York City and most European cities to Madrid, Malaga, Tenerife, and Santiago. Discounts available for youth under 22. **SpanAir** (in U.S. tel. (888) 545-5757; in Spain (902) 13 14 15; fax (971) 49 25 53; http://www.spanair.com) also offers international and domestic flights out of Spain.

BY TRAIN

Spanish trains are clean, relatively punctual, and reasonably priced, although they bypass many small towns. Spain's national railway is **RENFE** (**RE**d **N**acional de los **F**errocarriles **E**spañoles). The **Spain Flexipass** offers any three days of travel in a two-month period for US$180; additional days cost $40. The **Iberic Flexipass** offers any three days of unlimited travel in Iberia for a two-month period for US$198; additional

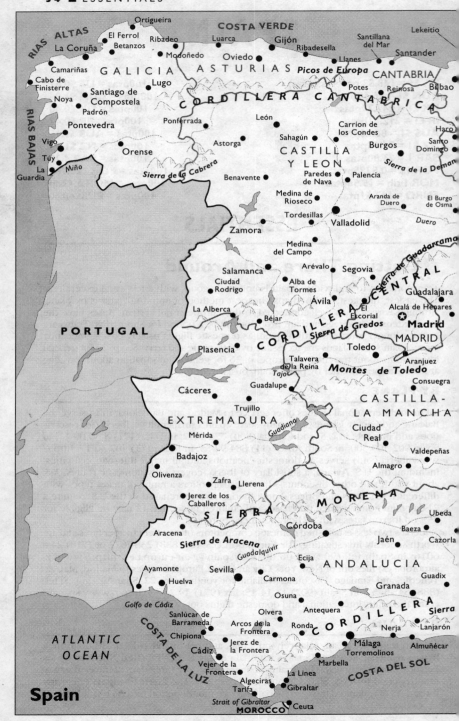

Spain

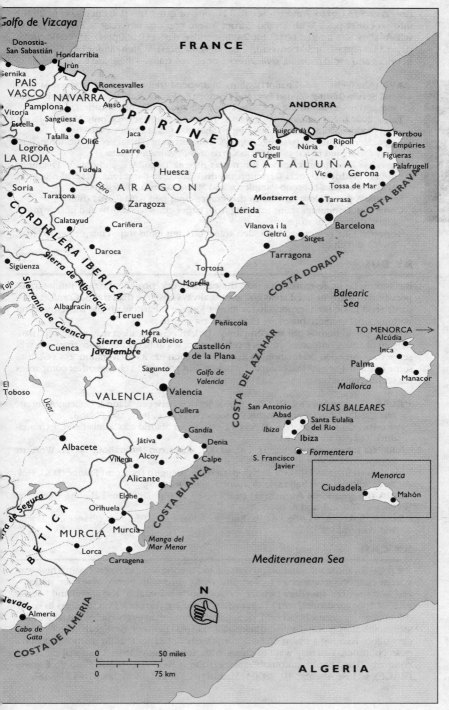

Golfo de Vizcaya

Donostia-
San Sebastián
Hondarribia
Irún
Gernika
PAIS
VASCO
NAVARRA
Roncesvalles
Ansó
Vitoria
Pamplona
Sangüesa
Estella
Tafalla
Olite
Jaca
Logroño
Tudela
Loarre
LA RIOJA
Soria
Huesca
Tarazona
CORDILLERA IBERICA
Zaragoza
Calatayud
Cariñera
Sigüenza
Daroca
Tajo
Sierra de Albaracin
Sierranía de Cuenca
Albarracín
Teruel
Cuenca
Mora
de Rubielos
El
Toboso
Sierra de
Javalambre
Peñíscola
Castellón
de la Plana
Sagunto
Golfo de
Valencia
Ucar
VALENCIA
Valencia
Cullera
Albacete
Játiva
Gandía
Villena
Alcoy
Denia
BÉTICA
Alicante
Calpe
Eldhe
COSTA BLANCA
Orihuela
ra de Segura
Murcia
MURCIA
Manga del
Mar Menor
Lorca
Cartagena
Nevada
Almería
Cabo de
Gata
COSTA DE ALMERIA

FRANCE

PIRINEOS

ANDORRA

Puigcerdà
Seu
d'Urgell
Núria
Ripoll
Portbou
Empúries
Figueras
Palafrugell
CATALUÑA
Vic
Gerona
Montserrat
Tarrasa
Tossa de Mar
COSTA BRAVA
Lérida
Vilanova i la
Geltrú
Barcelona
Sitges
Tarragona
COSTA DORADA
Morella
Tortosa
Ebro
ARAGON

Balearic
Sea

TO MENORCA →
Alcúdia
Inca
Palma
Manacor
Mallorca

COSTA DEL AZAHAR

San Antonio
Abad
Ibiza
Santa Eulalia
del Rio
Ibiza
S. Francisco
Javier
Formentera

ISLAS BALEARES

Menorca
Ciudadela
Mahón

Mediterranean Sea

N

0   50 miles
0   75 km

ALGERIA

days cost $43 (up to 7 more). See Rail Europe or other travel agencies on p. 29 for info on either pass. With a valid Carnet Joven, one can purchase a **Tarjeta Joven,** which allows unlimited travel for 7 consecutive days (19,000ptas), 15 consecutive days (23,000ptas), or 30 consecutive days (30,000ptas). Watch out for big differences in prices and avoid *tranvía, semidirecto,* or *correo* trains—these are turtle slow.

SPAIN

AVE (Alta Velocidad Española): Shiny high-speed trains that dart between Madrid and Sevilla (hitting Ciudad Real and Córdoba). AVE soars above other trains in comfort and price, not just speed. The 10am and noon trains are cheapest.

Talgo 200: *Talgo* trains on AVE tracks. These currently service only Madrid-Málaga and Madrid-Cádiz-Huelva. Changing a Talgo 200 ticket carries a 20% fine.

Talgo: Sleek trains zip passengers in A/C compartments. It's more comfortable, possibly faster, and twice as pricey as *Cercanías-Regionales* trains.

Intercity: Few stops, cheaper, but not as nice as Talgo. A/C and comfy. Five lines cover: Madrid-Valencia-Castellón, Madrid-Zaragoza-Barcelona, Madrid-Alicante, Madrid-Zaragoza-Logroño-Pamplona, and Madrid-Murcia/Cartegena.

Estrella: A pretty slow night train that comes equipped with *literas* (bunks).

Cercanías: Commuter trains traveling from larger cities to suburbs and nearby *pueblos,* with frequent stops.

Regional: Like *cercanías,* but older; trains offering multi-stop, cheap rides to small towns and cities.

BY BUS

Bus routes, far more exhaustive than the rail network, provide the only public transportation to many isolated areas and almost always cost less than trains. Comfort standards tend to be high, especially for longer journeys. Particularly for those traveling within a single region, buses are likely the best way to go.

Spain has numerous private companies; lack of centralization may make trip planning an ordeal. Companies' routes rarely overlap; it's unlikely that more than one will serve your intended destination. In many cities, each has its own station. *Let's Go* lists some of the major national companies below, but you will likely use other companies for within-region travel.

ALSA, Estacion Sur (tel. 91 528 28 03). Service between Madrid, Galicia, Asturias, and Castilla-León. Also to Portugal, Morocco, France, Italy, and Poland.

Auto-Res/Cunisa, S.A. (tel. 91 551 72 00). From Madrid to Castilla-León, Extremadura, Galicia, and Valencia.

Julia Via Internacional (tel. 91 490 40 00). Buses run throughout Iberia, Western Europe, and to Morocco.

Linebús (tel. 93 265 07 00). Serves passengers going to (or from) France, U.K., Holland, Belgium, and Italy; also to, from, and in Morocco.

SAIA (International Autocares) (tel. 91 530 76 00). Drives to Belgium, Germany, France, Holland, and Andorra.

Samar, S.A. (tel. 91 468 48 39). Runs to Aragón and Toulouse (France), Andorra, and Portugal.

BY CAR

See p. 39 for more information on renting and driving a car in Spain. Spain's highway system connects major cities by four-lane *autopistas* with plenty of service stations. Fast is vogue, but **speeders** beware: police can "photograph" the speed and license plate of your car, issuing you a ticket without pulling you over. Purchase **gas** in super (97 octane), normal (92 octane), diesel, and—more than ever—unleaded. Prices are astronomical by North American standards: 115ptas per liter, or slightly over US$3.50 per gallon. **Renting** a car in Spain is considerably cheaper than in many other European countries. You may want to check with Atesa, Spain's largest national car rental company. The Spanish automobile association is **Real Automóbil Club de España (RACE),** C. Jose Abascal, 10, 28003, Madrid (tel. 91 447 32 00; fax 91 447 79 48).

■ Accommodations

YOUTH HOSTELS

Red Española de Albergues Juveniles (REAJ), C. Jose Ortega y Gasset, 71, Madrid 28006 (tel. 91 347 77 00; fax 91 401 81 60), the Spanish Hostelling International (HI) affiliate, runs 165 youth hostels year-round. Prices depend on location (typically some distance away from town center) and services offered, but generally remain between 1000-2000ptas. Rates tend to be higher for guests ages 26 or older. Breakfast is usually included, lunch and dinner occasionally offered. Hostels usually lock out around 11:30pm, and have curfews between midnight and 3am. As a rule, don't expect much privacy. To reserve a bed in high season (July-Aug. and during *fiestas*) call well in advance. A national **Youth Hostel Card** (valid for your country and the HI network), is usually required (see **Hostelling Prep,** p. 9). HI cards are also usually available in Spain's main youth and/or travel company, TIVE. Occasionally, you can stay in a hostel without one and pay extra.

PENSIONES AND HOSTALES

Spanish accommodations have many aliases, distinguished by the different grades of rooms. The cheapest and barest options are **casas de huéspedes** and **hospedaje,** while **pensiones** and **fondas** are a bit nicer. All are basically boarding houses, occasionally with curfews. Higher on the ladder, **hostales** have sinks in their bedrooms, whereas **hostal-residencias** rival *hoteles* in overall quality. The government rates *hostales* on a two-star system; even one-star places in this category are typically quite comfortable. The system also fixes each *hostal*'s prices, posted in the lounge or main entrance. *Hostal* owners invariably dip below the official rates, especially when tourism sags. In all of these different types, the owner usually lives in the same building.

The highest-priced accommodations are **hoteles** which have a bathroom in each room but often overwhelm budget travelers' budgets. The cream of the accommodation crop are the beautiful **Paradores Nacionales**—castles, palaces, convents, and historic buildings since converted into luxurious hotels that often are interesting sights in their own right. 12,000ptas a night is a bargain for a *parador*.

Frequently you'll have to hand over your passport for the night; foot the bill the next morning to get it back. Before doing anything drastic (like choosing to stay), ask to see a room and verify the price, which proprietors are required by law to post visibly in every room and by the main entrance. Haggling for prices, especially in small inns, is common practice. Single rooms in a few cities are hard to come by, so solo travelers should be ready to occasionally pay for a double.

If you have any troubles (with rates or service), ask for the **libro de reclamaciones** (complaint book), which by law must be produced on demand. The argument will usually end immediately, since all complaints must be forwarded to the authorities within 48 hours. Report any problems to tourist offices who may help resolve disputes for you. In the text, **full bath** or **bath** refers to a shower and toilet, while **shower** means just a shower stall. Most rooms that *Let's Go* lists have winter heating, as Spanish winters (particularly in the north and the mountains) can be chilly; on the brighter, hotter side, A/C is documented in *Let's Go* on a case-by-case basis.

ALTERNATIVE ACCOMMODATIONS

To promote tourism in rural areas, tourist authorities may suggest alternative (perhaps more traditional) accommodations. **Casas particulares** (private residences) may sometimes be the only choice in less touristed towns. **Casas rurales** (rural cottages) and **casas rústicas** (farmhouses), officially referred to as *agroturismo,* have overnight rates from 1000 to 3500ptas. Both are somewhat common in northern Asturias and Castilla y León. **Refugios** are rustic mountain huts most frequented by hikers.

SPAIN

Colegios mayores (state university dorms) open their doors to summer travelers; the Consulate General of Spain (see **Embassies and Consulates,** p. 4) should have more info. Likewise, many private universities rent out rooms in their **residencias** (dorms); ask the closest tourist office for details. **Monasteries**—Benedictine and Cistercian—and **convents** house less rowdy travelers. Impressive architecture and unmatched tranquility often accompany this experience—though silence, prayer, and seclusion are the rule. Some of these lodgings are single-sex. Several monasteries refuse to charge, instead suggesting a donation (about 1700ptas). Both national and local tourist offices keep lists of holy lodgings broken down by religious order, number of rooms, and gender stipulations. Make reservations well in advance.

CAMPING

In **Spain,** campgrounds are generally the cheapest choice for two or more people. They either charge separate per person, per tent, and per car fees, or for a *parcela*—a small plot of land—plus possible per person fees. Prices can add up for lone travelers, and even for pairs. The law is on your side: campgrounds are categorized on a three-class system, with rating and pricing based on amenity quality. Like *hostales,* they must post fees within view of the entrance. They must also provide sinks, showers, and toilets. Ritzier ones may even have a playground, grocery store, cafe, restaurant, post office, bike or moped rentals, car wash, and/or pool. Most tourist offices provide info on official camping areas, including the hefty *Guía de campings.* It's wise to schedule reservations and arrive early, especially in high season.

▓ Tipping, Taxes, and Bargaining

Tipping is customary in Spain except when service is included. In restaurants, all menu prices include service charges and tipping is optional. Satisfied customers usually toss in some spare change but nearly always less than 5%. At bars and cafes, it is standard to leave small change. Personal services are also tipped: train or airport porters (100-150ptas per bag), taxi drivers (5-10% of the fare if they're nice), and hotel porters (100-150ptas per bag) are among those who should be tipped.

Spain has a 7% **value-added-tax** known as IVA on all restaurant and accommodations. The prices listed in *Let's Go* are inclusive of IVA unless otherwise mentioned. Retail goods bear a much higher 16% IVA, although listed prices are usually inclusive. Foreigners (non-EU), who have stayed in the EU less than 180 days can claim back the tax paid on purchases at the airport. Ask the shop where you have made the purchase to supply you with a tax return form.

Opportunities for **bargaining** are limited. Try in small hotels and inns, especially in the off season or for longer stays, and at flea markets.

▓ Keeping in Touch

Most useful communication information (including **international access codes, calling card numbers, country codes, operator** and **directory assistance,** and **emergency numbers**) is listed on the **inside back cover.**

Telefónica is the central phone company in Spain, with calling services throughout the world (and Spain). Staffed telephone **offices** are scattered everywhere, but there is little reason to use them; pay phones offer all the services you could possibly want. The offices do have a complete set of phone books for all of Spain and accept Visa credit cards. **Phone booths** are marked by signs that say *Teléfono público* or *Locutorio;* most bars have pay phones, usually coin-operated. Local calls cost 20ptas. International calls are pricey and the best way to call home is probably with a calling card; see p. 44 for details on calling card and call-back services. Numbers for major international calling cards (AT&T, MCI, Canada Direct, BT Direct, Ireland Direct, Australia Direct, New Zealand Direct, and South Africa Direct) are listed on the back cover. **Phone cards** in 1000 and 2000ptas denominations are more convenient than feeding coin after coin into a pay phone; they're sold at tobacconists (*estancos* or *tabacos;* identified by the brown sign with yellow lettering and an icon of a tobacco leaf) and most post offices. American Express and Diner's Club cards now also work as phone card substitutes in most pay phones.

Collect calls *(cobro revertido)* are billed according to pricier person-to-person *(persona a persona)* rates but may still be cheaper than calling from hotels. (1) Dial 005. (2) State the number you want to call and your name. (3) Hang up the phone. (4) The phone magically rings when your call is accepted.

Most Spanish post offices have **fax services.** Some photocopy shops and some telephone offices *(Telefónica)* also offer fax service, but they tend to charge more than the post office (whose rates are standardized by the government), and faxes can only be sent, not received. To send to North America, expect to spend around 1600ptas for the first page, 500ptas for each additional page. Prices do not include 16% IVA.

Air mail *(por avión)* takes four to eight business days to reach the U.S. and Canada; service is faster to the U.K. and Ireland and slower to Australia and New Zealand. Standard postage is 87-120ptas. **Surface mail** *(por barco)*, albeit considerably less expensive than air mail, takes one month or more, and some packages take two to three months. **Registered** or **express mail** *(registrado* or *certificado),* the most reliable way to send a letter or parcel home, takes four to seven business days (letter postage 237ptas). Spain's **overnight mail** is not worth the added expense nor does it work much more quickly. For similar rates and better service than the post office for big packages, try private companies such as DHL, UPS, or the Spanish company SEUR; look under *mensajerías* in the yellow pages. Yellow mail boxes are scattered through main streets. **Stamps** are sold at post offices and tobacconists (*estancos* or *tabacos;* identified by the brown sign with yellow lettering and an icon of a tobacco leaf; they always have postal scales). *Let's Go* lists post offices, including phone and address.

Email is easily accessible within Spain and much quicker and more reliable than the mail system. Cybercafes are listed in most major Spanish cities; for a complete list, consult the index under Internet access. To set up a free email account, see p. 44.

LIFE AND TIMES

With a history that spans over 50 constitutions, an endless array of amorphous kingdoms controlled by indigenous Iberians, Celts, Visigoths, Arabs, Germans, and French, and an empire that spread to the Americas, Spain can only be described imprecisely, as a *mestizo* culture.

■ History and Politics

Spain was colonized and came to be characterized by a succession of civilizations— **Basque** (considered indigenous), **Tartesian, Iberian, Celtic, Greek, Phoenician,** and **Carthaginian**—before the **Romans** dropped by with a vengeance in the 2nd century BC. In close to nine centuries, the Romans drastically altered the face of Spain, particularly by introducing Rome's own language, architecture, roads, irrigation techniques, and use of grapes, olives, and wheat. A slew of Germanic tribes, including Swabians (in Galicia) and Vandals, swept over Iberia in the early 700s AD, but the **Visigoths,** newly converted Christians, emerged above the rest. Truthfully, many argue that their influence has been exaggerated by the Orthodox Right (nicknamed the *godos* or Goths), who deemed their reign as a long-awaited period of Christian purity and national unity.

Moors in Store

Following Muslim unification and their victory tour through the Middle East and Africa, a small force of Arabs, Berbers, and Syrians invaded Spain in 711. Practically welcomed by the divided Visigoths, the Moors encountered little resistance, and the peninsula soon fell under Damascus's dominion. These events precipitated the infusion of Muslim influence (although Catholics and Jews were tolerated for the most part), which peaked in the 10th century. The Moors set up their Iberian capital in Córdoba. During Abderramán III's rule, some considered Spain the wealthiest and most cultivated country in the world. Abderramán's successor, the dictator Almanazor, who turned to one of the 40 poets in his retinue, snuffed out all opposition with his extravagant court, and undertook a series of military campaigns that climaxed with the destruction of Santiago de Compostela, a Christian holy city, in 997.

Tension between Moors and Christians was never continuous; most of the time, in fact, both peoples lived in peace. The turning point in Muslim-Christian relations came when Almanazor died, leaving a power vacuum in Córdoba. At this point, caliphate holdings shattered into petty states called *taifas*. With power less centralized, Christians soon got the upper hand. Christian policy was officially (though not always *de facto*) tolerated Muslims and Jews, a policy that fostered a syncretic culture and even a style of art, **Mudéjar.** Later, though, countless Moorish structures were ruined in the Reconquista, at the expense of many Muslims. In this game of life-and-death and convert-or-get-out, relations were not cordial.

The Catholic Monarchs: Dispersal and Discovery

In 1469, the marriage of **Fernando** de Aragón and **Isabel** de Castilla joined Iberia's two mightiest Christian kingdoms. By 1492, the dynamic duo had captured Granada (the last Moorish stronghold) and shuttled off Columbus, and later many others, to explore the New World. By the 16th century, the duo's strong leadership made Spain's empire the world's most powerful. The Catholic Monarchs introduced the **Inquisition** in the 1480s, executing and then burning Jews who were earlier forced to convert. The Spanish version had dual aims: to strengthen the authority of the Church and to better unify Spain. In approximately 90 years of rule, the Catholic Monarchs greatly heightened Spain's position as a world economic, political, and cultural power—made all the more enduring by conquests in the Americas. Spain proved braver than neighboring countries in financing such risky endeavors and—over the next 300 years—would reap the rewards.

Habsburgs in the House

The daughter of Fernando and Isabel, **Juana la Loca** (the Mad), married **Felipe el Hermoso** (the Fair) of the powerful Habsburg dynasty. Mr. Handsome (who died playing *cesta punta*, or "jai alai") and Mrs. Crazy (who refused to believe he died and dragged his corpse through the streets) spawned **Carlos I** (Charles V, 1516-1556), who reigned over an immense empire (as the last official Holy Roman Emperor) compris-

---

Estranged People in a Spain Place

For some time, **Jews** were peacefully settled throughout Iberia. A 15th-century rabbi noted that the Jews in Castile "have been the most distinguished in all the realms of the dispersion: in lineage, in wealth, in virtues, in science." Yet in 1369, **Enrique de Trastámara** defeated his half-brother **Pedro el Cruel** (a legendary Richard III type) at Montiel, inaugurating the Trastámara dynasty that was to spawn **Isabel la Católica.** Always a bit precarious, tolerance in Castile was substituted by Christian rigidity akin to the scene in 14th-century France. The 1391 pogroms started soon after, as thousands of Jews were massacred and many more forcibly converted. Even those who did convert, *conversos,* were persecuted and tortured. Paradoxically, *converso*s could rise to the high ranks of political, ecclesiastical, and intellectual institutions and become connected with Christian aristocratic and merchant classes. Catholic saint and author **Teresa of Avila** (1515-1582), for example, was the daughter of a *converso*, as was **Luis de Santángel,** the secretary of Isabel and a big promoter of Columbus. The mass conversion led to a complex situation as a "tainted" upper class desperately disavowed its Semitic heritage by devising false genealogies, among other tactics. As a result, *converso* culture became neither entirely Jewish nor Christian.

ing modern-day Holland, Belgium, Austria, Spain, parts of Germany and Italy, and the American colonies. Fortunately, he spent more time in Spain than any other country, but the task of maintaining political stability was monumental. Carlos did his part: as a good Catholic, he embroiled Spain in a war with Protestant France; as an art patron of superb taste, he nabbed Titian as his court painter; as a fashion plate, he introduced Spain to the Habsburg fashion of wearing all black.

But trouble was a-brewing in the Netherlands (then called the Low Countries and Flanders). After Carlos I died, his son **Felipe II** (Philip II, 1556-1598) was left holding the bag full of rebellious territories. More conservative (and faithful to Spain) than his father, he still would not stand still, sweeping Portugal after the ailing King Henrique died in 1580. One year later the Dutch declared their independence from Spain and Felipe began warring with the Protestants, spurring an embroilment with England. The war with the British ground to a halt when Sir Francis Drake and bad weather buffeted the **Invincible Armada** in 1588. His enthusiasm (and much of his empire) sapped, Felipe retreated to his grim, newly built palace, El Escorial, and remained there through the last decade of his reign.

Felipe III (1598-1621), preoccupied with many of the finer aspects of life, allowed his adviser, the Duque de Lerma, to pull the governmental strings. Shortly thereafter, Felipe III and the Duke expelled nearly 300,000 Moors. Mustached **Felipe IV** (1621-1665) painstakingly held the country together through his long, tumultuous reign. In the beginning of his rule, the **Conde Duque de Olivares** manipulated the impressionable young king, but Felipe's wisened up as he settled in (and set Olivares out). Emulating great-grandpa Carlos I, he discerningly patronized the arts (painter Diego Velázquez and playwrights Lope de Vega and Calderón de la Barca were in his court) and architecture (the Buen Retiro in Madrid), and donned extravagant black garb. Then the Thirty Years' War (1618-1648) broke out over Europe, and defending Catholicism sapped Spain's resources. It ended with the marriage of Felipe IV's daughter and Louis XIV. His successor **Carlos II,** the *"hechizado"* (bewitched), was epileptic and impotent, the product of generations of inbreeding. From then on, little went right: Carlos II died, Spain fell into a depression, and cultural bankruptcy ensued.

From France: Bourbons and Constitutions

The 1713 Treaty of Utrecht seated **Felipe V,** a Bourbon grandson of **Louis XIV,** on the Spanish throne. The king built huge, showy palaces (to mimic Versailles in France) and cultivated a flamboyant, debauched court. Despite his hardly disciplined example, the Bourbons who followed Felipe ably administered the Empire, at last beginning to regain control of Spanish-American trade lost to northern Europeans. They also constructed scores of new canals and roads, organized settlements, instituted agricultural reform and industrial expansion, and patronized the sciences and arts (via centralized academies). Next up, **Carlos III** was probably Madrid's finest "mayor," radically transforming the capital. Spain's global standing recovered enough for it to team with France to aid the 13 Colonies' independence from Britain, symbolized by Captain Gálvez' heroically engineered victories in the American South.

Napoleon then invaded Spain as part of his world domination kick. The French occupation ended, ironically enough, when the Protestant Brits beat up the Corsican's troops at Waterloo. This victory led to the restoration of arch-reactionary **Fernando VII,** who sought to revoke the progressive Constitución de Cádiz of 1812. As a result of Fernando's ineptitude and inspired by liberal ideas in the new constitution, most of Spain's Latin American empire soon threw off its yoke. Domestically, Parliamentary Liberalism was restored in 1833 upon Fernando VII's death; it would predominate Spanish politics until **Primo de Rivera's** mild dictatorship in the 1920s. Rapid industrialization and prosperity marked 19th century Spain. It was during this period that the wealth produced by Catalunya's industrial-inspired Renaixença (Renaissance) produced the **Modernista** movement in architecture and design and deliberate construction projects for Barcelona's bourgeoisie. But Spain's defeat to the U.S. in the 1898 Spanish-American War cost them Cuba, the Philippines, and Puerto Rico. Meanwhile, most of Spain remained indigent and agricultural.

The Civil War of the 1930s

In April 1931, **King Alfonso XIII** ignominiously fled Spain, thus giving rise to the Second Republic. Republican Liberals and Socialists established safeguards for farmers and industrial workers, granted women's suffrage, assured religious tolerance, and chipped away at traditional military dominance. National euphoria, however, faded fast. The 1933 elections split the Republican-Socialist coalition, in the process increasing the power of right wing and Catholic parties in the parliamentary *Cortes*. Military dissatisfaction led to a heightened profile of the Fascist *Falange,* which further polarized national politics. By 1936, radicals, anarchists, Socialists, and Republicans had formed a loose, federated alliance to win the next elections. But the peace was a tease. Once **Generalísimo Francisco Franco** snatched control of the Spanish army, militarist uprisings ensued, and the nation plunged into war. The three-year **Civil War** ignited worldwide ideological passions. Germany and Italy dropped troops, supplies, and munitions into Franco's lap, while the stubbornly isolationist U.S. and liberal European states were slow to aid the Republicans. Although Franco enjoyed popular support in Andalucía, Galicia, Navarra, and parts of Castilla, the Republicans controlled population and industrial centers. The Soviet Union, somewhat indirectly, called for a so-called **Popular Front** of Communists, Socialists, and other leftist sympathizers to stave off Franco's fascism. But soon after, the West abandoned the coalition, and aid from the Soviet Union waned as Stalin, disgruntled by the Spanish left's insistence on ideological autonomy and increasingly convinced that he might actually benefit from an alliance with Hitler, lost interest. All told, bombing, executions, combat, starvation, and disease took 600,000 lives.

Transition to Democracy

Brain-drain (as leading scientists, artists, and intellectuals emigrated or were assassinated en masse), worker dissatisfaction, student unrest, regional discontent, and international isolation characterized the first decades of Franco's dictatorship. Several anarchist and nationalist groups, notably the Basque ETA, resisted the dictatorship throughout Franco's reign, often via terrorist acts. In his old age, Franco tried to smooth international relations by joining NATO and encouraging tourism, but the "national tragedy" (as it was later called) did not officially end until Franco's death in 1975. **King Juan Carlos I,** grandson of Alfonso XIII and officially a Franco protégé, carefully set out to undo Franco's damage. In 1978, under centrist premier Adolfo Suárez, Spain adopted a new constitution in a national referendum that led to the restoration of parliamentary government and regional autonomy. The post-Franco years have been marked by progressive social change. Divorce was finally legalized in 1981 and women now vote more and comprise over 50% of universities' ranks. Problems may still plague Spain, but violent regionalists remain in the minority. Most, in fact, seem satisfied with the degree of regional cultural autonomy. By the early 1980s, many regions controlled everything but foreign relations.

Charismatic **Felipe González** led the PSOE (Spanish Socialist Worker's Party) to victory in the 1982 elections. González opened the Spanish economy and championed consensus policies, overseeing Spain's integration into the EU in 1986. Despite his support for continued membership in NATO (he had originally promised to withdraw if he won) and unpopular economic stands, González was reelected in 1986 and continued a program of massive public investment. The years 1986 to 1990 were outstanding for Spain's economy, as the nation enjoyed an average growth rate of 3.8% a year. By the end of 1993, recession set in. In 1993, González and the PSOE only barely maintained a majority in Parliament by allying with the Catalan nationalist party, Convergencia i Unió (CiU), against the increasingly popular conservative Partido Popular (PP). Revelations of large-scale corruption led to a resounding Socialist defeat in the 1994 European parliamentary elections at the hands of the Partido Popular. Negative attention triggered losses in regional elections in the President's homeland and traditional Socialist stronghold, Andalucía. A second cascade of high-profile scandals in late 1994 further destabilized the PSOE government. Most damaging of these scandals was the arrest of four interior ministry officials charged with organizing an illegal clandestine organization, GAL (Anti-terrorist Liberation Groups), in the 1980s to combat Basque separatists; González was eventually pestered into admitting his complicity in GAL "death squads." **José María Aznar** led the PP into power after González's support eroded and has managed to maintain his delicately balanced coalition while leading the Spanish economy to its best performance in years. While doing so, fears of a rightist reversion seem to have faded and most Spaniards seem pleased with the process of Parliamentary Democracy, if not always with its results and policies. Despite notable exceptions, most regional movements have been more cooperative than subversive to the central government in Madrid.

Current Events

Overall the nation is in good shape, spiritually and physically. With the unveiling of the new Guggenheim in Bilbao, northern Spain seized the cultural spotlight and resolidified its image as uniquely modern and forward looking. Spain's economy, meanwhile, continues to boom and even inflation has remained remarkably low during the expansion. Even its notoriously high levels of unemployment have begun to drop, although they remain the highest in Western Europe. With most of its populace approving the European Union's increasing integration, Spain is in lockstep with the majority of Europe before the dawn of the European Monetary Union.

Politically, however, things appear more unstable. ETA, now Europe's oldest active terrorist group, shows no signs of wanting peace and has killed six members of the ruling Partido Popular in 1998 alone; in response, the government has thrown several members of ETA's political wing into jail for their involvement. But the PP faces a more serious threat from an apparently resurgent socialist party, led by the charismatic *catalán*, Josep Borrell. The former head of the socialists, Felipe González, is meanwhile busy preparing his bid for the presidency of the EU while fighting off charges that he bears political responsibility for the activities of the GAL. Despite the turmoil, Spaniards, in traditional fashion, don't appear to bother themselves with much of this fuss, but rather focus on the more important and pressing matters, such as the day's lunch, the afternoon's rest, and the night's *fiesta*.

■ Language(s)

Spain's four regional languages and their various dialects differ far more than cosmetically, although some spelling variations are but superficial compared to their Castilian counterparts. **Castilian** *(castellano)*, almost always spoken, is as sure a ticket as you'll get. **Catalan** *(català)* is spoken in all of Catalunya and has given rise through permutations to **Valencian** *(valenciá)*, the regional tongue of Valencia in the east, and **Mallorquín,** the dialect of the Balearic Islands. The once-Celtic northwest corner of Iberia gabs in **Galician** *(gallego)*, closely related to Portuguese. Although more prevalent in the countryside than cities, Galician is now spreading among the young, as is **Basque** *(euskera)*, spoken in País Vasco and northern Navarra. These languages have standardized grammars and ancient literary traditions, both oral and written. Regional television broadcasts, native film industries, strong political associations, and extensive schooling have saved these from extinction.

City and provincial names in this text are usually listed in Castilian first, followed by the regional language in parentheses, where appropriate. We have found it most useful, however, to adhere to common usage, and if a town is almost exclusively referred to according to its regional name, then we have written it as such. Info within cities (i.e. street names or plaza names), on the other hand, is listed in the regional language. Generally when traveling throughout Spain, Castilian names will suffice and are universally understood. However, it is wise within the specific regions to exercise politeness and respect to the home language.

Let's Go provides a **phrasebook, glossary,** and **pronunciation guide** in the back of the book for all terms used recurrently throughout the text (see p. 649).

■ The Arts

PAINTING

Residents of the Iberian peninsula have been creating art since about 13,000 BC, the birthdate of the fabulous cave paintings at **Altamira.** Over this long stretch, Spanish painting has known a series of luminaries separated by several lulls. Although Flemish, French, and Italian influences have often predominated, such heavy hitters as El Greco, Diego Velázquez, Francisco Goya, and Pablo Picasso have forged a dazzling, distinctive, and hugely influential body of work.

In the 11th and 12th centuries, fresco painters and manuscript illuminators decorated churches and their libraries along the Camino de Santiago and in León and Toledo. **Pedro Berruguete's** (1450-1504) use of traditional gold backgrounds in his religious paintings exemplifies the Italian-influenced style of early Renaissance works. Not until after Spain's imperial ascendance in the 16th century did painting reach its **Golden Age** (roughly 1492-1650). Felipe II imported foreign art and artists in order to jumpstart native production and embellish his Escorial palace. Although he supposedly came to Spain seeking a royal commission, Cretan-born Doménikos Theotokópoulos, known as **El Greco** (1541-1614), was rejected by Felipe II for his shocking and intensely personal style. Confounding his contemporaries, El Greco has since received newfound appreciation in the 20th century for his haunting, elongated figures and dramatic use of light and color. Setting up camp in Toledo, El Greco graced the Church of Santo Tomé with his masterpiece *The Burial of Count Orgaz.*

Philip II's foremost court painter, **Diego Velázquez** (1599-1660), stands tall as one of the world's greatest artists. Whether representing Philip IV's family or lowly court jesters and dwarves, Velázquez painted with the same naturalistic precision. Working slowly and meticulously, he captured light with a virtually photographic quality. Nearly half of this Sevillian-born artist's works reside in the Prado, notably his famous *Las Meninas* (see **Museo del Prado,** p. 90).

Other noteworthy Golden Age painters include **José de Ribera** (1591-1652), **Francisco de Zurbarán** (1598-1664), and **Bartolomé Estebán Murillo** (1618-1682). Each treated religious subjects with distinctive flair: Italian-born Ribera took a realistic and even crude approach, Sevillian Zurbarán painted for monastic orders in a fittingly austere style, and Murillo depicted Catholic dogma with typical Baroque sentimentality.

During the era of Spain's waning power, **Francisco de Goya** (1746-1828) ushered European painting into modern times. Hailing from provincial Aragón, Goya rose to the position of official court painter under the degenerate Carlos IV. Not bothering with flattery, Goya's depictions of the royal family come closer to caricature, as Queen María Luisa's haughty, cruel jawline in Goya's famous *The Family of Charles IV* can attest. After an earlier Neoclassical period during which Goya stuck to smiling scenes of upper class gaiety, his later paintings graphically protest the lunacy of warfare. His series of etchings *The Disasters of War* and his landmark *El dos de mayo* and *El tres de mayo* record the horrific Napoleonic invasion in 1808. Deaf in his later years, Goya painted more nightmarish and wildly fantastic visions, inspiring expressionist and surrealist artists of the next century. The Prado museum houses an entire room of his chilling *Black Paintings.*

It is hard to imagine an artist who has had so profound effect upon 20th-century painting as Andalucían-born **Pablo Picasso** (1881-1973), the founder of Abstractionism. A youthful prodigy, Picasso headed for Barcelona, then a hothouse for Modernist architecture and political activism. Bouncing back and forth between Barcelona and Paris, Picasso inaugurated his Blue Period in 1900, characterized by somber depictions of society's outcasts. His permanent move to Paris in 1904 initiated his Rose Period, during which he probed into the curiously engrossing lives of clowns and acrobats. With his French colleague Georges Braque, he founded **Cubism,** a method of painting objects simultaneously from multiple perspectives. His 1937 Surrealist mural *Guernica* portrays the bombing of that Basque city by Nazi planes in cahoots with Fascist forces during the Spanish Civil War. A vehement protest against violence and fascism, *Guernica* now resides in the Centro de Arte Reina Sofia in Madrid.

Catalunyan painter and sculptor **Joan Miró** (1893-1983) created simplistic, almost child-like shapes in bright, primary colors. His haphazard, undefined squiggles became a statement against the authoritarian society of the post-Civil War years. By contrast, fellow Catalan **Salvador Dalí** (1904-1989) scandalized both high society and leftist intellectuals in France and Spain by supporting the Fascists. Dalí's name is virtually synonymous with **Surrealism.** The wildly mustached painter tapped into dreams and the unconscious for odd images like the melting clocks in *The Persistence of Memory.* His haunting *Premonition of the Civil War* (1936), subtitled *Soft Construction with Boiled Beans,* envisioned war as a distorted monster of putrefying flesh. A self-congratulatory fellow, Dalí founded the Teatro-Museo Dalí in Figueres, the second-most visited museum in Spain after the Prado.

Since Franco's death in 1975, a new generation of artists has thrived. With new museums in Madrid, Barcelona, Valencia, Sevilla, and Bilbao, Spanish painters and sculptors once again have a national forum for their work. Catalan **Antonio Tapiès** constructs collages out of unusual and unorthodox materials, **Antonio Saura** paints at the fore of the self-proclaimed "Abstract Generation" based in Cuenca, and **Antonio López García** has distinguished himself for his hyperrealist paintings. Upstarts include abstract artist **José María Sicilia,** sculptor **Susana Solano,** and **Miguel Barceló,** whose portraits resemble swarms of black flies.

ARCHITECTURE

Spanish architecture is as impressive and wildly diverse as the various civilizations that have called the Iberian peninsula home. Continental trends tended to arrive here late, only to be transformed into distinctively Spanish shapes and forms.

Scattered **Roman ruins** testify to six centuries of colonization. Highlights include some of the finest remains around: the aqueduct in Segovia, the theater in Mérida, and the town of Tarragona. Other vestiges of conquerors past lie at the ruined towns of Itálica (near Sevilla), Sagunto (near Valencia), and Empúries (near Palafrugell).

After the invasion of 711, the **Moors** constructed mosques and palaces throughout southern Spain. The Quran forbade human and animal representation. Instead, architects lavished their buildings with stylized geometric designs, red-and-white horseshoe arches, ornate tiles, courtyards, pools, and fountains. The spectacular 14th-century **Alhambra** in Granada and the **Mezquita** in Córdoba, one-time capital of the Muslim empire, epitomize the Moorish style.

The combination of Islam and Christianity created two architectural movements unique to Spain: **Mozarabic** and Mudéjar. The former describes Christians under Muslim rule, or Mozarabs, who adopted an Arab-influenced style. The more common **Mudéjar** architecture was created by Moors who stayed on after the Reconquista and constructed Christian edifices. Extensive use of brick and elaborately carved wooden ceilings typify Mudéjar style, which reached its height in the 14th century with **alcazars** (palaces) in Sevilla and Segovia and **synagogues** in Toledo and Córdoba.

In the 11th and 12th centuries, the **Romanesque** style spread from Italy and France, especially along the pilgrimage route to Santiago de Compostela. Constructed of heavy hewn stone and decorated with spindly, flat human and animal figures, Romanesque churches and monasteries are distinguished by their rounded arches and few windows. Militaristic architecture such as the walled town of Ávila also echoes Roma-style imperial fortifications.

The first Gothic cathedral in Spain was Burgos (1221), followed closely by Toledo and León. As elsewhere in Europe, the **Spanish Gothic** style brought experimentation with pointed arches, flying buttresses, slender walls, airy spaces, and stained-glass windows. There were variations, though: the Catalan style, for example, employed internal wall supports rather than external buttresses. Other Spanish riffs on the French original include centrally placed *coros* (choirs) and oversized *retablos,* or brightly colored carved pieces placed above the high altar. The Gothic period also birthed many of the various castles throughout the countryside.

New World riches inspired the **Plateresque** ("in the manner of a silversmith") style, a flashy extreme of Gothic that transformed wealthier parts of Spain. Intricate stonework and extravagant use of gold and silver splashed 15th- and 16th-century buildings, most notably in Salamanca, where the university practically drips with ornamentation. **Italian Renaissance** innovations in perspective and symmetry arrived in Spain to sober up the Plateresque style. **El Escorial,** Philip II's grand palace near Madrid, best exemplifies unadorned Renaissance buildings.

Opulence seized center stage once again in 17th- and 18th-century **Baroque** Spain. The Chirruguerra brothers pioneered the eponymous **Chirrugueresque** style, which is equal parts ostentatious, showy, and difficult to pronounce. Wildly elaborate works with extensive sculptural detail and twisted columns, like the altar of the Toledo cathedral, help set Spanish architecture apart.

In the late 19th and early 20th centuries, Catalan's **Modernistas** burst on the scene at Barcelona, led by the eccentric genius of **Antoni Gaudí, Luis Domènich i Montaner,** and **José Puig y Caldafalch.** Modernista structures defy any and all previous standards and are trademarked by voluptuous curves and abnormal textures. The new style was inspired partly by Mudéjar relics, but far more so by organic forms and unbridled imagination. Spain's outstanding architectural tradition continues to this day with such trendsetters as **Josep María Sert, Ricardo Bofill,** and **Rafael Moneo.**

LITERATURE

Spain's literary tradition first blossomed in the late Middle Ages, from 1000 to 1500. The 12th-century *Cantar de Mío Cid* (Song of My Cid), an epic poem and Spain's oldest surviving work, chronicles national hero El Cid's life and military battles, from his exile from Castilla to his return to grace in the king's court. Fernando de Rojas's *La Celestina,* a dialogue about a strong witch-like female character, helped pave the way for the picaresque novel (like *Lazarillo de Tormes, Guzmán de Alfarache*), American Dream-type stories about poor boys *(pícaros)* who overcome huge odds to attain great wealth. This literary form surfaced during Spain's **Golden Age.** Poetry particularly thrived in this era. Some consider the sonnets and romances of **Garcilaso de la Vega** the most perfect ever written in Castilian. Along with friend **Joan Boscán,** Garcilaso introduced the "Italian" style (Petrarchan love conventions) to Iberia. The reverent **Santa Teresa de Ávila** and **San Juan de la Cruz** blessed Spain with mystical autobiographical writings. This period also bred outstanding dramas, including works from **Calderón de la Barca** and **Lope de Vega,** who personally wrote over 2000 plays. Both espoused the Neoplatonic view of love, claiming it always changes one's life dramatically and eternally. **Francisco de Quevedo** contributed to the rebirth of sonnets, treating erotic themes with a sardonic twist. **Miguel de Cervantes'** two-part *Don Quixote de la Mancha*—often considered the world's first novel—is the most famous work of Spanish literature. Cervantes relates the hilarious parable of the hapless, marble-missing Don and his sidekick, Sancho Panza, who think themselves bold *caballeros* (knights) out to save the world.

The 19th century inspired contrast, from the biting journalistic prose of **Larra,** to **Zorrilla's** romantic *Don Juan Tenorio,* to the classic *La Regenta* by **Leopoldo Alas "Clarín."** The modern literary era began with the **Generación del '98,** a group led by essayist **Miguel de Unamuno** and cultural critic **José Ortega y Gasset.** Reacting to Spain's embarrassing defeat in the Spanish-American War (1898), these nationalistic authors argued, through essays and novels, that each individual must spiritually and ideologically attain internal peace before society can do the same. This new group coalesced into the **Generación del 1927,** a group of experimental lyric poets who used Surrealist and vanguard poetry to express profound humanism. This group included **Pedro Salinas, Federico García Lorca** (assassinated at the start of the Civil War), **Rafael Alberti,** and **Vicente Aleixandre.** In the 20th century, the Nobel Committee has honored playwright and essayist **Jacinto Benavente y Martínez,** poet **Vicente Aleixandre,** and novelist **Camilo José Cela** (author of *La Familia de Pascual Duarte*). Female writers, like **Mercè Rodoreda** and **Carmen Martín Gaite,** have earned critical acclaim. As Spanish artists are again flocking to Madrid, like they were in the early part of the century, a new avant-garde spirit has been reborn in the capital. **Ana Rossetti** and **Juana Castro** led a new generation of women erotic poets into the 80s. The newest group of poets represents the first time in panorama of Spanish literature that women are at the forefront.

MUSIC

Flamenco, the combination of *cante jondo* (melodramatic song), guitar, and dancing remains extremely popular into the 1990s. **Paco de Lucía,** an internationally renowned guitarist who experiments in jazz-flamenco crossover, rattles flamenco purists. Singer **Camerón de la Isla,** who died young in 1992, maintains a devoted following throughout the peninsula. (As to flamenco's dance side, see **below.**) Singer-songwriters voiced underground discontent during the Franco years voiced and became outwardly famous for it afterwards. **Joan-Manuel Serrat** is perhaps the biggest name; other singers of note are **Albert Pla, María del Mar Bonet, Lluis Llach,** and **Ana Belén.** American rock is ubiquitous in Spain, but Spanish rock sometimes gives it a run for its money. **Mecano** hypnotizes audiences beyond peninsular bounds, and Barcelona band **El Último de la Fila** and big-forum **Héroes del Silencio** are well worth a listen. Other popular groups and soloists are **Presuntos Implicados, Los Rodríguez,** and **Manolo Tena.** Barcelona-born José Carreras, of "three Tenors" fame, is recognized the world's finest opera singers. And we cannot forget Julio Iglesias, loved the world over.

Flamenco Frills and Drills

Few things are more exciting than a free-wheeling *sevillana,* part of why the feisty flamenco dancer is Spain's beloved cultural icon. The woman's *bata de cola*—a colorful 19th-century style dress with trains, frills, ribbons, and polka-dots—immediately catches the eye. But flamenco is not limited to *sevillanas;* numerous variations form the core of any master's repertoire. What follows is hardly complete; think of it as a mere sampling:

Soleares (Soléas): One of the oldest and most dignified flamenco forms, it reduces even stoic onlookers to tears. **Bulerías:** Near the end of a performance, the rhythm picks up and the entire company gets down in this—the *bulería.* **Alegrías:** The brisk pace and liveliness of *alegrías* (joy) make them crowd-pleasers. **Fandango:** The *fandango* dance may have originated in Huelva, but nearly every town in Andalucía has added a twist. **Farruca:** Boundless strength and refined beauty generally make strange bed-fellows, but not in the *farruca.*

FILM

One of the greatest influences on Spanish film was not a filmmaker, but a politician. Franco's regime of censorship (1939-1975) defined Spanish film both during and after his rule. Early success, at least, did not elude Spanish cinema. Spain's first film dates to 1897 and the Surrealist **Luis Buñuel,** close friends with **Salvador Dalí,** produced several early classics, most notably *Un Chien Andalou* (1929). Later, and in exile from Francoist Spain (1939-1975), he produced scores of brilliantly sardonic films including *Belle du Jour* (1967).

Meanwhile, in Spain itself, Franco's censorship stifled most creative tendencies and left the public with nothing to watch but cheap westerns *(chonzos)* and bland spy flicks. As government supervision slacked in the early 1970s, Spanish cinema showed signs of life, led by **Carlos Saura's** dark and subversive hits such as *El Jardin de las Delicias* (1970) and *Cría Cuervos* (1975).

In 1977, in the wake of Franco's death, domestic censorship laws were revoked, bringing artistic freedom along with financial crisis for Spanish filmmakers, who found their films shunned domestically in favor of newly permitted foreign films. Internationally, however, depictions of the exuberant excesses of a super-liberated Spain found increasing attention and respect. **Pedro Almodovar's** *Law of Desire* (1986), featuring **Antonio Banderas** as a homosexual, perhaps best captures the risqué themes of transgression and sexuality most often treated by contemporary Spanish cinema. His *Women on the Verge of a Nervous Breakdown* (1988) expresses post-Franco disillusion in a kitschy fashion-conscious Madrid. Other directors to look for in Spain include **Bigas Luna,** director of scatological *Jamón Jamón,* **Fernando Trueba, Vicente Aranda,** and **Victor Érice.** Trueba's *Belle Epoque* won an Oscar in 1994, exemplifying its artistic rise in respect and strength globally. Hopefully, such international recognition and popularity will help assuage some of the economic woes plaguing the Spanish film industry.

LORDS OF THE RING

Bullfighting as we know it started in the 17th century, to the partial dismay of the Church, which feared the risks made the activity tantamount to suicide (ergo sinful). Although anti-bullfighting arguments have persisted and evolved (in the Age of Reason they bemoaned the irrational use of land to raise bulls; now animal rights activists chain themselves to ring entrance gates), the fascination with the "spectacle" or "rite" (it's not considered a sport) prevails. The activity has been analyzed as everything from a mythical to psycho-sexual to Nationalist phenomenon. The recent bullfighting renaissance has been accompanied by books by English-speakers. We would be negligent not to plug Ernest Hemingway's accounts (and *machismo*) in *The Sun Also Rises* and *Death in the Afternoon.*

■ Food and Drink

The Spanish prize fresh ingredients, light sauces, and pig products. Each region has its own repertoire of dishes based on indigenous produce, meats, and fish. While the best-known Spanish dishes—paella, *gazpacho,* and *tortilla española*—are from Valencia, Andalucía, and Castilla respectively, País Vasco, Navarra, Catalunya, and Galicia traditionally cook up many of Spain's most intriguing dishes.

TYPICAL FARE

The wilds of the sea are tamed deliciously and distinctively throughout the Spanish rim. **País Vasco** masters *bacalao* (cod), *chipirones en su tinta* (squid in its own ink), *sopa de pescado* (fish soup), mouthwatering *angulas a la bilbaína* (baby eels in garlic), earthier *pimientos del piquillo* (roasted red peppers), and sumptuous *rellenos* (stuffed peppers). **Galicians** savor *empanadas* (pastry) with particularly tasty *bonito* (tuna), *pulpo* (octopus), *mejillones* (mussels), and *santiaguiños* (spider crabs). **Catalunya,** renowned for its cuisine, has blessed the world with *zarzuela,* a seafood and tomato bouillabaisse, and its own brand of *langosta* (lobster). One favorite includes *torradas,* hearty toast spread with crushed tomato and often topped with *butifarra* (sausage) or ham. **Menorca** miraculously whips up mayonnaise (named for its capital Mahón), while **Mallorca's** *ensaimada,* angel hair pastry smothered in powdered sugar, sweetens breakfasts. **Islas Baleares's** chefs also stir up various fish stews, while **Andalucíans** have famously—and lightly—mastered the art of frying fish.

Valencia glories in countless uses of rice; its paella, the saffron-seasoned dish made with meat, fish, poultry, vegetables, or snails, is world famous (there are over 200 varieties alone throughout the region). In the north, **Asturias** warms to *fabada* (bean stew), complemented by *queso cabrales* (blue cheese). Landlocked **Castilla** churns out a dense *cocido* (stew) of meats, sausage, and chick-peas, as well as *chorizo,* a seasoned savory sausage. For pork lovers, oh-so-tender *cochinillo asado al horno* (roast suckling pig) is a glutton's delight. Adventurers shouldn't miss **Navarra's** quirky *perdiz con chocolate* (partridge in chocolate).

Spain's most omnipresent edible manifestation crosses all regional bounds: *jamón serrano* or *jamón del país* (the best of which comes from pigs fed only acorns) is cured and zestier than regular ham, itself known as *jamón york* or *jamón dulce.* Or, you may enjoy sinking your teeth into *queso* (cheese). The best known is *queso de Burgos,* a soft, mild cheese thought to better the invalid (and pamper the healthy), and *queso manchego*, a fairly sharp brand made from sheep's milk. **Vegetarians beware**—not only is ham omnipresent, but Spanish chefs often take a "vegetarian" meal request to mean "with tuna" and will supplement this canned catch for other kinds of meat.

Consumed in bars and *tascas* (*tapas* bars), *tapas* tantalize taste buds all around Spain. *Tapas* are bite-sized servings, while **raciones** are bigger portions (sometimes equal in size to entrees). These munchables (*pintxos* in Basque) come in countless varieties, often region-specific. Served around dinner time, they are appetizers and the main course in one. *Tabernas* serve *tapas* from a counter, while *mesones* bring them to the table. *Tortilla de patata* (potato and egg omelette) and *tortilla francesa* (plain omelette) are ubiquitous. *Bocadillos* (thick baguette sandwiches) and *sand-wiches* (the flimsier white bread version, often grilled) are abundant. Our **Glossary of Food and Restaurant Terms** lists helpful food terms and translations (see p. 651).

MEALS AND DINING HOURS

Spaniards start their day with a continental breakfast of coffee combos or thick, liquid chocolate and *bollos* (rolls), *churros* (lightly fried fritters), or other pastries. As in most of Europe, Spaniards devour their biggest meal, dinner ("lunch" to Americans), at midday (around 2-3pm). This traditionally consists of several courses: an *entrem-esa* (appetizer) of soup or salad; a main course of meat, fish, or a twist like paella; and a dessert of fruit, *queso* (cheese), or some sweets. Supper at home is light, consumed near 8pm. Eating out time is after 9pm, and in some restaurants as late as midnight. Rendezvous at one or more *tascas*—featuring *tapas* and drinks—are common sup-per substitutes. Dessert lovers will also enjoy the famed *turrón* (almond nougat), marzipan, and other candied fruits and cakes served throughout the country.

RESTAURANTS

While some restaurants open from 8am to 1 or 2am, most serve meals from 1 or 2 to 4pm only and in the evening from 8pm until midnight. Some hints: eating at the bar is cheaper than at tables, and the check won't be brought to your table unless you request it. Most city tourist offices rate nearby *restaurantes* on a fork system, five forks meaning gourmet. Full *restaurante* meal prices range from about 800ptas to perhaps 1800ptas in a four-forker. *Cafeterías* are ranked by cups, one to three. Also, many *bar-restaurantes* (and some *hostales*) have cozy *comedors* (dining rooms) on the premises. Diners will repeatedly come across three options. **Platos combinados** (combination platters) include a main course and side dishes on a single plate, plus bread and sometimes a drink. The **menú del día**—two or three dishes, bread, wine/beer/mineral water, and dessert—is Spaniards' common choice for the *comida* (mid-day meal), at roughly 800-1500ptas. Generally, you'll have several options, although advertised items are periodically not available. Those dining **a la carte** choose from individual entrees. A full meal ordered this way typically runs twice as much, if not more, than the *menú*.

DRINKS

Spanish **wine** is uniformly good. When in doubt, the *vino de la casa* (house wine) is an economical, often delectable choice. Also good is *vino tinto* (red wine), *vino blanco* (white wine), or *rosado* (rosé). For a taste, get a *chato* (small glass). Mild, fra-grant reds are Spain's best vintages, but the corps of fine wines is vast. La Mancha's Valdepeñas are light, dry reds and whites, drunk young. Catalunya's whites and **cavas** (champagnes) and Aragón's Cariñena wines pack bold punches. The fresh Ribeiro and delicate Albariño from Galicia, the muscatel of Málaga, and Castilla's Valle de Duero all pleasingly quench the palate. **Sidra** (alcoholic cider) from Asturias and País Vasco, and **sangría** (a red-wine punch with sliced peaches and oranges, seltzer, sugar, and a dash of brandy) are delicious alcoholic options. A light drink is *tinto de verano*, a cool mix of red wine and carbonated mineral water.

Jerez (sherry), Spain's most famous wine, hails from Jerez de la Frontera in Andalucía. Tipple the dry *fino* and *amontillado* as aperitifs, or finish off a rich supper with the sweet *oloroso* or *dulce*. The *manzanilla* produced in Sanlúcar (near Cádiz) has a salty aftertaste, ascribed to the region's salt-filled soil.

Wash down your *tapas* with a *caña (de cerveza),* a normal-sized draft-beer. A *tubo* is a little bigger than a *caña,* and small beers go by different names—*corto* in Castilla, *zurito* in Basque. Pros refer to **mixed drinks** as *copas.* Beer and Schweppes is a **clara.** A **calimocho,** popular with young crowds, mixes Coca-Cola and red wine. Older drinkers prefer **sol y sombra** (literally sun and shade—brandy and anise).

Spain whips up numerous non-alcoholic quenchers, notably **horchata de chufa** (made by pressing almonds and ice together) and the flavored crushed-ice **granizados.** Shun the machine-made versions of either drinks—they don't do either justice. Coffee and milk *do* mix. *Café solo* means black coffee; add a touch of milk for a *nube;* a little more and it's a *café cortado;* all's fair with *café con leche*—half coffee, half milk—often imbibed at breakfast; savor steamed milk with a dash of coffee, a *leche manchada;* and top it off with a *blanco y negro,* an ice cream and coffee float.

■ The Media

NEWSPAPERS AND MAGAZINES

ABC, palpably conservative and pro-monarchist, is the oldest national daily paper. It jostles with the more liberal *El País* for Spain's largest readership. *El Mundo* is a younger left-wing daily renowned for its investigative reporting. Barcelona's *La Vanguardia* maintains a substantial Catalan audience, while *La Voz de Galicia* dominates the northwest. *Diario 16,* the more moderate counterpart to *El Mundo,* publishes the popular newsweekly *Cambio 16,* whose main competition is *Tiempo. Hola,* the original *revista del corazón* (magazine of the heart), caters to Spaniard's love affair with aristocratic titles, Julio Iglesias, and "beautiful" people. The nosier, less tasteful tabloid *Semana* has gossip galore and readers aplenty.

TELEVISION

Channel surf to the state-run TVE1 and La2 or private stations Tele5 and Antena3. Each region has its own network, broadcast in the local vernacular. In Madrid, the local channel is TeleMadrid (TM3). Canal Plus is Spain's top-notch HBO equivalent. It appears scrambled during movies but features free sit-coms and music videos on Sunday mornings. Tune in to news at 3 and 8:30pm on most stations. Programming includes well-dubbed American movies, sports, steamy Latin American *telenovelas* (soaps), game shows, jazzed-up documentaries, and cheesy three-hour variety extravaganzas. View fab American series like *Baywatch* and *Fresh Prince of Bel Air* and Spanish equivalents. If all else fails, *fútbol* games and bullfights are guaranteed to hold your attention. Check newspapers for listings.

■ Sports

¡Viva España! True to form, the beat—and the glory—go on for Spanish sports. Miguel Indurain, a Basque hero and Spain's most decorated athlete, may not have been able to win a sixth straight *Tour de France* title before his retirement, but he is remembered fondly by his fanatical fans. Spaniards, like Aranxta Sanchez Vicario and Conchita Martinez, star in tennis. Seve Ballesteros, the country's ace on the golf links, putts with the best of 'em despite his age. As with cuisine, regional specialties spice the sports scene, including *cesta punta* (known internationally as *jai alai*) from Basque country, wind surfing along the south coast, and skiing in the Sierra Nevadas and the Pyrenees. *Fútbol* pumps the blood of this country, uniting Spaniards who agree to disagree, vehemently, on local teams' fates. Their pro game ranks with the finest in Europe, featuring clubs such as F.C. Barcelona and Real

SPAIN

Madrid whose rosters read like a world all-star scroll. On top of that, the entire country revels in the travails of the national team. Despite having one of their best squads in years, the Spanish team was embarrassingly knocked out of World Cup '98 in the first round. Only Real Madrid fans had any solace with their team's surprising European Champions Cup win. Should an entire city seem desolate one Saturday afternoon, don't fret—go to a bar and prepare for the ensuing emotional eruptions as the game unfolds.

■ Further Sources

Travel Literature

English scribes have penned several top-notch Spanish travel narratives. Richard Ford's witty, 19th-century account, *Handbook for Travellers in Spain and Readers at Home,* remains a fan-favorite. Most time-honored classics are region-specific, including Washington Irving's *Tales of the Alhambra,* Bloomsbury Circle-expatriate Gerald Brenan's *South from Granada,* Robert Graves' Mallorcan stories, and Laurie Lee's *As I Walked Out One Midsummer Morning.* For native flavor, read Nobel prize-winning Camilo José Cela's *Journey to the Alcarria,* based on rural Castilla.

Fiction, Spanish and Foreign

Start with *Poema del Mío Cid* and Cervantes' *Don Quixote.* Among the most popular modern novelists are the moving Carmen Laforet *(Nada),* post-modern Juan José Millás *(El desorden de tu nombre),* lyrical Esther Tusquet *(El mismo mar de todos los veranos),* and amusing Manuel Vázquez Montalbán *(Murder in the Central Committee).* Spain has also inspired a number of prominent American and British authors. Ernest Hemingway immortalized bullfighting, *machismo,* and Spain itself in *The Sun Also Rises* and *For Whom the Bell Tolls.* Graham Greene takes a walk (via a priest, all around Spain) on the lighter side in the humorous *Monsignor Quixote.*

Art and Architecture

The standard work on Spanish architecture is Bernard Bevan's *History of Spanish Architecture.* For the latest (1980s and 90s) scoop, peruse Anatzu Zabalbeascoa's *The New Spanish Architecure.* Fred Licht's collection of essays, *Goya,* is a must-read for fans of the artist, and books on Picasso, Dalí, and Gaudí can be had with minimal fuss.

History and Culture

Written in 1968, James Michener's best-seller *Iberia* continues to captivate audiences for its thoroughness, insight, and style. *Barcelona,* by Robert Hughes, delves deep into the culture of Catalunya. George Orwell's *Homage to Catalonia,* a personal account of the Civil War, rivals *Iberia* and *Barcelona* in quality and fame. A handful of other historians stand out—Richard Fletcher on Moorish Spain, J.H. Elliot's work *Imperial Spain 1469-1716,* and Raymond Carr and Stanley Payne on the modern era.

Madrid

The stately grandeur of Old Madrid's palaces and museums rapidly dissipates as one enters the smaller avenues and encounters the libertarian *joie de vivre* of its transplanted citizens (pop. 4,500,000). After decades of totalitarian repression under Franco, Madrid's youth burst out laughing and crying during the 1980s, an era known as *la Movida* ("Shift" or "Movement"), and they have yet to stop.

Although it witnessed the coronation of Fernando and Isabel, Madrid was of no great importance until Habsburg King Felipe II moved the Spanish court here permanently in 1561—an unlikely choice for a capital considering the city's distance from vital ports and rivers. Nonetheless, from that moment the city became a seat of wealth, culture, and imperial glory, overseeing Spain's 16th- and 17th-century Golden Age of literature, art, and architecture. In the 18th-century, Madrid witnessed a Neoclassical redecoration providing it with wide, leafy boulevards and scores of imposing buildings that still define much of its space.

Even before Franco's totalitarian repression, Madrid was passionately hostile to his nationalists and was the last city save Valencia to fall during the civil war. But nothing can explain the explosion that was *la Movida*. Life poured into Madrid's streets and soul, achieving the whirlwind-like-state exemplified by Pedro Almodóvar's cinematic portrayals of frenetic lives and passionate colors. Madrid's cultural renaissance, however, did not stand behind a totemic figure like Almodóvar. Rather, a 200,000-strong student population took to the streets and have stayed there, shedding the decorous, if forced, reserve of their predecessors, and capturing the present. The students seem neither cognizant of their city's historic landmarks nor preoccupied with the future, even with unemployment rates reaching twenty percent.

One might expect a generational chasm between this radical youth and their parents and grandparents, but these young people are clearly affected by the countryside disposition of their elders. Because Madrid is a city of migrants—one rarely meets a *madrileño* who is more than two generations removed from the outlying regions of Spain—Madrid does not exemplify the chaos of more experienced European capitals. Like the residents of any Spanish town, *madrileños* rush home for the afternoon meal and flood the streets for their ritualistic evening stroll. But unlike most people of the world, *madrileños* do not live to work; they work so that they may live.

🏛 HIGHLIGHTS OF MADRID

- Three of the world's great museums: the **Museo del Prado** (see p. 103), the **Centro de Arte Reina Sofía** (see p. 105), and the **Museo Thyssen-Bornemisza** (see p. 105).
- The **cafes** along Po. Prado by day (see p. 99); the **bars** in Pl. Santa Ana by night; the throbbing **clubs** in El Centro, Malasañas, and Chueca by morning (see p. 108).
- The **Palacio Real's** Baroque elegance and beautiful gardens (see p. 98).
- The somber and majestic **El Escorial** (see p. 122).

■ Arrivals and Departures

BY PLANE

All flights land at **Aeropuerto Internacional de Barajas,** 30 minutes northeast of Madrid by car. In the international arrivals area of the airport, a branch of the **regional tourist office** (tel. 91 305 86 56) has **maps** and other basics (open M-F 8am-8pm, Sa 9am-1pm). Branches of the **Brújula** accommodations service, located in the airport and at the Bus-Aeropuerto stop, can immediately find visitors places to stay (see **Accommodations,** p. 85).

The green **Bus-Aeropuerto** (look for EMT signs just outside the doors) leaves from the national and international terminals and runs to the city center (1 per hr. 4:45-6:17am, departs every 15min. 6:17am-10pm, departs every 25min. 10pm-1:45am, 380ptas). The bus stops underground beneath the Jardines del Descubrimiento in **Plaza de Colón** (M: Colón). After resurfacing in Pl. Colón, walk toward the neo-Gothic statue on the opposite side of the Jardines. The statue overlooks **Paseo de Recoletos**. The Colón Metro station (brown line, L4) is across the street.

Fleets of **taxis** swarm the airport. The fare to central Madrid should cost no more than 3000ptas with the 350ptas airport surcharge, so beware of conniving drivers.

Airlines

Iberia: Santa Cruz de Marcenado, 2 (tel. 91 587 81 56). M: San Bernardo. Open M-F 9:30am-2pm and 4-7pm. Reservations and info (tel. 902 400 500) open 24hr. **Aviaco,** C. Maude, 51 (tel. 91 554 36 00), is a domestic Iberia affiliate. **Tap Air Portugal** (tel. 91 542 06 02) and **Portugália** (tel. 902 100 145) fly to Portugal.

Air France: Pl. España, 18, 5th fl. (tel. 91 330 04 02). M: Pl. España. Open M-F 9am-5pm. Reservations (tel. 91 330 04 40) open M-F 9am-5pm.

American Airlines: C. Pedro Texeira, 8, 5th fl. (tel. 91 597 25 85). M: Santiago Bernabeu. Open M-F 9am-5:30pm. Reservations (tel. 91 597 20 68) open M-F 9am-6:30pm, Sa 9am-2pm.

British Airways: C. Serrano, 60 (tel. 91 577 69 59). M: Serrano. Open M-F 9am-5pm. Reservations (tel. 902 111 333) open M-F 9am-7pm.

Continental: C. Leganitos, 47, 9th fl. (tel. 91 559 27 10). M: Pl. España. Open M-F 9am-6pm. Reservations accepted M-F 9am-7pm.

Lufthansa: Cardenal Marcelo Española, 2 (tel. 91 302 94 26). Office outside city limits. Reservations (tel. 902 220 101).

USAir: Santa Cruz de Marcenado, 31 (tel. 91 541 55 58). M: San Bernardo.

BY TRAIN

Two *Largo Recorrido* (long distance) **RENFE** stations, **Madrid-Atocha** and **Madrid-Chamartín,** connect Madrid to the rest of the world. Two intermediate stations, **Recoletos** and **Nuevos Ministerios,** connect Atocha and Chamartín. You can purchase tickets for RENFE **Cercanías-Regionales** (commuter rails) and board trains at the following Metro stations: Embajadores, Méndez Alvaro, Laguna, Aluche, and Principe Pío (access via M: Ópera). Self-service machines vend tickets for *Cercanías-Regionales.* Prices are determined by the number of zones crossed; Madrid's stations are in the middle zone (100ptas to travel within zone C-1). These trains are generally comfortable and have A/C. Hold on to your ticket. Principe Pío also has separate lines running to northern Spain. Call RENFE (tel. 91 328 90 20) for reservations and info. **RENFE Main Office,** C. Alcalá, 44, at Gran Vía (M: Banco de España) sells tickets for departures from Chamartín. Schedules and **AVE** (Alta Velocidad Española; tel. 91 534 05 05) and **Talgo** tickets are also available. Open M-F 9:30am-8pm.

Estación Chamartín: Agustín de Foxá (24hr. tel. 91 328 90 20; Spanish only). M: Chamartín. Bus #5 runs to and from Sol (45min.); the stop is just beyond the lockers. Ticket windows open 6:45am-10:30pm. Chamartín services towns throughout Spain—mostly northeast and south. International destinations include Lisbon and Paris. Most Cercanías trains can be boarded here. Chamartín has a **tourist office** (tel. 91 315 99 76; open M-F 8am-8pm, Sa 9am-1pm), **currency exchange,** accommodations service, post office, **telephones,** car rental, **lockers** (400-600ptas), bookstores, *cafeterías,* and police.

Estación Atocha: (tel. 91 328 90 20). M: Atocha-Renfe. Ticket windows open 6:30am-11:30pm. No international destinations. Trains head to: Andalucía, Castilla-La Mancha, Extremadura, Valencia, Castilla y León, and El Escorial. **AVE** service (tel. 91 534 05 05) to Sevilla via Córdoba. The cast-iron atrium of the original station has been turned into a simulated rainforest; the sound of sprinklers behind the station's Art Deco facade makes for a soothing, if humid, wait between trains. Art galleries, boutiques, restaurants, and cafes are additional diversions. **Luggage storage** (400-600ptas) is by the rainforest.

MADRID

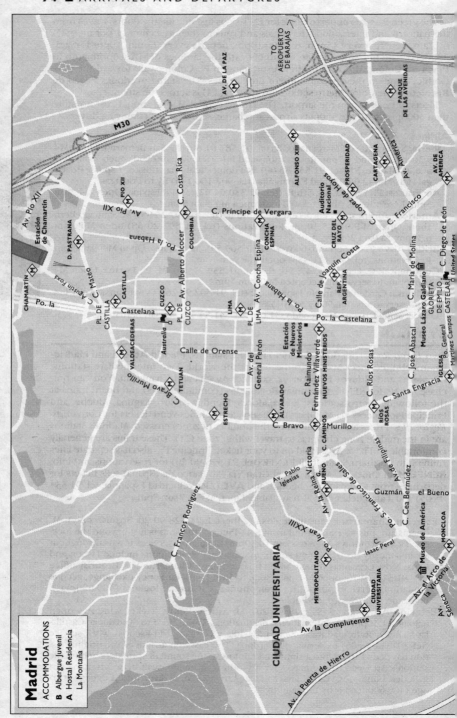

Madrid

ACCOMMODATIONS

B Albergue Juvenil
A Hostal Residencia
La Montaña

TO
AEROPUERTO
DE BARAJAS

PARQUE
DE LAS AVENIDAS

M30

AV. DE LA PAZ

ALFONSO XIII

PROSPERIDAD

Lopez de Hoyos

CARTAGENA

Av. América

AV. DE AMÉRICA

Av. Pío XII

Estación
de Chamartín

Av. Pío XII

C. Costa Rica

C. Príncipe de Vergara

Auditorio
Nacional

CRUZ DEL
RAYO

C. Francisco

Po. la Habana

COLOMBIA

CONCHA
ESPIÑA

CHAMARTÍN

D. PASTRANA

Agustín Foxá

PL. DE C. Mateo

Av. Alberto Alcocer

Av. Concha Espiña

C. María de Molina

C. Diego de León

United States

CASTILLA

CUZCO

CUZCO

LIMA

Calle de Joaquín Costa

Museo Lázaro Galdiano

GLORIETA
DE EMILIO
CASTELAR

Po. la

Castellana

Australia

PL. DE
CASTILLA

PL. DE
LIMA

Av. Habana

REP.
ARGENTINA

IGLESIA

Po. General
Martínez Campos

VALDEACEDERAS

Calle de Orense

Po. la Castelana

C. José Abascal

Bravo Murillo

C. TETUÁN

Av. del
General Perón

Estación
de Nuevos
Ministerios

C. Raimundo
Fernández Villaverde

C. Ríos Rosas

C. Santa Engracia

ESTRECHO

NUEVOS MINISTERIOS

RÍOS
ROSAS

ALVARADO

C. Bravo

Murillo

C. CAMINOS

Av. de Filipinas

Av. Pablo
Iglesias

Av. la Reina Victoria

G. BUENO

Po. de S. Francisco de Sales

C. Guzmán el Bueno

C. Cea Bermúdez

C. Francos Rodríguez

Po. Juan XXIII

METROPOLITANO

C.
Isaac Peral

Museo de América

MONCLOA

CIUDAD UNIVERSITARIA

CIUDAD
UNIVERSITARIA

Av. el Arco de
la Victoria

Av.
Séneca

Av. la Complutense

Av. la Puerta de Hierro

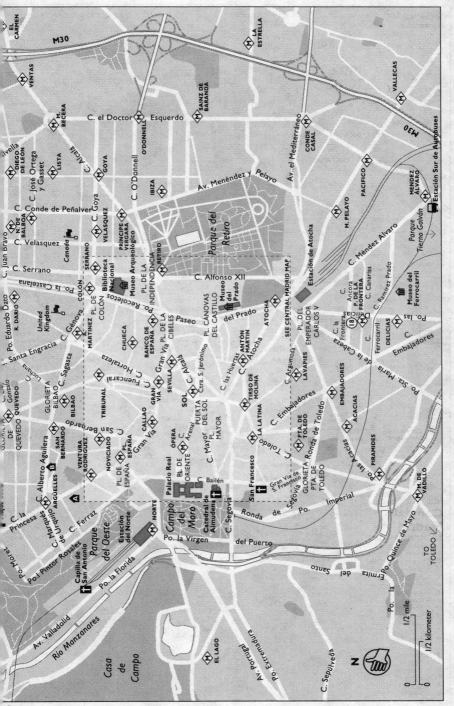

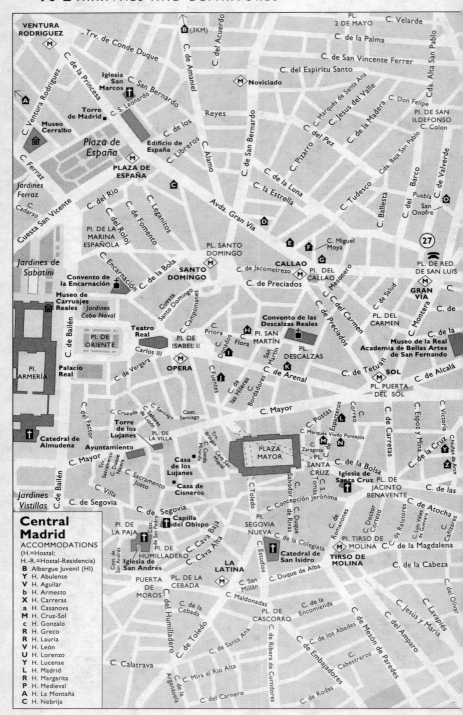

Central Madrid

ACCOMMODATIONS
(H.=Hostal;
H.-R.=Hostal-Residencia)

B Albergue Juvenil (HI)
Y H. Abulense
V H. Aguilar
b H. Armesto
X H. Carreras
a H. Casanova
M H. Cruz-Sol
c H. Gonzalo
R H. Greco
R H. Lauria
V H. León
U H. Lorenzo
Y H. Lucense
L H. Madrid
R H. Margarita
P H. Medieval
A H. La Montaña
C H. Nebrija

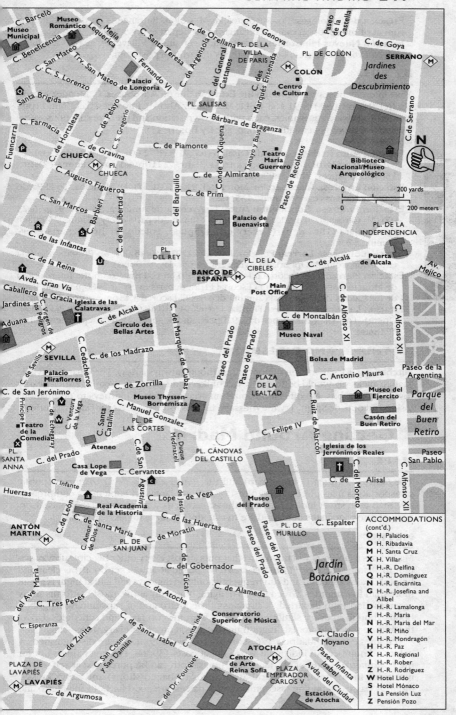

C. Barceló
Museo Romántico
Museo Municipal
C. Beneficencia
C. Mejía Lequerica
C. Santa Teresa
C. San Mateo
Trv. San Mateo
C. C. S. Lorenzo
Santa Brigida
C. Fernando VI
Palacio de Longoria
C. de Pelayo
C. de Orellana
C. del General Castaños
PL. DE LA VILLA DE PARIS
C. des Marqués Ensenada
C. de Genova
PL. DE COLÓN
COLÓN
Centro de Cultura
SERRANO
Jardines des Descubrimiento
C. de Goya

C. Farmacia
C. de Hortaleza
C. S. Gregorio
CHUECA
PL. CHUECA
C. Augusto Figueroa
C. San Marcos
C. de Gravina
PL. SALESAS
C. Bárbara de Braganza
C. de Piamonte
Teatro María Guerrero
C. de Almirante
Biblioteca Nacional/Museo Arqueológico
C. de Serrano
N

C. de las Infantas
C. de la Reina
Avda. Gran Via
Caballero de Gracia
Jardines
Aduana
C. Barbieri
C. de la Libertad
C. del Barquillo
C. de Prim
PL. DEL REY
Palacio de Buenavista
PL. DE LA CIBELES
C. de Alcalá
PL. DE LA INDEPENDENCIA
Puerta de Alcala
Av. Mejico

0   200 yards
0   200 meters

Iglesia de las Calatravas
C. de Alcalá
Circulo des Bellas Artes
C. de los Madrazo
SEVILLA
Palacio Miraflores
C. Cedacheros
C. de Zorrilla
C. Virgen de los Peligros
C. de Sevilla
C. del Marques de Cubas
Paseo del Prado
Paseo del Prado
BANCO DE ESPAÑA
Main Post Office
C. de Montalbán
Museo Naval
Bolsa de Madrid
C. Antonio Maura
C. de Alfonso XI
C. Alfonso XII
Paseo de la Argentina

C. de San Jerónimo
Principe
Teatro de la Comedia
PL. SANTA ANNA
C. del Prado
Casa Lope de Vega
C. Infante
Huertas
Museo Thyssen-Bornemisza
C. Manuel Gonzalez
PL. DE LAS CORTES
Ateneo
C. Cervantes
C. Santa Catalina
C. Ventura de la Vega
C. de Echegaray
C. de San Agustin
C. Duque Medinaceli
PLAZA DE LA LEALTAD
PL. CÁNOVAS DEL CASTILLO
C. Felipe IV
Museo del Ejercito
Casón del Buen Retiro
Iglesia de los Jerrónimos Reales
Parque del Buen Retiro
Paseo San Pablo
C. Ruiz de Alarcón
C. del Moreto

Real Academia de la Historia
C. de León
C. de Santa María
C. Amor de Dios
PL. DE SAN JUAN
C. de Moratin
ANTÓN MARTIN
C. Lope de Vega
C. de las Huertas
C. de Jesús
Museo del Prado
PL. DE MURILLO
C. Espalter
Alisal
C. de
C. Alfonso XII

C. del Ave María
C. Tres Peces
C. Esperanza
C. de Zurita
C. del Gobernador
C. de Fúcar
C. de Alameda
C. de Atocha
Paseo del Prado
Jardín Botánico
C. Claudio Moyano

PLAZA DE LAVAPIÉS
LAVAPIÉS
C. de Argumosa
C. San Cosme y San Damián
C. de Santa Isabel
C. Santa Inés
Conservatorio Superior de Música
Centro de Arte Reina Sofia
ATOCHA
PLAZA EMPERADOR CARLOS V
C. Infanta Isabel
Avda. del Ciudad
Estación de Atocha

Estación de Recoletos: Po. Recoletos, 4. M: Colón. Entrance is on the middle segment of the split boulevard. Cercanías trains depart every 5-10min.
Estación Nuevos Ministerios: C. Raimundo Fernández Villaverde, at Po. Castellana. M: Nuevos Ministerios. Cercanías trains depart every 5-10min.

BY BUS

Most intercity buses pass through the **Estación Sur de Autobuses,** C. Méndez Alvaro, s/n (tel. 91 468 42 00 or 91 468 45 11; M: Méndez Álvaro); info open daily 7am-11pm. Numerous private companies, each with its own station and set of destinations, serve Madrid (for more general information, see **By Bus,** p. 47).

Estación Auto Res: Pl. Conde de Casal, 6 (tel. 91 551 72 00). M: Conde de Casal. To Salamanca (3¼hr., 1440ptas; express 2½hr., 2210ptas) and Cuenca (2½hr., 1305ptas; express 2hr., 1600ptas).
Estación Empresa Alacuber: Po. Moret (tel. 91 376 01 04). M: Moncloa. To El Pardo (20min., departs every 13min., 135ptas).
Estación Empresa Continental Auto: C. Avenida de América, 34 (tel. 91 356 23 07). M: Cartagena. To: Alcalá de Henares (40min., departs every 15min., 250ptas); Guadalajara (1hr., departs every hr., 475ptas); Toledo (1½hr., departs every 30min., 570ptas).
Estación Empresa Larrea: Po. Florida, 11 (tel. 91 530 48 00). M: Príncipe Pío (via extension from M: Ópera). To Ávila (2hr., 4 per day, 910ptas).
Estación Herranz: (El Escorial tel. 91 890 41 00) on C. Princesa, in the Intercambio de Moncloa. M: Moncloa. To El Escorial (1hr., departs every hr., 380ptas) and Valle de los Caídos via El Escorial (20min., departs El Escorial 3:15pm, returns 5:30pm).
Estación La Sepulvedana: Po. Florida, 11 (tel. 91 530 48 00). M: Príncipe Pío (via M: Ópera). To Ávila (2hr., 3 per day, 910ptas) and Segovia (1½hr., departs every hr., 775ptas).

BY THUMB AND RIDESHARE

Hitchhiking is legal only on minor routes (though always a risk). The Guardia Civil de Tráfico picks up would-be highway hitchhikers and deposits them at either nearby towns or on a bus. No official organization arranges shared journeys to destinations inside and outside Spain. Try the **message boards** listed on p. 82 for rideshare offers.

■ Getting Around Madrid

MAPS

The *Plano de Madrid* (street map) and the *Plano y Guía de Transportes* (public transportation map), free at city tourist offices, are fantastic. For a more comprehensive map with street index, purchase the *Almax* map at a newsstand (650ptas). Convenient one-page maps of Madrid are free at any **El Corte Inglés** (see p. 82).

METRO

Madrid has a fabulous and fun metro that puts almost every other big-city subway system to shame. The free *Plano del Metro* (available at any ticket booth) is clear and helpful. Trains are clean and run frequently; only on Sundays and late at night is a wait more than five minutes. Green timers hanging boastfully above most platforms show when the last train departed. Wall maps of the Metro and of surrounding neighborhoods abound in every station, as do signs with info on fares and schedules. Up-to-the-minute schedules for late-night trains list arrival times for every stop.

Ten lines connect Madrid's 126 stations (164 by 1999). Lines are distinguished by color and number. An individual Metro ticket costs 130ptas, but savvy riders opt for the *bonometro* (ticket of 10 rides) at 670ptas. Both can be purchased at self-service machines in any metro stop and at *estancos* (tobacco shops) and news kiosks. Monthly passes, including discounted youth passes, are good for both the Metro and city buses. For more details, call **Metro info** (tel. 91 552 59 09) or ask at any ticket booth. Remember to hold on to your ticket or pass until you leave the Metro—riding without a receipt incurs an outrageous fine.

Trains run everyday from 6am to 1:30am, not late enough on Madrid time to be deserted. Violent crime in the Metro stations is almost unheard of, and women usually feel safe traveling alone. Do watch out for pickpockets in crowded cars. Ride in the first car where the conductor sits if you feel uncomfortable and avoid empty cars at night. Some stations, particularly those connected to two or more lines, have long tunnels and series of escalators; exercise caution here and stick with other people. Stations to the north are less frequented at night than most other stations and are often deserted by midnight. Metro stations Chueca, Gran Vía, Sol, Tirso de Molina, La Latina, and Plaza de España surface in areas that can be intimidating after midnight. Still, to reiterate, generally the Metro is clean, efficient, and worry-free.

BUS

Unlike the Metro, buses provide you with a view of Madrid and a sense of direction. Like the Metro, the system is exceptional. Most stops are clearly marked. For extra guidance in finding routes and stops, try the handy *Plano de Los Transportes,* available at newsstands (200ptas), or the free *Madrid en Autobús,* available at bus kiosks.

The fare is 130ptas and a 10-ride *bonobus* pass, sold at newsstands and *estancos* (tobacco shops), costs 670ptas. Buses run from 6am to 11:30pm. From then until 3am, nocturnal buses travel from Pl. Cibeles to the outskirts every 30 minutes; after that, every hour until 6am. Nocturnal buses (N1-N20) are listed on a special section of the *Plano* (cut it out and keep it with you). Buses stop all along the marked routes, not just in Pl. Cibeles, but make sure to signal your stop. For more info, call **Empresa Municipal de Transportes (EMT)** at 91 406 88 10 (Spanish only).

TAXI

Zillions of taxis zip around Madrid at all hours. If by some freak chance one does not appear when you need it, or if you want to summon one to your door, call 91 445 90 08 or 91 447 32 32. A green *libre* sign in the window or a lit green light indicates availability. Taxis are affordable for groups of two to four people and are particularly useful late at night when only night buses run. The base fare is 170ptas, plus 50-75ptas per kilometer. Common fare supplements include: airport (350ptas); bus and train stations (150ptas); luggage charge (50ptas per bag); Sundays and holidays (6am-11pm, 150ptas); nighttime (11pm-6am, 150ptas). The fare from the city center to the airport is about 3000ptas. To Estación Chamartín from Pl. Colón costs about 900ptas.

Taxi drivers in Madrid rarely cheat passengers unless you've got foreigner written all over you. You can, however, request an estimate before entering the cab and make sure that the driver turns on the meter. Also, don't rely on a driver's hostel, restaurant, or club recommendations, as they sometimes have deals going with the owners of such establishments. If you have a complaint or think you've been overcharged, demand a *recibo oficial* (official receipt) and *hoja de reclamaciones* (complaint form), which the driver is required to supply. Take down the license number, route taken, and fare charged. Drop off the forms and info at the Ayuntamiento (City Hall), Pl. Villa, 4 (tel. 91 447 07 15 or 91 447 07 14), to possibly get a refund.

To request **taxi service for the disabled,** call 91 547 82 00, 91 547 85 00, or 91 547 86 00. Rates are identical to those of other taxis. If you leave possessions in a taxi, visit or call the **Negociado de Objetos Perdidos,** Pl. Legazpi, 7 (tel. 91 588 43 46), between 9am and 2pm. Drivers are obligated to turn in any items within 48 hours.

CAR RENTAL

Why on earth do you want to rent a car? If congested traffic and nightmarish parking doesn't unnerve you, aggressive drivers and bratty moped maniacs will. Don't drive unless you're planning to zoom out of the city. To rent a car you must be over 21 and

MADRID

have an International Driver's Permit and major credit card (or leave a deposit equal to the estimated rental fee). Gas is not included in the price and averages 150ptas per liter. Per kilometer surcharges apply to rentals of less than a week. Tobacco shops sell parking permits. If driving outside Spain, a larger car rental chain is your best bet. The tourist office has a complete list of car rental companies, including **Avis** (tel. 91 305 42 73 or 91 547 20 48) and **Hertz** (tel. 91 393 60 00).

> **Autos Bravo:** C. Toledo, 136 (tel. 91 474 80 75). M: Puerta de Toledo. Medium car 12,670ptas per day, 74,950ptas per week. Unlimited mileage, insurance included. Also offers cheaper cars. Open M-F 9am-2pm and 4:30-8pm, Sa 9am-1:30pm.
>
> **Autos Viaducto:** C. Segovia, 26 (tel. 91 548 48 48), C. Martín de los Héroes, 23 (tel. 91 541 55 41), and Av. Mediterráneo, 4 (tel. 91 433 12 33 or 91 552 10 44). Cheapest rate at 5452ptas per day, including insurance, 100km free, 18ptas per every km over 100km. 16% IVA not included. Open M-F 9am-1:30pm and 4-7:30pm.

MOPED RENTAL

Popular with Madrid's residents, mopeds are swift and easy to park. A lock and helmet are needed. Try **Motocicletas Antonio Castro,** C. Conde Duque, 13 (tel. 91 542 06 57; M: San Bernardo). A 49cc Vespino costs 4500ptas per day (8am-8pm), 19,500ptas per week; unlimited mileage and insurance included. Deposit is 75,000ptas. 16% IVA is not included. Renters must be at least 18 and have an International Driver's Permit and photo ID. (Open M-F 8am-1:30pm and 5-8pm.)

■ Orientation

The "Kilómetro 0" marker in front of the police station signals the city's epicenter at **Puerta del Sol,** an intersection of eight major streets. Sol is the city's transportation hub. Below ground, three Metro lines (blue L1, red L2, and yellow L3) converge and transport people to within walking distance of any point in the city. Above ground, buses and taxis do the same. Sol is packed with restaurants, *cafeterías,* shops, banks, *hostales,* tourists, and their counterpart, thieves.

Most of Madrid's prominent points of interest surround Sol, each in a different direct compass direction and within walking distance. West of Sol, close to the metro station and to the heart of Sol, is the **Plaza Mayor.** This plaza has been happening since the 17th century as a hub of activity for both tourists and *madrileños* alike; it shares time and space with both contemporary cafes and the churches and historical houses of Habsburg Madrid, the **Madrid de los Asturias.** Farther west of Sol, via C. Arenal, lies the reigning monument of the **Madrid de los Borbones** (Bourbon Madrid), the **Palacio Real.** This section of Madrid, also known as **Ópera,** hosts fantastic gardens and churches; in summer, it also attracts various music festivals.

To the east of Sol, the **Museo del Prado,** on **Paseo del Prado,** may be reached by way of Carrera de San Jerónimo. The museum lies in the region of **Huertas,** once the literary district of Madrid and now the theater district. Huertas is bordered by **Calle Alcalá** to the north, Po. Prado to the east, Sol to the west, and C. Atocha to the south. Centered around **Plaza Santa Ana,** Huertas is crowded with some of the best hostel values in the city, as well as some of the best bars and cafes. East of the Po. Prado and behind the Museo del Prado, the lush **Parque del Buen Retiro** awaits.

South of Sol lies another world-renowned center of art, the **Museo Reina Sofía.** Also south of Sol, the area around Metro stops **La Latina** and **Tirso de Molina** has less wealth and prestige than the rest of Old Madrid, and consequently fewer tourists. **El Rastro,** a gargantuan ancient flea market, is staged here every Sunday morning. Farther south lies **Lavapiés,** a working-class neighborhood.

Finally, the area north of Sol is bordered by the grand avenue **Gran Vía,** running northwest to **Plaza de España.** The tall **Torre de Madrid** is the pride of 1950s Spain. Farther northwest of Sol lies **Argüelles,** an energetic neighborhood of families and students spilling over from **Moncloa,** the student district, whose nerve center is the McDonald's on C. Isaac Peral. Straight north of Gran Vía, linked by **Calle de Fuencar-**

ral, are the three hyper-cool club and bar-hopping districts of **Malasaña, Bilbao,** and **Chueca,** where the nightlife never stops. Beyond Gran Vía lies modern Madrid. Running the length of Madrid from **Atocha** in the south to **Plaza de Castilla** in the north, **Paseo de la Castellana-Paseo de Recoletos-Paseo del Prado** passes the Prado, the fountains at the plazas of **Cibeles** and **Colón,** and the elaborate skyscrapers beyond Pl. Colón, including the twin towers of the **Puerta de Europa.** Forever unfinished, they epitomize the unending growth of modern Madrid.

Madrid is much safer than most other major European cities, but the Sol, Pl. Dos de Mayo in Malasaña, Pl. Chueca, and Pl. España are still intimidating late at night. As a general rule, avoid the parks and quiet residential streets after dark. Watch out for thieves and pickpockets in crowds, and be wary of opportunists who target tourists with their clever scams; con artists are a tradition here.

Publications About Madrid

Because you will be a lost puppy without it, the weekly entertainment magazine **Guía del Ocio should be your first purchase in Madrid** (125ptas). It has concert, theater, sports, cinema, and TV schedules, as well as sections listing exhibits, restaurants, bars, and clubs under various specific categories. Brief articles highlight new establishments and special events. The *Guía* comes out on Thursday or Friday for the week beginning the following Monday, so be careful which edition you buy on Friday for information on weekend entertainment tips. The *Guía* is available behind the counter of any news kiosk. For a good supplement with articles on new finds in and around the city, pick up *In Madrid,* an interesting English monthly distributed free at tourist offices and many restaurants and bars. *En Madrid,* a monthly available at the tourist office, lists up-to-date hours and telephone numbers of monuments and some practical information, as well as a calendar of events. *The Broadsheet,* free at bookstores, is a no-frills listing of English classifieds with headings like "For Sale" and "Wanted." This self-proclaimed "lifesaver for English speakers in Madrid" is geared toward long-term residents of Madrid. The weekly *Segundamano,* on sale at kiosks, is essential for apartment or roommate seekers. The best full-length city guides to Madrid are *Time Out: Madrid* and the *Guía del Trotamundos: Madrid* (in Spanish).

■ Practical Information

TOURIST AND FINANCIAL SERVICES

Tourist Offices: English spoken at all tourist offices. Those planning trips outside the Comunidad de Madrid can visit region-specific offices within Madrid; ask the tourist offices below for their addresses. **Municipal,** Pl. Mayor, 3 (tel. 91 366 54 77 or 91 588 16 36; fax 91 366 54 77), on the Pl. Mayor. M: Sol. Hands out indispensable city and transportation maps, a complete guide to accommodations, as well as *En Madrid,* a monthly activities and information guide. Open M-F 10am-8pm, Sa 10am-2pm. **Oficinas de Información,** C. Princesa, 1 (tel. 91 541 23 25), off Pl. España. M: Pl. España. Has the same fabulous maps as the Municipal office. **Regional/Provincial Office of the Comunidad de Madrid,** Mercado Pta. de Toledo, Ronda de Toledo 1, stand #3134 (tel. 91 364 1876). M: Pta. de Toledo. In a gallery with large banners on a plaza across from the metro station. Brochures, transport info, and maps for towns in the Comunidad. Also has brochures about towns, campsites, highways, daytrips, and *paradores* throughout the Comunidad de Madrid. Open M-F 9am-7pm, Sa 9:30am-1:30pm. **Second office,** C. Duque Medinaceli, 2 (tel. 91 429 49 51), is just off Pl. Cortés. M: Sol. Open M-F 9am-7pm, Sa 9am-1pm. Other offices at **Estación Chamartín** (see **By Train,** p. 73) and the **airport** (see **By Plane,** p. 72). **El Corte Inglés** has **free maps** and info (see below).

General Info Line: Dial 010. Minute deposit 20ptas. Run by the Ayuntamiento. They'll tell you anything about Madrid, from the nearest police station's address to zoo hours. **Telephone Info:** Dial 1003. No English spoken. Minute deposit 10ptas.

Tours: Read the fine print before pledging to pay an arm and a leg. The following are given in English and geared toward tourists. **Pullmantur,** Pl. Oriente, 8 (tel. 91 541

18 05 or 91 541 18 06). M: Ópera. Several tours of Madrid, averaging around 4000ptas. Also excursions to outlying areas. **Trapsatur,** San Bernardo, 23 (tel. 91 542 63 20). M: Santo Domingo. **Juliá Tours,** Gran Vía, 68 (tel. 91 559 96 05). M: Pl. de España. Also offers tours of Andalucía, Portugal, and Morocco.

Budget Travel: Viajes TIVE, C. Fernando el Católico, 88 (tel. 91 543 02 08 or 91 543 74 12; fax 91 544 00 62). Exit M: Moncloa at C. Isaac Peral, walk straight down C. Arcipreste de Hita, and turn left on C. Fernando el Católico, across from the double underpass; the office is on your left. ISIC 700ptas, HI cards 1800ptas. Organizes group excursions and language classes. Lodgings and student residence info. English spoken. Arrive early, or count on long lines. Open M-F 9am-2pm, Sa 9am-noon. **Comunidad de Madrid, Dirección General de Juventud,** C. Alcalá, 30 and 32 (tel. 91 580 40 00 or 91 580 42 42). M: Banco de España. Same type of documentation as TIVE, though no tickets sold here. **Viva,** Pl. Callao, 3 (tel. 902 32 52 75; fax 91 531 76 95). Arranges trips, car rentals, and documentation. **Viajes Lanzani,** Gran Vía, 88 (tel. 91 541 47 32). M: Gran Vía. Info on discount and student airfare, bus and train tickets, discounted tours, excursion packages, and accommodations.

Consulates: See **Spain: Essentials: Embassies and Consulates,** p. 35.

Currency Exchange: Banco Central Hispano charges no commission on cash or traveler's checks and offers the best rates on AmEx traveler's checks. Open in summer M-F 8:30am-2:30pm; in winter M-Th 8:30am-2:30pm, F-Sa 8:30am-1pm. Banks (1-2% commission, 500ptas minimum charge), El Corte Inglés, and 4- and 5-star hotels offer exchange services at varying rates. Booths in Sol and Gran Vía, open as late as 2am and on weekends, have poor rates and are not a good deal for cashing traveler's checks, despite having no commission. On the other hand, for small-denomination bills (US$20 or US$50) they may be the best option. **ATMs** are plentiful in Madrid. **Servi Red, Servi Caixa,** and **Telebanco** machines accept bank cards with one or more of the Cirrus, PLUS, EuroCard, and NYCE logos. Be forewarned: use only the first 4 digits of your PIN code. For more info, see **Cash Cards,** p. 13. ATM-inspired crime is on the rise, so avoid nighttime ATM sprees.

American Express: Pl. Cortés, 2 (tel. 91 322 55 00; main info line (tel. 91 572 03 03). M: Sevilla. From M: Sevilla, go down C. Seducers and turn left on C. San Jerónimo; office is on the left. The office has *Agencia de Viajes* written in big letters on the windows. In addition to currency exchange (1% cash and 2% traveler's check commission; no commission on AmEx traveler's checks; no minimum charge), they'll hold mail for 30 days and help send and receive wired money. In an emergency, AmEx cashes personal checks up to US$1000 for cardholders only. Open M-F 9am-5:30pm, Sa 9am-noon. 24hr. Express Cash machine outside. To report or cancel lost traveler's checks, call toll free 900 99 44 26. To report other problems, call toll free 900 94 14 13. Both lines available 24hr.

LOCAL SERVICES

Message Boards: At **Librería Turner** and **Booksellers** (see **Shopping: Books,** p. 115); **TIVE** travel agency (see above), with tons of cheap travel tickets and rideshare offers; and **Albergue Juvenil Santa Cruz (HI),** with fewer of the same type of notices (heavy on the rideshare offers). Also check the message boards at foreign language schools and the classifieds in *En Madrid.*

Luggage Storage: Estaciones Chamartín, self-serve, automatic lockers in the *consigna* area by the bus stop. Lockers 400-600ptas per day. Open daily 6:30am-12:30am. Lockers opened once with each payment. **Estación Atocha,** same services, prices, and hours. Exiting the *largo recorrido* area, lockers are to the left of the rainforest display. **Estación Sur de Autobuses,** bags checked (800ptas).

El Corte Inglés: C. Preciados, 3 (tel. 91 379 80 00). M: Sol. **C. Goya, 76** (tel. 91 432 93 00). M: Goya. **C. Princesa, 42** (tel. 91 454 60 00). M: Argüelles. **C. Raimundo Fernández Villaverde, 79** (tel. 91 556 23 00). M: Nuevos Ministerios. Giant chain of department stores. "A place to shop. A place to dream." Good **maps,** haircutting, cafeteria-restaurant, **supermarket, telephones,** tapes and CDs, **books in English,** electronics, and sycophantic salespeople. **Currency exchange** with no commission, but mediocre rates. Open M-Sa 10am-9pm, Su 10am-2pm.

English Bookstores: See **Shopping: Books,** p. 115.

English-Language Periodicals: International edition dailies and weeklies available at kiosks everywhere, especially on the Gran Vía, Paseos del Prado, Recoletos, and Castellana and around Pta. Sol. If you're dying for the *New York Times* (425ptas), try one of the **VIPS** restaurants (see **Red-Eye Establishments,** p. 91).

Language Service: Forocio (*For*eign *Ocio*), C. Mayor, 6, 4th fl. (tel. 91 522 56 77). An organization dedicated to bringing foreigners and natives together to share languages (and anything else). Sponsors weekly international parties and organizes group trips to other parts of Spain. Open daily 10am-8pm.

Libraries: Bibliotecas Populares (info tel. 91 445 98 45). A big, airy branch is at M: Puerta de Toledo (tel. 91 366 54 07). English-language periodicals. If you bring your passport and two ID-size photos, they'll issue a card on the spot. Open M-F 8:30am-8:45pm. Free. **Biblioteca Nacional** (tel. 91 580 78 23) on C. Serrano next to the Museo Arqueológico. M: Serrano. Limited to scholars doing doctorate and post-doctorate research. To use the facilities, bring letters of recommendation and a project proposal, and overinflate your importance. Open M-F 9am-9pm, Sa 9am-1pm. **Washington Irving Center,** C. Marqués Villamagna, 8 (tel. 91 587 22 00). M: Serrano or Colón. From the station, walk up C. Serrano and turn left on C. Marqués de Villamagna. Good selection of U.S. magazines and books. Anyone over 16 can check books out for 2 weeks by filling out a form. Allow about 1 week for processing. Open M-F 2-6pm.

Religious Services: Our Lady of Mercy English-Speaking Parish, C. Alfonso XIII, 165 (morning tel. 91 533 20 32; afternoon tel. 91 554 28 60), on the corner of Pl. Habana. Mass in English daily 11:30am. **Immanuel Baptist Church,** C. Hernández de Tejada, 4 (tel. 91 407 43 47). English services Su 11am and 7pm. **Community Church of Madrid,** C. Bravo Murillo, 85. M: Cuatro Caminos. At the Colegio El Porvenir. Multi-denominational Protestant services in English Su 10am. **British Embassy Church of St. George,** C. Núñez de Balboa, 43 (tel. 91 576 51 09). M: Velázquez. Services Su 8:30, 10, and 11:15am. **Sinagoga Beth Yaacov,** C. Balmes, 3 (tel. 91 445 98 43 or 91 445 98 35), near Pl. Sorolla. M: Iglesia. Services F 8pm, Sa 9:15am. Kosher restaurant can be reserved. Passport sometimes required. Spanish only. **Centro Islámico,** C. Alonso Cano, 3 (tel. 91 448 05 54). M: Iglesia. Services and language classes. Open M-F 9am-2pm and 5-8pm.

Women's Services: Librería de Mujeres, C. San Cristóbal, 17 (tel. 91 521 70 43), near Pl. Mayor. M: Sol. Walk down C. Mayor and make a left on C. Esparteros, take the first right on C. Postas, and then the first left onto C. San Cristóbal. Gloria Steinem and Susan Faludi in translation. The shop's motto: *"Los libros no muerden, el feminismo tampoco."* ("Books don't bite, neither does feminism.") Books and gifts, but more of a resource for Spanish speakers. Open M-F 10am-2pm and 5-8pm. **Women's Issues** (tel. 900 19 10 10 or 91 347 80 00).

Gay and Lesbian Services: Colectivo de Gais y Lesbianas de Madrid (COGAM), C. Fuencarral, 37 (tel./fax 91 523 00 70), directly across from the Ministry of Justice. M: Gran Vía. Provides a wide range of services and activities of interest to gays, lesbians, and bisexuals. English usually spoken. Free screenings of gay-interest movies, COGAM youth group (25 and under), and HIV-positive support group (tel. 91 522 45 17; M-F 6-10pm). Reception daily M-F 5-9pm. Free counseling M-Th 7-9pm. Library open daily 7-9pm. COGAM also publishes the semi-monthly *Entiendes...?,* a magazine in Spanish about gay issues, as well as the *Pink and Black Pages* listing gay services, groups, activities, and personals (magazine available at many kiosks and bookstores). Their cafe, **Urania,** is unaffiliated, but is used as a social gathering center. **Berkana Librería Gai y Lesbiana** has good guides, contact information, and listings (see **Books,** p. 116). Most entertainment guides list gay and lesbian clubs. **GAI-INFORM,** a gay info line (tel. 91 523 00 70), provides info in Spanish (and sometimes French and English) about gay associations, leisure activities, and health issues. The same number has info on sports, workshops in French and English, dinners, and on Brujulai, COGAM's weekend excursion group. Open daily 5-9pm.

Laundromats: All laundromats have drying services—price varies depending on size of load or drying time (about 100ptas). **Lavandería Donoso Cortés,** C. Donoso Cortés, 17 (tel. 91 446 96 90). M: Quevedo. From the Metro, walk down C. Bravo Murillo to C. Donoso Cortés. Self-service. Wash 600ptas, detergent 60ptas. Open M-F 9am-2pm and 3:30-8pm, Sa 9am-2pm. **Lavandería Automática SIDEC,** C. Don

Felipe, 4. M: Tribunal. Wash 600ptas, detergent 25ptas. Open M-F 10am-9pm. **Maryland,** C. Meléndez Valdés, 52 (tel. 91 543 30 41). M: Argüelles. Go up C. Princesa, turn right on C. Hilarión, which then intersects C. Meléndez Valdés. Self service. Wash and detergent 725ptas. Open M-F 10:30am-8pm, Sa 10am-2pm.

EMERGENCY AND COMMUNICATIONS

Emergency: Dial 091 (national police) or 092 (local police). **Police:** C. Luna, 17 (tel. 91 521 12 36). M: Callao. From Gran Vía, walk down C. Arenal. This station has forms in English. To report crimes committed in the Metro, go to the office in the Sol station (tel. 91 521 09 11). Open daily 8am-11pm. **Guardia Civil** (tel. 062 or 91 534 02 00). **Protección Civil** (tel. 91 537 31 00).

Crisis Lines: Poison Control (24hr. tel. 91 562 04 20). **Rape Hotline** (tel. 91 574 01 10). Open M-F 10am-2pm and 4-7pm (other times machine-recorded instructions).

Help Lines: 20ptas minimum charge for all non-900 numbers. **AIDS Info Hotline** (tel. 900 11 10 00; M-F 9am-2pm). **Detox** (tel. 900 16 15 15). English spoken. 9am-9pm daily. **Alcoholics Anonymous,** C. Juan Bravo, 40-bis, 2nd fl. (English tel. 91 309 19 47; crisis line in Spanish tel. 91 341 82 82). M: Núñez de Balboa. **English-Language Helpline** (tel. 91 559 13 93) for confidential help from trained volunteers (ask for Ethan). Open daily 7-11pm.

Late-Night Pharmacy: (info tel. 098). Check *Farmacias de Guardia* listings in local papers to find pharmacies open after 8pm. Listings of the nearest on-duty pharmacy are also posted in all pharmacy windows. Contraceptive products are sold over the counter in most Spanish pharmacies.

Hospitals: Prompt appointments are hard to obtain, but public hospitals don't require advance payment. Emergency rooms are the best option for immediate attention. **Anglo-American Medical Unit,** Conde de Aranda, 1, 1st fl. (tel. 91 435 18 23). M: Serrano or Retiro. Doctors, dentists, and optometrists. Run partly by British and Americans. Regular personnel on duty 9am-8pm. *Not* an emergency clinic. 8000ptas for initial visit. Credit cards accepted. Embassies and consulates also keep lists of English-speaking doctors in private practice. **Hospital Clínico San Carlos,** Pl. Cristo Rey (tel. 91 330 30 00). M: Moncloa. Open 24hr.

Emergency Clinics: In a **medical emergency,** dial 061. **Equipo Quirúrgico Municipal No. I,** C. Montesa, 22 (tel. 91 588 51 00). M: Manuel Becerra. **Hospital Ramón y Cajal,** Ctra. Colmenar Viejo (tel. 91 336 80 00). Bus #135 from Pl. Castilla.

Internet Access: Net Café, C. San Bernardo, 81 (tel. 91 594 09 99). M: San Bernardo. One drink buys one hour of net use. Open M-Th 6pm-2am, F-Su 4pm-3am. **La Ciberteca,** C. General Perón, 32 (tel. 91 556 56 03). M: Santiago Bernabeu. Open M-Sa 4-11pm. Also **Cybercafe Comercial** (see p. 95).

Post Office: Palacio de Comunicaciones, Pl. Cibeles (tel. 902 19 71 97). M: Banco de España. Enormous, ornate palace on the far side of the plaza from the Metro. Info (main vestibule) open M-F 8am-10pm or call the useful info line (tel. 91 537 64 94). Open for stamp purchase and certified mail (main door) M-F 8:30am-10pm, Sa 8:30am-8pm, Su 9:30am-1:30pm. **Lista de Correos** (window 80) open M-F 8:30am-9:30pm, Sa 8:30am-8pm. Sending packages (door N) open M-F 8:30am-9pm, Sa 8:30am-1:30pm. Telex and **fax** service (door H, right of main entrance) open M-F 8am-midnight, Sa-Su 8am-10pm. Windows may change. English and French spoken at info desk. **Postal Code:** 28080.

Telephones: See **Keeping in Touch,** p. 49.

■ Accommodations and Camping

The demand for rooms is always high and it increases dramatically in summer. Never fear—Madrid is inundated with *hostales.* Prices average about 2400ptas per person for a basic *hostal* room, a bit more for a two-star *hostal,* slightly less for a bed in a *pensión,* and even less when visiting during the off season. Bargaining is a good idea, and perfectly acceptable, especially if you are sharing a room with two or more friends or are planning to stay for more than a few days.

ACCOMMODATIONS SERVICE

Viajes Brújula: Torre de Madrid, 14, 6th fl. (tel. 91 559 97 04 or 91 559 97 05; fax 91 548 46 24). M: Plaza España. Located in a huge building with signs for Alitalia on the ground floor. For 300ptas, they make reservations for any participating locale in Spain. *You must go in person.* You pay a deposit of one-third of the room price, which is then subtracted from the price of the accommodation. Not every establishment is signed up with Brújula (no HI youth hostels); nevertheless, it's a good deal if you are tired and need a bed. English spoken. Open M-F 9am-7pm. **Branch offices** at: Estación Atocha (tel. 91 539 11 73), at the AVE terminal (open daily 8am-10pm); Estación Chamartín (tel. 91 315 78 94; open daily 7am-11:30pm); and the airport bus terminal (tel. 91 575 96 80), in Pl. Colón (open daily 8am-10pm).

HOSTALES, PENSIONES, AND YOUTH HOSTELS

In Madrid, the difference between a one-star **hostal** and a *pensión* is often minimal. A room in a one- or two-star *hostal* has at least the basics: bed, closet space, desk with chair, sink and towel, window, light fixture, fake flowers, and a lock on the door (religious icons are popular, but not standard). Winter heating is standard, air-conditioning is not. Unless otherwise noted, communal bathrooms (toilet and shower) are the rule. Most places accept reservations, but they're never required. Reservations are recommended in summer and on weekends year-round, especially in the Puerta del Sol area and at our top listings in each district. Generally, in Madrid, especially in competitive central zones, *hostales* are well kept and comfortable. Owners are usually accustomed to opening the doors, albeit groggily, at all hours or providing keys for guests, but ask before club-hopping into the wee hours; late-night lockouts or confrontations with irate owners are never fun.

Pensiones are like boarding houses: they sometimes have curfews and often host guests staying for longer periods of time *(estables)*. Towels and sheets are provided but not always changed daily. The same goes for *casas de huéspedes* or simply *casas*. The best deals are found outside central locations, but Madrid's stellar public transportation makes virtually any locale central.

Madrid has two **HI hostels.** While neither is centrally located, the **Albergue Juvenil Richard Schirrman** in the Casa de Campo is located in an isolated and reputedly dangerous spot. For more information on the other HI hostel, see p. 89.

SOL AND ÓPERA

Puerta del Sol is the center of the city in the center of the country. All roads converge here (it's Spain's km 0) and all tourists ramble through at least once. Signs indicating *hostales* and *pensiones* stick out from flower-potted balconies and decaying facades on narrow, sloping streets. For better deals, stray several blocks from Sol. The following listings fall in the area west of Sol, between Sol and the Palacio Real. Buses #3, 25, and 39 serve Ópera, buses #5 (from Atocha), 15, 20, 50, 51, 52, 53, and 150 serve Sol.

Hostal Paz, C. Flora, 4, 1st and 4th fl. (tel. 91 547 30 47). M: Ópera. On a quiet street parallel to C. Arenal, off C. Donados or C. Hileras. Firm beds in 10 brilliant rooms—some overlooking a courtyard, others with access to a terrace. Satellite TV. Singles 2400ptas; doubles 3600ptas, with shower 4200ptas; triples with shower 5400ptas. Laundry 1000ptas. Reservations encouraged. A/C. Visa, MC.

Hostal-Residencia Luz, C. Fuentes, 10, 3rd fl. (tel. 91 542 07 59). M: Ópera. 12 sunny, inviting rooms in an elegant old building off C. Arenal. The bathrooms sparkle so much you won't mind sharing. Satellite TV, fax service, and public phone. Singles 2500ptas; doubles 3700ptas; triples 5300ptas. Laundry 1000ptas. Discounts for stays of 15 days or more. 7% IVA not included.

Hostal Portugal, C. Flora, 4, ground fl. (tel. 91 559 40 14). M: Ópera. Bright rooms, great location, and *cheap*. 2000ptas per person.

Hostal Madrid, C. Esparteros, 6, 2nd fl. (tel. 91 522 00 60; fax 91 532 35 10). M: Sol. Off C. Mayor. Spacious rooms with shiny wood floors and large windows. All have

TVs and new bathrooms. Telephones, A/C. Cold drinks 150ptas. Singles 5000ptas; doubles 8000ptas; triple with balcony 9000ptas. Reservations recommended. Visa.

Hostal-Residencia María del Mar, C. Marqués Viudo de Pontejos 7, 2nd and 3rd fl. (tel. 91 531 90 64). M: Sol. Off C. Correo from Pta. Sol. 30 recently renovated rooms with high ceilings, shiny floors, and shapely furniture—just don't get stuck in one of the 2 windowless singles. Lounge with TV. No smoking in common areas. 2am curfew. Singles with sinks (no hot water) 1800ptas; doubles 3000ptas, with bath 4500-5000ptas; triple with bath 6500ptas. Hot showers 200ptas.

Hostal-Residencia Cruz-Sol, Pl. Santa Cruz, 6, 3rd fl. (tel. 91 532 71 97). M: Sol. Ample rooms with parquet floors and cavernous ceilings. Many overlook the plaza. A warm beige interior with sudden bursts of red and sweet baby blue. Singles 2000ptas; doubles 2500ptas, with bath 4500ptas; triples 3000-5000ptas. Showers 200ptas per person, free for guests in singles. No winter heating.

Hostal-Residencia Santa Cruz, Pl. Santa Cruz, 6, 2nd fl. (tel./fax 91 522 24 41). M: Sol. Sky-high ceilings and a palatial lounge. Tiny, sinkless singles 2800ptas, with shower 3200ptas; doubles with shower 4200ptas, with bath 4800ptas; triples 5000ptas, with bath 6000ptas. Reservations accepted by fax.

Hostal-Residencia Miño, C. Arenal, 16, 2nd fl. (tel. 91 531 50 79). M: Ópera. A melting pot of rooms ranging from large with hardwood floors and balconies to tight quarters with vinyl underfoot. Some rooms overlook busy C. Arenal, others a quieter but darker patio. Singles 2200ptas, with shower 2900ptas; doubles with shower 3900ptas, with bath 4500ptas; triples 5400ptas.

Hostal-Residencia Rober, C. Arenal, 26, 5th fl. (tel. 91 541 91 75). M: Ópera. The hodge-podge of rugs and bed coverings give that grandparent feel. Smoking is strictly prohibited. All 14 pristine rooms have their own tiny TVs. Singles with shower 3000ptas, with bath 3500ptas; doubles with bath 4500ptas; triples with bath 6000ptas. Prices don't include 7% IVA. A/C. Visa, MC, AmEx.

Hostal-Residencia Encarnita, C. Marqués Viudo de Pontejo, 7, 4th fl. (tel. 91 531 90 55). M: Sol. Above the María del Mar. Standard *hostal* charm: claustrophobic rooms, soft beds, dim halls, cheap nature posters. Singles 1500ptas; doubles 2600ptas, with bath 2900ptas; triples 3900. Hot showers 200ptas, cold 100ptas.

HUERTAS

Although *madrileños* have never settled on a nickname for this neighborhood, it's generally referred to as Huertas and is known as Madrid's theater district. It rings all day and night with bar-crawlers nibbling on *tapas,* especially on Wednesdays when show tickets are discounted. Sol, Pl. Mayor, *El triángulo de arte,* and Atocha train station are all within walking distance. Sol-bound buses stop near accommodations on C. Príncipe, C. Nuñez de Arce, and C. San Jerónimo; buses #14, 27, 37 (passing Est. Atocha and Est. Sur de Autobuses), and 45 run along Po. del Prado.

Hostal Gonzalo, C. Cervantes, 34, 3rd fl. (tel. 91 429 27 14). M: Antón Martín. Off C. León, which is off C. Atocha. Newly renovated by friendly proprietors. All rooms with TV, fans in summer. Singles 4000ptas; doubles 5200ptas. Ask about discounts.

Hostal Villar, C. Príncipe, 18, 1st-4th fl. (tel. 91 531 66 00; fax 91 521 50 73; email hvillar@arrakis.es). M: Sol. From Sol, walk down C. San Jerónimo, and turn right on C. Príncipe. The 1970s stormed through this old building, leaving in their wake 46 comfortable rooms with TVs, telephones, and a whole lotta brown. Singles 2300ptas, with bath 3000ptas; doubles 3350ptas, with bath 4250ptas; triples 4650ptas, with bath 5900ptas; quads 6000ptas, with bath 7600ptas. A/C. Visa, MC.

Hostal Aguilar, C. San Jerónimo, 32, 2nd fl. (tel. 91 429 59 26 or 91 429 36 61; fax 91 429 26 61). M: Sol. More than 50 very, very clean, modern rooms, all with telephone, A/C, coin-operated TV, and bath. Singles 3500ptas; doubles 5500ptas; triples 7000ptas. 1500ptas per extra person. Visa, MC.

Hostal R. Rodríguez, C. Nuñez de Arce, 9, 3rd fl. (tel. 91 522 44 31), off Pl. Santa Ana. M: Sol. Alluring rooms, including 2 snazzy triples with classic columns and wispy curtains. English spoken. Singles 2500ptas; doubles 3500ptas; triples 4500ptas. Shared baths only. Reception 24hr.

Hostal-Residencia Sud-Americana, Po. Prado, 12, 6th fl. (tel. 91 429 25 64). M: Antón Martín or Atocha. Across from the Prado. 8 rooms total—all with faux-leather armchairs and some with balconies. Face the Po. de Prado and enjoy a magnificent view. Singles 2500ptas; doubles 4800ptas; one triple 6000ptas.

Hostal Armesto, C. San Agustín, 6, 1st fl. (tel. 91 429 90 31). M: Antón Martín. In front of Pl. Cortés. A small establishment with well-coordinated furniture, wallpaper, curtains, and carnation-pink bedspreads. Several rooms look out onto a garden. All rooms with bath and TV. Singles 4600; doubles 5600ptas; triples 7500ptas.

Hostal-Residencia Carreras, C. Príncipe, 18, 3rd fl. (tel. 91 522 00 36). M: Antón Martín, Sol, or Sevilla. Off San Jerónimo, between Pl. Santa Ana and Pl. Canalejas. Spacious rooms lit with fluorescent bulbs. A more modern **annex,** C. Príncipe, 20, is equipped with full modern baths and fewer fluorescent bulbs. Singles 2000ptas, with shower 3000ptas; doubles 3500ptas, with shower 4000ptas, with bath 4500ptas; triples 4500ptas; quads 6000ptas. House rules are posted throughout, including no noise after midnight. Advance payment required.

Hostal-Residencia Regional, C. Príncipe, 18, 4th fl. (tel. 91 522 33 73). M: Antón Martín, Sol, or Sevilla. Same building as Carreras. If you're lucky (and pay more), you'll get a futuristic shower pod. Singles 2400ptas, with shower 3400ptas; doubles 3400ptas, with shower 4400ptas; triples 4400ptas, with shower 5400ptas.

Hostal Lucense, C. Núñez de Arce, 15, 1st fl. (tel. 91 522 48 88) and **Pensión Poza,** C. Núñez de Arce, 9, 1st fl. (tel. 91 522 48 71). M: Sol. Go down C. San Jerónimo, turn right on C. Cruz, and left on C. Nuñez de Arce. The sign outside reads "Speaking Englisch," which turns out to be about right. Best for skinny people with lots of clothes—narrow rooms with huge closets. Poza has larger rooms for the same price. Singles 1300-1400ptas; doubles 2000-2400ptas; triples 3600ptas. Showers 200ptas, but shower times restricted.

Hostal Abulense, C. Nuñez de Arce, 15, 3rd fl. (tel. 91 522 81 44). M: Sol. Upstairs from the Hostal Lucense, a friendly proprietress runs this simple and slightly cramped *hostal* at very cheap rates. The doorbell chimes "Jingle Bells" and Beethoven's Fifth. Communal bathroom. Small singles 1400ptas; fair-sized doubles 2400ptas; triples 3300ptas. Showers 150ptas. Cheaper for longer stays.

Hostal-Residencia Mondragón, C. San Jerónimo, 32, 4th fl. (tel. 91 429 68 16). M: Sol. In the same building as the Aguilar and several other *hostales*. Spain's first motion picture was filmed in this building in 1898. Some rooms open on to a gardenia-filled terrace. Hot water runs only in communal bathrooms. Singles 2000ptas; doubles 2800ptas, with shower 3000ptas; triples 3900ptas.

Hostal-Residencia Lido, C. Echegaray, 5, 2nd fl. (tel. 91 429 62 07). M: Sol. Off C. San Jerónimo near Pl. Canalejas. The rickety steps don't seem to keep guests away. Smallish rooms, some without windows, others with big, arboreal balconies. Long-term guests are preferred and can use kitchen. Singles 2000ptas; doubles 3500ptas. Monthly: singles 35,000ptas; doubles 65,000ptas. Breakfast 350ptas.

Hostal León, C. San Jerónimo, 32, 4th fl. (tel. 91 429 67 78). M: Sol. On the same floor as the Mondragón. Cupid carvings adorn the ceilings of this simple *hostal*. Authentic 1970s decor and attractive tiling in the common bathroom. Not the most hygienic, but dirt cheap. Singles 1800ptas; doubles 2800ptas; triples 3900ptas.

GRAN VÍA

Screaming lights, flashing cars, swishing skirts, and heavy-heeled shoes swirling in cigar smoke and exhaust fumes. The Gran Vía is macro-Madrid, its Broadway or Champs-Elysées—busy and international. It has sex shops, McDonald's, ritzy theaters, and steel chairs reflecting the neon glow. It is vertical and cosmopolitan in a city that spreads outward, neighborhood by neighborhood. *Hostal* signs scatter the horizon. Accommodations tend to be expensive. If you're shown a streetside room, you might want to check it for well-fortified windows. Buses #44, 75, 133, 146, 147, and 148 reach Callao; buses #1, 2, 44, 46, 74, 75, and 133 service both Pl. España and Callao.

Hostal Lauria, Gran Vía, 50, 4th fl. (tel. 91 541 91 82; fax 91 541 91 88). M: Callao. Stucco walls, light wood shutters and baby blue beds create an airy, California-ranch house feel. Rooms are tastefully sparse, with big windows, pretty little bath-

MADRID

rooms, TVs, and telephones. The owner is eager to please—show him your *Let's Go*. Singles 4000ptas; doubles 5200ptas; triples 7000ptas. 20% off stays longer than a week. Laundry service available.

Hostal Margarita, Gran Vía, 50, 5th fl. (tel./fax 91 547 35 49). M: Callao. Ultra-comfortable rooms have oriental rugs and random artwork. Homey *salón* with stereo and TV. Use of kitchen and refrigerator. English spoken. All rooms with shower. Singles 4000ptas; doubles 4800ptas, with bath 5100ptas; triples 6750ptas. Laundry 1200ptas. Reservations recommended a week in advance. Visa, MC.

Hostal A. Nebrija, Gran Vía, 67, 8th fl., elevator A (tel. 91 547 73 19). M: Pl. España. Pleasant and spacious rooms, heavily furnished in medieval style and with huge windows revealing great views; a great place to read. Singles 3100ptas; doubles 4100ptas; triples 6100ptas. TV. Visa, AmEx.

Hostal-Residencia Alibel, Gran Vía, 44, 8th fl. (tel. 91 521 00 51). M: Callao. Well-lit rooms with great views and polished armoirs; a column here, an archway there. French spoken. Singles 3000ptas; doubles with shower 4500ptas; triples with shower 6000ptas. Laundry service, drinks available. Credit cards accepted.

Hostal Delfina, Gran Vía, 12, 4th fl. (tel. 91 522 64 23 or 91 522 64 22). M: Gran Vía or Sevilla. Old-fashioned charm in a stately building is spiced with parquet floors and lime green walls. All rooms have bath, telephone, TV, and A/C. Singles 3500ptas; doubles 5500ptas; triples 7000ptas. Slightly cheaper in winter.

Hostal-Residencia María, Miguel Moya, 4, 2nd fl (tel. 91 522 44 77). M: Callao. Located just off Pl. Callao, set 20m back from the noisy Gran Vía. Airy, spacious rooms, all with TVs and some with fans or attractive cut-glass fixtures. Whole place has a neutral, yellow-beige color. Singles with bath 3100ptas; doubles with bath 4500ptas; triple with bath 6000ptas. 7% IVA not included. Visa, MC.

Hostal-Residencia Lamalonga, Gran Vía, 56, 2nd fl. (tel. 91 547 26 31 or 91 547 68 94). M: Santo Domingo. Crowded TV lounge with a neat row of fancy chairs, stained-glass windows, and ubiquitous fake flowers. Walls meet at odd angles. All rooms have TV and private bath. Singles 4100ptas; doubles 6000ptas; triples 8000ptas. Cheaper in winter. 10% discount for stays over 5 days. Visa, MC.

Hostal Josefina, Gran Vía, 44, 7th fl. (tel. 91 521 81 31). M: Callao. Heavy gray drapes, peeling paint, and dramatic candelabra give the hallways a mysterious feel. The rooms, however, all have happy colors; most have balconies, although some have only a view of a dark gray wall. Room 15 is a dream triple with a spacious lounge. Common bathrooms. Singles 2700ptas, with shower 3000ptas; doubles with shower 4000ptas; triples with shower 6000ptas.

MALASAÑA AND CHUECA

Malasaña and Chueca, both hard-core party pits for the *jóvenes* (youth) of Madrid, is cut down the middle by C. Fuencarral. Though noisier and more odoriferous than the Gran Vía, C. Fuencarral, north of Sol between metro stops Gran Vía and Tribunal, is less expensive, and *hostales* and *pensiones* reside in practically every portal. Chueca is hip and fun but can be dangerous, especially for solo travelers. Buses #3, 40, and 149 run south along C. Fuencarral.

Hotel Mónaco, C. Barbieri, 5 (tel. 91 552 46 30; fax 91 521 16 01). M: Chueca or Gran Vía. A former brothel catering to Madrid's high society (Alfonso XIII, the king's grandfather, is rumored to have been a frequent visitor), the hotel's decor still encourages naughtiness. Frescoes of Eve-like temptresses prod and pry the imagination while hundreds of mirrors keep watch to ensure the realization of fantasy. Each room is a different adventure. Ostentatiously risquée first-floor bedrooms—welcome to Monaco, room 34. All rooms with bath. Lively bar area. Simple singles 7000ptas; doubles 10,000ptas; triples 13,500ptas; quads 15,000ptas. Treat yourself. Accepts all major credit cards.

Hostal Lorenzo, C. las Infantas, 26, 3rd fl. (tel. 91 521 30 57; fax 91 532 79 78). M: Gran Vía. Tasteful rooms with TVs, telephones, A/C, real plants on real balconies, and sound-proof windows. Turn the knob by the bed to hear music through ceiling speakers. All rooms with bath. Singles 4400ptas; doubles 6400ptas; triples 8000ptas. Breakfast 300ptas. Reservations recommended. Credit cards accepted.

Hostal Palacios and Hostal Ribadavia, C. Fuencarral, 25, 1st-3rd fl. (tel. 91 531 10 58 or 91 531 48 47). M: Gran Vía. Both *hostales* are run by the same cheerful family. **Ribadavia** (3rd fl.) has pleasant, bright rooms with old furniture. **Palacios** (1st and 2nd fl.) flaunts brand new rooms, all with TV. Singles with private bath just outside room 2600ptas, with bath inside 3000ptas; doubles with shower 3800ptas, with bath 4600ptas; triples with bath 6900ptas; quad with bath 7500ptas.

Hostal Abril, C. Fuencarral, 39, 4th fl. (tel. 91 531 53 38). M: Tribunal or Gran Vía. Nice and simple—light wood, low prices, and random baby posters. Renovated in 1994. Singles 1900ptas, with shower 2200ptas, with bath 2500ptas; doubles 2900-3200ptas, with bath 3400ptas; triples 3100ptas, with bath 4300ptas.

Hostal-Residencia Domínguez, C. Santa Brígida, 1 (tel. 91 532 15 47). M: Tribunal. Go down C. Fuencarral toward Gran Vía, turn left on C. Santa Brígada, and go up one flight of dark steps. Modern bathrooms almost as big as the quiet, spartan rooms (with TV). Narrow hallways lead to a free luggage storage area. Singles 1900ptas, with bath 2200ptas; doubles with bath 3800ptas. Reservations recommended.

Hostal Medieval, C. Fuencarral, 46, 2nd fl. (tel. 91 522 25 49). M: Tribunal. On the corner of C. Augusto Figueroa. Don't think Dark Ages, think pink. The lounge honors the Spanish royal couple and Real Madrid (*¡Hala Madrid! ¡Hala Vikingos!*). Singles with shower 3000ptas; doubles with shower 4000ptas, with bath 5000ptas; triples with shower 6200ptas.

ELSEWHERE

Near the **Chamartín** train station budget lodgings are rare, as they are in nearly all the residential districts located away from the center. Near the **Madrid-Atocha** train station are a handful of *hostales,* the closest down Po. Santa María de la Cabeza. The tourist office in Pl. Mayor has a full list of accommodations.

Albergue Juvenil Santa Cruz de Marcenado (HI), C. Santa Cruz de Marcenado, 28 (tel. 91 547 45 32; fax 91 548 11 96). M: Argüelles. From the Metro, walk 1 block down C. Alberto Aguilera away from C. Princesa, turn right at C. Serrano Jóve, and then left on C. Santa Cruz de Marcenado. Modern, recently renovated facilities near the student district. 72 firm beds in airy rooms fill quickly, even in winter. Message board and English spoken. Rooms have cubbies; lockers (outside rooms) 200ptas extra. An HI card is required and can be purchased for 1800ptas. Dorms 950ptas, over 26 1300ptas. Breakfast included. Sheets, but not towels, provided. 3-day max. stay. Silence after midnight; curfew 1:30am (strictly enforced). Reception daily 9am-1:30pm. Reserve a space (by person, mail, or fax only) in advance, or arrive early and pray. Closed Christmas and New Year's.

Hostal-Residencia La Montaña, C. Juan Álvarez Mendizábal, 44, 4th fl. (tel. 91 547 10 88), a short jaunt from the youth hostel. From the HI, cross the busy C. Princesa, turn left, go right on C. Rey Francisco, then go left on C. J.A. Mendizábal. From M: Ventura Rodríguez, facing the park (green shrubbery), walk 3 blocks up C. Princesa (to your left) to C. Rey Francisco, go 3 blocks to J. A. Mendizábal, and turn left again. Rooms are immaculate, ample, sunny, and in relatively low demand. Single by the front door is a bit cramped. Singles 1800ptas, with shower 2000ptas; doubles with shower 3400ptas, with bath 3700ptas; triples 5100ptas.

CAMPING

Tourist offices can provide info about the 13 or so campsites within 50km of Madrid. Similar info is in their **Guía Oficial de Campings** (official camping guide) a big book which they gladly let you look through, but don't give away (most bookstores carry it). The **Mapa de Campings** shows the location of every official campsite in Spain. Also ask for the brochure **Hoteles, Campings, Apartamentos,** which lists and describes hotels, campsites, and apartments in and around Madrid. For further camping info, contact the Consejería de Educación de Juventud (tel. 91 522 29 41).

Camping Osuna (tel. 91 741 05 10; fax 91 320 63 65) is located on Av. Logroño. Take the Metro to Canillejas, then cross the pedestrian overpass, walk through the parking lot, and turn right along the freeway. Pass under two bridges (the first a freeway and the second an arch) and look for campground signs on the right (630ptas per person, per tent, and per car, plus 7% IVA). **Camping Alpha** (tel. 91 695 80 69) hides on a shady site 12.4km down the Ctra. de Andalucía in Getafe. From the Legazpi Metro station take bus #447, which stops next to the Nissan dealership (10min., every 30min. until 10pm). Ask the driver to let you off at the pedestrian overpass near the Amper building. After crossing the bridge, take an enchanting 1.5km walk back toward Madrid along the edge of the busy highway. Alpha has a pool (590ptas per person and car, 640ptas per tent; plus IVA). Both campgrounds could pass as autonomous cities: each has phones, hot showers, washers and dryers, saves, currency exchange, medical care, a playground, a bar, and a restaurant.

■ Food

In Madrid, it's not hard to fork it down without forking over too much. Between *churro*-laden breakfasts, two-hour lunches, *meriendas* (snacks), dinner, and *tapas*, it's a wonder Madrid gets anything done at all. You can't walk a block without tripping over at least five *cafeterías*, where a sandwich, coffee, and dessert sell for around 600ptas. Fresh produce in Madrid's center is scarce. There's **Mercado San Miguel**, listed below, as well as some fruit stands north of Sol, in Pl. Carmen, but neighborhood markets lie in more residential areas. Vegetarians may shrink a size: this book alone lists most of the vegetarian restaurants available. For a full meal at a *restaurante* or *casa*, one step up from the hegemonic *cafetería*, expect to spend at least 1100ptas. Keep in mind the following essential buzz words for quicker, cheaper *madrileño* fare: *bocadillo* (a sandwich on hard role, 350-400ptas); *sandwich* (a sandwich on sliced bread, ask for it *a la plancha* if you want it grilled, 300ptas); *croissant* (with ham and cheese, 250ptas); *ración* (a large *tapa*, served with bread 300-600ptas); and *empanada* (a puff pastry with tuna, hake, or other fillings, 200-300ptas). See the **Glossary of Food Terms**, p. 651, for additional useful translations.

In general, *restaurantes* are open from 1 to 4pm and 8pm to midnight; in the following listings, such is the case unless otherwise noted. More casual establishments such as *mesones, cafeterías, bares, cafés, terrazas,* and *tabernas* serve drinks and foodstuffs all day until midnight; some are closed on Sundays. For a nibble, pop into any local food shop or **Rodilla**, an all-purpose food chain notable for its green decor. Rodilla sells sticky tarts, sandwiches for 85ptas, coffee, and croissants.

Groceries: %Dia and **Simago** are the cheapest city-wide supermarket chains. More expensive are **Mantequerías Leonesas, Expreso,** and **Jumbo.** Every **El Corte Inglés** has a huge food market with an excellent selection (it shows in the price), located either on the basement or top floor. Open M-Sa 10am-9:30pm. See **Practical Information,** p. 91, for addresses.

Markets: Mercado de San Miguel, a covered market on Pl. San Miguel, off the northwest corner of Pl. Mayor, sells the finest seafood and produce in the city at high prices. Open M-Th 9:30am-2pm and 5:30-8:30pm, F-Sa 9am-2:30pm and 5:30-9pm. Right behind lies a **%Dia. Mercado de la Cebada,** at the intersection of C. Toledo and C. San Francisco, is less expensive. Open M-Sa 8am-2pm and 5:30-8pm. **Mercado Antón Martín** is south of M: Antón Martín. Open M-Sa 8am-2pm and 6-8pm.

Specialty Shops: Excellent pastry shops abound in Madrid's streets. The sublime **Horno La Santiaguesa,** C. Mayor, 73, hawks everything from *roscones de reyes* (sweet bread for the Feast of the Epiphany) to *empanadas* to chocolate and candy. Open M-Sa 8am-9pm, Su 8am-8pm. **Horno San Onofre,** C. San Onofre, 4, off C. Fuencarral, serves sumptuous fruit tarts and *suspiros de modistilla* (seamstress's sighs), a *madrileño* specialty. Open M-Sa 9am-9pm, Su 9am-8pm. A super mouth-watering, tooth-rotting candy store is **Caramelos Paco,** C. Toledo, 53 (tel. 91 365 42 58). **El Gourmet de Cuchilleros,** just through Pl. Mayor's Arco de Cuchilleros, is a gourmet store stocking Spanish jams, honey, candy, and cheese. For goofy mugs and **Velveeta,** try **Taste of America,** Po. Castellana, 28 (tel./fax 91 435 70 39), an American grocery store also offering barbecue and Tex-Mex products, along with brownie mix. Open M-Sa 10am-9pm, Su 10:30am-9pm.

Red Eye Establishments: *Guía del Ocio* lists late-night eateries under *Cenar a última hora.* The chain **VIPS,** on **Gran Vía, 43** (tel. 91 542 15 78; M: Callao), **Serrano, 41** (M: Serrano), **Calle Princesa, 5** (M: Ventura Rodríguez), and other scattered locations is a standard late-night option, with an American twist. In other words, it's a diner with cushioned booths, serving average, overpriced Hawaiian burgers with cheese fries. VIPS also carries English books and magazines, records, chocolate, and canned food. Open daily 9am-3am. **7-Eleven** stores are scattered about in Ópera, Alonso Martinez (C. Mejía Lequerida), and Av. America, selling **Don Simón** *sangría* for about 169ptas. **Hot & Cool,** C. Gaztambide, in Moncloa-Argüelles, stays cool and hot with fresh *bocadillos* until 3am on weekends.

SOL AND PLAZA MAYOR

Choose carefully, although you'll inevitably pay for ambience. This area is overrun by tourists, *típico* fare abounds, and prices run fairly high. Cruise to nearby Pl. Santa Ana for better deals, but don't miss the Museo del Jamón.

Museo del Jamón, C. San Jerónimo, 6 (tel. 91 521 03 46). M: Sol. 5 other much-loved locations throughout the city, including one on Gran Vía. If for some reason the pork perfume and the in-your-face slabs of *jamón serrano* are rattling your nerves, head upstairs to the dining room (opens at 1pm). Succulent Iberian ham is served up in any and every form your piggish little heart could possibly desire: *bocadillo* (200ptas), *chiquito* (100ptas), *croissant* (200ptas), *ración* (600ptas). *Tapas maestro* and cold, frothy mugs of Mahou beer. It's noisy by sundown. Open M-Sa 9am-12:30am, Su 10am-12:30am. Visa, AmEx.

El Estragón, Pl. de la Paja, 10 (tel. 91 365 89 82). M: La Latina. Uphill off C. Segovia, facing La Capilla del Obispo. **Vegetarian** food that will make die-hard meat-eaters reconsider. An all-out pleasant dining experience, delicious platefuls of beautiful food; give a go at the zesty lentil salad (with yogurt sauce), included in the *menú* (1750ptas). Open daily 1-5pm and 8:30pm-midnight.

Casa Botín, C. Cuchilleros, 17 (tel. 91 366 42 17). Looks, smells, and is expensive— but in a good way. Four floors of *comedores* (each with its own name) are guaranteed to make you gasp in delight and sigh romantically, although spending 4165ptas on the *menú* (includes the house specialty—*cochinillo asado*) may make you gasp and sigh in a different way. Potentially the best restaurant in Madrid, maybe in all of Spain, and worth the ducats. Founded in 1725, it's the **oldest restaurant in the whole wide world,** according to Guinness. Hemingway loved it, and wrote about it in *A Clean, Well-lighted Place.* Reservations recommended.

Casa Lhardy, C. San Jerónimo, 8 (tel. 91 521 33 85 or 91 52 22 07), at C. Victoria. M: Sol. 1839-style dining at 2039-style prices in one of Madrid's oldest restaurants. The 3600ptas house specialty *cocido* is guarded by uniformed men. Former Prime Minister Felipe González comes here on occasion for power lunches. Budget hounds congregate in the ground floor store for cognac, sherry, *consomé* (200ptas each), and the best hors d'oeuvres in town. Gourmet foodstuffs for sale. Open M-Sa 1-3:30pm and 9-11:30pm, Su 1-3:30pm. Visa, MC, AmEx.

Taqueria La Calaca, C. Fuentes, 3 (tel. 91 541 74 23), off C. Arenal. M: Sol. Save yourself a flight to Mexico. Delicious nachos 875ptas and *tamales* 800ptas. Entrees 1150ptas. Open Su-Th 1-4:30pm and 8pm-1am, F-Sa 1-4:30pm and 8pm-2:30am.

Can Punyetes, C. Señores de Luzón, 5 (tel. 91 542 09 21), off C. Mayor. M: Ópera. Simple Catalan cuisine. Locals gather here for *tostadas* (grilled meat, pâtés, and cheeses on toast). A/C. *Menú* 1350ptas. Open M-Sa 1-5pm and 8pm-12:30am.

Bar-Restaurante Sabatini, C. Bailén, 15 (tel. 91 547 92 40), opposite the Sabatini Gardens, which are next to the Palacio Real. M: Ópera. Come at sunset and bring a date—sidewalk tables face some of Madrid's most famous (and romantic) sights. Portly portions of *paella* (900ptas) and garlic chicken (900ptas). *Menú* 1300ptas. Open daily 8am-11pm. Dinner served 8-11pm.

SANTA ANA

Plaza Santa Ana is a favorite spot to kill a couple hours with a beverage and a snack. It's green, shady, and generally a happy place. Unlike Puerta del Sol, you might sit next to a real live Spanish person. **Calles Echegaray, Ventura de la Vega,** and **Manuel Fernández González** are the budget streets. Quality is high and prices are low.

Gula Gula, C. Infantes, 5 (tel. 91 522 87 64), off C. Echegaray near C. Huertas. M: Antón Martin. Food is fun! Your waiter/waitress may be wearing a bikini. All you can eat from the exotic salad bar 1500ptas (the banana dish is particularly delectable). *Spectáculos* Sunday at 11pm might include storytellers or drag queens. Another Gula Gula is at Gran Via, 1 (tel. 91 522 8764), near C. Accacá. Both open for lunch and dinner. Make reservations on weekends.

Restaurante Integral Artemisa, C. Ventura de la Vega, 4 (tel. 91 429 50 92), off C. San Jerónimo. M: Sol. Tasty **veggie** food unspoiled by nicotine (no smoking). Its sibling, Tres Cruces, 4 (tel. 91 521 8721), off the Gran Vía, is even more politically correct. All proceeds from Wednesday dinners go to humanitarian organizations. Luscious salads. Entrees 1175-2595ptas. *Menú* 1200ptas. Non-vegetarian entrees 1200-1600ptas. Open daily 1:30-4pm and 9pm-midnight. A/C. Visa, MC, AmEx.

Taberna D'a Queimada, C. Echegaray, 17 (tel. 91 429 32 63 or 91 429 58 81), 1 block down from C. San Jerónimo. M: Sol. Nuggets and knickknacks from all over Spain. A cauldron of *paella* waits by the door. *Menú* 1500ptas. Entrees 900-2700ptas. Across the street is the identical **Taberna D'a Queimada II,** under the same management. A/C. Both open daily noon-5pm and 7:30pm-midnight.

Mesón La Caserola, C. Echegaray, 3 (tel. 91 429 39 63), off C. San Jerónimo. M: Sol. Bustling, crowded joint serves a solid *menú* (975-1500ptas) to ravenous locals. Despite its proximity to Sol, La Caserola's prices and atmosphere remain more *madrileño* than *turístico.* Also serves breakfast, *tapas,* and hefty *bocadillo-*and-beer combos named after relatives (you can eat your *suegra,* or mother-in-law, in the form of pork loin and lettuce). Many entrees around 900ptas. A/C. Open M noon-1:30am, Tu-Su 7:30-1:30am. Visa, MC, DC.

LAVAPIÉS-LA LATINA-ATOCHA

The neighborhoods south of Sol, bounded by C. Atocha and C. Toledo, are residential and working class. No caviar or champagne here, but plenty of *menús* for around 1000ptas. A la carte is often a better bargain. *Bocadillo* joints along **Calle Santa Isabel,** by Madrid-Atocha and the Reina Sofía, slap together greasy sandwiches and garlic-laden *tapas* at scrumptious prices.

El Granero de Lavapiés, C. Argumosa, 10 (tel. 91 467 76 11). M: Lavapiés, off the plaza. Old world charm and new world food on a tranquil tree-lined street. Gazpacho 475ptas. **Vegetarian** *menú* 1200ptas. Open daily 1-4pm.

La Biotika, C. Amor de Diós, 3 (tel. 91 429 07 90), at C. Santa María. An intimate haven for the **tofu** and **macrobiotic-**deprived. *Menú* (1100ptas) served until midnight. Open M-F 1-4pm and 8-11:30pm, Sa-Su 1:30-4pm and 8-11:30pm.

La Farfalla, C. Santa María, 17 (tel. 91 369 46 91). M: Antón Martín, 1 block south following C. Huertas. La Farfalla's specialty is Argentine-style grilled meat (1100-1750ptas), but true love is one unforgettable mouthful of their thin-crust pizza: *erótica* or *exquisita* 700ptas. Open for dinner Su-Th until 3am, F-Sa until 4am. Visa.

GRAN VÍA

If you came to Spain to escape fast-food chains, run away from the Gran Vía. Luckily, **Calle Fuencarral** is lined with cheap *mesones.*

Costa Del Sol (tel. 91 522 02 82 or 91 531 01 79). M: Gran Vía. Opposite C. Valverde. A well-kept secret. Its worn front hides a ship-shape restaurant with deliciously inexpensive meat and loads of it. Salads 250-450ptas. *Carnes* 400-875ptas. Lunchtime *menú* 1000ptas.

CHUECA

Chueca is a fantastically gay district, where the only thing in the closet is a cabaret of clothes and glam, glam, glam. Lots of good places to wine and dine.

El 26 de Libertad, C. Libertad, 26 (tel. 91 522 25 22), off C. las Infantas. M: Chueca. Spectacular food featuring innovative and exotic Spanish cuisine. The lunchtime *menú* (1250ptas) is fantastic. Dinner *menú* is double the price. Open M-F 1-4pm and 8pm-midnight, Sa 1-4pm and 9pm-1am.

Nabucco, C. Hortaleza, 108 (tel. 91 310 06 11), a few blocks off Pl. Santa Bárbara. M: Alonso Martínez or Chueca. Upscale clientele, excellent Italian food, and affordable prices, all with a burnt-orange backdrop, inspired by the dirt of Sevilla's Plaza de Toros. Pizzas 730-935ptas. Pasta 825-975ptas. Salads 590-875ptas. Open M-F 1:30-4pm and 8:45pm-midnight, Sa-Su 8:45pm-1am. Visa, MC, AmEx.

La Carreta, C. Barbieri, 10 (tel. 91 532 70 42 or 91 521 60 97), off C. las Infantas. M: Gran Vía or Chueca. Specializes in Argentinian, Uruguayan, and Chilean meals; lots of meat on wooden platters. Lunch *menú* 1500ptas. Entrees around 900ptas. If your budget allows, try the delicious Martín Fierro dessert (890ptas), named after the Argentinian national novel, or skip dessert and **tango.** Classes and performances offered M-Tu 7pm. Performances Sa-Su 8:30pm-5am. Reservations recommended. Open daily 1:30-5pm and 9pm-5am. Visa, MC, AmEx.

Restaurante Zara, C. las Infantas, 5 (tel. 91 532 20 74), off C. Hortaleza. M: Gran Vía. An island of colorful and delicious Cuban cuisine. Daily "tropical" specials 1400ptas. Meat entrees 700-1100ptas. Open M-F. Visa, MC, AmEx.

Chez Pomme, C. Pelayo, 4 (tel. 91 532 16 46), off C. Augusto Figueroa. M: Chueca. **Vegetarian** food and a pretty good *menú* 800ptas. Salads 500-900ptas. Entrees 700-800ptas. Open M-Sa 1:30-4pm and 8:30-11:30pm.

Taberna Carmencita, C. San Marcos, 36 (tel. 91 531 66 12), at C. Libertad. M: Chueca. Popular with tourists and businesspeople, this classic restaurant, founded in 1850, evokes pre-Civil War Madrid: brass fixtures, black and white photos of bullfighters, polychrome glazed tiles, lace curtains, and iron and marble tables. Lunchtime *menú* 1070ptas, dinnertime *menú* 1400ptas. Entrees 900-2600ptas. Open M-F 1-4pm and 9pm-midnight, Sa 9pm-midnight. Visa, MC, AmEx.

Tienda de Vinos, C. Augusto Figueroa, 35 (tel. 91 521 70 12), off C. Hortaleza. M: Chueca. Look for the red doors facing Mercado de San Antón. Once a major leftist hangout, now a good place for cheap food. Entrees 500-900ptas.

MALASAÑA

Streets radiating from **Plaza 2 de Mayo** drown in a sea of *cafeterías,* bars, restaurants, and pubs. **Calle San Andrés** is the most densely populated, but **Calles San Bernardo** and **Manuela Malasaña,** on the fringes of this neighborhood, shouldn't be overlooked. Many spots here are more imaginative in their cuisine and setting than those serving "regional specialties," and more likely to offer vegetarian options. Watch the colorful characters who fill the maze of tiny streets; watch them closely after dark.

El Tazumal, C. Madera, 36 (tel. 91 522 79 82). M: Tribunal. From the station, walk down to C. Espiritú Santo, turn right, then turn left at C. Madera. Tasty and unique cuisine from El Salvador in a down-home setting. Try the national favorite, *pupusas* (loosely described as small, thick tortillas) with cheese or meat (275ptas). Entrees 275-1300ptas. Open W-M 1:30-4:30pm and 8pm-midnight.

La Gata Flora, C. 2 de Mayo, 1, and across the street at C. San Vicente Ferrer, 33 (tel. 91 521 20 20 or 91 521 27 92). M: Noviciado or Tribunal. Huge servings. Pizzas and pastas 825-1000ptas. Luscious salads 550-700ptas. *Sangría* 600-900ptas. Open Su-Th 2-4pm and 8:30pm-midnight, F-Sa 2-4pm and 8:30pm-1am. Visa, MC.

La Granja Restaurante Vegetariano, C. San Andrés, 11 (tel. 91 532 87 93), off Pl. 2 de Mayo. M: Tribunal. Candles and incense lead to a romantic **vegetarian** encounter. Salads 650ptas. Entrees like *arroz con algas* (rice with seaweed) 600-750ptas. Lunchtime *menú* 975ptas. Open W-M 1:30-4:30pm and 9pm-midnight. Visa.

MADRID

El Restaurante Vegetariano, C. Marqués de Santa Ana, 34, off Pl. Juan Pujol, at C. Espíritu Santo. M: Tribunal. Another sanctuary for **vegetarians,** though smaller and a tad pricier than La Granja. Homemade bread. Soups 500-600ptas. Salad bar 550-775ptas. Main dishes 1000ptas. Open Tu-Su. Visa, MC.

BILBAO

The area north of Glorieta de Bilbao (M: Bilbao), in the "V" formed by **Calles Fuencarral** and **Luchana** and including **Plaza de Olavide,** is swarming with bars, clubs, cafes, and restaurants. Most bars and *mesones* purvey splendid, cheap *tapas* to feed an energized crowd that cruises the streets come evening. Lunch gets pricier farther north in a more gentrified area.

La Tarterie, C. Cardenal Cisneros, 24 (tel. 91 593 85 27), right off C. Luchana, which is off Glorieta de Bilbao. M: Bilbao. This restaurant/art gallery likes to consider itself an art gallery/restaurant and features temporary exhibits of experimental art. The not-so-great interior is full of skinny artists. Great quiches (675ptas), salads (650ptas), and pizzas (775-1050ptas).

Pizza Buona, C. Hartzenbusch, 19 (tel. 91 445 78 68), off C. Cardenal Cisneros, which is just off C. Luchana. M: Bilbao. An Italian restaurant decked out in patriotic green, red, and white on a German-named street in the heart of Spain. Tasty pizzas 575-895ptas. A/C. Open daily 1-5pm and 8pm-1am. Credit cards accepted.

Bar Samara, C. Cardenal Cisneros, 13 (tel. 91 448 80 56). M: Bilbao. Bills itself as Egyptian, but offers Middle Eastern staples. Hummus, baba ghanoush, and tahini salads 475-525ptas. Kebabs and other entrees from 1500ptas. Gets crowded after dark. A/C. Open Su and Tu-Th until midnight, F-Sa until 1am.

ARGÜELLES

Argüelles is a middle-class *barrio* near the Ciudad Universitaria. It's full of inexpensive markets, moderately priced restaurants, and unshaven neighborhood bars.

Cáscaras, C. Ventura Rodríguez, 7 (tel. 91 542 83 36). M: Ventura Rodríguez. Sleek interior that kind of looks like a tortilla, which, coincidentally, is also what they serve. Vegetarian dishes 675-975ptas. Tortillas 745-955ptas. Salads 675-935ptas. Non-vegetarian fare as well. Popular for *tapas, pinchos,* and ice-cold Mahou beer in the early afternoon and evening. The Fugees ate here. A/C. Open M-F 7am-1am, Sa-Su 10am-2am. Visa, MC, AmEx.

La Vaca Argentina, Po. Pintor Rosales, 52 (tel. 91 559 66 05). M: Moncloa or Argüelles. Near the Rosaleda. A haven for meat-lovers and for those seeking an afternoon break on their popular *terraza.* Other locations at C. Baileú, 20, and Po. Castellana, 206-208. Salads 450-750ptas. Pastas 700-900ptas. Grilled meats 1100-4500ptas. Open daily 1-4:30pm and 9pm-12:30am. Visa, MC, AmEx.

La Crêperie, Po. Pintor Rosales, 28 (tel. 91 548 23 58). M: Ventura Rodríguez. Affordable crepes (360-785ptas) on the chic Po. Rosales (has *terraza*). Open daily for lunch 1:30-4:15pm, for dinner Su-Th 8pm-1am.

Ristorante Capriccio, C. Rodriguez San Pedro, 66 (tel. 91 549 91 16). M: Argüelles. Exit at C. Alberto Aguilera. Italian countryside meets urban pastel decor. Homemade rolls. Fresh pasta 650-1100ptas. Gourmet pizzas 700-950ptas. A/C. Delivery. Open M-F 1-4pm and 9pm-1am, Sa-Su 1-4pm and 9pm-late. Visa, MC, AmEx.

TAPAS

Not so long ago, bartenders in Madrid used to cover *(tapar)* drinks with saucers to keep the flies out. Later, servers began putting little sandwiches on top of the saucers, and there you have it: *tapas.* Hopping from bar to bar gobbling *tapas* is an active alternative to a full sit-down meal and a fun way to try food you would normally never dream of putting near your mouth. Most *tapas* bars (a.k.a. *tascas* or *tabernas*) are open noon to 4pm and 8pm to midnight or later. Some double as restaurants, like **Museo del Jamón,** and many cluster around **Plaza Mayor** (tourist alert!) and **Plaza Santa Ana,** which is very hip on Sundays. But never fear, *tapas* bars are everywhere.

La Toscana, C. Manuel Fernández González, 10-17 (tel. 91 429 60 31), at C. Ventura de la Vega. M: Sol. Friendly *mesón* with a friendly bull's head and dangling crockery. Beautiful *tapas* like *morcilla* (250ptas). Jam-packed on weekends. Open Th-Tu noon-4pm and 8pm-midnight.

La Trucha, C. Nuñez de Arce, 6 (tel. 91 429 58 33). M: Sol. Cramped but cheap, and popular with locals. Open M-Sa 12:30-4pm and 7:30pm-midnight. Visa, MC, AmEx.

Los Caracoles, Pl. de Cascorro, 18 (tel. 91 365 94 39). M: La Latina. Use whatever money wasn't stolen during El Rastro to dine on *caracoles* (snails, 675ptas) in the company of old men and one particularly loud one (the owner). Open daily 10:30am-4pm and 7-11:30pm.

La Princesita, C. Princesa, 80 (tel. 91 543 30 47). M: Argüelles. Finding a seat is impossible, but bar fare is cheaper anyway. Specialties are *queso de Cabrales* (goat cheese, 100ptas) and *empanada asturiana* (250ptas). Open M-Sa 10am-11:30pm.

Cafetería-Restaurante El Encinar del Bierzo, C. Toledo, 82 (tel. 91 366 23 89). M: La Latina. Recent renovations now match the quality of the food. House specialties: *conejo al ajillo* (rabbit with garlic, 2000ptas) and *gambas a la plancha* (fried shrimp, 1100ptas). *Menú* 1300ptas. Open daily 1-4:30pm and 9pm-midnight.

CLASSIC CAFES

Coffee at these places is expensive (200-450ptas), but the price includes atmosphere. It's customary to linger for an hour or two in these historic cafes, an economical way to soak up a little of Madrid's culture (and a lot of secondhand smoke).

Café Círculo de Bellas Artes, C. Alcalá, 42 (tel. 91 360 54 00). M: Banco de España. Tourists rest weary museum feet outside (no cover charge there). For a 100ptas cover, you can lounge on leather couches beneath high frescoed ceilings among nude sculptures and clothed sculptors from the Círculo. Feel like a real-live artist. Coffee or tea 200ptas inside. Open M-F 9am-1am, Sa-Su 9am-3am. Credit cards accepted.

Café Gijón, Po. Recoletos, 21 (tel. 91 521 54 25). M: Colón. On its 100th anniversary in 1988, the Ayuntamiento designated Gijón a historic site, easing the blow of the expensive coffee (300ptas). If you want something to eat, forget about sending your kids to college. Choose between the breezy terrace and smoky bar-restaurant. White-uniformed waiters. Long a favorite of the literati. Open daily 9am-1:30am.

Café de Oriente, Pl. Oriente, 2 (tel. 91 547 15 64). M: Ópera. A beautiful, old-fashioned cafe catering to a ritzy, older crowd. Spectacular view of the Palacio Real from the *terraza,* especially at night when a spotlight illuminates the palace. Quite pricey (coffee on the terrace 400ptas, entrees from 1500ptas), so sneak a lot of free peeks at the palace. Open daily 8:30am-1:30am.

Nuevo Café Barbieri, C. Av. María, 45 (tel. 91 527 36 58). M: Lavapiés. Intellectuals lurk here, fingering stiff drinks and specialty coffees on balding velvet cushions. Art films some nights in the back room—pick up a schedule. Drinks 500-600ptas.

Café Comercial, Glorieta de Bilbao, 7 (tel. 91 531 34 52). M: Bilbao. Traditional cafe with high ceilings and huge mirrors. Frequented by artists and Republican aviators. Anti-Franco protests started here. Plays host to frequent *tertulias* (gatherings of literati and intellectuals). Sandwiches from 240ptas. Beer 300ptas. Upstairs, it joins the 21st century as **Cybercafe Comercial,** complete with coin-operated computers (100ptas for 8min., 500ptas per hr.). A/C. Open Su-Th 7am-1am, F-Sa 7am-3am.

■ Sights

> *You need good shoes to walk around in.*
>
> — A shoemaker

Madrid, large as it may seem, is a walker's city. It has a fantastic public transportation system, but you should use it as little as possible. In fact, while the word *paseo* refers to a major avenue—like *Paseo de la Castellana* or *Paseo del Prado*—it more literally means a "stroll." We recommend that you do just that from Sol to Cibeles and from the Plaza Mayor to the Palacio Real—sights will kindly introduce themselves. The city's art and architecture and its culture and air will convince you heartily that it was once the capital of the world's greatest empire. Madrid is a lounger's city, too—it offers some of the world's best places to stop strolling. When you're panting for a break after perusing the Triángulo de Arte or suffering from a hangover after a rough night in Chueca, you can head for Schweppes and shade at any sidewalk cafe.

For hard-core sightseers with a checklist of destinations, the municipal tourist office's *Plano de Transportes* map, marking monuments as well as bus and Metro lines, is indispensable. For everyone else, it's just damn useful. In the following pages, sights are arranged by a combination of geographical location and historical consistency. The first section, Puerta del Sol, is the heart of the city. Four of the nine neighborhoods that follow—Madrid de los Austrias, Madrid de los Borbones, Huertas, and Gran Vía—bud directly off Sol. A walking tour of any of those five areas can naturally begin there. Prado-Recoletos, Retiro, and Argüelles-Moncloa are each just a step away from Sol, linked to the magnificent plaza by one of the other four zones. El Pardo falls last, and buses destined for its palace and pastures leave from the penultimate neighborhood, Moncloa.

PUERTA DEL SOL

Kilómetro 0—the origin of six national highways fanning out to the rest of Spain—marks the physical and psychological center of the country in the most chaotic of Madrid's infinite plazas, **Puerta del Sol.** Sol races all day and night with taxis and pickpockets, lottery vendors and newsstands. The sunset here is spectacular, as the Tío Pepe sign begins to glow. A web of pedestrian-only tributaries originating at the Gran Vía lead a rush of consumers down a gallery of shoe boutiques and department stores and funnel them into Sol. The broad alleyways culminate at **El Oso y el Madroño,** the bronze symbol of Madrid and the city's universal meeting place. On New Year's Eve, citizens congregate in Sol to gobble a dozen grapes as the clock strikes midnight, one per strike. Literally the "Sun's Gateway," the giant plaza derives its name from an old gateway to the Alcázar that faced the Orient.

MADRID DE LOS AUSTRIAS

Also known as Habsburg Madrid and Old Madrid, the center of the city is the most densely packed with monuments and tourists. The Habsburgs (1516-1700) built the Pl. Mayor and the Catedral de San Isidro from scratch, but many of Old Madrid's buildings date much earlier than the 16th century, some to the age of the Moors (c. 860-1086). After Phillip II moved the seat of Castile from Toledo to Madrid (then only a town of 20,000) in 1561, he and his descendants commissioned the court's architects to update many of these edifices so that they fit the latest mode. The architects updated, for example, the Iglesia de San Francisco el Grande to Neoclassicism. **Plaza de la Villa** is the last sight listed, but you may wish to design your own walking tour of Habsburg Madrid to begin there. Geographically, Pl. Villa fits more snugly into a tour of Madrid de los Borbones (see p. 98), but for historical consistency, it belongs with Madrid de los Austrias.

Plaza Mayor

With lances of exaggerated length, 17th-century nobles on horseback spent Sunday afternoons chasing bulls in the **Plaza Mayor** (M: Sol). The nobility had such a jolly time giving it a go that eventually everyone joined in the fun. Citizens, on foot and armed with sticks, also began running hither and thither after those pesky bulls. The tradition came to be known as the *corrida*, from the verb *correr* (to run), which is why bullfights and Pamplona-like street frenzies are called *corridas de toros.* When they tired of the bulls, the commoners would relax with a good public execution.

The plaza, like Sol, is an easy orientation point for any walking expedition through Madrid. It is elegantly arcaded and topped with Habsburg *herrerense* (black slate roofs named after architect Juan de Herrera), spindly towers, and iron verandas, all properties that define "Madrid-style" architecture and inspire every peering *balcón* constructed in Spain and abroad. The plaza was completed in 1620 for Felipe III. His statue, installed in 1847, graces Pl. Mayor's center. Just east of Pl. Mayor via C.

Gerona, Pl. Santa Cruz cradles the **Palacio de Santa Cruz,** a former prison. The palace's alternation of red brick, granite corners, and black-slate towers exemplify the Habsburg style.

Toward evening, Pl. Mayor awakens as *madrileños* resurface, tourists multiply, and cafe tables fill with lively patrons. During the annual **Fiesta de San Isidro** (May 15-22), the plaza explodes. The plaza's surrounding streets, especially those through the **Arco de los Cuchilleros** on the southwest corner of Pl. Mayor, house old specialty shops and renowned *mesones,* where you can enjoy garlicky *tapas* and pitchers of *sangría* in a festive, albeit touristy, atmosphere.

La Latina

The **Catedral de San Isidro** (M: Latina), on C. Toledo directly south off Pl. Mayor, commemorates Madrid's patron saint. *(Open for mass only.)* The cathedral was designed in Jesuit Baroque style at the beginning of the 17th century; San Isidro's remains landed here in 1769. It reigned as the cathedral of Madrid from the late 19th century until the Catedral de la Almudena was consecrated in 1993. In 1936, rioting workers burned the exterior; it has since been restored.

Continuing down C. Toledo, turn right on the **Plaza de la Cebada** (M: Latina) and pass the Mercado de la Cebada on your left. Turning right up Cost. San Andrés leads to **Iglesia de San Andrés,** currently being renovated. *(Open for mass only.)* Muslims originally constructed the Gothic-Mudéjar red brick and granite building as a mosque. Its 17th-century overhaul infused Baroque intricacies and posited the sarcophagus of San Isidro in the **Capilla de San Isidro.** The **Museo de San Isidro** sits next door.

Continuing up Cost. San Andrés, turning left on C. Redonilla, and taking the third right onto C. Don Pedro will soon lead you to Pl. Gabriel Miró and the **Parque de las Vistillas** (so called for the tremendous *vistillas,* or little views of Palacio Real, Nuestra Señora de la Almudena, and the countryside). It's wise not to venture here after dark.

San Francisco El Grande and Puerta de Toledo

Doubling back along C. Don Pedro, turn right on C. Bailén to reach the **Plaza de San Francisco** and its **Iglesia de San Francisco el Grande** (St. Francis of Assisi), whose most outstanding feature is its Neoclassical facade. *(Open in summer Tu-Sa 11am-1pm and 5-8pm.)* Carlos III commissioned the fructiferous Francisco Sabitini, the third of four architects to work on the church since its inception in the 12th century, to reconstruct the facade in its present form (M: Puerta de Toledo or Latina). Inside, Goya's *Saint Bernard of Siena Preaching* hangs alongside Velázquez's *Aparition of the Virgin before Saint Anthony.* Saint Francis himself allegedly built a convent next door in the 13th century, where the **Capilla de Cristo de los Dolores** stands today. Follow Gran Vía de San Francisco downhill to reach Pl. Puerta de Toledo, where the **biblioteca pública** resides. Across the plaza sprawls the **Mercado de Puerta de Toledo;** inside is the **tourist office.**

Río Manzanares

Past the Pta. Toledo, the **Río Manzanares,** Madrid's notoriously dinky river, snakes its way around the city. The broad Baroque **Puente de Toledo** makes up for the river's inadequacies. Sandstone carvings on one side of the bridge depict San Isidro rescuing his son from a well, and on the other side depict his wife, Santa María de la Cabeza. Renaissance **Puente de Segovia,** which fords the river from C. Segovia, was conceived by Juan de Herrera, the talented designer of El Escorial. Both bridges afford gorgeous views (and fertile ground for the blossoming of young love/lust).

Plaza de la Villa

When Felipe II made Madrid the capital of his empire in 1561, most of the town huddled between Pl. Mayor and the Palacio Real, stretching north to today's Ópera and south to Pl. Puerta de Moros. Only a handful of medieval buildings remain, but the labyrinthine layout is unmistakable. **Plaza de la Villa**—west of Pl. Mayor on C. Mayor (M: Ópera)—marks the heart of what was old Madrid. The **Torre de los Lujanes,** a 15th-century building on the eastern side of the plaza (left side if looking from C.

Mayor), is the sole remnant of the once lavish residence of the Lujanes family. Note the original horseshoe-shaped Gothic door on C. Codo (there aren't many examples of Gothic-Mudéjar left in Madrid). Across the plaza, the characteristically Habsburg 17th-century **Ayuntamiento** (Casa de la Villa) was both the mayor's home and the city jail. As Madrid (and its bureaucracy) grew, officials annexed the neighboring **Casa de Cisneros,** a 16th-century Plateresque house (Cisneros was the architect).

MADRID DE LOS BORBONES

Weakened by plagues and political losses, the Habsburg era in Spain ended with the death of Carlos II in 1700. Felipe V, the first of Spain's Bourbon Monarchs, ascended the throne in 1714 after the 12-year War of Succession. The Decree of Nova Plata (1715) dissolved the remaining Aragonese territories into Castile. The move essentially solidified the territory now known as Spain. Bankruptcy, industrial stagnation, military incompetence, and widespread moral disillusionment compelled Felipe V to embark on a crusade of urban renewal. His successors Fernando VI and Carlos III fervently pursued the same ends, with wonderful results.

Palacio Real

Palace open, except during royal visits, Apr.-Sept. M-Sa 9am-6pm, Su 9am-3pm; Oct.-Mar. M-Sa 9:30am-5pm, Su 9am-2pm. 950ptas, students 850ptas, with 40min. guided tour in Spanish 950ptas. Wednesdays free for E.U. citizens. Arrive early to avoid lines.

At the end of C. Mayor, the impossibly luxurious **Palacio Real** (M: Ópera) lounges at the western tip of central Madrid, overlooking the **Río Manzanares.** Felipe V commissioned Giovanni Sachetti to replace the burned Alcázar with a palace that would dwarf all others. Sachetti died and Filippo Juvara took over the project, basing his new facade on Bernini's rejected designs for the Louvre. Although only a fragment is complete, it's still one of Europe's most grandiose residences. The shell took 40 years to build and the decoration of its 2000 rooms with 20 sq. km of tapestry dragged on for a century. The Monarchy abandoned the venture in the war-torn 1930s, having accumulated vast collections of porcelain, tapestries, furniture, armor, and art.

The palace's most impressive rooms include the raucously Rococo **Salón de Gasparini,** with a Mengs ceiling fresco, and the **Salón del Trono** (Throne Room), with a Tiepolo ceiling fresco. Hundreds of ornate timepieces, collected mainly by Carlos IV, are strewn about the palace. The **Real Oficina de Farmacia** (Royal Pharmacy) features crystal and china receptacles used to cut royal dope. The **Biblioteca** shelves first editions of *Don Quijote* and a Bible in the gypsy language Romany. The **Real Armería** (Armory) displays El Cid's swords, the armor of Carlos I and Felipe II, and other instruments of medieval warfare and torture.

Around the Palace

Beautiful gardens and parks swathe the Palacio Real. The **Plaza de Oriente** spans the foreground, a semicircular space lined with statues of monarchs. The sculptures were originally intended for the palace roof, but planners feared that the objects would fall off and hit the Queen. To the northwest are the **Jardines de Sabatini,** the park of choice for romantics. King Juan Carlos I opened **Campo del Moro** (facing the canal) to the public only 13 years ago; the view of the palace rising majestically on a dark green slope is straight out of a fairy tale. The **Catedral de la Almudena** rises from behind a stone pavilion, south of Campo del Moro. *(Open M-F 10am-1:30pm and 6-8:45pm, Su 10am-2pm and 6-8:45pm. Closed during mass.)* The reasons for the controversy surrounding the cathedral's face-lift after a 30-year hibernation is immediately apparent. The new psychedelic stained-glass windows clash jarringly with the more conventional altar. If relics are your style, the **Convento de la Encarnación,** with 700 saintly bones, awaits just to the north (see **Other Museums,** p. 106).

PRADO-RECOLETOS-CASTELLANA

The most striking feature on any map of Madrid is the one grand avenue that splits the city in two, running from the city's northernmost tip at Madrid-Chamartín to its southern extreme, Madrid-Atocha. Madrid's great thoroughfare is really three fused segments that represent three eras of urban expansion. Carlos III, the city's urban visionary, laid the Po. Prado from 1775 to 1882 to espouse community among the elite. The road connects Atocha to Pl. Cibeles, passing the Museo del Prado, Thyssen-Bornemisza, and the Ritz along the way. Along Po. Recoletos, extending from Cibeles to Pl. Colón, the newest members of the *clase alta* (upper class) congregate at the luxuriously shaded *terrazas*. Contemporary Madrid stretches along Paseo de la Castellana, lined with the bank buildings commissioned during the 1970s and 1980s and culminating with Pl. Castilla's twin towers (Puerta de Europa). If you're designing a walking tour around central Madrid over the span of a few days, the Castellana sights may be out of reach; however, the pleasant stroll is not one to miss. Recoletos and Prado tours combine well with the Huertas section and the Retiro route to form a manageable axis of sights.

Paseo del Prado

With virtually every major museum in the vicinity, this "museum mile," or Triángulo de Arte, is the cultural center of Madrid. Beginning from **Estación de Atocha's** iron-framed atrium, you'll see the ceramic tiles and stained glass of Ministerial de Agricultura on Po. Infanta Isabel. Home to Picasso's *Guernica*, the **Centro de Arte Reina Sofía** (see p. 105) and its glass-enclosed elevators vogue directly across from the station on Pl. Emperador Carlos V.

Walking up Po. Prado, you'll pass the **Jardín Botánico** on the right. Next to it sits the **Prado** (see p. 103), and behind it, on C. Ruiz de Alarcón, stands the **Iglesia de San Jerónimo,** built by Hieronymite monks and re-endowed by the Catholic Monarchs. *(Open daily 8am-1:30pm and 5-8:30pm.)* The church has witnessed a few joyous milestones: Fernando and Isabel were crowned here and it saw the marriage of King Alfonso XIII. Back on Po. Prado, to the north in Pl. Lealtad stands the **Obelisco a los Mártires del 2 de Mayo,** filled with the ashes of those who died in the 1808 uprising against Napoleon. Its four statues represent Constance, Virtue, Valor, and Patriotism, and the flame burns continuously in honor of the patriots. Behind the memorial sits the colonnaded Greco-Roman-style Bolsa de Madrid (Stock Exchange), a work by Repullés. Ventura Rodríguez's **Fuente de Neptuno,** Pl. Cánovas de Castillo, is one of three aquatic masterpieces along the avenue.

Plaza de la Cibeles

The tulip-encircled **Fuente de la Cibeles** (Fountain of Cybele) springs forth at the intersection of Recoletos and C. Alcalá (M: Banco de España). It depicts the fertility goddess's triumphant arrival in a carriage drawn by lions. Myth has it that the fleet-footed Atalanta would take as her lover only the man who could outrun her. No man was up to the challenge until one cunning suitor instructed his cohorts to scatter golden apples in Atalanta's path to distract her from running. The goddess Cibeles, watching the prank, was overcome with wrath at men's evil ways. She punished the plotters by turning them into lions and made them pull her carriage. Madrid residents successfully protected this emblem of their city (best viewed at dusk) during Franco's bomb raids by covering it with a pyramid of sandbags.

To the right are the **Museo Naval** (see **Museums,** p. 103) and the eye-popping **Palacio de Comunicaciones,** where you can mail your letters in true style. Antonio Palacios and Julián Otamendi of Otto Wagner's Vienna School designed the neo-Baroque structure in 1920. On the northeastern corner of the intersection (behind black gates) is the former **Palacio de Linares,** a 19th-century townhouse built for Madrid nobility. Long abandoned by its former residents and proven by a team of "scientists" to be inhabited by ghosts, it was transformed into the **Casa de América,** with a library and lecture halls for the study of Latin American culture and politics. It sponsors art exhibitions, tours of the palace, and guest lectures.

Paseo de Recoletos

Continuing north toward the brown **Torres de Colón** (Columbus Towers), you'll pass the **Biblioteca Nacional** (library; entrance at #20), whose sleek **Museo del Libro** (book museum) displays treasures from the monarchy's collection, including a first-edition copy of *Don Quijote de la Mancha. (Open Tu-Sa 10am-9pm, Su 10am-2pm. Free.)* Behind it the lies huge **Museo Arqueológico** (see **Museums,** p. 103). The museum is on C. Serrano, a thoroughfare lined with expensive boutiques set in the posh neighborhood Barrio de Salamanca.

The museum and library huddle just south of the **Plaza Colón** (M: Colón) and the adjoining **Jardines del Descubrimiento** (Gardens of Discovery). Huge clay boulders loom at one side (near C. Serrano), inscribed with odd trivia about the New World, like Seneca's prediction of the discovery, the names of all the mariners on board the caravels, and citations from Columbus's diary. A neo-Gothic monument to Columbus rises from a thundering fountain, whose spray can be very refreshing in Madrid's dry summer heat. Concerts, lectures, ballet, and plays are performed in the **Centro Cultural de la Villa** (tel. 91 575 60 80), beneath the statue and the waterfall.

Paseo de la Castellana

Nineteenth- and early 20th-century aristocrats dislocated themselves from Old Madrid to settle along **Paseo de la Castellana.** During the Civil War, Republican forces used the mansions as soldiers' barracks; and most were torn down in the 60s by the banks and insurance companies who would commission new and innovative structures in the following decade. Competition begot architectural excellence, offering the lowly pedestrian a rich man's spectacle of architecture and fashion (rose aluminum with pink glass, pink granite with green glass, and so on). Some notables include Moneo's **Bankinter** at #29, the first to integrate rather than demolish a townhouse; **Banco Urquijo,** known as "the coffeepot"; **Banca Catalana Occidente,** #50, the delicate ice cube on a cracker on Glorieta de Emilio Castelar near the American Embassy; the oh-so-pink **Edificio Bankunion,** #46; **Edificio La Caixa,** #61; and the Sevillian-tiled **Edificio ABC** at #34, the conservative, monarchical newspaper's former office.

Just south of the American Embassy, between Pl. Colón and Glorieta de Emilio Castelar and under the C. Juan Bravo overpass, is an **Open-air Sculpture Museum** with works by Miró, González, and Chillida (hanging from the bridge).

Much farther north of Pl. Emilio Castelar squats the **Museo Nacional de Ciencias Naturales.** Turning right on C. Juan Bravo you'll find the elaborate **Museo Lázaro Galdiano.** Left on Po. General Martínez Campos is the **Museo Sorolla** (see p. 106). Much, much farther north, past Torres Picasso and Europa at **Plaza de Lima,** squats the 110,000-seat **Estadio Santiago Bernabéu** (M: Nuevos Ministerios, Lima, or Cuzco), home to **Real Madrid,** champions of *La Copa de Europa* in 1998 (for more info, see **Fútbol,** p. 117). Still farther north, two 27-story leaning towers connected by a tunnel dominate Pl. Castilla (M: Pl. Castilla). American John Bergee designed the **Puerta de Europa** to look like a doorway to the city.

RETIRO

Felipe IV originally intended the 300-acre **Parque del Buen Retiro** (M: Retiro) to be a *buen retiro* (nice retreat). Before that it was hunting territory, and now it's a place to get your palm read, play a soccer or basketball match, or soak up the rays reflecting off the **Estanque Grande,** a rectangular lake in the middle of the park. *(Boat rentals open daily 9:30am-8:30pm. Cool paddle boats 550ptas for 4 people, less-cool motorboat 150ptas per person.)* The lake has been the social center of the Retiro ever since aspiring caricaturists, fortune-tellers, Michael Jackson impersonators, sunflower-seed vendors, and drug pushers parked their goods along its marble shore.

Ricardo Velázquez built the steel-and-glass **Palacio de Cristal,** south of the lake by the boat rental center, to exhibit Philippine flowers; it now hosts a variety of art shows with subjects from Bugs Bunny to Spanish portraiture. *(Open Tu-Sa 11am-2pm and 5-8pm, Su 10am-2pm. Admission varies, but often free.)* A few steps away, the **Palacio de Velázquez** (named after the Ricardo; tel. 91 573 62 45), north of the *estanque,* exhibits works in conjunction with the Museo de Arte Reina Sofía. The northeast corner of the park swells with medieval monastic ruins and waterfalls. At nightfall during the summer (when only the north gate remains open), Retiro becomes a lively bar and cafe hangout; however, avoid venturing into the park alone after dark.

Bullets from the 1921 assassination of prime minister Eduardo Dato permanently scarred the eastern face of **Puerta de Alcalá** (1778), outside Retiro's Puerta de la Independencia. The imposing five-arch monument honoring Carlos III has come to symbolize Madrid's grandeur. The area south of C. Alcalá and to the west of Retiro is littered with popular museums. Farther south, the **Casón del Buen Retiro** faces the park (see p. 105); behind it sits the **Museo del Ejército** (see p. 107). The three buildings are remnants of Felipe IV's palace, which burned down in 1764. South of Retiro, on Av. Alfonso XII, the 18th-century **Observatorio Astronómico** is considered one of the most elegant examples of Spanish Neoclassicism. *(Open M-F 9am-2pm.)*

HUERTAS

The area east of Sol is a wedge bounded by **Calle de Alcalá** to the north, C. Atocha to the south, and Po. Prado to the east. From the wedge's western apex at Sol, a myriad of streets slope downward, outward, and eastward toward various points along Po. Prado. **Carrera de San Jerónimo** splits the wedge a bit north of center, running directly from Sol down to Pl. Cánovas de Castillo. **Plaza de Santa Ana** is nestled below C. Nuñez de Arce and off **Calle del Prado** (not to be confused with Po. Prado).

Alcalá

The grand C. Alcalá leads from Sol northeast and dips down to Po. Recoletos at Pl. Cibeles before ascending again to the Pta. Alcalá and Parque del Buen Retiro (see above). Banks inhabit most of its beautiful statue-festooned Baroque buildings. Also on C. Alcalá is Churriguera and Diego Villanueva's **Museo de la Real Academia de Bellas Artes de San Fernando** (see **Museums,** p. 107). The **Círculo de Bellas Artes** has undergone a recent resurgence (see **Classic Cafes,** p. 95). Designed by Antonio Palacios, the building encloses two stages and several salons and studios for lectures and workshops run by prominent artists. Many facilities are for *socios* (members) only, but exhibition galleries for all media are open to the public. If you've a few hours to spare and some spiffy threads stashed away, the extra few hundred *pesetas* will buy you a cup of coffee and reward you with a sublime taste of decadent lifestyle.

San Jerónimo and Plaza Santa Ana

Looping back westward toward Sol on C. San Jerónimo (off Pl. Neptuno) will take you through the center of Madrid's foregone literary district. Home to Cervantes, Góngora, Quevedo, Calderón, and Moratín at its heyday during the Siglo de Oro, it enjoyed a fleeting return to literary prominence in the late 19th and early 20th centuries when Hemingway frequented the neighborhood. At C. San Jerónimo, 15, is the **Palacio Miraflores,** designed by the premier 18th-century architect, Pedro de Ribera. On the left rises Ribera's fantastic **Palacio del Marqés de Ugena,** Pl. Canalejas, 3.

Follow C. Príncipe downhill to the enchanting **Plaza Santa Ana** and its hopping bar and cafe scene (see p. 92). Calle del Prado on the southeast (left) side of the plaza leads to the **Ateneo,** C. Prado, 21, a hangout for intellectual Madrid at the close of the 19th century and again during the Second Republic following the Dictatorship of Primo de Rivera. The Ateneo is a private library, but its evening concerts and symposia are often open to the public. Two blocks south, at C. Huertas and C. León, Juan de Villanueva's austere **Real Academia de la Historia** houses a magnificent old library of its own, another exemplar of Madrid-style architecture. Although Golden Age playwright Lope de Vega and Miguel de Cervantes were bitter rivals, the 17th-century **Casa de Lope de Vega** (tel. 91 429 92 16) is ironically located at C. Cervantes, 11 (off C. León, south of C. San Jerónimo). *(Open Tu-F 9:30am-2pm, Sa 10am-1:30pm. 200ptas, students 100ptas. Wednesdays free.)* The prolific playwright and poet spent the last 25 years of his life here. Odder still, Cervantes is purportedly buried on C. Lope de Vega.

MADRID

GRAN VÍA

Urban planners paved the Gran Vía in 1910 to link **Calle de Princesa** with Cibeles. After Madrid won new riches as a neutral supplier during World War I, the city funneled its earnings into developing the Gran Vía into one of the world's great thoroughfares. At Gran Vía's highest elevation in **Plaza de Callao** (M: Callao), C. Postigo San Martín splits off southward, where you'll find the famed **Convento de las Descalzas Reales** (see **Museums,** p. 103). Returning to Pl. Callao and proceeding westward (left facing the conspicuous sex shop), the Gran Vía makes its descent toward **Plaza de España** (M: Pl. España). Next to the plaza are two of Madrid's tallest skyscrapers, the **Telefónica** (1929) and the **Edificio de España** (1953). Louis S. Weeks of the Chicago School designed the former, which was the tallest concrete building in existence at the time (81m), and Franco designed the latter. There's a **cafe** on the 26th floor of the Edificio (cover 100ptas). Tucked between the two skyscrapers on C. San Leonardo is crafty, little **Iglesia de San Marcos,** a Neoclassical church composed of five intersecting ellipses—a Euclidean dream, there's not a single straight line in sight. **Museo de Cerralbo** lingers nearby (see p. 107).

CHUECA

By night, Chueca bristles with Madrid's alternative scene of tourists, immigrants, gays, and the hopelessly fashion conscious in search of a common end—fun. By day, the area between **Calle de Fuencarral** and **Calle de San Bernardo** beholds some of the most avant-garde architecture and current art exhibitions in the city. Bourbon King Fernando VI commissioned the **Iglesia de las Salesas Reales** (1758), Pl. Salesas (M: Colón or Alonso Martínez), at the request of his wife Doña Bárbara. The Baroque-Neoclassical domed church is clad in granite, with facade sculptures by Alfonso Vergaza and a dome painting by the brothers González Velázquez. Its ostentatious facade and interior prompted critics to pun on the queen's name: "Barbaric queen, barbaric tastes, barbaric building, barbarous expense," giving rise to the expression *"¡qué bárbaro!"*, which can express absurdity, extravagance, or just plain "coolness." Bárbara and Fernando are buried in the *iglesia*.

ARGÜELLES-MONCLOA

The 19th century witnessed the growth of several neighborhoods around the core of the city, north and northwest of the Palacio Real. Today, the area known as **Argüelles** and the zone surrounding **Calle San Bernardo** form a cluttered mixture of elegant middle-class and student housing, bohemian hangouts, and cultural activity. Heavily bombarded during the Civil War, Argüelles inspired Chilean poet Pablo Neruda, then a resident, to write *España en el corazón*.

A prime example of Fascist Neoclassicism, the arcaded **Cuartel General del Aire** (Ejército del Aire) commands the perspective on the other side of Arco de la Victoria by the Moncloa Metro station. The complex was to form part of the "Fachada del Manzanares" urban axis linking Moncloa, the Palacio de Oriente, San Isidro, and the Iglesia de San Francisco. The building looks suspiciously like El Escorial. **Museo de América** (see p. 106) is a bit farther down the avenue, past the **Arco de Moncloa,** by the **Faro de Moncloa,** a 92m-high metal tower that you can pay to ascend. *(200ptas.)* You can see El Escorial on a clear day.

Parque del Oeste is a large, sloping park noteworthy for the **Rosaleda** (rose garden) at the bottom of the park (M: Argüelles or Moncloa). *(Open daily 10am-8pm.)* A yearly competition determines which award-winning rose will be added to the permanent collection. Nearby, on Po. Pintor Rosales in **Parque de la Montaña,** stands the 4th-century BC **Templo de Debod** (tel. 91 409 61 65). *(Currently closed for renovations. Open in summer Tu-F 10am-2pm and 6-8pm, Sa-Su 10am-2pm; in winter Tu-F 10am-2pm and 4-6pm, Sa-Su 10am-2pm. 300ptas, students 150ptas. Wednesdays free.)* Built by Pharaoh Zakheramon, it's the only Egyptian temple in Spain. The Egyptian government shipped the temple stone by stone from the banks of the Nile in appreciation of Spanish archaeologists who helped rescue a series of monuments from rising waters near the Aswan dam.

On **Paseo Rosales,** away from the city center and past the *terrazas,* is the *teleférico* (cable car), running between Po. Rosales and **Casa de Campo,** the city's largest park (M: Batán). *(Open in summer daily 11am-9pm; in winter Sa-Su noon-8pm. 360ptas.)* Inside the park, the "amusement" park **(Parque de Atracciones)** can be traced to its roller-coaster's pathetic creak. *(Open Su-F noon-11pm, Sa noon-midnight.)* The **Zoo/Aquarium** is five minutes away.

Ermita de San Antonio de la Florida (tel. 91 542 07 22; M: Príncipe Pío), containing Goya's pantheon, is close to Parque del Oeste at the end of Po. Florida. *(Open Tu-Su 10am-2pm. Free.)* Goya's frescoed dome arches above his own buried corpse—but not his skull, which was missing when the remains arrived from France (it was apparently stolen by a phrenologist). Be cautious walking here from Rosaleda.

EL PARDO

Open Apr.-Sept. M-F 9:30am-6pm, Su 9:25am-1:40pm; Oct.-Mar. M-F 10:30am-5pm, Su 9:55am-1:40pm. Compulsory 45min. guided tour in Spanish. 650ptas, students 250ptas, Wednesday free for E.U. citizens. Catch bus #601 from the stop in front of the Ejército del Aire building above M: Moncloa. 15min., 150ptas each way.

Built as a hunting lodge for Carlos I in 1547, **El Pardo** was enlarged by generations of Habsburg and Bourbon royalty into a magnificent country palace. Franco resided here from 1940-1975. Although politics have changed, the palace is still the official reception site for distinguished foreign visitors who wine, dine, and politic amid gorgeous Renaissance and Neoclassical furniture, chandeliers, and other works. Renowned for its collection of tapestries—several of which were designed by Goya—the palace also holds a little-known Velázquez and Ribera's *Techo de los hombres ilustres (Ceiling of the Illustrious Men).* During his stay, Franco fitted the palace with modern amenities such as TVs and air conditioning, which are cunningly camouflaged so as not to clash with the elegant decor. You can also see the bedroom cabinet in which he kept Santa Teresa's silver-encrusted hand. The palace's **capilla** and the nearby **Casita del Príncipe,** created by Villanueva of El Prado fame, are both free.

■ Museums

Don't miss the **Paseo del Arte** ticket that grants admission to the Museo del Prado, Colección Thyssen-Bornemisza, and Centro de Arte Reina Sofía for 1050ptas. Passes are available at the three museums.

MUSEO DEL PRADO

Tel. 91 420 37 68. Po. Prado at Pl. Cánovas del Castillo. M: Banco de España. Open Tu-Sa 9am-7pm, Su 9am-2pm. 500ptas, students 250ptas. Saturdays 2:30-7pm and Sundays all day free.

The Prado is Spain's premier museum and one of Europe's finest. Toward the end of the 18th century, Carlos III commissioned Juan de Herrera to construct the Neoclassical building as the Museum of Natural Sciences. In 1819, Fernando VII, who cared precious little for art and rather more about making an impression at home and abroad, transformed it into a striking display of the royal painting collection. The modern-day Prado's collection of 7000 paintings, many collected by Spanish monarchs between 1400 and 1700, includes Spanish and foreign masterpieces, with particular strengths in the Flemish and Venetian Schools.

Hours of jostling through herds of schoolchildren will not allow every canvas in the Prado its due. Don't feel bad about striding through rooms full of imitation Rubens. The museum is laid out in a logical fashion with rooms numbered and indexed in a free brochure. Nevertheless, once inside it's easy to lose sight of the forest through the groves of Goyas and Velázquezes. Guidebooks can be helpful and informative. They vary in size and detail, ranging from 150ptas "greatest hits" brochures to weighty 2000ptas tomes packed with serious art criticism.

Diego Velázquez

The second floor houses Spanish and Italian works from the 16th and 17th centuries, most notably an unparalleled collection of works by Diego Velázquez (1599-1660), court painter and interior decorator for Felipe IV. Within are several of his most famous paintings, including *Las hilanderas (The Tapestry Weavers), Los borrachos (The Drunkards),* and *La fragua de Vulcano (Vulcan's Forge).* To achieve what some consider to be an effect of continuous movement with the viewer, Velazquez repositioned the horse in *Las lanzas (The Spears or The Surrender of Breda)* several times before its completion. The complex and oft-imitated *Las meninas (The Maids of Honor),* widely considered Velázquez's magnum opus, occupies an entire wall. The layered web of stares and glances has led many critics to insist that it's not a painting but an "encounter." Exquisite portraits of the royal family, including Velázquez's affectionate renderings of the foppish and fey Felipe IV, are legion. Velázquez is renowned for his masterful manipulations of light and perspective and is credited with radicalizing portraiture with his unforgiving realism.

Francisco Goya

The far-reaching influence of Velázquez's technique is evident in the work of Francisco de Goya y Lucientes (1746-1828), especially in his two hilariously unflattering depictions of Carlos III and his satirical masterpiece *La familia de Carlos IV.* Many wonder how he got away with depicting the royal family the way he did. Some suggest that in *La familia de Carlos IV* he manipulated light and shadow to focus the viewer's gaze on the figure of the queen, despite the more prominent position of the king, thus supporting contemporary popular opinion about who truly powered the monarchy without violating protocol. The stark terrors depicted in *Dos de Mayo* and *Fusilamientas de Tres de Mayo,* street scenes from the Revolution of 1808, may be his most recognized works. Gossipers, however, focus on Goya's mysteriously expressionless women in *La maja vestida (Clothed Maja)* and *La maja desnuda (Nude Maja),* arguing that the paintings depict the Duchess of Alba. That speculation has been ruled out by experts, but Velázquez and the Duchess did have a hot affair. Don't miss the large room downstairs devoted to Goya's *Pinturas Negras (Black Paintings). Saturno devorando a su hijo (Saturn Devouring His Son)* is an especially graphic image capturing the moment when Saturn, upon hearing a prophesy that one of his children would soon overthrow him, eats them all (in vain). These works date from the end of Goya's life, when the artist was in declining health and living in a small country house outside Madrid, since nicknamed the "Quinta del Sordo" (deaf man's house). Goya painted these chillingly macabre scenes on the walls of his house; years after his death they were transferred to canvases and restored.

Italian, Flemish, and Other Spanish Artists

Of the other **Spanish** works in its collection, the Prado displays many of **El Greco's** (Doménikos Theotokópoulos, 1541-1614) religious paintings. *La Trinidad (The Trinity)* and *La adoración de los pastores (The Adoration of the Shepherds)* are characterized by El Greco's remarkably luminous colors, elongated figures, and mystical subjects. On the second floor you can find **Murillo's** *Familia con pájaro pequeño (Family with Small Bird),* **Ribera's** *El martirio de San Bartholomeo (Martyrdom)* and *La Trinidad,* and **Zurbarán's** *La inmaculada.*

The Prado has a formidable collection of **Italian** works, including **Titian's** portraits of Carlos I and Felipe II and **Raphael's** *El cardenal desconocido (The Unknown Cardinal).* **Tintoretto's** rendition of the homicidal seductress Judith and her hapless victim Holofernes, as well as his *Washing of the Feet* and other works, are here. Some minor **Botticellis** and a slough of his imitators are also on display. Among the works by **Rubens,** *Un Satiro (A Satyr)* stands out.

Because the Spanish Habsburgs once ruled the Netherlands, the **Flemish** holdings are also top-notch. **Van Dyck's** *Marquesa de Legunes* is here, as well as **Hieronymus Bosch's** harrowing triptych, *The Garden of Earthly Delights,* and works by **Albrecht Dürer** and **Peter Breughel the Elder.**

Jardín Botánico and Casón del Buen Retiro

Next to the Prado, the lush and shady **Jardín Botánico** awaits with 30,000 species of plants. *(Open daily in summer 10am-9pm; in winter 10am-6pm; in spring and fall 10am-7pm. 200ptas, students 100ptas.)* The vast collection of imported trees, bushes, and flowers from occident to orient pleases just about everyone. Three minutes from the Prado at C. Alfonso XXII, 28 (tel. 91 330 28 60), sits the **Casón del Buen Retiro.** *(Closed for renovations until at least 2002.)* Once part of Felipe IV's Palacio del Buen Retiro, the Casón was destroyed in the Napoleonic wars. The rebuilt version has a great collection of 19th-century Spanish paintings.

MUSEO NACIONAL CENTRO DE ARTE REINA SOFÍA

Tel. 91 467 50 62. Calle Santa Isabel, 52, opposite Estación Arocha at the south end of Po. Prado. M: Atocha. Open M and W-F 10am-9pm, Su 10am-2:30pm. 500ptas, students 250ptas. Saturdays after 2:30pm and Sundays all day free.

Two floors of this renovated hospital house a marvelous permanent collection of 20th-century art. The Reina Sofía also hosts rotating exhibits, a library and archives specializing in 20th-century art, photography archives, a music library, a repertory cinema, a cafe, a gift shop, a gorgeous courtyard, and a sculpture garden.

Set apart and cordoned off from the public, **Picasso's** master work *Guernica* is the centerpiece of the Reina Sofía's permanent collection. When the Germans bombed the Basque town of Guernica as a military exercise at the behest of Franco during the Spanish Civil War, Picasso painted this huge colorless work of contorted, agonized figures to denounce the bloodshed. The screaming horse in the center represents war, and the twisted bull, an unmistakable national symbol, places the scene in Spain. When asked by Nazi officials whether he was responsible for this work, Picasso answered, "No, you are." He gave the canvas to New York's Museum of Modern Art on the condition that the museum return the painting to Spain when democracy was restored. In 1981, five years after Franco's death, *Guernica* was brought to Madrid's Casón del Buen Retiro. The subsequent move to the Reina Sofía sparked an international controversy—Picasso's other stipulation had been that the painting hang only in the Prado, to affirm his equivalent status with Titian and Velázquez. The masterpiece is currently accompanied by a large, fascinating array of preliminary sketches and drawings. The bullet-proof glass that once shielded the enormous work and created disturbing reflections has recently been removed.

Spain's contribution to early avant-garde art and the essential role of Spanish artists in the Cubist and Surrealist movements are also illustrated by the works of **Miró, Julio González, Juan Gris,** and **Dalí** in the Reina Sofía's permanent collection. The increasing prominence of abstract movements is well chronicled. Particularly impressive are the exhibits of Dali's work as a young artist and Miró's paintings from the 1970s.

MUSEO THYSSEN-BORNEMISZA

Tel. 91 369 01 51. Located on the corner of Po. Prado and C. San Jerónimo. M: Banco de España. Bus #6, 14, 27, 37, or 45. Open Tu-Su 10am-7pm. No one admitted after 6:30pm. Permanent collection 600ptas, seniors and students with ISIC 400ptas, under 12 free. Stamps available for same-day re-entry.

Without missing a step, the 775-piece Thyssen-Bornemisza collection surveys over 600 years of art in the world's most extensive privately owned showcase. The 18th-century Palacio de Villahermosa houses Baron Hans-Heinrich Thyssen-Bornemisza's collection. Rafael Moneo remodeled its interior in 1992, adding marble floors and blushing terra-cotta walls and retaining a flat, spacious layout. Madrid won the bidding for the baron's collection largely because the magnificent space was available.

MADRID

After passing by portraits of the royal couple on the bottom floor, the tour begins on the top floor with a brief look at the Middle Ages. The **Old Masters collection,** including a Van Eyck diptych and Holbein's portrait of *Henry VIII,* stands out where the Prado is relatively weak. Domenico Ghirlandaio's profile portrait of Giovanni Tornabuoni has graced the cover of a few publications (another portrait of her, by Botticelli, hangs in the Louvre). Jan de Beer's *The Birth of the Virgin* is a marvel of old period techniques. Works by Derick Bagert stand out among the **16th-century German** paintings. The Titians and Tintorettos surpass those at the Prado, as do works from the early **Baroque** period, especially those by Caravaggio.

Winding through the centuries, one eventually meets more vibrant splashes of color. **Impressionist** and **Post-Impressionist** collections include works by Manet, Pisarro, Gauguin, Van Gogh, Monet, Renoir, Degas, and Cezanne and drawings by Toulouse-Lautrec (famous from their days as Parisian theatre posters). A Modigliani work hangs out among other Fauvists, and Feiningu's *White Man* lights up the **Expressionist** section. The collections of **17th-century Dutch** (including work attributed to Frans Hals) and **19th-century North American** paintings are also excellent.

The breadth of the **20th-century collection** is a wonder to behold. A great many of the towering names of this century are represented: Picasso, Chagall, Max Ernst, Paul Klee, Miró, Léger, Juan Gris, Mondrian, Maholy-Nagy, Magritte, Giacometti, Kandinsky, Lichtenstein, David Hockney, Hopper, Rauschenberg, Stella, Dalí, Tanguy, O'Keefe, Andrew Wyeth, Rothko, Jackson Pollock...and the list goes on. Among the standouts of this brilliant group are Richard Estes's *Telephone Booths,* Mondrian's *New York City, New York,* and Domenico Gnoli's *Armchair.* Ben Shahn contributes two excellent pieces: *Four Piece Orchestra* and *Carnival.* The array of Cubist works includes important Picassos and Braques. Hockney's coffin-shaped *In Memory of Cecchino Bracci* and Richard Lidner's *Moon Over Alabama* are also here.

OTHER MUSEUMS

Monasterio de las Descalzas Reales, Pl. Descalzas (tel. 91 559 74 04), between Pl. Callao and Sol. M: Callao or Sol. Juana of Austria, daughter of Carlos I, converted the former royal palace into a monastery in 1559. La Roldana, one of the few known 17th-century female artists, designed a chapel in the upper cloister. The Salón de Tapices contains 10 renowned tapestries woven from cartoons by Rubens (some of which hang in the Prado), as well as Santa Ursula's jewel-encrusted bones and a depiction of *El viaje de Santa Ursula y las once mil vírgenes (The Journey of Santa Ursula and the Eleven Thousand Virgins).* Zurbarán, Titian, and Rubens are all represented in the museum. The convent is still home to 26 Franciscan nuns. Open Tu-Th and Sa 10:30am-12:45pm and 4-6pm; F 10:30am-12:45pm, Su 11am-1:45pm. 650ptas, students 250ptas, E.U. citizens free Wednesdays. 45min. tours conducted in Spanish (30min. max. wait while a tour group assembles). Convent's church free during mass (M-Sa 8am and 7pm, Su 8am and noon).

Convento de la Encarnación (tel. 91 542 00 59), in Pl. Encarnación, off C. Bailén just east of Palacio Real. M: Ópera. Juan de Herrera's disciple Juan de Gómez constructed the convent with representative *herrerense* austerity. The macabre *relicuario* houses about 1500 relics of saints, including a vial of San Pantaleón's blood, believed to liquify every year on July 27. In 1995 alone, 30,000 people showed up to gawk. The *Exchange of Princesses on the Bidasoa* depicts the swap weddings of French King Louis XII's sister Isabel to Felipe IV, and Felipe IV's sister Anne to Louis XII. Open W and Sa 10:30am-12:45pm and 4-5:45pm, Su 11am-1:30pm. 425ptas, students 225ptas, E.U. citizens free Wednesday.

Museo de América, Av. Reyes Católicos, 6 (tel. 91 549 26 41), near Av. Puerta de Hierro and next to the conspicuous *Faro de Moncloa,* the futuristic metal tower. M: Moncloa. This under-appreciated museum recently reopened after painstaking renovations and is now a can't-miss. It documents the societies and cultures of pre-Columbian civilizations of the Americas, as well as the Spanish conquest. Newly renovated to include state-of-the-art multimedia exhibits. Open Tu-Sa 10am-3pm, Su 10am-2:30pm. 500ptas, students 200ptas. Sunday free.

Museo Cerralbo, C. Ventura Rodríguez, 17 (tel. 91 547 36 46). M: Ventura Rodríguez. Once home to the Marquis of Cerralbo XVII (1845-1922), the palatial residence-turned-museum displays an eclectic assemblage of period furniture and ornamentation. Beautiful Venetian glass chandeliers and a so-called "mysterious" clock by Barbedienne stand out within a labyrinth of marble and mirrors. The ballroom is an aesthetic feast, the music room has a Louis XVI-style French piano, and the chapel houses El Greco's *The Ecstasy of Saint Francis.* Open Tu-Sa 9:30am-2:30pm, Su 10am-2pm. 400ptas, students 200ptas. Wednesday and Sunday free.

Museo de la Real Academia de Bellas Artes de San Fernando, C. Alcalá, 13 (tel. 91 522 14 91). M: Sol or Sevilla. A beautiful museum with an excellent collection of Old Masters surpassed only by the Prado. The Royal Academy of Fine Arts was founded in 1752 by Ferdinand VI and served as a pedagogical institution ever since. Goya was a director, and famous prodigies include Dalí and Picasso. Velázquez's portraits of Felipe IV and Mariana de Austria and Goya's *La Tirana* are masterpieces; the Raphael and Titian collections are also strong. Other notable works are the Italian Baroque collection and 17th-century canvases by Ribera, Murillo, Zurbarán, and Rubens. Large collection of Picasso prints. Open Tu-F 9am-7pm, Sa-M and holidays 9am-2:30pm. 400ptas, students 200ptas. Saturday and Sunday free. The **Calcografía Real** (Royal Print and Drawing Collection) in the same building houses Goya's studio and some of his equipment and organizes temporary exhibitions (free with museum admission).

Museo Arqueológico Nacional, C. Serrano, 13 (tel. 91 577 79 12), behind the Biblioteca Nacional. M: Serrano. The history of the entire western world is on display in this huge museum. Amid other astounding items from Spain's distant past is the country's most famous archaeological find, *Dama de Elche,* a 4th-century funeral urn. Museum also houses a replica of the Cantabrian *Cuevas de Altamira,* ivories from Muslim Andalucía, Romanesque and Gothic sculpture, and Celtiberian silver and gold. Call ahead for a schedule of exhibits. Open Tu-Sa 9:30am-8:30pm, Su 9:30am-2:30pm. 500ptas, students 250ptas. Saturday free after 2:30pm.

Museo Sorolla, Po. General Martínez Campos, 37 (tel. 91 310 15 84). M: Gregorio Marañón. Former home and studio of Joaquín Sorolla, the acclaimed 19th-century Valencian painter. Tranquil garden and uncrowded halls are a change from most museums. Sensual paintings of the Valencian shores, sunbathers, and society portraits. Open Sept.-July Tu-Sa 10am-3pm, Su 10am-2pm. 400ptas, students 200ptas.

Museo Lázaro Galdiano, C. Serrano, 122.(tel. 91 561 60 84). M: Rubén Dario. Beautiful interior with frescoed walls. Among the riches are an overwhelming display of Italian Renaissance bronzes, ancient jewels, Gothic reliquaries, and Celtic and Visigoth brasses. Array of paintings includes canvasses by Velázquez, Zurbarán, Ribera, El Greco, Bosch, and Goya, plus a da Vinci. Brits are well represented— Gainsborough, Reynolds, Constable, Turner, and T.H. Lawrence. Open Sept.-July Tu-Su 10am-2pm. 300ptas. Sundays free.

Museo Romántico, C. San Mateo, 13 (tel. 91 448 10 71). M: Alonso Martínez. Housed in a 19th-century mansion built by a disciple of Ventura Rodríguez, this museum is an exquisite time capsule of the Romantic period (early 19th century) decorative arts and painting. Open Sept.-July Tu-Sa 9am-3pm, Su 10am-2pm. 400ptas, students 200ptas. Sundays free.

Museo del Ejército, C. Méndez Núñez, 1 (tel. 91 522 89 77), just north of Casón del Buen Retiro. M: Retiro or Banco de España. Vast collection of military paraphernalia in a stately fragment of the Palacio del Buen Retiro. Open Tu-Su 10am-2pm. 100ptas, students 50ptas, under 18 and Saturdays free.

Museo Naval, C. Montalbán, 2 (tel. 91 379 52 99), across from Palacio de Comunicaciones. M: Banco de España. Models of ships from the golden days. A 1693 globe of the sky gives a taste of 17th-century cosmology, and an enormous map charts historic Spanish expeditions. Open Sept.-July Tu-Su 10am-1:30pm. Free.

Museo Municipal, C. Fuencarral, 78 (tel. 91 588 86 72). M: Tribunal. Exhibit traces the evolution of Madrid from ancient times, with an enormous diorama of the city in 1830, a model of 17th-century Pl. Mayor, and a variety of documents. Open Tu-F 9:30am-8pm, Sa-Su 10am-2pm. 300ptas. Wednesdays and Sundays free.

Art Galleries

Calle de Claudio Coello (M: Goya), **Calle de Barquillo** (M: Chueca), and **Calle de Galileo** (M: Quevedo) pack in the most art galleries. (Generally open M 5-9pm, Tu-F 11am-2pm and 5-9pm; free.) Again, *Guía del Ocio* is vital.

■ La Marcha (Nightlife)

In Madrid, a perpetual stream of automobile and pedestrian traffic blur the distinction between 4pm and 4am. In summer, after the sun has mellowed, *terrazas* (a.k.a. *chiringuitos,* outdoor cafes) sprawl across sidewalks all over Madrid. Colder weather sends *madrileños* scrambling into bars and *discotecas.*

Madrid's nightlife is without peer. *La marcha,* as students call it, is concentrated in several distinct neighborhoods. Everyone has a favorite neighborhood, and while hip clubs change with season, year, and time of day (night or morning), the personality of each zone evolves slowly. Once you've found the neighborhoods that suit your tastes, you'll find there's plenty of night to be spent hopping from place to place and *barrio* to *barrio.* For current info on the goings on, scan Madrid's entertainment guides (see p. 81). **Forocio** (tel. 91 522 56 77) organizes special events for visitors. The *Guía del Ocio* runs features on the hottest locales and lists basic information on practically every nightspot.

Spaniards get an average of one hour less sleep than other Europeans. People in Madrid claim to need even less than that. Proud of their nocturnal offerings (they'll tell you with a straight face that they were bored in Paris or New York), *madrileños* insist that no one goes to bed until they've "killed the night"—and a good part of the following morning. Some clubs don't even bother opening until 4 or 5am. **Goa After Club** (M: Gran Vía), **Heaven** (M: Centro), and **Midday** (M: Malasaña) are the top after-hours clubs. The only (relatively) quiet nights of the week are Sunday and Monday.

For clubs and discos, life begins around 2am. Many discos have "afternoon" sessions for teens (7pm-midnight; cover 250-1000ptas). But the "night" sessions (lasting until dawn) are when to really let your hair down. Don't be surprised if at 5:30am there's a line of people waiting to get into a hipster club. The *entrada* (cover) often includes a drink and can be as high as 2000ptas; men may be charged up to 500ptas more than women, if women are charged at all. Keep an eye out for *invitaciones* and *oferta* cards—in stores, restaurants, tourist publications, tourist offices, or in the streets—that offer discounts or free admission.

Plaza 2 de Mayo in Malasaña, Plaza Chueca, Plaza de España, and the Gran Vía can be intimidating; their smaller streets can be sleazy. But they also provide laid-back chill time for many a university student—bring a box of *sangría* and bond with the *jóvenes.* Madrid is fairly safe for a city of its size, but one should always exercise caution. The only really fearsome places late at night are the parks.

CENTRO

The area of El Centro encompasses Sol, Atocha, Ópera, and Tirso de Molina. The imposition of high prices and tourists are nuisances only to those who aren't in the know. Here's the scoop:

Kapital, C. Atocha, 125 (tel. 91 420 29 06). M: Atocha. A block off Po. Prado. One of the most extreme results of *La Movida,* this *macro-discoteca* tries really hard to impress. 2 dance floors, a sky-light lounge, and tons of bars amount to seven floors of macro-pseudo-fun. Packed with 20-year-olds willing to pay the 1200ptas cover, including 2 drinks if you have their invite from the tourist office, 1 drink without. Don't lose your ticket or they'll fine you 5000ptas on leaving. Drinks 800-1000ptas. Thursday parties. Open Th 12:30-6am, F-Su 6-11pm and 12:30-6am.

Joy Eslava, C. Arenal, 11 (tel. 91 366 37 33). M: Sol or Ópera. 3-tiered theater turned disco featuring 3 bars, laser lights, video screen, and live entertainment. Diverse young crowd grooves to sets of disco, techno, R&B, and salsa. Watch out for the rising stage—you might end up a superstar. Cover 1500-2000ptas includes 1 drink. Open M-Th 11:30pm-dawn, F-Sa 7-10:15pm and 11:30pm-5:30am.

Las Noches de Babel, Ronda de Toledo, 1 (tel. 91 366 49 23). M: Puerta de Toledo. *Pijolandia*—where sleek, chic, and young (23-28 year-old) "beautiful people" wiggle around in tight clothes to light funk and house. Open daily 10pm-6am.

Refugio, C. Dr. Cortezo, 1. M: Tirso de Molina. An outrageous gay men's scene. Famous for *fiestas de espuma* (suds parties) and racy F-Sa night "shows," like the *concurso de pollas* (penis competition). It's got a dark room for the shadiest of affairs. Cover 1000ptas includes a drink. Open Tu-Su midnight-morning.

Heaven, C. Veneras, 2 (tel. 91 548 20 22). M: Santo Domingo. Heavenly party at 8am. **After-hours.** Cover 1000ptas. Drinks 600-900ptas. Open Sa-Su 6-10:30am.

Azúcar, Po. Reina Cristina, 7 (tel. 91 501 61 07). M: Atocha. The only place up to date on top Latin American rhythms. Leave your Air Jordans in the hostel—no sneakers. Salsa classes daily 9:30-11pm. Cover 1200ptas, Sa 1500ptas includes 2 drinks. Open M-Th 11pm-5am, F-Sa 11pm-6:30am, Su 8pm-5am.

Torero, C. Cruz, 26 (tel. 91 523 11 29). M: Sol or Sevilla. Crowds in their late 20s to early 30s. A little off from the cutting edge and all the more festive for being a little out of sync. Spanish pop, Latin rhythms, and house. Thursday a veritable cabaret, with drag queens and wacky theater spectacles. Open daily 11pm-6am.

Kathmandú, C. Señores de Luzón, 3 (tel. 91 541 52 53), off C. Mayor, facing the Ayuntamiento. M: Sol. A hole in the wall offering high-energy techno and acid jazz. Cover 600-1000ptas includes 1 drink. Open Th 11pm-5am, F and Sa 11pm-6am.

Palacio Gaviria, Arenal, 9 (tel. 91 526 60 69/70/71). Former palace turned ballroom haven for Chachachá. Fun Thursdays when **Forocio** (see p. 83) throws its international festivals. Pick up an invitation at the tourist office on C. Mayor, 6.

La Movida

Forty years of Franco-imposed repression were bound to end in an explosion—and indeed, his death proved quite the catalyst. Not so much as a day had passed before every newspaper had printed a pornographic photo on its front page. This period is known commonly as "*el destapeo*" (the uncorking or uncovering). Then came the 80s and *la Movida* (the Movement) and Pedro Almodóvar's films about loony grandmothers, outgoing young women, typified animated homosexuals, and electric students. Nightlife was given a dose of the movement, but in many areas it was still a bit too much a bit too fast, resulting in today's golden age of overly ambitious clubs and gimmicky bars. The legendary nightlife, however, existed *before* Franco's rule. Royal fiestas filled Parque del Retiro's lake with silver gondolas and chaotic reenactments of naval battles, while El Capricho Park near the airport almost surely hosted some of the Queen's orgies.

GRAN VÍA

This street just won't go away. "Hello, it's me again," Papa Vía says, and you think to go run and hide. These night spots, just a skip away from Papa, provide great shelter, but don't wander excessively around dark side streets hereabouts looking for a bar.

Tierra, Cabarello de Gracia, 20 (tel. 91 532 72 71). M: Gran Vía. Off C. Montera, but best to go over 1 block to C. Peligios. Cow-patterned upholstery. Black interior with psychedelic glow-in-the-dark design plays host to wicked good house. Beer 500ptas. Open Th-Sa midnight-4:30am.

Soul Kitchen, Mesoneros Romanos, 13 (tel. 91 532 15 24). M: Gran Vía or Callao, where *"la música es funky."* The only real hip-hop club in town. Considered a bit sketchy, but a fave watering hole for American basketball players in Madrid. Cover 1000-2000ptas includes 1 drink. Open W-Sa midnight-5:30am.

Goa After Club, C. Mesonero Romanos, 13 (tel. 91 531 48 27). M: Callao or Gran Vía. "Psychedelic trance atmosphere." **After-hours** party for the artificially energized. Cover 1000ptas includes 1 drink. *Copas* 700-1000ptas. Open Sa-Su 6-10am.

SANTA ANA

Plaza Santa Ana's many bars and small *terrazas* are the preferred jumping-off point for an evening of bar- and club-hopping. Tourists and *madrileños* mingle, chat, smoke, and drink here, the heart of Huertas, Madrid's erstwhile literary district and now the cafe spot for the theater crowd. It's also a place for first-session dance clubs.

Discotecas

No Se Lo Digas a Nadie, C. Ventura de la Vega, 7, next to Pl. Santa Ana. M: Sevilla. Not the best-kept secret in Madrid. This place, with its bright blue sign and bright blue garage doors, is conspicuous. Billiards upstairs. Drinks 500-800ptas. Live mellow music starts around 12:15am.

Angels of Xenon, C. Atocha, 38 (tel. 91 369 38 81). M: Antón Martín. Black walls enclose a mostly gay crowd, under two big-ass disco balls. Too cool for the likes of you. Cover 1200ptas includes 1 drink. Open F-Sa midnight-7am.

Bar-Musicales

La Comedia, C. Príncipe, 16 (tel. 91 521 51 64). M: Sevilla. Chill place for the R&B trendoid. Cheaper than Soul Kitchen, but the music is older. **After hours** daily 5-9am. Cover 1000ptas includes 1 drink. Open Su-Th 3pm-4am, F-Sa 3pm-5am.

Kasbah, C. Santa María, 17. M: Antón Martín. Dazed aliens and other funked-out decorations look on as house DJs spin some of the best jungle and techno in Madrid. On Sunday, amateurs are invited to give it a whirl. Beer 300ptas. No cover.

Café Jazz Populart, C. Huertas, 22 (tel. 91 429 84 07). Jazz aficionados (to some extent) in a smoky bar decorated with brass instruments. Live music daily except Thursday: jazz, blues, swing, reggae, flamenco, and Latin jazz. Shows Su-W 11pm, F-Sa 11pm and 12:30am. No cover. Open Su-Th 6pm-12:30am, F-Sa 6pm-3am.

Café Central, Pl. Angel, 10 (tel. 91 369 41 43), off Pl. Santa Ana. M: Antón Martín or Sol. Jazz club of such high class that the middle-aged audience has no rhythm whatsoever. Beer 300-500ptas. Cover 700-1500ptas. Open 1:30pm-3:30am.

El Mosquito, Torrecilla de Leal, 13. M: Antón Martín. Rap, soul, and funk draw a lesbian and gay crowd. Drinks 300-700ptas. Open Su-Th 6pm-12:30am, F-Sa 6pm-3am.

Bars

Mauna Loa, Pl. Santa Ana, 13 (tel. 91 429 70 62). M: Sevilla or Sol. Hawaiian bar with romantic nooks ideal for couples. *Superguay* (supercool) volcano drinks with eye-poking straws. Open Su-Th 7pm-2am, F-Sa 7pm-3am.

Naturbier, Pl. Santa Ana, 9 (tel. 91 429 39 18). M: Sol or Sevilla. Locally brewed *bier,* inspired by the credo: "beer is important to human nutrition." Superior lager 225-500ptas. Open Su-Th 11:30am-1am, F-Sa 11am-3am.

Viva Madrid, C. Manuel Fernández González, 7 (tel. 91 429 36 40), next to Pl. Santa Ana. M: Sol or Sevilla. Tiled and classy U.S. expat hangout. You'll still hear Spanish, though, because they're louder. Packed. Beer 300-400ptas, mixed drinks 700-800ptas. Open 1pm-7am.

Cervecería Alemana, Pl. Santa Ana, 6 (tel. 91 429 70 33). M: Sol or Sevilla. Naturbier's neighbor. A former Hemingway hangout with a slightly upscale crowd. Open Su-Th noon-2am, F-Sa noon-4am.

Punto y Coma, Pl. Santa Ana, at corner of C. Prado. M: Sol or Sevilla. Popular local hangout, the "pearl of the plaza." Beer 300ptas. Open nightly until 1am.

El Oso y el Madroño, C. Volsa, 4 (tel. 91 522 77 96). M: Sol. A hand organ and old photos of Madrid. Try the potent Licor de Madroño, an arbutus-flavored Spanish liquer (150ptas). Open M-Sa 10am-midnight.

El Café de Sheherezade, C. Santa María, 18, a block south of C. Huertas. M: Antón Martín. Recline on opulent pillows as you sip exotic infusions (tea 350ptas). Moorish arches and Persian rugs in a dark, mellow, bohemian atmosphere. Thursday features Middle Eastern music. Offers *pira* (pipe 600-1000ptas).

LA CASTELLANA

The fashionable *terrazas* lining Madrid's most modern drag come alive every night around 11:30pm in July and August. Drinks can be quite pricey, reaching 600ptas for beer, 1000ptas for mixed drinks. There's no cover, but if you want anybody to talk to you, you'll have to spend a few extra *pesetas* on clothes.

Bolero Terraza, Po. Castellana, 33 (tel. 91 554 91 51). M: Rubén Darío. An ultra-fashionable *terraza*. Claw your way to the bar with your exquisitely manicured hands. Drinks 1000ptas. Open nightly 7:30pm-3am.

Boulevard Terraza, Po. Castellana, 37 (tel. 91 308 52 58). M: Rubén Darío. *Gente guapa* (beautiful people); loud music. Drinks 1000ptas. Open nightly 7pm-3am.

BagëLus, C. María de Molina, 25 (tel. 91 561 61 00). M: Av. América. 3 sumptuous floors of *pijolandia* (rich kid land)—restaurant, cafe, art gallery, club (techno on one floor, Latin on another), *terraza,* and even a travel agency. Be forewarned that *bagëlus* means "virility." Beer 600ptas, mixed drinks 800ptas.

CHUECA

Chueca is home to an outrageous, mostly male, gay scene, but Pl. Chueca's *terrazas* are becoming more and more popular among all youths. Clubs may come and go, but **Calle de Pelayo** is clearly the main drag. Beers cost about 400ptas. Generally the safest walking route at night is up C. Fuencarral from Gran Vía and right on C. Augusto Figueroa, although you should still take proper precautions.

Rick's, C. Clavel, 8. M: Chueca. Chueca's hottest bar is sure to be fired up for the new century. Mostly gay men, but women mingle comfortably in a bar of multifaceted tastes, where you can dance, schmooze, smooch, or knock around a foosball. Look good, be happy. Beer 600-900ptas. Open daily 11:30am-morning.

Black & White, C. Libertad, 34 (tel. 91 531 11 41). M: Chueca. Top and bottom floors are stark contrasts. Upstairs a more mature crowd mingles and downstairs the young ones whoop it up on the dance floor. Gays and lesbians, but not exclusively. Beer 500ptas, mixed drinks 800ptas. Open daily 8pm-5am.

Finnegan's Irish Pub, Pl. Salesas, 9 (tel. 91 310 05 21). M: Chueca. Welcoming scene popular with Americans. Open daily M-Th 10:30pm-5am, Sa-Su 1pm-morning.

Café Figueroa, C. Augusto Figueroa, 17 (tel. 91 521 16 73), on the corner of C. Hortaleza. M: Chueca. Smoke-filled, dimly lit cafe is otherworldly. Low lounge-couches and lacy curtains emanate a dream-like elegance. Gay clientele. Beer 300-425ptas. Coffee 250-450ptas. Open Su-Th 3pm-1am, F-Sa 3pm-2:30am.

Acuarela, C. Gravina, 8, off C. Hortaleza. M: Chueca. Very chill cafe—an alternative to the cruising scene. Crowded. Beer 400ptas. Open daily 4pm-4am.

Ambient, C. San Mateo, 21 (tel. 91 448 80 62), off C. Hortaleza. M: Chueca or Alonso Martínez. A lesbian *bar-pizzería* that takes pool very seriously. Look out for the Pool Championships in March.

El Truco, C. Gravina, 10 (tel. 91 532 89 21). M: Chueca. Classy bar featuring local artists' works. Lesbian-friendly. Open Su-Th 8pm-2am, F-Sa 9pm-4am. Same owners run **Escape,** a club down the street. Both are strong enough for a man, but designed particularly for a woman. Open F-Sa midnight-7am.

ALONSO MARTÍNEZ-BILBAO

Plenty of discos and bars shake around **Glorieta de Bilbao,** especially along and between **Calles Fuencarral** and **Luchana.** *Terrazas* on **Plaza Olavide** have a mellower drink-sipping scene (drinks outside 150-250ptas). Being frugal is no trouble in these high school and college student-filled streets. Bars and clubs are boisterous and packed year-round. In **Alonso Martínez,** the university crowd sweats out strong drinks in tight spaces.

Barnon, C. Santa Engracia, 17 (tel. 91 447 38 37). M: Alonso Martínez Tribunal. Real Madrid's stud forward Raúl owns this hip-hop bar of VIPs that attracts *vikingos,* his teammates, and American hoops players. High fashion crowd jets to Soul Kitchen once they get their buzz on. No cover. Open Su-Th 10pm-3am, F-Sa 10pm-4am.

Vaivén, Travesía de San Mateo, 1. M: Tribunal. The most exclusive salsa club in the city. If you've got the goods, it's a great place to meet someone of the opposite sex. Mid-week concerts. Beer 600ptas, mixed drinks 900ptas. Open daily 9pm-4am.

Clamores Jazz Club, C. Albuquerque, 14 (tel. 91 445 79 38), off C. Cardenal Cisneros. M: Bilbao. Swanky (pink neon) setting and some of Madrid's more interesting jazz. The cover (600-1200ptas) gets slipped into the bill. Live jazz daily except for Monday. Open July-Aug. M-Th 7pm-3am, F-Sa 7pm-4am; Sept.-June Su-Th 7pm-3am, F-Sa 7pm-4am.

Archy, C. Marqués de Riscal, 11 (tel. 91 308 31 62), off C. Almagro from Pl. Alonso Martínez. M: Ruben Darío. Dress to kill or the fashion police at the door might point and laugh. Beautiful people only. Also a fancy restaurant. No cover, but drinks cost 700-900ptas. Open Th-Sa 11pm-morning.

Cambalache, C. San Lorenzo, 5 (tel. 91 310 07 01). M: Alonso Martínez or Tribunal. Argentine food served 6-11pm, tango classes 7-9pm, live tangos 11pm-midnight. You might want to reserve ahead. Open daily 8:30pm-5am.

Big Bamboo, C. Barquillo, 42 (tel. 91 562 88 38) M: Alonso Marínez. 3 blocks east of C. Pelayo down C. Gravina, and left on C. Barquillo. It's not who you dance with, it's what you dance to: reggae all the way. African immigrants and tons of tourists. Usually no cover. Open Tu-Th 10pm-6am, F-Sa 10pm-7am.

Cervecería Ratskeller's, C. Luchana, 15 (tel. 91 447 13 40), at C. Palafox (by the cinema Palafox). M: Bilbao. Barfing, pinching, white hats, jams, flannels, and Bud t-shirts. You're in Cancún all over again. Open daily 5pm-3am.

MALASAÑA

Malasaña is darker, more bohemian, and more sedate(d) than Pl. Santa Ana. Entertainment guides don't list the heaps of small, crowded pubs in this area, most of which play great music (jazz and blues). Hippies, intellectuals, junkies, and hippy-intellectual-junkies check each other out in **Plaza 2 de Mayo. Calle San Vincente Ferrer,** with its tattoo parlors, secondhand clothing, leather stores, motorcycle repair shops, and countless pubs, is prime Malasaña. On **Calle Barceló,** kids run an open-air narcotics market. Most people in Masalaña are drunk, high, or both. Be wary here at night.

Café la Palma, C. La Palma, 62 (tel. 91 522 50 31). M: San Bernardo or Noviciado. Rugs and throw pillows in a Moroccan-style atmosphere, or air, or aura, or cloud. Open daily 4pm-morning.

Midday, C. Amaniel, 13 (tel. 91 547 25 25). M: Noviciado. *The* **after-hours** club for Madrid's *gente guapa.* Techno and house and very exclusive. Open Su 9am-3pm.

Vía Láctea, C. Velarde, 18 (tel. 91 466 75 81). M: Tribunal. This deservedly famous club is almost always jam-packed. The "Milky Way's" loudspeakers and slightly expensive drinks will make you think you're a comet. Open Tu-Su 7:30pm-3am.

La Tetera de la Abuela, C. Espíritu Santo, 19. "Granny's Teapot" attracts a young and angsty pseudo-intellectual crowd. Open Su-Th 7:30pm-1am, F-Sa 7:30pm-2am.

Manuela, C. San Vicente Ferrer, 29 (tel. 91 531 70 37). M: Bilbao or Tribunal. Old-looking cafe-bar with dirty mirrors is elegant in a "this-must-have-been-elegant-quite-some-time-ago" sort of way. Live music (usually folksy) begins at 10pm. Cover for performances 300-400ptas. Open daily 6pm-3am.

ARGÜELLES-MONCLOA

"Los jóvenes, los jóvenes" (the kids, the kids). Young aspiring high-school students inundate the streets wearing banana-peel-tight jeans, halter tops, denim jackets, and pony tails. This place will make you feel sorry for Spanish mothers. The area clears out weekdays in June (when exams hit) and everyday in August (when they leave town for vacation). In July, the weekend is a call to arms.

Chapandaz, C. Fernando Católico, a block from Arcipreste de Hita, down the stairs to the right. M: Moncloa. Strip mall by day, student hub by night (F-Sa). Lined with several bars and clubs, but only Chapandaz has stalactites and the mysterious *leche de pantera* (panther's milk). Large mixed drinks 500ptas. Open daily until 2am.

MADRID

Galileo Galilei, C. Galileo, 100 (tel. 91 534 75 57 or 91 534 75 58). M: Moncloa or Quevedo. Off C. Alberto Aguilera. Soft 80s decor hosts some of Madrid's most fervent pop bands. Cover free-1500ptas. Open Su-Th 6pm-3am, F-Sa 6pm-5am.

Patato Bar, C. Hilavion Eslava, at C. Fernando El Católico. M: Movidoa. A great place to start the night. *Patatas bravas* and *minis* (huge mugs of beer) or *sangría* (500ptas) go well together. Open daily until 1am.

Palio, Isaac Peral, 38 (tel. 91 543 13 49). M: Moncloa, up C. Peral on the right. Glowing fluorescence of the zodiac is only just the entryway. Beer 500ptas. No cover.

■ Entertainment

MUSIC

In summer the city sponsors free concerts, ranging from classical and jazz to bolero and salsa, at **Plazas Mayor, Lavapiés, Oriente,** and **Villa de París.** See **Publications about Madrid,** p. 81, for informative publications, and check out the preceding clubs and bars for live rock and jazz performances.

The **Auditorio Nacional,** C. Príncipe de Vergara, 146 (tel. 91 337 01 00; M: Cruz del Rayo), is home of the National Orchestra and features the best classical performances in Madrid (800-4200ptas). The **Fundación Juan March,** C. Castelló, 77 (tel. 91 435 42 40; M: Núñez de Balboa), sponsors free weekly concerts (F-Su) and hosts a university lecture series (Tu-W 7:30pm). The **Conservatorio Superior de Música** (M: Atocha), next door to the Centro Reina Sofía, hosts free student performances, professional traveling orchestras, and celebrated soloists. **Teatro Monumental,** C. Atocha, 65 (tel. 91 429 81 19; M: Antón Martín), is home to Madrid's Symphonic Orchestra. Reinforced concrete—a Spanish invention—was first used in its construction in the 1920s; prepare for unusual acoustics. Most of the above organizations shut down in July and August.

For opera and *zarzuela* (Spanish light opera), head for the ornate **Teatro de la Zarzuela,** C. Jovellanos, 4 (tel. 91 524 54 00; M: Banco de España), modeled on La Scala. The grand 19th-century granite **Teatro de la Ópera** (tel. 91 559 35 51), on Pl. Ópera, is the city's principal venue for classical ballet.

Flamenco in Madrid is tourist-oriented and expensive. It's like looking for pasta at McDonald's. **Café de Chinitas,** C. Torija, 7 (tel. 91 547 15 01 or 91 547 15 02; M: Santo Domingo), is as overstated as they come. Shows start at 10:30pm and midnight; the memories last forever (they'd better—the 4300ptas cover includes one drink). At **Corral de la Morería,** C. Morería, 17 (tel. 91 365 84 46 or 91 365 11 37; M: La Latina), by the Viaducto on C. Bailén, shows start at 10:45pm and last until 2am. The 4000ptas cover includes one drink. **Casa Patas,** C. Cañizares, 10 (tel. 91 369 04 96; M: Antón Martín), is a more down-to-earth flamenco club. Shows start at midnight Thursday to Saturday. The cover charge varies. (Open M-Sa 8pm-2:30am.) **Teatro Albéniz,** C. Paz, 11 (tel. 91 521 99 98; M: Sol), hosts a yearly *Certamen de Coreografía de Danza Española y Flamenco* that features original dance and music, including a good portion of extraordinary flamenco (tickets 700-2000ptas).

The **Johnnie Walker Music Festival** in June and July brings big-name musicians from around the world. Madrid's big rock 'n' roll stadium, **Palacio de los Deportes,** Av. Felipe II (tel. 91 401 91 00; M: Goya), generally brings in American groups. More alternative groups play at **Aqualung Universal,** Po. Ermita del Santo, 45 (tel. 91 470 23 62). For information and tickets, try **FNAC** (tel. 91 595 62 00), **Madrid Rock** (tel. 91 523 26 52), **Virgin Megastore** (tel. 91 431 74 44), **Libreria Crisol** (tel. 91 322 47 00), or **TelEntrada** (tel. 902 38 33 33).

FILM

In summer, the city sponsors free movies and plays, all listed in the *Guía del Ocio* and entertainment supplements in all Friday papers. Look out for the **Fescinal,** a film festival at the Parque de la Florida in July. The **Parque del Retiro** sometimes shows free movies at 11pm. The **Centro Reina Sofía** has a repertory cinema of its own. The university's **colegios mayores** sponsor film series and jazz concerts.

Most cinemas show three films per day at around 4:30, 7:30, and 10:30pm. Tickets cost 600 to 700ptas. Some cinemas, like the Princesa, offer weekday-only matinee student discounts for 550ptas. Wednesday is *día del espectador*. Tickets cost around 500ptas—show up early. Check the *versión original* **(V.O. subtitulada)** listings in entertainment guides for subtitled movies. Most Spanish theaters will not allow entrance to a movie past showtime. You can't go wrong if you hop off at M: Ventura Rodríguez, between Pl. España and Argüelles, site of three excellent theaters. **Princesa,** C. Princesa, 3 (tel. 91 541 41 00), shows mainstream Spanish films and subtitled foreign films. **Alphaville,** C. Martín de los Heros, 14 (tel. 91 559 38 36), behind Princesa passing underneath the large patio, has a bar and shows films suited to alternative tastes and current Spanish titles. (**Lumière,** in the underpass, shows V.O. films but the crowd is less hip.) **Renoir,** C. Raimundo Fernández Villaverde, 10 (tel. 91 541 41 00), is a few doors down by the popcorn vendor, but the erudite theater won't let you eat inside. Renoir shows highly acclaimed recent films, many foreign and subtitled. The state-subsidized *filmoteca española* in the Art Deco **Ciné Doré,** C. Santa Isabel, 3 (tel. 91 369 11 25; M: Antón Martín), is Madrid's finest repertory cinema (tickets 200-400ptas). Subtitled films are shown in many private theaters, including **Multicines Ideal,** C. Dr. Cortezo, 6 (tel. 91 369 25 18; M: Sol), an anglophile favorite with nine screens. To experience Spain's flawless dubbing industry, renowned worldwide, change over to **Gran Vía's** plush cinemas.

THEATER

In July and August, **Plazas Mayor, Lavapiés,** and **Villa de París** frequently host plays; some *teatros* close for vacation. During the rest of the year, theater-goers can consult the well-illustrated magazines published by state-sponsored theaters—which also sell posters of their productions for next to nothing—such as **Teatro Español, Teatro de la Comedia,** and the superb **Teatro María Guerrero.** Buy tickets at theater box offices or at agencies (**FNAC** tel. 91 595 62 00; **Librería Crisol** tel. 91 322 47 00; **TelEntrada** tel. 902 38 33 33). **Huertas,** east of Sol, is the theater district (see p. 101). For a complete listing of theaters and shows, consult the *Guía del Ocio.*

Main Stages

Centro Cultural de la Villa, Pl. Colón (tel. 91 575 60 80). M: Colón or Serrano. Performance center showing ballet and plays. Tickets 2000ptas. Summer venue.

Sala Olimpia, C. Valencia (tel. 91 527 46 22). M: Lavapiés. National troupe produces avant-garde theatrical works. Tickets 2200-2600ptas, 30% student discounts. Summer venue.

Teatro Bellas Artes, C. Marqués de Casa Riera, 2 (tel. 91 532 44 37). M: Banco de España. Private theater devoted to staging new works. Tickets 2000-3500ptas.

Teatro de Cámara, C. San Cosme y San Damián, 3 (tel. 91 527 09 54). M: Atocha or Antón Martín. Classic repertory theater company produces canonical dramas and comedies by the likes of Gogol, Cervantes, Chekhov…and Raymond Carver. Poetry recitals. Tickets 1000-1500ptas. Summer venue.

Teatro de la Comedia, C. Príncipe, 14 (tel. 91 521 49 31). M: Sevilla. The traveling *Compañia Nacional Teatro Clásico* often performs classical Spanish theater here. Tickets 1300-2600ptas, reduced prices Thursdays. Ticket office open daily 11:30am-1:30pm and 5-9pm.

Teatro Español, C. Príncipe, 25 (tel. 91 429 62 97 or 91 429 91 93). M: Sol. Site of 16th-century Teatro de Príncipe, the Teatro Español dates from the 18th century. Established company regularly showcases winners of the prestigious Lope de Vega award. Tickets 200-2000ptas, 50% discount on Wednesday. Summer venue.

Teatro La Latina, Pl. Cebada, 2 (tel. 91 365 28 35). M: Latina. A varied repertoire of works by new and established playwrights. Tickets 1500-2800ptas. Ticket office open daily 11am-1pm and 6:30-8pm. Summer venue.

Teatro María Guerrero, C. Tamayo y Baus, 4 (tel. 91 319 47 69). M: Colón or Banco de España. Excellent state-supported repertory company. Tickets 1650-2600ptas. Ticket office open daily 11:30am-1:30pm and 5-6pm. Summer venue.
Teatro Nacional Clásico, C. Príncipe, 14 (tel. 91 521 49 31). Works by great Spanish dramatists of the past. Tickets 1300-1600ptas. Visa, AmEx.

Alternative Theater

Teatro El Canto de la Cabra, C. San Gregorio, 8 (tel. 91 310 42 22). M: Chueca. Avant-garde troupe, offering interesting open-air performances in July and August. Tickets 1700ptas, students 1200ptas. Summer venue.
Teatro Cuarta Pared, C. Ercilla, 17 (tel. 91 517 23 17). M: Embajadores. Storytelling performances and experimental theater. Tickets 1200ptas.
Teatro Estudio de Madrid, C. Cabeza, 14 (tel. 91 539 64 47). M: Tirso de Molina. Amateur studio theater; avant-garde works and performance art. Tickets 1200ptas, students 800ptas. Summer venue.
Teatro Maravillas, C. Manuela Malasaña, 6 (tel. 91 446 71 94). M: Bilbao. Popular theater; mostly musicals and comedies. Tickets 1500-2500ptas, under 20 1000ptas.
Teatro Triángulo, C. Zurita, 20 (tel. 91 530 68 91). M: Lavapiés. Mainly theater of the absurd. Tickets 1400ptas, students 800ptas. Summer venue.

SHOPPING

Most shops open in the morning, roll up their awnings and drop their metal grates for *siesta* from 2 to 5pm, and then re-open until 8pm. Major department stores, like **El Corte Inglés** and **FNAC** (see p. 82), are open from 10am to 9pm. Some shops have begun to stay open on Saturday afternoons and during lunch. By law, *grandes almecenes* (department stores) may only open the first Sunday of every month, a law that reflects the State's reluctance to make the capitalistic plunge. Many close in August, when practically everyone flees to the coast. **Inal** publishes a yearly *Guía Esencial para vivir en Madrid,* which includes descriptions of most stores.

El Rastro (Flea Market)

Every Sunday morning for hundreds of years, **El Rastro** has been *the* place to sell stolen watches and buy battered birdcages. Old shoes and cheap jewelry abound, but the intrepid shopper will find good deals on second-hand leather jackets, leather bags, and canaries (on their own special sidestreet). Students and their propaganda of discontent congregate around *Tirso de Molina.* Antiquarians contribute their peculiar mustiness to Calle (not Salón or Paseo) del Prado and adjacent streets—some Spaniards pride themselves on equipping an entire apartment with antique sideboards and cauldrons from the Rastro. From Pl. Mayor, walk down C. Toledo to Pl. Cascorro (M: La Latina), where the market begins, and follow the rest of the world to the end, at the bottom of C. Ribera de Curtidores. Unless you enjoy being crushed in a river of solid flesh, arrive no later than 10am and drift off to an air-conditioned bar when you get sticky. The flea market is a den of **pickpockets**, so wear your backpack backwards (that is, frontwards) and be very discreet when taking out your wallet or money. El Rastro is open Sunday and holidays from 9am to 2pm.

Boutiques

From Sol to the Gran Vía and along C. Princesa, the main department stores float in a sea of smaller discount stores. Budgeters with weary spirits and scraped soles shop at **Los Guerrilleros** (a very big store with very low prices), Puerta del Sol, 5, diagonally across from El Corte Inglés.

Lines of outlets with wholesale prices mingle with young designer boutiques on **Calle Conde de Romanones** (M: Tirso de Molina). Shopping here means fishing through a sea of funky to undesirably tacky clothes to find what fits your fancy. For die-hard club gear, head to **Glam,** C. Fuencarral, 35 (tel. 91 522 80 54; M: Gran Vía), or the naughtier **Come,** C. Hortaleza, 38—nothing but platforms and vinyl here. At Almirante, 22, is crazy, modern, unisex **Plan 2** (tel. 91 522 33 11; M: Chueca).

Shall we shop?

With almost 200 of them throughout Spain, Zara stores are hard to miss. In Madrid, they virtually line the streets near Puerta del Sol; in Barcelona, they show up about every other block; and in Sevilla, two sit right next door to each other. So, what is Zara? Part clothing chain, part national phenomenon. This home-grown Spanish clothing retailer sells men and children's attire, but it's the women's clothing that inspires frenzies: stylish yet cheap, classy yet sexy—Zara's fans can't praise the stores enough. Maybe the clothes won't last forever (at the most heavily trafficked stores, sweaters sometimes pill and seams can strain even before clothes are bought), but Zara's reputation might. Stock changes constantly, weekly if not hourly. Mounds of sparkly tank tops, almost sheer dresses, baggy khakis, wool sweaters in every color, belts, bags, boots, and bathing suits are just a few of the items that immediately convert first-time visitors to the wonders of Zara's.

Be warned that during seasonal sales, waiting in line for dressing rooms and paying for your purchase could take the better part of a day. But don't worry—the museums and the beach are not going anywhere, but cheap tube tops and knee-length skirts are in high demand. Just shop.

For a designer look and semi-affordable prices, there's **Zara,** a retail store found throughout Madrid (C. Fuencarral, 126-128; Gran Vía, 32; and C. Princesa, 45). Zara's factory reject branch, **Lefties,** is cheap-cheap-cheap, and located at C. Carretas, 10, a block and a half off Sol. **Kameleón,** Arenal, 8 (tel. 91 523 21 63), and Postas, 1 (tel. 91 522 35 93), sells secondhand clothes.

The embassy quarter north of C. Génova is decidedly more haughty. Madrid's posh-est shopping areas are Jerónimos and Salamanca. In the latter, couture and near-cou-ture boutiques vogue on **Calles Serrano, Príncipe de Vergara, Velázquez, Goya, Ortega y Gasset, Coello,** and **Alfonso XII** (M: Serrano or Velázquez).

Malls

La Vaguada (M: Barrio del Pilar; bus #132 from Moncloa), in the northern neighbor-hood **Madrid-2,** is Madrid's first experiment with Americana. It offers everything the homesick could want: 350 shops, including the Body Shop, Springfield, Burberry's, and confectionery bazaars; a food court with Colonel Sanders and Ronald McDonald; multicinemas; and a bowling alley/arcade. (Open daily 10am-10pm.)

By far the poshest shopping mall belongs to the **Galería del Prado,** Pl. Cortes (M: Banco de España), located beneath the crusty Hotel Palace and across the Castellana from the Ritz, no less. Let's face it—handling furs and suedes you could never afford is fun. (Open M-Sa 10am-9pm.) Of course, don't forget El Corte Inglés (see **Tourist and Financial Services,** p. 81).

Books

FNAC, C. Preciados, 28 (tel. 91 595 62 00). M: Callao. The best music and book selection in town. Books in English. Open M-Sa 10am-9:30pm, Su noon-9:30pm.

Librería Crisol, C. Juan Bravo, 38 (tel. 91 322 48 00). A high-powered place with futuristic interior design; service and prices to match. Great hours: open M-Sa 10:30am-10:30pm, Su 11am-3pm and 5-9pm. Many other locations around Madrid.

Booksellers, C. José Abascal, 48 (tel. 91 442 79 59 or 91 442 81 04). M: Gregorio Marañón. A vast array of new books in English, plus American and English maga-zines. Open M-F 9:30am-2pm and 5-8pm, Sa 10am-2pm.

Librería de Mujeres (Women's Bookstore), C. San Cristóbal, 17 (tel. 91 521 70 43), near Pl. Mayor. International bookstore. English spoken. (See **Practical Informa-tion,** p. 83).

Berkana Librería Gai y Lesbiana, C. Gravina, 11 (tel./fax 91 532 13 93). M: Chueca. Gay and lesbian bookstore. Also offers space for young artists, book presentations, and loads of contact information for gay/lesbian foreigners. Free map of gay Madrid. Open M-F 10:30am-2pm and 5-8:30pm, Sa noon-2pm and 5-8:30pm.

Cuesta de Moyano, along the southern border of the Jardín Botánico (M: Atocha). 30 open-air stalls hawk paperbacks and rare books. Best buying day is Sunday.

Librería Felipe, C. Libreros, 16, off Gran Vía. M: Callao or Pl. España. The entire street is books, but only Felipa gives a 20% discount off list price. Open M-F 9:30am-1:30pm and 4:30-8pm, Sa 9:30am-1:30pm.

English Editions, Pl. San Amaro, 5 (tel. 91 571 03 21). M: Estrecho. In the tiny Pl. San Amaro, off C. General Perón. Used novels bought and sold—excellent selection. Also a mini-mart featuring English and American food specialties. Call for hours.

Altair, C. Gaztambide, 31. M: Argüelles. New travel-book bookstore. Carries guides to almost everywhere. Open M-Sa 10am-2pm and 4:30-8pm.

VIPS mega-convenience-stores also stock novels and guidebooks in English. See **Red-Eye Establishments,** p. 91

El Corte Inglés, granted (see **Practical Information,** p. 91), sells books and CDs.

ATHLETICS

Fútbol

Spaniards obsess over **fútbol** (soccer). If either **Real Madrid** or **Atlético de Madrid** wins a match, count on streets being clogged with honking cars (more so than is usual) and, on Pl. Cibeles, being filled with wet fans. Every Sunday and some Saturdays between September and June, one of these two teams plays at home. *Los vikingos,* fans of El Madrid, supported Raúl and the boys to the European Cup in 1998, although they had a disappointing year within the Spanish league (won by their hated rival, F.C. Barcelona). Real Madrid plays at **Estadio Santiago Bernebéu,** Po. Castellana, 104 (tel. 91 457 11 12; M: Lima). Atlético de Madrid plays at **Estadio Vicente Calderón,** C. Virgen del Puerto, 67 (tel. 91 366 47 07; M: Pirámides or Marqués de Vadillos). Tickets for seats cost 3000-7000ptas. If tickets are sold out, shifty scalpers lurk around the stadium during the afternoon or evening a few days before the game. These tickets cost only 25-50% more, whereas on game day prices become astronomical. For the big games—Atlético vs. Real, either team vs. F.C. Barcelona *(La Barça),* key matches in April and May, summer *Copa del Rey* and *Copa de Europa* games—scalpers are really the only option, so be wary. Betting is legal with the state-run lottery; department stores and *éstancos* distribute gamecards.

Recreation

For **cycling** info and bicycle repair, spin over to **Ciclos Muñoz,** C. Pablo Ortiz (tel. 91 475 02 19; M: Usera; open M-F 9am-2pm and 5-8pm, Sa 9am-2pm). **Swimmers** splash in the outdoor pools at: **Casa de Campo** (tel. 91 463 00 50) on Av. Angel (M: Lago); the indoor **Municipal de La Latina,** Pl. Cebada, 2 (M: La Latina); **Aluche** (tel. 91 706 28 28) on Av. General Fenjul (bus #17, 34, or 139); and **Peñuelas,** C. Arganda (tel. 91 474 28 08; M: Delicias or bus #18). (All pools open daily 10:30am-8pm; 500ptas, ages 4-13 225ptas.) Gallop over to the **Hipódromo de Madrid,** Ctra. de La Coruña, km 7800 (tel. 91 357 16 82), for **horse-racing.** Call the **Oficina de Información Deportiva** (sports information; tel. 91 463 55 63) for more info. For information and tickets for Madrid's two basketball teams' games (Real Madrid and Estudiantes Madrid), call the **Palacio de Deportes** (tel. 91 401 91 00; M: Goya).

La Corrida (The Bullfight)

Bullfighters are loved or loathed. If the crowd thinks the *matador* is a man of mettle and style, they exalt him as an emperor. If they think him a coward or a butcher, they whistle cacophonously, chant *"Vete"* (Get out!), throw their seat cushions (40ptas to rent) at him, and wait outside the ring to stone his car. A bloody killing of the bull, instead of the swift death-stab, can upset the career of even the most renowned *matador* or *matadora*—in 1996, **Cristina** entered the ring as Spain's first female bullfighter of premier rank.

Corridas (bullfights) are held during the Festival of San Isidro and every Sunday in summer, less frequently the rest of the year. The season lasts from March to October, signalled by posters in bars and cafes (especially on C. Victoria, off C. San Jerónimo).

Plaza de las Ventas, C. Alcalá, 237 (tel. 91 356 22 00; M: Ventas), east of central Madrid, is the biggest ring in Spain. A seat runs 450-15,200ptas, depending on whether it's in the *sombra* (shade) or the blistering *sol*. Tickets are usually available the Friday and Saturday before and the Sunday of the bullfight. If you're intrigued by the lore but not the gore, head to the **Museo Taurino,** C. Alcalá, 237 (tel. 91 725 18 57), at Pl. Monumental de Las Ventas. The museum displays a remarkable collection of *trajes de luces,* capes, and posters of famous *corridas.* (Open Tu-F 9:30am-2:30pm, on fight days 10am-1pm: free.) The bullfighting school (tel. 91 470 19 90; M: Batán), by the amusement park, often has its own *corridas* for free.

From May 15 to 22, the **Fiestas de San Isidro** bring a bullfight every day with the top *toreros* and fiercest bulls. The festival is nationally televised, and most of those without tickets crowd into bars. **Bar-Restaurante Plata,** C. Jardines, 11 (M: Sol), has cheap *tapas* and a loud television. **Bar El Pavón,** C. Victoria, 8, at C. Cruz (M: Sol); **El Abuelo,** C. Núñez de Arce, 5, where aficionados brandish the restaurant's famous shrimp during arguments over bullfighters; and **Bar Torre del Oro,** Pl. Mayor, 26 (M: Sol or Ópera), are all local favorites. The bar of ritzy **Hotel Wellington** on C. Velázquez is also known to have its share of *matadores* and their groupies. During the *fiestas* it's unusual to enter a bar and *not* find the TV tuned to the bullfight.

FESTIVALS

The brochure *Las Fiestas de España,* available at tourist offices and the bigger hotels, contains historical background and general info on Spain's festivals. Madrid's **Carnaval** was inaugurated in the Middle Ages then prohibited during Franco's dictatorship. Now the city bursts with street fiestas, dancing, and processions, and the Fat Tuesday celebration culminates with the mystifying "Burial of the Sardine." In late April, the city bubbles with the high quality **International Theater Festival.** The May **Fiestas de San Isidro,** in honor of Madrid's patron saint, bring concerts, parades, and Spain's best bullfights. Throughout the summer, the city sponsors the **Veranos de la Villa,** an outstanding and varied set of cultural activities, including free classical music concerts, movies in open-air settings, plays, art exhibits, an international film festival, opera, *zarzuela* (Spanish operetta), ballet, and sports. In August, the neighborhoods of **San Cayetano, San Lorenzo,** and **La Paloma** have their own festivities in a flurry of *madrileñismo:* processions, street dancing, traditional games, food, and drink are combined with home-grown hard rock and political slogans. The **Festivales de Otoño** (Autumn Festivals) from September to November also conjure an impressive array of music, theater, and film. On November 1, **Todos los Santos** (All Saints' Day), an International Jazz Festival brings great musicians to Madrid. The **Día de la Constitución** (Day of the Constitution, or National Day) on December 6 heralds the arrival of the National Company of Spanish Classical Ballet in Madrid. Tourist offices in Madrid have all the information.

COMUNIDAD DE MADRID

The Comunidad de Madrid is an autonomous administrative region, shaped like an arrowhead and pointing right at the heart of Castilla y León. Historically, Madrid and Castilla La Mancha were known as Castilla La Nueva (New Castile), while the area north of Madrid was called Castilla La Vieja (Old Castile, now part of Castilla y León).

▓ Alcalá de Henares

The people of Alcalá (pop. 165,000) pride themselves on their town's most distinguished offspring—Miguel de Cervantes—as well as their university's many famed alumni, among them Golden Age authors Francisco de Quevedo and Lope de Vega. Exceptional Renaissance architecture, especially the university's 16th-century facade and the Capilla de San Ildefonso, draw daytrippers from nearby Madrid.

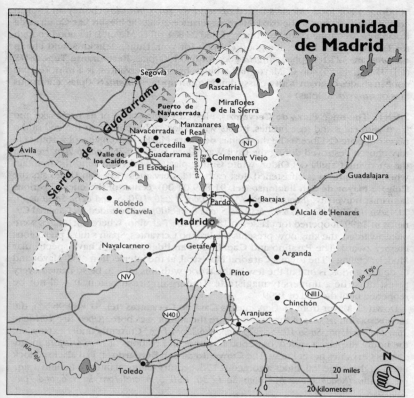

Comunidad de Madrid

ORIENTATION AND PRACTICAL INFORMATION Plaza de Cervantes is the main square. To get there from the train station, turn left as you exit and then bear right onto Po. Estación. After Vía Complutense (about 5 blocks down), take the first right onto C. Libreros and the plaza will be on your left.

The **train station** (tel. 91 563 02 02) is located on Po. Estación. Cercanías trains run from Madrid's Atocha and back about every 15 minutes (35min., round-trip 610 ptas). The **Continental-Auto bus station,** Av. Guadalajara, 5 (tel. 91 888 16 22), runs buses every 15 minutes between Alcalá and Madrid (35min., 250ptas). To reach the city center from the bus station, turn right on Av. Guadalajara and continue as it turns into C. Libreros. The helpful **tourist office,** Callejón de Santa María, 1 (tel. 91 889 26 94), at Pl. Cervantes, has a list of tourist sites and a detailed map of Alcalá. (Open daily June and Aug. 10am-2pm and 5-7:30pm; Mar.-May 10am-2pm and 4-6:30pm; July and Sept. Tu-Su 10am-2pm and 5-7:30pm.) **Banco Central Hispano,** Pl. Cervantes, 4, has an **ATM.** For an **ambulance,** dial 061. The **Red Cross,** Pl. Cervantes, 12 (tel. 91 883 60 63 or 91 881 40 83), has a 24-hour emergency line (tel. 91 522 22 22). The **police** answer at 91 881 92 63. Call 091 or 092 in an **emergency.** The **post office** (tel. 91 219 71 97) is located at Pl. Cervantes, 5, inside Banco Argentina (open M-F 8:30am-7pm, Sa 9:30am-1pm). The **postal code** varies by street between 28801 and 28807.

ACCOMMODATIONS AND FOOD Some of the least-expensive rooms lie within **Hostal Jacinto,** Po. Estación, 2, 2nd staircase, 1-D (tel. 91 889 14 32), three blocks from the train station. Firm beds, floral bedspreads, TVs, and an unusual selection of art grace this hostel. (Singles 2400ptas; doubles 4000ptas, with bath 4500ptas; triples

5000ptas.) For food, Alcalá's famed *almendras garrapiñadas* (honey and sugar-coated almonds) beg to be tried. More sustenance awaits at **Mesón Las Cuadras de Rocinante,** C. Carmen Calzado, 1 (tel. 91 880 08 88), off C. Mayor. If it's good enough for Don Quijote's horse, it's good enough for you. Huge, delicious, and cheap *raciones* are 325-1000ptas; *sangría* goes for 650-1300ptas. **Restaurante Topeca '75** (tel. 91 888 45 25), on C. Mayor half a block from Pl. Cervantes, is a mirrored bar done in shades of green with a classy dining room upstairs (*menú* 850ptas, enormous jugs of *sangría* 500ptas).

SIGHTS The huge **Plaza de Cervantes,** blessed with a statue of its namesake and filled with cafes and rose bushes, bursts with color each summer. At the end of the plaza opposite C. Libreros lie the **Ruinas de Santa María,** the remains of a 16th-century church destroyed during the Civil War. *(Open T-Su noon-2pm and 6-9pm. Free.)* In the surviving Capilla del Oidor, white Gothic plaster works surround the fountain where Cervantes was christened. Just east of Pl. Cervantes in Pl. San Diego sits the **Colegio Mayor de San Ildefonso** (tel. 91 889 04 00), center of the once illustrious humanist university. *(Required tour M-F 11:30am, 12:30, 1:30, 5, and 6pm; Sa-Su at 11, 11:45am, 12:30, 1:15, 2, 5, 5:45, 6:30, 7:15, and 8pm. 300ptas.)* Founded by Cardinal Cisneros in 1499, it opened for classes in 1508. In the **Parafino,** where doctorates were once awarded, the king now presents the Premio Cervantes, Spain's most prestigious literary award. The Parafino and **Capilla de San Ildefonso** both have spectacular Mudéjar ceilings. The town's **Catedral Magistral,** at the intersection of C. Mayor and C. de Escritorios, is one of the few in the world with this title; to be so named every priest must be a university magistrate. Undergoing restoration, it will not be reopened until the end of 1999.

Down C. Mayor from Pl. Cervantes is **Casa de Cervantes** (tel. 91 889 96 54), the reconstruction *in situ* of the house where the author was born. *(Open Tu-F 10:15am-2pm and 4-6:45pm, Sa-Su 10:15am-2pm and 4-6:30pm. Free.)* Currently under expansion, the house displays a variety of period furniture and editions of *Don Quijote* in languages Cervantes never knew. The **Convento de San Bernardo,** at Pl. Palacio a block north of the cathedral, hides a gorgeous 17th-century elliptical interior behind a simple facade. *(Required tour M-F 6pm, Sa 12:30, 1:30, 5, 6, and 7pm, Su 5, 6, and 7pm. 350ptas.)*

■ Sierra de Guadarrama

The Sierra de Guadarrama is a pine-covered mountain range halfway between Madrid and Segovia. Its dark geological shapes loom large in local imagination, as well as the local economy. With *La Mujer Muerta* (The Dead Woman) to the west, the *Sierra de la Maliciosa* (Mountain of the Evil Woman) to the east, and, between the two, the *Siete Picos* (Seven Peaks), it's a bit scary out there. Yet none of these portents of doom deter the influx of summer and winter visitors who come to hike and ski.

■ Cercedilla

Cercedilla sucks in city slickers yearning for fresh air. A picturesque town of Alpine chalets, Cercedilla's attractions change with the seasons: in summer, vacationers seek the cooler, more relaxed living of the Sierra; in winter, skiers crowd nearby resorts.

ORIENTATION AND PRACTICAL INFORMATION Cercedilla is the easiest town in the Sierras to reach by **train** as a daytrip from Madrid or Segovia. Frequent **buses** from Madrid drop you off in the center of town. To get to town from the station, go uphill, fork right at the top, and continue straight on at the train track (15-20min.). The **train station** (tel. 91 852 00 57) is at the base of the hill on C. Emilio Serrano across from a place to **rent bikes.** There's service to: Madrid (1½hr., over 30 per day, 475ptas); Segovia (45min., 9 per day, 290ptas); Los

Cotos (45min., 9 per day, 475ptas, round-trip 740 ptas); and Puerto de Navacerrada (30min., 9 per day, 130ptas, round-trip 450ptas). The **bus station,** Av. José
Antonio, 2 (tel. 91 852 02 39), is across the street and to the left of the Ayuntamiento. In an **emergency,** dial 091. The **police** are at 91 852 02 00 or 91 852 04
25. For **medical assistance,** call **Centro Médico** (tel. 91 852 04 97).

ACCOMMODATIONS AND FOOD
On Ctra. Las Dehesas, two **HI youth hostels** have
views of the Sierra, group meals, and lockout. The **Villa Castora (HI)** (tel. 91 852 03
34) is closest to the train station, about 1½km up Ctra. Las Dehesas on the left. The
pool is open in summer. Rooms have baths and the first floor has a terrace. (Doubles
2550ptas, over 26 3450ptas; quads 3800ptas, over 26 5200ptas. Breakfast included.
Reception daily 8am-10pm. Reservations 15 days in advance recommended.) The
same prices and hours can be found at **Las Dehesas (HI)** (tel. 91 852 01 35), along
with spartan but sunny and clean rooms, tucked back among the trees just beyond
the Agencia del Medio Ambiente on Ctra. las Dehesas. It's closer to the hiking trails
and farther from the highway. (Curfew midnight. Make reservations one week ahead.
HI cards, required at both, are available on the spot for 1800ptas.) **Camping** is strictly
controlled throughout the Sierra de Guadarrama and is no longer allowed within Cercedilla's town limits, which extend far beyond the town. A list of campsites is available at the Agencia del Medio Ambiente.

Supermarket **Maxcoop,** C. Docta Cañados, 2 (tel. 91 852 00 13), is in the town center off Av. Generalísimo (open M-Sa 9:30am-2pm and 5:30-9pm, Su 9:30am-2pm).
Hordes of bars peddle inexpensive *bocadillos* and *raciones* in the town proper.

HIKING AND SIGHTS
The **Consejería de Medio Ambiente,** Ctra. las Dehesas (tel.
852 22 13), a wooden chalet 2km up the road (30min. from the train station), functions as a tourist office and offers hiking info. The free leaflet *Sendas* (self-guided
trails) is especially good. From July to October, free guided tours of the valley depart
from the shelter across the road from the chalet at 10am (open daily 10am-6pm).
Most of the hiking action begins up the **Carretera las Dehesas,** beyond the intersection, uphill from the train station. A strenuous hike leads past the Hospital de Fuen-
frías to the meadow of Navarrulaque. The **Calzada Romana,** atop the Carretera,
offers hiking along an ancient Roman road that once connected Madrid to Segovia.

■ Puerto de Navacerrada and Los Cotos

A magnet for outdoorsy types year-round, **Puerto de Navacerrada** (tel. 91 262
1010) offers bland **skiing** in the winter and beautiful **hiking** in the summer—backpackers often use Navacerrada as a starting point to roam the surrounding peaks.
The ski season lasts from December to April; there are areas just for beginners
and competitions for the more advanced. For hiking, exit the train station, turn
left at the highway, and turn left again (off the road) at the large intersection
marking the pass. The dirt path leads uphill. Many hiking routes lead through the
pine forests; the **Vía de Schmidt** (or Smit) to the left leads back to Cercedilla. A
little **train** leaves for Navacerrada from the Cercedilla station. In addition, the
same Cercanías line that travels from Madrid to Cercedilla passes through Navacerrada a few stops later (1¾hr., 445ptas).

Los Cotos is another popular winter resort. Nearby **Rascafría** in Los Cotos has
two well-regarded ski stations: **Valdesqui** (tel. 91 515 5939) and **Valcotos** (tel. 91
435 15 48). Both are open daily in winter roughly 10am to 5pm. For more
detailed info on winter sports, consult the tourist office in Madrid or call the
resorts. Cercanías **trains** run from Madrid to Los Cotos, through Cercedilla and
Navacerrada (2hr., 475ptas).

■ San Lorenzo del Escorial

In the shadow of Felipe II's somber colossus El Escorial—half monastery and half mausoleum—the town of San Lorenzo is usually neglected by daytrippers from Madrid, although it is within easy striking distance. Arrive early and stay late to make the most of the Spanish "eighth wonder of the world," a fascinating, severe complex including a monastery, two palaces, a church to die for, two pantheons, a magnificent library, and innumerable artistic treasures. Above all, **don't come on a Monday**, when the whole complex and most of the town is closed.

ORIENTATION AND PRACTICAL INFORMATION

Autocares Herranz **bus** is the easiest way to travel between El Escorial and Madrid. Buses leave from the Moncloa Metro station and whisk travelers to El Escorial's **Plaza Virgen de Gracia.** The Autocares Herranz office, C. Reina Victoria, 3 (tel. 91 890 41 00, 91 890 41 22, or 91 890 41 25), and the bar/casino at C. Rey, 27, sell tickets to Madrid (1hr., M-F over 40 per day, Sa-Su 10 per day, round-trip 740ptas). Confirm your return ticket before boarding the bus for Madrid at the bar/casino. El Escorial's train station, on Ctra. Estación (tel. 91 890 07 14; RENFE info tel. 91 328 90 20), is 2km from town. Shuttle buses run frequently between the station and Pl. Virgen de Gracia. Trains run to Madrid-Atocha and Madrid-Chamartín (1hr., departs every 20min. 9am-3pm, round-trip 780ptas). From the bus stop exit left and turn right up C. Florida Blanca to get to the tourist office, C. Floridablanca, 10 (tel. 91 890 15 54), where you can pick up a map (open M-Sa 10am-6pm). The police, C. Gobernador, 2 (tel. 91 890 52 23), have an emergency line (tel. 091). Those with medical problems should call an ambulance at 91 896 11 11.

ACCOMMODATIONS, FOOD, AND FIESTAS

Although San Lorenzo makes an ideal daytrip, rooms fill up quickly in July and August and the situation gets dire during the festivals (Aug. 10-20). To reach the **Residencia Juvenil "El Escorial" (HI),** C. Residencia, 14 (tel. 91 890 59 24; fax 91 890 06 20), from C. Rey turn right at C. San Pedro Regalado, and go up the steps with the stone balls. When the road forks, take the middle path (C. San Milán); when it forks again, take C. Residencia (15min.). (Singles 1275ptas, over 26 1725ptas; doubles 2550ptas, over 26 3450ptas; quads 3800ptas, over 26 5200ptas. Breakfast included; lunch, and dinner available. HI card required. Reservations accepted.) From the bus stop to **Hostal Vasco,** Pl. Santiago, 11 (tel. 91 890 16 19), walk up C. Rey two blocks and turn right. The hostel has a terrace on the plaza. Some rooms sport small balconies and excellent views of the monastery. (Singles 3000ptas; doubles with shower 4500ptas, with full bath 4700ptas; triples 5700ptas. Breakfast 425ptas.) To sleep under the stars, go to **Camping Caravaning El Escorial** (tel. 91 890 24 12), 7km away on Ctra. de Guadarrama, km 14.8 al Escorial. (650ptas per person, per tent, and per car). The center's many cafes are busy throughout the day. Purchase *pan, queso, y vino* (bread, cheese, and wine) at the **Mercado Público,** C. Rey, 7, two blocks off C. Floridablanca (open M-Sa 9am-2pm and 6-9pm).

During the **Festivals of San Lorenzo** (Aug. 10-20), parades of giant figures line the streets and fireworks fill the sky. Folk dancing contests and horse-drawn cart parades mark **Romería a la Ermita de la Virgen de Gracia,** the second Sunday in September. Ceremonies are held in the forest of Herría.

EL ESCORIAL

Tel. 91 890 59 03, 91 890 59 04, or 91 866 02 38—it's that big. The entire El Escorial complex is open Apr.-Sept. Tu-Su 10am-7pm; Oct.-Mar. Tu-Su 10am-6pm. Last admission to palaces, pantheons, and museums is 1hr. before closing. Monastery 850ptas, students 350ptas, guided tour 950ptas, E.U. citizens free Wednesdays. Casitas 325ptas.

The Monastery

The **Monasterio de San Lorenzo del Escorial** was a gift from Felipe II to God, the people, and himself, commemorating his victory over the French at the battle of San Quintín in 1557. It was a jubilant occasion, but Felipe squelched any frivolous exuberance in the design of what was to be first his royal monastery and then his mausoleum. Juan Bautista de Toledo was commissioned to design the complex in 1561; when he died in 1567, Juan de Herrera inherited his mantle. Except for the Panteón Real and minor additional work, the monastery was finished in a speedy 21 years. According to tradition, Felipe oversaw much of the work from a chair-shaped rock 7km from the construction site. That stone is now known as **Silla de Felipe II** (Felipe's Chair) and still provides a regal view.

Considering the resources that Felipe II—son of Carlos I, who had ruled the most powerful empire in the world—commanded, the building is noteworthy for its austerity, symmetry, and simplicity; in Felipe's words, "majesty without ostentation." Four massive towers pin the corners, and the towers of the basilica that rise from the center are surmounted by a great dome, giving the ensemble a pyramidal shape. At Felipe II's behest, steep slate roofs were introduced from Flanders—the first of their kind in Spain. Slate spires lend grace to the grim structure, further mellowed by the glowing *piedra de Colmenar,* a stone hewn from nearby quarries. Variations of this Habsburg style (or *estilo herrerense*) of unadorned granite and red brick, slate roofs, and corner towers, appear throughout Spain—particularly in Madrid and Toledo.

To avoid the worst of the crowds, enter El Escorial by the traditional gateway on the west side (C. Floridablanca). You should encounter a collection of Flemish tapestries and paintings, including El Greco's *Martirio de San Mauricio y la Legión.* The adjacent **Museos de Arquitectura and Pintura** has an outstanding exhibition on the construction of El Escorial, comparing it to other related structures and with wooden models of 16th-century machinery and of the buildings themselves. The Museo de Pintura features masterpieces by Bosch, Dures, El Greco, Titian, Tintoretto, Velázquez, Zurbarán, Van Dyck, and others.

The **Palacio Real,** lined with 16th century *azulejos* (tiles) from Toledo, includes the **Salón del Trono** (Throne Room) and two **dwellings**—Felipe II's spartan 16th-century apartments and the more luxurious 18th-century rooms of Carlos III and Carlos IV. The Bourbon half is distinguished by the sumptuousness of its furniture and **tapestries.** Copies of works by Goya, El Greco, and Rubens done in intricate detail and brilliant wool yarn cover the walls. Pastoral images cover the **Puertas de Marguetería,** German doors made from 18 different types of trees—some from as far as America.

The long **Sala de Batallas** (Battle Room) links the two parts of the palace. A huge fresco here depicts some of Castile and Spain's greatest victories: Juan II's 1431 triumph over the Muslims at Higueruela (note the fleeing townsfolk), Felipe II's two successful expeditions to the Azores, and the battle of San Quintín. Downstairs, in the royal chambers, Felipe II's miniscule bed attests to his (relative) asceticism.

Death Royale

The **Panteón Real** was another brainchild of Felipe II. Although he didn't live to see it finished, he's buried here along with Carlos I and most of their royal descendants. Servants dumped bygone nobles in the small adjoining rooms so that the bodies could dry before being stuffed into their permanent tombs; drying time varied based on climate conditions and fat content (about 15-20 years).

The stairway and the crypt are elegantly adorned with black and red marble and jasper—a colorful combination that, combined with the gold cherubs and high ceiling, resembles a deathly *discoteca.* Of the 26 gray marble sarcophagi, 23 contain the remains of Spanish monarchs, and three are still empty. All the late Spanish kings except for Felipe V and Fernando VI are buried here—only those whose sons become monarchs can join the macabre club.

MADRID

The **Biblioteca** (library) on the second floor holds numerous priceless books and manuscripts despite several fires that have reduced the collection. Alfonso X's *Cantigas de Santa María*, the Book of Hours of the Catholic monarchs, Saint Teresa's manuscripts and diary, the gold-scrolled *Aureus Codex* (by German Emperor Conrad III, 1039), and an 11th-century *Commentary on the Apocalypse* by Beato de Liébana are just a small selection of the choice readings.

The lower main cloister is segues into the cool and magnificent **basílica.** Marble steps lead to an altar adorned by two groups of elegant sculptures by Pompeo Leoni. The figures on the left represent assorted relatives of Felipe II: parents Carlos I and Isabel, daughter María, and sisters María (Queen of Hungary) and Leonor (Queen of France). Those on the right depict Felipe II with three wives and his son Carlos. The **Coro Alto** (High Choir) has a magnificent ceiling fresco of heaven filled with choirs of angels. The **cloister** shines under Titian's fresco of the martyrdom of St. Lawrence.

Casitas

Commissioned by the Prince of Asturias, who later became Carlos IV, the **Casita del Príncipe** has a splendid collection of ornaments, including chandeliers, lamps, rugs, furniture, clocks, tapestries, china, and engraved oranges. The French roughed up the *casita* during the Napoleonic invasions, but many rooms were redecorated by Fernando VII in the then-popular Empire style. To get to the *casita,* follow the right side of the Ctra. Estación to the corner of the monastic complex, turn the corner, and fork left (15min.). Three kilometers toward Avila sits the simpler **Casita del Infante,** commissioned by Gabriel de Borbón, Carlos's brother, in the mid-16th century.

■ Near El Escorial: El Valle de los Caídos

Mass daily at 11am. Open in summer daily 9:30am-7pm; in winter 10am-6pm. 650ptas, seniors and students 250ptas, E.U. citizens free Wednesdays. Funicular to the cross 350ptas.

In a previously untouched valley of the Sierra de Guadarrama, 8km north of El Escorial, Franco built the overpowering monument of **Santa Cruz del Valle de los Caídos** (Valley of the Fallen) as a memorial to those who gave their lives in the Civil War. Naturally, the massive granite cross (150m tall and 46m wide) was meant to honor only those who died "serving *Dios* and *España,*" i.e. the fascist Nationalists. Apocalyptic tapestries line the cave-like **basilica,** which is also decorated with death-angels with swords and angry light fixtures. Behind the chapel walls lie a multitude (nine levels) of dead. The high altar is located directly underneath the mammoth cross with its mammoth statues, and is testimony to modern Spain's view of Franco; despite the fact that Franco lies buried underneath, there is no mention of his tomb in tourist literature. El Valle de los Caídos is accessible only via El Escorial. **Autocares Herranz** runs one **bus** to the monument (15min., leaves El Escorial Tu-Su 3:15pm and returns 5:30pm, round-trip plus admission 870ptas, funicular not included).

■ Aranjuez

Two rivers converge at the heart of green Aranjuez (pop. 48,900), a getaway for generations of Habsburg and Bourbon royalty, now a perfect place for more common folk to stroll through wondrous gardens and dazzling palaces. Famed for its delicious —though arguably overrated—strawberries and asparagus, Aranjuez makes a great daytrip from Madrid for treating the eyes and tummy.

PRACTICAL INFORMATION From the **train station** (tel. 91 891 02 02), it's a pleasant 10 minute walk to the town center. With your back to the station, turn right, walk to the end of the street, and then turn left onto tree-lined Ctra Toledo. Municipal bus L2 stops outside the station and on C. Stuart (M-F departs every 30min., Sa-Su departs every hr., 75ptas). **Trains** roll to: Madrid (45min., 46 *cercanías* per day to Atocha, 8 *regionales* to Chamartín, 480ptas); Toledo (30min., 8 per day,

320ptas); and Cuenca (2hr., 5 per day, 820ptas). AISA parks in Aranjuez's **bus station,** C. Infantas, 8 (tel. 91 891 01 83) and goes to Madrid's Estación Sur de Autobuses (45min., M-Sa 20-30 per day, Su 10 per day, 390ptas). For **taxis,** call 91 891 11 39. The **tourist office** (tel. 91 891 04 27), in Pl. San Antonio, supplies maps and brochures (open M-F 10am-2pm and 4-6pm). The **emergency** number is 091. Contact the municipal **police** at C. Infantas, 36 (tel. 91 891 00 22). The **post office** (tel. 91 891 11 32) is at C. Peña Redonda, 3, off C. Capitán Gómez (open M-F 8:30am-2:30pm, Sa 9:30am-1pm). The **postal code** is 28300.

ACCOMMODATIONS AND FOOD Accommodations in Aranjuez tend to be costly and luxurious. **Hostal Rusiñol,** C. San Antonio, 76 (tel./fax 91 891 01 55) at C. Stuart offers rooms with TVs (singles 1850ptas; doubles 2900ptas, with shower 4200ptas; Visa). **Camping Soto del Castillo** (tel. 91 891 13 95), across Río Tajo and off the highway to the right (2km from palace, watch for the signs), is a first-class site amid lush fields (600ptas per person, 500ptas per car, 525-650ptas per tent, electricity 500ptas).

The town's **strawberries** and **asparagus** have been famous for centuries. Nowadays, many of Aranjuez's strawberries are actually grown in other areas of Spain to be sold (to unsuspecting tourists) as *fresón con nata* (strawberries with cream 350-450ptas) at kiosks and cafes throughout town. Imitations are huge—real Aranjuez strawberries are on the smaller side. Aranjuez's restaurants, with views of the Tajo, are plentiful and expensive. For cheaper fare, hit **Bar-Restaurante Infantas** at the corner of C. Stuart. (*Bocadillos* 300-500ptas, *tapas* 125-300ptas, *pulpo a la gallega* 1100ptas. Open daily 6:30am-10pm.)

SIGHTS The Tajo and its tributary, the Jarama, water the palace's beautiful gardens (and also add undesirable humidity to the summer air). River walkways run from the **Jardín de la Isla,** which sprouts banana trees and a mythological statue garden, to the huge **Jardín del Príncipe,** originally created for the amusement of Carlos IV. (*Both gardens open daily June-Sept. 8am-8:30pm; Oct.-May 8am-6:30pm. Free.*) Inside the park, the **Casa del Labrador** (tel. 91 891 03 05), a mock laborer's cottage, is a treasure trove of Neoclassical decorative arts destined for courtly galas. It also houses the queen's private quarters, overflowing with such knick-knacks as Roman mosaics from Mérida and views of Madrid embroidered in silk. Also in the park, the **Casa de Marinos,** once the quarters of the Tajo's sailing squad, stores royal gondolas. (*Both casas open Tu-Su 10am-6:15pm. Casa del Labrador 500ptas, students 225ptas. Call for reservations. Casa de Marinos 325ptas, students 225ptas.*)

The stately **Palacio Real,** a marvel in white brick, was originally designed by Juan de Herrera—chief architect of El Escorial—under the aegis of Felipe II. (*Open June-Sept. Tu-Sa 10am-6:15pm; Oct.-May Tu-Sa 10am-5:15pm. Compulsory 30min. tour in Spanish. 500ptas, students 250ptas. Free on Wednesdays for EU citizens.*) In the years to come, both Felipe VI and Carlos III had their minions enlarge and embellish the palace. Now, room after opulent room displays Vatican mosaic paintings in marble, crystal chandeliers and mirrors from La Granja. Flemish tapestries and ornate French clocks also adorn the palace. The Oriental porcelain room, with 3-D wallpaper and Rococo ceramic work, and the Mozarabic smoking room, a striking reminder of the Alhambra palace, are particularly remarkable.

■ Near Aranjuez: Chinchón

Ordinarily dusty and deserted, tiny, tranquil **Chinchón** lies 45 minutes away by bus from Aranjuez. Considered an enchanting visit, the town is a favorite weekend getaway for Spanish tourists who relax by the picturesque **Plaza Mayor** and imbibe the local *anís,* a savory liquor famed in the region. Chinchón also boasts a castle, a frescoed parador, a clocktower, and charming views.

Although Chinchón is perhaps best as a half-day excursion, travelers looking to stay the night can check into dreamy **Hostal Chinchón,** C. José Antonio, 12 (tel. 91 893 53 98; fax 91 894 01 08). With a summer pool, garden, and rooms overlooking the Pl. Mayor, the hostel is a great escape for tired *madrileños* (singles with bath 4000ptas; doubles with bath 6000ptas; Visa, MC). Farther up C. José Antonio is **Bar-Restaurante Belle Epoque,** serving Spanish dishes at low prices. **Buses** run to Chinchón four times a day on weekdays and twice on Saturdays, but beware—only two buses return daily. The **MOSAMO** bus (tel. 91 891 39 37) leaves Aranjuez on C. Almíbar near the Pl. de Toros (200ptas). The bus schedule and a map of Chinchón are available at the Aranjuez tourist office; Chinchón still does not have one.

Strawberries and Steam

Spain's second locomotive, which first ran from Madrid to Aranjuez on February 9, 1851, was dubbed the **strawberry train.** Built during the reign of Isabel II, it became all the rage, carting Aranjuez strawberries to Madrid during the week and *madrileños* to Aranjuez on weekends. For the past 10 years, tourists have relived those bygone days in an exact replica of that first steam train, complete with officious costumed porters. (For info call 902 22 88 22. Train runs Apr. 18-Oct. 18 Sa-Su and holidays only. Leaves from Madrid-Atocha at 10am, arrives in Aranjuez an hour later. Returns at 7:30pm. Round-trip fare, including admission to all sights and plenty of strawberries, 3100ptas, children 1900ptas.)

MADRID

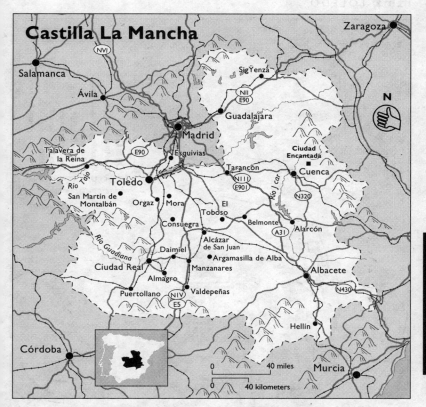

Castilla La Mancha

Cervantes chose to set Don Quijote's adventures in La Mancha (*manxa* is Arabic for parched earth) to evoke a cultural and material backwater. No overworked fantasy of the Knight of the Sad Countenance is needed to transform the austere beauty of this battered, windswept plateau. Its tumultuous history, gloomy medieval fortresses, arid plains, and awesome crags provide grist for the imagination. The 500 castles that lend the region its name served as models for Disney World's medieval castle.

Long, long ago, this area was the battleground for conflicts between Christians and Muslims. The Christians captured Toledo in 1085 by plowing through Magerit, which would later be called Madrid. As Christian forces pranced into Muslim Spain (Toledo was captured in 1085), La Mancha became the domain of the military orders Santiago, Calatrava, Montesa, and San Juan, which were modeled after crusading institutions such as the Knights Templar, a society of powerful warrior-monks. In the 14th and 15th centuries, the region bore fearsome struggles between the kingdoms of Castilla and Aragón. All this warring left the region looking like the mess left over from a child's toy battleground: castles, fortresses, churches, walls, and ramparts scattered hither and yon, with a few windmills thrown in for good measure.

The region is Spain's largest wine-producing area (Valdepeñas and Manzanares are common table wines), and its abundant olive groves and excellent hunting provide for many local repasts. Stews, roast meats, and game are *manchego* staples. *Gazpacho manchego,* a hearty stew of rabbit, lamb, chicken, and pork, and *queso manchego,* Castile's beloved cheese, are indigenous specialties.

CASTILLA LA MANCHA

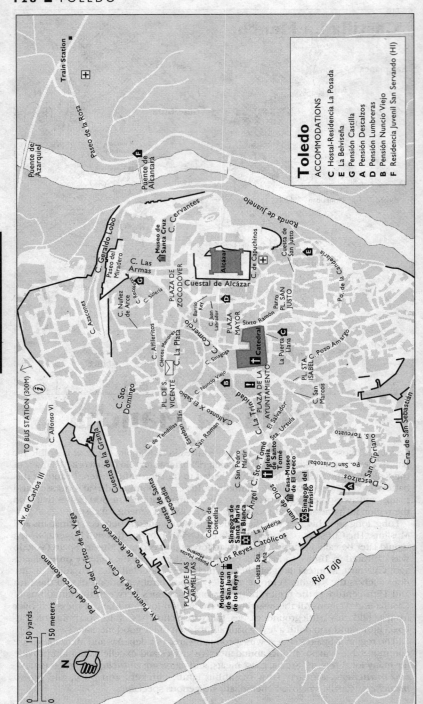

Toledo

ACCOMMODATIONS

C Hostal-Residencia La Posada
E La Belviseña
G Pensión Castilla
A Pensión Descalzos
D Pensión Lumbreras
B Pensión Nuncio Viejo
F Residencia Juvenil San Servando (HI)

🗺️ *HIGHLIGHTS OF CASTILLA LA MANCHA*

- **Toledo,** glorious former capital of Holy Roman, Visigothic, and Muslim empires.
- **Cuenca's** famed **casas colgadas** (hanging houses; see p. 135).

■ Toledo

For Cervantes, Toledo was a "rocky gravity, glory of Spain and light of her cities." To Cossío, it was "the most brilliant and evocative summary of Spain's history." Successively a Roman settlement, capital of the Visigoth kingdom, stronghold of the Emirate of Córdoba, and imperial city under Carlos V, Toledo (pop. 65,000) may be marred by armies of tourists and caravans of kitsch, but it remains a treasure-trove of Spanish culture. Or, stated a little less optimistically in the words of another novelist-playwright, Benito Pérez Galdos, Toledo is a "town with a great history, but only a history." Emblematic of a past *convivencia,* when Spain's three religions peacefully coexisted, are the numerous churches, synagogues, and mosques that share twisting alleyways. Visitors pay monetary homage to Toledo's damascene swords and knives, colorful pottery, and almond-paste marzipan. Many streets clank with junky gift shops, selling everything from miniature suits of armor to tacky ceramic pigs. Accordingly, prolonged stays and winter visits afford a more authentic sense of Toledo.

ORIENTATION AND PRACTICAL INFORMATION

Toledo is an almost unconquerable maze of narrow streets where pedestrians and cars battle for sovereignty. To get to **Plaza de Zocodóver** in the town center, take bus #5 or 6 (115ptas) from the stop to the right after you exit the **train station** or from the stop directly outside the **bus station.** Alternatively, it's not a bad walk from either station, albeit completely unshaded and mostly uphill (20-30min.). From the bus station, exit on the side with trees, walk right, and take the first right along the steep highway that surrounds the city. From the train station, *do not* take the big bridge across the Tajo; it's a long and unpleasant route. Instead, turn right leaving the station and follow the left fork uphill to a smaller bridge, **Puente de Alcántara.** Cross the bridge to the *puente's* stone staircase (through a set of arches); after climbing the stairs, turn left and continue upwards, veering right at C. Cervantes and directly to Pl. Zocodóver. Despite the well-labeled streets and the map dispensed by the tourist office, **you will get lost** in Toledo; the city could not be more labyrinthine if it contained an actual Minotaur. Accept it as part of the package; it's the best way to discover the town's beauty.

Trains: Po. de la Rosa, 2 (tel. 925 22 30 99), in a simply exquisite neo-Mudéjar building opposite the Puente de Azarquiel. Its only line runs to Madrid's Atocha (1½hr., 7-9 per day M-F 7am-9pm, Sa-Su 8:30am-9pm, 630ptas), passing through Aranjuez (35min., 320ptas). To get elsewhere, transfer in Madrid or Aranjuez.

Buses: (tel. 925 21 58 50), 5min. from the city gate (from Pl. Zocodóver, take C. Armas). Serviced by various companies. To Madrid (1½hr., departs every 30min., M-Sa 5:30am-10pm, Su 8:30am-11:30pm, 580ptas) and Cuenca (3hr., departs M-F at 5:30pm, 1300ptas). Call **SAMAR** for buses to Valencia (tel. 925 22 39 15 or 925 22 12 17).

Public Transportation: Buses 115ptas. #5 and 6 stop to the right of the train station and directly outside the bus station and head straight to Pl. Zocodóver. The stop in Pl. Zocodóver is on C. Cuesta del Alcázar.

Taxis: Call 925 25 50 50.

Car Rental: Avis (tel. 925 21 45 35 or 925 21 57 94), on C. Nancio González, and **Hertz** (tel. 925 25 38 90), on Po. de la Rosa near the train station.

Tourist Office: (tel. 925 22 08 43; fax 925 25 26 48), just outside the Puerta Nueva de Bisagra, on the north side of town. From Pl. Zocodóver, take C. Armas, the main street with many name changes, downhill and through the gates (Puertas de Bisagra); the office is across the intersection (15min.). From the train station, turn right and take the busy right-hand fork across the bridge (Puente de Azarquiel); follow the city walls until you reach the plaza. The office is across the road, outside the walls. Open M-F 9am-6pm (until 7pm in summer), Sa 9am-7pm, Su 9am-3pm.

Luggage Storage: At the bus station (100-200ptas) and train station (400ptas).

Emergency: Dial 092. **Police:** (tel. 925 21 34 00) Avda. Portugal.

Pharmacy: (tel. 925 22 17 68) on Pl. Zocodóver. List of late-night pharmacies posted. Open daily 9:30am-2pm and 5-8pm.

Hospital: Hospital Virgen de la Salud (tel. 925 26 92 00), toward the Ávila highway on Av. Barber.

Internet Access: Scorpions (tel. 925 21 25 56), on Pintor Matías Moreno next to Monasterio San Juan de los Reyes, has 2 space-age computers for surfing or email. 7min. runs 100ptas. Open M-F 10am-2:30am, Sa-Su noon-2:30am. Visa, MC, AmEx.

Post Office: C. Plata, 1 (tel. 925 22 36 11), off Pl. Zocodóver via C. Comercio and then C. Toledo. All services, including *Lista de Correos*. Open M-F 8:30am-9pm, Sa 9am-2pm. **Postal Code:** 45070.

ACCOMMODATIONS AND CAMPING

Toledo is chock-full of accommodations, but finding a bed during the summer, especially on weekends, can be a hassle. The tourist office provides an invaluable list of *hoteles, hostales,* and *pensiones.*

Residencia Juvenil San Servando (HI), Castillo San Servando (tel. 925 22 45 54), uphill from the train station (10min.). Cross the street from the station, turn left and immediately right up Callejón del Hospital. When the steps reach a road, turn right and then right again following the signs to Hospital Provincial. The steep walk uphill just past the hospital leads to a 14th-century castle—that's not for you; you're going to the annex. If alone at night, take a cab. 48 rooms, each with 4 bunk beds, some with views. Dorms 1100ptas, over 26 1350ptas. No lockers. Laundry 500ptas. Pool in summer, TV room. Reception 7am-11:50pm. Curfew 11:50pm. No reservations accepted. Closed various times throughout the year, so call ahead.

Pensión Nuncio Viejo, C. Nuncio Viejo, 19, 3rd fl. (tel. 925 22 81 78), on a street leading off the cathedral. Sweet-smelling entrance by a flower shop. Only 6 rooms—you'll feel like one of the family. Rooms are a bit cramped and dim, but your new mom is a great cook. Singles 1300ptas; doubles 2900ptas, with bath 3200ptas. Breakfast 225ptas. Lunch and dinner 850ptas each. TV room.

Pensión Castilla, C. Recoletos, 6 (tel. 925 25 63 18), up an alley off C. Armas. Comfortable and spacious doubles make you feel right at home, as does owner Teresa. Singles 2200ptas; doubles with bath 3900ptas.

Pensión Descalzos, C. Descalzos, 30 (tel. 925 22 28 88), down the steps off Po. San Cristóbal or down the Bajada Descalzos near the Casa del Greco. A chill abode with views of San Martín Bridge (for extra *pesetas*). Singles 2500ptas; doubles 3500ptas, with bath or shower 5600ptas; triples with bath 7290ptas. Low season: 2200ptas; 3200ptas; 5400ptas; 7560ptas. Rooms with bath have TVs. Closed Feb. Visa, MC.

La Belviseña, Cuesta del Can, 5 (tel. 925 22 00 67). From Pl. Zocodóver, walk down Cuesta Carlos V (a.k.a. Cuesta del Alcázar), past the Alcázar and through the small plaza beyond. Take C. Gran Moscardo, the street left of the hotel, and turn right on C. Soledad. Veer right and go left on C. San Miguel until you get to C. San Justo. Turn left and go uphill. Cuesta del Can is on the right. The cheapest *pensión* in Toledo. The Ritz it's not, but it's still clean. Singles 1200ptas; doubles 2300ptas.

Hostal-Residencia la Posada, Callejón de San Pedro, 2 (tel. 925 21 47 34), near the cathedral's Puerta Llana. Simple and clean (take a sniff) with pink curtains to boot. Singles 2000ptas; doubles 3000ptas; triples 4000ptas, with bath 5000ptas. Breakfast 200ptas. Lunch *menú* 800ptas.

Camping: Camping El Greco (tel. 925 22 00 90), 1.5km from town on the road away from Madrid (C-502). Bus #7 (from Pl. Zocodóver) stops at the entrance. Wooded and shady 1st-class site between the Tajo and an olive grove. 575ptas per person (children 475ptas), 590ptas per tent, 550ptas per car. 7% IVA not included. **Circo Romano,** Av. Carlos III, 19 (tel. 925 22 04 42). 2nd-class site. Closer but noisier. 575ptas per person (children 475ptas), 590ptas per tent, 550ptas per car.

CASTILLA LA MANCHA

FOOD

Toledo grinds almonds into marzipan delights of every shape and size, from colorful fruity nuggets to half-moon cookies; *pastelerías* beckon on every corner. If your pocket allows, dining out in Toledo can be an ecstatic culinary experience (*menús* 1400-1600ptas). Regional specialties include *perdiz* (fowl), *cuchifritos* (a melange of sheep, eggs, tomato, and white wine), *venado* (venison), and *carcamusas* (mystery meat). Buy fresh fruit and basics at **Frutería-Pan,** C. Real Arrabal, opposite the tourist office (open daily 9am-10pm). The smelly **mercado** (market) is in Pl. Mayor, behind the cathedral (open M-Sa 8:30am-2pm). **Udaco** is a mini-market on Pl. San Justo, southeast of the cathedral, down C. Sixto R. Parro from Puerta Llana (open M-F 8am-2pm and 5-9pm, Sa 9am-2pm).

Restaurante Armiño, C. Tendillas, 8 (tel. 925 22 22 73). From C. Comercio, near the cathedral, head up C. Nuncio Viejo past the plaza. At the intersection, steer left and make an immediate right (watch for the Pizzeria sign). Serves Spanish *menús* for lunch and Italian specialties for dinner. A vegetarian's delight. *Menú* 875ptas. Pasta 750-800ptas. Pizza 900ptas. A/C. Open daily 1-5pm and 8pm-midnight. Visa, MC.

Pastucci, C. Sinagoga, 10 (tel. 925 21 48 66). From Pl. Zocodóver take C. Comercio. Keep to the right of the Lacoste store and turn right through an underpass. A colorful and popular Italian eatery. Pizza priced by size (900-2300ptas). Pasta 850-945ptas. Salads 600-950ptas. Open daily noon-midnight. Visa, MC.

Restaurante El Zoco, C. Barrio Rey, 1 (tel. 925 22 20 51), off Pl. Zocodóver. Attractive and reasonably priced and your countrymen know it! Expect to hear English at lunch. *Menú* 800-1500ptas. A/C. Open daily 1:30-4pm and 8-10:30pm.

SIGHTS

Toledo has an excellent collection of museums, churches, synagogues, and mosques, making the city almost impossible to see in just one day. Within the city's fortified walls, attributed to the 7th-century King Wamba, Toledo's major attractions form a belt around its fat middle. An east-west tour, beginning in Pl. Zocodóver, is mostly downhill. Be aware that most sights are closed on Mondays.

Catedral

In the city center, southwest of Pl. Zocodóver. **Open** *July-Aug. M-Sa 10:30am-1pm and 3:30-7pm, Su 10am-1:30pm and 4-7pm; Sept-June M-Sa 10:30am-1pm and 3:30-6pm, Su 10am-1:30pm and 4-6pm. Sala Capitular, Capilla del Rey, tesoro, coro, and Sacristía 500ptas.* **Buy tickets** *at the store, open daily 8am-8pm, opposite the entrance.*

Built between 1226 and 1498, the grandiose cathedral, with five naves, delicate stained glass, and ostentation throughout, is the seat of the Primate of Spain. Noteworthy pieces are the 14th-century Gothic **Virgen Blanca** by the entrance and, above all, Narciso Tomés's **Transparente** (1732), a Spanish Baroque whirlpool of architecture, sculpture, and painting showing the way to heaven. In the **Capilla Mayor,** the enormous Gothic altarpiece stretches to the ceiling. Cardinal Mendoza, private confessor to a queen and a Head Inquisitor, lies dead on the left. Beneath the dome is the **Capilla Mozárabe,** the only venue where the ancient Visigoth mass (in Mozarabic) is still held. The **tesoro** flaunts worldly accoutrements, including a 400-pound, 16th-century gold monstrance lugged through the streets during the annual Corpus Christi procession. The **Sacristía** holds 18 El Grecos and two Van Dycks, along with the portraits of every archbishop of Toledo that hang in the **Sala Capitular.**

Alcázar

Open *Tu-Su 10am-2pm and 4-6pm. 125ptas. Wednesdays free for EU citizens.*

South and uphill from Pl. Zocodóver sits the **Alcázar,** Toledo's most formidable landmark. The site was a stronghold of Visigoths, Muslims, and Christians, who each rebuilt it in their own style. Little remains of Carlos V's 16th-century structure; the building was reduced to rubble during the Civil War as besieged Fascist troops held out against an acute Republican bombardment. Don't miss the room where the father-son drama of the Moscardós took place—it records Colonel Moscardó's refusal to surrender the Alcázar, even at the cost of losing his son. You can also visit the dark, windowless basement refuge where over five hundred civilians hid during the siege. The rooms above ground are now a nationalistic military museum with armor, swords, guns, knives…and dried plants.

El Greco

Greek painter Doménikos Theotokópoulos (a.k.a. El Greco) lived most of his life in Toledo, churning out eerie canvases and portraits of willowy saints. Many of his works are displayed throughout town, but the majority of his masterpieces have long since been carted off to the Prado and elsewhere. On the west side of town the **Iglesia de Santo Tomé** houses El Greco's famous *El entierro del Conde de Orgaz (Burial of Count Orgaz)*. *(Open Tu-Sa 10am-6:45pm. 150ptas.)* The stark figure staring out from the back is El Greco himself, and the boy is his son, Jorge Manuel, who built Toledo's city hall. Downhill and to the left lies the **Casa Museo de El Greco**, C. Levi, 3. *(Open Tu-Sa 10am-2pm and 4-6pm, Su 10am-2pm. 200ptas, students free. Sa and Su afternoons free.)* This oddly arranged museum has 19 works by El Greco, including a copy of the *Vista y plano de Toledo (Landscape of Toledo)*. Outside handsome Puerta Nueva de Bisagra on the way to Madrid, 16th-century **Hospital Tavera** displays five El Grecos and some Titians. *(Open daily 10:30am-1:30pm and 3:30-6pm; 500ptas.)* The impressive and untouristed **Museo de Santa Cruz** (1504), C. Cervantes, 3 (tel. 925 22 14 02), off Pl. Zocodóver, exhibits a handful of El Grecos in its eclectic art collection (1504). *(Open M-Sa 10am-6pm, Su 10am-2pm. 200ptas, students 100ptas.)* Oddly enough, it also holds the remains from archaeological digs throughout Toledo province.

The Old Jewish Quarter

Samuel Ha-Leví, diplomat and treasurer to Pedro el Cruel, built the **Sinagoga del Tránsito** (1366). Its simple exterior hides an extraordinarily ornate sanctuary with Mudéjar plasterwork and an *artesonado* (intricately designed wood) ceiling. The walls are crawling with Hebrew inscriptions, mostly taken from psalms. Inside, the **Museo Sefardí** (Jews of Spanish descent) is packed with artifacts, including a torah (parts of which are over 400 years old) and a beautiful set of Sephardic wedding costumes. *(Open Tu-Sa 10am-1:45pm and 4-5:45pm, Su 10am-1:45pm. 400ptas, students and under 18 200ptas. Free Sa after 4pm and Su.)* **Sinagoga de Santa María la Blanca** (1180), down the street to the right, was originally built to be a mosque, but was then purchased by Jews, used as the city's principle synagogue, and in 1492 was converted into a church. *(Open 10am-1:45pm and 3:45-5:45pm. 150ptas.)* Now secular, the Moorish arches and a tranquil garden make a welcome retreat.

Elsewhere

At the far western bulge of the city, with views of the surrounding hills and Río Tajo, stands the Franciscan **Monasterio de San Juan de los Reyes** (tel. 925 22 38 02), commissioned by Isabel and Fernando to commemorate their victory over the Portuguese in the Battle of Toro (1476). *(Open daily 10am-1:45pm and 2:30-6:45pm; closes 1hr. earlier in winter. 150ptas.)* The light-filled cloister, covered with the initial of the *Reyes Católicos*, mixes Gothic and Mudéjar architecture, in contrast to the super-Gothic Platteresque church interior. The Catholic monarchs had planned to use the church as their burial place but changed their minds after their victory over Granada.

Toledo was the seat of Visigoth rule and culture for three centuries prior to the 711 Muslim invasion. The **Museo del Taller del Moro**, on C. Bulas near Iglesia de Santo Tomé, features outstanding woodwork, plasterwork, and tiles. The exhibits at the **Museo de los Concilios y de la Cultura Visigótica**, C. San Clemente, 4 (tel. 925 22 18 72), pale in comparison to their beautiful setting in a 13th-century Mudéjar church. *(Both open Tu-Sa 10am-2pm and 4-6:30pm, Su 10am-2pm. 100ptas, students 50ptas.)*

Tolerance in Sepharad

Toledo fell to Alfonso VI in 1085, and Jewish culture blossomed under his tolerant reign. Jewish poets (including Yehuda Ha-Leví), doctors, translators, and bankers rose to prominence, even intermarrying with noble Christian families and serving in royal courts. This period of *toledancia*—a pun on Toledo and tolerance—would not last, however. Mounting nationalism and anti-semitism led to the persecution, forced conversion, expulsion, and, at times, killing of Jews during the 1492 Inquisition. Today, only two of eight synagogues remain in what was once Spain's (Sepharad in Hebrew) largest Jewish community. Jews of *toledano* descent, some of whom still speak *Ladino*, a variation on 15th-century Spanish, have returned to visit in recent years. An American Jewish woman made headlines when she entered a Toledo home with the same key her ancestors had used 500 years ago.

ENTERTAINMENT

The best area for the city's trademark souvenirs is **Calle de San Juan de Dios**, by the Iglesia de Santo Tomé. The shop owners are aggressive but willing to haggle. The town goes crazy for **Corpus Christi**, celebrated the eighth Sunday after Easter—citizens parade through the streets with the cathedral's weighty gold monstrance. Most spots cater to tourists—local nightlife tends to disappear down the following streets:

Calle de Santa Fe, east of Pl. Zocodóver, through the arch. Filled to the brim with beer and youth. Look for **Bar Black and Blue** (tel. 925 22 21 11), a busy blues bar, on the small Pl. Santiago Caballeros off C. Cervantes. Beer 300ptas. Performances Th 10:30pm. No cover. Open until 3am.

Calle de la Sillería and **Calle de los Alfileritos**, west of Pl. Zocodóver. Twenty-something crowd. Home to more upscale bars and clubs, including **Bar La Abadía**, Nuñez de Arce, 5 (tel. 925 25 11 40), whose cavernous basement makes for great hide-and-seek. Open M-Th 8am-midnight, F-Su noon-midnight.

Centro Comercial Miradero, downhill on C. Armas. **Zaida** is a perennial hot spot for dancing.

■ Near Toledo

Cervantes freaks come to **La Mancha** to follow his footsteps and those of his most famous creations, Don Quijote and the faithful Sancho Panza. Cervantes met and married Catalina de Palacios in the main church in **Esquivias** in 1584. He supposedly began writing his masterpiece while imprisoned in the **Cueva del Medrano**, in the town of **Argamasilla de Alba**. It was in **El Toboso**, 100km southeast of Toledo, that Quijote fell nobly in love with Dulcinea. El Toboso holds the **Museo Cervantino**, which displays a fine collection of Cervantes ephemera, including translations of *Don Quijote* into 30 different languages.

A hop, skip, and a jump south of Toledo lands you at the small but fierce **San Martín de Montalbán**, home to an amazing castle poised on an enormous pile of gray granite rocks and leaning out over an abysmal gorge of the River Torión. It was first a Visigothic, then an Arab, fortress and later an enclave of the cabalistic Knights Templar. Legend has it that somewhere inside its walls lies a cache of buried treasure.

Of all Manchegan villages, tiny **Consuegra** provides perhaps the most raw material for an evocation of Quijote's world. The **castle**, called the *Cresteria Manchega* by locals, was a Roman, then Arab, then Christian fortress. The castle keeps erratic hours, but the view of the surrounding plains justifies a climb anytime. El Cid's only son, Diego, died in the stable; you can visit a lavish monument in his honor near the Ayuntamiento. Diminutive Consuegra remarkably also holds a palace, a Franciscan convent, and a Carmelite monastery. Learn more at the **Museo de Consuegra** (tel. 925 47 37 31), next to the Ayuntamiento (museum hours not fixed; 100ptas). Plan around inconvenient bus departure times so you don't spend the night where you only wanted to stay several hours. For greater flexibility, rent a car and use Toledo as a base for excursions into this region. **Samar buses** (tel. 925 22 39 15) depart from the Toledo bus station (10 per day, 535ptas). Buses return to Toledo from C. Castilla de la Mancha (7 per day). Purchase tickets from the driver when returning from Consuegra; when coming from Toledo, purchase them at the bus ticket office.

■ Almagro

Classical theater buffs and city slickers seeking solace will find sleepy Almagro (pop. 9000) appealing. A famed theater festival attracts hundreds of visitors in July, while cobble-stoned streets, whitewashed houses, and immaculate monuments, dating from the 16th century, attract people year-round. Infrequent bus and train services, however, pose a challenge to potential visitors.

ORIENTATION AND PRACTICAL INFORMATION   The **train station** (tel. 926 86 02 76) awaits at the end of the tree-lined Po. Estación. To get from the station to the **Plaza Mayor,** walk down Po. Estación and turn left onto C. Rondo de Calatrava (a sign points to the **Centro Urbano**); turn right onto C. Madre de Dios (another Centro Urbano sign), which becomes C. Fería and leads to the plaza (10min.). Trains run to: Madrid-Atocha (2½hr., 1 per day, 1760ptas); Ciudad Real (15min., 4 per day, 245ptas); Alcázar de San Juan (1hr., 4 per day, 695ptas); Aranjuez (2hr., 2 per day, 1355ptas). Change at Aranjuez, Ciudad Real, or Alcázar de San Juan for connections to other cities. **Buses** (tel. 926 86 02 50) stop at the brick building, which doubles as a bar, at the far end of Ejido de Calatrava across from the Hospedería Municipal. To get to Pl. Mayor, turn left on C. Madre de Dios (follow the sign to the Centro Urbano) and take the road until the plaza (5 min.). **Aisa** buses leave for Madrid (2¼hr., 3 per day, 1505ptas) and Ciudad Real (20min., 6 per day, 230ptas), the latter for connections to Toledo. **Sepulvedena** goes to Jaén on weekdays (2hr., departs 9:45am, 1455ptas). All service is less frequent or non-existent on weekends, so check the bus schedule ahead of time. The bus station is closed on Sundays. Some try **hitching** to Valdepeñas (36km), where buses to Andalucía down highway Nacional IV are more common.

The **tourist office,** C. Bernardas, 2 (tel. 926 86 07 17), sits inside the Palacio del Conde de Valdeparaíso. From Pl. Mayor, take a right on C. Mayor de Carnicerías and another right on C. Bernardas. They have a helpful brochure with a map and descriptions of all the sights in Almagro. (Open Tu-F 10am-2pm and 5-8pm, Sa 10am-2pm and 5-7pm; holidays 11am-2pm.) A **Banco Central Hispano** (tel. 926 86 00 04) sits alongside Pl. Mayor. (Open May-Sept. M-F 8:30am-2:30pm; Oct.-Apr. M-F 8:30am-2:30pm, Sa 8:30am-1pm.) The **police** (tel. 926 86 00 33) survey Almagro from the Ayuntamiento in Pl. Mayor. Dial 006 in an **emergency. Centro de Salud (health clinic),** C. Mayor de Carnicerías, 11 (tel. 926 86 10 26 or 926 88 20 16), heals on the site of a 10th-century jail. The **post office** (tel. 926 86 00 52) is on C. Mayor de Carnicerías (open M-F 8:30am-2:30pm, Sa 9am-1pm). The **postal code** is 13270.

ACCOMMODATIONS AND FOOD   The dark hallways and ancient furnishings of **Hospedería Municipal de Almagro,** Ejido de Calatrava, s/n (tel. 926 88 20 87; fax 926 88 21 22), testify to the massive building's 500-year history. Firm beds, telephones, and TVs provide modern creature comforts. (Singles with bath 2500ptas; doubles with shower 3500ptas, with full bath 4000ptas. Breakfast 250ptas. Lunch and dinner 1100ptas each. Call ahead for reservations. For the theater festival in July, when prices rise significantly, make reservations 2-3 months in advance.) The Plaza Mayor has several *terrazas* with *menús* featuring typical Manchegan dishes. One such establishment is the lively **Restaurante Airén** (tel. 926 88 26 56). The *menús* start at 1200ptas, but it's hard to resist extra dishes when the bartender offers them as "something my Grandma made."

SIGHTS AND ENTERTAINMENT Every July, Spain's most prestigious theater companies and players from around the globe descend on Almagro for the **Festival Internacional de Teatro Clásico de Almagro.** Daily performances of Spanish and international theater classics take place in the Corral de Comedias, the Hospital de San Juan de Dios, and the Claustro de los Domínicos. The **box office** (tel. 926 86 14 12) is at the Teatro municipal. *(Open Tu 11am-2pm. Shows at 10:45pm. Tickets 1600-2300ptas, Tuesdays ½-price. Free outdoor performances in Pl. Mayor. Tickets should be purchased before the festival. Call 926 902 38 33 for credit card purchase.)*

In the 13th century, tiny Almagro became the seat of the vast and powerful Orden de Calatrava, the oldest fraternity of monks-turned-soldiers that fueled the *Reconquista.* Connected to the Hospedería Municipal (see **Accommodations and Food,** above) is the **Convento de la Asunción de Calatrava,** home of the order. Its cloistered courtyard was built in 1519; renovations are still underway and no set open hours exist. Visit in the morning, and one of the Dominican fathers, who own the convent, can admit you.

The centerpiece of Almagro is its **Plaza Mayor,** whose long balconies with green window frames are characteristic of Fugger-style architecture. The Fuggers were a 16th-century family of German bankers who lent money to the monks of Calatrava and Emperor Carlos V. The **Fugger house,** C. Arzobispo, 6, is also the Universidad Popular and is open to the public. From Pl. Mayor, take C. Fería and make a left onto C. Arzobispo. The other hometown hero is, of course, Diego de Almagro, hailed as the conquistador of Chile, but less patriotic accounts reveal that he was executed for conspiracy against fellow conquistador Francisco Pizarro.

In the great Pl. Mayor stands the **Corral de Comedias,** an open-air multilevel theater resembling Shakespeare's Globe. *(Open Tu-F 10am-2pm and 5-8pm, Sa 10am-2pm and 5-7pm, Su 11am-2pm and 5-7pm.)* This theater is the only one left intact from the Golden Age *(Siglo de Oro)* of Spanish drama. Here, performers act out the works of Cervantes and Lope de Vega, once fierce literary rivals. Directly across the plaza from the *corral* and through some arches, the new **Museo del Teatro** displays the history of Spanish drama. *(Open Tu-F 10am-2pm and 5-8pm, Sa 10am-2pm and 5-7pm, Su 11am-2pm. 400ptas, students 200ptas, seniors and under 18 free. Sa afternoons and Su mornings free.)* Your ticket to the museum allows access to the Corral de Comedias and the **Teatro Municipal** (up C. San Agustín, from the plaza on the right), a crimson building that houses a renovated theater. Inside there's a collection of elaborate costumes.

▓ Cuenca

Cuenca (pop. 43,500) is up there, perched sky-high due to a lack of space. Atop a hill, the vertical city overlooks the two rivers that confine it and the stunning rock formations those rivers created. These natural boundaries have served the city well; Muslims and then Christians settled in Cuenca because it was nearly impenetrable. Cuenca strains against these borders, forcing much of the city's modern commercial life to spill down the hill into New Cuenca. The enchanting old city, however, safeguards most of Cuenca's unique charm, including the famed *casas colgadas* (hanging houses) that dangle high above the Río Huécar.

ORIENTATION AND PRACTICAL INFORMATION

When you exit the train station, the back of the bus station is right in front of you—go up the steps to **Calle Fermín Caballero** and turn right. To get to **Plaza Mayor** in the old city from either station, go left until you hit the first bus shelter and catch bus #1 or 2—the old city's the last stop (#1 departs every 30min., 80ptas). On foot to Pl. Mayor, walk left from the bus station along C. Fermín Caballero, which becomes C. Cervantes, then C. José Cobo, and finally (after passing through Pl. Hispanidad), **Calle Carretería,** the town's main drag. From here, turn right on any street (C. Fray Luis de León is the most direct) and trudge upward; it's a grueling and twisty walk (20-25min.) to the plaza and the old city.

Trains: Po. del Ferrocarril, (tel. 969 22 07 20), in the new city. To: Madrid, Estación Atocha (2½-3hr., 8 per day, 1355ptas); Aranjuez (2hr., 5 per day, 980ptas); Valencia (3-4hr., 4 per day, 1490ptas). To get to Toledo, transfer in Aranjuez; to get anywhere else, transfer in Madrid.

Buses: C. Fermín Caballero (tel. 969 22 70 87 for departure times; call **Auto Res** at 969 22 11 84 for their prices). To Madrid (2½hr., 7 per day, 1305-1600ptas). To Toledo, buy a ticket on the AISA (3hr., departs M-F at 5:30am, 1600ptas). **SIAL** goes to Barcelona (3½hr., departs M and Th-F at 9:30am, 4295ptas).

Taxis: Radio-Taxi Cuenca (tel. 969 23 33 43). 24hr. service. Fare from RENFE station to Pl. Mayor: 500-600 ptas.

Tourist Office: C. González Palencia, 2 (tel. 969 17 88 00), in the new city near C. Carretería. No English. Supposedly open daily 9am-2pm. You'll do better at the **Municipal Tourist Office,** Pl. Mayor (tel. 969 23 21 19), opposite the Ayuntamiento. Brochures, maps, a video, hiking and excursion routes, an interactive computer, and lots of info about the goings on about town. Open daily 9:30am-2pm and 4-6 pm.

Currency Exchange: ATMs abound in the new city on C. Fermín Caballero and C. Carretería. **Caja de Madrid** on C. Carretería has a 24hr. ATM and no commission on cash exchanges below 100,000ptas. Open M-F 8:15am-2:30pm.

Luggage Storage: train station (400ptas per day) or bus station (200ptas per day).

Emergency: tel. 091. **Police:** C. Astrana Marín, 2 (tel. 969 23 23 02). **Municipal Police,** C. Martínez Kleyser, 4 (tel. 969 22 48 59), an immediate left off C. Sánchez Vera.

Pharmacy: Farmacia Castellano, C. Cervantes, 20 (tel. 969 21 23 37), at the corner of C. Alferez Rubianes. List of late-night pharmacies in the window.

Post Office: Parque de San Julián, 16 (tel. 969 22 10 42). Open M-F 8:30am-8:30pm, Sa 9:30am-2pm. Smaller **branch** with fewer services up the street from the RENFE station. Open M-F 9am-2pm. **Postal Code:** for the large post office, 16002.

ACCOMMODATIONS

Although there are no cheap accommodations in the old part of town, lots of cheap, adequate rooms collect in the new city. Rooms on the hill with spectacular views of the old town and gorge extract a bit more money. The tourist office has a complete list of places to stay.

Hostal-Residencia Posada de San José, C. Julián Romero, 4 (tel. 969 21 13 00; fax 969 23 03 65), just up the street from the cathedral. Cash in a few extra *pesetas* for cushy beds, amazing water pressure, historic echoes (it's a 17th-century convent), and gorgeous views of the Puente de San Pablo. And why not let loose with *sangría* (750-800ptas) on the cafe's terrace? Singles 2600ptas, with shower 4300ptas; doubles 4300ptas, with shower 7400ptas, with bath 8400ptas; triples 5800ptas, with bath 11,000ptas. Prices vary by season and are higher on weekends. Reserve 2-3 weeks in advance. Visa, MC, AmEx, Diners. See below for cafe.

Pensión Cuenca, Av. República Argentina, 8, 2nd fl. (tel. 969 21 25 74), in the new city. Take C. Fermín Caballero from the bus station until you hit the busy intersection. The street to the left is C. Hurtado de Mendoza, which becomes Av. República Argentina. Matching, shiny new furniture and amiable owners. Singles 1600ptas, with shower 1900ptas; doubles 2300ptas, with shower 3500ptas. TV lounge.

Pensión Central, C. Alonso Chirino, 7, 2nd fl. (tel. 969 21 15 11), off C. Carretería. Clean rooms with huge beds and high ceilings. Freaky neon green patio light. Singles 1400ptas; doubles 2500ptas, without running water 2100ptas; triples 3450ptas. Breakfast 220ptas. Lunch or dinner 800ptas.

Pensión La Mota, Pl. Constitución, 7, 1st fl. (tel. 969 22 55 67), at the end of C. Carretería. Attractive, sparkling, and huge new bathrooms in a *hostal* catering to pairs. Doubles 3300ptas, with bath 4600ptas. Breakfast 200ptas. Shower 200ptas. Solo travelers get small discount.

FOOD

Cuenca's inexpensive restaurants are mediocre; around **Plaza Mayor,** they're expensive and mediocre. Budget eateries line **Calle Cervantes** and **Calle República Argentina,** while the bar-cafes in the plaza off C. Fray Luis de León are even cheaper. A few places still dish out *zorajo* (lamb tripe) and *morteruelo* (a pâté dish), rare regional specialties. Smile about *resoli,* a typical liqueur of coffee, sugar, orange peel, and eau-de-vie, and *alajú,* a sticky sweet nougat made with honey, almonds, and figs. The **market** is on C. Fray Luis de León (open daily 8:30am-2pm). **Heladerías Italianas** scoop out excellent *gelato* (small scoop 100ptas); there are two within a block of each other on C. Carretería (open daily 9:30am-midnight, F-Sa until 9:30am-3am). Groceries are at **Supermercado Alconsa,** C. Fermín Caballero at C. Teruel, a two minute walk from either station (open daily 9:30am-2pm and 5-8pm; Visa, MC). Or try discount supermarket **%Día,** Av. Castilla La Mancha at Av. República Argentina (open M-Th 9:30am-2pm and 5:30-8:30pm, F-Sa 9am-2:30pm and 5:30-9pm).

Posada de San José, C. Julian Romero, 4 (tel. 969 21 13 00). The cafe at this former convent boasts spectacular views and delicious regional *tapas.* Great *ensalada mixta* for two (850ptas). Wonderful *pisto* (stew made of tomatoes, peppers, and onions, 550ptas). *Raciones* about 750ptas. Open Tu-Su 6-10pm.

Restaurante Italiano Piccolo, Av. República Argentina, 14 (tel. 969 23 20 35). Waiters and waitresses are eager to tell the stories at which the black and white family photos on the walls only hint. Ask Pica for the real scoop. Lots of vegetarian starters. Great pizzas 700-975ptas. Pasta 750-975ptas. *Menú* 1350ptas. Visa, MC, AmEx.

Mesón Casas Colgadas, C. Canónigos (tel. 969 22 35 09), to the left of the Museo de Arte Abstracto. It's the best you'll ever eat in an original, 14th-century *casa colgada* (hanging house). Bypass the expensive restaurant for the bar (opens at 1pm); it's the same fabulous view with simpler fare and affordable prices. *Raciones* 200-1000ptas. *Bocadillos* 350-1100ptas. Coffee or tea 150-175ptas. Visa, MC, AmEx.

SIGHTS

Picturesque Cuenca's **cathedral** is one of the most original works of the Spanish Gothic, but the city has drawn its fame from its gravity-defying **casas colgadas.** Down C. Obispo Valero from the Pl. Mayor, they dangle over the riverbanks as precariously today as they did six centuries ago. In his memoirs, Surrealist filmmaker Luis Buñuel recalled a pre-war visit to one of the *casas,* in which he spied birds flying beneath the toilet seat. Walk carefully across the terrifying Puente de San Pablo (not for those afraid of heights) to the **Hoz del Huécar** to get a spectacular view of the *casas* and the surrounding cliffs. Even better, do it at sunset. Two hiking trails along the **Hoz del Júcar** and Hoz del Huécar present fantastic views of the old city and the gorges that isolate it. Maps are available from the municipal tourist office.

Inside one of the *casas* at Pl. Ciudad de Ronda, the award-winning **Museo de Arte Abstracto Español** (tel. 969 21 29 83; fax 969 21 22 85) displays important works by the wacky and internationally known "Abstract Generation" of Spanish painters.

CASTILLA LA MANCHA

Livin' on the Edge

Very little is known about Cuenca's unique 14th-century *casas colgadas.* Supposedly, they were originally built to house kings, giving name to **Casa del Rey. Casa de la Sirena,** the only other remaining original hanging house, got its name from the siren-like screams emitted by a Cuenca *señorita* when she flung herself out of the window after her lover, Enrique Trastamara, killed their son. Despite legendary conjectures and the *casas'* striking appearance, these architectural phenomena did not become famous until recently. Indeed, the *casas* were completely run down when the city of Cuenca decided to rehabilitate them early in this century, transforming them into magnificent museums—and tourist attractions that draw thousands of visitors each year.

(Open M-F and holidays 11am-2pm and 4-6pm, Sa 11am-2pm and 4-8pm, Su 11am-2:30pm. 500ptas, students 250ptas.) All pieces were chosen by artist Fernando Zóbel, a major figure in the school. The well-designed museum exhibits works by Zóbel himself, Canogar, Tápies, and Chillida. Don't miss the "White Room" upstairs. Striking views of the gorge are also on display.

The 18th-century **Ayuntamiento** is built into a Baroque arch at the Pl. Mayor's southern end; the **cathedral,** constructed under Alfonso VIII six years after he conquered Castile·(1183), dominates the other side. *(Open daily in summer 10:30am-2pm and 5-8pm.; in winter 10:30am-2pm and 4-6pm. Mass 9:20am.)* A perfect square, 25m on each side, this building is the only Anglo-Norman Gothic cathedral in Spain. A Spanish Renaissance facade and tower were added in the 16th and 17th centuries, only to be torn down when deemed inappropriate. A 1724 fire cut short the latest attempt to build a front, leaving the current exterior incomplete and strangely reminiscent of a Hollywood set. Psychedelic contemporary stained-glass windows complete the jumble. Inside, the **Museo del Tesoro** houses some late medieval Psalters and a great deal of gold jewelry. More impressive is the **Sala Capitular** and its delightful ceiling. *(Open Tu-Su 11am-2pm and 4-6pm; 200ptas.)*

Down C. Obispo Valero, the **Museo de Cuenca** (tel. 969 21 30 69) is a treasure-trove of archeological finds, including Roman mosaics, ceramics, coins, and other items from local excavations, like excellent Visigoth jewelry. *(Open Tu-Sa 9am-2pm and 4-6pm, Su 11am-2pm. 200ptas, students 100ptas.)* Perhaps the most beautiful of the museums along this short street is the **Museo Diocesano** (tel. 969 22 92 10). *(Open Tu-F 11am-2pm and 4-6pm, Sa 11am-2pm and 4-8pm, Su 11am-2pm. 200ptas.)* Exhibits are imaginatively displayed and include Juan de Borgoña's altarpiece from local Convento de San Pablo, many colossal Flemish tapestries, splendid rugs, and two El Grecos *(Oración del huerto* and *Cristo con la cruz).*

ENTERTAINMENT

Nightlife in New Cuenca is basically a bar scene that extends into the wee hours. Several bars with loud music and young, snazzily dressed crowds line small **Calle Galíndez,** off C. Fray Luis de León, a long and dark but sweet walk down the hill from Old Cuenca; a taxi will cost about 500ptas. The Pl. Mayor boasts several pleasant, if touristy, cafes. For more bars and nightclubs, take the winding street/staircase just off Pl. Mayor across from the cathedral down toward the Río Júcar, where you'll encounter an army of empty bottles.

Cuenca rings with song during the **Festival of Religious Music.** This famous international celebration occurs the week before Holy Week. The **Teatro-Auditorio de Cuenca** (tel. 969 23 27 97) hosts several concert series throughout the year.

■ Sigüenza

The sleepy town of Sigüenza (pop. 5,000) perches on a hill halfway between Madrid and Zaragoza. Pinkish stone buildings and red-roofed houses cluster around a storybook Gothic cathedral and castle. During the Civil War, the Republicans seized the cathedral and the Nationalists the castle, making for one hell of a shoot-out. Despite heavy damages, Sigüenza's medieval architecture has been painstakingly restored, and peace has returned to this tranquil town.

PRACTICAL INFORMATION The **train station** (tel. 949 39 14 94) is at the end of Av. Alfonso VI. At least 12 trains pass through daily heading either to Madrid (1½-2hr., round-trip 1960ptas) or toward Soria and Zaragoza. Call a **taxi** at 949 39 14 11. To get to the **tourist office** (tel. 949 39 32 51), follow Av. Alfonso VI past el Parque de la Alameda to the first intersection. The office is be on the left in the restored Ermita del Humilladero. (Open Tu-F 10am-2pm and 4:30-7pm, Sa-Su 9am-2:30pm and 4:30-7pm). Across the intersection sits **Banco Hispano Central,** which also has an **ATM.** **Luggage storage** is available at the train station until midnight (300ptas). The **Red Cross** (tel. 949 39 13 33) is on Cra. Madrid. The **police,** Carretera de Atienzo, can be

CASTILLA LA MANCHA

reached at 949 39 01 95. In an **emergency,** dial 949 30 00 19; 091; or 092. The **post office** (tel. 949 39 08 44) is on C. Villaviciosa off Pl. Hilario Yabén (open M-F 8:30am-2:30pm, Sa 9:30am-1pm). The **postal code** is 19250.

ACCOMMODATIONS AND FOOD Although you can "do" Sigüenza in a couple of hours, it's pleasant to loiter for a while or even spend the night. **Pensión Venancio,** C. San Roque, 3 (tel. 949 39 03 47), is charming. From the station follow Av. Alfonso VI, turn left at the first intersection onto Av. de Pio XII, then take the first right. The spacious and airy rooms sport mirrors for the glam backpacker (singles 2000ptas; doubles 3600ptas). Cheap places to eat are not hard to come by. **Restaurante El Mesón,** Roman Pascual, 14 (tel. 949 39 06 49), sells veggie and egg options for 400-750ptas; meat and fish entrees go for 800-1700ptas (Visa).

SIGHTS From the bottom of the hill, two buildings jut out from Sigüenza's low skyline: the cathedral and the fortified **castillo,** a 12th-century castle-turned-parador. Restored in the 1970s, the castle merits an uphill stroll through the cobblestone streets, if just to peek in the luxuriously decorated *parador.* To get to the magnificent **cathedral,** follow Av. Alfonso VI uphill (it changes to C. Humilladero) then take a left onto C. Cardenal Mendoza. *(Open May-Nov. M-F 11am-1pm and 4-6pm; Sa-Su 10:30am-1:30pm and 5:30-6:30pm. Ask a cathedral employee for a tour. 300ptas. No entry during services unless you wish to participate.)* Work on the cathedral began in the mid-12th century and continued until the 16th century. The building combines Romanesque, Mudéjar, Plateresque, and Gothic styles. One of the structure's most renowned features is the 15th-century **Tumba del Doncel,** commissioned by Isabel la Católica in memory of a favorite page who died fighting the Muslims in Granada. The young man rests contentedly dead, reading a book. The **sacristry's** elaborate Renaissance ceiling boasts 304 stone portraits carved by Covarrubias. The staring faces, both Christians and Moors, hail from all walks of life: monks, countesses, dandies, and dames. The adjoining chapel houses an El Greco *Anunciación* and a ceiling so magnificent that the church thoughtfully provides a mirror on the floor to help you view it. Opposite the cathedral, the small **Museo de Arte Antiguo,** a.k.a. Museo Diocesano (tel. 949 39 10 23), exhibits medieval and early modern religious works, including a Ribera and Zurbarán. *(Open Apr.-Sept. Tu-F noon-2pm and 4-5pm, Sa-Su 11am-2pm and 5-7pm. 200ptas.)*

CASTILLA LA MANCHA

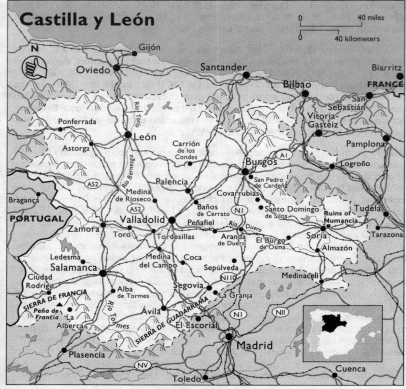

Castilla y León

Castilla y León's cities emerge like islands from a sea of burnt sienna. Reigning strong in the region, these urban personages survey their surroundings from splendid cathedrals and sumptuous palaces. The monuments—the majestic Gothic cathedrals of Burgos and León, the slender Romanesque belfries along the Camino de Santiago in León, the intricate sandstone of Salamanca, and the proud city walls of Ávila—have emblazoned themselves as national as well as regional images.

Well before Castilla's famous 1469 confederation with Aragón, when Fernando of Aragón and Isabel of Castilla were united in world-shaking matrimony, it was clear that Castilla had its act together. In the High Middle Ages, the region emerged from obscurity to lead the Christian charge against Islam. Castilian nobles, sanguine from the spoils of combat, introduced the concept of a unified Spain (under Castilian command, of course), and *castellano* ("Spanish") became the dominant language throughout the nation. Imperious León, Castilla's comrade at arms, though chagrined to be lumped with Castilla in a 1970s provincial reorganization, has much in common with its co-province. Neither has been as economically successful as their more high-tech northeastern neighbors.

Castilian gastronomy favors red meats and vegetables that can be grown in relatively cold climates, such as potatoes. *Cocido castellano* is beef, ham, potatoes, sausage, carrots, and garlic stewed together. Castilians also tend to get hyperbolically excited about their lamb dishes.

🐾 HIGHLIGHTS OF CASTILLA Y LEÓN

- Segovia's impressive **Alcázar** (palace) and hulking **Roman aqueduct.**
- **Ávila** (see p. 147), the best preserved medieval walled city in Europe.
- The lovely Plateresque architecture at the **University of Salamanca** (see p. 154).
- Burgos's imposing **Gothic cathedral,** Spain's biggest and best (see p. 171).

■ Segovia

Legend has it that Segovia's famed *acueducto* was built in a single day—by the Devil, trying to win the soul of a Segovian water-seller named Juanilla. When the shocked Juanilla woke up to find the aqueduct almost completed, she prayed to the Virgin Mary, who made the sun rise a bit earlier in order to foil the Devil's scheme. Segovia's aqueduct may not have won Juanilla's soul, but it has intrigued visitors ever since Roman times. The town (pop. 55,000) represents Castilla at its best—a magnificent castle, an impressive cathedral, and twisting alleyways filled with the aroma of *sopa castellano* and *cochinillo asado* (roast suckling pig). As always, pleasure has its price: *peseta* tags on food and accommodations are much higher than in Madrid.

ORIENTATION AND PRACTICAL INFORMATION

On the far side of the Sierra de Guadarrama, 88km northwest of Madrid, Segovia is close enough to the capital to be a daytrip but definitely warrants a longer stay.

To get to **Plaza Mayor,** the city's historic center and site of the **tourist office,** take any bus from the train station (100ptas). On weekdays some go only as far as **Paseo del Salón,** in which case go left up the steps on **Puerta del Sol,** turn right, and make the first left up to the plaza. For the fastest route from the **bus station** to Pl. Mayor, make a left from the station onto C. Ezekiel González and walk until you get to the first round intersection with a statue. Turn right, cross the Puente de Sancti Spiritus, and take the stairs up to the park. Cross the park and go up the steps of the Puerta del Sol. Turn right on C. Judería Vieja, then make a sharp left at the first corner (15min.).

The city is impossible to navigate without a map. It may help to think of the old city, high above the newer *barrios,* as a ship, with the Alcázar acting as bow, the aqueduct as stern, and the cathedral tower as mainmast. Both Pl. Mayor (10min.) and the Alcázar (20min.) are uphill from **Plaza de Azoguejo,** next to the **aqueduct.** Running between Pl. Mayor and Pl. Azoguejo is **Calle Isabel la Católica-Calle Juan Bravo-Calle Cervantes,** a busy pedestrian thoroughfare.

Trains: (tel. 921 42 07 74), Po. Obispo Quesada. Only one line: the Segovia-Madrid *regional.* To Madrid (2hr., 9 per day, 765ptas) and Villalba (1hr., 500ptas, halfway along the same line, transfer point for El Escorial, Ávila, León, and Salamanca). The bus is often a better bet unless you're coming directly from the Madrid airport.

Buses: Estacionamiento Municipal de Autobuses, Po. Ezequiel González, 12 (tel. 921 42 77 25), at the corner of Av. Fernández Ladreda. To: Madrid (1¾hr., departs every hr., 765ptas); Ávila (1hr., M-F 6 per day, Sa-Su 1 per day, 555ptas); Salamanca (3hr., 3 per day, 1245ptas); Valladolid (2hr., M-F 13 per day, Sa-Su 7-9 per day, 855ptas); La Granja (20min., 7-11 per day, round-trip 200ptas).

Public Transportation: Transportes Urbanos de Segovia, Pl. Mayor, 8 (tel. 921 46 03 29). Buses 85-100ptas.

Taxis: Taxis pull up by the train and bus stations. **Radio Taxi:** tel. 921 44 50 00.

Car Rental: Avis (tel. 921 42 25 84) and **Europcar** (tel 921 43 41 70).

Tourist Office: Municipal Office, Pl. Mayor, 10 (tel. 921 46 03 34), in front of the bus stop on the corner opposite the cathedral. Complete info on accommodations, bus and train schedules, and sights posted in the windows. Indispensable **map.** Some English and French spoken. Open daily 10am-2pm and 5-8pm. **Regional Tourist Office,** Pl. Azoguejo, 1 (tel. 921 44 03 02), at the foot of the steps leading to the top of the aqueduct. Less crowded. Piles of glossy brochures. Open daily 10am-8pm.

CASTILLA Y LEÓN

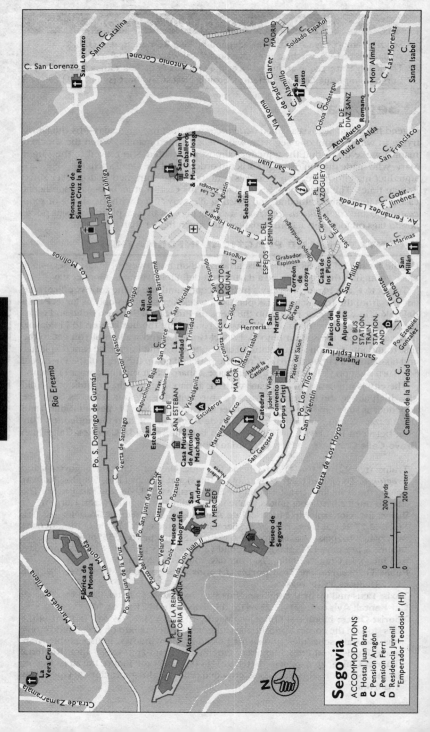

CASTILLA Y LEÓN

Segovia

ACCOMMODATIONS
B Hostal Juan Bravo
C Pension Aragón
A Pension Ferri
D Residencia Juvenil
"Emperador Teodosio" (HI)

Currency Exchange: Banks and **ATMs** surround Pl. Azoguejo and Pl. Mayor.
Luggage Storage: Lockers at the train station. 400ptas. Open daily 5:45am-10pm.
Emergency: dial 091. **Police:** Po. Ezequiel González (tel. 921 42 51 61), across from the bus station. **Municipal,** C. Guadarrama (tel. 921 43 12 12).
Medical Services: Hospital Policlínico, C. San Agustín, 13 (tel. 921 41 90 65). **Hospital General,** Crta. de Ávila (tel. 921 41 91 00). Either one for **emergencies.**
Internet Access: Ludos, C. José Zorilla, 26 (tel 921 44 44 69). 600ptas per hr. Open daily 1pm-3am.
Post Office: Pl. Dr. Laguna, 5 (tel. 921 43 16 11), up C. Cronista Lecea from Pl. Mayor. Open for stamps and Lista de Correos M-F 8:30am-8:30pm, Sa 9:30am-2pm. **Postal Code:** 40001.

ACCOMMODATIONS AND CAMPING

Finding a *hostal* during the summer can be a nightmare. The regional tourist office's list of accommodations is valuable, but be prepared to pay 2500ptas or more for a single, unless you're hip to a windowless, sinkless space.

Residencia Juvenil "Emperador Teodosio" (HI), Av. Conde de Sepúlveda (tel. 921 44 11 11 or 921 44 10 47). Look for its huge red fire escape. From the train station, go right, cross the street, and walk along Po. Obispo Quesada, which soon becomes Av. Conde de Sepúlveda (10min.). The hostel is on the left. From the bus station, go right on C. Ezequiel González, which becomes Av. Conde de Sepúlveda (10min.). Hostel is on the right. Open to travelers July-Aug., when modern amenities and hotel-like doubles and triples, all with private baths, make it nearly impossible to get a room. Dorms 1000ptas, with full meals 2200ptas; over 26 1450ptas, with full meals 3000ptas. 3-night max. stay. Curfew varies.
Hostal Juan Bravo, C. Juan Bravo, 12, 2nd fl. (tel. 921 46 34 13), on the main thoroughfare in the old town, near Iglesia de San Martín. Bright, carpeted rooms with schmaltzy pictures are cool in summer. Doubles 3800ptas, with bath 4800ptas; triples 5000ptas, with bath 6500ptas. Visa, MC.
Pensión Ferri, C. Escuderos, 10 (tel. 921 46 09 57), off Pl. Mayor. Central and clean. Only single 1400ptas; doubles 2300ptas. Showers 300ptas.
Pensión Aragón, Pl. Mayor, 4 (tel. 921 46 09 14), directly across from the tourist office. Cheap and central. Singles 1300ptas; doubles 2500ptas; triples 2800ptas. Hot shower 200ptas.
Camping: Camping Acueducto, Ctra. Nacional, 601, km 112 (tel. 921 42 50 00), 2km toward La Granja. Take the AutoBus Urbano from Pl. Azoguejo to Nueva Segovia (100ptas). 2nd-class campsite shaded by the Sierra de Guadarrama. Hot water. 500ptas per person and per tent, children 450ptas. Open all year.

FOOD

Choosing a restaurant in Segovia is a crap shoot. In general, steer clear of Pl. Mayor, Pl. Azoguejo, and all signs simulating worn medieval parchment. *Cochinillo asado* (roast suckling pig), lamb, and *croquetas* have always been favorites. **Panaderías** around C. Juan Bravo and off Pl. Azoguejo sell goodies for reasonable prices. **Fruit and vegetable stands** crowd C. Juan Bravo and its neighboring streets. **%Día,** C. Fernández Jimenez, 3, off C. Fernández Ladreda, is a discount supermarket (open M-Th 9:30am-2pm and 5:30-8:30pm, F-Sa 9am-2:30pm and 5:30-9pm).

Bar-Mesón Cueva de San Esteban, C. Valdeláguila, 15 (tel. 921 46 09 82), off Pl. San Esteban and C. Escuderos. Local budgeters eat at this stone- and mortar-walled retreat, complete with wooden pygmy footstools for seats. Entrees start at 675ptas. *Menú* 900ptas. Open daily 10am-midnight.
Restaurante La Almuzara, C. Marqués del Arco, 3 (tel. 921 46 06 22), past the cathedral toward the Alcázar. Excellent vegetarian restaurant with greenery-inspired frescoes. Big salads (400-900ptas), *platos combinados* (700-1300ptas), pizzas, pasta, and some hefty entrees. Open Tu-Su for dinner only.
Restaurante-Mesón Alejandro (tel. 921 46 00 09), at the end of C. Carbitrería. Take the first left off C. Cronista Lecea, which is off Pl. Mayor to the left of the tourist

office. Excellent and inexpensive. Delicious *paella* for 2, and a good *menú del día*
(900ptas). Open daily 1:30-4pm and 8:30-10:45pm. Visa, MC, AmEx.

La Concepción, Pl. Mayor, 15 (tel. 921 46 09 30). Cheap for Pl. Mayor, this popular
cafe tempts passersby with its huge portions of delectable *croquetas* (750ptas) and
aesthetically pleasing desserts (850-900ptas). Open daily 9am-2am. Visa, AmEx.

SIGHTS

Segovia rewards the wanderer. Whether palace, church, house, or sidewalk, almost
everything deserves close consideration. Look for *esgrafía*, lacy patterns on the
facades of buildings. Also, be sure to explore the northern parts of town, away from
the Alcázar and aqueduct.

The Alcázar

Open daily Apr.-Sept. 10am-7pm; Oct.-Mar. 10am-6pm. 375ptas, seniors 250ptas.

The Alcázar (tel. 921 46 07 59), an archetypal late-medieval castle, audaciously juts
into space at the far north end of the old quarter, where the surrounding countryside
provides a Kodak moment. Alfonso X, who allegedly thought himself greater than
God, beautified the original 11th-century fortress. He was later struck by lightning.
Successive monarchs added to the Alcázar's grandeur, befitting it for the 1474 coronation of Isabel I as Queen of Castilla. In succeeding centuries, the Alcázar served as a
prison, while in 1764 Carlos III converted it into Spain's most prestigious artillery
academy, graduating tough and educated **Caballeros Cadetes.** A small but marvelous
museum inside the Alcázar explains the role of science in the "enlightened" military.

Trappings from an illustrious past fill the rest of the castle: tapestries, armor,
thrones, sculpture, and paintings. The walls of the **Sala de Reyes** (royal room) are
adorned with wood-and-gold-inlaid sculptures of the monarchs of Asturias, Castilla,
and León. In the **Sala de Solio** (throne room), the inscription above the throne reads:
"tanto monta, monta tanto" (she mounts, as does he). This popular saying signifies
not what your dirty mind suggests but rather Fernando and Isabel's equal authority as
sovereigns. The **Sala de Armas** holds an arsenal of medieval weaponry.

If you feel strong, climb the 140 steps up a nausea-inducing spiral staircase to the
top of the **torre,** where you will be rewarded with a marvelous view of Segovia and
the surrounding amber plains. Prince Pedro, son of Enrique IV, slipped form his
nurse's arms, fell off the balcony, and crashed onto the ramparts to his bloody death;
out of desperation his nurse leapt after him and ended her own life.

The Cathedral

Open daily Apr.-Oct. 9:15am-6:45pm; Nov.-Mar. 9:30am-5:45pm. 250ptas.

Commissioned by Carlos I in 1525 to replace a 12th-century cathedral damaged during the "Comunidades" war, Segovia's huge Gothic cathedral towers over Pl. Mayor.
With 23 **chapels** and a silver and gold **tesoro,** the cathedral has earned its nickname
as "The Lady of all Cathedrals." The **Sala Capitular,** hung with well-preserved 17th-

---

La Mujer Muerta

According to local folklore, a picturesque mountain silhouette south of Segovia
known as **La Mujer Muerta** (The Dead Woman) commemorates a bloody but stir-
ring turn of events. **La mujer,** the wife of a chief, was widowed when her twin
sons were but young boys. As only one of the two could inherit his father's rule,
the mother grew fearful of impending fratricide once the children came of age.
Stoically, she offered her life to God as a sacrifice, hoping this act would save both
her sons. On a summer's day years later, as the two young men prepared to fight
each other for supremacy, torrents of snow miraculously fell throughout the land.
By the time the storm dissipated, a snow-capped mountain had materialized upon
the scene of the proposed battleground. As all soon acknowledged, it was the
resting body of the twins' mother. *Segovianos* insist that two small clouds float
closer to the mountain at dusk—the two sons kissing their mother good night.

century tapestries, displays a silver and gold chariot, an ornate *artesonado* ceiling, and an incredible number of crucifixes, chalices, and candelabras. The **museum** (tel. 921 46 22 05) holds an excellent collection, including Coello's 16th-century painting *La duda de Santo Tomás* (Doubt) and a series of 17th-century paintings on marble depicting the Passion of Christ. Here also lies Prince Pedro. Upstairs, valuables include ceremonial robes, dazzling 16th-century manuscripts, and little saintly pieces.

The Aqueduct

The serpent-like **acueducto romano,** built by the Romans around 50 BC to pipe in water from the Rio Frío 18km away, towers over the entrance to the old city. Supported by 128 pillars that span 813m, the two tiers of 163 arches are constructed of some 200,000 blocks of granite—without any mortar to hold them together. This spectacular feat of engineering, restored by the monarchy in the 15th century, was still in use 50 years ago, and construction to restore the aqueduct's function has begun again. The grand structure reaches its maximum height of 28.9m beside Pl. Azoguejo, but there is no reason to limit your viewing to that particular spot.

Churches and Palaces

Segovia's 12th- and 13th-century Romanesque churches hold erratic afternoon hours, a hindrance to whirlwind touring. Most are open for visits roughly 11am to 2pm and 4 to 7pm, but their exteriors make a worthwhile visit themselves. **San Millán,** C. Fernández Ladreda (near the bus station), is the finest example of Romanesque architecture in the city. *(Open daily during mass only, 8pm.)* Its medieval frescoes were discovered under a layer of paint about 30 years ago. Tenth-century **San Martín,** Pl. San Martín, off C. Juan Bravo, is livened by *mozárabe* touches, a Baroque *retablo* (altarpiece), and sepulchres of 17th-century Segovians. Nearby **San Andrés,** C. de Daoiz, past the cathedral, is also worth a visit. Thirteenth-century **San Esteban,** to the west on Pl. Esteban, has one of the highest towers of any church in Spain. Restored in the early 20th century, the building houses a calvary from the 1800s. **La Trinidad,** west of San Esteban, is relatively well preserved. The walk around and between **San Esteban** and **La Trinidad** reveals Segovia at its subtle best. Other outstanding churches include **San Justo** and **San Sebastián,** near the aqueduct.

A 14th- and 15th-century wave of palaces also adorn historic Segovia. **Torreón de Lozoya,** Pl. San Martín, off C. Juan Bravo, is a dandy *palacio* hosting art exhibitions. *(Open M-F 7-9:30pm, Sa noon-2pm and 7-9:30pm. Free.)* The 16th-century **Casa de los Picos,** down C. Juan Bravo from Pl. San Martín, has an intriguing facade studded with rows of diamond-shaped stones. The **Palacio del Conde Alpuente,** up C. Juan Bravo in an alley to the left, epitomizes Segovian *esgrafía.* Though significantly more humble than a *palacio,* the **Casa-Museo de Antonio Machado** (past the cathedral, make a right on C. Desamparados) still holds its own among Segovia's historic treasures. *(Open daily 4-7pm. Free.)* The poet's 13-year residence (1919-1932) has been left untouched. Go even if only to look out the windows.

Outside the Walls

The walk north away from the city offers an escape from the urban environment. The meandering Eresma River and lush greenery offer a welcome change of pace, and there are several sights of interest. However, such pleasure comes at a cost—be prepared for a grueling uphill trek back to the city. If you follow C. Pozo de la Nieve (on the left with your back to the Alcázar) and head down the second stone staircase, you'll be on Po. San Juan de la Cruz. A green 20-minute walk leads to **Iglesia de la Vera Cruz,** a mysterious 12-sided basilica built by the cabalistic Knights Templar in 1208. *(Open Apr.-Sept. Tu-Su 10:30am-1:30pm and 3:30-7pm; Oct.-Mar. Tu-Su 10:30am-1:30pm and 3:30-6pm. 200ptas.)* Beneath its lofty vaults are two hidden chambers where clergymen guarded their lives and their valuables from robbers and highwaymen. The Knights Templar gathered to perform initiation ceremonies in these same rooms—step into the center for an auditory adventure.

CASTILLA Y LEÓN

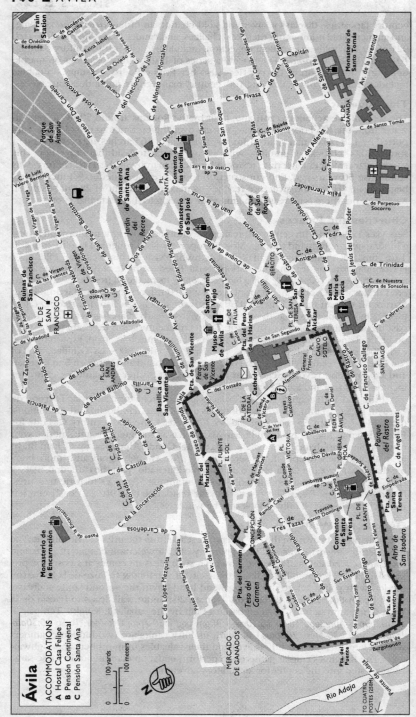

CASTILLA Y LEÓN

Ávila

ACCOMMODATIONS
A Hostal Casa Felipe
B Pensión Continental
C Pensión Santa Ana

0   100 yards
0   100 meters

ENTERTAINMENT

Packed with bars and cafes, **Plaza Mayor** and its tributaries are the center of Segovian nightlife for the older crowd. **Plaza Azoguejo** and **Calle Carmen,** near the aqueduct, are filled with bars as well, where those under 20 (and way under 20) gather. Club headquarters are at **Calle Ruiz de Alda,** off Pl. Azoguejo. Disco-goers shuffle their feet at **Sabbat,** Po. del Salón. **Las Aguas Blancas,** C. Judería Vieja, 17 (tel. 921 46 21 67), up from Po. del Salón, pleasantly reminisces with music from the 80s (beer 300ptas).

In July, Segovia hosts two classical music festivals. From June 24-29, Segovia celebrates its *fiestas* in honor of San Juan and San Pedro. Look for free concerts on Pl. Azoguejo and a fireworks display on June 29.

Three kilometers northwest of Segovia, **Zamarramala** hosts the **Fiestas de Santa Agueda** in February. Women take over the town's administration for a day (Feb. 5), dress up in beautiful, old-fashioned costumes, and parade through the streets. They parody men to commemorate an abortive sneak attack on the Alcázar in which the women of Zamarramala tried to distract the castle guards with wine and song.

■ Near Segovia: La Granja de San Ildefonso

The royal palace and grounds of **La Granja** (tel. 921 47 00 19), 9km southeast of Segovia, are the Versailles of Spain. (*Open daily June-Sept. Tu-Su 10am-1:30pm; Oct.-Mar. Tu-Sa 10am-1:30pm and 3-5pm, Su 10am-2pm; Apr.-May Tu-F 10am-1:30pm and 3-5pm, Sa-Su 10am-6pm. 650ptas, students 250ptas, Wednesdays free for E.U. citizens.*) One of four royal summer retreats (with El Pardo, El Escorial, and Aranjuez), La Granja is the most extravagant. Marble fortifications, antique lace curtains, ceiling frescoes, and lavish crystal chandeliers (made in San Ildefonso's renowned crystal factory) are its ornaments. Felipe V, the first Bourbon King of Spain and grandson of Louis XIV, detested the Habsburgs' austere El Escorial. Nostalgic for Versailles, he commissioned La Granja in the early 18th century. The guided tour (in Spanish) is mandatory for visitors but worth enduring—the best exhibits come last. A mysterious fire destroyed the living quarters of the royals and their servants in 1918. The rubble was rebuilt to house one of the world's finest collections of Flemish **tapestries.** Woven in the 16th and 17th centuries, they covered the walls of Habsburg kings Carlos I and Felipe II. The peach **iglesia** flanking the palace has a red marble interior, gilded woodwork, and an impressive display of various saints' and martyrs' bones.

Outside, the cool and expansive **jardines** are surrounded by a forest with statues of children and animals. The flamboyant **Cascadas Nuevas,** an ensemble of illuminated fountains and pools, represents the continents and four seasons. People even yell in ecstasy when the fountain turns on. (*Gardens free except W and Sa-Su after 3pm; 325ptas, students 200ptas. Fountains turned on W and Sa-Su at 5:30pm.*)

Along with water, glass is another celebrated transparency in La Granja. Follow the evolution of the wine bottle and stare wide-eyed at the collection of contemporary glass art in the **Real Fabrica de Cristales.** (Tel. 921 47 17 12; fax 921 47 15 72; http://www.fcnv.es). (*Open daily Apr.-Sept. 11am-8pm; Oct.-Mar. 11am-7pm. 400ptas, seniors and students 200ptas.*) Frequent **buses** leave Segovia's bus station for La Granja (20min., 10-13 per day, 200ptas round-trip).

■ Ávila

Oh, if the walls had ears, what stories Ávila's medieval *murallas* could tell. One of Castilla's most important provincial capitals, Ávila (pop. 50,000) is renowned for the 2.5km of magnificently preserved 12th-century stone walls that encircle its old city. Santa Teresa de Jesús and San Juan de la Cruz, famed 16th-century mystics, writers, and religious reformers, lived out their spiritual days here, penning mystical tracts and founding monastic communities. Poor San Juan got a bit lost in the shuffle—Ávila is crazy for Santa Teresa. Museums and monuments depict in exhaustive detail her divine visitations and ecstatic visions, and Ávila's inhabitants have taken the heroine as their patron saint, naming everything from pastries to driving schools after her.

CASTILLA Y LEÓN

The city sits on a rocky escarpment high above the Río Adaja valley. It stays cool in the summer, unlike the sweltering plain below, but gets freezing in the winter. Just west of Segovia and northwest of Madrid, Ávila is a reasonable daytrip from either.

ORIENTATION AND PRACTICAL INFORMATION

The city has two central squares: **Plaza de la Victoria** (known to locals as the **Plaza del Mercado Chico**) inside the city walls, and **Plaza de Santa Teresa,** just outside. The cathedral sits between the two plazas, in the eastern half of the old city. To get to the city center from the **bus station** (east of the center), cross the intersection, turn right down C. Duque de Alba (keeping the small park to the right), and follow the street past the Iglesia de San Pedro to cafe-filled Pl. Santa Teresa (10min.). To reach Pl. Santa Teresa from the **train station** (northeast of the center), follow Av. José Antonio until it ends in a tangle of streets at Pl. Santa Ana. There you will find C. Isaac Peral, which leads to C. Duque de Alba; turn left and continue on to Pl. Santa Teresa (15min.). Municipal bus #1 (75ptas) runs to Pl. Victoria from the bus stop one block toward town, near the train station.

Trains: Av. José Antonio (tel. 920 25 02 02), on the northeast side of town. To: Madrid (1½-2hr., 20-25 per day, fewer on weekends, 835-1500ptas); Villalba, for transfer to Segovia (1hr., 16 per day, 980ptas); Salamanca (1¾hr, 3 per day, 835ptas); Valladolid (1½hr., 7 per day, 965-1500ptas); El Escorial (1hr., 7 per day, 500ptas).

Buses: Av. Madrid, 2 (tel. 920 22 01 54), at Av. Portugal on the northeast side of town. To: Madrid (1½hr., 3-7 per day, 910ptas); Segovia (1hr., M-F 7 per day, Sa-Su 2 per day, 555ptas); Salamanca (1½ hr., M-Sa 4 per day, Su 2 per day, 700ptas).

Taxis: Pl. Santa Teresa (tel. 920 21 19 59), also at the train station (tel. 920 22 01 49). From train station to Pl. Santa Teresa 350ptas plus 25ptas per piece of luggage.

Tourist Office: Pl. Catedral, 4 (tel. 920 21 13 87), opposite the cathedral entrance. From Pl. Santa Teresa, go through the main gate and turn right on C. Alemania (the 2nd street). Friendly, bilingual staff. Open daily 10am-2pm and 4-7pm.

Emergency: tel. 092. **Police:** Av. Inmaculada, 11 (tel. 920 21 11 88).

Medical Services: Hospital Provincial: Jesús del Gran Poder (tel. 920 35 72 00). **Ambulance:** tel. 920 22 14 00.

Post Office: Pl. Catedral, 2 (tel. 920 21 13 54), to the left of cathedral when facing the main entrance. Lista de Correos and all services open M-F 8:30am-8:30pm, Sa 9:30am-2pm. **Postal Code:** 05001.

ACCOMMODATIONS

Accommodations are plentiful and reasonably priced, although some fill up in summer. Ávila's only *albergue*, **Residencia Juvenil "Duperier" (HI)** has only very limited beds available and sits far from the city center in a less safe neighborhood; the following are recommended by *Let's Go*:

Pensión Continental, Pl. Catedral, 6 (tel. 920 21 15 02; fax 920 25 16 91), next to the tourist office. Beautiful ex-hotel in excellent location. Bright rooms with bouncy beds and phones. Singles 2200ptas; doubles 3700ptas, with bath 4500ptas; triples 5500ptas, with bath 6700ptas; 6 room suite 8500ptas. 7% IVA not included. Visa, MC, AmEx.

Pensión Santa Ana, C. Alfonso Montalvo, 2, 2nd fl. (tel. 920 22 00 63), from the train station, down Av. José Antonio and off Pl. Santa Ana. Spacious rooms and immaculate bathrooms. Singles 2500ptas; doubles 4000ptas; triples 4500ptas.

Hostal Casa Felipe, Pl. Victoria, 12 (tel. 920 21 39 24), on the side of the plaza closest to cathedral. Conveniently located above the bar. TVs and sinks standard; many rooms have balconies. Singles 2200ptas; doubles with shower 4000ptas, with bath 5000ptas. Prices lower in June and winter.

CASTILLA Y LEÓN

FOOD

Budget sandwich shops cluster around **Plaza Victoria. Calle San Segundo,** off Pl. Sta. Teresa, is Ávila's most affordable restaurant row. The city has won fame for its *ternera de Ávila* (veal) and *mollejas* (sweetbread). The *yemas de Santa Teresa* or *yemas de Ávila,* local confections made of egg yolk and honey, and *vino de Cebreros,* a smooth regional wine, are delectable. Every Friday, the **mercado** in Pl. Victoria sells foodstuffs at low prices (open 10am-2pm). **El Arbol,** C. Alfonso de Montalvo, 1, off Pl. Santa Ana, is a decent supermarket. (Open in summer M-Sa 9:30am-2pm and 5:30-8:30pm; in winter M-Sa 9:30am-2pm and 5-8pm.) Bars and local culture can be enjoyed on **Conde de Vallespin** (off Pl. Victoria) and its side streets.

Restaurante El Grande, Pl. Santa Teresa, 8 (tel. 920 22 30 83). A festive family-style restaurant with outdoor seating. Specialty croissant sandwiches (285-335ptas). *Raciones* 375-800ptas; *menú* 765ptas. Open daily noon-4pm and 8pm-midnight.

Gran Muralla, C. San Segundo, 18. This flashy Chinese restaurant is a safe bet for cheap, plentiful, and downright tasty servings. Lunchtime *menú* 765ptas, combination plates 490-940ptas. Open daily 11:30am-4:30pm and 7:30pm-12:30am.

Bocatti, C. San Segundo, 26 (tel. 920 25 10 80). A bright 50s-inspired sub shop with checkered tiles, Americana on the walls, and Elvis on the jukebox. Cold and hot sub sandwiches on freshly baked bread 295-490ptas. Open daily noon-midnight.

Casa Patas, C. San Millán, 4 (tel. 920 21 31 94), off Pl. Santa Teresa. A small, colorful restaurant with few tables and a cheap lunchtime *menú* (1200ptas). Entrees 400-2000ptas. Open daily 9:30am-11:30pm. Visa.

Ristorante Italiano, C. San Segundo, 28 (tel. 920 25 28 90). Wide selection of pricey wines behind a bar decorated with cowhide. Salads (600-1200ptas), pastas (700-1000ptas), and pizzas (1200ptas). Open daily noon-4pm and 8pm-midnight.

SIGHTS

City Walls (Las Murallas)

Ávila's inner city is surrounded by Spain's oldest and best-preserved medieval walls. Construction of the **murallas medievales** began in 1090, and most were completed in the next century. It was this concentrated burst of activity that gave the walls their unusual uniformity. Mudéjar features suggest that *morisco* citizens helped fortify Christian Ávila. Eighty-two massive towers reinforce walls whose thickness averages 3m. The most imposing of the towers, **Cimorro,** is also the cathedral's bold apse. On the inside, in the corner to the right of the cathedral, are the outlines of two windows and two balconies—all that remains of a former Alcázar. If you wish to walk on the walls (200m are open to the public), start from the **Puenta del Alcázar.** *(Open Tu-Su 11am-1:30pm and 5-7:30pm; in winter Tu-Su 10:30am-3:30pm. 200ptas.)*

The best view of the walls and of Ávila itself is from the **Cuatro Postes,** a tiny four-pillar structure past the Río Adaja on the highway to Salamanca, 1.5km northwest of the city. At this very spot, Santa Teresa was caught by her uncle while she and her brother were trying to flee to the Islamic south to be martyred.

Inside the Walls

Some believe that the profile of the huge **cathedral** (tel. 920 21 16 41) looming over the watchtowers inspired Santa Teresa's metaphor of the soul as a diamond castle. *(Open daily Apr.-Oct. 10am-1pm and 3:30-6pm; Nov.-Mar. 10am-1:30pm and 3:30-5:30pm. 250ptas.)* Begun in the second half of the 12th century, it is the oldest Spanish cathedral in the transitional style from Romanesque to Gothic, testifying to the long, turbulent years of the *Reconquista.* View the **Altar de La Virgen de la Caridad,** where 12-year-old Santa Teresa prostrated herself after the death of her mother. Behind the main altar is the alabaster **tomb** of Cardinal Alonso de Madrigal, an Ávilan bishop and prolific writer whose dark complexion won him the label "El Tostado" (the Toasted). In fact, it became popular during the Golden Age to refer to all literary windbags by

CASTILLA Y LEÓN

this nickname. The museum displays an enormous *libros de canti* (hymnals) and Juan de Arfe's silver, six-leveled **Custodia del Corpus** with bells that still swivel.

Santa Teresa's admirers built the 17th-century **Convento de Santa Teresa** on the site of her birthplace and childhood home. *(Open daily May-Sept. 9:30am-1:30pm and 3:30-9pm; Oct.-Apr. 9:30am-1:30pm and 3:30-8:30pm.)* To the right of the convent, the small **Sala de Reliquias** holds some great Santa Teresa relics, including her right ring finger, the sole of her sandal, and the cord with which she flagellated herself. *(Open daily 9:30am-1:30pm and 3:30-7:30pm. Free.)*

Outside the Walls

A short distance outside the city walls on Po. Encarnación is the **Monasterio de la Encarnación** (northwest of the city), where Santa Teresa lived for 30 years. *(Open daily in summer 10am-1pm and 4-7pm; in winter 10am-1pm and 3:30-6pm. 150ptas.)* The mandatory guided tour in Spanish (10-15min.) visits Santa Teresa's tiny cell and the small rooms where nuns peered at their guests through little barred windows. On the main staircase, Santa Teresa had her mystical encounter with the child Jesus. Ask for the informational brochure for a dramatic re-creation of the scene and a transcript of their dialogue. Upstairs from the cloister, a museum features a collection of furnishings, letters, and other personal effects given to the convent by wealthier nuns as bribes (dowries, if you prefer) to procure entrance. Currently, 27 nuns live in the monastery.

Casa de los Deanes, a mansion in Pl. Nalvillos with a Renaissance facade, houses the remarkable **Museo de Ávila** (tel. 920 21 10 03). *(Open Tu-Su 10am-2pm and 4:30-7:30pm. 200ptas, students free, Sa-Su free.)* The museum exhibits beautiful artifacts from Ávila's past, including *verracos,* pre-Roman granite works abstractly representing bulls and hogs. Entrance also gets you into the new Iglesia de Santo Tomé (across the plaza), which displays even more archaeological finds.

Basílica de San Vicente, a large 12th-century Romanesque and Gothic building, is dedicated to Vicente, Sabina, and Cristeta, three martyred saints buried in a triple-decker sepulchre. *(Open daily 10am-2pm and 4-7:30pm. 50ptas.)*

Monasterio de Santo Tomás, Pl. Granada, 1, some distance from the city walls at the end of C. Jesús del Gran Poder (or Av. de Alférez Provisional), was the summer palace of the Catholic Monarchs, Fernando and Isabel, and a seat of the Inquisition. Inside the church and in front of the *retablo* (altarpiece) is the tomb of Prince Don Juan, Fernando and Isabel's only son, who died in 1497 at the age of 19. To the right (when facing the altar) is the **Capilla del Santo Cristo,** where Santa Teresa came to pray and confess. Also here are the Tuscan **Cloister of the Noviciate,** the Gothic **Cloister of Silence,** and the Renaissance-Transition **Cloister of the Kings.** *(Church open daily 8am-1pm and 4-8pm. Museum open daily 11am-12:45pm and 4-7pm. Cloisters 100ptas, museum 200ptas, church free.)*

Fairs and parades of *gigantes y cabezudos* (giant effigies) pass through when the city gets a little crazy to honor Santa Teresa (Oct. 7-15). In the second or third week of July, the **Fiestas de Verano** bring exhibits, folk-singing, dancing, pop groups, fireworks, and a bullfight.

Bullboards

Staring glassy-eyed out of the window of your preferred mode of transportation, you may notice rather unusual monuments along the highway: massive, black paper cut-outs of a solitary bull. Once upon a time (in the 1980s) these cut-outs were advertisements for *Soberano Coñac* (cognac). In the early 1990s, however, billboards were prohibited on national roads. A plan was drafted to take the bulls down, but the Spaniards protested, as the lone bull towering along the roadside had become an important national symbol. After considerable clamoring and hoofing, the bulls were painted black and left standing, looming proudly against the horizon. Now the familiar shape decorates t-shirts and pins in souvenir shops, but the real thing is still impressive. Keep your eyes peeled as you whiz through the countryside.

■ Salamanca

For centuries the "hand of Salamanca," a style of brass knockers found in Salamanca, has welcomed students, scholars, rogues, royals, and saints. Salamanca boasts the features of a great medieval city—cathedral, university, and river—all in grandiose proportions. Burning sandstone forms the gargoyles, arches, walls and bell towers of everything from its 13th-century university to Alberto Churriguera's Plaza Mayor.

During medieval times, Salamanca's university joined Bologna, Paris, and Oxford as "the four leading lights of the world." Countless eminent Spanish intellectuals, including Antonio de Nebrija, Fernando de Rojas, and Miguel de Unamuno, have trod its hallowed halls. The perfect balance of the active and the contemplative life is the hallmark of the Salamantine way. Foreign students, especially Americans, invade year-round, while in winter occasional snowfalls accent its heavy, haunting buildings.

ORIENTATION AND PRACTICAL INFORMATION

The beaming **Plaza Mayor** is the social and geographic center of town. Most sights and budget accommodations lie south of the plaza. Areas directly to the north tend to be newer and more expensive. Farther north, beyond the **Plaza de España,** are working-class districts. The **universidad** is south of Pl. Mayor, near the **Plaza de Anaya.** From the **train station** (northeast of the center), either catch bus #1 (75 ptas) to the Gran Vía, a block from Pl. Mercado (next to Pl. Mayor), or, with your back to the station, turn left down Po. Estación to Pl. España and walk down C. Azafranal (or C. Toro) to Pl. Mayor (30min.). From the **bus station,** either catch bus #4 to Gran Vía or walk down C. de Filiberto Villalobos, cross busy Av. Alemania/Po. San Vincente, and go down C. Ramón y Cajal. Keep the park on your left; at the end (just after the Iglesia de la Purís), head left and go up C. Prior, which runs to Pl. Mayor (20min.). Avoid the southwest section of town after dark unless you are accompanied by a friend or bodyguard—Salamanca's drug scene is notorious.

Transportation
Trains: (tel. 923 12 02 02), Po. Estación Ferrocarril, northeast of town. **RENFE,** Pl. Libertad, 10 (tel. 923 21 24 54; open M-F 9am-2pm and 5-8pm). 2 regional lines. To: Ávila (2hr., 3 per day, 835ptas); Palencia (2hr., 2 per day, 1800ptas); Valladolid for transfers (2hr., 10 per day, 1400ptas); Burgos (3hr., 5 per day, 2300ptas); Madrid (3½hr., 4 per day, 1625ptas); Lisbon (6hr., 1 per day, 5000ptas); Barcelona (11½hr., 2 per day, 6000ptas).
Buses: Av. Filiberto Villalobos, 71-85 (tel. 923 23 67 17). Info open M-F 8am-8:30pm, Sa 9am-2:30pm and 4:30-6:30pm, Su 10am-2pm and 4-7pm. To: Ciudad Rodrigo (1hr., 3-11 per day, 715ptas); Zamora (1hr., 9-25 per day, 515ptas); Ávila (1-2hr., 2-7 per day, 820ptas); Valladolid (2hr., 6 per day, 915ptas); Segovia (3hr., 1-3 per day, 1245ptas); Madrid (regular 3hr., 7-10 per day, 2210ptas; express 2½hr., 12-15 per day, 2690ptas); León (3hr., 1-3 per day, 1675ptas); Cáceres (4hr., 3-8 per day, 1700ptas); Barcelona (11½hr., 3 per day, 6425ptas). Also to: La Alberca, Bilbao, Burgos, Cuenca, Valencia, Sevilla, Mérida, Trujillo, Badajoz, Zafra, and Santander.
Taxis: Tele-taxi (24hr. tel. 923 25 00 09) and **Radio Taxi** (24hr. tel. 923 27 11 11).
Car Rental: Avis, Po. Canalejos, 49 (tel. 923 26 97 53). Open M-F 9:30am-1:30pm and 4-7pm, Sa 9am-1:30pm. **Europcar,** Maestro Avila, 3 (tel. 923 26 23 34; open M-F 9:30am-1:15pm and 4:30-7:30pm, Sa 9:30am-1:15pm).

Tourist, Financial, and Local Services
Tourist Office: Municipal, Pl. Mayor, 14 (tel. 923 21 83 42). Big, helpful office. Open M-Sa 9:30am-2pm and 4:30-6:30pm, Su 10am-2pm and 4:30-6:30pm. **Provincial** (tel. 923 26 85 71), C. Rua Mayor, at the Casa de las Conchas. Open M-F 10am-2pm and 5-8pm, Sa-Su 10am-7pm. **Info booths** open occasionally July-Sept. Students distribute maps, info, and accommodations listings from booths in Pl. Anaya, the train station, and the bus station. **Café Alcaraván,** C. Compañía, 12, and **Restaurante El Bardo** (see **Food,** p. 154) both have crowded message boards offering rideshares, language trades, and rooms to rent.

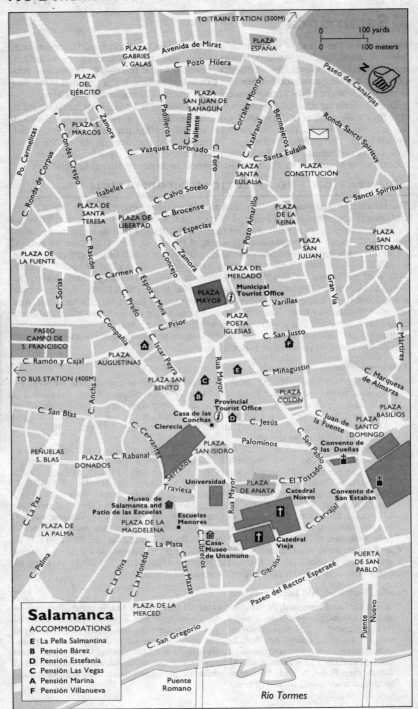

TO TRAIN STATION (500M)

PLAZA GABRIES V. GALAS
Avenida de Mirat
PLAZA ESPAÑA
C. Pozo Hilera
Paseo de Canalejas
PLAZA DEL EJÉRCITO
C. Padilleros
PLAZA SAN JUAN DE SAHAGUN
Corrales Monroy
C. Azafranal
C. Bermejeros
Ronda Sancti Spiritus
C. Zamora
PLAZA S. MARCOS
C. Condes Crespo
C. Frutos Valiente
C. Vazquez Coronado
C. Toro
C. Santa Eulalia
PLAZA SANTA EULALIA
PLAZA CONSTITUCIÓN
Po. Carmelitas
C. Ronda de Corpus
Isabeles
C. Calvo Sotelo
PLAZA DE SANTA TERESA
PLAZA DE LIBERTAD
C. Brocense
C. Especias
C. Pozo Amarillo
PLAZA DE LA REINA
C. Sancti Spiritus
PLAZA SAN CRISTOBAL
PLAZA DE LA FUENTE
C. Rascón
C. Zamora
C. Concejo
PLAZA SAN JULIAN
C. Sorias
C. Carmen
C. Espoz y Mina
C. Prado
C. Prior
PLAZA DEL MERCADO
Gran Via
PASEO CAMPO DE S. FRANCISCO
C. Compañía
PLAZA MAYOR
Municipal Tourist Office
C. Varillas
← C. Ramón y Cajal
PLAZA AUGUSTINAS
C. Iscar Peyra
PLAZA POETA IGLESIAS
C. San Justo
F
TO BUS STATION (400M)
Rua Mayor
E
C. Miñagustin
C. Mártires
PLAZA SAN BENITO
C
B
PLAZA COLÓN
C. Marquesa de Almarza
C. Ancha
Casa de las Conchas
Provincial Tourist Office
D
C. Jesús
PLAZA BASILIOS
C. San Blas
Clerecía
C. Juan de la Fuente
PLAZA SANTO DOMINGO
PEÑUELAS S. BLAS
PLAZA DONADOS
C. Rabanal
C. Cervantes
PLAZA SAN ISIDRO
Palominos
C. San Pablo
Convento de las Dueñas
Serranos
Universidad
PLAZA DE ANAYA
C. El Tostado
Catedral Nuevo
Convento de San Esteban
C. La Paz
Traviesa
Museo de Salamanca and Patio de las Escuelas
Rua Mayor
C. Carvajal
PLAZA DE LA PALMA
PLAZA DE LA MAGDALENA
Escuelas Menores
Catedral Vieja
C. Palma
C. La Plata
Casa-Museo de Unamuno
PUERTA DE SAN PABLO
C. La Oliva
C. La Moneda
C. Las Mazas
C. Gibraltar
Paseo del Rector Esperaeé
Puente Nuevo
PLAZA DE LA MERCED
C. San Gregorio
Puente Romano
Río Tormes

0 ___ 100 yards
0 ___ 100 meters
N

CASTILLA Y LEÓN

Salamanca
ACCOMMODATIONS
E La Pella Salmantina
B Pensión Bárez
D Pensión Estefanía
C Pensión Las Vegas
A Pensión Marina
F Pensión Villanueva

Budget Travel: TIVE, Po. Carmelitas (a.k.a. Av. Alemania), 83 (tel. 923 26 77 31). Student services, but no ticket sales. Long lines—go early. Open M-F 9am-2pm. **Juventus Travel,** Pl. Libertad, 4 (tel. 923 21 74 07; fax 923 21 74 08). Ticket sales. Open M-F 9:45am-1:45pm and 4:30-8pm, Sa 10am-1:30pm.
Currency Exchange: ATMs on C. Toro. **Banco Central Hispano** is on R. Mayor.
Luggage Storage: At the train station (300ptas) and bus station (75ptas per item).
English Bookstores: Cervantes (tel. 923 21 86 02; fax 923 26 18 95), Pl. Santa Eulalia, near C. Azafranal. Enormous bookstore with 3 entrances, all within a block of each other. Open M-F 9:45am-1:30pm and 4:30-8:30pm, Sa 9:45am-1:45pm. **Portonaris,** R. Mayor, 35 (tel. 923 26 58 21), opposite the Casa de Conchas. Open M-F 10am-2pm and 5-8:30pm, Sa 10am-1:30pm.
Gay and Lesbian Services: Colectivo de Gais y Lesbianas de Salamanca has a telephone line (tel. 923 24 64 71) staffed M 7-9pm.

Emergency and Communications

Emergency: dial 091 or 092. **Police:** (tel. 923 27 91 38), in the Ayuntamiento, Pl. Mayor, or at Ronda de Sancti-Spiritus, 8 (tel. 923 26 53 11).
Hospital: Hospital Clínico Universitario, Po. San Vicente, 108 (tel. 923 29 11 00).
Internet Access: Informática Abaco Bar, C. Zamora, 7 (tel. 923 26 15 89; fax 923 26 15 87), near Pl. Mayor. 150ptas per 15min. until 11pm, 150ptas per 30min. after. Open M-F 9:30am-1am, Sa noon-2:30pm and 4pm-1am, Su 4pm-1am. **Campus Cibermático,** Pl. Mayor, 10, 1st fl. (tel. 923 27 11 31), down from the tourist office. 250ptas per 30min. Open M-F 11am-1:30pm and 5-7pm.
Post Office: Gran Vía, 25 (tel. 923 26 06 07). Open for stamps and Lista de Correos M-F 8:30am-8:30pm and Sa 9:30am-2pm. **Postal Code:** 37001.

ACCOMMODATIONS AND CAMPING

Thanks to floods of students, *hostales* and *pensiones* flourish in Salamanca, and prices tend to be quite reasonable. Accommodations often fill up in August, so call ahead. A tourist office brochure lists all of them. There are plenty of cheap *pensiones* on side streets off Pl. Mayor, especially on **Calle Meléndez,** just south of the plaza.

Pensión Marina, C. Doctrinos, 4, 3rd fl. (tel. 923 21 65 69), between C. Compañía and C. Prado. A plant-filled paradise with an elevator soon to come. One of the best values in town—comfortable bedrooms, gregarious owners, and 2 mammoth TV lounges. Can get chilly in winter. Doubles 2700ptas. Showers 200ptas.
Pensión Las Vegas, C. Meléndez, 13, 1st fl. (tel. 923 21 87 49), down C. Corrillo. Cushy beds, TV, and tons of plants. Singles 1300-1500ptas; doubles 2500ptas, with bath 3000ptas; triples 4000ptas, with bath 4500ptas. Hot showers 150ptas.
Pensión Bárez, C. Meléndez, 19 (tel. 923 21 74 95). Romantic windows in several sparkling clean rooms. Generous owners provide TV lounge. Singles 1400ptas; doubles 2600ptas; triples 3000-3600ptas. Showers 150ptas.
Pensión Estefanía, C. Jesús, 3-5 (tel. 923 21 73 72 or 923 24 87 48). Floral bedspreads grace rooms on a quiet street off bustling Pl. Mayor. Singles 1750ptas; doubles with shower 3400ptas; triples 4600. Showers 150ptas. No winter heating.
Pensión Villanueva, C. San Justo, 8, 1st fl. (tel. 923 26 88 33). Exit Pl. Mayor via Pl. Poeta Iglesias, cross the street, and take the first left. Funky beds and spacious rooms. Singles 1300ptas, with shower 1700-1800ptas; doubles 2700ptas, with shower 3200ptas; triples 4200ptas. Less expensive on weekdays.
Hostal La Perla Salamantina, Sánchez Barbero, 7 (tel. 923 21 76 56). Exit Pl. Mayor via Pl. Poeta Iglesias, cross the street, and take the first right. Everything sparkles. Plenty of rooms with plenty of room. Singles 2000ptas, with shower 2500ptas; doubles with shower 3800ptas, with bath 4800ptas.
Camping: Regio (tel. 923 13 88 88), on Ctra. Salamanca, 4km toward Madrid. Albertur buses leave from the Gran Vía every 30min. A 1st-class site with all the amenities: nature, hot showers, nearby public transportation, pool, tennis courts, and currency exchange, in a luxury tourist complex with a 4-star hotel, restaurants, *terrazas,* and bars. 425ptas per person, per tent, and per car, 375ptas for a one-person tent. Visa, MC. **Don Quijote** (tel. 989 18 92 73), on the Ctra. Salamanca, 4km toward Aldealengua. Minivans leave from the Gran Vía. A small, 2nd-class campsite. 325ptas per person, 350ptas per car, 375ptas per tent. Open Mar.-Oct.

FOOD

Every clique has its favorite cafe in **Plaza Mayor.** All serve the same decent food at slightly inflated prices. Students meet at *bar-restaurantes* lining the streets between the plaza and the university, where a full meal costs under 1000ptas. **Simago,** C. Toro, 82, has a downstairs **supermarket** with a large selection of fresh produce (open M-Sa 9:30am-8:30pm). Cheap markets abound north of Av. Mirat.

Restaurante El Bardo, C. Compañía, 8 (tel. 923 21 90 89), between the Casa de Conchas and the Clerecía. A traditional Spanish restaurant crowded with Americans. Lively bar downstairs. Meat entrees 1000-1800ptas. Salads 600-850ptas. Vegetarian *menú* (1000ptas). Open daily 10am-5pm and 7pm-1am. Visa, MC.

El Ave, C. Libreros, 24. Spacious, tiled, and bustling. Big-screen TV and lighter Spanish specialties. *Platos combinados* 675-725ptas, *menú* 1100ptas. Open M-F 8am-midnight, Sa-Su 8am-2am.

Pans & Company, C. Rua Mayor, 26. The Spanish fast food chain many travelers grow to love. Selection of tasty *bocadillos,* including some vegetarian (395-485ptas). Open M-F 10am-midnight, Sa-Su 11am-1am.

La Luna, C. Libreros, 4. The bright red sign and lively music will make you happy. Veggie burgers, vegetarian *platos combinados* (875-975ptas). Meat meals 975-1800ptas, salads 900ptas, *menú* 1100ptas. Open daily 10am-1am.

SIGHTS

Plaza Mayor and Environs

Pick a style, any style—they're all here from Roman to Romanesque, Gothic, Renaissance, and Baroque, and all in sandstone. Between the arches of the Baroque **Plaza Mayor** hang medallions with bas-reliefs of famous *españoles,* from El Cid to Franco. The plaza is Alberto Churriguera's *tour de force,* and the pinnacle of Churrigueresque architecture. Andrés García de Quiñones designed the **Ayuntamiento's** facade. Churriguera's **Pabellón Real** is to its left.

The cafe-lined R. Mayor runs to the south of the plaza (the clock lies on the north side). On this road is one of Salamanca's most famous landmarks, the 15th-century **Casa de las Conchas** (House of Shells; tel. 923 26 93 17), adorned by scallop shells chiseled in sandstone. *(Open M-F 9am-9pm, Sa 9am-2pm and 4-7pm, Su 10am-2pm and 4-7pm. Free.)* Pilgrims who journeyed to Santiago de Compostela wore shells to commemorate their visit to the tomb of St. James the Apostle, and the owner of the *casa,* a knight of the Order of Santiago, wanted to create a monument to the renowned pilgrimage site. The building is now a public library and home to the Provincial Tourist Office. There are occasional art exhibits here, and the courtyard is open to visitors. The **Clerecía** (a.k.a. Real Colegio del Espíritu Santo; tel. 923 26 46 60), across the street, is a Baroque complex that was, until recently, used by a Jesuit community. *(Open for mass M-Sa 1:15pm and 7:30pm, Su 12:30pm. Free.)* It has a church, a school, and what was the community's old living quarters: 300 rooms with 520 doors and 906 windows. The narrow street prevents full appreciation of the wonderful facade. A few wealthy believers once offered a large sum of money to widen the street.

The University

Tel. 923 29 44 00. University and museum open M-F 9:30am-1:30pm and 4-7:30pm, Sa 9:30am-1:30pm and 4-7pm, Su 10am-1:30pm. Admission to university and museum 300ptas, seniors and students 150ptas. Tickets sold until 30min. before closing.

The focal point of Salamanca, the great **universidad,** established in 1218, is best entered from the **Patio de las Escuelas,** off C. Libreros. The statue here represents **Fray Luis de León,** a university professor and one of the most respected literati of the Golden Age. A Hebrew scholar and a classical Spanish stylist to boot, Fray Luis was arrested by the Inquisition for translating Solomon's *Song of Songs* into Castilian and

CASTILLA Y LEÓN

for preferring the Hebrew version of the Bible to the Latin one. After five years of imprisonment, he returned to the university and began his first lecture: *"Decíamos ayer..."* ("As we were saying yesterday...").

The university's entryway is one of the best examples of Spanish Plateresque, a style named after the filigree work of *plateros* (silversmiths). The central medallion represents King Fernando and Queen Isabel. The small frog atop a skull is Salamanca's "gray eminence," said to represent the dankness of prison life and bring good luck on exams. If you spot the frog without assistance you will be married within the year. The walls are marked with students' initials, painted upon graduation in an ink of bull's blood, olive oil, and herbs.

The old lecture halls inside are open to the public. **Aula Fray Luis de León** has been left in more or less its original state. The hard benches were considered luxurious by medieval standards, as most students then sat on the floor. A plaque bears Unamuno's famous love poem about the students of Salamanca. The sumptuous **Paraninfo** (auditorium) contains Baroque tapestries and a portrait of Carlos IV attributed to Goya. Fray Luis is buried in the 18th-century **chapel.** The **Antigua Biblioteca** (old library) is the most spectacular of all, located atop a magnificent Plateresque staircase whose statues and historic books can be seen through a glass cube. The sign in the library that threatens excommunication for those who steal or damage books has been oft reproduced Salamanca's souvenir shops. (Don't miss the room of fossilized turtles, apparently the second most important of such collections in the world.)

Also on the exterior patio are the **Escuelas Menores,** with a smaller version of the main entryway's Plateresque facade. There the **University Museum** (tel. 923 29 12 25) preserves the **Cielo de Salamanca,** the library's famous ceiling, whose 15th-century fresco of the zodiac was painted by the celebrated Gallego brothers, Francisco and Fernando. Take a peek at the intricate strongbox with its many locks.

The **Museo de Salamanca** (tel. 923 21 22 35) occupies a beautiful 15th-century building once home to Álvarez Albarca, physician to the *Reyes Católicos. (Open Tu-F 9:45am-1:45pm and 4:45-7:15pm, Sa 10:15am-1:15pm and 4:45-7:45pm, Su 10:15am-1:45pm. 200ptas.)* Along with the *Casa de las Conchas,* this structure is among Spain's most important examples of 15th-century architecture. The museum has an intriguing collection of painting and sculpture as well as some temporary exhibits in archaeology and ethnology. Its most important canvases are Juan de Flandes' portrait of Saint Andrew and Luis de Morales's *Llanto por Cristo Muerto,* both from the 16th century, and Vaccaro's ethereal *Inmaculada.*

To the right of the university's main entrance is the absorbing **Casa-Museo de Unamuno** (tel. 923 29 44 00, ext. 1196). *(Open July-Sept. Tu-F 9:30am-1:30pm, Sa-Su 10am-noon; Oct.-June Tu-F 9:30am-1:30pm and 4-6pm, Sa-Su 10am-2pm. Research room open M-F 8:30am-2:30pm. Mandatory guided tour in Spanish every 30min., 300ptas. Ring the bell if the house appears closed.)* Miguel de Unamuno, Rector of the University at the begin-

Just Another Manic Monday

In days of old, students age 14-25 traveled from all over Spain—by foot, mule, or wagon—to study in Salamanca, one of medieval Europe's greatest universities. In order to be admitted, one had to pass a difficult set of exams and show proof of "pure blood." No trace of Moorish or Jewish ancestry was permitted. As evidenced by the university's spartan Aula de Fray Luis de León, students studied under strict ecclesiastical authority and were expected to exhibit "composure, discipline, silence, piety, confinement, chastity, humility, and obedience," and "refrain from sport." Well, that was the theory anyway.

Campus activities drew vigor from "fraternal brotherhoods," whose rivalries climaxed in duels at the Escuelas Menores. Rising pheromone levels drew prostitutes from nearby lands—so many that a *fiesta* celebrated them. Banished to the other side of the Río Tormes during Lent, the prostitutes were led back to the city in triumph on the second Monday following Lent. The post-festival was named *Lunes de Agua* (Water Monday), and is still celebrated.

ning of this century, is revered as one of the founding figures of the Spanish literary movement known as the "Generation of '98." Unamuno passionately opposed dictatorship and encouraged his students to do so also. His stand against General Primo de Rivera's 1923 *coup d'état* led to his dismissal from the rector's post; he was triumphantly reinstated some years later. Among the more charming exhibits in the residence are Unamuno's ruminations about his birth and his intricate origami.

Cathedrals

Cathedrals open daily Apr.-Sept. 9am-2pm and 4-8pm; Oct.-Mar. 9am-1pm and 4-6pm. Old cathedral, cloister, and museum 300ptas. New cathedral free.

Begun in 1513 to accommodate the growing number of believers, the Catedral Nueva and its spires were not finished until 1733. While several later architects decided to retain the original late Gothic style, they could not resist adding touches from later periods, notably its Baroque tower. Restorers from the 20th century succumbed to the same temptation, adding an astronaut, a bull, and a demon eating ice cream to the side entrance's facade. The *Cristo de las Batallas*, carried by El Cid in his campaigns, is in the central chapel on the wall behind the main altar.

The smaller **Catedral Vieja** (1140) was built in the Romanesque style. Apocalyptic angels separate the sinners from the saved inside the striking cupola. On the outside of the cupola is the scaled **Torre del Gallo** (Tower of the Rooster). Named for the shape of its weathervane, it is best seen from the cloister courtyard. The oldest part of the cathedral is the **Capilla de San Martín,** with brilliantly colored frescoes dating from 1242. Off to one side is the 12th-century cloister, rebuilt after the earthquake of 1755. Here, the **Capilla de Santa Bárbara,** also called the Capilla del Título, was once the site of final exams. The **cathedral museum** (tel. 923 21 74 76) features a paneled ceiling by Fernando Gallegos and houses the Mudéjar Salinas organ (one of the oldest in Europe). Outside the older cathedral is the famed **Patio Chico,** which offers a beautiful view of the two cathedrals.

Convents

Christopher Columbus might have spent time in one of Salamanca's most dramatic monasteries, the **Convento de San Esteban,** downhill from the cathedrals. During the afternoon, its facade becomes a solid mass of light depicting the stoning of St. Stephen and the crucifixion of Christ. The beautiful **Claustro de los Reyes** (Kings' Cloister; tel. 923 21 50 00) is a medley of Gothic and Plateresque. *(Open daily Apr.-Sept. 9am-1pm and 4-8pm; Oct.-Mar. 9am-1pm and 5-6:30pm. 200ptas.)* Churriguera's central altarpiece in the church (1693) is a masterpiece of the Spanish Baroque.

The nearby **Convento de las Dueñas** (tel. 923 21 54 42) was formerly the Mudéjar palace of a court official. *(Open daily Apr.-Sept. 10:30am-1pm and 4:30-7pm; Oct.-Mar. 10:30am-1pm and 4:30-5:30pm. 200ptas, students 100ptas. A shop selling (holy) candies, made by the 29 nuns themselves, is on the 1st floor.)* The elegant cloister is perhaps the most interesting, and most beautiful, in Salamanca. Medallions adorning the walls depict real Salamantines, and exuberantly gargoyled columns line the second floor.

Elsewhere

Take a stroll down C. Rua Mayor from Pl. Mayor to the **Puente Romano,** a 2000-year-old Roman bridge spanning the scenic Río Tormes. The bridge was part of an ancient Roman road called the *Camino de la Plata* (Silver Way) that ran from Mérida in Extremadura to Astorga, near León. Legend has it that Hannibal and his elephants once crossed it. The pre-Roman **Toro Ibérico** stands on the near end of the bridge, a headless granite bull. The old bull figures in one of the most famous episodes of *Lazarillo de Tormes,* the prototype of the 16th-century picaresque novel and a predecessor to *Don Quijote,* when the diminutive hero finds his head slammed into the bull's stone ear after cheating his employer.

ENTERTAINMENT

The **Plaza Mayor** is the town's social center. Locals, students, and tourists come at all hours to lounge in its cafes or to take a stroll. At night, members of various local college or graduate school **tunas** (medieval-style student troubadour groups) often finish their rounds here. Dressed in traditional black capes, they strut around the plaza serenading women with guitars, mandolins, *bandurrias,* and tambourines. When the show is over, they make excellent drinking partners, doing their best to emulate Don Juan. People overflow from the plaza as far west as **San Vicente.** Student nightlife is also concentrated on the **Gran Vía, Calle de Bordadores,** and side streets. Bars blast music ranging from reggae to vintage rock to modern ballads. **Calle Prior** and **Calle Rua Mayor** are full of bars, and a few charming *terrazas* (and fewer Americans) gather in **Plaza de la Fuente,** off Av. Alemania. More intense partying occurs off **Calle Varillas.** Cafes and bars initiate those heading for the club scene and then reclaim them later in the evening.

Camelot, C. Bordadores, 3. Medieval chic. This monastery-turned-club is one of the stops on the **Gastby** (no, not Gatsby) and **Cum Laude** (C. Prior) club-hopping route. On weekends, places are packed by 2am. No cover.

El Corrillo Café, C. Meléndez, 14-18. Live jazz (or hip hop on the radio) for the ultra-hip in a chill setting with a Hollywood theme. Performances 1000ptas. No cover.

Birdland, C. Azafranal, 57, by Pl. España. Drink (500ptas) to jazz greats. Open nightly 5pm-4:30am.

Submarino, C. San Justo, 27 (crossing Gran Vía). Built in an old boat—get hip with life vests. A gay and straight clientele grooves under black lights.

Café Novelty, on Pl. Mayor. The oldest cafe in town and a meeting place for students and professors. Miguel de Unamuno was a regular. Open until 2am.

Pub Rojo y Negro, C. Espoz y Mina, 22. Scrumptious coffee, liqueur, and ice cream concoctions (200-1100ptas) in an old-fashioned setting (with a dance floor) catering to couples. Open M-F noon-2:30am, Sa-Su noon-4:30am.

Lugares, a free, slim pamphlet distributed at the tourist office and at some bars, lists everything from movies and special events to bus schedules. Posters at the **Colegio Mayor** (Palacio de Anaya) advertise university events, free films, and student theater. During the summer, Salamanca sponsors the **Verano Cultural de Salamanca,** with silent movies, contemporary Spanish cinema, pop singers, and theater groups. On June 12, in honor of San Juan de Sahagún, there is a **corrida de toros** charity event. September 8 to 21, Salamanca indulges in festivals and exhibitions, most with bull themes. The **Semana Santa** activities are also quite famous.

■ Near Salamanca: Ciudad Rodrigo

A medieval town 21km from Portugal, Ciudad Rodrigo's honey-colored stonework glistens from above the surrounding plains. The old city's medieval walls enclose intricate 18th-century defenses and other masonry treasures. These stone features and a quirky cathedral lure daytrippers from nearby Salamanca (1¼hr.).

PRACTICAL INFORMATION Ciudad Rodrigo is easily accessible by bus from Salamanca; trains are infrequent and the station is 35 minutes from the old city. The **bus station** (tel. 923 46 10 09) is on C. Campo de Toledo, and buses go to Salamanca (1¼hr., M-F 8 per day, Sa 5 per day, Su 3 per day, 715ptas). Go left out of the bus station, take the second right (uphill) and pass through the stone arch ahead; the **tourist office,** Pl. Amayuelas, 5 (tel. 923 46 05 61), is on the left, less than one block from the cathedral and three blocks from Pl. Mayor. (Open M-F 10am-2pm and 5-8pm, Sa 10am-2pm and 4-7pm). Municipal **police** patrol from Pl. Mayor, 27 (tel. 923 46 04 68). The **post office,** C. Dámaso Ledesma, 12 (tel. 923 46 01 17), in Pl. Mayor, rests in a bizarre 16th-century building also known as **Casa de los Vásquez.** The interior definitely warrants a gander. (Open M-F 8:30am-2:30pm, Sa 9am-1pm.)

ACCOMMODATIONS AND FOOD **Pensión Madrid,** C. Madrid, 20 (tel. 923 46 24 67), off Pl. Mayor on the side perpendicular to the Ayuntamiento, has well-ventilated rooms (doubles 3000ptas; a super triple with bath and kitchenette 6000ptas). Cafes on Pl. Mayor serve inexpensive *platos combinados* (450-575ptas). Alternatively, try hiking out to **Pizzería Gepetto,** Av. Conde Foxá, 39 (tel. 923 48 14 34). Go right exiting the city walls and walk about four blocks past the rotary, continuing along the road that's on the right side of the Insalud building. There's a variety of cheap pizzas from which to choose (individual 500ptas, small 850ptas, large 1800ptas).

SIGHTS The **cathedral** is the town's masterpiece. *(Open daily 9:30am-1:30pm and 4-8pm. Free.)* Originally a Romanesque church commissioned by Fernando II of León, it was substantially modified in the 16th-century Gothic style. The **coro** (chorus) was the master work of Rodrigo Alemán from 1498 to 1504 and includes the sculptor's signature—a carving of his head. The two 16th-century organs star in a series of concerts every August. The **claustro** alone merits a trip to Ciudad Rodrigo. Fascinating figures decorate the columns—making love, playing peek-a-boo, and flirting with cannibalism. Ears, cheeks, and breasts are all subject to nibbling. At one corner, monsters devour Muslims; while above the courtyard entrance a choir of angels all shape their mouths for the appropriate note (*do, re, mi*). The cathedral's **museum** is filled with strange and thrilling pieces, including an ancient clavichord, the "ballot box" used to determine the cathedral's hierarchy, richly embroidered robes and slippers worn by bishops and priors, and Velázquez's *Llanto de Adam y Eva por Ariel muerto. (Cloister and museum open daily 10am-1pm and 4-6pm. 200ptas. Great tour in Spanish.)*

Few structures have appeared in Rodrigo since the days when the ornate buildings served as palaces for noble families. The 14th- and 15th-century **Castillo de Enrique de Trastámara,** by Gonzalo Arias de Genizaro, crowns the battlements and surveys the surrounding countryside and the Agueda River. A road on the right leads to Portugal. It is now a *parador de turismo* (luxury hotel).

■ Near Salamanca: Alba de Tormes

Santa Teresa left her heart in Alba de Tormes. In fact it's in a big urn, along with her body, in the lovely **Convento de la Anunciación,** which she founded in 1571. In her autobiography, she writes that her heart was pierced by an angel of the Lord with a fiery dart and after repeated stabbings, she was left "on fire with the great love of God." The convent is in the Plazuela de Santa Teresa, two blocks from the peaceful Plaza Mayor. If you'd like a tour, ask a guide at the **Museo Teresiano** across the street. *(Open Tu-Sa 10am-1:30pm and 4-7:30pm, Su 10am-2pm. Donation requested.)* The museum holds other parts of Santa Teresa and bits of San Juan de la Cruz. A few blocks down from the Pl. Mayor is the **Castillo de los Duques de Alba,** remnants of a 15th- to 16th-century structure excavated in 1991-1993. *(Open July-Aug. Sa-Su; Sept.-June tourist office staff can let you in.)* Renaissance frescoes and an archaeological exhibit of the remains are displayed. Tiny Alba de Tormes also boasts seven churches, monasteries, and convents, plus a neo-Gothic basilica. The **tourist office,** C. Lepanto, 4 (tel. 923 30 08 98), aids visitors when it's open. (Hours not fixed, but open daily in summer about 10am-2pm and 4:30-8:30pm; in winter 10:30am-2pm and 4-6:30pm.) Alba de Tormes makes an easy daytrip by **bus** from Salamanca (30min., 8-12 per day, 175ptas).

■ Near Salamanca: La Alberca and Peña de Francia

Three mountain ranges to the south conceal some delightful small towns between the plains of Castilla y León and Extremadura. **La Alberca,** a charming, rustic village, was the first rural town in the country to be named an official National Historic-Artistic Monument (1940). Above La Alberca in the Sierra de Francia rises the province's highest peak, the **Peña de Francia** (1723m). Determined souls can scale the mountain from La Alberca. **Empresa V. Cosme** (tel. 923 30 02 71) runs **buses** from Salamanca to La Alberca (1½hr., M-F 2 per day, Sa-Su 1 per day, 600ptas). For more info about La Alberca or Peña de Francia, contact the **tourist office** (tel. 923 41 52 91, ext. 15; open June-Sept. M-Sa 10am-1pm and 5-7pm, Sa 10am-1pm and 4-6pm, Su 10am-1pm).

■ Zamora

Provincial Zamora (pop. 65,000) is a lazy crossroads of human and animal life. Dogs trot leashless past the cathedral, and white storks fashion nests atop the city's eight Romanesque churches. Zamora has not seen much action since the 12th century, when Sancho II died here during his attempt to subdue his errant sister Doña Urraca and consolidate his hold on the House of Castile. Although she had been passed over in her father's will in favor of Sancho and another brother, Urraca managed to steal away her brothers' inheritance by threatening to sleep with every man in the House of Castile if the kingdom was not passed to her. Vestiges of this illustrious and shocking past attract history buffs, but not too many of them.

ORIENTATION AND PRACTICAL INFORMATION Modern train and bus stations lounge in the northeast corner of the city, a 15-minute walk from **Plaza Mayor.** To get to the center from the train station, turn left onto C. Alfonso Peña (which becomes Av. Tres Cruces) and continue to Pl. Alemania; turn left onto C. Alfonso IX and go two blocks to **Calle de Santa Clara,** a major pedestrian street that leads to Pl. Mayor. From the bus station, turn left on C. Alfonso Peña and follow the same directions.

   Trains leave from the station (tel. 980 52 19 56; 24hr. tel. 980 52 11 10), at the end of C. Alfonso Peña, 100m down from the bus station, and go to: Valladolid (1½hr., 3 per day, 985ptas); Madrid (4hr., 5 per day, 2150ptas); La Coruña (7hr., 3 per day, 3700ptas); and Barcelona (12hr., 5 per week, 7600ptas). **Buses** depart from C. Alfonso Peña, 3 (tel. 980 52 12 81 or 980 52 12 82), to: Valladolid (1½hr., 7 per day, 780ptas); León (2hr., 6 per day, 1160ptas); Madrid (3½hr., 5 per day, 1600-2300ptas); La Coruña (7hr., 3 per day, 3125ptas); Barcelona (12hr., 3 per day, 6785ptas); and Bragança, Portugal (2hr., 2 per day, 1495ptas). **Empresa F. Ledesma** runs to Zamora from Bragança (M, W, Sa 4pm, 1495ptas).

   The municipal **tourist office,** C. Santa Clara, 20 (tel. 980 53 18 45; fax 980 53 38 13), hands out multilingual brochures, maps, and a hostel guide (open M-F 10am-2pm and 5-8pm, Sa 9am-2:30pm and 5-8pm). **Luggage storage** is in the bus station (90ptas per bag; open daily 7am-midnight) and train station (300ptas per bag; open 24hr.). The **municipal police** can be reached at 980 53 04 62. In an **emergency,** call 091 or 092. The **post office,** C. Santa Clara, 15 (tel. 980 51 33 71 or 980 51 07 67; fax 980 53 03 35), just past C. Benquente, offers stamps, Lista de Correos, and **fax** service (open M-F 8:30am-8:30pm, Sa 9am-2pm). The **postal code** is 49080.

ACCOMMODATIONS AND FOOD For simple rooms at reasonable prices, investigate the streets off **Calle de Alfonso Peña** by the train station or off C. Santa Clara near Pl. Mayor. Call ahead during the fiestas the last week of June, and try negotiating prices in the off-season. Catch some winks at **Pensión Fernando III,** Pl. Fernando III, 2 (tel. 980 52 36 88). From the bus station, take the first right uphill off C. Alfonso Peña. The large, sunlit rooms are a bargain and close to the stations. All rooms have sinks; bathrooms are down the hall. (Singles 1000-1300ptas; doubles 2000-2500ptas; triples 2900ptas. Meals available.) **Pensión Gemi,** C. Juan II, 10 (tel. 980 51 96 88), has similar rooms, some with showers (singles 1000-1300ptas; doubles 2000-2500ptas; triples 2900ptas). Head up C. Alfonso Peña three blocks from the bus station and turn left.

   Dining in Zamora tends to be expensive. Restaurants rub elbows near C. Santa Clara and around Pl. Mayor, particularly on **Calle de los Herreros.** Roast meats, particularly *preses de ternera* (veal) and *bacalao a la tranca* (cod), are regional specialties. The **Mercado de Abastos,** in a domed building just to the left off C. Santa Clara after the tourist office, provides all the basics (open M-Sa 7am-3pm). Steer a shopping cart at trusty **Supermarket Simago,** on C. Victor Gallego, north of Pl. Alemania off Av. Tres Cruces (open M-Sa 8:30am-9pm). **Mesón Los Abuelos,** the local hangout, is at C. Herreros, 30. More kids than *abuelos* (grandfathers) gather here, where *bocadillos* run 300-450ptas and *raciones* cost 700-900ptas. (Open daily noon-2am.)

SIGHTS Zamora's foremost monument is its mostly Romanesque **cathedral,** begun in 1135, a stocky building topped with a Byzantine dome. *(Open daily 10am-1pm and 5-8pm. Free.)* Around the main altar swarm hosts of angels painted blue and gold with an unusual, child-like hand. Inside the cloister, the **Museo de la Catedral** features the priceless 15th-century Black Tapestries. *(Open Apr.-Sept. Tu-Sa 11am-2pm and 5-8pm, Su 11am-2pm; Oct.-Mar. Tu-Sa 11am-2pm and 4-6pm, Su 11am-2pm. 300ptas.)* In these gruesome Trojan War tapestries, the artist captures numerous warriors and princesses at the very moment of their decapitation. Just uphill from the cathedral, a **medieval castle** (or what's left of it) reigns over a beautiful garden. The neighboring **Roman walls** command a fine view of the mighty Río Duero. From the castle's segment with the moat, look back toward the city center at the **Iglesia de San Isidoro;** elegant white storks often perch there.

Eight handsome **Romanesque churches** remain within the walls of the old city, each gleaming in the wake of recent restoration. *(Open Tu-Sa 10am-1pm and 5-8pm; Nov.-June only during mass. Free.)* If you suspect they'll all begin to look the same, at least drop by the intricately carved porch of **La Magdalena.** The luminescent marble-veined windows in **Iglesia San Juan** and the bright green-and-orange organ in **Iglesia San Ildefonso** are also worth a look.

The **Museo de Semana Santa,** in sleepy Pl. Santa María la Nueva, is a rare find. *(Open M-Sa 10am-2pm and 5-8pm, Su 10am-2pm. 300ptas.)* Hooded mannequins stand guard over elaborately sculpted floats from the turn of the century. To reach the museum from Pl. Mayor, take C. Sacramento and turn right on C. Barandales.

■ León

León is a bustling provincial capital and university town, home to a cathedral whose spectacular blue stained-glass windows have earned the city the nickname *La Ciudad Azul* (The Blue City). Proud *leoneses* (literally "lions") roar that their cathedral is the finest in of all Spain. León was founded in AD 68 by the Seventh Roman Legion—hence the name (León stems from *legio,* Latin for legion). The lions emblazoned everywhere postdate the naming of the city and are actually an inspired misreading. Formerly the seat of the Asturian-Leonese kingdom and a springboard for the *Reconquista,* León's material ease today comes from its fertile agricultural hinterland and the deposits of iron and cobalt mined throughout the province.

ORIENTATION AND PRACTICAL INFORMATION

Most of León lies on the east side of the **Río Bernesga,** while the bus and train stations are in the west end. Across the river from the stations is the modern commercial district, directly before the old city. **Avenida de Palencia** (take a left out of the bus station or a right out of the train station) leads across the river to **Plaza Guzmán el Bueno,** where it becomes **Avenida de Ordoño II** and leads to the cathedral. The road then bisects the new city and becomes **Avenida del Generalísimo Franco** in the old town, on the other side of **Plaza Santo Domingo,** splitting the old town in two.

Transportation

Trains: RENFE, Av. Astorga, 2 (info. tel. 987 27 02 02; station tel. 987 22 37 04), across the river from Pl. Guzmán el Bueno, at the bend in Av. Palencia. Info open 24hr. **Ticket office,** C. Carmen, 4 (tel. 987 22 05 25). Open M-F 9:30am-2pm and 5-8pm, Sa 10am-1:30pm. To: Astorga (45min., 8 per day, 400ptas); Palencia (1½hr., 14 per day, 1100-1400ptas); Valladolid (2½hr., 12 per day, 1370-1800ptas); Oviedo (2½hr., 7 per day, 900-1400ptas); Madrid (4½-5½hr., 12 per day, 3190-3500ptas); La Coruña (7hr., 5 per day, 3200-4400ptas). **FEVE,** Est. de Matallana, Av. Padre Isla, 48 (tel. 987 22 59 19), north of Pl. Santo Domingo. Trains to local destinations. A full bus and train schedule is printed daily in *Diario de León* (110ptas).

Buses: Estación de Autobuses, Po. Ingeniero Saenz de Miera (tel. 987 21 00 00). Info open M-Sa 7:30am-9pm. To: Astorga (45min., 16 per day, 405ptas); Valladolid

CASTILLA Y LEÓN

(2hr., 8 per day, 1060ptas); Zamora (2½hr., 6 per day, 1135ptas); Madrid (4½hr., 12 per day, 2550ptas); Santander (5hr., 1 per day, 2800ptas).
Taxis: Radio Taxi (tel. 987 24 24 51).
Car Rental: Hertz (tel. 987 23 19 99) on C. Sampirosh. Must be over 25 and have had license for one year. Open M-F 9am-2pm and 4-7pm, Sa 9am-1pm.

Tourist and Financial Services

Tourist Office: Pl. Regla, 3 (tel. 987 23 70 82; fax 987 27 33 91), in front of the cathedral. Free city maps, regional brochures, and lodgings guide. English spoken. Open M-F 10am-2pm and 5-7:30pm, Sa 10am-2pm and 4:30-8:30pm, Su 10am-2pm.
Budget Travel: TIVE, C. Arquitecto Torbado, 4 (tel. 987 20 09 51), just off Pl. Cortes. ISIC 500ptas. HI cards 1800ptas. Open M-F 9am-2pm.
Currency Exchange: Banco Central Hispano, Pl. Santo Domingo. Follow Av. Ordoño II into the plaza. Open M-F 8:30am-2:30pm. No commission.

Local Services

Luggage Storage: At the **train station** (lockers 400ptas). Open 24hr. At the **bus station** (25ptas per bag). Open M-F 9am-2pm and 6-8pm, Sa 9am-2pm.
English Bookstore: Pastor, Pl. Santo Domingo, 4 (tel. 987 22 58 56). Substantial selection. Open M-F 10am-12:30pm and 4:30-8pm, Sa 10am-1:45pm.

Emergency and Communications

Emergency: call 091 or 092. **Police:** C. Villa Benavente, 6 (tel. 987 20 73 12 or 091).
Medical Services: Hospital Virgen Blanca (tel. 987 23 74 00).
Telephones and Internet Access: Locutorio La Rúa, C. La Rúa, 8 (tel. 987 23 01 06; fax 987 23 01 91). Take C. Ancha from Pl. Santo Domingo and turn right on C. La Rúa. Open M-F 9:30am-2:30pm and 4:30-11pm, Sa 9:30am-2:30pm.
Post Office: Jardín San Francisco (tel. 987 23 42 90; fax 987 23 47 01). From Pl. Santo Domingo, down Av. Independencia and opposite Parque San Francisco on the left. Stamps, Lista de Correos, and **faxes.** Open M-F 8:30am-8:30pm, Sa 9:30am-2pm. **Postal Code:** 24071.

ACCOMMODATIONS

Budget beds are not scarce in León, but *hostales* and *pensiones* often fill during the June *fiestas*. Look on **Avenida de Roma, Avenida de Ordoño II,** and **Avenida de la República Argentina,** which lead into the new town from Pl. Guzmán el Bueno. *Pensiones* are also scattered on the streets by the train and bus stations, but these establishments are less centrally located and are a bit intimidating at night. Check the black tourist office map for more *hostal* locations.

Consejo de Europa (HI), Po. Parque, 2 (tel. 987 20 02 06), behind Pl. Toros. Recently renovated *albergue*. Dorms 850ptas, over 26 1000ptas. Breakfast 300ptas. Often booked, so call ahead. Open late June-Aug.
Hostal Oviedo, Av. Roma, 26, 2nd fl. (tel. 987 22 22 36). Funky iron headboards jazz up cozy beds. Chatty proprietors offer huge rooms, many with sinks and terraces. Singles 1900ptas; doubles 3000ptas; triples 4500ptas.
Hostal Europa, Av. Roma, 26, 1st fl. (tel. 987 22 22 38). There must have been a sale on iron beds way back when. Bath down the hall; hot water faucet doesn't always work. Singles 1500ptas; doubles 2700ptas; triples 3500ptas.
Condado, Av. República Argentina, 28 (tel. 987 20 61 60). Airy rooms in shades of beige, brown, and lumberjack red. Fuzzy kitty bathmat in huge bathroom. Singles 1500-1800ptas; doubles 2000-2400ptas. Showers 250ptas. Meals available.

FOOD

Inexpensive eateries cluster near the cathedral and on the small streets off Av. Generalísimo Franco; also check **Plaza de San Martín,** near Pl. Mayor. Nearly all cafes come equipped with slot machines. Pork in all possible guises tops the local menus, while roast suckling lamb is almost equally popular. Thirty-five hundred kilometers of trout-fishable streams invite the wild, avant-garde **International Trout Festival** in June.

Fresh produce and eels in all shapes and sizes are sold at the **Mercado Municipal del Conde,** Pl. Conde, off C. General Mola (open M-Sa 9am-3:30pm). **Markets** in Pl. Mayor provide vegetables (open W and Sa 9am-2pm). For everyday groceries try **Consum** on Av. de José Antonio (open M-Sa 9:30am-6:30pm).

Calle Ancha, C. Generalísimo Franco, on the block between C. General Mola and C. Conde Luna. Fill your belly with fresh veggies, quiche, and fish. Gourmet vegetarian *menú* 900ptas; non-vegetarian *menú económica* 950ptas. Both *menús* come with a bottle of wine. Open daily 8am-1:30am.

Cafetería-Restaurante Catedral, C. Mariano Domínguez Berrueta, 17 (tel. 987 21 59 18), to the right of the cathedral. Monumental portions make the 1100ptas *menú* a great bargain. Chomp down on a *bocadillo* at the mile-long bar (400-600ptas). Open M and Th-Sa 1-4 and 8-11pm, Tu-W 8-11pm.

Lleras, 38, C. Burgos Nuevo, less than a block from its intersection with Av. República Argentina. Jazzy restaurant offering everything from spaghetti and trout to melon and tongue. *Menú* 1050ptas. Open daily 1-5pm and 8pm until it's empty.

SIGHTS

The 13th-century Gothic **cathedral,** La Pulchra Leonina, is arguably the most beautiful in Spain. *(Open daily 8:30am-1:30pm and 4-8pm.)* Its exceptional facade depicts smiling saints in heaven side by side with bug-eyed monsters munching on the damned. But the real attractions are the glorious rose windows with their spirals of saints, the vivid stained-glass interior, and the glass gardens of tiny faces amid luminous petals. The cathedral's **museo** (tel. 987 23 00 60) includes gruesome wonders like a skeleton statue of Death and a sculpture depicting the skinning of a saint. *(Open in summer M-F 9:30am-2pm and 4-7:30pm, Sa 9:30am-2pm; in winter M-F 9:30am-1:30pm and 4-7pm, Sa 9:30am-1:30pm. 450ptas.)*

The **Basílica San Isidoro** was dedicated in the 11th century to San Isidoro of Sevilla, whose remains were brought to León while Muslims ruled the south. The corpses of countless royals rest in the impressive **Panteón Real,** with ceilings covered by vibrant 12th-century frescoes. *(Open daily July-Aug. 9am-2pm and 3-8pm; Sept.-June 10am-1:30pm and 4-6:30pm. 350ptas.)* The unusual Annunciation and medieval agricultural calendar are particularly noteworthy. Admission to the pantheon allows entrance to the library, which includes a 10th-century handwritten Bible, and to the treasury, home of Doña Urraca's famous agate chalices. While visiting the cathedral and San Isidoro, keep an eye out for some of the city's **Roman walls.**

The **Museo de León** (tel. 987 24 50 61), Pl. San Marcos, holds an extensive archaeological collection with pieces dating from the Paleolithic era. *(Open Tu-Sa 10am-2pm and 5-8:30pm, Su 10am-2pm. 200ptas, students and over 65 free, weekends free.)* Next door to the *museo,* the **Monasterio San Marcos,** once a rest stop for pilgrims en route to Santiago, is León's only five-star hotel and sports a Plateresque facade. **Los Botines,** Pl. Santo Domingo, is one of the few buildings outside of Catalunya designed by *Renaixançista* Antoni Gaudí. The relatively restrained structure displays only hints of the wild stuff to come later in his life (see **Barcelona,** p. 296).

ENTERTAINMENT

For the early part of the night the *barrio húmedo* (drinker's neighborhood), around **Plaza de San Martín,** sweats with bars, discos, and techno-pop. **El Bacanal** attracts a primarily gay crowd to its Caravaggio-covered walls. Mellower music, pastel walls, and actual breathing space characterize **El Robote** (across the square). After 2am, the crowds weave to **Calle Lancia** and **Calle Conde de Guillén,** both heavily populated with discos and bars. Plenty of cool cafes line Av. Generalísimo Franco. **La Gargola** has cushy yellow-striped sofas and a starry night painted on the ceiling. **El Gran Café,** on C. Cervantes one block off Av. Generalísimo Franco, delivers live jazz nightly to its chic clientele. For more romantic, secluded spots, explore C. La Paloma and other narrow streets around the cathedral, which harbor quieter candle-lit cafes.

Fiestas commemorating St. John and St. Peter occur from June 21-30, as does a *corrida de toros* (bullfight). Highlights are the feast days of San Juan on June 25 and San Pedro on June 30. King Juan Carlos I and his wife Sofía attend the fiestas and the cathedrals's **International Organ Festival** on a yearly basis.

■ Near León: Astorga

Antoni Gaudí responded to a request from his friend, the bishop of Astorga, to design a new episcopal residence with converging arches, elaborate stained glass, and jutting turrets of a fanciful **Palacio Episcopal** (Bishop's Palace). As the construction dragged on for 20 years after the bishop's death, the expense proved enormous for the poor parish, whose original residence had burned in 1886. Sadly, no bishop dared occupy the fairy-tale home upon its belated completion. Today the palace houses the fascinating but decidedly eclectic **Museo de los Caminos** (tel. 987 61 88 82), whose ostensible purpose is to illustrate the various *caminos* (paths) that have passed through 2000-year-old Astorga. *(Open daily in summer 10am-2pm and 4-8pm; in winter 11am-2pm and 3:30-6:30pm. 250ptas. 400ptas gets you into the cathedral museum as well.)* On the second floor, Gaudí's candy-bright stained-glass windows dazzle and awe, especially those in the effervescent chapel and dining room.

The **cathedral,** opposite Gaudí's *palacio,* is worth at least a glance. *(Open daily June-Sept. 9am-noon and 5-6:30pm; Oct.-May 9am-noon and 4:30-6pm. Free.)* Though not as spectacular as León's cathedral, the ornate 18th-century facade and beautiful choir loft in Astorga's are impressive. The cathedral's **museum** has ten rooms of relics and votive objects. *(Open daily 10am-2pm and 4-6pm. 250ptas, 400ptas for Caminos museum as well.)*

The **tourist office** is inside the small stone church between the cathedral and the palace (open June-Oct. M-Sa 10am-2pm and 4-8pm). **Luggage storage** is at the train station (400ptas). **Police** (tel. 987 61 60 80) are at Pl. San Miguel; for **ambulances** call 987 61 85 85. The **post office** is on C. Alfereces.

Rooms tend to be expensive. **Pensión García,** C. Bajada de Postigo, 6, has the best deals in town (singles 2150ptas; doubles 3400ptas). Take the main street that runs past the cathedral and Gaudí's palace until you reach Pl. Mayor, the fourth plaza, also called Pl. España. Then take C. Bañeza, to the right as you face the Ayuntamiento, which becomes C. Bajada de Postigo just down the hill. **Restaurants** abound around the cathedral and on Av. Murallas, near the bus station. In addition to the famous *mantecadas* (little sponge cakes), Astorga is also home to the hefty stew *cocido maragato,* which is traditionally eaten in "reverse order" (meat to broth).

To get to the town center from the RENFE **train station,** Pl. Estación (tel. 987 61 64 44), walk uphill along C. Pedro de Castro to Pl. Obispo Alcolea; turn right here and continue to walk up. The **bus station** (tel. 987 61 91 00), on Av. Ponferrada across from the Palacio Episcopal, is close to the town's sights. Sixteen buses make the 45-minute journey to and from León daily (405ptas), as do 8 trains (400ptas).

■ Valladolid

Wealth, political prominence, and architectural grandeur once came easily to Valladolid. In 1469 Fernando and Isabel were joined here in momentous matrimony. Close to a century later, shady dealings by minister Conde Duque de Lerma snuffed out the glory days. The beneficiary of a whopping bribe, Lerma squeezed Valladolid (already the capital of Castilla) out of the running for capital of Spain. Madrid won, Valladolid lost, and history moved on. Yet today, the city makes up for a lack of national status with an impressive Museo de la Escultura (sculpture) as well as a number of endearing quirks. Fountains are lit in day-glo pink and green, seventies architecture challenges graceful Renaissance forms, and Supermarket Simago blasts American music up and down the main pedestrian thoroughfare while the locals hum along.

ORIENTATION AND PRACTICAL INFORMATION

Valladolid occupies a central position between León (133km) and Segovia (110km) and between Burgos (122km) and Salamanca (114km). The bus and train stations sit on the south edge of town. To get from the bus station to the **tourist office,** turn right on C. San José and take the first left onto C. Ladrillo. Angle to the right onto C. Arco de Ladrillo, which cuts through the wooded park **Campo Grande** and ends at **Plaza Zorrilla** and the tourist office. From there, walk down **Calle Santiago** to get to **Plaza Mayor.** The **cathedral** is a 10-minute walk east from Pl. Mayor (right as you face the Ayuntamiento). **Plaza del Val** is just behind Pl. Mayor, off the northeast corner.

Transportation

Flights: Villanubla Airport, León Highway (N-601), km 13 (tel. 983 41 54 00). Daily trips to Barcelona, Madrid, and Paris. Service to Islas Baleares in summer. Info open daily 12:30-7:30pm. **Iberia,** C. Gamazo, 17 (tel. 983 30 06 66 or 983 30 26 39). Open M-F 9:30am-1:30pm and 4-7pm, Sa 9:30am-1:30pm. Taxi to airport 1800ptas.

Trains: Estación del Norte, C. Recondo (tel. 983 30 35 18 or 983 30 75 78), at the end of Campo Grande. Info (tel. 983 20 02 02) open daily 7am-11pm. To: Zamora (1½hr., 1 per day, 980ptas); Burgos (1½hr., 14 per day, 900ptas); Salamanca (1¾hr., 11 per day, 830ptas); León (1½hr., 10 per day, 1225ptas); Madrid (4hr., 19 per day, 1825ptas); Santander (4¾hr., 7 per day, 1855ptas).

Buses: Puente Colgante, 2 (tel. 983 23 63 08). Info open daily 8:30am-8:30pm. From the train station, turn left and follow C. Recondo, which becomes C. Puente Colgante (5min.). To: Tordesillas (30min., 25 per day, 250ptas); Zamora (1½hr., 7 per day, 795ptas); Burgos (2hr., 5 per day, 1600ptas); León (2hr., 9 per day, 1600ptas); Madrid (2½hr., 18 per day, 1470ptas); Oviedo (4hr., 4 per day, 2125ptas); San Sebastián (5hr., 2 per day, 2785ptas); Barcelona (9hr., 3 per day, 5975ptas).

Taxis: Radio Taxi (tel. 983 29 14 11) is on call 24hr.

Tourist and Local Services

Tourist Office: Pl. Zorrilla, 3 (tel. 983 35 18 01). Maps, museum info, and a useful hotel info booklet. English spoken. Open daily 10am-2pm and 5-8pm.

Budget Travel: TIVE, Edificio Administrativo de Uso Múltiple, 3rd fl. (tel. 983 35 45 63). From Pl. Zorrila, take C. María de Molina to C. Doctrinos, and follow it across Puente Isabel la Católica, then past the parking lot. Open M-F 9am-2pm.

Currency Exchange: At the **bus station** and **Banco Central Hispano,** corner of Acera de Recoletos and C. Perú. No commission. Open M-F 8:30am-2:30pm.

El Corte Inglés: (tel. 983 27 23 04 or 983 47 83 00) on C. Constitución. Take a left off C. Santiago walking away from Pl. Mayor. Great **maps,** novels, and guidebooks in English; **currency exchange.** Open M-Sa 10am-9pm.

Luggage Storage: Estación del Norte has lockers. Counters are available at the ticket window (300ptas). Baggage check at the **bus station** (50ptas per bag; open M-Sa 9am-10pm).

Emergency and Communications

Emergency: dial 091 or 092.

Crisis Lines: Women's Info Line (tel. 983 30 08 93). **De la Esperanza** (tel. 983 30 70 77) and **Voces Amigas** (tel. 983 33 46 35) for depression. Limited English.

Late-Night Pharmacy: Check local papers *El Norte de Castilla* (115ptas) or *El Mundo de Valladolid* (125ptas) for listings.

Medical Services: Hospital Pío del Río Hortega, C. Santa Teresa (tel. 983 42 04 00 10pm-9am). Some doctors speak English.

Post Office: Pl. Rinconada (tel. 983 33 06 60; fax 983 39 19 87). C. Jesús, on the left of the Ayuntamiento in Pl. Mayor, leads to Pl. Rinconada. Stamps, **faxes,** and Lista de Correos. Open M-F 8:30am-8:30pm, Sa 8:30am-2pm. **Postal Code:** 47001.

ACCOMMODATIONS

Cheap lodgings, all with winter heating, are abundant. The streets off the right side of **Acera de Recoletos** as you leave the train station—though a little dark and scary— and those near the cathedral and behind Pl. Mayor at **Plaza del Val,** are packed with

CASTILLA Y LEÓN

pensiones and *hostales*. **Albergue Juvenil Río Esgueve (HI),** Camino Cementerio (tel. 983 25 15 50), is currently undergoing renovations and will be open in August 1999. In a pinch, the tourist office's guidance is invaluable.

Pensión Dos Rosas, C. Perú, 11, 2nd fl. (tel. 983 20 74 39). From the train station, walk up Av. Acera Recoletos and turn right on C. Perú. A good bargain only 2 blocks from Pl. Zorrilla. Tiny singles with shiny crimson bedsheets and hieroglyphics in some rooms. Doubles are spacious and sunny. Bathrooms down the hall. Portable heaters in winter. Singles 1450ptas; doubles 2600ptas; triples 3800ptas.

Pensión Dani, C. Perú, 11, 1st fl. (tel. 983 30 02 49), downstairs from Dos Rosas. Clean, narrow rooms. Modern baths down the hall. Singles 1450ptas; doubles 2600ptas.

Pension Angustias, C. Angustias, 32 (tel. 983 25 40 25). Take C. Ferrari from Pl. Mayor to Bajada Libertad, which becomes C. Angustias. The seventy-something owners are rightfully proud of their spacious, clean quarters with shared baths. Singles 1700ptas; doubles 2500ptas; triples 3600ptas.

Pensión Mary, C. Angustias, 32 (tel. 983 26 17 74), 5min. from Pl. Mayor. Follow the directions for Pensión Augustias. Newly painted rooms with dark wood furniture. Singles 1000ptas; doubles 2000ptas; triples 3000ptas. Open July-Dec.

FOOD

Stiff competition keeps prices down, making many elegant restaurants accessible to budget diners. Restaurants abound between Pl. Mayor and Pl. Val. Explore the **universidad** area, near the cathedral, for *tapas*. The **Mercado del Val,** on C. Sandoval in Pl. Val, has fresh foods (open M-Sa 6am-3pm). Go to **Supermarket Simago,** on the corner of C. Santiago and C. Montero Calvo, for groceries (open M-Sa 9:30am-9pm).

Casa San Pedro Regalad, Pl. Ochavo, 1 (tel. 983 34 45 06), on the corner of C. Platerías. Facing the Casa Consistorial, it's two jagged blocks off the far right corner of Pl. Mayor in Pl. Dorada. Meat hangs from the rafters and is roasted over coals to the delight of over 300 patrons, many of whom are seated downstairs. *Menú del día* M-F 1000ptas, Sa-Su 980ptas. Open daily 1:30-4pm and 8-11pm. Visa, MC, AmEx.

Restaurante Covadonga, C. Zapico, 1 (tel. 983 33 07 98), up the street from Pl. Val. As elegant as a restaurant can be and still have "Polly," the talking stuffed parrot hanging in the *comedor*. *Menú* 950ptas. Lots of meat and fresh vegetables. Open Aug.-June M-Sa 1-4 and 9-11:30pm, Su 1-4pm.

Restaurante Chino Gran Muralla, C. Santa María, 1 (tel. 983 34 23 07). Look for the hanging dragons half a block off C. Santiago, north of Pl. Zorrilla. *Menú* M-Th 800ptas, F-Su 950ptas. Open daily approximately 1-4pm and 7-11:30pm.

SIGHTS

The **Museo Nacional de Escultura** in the **Colegio de San Gregorio**—probably Valladolid's most fascinating visit—offers the thrill of 20 churches in one convenient location. *(Open Tu-Sa 10am-2pm and 4-6pm, Su 10am-2pm. 400ptas, students 200ptas, Saturday afternoon and Sundays free.)* The twenty-plus rooms chart the region's religious art history through transplanted segments of now-destroyed monasteries and churches, including figurines, tableaux, sculpted choir lofts, and intricate ceilings.

The **cathedral** (1580), Pl. Universidad, was designed by Juan de Herrera, also responsible for El Escorial. Its interior is typically imposing and severe, with light gray stone and large, colorless windows. Only the gold of the *retablo* interrupts the stolidly monochromatic interior. The extensive **Museo Diocesano** (tel. 983 30 43 62), inside, is worth a look for its model of the basilica's original design, its many statues of Jesus, Mary, and the saints, and its gruesome Jesus with real matted hair. *(Open Tu-F 10am-1:30pm and 4:30-7pm, Sa-Su 10am-2pm. Cathedral free, museum 350ptas.)* Behind the cathedral is the Romanesque **Tower of Santa María la Antigua.**

Plush **Casa de Colón** (tel. 983 29 13 53), on C. Colón, now part research library and part museum. *(Open Tu-Sa 10am-2pm and 5-7pm, Su 10am-2pm; shorter hours in winter. Free.)* From the looks of **Casa de Cervantes,** off C. Castro, one might conclude that the writer died of boredom. *(Open Tu-Sa 10am-3:30pm, Su 10am-3pm. 400ptas, students 200ptas, Sundays free.)* There is an amusing collection of old books and furniture, but the medieval bed-warmer is the real highlight.

ENTERTAINMENT

Valladolid's cafes and bars are lively, though nothing to write home about. A young, mainly university crowd fills the countless bars on **Calle del Paraiso.** Later in the night, the youth movement heads to pubs in **Plaza de San Miguel.** Cafes on **Calle de Vincente Meliner,** near Pl. Dorado, draw an older crowd. At **Roma es Azul,** people reading newspapers by the entrance are no indication of the mayhem inside.

Schedules for movies, as well as for Valladolid's first-division soccer team, **Real Valladolid,** can be found in *El Monde de Valladolid* or *El Norte de Castilla.* Valladolid's **Semana Santa** (Holy Week) is, as in every other city, a fascinating festival. The week of September 21 marks the **Fiesta Mayor** celebrations, featuring bullfights, carnivals, and parades.

■ Palencia

Palencia (pop. 82,000) is a town where people and cows cross paths with surprising frequency. The city's laid-back residents may ask you flatly why you have come. Though low on pizazz, Palencia may please travelers craving a healthy dose of Romanesque and Visigothic architecture.

ORIENTATION AND PRACTICAL INFORMATION The train and bus stations, next to the park **Los Jardinillos,** are north of **Calle Mayor,** the main pedestrian artery and shopping zone. C. Mayor runs north-south beginning at **Plaza de León,** a traffic rotary adjacent to the park. **Plaza Mayor** lies five blocks south, midway on C. Mayor. The **tourist office** is a 10-minute walk farther, at the southern end of C. Mayor, on the left before Av. José Antonio Primo de Rivera (where the pedestrian zone ends). Thereafter, C. Mayor becomes **Avenida de la República Argentina.** To reach the **cathedral,** take the first right off C. Mayor after leaving Pl. León and walk three blocks.

Trains (tel. 979 74 30 19) steam from Los Jardinillos park to: Madrid (4hr., 16 per day, 1985-2280ptas); Valladolid (45min., 22 per day, 385-445ptas); Burgos (1hr., 11 per day, 490-565ptas); and León (1¼hr., 15 per day, 890-1025ptas). The **bus station** (tel. 979 74 32 22) is also at Los Jardinillos, to the right of the train station (info booth open daily 9:30am-8pm). To: Madrid (3½hr., 7 per day, 1885ptas); Valladolid (45min., 7 per day, 385ptas); Burgos (1½hr., 3 per day, 720ptas); and Carrión (30min., 3 per day, 315ptas). The bus station has **luggage storage** (70ptas per day; open M-F 9:30am-7pm, Sa 9:30am-2pm), as does the train station (300ptas per day; accessible 24hr.) To get to Pl. León and C. Mayor, exit the station and turn right, then turn left onto Av. Dr. Simón Nieto, which hits Pl. León.

The **tourist office,** C. Mayor, 105 (tel. 979 74 00 68; fax 979 70 08 22), distributes free maps and posters (open M-Sa 10am-2pm and 5-7pm). Change currency at **Banco Central Hispano,** C. Mayor, 37 (open M-F 8:30am-2:30pm; no commission). In an **emergency,** dial 092 or 091. Mail services are divided between two **post offices:** Pl. León, 1 (tel. 979 74 21 80; fax 979 74 22 60), sends and receives **faxes;** the second office (tel. 979 74 21 77), next to the train station, provides Lista de Correos (both offices open M-F 8:30am-8:30pm, Sa 9:30am-2pm). The **postal code** is 34001.

ACCOMMODATIONS AND FOOD Plenty of reasonably priced *hostales* with clean, plain rooms line side streets running from C. Mayor toward the Río Carrión. The youth hostel, **Victorio Macho (HI),** C. Dr. Fleming, s/n (tel. 979 72 04 62), is only open during the summer (July -Aug. 15). Prospective hostelers should call ahead, as groups often take over. (Members only. 1000ptas, over 26 1450ptas). Bus B from Los Jardinillos (every 12min., 45ptas) saves trekkers a hike. **Pensión Gredos,** C. Valentin Calderon, 18 (tel. 979 70 28 33), three blocks down and a left off C. Mayor from Pl. León, feels homey with comfy beds, a backyard patio, and red-checked tablecloths (singles 1800ptas; doubles 3500ptas; breakfast 275ptas). **El Salón,** Av. República Argentina, 10 (tel. 979 72 64 42), has sweet owners and miniature velvet chairs. Most rooms don't have running water and the beds are a little springy, but there are four spotless bathrooms. (Singles 1800ptas; doubles 3000ptas.)

Numerous restaurants and *tapas* bars—most of similar price and quality—line the streets just off C. Mayor. At **Bar-Restaurante El Coso,** Eduardo Dato, 8 (tel. 979 74 67 58), off Pl. de Leon, posters of matadors line the walls and a stuffed bull's head watches you eat. **Papareschi Restaurante-Pizzeria,** Av. Comandante Velloso, 1 (tel. 979 72 80 10), a continuation of Av. José Primo Antonio de Rivera, serves up authentic Italian pizzas (700-825ptas), standard pastas, and Budweiser (open W-M noon-midnight; Visa, MC).

SIGHTS Palencia's biggest attraction is its 14th-century Gothic cathedral, **Santa Iglesia de San Antolín** (tel. 979 70 13 47), where 14-year-old Catherine of Lancaster married 10-year-old Enrique III in 1388. *(Open M-Sa 9:30am-1:30pm and 4-6:30pm, Su 9:30am-1:30pm. Free. Short guided tours in Spanish 100ptas.)* During the tour, guides illuminate (literally) the various altars and then lead you way, way down a stone staircase to the spooky **Cripta de San Antolín,** a 7th-century sepulchre. The cathedral's **museum** houses El Greco's famed *San Sebastián* and some spectacular 16th-century Flemish tapestries—not to mention a tiny caricature of Carlos V. *(Open M-Sa 9:30am-1pm and 4-6pm. Admission 300ptas.)*

Of the other churches in town, the favorite of El Cid fans is **Iglesia de San Miguel** (tel. 979 74 07 69), on C. General Mola, which runs parallel to the river. *(Open daily 9:30am-1:30pm.)* As legend has it, it is here that El Campeador wed Doña Jimena.

■ Near Palencia: Carrión de los Condes

Forty kilometers north of Palencia on the **Camino de Santiago,** tiny riverside beauty Carrión (pop. 1000) safeguards some incredible sights. On the south side of the **Iglesia de Santa María** (tel. 979 88 00 72), a 12th-century temple, is a depiction of the legendary tribute of four Carrión maidens to Moorish conquerors. *(Open daily 9am-2pm and 4:30-6:30pm. Mass held daily at 8:30am, holidays 10:30am and noon.)* Supposedly, Santa María foiled the transaction by sending four menacing bulls to gore the Moors.

On the far side of the Río Carrión looms the secularized **Monasterio de San Zoilo** (tel. 979 88 00 49 or 979 88 01 35). *(Open Tu-Su 10:30am-2pm and 4-6pm. 200ptas.)* Faces of saints and popes stare down from the ornate arches of its Renaissance cloister, partially open to the public. Situated near the exit are the tombs of the notorious Infantes de Carrión. In the *Cantar del Mío Cid,* they married El Cid's daughters, deflowered them, beat them, and then abandoned them in the middle of the forest.

Carrión's hidden treasure is the **Convento de Santa Clara,** also known as Las Clarisas. The *repostería* (pastry shop) bakes scrumptious cookies. To see the **museo** (tel. 979 88 01 34), ring the bell and ask for Sr. Antonio to let you in. *(Open Tu-Su 10:30am-1pm and 4:30-7pm. 200ptas.)* The eclectic one-room collection includes shepherds' nutcrackers, a statue of baby Jesus with a toothache, and numerous baby-doll clothes made especially for *el Niño.*

Carrión's **tourist office** (not a government office, so hours vary) is in a wood-frame hut across the street from **Café-Bar España,** where the bus drops you off. **Hostal La Corte,** C. Santa María, 34 (tel. 979 88 01 38), provides luxurious, spotless rooms, and an elegant restaurant (singles 2000-2500ptas; doubles 3500-5000ptas). Or, stay with the nuns at **Convento Santa Clara** (singles 1000ptas, free for pilgrims). **El Edén Camping** (tel. 979 88 01 85), hugs the river two blocks from the central Café-Bar España (300ptas per person, 300-400ptas per tent). Three **buses** per day (tel. 979 74 32 22) carry day- (or half-day-) trippers from Palencia to Carrión (30min., 315ptas).

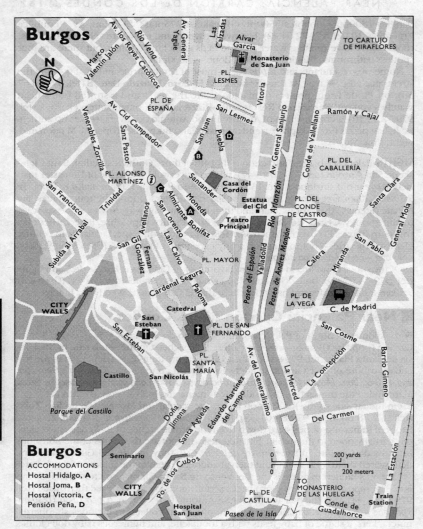

Burgos

N

TO CARTUJO
DE MIRAFLORES

Av. los Reyes Católicos
Río Vena
Av. General Yagüe
Marco Valentín Jalón
Las Calzadas
Alvar Garcia
Monasterio de San Juan
PL. LESMES
Vitoria
Ramón y Cajal
Av. Cid Campeador
PL. DE ESPAÑA
San Lesmes
San Juan
Puebla
D
Sanz Pastor
Santander
Conde de Vallellano
PL. DEL CABALLERÍA
Venerables Zorrilla
PL. ALONSO MARTÍNEZ
i
B
Casa del Cordón
Av. General Sanjurjo
Santa Clara
San Francisco
C
Moneda
Estatua del Cid
Río Arlanzón
PL. DEL CONDE DE CASTRO
General Mola
Trinidad
Almirante Bonifaz
San Lorenzo
A
Teatro Principal
Subida al Arrabal
San Gil Avellanos
Laín Calvo
Fernán González
PL. MAYOR
Paseo del Espolón
Valladolid
Paseo de Andrés Manjón
Calera
Miranda
San Pablo
Cardenal Segura
Paloma
PL. DE LA VEGA
C. de Madrid
CITY WALLS
Catedral
PL. DE SAN FERNANDO
San Cosme
San Esteban
San Esteban
PL. SANTA MARÍA
Av. del Generalísimo
La Concepción
Barrio Gimeno
Castillo
San Nicolás
La Merced
Parque del Castillo
Doña Jimena
Santa Agueda
Eduardo Martínez del Campo
Del Carmen
Burgos
ACCOMMODATIONS
Hostal Hidalgo, **A**
Hostal Joma, **B**
Hostal Victoria, **C**
Pensión Peña, **D**
Seminario
CITY WALLS
Po. de los Cubos
Hospital San Juan
PL. DE CASTILLA
Paseo de la Isla
TO MONASTERIO DE LAS HUELGAS
Conde de Guadalhorce
La Estación
Train Station

0   200 yards
0   200 meters

CASTILLA Y LEÓN

■ Burgos

Despite its somewhat small dimensions, Burgos (pop. 180,000) has figured prominently in Spain's history, largely as a conservative citadel. For 500 medieval years it
was the seat of *Castilla Vieja* (Old Castile). During its reign, the city built an extraordinary Gothic cathedral and witnessed the exploits of nobleman Rodrigo Díaz de
Vivar, better known as El Cid Campeador, the national hero of Spain.

Nine centuries after El Cid's banishment from town, General Franco stationed
nationalist headquarters here in a revival of hard-line politics. But today's Burgos is
significantly more relaxed. During the day natives share the streets with history-seek-
ing tourists and international pilgrims backpacking along the Camino de Santiago. At
night, folks head for the myriad bars with what seems a determination to leave Burgos's gloomy, somber reputation in the past.

ORIENTATION AND PRACTICAL INFORMATION

Burgos lies about 240km north of Madrid on the main route between Madrid and the French border. The Río Arlanzón splits the city into north and south sides. The **train** and **bus stations** are on the south side, while the **cathedral** and all other sights of interest are located on the north side. From the train station, follow **Avenida Conde de Guadalhorce** across the river and take the first right onto **Avenida del Generalísimo Franco,** which turns into **Paseo del Espolón** farther down. From the bus station, follow **Calle de Madrid** through **Plaza de la Vega** and across the river, and then turn right on **Paseo del Espolón.** The cathedral's massive gray spires touch ground several hundred meters north. Upstream, along the *paseo,* at C. Santander, stands a large statue of El Cid. A short walk up C. Santander leads to **Plaza de España.** Look here for signs to the tourist office, on **Plaza de Alonso Martínez.** The **Plaza José Antonio** (or **Plaza Mayor**) is between the cathedral and the tourist office, just east of the former.

Transportation

Trains: (tel. 947 20 35 60), at the end of Av. Conde de Guadalhorce across the river from Pl. Castilla. A 10min. walk southwest of the city center, or a 300-500ptas taxi ride. Info open daily 7am-10pm. **RENFE,** C. Moneda, 21 (tel. 947 20 91 31). Open M-F 9am-1pm and 4-7pm, Sa 9am-1pm. To: Palencia (1hr., 11 per day, 500-1200ptas); Valladolid (1½hr., 16 per day, 910-1500ptas); Logroño (2hr., 4 per day, 1120ptas); León (2hr., 8 per day, 2000ptas); Madrid (3½hr., 10 per day, 2945ptas); San Sebastián (4hr., 8 per day, 2180ptas); Bilbao (4hr., 5 per day, 1800ptas); Santiago (8hr., 3 per day, 4500ptas); Barcelona (8hr., 12 per day, 4800ptas).

Buses: C. Miranda, 4 (tel. 947 28 88 55), just off Pl. Vega, on the south side of the river directly south of the cathedral. To: Madrid (3hr., 12-15 per day, 1920ptas); Barcelona (7½hr., 4 per day, 4960ptas); Bilbao (2-3hr., 8 per day, 1420ptas); Valladolid (2hr., 3 per day, 1060ptas); Santander (2¾hr., 4 per day, 1350ptas); León (3½hr., 2 per day, 1700ptas); Vitoria (1½hr., 8 per day, 940ptas); San Sebastián (3¼hr., 5 per day, 1825ptas); and Pamplona (3½hr., 5 per day, 1900ptas).

Taxis: Abutaxi (tel. 947 27 77 77) and **Radio Taxi** (tel. 947 48 10 10). 24hr. service.

Car Rental: Hertz, C. General Mola, 5 (tel. 947 20 16 75), on the block parallel to C. Miranda near Pl. Vega. Must be at least 25. A small car with unlimited mileage is 11,000ptas for one day, cheaper for longer rentals. Accepts all major credit cards. Open M-F 9am-2pm and 4-7pm, Sa 9am-1pm. **Avis,** C. Maestro Justa del Río, 2-4 (tel. 947 20 06 06). Must be at least 23. Special weekend rate of 21,425ptas for 3 days. Open M-F 8:30am-1:30pm and 4-7pm, Sa 9am-1pm.

Hitchhiking: To Madrid, hitchers walk south along C. Madrid from Pl. Vega until highway N-1; to Santander, hitchers walk north on Av. General Vigón. But remember, your mother, the tourist office, and *Let's Go* do not advocate hitching.

Tourist, Financial, and Local Services

Tourist Office: Pl. Alonso Martínez, 7 (tel. 947 20 31 25), next to the Capitanía General building. A variety of multilingual brochures and maps. English spoken. Open M-F 9am-2pm and 5-7pm, Sa-Su and holidays 10am-2pm and 5-8pm.

Budget Travel: Viajes TIVE, C. General Yagüe, 20 (tel. 947 20 98 81), off Pl. de España. Student IDs 700ptas. English spoken. Open M-F 9am-2pm.

Currency Exchange: Banco Central Hispano sits at C. Vitoria, 6, next to El Cid, and at Pl. Vega near the bus station. Open May-Sept. M-F 8:30am-2:30pm, Oct.-Apr. M-F 8:30am-2:30pm, Sa 8:30am-1pm. For **ATMs,** hunt down Telebanco or SirviRed signs.

Luggage Storage: Lockers at the **train station** 400ptas. Accessible 24hr. Check your bag at the **bus station** (100-150ptas per bag). Open M-F 9am-8pm, Sa 9am-6pm.

Emergency and Communications

Emergency: Police (tel. 091 or 092).

Late-Night Pharmacy: Check the listings in the local paper *El Diario de Burgos* (125ptas) or the sign posted in every pharmacy.

Medical Services: Ambulance: (tel. 947 28 18 28).

CASTILLA Y LEÓN

Telephones: Locutorio Telefónico, Pl. Alonso Martínez (tel. 947 26 42 28; fax 947 27 93 59), near the tourist office. **Fax** service. Open daily 10am-3pm and 4-11pm.

Internet Access: Cafe Cabaret Ciber-Cafe, C. Puebla, 21 (tel. 947 20 27 22; http://www.render.es/cabaret). 30min. of surfing for 500ptas, each additional 30min. 300ptas. Printing for 10ptas per page. Open Su-Th 4pm-2am, F-Sa 4pm-4am.

Post Office: Pl. Conde de Castro, 1 (tel. 947 26 27 50; general info 947 20 41 20). El Cid points the way across the river from Pl. Primo de Rivera; the post office is the big building at the first intersection. Open for stamps and Lista de Correos M-F 8:30am-8:30pm, Sa 9:30am-2pm. **Postal Code:** 09070.

ACCOMMODATIONS AND CAMPING

For rousing nightlife and good *hostal* prices, scout the streets near **Pl. Alonso Martínez** on the north side of the river. The **Calle San Juan** area is also dotted with reasonably priced *hostales*. Reservations are crucial for the last week of June and the first week of July (holidays of St. Paul and St. Peter) and are advisable in August. The "Fuentes Blancas" bus leaves from Pl. España (only runs July to mid-September 9:30am, 12:30, 4:15, and 7:15pm; 75ptas) and voyages to **Camping Fuentes Blancas,** 3.5km outside Burgos. (Open Apr.-Sept. 575ptas per person, per tent, and per car, plus 7% IVA.)

Pensión Peña, C. Puebla, 18 (tel. 947 20 63 23). From Pl. España, take C. San Lesmes; C. Puebla is the 3rd right. Small, elegant rooms with big windows. Family-owned for nearly 50 years. Singles 1500ptas, with sink 1600ptas; doubles 2700ptas, with sink 2800ptas. Laundry service and storage of luggage and bicycles.

Hostal Victoria, C. San Juan, 3 (tel. 947 20 15 42). From El Cid's statue, walk up C. Santander past Pl. Calvobotelo and turn right onto C. San Juan. Simple, attractive rooms with sinks. Mostly tenanted by students from mid-Oct. to late June. English and French spoken. Singles 2300ptas; doubles 3500ptas; triples 4500ptas; quads 6000ptas. Luggage storage available.

Hostal Hidalgo, C. Almirante Bonifaz, 14 (tel. 947 20 34 81), one block from Pl. Alonso Martínez. Off C. San Juan. A dim stairway leads to a warm and friendly *hostal*. High ceilings, hardwood floors. Singles 1800ptas; doubles 3200ptas; triples 4500ptas; quads 6000ptas. Primarily available from the end of June to Sept.

Hostal Joma, C. San Juan, 26 (tel. 947 20 33 50). From El Cid's statue, walk up C. Santander past Pl. Calvo Sotelo and turn right on C. San Juan. The poorly marked *hostal* is opposite a pharmacy. Climb two dim flights of stairs to the smoky reception area. The rooms are small and bare, but it's one of the cheapest places in Burgos. Singles 1700ptas; doubles 2800ptas. Extras include shower (200ptas), breakfast (250ptas), dinner (750ptas), and laundry (400ptas per load).

FOOD

Vegetarians take heed—Burgos specializes in meat, meat, and more meat. Carnivores can try *picadillo de cerdo* (minced pork), *cordero asado* (roast lamb), or, for a taste of everything, *olla podrida*, a stew in which sausage, beans, pork, cured beef, bacon, and heart disease mingle as one. Burgos natives take pride in *morcilla*, a sausage concocted from blood and rice and the delicious *queso de Burgos* (cheese). The area around Pl. Alonso Martínez teems with restaurants serving these staples. Calle San Lorenzo is *tapas* heaven. At **Mercado de Abastos (Norte),** near Pl. España, and the smaller **Mercado de Abastos (Sur),** on C. Miranda next to the bus station, the scents of raw meat and fresh bread collide (markets open M-Sa 7am-3pm; Mercado Norte reopens F 5:30-8pm). **Spar Supermercado,** on C. Concepción, midway on the block between C. Hospital Militar and C. San Cosme, prepares you for picnics (open M-F 9am-2pm and 5-8pm, Sa 9am-2pm).

Gaia Comedor Vegetariano, C. San Francisco, 31 (tel. 947 23 76 45). A little bit of Berkeley, California, on C. San Francisco. Gazpacho, fresh salads, asparagus crepes, and creamy vegetable *pasteles,* as well as desserts and wine, make for a light, flavorful *menú*. Fresh roses and soothing sitar music. Gaia also posts info about tai chi, yoga, and the environment. Open M-Sa 1:30-4pm.

La Riojana, C. Arellanos, 10 (tel. 947 20 61 32). A haven for the famished. The 900ptas *menú* will fill the emptiest of stomachs with heaping platefuls of paella, codfish, pork, and local specialties. The small, wood-paneled *comedor* hums with the chatter of local teens and the TV overhead. Open daily noon-1am.

Mesón la Amarilla, C. San Lorenzo, 26, between Pl. Mayor and Pl. Alonso Martínez. Snack at the bar or head upstairs to dine. *Patatas bravas* (French fries in spicy orange-colored sauce) is a specialty. *Raciones* 500-750ptas, *platos combinados* 1100ptas. Open daily 9am-4pm and 7pm-2am.

Casa Pancho, C. San Lorenzo, 13 (tel. 947 20 34 05). A good place to sample *morcilla* (175ptas) or *calimares a la romana* (fried squid, 650ptas). Or make a meal out of the generous servings of tasty *tapas* (200-600ptas) at this friendly bar-restaurant. Open Su-F 10am-2:30am, Sa 10am-1am.

SIGHTS

Cathedral

The spires of Burgos's magnificent Gothic **cathedral** (tel. 947 20 47 12) rise high above the city. *(Open daily 9:30am-1pm and 4-7pm. Admission to sacristy, museum, and Capilla Mayor 400ptas, students 200ptas.)* Although begun in the 13th century by *Reconquista* hero Fernando El Santo (Fernando III), when it was funded by gentlemen sheep farmers, the cathedral has been a work in progress for centuries. The north facade in 13th-century Gothic style is stark in comparison to the intricate 15th-century towers and the beautiful 16th-century stained-glass dome of the **Capilla Mayor.** Here, El Cid's body (or parts of it) lies with his wife Doña Jimena; his coffin hangs several meters overhead in the 18th-century Baroque sacristy. Another curious inhabitant of the cathedral is the eerily lifelike **papamoscas** (fly-catcher), high up near the main door in the central aisle. As it tolls the hours, the strange creature opens its mouth and gulps, much to the joy of onlookers below.

Near the Cathedral

Across from the cathedral, in the Pl. Santa Maria, stands the **Iglesia de San Nicolás,** home to 15th and 16th-century Hispano-Flemish paintings and altarpieces. *(Open July-Sept. M 9am-8pm, Tu-Su 9am-2pm and 4-8pm; Oct-June Tu-F 6:30-7:30pm, Sa 9:30am-2pm and 5-7pm, holidays 9am-2pm and 5-6pm. Free.)* If you're an altarpiece fan, continue up Pozo Seco to the **Museo del Retablo/Iglesia de San Esteban.** Eighteen 16th- to 18th-century *retablos* (altars) depict the life of Christ and various saints. *(Open in summer Tu-Sa 10:30am-2pm and 4:30-7pm, Su 10:30am-2pm; in winter Sa 10:30am-2pm and 4:30-7pm, Su 10:30am-2pm. Admission 200ptas, students 100ptas, under 11 free.)*

CASTILLA Y LEÓN

El Cid Campeador

Although Rodrigo Díaz de Vivar (a.k.a. El Cid), Spain's real-life epic hero, was not born in Burgos, some of the most celebrated incidents of his life took place here. After the cathedral, the **Estatua del Cid** in Pl. General Primo de Rivera is Burgos's most revered landmark. Rodrigo Díaz de Vivar ("Cid" comes from the Arabic for lord) won his fame through bold exploits at home and in battle against Moors and Christians. Despite the statue's inscription and the stories often told about him, El Cid was no traditional Christian hero. A particularly successful mercenary, he spent much of his life exiled from a number of Christian states whose nobles he had outraged; from time to time, he even allied himself with various Muslims. All the same, El Cid is thought by many to be the most famous Castilian of all time, and the medieval epic poem celebrating his life, *Cantar de Mío Cid* (c. 1140), is considered the first great work of Castilian literature. Tradition compels Burgos's youngsters to climb the statue and fondle the testicles of El Cid's horse, thus ensuring their own strength, courage, and fame.

The ruins of a **medieval castle** preside over Burgos from a hill high above the cathedral. From the Museo del Retablo, it takes about 15 minutes to climb the 200 steps that rise through spruces and bright red poppies. Atop the bleached castle rocks, an astounding view of the red roofs of Burgos and the surrounding countryside awaits.

Elsewhere within City Limits

Just up C. Santander on the other side of the statue of El Cid and on the right lies the restored **Casa del Cordón,** reincarnated as the Savings Bank of Burgos. Here Columbus met with Fernando and Isabel after his second trip to America. Felipe el Hermoso (the Handsome) died here after an exhausting game of *pelota* (jai-alai), provoking his wife Juana la Loca (the Mad), who later dragged his corpse through the streets.

The renovated **Museo de Pintura Marceliano Santa María** (tel. 947 20 56 87) stands among the ruins of the **Monasterio de San Juan,** whose cloister it occupies. *(Open Tu-Sa 10am-2pm and 5-8pm, Su 10am-2pm. Closed holidays. Free.)* Today one of the eponymous museum's galleries is devoted to the work of the Castilian Romantic painter, while the other displays contemporary exhibits. To reach the monastery and museum, follow C. Vitoria away from El Cid's statue and take the second left.

Other Excursions

The **Museo-Monasterio de las Huelgas Reales** (tel. 947 20 16 30), while not centrally located, is worth the trek. Once a summer palace for Castilian kings and later an elite convent for Cistercian nuns, the monastery has been closely associated with Spanish royalty since the Middle Ages; the abbess of Las Huelgas traditionally served as a personal advisor to the king. Today, 40 *monjas* (nuns) live here amid Gothic splendor. Inside the monastery, the **Museo de Telas** (Textile Museum) houses the burial wardrobe of Fernando de Cerda (1225-1275) and family. *(Open Apr.-Sept. Tu-Sa 10:30am-1:15pm and 4-5:45pm, Su and holidays 10:30am-2:15pm; Oct.-Mar. Tu-F 11am-1:15pm and 4-5:15pm, Sa 11am-1:15pm and 4-5:45pm, Su and holidays 10:30am-2:15pm. 650ptas, students with ID and children under 14 250ptas, children under 5 free.)* After Napoleon's troops snatched the entombed corpses' jewelry, Spaniards later stripped the bodies to put their stunning gold-silk smocks and beaded hats on display. To get here, take the "Barrio del Pilar" bus from Pl. España to the Museo stop (65ptas).

The **Cartuja de Miraflores** is a Carthusian monastery that houses a dozen or so monks and the intricate tombs of King Juan II of Castile, Queen Isabel of Portugal, and their son Don Alfonso. *(Open M-Sa 10:15am-3pm and 4-6pm, Su and holidays 11:20am-12:30pm, 1-3pm, and 4-6pm, but sometimes the monks wake up late. Free. Open for mass M-Sa 9am, Su and holidays 7:30 and 10:15am.)* To get there, take the "Fuentes Blancas" bus and either walk 300m up the road that angles to the right, along the red-dirt path that runs parallel through the woods, or walk 3km upstream along Po. Quinta. (Bus runs only July to mid-Sept. 9:30am, 12:30, 4:15, and 7:15pm; 75ptas.)

ENTERTAINMENT

Party-seekers inundate the city of Burgos after dark. Bars on C. San Juan and C. Puebla fill up with merrymakers aiming for an early start soon after dinner (try **Marmedi** or **Rebotica** on C. Puebla). By 11pm a steady hum rises up from **La Pécora,** where startling numbers of teenagers swarm in search of nectar and solid rock 'n' roll. To investigate the somewhat limited gay scene, head to **Arco** on C. San Gil. Across the river at the tiny bar **Patillas,** on C. Calere near the post office, ultra-cool locals have been known to break into impromptu flamenco concerts. By 2am the crowd has matured; when the "early" bars close at 4 or 5am, head to the slightly more upscale **Las Bernardas** (the general area circumscribed by C. Las Calzadas, C. Belorado, and Av. General Yagüe) for "la penúltima"—the perpetual second-to-last drink.

Nightlife switches into highest gear the last week in June, when Burgos honors patron saints Peter and Paul with concerts, parades, fireworks, bullfights, and dances. The day after Corpus Christi, citizens parade through town with the *Pendón de las Navas,* a banner captured from the Moors in 1212. The recently restored **Teatro Principal,** at the end of Po. Espolón, next to El Cid, offers international concerts, plays, and dance performances (100-500ptas for the cheapest tickets).

■ Near Burgos: Santo Domingo de Silos

Located amid rolling hills 60km north of Burgos, the little town of **Santo Domingo de Silos** (pop. 380) draws visitors to its monastery of Benedictine monks, who since 1993 have sold 5 million recordings of Gregorian chants, reaching #1 on global pop charts. Call them international recording artists. In the **Abadía de Santo Domingo de Silos** (tel. 947 39 00 68), listeners are transported back in time as the black-cloaked monks chant along with the organ and the soothing echoes of their own voices. *(Abbey open Tu-Sa 10am-1pm and 4:30-6pm. Admission 200ptas, under 14 free.)* You can sit in at morning song at 7:30am, high mass at 9am, *sexta* at 1:45pm, and vespers at 7pm (8pm in summer). More interesting than the church itself is the Romanesque **cloister** next door, whose highlights include an ancient pharmacy of 300-year-old chemicals, skulls, and preserved animal parts. Beyond the monastery, the sole option for entertainment is hiking in the hills. To live on the wild side, ask for directions to **La Yecla** (2.5km from Silos) where a precarious walkway leads through a narrow gorge above a small waterfall. Rooms are a cinch to find in this friendly little town. **Hostal Cruces** (singles 3000ptas) and **Hostal Santo Domingo de Silos** (singles 2500ptas, discount for more than 1 night) have cozy restaurants and the best rates. A **bus** for Santo Domingo leaves the Burgos station Monday to Thursday 5:30pm, Friday 6:30pm, and Saturday 2pm and returns Monday to Thursday and Saturday at 8:30am (610ptas). Because of the monastery's hours, the bus-bound should consider a two-night stay.

■ Soria

Modern development has encroached upon the provincial capital of Soria (pop. 33,000), but the city retains a leisurely pace. Black-bereted men tote bundles of local bread past reddish Romanesque churches, and Soria's inhabitants still religiously observe the evening *paseo*, strolling and chatting with friends and neighbors every, evening before dinner. Although the city proper probably best serves as a base for exploring surrounding towns, on the outskirts of Soria two intriguing architectural anomalies await: the **Monasterio de San Juan de Duero** and the **Ermita San Saturio**.

ORIENTATION AND PRACTICAL INFORMATION

To get to the city center from the **bus station** (northwest of downtown), either take the shuttle bus (see **Buses,** below) or walk for 15 minutes. From the traffic circle outside the station, signs on Av. Valladolid point the way downhill to the *centro ciudad.* Keep walking for about five blocks, and then bear right at the traffic light onto **Paseo Espolón,** which borders the **Parque Alameda.** When the park ends you'll see the central **Plaza Mariano Granados** directly in front of you. To get to the center from the **train station** (south of the center), either take the shuttle (see **Trains,** below) or turn left onto C. Madrid and follow the signs to *centro ciudad.* Continue on C. Almazán as it bears left and becomes Av. Mariano Vicen; follow for about six blocks (veering left on C. Alfonso VIII at the next fork) until you reach Pl. Mariano Granados (20min.). From the side of the plaza opposite the park, C. Marqués de Vadillo leads to the pedestrian walkway **Calle El Collado,** the main shopping street that cuts through the old quarter past **Plaza San Esteban** to **Plaza Mayor.**

Trains: Estación El Cañuelo, Carretera de Madrid (tel. 975 23 02 02). Shuttle buses run from Pl. Mariano Granados to the train station 20min. before each departure (50 ptas). To Alcalá de Henares (2¾hr., 2-3 per day, 1490ptas) and Madrid (3hr., 2-3 per day, 1760ptas).

Buses: Av. Valladolid (tel. 975 22 51 60), at Av. Gaya Nuño. Shuttle bus from Pl. Mariano Granados (every hr. on the ½hr., 9:30am-2:30pm, 30ptas). Info open 9am-7pm and 8-10pm. Most tickets may be purchased 30min. before departure, except on holidays when seats may be reserved days before. **Therpasa** (tel. 975 22 20 60) to Tarazona (1hr., 5 per day, 540ptas) and Zaragoza (2¼hr., 5 per day, 1075ptas). **La Serrana** (tel. 975 24 09 13) to Burgos (2½hr., 4 per day, 1240ptas). **Linecar** (tel.

975 22 51 50) to Zaragoza (2½hr., 2-3 per day, 1100ptas) and Valladolid (3hr., 2-3 per day, 1460ptas). Double-decker **Continental Auto** (tel. 975 22 44 01) to: Pamplona (2hr., 6 per day, 1460ptas); Madrid (2½hr., 6-8 per day, 1680ptas); Logroño (1½hr., 7-8 per day, 825ptas). **RENFE-Iñigo** (tel. 975 22 89 89) to Salamanca (5hr., 2-3 per day, 2580ptas) and Barcelona (6hr., 2-3 per day, 3885ptas).

Taxis: (tel. 975 21 30 34 or 975 22 17 18). Stands at Pl. Mariano Granados and bus station. To bus station (350ptas) and ruins of Numancia (negotiable 1000ptas).

Car Rental: Europcar, C. Angel Terrel, 5, (tel. 975 22 05 05), off C. Sagunto. 6270ptas plus IVA per day; 47,000ptas per wk. Open M-F 9:30am-1:30pm and 4:30-8pm.

Tourist Office: Pl. Ramón y Cajal (tel./fax 975 21 20 52), on the side of Pl. Mariano Granados opposite the park. It's the glass hut set back from the street. Ask for the *Ruta de los poetas* map. Open daily 10am-2pm and 5-8pm.

Budget Travel: TIVE, C. Campo, 5 (tel./fax 975 22 26 52), up the hill along C. Ferial from the corner of Pl. Mariano at C. Mesta. ISIC 700 ptas, HI card 500 ptas. Open M-F 8am-3pm.

Currency Exchange: **Banco Hispano Central,** off Pl. Ramon Bento Aceño on C. Collado. No commission. **ATMs.** Open May-Sept. M-F 8:30am-2:30pm; Oct.-Apr. M-F 8:30am-2:30pm, Sa 8:30am-1pm.

Luggage Storage: Bags checked at the bus station (75ptas first day, 25ptas per day after that). Open daily 9am-7pm and 8-10pm.

Emergency: Dial 091 or 092. **Police: Municipal Police** (tel. 975 21 18 62).

24-Hour Pharmacy: Check the door of any pharmacy, call the police, or consult the local newspapers *Soria 7 Días* or *Diario Soria.*

Medical Services: Emergencies: (tel. 975 22 22 22). **Hospital General,** Ctra. Logroño (tel. 975 22 08 50).

Post Office: Po. del Espolón, 6 (tel. 975 22 41 14), straight ahead facing Parque Alameda from Pl. Mariano Granados. Open M-F 8:30am-8:30pm, Sa 9:30am-2pm. **Postal Code:** 42070.

ACCOMMODATIONS AND CAMPING

Affordable *pensiones* are sprinkled in the streets around **Pl. Olivo** and **Pl. Salvador,** both near Pl. Mariano Granados. Reservations, necessary during the *fiestas* in the last week of June, are also wise mid-July through mid-September.

Residencia Juvenil Antonio Machado (HI), Pl. José Antonio, 1 (tel. 975 22 00 89), a seasonal hostel. From Pl. Mariano Granados take C. Nicolás Rabal until you reach Pl. José Antonio. A modern college dorm open to tourists July-Aug. 15. Often filled with youth groups, but 20 beds held for independent travelers. Members only. Dorms 950ptas, over 26 1350ptas. Cafeteria. 3-night max. stay. Must check-in by 8pm. Curfew 11:30pm. Reservations not accepted.

Pension Ersogo, C. Alberca, 4 (tel. 975 21 35 08). From the tourist office, head up C. Caballeros and take the first right. Ring the bell on the right-hand door on the 2nd floor. Friendly owners and well-lit, clean, simple rooms, some with nice big windows. Singles 1800ptas; doubles 3200ptas; triples 4000ptas.

Casa Diocesana Pío XII, C. San Juan, 5 (tel. 975 21 21 76). From Pl. Marciano Granados, head up C. El Collado past Pl. San Blas, and then turn right on C. San Juan; enter through iron gates at the corner. Be prepared to see priests wandering the halls. Nice rooms with bath and crucifix. July-Aug.: singles 2800ptas; doubles 3850ptas. Sept.-June: singles 2380ptas; doubles 3370ptas.

Camping: Camping Fuente la Teja (tel. 975 22 29 67), 2km from town on Cra. Madrid (km 233). Swimming pool. 500ptas per person, 525ptas per car, 600ptas per tent plus IVA. Open from Semana Santa-Sept.

FOOD

Soria's specialties include *chorizo* and *migas* (fried bread crumbs), and the region's butter is celebrated throughout Spain. *Paciencias* (local pastries) are hard little cookies meant to be held in the mouth, not in the hand, until they soften up. **Calle M. Vincente Tutor** is spiced with bars and inexpensive restaurants. Merchants sell fresh produce, meat, and fish at the **market** in Pl. Bernarda Robles on C. Estudios, left off C. Callado (open M-Sa mornings). Cruise the **supermarket** aisles at **%Dia-Autoservicio Descuento,** Av. Mariano Vicen, 3½ blocks from Pl. Mariano Granados toward the train station (open daily 9am-2pm and 5-8pm).

Nueva York, C. Collado, 14 (tel. 975 21 27 84), one block past Pl. San Esteban. You'll want to be a part of breakfast (served until 12:30pm) with coffee, fresh orange juice, and buttery toast or croissants (310ptas). An array of cookies and chocolate beckons. Open daily in summer 8am-10pm; in winter 8am-9:30pm.

Bar Restaurante Regio, Pl. Ramón y Cajal, 7 (tel. 975 21 30 76). A fine selection of *bocadillos* (275-650ptas), *raciones* (350-1600ptas), and *menús del diá* (1300ptas). The mammoth *tortilla de patata* is a steal at 300ptas. Open daily 7am-midnight.

Chinatown II, C. Nicoás Rabal, 5 (tel. 975 21 18 35). For a change of taste, sample the generous and cheap *menú* (795ptas). Plates of rice, noodles, and bean sprouts start at 455ptas. Enjoy deciphering the English translation of the Spanish description of the Chinese food. Open daily noon-4pm and 8pm-midnight. MC, Visa.

SIGHTS AND ENTERTAINMENT

The **Río Duero,** which the great 20th-century poet Antonio Machado likened to a drawn bow, forms an arc around Soria. To find the river from Pl. Mariano Granados, walk past the sign for Nueva York and straight down C. Zapatería. Halfway down the hill, C. Zapatería changes to C. Real. Follow this road to Pl. San Pedro. The erratically open **Concatedral de San Pedro** is on the left; the bridge lies straight ahead.

Soria's biggest draw, however, lies across the river. The 17th-century **Ermita de San Saturio,** 1.5km downstream, was built into the side of a cliff. *(Turn right with the road after crossing the bridge. Open daily May-Sept. 10am-2pm and 4:30-8pm; Oct.-Apr. 10:30-6:30pm.)* A heavenly retreat where light seeps into the caves through stained-glass windows. Note the window from which a 6-year-old child fell in 1772, landing on his knees unharmed—supposedly saved by San Saturio. It's well worth the riverside trek. The **Monasterio San Juan de Duero** sits tranquilly amid cottonwoods and green, green grass by the river. *(Turn left after crossing bridge. Open June-Aug. Tu-Sa 10am-2pm and 5-9pm, Su 10am-2pm; Sept.-Oct. and Apr.-May Tu-Sa 10am-2pm and 4-7pm, Su 10am-2pm; Nov.-Mar. Tu-Sa 10am-2pm and 3:30-6pm, Su 10am-2pm. 200ptas; under 18, over 65, and students free; Sa and Su free for everyone.)* The church itself, dating from the 12th century, is quite simple. The remarkable and graceful arches, combining Romanesque and Islamic styles, are all that remain of the 13th century cloister. Inside, a small museum displays medieval artifacts.

The **Museo Numantino,** Po. Espolón, 8 (tel. 975 22 13 97), shows off the impressive Celto-Iberian and Roman artifacts excavated from nearby Numancia. *(Open June-Sept. Tu-Sa 9am-2pm and 5-9pm, Su 9am-2pm; Oct.-May Tu-Sa 9am-8:30pm, Su 9am-2pm. 200ptas. Under 18, over 65, student with ID or youth card, and everyone on Sa and Su free. Wheelchair accessibility from Pl. Rey el Sabio.)*

When work's over, everybody in Soria heads for the old town. Early evening finds them in either Pl. Ramón Benito Aceña or Pl. San Clemente, both off C. Collado. There locals order drinks and nibbles from bar windows and loiter outside. Late-night festivities center at the disco-bars grouped around the intersection of **Rota de Calatañazer** and **Calle Cardenal Frías** near Pl. Toros.

Many Spanish fiestas involve watching bulls and eating, but Soria ingeniously combines the two. The **Fiesta de San Juan** (the last week in June) starts each day with a running of the bulls and ends each day with an ingestion of them.

■ Near Soria: Ruins of Numancia

Die-hard archeology fans should check out the architectural ruins of **Numancia** (tel. 975 18 07 12), a hilltop settlement 7km north of Soria dating back more than 4000 years. *(Ruins open T-Sa 10am-2pm and 5-9pm. 200ptas.)* The Celto-Iberians had settled here by the 3rd century BC and tenaciously resisted Roman conquest. It took 10 years of the Numantian Wars and the direction of Scipio Africanus to dislodge them. Scipio erected a system of walls 9km long, 3m tall, and 2.5m thick to encircle the town and starve its residents. High off his victory, he saved 50 survivors as trophies, sold the rest into slavery, burned the city, and divided its lands among his allies. Numancia, however, lived on as a metaphor for patriotic heroism in Golden Age and Neoclassical tragedies. The ruins, though battered, are still worth a visit. Check out the foundations of the Roman houses and the underground wells. All excavated artifacts now hang at the Museo Numantino in Soria.

Getting to Numancia can be a problem for the carless. A **bus** runs to Garray (15min., 1km from the ruins, M-F at 3 and 5:45pm, 90ptas). Getting back from Numancia is even tougher; the buses don't pass by again until 2:15 the next day. Happy hiking (or call a cab).

■ Near Soria: El Burgo de Osma

El Burgo de Osma (pop. 5100) is probably worth the trip only if you have your own wheels, but medievalists who persevere past its gritty exterior and venture into the back streets around the cathedral will be richly rewarded. Two of the more attractive buildings are **Hospital de San Agustín** and the **Casas Consistoriales** in Pl. Mayor. Fulfilling a vow, the Cluniac monk Don Pedro de Osma erected the magnificent 13th-century Gothic **cathedral** (tel. 975 34 03 22) on the site of an earlier church. *(Open Tu-Su 10am-1pm and 4-7pm. Guided tour of museums 350ptas. Cathedral free.)* The cathedral's two **museums** have an important collection of codices, including a richly illuminated Beato de Liébana commentary on the Apocalypse and a 12th-century charter, thought to be one of the earliest written examples of Castilian vernacular.

Calle Universidad is a good place to look for some affordable beds. Next to a gas station, the **Hostal Residencia La Perdiz,** C. Universidad, 33 (tel. 975 34 03 09), on the edge of town, has frumpy rooms with baths, phones, and TVs (singles 3500ptas; doubles 6500ptas; 7% IVA not included). The **campground's** ownership has changed and its future is unclear; contact the tourist office for an update. **Gonzalo Ruiz** (tel. 975 22 20 60) sends **buses** to and from Soria (50min., M-Sa 2 per day, 455ptas).

Galicia (Galiza)

If, as the old Galician saying goes, "rain is art," then there is no gallery more beautiful than the misty skies of northwestern Spain. An anomaly to international conceptions of Spain, Galicia looks and feels like no other region in the country. Often veiled in a silvery drizzle, its fern-laden eucalyptus woods and slate-roofed fishing villages rest beside long white beaches. Rivers wind through hills and gradually widen into the famed *rías* (estuaries) that empty into the Cantabrian Sea and Atlantic Ocean.

A rest stop on the Celts' journey to Ireland around 900 BC, the region of Galicia displays enduring Celtiberian influences. Ancient *castros* (fortress-villages), inscriptions, and bagpipes testify to this Celtiberian past, while lingering lore about witches, fountain fairies, and buried treasures maintains Galicia's reputation as a land of old magic.

Galicia's harsh landscape of daunting mountain barriers and weaving rivers, once a blessed defense against Moorish invasion, now hinders economic growth. The terrain sustains few cash crops and hampers potential trade routes, while Galicia's renowned fishing industry and net-and-plow farming methods do not provide enough support for the region. National and regional governments are trying to upgrade Galicia's inadequate roads, in part to perpetuate a recent surge in tourism that has permeated even smaller towns. Thanks in part to their efforts, Santiago de Compostela, the final destination on the Camino de Santiago, continues to be one of the most popular Spanish cities among backpackers. Although transportation between towns may be limited, those with patience and flexible itineraries are duly rewarded.

GALICIA

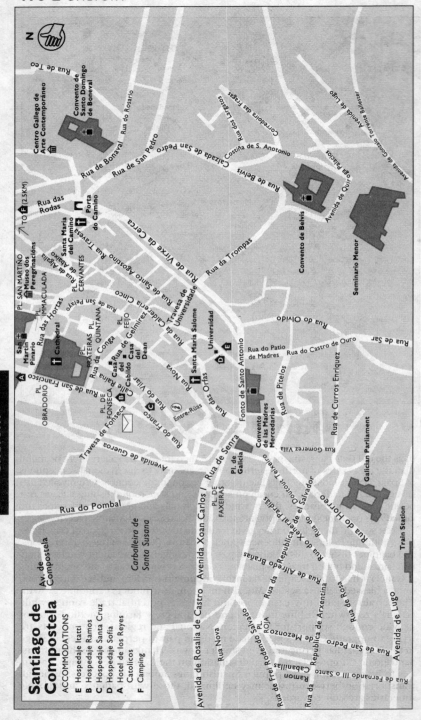

Santiago de Compostela

Av. de Compostela

ACCOMMODATIONS
E Hospedaje Itatti
B Hospedaje Ramos
C Hospedaje Santa Cruz
D Hospedaje Sofía
A Hotel de los Reyes Catolicos
F Camping

Galicians speak *gallego,* a language related to Castilian and Portuguese. In fact, *gallego* is a linguistic missing link of sorts between the two languages. On the most basic level, *gallego* differs from Castilian by replacing "La" and "El" with "O"; "J's" with a preponderance of "X's"; and "LL" with "L." For example, *"En el pueblo"* becomes *"No poblo."* Since most Galicians are bilingual, save for townspeople in remote areas, conversation tends to proceed in Castilian. Newspapers and street signs, however, alternate between languages. Regional cuisine features *caldo gallego* (a vegetable broth), *vieiras* (scallops, the pilgrim's trophy), the *empanada* (turnover/pastry stuffed with tomato and tuna, among other fillings), and *tetilla* (a creamy, tangy cheese). Although regionalism in Galicia fails to make the headlines that nationalism makes in Basque and Catalan areas, you will find some graffiti calling for *"liberdade."*

🚲 HIGHLIGHTS OF GALICIA (GALIZA)

- Camping on the idyllic, undeveloped **Islas Cíes** (see p. 187).
- Arriving amid mobs of pilgrims at **Santiago de Compostela's** breathtaking cathedral.

■ Santiago de Compostela

Ever since the remains of the Apostle St. James were supposedly discovered here in 813, Santiago has drawn a myriad of pilgrims, many walking for years to worship at its cathedral. Built over the saint's alleged remains, the cathedral marks the end of the Camino de Santiago, an 800-year-old, 900km pilgrimage believed to halve one's time in purgatory (see **Pilgrim's Progress,** p. 183) and the force lifting Santiago into the ranks of Christianity's holiest cities, even alongside Rome and Jerusalem. Today, sunburnt pilgrims, street musicians, and hordes of tourists fill the granite streets by the cathedral. Students at the city's renowned university enjoy the city's modern art gallery and state-of-the-art concert hall as well as an active nightlife.

ORIENTATION AND PRACTICAL INFORMATION

Street names in Santiago can be confusing since languages do not always coordinate between street signs and maps: *calle* in Castilian becomes *rúa* in Galician, *del* becomes *do.* The **cathedral** marks the center of the old city, which sits up higher than the new city. From the train station in the southern end of town, three main streets lead to the cathedral: **Rúa do Franco** (Calle del Franco), **Rúa do Vilar** (Calle del Vilar), and **Rúa Nova** (Calle Nueva).

From the **train station,** turn right at the top of the stairs and take C. Hórreo to **Praza de Galiza** (do *not* take Av. de Lugo), then go one more block to **Calle Bautizatos,** where three cathedral-bound streets originate. From the **bus station,** take bus #10 to Pr. Galizia (departs every 15-20min., 90ptas). On foot, exit the station onto R. Angel Castro and turn left onto R. Pastoriza; continue for 20min. as the street changes names like a chameleon. Turn right onto R. Atalia then left after one block onto Pr. Pena. Follow this road through Pr. San Mariño right into the cathedral's Pr. Immaculada.

Transportation

Flights: Aeropuerto Lavacolla (tel. 981 59 74 00), 10km away on the road to Lugo. A bus connects it to Santiago, stopping at the bus station, train station, and C. General Pardiñas, 26 (8 per day, 125ptas). Schedule printed in the daily paper *El Correo Gallego* (daily paper, 125ptas). **Iberia,** C. General Pardiñas, 36 (tel. 981 57 20 24). Open M-F 9:30am-2pm and 4-7:15pm.

Trains: (tel. 981 52 02 02), Itòrreo. Open M-Sa 7am-9pm, Su 7am-1pm. To: La Coruña (1hr., 16 per day, 500-575ptas); Pontevedra (1½hr., 14 per day, 490-565ptas); Vigo (2hr., 13 per day, 750-865ptas); León (6½hr., 2 per day, 2800-3300ptas); Madrid (8hr., 2 per day, 4600-5600ptas). Schedule printed daily in *El Correo Gallego.*

Buses: Estación Central de Autobuses (tel. 981 58 77 00), C. San Cayetano. Nothing central about it: a 30min. walk from downtown. Bus #10 leaves from the R.

Montero Río side of Pr. Galiza for the station (departs every 15-20min., 90ptas). Info open daily 6am-10pm. **ALSA** (tel. 981 58 61 33). To: San Sebastián (6hr., 2 per day, 6910ptas); Madrid (8-9hr., 3 per day, 5010ptas); Bilbao (9½hr., 3 per day, 6300ptas). **Castromil** (tel. 981 58 90 90) to: Noya (1hr., 12 per day, 630ptas); La Coruña (1½hr., 6-10 per day, 650-820ptas); Pontevedra (1½hr., 15 per day, 620ptas); El Ferrol (2hr., 4 per day, 950ptas); Muros (2hr., 12 per day, 765ptas); Vigo (2hr., 15 per day, 900ptas). **Finisterre** (tel. 981 58 73 16) to Camariñas (2hr., 3 per day, 1025ptas) and Finisterre (2½hr., 3 per day, 1360ptas). **Empresa Freire** (tel. 981 58 81 11) to Lugo (2hr., 9 per day, 890ptas).

Public Transportation: (tel. 981 58 18 15). Bus #6 (daily 10am-10:30pm) to the train station, #9 to the campgrounds (daily 10am-8pm), #10 to the bus station. All buses stop in Pr. Galicia—check the signs to see which side (90ptas). Except for bus #6 and 9, buses run daily 7am-10:30pm.

Taxis: call 981 59 84 88 or 981 58 24 50.

Car Rental: Autotur, C. General Pardiñas, 3 (tel. 981 58 64 96), 2 blocks from Pr. Galicia in the new town. Must be at least 21 and have had a license at least 1 year. Rent a small car with unlimited mileage from 7600ptas per day (price depends on duration of rental and time of week). Open M-F 9am-2pm and 4-8pm.

Tourist and Financial Services

Tourist Office: (tel. 981 58 40 81). Take your pick of two. One **branch** on R. Vilar in the old town under the arches of a colonnade. Open M-F 10am-2pm and 4-7pm, Sa 11am-2pm and 5-7pm, Su and festivals 11am-2pm. Or try the **little Modernist structure** in the center island of Pr. Galicia. Open in summer M-F 10am-2pm and 5-8pm, Sa 11am-2pm; in winter M-F 10am-2pm and 5-8pm.

Budget Travel: TIVE (tel. 981 57 24 26), Pl. Matadero. Turn right up R. Fonte Santo Antonio from Pr. Galiza. Train, bus, and plane tickets for international destinations. ISIC 700ptas, HI card 500ptas. Open M-F 9am-2pm.

Currency Exchange: Banco Central Hispano, R. Vilar, 30 (tel. 981 58 16 12). No commission. Open May-Sept. M-F 8:30am-2:30pm; Oct.-Apr. M-F 8:30am-2:30pm, Sa 8:30am-1pm.

American Express: Ultratur Viajes, Av. Figueroa, 6 (tel. 981 58 70 00). Open M-F 9:30am-2pm and 4:30-7pm, Sa 10am-12:30pm.

Local Services

Luggage Storage: At the train station (lockers 400ptas). Open 7:30am-11pm. At the bus station (80ptas per bag). Open daily 8am-10pm.

Laundromat: Lavandería Lobato, C. Santiago de Chile, 7 (tel. 981 59 99 54), 1 block from Pr. Vigo in the new city. Self-service wash and dry 700ptas per 4kg load. Full service 800ptas per load. Open M-F 9:30am-2pm and 4-8:30pm, Sa 9am-2pm.

English Bookstore: Librería Galicia, Pr. Universidad, 2 blocks east of R. Nova. Excellent selection of classic English novels and some poetry. Open M-F 9:30am-2pm and 4-8pm. Stores in the cathedral-university area also carry English books.

Religious Services: Mass in the cathedral M-Sa 9:30am and noon, Su 9, 10:30am, 1, 5, and 7pm. A special **pilgrim's mass,** featuring the *botafumeiro* (an incense burner on steroids) M-F 7:30pm, Sa 6 and 7:30pm.

Emergency and Communications

Emergency: call 091 or 092. **Police: Guardia Civil,** call 981 58 22 66 or 981 58 16 11.

Late-Night Pharmacy: Bescansa, Pr. Toural, 10 (tel. 981 58 59 40), 1 block toward the cathedral from Pr. Galicia.

Medical Assistance: Hospital Xeral, C. Galeras (tel. 981 54 00 00).

Internet Access: Zum Zum, C. Rep. de El Salvador, 28 (tel. 981 59 97 45). A friendly cybercafe in the heart of the new city. 200ptas per 30min. Open daily noon-3am.

Post Office: Travesa de Fonseca (tel. 981 58 12 52; fax 981 56 32 88), on the corner of R. Franco. Open for stamps, Lista de Correos (around the corner, R. Franco, 6), and **faxes** M-F 8:30am-8:30pm, Sa 9:30am-2pm. **Postal Code:** 15080.

GALICIA

ACCOMMODATIONS AND CAMPING

Santiago's rooms are not the cheapest, but they are plentiful. *Hospedajes* and *pensiones* conglomerate around **Rúa Vilar** and **Calle Raíña** (between R. Vilar and R. Franco), and hand-drawn *habitaciones* signs are just about everywhere else.

Hospedaje Itatti, Pr. Mazarelos, 1 (tel. 981 58 06 29). At Pr. Galicia, take a right onto R. Fonte San Antonio, and then the 1st left up a granite street. Huge, sunny rooms with classy ambiance and sweet prices. Doubles with hall bath 1150ptas, with private bath 3500ptas. Call ahead in winter when students occupy most rooms.

Hospedaje Ramos, C. Raíña, 18, 2nd fl. (tel. 981 58 18 59), above O Papa Una restaurant. Spacious and sparkling clean rooms (some with views of a cathedral tower—stick your head *way* out the window) with pilgrim shell decor. Singles 1600ptas, with bath 1750ptas; doubles 3000ptas, with bath 3500ptas.

Hospedaje Sofia, C. Cardenal Paya, 16 (tel. 981 58 51 50). Within sight of Hospedaje Ittati, off Pr. Mazarelos. Enter the restaurant on the ground floor, but head directly upstairs (*hospedaje* and restaurant are not related) for spic 'n' span, spacious rooms, some with balconies and flowers. Practice your French with the warm owners. Singles 2500ptas; doubles 3600-4000ptas. Bath down the hall. Prices drop in winter.

Hospedaje Santa Cruz, R. Vilar, 42, 2nd fl. (tel. 981 58 28 15). Large, simple rooms have big windows overlooking the most popular street in Santiago. In summer singles 2000ptas; doubles 2500ptas; in winter singles 1500ptas; doubles 3000ptas.

Camping: Camping As Cancelas, R. 25 de Xullo, 35 (tel. 981 58 02 66), 2km from the cathedral on the northern edge of town; take bus #6 or 9. Souvenirs, laundry, supermarket, and pool make this place the Club Med of camping. 475ptas per person, per car, and per tent. Electricity 450ptas. Open year-round.

FOOD

Let's Go disciples breathe—and eat—easy in Santiago. Bars and cafeterias line old town streets, proffering a glorious variety of finned *raciones* and remarkably inexpensive *menús*. Most restaurants are south of the cathedral, notably on **Rúa do Vilar, Rúa Franco,** and **Calle Raíña.** In the new city, try the streets radiating from Pr. Roxa. End your meal with a *tarta de Santiago,* rich almond cake emblazoned with a stylized cross. Santiago's **market** is a sight in its own right. From Pr. San Felix to Convento de San Augustín, the streets are lined with produce carts, meat stalls, fresh cheese baskets, flowers, and...baby clothes (open M-Sa 7:30am-2pm). **Supermercados Lorenzo Froiz,** Pr. Toural, is one block into the old city from Pr. Galicia, and does not have peanut butter (open M-Sa 9am-3pm and 5-9pm).

O Cabaliño do Demo, R. Aller Ulloa, 7 (tel. 981 58 8146). A chic and cheery **vegetarian** restaurant in Pota de Camiño, with creative, mostly organic recipes. Specialty house salad (300ptas), *menú del dìa* (850ptas), and organic wines (from 650ptas.) Menu in *gallego* but English spoken. Open daily 2-4pm and 9pm-midnight.

Casa Manolo, R. Traviesa, 27 (tel. 981 58 29 50). By the market and Pr. San Augustín. Come early and often to sample the many combinations on their *menú* (includes homemade *flan,* but not wine, 750ptas). Open M-F 1-4pm and 8pm-midnight.

La Crepe, Pr. Quintana (tel 981 57 76 43). Head upstairs to this *cozy comedor* hidden above terrace cafes. Tasty crepes (700-900ptas) and *platos combinados* (700-950ptas) made all the tastier by a gorgeous view of Pr. Quintana.

Entre-Rùas, Ruela de Entre-Rùas, 2 (tel. 981 58 61 08), off of R. Nova. Intimate little restaurant, popular with locals, students, and professors alike because of its simple and economical dishes. Entrees 625ptas. Open daily 9am-midnight.

Pizzeria Oasis, R. Nova de Abaixo, 3 (tel. 981 59 98 55). In the quiet downstairs dining room, a plaque recognizes the restaurant as a Galician pizza champion (the competition was, no doubt, fierce). Pizzas 600-900ptas, hearty calzones 750-850ptas. Open M 8pm-midnight, W-Su 1-4:30pm and 8pm-midnight.

GALICIA

Café-Bar El Metro, R. Nova, 12 (tel. 981 57 65 38). Snag a table under the archway outside. *Menú del día* (825ptas). *Menú del estudiante,* with a main *plato* of hake or steak 650ptas. Entrees 350-600ptas. Open daily 1-5pm and 8-10pm. Closed Christmas week and Semana Santa.

SIGHTS

The Cathedral

Offering a cool, quiet sanctuary to priest, pilgrim, worshiper, and tourist alike, Santiago's **cathedral** rises above the center of this lively old city. The cathedral comes gloriously to life during mass, when every candle is lit and every pew bursts. Pilgrims in t-shirts and shorts speak at the altar during services and hug the jewelled bust of St. James with special fervor. The cathedral has four facades, each a masterpiece from a different time period, with entrances opening to four different *prazas:* Platerías, Quintana, Obradoiro, and Azabaxería. From the southern **Praza de Platerías** (with the spitting sea horse), enter the cathedral through the Romanesque arched double doors. Columns and assorted icons in various stages of undress cover this side of the cathedral, the oldest of the four facades. The **Torro do Reloxio** (clock tower), Pórtico Real, and Porta Santa face the **Praza da Quintana,** to the west of the cathedral. To the north, a blend of Doric and Ionic columns grace the **Praza de Azabaxerìa** (also called Pl. Inmaculada), combining Romanesque and Neoclassical styles.

Consecrated in 1211, the cathedral later acquired Gothic chapels in the apse and transept, a 15th-century dome, a 16th-century cloister, and the Baroque **Obradoiro** facade with its two grand towers that soar above the city. This facade faces **Praza da Obradoiro** (to the west), an immense plaza scattered with camera-snappers, souvenir hawkers, and *tunas* (young men in medieval garb strumming lutes). Encased in the Obradorio facade, the **Pórtico de la Gloria** by Maestro Mateo is considered the crowning achievement of Spanish Romanesque sculpture. This unusual 12th-century amalgamation of angels, prophets, saints, sinners, demons, and monsters forms a compendium of Christian theology. Unlike most rigid Romanesque statues, those in the *Pórtico* smile, whisper, lean, and gab, leaving Galician author Rosalía del Castro to proclaim, "It looks as if their lips are moving...might they be alive?" The cathedral includes a bust of Mateo—unusual considering artists in the Middle Ages were rarely recognized in sculpture. Visitors knock their heads three times against Mateo's head, hoping that some of his talent will rub off in the process.

St. James's revered remains lie beneath the high altar in a silver coffer, while his bejeweled bust, polished by thousands of pilgrim embraces, sits above the altar. The **botafumeiro,** an enormous silver censer supposedly intended to overpower the pilgrims' stench, swings from the transept during high mass and major liturgical ceremonies. The **museum** and **cloisters** have gorgeous and intricate 16th-century tapestries and two especially poignant statues of the pregnant Virgin Mary with her hand on her expanding belly. *(Museum open June-Sept. M-Sa 10am-1:30pm and 4-7:30pm, Su and holidays 10am-1:30pm and 4-7pm; Oct.-May M-Sa 11am-1pm and 4-6pm, Su and holidays 10am-1:30pm and 4-7pm. Museum and cloisters 500ptas.)* The museum also houses manuscripts from the *Códice Calixtino* and Romanesque remains from one of many archaeological excavations conducted in the cathedral. The early 12th-century *Códice,* five volumes of manuscripts on the stories of the Apostles, includes traveling information for pilgrims.

Much older than the towers that house them, the **bells** of Santiago were stolen as souvenirs by Moorish invaders and transported to Córdoba on the backs of Christian slaves. Centuries later, when Spaniards conquered Córdoba, they took back their bells, using some unlucky Moors as pack horses to complete their revenge.

Architecture Elsewhere

Indulge your art-historian heart in the old town, all of which has been designated a national monument. Across Pr. Obradoiro, facing the cathedral, the majestic facade of the former **Pazo de Raxoi** shines with gold-accented balconies and monumental Neoclassical columns. Once a royal palace, it now houses the Ayuntamiento and office of

Pilgrims' Progress

One starry night in the year 813, a lonely hermit trudged through the hills on the way to his hermitage. Suddenly, miraculously, bright visions flooded the scene, revealing the long-forgotten tomb of the Apostle James ("Santiago" in Spanish). Around this *campus stellae* (Latin for "field of stars"), the cathedral of Santiago de Compostela was built, and around this cathedral, a world-famous sacred pilgrimage was born.

Since the 12th century, thousands of pilgrims have traveled the 900km of the **Camino de Santiago.** Many have made the pilgrimage in search of spiritual fulfillment, most as true believers, some to adhere to a stipulation of inheritance, others as an alternative to prison, and many even to find romance—the wife of Bath in Chaucer's *Canterbury Tales* sauntered to Santiago in bright, red stockings to find herself a husband! Clever Benedictine monks built monasteries to host pilgrims along the *camino,* giving rise to the first large-scale, international tourism, and making Santiago's cathedral the most frequented Christian shrine in the world. In the 12th century, an enterprising French monk created *Codex Calixtus,* the first known travel guide, filled with information on the quality of water at various rest stops and descriptions of villages and monuments along the most common route, *La Ruta Francesa* (beginning near the French border in Roncevalles, Navarra). Pilgrims flowed into Santiago, introducing Romanesque art and architecture, Provençal lyrics, epics, legends, and music to Spain.

The scallop-edged conch shell, used for dipping water from streams along the way, has become a symbol of the Camino de Santiago. Pilgrims are easily spotted by the shells tied onto their weathered backpacks and by their crook-necked walking sticks and tanned bodies. True *peregrinos* (pilgrims) must cover 100km on foot or horse, or 200km on bike, to receive *La Compostela* an official certificate of pilgrimage completion, issued by the cathedral. A network of *refugios* (refuges) and *albergues* (shelters) offer free lodging to pilgrims on the move and stamp the requisite "pilgrims' passports" to provide evidence of completion of the full distance. For more information and free guides to the Camino de Santiago, contact the **Officinal de Acogida del Peregrino,** R. Vilar, 1 (tel. 981 56 24 19), in the Casa del Deán. At a rate of 30km per day, walking the entire *camino* takes about a month. For inspiration along the way, keep in mind that you are joining the ranks of such illustrious pilgrims as King Ferdinand and Queen Isabella, Francis of Assisi, Pope John Paul II, and Shirley MacLaine.

The year 1999 has been designated an **Año Santo** for Santiago, which means that various special activities will be scheduled throughout the year, culminating on July 24, when the Pope comes to open the *puerta sacra.*

the president of the Xunta de Galicia. At night, floodlights illuminate the remarkable bas-relief of the Battle of Clavio, achieving maximum dramatic effect.

The 15th-century Renaissance **Hospital Real,** now **Hotel dos Reyes Católicos,** a ritzy *parador,* is also in Pr. Obradoiro. *(Open daily 10am-2pm and 4-7pm. Free.)* It upholds an ancient tradition of feeding 10 pilgrims per day (in the employee dining hall). Try to catch one of three splendid art exhibitions given occasionally in the lobby, or linger long enough and you may be let in to see its four courtyards, chapel, and sculpture. In Pr. San Martín (across from the cathedral in Pl. Inmaculada) stands the impressive **Monasterio de San Martín Pinario,** once a religious center almost as powerful as the cathedral. A mixture of Romanesque cloisters, Plateresque facades, and Baroque sculpture, the monastery displays a composite style that is the most outstanding architecture of its type in Santiago.

Off Pr. Platerías, residential architecture holds its own in the Baroque **Casa del Deán** and **Casa del Cabildo,** now the pilgrim info headquarters. West of the old town, a Neoclassical **universidad** weaves into an otherwise Romanesque and Baroque warp. Located 1km from the cathedral, the 15th-century **Colexiata de Santa María do Sar** has a disintegrating Romanesque cloister—it started crumbling in the 12th century and never stopped. *(Open M-Sa 10am-1pm and 4-7pm. Free.)* Inside, foreboding pillars lean at frightening angles, making visitors wary.

GALICIA

Three Museums and a Park

Those still curious about the Camino de Santiago should head to the comprehensive **Museo das Peregrinacións** (tel. 981 58 15 58), in the Pl. San Miguel. *(Open Tu-F 10am-8pm, Sa 10:30am-1:30pm and 5-8pm, Su 10:30am-1:30pm. 400ptas, students 200ptas.)* This three-story Gothic building is chock-full of creatively displayed historical information about the *camino,* including exhibits on the rites and rituals of pilgrimage, the iconography of St. James, and statues of the Virgin as a baby-Jesus-toting pilgrim.

You will find out everything you have ever wanted to know (and possibly more) about traditional Galician living at the **Museo de Pobo Gallego** (tel. 981 58 36 20), just past the Porto de Camino, inside the Gothic Convento de Santo Domingo de Bonavad. *(Open daily 10am-1pm and 4-7pm. 200ptas. Sundays free.)* Documentary exhibits on shipbuilding, pottery, house construction, and bagpipe making (just to name a few) are the highlights, but the museum also includes several rooms dedicated to Galician painting. Next door, the expansive galleries and rooftop *terraza* of the sparkling new, white stone **Centro Gallego de Arte Contemporáneo (CGAC)** house bizarre, multi-media exhibitions on international modern art. *(Open Tu-Sa 11am-8pm, Su 11am-4pm. Free. Small selection of striking, dirt-cheap posters.)* A walk in the **Caballeira de Santa Susana,** between the new and old cities, is a lovely way to stave off monument overdose. Its manicured gardens and eucalyptus-lined walkways open onto gorgeous views of the cathedral, the university, and rolling farmland.

ENTERTAINMENT

The local newspaper *El Correo Gallego* (125ptas) lists art exhibits and concert information. Consult any of three local monthlies, *Santiago Dias Guía Imprescindible, Compostelán* (both available at the tourist office), or *Modus Vivendi* for updates on the live music scene. *La Voz de Galicia* (125ptas) offers a more regional focus.

At night, crowds flood cellars throughout the city. Bars on **Rúas Nova, Vilar,** and **Franco** are packed all night. Clubs are open roughly from 11pm to 4am, although the most heavenly action starts well after midnight. Women generally get in for free; men pay 500 to 800ptas for cover. At **Cervecería Dakar,** R. Franco, 13, rich *batidos* (milkshakes 350ptas) of nutmeg and delicious liqueurs (five flavors) entice students, who spread their papers all over the tables (open daily 8am-midnight). **Modus Vivendi,** in Pr. Feixoo, five minutes from Pr. Praterías on R. Conga, was a hangout for revolutionary Galician youth in the 1970s and now plays the headquarters for Santiago's nightlife. Striking an eclectic balance between Galician bagpipes, Aretha Franklin, and local art, Modus's intimate setting often features concerts or debates. Check the entryway for listings of *música en directo* (live music) at other local spots, like **Borriquita de Belén,** R. San Pelayo, 22 (mostly jazz), **Crechas,** San Pelayo (folk music), **Joam Airas,** R. Traviesa, or **Retablo,** R. Nueva. If you prefer music from a can, spin over to slightly preppy **Casting Araguaney,** C. Montero Rios, 25 (tel. 981 59 96 72), a few blocks west of Pr. Galicia, in Hotel Araguaney. **Discoteca Libertí** rumbles salsa and merengue just across the street. People of all ages kiss sanity goodbye at **Discoteca Black,** C. Rosalía de Castro, a popular, primarily gay club inside Hotel Peregrino. The *galerías* on R. Nova de Abaixo, in the new city, are mobbed with students on Friday nights.

Ten minutes from the old town, the recently unveiled **Auditorio** schedules classical music interrupted by an occasional Santana concert (shows Oct.-June; check the tourist office and newspaper for more info). The **Teatro Principal,** R. Nova, 21 (tel. 981 58 19 28), lines up a mix of puppet shows, ballet, and Shakespeare (tickets at the box office daily 12:30-2pm and 6pm-showtime). To check out schedules before you come, visit http://www.xunta.es/consello/cultura. For less highbrow, more funky theater, head to **Sola Galan** on the corner of R. Gomez Ulla and R. Curros Enriquez, where contemporary dance and drama performances are held. They also host an outdoor theater festival in late June. August brings an international folk music festival to town; Santiago's major **fiestas** occur from July 18 to 31.

RÍAS BAJAS (RÍAS BAIXAS)

According to Gallegan lore, the Rías Bajas (Low Estuaries) were formed by God's tremendous handprint. Each *ría*, or estuary, stretches like a finger through the territory. Coves and picturesque islands lure Galicians for weekend visits. Foreign tourists have recently caught on, and tourism may soon eclipse fishing as the region's top industry. Public transportation between towns is often sparse, so rent a car or plan ahead.

■ Vigo

After its beautiful harborside view, the most enticing characteristic of Ria de Vigo's major port city is a Vigo's biggest attraction is a well-developed service economy. The sprawling city (pop. 300,000) is noisy and polluted, but ferries, buses, and trains mercifully and efficiently shuttle visitors to the surrounding Ría de Vigo and nearby Río Miño, while a network of hotels and shops pamper tourists between excursions. Elegant cafes near the water provide soothing spots to while away an evening.

ORIENTATION AND PRACTICAL INFORMATION

The **Gran Vía** is Vigo's main thoroughfare, stretching south to north from **Praza de América**, through **Praza de España,** and ending at the perpendicular **Rúa Urzáiz.** A left turn (west) onto R. Urzáizone leads to **Porta do Sol** and into the **casco antiguo.**
As you exit the **train station** on to R. Urzáiz, go right two blocks to reach the central Gran Vía-Urzáiz. The city center is a 25-minute trek from the **bus station.** Exit left then turn right on Av. Madrid, the third intersection. Eventually, a right on Gran Vía at Pr. España leads to the intersection with R. Urzáiz (marked by the sculpture of a naked man). The R4 bus from the bus station also goes to R. Urzáiz (110ptas).

Transportation

Flights: Aeropuerto de Vigo, Av. Aeroporto (tel. 986 48 74 09). Daily flights to Madrid, Barcelona, Bilbao, and Valencia. The R9 **bus** runs regularly from R. Urzáiz near R. Colón to the airport (110ptas). **Iberia's** office is at Marqués de Valladares, 17 (tel. 986 22 70 05).

Trains: RENFE, Pr. Estación (tel. 986 43 11 14), downstairs from C. Lepanto. Info open daily 10am-11pm. To: Pontevedra (35min., 21 per day, 245ptas); Valladolid (change at Medina del Campo, 2 per day, 4300ptas); Túy (45min., 4 per day, 315ptas); Santiago de Compostela (2hr., 20 per day, 800ptas); La Coruña (3hr., 17 per day, 1200ptas); Madrid (8-9hr., 3 per day, 4800-5600ptas); Porto, Portugal (2½hr., 3 per day, 1675ptas).

Buses: Estación de Autobuses, Av. Madrid (tel. 986 37 34 11), on the corner with R. Alcalde Gregorio Espino. **Castromil** (tel. 986 27 81 12). To: Santiago de Compostela (2hr., 27 per day, 900ptas); La Coruña (2½hr., 9 per day, 1695ptas); Pontevedra (45min., 31 per day, 315ptas). For **ATSA buses** (tel. 986 61 02 55), buy tickets upon boarding. To: Túy (45min., departs every 30min., 320ptas); La Guardia (1hr., departs every 30min., 595ptas); Bayona (50min., departs every 30min., 245ptas). **Auto Res, S.A.** (tel. 986 37 78 78). To Madrid (9hr., 4 per day, 450ptas).

Ferries: Estación Ría, Av. Avenidas (tel. 986 43 77 77), just past the nautical club. To: Cangas (20min., departs every 30min., 225ptas); Moaña (30min., departs every hr., 175ptas); Islas Cíes (50min., 5 per day, round-trip 2000ptas).

Public Transportation: Red and green **Vitrasa buses** (tel. 986 29 16 00) run to every corner of the city (110ptas).

Taxis: Radio Taxi (tel. 986 47 00 00).

Car Rental: Atesa, R. Urzáiz, 84 (tel. 986 42 10 33). Must be at least 21 and have had license one year. Open M-F 9am-1:30pm and 4:30-7pm, Sa 10am-noon.

Tourist, Financial, and Local Services

Tourist Office: Av. Avenidas (tel. 986 43 05 77). Take R. Urzáiz to R. Colón, follow R. Colón to the water, turn left onto R. Montero Ríos and walk 6 blocks. The office is in the long cement building next to the ferry station. Lots of brochures and maps. English spoken. Open M-F 9am-2pm and 4:30-6:30pm, Sa 10am-12:30pm.

Currency Exchange: Banco Central Hispano, R. Urzáiz, 20. No commission. Open M-F 8:30am-2:30pm.

Luggage Storage: Lockers at the **train station** (400ptas). Open daily 7am-9:45pm. At the **bus station** (60ptas per bag). Open M-F 9:30am-1:30pm and 3-7pm, Sa 9am-2pm. The train station is infinitely more convenient.

El Corte Inglés: Gran Vía, 25-27 (tel. 986 41 51 11). 3 blocks uphill from R. Urzáiz. Novels and guidebooks in English, haircutting, cafeteria, restaurant, **telephones,** and **maps.** Open M-Sa 10am-9:30pm.

Emergency and Communications

Emergency: Dial 091 or 092. **Police:** Pr. do Rey (tel. 986 43 22 11).

24hr. Pharmacy: Check *Farmacias de Guardia* listings in the newspaper *Faro de Vigo* (120ptas) or the sign posted in all pharmacy windows.

Hospitals: Hospital Municipal, C. Camelias, 109 (tel. 986 41 12 44). **Ambulance:** (tel. 986 41 62 26).

Internet Access: La Red Cibercafé, C. Argentina, 24 (tel. 986 43 01 89). 200ptas for 15min.

Post Office: Pr. Compostela, 3 (tel. 986 21 70 09 or 986 43 40 09; fax 986 37 47 26). Open for stamps and Lista de Correos M-F 8:30am-8:30pm, Sa 9am-2pm; for **faxes** M-Sa 9am-9pm. **Postal Code:** 36200.

ACCOMMODATIONS AND FOOD

Vigo's inexpensive rooms make the city a logical base for exploring surrounding areas. **Calle Alfonso XIII** (to the right upon exiting the train station) is full of cheap sleeps, as are streets around the **port,** particularly **Calle Carral** and **Calle Urzáiz**. The **Gran Vía** and **Calle Venezuela** are brimming with bright *cafeterías* and *terrazas*. Streets leading away from the port hide a seafood paradise. For **groceries,** El Corte Inglés is a sure bet (see **Local Services,** above).

Hostal Ría de Vigo, C. Cervantes, 14 (tel. 986 43 72 40), left off C. Alfonso XIII. Spacious and squeaky clean with balconies and private bathrooms. Sept.-June: singles 1500ptas; doubles 2000ptas. July-Aug.: singles 2000ptas; doubles 3000-3500ptas.

Barcia Casa de Huespedes, C. Mexico, 2 (tel. 986 42 51 45). Right off R. Urzáiz, 2min. from the train station. Convenient location plus spacious, super clean and comfy rooms with TVs and balconies. Huge bathrooms down the hall. Singles 2000ptas; doubles 3200ptas. Look for the "CH" sign outside.

Luces de Bohemia, C. Colón, 34 (tel. 986 43 00 20). A bright, mirrored interior and plenty of good eats. *Platos combinados* (500-1200ptas), salads (250-650ptas), and several *menús* from which to choose. Delicious desserts and specialty drinks.

Mesón Don Sancho, C. García Olloqui, 1 (tel. 986 22 76 46), at the end of Pr. Compostela, and 1 block up from R. Montero Ríos. Almost as good as being on a boat; fresh seafood includes grilled shrimp (600ptas) and clams steamed in wine and garlic (650ptas). Open daily 11:30am-4pm and 8:30pm-midnight.

SIGHTS AND ENTERTAINMENT

In honor of its notorious past as a center for witches (good and evil), Vigo hosts *Expomagia,* a celebration of all things occult, in mid-June. Tantric yogis and *umbanda* (a Brazilian cult similar to voodoo) practitioners demonstrate and sell their wares down at the port. Watch for the **Fiesta de San Juan** (Xuan) in late June, when neighborhoods light huge cauldrons of *aguardiente* (firewater—the best are in the *casco antiguo*) and revel in traditional song and dance. A final summer festival, **Romería Vikinga,** sails into town the first week in August when locals enact a simulation of the Vikings' landing with period ships and costumes.

Hitting the sack early to dream of Madrid's nightlife may be your best option. Starting in the late afternoon, students pack the *casco antiguo*. Cafes, bars, and discos abound just off the steep, mossy steps. You can always catch a flick at **Multicines Centro** (tel. 986 22 63 66), at the base of C. Maria Berdiales.

■ Near Vigo

Ría de Vigo's wide-open mouth (as if, according to one brochure, "it were about to swallow up a big piece of ocean") is home to several lively coastal towns. Cangas and Bayona, as well as the beautiful Islas Cíes, are all easy daytrips from Vigo. Farther south but equally accessible, La Guardia and Túy lie along the Ría Miño, the quiet and porous border with **Portugal.** From there, it doesn't take long to reach more of the same gorgeous beaches that have recently led to thriving tourism closer to Vigo.

■ Islas Cíes

Guarding the mouth of the Ría de Vigo, the Islas Cíes offer irresistible beaches and cliff-side hiking trails for tourist-weary travelers. Believe it or not, there's no tourist office on these islands. Because of the islands's natural refuge status, only 2200 people are allowed in per day, ensuring wide stretches of uncrowded beach. **Playa de Figueiras** and **Playa de Rodas** gleam with fine sand and sheltered turquoise waters. For smaller, wavier, and more secluded spots, walk along the trail beyond Playa de Figueiras leading to a plethora of coves and rocky lookouts. A 4km hike to the left of the dock on the main "road" leads to a bird conservatory, a lighthouse, and breathtaking views. Watch out for territorial seagulls that dive-bomb hikers walking too close to the birds's spotted chicks.

For budget food (*bocadillos* and ice cream), head to **Restaurante Playa de Rodas** (tel. 986 68 75 11) or **Restaurante Camping** (tel. 986 68 75 04), on the other side of the Playa de Rodas. Octopus, chicken, and *calamares* come cheaply considering the restaurants' prime location. A **mini-market** is next door, as are **campsites** (tel. 986 43 83 58). Space is limited, so call in advance for reservations (535ptas per person and 550ptas per tent). From June to September, five **ferries** per day make the 50-minute trip to and from the island, sometimes more in nice weather. Though fairly expensive, the trip is worth every *peseta*, especially when you chance on schools of dolphins leaping in the waves at the *ría*'s mouth. (2000ptas per adult, 1000ptas per child.)

■ Cangas

A 20-minute ferry ride across the Ría de Vigo, Cangas is hardly unspoiled paradise, but its attractive **beach** and small-town feel do offer respite from the urban bustle of Vigo. Inexpensive lodging is scarce—spending the night in Vigo is the best way to go. A central, relatively cheap option in Cangas is **Hostal Belén** (tel. 986 30 00 15), on C. Antonio Nores, a tiny alley off C. Baiona before it intersects with Av. Marin. Ask for the restaurant owner. (Doubles 4000ptas; mid-September to June 3200ptas.) **Camping Cangas** (tel. 986 30 47 26), on Playa de Limens, has beach-front sites for tent-pitching (525ptas per person and per car; open May-Sept. 9). **Mesón O Batel,** half a block behind the market, off Pr. Constitución on R. Real, is popular with locals (*platos combinados* 850ptas). Simple, cheap *cafeterías* scatter along Av. Ourense behind the path to the beach. **Ferries** travel from Vigo to Cangas and back again (20min., departs every 30min., round-trip 400ptas). The **tourist office** *(turismo)* welcomes visitors upstairs from the ferry ticket office (open M-F 10:30am-2pm and 4-8pm).

GALICIA

■ Bayona (Baiona)

Twenty-one kilometers southwest of Vigo, snug in its own mini-estuary, Bayona (pop. 10,000) was the first European town to receive word from the New World when Columbus returned to port in March 1493. You can visit a reconstructed version of the famous globe-trotting ship **La Carabela Pinta** in Bayona's harbor (115ptas), but the town's main attractions are its seductive **beaches** and the 16th-century **Fortress of Monte Real**, now a *parador nacional* (luxury hotel). A 2km *paseo peatonil* (foot path) loops around the grounds along the shore, passing barrier rocks for picnics and sunbathing. A **tourist office** camps out in the stained wood shack just before the *parador* gates (open July-Aug. M-Sa 9am-2pm). During other months, get info in the Ayuntamiento (open M-Sa 9am-1pm).

Buses run to and from Vigo (1hr., departs every 30min., 245ptas). Bayona's budget accommodations may not live up to *parador* splendor, but affordable **Hospedaje Kin,** C. Ventura Misa, 27 (tel. 986 35 56 95), has TVs, sinks, and knit bedspreads. (Singles 1200-1500ptas; doubles 2500-3000ptas, with bath 3800ptas. Prices may be flexible.) **Camping Bayona Playa** (tel. 986 35 00 35) is open June to September (670ptas per person; 680ptas per tent and per car). For *comida*, check out **Calle Ventura Misa** (parallel to C. Eldouayan, one block inland), lined with *mesones* and *cafeterías*.

■ Túy (Tui)

The charming border town of Túy (pop. 16,000) offers tourists the opportunity to walk into Portugal. The 1km stroll to Valença do Minho across a metal walkway over the Río Miño ends on the Portuguese side, which looks remarkably similar to the Spanish side. Túy also has a small but pretty **cathedral,** a mix of Gothic and Romanesque styles and home to the relics of San Telmo, patron saint of sailors. One ticket gets you into the cathedral's **museo** and the **Museo Diocesano** as well. (Both open daily July-Aug. 9:30am-2pm and 3:30-9pm; Sept.-May 9:30am-2pm. 250ptas.)

An ATSA **bus** (tel. 986 60 00 22) from Vigo stops on C. Calvo Sotelo at Hostal Generosa and returns to Vigo from the other side of the street (45min., departs every 30min., 320ptas). Three **trains** per day (tel. 986 60 08 13) run from Vigo to Túy then on to Valença and Viana do Castelo, Portugal. They stop for 15 minutes on each side for customs and passport inspections. The train stations in each town are far from the border and the center of town; taking the bus or walking across makes more sense.

■ La Guardia (A Guarda)

Perched between the mouth of the Río Miño and the Atlantic Ocean, La Guardia (pop. 11,000) thrives on an active fishing industry and the 500,000 tourists who annually invade its little beach and large mountain. The **bus** stops at the corner of C. Domínguez Fontela and C. Concepción Arenal. Take C. Domínguez Fontela to reach C. José Antonio, on your way to the majestic **Monte Santa Tecla.** From C. José Antonio, bear right onto C. Rosalía de Castro, which continues to the top (6km). Alternatively, hike five minutes up the road and look for the steps off to the left after the park that mark the start of a shorter, steeper 3km pathway through the woods. Halfway up lie the ruins of an old Celtic village, while near the peak is a **chapel** dedicated to Santa Tecla, the patron saint of headaches and heart disease. The wax body parts inside (hearts, heads, and feet) are thank-you gifts to Sta. Tecla from cured worshipers. A beautiful view and the melodious tones of a bagpiper greet tourists at the very top, along with booths of trinkets and aggressive vendors that will delight diehard souvenir hunters but disgust everyone else.

Buses run to and from La Guardia from Vigo (1hr., departs every 30min., 595ptas). La Guardia's **tourist office** (tel. 986 61 18 50) sits in the cultural center on C. Rosalía de Castro during the summer (mid-June to mid-Sept. open M-Sa 11am-2pm and 5-8pm) and in the Ayuntamiento (tel. 986 61 00 00) in Pr. España the rest of the time (open M-Sa 8am-3pm). Change lead into gold at **Banco Central Hispano,** C. José ntonio, 11 (open M-F 8:30am-2:30pm). In La Guardia proper, **Hostal Martírrey**, C. osé Antonio, 8 (tel. 986 61 03 49), doubles as a beer stein mausoleum. It offers posh ooms, many with TV. (Singles 2000-2500ptas; doubles 4000-4600ptas. Breakfast 00ptas.) The lone hotel on the mountain, **Hotel Pazo Santa Tecla** (tel. 986 61 00 2) justifies its prices with a spectacular view of the valley. (In-season singles with ath 3400ptas; doubles with bath 4650ptas. Off-season singles with bath 3100ptas; oubles with bath 4200ptas. Breakfast 350ptas. Open Semana Santa-Oct.) The **mar- et** is on C. Concepción Arenal, but those hungry for seafood should try **Bar Bode- ón Puerto Guardés**, 1 (tel. 986 61 16 47), at the port. Specials nclude salmon and *balacas* (700ptas). (Open daily 10am-3pm and 7-10:30pm.) La uardia hosts a **lobster festival** the last Sunday in June, as well as the mysterious Burial of the Swordfish" during *Carnaval*. Pilgrimages, *fútbol*, and folk festivals mark he **Feria de Monte de Santa Tecla** in the second week of August.

▌Ría de Pontevedra and Pontevedra

ccording to legend, Pontevedra (pop. 74,000) was founded by the Greek archer eucro as a place to convalesce after his Trojan War exploits. Its name derives from n old Roman bridge (Pontus Veteri), and since medieval times it has been an impor- ant stopover on the southern (Portuguese) Camino de Santiago. Centrally located in he Ría Bajas, Pontevedra continues to provides transportation to wayfarers heading lsewhere—it's less of a destination in itself. To its credit, though, this regional capital laims a wealth of beautiful parks and plazas, easy transportation to nearby villages nd beaches, and the only bull ring in all of Galicia.

▌RIENTATION AND PRACTICAL INFORMATION

ix streets radiate out from the center of town, **Praza Peregrina**. The main streets are **alle de la Oliva, Calle Michelena, Calle Benito Corbal,** and **Calle de la Peregrina. raza Galiza** is a five-minute walk south of Pr. Peregrina (from Pr. Peregrina, down C. eregrina one block and right onto C. Andrés Muruais). The **train** and **bus stations,** ocated across from each other, are about 1km from town. To get to the city **center,** urn left exiting the bus station (go with the flow of buses). Continue on this street for 2 minutes as it changes from Av. Alféreces Provisionales to Av. de Vigo to C. Pereg- ina, which deposits you in Pr. Peregrina.

Trains: Av. Alféreces Provisionales (tel. 986 85 13 13 or 986 43 11 14). A lengthy walk from town. Info open daily 7:30am-1:30pm and 3:30-9:30pm. To: Madrid (11hr., 2 per day, 5200ptas); Santiago (1½hr., 16 per day, 575ptas); La Coruña (3hr., 16 per day, 1110ptas); Vigo (30min., 16 per day, 285ptas).

Buses: Av. Alféreces Provisionales (tel. 986 85 24 08; fax 986 85 25 30). Info open M-Sa 8:30am-9pm. Service is more frequent than rail service. To: Santiago (1hr., departs every hr., 620ptas); La Coruña (2½hr., 10 per day, 1400ptas); Cambados (1hr., 10 per day, 300ptas); Sangenjo (30min., departs every 30min., 235ptas); El Grove/La Toja (1hr., departs every 30min., 435ptas); Marin (30min., departs every 15min., 120ptas); Madrid (8hr., 4 per day, 3445ptas).

Taxis: (tel. 986 85 12 85 or 986 85 12 00), 350ptas from the stations to downtown.

Car Rental: Avis, C. Peregrina, 47 (tel. 986 85 20 25). Rates vary with duration of rental. One day unlimited mileage 11,950ptas. Must be over 22 and have had a license for at least 1 year. Open M-F 9am-1pm and 4-7pm, Sa 9am-12:45pm.

Tourist Office: There are 2 offices, but only 1 open per season. In summer, look for the little wooden building in Pl. de España. Tons of slick brochures and maps. In winter, head to C. General Mola, 3 (tel. 986 85 08 14), one block from Pr. Pereg- rina, left off C. Michelena. English spoken. Both open Sa-Su 11am-2pm and 5-8pm.

Budget Travel: TIVE, C. Benito Corbal, 47, 2nd fl. (tel. 986 80 55 32), hidden inside a larger regional office. Open M-F 9am-2pm.

Currency Exchange: Banco Central Hispano (tel. 986 85 38 12), Pl. Peregrina. No commission. Open M-F 8:30am-2:30pm.

GALICIA

Luggage Storage: Lockers at the train station 400ptas; at the bus station 80ptas per piece. Both open daily 8am-10pm.

English Bookstore: Librería Michelena, C. Michelena, 22 (tel. 986 85 87 46). Sizeable selection of classics and contemporary works in Spanish, French, and English. Austen to Morrison to Pynchon. Open daily 9am-1:30pm and 4:30-8pm.

Emergency: dial 091 or 092. **Medical Emergencies:** dial 061. **Police:** C. Joaquín Costa, 19 (tel. 986 85 38 00).

Hospital: Hospital Provincial, C. Doctor Loureiro Crespo, 2 (tel. 986 85 21 15).

Post Office: C. Olivia, 21 (tel. 986 54 53). For stamps and Lista de Correos open M-F 8:30am-8:30pm, Sa 9am-2pm. **Postal Code:** 36001.

ACCOMMODATIONS AND FOOD

Calle Michelena, Calle Peregrina, and the area around **Praza Galiza** are dotted with *fondas* and *pensiones*. Like many towns in Galicia, Pontevedra prides itself on seafood. In the evenings, locals crowd tiny bars on **Calle Figueroa** to munch on an endless variety of fishy *tapas,* washed down with the local Albariño wine. For land-based goods, there's **Supermercado Froiz,** C. Benito Corbal, 28 (tel. 986 52 51), at the corner of C. de Sagasta (open M-Sa 9am-9pm).

Pensión Florida, C. García Camba (tel. 986 19 79), just off C. Peregrina. Clean, modern, high-altitude rooms compensate for the long flights of stairs. Singles 1800ptas; doubles 2500-3500ptas.

Pensión La Cueva, C. Andrés Mellado, 7 (tel. 986 12 71), in Pr. Galiza. Aptly named, with large, dim rooms. It's not the Ritz, but the price is right. Singles 1000ptas; doubles 1500-2500ptas. Bathrooms down the hall.

Bodegón Micota, C. Peregrina, 4 (tel. 986 59 17). This intriguing alternative to the cafe-bar scene borders on "cuisine," the great temptress of the budget traveler. Carrot soup (385ptas), cheese plates (385ptas), barbecued ribs (1250ptas), mango pie (425ptas), and *bocadillos* (585ptas). Open daily 1:30-6pm and 7pm-2am.

Mesón Pontesampaio, C. Joaquín Costa, 24 (tel. 986 40 77). From C. Peregrina turn onto C. Sagasta, then take the 2nd right onto C. Joaquín Costa. Greasy regional specialties in an 800ptas *menú* (1100ptas at night). Open daily 7:30am-2am.

SIGHTS AND ENTERTAINMENT

Pontevedra proper's best sight is the extensive **Museo Provincial,** which starts in Pr. Leña. *(Open Tu-Sa 10am-2:15pm and 5-8:45pm, Su 11am-1pm. 200ptas, EU members free.)* Exhibits in the five-building collection embrace a wide range of themes, including traditional Galician cooking, both sacred and contemporary art, archaeology, and glasswork. A highlight is the reproduction of the cabin of Admiral Méndez-Núñez's *Numancia,* the first battleship to sail around the world. The museum also includes the Gothic **Ruinas de Santo Domingo** in Pl. de España. More off the beaten tourist track, the funky **Sala de Explosiones Teucro** on C. Javier Puig (around the corner from TIVE) holds international modern art shows in its tiny two-room gallery. *(Open M-F 7-9:30pm, Sa noon-2pm and 7-9:30pm. Free.)*

If it's sunny, there's sure to be a crowd at the **beaches** of nearby **Marin.** A fleet of red APSA buses makes the 30-minute journey from Pr. Galicia (departs every 15min., 115ptas). You'll endure the horrid stench of a paper mill along the way, but the beaches are clean and inviting. From the bus stop in Marin, facing the water, head left on C. Angusto Miranda around the track and up the hill. To arrive at Playa Porticelo, turn right on C. Tiro Naval Janer, continue for 15 minutes bearing right where the road splits. Another seven minutes on foot brings you to the larger **Playa Mogor.** Both beaches come equipped with bar-cafes.

In the evening, the granite walls and arcades of Pontevedra's old town emit a luminescent glow. The 18th-century **Capilla de la Virgen Peregrina** is dedicated to Pontevedra's patron saint, a pilgrim version of the Virgin Mary, and is modeled after the scallop shell associated with Santiago. The **Basílica Menor de Santa María** (from Pl. España take Av. Santa María, on the left of the Ayuntamiento) features a golden Plater-

GALICIA

esque door that's illuminated by flood-lights at night. It's worth checking out because a) it's pretty and b) it may be the most happening thing in town.

Pontevedra's modest **nightlife,** centered around bars near the Basílica de Santa María, supposedly picks up during the **festivals** of **Santiago de Burgos** (July 25) and **La Peregrina** (2nd Sunday in August). Should you hanker for dubbed American flicks, a movie theater sits on C. Fray Juan de Navarrete where it splits from C. Peregrina *(Tickets 575ptas; check local papers for other theaters and daily listings.)*

■ Ría de Arousa

The following towns are perfect daytrips from Pontevedra, as frequent bus service covers this area from Pontevedra. The train from Santiago in the north swings towards the coast at Vilagarcía de Arousa, the commercial center of central Galicia.

■ El Grove (O Grove) and La Toja (A Toxa)

Every July and August, vacationing Europeans come in Land Rovers and BMWs to seaside El Grove (pop. 11,000) and its island partner, La Toja. Charming El Grove, west of Pontevedra on a tranquil strait, is lined with mussel farms, colorful boats, and clam-diggers. La Toja, across the bridge, lures the wealthy with a casino, aggressive vendors in "typical Galician dress," and a decent beach. The unusual seashell-covered church and heavy, distinctive-smelling soap (Magno) produced in La Toja lend the town some redeeming value.

Buses run from El Grove to Pontevedra (1hr., 17 per day, 435ptas) and to Cambados on the way to Vilagarcía (30min., 4 per day, more in July-Aug., 235ptas). Schedules are posted inside and on the door of the bus office, 50m left. From July to mid-October the **tourist office** in El Grove has its own little office in the square near the Ayuntamiento and the bus stop. The rest of the year, brochures are dispensed on the second floor of the Ayuntamiento. (Open July-Oct.15 M-Sa 10am-9pm; Oct. 16-June M-F 8am-3pm.) All buses depart from the end of the waterfront.

Rooms in El Grove are not cheap, and you'll need a royal flush at the casino to stay in La Toja. **Hostal Miramar** (tel. 986 73 01 11), on R. Teniente Dominguez one block from the bridge to La Toja, offers TVs and private bathrooms (singles 2000-2500ptas; doubles 3600-5000ptas). The **mercado** sits along the water's edge (open M-Sa 9am-1:30pm). A lively local restaurant, **Taberna O Pescador,** C. Pablo Iglesias, 9, serves heaping sea specialties including *chipirones* (400ptas) and *pulpo* (750ptas; open daily 11am-midnight). **Gadis Supermercado,** Rúa Castelao, 73, has the staples (open M-Sa 9am-2pm and 5-9pm).

■ La Lanzada

Five kilometers toward Pontevedra from El Grove, La Lanzada's **beach** lures topless bathers with its fine white sands and irresistible waves. Home to the pagan cult of the "Ninth Wave," this area's mysterious methods of ensuring romance and fertility will either baffle or entice you. Two hundred meters past the end of La Lanzada sits **Restaurante La Lanzada,** accessible by beach or road, a white *cabaña* with simple, spacious rooms 50m from the surf. (Doubles with one large bed 3000ptas, with two beds 4000ptas, with large bed and bath 5000ptas.) **Camping Muiñeira** (tel. 986 73 84 04) is a short way past Restaurante La Lanzada. Sites with soft grass and wildflowers are not particularly private, but a gorgeous beach is just a street-crossing away. (500ptas per person and per tent; 400ptas per car.) To get to La Lanzada, take the same **bus** as to El Grove/La Toja, but make sure the driver knows that you want to get off 10 minutes before the El Grove/La Toja stop.

GALICIA

■ Cambados

For a glimpse of small-town life and a glass of good wine, head to harborside Cambados (pop. 14,000), 26km northwest of Pontevedra. Lack of a beach has left Cambados out of the tourist loop—its taxi drivers play cards all afternoon. On a quiet hill 15 minutes from the center, the beautiful ruins of the **Iglesia Santa María** watches over the town's cemetery. For a lovely view of the town and the *ría,* climb the steps to the left of the ruins up to the small park.

The **Pazo de Fefiñanes,** an attractive 16th-century palace-turned-*bodega,* brims with gigantic, sweet-smelling barrels of wine. The lively **Praza de Fefiñanes** is filled with bar-restaurants serving the pride of Cambados. Cambados throws a *fiesta* virtually every night in mid-summer, beginning with the July celebration of **Santa Mariña** and culminating the first weekend in August with an official tasting of the previous year's local Albariño, a light and fruity wine.

Plus Ultra **buses** trek to Pontevedra from the new bus station near Pr. Concello (1hr., 9 per day, 300ptas). The last bus leaves at 7pm. A new **tourist office** (near the bus station) serves the town's visitors (open M-Sa 10am-1:30pm and 4:30-7pm). Marble-floored, shiny rooms with baths can be found at **Hostal Pazos Feíjoo,** C. Curros Enríquez, 1 (tel. 986 54 28 10), 1 block behind the bus stop off Pr. Concello (doubles 3000-4000ptas). For food head to the **Plaza de Fefiñanes.** Walk toward Pontevedra, turn right on Av. Vilariño, and then left on Av. Madrid, which becomes R. Real to reach the friendly folks at **Los Amigos Hamburguesería-Pizzería,** who stuff patrons with pizza (600-1000ptas) and cheap *bocadillos.* **Supermercado Vego** vends various goodies on R. Nova (open M-Sa 9am-2pm and 5-9pm).

■ Ría de Muros y Noya

Although the northern areas of the Rías Bajas don't see too many tourists, **Muros** and Noya have plenty to offer the visitor. These little towns boast beautiful, granite old cities and popular beaches. The region's real gem, however, is the ancient Celtic castle, O Castro de Baroña. Frequent buses make these towns easy daytrips from Santiago, although transportation should be planned carefully.

■ Muros and Louro

Sitting pretty 65km west of Santiago, on the northern side of the *ría,* Muros combines exquisite mountain views with the warmth and friendliness of a fishing village. Stone houses, winding, hilly streets, and several chapels characterize this lively little town set in the wilds of Galicia. Historically, Muros served as a leper hospital and pilgrim pit-stop before Cabo Finisterre (see p. 194). The town's church, the **Colexiata do Santa María,** sports Romanesque and Gothic stylistic influences, thanks to Lope de Mendoza's refurbishing in 1400. The **Paseo Marítimo,** along the port where the bus stops, crackles with action in summer. Watch for the **Fiesta de San Pedro** during the last few days in June, with an outdoor theater and traditional Galician music in the central square, and firecrackers, merry-go-rounds, and ferris wheels at the port.

Buses to Muros stop in front of Banco Pastor on R. Castelao. Castromil **buses** run from Santiago (2hr., 12 per day, 750ptas). **Transportes Finisterre** buses (tel. 986 82 69 83) serve Muros and nearby towns, passing the **Playa San Francisco,** 3km away, en route to Cée (10min., 10 per day, 60ptas). The **Ayuntamiento,** at the right end of the street as you face the water, has maps and brochures (open M-F 8:30am-2:30pm). The **municipal police** (tel. 986 82 72 76) hide out in the same building. In an **emergency,** call 091 or 092.

Hostal Ría de Muros, R. Castelao, 53 (tel. 986 82 60 56), located where the bus stops, offers huge rooms, big baths, TVs, and swell views (June-Sept. doubles with bath 5300ptas; Sept.-May doubles with bath 3210ptas). Up the street, **Hospedaje A Vianda,** R. Castelao, 47 (tel. 986 82 63 22), has airy rooms, most with bath, some with TVs (singles 1500-2000ptas; doubles 3000-4000ptas). Downstairs, the owners serve a

GALICIA

menú for 1000ptas. More restaurants line R. Castelao. Try the egg, tuna, and aspara-gus pizza at **Pizzería Pulpería** (*pulpo* 800ptas, pizzas 600-800ptas). On Friday morn-ings, you can buy that beachwear you forgot to pack for low prices at the **outdoor market** behind R. Castelao.

Four kilometers from Muros, the **beaches** of little **Louro,** which sit on the edge of an untamed forest, attract the majority of Muros' tourists. Some say these are the most virginal beaches in the Rías Bajas. To get to Louro, take the Finisterre **bus** from Muros to Cée (see above), and then take a Finisterre bus to Louro from Cée (5min.). If you choose to spend a night in Louro, **Camping A Bouga** (tel. 986 82 60 25), with a **supermarket** and free hot showers, packs you in right near the water (435ptas per adult, per tent, and per car; electricity 400ptas; open year-round).

■ Noya (Noia)

Nicknamed "the little Compostela" for its density of monuments, Noya is distin-guished by the Gothic arcades and 15th-century stone houses that surround its many small squares. The 14th-century **Igrexa de Santa María** houses a bulky collection of tomb-lids; the 16th-century **Igrexa de San Francisco** keeps the **Ayuntamiento** com-pany while the latter undergoes construction. Well-preserved statues of curly-bearded saints compose the Galician Gothic facade of **Igrexa de San Martín.** The Cas-tromil **bus** (in Santiago tel. 986 58 90 90; in Noya tel. 986 82 05 19), which runs from Santiago to Muros, stops in Noya (1hr., departs every hr., 680ptas). Fourteen buses return from Noya to Santiago daily. The bus station has **luggage storage** (75ptas; open M-F 9am-2:30pm and 3:30-8pm). The **tourist office** (open M-Sa 9am-2pm) and local **police** (tel. 986 82 27 03) are in the Ayuntamiento. For **medical emergencies,** call 986 82 33 10. **Hostal Valadares** (tel. 986 82 04 36), Rúa Edgar Moniz, is a two-minute walk from the bus station. With shiny rooms and private sinks, it's the best deal in town. (Singles 1600ptas; doubles 2600ptas; cheaper when staying for more than one night.) The restaurant downstairs serves up an *menú* for 1000ptas.

■ O Castro de Baroña

Nineteen kilometers south of Noya lies a little-known treasure of historical intrigue and mesmerizing natural beauty—the seaside remains of a 5th-century Celtic fortress known as O Castro de Baroña. The circular foundations of the houses dot the neck of an isthmus, ascending to a rocky promontory above the sea and descending to a cres-cent **beach** (clothing very optional). Catch the sunset, then pitch a tent at the free public campsite in the forest just 300m from shore. **Café-Bar O Castro** (tel. 986 76 74 30), the single building of the O Castro bus stop, offers spotless rooms upstairs (doubles in summer 3000-3500ptas; in winter 2500-3000ptas). There are bathrooms down the hall and bargains for longer stays. The restaurant downstairs has a *menú* for 800ptas (not including dessert or coffee). Ten **Hefsel buses** run daily between Noya and Riveira, stopping (but often passing—tell the driver where you are going) on the road in front of Café-Bar O Castro (30min., 250ptas). Catch the bus across the road on the way back. The nearest town, **Baroña,** 1km north, has a small supermarket, a res-taurant, and a bus stop. Five kilometers north of Baroña basks more populous **Porto do Son,** with an exquisite beach of its own.

SOUTH RÍAS ALTAS

If Galicia is the forgotten corner of Spain, then the small *rías* of the Costa de la Muerte are the forgotten corner of Galicia. Beaches here are arguably the emptiest, cleanest, and loveliest in all of Spain. The local population still plows with oxen, and women tote homegrown produce to market in head-held baskets.

Although its appellation "Coast of Death" refers to the many shipwrecks along the rocky coast, it could just as well apply to tragedy bred by gourmet tastes. Several fishermen pass away each year while attempting to extract the expensive and highly sought-after delicacies, *percebes* (barnacles), from sharp rocks on the coast. The fiercest challenge for travelers, thankfully, is finding quick transportation to this remote Elysian region. Both Cabo Finisterre and Camariñas can be reached by bus from Santiago and La Coruña, but bus service to the smaller towns and isolated beaches is infrequent. The roads, tortuous and sometimes poorly paved, have vague signs, and thick mists often settle in the morning. Campgrounds along the coast tend to be overpriced, dirty, and amenity-free—but maybe that's part of the charm.

■ Cabo Finisterre (Cabo Fisterra)

For pilgrims in the middle ages, a trip to Finisterre was almost obligatory; after completing the entire Camino de Santiago, it was the icing on the cake to catch a glimpse of what was then considered the end of the world (*finis terrae*). To the left of Cabo Finisterre spreads the Ría de Corcubión and its attractive **beaches,** Sardineiro and Langosteira; to the right, jagged mountains meet the unforgiving landscape of the open sea. Straight ahead and 4km from town stands the lighthouse that has beckoned ships for years, offering stunning views. Hidden turquoise beaches here have seduced such travelers as Spain's Nobel Prize winning novelist Camilo José Cela.

Besides glorious views from the lighthouse, there's not much in town. The **Capilla de Santa María das Areas** contains a painting of the "Christ of the Golden Beard," purportedly thrown off a British ship and found by a local fisherman. A 12th-century **church** stands beside the road to the cape. To reach the beach, proceed uphill from the statue at the port past C. Carrasqueira, then turn right at the first dirt road. After about 50m, turn left at the white house with blue trim onto the seaward path.

PRACTICAL INFORMATION Finisterre **buses** make daily trips between Finisterre and Santiago (2½hr., 2 per day to Santiago, 3 per day from Santiago to Finisterre, 1360ptas). Buses often require a transfer in Vimianzo, but there is rarely a wait. If you plan to see Finisterre as a daytrip from Santiago, check return times carefully—the last bus may leave during mid-afternoon. Finisterre buses also travel daily to Cée, a good place for connections to towns south along the coast (8 per day). The **Casa do Concello** (tel. 981 74 00 01), C. Santa Catalina, has nice stickers but only the barest minimum of **tourist information.** As you head uphill from the statue, turn right and walk two blocks. (Open June-Sept. M-F 8:30am-2:30pm, Sa 8am-1pm; Oct.-May M-F 9am-2pm and 5-7pm, Sa 9am-2pm.) An **ATM** hides out in Caixa Galicia, in the main square off C. Santa Catalina (left turn coming from the statue). In an **emergency,** call 091 or 092. The Casa del Mar Clínica (tel. 981 74 02 52), next door to the tourist office, offers **medical assistance.**

ACCOMMODATIONS AND FOOD While Finisterre is a feasible daytrip from Santiago, **Hospedaje López,** C. Carrasqueira, 4 (tel. 981 74 04 49), has cheap, immaculate, light-filled rooms (some with ocean views) and Disney cheer. Head uphill away from the main statue at the port, turn right onto C. Carrasqueira, and walk for five minutes. (Singles 3000ptas; doubles 2500-3500ptas; triples 4500ptas. Prices lower in winter.) Plump lobsters wave from the mirrored tanks at the entrance to **Hotel Cabo Finisterre** (tel. 981 74 00 00), C. Santa Catalina, 50m uphill from the statue at the port. Rooms come with bath, telephone, and TV (doubles 6000ptas). For organized camping and more temperate water, head to the opposite side of the isthmus connecting Finisterre with the mainland. **Camping Ruta Finisterre** (tel. 981 74 63 02), Ctra. Coruña, is east of Finisterre on the Playa del Estorde in Cée (465ptas per person, per tent, and per car; open Apr.-Sept. 15). A small supermarket sits on C. Santa Catalina. **Supermercado Froiz,** a five-minute walk left of the statue along the shore, is the big fish (open M-Sa 9am-

GALICIA

2pm and 5-9pm). Although most restaurants along the dock are overpriced, **Restaurante O Centalo** (tel. 981 74 04 52) serves a *menú* for 1100ptas and many good *raciones* for 300 to 900ptas (open daily1-4:30pm and 9pm–midnight.)

■ Camariñas

Showing shades of Penelope, who wove and wove as her husband Odysseus sailed the seas, the women in Camariñas (pop. 3250; north of Cabo Finisterre on the other side of the *ría*), knit the intricate, expensive, and delicate *encaje de bolillos* lace, an activity introduced by the Celts. The difference is that these women are not waiting for their seafaring husbands; rather, they are keeping this whitewashed town afloat economically. The *palilleiras* (lace-makers) are the town's secret weapon; they are honored by a statue in the town square.

To the left of the port, the **faro** (lighthouse) looms on a wind-swept cliff 5km above frothy waves, a one-hour walk up a windy road through fields of wildflowers and space-age windmills (hold on to your hat and lightweight loved ones). Toward Ctra. General (the main highway) are **Area da Vila** and **Lingunde,** two virtually untouched beaches, approachable only via a sandy, rocky cliffhanger of a path (off the road to the lighthouse). Across the *ría* from Camariñas on a rocky point in **Muxía,** historic model ships hang from the ceiling of the **Igrexa de Nossa Señora da Barca** (Our Lady of the Ship). The rocks in front of the church supposedly hum when innocent people walk by (although they didn't hum for us…).

PRACTICAL INFORMATION, ACCOMMODATIONS, AND FOOD Transportes Finisterre **buses** (tel. 981 74 51 71) run between Camariñas and Santiago (2hr. 2 per day to Santiago, 3 per day from Santiago to Camariñas 1200ptas). Buses also travel from La Coruña (2 per day). Camariñas can be reached from Finisterre, but if you leave Finisterre in the morning, you'll have to wait 1½ hours in the tiny town of Vimianzo for a transfer. Behind the statue of the *palilleira* stands the **Casa Consistorial** (tel. 981 73 60 00 or 981 73 60 25), purveyor of tourist tips (open M-F 8am-2pm, Sa 9am-2pm). The **Guardia Civil,** C. Generalísimo Franco, 5 (tel. 981 73 62 62, or 981 66 86 02), are also behind the statue (open daily 9am-2pm and 4-7pm). In **emergencies,** call 062.

Hostal La Marina, Cantón Miguel Freijo, 4 (tel. 981 73 60 30), offers large rooms, many with views of the water. (Singles 1600-2000ptas, with bath 2100-2700ptas; doubles 2450-3350ptas, with bath 3100-4200ptas.) La Marina's restaurant downstairs serves a filling *menú* (850ptas). Restaurants serving fresh seafood line the dock along C. Miguel Freijo. **Supermercados Más y Más,** on Pr. Insuela by the *palilleira* statue, sells picnic fixings (open M-F 9am-2pm and 4:30-8:30pm).

■ Near Camariñas

A minor coastal road passes isolated beaches such as **Praia Traba** on its way to the Ría de Laxe-Corme. At **Laxe,** on the west side of the *ría*, a vast, open stretch of sand separates the geological institute at one end from the fishing fleet at the other.

Corme, on the other side of the *ría*, is famous for its delicious *percebes* (barnacles), which are pried off rocks in treacherous waters. Try them or whatever else is swimming in the tanks at **O Biscoiteiro** (tel. 981 73 83 76), on C. Remedios. But don't pass up the freshly baked tart bread and bountiful entrees (600-900ptas).

■ La Coruña (A Coruña)

While the newer parts of La Coruña are gray and mundane, recent massive efforts by the city have made the *ciudad vieja* (old city) and port areas more attractive to visitors. Sailboats line the north end of the port, and gardens and parks lie tucked within the old city. Many of La Coruña's 250,000 residents while away afternoons at pleasant

La Coruña

ACCOMMODATIONS
B Hospedaje María Pita
A Hostal Castelos
C Pensión la Alianza

Puerto de la Coruña

waterfront cafes along the brand new Paseo Marítimo, which winds around the isthmus along marinas, rocky cliffs, and beaches. An excellent base for exploring the Rías Altas, La Coruña's stellar nightlife, historic old town, and pleasant beaches more than make up for the dingier parts of town.

ORIENTATION AND PRACTICAL INFORMATION

La Coruña's new city sprawls across the mainland; an isthmus and peninsula contain the *ciudad vieja*. **Avenida de la Marina** leads past the tourist office into the old city, with shaded streets filling the peninsula's southern tip overlooking the port. Surfboard haven **Praia del Orzán** and **Praia de Riazor** are 10-minute walks northwest from the tourist office, on the other side of the peninsula's neck. From the bus station, take bus #1 or 1A straight to the **tourist office,** on the **Dársena de la Marina** (105ptas). To get to the bus station from the train station, walk in the direction of El Corte Inglés, and take the pedestrian overpass, which leads to the bus station (5min.). Catch bus #1 or 1A into town, or brave the long, long walk from the bus station to the tourist office. Go down C. Ramón y Cajal, take a left at the commercial train station on Av. Primo de Rivera, and follow it through five name changes up to the port. Walk (with the water on your right) until you reach the tourist office (40min.). **Praza de María Pita** is one block from the port.

Transportation

Flights: Aeropuerto de Alvedro (tel. 981 18 72 00), 9km south of the city. Served only by Aviaco. **Iberia/Aviaco,** Pr. Galiza, 6 (tel. 981 22 56 36). Open M-F 9:30am-1:30pm and 4:30-8pm, Sa 9:30am-1:30pm.

Trains: (tel 981 15 02 02), in Pr. San Cristóbal. Info open 7am-11pm. To: Santiago (1hr., 13 per day, 500-565ptas); El Ferrol (1¾hr., 2 per day, 495ptas); Pontevedra (2½hr., 13 per day, 1060-1215); Vigo (3hr., 13 per day, 1200-1370ptas); Madrid (11hr., 3 per day, 5000-7700ptas); Barcelona (16-17hr., 2 per day, 6600ptas). **RENFE office,** C. Fonseca, 3 (tel. 981 22 19 48).

Buses: (tel. 981 23 96 44), on C. Caballeros, across Av. Alcalde Molina from the train station. **ALSA-Intercar** (tel. 981 23 70 44). To: Oviedo (5hr., 4 per day, 3600ptas); Madrid (8½hr., 4 per day, 4850ptas); San Sebastián (14hr., 1 per day, 6300ptas).

GALICIA

Castromil runs to Santiago (1½hr., 7-10 per day, 650-900ptas). **IASA** (tel. 981 23 90 01). To: Betanzos (45min., departs every 30min., 245ptas); El Ferrol, with transfer to Cedeira (2hr., departs every hr., 700ptas); Vivero, with stops at O Barqueiro, Ortigueiro, El Ferrol, Vicedo, and Betanzos (4hr., 3-4 per day, 1600ptas). Other companies have routes to Vigo, Camariñas, and other destinations.

Public Transportation: Red buses of the **Compañía de Tranvías de la Coruña** (tel. 981 25 01 00) run frequently throughout the day (7am-11:30pm, 105ptas). Bus stops post full itineraries.

Taxis: Radio Taxi (tel. 981 24 33 33). **Tele Taxi** (tel. 981 28 77 77).

Car Rental: Autos Brea, Av. Fernández Latorre, 110 (tel. 981 23 86 45). Must be at least 21 and have had license at least 1 year. 3-day min. rental, from 2075ptas per day with unlimited mileage. Open M-F 9am-1pm and 4-7pm, Sa 9am-2pm.

Tourist, Financial, and Local Services

Tourist Office: (tel. 981 22 18 22) on Dársena de la Marina, connecting the peninsula and mainland, near the waterfront. Full of tips on daytrips. Has brochures and an accommodations guide. Open M-F 9am-2pm and 4:30-6:30pm, Sa 10:30am-1pm.

Currency exchange: Banco Central Hispano, Canton Grano, 9-12. No commission. Open M-F 8:30am-2:30pm.

El Corte Inglés: C. Ramón y Cajal, 57-59 (tel. 981 29 00 11). A sharp right from the bus station exit. **Currency exchange,** maps, novels and guidebooks in English, haircutting, cafeteria, **supermarket,** restaurant, and **telephones.** Open M-Sa 10am-9:30pm.

American Express Travel: Viajes Amado, C. Compostela, 1 (tel. 981 22 99 72). Open M-F 9:30am-2pm and 4:30-8pm, Sa 9:45am-1:30pm.

Luggage Storage: At the train station (lockers 400ptas). Open daily 6:30am-1:30am. At the bus station (75ptas per checked bag). Open daily 8am-10pm.

English Bookstore: Librería Colón, C. Real, 24 (tel. 981 22 22 06), a few blocks from the tourist office. Assorted novels and a large selection of international newspapers. Open M-F 10am-1:45pm and 5-8:30pm, Sa 10am-2pm and 5-8pm.

Laundromat: Lavandería Glu Glu, C. Alcalde Marchesi, 4 (tel. 981 28 28 04), off Pr. Cuatro Caminos. Wash and dry self-serve 800ptas per 5kg load. Full service 950ptas per load. Open M-F 9:30am-8:30pm, Sa 9:30am-6pm.

Local Services

Emergency: dial 091 or 092. **Police: Municipal** (tel. 981 18 42 25), C. Miguel Servet.

Late-Night Pharmacy: Check listings in *La Voz de Galicia* (125ptas) or in any pharmacy window.

Medical Services: Ambulatorio San José, C. Comandante Fontanes, 8 (tel. 981 22 63 35).

Internet Access: Paizon E.D., C. San Nicolas, 37 (tel. 981 20 55 24), 1 block up from C. Riegode Agua. 250ptas per 30min. Open daily 9am-11pm.

Post Office: (tel. 981 22 19 56) on C. Alcalde Manuel Casas, past Teatro Colón off Av. Marina. Open for stamps, Lista de Correos, and **faxes** M-F 8:30am-8:30pm, Sa 9:30am-2pm. **Postal Code:** 15070.

ACCOMMODATIONS

The best and most convenient area for lodging is one block back from **Avenida de la Marina,** near the tourist office. **Calle Riego de Agua** and the surrounding area (from Pr. María Pita down to Pr. San Agustín) always have available rooms. There are many *pensiones* near the stations, though miles away from the *ciudad vieja.* HI hostels are fairly inconveniently located; the cost of transportation to La Coruña proper will most likely cancel out any actual savings.

Marina Española (HI) (tel. 981 62 01 18), in Sada, about 20km east of La Coruña. The Empresa Calpita bus (tel. 981 23 90 72) runs to Sada (30min., 240ptas). Dorms 750ptas, over 26 1100ptas. 3-day max. stay. Call first, especially in summer.

Albergue Xuvenil "Gandario" (HI) (tel. 981 79 10 05) in Gandario, 19km outside La Coruña. Take the bus to Gandario (30min., 215ptas). They pack 'em in 6 per single-sex room. Dorms 750ptas, over 26 1100ptas. 3-day max. stay.

Hospedaje María Pita, C. Riego de Agua, 38, 3rd fl. (tel. 981 22 11 87), above Hospedaje Moran. White lace curtains, cheery rooms, and pristine bathrooms. There are 3 other *hostales* in this building. Doubles 2700ptas; off-season 2200ptas. Arrangements for singles may be made if you're willing to be persuasive.

Hostal Castelos, C. Real, 14 (tel. 981 22 29 06), 1 block behind Av. Marina. Original 1890s mahogany wainscoting and velvet armchairs. Sashay into cavernous rooms through hand-carved door frames. Doubles 3300-3800ptas.

Pensión la Alianza, C. Riego de Agua, 8, 1st fl. (tel. 981 22 81 14). Dark wood and home-made oil paintings in quiet, simple rooms. Some have no windows. Spotless gray-tiled bathroom down the hall. Singles 1500-2000ptas; doubles 2500-3500ptas.

FOOD

Cheap eats abound in *mesones* on **Calle Estrella, Calle de la Franja,** and nearby streets. For snazzier cafes and pizzerias, head to the area around C. Rubine off Playa de Raizor. Fresh fruit and vegetables are in the **market** in the oval building on Pr. San Agustín, near the old town (open M-Sa 8am-3pm). When the market closes, buy your groceries downstairs at **Supermercados Claudio** (open daily 9am-3pm and 5-9pm).

Mesón Trotamundos, Pr. España, 9 (tel. 981 22 16 09). Sit at wooden tables under hunks of beef and hundreds of wine bottles, and watch the staff snip arms off octopi to make *pulpo a la gallega.* A *ración* of 6 grilled sardines costs just 450ptas. Other *raciónes* 250-1100ptas. *Menú* M-Sa 800ptas. Open daily 10am-2am.

Cafetería SouSantos, C. Fransisco Mariño, 10 (tel. 981 22 76 09). Near Pl. de Pontevedra and Pl. de Riazor. During mid-afternoon, seemingly half of La Coruña crowds this classy cafeteria for *raciónes* of clam pasta (650ptas), lasagna (650ptas), and *croquetas* (300ptas). Vegetarians will rejoice over the *gazpacho* (300ptas). Open July-Aug. daily 8am-3am; Sept.-June F-W 8am-3am.

Pizzería Bingo, Av. de Rubine, 11 (tel. 981 26 18 00). No numbers or door prizes here, but you may shout "Bingo!" when you sink your teeth into their shrimp, salmon, and caviar pizzas (700-1000ptas). Open daily 1:30-4pm and 8pm-midnight.

Gastof, Av. Marina, 6 (tel. 981 22 10 27). Mature folk will enjoy sitting outside in the tranquil terrace; the rest of us can delight in the cartoon decor indoors. Sandwiches 300-480ptas, *platos combinados* 600-800ptas.

SIGHTS

La Coruña's famous tourist magnet, the 2nd-century **Torre de Hércules,** towers over rusted ship carcasses on the west end of the peninsula. *(Open daily July-Sept. 10am-7pm; Oct.-June 10am-6pm. 250ptas, seniors and children free.)* Hercules allegedly erected the tower, now the world's oldest working lighthouse, upon the remains of his defeated enemy Gerión. Enter through the lower of two entrances to creep around the original foundation, then climb a claustrophobic 237-step tunnel to the pinnacle. To get there, take the seaside path from the popular **Orzán** and **Riazor beaches,** which pack in their share of surfers, volleyball players, sunbathers, and strollers, on the northwest side of the isthmus (2km). Or, take bus #9 or 13 (105ptas).

Just up the **esplanade,** connecting Playa Orzán to Playa Riazor, the brand-new **Museo Domus** (Museum of Man; tel. 981 22 89 47) houses three floors of interactive, high-tech exhibits on the human body. *(Open July-Aug. Tu-Sa 11am-9pm; Sept.-June Tu-Sa 10am-7pm, Su and festivals 11am-2:30pm. 400ptas, with student ID 100ptas.)* Watch "blood" spurt at 30mph from a pretend heart; hear "Hello, I love you" in over 30 languages (sadly, from a computer); and spend hours playing with microscopes, computers, and other fun gizmos. The entrance fee gets also you into the **Science Museum/Planetarium** (tel. 981 27 91 56) in Parque de Santa Margarita.

In the *ciudad vieja*, simple arches and windows surround the cobbled **Praza de María Pita**, named for the heroine who held off attacking Brits in 1589. The three domes of the **Pazo Municipal** rise majestically from the north side. Close by, **Prazuela Santa Bárbara** borders a 15th-century convent of the same name. A small Gothic doorway opens to **Igrexa de Santa María del Campo**, with granite columns and a rose window. The **Real Academia Gallega** (Royal Galician Academy; tel. 981 20 73 08) makes its headquarters at the former family seat of 19th-century novelist Condesa Emilia Pardo Bazán; its library contains 25,000 volumes on Galician literature, history, and culture. *(Open July-Sept. M-F 10am-1pm; Oct.-June M-F 10am-noon. Free.)* Next door, at C. Tabernas, 11, the academy devotes part of a museum to Pardo Bazán's work and part to a rotating exhibition of modern and 19th-century Galician art.

Sandwiched between Av. Marina and the dock, the elegant **Jardín Méndez Núñez** has a clock snipped to botanical perfection, with arms that really do tell the correct time. Soothing **Jardín de San Carlos**, in the old part of the city, was originally planted in 1843 on the site of the old Forte San Carlos—it still shelters the tomb of Sir John Moore. Local lore has it that killing this incompetent general cost Napoleon his crown, since Wellington took over Moore's command. Take a stroll and smell the eucalyptus in the **Parque de Santa Margarita**.

ENTERTAINMENT

Summer nightlife in La Coruña reflects the cheerful nature of the peninsula. **Cafe-Bar La Barra**, C. Riego de Agua, 33, offers innocent entertainment all day long. After about 10am, students and old men gather around its wooden tables to play cards, dominoes, and parcheesi. (Open daily 9am-2am.) The **Teatro Principal** on Av. Marina, next door to the post office, stages local plays and international productions. Residents bar-hop around **Calles Franja, La Florida,** and **San Juan** and around the surrounding side streets. When bars die down at around 2am, **discos** along the two beaches start making a ruckus. Also try the discos and cafes on **Calles Juan Florez** and **Sol. Pirámide,** Juan Florez, 50 (tel. 981 27 61 57), plays dance music to rouse the dead, while **Picasso** and **Lautrec,** opposite each other on C. Sol, attract the artistically inclined.

Although celebrated in many parts of Europe, **La Noche de San Juan** (June 23) is greeted with particular fervor in La Coruña since it coincides with the opening of sardine season. Locals light the traditional *aguardiente* bonfires and spend the night leaping over the flames (contrary to the image that comes to mind, the rite ensures fertility) and gorging on sardine flesh. If you drop an egg white in a glass of water on this night, it will assume the form of your future spouse's occupation; many are led to believe they'll marry a dairy farmer or a cow. The last two weeks of August bring concerts, parades, folk dancing, and a mock naval battle to honor María Pita.

La Coruña's **fútbol** team, Deportivo de La Coruña, the 1995 Spanish first-division champions, plays by the beach in **Estadio de Riazor** from April through June; check local papers or any bar for information.

■ Near La Coruña: Betanzos

A provinicial capital of ancient Galicia, the modern-day city of **Betanzos** (pop. 12,000) assumes a low profile despite its position at a crucial transportation intersection, 23km east of La Coruña and 38km south of El Ferrol. Cafes line the central **Praza García Hermanos,** home to a statue of the brothers García, the city's great benefactors. **Igrexa de San Fransisco,** located several blocks down the hill from Praza Hamanos, features the image of San Fransisco de Betanzos resting on the backs of a huge bear and boar and surrounded by his faithful puppies. At the bottom of the hill, across R. Cruz Verde, lies the old **Jewish quarter.** All houses here have two or three floors, as the first floor was used as a stable. Betanzos's great **festival** involves the launching of the world's largest paper balloon (about 25m high) on August 16, the night of San Roque. On August 18 and 25, watch for the boat festival, *Romería*, during which Betanzos's natives adorn their tiny fishing boats with flowers and float down the river Mandeo to Canarias for feasts, wine, and gleeful insanity.

Betanzos makes a good half-day trip from La Coruña and is most easily reached by bus. **IASA buses** (tel. 981 23 90 01) run from La Coruña and El Ferrol (45min., M-Sa departs every 30min., Su departs every hr., 230ptas), and elsewhere along the *rías*. Two **trains** per day stop in Betanzos on the way from La Coruña to El Ferrol. The train station sits across the river.

In Pr. García Hermanos' *bilblioteca-museo,* one block behind the statue to the left, the **tourist office** offers a map with a walking tour of the old city (open July-Sept. M-F 10am-1pm and 4-8pm, Sa-Su 10am-1pm). For **currency exchange** and **ATM** access, try **Banco Central Hispano,** on the Central Plaza (open M-F 8:30am-2:30pm). **Police** answer at tel. 981 77 06 02. Eggs, cheese, and produce arrive in wheelbarrows at the plaza's **market** (open M, Th, and Sa 9am-1pm).

Some think **Miño,** 12km north of Betanzos, has the nicest beach in the Rías Altas. On Saturday afternoons in **Pontedeume,** 22km from Betanzos, workers at the town market cook *pulpo* (octopus) in huge copper urns and mock the citizens of Betanzos for making that ridiculously huge balloon. You can reach both towns on the bus lines heading to El Ferrol (departs every 30min., 280ptas).

NORTH RÍAS ALTAS

Not as isolated as the Costa de la Muerte, these urbane *rías* become calmer as they move eastward. Old lighthouses, churches, and the remains of an ancient wall or two dot the green countryside. In the misty mountains of Galicia, the weather is anything but predictable, but views are spectacular year-round. Thanks to increasing popularity among vacationing Spaniards, the north Rías Altas have accumulated enough capital resources to create a transportation system, rendering the unspoiled coastline easily accessible (see **La Coruña: Buses,** p. 195).

■ Rías de Cedeira and Vivero

Where the average tourist seldom treads, rainforests covered with ferns give way to soft, empty beaches. Welcome to Cedeira and Vivero. Thick mists veil the valleys of these northernmost *rías*. Buses and FEVE trains run inland to Vivero from El Ferrol, but the sporadic coastal bus is preferable, allowing you to hop off anytime.

■ Cedeira

When cuckolding Lancelot fled England to escape the ire of King Arthur, he allegedly landed in Cedeira (pop. 8000), founding the town and sowing his seed. Set on its own *ría* 32km northeast of El Ferrol and 84km northeast of La Coruña, this small town offers pretty beaches and breathtaking scenery. There's not much to do except watch the tide, but no one seems to mind.

Bus service in Cedeira is fairly sparse. To get to Vivero or Ortigueira, take an **IASA** bus from C. Ezequiel Lopez, 28, to Campo do Hospital (15min., 5 per day, 120ptas), where you can change to the Campo do Hospital-Viviero IASA bus line. **RIALSA** buses run from Cedeira to El Ferrol (1hr., 7 per day, 490ptas), where connections can be made to La Coruña and elsewhere. Near the second bus stop, the **tourist office,** C.

Ezequiel Lopez, 22 (tel. 981 48 21 87), hands out brochures (open July-Aug. M-F 10:30am-2pm and 6-9pm, Su and holidays noon-2pm; May-June and Sept. M-F 10:30am-2pm and 4:30-8pm, Sa 10:30am-2pm, Su and holidays noon-2pm). In an **emergency,** call 981 48 07 25 for the **police.** The **post office** is at Av. Zumalacárrequi, 17 (tel. 981 48 05 52; open M-F 8:30am-2pm, Sa 9am-2pm). The **postal code** is 15350.

Hostal Chelsea, Pr. Sagrado Corazón, 9 (tel. 981 48 23 40), hosts guests in light-filled rooms around the corner from the first bus stop and near the beach (doubles with shower and TV 3600-3800ptas). For a small town, Cedeira has amassed a surprising number of local specialties. Open-faced *empanadas* are unique to the town, and locals love to snack on S-shaped sugar cookies (*"eses"*). Commendable *bodegas* and *mesones* line both sides of the *ría.* **Taberna da Calexa,** Tras. Elrexa, 7 (tel. 981 48 20 09), up a tiny staircase off the road leading to the church, serves Galician wine (100ptas per glass) behind medieval stone walls, complemented by a wide variety of homemade *raciones* (mussels in vinaigrette, 400ptas).

The **Santuario de San Andrés de Teixido** (a steep 12km hike from town) provides a 620m-high vista overlooking the sea. The highest coastline in Europe, the Santuario still hosts pagan cults with thriving rituals involving stone and water and the worship of the *herba de enamorar* (love herb). Closer to town lies the hermitage of **San Antonio de Corbeiro,** an easy 2km walk up a gentle slope. From the tourist office, turn left and follow signs to the turnoff (0.5km farther on the left). Then, it's up, up, and away. The hermitage is a white structure above the *ría,* high enough to send any acrophobe into a cold sweat. A steep tortuous 6km climb past the turnoff for San Antonio is the lighthouse **Faro de Punta Candieira.** The **Curro festival,** on the fourth Sunday in June, involves rounding up the wild horses living nearby. Mid-August is devoted to the **Feria de la Virgen del Mar.**

■ Vivero (Viveiro)

The tourist brochure's assertion *"No es un sueño. Existe."* ("It's not a dream. It exists.") may seem a bit much, but seaside Vivero (pop. 14,000) does have a timeless quality. Known throughout Spain for its beautiful, tiny old city at the forest's edge, Vivero's peaceful atmosphere, nearby beaches, and July *fiestas* draw a flotilla of Spanish tourists every summer. The nearest beach is in the resort town of **Covas,** 1km across the river from Vivero. If you tire of Covas, **Playa de Area** suns itself 4km from Vivero, and **Playa de Sacido** is not much farther away (6km). The first weekend of July is marked by the *Rapa das Bestas,* a festival celebrating the capture of wild horses. The main *fiestas* take place the last week in July. Vivero's *encierro* (running of the bulls) cures even the worst hangover.

PRACTICAL INFORMATION FEVE **trains** (tel. 981 55 07 22), down Trav. Marina past Pr. Lugo, chug twice daily to: Ribadeo, with connections to Ortigueira, Barqueiro, and Vicedo (1hr., 3 per day, 485ptas); El Ferrol (2hr., 3 per day, 6750ptas); and Oviedo (5hr., 2 per day, 1805ptas). **Bus** companies **IASA** (tel. 981 56 01 03), on Trav. Marina, and **ERSA,** Pr. Lugo, 2 (tel. 981 56 03 90), recently merged. Together, they run to: Ribadeo (1½hr., 2 per day, 575ptas); El Ferrol (2hr., 5 per day, 960ptas); Lugo (2½hr., 5 per day, 1200ptas); and La Coruña (4hr., 5 per day, 1600ptas). **ALSA** buses go from Ribadeo to Oviedo. Rent **cars, bikes,** and **motorcycles** at **Viajes Arifran,** C. Rosalía de Castro, 54 (tel. 981 56 04 97). Motorcycles run about 9000ptas per day and bicycles 1000ptas per day. (Open July-Aug. M-F 9:30am-1pm and 4-7pm, Sa 9:30am-1:30pm.) Vivero's **tourist office** (tel. 981 56 08 79), on Av. Ramón Canosa, hands out maps and brochures and posts information about *pensiones* (open daily 11am-2pm and 5-7pm). **Banks** and **ATMs** line Av. Galicia. In an **emergency,** dial 091 or 092. For the **police,** call 981 56 29 22. The **post office** (tel. 981 56 09 27) is 20m past the market away from town (open M-F 8:30am-2pm, Sa 9:30am-1pm).

G
A
L
I
C
I
A

ACCOMMODATIONS AND FOOD Fonda Bossanova, Av. Galicia, 11 (tel. 981 56 01 50), one block from the bus station in the direction of Covas, has small, mostly interior rooms (singles 2000ptas; doubles 3000ptas). On the first floor, the owner pleases locals with a *menú* for 1000ptas and delicious desserts. More picturesque (but pricier) lodgings are tucked in various corners throughout the old city. For spacious rooms with balconies and a view of the Igrexa de Santa María, try **Fonda Nuevo Mundo** (tel. 981 56 00 25), off Pr. Maior (singles 2000ptas; doubles 3500ptas). On the same road heading toward Vivero is **Camping Vivero** (tel. 981 56 00 04). Follow the signs to the flagged reception hut. A cafe and broad beach are just steps away from this second-class campsite. (425ptas per person, per tent, per car. Electricity 425ptas. Reception daily 9am-11pm. Open June-Sept.)

The huge Mega-Claudio **supermarket** looms beside the bus station (open M-Sa 9:30am-9pm), and budget *mesones* proliferate around Pr. Maior. **Mesón Xoaquín,** R. Irmans Vilarponte, 19 (tel. 981 56 27 56), up from the square, serves a *menú* for 850ptas in a stone *comedor* with stuffed boars and snazzy red tablecloths (open daily 1-4pm and 8-10pm). **A Cepa,** R. Fernández Victorio, 7, dishes out cheap *tapas: chipirones* 200ptas, *patatas bravas* 110ptas, and the mysterious *bikini* 150ptas (open daily noon-3pm and 7:30pm-midnight).

■ Ría de Ribadeo

Even when inundated with summer residents, Ribadeo's stunning Galician scenery gives the town a ghostly, deserted air. It is the last *gallego* outpost before the Asturian border. Choose your mountain, *ría,* or Cantabrian Sea view, then pray for a clear day—the town has little else to offer.

At the water's edge, both the **Paseo Marítimo** and the **Praia Os Bloques,** just past the dock, harbor spectacular views. High above the *ría,* a 3km walk from town through farm land (follow the signs), sits the **Igrexa de Santa Cruz.** If the climb doesn't take your breath away, the view of the eucalyptus countryside and crazy-blue ocean will. Three kilometers in the other direction, at the **Praia de Rocas Blancas,** a red and white *faro* (lighthouse) towers above the water.

Getting in and out of Ría de Ribadeo isn't that hard. The **FEVE train station** (tel. 982 13 07 39) is a 15-minute walk from Pr. España straight along R. Villafranco Bierzo, which changes names four times (info open daily 6am-9pm). Trains crawl along the coastal route connecting Ría de Ribadeo to: El Ferrol (3½hr., 3 per day, 1145ptas); Oviedo (4hr., 2 per day, 1290ptas); Ortigueira; and Vivero. **IASA buses** (tel. 982 22 17 60) run to: Vivero (2 per day, 1250ptas); La Coruña (3hr., 10 per day, 1000ptas); and El Ferrol (4 per day, 1030ptas). The **ALSA** station off Pr. España runs buses to Oviedo (4hr., 4 per day, 550ptas). Buses leave from Av. Rosalía de Castro, in front of Viajes Terra y Mar. From Pr. España, take C. San Roque (the upper left corner), head left for two blocks, turn right, go downhill, and walk about 150m to the travel agency.

The **tourist office** (tel. 982 12 86 89), in the center of Pr. España, distributes a decent map. (Open in summer M 4-7pm, Tu-Sa 9:30am-1:30pm and 4-7pm, Su and holidays 11am-1pm; in winter M-F 4-7pm, Su and holidays 11am-1pm.) Change money at **Banco Central Hispano,** C. San Rogue, 17. In an **emergency,** call 091 or 092. The **post office** sits at Av. Asturias, 17 (tel. 982 12 82 48; open M-F 8:30am-2:30pm, Sa 9:30am-1pm). The **postal code** is 27700.

Several hostels sit on C. San Roque, on the way from the train station. On Pr. España across from the church is **Hostal Costa Verde,** 13 (tel. 982 12 86 81). Its rooms and bathrooms are pristine, and some rooms have balconies. (Singles 1600ptas; doubles 3000-4500ptas. Inquire in the bar downstairs.) **Camping Ribadeo** (tel. 982 13 11 67) charges 425ptas per person, tent, and car. **Supermercado El Arbol** (tel. 982 72 58 50), on Av. Galicia, is well stocked (open Tu-Sa 9am-

2pm and 5-8pm, M 9:30am-2pm), and low-priced *cafeterías* pepper Pr. España.
Restaurante Ros Mary, C. San Francisco, 3, has a *menú* of hake, steak, and *faba-das* for 950ptas (open daily 8am-2pm).

No More Bull

Instead of typical Spanish *corridas* (bullfights), Galician *pueblos* Vivero and San Lorenz host an event in the first weekend of July called *La Rapa das Bestas.* This spectacle involves capturing and breaking in wild mountain horses. A dozen or so men attempt to brand and cut hair from the manes and tails of galloping, bucking, kicking equines in a ring much smaller than a *plaza de toros.* Both horses and men frequently suffer serious injuries. A famous picture depicts a fiery one-armed man biting the horse's mane with his teeth—mmm, mmm good.

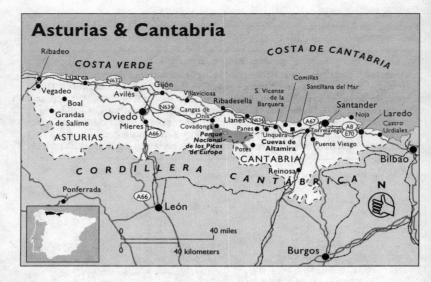

Asturias and Cantabria

Seething cliffs and hell-reaching ravines lend an epic scope to the tiny lands of Asturias and Cantabria, tucked away between País Vasco and Galicia. With the decline of Asturias's traditional craftsmaking production, and of the region's mining, steel, and shipping industries, the economic livelihood of Asturias and Cantabria has come to rely upon scientific research and green tourism. Now an extensive network of quaint tourist towns, cottages, and country inns in old *casas de indianos* (rambling Victorian mansions built by settlers who scored big in the Americas) provides the residents of Asturias and Cantabria a means to get rich off the vacation plans of the modern-day Spanish elite. Besides its industrial centers, the area is also known for its prosperous dairy farms and the National Parks, especially the Picos de Europa, that make Asturias and Cantabria popular spots for hunting, fishing, and hiking.

Agricolar Moors had little use for the region's rough terrain, enabling the Christians to make the land their northern base. The reconquest officially began in Asturias, while Cantabria was the only region never to fall to the Moors, a source of pride to this day. Centuries later, this historical defiance translated into a legendary, blue-collar resistance to the Fascists in the Civil War that inspired Republican forces throughout the peninsula.

Because of the variegated terrain and unpredictable weather, public transportation in the Asturias and Cantabria regions can be erratic. But the roads are striking, winding through alpine forests or green valleys quilted with cornfields and pastures.

HIGHLIGHTS OF ASTURIAS AND CANTABRIA

- **Picos de Europa,** a spectacular range of jagged peaks and beautiful scenery, for every outdoor activity imaginable (p. 208).

ASTURIAS

■ Oviedo

Smack in the middle of Asturias's plunging green valleys sits the region's capital and transportation hub—colorful, cosmopolitan Oviedo (pop. 200,000), where cars roar down the four-lane streets of the new city and Victorian architecture presides over a plethora of parks. Oviedo's monastic origins may be partly buried beneath cement and smokestacks, but the old city is lively and packed in the summertime. Stock up on info and supplies for your trip to the Picos de Europa, then wander through the *sidrería*-lined streets and look in on the city's celebrated cathedral.

ORIENTATION AND PRACTICAL INFORMATION

Calle de Uría bisects the city, running northwest to southeast from its origin at the **RENFE station.** On the west side of C. Uría is the leafy, luscious **Campo de San Francisco;** on the east side is the old city, with **Plaza Mayor** and **Plaza de Alfonso II,** known to locals as **Plaza de la Catedral** and to tourists as site of the tourist office.

The **first FEVE train station** (serving Cantabria and País Vasco) is to the left as you leave RENFE, on **Avenida Santander.** To reach the **bus stations** from FEVE, take **Calle Jerónimo Ibrán,** on which Económicos (EASA) and Turytrans buses stop, to **Plaza General Primo de Rivera,** where the ALSA bus has its unmarked station; the station's info office has a good **map** on the wall. To reach C. Uría from Pl. General Primo de Rivera, take a soft left onto C. Fray Ceferino, which ends at C. Uría.

The **second FEVE train station** (serving the Galicia-Asturias route) is way east of the bus stations on **Calle Víctor Chávarri.** To reach C. Uría from here, take C. Víctor Chávarri, which becomes Alcalde García Conde and ends at Pl. Carbayón. On the far side of the plaza, pick up C. Argüelles and you'll hit C. Uría.

Transportation

Flights: Aeropuerto de Ranón/ Aeropuerto Nacional de Asturias (tel. 98 555 18 33), in Avilés, northwest of Oviedo. **Aviaco** (tel. 98 512 76 03) flies to Madrid, Barcelona, and London. **Prabus,** C. Marqués de Pidal, 20 (tel. 98 525 47 51), runs frequent buses from the ALSA station to the airport. **Iberia** (tel. (985) 12 76 07).

Trains: RENFE, C. Uría (tel. 98 524 33 64 or 98 525 02 02), at the junction with Av. Santander. Pay attention to the kind of train; a slow local train through the mountains can double your travel time. Info open daily 7:45am-11:15pm. To: Gijón (30min., departs every 30min., 300-350ptas); León (2½hr., 8 per day, 850-1470ptas); Madrid (6½-8hr., 6 per day, 4200ptas); Barcelona (13hr., 2 per day, 6000ptas). **FEVE,** Av. Santander (tel. 98 528 40 96 or 98 529 76 56), is left from the RENFE exit and downhill (2min.). To: Llanes (4½hr., 3 per day, 875ptas); Santander (5-8hr., 2 per day, 1650ptas); Bilbao (7hr., departs at 8:15am, 2570ptas). Another **FEVE,** C. Víctor Chavarri, 19 (tel. 98 521 90 26), is for trains running west as far as Ferrol. To Ribadeo (4hr., 2 per day, 1295ptas) and Ferrol (7½hr., 2 per day, 2420ptas).

Buses: ALSA, Pl. General Primo de Rivera, 1 (tel. 98 528 12 00), unmarked, on the lower level of a shopping arcade. To: León (2hr., 8 per day, 1010ptas); Santander (3hr., 1 per day, 1755ptas); Burgos (4hr., 2 per day, 1640ptas); La Coruña (6hr., 3 per day, 1360ptas); Madrid (6hr., 7 per day, 3700-5800ptas); Vigo (9hr., 2 per day, 4210ptas); Santiago (8hr., 3 per day, 3620ptas); Barcelona (12hr., 2 per day, 4850ptas). **Económicos (EASA),** C. Jerónimo Ibrán, 1 (tel. 98 529 00 39). To: Cangas de Onís (1½hr., 12 per day, 670ptas); Covadonga (1¾hr., 5 per day, 790ptas); Arenas de Cabrales (2¼hr., 4 per day, 950ptas); Llanes (2½hr., 11 per day, 1000ptas). Significantly fewer buses on weekends.

Public Transportation: TUA (tel. 98 522 24 22) runs **buses** (110ptas) 8am-10pm. #4 goes to bus, FEVE, and RENFE stations; #2 goes to the youth hostel/hospital; #2, 3, 5, and 7 run from RENFE to near the old part of the city.

Taxis: Radio Taxi (tel. 98 525 00 00 or 98 525 25 00).
Car Rental: Avis, C. Ventura Rodríguez, 12 (tel. 98 524 13 83). From 9600ptas per day. Weekend specials. Open M-F 9am-1pm and 4-7:30pm, Sa 9am-1pm.

Tourist and Financial Services

Tourist Office: Pl. Alfonso II (tel. 98 521 33 85). Busy staff has a handy guide to the city (maps included) and advice on Picos treks. English spoken. Open M-F 9:30am-1:30pm and 4:30-6:30pm, Sa 9am-2pm, Su 11am-2pm.
Budget Travel: TIVE, C. Calvo Sotelo, 5 (tel. 98 523 60 58), past the Campo San Francisco, up from C. Marqués de Santa Cruz. Info on nearby hiking and travel; excursions. ISIC 750ptas. HI card 500ptas, over 26 1000ptas. Open M-F 8am-3pm.
Currency Exchange: Banco Central Hispano, on the corner of C. Uría and C. Argüelles. Open June-Sept. M-F 8:30am-2:30pm; Oct.-May 8:30am-4:30pm.

Local Services

El Corte Inglés: The feudal lord of superstores, now at 2 convenient locations: C. General Alorza, opposite the ALSA station, and C. Uría. **Currency exchange, telephones,** and groceries. Open M-Sa 10am-9:30pm.
Luggage Storage: At RENFE station (lockers 300ptas). Open daily 7am-11pm. At ALSA bus station (lockers 200-300ptas). Open daily 7am-11pm.
Trekking: Dirección Regional de la Juventud, C. Calvo Sotelo, 5 (tel. 98 523 11 12). A comprehensive pamphlet on camping, youth hostels, and hiking plus info on cultural activities. Open M-F 10am-1pm. **Federación Asturiana de Montaña,** C. de Julián Clavería (tel. 98 525 23 62), a 30min. walk from the city center near the bull ring, or take bus #2. Call first; if you walk, get the big map from the tourist office. Organizes excursions, stocks good trail maps, and provides mountain guides, info about weather conditions, and the best hiking routes. Open M-F 6-8:30pm.

Emergency and Communications

Emergency: dial 091 or 092. **Police: Policía Municipal,** C. Quintana (tel. 98 521 80 29).
Late-Night Pharmacy: Check listings in *La Voz de Asturias* (110ptas), or *La Nueva España* (110ptas).
Hospital: Hospital General de Asturias (tel. 98 510 61 00), C. J. Clavería.
Internet Access: Laser Internet Center, C. San Francisco, 9 (tel. 98 520 00 66). 400ptas per 30min.
Post Office: C. Alonso Quintanilla, 1 (tel. 98 521 41 86). From C. Uría, turn left onto C. Argüelles and then left again. Open for stamps and Lista de Correos M-F 8:30am-8:30pm, Sa 9:30am-2pm. **Postal Code:** 33060.

ACCOMMODATIONS

A plethora of *pensiones* pack the new city near the transport stations. Try **Calle Uría, Calle Campoamor** (1 block east), and **Calle Nueve de Mayo** (a continuation of C. Manuel Pedregal, 1 block farther east). Near the cathedral, try C. Jovellanos.

Residencia Juvenil Ramón Menéndez Pidal, C. Julián Clavería, 14 (tel. 98 523 20 54), across from the hospital. Take bus #2 from C. Uría. TV room, library, and dining room. Few beds in summer; call first. Dorms 750ptas, over 26 1000ptas.
Pensión Pomar, C. Jovellanos, 7 (tel. 98 522 27 91). Super-clean, airy rooms with big windows and blue sinks in a spacious old building. Singles 1500-2000ptas; doubles 3000-3500ptas; triples 4500ptas. Prices fluctuate with demand.
Pensión Martinez, C. Jovellanos, 5 (tel. 98 521 53 44). Clean rooms with sinks. Communal bathrooms. Singles 1600ptas; doubles 3000ptas; triples 3000ptas.
Pensión Riesgo, C. Nueve de Mayo, 16, 1st fl. (tel. 98 521 89 45). Long oriental rug in foyer leads to clean, simple rooms with cool, bedside lamps. Singles 1800ptas; doubles 3500ptas.

ASTURIAS & CANTABRIA

FOOD

Order *sidra* by the bottle (usually 250ptas)—it goes fast, and much of it ends up on the floor. For the best *sidra* experience, head to the wooden-beamed, ham-hung **sidrerías** where waiters pour *sidra* from above their heads into your glass to release its aroma. Asturias's typical dish is the meaty, bean-based *fabada*, with chunks of sausage and ham, while *carbayon* is a sweet and tangy almond and egg yolk delight. Cheap restaurants line **Calle Fray Ceferino,** running between the bus and train stations. The posh indoor **market** (with an **ATM**) is on C. Fontán, off Pl. Mayor (open M-Sa 8am-8pm). For groceries, try **El Corte Inglés** (see p. 206) or C. La Lila.

Mesón Luferca, a.k.a. **La Casa Real del Jamón,** C. Covadonga, 20 (tel. 98 521 78 02). You may be used to those hanging hams, but nothing can prepare you for the sheer quantity and density of the pig parts in this place. Many meaty *tapas* from 500ptas. Open M-Sa 8:30am-11:30pm.

Sidrería Astoria (tel. 98 521 16 09), on C. Santa Clara. There's ham hanging from the ceiling and *sidra*-drenched sawdust on the floor. Ham, pork, or sausage, and— of course—*sidra* for 500ptas. *Menú* 950ptas. Open daily 9am-3am.

Restaurante Pinocchio (tel. 98 522 35 21), on C. Altamirana, a block up from the cathedral heading toward Pl. Mayor. A giant Pinocchio (honestly) watches the airy *comedor*. 1100ptas *menú* includes steak topped with cheese and a delicious nut tart. An array of Italian specialties. Open Tu-Su 1-4pm and 8pm-midnight.

Casa Albino, C. Gascona, 15 (tel. 98 521 04 45), a right turn from the FEVE-Galicia station. Bullfights on TV and a few Real Madrid photos for atmosphere, but the 990ptas *menú* extends to *fabada* and braised lamb. Two dozen shrimp and *sidra* for an unbelievable 600ptas. Open daily 9:30am-5pm and 7pm-1am.

SIGHTS

In Clarín's 19th-century novel *La Regenta,* Ana Osorio throws herself at the feet of her ecclesiastical lover in Oviedo's **cathedral** (tel. 98 522 10 33), Pl. Alfonso II. *(Open daily 10am-1pm and 4-7pm. Free.)* Finished for the most part in 1388, the cathedral's 80m **tower** offers great views of the city's rooftops. The exterior seems charred due to excessive pollution, but glowing stained-glass windows illuminate the stone interior. Painted with crushed lapis lazuli stone, the brilliant blue ceiling above the altar seems to shed its own light. In the north transept, the **Capilla del Rey Castro** houses the royal pantheon, designated by Alfonso II as the resting place of Asturian monarchs. The more unusual **Capilla de San Pedro** houses an intense sculpture in metal relief depicting Simon Magnus being dropped from the sky by hideous demons. The cathedral complex also houses a **museum**, a *cámara santa* (holy chamber), and a **cloister.** *(Museum, chamber, and cloister open M-F 10am-8pm, Sa 10am-6:30pm. 400ptas, children 300ptas. Thursdays free.)* The museum holds a fine collection of scepters, chalices, candelabras, processional crosses, and liturgical formal wear.

Just up C. Santa Ana from Pl. Alfonso II is the **Museo de Bellas Artes,** C. Santa Ana, 1, and C. Rúa, 8 (tel. 98 521 30 61). *(Open Tu-F 10:30am-1:30pm and 5-8pm, Sa-Su and holidays 11am-2pm. Free.)* The two-building, three-story complex displays a wide range of Asturian art and a small collection of 16th- to 20th-century (mainly Spanish) art. For a change of pace, check out the temporary exhibits at the **Centro de Arte Moderno,**

Resurrecting a Tower of Bable

Galicians have Gallego, Catalans have Catalan, and Asturians have...Bable? Though it's not an official language, the dialect has returned with the sweeping post-Franco reassertion of regional tradition. Although it is not spoken on the street, Bable is taught to children in at school. A codification of a hodge-podge of more than 10 distinct traditional dialects originating in different corners of Asturias, Bable's grammar borrows from many but belongs to none. As a result, almost no one is fluent in the tongue, and more than a handful of grandmothers express bewilderment at their grandchildren's *bable*-ing.

C. Alonso Quintanilla, 2, opposite the post office. *(Open M-Sa 5:30-9pm.)* Asturian Pre-Romanesque—the first European attempt to blend architecture, sculpture (including human representations), and mural painting since the fall of the Roman Empire—was developed under Alfonso II (789-842) and refined under his son Ramiro I, for whom the *Ramirense* style is named. Two beautiful examples of *Ramirense*, **Santa María del Naranco** and **San Miguel de Lillo,** tower above Oviedo on **Monte Naranco.** *(Both buildings open May-Sept. M-Sa 9:30am-1pm and 3-7pm, Su 9:30am-1pm; Oct.-Apr. M-Sa 9:30am-1pm and 3-5pm, Su 10am-1pm. 200ptas, Mondays free.)*

HIKING

A good **English guidebook** to the trails and towns of the area is Robin Walker's *Picos de Europa.* If you read *castellano,* check out the many publications of **Miguel Ángel Andrados.** Helpful organizations and businesses are listed below, all based in Oviedo unless otherwise noted. Most base towns in the Picos support excursion-organizers; check specific towns for listings. Oviedo is the place to buy all of your supplies—stores closer to the mountains get smaller and more expensive.

ICONA, C. Arquitecto Reguera, 13, 2nd fl. (tel. 98 524 14 12). Excursions, camping and trail info, and a 30min. video on flora, fauna, and cheese. The office in **Cangas de Onís,** Av. Covadonga, 35 (tel. 98 584 91 54), is the best place to get detailed (free) info on the Picos.

Federación Asturiana de Montaña, Dirección Regional de la Juventud, and **TIVE** travel agency (see p. 206 for addresses and phone numbers). Referral to mountain guides, organized tour groups, and instructors in everything from paragliding to kayaking and spelunking.

Dirección Regional de Deportes (tel. 98 527 23 47), in Pl. España. Info and referrals for outdoor sports and mountaineering.

Oxígeno (tel. 98 522 79 75), on C. Manuel Pedregal, a continuation of C. Nueve de Mayo, past C. Fray Ceferino, heading toward RENFE. A hardcore mountaineer shop with 2 walls of maps and guides and Andrados's hiking books. Staff of Picos veterans enthusiastically doles out advice. Open M-Sa 10am-1:30pm and 4:30-8:30pm.

Deportes Tuñon, C. Campoamor, 8. Sells camping gear on the block between C. Dr. Casal and C. Fray Ceferino. Extensive selection of camping and rock-climbing gear, long underwear, and a few maps. Open M-Sa 10am-1:30pm and 4:30-8:30pm.

ENTERTAINMENT

The streets south of the cathedral, around **Plazas Riego, da Fontán,** and **del Paraguas,** teem with noisy *sidrerías* and clubs. Stylish **Bar Riego,** on Pl. Riego, serves rich *batidos* (milkshakes) on a breezy *terraza.* Wine connoisseurs follow **la ruta de los vinos,** from *bodega* to *bodega* along C. Rosal, with *copas* 100-200ptas. On C. Cuna, between Alcalde García Conde and C. Jovellanos, **Danny's Jazz Café** soothes guests lounging on red velvet couches with a cool dose of jazz recordings and videos. The **Teatro Filarmónica,** C. Mendizábel, 3 (tel. 98 521 27 62), hosts dramatic productions in September and musical concerts the rest of the year. Check the local paper for playhouse listings. Oviedo celebrates its **patronal fiesta** in honor of San Mateo on September 19 to 21.

PICOS DE EUROPA

As the crow flies, it is a scant 25km from sea level to the 2600m heights of the Picos de Europa. Other European mountain ranges may be higher, but few match the beauty of the Sierra's abrupt, jagged profile. Intrepid mountaineers, novice trekkers, and even idle admirers flock to the Picos, which compose the most notable section of the Cordillera Cantábrica, a larger range that extends across northern Spain.

The land's myriad caves and caverns, the legacy of ancient glacial abuse, make it a modern-day haven for spelunkers. Other popular activities include paragliding, whitewater rafting, kayaking, salmon and trout fishing, and rock-climbing. Many hik-

ASTURIAS & CANTABRIA

Picos de Europa

ing and mountain bike trails follow old mule tracks from the time (centuries ago) when the Picos' valleys were man-made haymeadows; now the region contains (in addition to hay), some 800 species of plants and wildflowers—including 40 species of wild orchids. Herds of wild horses run free here, and wild boar and *chamois* (a goat-type animal) can also be spotted. Songbirds and raptors fill the air, while salmon and trout populate the rivers.

Most of the Picos area has been granted environmental protection as the Picos de Europa National Park, but continental Europe's largest national park is nonetheless an increasingly popular vacation destination. The best time to head for the Picos is late summer, despite the crowds. The region is cold and often stormy through May and even June, while the autumn weather is chilly and unpredictable. Buses from Santander and León cover the range, but the best place to start is Oviedo, base-camp of many *federaciones* (hiking organizations).

■ Orientation

Spanning a region approximately 40 by 20km in area, the Picos de Europa are made up of three mountainous massifs: the **Occidental** (or Cornión), the **Central** (or Urrieles), and the **Oriental** (or Ándara). The Garganta del Cares (Cares Gorge) marks the dramatic division between the Central and Oriental massifs, and in this area lie the park's most popular trails and most famous peaks—the postcard-perfect Peña Vieja and Pico Tesorero, the stark Llambrión, and the mythic **Naranjo de Bulnes,** which has become a symbol for the region.

Route AS-114 runs along the north edge of the Picos from **Cangas de Onís** (10km north of **Covadonga**) through **Arenas de Cabrales,** and on to **Panes,** where it intersects Route N-621. N-621 runs 50km south and west to **Potes,** where a branch leads to **Fuente Dé.** Arenas de Cabrales is a prime base for serious hiking, while larger Potes is a bit more touristy and expensive take-off point. Covadonga and the Fuente Dé areas have excellent guided day **hikes** (free) of varying length and difficulty. Getting to the Picos is relatively easy, since **ALSA buses** link together the main towns, and highways are well maintained.

For a list of mountain **refugios** (usually cabins with bunks but not blankets) and general information on the park, contact the **Picos de Europa National Park Visitors Center** (tel. 985 84 86 14). Other lodging options include **albergues,** ancient, non-heated buildings with bunks and cold water, and **casas,** buildings with bunks, hot

ASTURIAS & CANTABRIA

water, and wood stoves. In both cases you should bring a sleeping bag. But often only campers can find beds during July and August, and even this endeavor can be touch and go—many campgrounds fill up in high season. Call *hostales* or *pensiones* in June or earlier to make reservations. *Refugios* can generally only be contacted by portable phone or short-wave radio (the Guardia Civil can often help). In a jam, tourist offices can help you find a bed in a private residence.

Plan ahead! Water sources and campsites are sprinkled infrequently across the range. Covadonga does not have an ATM or a supermarket. Arenas has an **ATM**, but its small shops are pricey and limited. Stock up in Oviedo or Cangas de Onís. If you set off alone (not recommended), leave a copy of your planned route so a rescue squad can be alerted if you don't return or call by a certain time. Always pack **warm clothes** and **rain gear**, since sudden changes in weather are not uncommon. If a heavy mist descends en route (as often happens), don't continue unless you know exactly where you're going.

■ Cangas de Onís

Founded after the Castilian victory over the Moors at Covadonga in 722, Cangas de Onís (pop. 6285) was the first capital of the Asturian monarchy and a launching pad for the *Reconquista*. Now known as the gateway to the Picos National Park, this town of many postcard racks is still 10km away from the edge of the actual park at Covadonga. Although not as central as Arenas de Cabrales, Cangas offers its own mini-hikes and is a great place to eat, sleep, and grocery shop between excursions.

PRACTICAL INFORMATION ALSA, (tel. 98 584 81 33) Av. Covadonga, across from the tourist office, regularly runs **buses** to: Arenas de Cabrales (30min., 4 per day, 285ptas); Llanes (40min., 1 per day, 500ptas); Oviedo (1¼hr., 10 per day, 680ptas); and Madrid (8hr., daily at 10:50am, 3635ptas). The **tourist office** (tel. 98 584 80 05), in a glass kiosk in the park by the Ayuntamiento (on Av. Covadonga) has a map but little else (open daily May-Sept. 10am-3pm and 4-9pm; Oct.-Apr. 10am-2pm and 4-7pm). One block toward Arenas de Cabrales from the tourist kiosk, the Picos de Europa National Park **Visitors Center,** in the Casa Dago, has a list of mountain *refugios*, **maps,** a short nature exhibit, and a vivid description of the park (open daily in summer 9am-9pm; in winter 9am-2pm and 4-6:30pm). Down the street in the opposite direction from the kiosk, **Librería Imagen** stocks guides and maps (open daily). **Aventura,** Av. Covadonga, s/n (tel. 98 584 92 61 or 98 584 85 76), sets up various expeditions, including hiking, canyoning, spelunking, canoeing, horseback riding, and bungee jumping (3000ptas per jump). **Municipal police,** in the Ayuntamiento, answer at tel. 98 584 85 58. The **Red Cross** (24hr. tel. 98 594 7310) is just above the **post office** (tel. 584 81 96). The **postal code** is 33550.

ACCOMMODATIONS AND FOOD A few clean *pensiones* welcome guests on the main street, Av. Covadonga. With a sign on Av. Covadonga, but with its entrance on Av. Castilla, is the recently remodelled **Pensión Labra,** Av. Castilla, 1, 1st fl. (tel. 98 584 90 47; doubles July-Aug. 5000ptas; Sept.-June 3000-4000ptas). **El Choffer** (tel. 98 584 83 05), C. Emilio Lareahas smallish, clean rooms, firm beds, Oriental rugs, and hall baths (ask in the restaurant about the *pensión*). In the bar downstairs hangs a cigar-smokin' boar's head with hat and sunglasses. (Singles 2500ptas; doubles 4000ptas.) Campers frequent the second-class **Camping Covadonga** (tel. 98 594 00 97), on Soto de Cangas about 4km up the road toward Covadonga (5-7 buses per day). Amenities include a cafeteria, bar, supermarket, and showers. (550ptas per person, 425ptas per car, 475ptas per tent. Open Semana Santa and June-Sept. 20.) Some people camp illegally in a secluded meadow by the river.

After a rousing hike, few pleasures surpass a substantial meal in the land of *fabes* (beans) and *sidra* (cider). Most restaurants on Av. Covadonga serve *menús* slightly over 1000ptas; cheaper places with fewer tourists hide on side streets. By the church off Av. Coratorga, **Mesón El Overtense,** C. San Pelayo, 15 (tel. 98 584 81 62), serves up a flexible 1000ptas *menú*. Left of the park, **Supermercados El Arbol** sells preparations for a do-it-yourself meal (open M-Sa).

SIGHTS AND EXCURSIONS Walking into Cangas from the Puente Romano—a medieval bridge masquerading otherwise—turn left opposite the park and cross a modern bridge to **Capilla de Santa Cruz.** This Romanesque chapel sits atop the town's oldest monument, a Celtic *dolmen* (monolith). Priests hid from invading Moors in a cave underneath. The **Cueva del Buxu** (BOO-shoo), with walls adorned by 15,000-year-old paintings, is 5km away. *(Open W-Su 10am-2pm and 4-6pm. 200ptas. Only 25 people are admitted to the cave each day, so arrive early.)* To reach the cave, follow the main road to Arenas de Cabrales for 3km until the sign for the *cueva* directs you left. From here, it's a gradual 2km climb past pastures and chicken coops. **Buses** to Covadonga, Llanes, and Arenas run near the Cueva del Buxu (ask to be dropped off at the Cruce de Susierra).

■ Covadonga

"This little mountain you see will be the salvation of Spain," prophesied Don Pelayo to his Christian army in 718, gesturing to the rocky promontory that soon would be the site of the first successful rebellion against the Moors. The *Reconquista* started in what is now the tiny town of Covadonga *(la donga)*, about 10km east of Arenas. Nationalistic legend claims that the Virgin interceded with God on behalf of Don Pelayo's forces. Covadonga has a few impressive sights, but the gorgeous lakes are what will occupy you for more than a couple of hours. With very few permanent residents, the area is primarily a tourist magnet and serves well as a starting point for hikes.

Don Pelayo prayed to the Virgin perched atop a gushing waterfall in the **Santa Cueva** (Holy Cave). It now beckons pilgrims who crawl up its 50 steps, sometimes on their hands and knees. The virgin changes her lovely cloak every few days in the summer. Pilgrims and tourists now crowd the sanctuary (open daily; free). The **Santuario de Covadonga,** a neo-Gothic basilica in fairy tale pink (1901), towers above the town (open daily). The *Corona de la Virgen,* a crown of gold and silver studded with 1109 diamonds and 2000 sapphires, is on display in the **Museo del Tesoro,** across the square from the basilica. Underneath lies Jesus's crown, encrusted with sparklers (open daily; 200ptas).

ALSA buses (tel. 98 584 81 33) from Oviedo (1¾hr., 7 per day, 785ptas) and Cangas (20min., 110ptas) grace Covadonga with two stops: one at the Hospedería and one uphill at the basilica. To reach Llanes or Arenas from Covadonga, you must backtrack to Cangas and catch a bus there. Head to Covadonga's **info office** (tel. 98 584 60 35) for information on local accommodations and sights. (Open in summer 10am-7pm; in winter 11am-5pm.) Those planning to do serious hiking should get trail info ahead of time from the visitor's center in Cangas de Onís. Spending the night in Cangas is cheaper than here *(la donga)*, but the light blue shutters of **Hospedería del Peregrino** (tel. 584 60 47), on the main highway downhill, open onto swoon-inducing views of the mountains and basilica (4000ptas per person). The only **groceries** in town arrive twice a week (W and Sa) by truck—buy them from the driver at the Hospedería del Peregrino. Knock on the last door on the right.

■ Near Covadonga: Los Lagos de Enol y Ercina

Buses run from Oviedo to Cangas and continue 12km higher, past Covadonga, en route to the sparkling **Lagos de Enol y Ercina** (Lakes of Enol and Ercina; July-Aug. 5 per day; Sept.-June 2 per day, 220ptas). Buses leave from the basilica at Covadonga and return from a mountain traverse on a spectacular road hemmed in by cliffs and precipitous pastures. Along the way, cows and striking rock formations surround the crystal blue lakes. Don't make the trip if it's cloudy or else you will be *in* the clouds, guided and misguided by invisible mooing cows. Monday through Friday there are free **guided hikes** of Los Lagos. Leaving from the Lake Enol parking lot (2½hr., departs 10:30am).

The **Refugio de Vega de Enol** (tel. 98 584 85 76) lies off the trails leading from the lakes. It has 30 spots open year-round, with meals and guides provided. To get there by car, take highway C-6312 (Cangas de Onís-Panes, *desvío hacia* Covadongas y Lagos), go right at Lago Enol, and keep going to the *refugio* (400-600ptas per person, *pensión completa* 2400-2700ptas).

▓ Arenas de Cabrales

If tourists valued natural beauty as much as paintings and monuments, Arenas (pop. 800) would be as packed as the Louvre in July. As it is, a fair number of outdoor enthusiasts come to this tiny town between Cangas and Potes in late summer to take advantage of the excellent hiking and climbing—Arenas makes an ideal, untouristed base for exploring the central Picos. It is also the place to try *queso de cabrales,* the local, pungent blue cheese created by mixing goat, cow, and sheep's milk, wrapping the mush in leaves, and stewing the whole mess in nearby caves for a few months.

PRACTICAL INFORMATION ALSA buses go west to Cangas de Onís and Oviedo (4 per day). They run twice a day in the other direction to Panes (45min., 220ptas), Unquera (1¼hr., 240ptas), and on to Santander (1½hr., 2 per day, 650-700ptas). **Palomera** buses leave from the center of Panes to Potes (2 per day, 45min., 220ptas). The **tourist office** (tel. 98 584 64 84) is small but helpful (open July-Sept. 20 Tu-Su 10am-2pm and 4-8pm). U.K. natives Jim and Peter at **Hotel Torrecerredo** (tel. 98 584 66 40) organize hiking/off-road excursions. They also dole out detailed trail guides for short hikes from Arenas; get one, because it's easy to get temporarily lost. Caja de Asturias has an **ATM.** For **police,** call the Guardia Civil in Carreña de Cabrales (tel. 98 584 50 04). The **post office** is up the street toward Cangas from the bus stop (open M-Sa mornings). The **postal code** is 33554.

ACCOMMODATIONS AND FOOD Since many of Arenas's visitors settle down in campsites, the town has few reasonable *hostales.* **El Castañeu** (tel. 98 584 65 73) is near the tourist office (singles 1500ptas; doubles 4000ptas; triples 4500ptas; cheaper in off-season). **Naranjo de Bulnes Camping** (tel. 98 584 65 78), 1km east on Crta. AS-14, has both a campsite (600 per person, 550 per car and per tent) and cabins (1-2 people 5500ptas; each additional person 1000ptas). It also has a cozy TV room, cafeteria, bar, shower facilities, and reams of info on hiking and assorted mountain sports. (Singles 3500ptas.) Spelunkers should ask about trips to **Cueva Jou de Alda,** a fascinating nearby cave.

A few grocery-*queso de Cabrales*-postcard shops make a killing selling essentials. For a *menú* (900ptas), try **Restaurante Castañeu,** under the pensión. For a lot of cozy after-dinner atmosphere, **Bar La Panera** has the look and the feel of an alpine lodge, perched on a small hill to the left of Banco Bilbao Vizcaya.

HIKES The area's hiking trails begin 6km away, in **Poncebos.** The walk to the trailhead is breathtaking, and after an all-day hike it's relatively easy to get a ride back to Arenas from tired fellow hikers. If you're looking to get an early start on the trail, two hostels in Poncebos, **Hostal Poncebos** (tel. 98 584 64 47) and **Hostal-Restaurante-Bar Garganta del Cares** (tel. 98 584 64 63), keep comfortable, scenic rooms. (Both *hostales:* singles 2000ptas, doubles 4000ptas.) Check with the tourist office about **refugio** options.

Poncebos marks the start of one of the Picos's most famous trails, the 12km **Ruta del Cares.** Hewn and blasted out of mountain and sheer rock faces, at points the gorges' vertical walls drop straight down to the Río Cares 150m below. After a steep, rocky climb, the trail descends gradually behind small waterfalls and through tunnels opening onto spectacular views of lush cliffs and the river far below. In July and August, start early to avoid crowds and to see (almost) tame mountain goats. **Poncebos-Bulnes** is a shorter and less-traveled path that leads south along the Río Tejo to **Bulnes,** a microscopic, roadless village. The blistering hike takes one-and-a-half hours out and one hour back, and is actually more difficult than the Ruta del Cares. If Bulnes

Trouts of the Trade

The pristine waters and shiny white creekbeds characteristic of the Picos may yield a few glimpses of fish cruising along in their natural state, but don't count on restaurants serving them up on your plate. Although *trucha* (trout) is a staple of every mountain *mesón menú*, it has probably been trucked in from afar. The eco-laws of the protected Picos region preclude large commercial takes. Restaurateurs claim to have access to black market local stock for "special occasions," but they don't advertise it, and they probably don't know you well enough to let you in on the deal. Sans local connections, the best way to sink your teeth into the real thing is to catch and cook them yourself. Otherwise, the trout on most *menús*, usually fried unless you request *a la plancha* (grilled), is still quite good.

seduces you, consider tucking in at the **Albergue de Bulnes** (tel. 98 536 69 32). It has 20 beds in three rooms, a bar, a library, games, showers, guides, and meals (1400ptas per person, with breakfast 2000ptas; reservations suggested). The **Poncebos-Camarmeña** path shoots straight up a cliff on the way to terrific views.

A killer 17km hike, the **Poncebos-Invernales de Cabao-Naranjo de Bulnes** route (10-12hr.), crawls to Invernales de Cabao, then inches 9km more to the Picos's most famous mountain, **Naranjo de Bulnes.** From here you can see all the major *picos* in the area as well as the blue waves of the Cantabrian Sea in the distance.

▓ Potes

The cobbled streets of Potes (pop. 2000), while quiet and snow-bound in winter, shimmer in summer with city-fleeing climbers. This way-station between excursions to the southeast and central Picos, though surrounded by beautiful peaks, overdoes its touristy charm. Typical Asturian specialty shops crowd the town center, tempting visitors with overpriced walnut honey and do-it-yourself *fabada* kits.

PRACTICAL INFORMATION Palomera **buses** (tel. 942 88 06 11) travel from Santander and back (2½hr., 3 per day, 900ptas), stopping along the way at San Vicente de Barquera. Buses run to and from Fuente Dé (45min., 3 per day, 185ptas), but the timing makes this trip almost a full-day adventure. Coming into town, Palomera buses stop twice—once in front of Hotel Rubio, and again farther into town across from Pl. Jesús de Monasterio and the tourist office. They leave from the *plaza* near the tourist office. The **tourist office,** C. Independencia, 30 (tel. 942 73 07 87), in the old church, has general info about the region, though very little on Potes itself. They have a list of mountain refugios with contact information. (Open daily in summer 10am-1pm and 4-7:30pm; in winter 10am-2pm and 4-6pm.)

Wentura (tel. 942 73 21 61), at the end of C. Dr. Encinas toward Panes, organizes expeditions. (One-day **mountain bike rental** 2200ptas; 3hr. horseback trip 4600ptas; Paragliding 7000ptas; Canyon descending—combining swimming, rappelling, and loads of adrenaline—5000ptas.) **Bustamante,** C. Dr. Encinas, 10, sells **maps** and guidebooks. **Change money** at Caja de Madrid, Pl. Jesús de Monasterio (open M-F). The **post office** is across from Pl. Jesús de Monasterio (open M-Sa mornings).

ACCOMMODATIONS AND FOOD Several *hostales* and *pensiones* line the main road. The cheapest rooms fill early in the day, so consider reserving in advance. **Hostal Lombraña,** C. el Sol, 2 (tel. 942 73 05 19), through a passageway off the main road, offers capacious rooms, some overlooking the river. (Singles 2600ptas, with bath 3200ptas; doubles 3200ptas, with bath 3900ptas; IVA not included.) **Casa Cayo,** C. Cántabra, 6 (tel. 73 01 50), has quaint rooms in its old wing, and bright modern ones in the new part. Enjoy in-room TVs, phones, bathrooms, and a cozy lounge with an even bigger tube. Look for their sign on your right as you walk from second bus stop to town. (Singles 3000ptas; doubles 6000ptas; triples 7000ptas. Cheaper in off-season.) Closer to Panes off C. Dr. Encinas and under the tweeting canaries, **Fogon de Cus** (tel. 942 73 00 60) has sunny, airy rooms (singles 2000ptas; doubles 4000ptas;

cheaper in off season). There are also several *casas de labranza* (farm houses for rent) in the area. Ask at the tourist office for details.

There's no official camping in Potes proper. The closest site is first-class **Camping La Viorna** (tel. 942 73 20 21), about 2km up the road to Monasterio Santo Toribio. Besides its restaurant, supermarket, and swimming pool, it also helps organize hiking, climbing, mountain biking, spelunking, and horseback excursions. (475ptas per person, car, and tent. Open Semana Santa-Oct. 30.) Five kilometers down the road from Potes to Fuente Dé is **Camping San Pelayo.**

The road through town brims with cafes and restaurants. Classy **Restaurante El Fogón de Cus** (tel. 942 73 00 60) is in a quiet corner below the eponymous *pensión.* Its *menú* (1150ptas) of soup, *fabada,* and macaroni nourishes famished hikers. **Supermercado Lupa** is near the second (main) bus stop (open M-Sa).

EXCURSIONS Lucky for the touristophobe, there are many different opportunities to get out of Potes and explore some of the fascinating surrounding areas. The first and most popular is **Fuente Dé,** where a mind-blowing 800m *teleférico* glides up the lunar-like mountain face to a fancy *parador* and spectacular views. (Open daily July-Aug. 9am-8pm; Sept.-June 10am-6pm. 800ptas, round-trip 1300. Under 10: 500ptas; 300ptas.) There are usually huge lines for the lift in the middle of summer. From the top, it's a 4km walk to **Refugio de Aliva** (tel. 942 73 09 99). Don't be fooled by the name—it's a *parador* (singles 5000ptas, doubles 7500ptas). To return to road-level, retrace your steps to the *teleférico* or walk (3hr.) to **Espinama.** In early July, a rowdy **festival** brings horse racing and dancing to Aliva. Three **buses** per day also traverse the 23km route from Potes to Fuente Dé.

Urdón, 15km north of Potes and on the road to Panes, is the start of a challenging hike to **Treviso,** a tiny town with far more chickens than humans. Trail details (steepness and turns) are on posters all over Potes. The town lies about 6km away (4hr.).

Another option for outings from Potes is **Peña Sagra,** about 13km east and a two-hour walk from the towns of **Luriezo** or **Aniezo.** From the summit, you can survey all the Picos and the sea 51km away. On your way down, visit **Iglesia de Nuestra Señora de la Luz,** where the beautifully carved patron saint of Picos lives 364 days a year. The Virgin, known affectionately as *Santuca* (tiny saint), is honored on May 2.

The town of **Panes,** on the routes to Santander and Cabrales, is near some spectacular scenery. The Potes-Panes drive through the **Desfiladero de Hermida** (a sharp gorge carved by the Río Deva) is stunning, but the terrifying continuation of that route to Cabrales has been reported to induce vomiting.

ASTURIAN COAST

Plunging eucalyptus forests in the west and rolling pastures in the east characterize calm Asturian coast. Summer brings swarms of suntan-seeking Spaniards to the beautiful beaches here. But the true Asturians can always be picked out by their spectacular *sidra*-pouring skills—much to every tourist's appreciation.

■ Llanes

The secluded, monument-speckled coves of Llanes are home to some of the most popular beaches on the Asturian coast. In the summer months, the entire town heads for the waterside as parties spread across its more than thirty beaches.

PRACTICAL INFORMATION The bus and train stations are at opposite ends of town. ALSA-Turytrans runs **buses** to: Cangas de Onís (1¾hr., 1 per day, 600ptas); Santander (2hr., 11 per day, 900ptas); Oviedo (2hr., 6 per day, 1000ptas); and Madrid (1 per day, 4000ptas). To reach the town center from the **bus station** exit, take a left and go down C. Cueto Bajo to the post office, then turn left and keep going. **Trains** chug from the FEVE station (tel. 98 540 01 24), at the end of Av. Estación, to Santander (2hr., 2 per day, 810ptas) and Oviedo (2½hr., 5 per day, 885ptas).

The busy **tourist office** (tel. 98 540 01 64) hands out maps in the 13th-century tower on C. Alfonso IX, around the corner from the yellow Ayuntamiento. (Open in summer M-Sa 10am-2pm and 5-9pm; Su 10am-3pm; in winter M-F 10am-2pm and 4-6:30pm, Sa 10am-1:30pm and 4:30-6:30pm.) Change money at **Banco Central Hispano,** C. Nemesio Sobrino, a block past the Ayuntamiento (open M-F 8:30am-2:30pm). In an **emergency,** dial 091 or 092. The **Policía Municipal** (tel. 98 540 18 87) is on C. Nemesio Sobrino. The **post office** (tel. 98 540 11 14) is on C. Pidal; from the tourist office, head left in the direction of the bus station. (Open M-F 8:30am-2:30pm, Sa 9:30am-1pm.) The **postal code** is 33500.

ACCOMMODATIONS AND FOOD

Rooms fill early in the day during the summer. **Casa del Río,** Av. San Pedro, 3 (tel. 98 540 11 91), is near the beach in a cute red house behind light blue iron gates. To get there, face the Ayuntamiento, hang a left to the first real street, San Pedro. Del Río has communal bathrooms and wonderful rooms, some with *two* balconies. (Singles 2000-2500ptas; doubles 4000-6000ptas; triples 6000-7000ptas.) **Pensión La Guía,** Pl. Parres Sobrino, 1 (tel. 98 540 25 77), lies beneath the stone archway in the thick of the action. (Singles 2500-3500ptas; doubles 4000-7000ptas; triples 6000-9000ptas; all rooms with bath; open Semana Santa-Oct.) **Campers** can pick and choose from nearby sites. First-class camping **Las Barcenas** (tel. 98 540 15 70), with showers and currency exchange, sits 200m past the bus station, heading toward Santander. The view of the Picos in the distance helps you forget your neighbor is four feet away. (July-Aug. 475ptas per person, 450ptas per car, 550ptas per tent. Sept. and June 425ptas per person, 400ptas per car, and 500ptas per tent. Reception daily 8am-11pm. Open June-Sept.) They also rent four-person *refugios* (cabins) with bunks but no blankets. **El Brao** (tel. 98 540 00 14), a large campsite with showers, currency exchange, cafeteria, and supermarket, is a mere 15m outside town, past the bus station; go past Las Barcenas, then turn left. (470ptas per person, per tent, and per car. Reception daily 8:30am-midnight. Open June-Sept.)

Besides many small grocery stores spotting the main street, the large **El Árbol** has a branch on the plaza at the intersection of C. Manuel Romano and C. Román Romano (open M-Sa). Next door, independent **Café del Árbol** bakes its own bread and serves an affordable *menú* on the *terraza*. Reasonably priced outdoor cafes cluster in Manuel Cué, a tiny street off C. Muelle that runs parallel to the river. **El Pescador, Colón,** and **Puerta del Sol** each serve a seafood-focused *menú*.

SIGHTS

No buts about it, the main attraction here is the beach. **Playa de Sablón** and **Playa Puerto Chico** host beach parties all summer long on their small, wavy shores. Ask at the tourist office for directions to other spots, or just wander on your own. **Paseo de San Pedro,** an elevated grassy path along a bluff above Playa Sablón, is perfect for a quiet picnic. Plateresque fans should peek at the **Iglesia de Santa María del Conceyu's** early 16th-century altar and ornate (but badly worn) portal. *(Open for mass M-F 7:30pm, Sa 11am, 8, and 9pm, Su 11:30am, 1, and 7pm.)* Violets creep across the walls of the white church in summer.

CANTABRIA

Picturesque fishing villages and popular beach towns await visitors on the soft, sandy shores of Cantabria. Quiet dairy farming towns plug away slightly inland. Served by La Cantábrica buses, all make pleasant excursions from Santander, the wealthy capital and transportation hub of Cantabria.

ASTURIAS & CANTABRIA

■ Santander

In 1941, an enormous fire gutted Santander (pop. 200,000), Cantabria's capital. Local visionaries rebuilt this peninsular city with cosmopolitan predilections. A slew of trendy beaches and promenades, a swanky casino, and an upscale shopping district helped them achieve their commercial dreams. The comfort of having a streamlined beach alongside modern facilities makes Santander a favorite seaside resort among European professionals, while an active fisherman's wharf adds a touch of urban charm to the blandness of Santander's more industrialized areas. Artists and scholars from the Universidad Internacional Menéndez Pelayo keep things lively in the off season.

ORIENTATION AND PRACTICAL INFORMATION

This slender, elongated city sits on the northwest side of a bay. The small **Plaza Porticada** is its heart. **Avenida de Calvo Sotelo** becomes **Paseo de Pereda** to the east and runs along the waterfront. Buses and trains arrive at **Plaza de Estaciones**, about six blocks west of Pl. Porticada. Beach activity centers in **El Sardinero**, a neighborhood in eastern Santander. The beach is bordered by lengthy **Avenida Reina Victoria** and **Avenida de Castaneda**. Midway along the Sardinero beachfront lies the **casino** in **Plaza de Italia**. The best way to navigate Santander's sprawling streets is to take the municipal bus; ask at the tourist office for a detailed schedule.

Transportation

Flights: Aeropuerto de Santander (tel. 942 25 10 07 or 942 25 10 04), 4km away. Daily to Madrid and Barcelona. Accessible by taxi only (1300-1500ptas). **Iberia,** Po. Pereda, 18 (tel. 942 22 97 00). Open M-F 9am-1:30pm and 4-7pm.

Trains: Pl. Estaciones, on C. Rodríguez. **RENFE station** (tel. 942 28 02 02). Info open 7:30am-11pm. Santander is the north terminus of one RENFE line. For service to points north, take FEVE to Bilbao and then pick up RENFE again. To: Palencia (2¼hr., 8 per day, 1455-2200ptas); Valladolid (5hr., 8 per day, 1855-2600ptas); Madrid (7hr., 3 per day, 3900-4200ptas); Salamanca, with a change at Valladolid (7hr., 5 per day, 3100-3900ptas). **RENFE ticket office,** Po. Pereda, 25 (tel. 942 21 23 87). Open M-F 9am-2pm and 5-7pm, Sa 9am-1:30pm. **FEVE station** (tel. 942 21 16 87). Info open 9am-2pm and 4-7pm. To Bilbao (2½hr., 3 per day, 910ptas) and Oviedo (5hr., 2 per day, 1610ptas).

Buses: (tel. 942 21 19 95), Pl. Estaciones, across C. Rodríguez from the train station. Info open M-Sa 8am-10pm, Su 9am-9pm. To: Santillana del Mar (45min., 7 per day, 270ptas); San Vicente (1½hr., 12 per day, 540ptas); Llanes (2hr., 10 per day, 825ptas); Bilbao (3hr., 24 per day, 900-1495ptas); León (3½hr., 1 per day, 2740ptas); Oviedo (4hr., 8 per day, 1710ptas); Madrid (6hr., 6-9 per day, 3255-4550ptas); La Coruña (12hr., 2 per day, 4750ptas).

Ferries: Brittany Ferries, Muelle del Ferrys, near the Jardines de Pereda. To Plymouth, England (2 per week, 13,000-15,000ptas, plus 1400ptas for seat reservation). Get tickets at Modesto Piñeiro (tel. 942 36 06 11), at the ferry station. Info open M-F 9am-3:30pm and 4:30-7:30pm. In summer reserve 2 weeks ahead. **Las Reginas** (tel. 942 21 66 19), from Embarcadero by the Jardines de Pereda. Across the bay to Pedreña and Somo (45min., in summer departs every 15min., round-trip 340ptas). Tours of the bay (1½hr., in summer 3-6 per day, 625ptas).

Public Transportation: Municipal buses run throughout the city (frequent service in July-Aug. from between 6 and 8am to midnight, in Sept.-June from between 6 and 8am to 10:30pm, 100ptas). Buses #1, 3, 4, 5, 7, and 9 run between the city center and El Sardinero (departs every 15min. from around 6am-midnight, 110ptas).

Taxis: Radio Taxi (tel. 942 33 33 33).

Car Rental: Avis, C. Nicolás Salmerón, 3 (tel. 942 22 70 25). Must be at least 23 and have had license for at least one year. From 9000ptas per day. Open M-F 8am-1pm and 4-7:30pm, Sa 9am-1pm.

Tourist and Financial Services

Tourist Office: (tel. 942 21 61 20), Jardines de Pereda. From the stations, follow C. Calderón de la Barca into the park; the office is off Po. Pereda. Maps and info on Santander and Cantabria. English spoken by a team of uniformed models. Open daily July-Sept. 9am-2pm and 4-9pm; Oct.-June 9am-1:30pm and 4:30-7:30pm. Other offices in the ferry station and El Sardinero across from Pl. Italia.

Budget Travel: TIVE, C. Canarias, 2 (tel. 942 33 22 15), a 20min. walk northwest from the center. Or take bus #5 just off Av. General Camilo Alonso Cela. Travel discounts and flights. ISIC 700ptas. HI card 1800ptas. Open M-F 9am-2pm.

Currency Exchange: Banco Central Hispano, on C. Calvo Sotelo across from the post office. Open May-Sept. M-F 8:30am-2:30pm; Oct.-Apr. M-F 8:30am-2:30pm, Sa 8:30am-1pm.

American Express: Viajes Altair, C. Calderón de la Barca, 11 (tel. 942 31 17 00; fax 942 22 57 21). Standard services and mail-holding for members. Open M-F 9:30am-1:30pm and 4:30-8pm, Sa 10am-1:30pm.

Local Services

Luggage Storage: At the train station, by the counter at the ticket window (lockers 400ptas). Open daily 7am-11pm. At the bus station (lockers 300ptas). Open daily 7:30am-10:30pm.

English Bookstores: Estudio Santander, C. Calvo Sotelo, 23. A random selection of English novels, not particularly cheap. **Hispano Argentina,** San Francisco, 13 (tel. 942 21 17 65). 2 small shelves of American "classics." Open M-F 9:45am-1:30pm and 4:30-8pm, Sa 9:45am-1:30pm.

Laundromat: El Lavadero, C. Mies del Valle, 1 (tel. 942 23 06 07), just off C. Floranes, west of the train station. Wash 350ptas. Dry 200ptas per 6kg load. Soap 50ptas. Open M-F 9:30am-1:30pm, Sa 5-8pm.

Emergency and Communications

Emergency: dial 091 or 092. **Police:** Pl. Verlade (tel. 942 33 73 00 or 942 22 07 44). **Hospital: Hospital Valdecilla-Cantabria** (tel. 942 20 25 20).

Internet Access: Libro Viejo, C. Perines, 19 (tel. 942 23 57 06). 500ptas for first 30min., 300ptas for each additional 30min. Open daily 6pm-2am.

Post Office: Av. Alfonso XIII (tel. 942 21 26 73; fax 942 31 02 99), near the Jardines de Pereda on the water. Open for stamps, Lista de Correos, and **fax** M-F 8:30am-8:30pm, Sa 9:30am-2pm. **Postal Code:** 39080.

ACCOMMODATIONS AND CAMPING

Santander offers very few accommodation options during July and August, especially during the July festivals. Call ahead to avoid getting stuck without a room. The highest hotel densities are near the market, around **Calle Isabel II,** across from the train station on **Calle Rodríguez,** and along elegant **Avenida Castros** in **El Sardinero.** If you've come with the beach in mind, the splendor is worth the schlep.

The Monolith at Calle Rodríguez, 9

Cross the street and turn right from the train station to reach this haven for backpackers. The *hóspedes* on the sixth floor offer more informal (no keys) lodging at the same prices as the *pensiones* below.

Fonda María Luisa, C. Rodríguez, 9, 5th fl. (tel. 942 21 08 81). Rustic, carved headboards and lively wallpaper. Singles 1500-2500ptas; doubles 3000-4500ptas.

Pensión Angelines, C. Rodríguez, 9, 1st fl. (tel. 942 31 25 84). Exuberant color scheme of tan, beige, or brown. Singles 1600-2000ptas; doubles 2500-4000ptas. Bath down the hall.

Pensión Fernando, C. Rodríguez, 9, 3rd fl. (tel. 942 31 36 96). Elmer Fudd fantasy land—beware the boar's head in the foyer and animal skin rugs in some of the newly tiled rooms. Singles 1600-2600ptas; doubles 3000-4500ptas; triples 4500-6000ptas. Bath down the hall.

City Center

Hostal Real, Pl. Esperanza, 1, 3rd fl. (tel. 942 22 57 87), in the peach building at the end of C. Isabel II. Curtained hallways lead to large doubles with wood-carved ceilings and balconies. Spartan, tiny singles upstairs. Singles 2000-3500ptas; doubles 3000-5000ptas; triples 5000-6750ptas.

Hostal Botín, C. Isabel II, 1, 1st fl. Satiny beds, huge rooms, and balconies overlooking the bustling market. Sept.-July singles 1900ptas; doubles 3200ptas; triples 4320ptas; quads 6720-8320ptas. Aug. singles 3100ptas; doubles 5200ptas; triples 7020ptas; quads 6720-8320ptas.

El Sardinero

Hostal-Residencia Luisito, Av. Los Castros, 11 (tel. 942 27 19 71), one block from the beach. Take bus #4 to Hotel Colón (Pl. Brisas); then walk on El Sardinero's rose-colored sidewalks to the beach (3min.). Spacious yellow rooms, many with huge balconies overlooking the owners' mini-orchard. Singles 2250ptas; doubles 3900ptas. Breakfast 205ptas. Baths in the hall. 7% IVA not included. Open July-Sept.

Pensión Soledad, Av. Castro, 17 (tel. 942 27 09 36), next door to Luisito. Simple, plain, large rooms with sinks. Breakfast in the dining room downstairs. Singles 2150ptas; doubles 3850ptas. Breakfast 200ptas. 7% IVA not included.

Camping: 2 back-to-back sites on the scenic bluff called Cabo Mayor, 3km up the coast from Playa de la Magdalena. Both are *enorme*. Take the Cueto-Santander bus (110ptas) from in front of the Jardines de Pereda. **Camping Bellavista** (tel. 942 39 15 36). A 1st-class site on the beach. 600ptas per person and per car, 650ptas per tent. Reception daily 8am-midnight. **Camping Cabo Mayor** (tel. 942 39 15 42). Pool and tennis courts. 500ptas per person and per car, 550ptas per tent. Prices rise in August. Reception daily 8am-11pm. Open mid-June to Sept.

FOOD

Seafood restaurants crowd the **Puerto Pesquero** (fishing port), grilling up the day's catch on a small stretch at the end of **Calle Marqués de la Ensenada.** From the train station, walk eight blocks down C. Castilla and turn left on C. Héroes de la Armada; cross the tracks and turn right after about 100m (20min.). Be cautious walking here alone at night—some areas are deserted. Closer to the city center, reasonable *mesones* and bars line **Calles Hernán Cortés** and **Daóiz y Velarde,** and **Plaza Cañadío.** The **Mercado de Plaza Esperanza,** C. Isabel II, sells produce near Pl. Generalísimo, behind the police station (open M-F 8am-2pm and 5-7:30pm, Sa 8am-2pm). There's a lively lingerie/sandal/bikini/clothes market here every Thursday. **Supermercado BM,** C. Calderón de la Barca, 12, is one block from the train and bus stations (open M-F 9am-1:30pm and 5:15-7:45pm, Sa 9am-2pm).

Bar Restaurante La Gaviota (tel. 942 22 10 06), on C. Marqués de la Ensenada, at the corner of C. Mocejón in the *barrio pesquero* (fisherman's neighborhood). Fresh grilled sardines (12 for 600ptas) and *paella de mariscos* (1000ptas) are delicious specialties. Watch your 1000ptas *menú* being prepared smack in the middle of the cavernous dining room. Open daily 1-4:30pm and 7:30-11:30pm.

La Cueva (tel. 942 22 20 87), on C. Marqués de la Ensenada, next door to La Gaviota. Cozier than its neighbors, with many options on its *menú* (900ptas). *Chipirones encebollados* (baby squid fried in onion, 675ptas). The gigantic frying pan outside brims with steaming *paella* and lures many a hungry sailor to blissful surrender. Open daily noon-5pm and 7:30pm-midnight.

Bar-Restaurante Silverio, Pl. Esperanza, 1 (tel. 942 21 31 25). *Raciones* at the bar are innovative and reasonable. Weird Egyptian statues. Stewed quail 400ptas. Garlic snails 500ptas. Open daily 12:30-4pm and 8pm-midnight.

Cervecería Aspy, C. Hernán Cortés, 22 (tel. 942 31 45 95), off C. Lope de Vega. Elegant dining room has it all: wine rack, paintings, and a signed photo of golf star Seve Ballesteros. *Platos combinados* 650-850ptas. *Menú* 1000ptas. Open daily 8am-1am.

Restaurante Cruz Blanca, C. Hernán Cortés, 16 (tel. 942 36 42 95), just up from Aspy. *Arroz a la cubana* and chicken breasts pack their 1000ptas *menú.* Prussiaphiles dig the Teutonic decor, *bier,* and bratwurst (450ptas). Open daily noon-4pm and 8pm-midnight. Standing room only after 9pm.

SIGHTS AND BEACHES

Santander's sights scene is small on architecture, big on seaside beauty, and balanced by pleasant free museums. Jutting into the sea between El Sardinero and Playa de la Magdalena, the **Península de la Magdalena** is crowned by an early 20th-century neo-Gothic fantasy **palacio.** *(Peninsula de Magdalena open daily 8am-10pm. The palacio does not have scheduled visiting hours.)* Originally Alfonso XIII's summer home, the cliff-top palace is a classroom building and dorm for the university. The peninsula is a **park** of beautiful lawns, hedges, and gardens overlooking the sea. A **mini-zoo** on the edge of El Sardinero has a polar bear, sleepy lions, pot-bellied penguins, and honking sea lions.

Santander's **beaches** are truly spectacular. **El Sardinero's** powdery sands seem to stretch on forever. But in July and August, every inch is covered by fluorescent tourist sardines marinating in cocoa butter. Less crowded beaches—**Playas Puntal, Somo,** and **Loredo**—line the other side of the bay. In summer, Las Reginas **boats** (tel. 942 21 56 19) run across to the beaches of Pedreña and offer 80-minute sailing tours around the bay (see **Practical Information: Ferries,** p. 216).

The **Museo Marítimo** (tel. 942 27 49 62), C. San Martín de Bajamar, stands beyond the *puerto chico* (little port). *(Open mid-June to mid-Sept. Tu-Sa 11am-1pm and 4-7pm, Su 11am-2pm; mid-Sept. to mid-June M-Sa 10am-1pm and 4-6pm, Su and holidays 11am-2pm. Free.)* The top floors chart regional fishing-boat evolution, while the bottom floor, quaking under mammoth whale skeletons, highlights the sea's living creatures. *Far Side*-esque formaldehyde fishes in contorted positions peer out from glass jars, and a small aquarium shows life at sea levels. Paleolithic skulls and tools rattle at the **Museo de Prehistoria y Arqueología,** C. Casimiro Sáinz, 4 (tel. 942 20 71 05). *(Open daily June 15-Sept. 15 10am-1pm and 4-7pm; Sept. 16-June 14 9am-1pm and 4-7pm, Su and holidays 11am-2pm. Free.)* Artifacts from and photographs of the Cuevas de Altamira (see p. 221) are truly spectacular, especially considering the sad fact that they're probably as close as you'll get to the real thing. The 1941 fire scorched the **cathedral's** facade (tel. 942 22 60 24), but the downstairs chapel is worth visiting for its unusually low Romanesque vaulting. *(Open M-F 10am-1pm and 4-7:30pm, Sa-Su and holidays 10am-1pm and 4:30-9pm.)*

ENTERTAINMENT

As night falls, Santander goes Bacchanalian. Students forget their studies in the area around **Plaza de Cañadío, Calle de Pedrueca,** and **Calle de Daóiz y Velarde,** and up the hill from Pl. Cañadío on **Pasadillo de Zorilla.** At **Blues** on C. Gomez Areña in Pl. Cañadío, jazz and blues fans mingle under the huge plastic statues of a jazz combo.

In **El Sardinero,** tourists, students, and spirits mingle all night long. **Plaza de Italia** and nearby **Calle de Panamá** are neighborhood hotspots. The **Gran Casino** on Pl. Italia brings out the card shark in everyone. Passport, proper dress (pants and shoes), and a minimum age (18 to gamble) are required. (Open daily 7pm-4am. 600ptas.) Students crowd bars **Gloria** and **Albatros** on C. Panamá. The **Cotton Pub,** set back in the hillside off C. Panamá, draws a thirtysomething crowd to its black and white *terraza.*

The August **Festival Internacional de Santander** brings myriad music and dance recitals. The events culminate in the **Concurso Internacional de Piano de Santander.** Daily classical **concerts** ring through Pl. Porticada; recent festivals have featured the London Symphony Orchestra and the Bolshoi Ballet. High-priced tickets are sold in booths on Pl. Pereda and Pl. Porticada; a precious few tickets are sold for under 1500ptas. For concert info, contact the Oficina del Festival, Palacio de Festivales de Cantabria (tel. 942 21 05 08 or 942 31 48 53; fax 942 31 47 67), on C. Gamzo. Concerts rock the **Palacio,** a grand pink- and white-striped auditorium. The

ASTURIAS & CANTABRIA

barrio pesquero celebrates its patron of fishing safety, Santiago, the third week in July with sardine fests, soccer tournaments, music, carnival rides, and fireworks. For info about concerts, festivals, and movies, check the local paper *El Diaro de las Montañas* (110ptas).

■ Near Santander

Since only a handful of people get into the Cuevas de Altamira each day, many spelunk in the lesser known town of **Puente Viesgo,** about 30km south of Santander. The **Cuevas del Castillo** (tel. 942 59 84 25) display paintings nearly as well preserved as those in Altamira. *(Open daily 10am-12:15pm and 3-7:15pm. 225ptas, E.U. citizens free.)* Continental-Auto **buses** stop in Puente Viesgo en route from Santander to Burgos. *(45min., 2 per day, 480ptas.)*

▓ Santillana del Mar

Known as the town of the three lies, Santillana del Mar is neither *Santa* (holy), *llana* (flat), nor *del mar* (on the sea), yet the entire town is still a national historical monument, crowded with stone houses and cobblestone streets. Opportunistic residents have converted their entryways into souvenir shops and offer *comida típica* (typical cuisine). The winding side passages, however, are blissfully quiet, save for the whistling of flirtatious parrots from geranium-covered balconies.

PRACTICAL INFORMATION Santillana is a short trip from Santander (26km away) by **bus.** La Cantábrica (tel. 942 72 08 22) sends buses from Pl. Estaciones in Santander (45min., 4-6 per day, 270ptas). The **tourist office,** Pl. Mayor, supplies a bus schedule, a map, and a frank opinion of the region's sights (open in summer daily; in winter M-Sa). When the bus drops you off (and continues to Comillas), go to Hotel Santillana on the corner, then head uphill. Change money at **Banesto,** also in Pl. Mayor (open M-F 9am-2pm). In **medical emergencies,** dial 942 82 06 94. Go left exiting the tourist office for the **post office** (open M-F 8:30am-2:30pm, Sa 9:30am-1pm). The **postal code** is 39330.

ACCOMMODATIONS AND FOOD Santillana's few budget rooms fill fast in July and August, so consider daytripping from Santander. Don't be lured by the *hostales* on the highway near the bus stop; **casas particulares** in town are sure to be cheaper. The tourist office can help find one. **Pensión Angélica,** C. Hornos, 3 (tel. 942 81 82 38), off Pl. Mayor (next to the post office, look for the crescent *habitaciones* sign), is as beautiful inside as out. Lacy blue rooms with animal rugs. (Singles 3500ptas; doubles 3500-4000ptas; triples 4500-5000ptas.) Nearby **Posada Santa Juliana,** C. Carrera, 19 (tel. 942 84 01 06), is equally endearing. Some rooms have exposed wood beams, and all have TVs, quilts, and down pillows. (Doubles July-Aug. 5000-8000ptas; Sept.-June 4000ptas.) Less than 1km away on the road to Comillas is **Camping Santillana** (tel. 942 81 82 50). It would be easy to mistake this deluxe first-class site for a *parador;* it boasts a panoramic view of the town, a supermarket, shiny cafeteria, pool, miniature golf, and tennis courts. (575ptas per person, 525ptas per tent and per car. Mini-golf 350ptas per person per hr., tennis 600ptas per person, per hr. Reception daily 8:30am-8:30pm.)

Most everyone who comes to **Casa Cossío** (tel. 942 81 83 55), Pl. Abad Francisco Navarro, across from the church, orders the 1100ptas *menú* for the ribs. Grilled with a tasty paprika sauce in the open fire downstairs, they're served in the shadows of stone walls and bubbly lobster tanks. (Bar open daily 10:30am-11:30pm. *Comedor* open daily 1-4pm and 8-11pm.) **Bodega El Porche,** Pl. Juan Infante, has sandwiches (300-500ptas) and *platos combinados* (600-800ptas; open daily 1-3:30pm and 8-10:30pm). The **SPAR** supermarket at Pl. Rey, near C. Jesús de Tagle heading away from Pl. Mayor, sells staples (open daily 9am-10pm).

SIGHTS Emblazoned above the door of virtually every house is a heraldic shield proclaiming the rank and honor of former noble residents. Many residents have converted their doorways into storefronts, selling ceramics and local delectable (if overpriced) sweet milk and *bizcocho* (sponge cake).

The **Colegiata de Santa Juliana,** a 12th-century Romanesque church, occupies one end of C. Santo Domingo. *(Open daily. 300ptas also gets you into the Museo Diocesano.)* The charming ivy-covered **claustro** has some fragmented capitals featuring a mixture of biblical figures and fantastical beasts. The 12th-century reform of the Cistercian Order prohibited the representation of any human form on pillars—hence the ropy vegetable patterns.

In a town that's a museum itself, the **Museo Diocesano** is one of only two official exhibits. *(Open daily. 100ptas.)* Religious art and artifacts are spread throughout the harmonious Romanesque cloister and corridors of the Monasterio Regina Coeli. The **Museo Regional,** in the Casa del Aguila y la Parra, across from the *parador,* is Santillana's other indoor exhibition. *(Open daily 10am-1:30pm and 4-7:30pm. Free.)* The eclectic collection contains everything from Roman artifacts to 19th-century tools, with a few stuffed boars' heads thrown in for good measure.

■ Near Santillana del Mar: Cuevas de Altamira

Bison roam, horses graze, deer prance, and goats butt heads on the ceilings of the limestone **Cuevas de Altamira** (2km from Santillana del Mar), sometimes called the "Sistine Chapel of Paleolithic Art." The large-scale (over 2m in length) polychrome paintings are renowned for their scrupulous attention to naturalistic detail (such as genitalia and the texture of hides) and resourceful use of the caves' natural texture; in 1985 the caves were declared a UN World Heritage site. The 25 animals are so realistic and carefully wrought that they were thought to be a hoax when first discovered at the end of the past century. To catch a glimpse, you must obtain written permission from the Centro de Investigación de Altamira, Santillana del Mar, Cantabria, Spain 39330 (tel. 942 81 80 05). **You must write one year in advance.** Send a photocopy of your passport. Since the caves have been debased by excessive tourism, only 20 people per day get to take the tour (15min., departs Tu-Su 9:30am-2:30pm). If you don't get in, join fellow unfortunates in the **museum** of prehistory (open M-Sa 10am-1pm and 4-6pm, Su 10am-1pm; free). To walk here, follow the signs from Santillana past the abandoned **Iglesia de San Sebastián,** a hotspot for picnickers. Make a detour through the streets of Herrán, and turn right into the corn field at the wooden barrier on the other side of town.

■ Comillas

Comillas is an understated resort favored by Spain's noble families, who retain their modest palaces along with their anachronistic titles. Among the few places in historically leftist northern Spain where people can legitimately refer to themselves as count or duchess, the town has a conservative nature diluted only by thousands of young people tracking sand through the streets each summer.

ORIENTATION AND PRACTICAL INFORMATION At 18km from Santillana del Mar and 49km from Santander, Comillas is an easy daytrip. La Cantábrica **buses** (tel. 942 72 08 22) run between Santander and San Vicente de la Barquera, stopping at Comillas, and an equal number return (6 per day, Sept.-June 3 per day, from Santander 275ptas, from San Vicente 105ptas). The **train** goes as far as Torrelavega, where you can catch a bus to Comillas.

The **tourist office** is on C. Maria del Piélago, 2 (tel. 942 72 07 68). From the bus stop near the Palacio, continue on the main road past the turn-off for the beach, into the plaza, and then uphill (still on the main road) one block, at which point a sign directs you left. If you got off the bus at the top of the hill, walk down 25m until the sign directs you right. The office stocks bus and excursion info, as well as a list of *hos-*

tales. Their only map costs 100ptas; stare at their copy for five seconds or pick one up at your *hostal*. (Open May-Sept. M-Sa 10am-1pm and 5-9pm, Su 11am-1pm and 5-8pm.) The **post office,** C. Antonio López, 6, is on the main road uphill from the tourist office turnoff (open M-Sa mornings). The **postal code** is 39520.

ACCOMMODATIONS AND FOOD Comillas's budget lodgings are few and fill quickly in summer. Call ahead, especially if you're coming during the *fiestas* in July. At **Pensión Bolingas** (tel. 942 72 08 41), C. Gonzalo de la Torre de Trassiera El Corro, downhill from the tourist office, the enthusiastic owner leads you through the lobby to relatively bare, clean rooms, some with gorgeous views of the hillside university. Enjoy a sack lunch at the tables in her garden. (Doubles 3400ptas; open June 15-Sept. 15.) **Pensión la Aldea** (tel. 942 72 10 46), one block off C. Infantas, opposite Supermercado Greyfuss, greets guests with more serene browns and grays (doubles with bath 3500ptas; cheaper off-season). **Camping de Comillas** (tel. 942 72 00 74) is a first-class site on the water. It has a supermarket, cafeteria, laundromat, and beautiful views. (500ptas per person, 1600ptas per *parcela.* Open June-Sept.) Nearby **Camping El Helguero** (tel. 942 72 21 24), 3km east in **Ruiloba,** rivals the Comillas site, parading the same amenities, plus a swimming pool (475ptas per person, per car, per tent; reception daily 9am-11pm. Open Semana Santa-Oct.). The La Cantábrica bus from Santander to San Vicente de la Barquera stops at the grounds.

While upscale restaurants dot the small streets of Comillas, less-expensive bars and *cafeterías* jockey for your business in Pl. Corro (1000ptas *menús*). The **Restaurante-Pizzeria Quo Vadis,** C. Marqués de Comillos, has *molto* Italian treats (pastas 650-900ptas, pizzas 600-1000ptas). **Supermercado Greyfuss,** at the turnoff to the beach, replenishes beachgoers with fluids and fruits (open M-Sa 9am-2pm and 4:30-8pm). **El Árbol,** on C. Cervantes near Pl. Joaquin de Piélago, has longer hours (open M-F 9am-9pm, Sa 10am-2pm).

SIGHTS AND ENTERTAINMENT The broad **Playa Comillas,** adjacent to the port, or the longer, quieter beach of **Oyambre,** 4km away with huge waves for surfers, are both part of a series of beaches in the **Parque Natural de Oyambre.** Ask for directions to various other quieter beaches.

Many petite **palaces** and an enormous Jesuit **university,** the site of summer classes, rise in Gothic splendor, framed by sea and the Picos de Europa. The neo-Gothic **Palacio de Sobrellano,** on the outskirts of town, dominates a pretty park. Inside, the **Capilla-Pantheon** contains furniture designed by Gaudí. *(Open W-Su. Free.)* More Gaudí awaits at multi-colored **El Capricho,** a small stone-and-sunflower-tiled palace that has metamorphosed into a fine (read: expensive) restaurant. It's one of only three Gaudí creations outside of Cataluña.

Between July 15 and 18, the **fiestas** go up in a blaze of fireworks and spur-greased pole-walking, goose-chasing, and dancing in the plaza.

■ San Vicente de La Barquera

The view from San Vicente's (pop. 4800) crescent beach scans a rapidly growing jigsaw of modern hotels and older houses, governed by a hillside castle framed by the Picos de Europa. It's truly gorgeous, but this might be as close as you want to get to San Vicente in July and August, when tourists crowd the town's every street and ring every postcard rack with clicking cameras and humming camcorders.

PRACTICAL INFORMATION Reaching this paradise/zoo is not that difficult, although traffic may be horrendous on warm weekends. **ALSA-Turytrans buses** (tel. 942 21 56 50) run between Santander and San Vicente in July and August (1½hr., 12 per day, 535ptas). **La Cantábrica** buses (tel. 942 72 08 22) travel between Santander and San Vicente (1½hr., July-Aug. 6 per day; Sept.-June 3 per day, 550ptas), stopping at Comillas (20min., July-Aug. 6 per day; Sept.-June 3 per day, 105ptas). For La Cantábrica buses, buy tickets on board. For ALSA-Turytrans buses, buy a ticket or scan a schedule at Fotos Noly, on C. Miramar next to the post office.

The **tourist office** (tel. 942 71 07 97), on Av. Generalísimo (the main street running perpendicular to the waterfront), helps with accommodations (open Semana Santa and July-Sept. W-Sa 9:30am-2pm and 4-9pm; closed in winter). For **medical** situations call the Centro de Salud (tel. 942 71 24 50 or 942 71 24 56). In an **emergency,** dial 091 or 092. The **post office,** C. Miramar, 16 (tel. 942 71 02 19), sits along the waterfront (open M-F 8:30am-2:30pm, Sa 9:30am-1pm). The **postal code** is 39540.

ACCOMMODATIONS AND FOOD Budget accommodations in San Vicente are a precious few, so in August it's best to make reservations weeks ahead. But even during peak season room-hawkers are sure to approach backpackers with *habitación* offers: just remember to ask for their prices (try bargaining) before following them. In town, **Hostal La Paz,** C. Mercado, 2 (tel. 942 71 01 80), off the plaza at the intersection of C. Miramar and C. Generalísimo, has big airy rooms with sinks and balconies. (Singles 2500-2800ptas; doubles 3000-4200ptas, with showers and TV 4000-5000ptas.) Along the port, awash in its own flower gardens, sprawls the *parador* of San Vicente's lodgings, **Hostal La Barquera** (tel. 942 71 00 75), which sports enormous rooms, some with balconies. Although you might feel as if you need a lantern in this nostalgic setting, this place has electricity, perfectly functional plumbing, and overlooks San Vicente's exquisite beach. (Doubles with bath 7000ptas; reception at Hotel Miramar.) **Camping El Rosal** (tel. 942 71 01 65) is near the beach. From the bus stop, cross the bridge and keep going (20min.). Stores surround the second-class site, including a lively *cafetería* and bar, supermarket, laundry, currency exchange, and camping equipment rental. They also provide info on excursions. (600ptas per person and per car, 500ptas per tent. Reception daily 10am-10pm. Open April-Oct.)

Most restaurants off C. Miramar and Av. Generalísimo serve 900-1000ptas *menús* featuring regional cuisine. Tiled **Café Bar Folia,** Av. Generalísimo, 7, serves fresh seafood *raciones* at reasonable prices. **Supermercado Greyfuss,** C. El Arenal, 9, a block off Av. Generalísimo, stocks picnic supplies (open M-Sa).

SIGHTS For those venturing downtown, the 12th-century church-fortress **Santa María de los Angeles** shows off a handsome Romanesque portico and the Renaissance tomb of Antonio Corro, the infamous 16th-century Grand Inquisitor. The 8th-century **castillo** above town can be seen from the outside only. For silicon-enhanced fun, try beaches **Merón** and **El Rosal.** From the expansive sands of Playa Merón, a 15-minute walk over the 15th-century stone Puente de la Maza leads to fabulous views of the Picos de Europa.

ASTURIAS & CANTABRIA

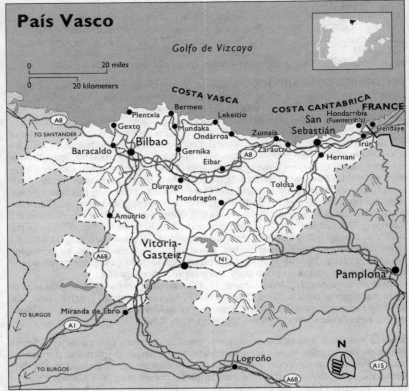

País Vasco

Golfo de Vizcaya

COSTA VASCA

COSTA CANTABRICA

FRANCE

Hondarribia (Fuenterribia)

San Sebastián

Hendaye

Plentxia

Bermeo

Lekeitio

Gexto

Mundaka

Ondárroa

Zumaia

Zarautz

Irún

Bilbao

Gernika

Eibar

Hernani

Baracaldo

TO SANTANDER

A8

A8

Durango

Tolosa

Mondragón

Amurrio

Vitoria-Gasteiz

N1

Pamplona

A68

TO BURGOS

Miranda de Ebro

A1

N

TO BURGOS

Logroño

A68

A15

0   20 miles

0   20 kilometers

País Vasco (Euskadi, Basque Country)

"Before God was God and the rocks were rocks, the Basques were Basque." País Vasco is officially composed of the provinces Guipúzcoa, Alava, and Vizcaya, but those who identify themselves as Basque are not restricted by political boundaries, extending Euskadi (Basque Country) into parts of Navarra and southwestern France. The varied landscape of País Vasco resembles a nation complete unto itself, combining large, cosmopolitan cities, verdant hills, industrial wastelands, and quaint fishing villages. The people are united by their deep attachment to the land, an almost spiritual appreciation of fine food and drink, and immense cultural and national pride.

Many believe that the Basques are the native people of Iberia, their culture and language dating back several millennia. Nationalistic sentiment runs back a number of centuries. The 18th-century abolition of the Basque *fueros* (or ancient rights of self-government), the Basques' military defeat in the late 19th-century Carlist wars, and more recently, Franco's attempts to suppress Basque identity were seen as threats to their traditional values, provoking a renewal of pre-modern identities.

During Franco's regime, Euskadi eta Askatasuna (ETA; Euskadi and Liberty) began an anti-Madrid terrorist movement that has lasted over 30 years. Most Basque Nationalists are critical of ETA and the affiliated party, Herri Batasuna (the United People), and instead prefer to seek independence through politics. Demonstrations and other forms of Nationalist activity do, however, occur. Although violence has generally been directed at Spanish government officials, in 1996 ETA targeted heavily touristed areas in order to arouse international attention.

The preservation of cultural identity is a universally shared sentiment of the Basques. Although Castilian Spanish is the predominant language, the Basque's *Euskera* has enjoyed a resurgence of popularity since Franco's death. Centuries-old sporting traditions such as rowing (*traineras*), *cesta punta* or *pelota vasca* (often known outside of Spain as *jai-alai*), and rural sports like log chopping continue to thrive. Each region also claims its own distinctive heritage in music and dance. Few traditions, however, match the breadth and sophistication of Basque cuisine. Spaniards prize *bacalao a la vizcaina* (salted cod in a tomato sauce), dishes *a la vasca* (in a delicate parsley-steeped white wine sauce), and *chipirones en su tinta* (baby squids in their own ink). *Tapas* in País Vasco, considered regional specialties, are called *pintxos*; locals wash them down with *sidra* (cider) and the local white wine, *txacoli*.

Tourist offices stock a guide for Compostelan pilgrims and art lovers called *Los Caminos de Santiago* (The Roads to Saint James) and the comprehensive *Guía de Recursos* (Guide to Tourist Resources). Rural tourism is being heavily promoted by regional authorities and tourist offices in Basque cities have brochures on *agroturismo*. In general, buses are faster and cheaper than trains in the region.

🖐 HIGHLIGHTS OF PAÍS VASCO

- Frank O. Gehry's shiny new **Guggenheim Museum Bilbao** (see p. 229).
- *Pintxos (tapas)* at **San Sebastián's** bars after a day at the beach (see p. 233).
- A wander along the marina in the refreshingly simple seaside town of **Hondarribia** (see p. 239).

■ Bilbao (Bilbo)

Graced with the marvelous new Guggenheim Museum, Bilbao (pop. 1,000,000) is finally overcoming its reputation as a bourgeois, business-minded industrial center. The economic engine of the Basque country, Bilbao has been making people wealthy since the 16th century, when its shipbuilding industries and coastal location made it a key trading link between Castile and Flanders.

The city has bought respectability by investing heavily in the arts and its own infrastructure. Economic booms in the 19th century bestowed wide boulevards lined by grandiose buildings, while 20th-century success has showered the city with a new subway system, an overhauled airport, a new bridge, and a stylish riverwalk project, all executed by renowned international architects. One of the finest collections of paintings in all of Spain resides in its Museo de Bellas Artes. It is the Guggenheim, though, that seems most likely to launch Bilbao's rise to international prominence. Although Bilbao will not win any beauty pageants for its urban sprawl, this up-and-coming city is quite a place to see.

ORIENTATION AND PRACTICAL INFORMATION

It's wise to get yourself a map, as Bilbao's sights are far-flung. The city's main artery, the **Gran Vía (de Don Diego López de Haro),** leads east from the oval **Plaza de Federico Moyúa** to the **Plaza de España (Plaza Circular),** the axis for many important stops and stations. Past Pl. España, you will cross **Ría de Bilbao** on **Puente del Arenal,** which deposits you on the **Plaza de Arriaga,** the entrance to the **casco viejo** and home of the tourist office.

Transportation

Flights: Airport (tel. 94 486 93 00), is 10km from Bilbao in Sondica (Sondika). Take the Bizkai Bus A-3247 from C. Sendeja next to the Ayuntamiento, on the left after crossing Puente Arenal into the old town (40min., departs every 40min., 125ptas).

Bilbao

ACCOMMODATIONS
D Hostal Arana
A Hostal-Residencia Jofra
E Pensión Ladero
F Pensión la Fuente
C Pensión Mardones
B Pensión Mendez

URIBARRI

Basílica de Begoña

Casa Consistorial

Puente del Ayuntamiento

Muelle del Arenal

Muelle de Ripa

Campo de Mallona

S. Nicolas

Plaza Nueva

CASCO VIEJO

Museo Vasco

Catedral de Santiago

Puente del Arenal

Teatro Municipal Arriaga

Mercado de la Ribera

Puente de S. Antón

Estación de Atxuri

BILBAO LA VIEJA

Puente de la Ribera

Puente de la Merced

Estación de Santander

Funicular de Monte Archanda

Paseo Campo Volantín

Muelle de Uribarte

Alameda de Mazarredo

Estación de Abando

Plaza de Toros

Estación de Amézola

Guggenheim Museum

Puente Príncipes de España

ABANDO

PL. DEL ENSANCHE

MOYUA

ABANDO

C. Elcano

Alhóndiga

Teatro Campos Elíseos

ANSA

Museo de Bellas Artes

La Unión

Parque de Doña Casilda de Iturriza

Paseo Clave

Gran Vía de Don Diego López de Haro

INDAUTXU

INDAUTXU

Alameda del Doctor Araliza

PL. DE SAGRADO CORAZÓN

Universidad de Deusto

Puente de Deusto

SAN PEDRO DE DEUSTO

Río de Bilbao

Astilleros Españoles Euskalduna

Campo de San Mamés

SAN MAMÉS

Cybercafe

Termibús

Avenida de Sabino Arana

PAÍS VASCO

300 yards
300 meters

What the Devil Are They Txpeaking?

Linguists still cannot pinpoint the origin of *Euskera,* an agglutinate non-Indo-European language. Its commonalities with Caucasian and African tongues in terms of root structures suggest that prehistoric Basques may have migrated from the Caucasus through Africa. Historically referred to by other Spaniards as *la lengua del diablo* (the devil's tongue), *euskera* has come to symbolize cultural self-determination. Only half a million natives speak the language, chiefly in País Vasco, the regions of Guipúzcoa and Vizcaya, and northern Navarra. Franco banned *euskera* and forbade parents to give their children Basque names. Nowadays usage spreads through *ikastolas* (all-Basque schools), TV, and Basque publications. As a result, mostly the young and elderly speak the language. The younger generations listen to rock music in *euskera,* conduct conversations in the language, and give their kids traditional names such as Iñaki and Idoya.

Served by all major European airlines. **Iberia office,** C. Ercilla, 20 (tel. 94 424 10 00; airport tel. 94 471 12 10), at C. Colón de Larreátegui. Open daily 6:30am-10:30pm.

Trains: Bilbao has 3 train stations, each with at least 2 names; the major ones huddle near Puente del Arenal. By 2005, the city hopes to have completed **Estación Intermodal,** which will house all major bus and train lines under one roof. Meanwhile...

RENFE: Estación de Abando/del Norte, Pl. España, 2 (tel. 94 423 86 23). Info open 7am-9pm. To: Salamanca (5½-6½hr., 2 per day, 3400ptas); Madrid (6-9hr., 2 per day, 4100-4300ptas); Barcelona (9½-11hr., 2 per day, 4800-5000ptas).

FEVE: Estación de Santander, C. Bailén, 2 (tel. 94 423 22 66). From Pl. España walk down C. Navarra toward the river and take a right just before the bridge. A huge gilded building on the water. FEVE is less convenient than RENFE. Info open M-F 7am-9pm. To Santander (2½hr., 3 per day, 910ptas).

Ferrocarriles Vascongados/Eusko Trenbideak (FV/ET; tel. 94 433 95 00). **Atxuri Station,** Cl. Atxuri, 6-8. Follow river south from Pl. Arriaga. To: Gernika (1hr., 17-20 per day, 300ptas). Also to the beach towns of Mundaka and Bermeo.

Buses: Most bus companies are based at the **Termibús terminal,** C. Gurtubay, 1, (tel. 94 439 50 77; M: San Mamés), on the west side of town. The tourist office can help unravel the sometimes confusing bus system. To get to Pl. Arriaga from the station take the Metro to Casco Viejo, exiting to Pl. Unamuno. Take a right on C. Sombreria and the first right onto C. Correo.

ANSA (GETSA, VIACAR), C. Autonomía, 17 (tel. 94 444 31 00). From Pl. España, go down C. Hurtado de Amézaga to Pl. Zabálburu, bearing right on C. Autonomía for 2 blocks; enter through Bar Ansa. To: Burgos (2hr., 4 per day, 1420ptas); Madrid (4½hr., 9-15 per day, 3245ptas); Barcelona (7hr., 4 per day, 4750ptas); León (7hr., 1 per day, 3125ptas).

Compañía Automóviles Vascongados (CAV), C. Hurtado de Amézaga, Túnel de RENFE (tel. 94 454 05 44). In Estación de Abando (see Trains, above). To Gernika (45min., departs every 15-30min., 300ptas).

ENATCAR, Termibús terminal (tel. 94 439 51 11). To Salamanca (5 hr., M-Sa 2 per day, 3110ptas).

PESA, Termibús terminal (tel. 94 424 88 99; info tel. (902) 10 12 10). To San Sebastián (1hr., 8-23 per day, 1060ptas).

La Unión, C. Henao, 29 (tel. 94 424 08 36). From Pl. España walk down Gran Vía to Pl. Federico de Moyúa, turn right on Alameda de Recalde and go 2 blocks to C. Henao. To: Vitoria-Gasteiz (1hr., 14-22 per day, 655ptas). Leaving from Termibús (tel. 94 439 50 77) to: Haro (1hr., 2-5 per day, 1020ptas); Logroño (1¾ hr., 3-5 per day, 1435ptas); Pamplona (2hr., 4-6 per day, 1535ptas).

ALSA Grupo, Termibús terminal (tel. 902 42 22 42). To: Santander (3½hr., 6 per day, 820ptas); Zaragoza (4hr., 4-6 per day, 2430ptas); La Coruña (5½hr., 4 per day, 3060ptas).

Public Transportation: Bilbao opened an attractive and user-friendly **metro** (tel. 94 425 40 25) in Nov. 1995. Look for 3 red circles, all interlocking, to find entrances. The system has 1 line with terminal points in the suburbs. Hang on to your ticket after entering—you'll need it again to exit. Travel within 1 zone 135ptas; 2 zones 160ptas; 3 zones 190ptas. 10-trip ticket within 1 zone 800ptas; 2 zones 950ptas; 3

zones 1150ptas. Trains run M-Sa 6am-2am, Su 7am-11pm. **Bilbobús** (tel. 94 475 82 00) runs 23 lines across the city (6am-11:30pm; 110ptas, 10-ride coupon 645ptas). **Bizkai Bus** connects Bilbao to suburbs and the airport in Sondica.

Taxis: Teletaxi (tel. 94 410 21 21). **Radio Taxi Bilbao** (tel. 94 444 88 88). Some cluster directly behind the Teatro Arriaga. To airport 2500ptas.

Car Rental: Europcar, C. Licenciado Poza, 56 (tel 94 442 22 26). Must be at least 21. 6000ptas per day. Open M-F 8am-1pm and 4-7:30pm, Sa 9am-1pm.

Tourist and Financial Services

Tourist Office: Oficina de Turismo de Bilbao, Pl. Arriaga (tel. 94 416 00 22; fax 94 416 81 68; http://www.bilbao.net). Fabulous English-speaking staff gives out an excellent map and tri-monthly bulletin of events. Open M-F 9am-2pm and 4-7:30pm, Sa 9am-2pm, Su 10am-2pm.

Currency Exchange: Banks and ATMs are everywhere. **Banco Central Hispano** sits in Pl. España. Open in summer M-F 9am-2pm; in winter M-Th 9am-5:30pm, F-Sa 9am-2pm.

American Express: Viaca, Alameda de Recalde, 68 (tel. 94 444 48 62), off C. Autonomía. Open M-F 9am-1:30pm and 4:30-7:30pm, Sa 10am-1pm.

El Corte Inglés: Gran Vía, 7-9 (tel. 94 424 22 11), on the east side of Pl. España. Distributes **maps.** They also offer novels, guidebooks, haircuts, a **supermarket,** a cafeteria, a restaurant, and **currency exchange.** Open M-Sa 10am-9pm.

Local Services

Luggage Storage: In Estación de Abando, small lockers are 400ptas, large 500ptas. Open daily 5am-11:30pm. In Termibús, 100ptas a day. Open daily 8:30am-8pm.

English Bookstores: Casa del Libro, C. Colón de Larreátegui, 41 (tel. 94 424 07 04). A terrific selection. Open M-F 9:30am-1:30pm and 4-8pm, Sa 9:30am-1:30pm.

Bisexual-Gay-Lesbian Organizations: EHGAM, Escalinatas de Solokoetxe, 4 (tel. 94 415 07 19). Open M-F 8-10pm. On weekends it's a gay and lesbian disco.

Youth Services: TIVE, C. Iparraguirre, 3. ISICs for sale. Open M-F 9am-2pm.

Emergency and Communications

Emergency: dial 088. **Police: Municipal** (tel. 94 420 50 00), C. Luis Briñas.

24hr. Pharmacy: Check any pharmacy's door, or call the municipal police.

Medical Services: Hospital Civil de Basurto, Av. Montevideo, 18 (tel. 94 441 88 00 or 94 442 40 51). **Ambulance:** tel. 94 473 16 34.

Internet Access: Cybercafé Antxi (tel. 94 441 04 48). Luis Briñas, 13. Great decor. 500ptas per hr., 250ptas per 30min. Open M-F 9am-1:30pm and 4-9:30pm.

Post Office: Main office, Alameda Urquijo, 19 (tel. 94 422 05 48; fax 94 443 00 24). Walk 1 block down Gran Vía from Pl. España and turn left after El Corte Inglés; it's on the corner of C. Bertendona. Open for info, **fax,** and Lista de Correos M-F 8:30am-8:30pm, Sa 9:30am-2pm. **Postal Code:** 48005.

ACCOMMODATIONS

At any time other than during the August festival season (when rates can be higher than those listed below), it shouldn't be hard to find a reasonably priced room. The tourist office has a list of recommended budget *pensiones,* most of which are in the *casco viejo.* Starting points are **Plaza Arriaga,** at the base of the bridge and down the stairs to the right, and **Calle Arenal,** which runs up to the left.

Pensión de la Fuente, C. Sombrería, 2 (tel. 94 416 99 89). From C. Arenal, turn right on C. Correo, follow it 2 blocks past Pl. Nueva, and then turn left. Friendly owner rents pleasant high-ceilinged rooms with big furniture. Singles 1700-2000ptas; doubles 3000ptas, with bath 4000ptas. Laundry service. Heating, TV extra.

Pensión Ladero, C. Lotería, 1, 4th fl. (tel. 94 415 09 32). From Pl. Arriaga, take C. Bidebarrieta and turn left onto C. Lotería. Very clean, all with TV and olive green bedspreads. Singles 2000ptas; doubles 3000ptas.

Pensión Mendez, C. Santa María, 13, 4th fl. (tel. 94 416 03 64). From the bridge, turn right on C. Ribera; C. Santa María is on the left as the street turns. 5 floors insulate the *pensión* from raging nightlife below. Some of the clean, comfy rooms are huge, most come with balconies and sinks. Singles 2000ptas, with bath 4000ptas; doubles 3000ptas, with bath 6000ptas; triples 4500ptas.

Hostal Mardones, C. Jardines, 4, 3rd fl. (tel. 94 415 31 05). From the bridge, turn right onto C. Bidebarrieta and right again. Lovely rooms, some with balconies, all with polished wood floors and marble sinks. Delightful owners. Singles 3000ptas, with bath 4000ptas; doubles 3500ptas, with bath 4500ptas. Prices vary; call ahead.

Hostal-Residencia Jofra, C. Elcano, 34, 1st fl. (tel. 94 421 29 49), in the new city. From Pl. España, walk 5 blocks down C. Hurtado de Amézaga past Estación de Abando and turn right. Pleasant rooms with flowered bedspreads and sinks off a quiet street. Singles 2200ptas; doubles 3300ptas. Open Sept.-June.

Hostal Arana, C. Bidebarrieta, 2 (tel. 94 415 64 11), at Pl. Arriaga. Faded red carpeted stairway and pastel hallways lead to clean rooms with sinks, some overlooking the river (for what it's worth). Singles 3000ptas, with bath 4000ptas; doubles 4500ptas, with bath 5500ptas. Prices don't include 7% IVA.

FOOD

Restaurants and bars in the *casco viejo* offer a wide selection of local dishes, plus *pintxos* and *bocadillos* aplenty; the modern city has more variety but less down 'n' dirty ambience. **Mercado de la Ribera,** on the bank of the river heading left from the tourist office, is the biggest indoor market in Spain. It's worth a trip even if you're not eating. Upstairs, on tables at the far end of the building, local farmers sell just-picked produce at lower, bargainable prices. (Open June 15-Sept. 15 M-Sa 8am-2pm; Sept. 16-June 14 M-F 8am-2pm and 4:30-7pm, Sa 8am-2pm.) Groceries are on the second floor of a massive **Simago,** Pl. Santos Juanes (open M-Sa 9am-9pm).

Casco Viejo

Aitxiar, C. María Muñoz, 8 (tel. 94 415 09 17). Ambrosial food in a lively setting. Try the *merluza a la vasca* (hake in a wine, garlic, and parsley sauce with clams) and you'll know why this dish is so popular. The *tostadas* dessert is the French toast of your dreams, with anis-scented cream. Lunch *menú* 1000ptas. Open Tu-Su 9am-2am. Meals served 1-3:30pm and 8-11pm. Visa.

Restaurante Kaltzo, C. Barrencalle Barrena, 5 (tel. 94 416 66 42). A super pick on a street lined with many inexpensive options. Sedate dining room. 1000ptas *menú del día* changes daily. Open M 1-4pm, Tu-Sa 1-4pm and 8-10:30pm. Visa, MC.

Restaurante Juanak, C. Somera, 10 (tel. 94 415 99 79). Snug bar with lively 20-something crowd and 54 *bocadillos* that include vegetarian options (350-500ptas). Available to go. Open daily noon-midnight.

New City

Restaurante Zuretzat, C. Iparraguirre, 7 (tel. 94 424 85 05), down the street from the Guggenheim. The 1100ptas *menú* (served 1-4pm) is a jewel that varies daily. Try the incredibly sweet and rich pudding *a la caramel.* Open M-F 7am-10:30pm, Sa-Su 8:30am-11pm. Meals served daily 1-4pm and 8:30-11pm.

Restaurante-Bar Al Jordan, C. Elcano, 26 (tel. 94 410 42 55), on a side street near the train station. Middle Eastern food with vegetarian options. Veg and non-veg *menú* 975ptas. Breakfast with mint tea, Arabic pastries, and fresh juice 300ptas. Open M-Th 8am-1am, F-Sa 10am-3am. Visa, MC, AmEx.

Café La Granja, Pl. España, 3 (tel. 94 423 08 13), opposite Estación de Abando. Cavernous classic cafe. Spanish breakfast with juice 400ptas. 1400ptas *menú* daily 1:30-4pm. Open M-F 7am-midnight, Sa 9am-2:30am, Su noon-midnight.

SIGHTS

The Guggenheim
Av. Abandoibarra, 2. Tel. 94 435 90 80. For pictures, see http://www.guggenheim.org/bilbao.html or our snazzy cover photo. Open Tu-Su 11am-8pm. 700ptas, seniors and students 350ptas, under 12 free. 900ptas includes entrance to Guggenheim and Museo de Bellas Artes. Free guided tours Tu-F 11:30am, 1 (English), 4 (English), and 6pm, Sa-Su 1 and 4pm (English). Sign up 30min. before tour at Info Desk.

Frank O. Gehry's **Guggenheim Museum Bilbao,** inaugurated in October of 1997, can only be described as breathtaking. Lauded in the international press with every superlative imaginable, it has catapulted Bilbao straight into cultural stardom. Constructed mainly out of titanium, limestone, and glass in a series of interconnected pieces, the US$100 million building, with its undulating curves and multiple levels, resembles something between a blossoming silver flower, a ship about to set sail on the river it sits aside, and a building. The amazingly light and airy interior features a towering atrium and a series of non-traditional exhibition spaces, including a gargantuan 130 by 30m hall. The museum currently hosts rotating exhibits drawn from the Guggenheim Foundation's collection but will gradually acquire its own international sampling of 20th-century works. Sleek black-suited staff slap hospital bracelets on the streams of visitors filing through the door—may you enjoy your stay.

Museo de Bellas Artes, Museo Vasco, and Elsewhere

Not to be overlooked by its flashier cousin, Bilbao's **Museo de Bellas Artes,** Pl. Museo, 2 (tel. 94 439 60 60), hoards aesthetic riches behind an unassuming facade. *(Open Tu-Sa 10am-1:30pm and 4-7:30pm, Su 10am-2pm. 400ptas, seniors and students 200ptas, under 12 free. Wednesdays free.)* An impressive collection ranges from the 12th to 20th century and features excellent 15th- to 17th-century Flemish paintings, works by El Greco, Zurbarán, Goya, Gauguin, Francis Bacon, Velázquez, Picasso, and Mary Cassatt, as well as numerous canvases by Basque painters. Follow C. Elcano to Pl. Museo, or take bus #10 from Puente del Arenal.

Dip into Basque culture and history at the **Museo Vasco,** C. Cruz, 4 (tel. 94 415 54 23). *(Open Tu-Sa 10am-1:30pm and 4-7pm, Su 10:30am-1:30pm. 300ptas, students 150ptas, seniors and under 12 free. Thursdays free.)* Housed in a 17th-century building with a beautiful cloister, its exhibits cover hand-weaving, blacksmiths, pastoral life, and the sea. The museum is in the old city; walk past Pensión de la Fuente away from C. Correo to Pl. Miguel de Unamuno, where C. Cruz appears.

The best view of Bilbao (which isn't saying a lot) is from the *mirador* on **Monte Archanda,** north of the old town. For the funicular to the top (departs every 15min., 100ptas), turn left from Pl. Arenal with your back to the new town and follow the riverside road past the Ayuntamiento. On Po. Campo de Volantin, turn right on C. Espalza and zig-zag left at its end.

A short Metro ride leads to beaches north of the city at **Plencia** (Plentzia) or at **Sopelana** along the way. Plencia's beach is a bit rough. **Getxo** lies just a little nearer to the surf; its illuminated **Puente Colgante** (suspension bridge) fords the river, leading to a spate of all-night bars. Revelers who miss the midnight train will find themselves obliged to taxi home (2000-2500ptas). The **surfing** mecca of **Mundaka** lies along the coast, past the Urdaibai Biosphere Reserve.

ENTERTAINMENT

Like most Spanish cities, Bilbao has a thriving after-dark bar scene especially (but not exclusively) on the weekends. In the **casco viejo** revelers spill out into the streets, sip their *txikitos* (small glasses of beer or wine characteristic of the region), especially on **Calle de Barrencalle (Barrenkale).** Teenagers and twenty-somethings also jam at **Calle de Licenciado Poza** off Av. Sabion Arana on the west side of town. For a mellower scene, people-watch at one of the city's elegant 19th-century cafes like **Café Boulevard,** C. Arenal, 3 (tel. 94 415 31 28), one of Miguel de Unamuno's old haunts. Upscale Bilbao retires to the **Jardines de Albia** to get its *copas.*

The massive blowout *fiesta* in honor of Nuestra Señora de Begoña takes place during **Semana Grande** (actually 9 days, beginning the weekend after Aug. 15). Music, theater, and bullfights climax with fireworks. Documentary filmmakers the world over gather from October to November for the **Festival Internacional de Cine Documental de Bilbao.** Until then, you can watch original version (not dubbed) movies regularly at **Cines Abra,** C. Nicolas Alcorta, 5 (tel. 94 443 65 21). During the summer, there are free **concerts** every Sunday evening at the bandstand in the Parque Arenal. For current goings-on, pick up *Bilbao Guide* from the tourist office.

PAÍS VASCO

¡Basta ya!

On July 10, 1997, at 4pm Miguel Ángel Blanco, 29, disappeared near his home-town from his city council seat of Ermua in the Basque province of Vizcaya. The kidnappers were members of the Basque separatist group ETA (Eskadi ta Askata-suna). ETA's plea was that the government stop incarcerating ETA members in the Canary Islands rather than in their home nation. The demand was not new, and the government was still adamant in refusing it. The dramatic circumstances of the act riveted the nation's attention and stirred its passions. On July 12, at 5pm, the news came: Ángel Blanco had been shot in the head and died soon after in the hospital. The anger over the murder was palpable. Heads of government in País Vasco expressed regret, outrage, and the solidarity of the Basque people against ETA. Millions took to the streets in an unprecedented display of outrage, and anti-ETA demonstrations even occurred in the País Vasco. The cry rose up across the nation: "¡Basta ya!" (Enough already!). Since then, sadly, the killings have not stopped: five Partido Popular councillors have been murdered by ETA since Blanco's death, including Manuel Zamarreño, Blanco's successor, killed by a car bomb in June of 1998. Although since Blanco's death these other incidents have failed to awaken the same unified response of outrage, the general consen-sus remains the same: violence is not the way to affect change and gain further autonomy. ETA graffiti continues to litter the walls, but occasionally it is scrawled out with writing that reads "Negotiation is the solution" instead of "Gora ETA," or "Long live ETA."

■ Gernika (Guernica)

On April 26, 1937, the Nazi "Condor Legion" released an estimated 29,000kg of explosives on Gernika, obliterating in three hours all but thirty percent of a city long considered the spiritual and historical center of the Basque country. Gernika's trag-edy marked the first mass civilian aerial bombing attack; the nearly 2,000 people who were killed that day were immortalized in Pablo Picasso's stark masterpiece *Guer-nica*, now in Madrid's Reina Sofía gallery. The eerily modern city (pop. 15,568) is in itself not much of an attraction, but for those interested in learning more about this infamous event that occurred here, it's a rewarding daytrip.

PRACTICAL INFORMATION **Trains** (tel. 94 625 11 82) journey to Bilbao (45min., 17-30 per day, 300ptas). Compañía de Automóviles Vascongados (Bizkaibus) (tel. 94 625 50 13) sends **buses** between Bilbao's Estación de Abando and Gernika (45min., departs every 15-30min., 300ptas). Hail a **taxi** by calling 94 625 10 02.

To reach the **tourist office,** C. Artekalea, 8 (tel. 94 625 58 92; fax 94 625 75 42), from the train station, walk straight two blocks up C. Adolfo Urioste and turn right onto C. Artekalea. The entrance is around the corner on C. Andra María. (Open July-Sept. M-Sa 10am-7:30pm, Su 10am-2pm; Oct.-June M-Sa 10am-1pm and 4-7:30pm, Su 10:30am-1:30pm.) In an **emergency,** call 088. **Municipal police** are on C. Artekalea, 6 (tel. 94 627 02 02). **Medical services** are on C. San Juan, 1 (tel. 94 625 42 46). The **post office** is on C. Iparragirre, 26 (tel. 94 625 03 87), immediately left as you exit the train station (open M-F 8:30am-2:30pm, Sa 9:30am-1pm). The **postal code** is 4830.

ACCOMMODATIONS AND FOOD Although there is little reason to stay the night, clean, comfortable rooms are available at **Hostal Iratxe,** C. Industria, 4 (tel. 94 989 70 71 33). If nobody's home, knock at Bar Frontón (tel. 94 625 31 34), down the street, with the same ownership as the hostal. (Singles 2000ptas, with bath 2500; doubles 3500, with bath and TV 4000.) From the train station, go up C. Urioste and turn left on C. Pablo Picasso, which becomes C. Industria.

Market mavens go to the huge round building on the pedestrian street next to the tourist office (open M-F 9am-1:30pm and 4:30-8:30pm, Sa 9am-1:30pm). **Supermer-cado Tutoricagüena** is at C. Ciudad de Berga, 2, across from the bus stop (open M-F

PAÍS VASCO

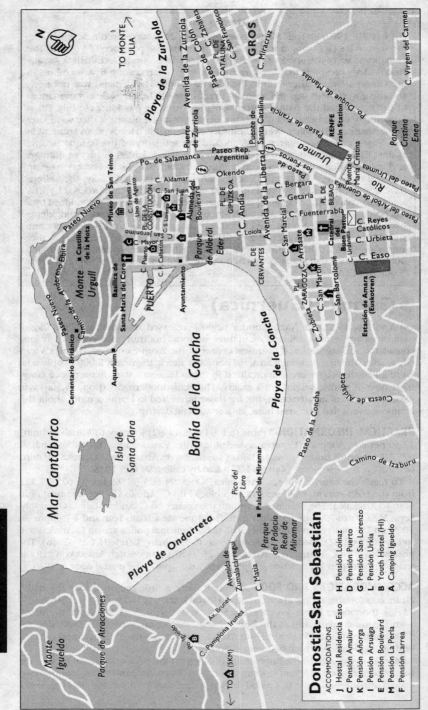

Donostia-San Sebastián

ACCOMMODATIONS

- J Hostal Residencia Easo
- C Pensión Amaiur
- K Pensión Añorga
- I Pensión Arsuaga
- E Pensión Boulevard
- M Pensión La Perla
- F Pensión Larrea
- H Pensión Loinaz
- D Pensión Puerto
- G Pensión San Lorenzo
- L Pensión Urkia
- B Youth Hostel (HI)
- A Camping Igueldo

PAÍS VASCO

9:30am-1:30pm and 5-8:30pm). Popular family-run **Restaurante Zallo Barri,** C. Juan Calzada, 79 (tel. 94 625 18 00), left off C. Urioste as you exit the train station, dishes out a tasty 900ptas *menú* (open daily 8:30am-11pm; Visa, AmEx).

SIGHTS The emotional focus of Gernika is **El Arbol.** The remains of this 2000-year old oak tree stands next to the **Casa de Juntas,** where the Vizkaya General Assembly meets. *(Casa open daily June-Sept. 10am-2pm and 4-7pm; Oct.-May 10am-2pm and 4-6pm. Free.)* For centuries the tree marked the political center of the region, where medieval Basques gathered to debate community issues and Castilian monarchs ritually swore their respect for the autonomy of the local governments and laws. The oak's off-spring, an equally august tree of 140 years, grows nearby.

Paintings and artifacts on display inside the **Museo de Euskal Herria** (tel. 94 625 54 51), on C. Allende Salazar, help fill visitors in on Basque history. *(Open Tu-Sa 10am-2pm and 4-7pm, Su 10am-1:30pm. Free.)* **Gernika Museoa,** Foru Plaza, 1 (tel. 94 627 02 13), has a moving exhibition chronicling the bombardment. *(Open daily 11am-2pm and 4-8pm. 200ptas, under 16 free.)*

Eduardo Chillida's dramatic sculpture **Gure aitaren etxea** (Our Father's House) was commissioned for the 50th anniversary of the city's bombing. It stands side by side with Henry Moore's voluptuous *Large Figure in a Shelter.* Both pose in the bucolic **Parque de los Pueblos de Europa.** *(Open daily in summer 10am-9pm; in winter 10am-7pm. Free.)* From the bus station, follow C. Adolfo Urioste as far as it goes. At the top, enter the park and cross the little wooden bridge to the right.

■ Donostia-San Sebastián

Glittering on the shores of the Cantabrian Sea, San Sebastián (pop. 180,000) is a coolly elegant city of garden avenues, ornate buildings, and radiant beaches. Ever since Isabel II chose San Sebastián as her vacation spot in 1845, it's been a popular town, particularly with Spaniards desperate to flee the heat of central Spain. The fan-shaped bay, encased by hills, floods with tan flesh in July and August, yet no tourist influx manages to dampen the city's genuinely warm, welcoming atmosphere. Locals and vacationers alike down *pintxos (tapas)* and drinks in the old quarter, which claims the most bars per square meter in the world.

Beneath its tranquil facade, San Sebastián is passionately involved with Basque Nationalism. *Euskera* is fairly widely spoken here, and there is a chance you will spot a Nationalist demonstration. Odds are better, though, that you'll encounter nothing more than a proud people preoccupied with having a good time. So just smile, try out a little *euskera,* and nod your *kaixos* and *agurs* (hellos and good-byes).

ORIENTATION AND PRACTICAL INFORMATION

Street and plaza signs are often in both *castellano* and *euskera.* The street guide on the tourist office map gives both versions in its index, so don't despair if you see "kalea" and "tx" everywhere. The **Río Urumea** splits San Sebastián in two. The city center, most monuments, and the two most popular beaches are on the peninsula on the west side of the river. The tip of the peninsula is **Monte Urgulla.** Inland is the **parte vieja** (old city), where nightlife rages and budget accommodations and restaurants cluster. South of the *parte vieja,* at the base of the peninsula, is the commercial district. In the heart of the district sits the **Catedral de Buen Pastar.** The **bus station** lies in the south of the city on Pl. Pío XII. **Avenida de Sancho el Sabio** runs to the right (north) straight toward the cathedral, ocean, and old town.

East of the river lies the **RENFE station, Barrio de Gros,** and **Playa de la Zurriola.** The west and east sides of the river are connected by three bridges: Puentes Zurriola, Santa Catalina, and María Cristina (listed from north to south). To get to the *parte vieja* from the train station, head straight to Puente María Cristina, cross the bridge, then turn right at the fountain and walk four blocks north to Av. Libertad. Turn left and follow it to the port; the *parte vieja* fans out to the right, La Concha to the left.

Transportation

Flights: Airport in Hondarribia (Fuenterrabía), 20km east of the city. **Interurbanos** buses to Hondarribia pass by the airport (45min., departs every 12min., 195ptas). Taxis cost 3200ptas. To Madrid (4 per day) and Barcelona (3 per day). **Iberia** office at the airport (tel. 943 64 12 67).

Trains: RENFE, Estación del Norte (tel. 943 28 30 89), on Po. Francia, on the east side of Puente María Cristina. Info desk open daily 7am-11pm. To: Vitoria-Gasteiz (1¾hr., 9 per day, 1500ptas); Pamplona (2hr., 2 per day, 1400ptas; take the bus—it costs half as much and takes half the time); Burgos (3½hr., 7 per day, 2500ptas); Zaragoza (4hr., 2 per day, 2700ptas); Madrid (8hr., 3 per day, 4800ptas); Barcelona (9hr., 1-2 per day, 4700ptas); Paris (8-11hr., 3 per day, 11,000ptas; change at Hendaye). **Estación de Amara (Euskotren),** Pl. Easo (tel. 943 45 01 31). Frequent commuter trains to Irún (30min., 125ptas) and Hendaye (35min., 125ptas).

Buses: Several private companies run from different points in the city. Most companies pass through the central station, on Pl. Pío XII, about 13 blocks south of Av. Libertad on Av. Sancho el Sabio. Public bus #28 goes to the center from the bus station. Buy tickets at each the office of each company. **PESA,** Av. Sancho el Sabio, 33 (tel. 902 10 12 10 or 943 47 30 85). To Bilbao (1¼hr., departs every 30min., 1060ptas) and Vitoria-Gasteiz (2hr., 1-4 per day, 1010ptas). **Continental Auto,** Av. Sancho el Sabio, 31 (tel. 943 46 90 74). To: Vitoria-Gasteiz (1½hr., 4-7 per day, 930ptas); Burgos (3-3½hr., 6-7 per day, 1825ptas); Madrid (6hr., 9-11 per day, 3685ptas). **La Roncalesa,** Po. Vizcaya, 16 (tel. 943 46 10 64). To Pamplona (1hr., 7 per day, 750ptas). **Irbarsa,** Po. Vizcaya, 16 (tel. 943 45 75 00). To Barcelona (7hr., 3 per day, 2450ptas). **Turytrans** (tel. 943 46 23 60). To Paris (11 hr., 3 per week, 7600ptas). **Interurbanos,** Pl. Guipozcoa (tel. 943 64 13 02). Pay on board. To Irún (35min., departs every 15min., 185ptas) and Hondarribia (45min., departs every 15min., 195ptas).

Public Transportation: List of routes (19 in all) available at the tourist office or call 943 28 71 00. Each trip costs 105ptas. Bus #16 goes from Alameda del Boulevard to the campground and beaches.

Taxis: Santa Clara (tel. 943 31 01 11) or **Donostia** (tel. 943 46 46 46).

Car Rental: Europcar, Estatión de RENFE (tel. 943 32 23 04; fax 943 29 07 00). Must be 21 or over. Open M-F 8am-1pm and 4-7:30pm, Sa 9am-1pm.

Mountain Bike Rental: Comet, Av. Libertad, 6 (tel. 943 42 66 37). Half-day 2000ptas, full day 3000ptas, additional day(s) 1000ptas. Open M-F 10am-1pm and 4-8pm, Sa 10am-1pm and 4-7:30pm.

Tourist, Financial, and Local Services

Tourist Office: Municipal: Centro de Atracción y Turismo, C. Reina Regente (tel. 943 48 11 66; fax 943 48 11 72), in the vast Teatro Victoria Eugenia. From the train station, turn right immediately after crossing Puente María Cristina. Continue until reaching Puente Zurriola; C. Reina Regente will be on the left. From the bus station, go down Av. Sancho el Sabio. At Pl. Centenario, bear right on C. Prim, continue for a ways, take a left on Av. Libertad, and follow it to the end. English-speaking staff, indexed map, transit and accommodations info, and a message bulletin board. Open June-Sept. M-Sa 8am-8pm, Su 10am-1pm; Oct.-May M-Sa 9am-2pm and 3:30-7pm, Sa 8am-8pm. **Regional: Oficina de Turismo del Gobierno Vasco,** Po. Fueros (tel. 943 42 62 82), is farther down the river from the above office, toward the train station. Info on Guipuzcoa, including *sidrerías* (see **Entertainment,** p. 238). Open in summer M-F 9am-1:30pm and 3:30-6:30pm, Sa-Su 9am-1pm; in winter M-F 9am-1:30pm and 3:30-6:30pm, Sa 9am-1pm.

Currency Exchange: Banco Central Hispano, Av. Libertad, 17. Open in summer M-F 8:30am-2pm; in winter M-F 8:30am-2pm, Sa 8:30am-1pm. **ATMs** dot the city.

Luggage Storage: Lockers at RENFE station, 400ptas per day. Open daily 7am-11pm. At Continental Auto, 300ptas per day. Open daily 7am-noon and 3-8:30pm.

English Bookstore: Donosti, Pl. Bilbo, 2 (tel. 943 42 21 38), 1 block west of Puente María Cristina near the cathedral. Excellent selection. Open M-F 9am-1pm and 4:30-8pm, Sa 9am-1pm. **Azoka,** San Martin, 3 (tel. 943 48 82 33), off Av. San Martín. Wordsworth Classics. Open M-Sa 10am-1:30pm and 4-8:30pm, Su 5-8:30pm.

PAÍS VASCO

Laundromat: Lavomatique, C. Iñigo, 13 (tel. 943 42 38 71), off C. San Juan. Self-service. 575ptas wash, 400ptas dry. Soap and ironing available. Open M-F 10am-1pm and 4-7pm, Sa-Su 10am-1pm.

Hiking Info: Club Vasco de Camping, San Marcial, 19 (tel. 943 42 84 79), 1 block south of Av. Libertad. Organizes excursions. Open M-F 6am-8:30pm. **Izadi,** Po. Ramón, 20 (tel. 943 29 35 20). Bookstore with hiking guides and maps, some in English. Organizes tours and rents skis, wetsuits, and hiking equipment. Open M-Sa 10am-1pm and 4-8pm.

Youth Services: TIVE, C. Tomás Gros, 3 (tel. 943 27 69 34; fax 943 32 04 94), 1 block off Pl. Euskadi, down C. Miracruz and then right. ISIC 700ptas. HI card 1800ptas. Open M-F 9am-2pm.

Emergency and Communications

Emergency: call 088. **Police: Municipal,** C. Easo (tel. 943 45 00 00).

Medical Services: Casa de Socorro, Bengoetxea, 4 (tel. 943 44 06 33). **Ambulance:** call 088.

24hr Pharmacy: Ask the **municipal police** or check p. 2 of *Diario Vasco*.

Internet Access: Elaurre Cibercafé, C. Urbiata, 12 (tel. 943 44 00 90). 250ptas per 15min., 400ptas per 30min., 700ptas per hr. Open M-Sa 10am-10pm.

Post Office: C. Urdaneta (tel. 943 46 49 14; fax 943 45 07 94), the street just south of the cathedral. Open M-F 8:30am-8:30pm, Sa 9:30am-2pm. Lista de Correos at window #3. **Postal Code:** 20007.

ACCOMMODATIONS AND CAMPING

Desperate backpackers must scrounge for rooms in July and August—particularly during San Fermines (July 6-14) and Semana Grande (starts Sunday during the week of Aug. 15). In September, while the film festival takes place, finding rooms can also be difficult. To make matters worse, many places don't take reservations in the summer. Budget options center in the **parte vieja** and around the **cathedral;** there are often a few per entryway—look for signs in doorways. The majority are excellent and reasonably priced. Solo travellers should be prepared to pay for a double; single rooms are virtually impossible to come by in the summer. The tourist office has lists of budget accommodations, and most *pensión* owners know of **casas particulares**—don't be afraid to ask for help. Owners of *casas particulares* often solicit guests at the RENFE. Be wary: such solicitations are illegal and filthy floors can go for stratospheric prices. The police will kick out those who attempt to sleep on the beach; the area is reputedly full of shifty characters anyways.

Albergue Juvenil la Sirena (HI), Po. Igueldo, 25 (tel. 943 31 02 68; fax 943 21 40 90), near the beach at the far west end of the city. Bus #24 runs from the train and bus stations to Av. Zumalacárregui (the stop in front of the San Sebastián Hotel). Bus #5 drops you off 1 street away on C. Matia. From Av. Zumalacárregui, take the street that angles toward the mountain (Av. Brunet) and turn left at its end. The hostel is the big pink building. Clean, modern, dorm-style rooms and a multilingual staff. HI members and ISIC-carriers only. In summer 1885ptas, over 26 2145ptas; in winter 1550ptas, over 26 1885ptas. Breakfast included. Lunch and dinner each 765ptas. Sheets 385ptas. Luggage storage, laundry facilities, and kitchen available. Lockout 11am-3pm. Curfew in summer daily 2am; in winter Su-Th midnight, F-Sa 2am. Reception daily 3pm-11am. Best to arrive before 11am. Visa.

In the Parte Vieja

A bit of a hike from both stations, the *parte vieja* is brimming with reasonably priced *pensiones*. Its proximity to Playa de la Concha and the port makes this area a prime nightspot; scores of *pensiones* offer a night's sleep above loud *pintxos (tapas)* bars. The smart money calls in advance. **Alameda del Boulevard,** just west of Puente Zurriola, marks the south border and is a major artery.

Pensión Amaiur, C. 31 de Agosto, 44, 2nd fl. (tel. 943 42 96 54). From Alameda del Boulevard, go up C. San Jerónimo to the end and turn left. You'll know it when you see the flower-obscured facade. The floral motif continues in pastel rooms, many with balconies facing the street or the mountains. Delightful owner is also a water conservationist—showers last 10min. Semana Santa and June 22-Sept. 21 doubles 5000ptas; triples 6500ptas. Apr.-June and Oct. doubles 3500ptas; triples 4700ptas. Nov.-Mar. doubles 3000ptas; triples 3800ptas. *Let's Go* discount 300ptas.

Pensión Loinaz, C. San Lorenzo, 17 (tel. 943 42 67 14), off C. San Juan. Attentive, English-speaking owners have bright rooms with big windows. July-Aug. doubles 4200-4700ptas; triples 6200ptas. Apr.-June doubles 3200ptas; triples 4500ptas. Sept.-Apr. doubles 2700ptas; triples 3800ptas. Singles sometimes available. 3-bedroom apartment available upstairs for groups. *Let's Go* discount. Laundry 1000ptas.

Pensión San Lorenzo, C. San Lorenzo, 2 (tel. 943 42 55 16), off C. San Juan. Cozy rooms and a fully equipped guests-only kitchen that's also a chatty community center. June-Oct. 1500-1700ptas per person. Nov.-May singles 2000ptas; doubles 2800ptas; triples 3900ptas; quads 4800ptas.

Pensión Larrea, C. Narrica, 21, 1st fl. (tel. 943 42 26 94). Simple, appealing rooms with big windows and sparkling bathrooms. July-Aug. singles 3000ptas; doubles 5000ptas; triples 6000ptas. Sept.-June singles 2500ptas; doubles 3500ptas; triples 5000ptas. Open Mar. 21-Oct.

Pensión Puerto, C. Puerto, 19, 2nd fl. (tel. 943 43 21 40), off C. Mayor. Clean rooms with big closets. Some rooms have balconies. 2000ptas per person.

Pensión Arsuaga, C. Narrica, 3, 3rd fl. (tel. 943 42 06 81), off Alameda del Boulevard. Charming, homey rooms. Doubles 4000ptas; triples 6500ptas. Breakfast 300ptas. Lunch and dinner each 1000ptas.

Pensión Boulevard, Alameda del Boulevard, 24 (tel. 943 42 94 05). Beautiful, modern rooms overlooking the leafy boulevard. Radios in all rooms, balconies in some, and a fireplace in one. In summer 2000ptas per person; in winter singles 2500ptas; doubles 3000ptas, with bath 4500ptas; triples 4000ptas.

Near the Cathedral

These *hostales* lie in the heart of the commercial zone. They tend to be quieter than those elsewhere in the city, yet still fairly close to buses, trains, port, beach, and within easy walking distance of all the action in the *parte vieja*.

Pensión Urkia, C. Urbieta, 12, 3rd fl. (tel. 943 42 44 36). Calle Urbieta borders the cathedral on the west side; the *pensión* is one block north at C. Arrasate. Polished knick-knacks and gilt mirrors in the foyer and rooms with lovely blue and white linens, full bathrooms, and TV. July-Sept. doubles 5300ptas. Oct.-June singles 3000ptas; doubles 3745ptas.

Pensión La Perla, C. Loiola, 10, 2nd fl. (tel. 943 42 81 23), on the street directly ahead of the cathedral. Grand stairway leads to attractive rooms with polished floors. All rooms have bath and TV; #7 is a gem. Friendly, English-speaking owner. July-Sept. singles 4000ptas; doubles 6000ptas. Oct.-June singles 3225ptas; doubles 3750ptas.

Pensión Añorga, C. Easo, 12, 1st fl. (tel. 943 46 79 45), at C. San Martín. Shares entryway with 2 other *pensiones*. Basic, but clean and breezy. Some rooms have TVs. July-Aug. singles 3000ptas; doubles 4000ptas, with bath 6000ptas. Sept.-June singles 2000ptas; doubles 3000ptas, with bath 4000ptas.

Hostal Residencia Easo, C. San Bartolomé, 24 (tel. 943 45 39 12). From C. San Martín, heading toward the beach, turn left on C. Easo and right on C. San Bartolomé. Near the beach. Prim beds in wooden-floored rooms with huge windows and TVs. July-Sept. 15 singles 5000ptas; doubles 5800ptas, with bath 8000ptas. Sept. 16-June singles 3000ptas; doubles 4000ptas, with bath 6000ptas.

Camping: Camping Igueldo (tel. 943 21 45 02), 5km west of town. The 268 *parcelas* (slots) fill in the blink of an eye. Bus #16 "Barrio de Igueldo-Camping" runs between the site and Alameda del Boulevard (departs every 30min., 105ptas). Keep in mind San Sebastián's quirky weather. Bar-restaurant and supermarket. *Parcela* (including tent and up to 2 people): summer and Semana Santa 2889ptas, extra person 425ptas; rest of year 1386ptas, extra person 357ptas. Reception daily in summer 8am-midnight; in winter 9am-1pm and 5-9pm.

PAÍS VASCO

FOOD

Pintxos (*pinchos* in *castellano*), chased down with the fizzy regional white wine *txacoli*, are a religion here; bars in the lively old city spread an array of enticing tidbits on toothpicks or bread. *Pintxos* rarely cost more than 175ptas each. Go crazy. In the harbor, many small places serve tangy sardines with strong, slightly bitter **sidra** (cider), another regional specialty. Custom insists on pouring it with one's arm extended upward so the force of the stream hitting the glass will release the *sidra's* bouquet.

Masses of restaurants and bars clamor for attention on **Calle Fermín Calbetón,** in the old quarter. In fact, the entire *parte vieja* seems to exist for no other purpose than to feed. The majority of restaurants offer their best deals on lunchtime *menús del día.* **Mercado de la Bretxa** on Alameda del Boulevard at C. San Juan sells fresh produce. **Mercado de San Martín** is on C. San Marcial, between C. Loyola and C. Urbieta. (Both markets open M-F 7:30am-2pm and 5-7:30pm, Sa 7:30am-2pm.) **Groceries** near the *albergue* await at **Todo Todo 3,** C. Serrano Anguta, between C. Zumalacárregui and C. Matia (open M-Sa 9am-9pm, Su 10am-2pm). Those staying in the old city will find **Super Todo Todo** on Alameda del Boulevard, around the corner from the tourist office (open M-Sa 8:30am-2:30pm and 5-9pm, Su 10am-2pm). Organic munchies are available at **Muerdago,** San Martin, 18 (open M-F 9:30am-1:30pm and 4:30-8pm, Sa 9:30am-1:30pm).

Pintxos in the Parte Vieja

Bar La Cepa, C. 31 de Agosto, 7-9 (tel. 943 42 63 94). Try the to-die-for peppers and a host of other delicacies. *Pintxos* 160-325ptas. *Bocadillos* 380-625ptas. *Menú del día* 1700ptas at lunch only. Open Tu-Su 10am-11:30pm.

Bar Intza, C. Esterlines, 12 (tel. 943 42 48 33). Outdoor seating and tasty *pintxos.* Mussels stuffed with spinach and cheese (150ptas each). Open Su-Th 10am-4pm and 6:30-11:30pm, later F-Sa. Closed May 15-June and Oct. 15-31.

Bar Juantxo, C. Embeltrán, 6 (tel. 943 42 74 05), in the *parte vieja.* Crammed with locals. *The* place for *bocadillos* (275-465ptas)—they sell an estimated 1000 a day! And with good reason. *Pintxos* 130ptas. Open daily 8:30am-midnight.

Ganbara, C. San Jerónimo, 21 (tel. 943 42 25 75). Extremely popular place. Sitting down may be out of the question (financially), but the affordable *pintxos* are exquisite. Don't miss the *gambas rebozadas* (shrimp, 160ptas). Open daily 11am-3:30pm and 6pm-midnight.

Restaurants in the Parte Vieja

Jatetxea Morgan, C. Narrica, 7 (tel. 943 42 46 61). Way more than you can afford, except for the scene-stealing *menú del día,* 1355ptas plus IVA (lunch only). Classy, *muy* classy. Open M-Sa 1:30-3:30pm and 9-11:30pm, Su 1:30-3:30pm. Visa, MC.

Pizzeria Trattoria Capricciosa, C. Fermín Calbetón, 50 (tel. 943 43 20 48). Italian basics done well. Pastas 650-1000ptas, pizzas 800-1100ptas. Open M-F 1-3:30pm and 8:30pm-11:15pm; Sa-Su 1:30-3:45pm and 8:30-11:30pm. Visa, MC.

Santa Lucia, C. Puerto, 6 (tel. 943 42 50 19). For big portions at low prices, this is the place. The "HungryMan" (#6), with lots of bacon, eggs, and toast, satiates for 500ptas. Open Su-Th 8:30am-9pm, later F-Sa.

Near the Cathedral

Rojo y Negro, C. San Marcial, 52 (tel. 943 42 61 46). Heavenly *pintxos* 150-175ptas. Sandwiches are 400ptas. Open daily 7am-2:30am.

Cachón, C. San Marcial, 40 (tel. 943 42 75 07), is a perfect stop on a creative, marine-inspired *pintxos* tour. Yum's the word. *Pintxos* 140-180ptas. Open daily 7:30am-11pm. Visa, MC, AmEx.

La Barranquesa, C. Larramendi, 27 (tel. 943 45 47 47), 2 blocks down C. Reyes Católicos from the cathedral to the right. One of the cheapest restaurants in town. *Lomo de cerdo* 450ptas, *bacalao a la vizcaína* 750ptas, *menú del día* 900ptas. Open M-Sa 1:15-3:30pm and 8:15-11:30pm.

Caravanseri Café, C. San Bartolomé, 1 (tel. 943 47 54 78). To the east of the cathedral. Salads, baked potatoes, burgers, and fabulous vegetarian options including tofu and veggie burgers (400ptas). Open M-Sa 8am-12:30am, Su 10am-midnight.

Casa Valles, C. Reyes Católicos, 10 (tel. 943 45 22 10). Tempting *pintxos* (140ptas). Well-trodden by locals. Open M-Su 9am-11pm. MC.

SIGHTS

San Sebastián's most attractive sight is its scenery—green walks and parks, grandiose buildings, and attractive hillsides encircle a placid, fan-shaped bay and the dreamy island of Santa Clara. Although the views from both mountains are spectacular, the vistas from **Monte Igueldo** are probably superior. By day you can see the countryside meet the ocean in a line of white and azure; by night Isla Santa Clara, lit by floodlights, seems to float on a ring of light. The sidewalk toward the mountain ends just before the base of Monte Igueldo with Eduardo Chillida's sculpture *El peine de los vientos* (Wind's Comb). The walk up is not too strenuous, but a funicular also climbs there.

At the other end of the bay, the gravel paths through the shady woods of **Monte Urgull** are peppered with monuments, blissful couples, and stunning vistas. The overgrown **Castillo de Santa Cruz de la Mota** crowns the summit with cannons and a chapel and is itself crowned by the statue of the Sagrado Corazón de Jesús, which blesses the city. *(Open daily in summer 8am-8pm; in winter 8am-6pm.)* Halfway up, the huge **Cementerio Británico** commemorates British soldiers who died defending the Spanish monarchy from the French during the Peninsular War in 1813.

On Paseo Nuevo, the **Museo de San Telmo** (tel. 943 42 49 70) resides in an erstwhile Dominican monastery. *(Open Tu-Sa 10:30am-1:30pm and 4-8pm, Su 10:30am-2pm. 350ptas, students 200ptas.)* The serene, overgrown cloister is strewn with Basque funerary relics. The main museum beyond the cloister comprises a fascinating array of Basque artifacts dating to prehistory, a couple of dinosaur skeletons, some El Grecos, and contemporary art. An **Aquarium**, Po. Muelle, 34 (tel. 943 44 00 99), lies on the edge of the port. *(Open July-Aug. 10am-10pm; Sept.-June 10am-1:30pm and 3:30-7:30pm. 700ptas, students 630ptas.)* A wander through the *parte vieja* reveals **Plaza Constitución,** with the ornate portal of Iglesia Santa María and numbered balconies dating from the plaza's days as a bull ring.

Once Isabel II started vacationing here in 1846, fancy buildings sprung up like wildfire. Even the railings on the boardwalk harken back to a time when the city belonged to the elite. **El Palacio de Miramar,** built on the land that splits Playa de la Concha and Playa de Ondarreta, passed through the hands of the Spanish court, Napoleon III, and Bismarck. *(Open daily in summer 9am-9pm; in winter 10am-5pm.)* Visitors can stroll through the grounds. Cuesta de Aldapeta leads up to the **Palacio de Ayete** (accessible by bus #19). The residence is closed to the public, but the trails are not. *(Grounds open in summer 10am-8:30pm; in winter 10am-5pm.)*

Thirty minutes from the town center between a lush hill and a dark, gray-green bay, lies the one-(cobbled)-street town of **Pasajes de San Juan.** The charming fishing village's wood-balconied houses and small bay crowded with colorful *chalupas* (little boats) make for an enchanting time warp. To get there, take the Areizaga **bus** (tel. 943 45 27 08) from C. Regina Regente in front of the tourist office to **Pasajes de San Pedro** (departs every 15-30min., 105ptas). From here, follow the road toward the sea until you can see Pasajes de San Juan across the bay. Steps lead down to the swift blue boat that will whisk you across for a small fee. A **Herribus** bus (tel. 943 49 18 01) also goes to Pasajes de San Juan from Pl. Gipúzkoa (departs every 20-30min., 105ptas).

ENTERTAINMENT

Nightlife and Drinking

The **parte vieja** pulls out all the stops after dark. **Calle Fermín Calbetón,** three blocks in from Alameda del Boulevard, sweats in a pool of bars. **Bar Tas-Tas,** C. Fermín Calbetón, 35 (tel. 943 43 06 12), attracts crowds, and a generous helping of international backpackers, with a Monday to Thursday two-drinks-for-one Happy Hour (open daily 3pm-3am). **Bars Sariketa,** C. Fermín Calbetó, 23, and **Txalupa,** C. Fermín Calbetó, 3, are human zoos and virtually impassable after dark. If you prefer to whisper intimately, listen for the background jazz of **Bar Kai,** C. Juan de Bilbao, 2 (open Su-Th 6pm-12:30am, later F-Sa). Locals and techno fans head to **Akerbeltz** and **Etxe Kalte,** both on C. Mari near the port. These bars are sleek, black, and cave-like.

At around 2am, San Sebastián's small but mighty disco scene starts thumping. Many discos crowd along the beach. **Bataplán,** Po. Concha, opens at midnight (cover 2000ptas includes one drink). **Kabutzia,** in Muelle, and **Ku,** atop Monte Igueldo, both open at 8pm. Covers can be exorbitant; the smart club-goer keeps an eye out for free invitations at bars, record shops, and elsewhere. Tune in to live jazz at **altxeri galeria,** C. Reina Regente, 2 (tel. 943 42 29 31; open Su-Th 5pm-2:30am, F-Sa 5pm-3:30am).

From January through April, the fastidious gourmands of San Sebastián turn their attention to **sidrerías,** where the slightly bitter *sidra* is brewed. The *sidrerías* are open to the public and all provide the same, standard meal (cod, beef chop, and cheese) to complement their own delicious *sidra.* Favorite local *sidrerías* are in nearby **Astigarraga.** The regional tourist office has transportation info and an extensive list of near, far, and isolated *sidrerías.*

The Beach and Outdoors

The gorgeous **Playa de la Concha** curves from the port to the **Pico del Loro,** the beak-shaped promontory dwelling of the Palacio de Miramar. Unfortunately, the virtually flat beach disappears during high tide and each year erosion narrows the beaches a little more. Crowds and parasols jam onto the smaller and steeper **Playa de Ondarreta,** beyond Miramar. East of Mt. Urguel, across the river, surfers crowd Playa de la Zurrida. Here Windsurf Donostia rents **windsurfing** equipment, surfboards, and kayaks in the summertime. Picnickers can head for the alluring **Isla de Santa Clara** in the center of the bay. Frequent motorboats leave for the island (5min., June-Sept. only, round-trip 250ptas), or power yourself and rent a rowboat. Check at the portside kiosk for info on both options.

Numerous sports-related groups offer short courses in a variety of activities all summer long. For **windsurfing** and **kayaking,** call the Real Club Nautico, C. Igentea, 9 (tel. 943 42 35 75). For **parachuting,** try Urruti Sport, C. José Maria Soroa, 20 (tel. 943 27 81 96). And for **surfing,** check out the Pukas Surf Club, C. Mayor, 5 (tel. 943 42 72 28). For info on all sports, pick up a copy of the *UDA-Actividades deportivas* brochure at the tourist office. Scuba Du, Muelle, 23 (tel. 943 42 24 26), rents **scuba** equipment and offers classes and certification.

Events and Festivals

The tourist office has a tri-monthly booklet of activities and events as well as *Guía del Ocio.* The city hosts a **marathon** in November; **El Día de San Sebastián** (Jan. 19-20) brings traditional parades; a **carnival** feasts in February; and **Festival Internacional de Danza** (dance festival; tel. 943 48 21 11) leaps in May.

San Sebastián's five-day **Festival de Jazz,** in mid to late July, is one of Europe's most ambitious. Such giants as Art Blakey, Wynton Marsalis, and Dizzy Gillespie have played here. For info on the 1999 festival, contact the Oficina del Festival de Jazz (tel. 943 48 11 79; email jazzaldia_donostia@donostia.org; http://www.jazzaldia.com). Movie stars and directors own the streets for a week in September during the **Festival Internacional de Cine,** deemed one of the four most important in the world (along with Venice, Cannes, and Berlin). For info about the 1999 film festival, call the Victoria Eugenia Theater (tel. 943 48 12 12; fax 943 48 12 18).

The week of August 15, **Semana Grande** (Big Week) is ablaze with concerts, movies, and an international fireworks festival. The **Fiestas de San Juan,** on and around June 24, bring their own share of folklore performances, Basque sports competitions, and general revelry. **La Quincena Musical,** in the Teatro Victoria Eugenia, C. Reina Regente, sponsors more than two weeks of classical music concerts in late August, most of them free.

■ Near San Sebastián: Hondarribia

Less than an hour east of San Sebastián by bus, Hondarribia (pop. 180,000) is a European beach town designed the way European beach towns should be. Stretching along the Txingudi Bay, the town flaunts a silky-smooth beach and brightly painted houses with flower-filled balconies. The gorgeous stone-and-timber *casco antiguo,*

PAÍS VASCO

centered around Carlos V's imposing palace in Pl. Armas (now a *parador*—peek inside), provides welcome relief from Coppertone fumes. The **Parroquia de Nuestra Señora de la Asunción** alongside the Pl. Armas is a lovely Gothic church that dates from the 15th century. Louis XIV of France married, by proxy, Spanish Habsburg Infanta María Teresa here. (Officially open for mass only; try the door and you might be able to sneak a visit.)

After the chic atmosphere of San Sebastián, Hondarribia is refreshingly simple. The beach, which lies at the far end of town past the fisherman's marina and at the end of a long seaside walk, can become ridiculously crowded with vacationers from Madrid and Barcelona in the peak days of summer, although it's still pleasantly calm through June. Spanish is still the predominant language, but you'll encounter plenty of Euskera (especially on street signs) and hear French as well.

PRACTICAL INFORMATION The entire bay, containing both Hondarribia and Irún, is called **Bidasoa. Interurbanos buses** (tel. 943 64 13 02) run to San Sebastián from C. Zuluaga (45min., departs every 15min. until 10pm, 195ptas). **AUIF** buses (tel. 943 64 27 91) go to Irún (10min., departs every 15min. until 10pm, 105ptas). The **airport** (tel. 943 66 85 00) is within walking distance of the town center. The regional **tourist office** is **Bidasoa Turismo,** C. Javier Ugarte, 6 (tel. 943 64 54 58), on Pl. San Cristobál. The English-speaking staff doles out maps and lodging lists. (Open July-Aug. daily 10am-8pm; Sept.-June M-F 9am-1:30pm and 4-6:30pm, Sa 10am-2pm.) Dial 088 in an **emergency.** The **police** are at 943 64 43 00. The **postal code** is 20280.

ACCOMMODATIONS AND FOOD Reservations are key in the summer; definitely call ahead. The modern **Albergue Juan Sebastián Elcano (HI),** Ctra. Faro (tel. 943 64 15 50; fax 943 64 00 28), sits on a hillside overlooking the sea. From the bus stop, head to the beach on C. Itsasargi, bearing left at the coast and continuing straight for several long blocks. At the traffic circle turn left and follow signs uphill to the hostel. Two hundred beds and a TV room wait for travelers, but still call a day ahead to reserve. (Members only; HI cards for sale. Dorms 1200ptas, over 30 1800ptas. Breakfast included. Sheets 110ptas. 3-night max. stay when full. Curfew midnight, but doors open at 1 and 2am. Reception daily 9am-noon and 4-7pm.) In the other direction from Pl. San Cristobál sits the darling **Hostal Txoko Goxoa,** C. Murrua, 22 (tel./fax 943 64 46 58), in the old quarter. Head up C. Javier Ugarte from the tourist office; take the second right, onto C. Juan Laborda, and follow the street until it ends at C. Murrua along the old walls. The *pensión* is on the right, with sweet rooms and big windows, all with bath. (July-Sept.: singles 3000ptas if available, doubles 6000ptas. Oct.-June: singles 2500ptas, doubles 5500ptas. Discounts for longer stays. Breakfast 475ptas. Visa, MC, Eurocard. IVA not included.) **Casas rurales** provide alternative accommodations (consult the tourist office). **Camping Jaizkibel** (tel. 943 64 16 79; fax 943 64 26 53) spreads 2km from town on Ctra. Guadelupe toward Monte Jaizkibel. They also rent bungalows. (540ptas per person, per tent, and per car. Reception daily 9am-11pm.)

Several **markets** spill onto C. San Pedro, three blocks inland from the port. **Market Goikoetxea** (tel. 943 64 10 29) includes flowers and fresh bread among its luscious outdoor offerings (open M-F 7:30am-2pm and 4-8pm, Sa 7am-2pm). Beach bums refuel at **Gaxen,** C. Matxin Arzu, 1 (tel. 943 61 14 62), a cafe six blocks from the beach and two from the bay. The cafe serves full breakfasts, fresh fruit shakes (325ptas), and 36 kinds of sandwiches (325-675ptas). (Open M-Th 8am-9pm, F-Su 8am-11pm.) There is a similar menu at **Kaiela,** C. Itxas Argi, 4 (tel. 943 64 42 12), a bit closer to the beach than Gaxen (sandwiches 325-500ptas, salads 375-500ptas). Try C. Mayor (Nagusia) in the **casco antiguo** for various *menus del día.*

EXCURSIONS Hondaribbia offers several excursion possibilities. Six kilometers up Av. Monte Jaizkibel, **Monte Jaizkibel,** the highest mountain on the Costa Cantábrica, guards the **Santuario de Guadalupe.** The environs offer mind-blasting views of the coast. On a clear day you can see as far as Bayonne, France, 45km away. **Boats** (tel. 943 61 64 47) shuttle travelers 5km to Hendaye, a French town with a bigger beach. Boats leave from the pier at the end of C. Domingo Egia, off La Marina (departs every 15min, reduced service in winter, 200ptas).

■ Near San Sebastián: Irún

As if Irún (pop. 53,000) meant what the word looks like in English, travelers who come here are usually rushing somewhere else. And with good reason—besides the transportation services that connect to Paris, Madrid, San Sebastián, and the French border, Irún has only a vast urban sprawl to recommend it.

RENFE **trains** (tel. 943 61 67 08) fan out to all of Spain; connections to San Sebastián are frequent (25min., 150ptas). The train station has **currency exchange,** a **post office,** and **luggage storage** (400ptas, ask for token at the bar; open daily 7am-11pm). Irún's **Ayuntamiento (SAC office),** C. Juan de la Cruz, 2 (tel. 943 64 92 00), on Pl. Zabaltza off Po. Colón, dispenses maps and free pens (open M-F 8:30am-2pm and 4-7:30pm, Sa 8:30am-1:30pm). In an **emergency,** dial 088. The **police** (tel. 943 64 92 00) are stationed in Pl. Ensanche.

Most overnighters in Irún arrived too late in the day to continue on to San Sebastián or elsewhere. Affordable *hostales* line C. Estación in front of the station. To find **Hostal Residencia Lizaso,** C. Aduana, 5 (tel. 943 61 16 00), follow C. Estación, bear right on Po. Colon, and take the first right. A TV room and clean, simple rooms await. (July-Aug.: singles 2300ptas; doubles 3750ptas, with shower 4750ptas, with full bath 5250-5450ptas. Sept.-June: singles 2500ptas; doubles 3200ptas, with shower 3700ptas, with full bath 4300ptas. IVA not included.) **Bar Restaurante Xavier,** C. Estación, 14, serves a 900ptas *menú* with lots of options. The **mercado** is at C. República de Argentina, 12 (open daily 8:30am-1:30pm).

■ Vitoria-Gasteiz

Oozing with prosperity, Vitoria-Gasteiz (pop. 217,000), like Bilbao and the rest of Basque Country, is clearly up-and-coming. It is the capital of País Vasco, but anomalously preserves its greener quarters and slow pace of life. The city boasts tree-canopied avenues, leafy parks, magnificent churches, and world-class museums, successfully retaining the charm of an old city packaged into a sleek cosmopolitan center.

Vitoria-Gasteiz's name game is indicative of the city's regional political and cultural sentiment. In 1181 King of Navarra Sancho "El Sabio" (the Wise) changed the town's name from Gasteiz to Villa de Nueva Vitoria, promoting it to city status in a single stroke. Eight centuries later, upon recovering regional autonomy in 1979, the Basques re-incorporated the original name. However, the name change is mainly symbolic, and the city is most often referred to as Vitoria.

As Castilla's commercial routes took on increasing importance in the 19th and 20th centuries, *castellano* began to replace *euskera* (the Basque language) in everyday discourse. Today, you're most likely to hear Castilian, although street signs and graffiti are written almost exclusively in *euskera.* With its broad boulevards and stone-and-timber houses, Vitoria feels more Northern European than Spanish, though less nationalist than other metropolises in the region.

ORIENTATION AND PRACTICAL INFORMATION

The medieval **casco viejo** (old city) is the egg-shaped epicenter of Vitoria-Gasteiz. At its base, **Plaza de la Virgen Blanca** marks the center of town. Wide tree-lined pedestrian streets surround the old city. From the **train station,** follow **Calle Eduardo Dato** to its end, turn left on C. Postas, and head straight to the plaza. The old **bus station** on C. Francia won't re-open for another year or so. Until then, buses park 'n' roll from a temporary glass building on **Calle de los Herrán,** between C. Prudencio María Verástegui and C. Arana. **All directions below will be given assuming you exit on its west side.** Facing the stores across the street (there are none on the east side), from the west side of the station, turn left and make an immediate right on to C. Verástegui; to get to Pl. Virgen Blanca, follow it to its end and turn left on C. Francia; follow C. Francia for four blocks as it becomes C. Paz and turn right onto C. Postas, which leads straight to the plaza.

PAÍS VASCO

Transportation

Flights: Aeropuerto Vitoria-Foronda (tel. 945 16 35 00), 9km out of town. Accessible only by car or taxi (2000ptas). Info open 7:30am-10pm. **Iberia** (tel. 945 27 40 00), info open 7am-11pm. Check back pages of *El Correo Español* (local paper) for current flights.

Trains: RENFE, Pl. Estación (tel. 941 23 02 02), at the end of C. Eduardo Dato, south of the old city. Info open 7:30am-10:30pm. To: Pamplona (1hr., 3-4 per day, 575-1100ptas); San Sebastián (2-2½hr., 8-9 per day, 1500ptas); Burgos (1½, 8-10 per day, 1000-1500ptas); Zaragoza (3hr., 1 per day, 2700ptas); Madrid (4½-7hr., 5-6 per day, 4000ptas); Barcelona (1 per day, 6½hr., 4400ptas).

Buses: C. Herrán, 50, on a traffic island east of the old city. General info (tel. 941 25 84 00), open M-F 8am-9pm, Sa-Su 8am-7pm. Tons of companies. **ALSA** (tel. 941 25 55 09) to: Pamplona (1½hr., 3-7 per day, 875ptas); Zaragoza (3hr., 5-8 per day, 2020ptas). **La Unión** (tel. 941 26 46 26), to Bilbao (1hr., 17-20 per day, 655ptas). **Continental Auto** (tel. 941 28 64 66), to: Burgos (1½hr., 8-9 per day, 940-1150ptas); San Sebastián (1½hr., 7-10 per day, 930ptas); Madrid (4½-5hr., 9 per day, 2800-4390ptas).

Public Transportation: (tel. 945 16 15 70) Buses cover the metropolitan area and suburbs (90ptas). The tourist office has a pamphlet with routes. Bus #2 goes from the bus station to C. Florida (home of many *pensiones*). City buses run approximately 6:30am-11pm.

Taxis: Radio-Taxis (tel. 945 27 35 00 or 945 25 30 33).

Car Rental: Avis, Av. Gasteiz, 53 (tel. 945 24 46 12), just past C. Adriano VI. From 9727ptas per day (includes mileage, insurance, and tax). Must be at least 23 and have had license for 1 yr. Open M-F 9am-1:30pm and 4-7pm, Sa 9am-1:30pm.

Tourist and Financial Services

Tourist Office: Parque de la Florida (tel. 945 13 13 21; fax 945 13 02 93), from the train station follow C. Eduardo Dato (go straight exiting the station) and take the 2nd left onto C. Florida; follow it to the edge of the *parque*. From the bus station, head towards Pl. Virgen Blanca, but follow C. Francia/Paz 2 blocks past C. Postas to C. Ortiz de Zárate on the right, which leads to C. Florida. In the park, follow the tree-lined path to the left; the tourist office is in a squat stone house. Trilingual staff gives out a great map and info on all of País Vasco. Open June-Oct M-F 9am-2pm, Sa 9am-1pm and 3-7pm; Nov.-May M-F 9am-1:30pm and 3pm-6pm. The **municipal tourist office** (tel. 945 16 15 98; fax 945 16 11 05) is on Av. Gasteiz, 53.

Currency Exchange: Banco Central Hispano is at C. Eduardo Dato, 26 at the intersection with C. San Prudencio. Has an **ATM**. Open M-F 8:30am-2:30pm. Open Saturdays in winter.

Local Services

Luggage storage: At the train station 400ptas. Buy token from the ticket counter 6am-1am. At the bus station 105ptas the first day, 87ptas each additional day. Open M-F 8am-9pm, Sa-Su 8am-7pm.

English Press: Study Librería, C. Fueros, 14 (tel. 945 14 37 80), left off C. Postas heading toward Pl. Virgen Blanca. Penguin classics, travel guides, and some pulp fiction. Open M-F 9:45am-1:30pm and 4:30-8pm, Sa until 8:15pm.

El Corte Inglés: (tel. 945 26 63 33), on the corner of C. Paz and C. Independencia, one block past C. Postas coming from bus station. English books, supermarket, currency exchange, and everything else your heart desires.

Youth Center: Centro Coordinador de Información y Documentación Juvenil de Euskadi, Duque de Wellington, 2, 4th floor (tel. 945 18 94 77 or 945 18 94 79). HI card available. Open 9am-2:30pm.

Emergency and Communications

Emergency: dial 088 or 092. **Police: Municipal:** (tel. 092).

Crisis Line: Women's Services (tel. 945 16 13 45).

24-Hour Pharmacy: Call tel. 945 23 07 21 for a recording. Check pharmacy doors (one at C. Eduardo Dato, 24, another at C. Postas, 34) or back pages of *El Correo Español.*

(go down in history)

and use **AT&T Direct**^{SM} Service
to tell everyone about it.

It's all within **AT&T** your reach.

Before you go exploring lost cultures, get an

AT&T Direct^{SM} Service wallet guide.

It's a list of access numbers you need to call home fast and clear from

around the world, using an AT&T Calling Card or credit card.

What an amazing culture we live in.

For a list of **AT&T Access Numbers,**
take the attached wallet guide.

It's all within  your reach.

w w w . a t t . c o m / t r a v e l e r

For credit card payment information call 1 888 259-3505. Payment terms subject to your credit card agreement.   ©1999 AT&T

For your
calling
convenience
tear off
and take
with you!

AT&T Direct℠ Service

WALLET GUIDE

Inside you'll find simple instructions on how to use AT&T Direct Service to place calling card or collect calls from outside the U.S.

All you need are the AT&T Access Numbers when you travel outside the U.S., because you can access us quickly and easily from virtually anywhere in the world. And if you need any further help, there's always an AT&T English-speaking Operator available to assist you.

www.att.com/traveler

Calling From Specially Marked Telephones

Throughout the world, there are specially marked phones that connect you to AT&T Direct℠ Service. Simply look for the AT&T logo. In the following countries, access to AT&T Direct Service is *only* available from these phones: Ethiopia, Mongolia, Nigeria, Seychelles Islands.

Public phones in Europe displaying the red 3C symbol also give you quick and easy access to AT&T Direct Service. Just lift the handset and dial ✱60 (in France dial M60) and you'll be connected to AT&T.

Pay phones in the United Kingdom displaying the New World symbol provide easy access to AT&T. Simply lift the handset and press the pre-programmed button marked AT&T.

NEW WORLD PAYPHONES

Customer Care

If you have any questions, call 800 331-1140, Ext. 707.

When outside the U.S., dial the AT&T Access Number for the country you are in and ask the AT&T Operator for Customer Care.

108-25   © AT&T 6/98

Printed in the U.S.A.
on recycled paper.

To Call the U.S. and Other Countries Using Your AT&T Calling Card* or credit card∞, Follow These Steps:

1. Make sure you have an outside line. (From a hotel room, follow the hotel's instructions to get an outside line, as if you were placing a local call.)

2. If you want to call a country other than the U.S., make sure the country *you are in* is highlighted in blue on the chart like this: [ ]
   Enter the AT&T Access Number listed in the chart for the country *you are in.*

3. Enter the AT&T Access Number listed in the chart for the country *you are in.*

4. When prompted, enter the telephone number you are calling as follows:

   - For calls to the U.S., dial the Area Code (no need to dial 1 before the Area Code) + 7-digit number.
   - For calls to other countries,† enter 01 + the Country Code, City Code, and Local Number.

5. After the tone, enter your AT&T Calling Card* or credit card number (not the international number). If you need help or wish to call the U.S. collect, hold for an AT&T Operator.

* You may also use your AT&T Corporate Card, AT&T Universal Card, or most U.S. local phone company cards.
† The cost of calls to countries other than the U.S. consists of basic connection rates plus an additional charge based on the country you are calling.
∞ Credit card billing subject to availability.

Special Features

Just dial the AT&T Access Number for the country *you are in* and follow the instructions listed below.

- To call U.S. 800 numbers: Enter the 800 number you are calling. (Note: Based upon the 800 number dialed, calls may be toll-free or AT&T Direct℠ Service charges may apply for the duration of the call; some numbers may be restricted.)

- To set up conference calls: Dial AT&T TeleConference Services at 800 232-1234. (Note: One conferee must be in the U.S.)

- To access language interpreters: Dial AT&T Language Line® Services at 408 648-5871.

- To record and deliver messages: Dial #123 if you get a busy signal or no answer, or dial AT&T True Messages® Service at 800 562-6275.

Here's a time-saving tip for placing additional calls: When you finish your conversation, or if there is a busy signal or no answer, don't hang up – press # and wait for the voice prompt or an AT&T Operator.

AT&T Access Numbers (Refer to footnotes before dialing.) From the countries highlighted in blue below, like this [ ], you can make calls to the U.S. location in the world; and from *all* the countries listed, you can make calls to virtually any

It's all within your reach.

Country	Access Number
Albania ●	00-800-0010
American Samoa	633 2-USA
Angola	0199
Anguilla +	1-800-872-2881
Antigua ▲	1-800-872-2881
(Public Card Phones)	#1
Argentina	0-800-54-288
Armenia ●▲	8◆10111
Aruba	800-8000
Australia	1-800-881-011
Austria ○	022-903-011
Bahamas	1-800-872-2881
Bahrain	800-000
Bahrain↑	800-001
Barbados+	1-800-872-2881
Belarus ✕⟶	8◆800101
Belgium●	0-800-100-10
Belize ▲	811
(From Hotels Only)	555
Benin●	102
Bermuda+	1-800-872-2881
Bolivia●	0-800-1112
Bosnia ▲	00-800-0010
Brazil	0800
British V.I. +	1-800-872-2881
Brunei●	800-1111
Bulgaria ■■▲	00-800-0010
Cambodia✴ (Outside Cairo)	#1
Canada	1 800 CALL ATT
Cape Verde Islands	112
Cayman Islands+	1-800-872-2881
Chile	800-800-311 or 800-800-288
(Easter Island)	800-800-311
China .PRC ▲	10811
Colombia	980-11-0010
Cook Island	09-111
Costa Rica	0-800-0-114-114
Croatia ▲	99-385-0111
Cyprus●	080-90010
Czech Rep. ▲	00-42-000-101
Denmark	8001-0010
Dominica ●	1-800-872-2881
Dom. Rep. ✕, □	1-800-872-2881
Ecuador ▲	999-119
Egypt○ (Cairo)	510-0200
(Outside Cairo)	02-510-0200
El Salvador ○	800-1785
Estonia	8-00-8001001
Fiji	004-890-1001
Finland ●	9800-100-10
France	0800 99 00 11
French Antilles	0800 99 0011
French Guiana	0800 99 0011
Gabon●	00•001
Gambia●	00111
Georgia ▲	8◆0288
Germany	0130-0010
Ghana	0191
Gibraltar	8800
Greece ●	00-800-1311
Grenada +	1-800-872-2881
Guadeloupe + ✴	0800 99 00 11
(Marie Galante)	
Guam	1 800 CALL ATT
Guantanamo Bay ↑ (Cuba)	935
Guatemala ○,✴	99-99-190
Guyana ✴	165
Haiti	183
Honduras	800-0-123
Hong Kong	800-96-1111
Hungary●	00◆800-01111
India ✕,▲⟶	000-117
Indonesia⟶	001-801-10
Ireland✓	1-800-550-000
Israel	1-800-94-94-949
Italy●	172-1011
Ivory Coast●	00-111-11
Jamaica ○	1-800-872-2881
Jamaica □	872
Japan IDC◆▲	0066-55-111
Japan KDD◆	005-39-111
Kazakhstan ✕	8◆800-121-4321
Korea◆	✴0072-911 or 0030-911
Korea↑	550-HOME or 550-2USA
Kuwait	800-288
Latvia (Riga)	7007007
(Outside Riga)	8◆7007007
Lebanon○ (Beirut)	426-801
(Outside Beirut)	01-426-801
Liechtenstein●	0-800-89-0011
Lithuania ✕ ⟶	8◆196
Luxembourg†	0-800-0111
Macao	0800-111
Macedonia, F.Y.R. of ●,○	99-800-4288
Malaysia○	1800-80-0011
Malta ●	0800-890-110
Marshall Isl.	1 800 CALL ATT
Mauritius	73120
Mexico▽	01-800-288-2872
Micronesia	288
Monaco●	800-90-288
Montserrat	1-800-872-2881
Morocco	002-11-0011
Netherlands Antilles ⊕	001-800-872-2881
Netherlands ●	0800-022-9111
New Zealand	000-911
Nicaragua	174
Norway	800-190-11
Pakistan ▲	00-800-01001
Palau	02288
Panama	109
(Canal Zone)	281-0109
Papua New Guinea	0507-12880
Paraguay■,▲	008-11-800
Peru ●	0-800-50000
Philippines●	105-11
Poland	0◆0-800-111-1111
Portugal▲	05017-1-288
Qatar	0800-011-77
Reunion Isl.	0800 99 0011
Romania	01-800-4288
Romania↑	01-801-0151
Russia●▲ (Moscow)	755-5042
(Outside Moscow)	8-095-755-5042
Russia●▲ (St. Petersburg)	325-5042
(Outside St. Petersburg)	8-812-325-5042
St. Kitts/Nevis & St. Lucia +	1-800-872-2881
St. Pierre & Miquelon	0800 99 0011
St. Vincent △,■	1-800-872-2881
Saipan ▲	1 800 CALL ATT
San Marino ●	172-1011
Saudi Arabia◇	1-800-10
Senegal	3072
Sierra Leone	1100
Singapore ■	800-0111-111
Slovakia ▲	00-42-100-101
Solomon Isl.	0811
So. Africa	0-800-99-0123
Spain	900-99-00-11
Sri Lanka ■	430-430
Sudan	800-001
Suriname △	156
Sweden	020-795-611
Switzerland●	0-800-890011
Syria	0-801
Taiwan	0080-10288-0
Thailand◄	001-999-111-11
Trinidad/Tob.	1-800-872-2881
Turkey●	00800-12277
Turks & Caicos +,■	1-800-872-2881
Uganda	800-001
Ukraine ▲	8◆100-11
U.A. Emirates ●	800-121
U.K.▲,✚	0800-89-0011 or 0500-89-0011
U.S. ▼	1 800 CALL ATT
Uruguay	000-410
Uzbekistan 8◆	641-7440010
Venezuela	800-11-120
Vietnam●	1-201-0288
Yemen	00 800 101
Zambia	00-899
Zimbabwe ▲	110-99890

● Public phones require coin or card deposit ✴ Press red button ■ Additional charges apply when calling outside of Moscow ■ AT&T Direct™ calls cannot be placed to this country from outside the U.S. ✕ Available from pay phones.
Phnom Penh and Siem Reap only. ✕ Not available from public phones.
✥ From St. Maarten or phones at Bobby's Marina, use 1-800-872-2881.

◇ From this country, AT&T Direct™ calls terminate to designated countries only.
↑ From U.S. Military Bases only. ⟶ Not yet available from all areas. ○ Select hotels.
+ May not be available from every phone/public phone. †Collect calling from public phones. ✕ Available from phones with international calling capabilities or from most Public Calling Centers. ✓ From Northern Ireland use U.K. access code.

● Collect calling only. ○ Public phones require local coin payment through the call duration. ◆ Await second dial tone. ✕ When calling from public phones, use phones marked "Lattel." If call does not complete, use 001-800-462-4240.
△ Available from public phones only. + Public phones and select hotels. ✕ When calling from public phones use phones marked Lenso.

□ Calling Card calls available from select hotels. ⟶ Use phones allowing international access. ▼ Including Puerto Rico and the U.S. Virgin Islands.
▼AT&T Direct™ Service only from Telephone calling centers in Hanoi and post offices in Da Nang, Ho Chi Minh City and Quang Ninh. ✚ If call does not complete, use 0800-013-0011.

WE GIVE YOU THE WORLD...AT A DISCOUNT

LET'S GO®

TRAVEL

LET'S GO TRAVEL

MERCHANDISE CATALOG FOR 1999

LET'S GO Travel Gear

World Journey

Equipped with Eagle Creek Comfort Zone Carry System which includes Hydrofil nylon knit on backpanel and lumbar pads. Parallel internal frame. Easy packing panel load design with internal cinch straps. Lockable zippers. Detachable daypack. Converts into suitcase. 26x15x9", 5100 cu. in., 6 lbs. 12 oz. Black, Evergreen, or Blue. $30 discount with railpass. **$225.00**

Continental Journey

Carry-on size pack with internal frame suspension. Comfort Zone padded shoulder straps and hip belt. Leather hand grip. Easy packing panel load design with internal cinch straps. Lockable zippers. Detachable daypack. Converts into suitcase. 21x15x9", 3900 cu. in., 4 lbs. 5 oz. Black, Evergreen, or Blue. $20 discount with railpass. **$175.00**

Security Items

Undercover Neckpouch Ripstop nylon with a soft Cambrelle back. Three pockets. 5 1/2" x 8 1/2". Lifetime guarantee. Black or Tan. **$10.50**

Undercover Waistpouch Ripstop nylon with a soft Cambrelle back. Two pockets. 12" x 5" with adjustable waistband. Lifetime guarantee. Black or Tan. **$10.50**

Travel Lock Great for locking up your World or Continental Journey. Two-dial combination lock. **$5.25**

Hostelling Essentials

Hostelling International Membership

Cardholders receive priority, discounts, and reservation privileges at most domestic and international hostels.

Youth (under 18)..................... free
Adult (ages 18-55)................$25.00
Senior (over 55)....................$15.00

European Hostelling Guide

Offers essential information concerning over 2500 European hostels. **$10.95**

Sleepsack

Required at many hostels. Washable polyester/cotton. Durable and compact. **$14.95**

International ID Cards 1999

Provide discounts on airfares, tourist attractions and more. Includes basic accident and medical insurance. **$20.00**

International Student ID Card (ISIC)
International Teacher ID Card (ITIC)
International Youth ID Card (GO25)

1-800-5LETSGO

http://www.hsa.net/travel

— Prices are in US dollars and subject to change.—

Eurailpass Unlimited travel in and among all 17 countries: **Austria, Belgium, Denmark, Finland, France, Germany, Greece, Holland, Hungary, Italy, Luxembourg, Norway, Portugal, Republic of Ireland, Spain, Sweden, and Switzerland.**

	15 days	21 days	1 month	2 months	3 months	10 days	15 days
First Class	*c o n s e c u t i v e d a y s*					*in two months*	
1 Passenger	$554	$718	$890	$1260	$1558	$654	$862
2 or More Passengers	$470	$610	$756	$1072	$1324	$556	$732
Youthpass (Second Class)							
Passengers under 26	$388	$499	$623	$882	$1089	$458	$599

Europass Travel in the five Europass countries: **France, Germany, Italy, Spain, and Switzerland.** Up to two of the four associate regions (Austria and Hungary; Benelux (Belgium, Netherlands, and Luxembourg); Greece; Portugal) may be added.

	5 days	6 days	8 days	10 days	15 days	first	second
First Class	*in two months*					*associate country*	
1 Passenger	$348	$368	$448	$528	$728	+$60	+$40
2 to 5 Passengers traveling together	$296	$314	$382	$450	$620	+$52	+$34
Youthpass (Second Class)							
Passengers under 26	$233	$253	$313	$363	$513	+$45	+$33

Pass Protection   For an additional **$10**, insure any railpass against theft or loss.

Discounts *with the purchase of a railpass*
- $30 off a World Journey backpack
- $20 off a Continental Journey backpack
- Any *Let's Go* Guide for 1/2 Price
- Free 2-3 Week Domestic Shipping

Call about Eurostar–the Channel Tunnel Train–and other country-specific passes.

Airfares
& Special Promotions

Call for information on and availability of standard airline tickets, student, teacher, and youth discounted airfares, as well as other special promotions.

Publications
& More

Let's Go Travel Guides—
The Bible of the Budget Traveler

USA • India and Nepal • Southeast Asia............22.99
Australia • Eastern Europe • Europe..................21.99
Britain & Ireland • Central America • France •
Germany • Israel & Egypt • Italy • Mexico •
Spain & Portugal...19.99
Alaska & The Pacific Northwest • Austria &
Switzerland • California & Hawaii • Ecuador
& The Galapagos Islands • Greece • Ireland.....18.99
South Africa • Turkey.......................................17.99
New York City • New Zealand • London •
Paris • Rome • Washington D.C. 15.99

Let's Go Map Guides
Know your destination inside and out!
Great to accompany your Eurailpass.

Amsterdam, Berlin, Boston, Chicago, Florence, London, Los Angeles, Madrid, New Orleans, New York, Paris, Rome, San Francisco, Washington D.C.   8.95

Michelin Maps

Czech/Slovak Republics • Europe • France • Germany • Germany/Austria /Benelux • Great Britain & Ireland • Greece • Italy • Poland • Scandinavia & Finland • Spain & Portugal 10.95

LET'S GO Order Form

Last Name* _____   First Name* _____   Home and Day Phone Number*
(very important)

Street* _____ (Sorry, we cannot ship to Post Office Boxes)

City* _____   State* _____   Zip Code* _____

Citizenship‡§□   School/College§   Date of Birth‡§   Date of Travel*
(Country)

Qty	Description	Color	Unit Price	Total Price

Shipping and Handling

2-3 Week Domestic Shipping	
Merchandise value under $30	$4
Merchandise value $30-$100	$6
Merchandise value over $100	$8
2-3 Day Domestic Shipping	
Merchandise value under $30	$14
Merchandise value $30-$100	$16
Merchandise value over $100	$18
Overnight Domestic Shipping	
Merchandise value under $30	$24
Merchandise value $30-$100	$26
Merchandise value over $100	$28
All International Shipping	$30

Total Purchase Price	
Shipping and Handling	+
MA Residents add 5% sales tax on gear and books	+
TOTAL	

□ Mastercard   □ Visa

Cardholder name:

Card number:

Expiration date:

When ordering an International ID Card, please include:

1. Proof of birthdate (copy of passport, birth certificate, or driver's license).
2. One picture (1.5" x 2") signed on the reverse side.
3. (ISIC/ITIC only) Proof of current student/teacher status (letter from registrar or administrator, proof of tuition, or copy of student/faculty ID card. FULL-TIME only).

* Required for all orders
‡ Required in addition for each Hostelling Membership
§ Required in addition for each International ID Card
□ Required in addition for each railpass

Prices are in US dollars and subject to change.

Make check or money order payable to:
Let's Go Travel
17 Holyoke Street
Cambridge, MA 02138
(617) 495-9649

1-800-5LETSGO

Hours: Mon.-Fri., 10am-6pm ET

Medical Services: Hospital General de Santiago, C. Olaguíbel (tel. 945 25 36 00). With your back to the bus station, go left 1 block after C. Francia becomes C. Paz.

Cybercafé: Acid Jazz Café, C. San Prudencio, 17. 100ptas for 3min. Open in summer Tu-Su 1pm-3am, winter Th-Su 1pm-3am.

Post Office: C. Postas, 9 (tel. 945 23 05 75; fax 23 37 80), on the pedestrian street leading to Pl. Virgen Blanca from the east. Open M-F 8:30am-8:30pm, Sa 9:30am-2pm. For Lista de Correos, walk around the corner to the C. Nuestra Señora del Cabello side of the building to the back door. **Postal Code:** 01008.

ACCOMMODATIONS AND CAMPING

There aren't many bargains in Vitoria-Gasteiz though slightly more deluxe hostals abound. If you plan to drop in during the *fiestas* from August 4 to 9th, make reservations at least a month in advance.

Casa 400, C. Florida, 46, 3rd fl. (tel. 945 23 38 87), a right turn off C. Eduardo Dato coming from the train station. A private college dormitory during the school year. Completely renovated with a youthful atmosphere. Almost all rooms have big balconies. Singles 2500ptas; doubles 3200ptas. Breakfast 250ptas. *Pension completa* (room and board) 3950ptas per person. Dining room, coffee machine, and laundry service. Rooms available only July 1-Sept. 30.

Hostal-Residencia Nuvilla, C. Fueros, 29, 3rd fl. (tel. 945 25 91 51), from the bus station follow directions to Pl. Virgen Blanca (see **Orientation,** p. 241) but take the first left off C. Postas. Large rooms with big windows. Rare singles 2500ptas; doubles 3500ptas; triples 5000ptas. Owner doesn't give out keys to room doors.

Pensión Zurine, C. Florida, 24 (tel. 945 14 22 40), across the street from Pensión Araba. Baby-pink rooms contrast with the ice-blue bathrooms. Low, firm beds. Singles 2300-2500ptas; doubles 3500-4000ptas. Some rooms unnervingly windowless.

Hostal Eguileta, C. Nueva Fuera, 32 (tel. 945 25 17 00 or 945 25 17 11, fax 945 25 17 22). From the bus station, take a right on C. Francia and the first left. Ask about rooms across the street in Hotel Desiderio. Clean rooms with windows, and pristine shared bathrooms. Singles 1900ptas plus 7% IVA; doubles 3200 plus 7% IVA.

Pensión Araba (2), C. Florida, 25 (tel. 945 23 25 88), on the road to the tourist office from the bus station; from the train station, turn right onto C. Florida. Très posh. Persian-style rugs, wood floors, dark furniture, and beautifully tiled bathrooms. Elevator and parking garage. TVs and sound systems for all. A few singles 2800ptas; doubles 3500ptas, with bath 4500ptas; triples 4725ptas, 6075ptas.

Camping Ibaya (tel. 945 14 76 20), 5km from town toward Madrid. Follow Portal de Castilla west from the tourist office intersection. Supermarket, cafe/restaurant, hot showers. 500ptas per person, per tent, and per car. Open year-round.

FOOD

Plunge into the **casco viejo** and the surrounding pedestrian streets, and you can hardly go wrong. **C. Cuchillería,** uphill from the post office off C. Francisco, offers many options. From the train station, take C. Eduardo Dato, turn right on C. Postas, then left past the post office and uphill, where C. Cuchillería and other old-town streets radiate from C. San Francisco. There are *tapas* galore in the streets around Pl. España. Fresh produce and red meat fill the two-level market, **Mercado de Abastos,** on Pl. Santa Bárbara off C. Paz (open M-F 9am-2pm and 5-8pm, Sa 8am-3pm). There's the **grocery** option at **Simago,** C. General Alava, 10, between C. Eduardo Dato and C. San Antonio (open M-Sa 9am-9pm).

Casco Viejo

Restaurant Hirurak, C. Cuchillería, 26 (tel. 945 28 81 47), off C. San Francisco on the right. Funky, young clientele bops to reggae and blues. *Menú del día* 1100ptas at lunch only, 1500ptas on sunday. Entrees 950-1400ptas. Open Tu-Su 1-3:30pm and 9-11pm.

Gasteiz-bi, Mateo Moraza, 23 (tel. 945 23 34 85). Turns into a hip bar after 11:30pm. *Bocadillos* from 400ptas and up. Open M-Th 7:30am-11pm, F-Sa 7:30am-3am.

Café bar Otxanda, Sierras de Jesús, 27 (tel. 945 27 96 97). Follow C. Postas as it curves around the *casco viejo.* Yummy *pinchos* from 135ptas up and *bocadillos* starting at 250ptas. Occasional art exhibitions. Open Su-Th 7am-11:30pm, F-Sa until 1:30 or 2am.

Elsewhere

Museo del Organo, C. Manuel Iradier, 80. Take C. Florida east from the park to the Pl. Toros, then turn right. Munch on vegetarian delights to soothing music. 4 course *menú* which changes daily, but usually includes a salad bar with fresh vegetables (1100ptas). Lunch only, open M-Sa 1-4pm.

Restaurante Bilbaína, C. Prudencio María Verástegui, 2 (tel. 945 25 44 00). Recommended by bus drivers and frequented by businessmen, so you know it's good. Exceptional *menú* includes a savory *merluza a la rancha* (ranch-style hake) and baked cinnamon apples for dessert (1150ptas plus 7% IVA). Open M-Sa 1-4pm and 9-11pm, Su 1-4pm.

Bar Restaurante Poliki, C. Fueros 29 (tel. 945 25 05 19). Tasty dishes populate the *menú del dia* (1100ptas) while the *tapas,* especially *boquerones en vinagres* (anchovies in vinegar 300ptas) and *patatas picantes* (spicy french fries, 300ptas) are delish. Open 1:30-4:30pm and 8-11:30pm. Visa, MC, AmEx.

SIGHTS

The tree-lined pedestrian walkways of the new city and steep narrow streets of the *casco viejo* make for pleasant wanderings. **Plaza de la Vírgen Blanca** is the focal point of the *casco viejo* and site of Vitoria-Gasteiz's *fiestas.* Beside Pl. Virgen Blanca is the broad, arcaded **Plaza de España,** marking the division of the old town from the new. **Los Arquillos,** a series of arches that rise above Pl. España were designed by architects Sefurola and Olaguíbel in 1802 to connect the hill of the *casco viejo* with the rapidly growing new town below. Many of the old quarter's Renaissance *palacios* are open to the public as museums. At C. Cuchillería, 24, the 15th-century **Casa del Cordón,** (tel. 945 25 96 73) so-called because of the stone *cordón* (rope) that embellishes its central arch, is open to all (M-Sa 7-9pm). Further down C. Cuchillería, the **Palacio de Bendaría,** that dates from 1525, houses the **Museo de Naipes** and its collection of playing cards that dates back six centuries. *(Open Tu-F 10am-2pm and 4-6:30pm, Sa 10am-2pm, Su 11am-2pm.)* Straight across over the hill, the **Casa-Torre de Doña Ochanda,** C. Siervas de Jesús, 24 (tel. 945 18 19 24), invites visitors inside the home of a medieval noble that now shelters the birds, butterflies, and bones of the **Museum of Natural Science.** *(Open Tu-F 10am-2pm and 4-6:30pm, Sa 10am-2pm, Su 11am-2pm.)* Construction of the Gothic **Catedral de Santa María** (also known as the Catedral Vieja, or Old Cathedral), at the top of the *casco viejo,* began in the 14th century, and today flaunts two especially expressive *portales* (doors)—it's a good thing, since the rest of the cathedral is closed for restoration. The 20th-century neo-Gothic **New Cathedral** is in the new part of town on C. Monseñor Cadena y Eleta.

The gorgeous **Palacio Augustín** on Po. Fray Francisco de Vitoria houses the **Museo de Bellas Artes,** with sculptures in the front garden, and works by Ribera, Miró, El Greco, and Picasso inside, as well as an interesting collection of paintings and sculptures by contemporary Spanish, and especially Basque, artists. *(Open Tu-Fr 10am-2pm and 4-6:30pm, Sa 10am-2pm, Su 11am-2pm. Free.)*

ENTERTAINMENT

You can't go wrong by heading to the *casco viejo* after nightfall in Vitoria-Gasteiz. On weekdays the action settles down by midnight, but the thrashing weekend scene rumbles till dawn, so lace up your platform sneakers and join the fun. Bars line **Calle Cuchillería** "La Cuchi," **Calle Herrería, Calle Zapatería,** and **Cuesta de San Francisco.** C. Dato also attracts a crowd, if slightly older. Check out **Bar Carajo** and **Gasteiz-bi,** #9 and #23, C. Mateo Moraza off Cuesta de San Francisco. Dancing types can head around 2am to **María,** on C. Florida, **Circulo,** on C. General Alava, or **Aural** on Po. Fray Francisco near Parque Florida. The more refined, if no less exotic, **El**

PAÍS VASCO

Jardín de Atras, C. Correría, is a Moroccan tea room that pipes in Arabic music and puts out delicious pastries. **Acid Jazz Cafe,** C. San Prudencio, 17 has live music on Sunday nights.

Pick up the **Gaceta Municipal** at the tourist office or newsstands for info on theater and special events. World class jazz grooves into Vitoria-Gasteiz in mid-July for the week-long **Festival de Jazz de Vitoria-Gasteiz.** Tickets for big name performers cost 500-2000ptas, but there are plenty of free performances on the street. For info call 945 14 19 19. The last weekend in July also brings an **International Folklore Festival** to Bilbao, with more free performances. The **Fiesta de la Virgen Blanca** (Aug. 4-9), is the big party launched by rockets in Pl. Virgen Blanca.

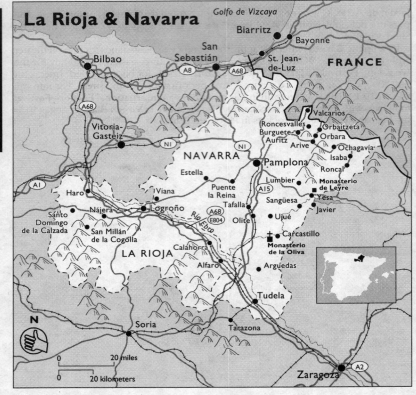

La Rioja & Navarra

Golfe de Vizcaya

La Rioja and Navarra

The Navarrese countryside slopes down from rustic Pyrenean villages on the French border, through bustling Pamplona, and to the dusty villages in the south. Bordered by Basque Country to the west and Aragón to the east, Rioja and Navarra's little-visited countryside greets tourists with varied landscapes and welcoming villages.

Navarra has long experienced the vicissitudes of Spain's on-again, off-again regionalism. In 1512 Fernando el Católico annexed the historically independent kingdom to a newly unified Spain but granted the Navarrese partial autonomy, permitting the continuation of *fueros* (traditional medieval laws). Their independent and active role in the Peninsular War ironically ushered in a period of centralism hostile to special regions such as Navarra, and their residual autonomy was revoked in 1833. Navarrese misfortune continued into the Modern Age when the regions supported the losing conservative and anti-centralist side in the 19th-century Carlist Wars. They sided with the "winners" in the 20th century by allying themselves with General Francisco Franco's Nationalist forces, victors of the Spanish Civil War, only to find themselves under a regime with no toleration for regional differences.

The Navarrese have continued to support regionalist causes since the fall of Franco and the subsequent reestablishment of provincial autonomy in 1983. Many of the region's northern inhabitants identify themselves as Basque and some align themselves with Basque independence movements. Basque Nationalists in Navarra are concerned with their regional exclusion both from País Vasco and the Basque independence movement.

In areas where Navarra sees few tourists, locals receive guests with exceptional warmth. An extensive network of government-approved *casas rurales* host tourists in lovely private homes, and home-cooked meals are often available. The region's epicurean specialty is *trucha a la Navarra* (trout stuffed with ham) but anything that finds its way onto your plate here is likely to be hearty and filling. The very helpful *Guía de turismo rural* (rural tourism guide) is available at any tourist office.

Tucked under Navarra, La Rioja is famous for great wine. "Rioja" is an internationally acclaimed wine classification with an 800-year tradition. The name derives from the Ebro tributary Río Oja, whose muddy waters trickle through the vineyards. Both the 1994 and 1995 grapes received the highest ratings possible. When ordering wine, know that asking for *"vino"* will get you the wine of the year, ordering *"crianza"* delivers higher-quality wine at least three years old, while a request for *"gran reserva"* brings the *crème de la crème* (and you'll pay for it). At home and abroad, look for the label of authenticity *denominación de origen calificada*.

Logroño, capital of La Rioja, lies in the region's center. The best *bodegas* (wine cellars) siphon off the lands in western Rioja Alta, around Haro. El Camino de Santiago (St. James' Way) passes through much of La Rioja, and tourist offices can provide useful information on the route. The mountainous Sierra region, with tranquil fields at the feet of lunar-like peaks, lines La Rioja's southern border, where dinosaur tracks have been discovered; ask at any tourist office about the *Ruta del dinosaurio*.

HIGHLIGHTS OF LA RIOJA AND NAVARRA

- Without a doubt, the world (in)famous **Fiestas de San Fermín** (Running of the Bulls) in Pamplona (see p. 257).
- The darling towns, inviting *casas rurales,* and prime hiking and skiing grounds of the **Valle del Roncal,** in the Navaresse Pyrenees (see p. 266).

■ Logroño

With characteristic hyperbole, the tourist office brochure proclaims that Logroño (pop. 124,000) feeds both the body and the soul. Although the Camino de Santiago makes a stop here, the soul finds little but bustling commerce and industry for spiritual nourishment; your body, however, will have plenty to be happy about. The best entry point into the vineyard towns of La Rioja, Logroño hosts even hole-in-the-wall bars in the pleasant *casco antiguo* that serve the region's fine wine, complemented with savory, inexpensive *tapas*.

ORIENTATION AND PRACTICAL INFORMATION

Both the old and new towns radiate from the **Parque del Espolón,** a tree-lined set of gravel paths with a large fountain at the center. The **casco antiguo** stretches between the park and the **Río Ebro,** on the far north side of the city.

To reach the park from the **train station,** cross the major traffic artery of **Avenida de Lobete** and angle left on **Avenida de España,** bearing right at the fork. Continue past the **bus station** at the next major intersection, connecting Av. España and **Calle del General Vara de Rey** (hereafter C. General Vara), which runs north-south. A right onto C. General Vara leads north to the park (8min.) and the *casco antiguo*.

Trains: RENFE, Pl. Europa (tel. 941 24 02 02), off Av. España on the south side of town. Note that bus service tends to be more frequent and thorough. Info open 7am-11pm. To: Haro (45min., 2 per day, 395-1100ptas); Calahorra (40min., 3-4 per day, 430ptas.); Burgos (2hr., 2-3 per day, 1800ptas); Zaragoza (2-2½hr., 5-6 per day, 1220-1800ptas); Bilbao (4hr., 2 per day, 1800ptas); Madrid (5½hr., 1 per day, 4000ptas); Barcelona (7hr., 3 per day, 4100ptas).

Buses: Av. España (tel. 941 23 59 83), on the corner of C. General Vara and Av. Pío XII. Several companies. Check info board for the appropriate counter. Info open daily 6am-11pm. To: Haro (1hr., 3-5 per day, 400ptas); Santo Domingo de la

Calzada (1hr., 3-9 per day, 360ptas); Soria (1½hr., 5 per day, 825ptas); Vitoria-Gasteiz (2hr., 4-6 per day, 970-1035ptas); Pamplona (2hr., 3-5 per day, 900ptas); Zaragoza (2hr., 4-6 per day, 1400ptas); Bilbao (2hr., 3-5 hr., 1500ptas); Burgos (2hr., 4-7 per day, 900ptas); Madrid (4¼hr., 5-6 per day, 2485ptas); Barcelona (6hr., 2-4 per day, 3900ptas).

Public Transportation: All buses run to Gran Vía del Rey Juan Carlos I, one block from Parque Espolón; lines #1 and 3 pass the bus station. All rides 75ptas.

Taxis: (tel. 941 22 42 99). Stands at the northwest corner of the park and the bus station. **Radio Taxi** (tel. 941 50 50 50).

Car Rental: Avis, Gran Vía del Rey Juan Carlos I, 67 (tel. 941 20 23 54), left off C. General Vara. Open M-F 9am-1:30pm and 4-7pm, Sa 10am-1:30pm. **Hertz,** Av. España, 1 (tel. 941 25 80 26), in the bus station. Open M-F 10am-2pm and 4-7pm.

Tourist Office: Po. Espolón (tel. 941 26 06 65; fax 941 25 60 45), at the south end of Parque Espoón, gives out **maps.** Take a left off C. General Vara coming from the bus and train stations. Open mid-June to Oct. M-Sa 10am-2pm and 4:30-7:30pm, Su 10am-2pm; Nov.-May M-F 9am-2pm.

Currency Exchange: Many banks crowd the broad avenues surrounding the park. Open M-F 8:30am-2:30pm. All have **ATMs.** A **Banco Central Hispano** is on C. General Vara at the corner of Parque Espolón.

Luggage Storage: At the bus station (200ptas; open 24hr.; tokens available 6am-11pm) and train station (400ptas; open 24hr.; tokens available 7am-11pm).

Emergency tel. 091, 092. **Police:** tel. 092.

Medical Services: Hospital de la Rioja, Av. Viana, 1 (tel. 941 29 11 94), on the edge of town in the direction of Pamplona.

Post Office: Pl. San Agustín (tel. 941 22 00 66 or 941 22 89 06), next to the museum. Open M-F 8:30am-8:30pm, Sa 9:30am-2pm. **Postal Code:** 26070.

ACCOMMODATIONS AND CAMPING

The *casco antiguo* brims with budget *pensiones* and *hostales*. Try **Calle San Juan,** the second left past Parque Espolón from the stations, and **Calle San Agustín** and **Calle Laurel,** a little deeper into the old quarter past the far corner of the park. Reservations are crucial for the *fiesta* week around September 21. There's an *albergue* for Santiago pilgrims only, on C. Ruavieja, 32, with space for 70.

Residencia Universitaria (HI), C. Caballero de la Rosa, 38 (tel. 941 29 11 45 or 941 26 14 22). From the stations, take a right off C. General Vara onto Mura de Cervantes, which becomes Av. Paz. Go about 10 blocks, and make a left on C. Caballero de la Rosa. Buses #1-A and 4 stop nearby. 15-20min. walk from the *casco antiguo*. Dorms 1000ptas, with sheets 1350ptas. Breakfast 200ptas. Open as *albergue* July-Sept. Call ahead.

Fonda Bilbaína, C. Capitán Eduardo Gallarza, 10, 2nd fl. (tel. 941 25 42 26). Take C. Sagasta into the *casco antiguo,* and turn left on C. Hermanos Moray and then right on C. Capitán Eduardo. High ceilings, shiny wooden floors, and bright rooms, some with balconies. Singles 1700ptas; doubles 3000ptas, with shower 3500ptas, with full bath 4000ptas.

Hostal Sebastián, C. San Juan, 21 (tel. 941 24 28 00). Large doubles with sinks and firm beds. Sparkling bathrooms. Front rooms have balconies looking out over the *tapas* scene. Singles 2000ptas; doubles 3500ptas; triples 4500ptas.

Pensión "El Revellín," C. Norte, 50 (tel. 941 22 02 31). From C. Sagasta take a left on C. Portales; after about 4 blocks go right on C. Once de Junio. It's 2 blocks ahead across the street. A friendly couple runs the *pensión* on the edge of the *casco antiguo.* Dim-but-clean doubles and triples without baths. Singles 2300ptas; doubles 3500ptas; triples 4500ptas.

Camping La Playa, Av. Playa, 6 (tel. 941 25 22 53), off the main highway across the river from the *casco antiguo.* Riverbank site with sandy beach. Laundromat, too. Municipal swimming pools next door, open after July 15 (free). 600ptas per person, per tent, per car. Open June-Sept.

FOOD

Logroñeses take their grapes seriously. Wine is the beverage of choice for everyone from patrons of the most elegant restaurants to the barflies pounding *chatos* (shot glasses of wine) in the street. Restaurants in the *casco antiguo* stock La Rioja's bite-sized delights, including *pimientos a la riojana* (sweet peppers with minced meat) and just about anything with mushrooms. Head to **Calle Laurel** and **Calle San Juan**, brimming with bars and cafes—many have little windows so giddy passers-by can sample all the goodies. The local market, **Mercado de San Blas,** is in the large concrete building on C. Capitán Eduardo Gallarza. Take a right off C. Mura de la Francisco de la Mata, along the park (open M-Sa 7:30am-1:30pm and 4-7:30pm). For half a block's worth of groceries, head to supermarket **Simago,** Av. La Rioja, a left off C. Miguel Villanueva past the tourist office (open M-Sa 9am-9pm).

Bar Soriano, Travesía de Laurel, 2 (tel. 941 22 88 07), where C. Laurel makes its 90° turn. Delish—it borders on the transcendent. Bartenders shovel shrimp and mushrooms out the window to eager crowds in the street. Specialty *pincho* is *champiñones con gambas* (sauteed mushrooms and shrimp on bread, with *chato* of wine or beer 140ptas). Open daily 11am-1am.

Bar Torrecilla, C. Laurel, 17. Try the *pincho moruños,* a slightly spicy beef kebab grilled as you wait. Perfect with a *chato* (150ptas). Open M-Th 10:30am-3pm and 7-11pm, F-Su 10:30am-3pm and 7pm-1am.

Restaurante Ruiz, C. San Juan, 11 (tel. 941 23 18 64). Delicious *menú* (1100ptas) includes a tasty *patatas a la Riojana* (starch with chorizo in a paprika-flavored broth). Open daily 1-3pm. Visa, MC.

Bocatas Riojas, C. Portales, 39 (tel. 941 25 40 55), across from the cathedral. Stuffs just about anything between two slices of hot bread—try the *logroñesa* with tomato, bacon, and cheese (350ptas) or the *cordobés* with tomato and a skewer of spicy grilled beef (400ptas). Long hours satisfy wandering youth with the munchies. Open M-Th 9am-11pm, F 9am-2am, Sa 11am-4am, Su 11am-midnight.

SIGHTS AND ENTERTAINMENT

The ornate Chirrugueresque towers of the **Catedral de Santa María de la Redonda** dominate the Pl. Mercado in the *casco antiguo. (Open daily 8am-1pm and 6-8:30pm. Free.)* From C. General Vara turn left on C. Portales; the cathedral is two blocks away on the right. Another three blocks along C. Portales sits the darling **Museo de La Rioja,** Pl. San Agustín, 23 (tel. 941 29 12 59), with an interesting collection that spans the 12th to 20th centuries and originates from the 1835 state seizure of regional monasteries' and convents' artwork and wealth, a move sanctioned by the Disentailment Law. *(Open Tu-Sa 10am-2pm and 6:30-9pm, Su 11:30am-2pm. Free.)*

The grassy knolls along the **Río Ebro** are good strolling ground. A pedestrian path and the bridges **Puente de Hierro** and **Puente de Piedra** cross the river.

At night, the **partying** begins in the *casco antiguo* along C. Laural and after midnight moves to C. Mayor along Pl. Mercado, C. Sagasta, and C. Carnicerias. Dusk-till-dawn revelry characterizes the **Fiestas de San Bernabé** (June 11), which is capped by an awesome fireworks display. The big party is September 20-26, around the **Fiesta de San Mateo** on September 21, which conveniently coincides with the **Fiestas de la Vendimia,** celebrating the grape harvest, when the bulls run and citizens make a ceremonial offering of crushed grapes to the Virgen de Valvanera.

■ Near Logroño: Santo Domingo de la Calzada

A symbolically important stop along the Camino de Santiago, Santo Domingo de la Calzada owes its existence to the pilgrimage. Eleventh-century Santo Domingo retired to the woods southwest of Logroño in search of ascetic solitude, but he didn't stay lonely for long. Seeing first-hand the trials and travails of pilgrims crossing the

A Little Something to Cock About

Wandering through the Cathedral of Santo Domingo, the visitor may be surprised to hear the crowing of a rooster, only to stumble upon said rooster and accompanying hen in an elegant pen in the cathedral wall. The birds are there to remember the tale of the miracle of Santo Domingo, known as "the cock that crows after it has been roasted." As the legend goes, an innkeeper's daughter fell madly in (unrequited) love with a pilgrim named Hugonell. The rejected, heart-broken girl slipped a silver cup into Hugonell's bag and reported the "robbery" to the mayor. Hugonell was found guilty and hanged. When his distraught parents visited the gallows, they heard their son's voice insisting that he was alive and that Santo Domingo had saved him. They rushed to the mayor's house and related the bizarre series of events. The skeptical mayor, his meal of fowl and greens interrupted, scoffed and insisted that Hugonell was as dead as the roasted chicken on his plate. The mayor ate his words when the cooked cock suddenly sprouted feathers and crowed Hugonell's innocence.

Tourists who wish to engage in their own culinary commemoration of the miracle can pick up bags of the local pastry, called *ahorcamientos,* or hangings.

river and being a good-hearted sort of chap, he built a bridge for them, drove a road (the *calzada,* or causeway) through the woods, and converted his hermitage into a hospice. Soon, business was booming in Santo Domingo (pop. 6000—now, not then). The town honors its founder during the week of May 10 with a series of rituals that re-enact episodes of his life.

King Alfonso VI noticed the work of this monastic reject and donated resources for the construction of the grand **Catedral de Santo Domingo**—he even set the first stone himself. *(Open M-Sa 10am-6:30pm. 250ptas, over 65 and pilgrims 150ptas, under 18 100ptas.)* The lavish *retablo* (altarpiece) was removed for restoration in 1994, and exquisite Romanesque pillars were discovered behind where the altarpiece had stood. Consequently the *retablo* has been moved to a side chapel to preserve the stylistic cohesiveness of the Romanesque church. To reach the cathedral from the **bus stop** at Pl. Beato Hermosilla, cross Av. Juan Carlos I and follow C. Alcalde Rodolfo Varona. Take the next left (unmarked C. Pinar) for one block, then turn right on C. Hilario Perez, which ends at the Plaza del Santo, bordered by the cathedral and pilgrim hospice-turned-parador. The **Casa del Santo,** C. Mayor, 42 (tel. 941 34 33 90), off the cathedral square, has info for pilgrims in the Federación de Asociaciones Jacobeas office. *(Open in summer M-Sa 9am-7pm, in winter M-Sa 9am-2pm.)* The *hospedería* upstairs has 41 beds and meals for free, but only for those heading to Santiago.

The town's **tourist office** sits in Casa de Trastámara, C. Mayor, 70 (tel. 941 34 33 34). The **postal code** is 26250. From Pl. Santo, facing the cathedral, go left onto C. Mayor (open daily 10am-2pm and 4:30-7:30pm). Unless you're planning to withdraw in contemplation, Santo Domingo is best as a daytrip. Persistent non-pilgrims can try **Hostal Miguel,** C. Juan Carlos I, 23 (tel. 941 34 32 52), which is clean and comfy with big windows (singles 2000ptas, with bath 3500ptas; doubles 4000ptas, with bath 6000ptas). Several restaurants hover near the cathedral on C. Mayor and adjoining plazas, luring hungry pilgrims with generous *menús*.

Buses run from Pl. Beato Hermosilla to Logroño (1hr., M-Sa 9 per day, Su 3per day, 360ptas) and Haro (20min., M-Sa 2-5 per day, 160ptas).

■ Near Logroño: Calahorra

Despite 200 years as a Roman metropolis and a smattering of monuments both religious and Roman, Calahorra's (pop. 19,500) minor claim to fame is its food. The city is known for its *huertas,* or market gardens that have taken place in the **Plaza del Raso** since the Middle Ages (every Thursday morning). Spring sprouts and asparagus are combined with artichokes, cauliflower, peas, carrots, green beans, and lamb to make *menestra de verduras,* a typical Calahorran dish. Food in Calahorra is, of course, best complemented by an array of local wines. Various **restaurants** along Po.

Mercadal and in Pl. Raso offer tasty regional delights in reasonably priced *menús*. **Viana,** C. Estrella, 18, (tel. 941 13 00 08), around the corner from the bus station, tempts tummies with meals concocted from the spring harvest (*menú* 1100 ptas).

The requisite 15th- and 16th-century Gothic **Catedral de Santa María** (tel. 941 13 12 52) lies buried within the *casco antiguo.* (Open daily 10:30am-12:30pm and 5-8:30pm. For guided tours call 941 13 21 20.) To get there, take C. Mayor from Pl. Raso, follow the signs and turn left on Cuesta de la Catedral. At its end, turn right downhill. The story behind the cathedral is perhaps more interesting than the structure itself: it's built on the site where the city's two patron saints, Emeterio and Celedonio, were reportedly killed. Their decapitated heads continued to preach Christianity so they were thrown into the Río Ebro. **Roman ruins** sprinkle the city, including a statue of **La Matrona,** by the parador on Po. Mercadal. When Hannibal besieged the city in AD 72, this woman was the lone survivor, having conquered starvation by eating human flesh.

A prospective **tourist office** (tel. 941 13 09 32, fax 941 14 63 27) in the Museo Municipal, just off Pl. Raso, will dispense maps, as will a summertime kiosk in front of the **Ayuntamiento,** and—in a pinch—the public officials inside (open M-F 8am-3pm, Sa 9am-2pm). To Pl. Raso from the Ayuntamiento, walk straight up C. Martires, which becomes C. Grande.

RENFE trains (tel. 941 13 19 46) run to Logroño (40min., 2-3 per day, 455ptas). The **bus station** (tel. 941 23 59 83) is on C. Miguel de Cervantes. The last bus to Logroño leaves at 8:45pm (1hr., 6-8 per day, 430ptas). To get to the Ayuntamiento from the train station, take a left at the end of the block and then right up the hill on Av. Estación, bearing right at the fork and continuing up along tree-lined Po. Mercadal. From the bus station, turn right out of the station and left onto C. Bebricio.

■ Haro

Seventeen *bodegas* overwhelm the town of Haro (pop. 9500), the heart of La Rioja's wine industry. Most offer free tours of their facilities in English and Spanish between 9am and 2pm, although reservations are almost always required. Only **Bodegas Muga** (tel. 941 31 04 98), across the river, can be visited without calling ahead. (Tours in summer M-F 10, 11am (English), and noon; in winter M-F 11am and 4pm. The tourist office has additional information on visiting *bodegas.*)

For those craving a little religion with their wine, the **Basílica de Nuestra Señora de La Vega** has beautiful stained-glass windows and a frescoed dome. To find the church from the tourist office, turn left and follow C. Vega for about three blocks (church open daily 8am-1pm and 5-8:30pm). Past the basilica, in the Estación Etnológica, the **Museo del Vino** has sleek exhibits on everything you wanted to know about wine and then some. (Open M-Sa 10am-2pm and 4-8pm, Su 10am-2pm. 300ptas, Wednesdays free.) The 16th-century **Iglesia Parroquial de Santo Tomás** is on Pl. Iglesia, a left from Pl. Paz as you face the Ayuntamiento.

PRACTICAL INFORMATION RENFE trains (tel. 941 31 15 97) run to Logroño (35min., 5 per day, 455-900ptas), Bilbao (2hr., 4 per day, 1000ptas), and Zaragoza (2½hr., 5 per day, 2400ptas). To reach Pl. Paz from the train station, take the road downhill, turn right and then left across the river, and let C. Navarra lead you uphill to the plaza. Haro's **bus station** is at C. Ventilla (tel. 941 31 15 53). Buses go to: Logroño (1hr., 6-7 per day, 345ptas); Vitoria (45min., 5-6 per-day, 550ptas); Bilbao (1hr., 4-6 per day, 1020ptas); and Santo Domingo de la Calzada (30min., 2-4 per day, 160ptas). To reach Pl. Paz from the bus stop, follow signs to *centro ciudad* along C. Ventilla and continue across Pl. Cruz on C. Victor Pradera; take the first left into Pl. Paz.

A helpful bilingual staff at the **tourist office,** Pl. Monseñor Florentino Rodríguez (tel. 941 30 33 66), dispenses information and maps. With your back to the Ayuntamiento, take C. Vega from the far left corner of Pl. Paz. The office is in the plaza to the left around the bend. (Open June-Oct. 15 M-Sa 10am-2pm and 4:30-7:30pm, Su 10am-2pm; Oct. 15-May Tu-F 10am-2pm, Sa 10am-2pm and 4:30-7:30pm.) The **postal code** is 26200.

LA RIOJA & NAVARRA

ACCOMMODATIONS AND FOOD Haro is a good daytrip from Logroño, but for those sticking around, **Hostal Aragón,** C. Vega, 9 (tel. 941 31 00 04), between the tourist office and Pl. Paz, has spacious old rooms with high ceilings and wood floors (singles 1600ptas; doubles 3200ptas). **Camping de Haro,** Av. Miranda (tel. 941 31 27 37), is on the train-station side of the river, left of the bridge from town (Jan.-June 15 410ptas per person, per tent, and per car; June 16-Dec. 485ptas; 7% IVA). For an excellent lunch and an even better bargain, join Haro's upper crust at **Mesón Ata-mauri,** Pl. Juan Garcia, Gato 1 (tel. 941 30 32 20), right off C. Vega on the way to the tourist office (*menú del día* 1350ptas). For cheaper eats, munch on *tapas* in **La Her-radura** quarter or on C. Vega. On C. Santo Tomás, many **wine shops** sell the region's fruit of the vine. The best vintages start at around 3500ptas per bottle, but others cost as little as 200-500ptas.

Join the locals and *ir de vinos* (literally, "go for wines") in the evening in *La Herra-dura* (the horseshoe), the area around C. St. Tomás off Pl. Paz. Ask for *vino* and you'll get the vintage of the year (about 50-75ptas); for higher quality, order *crianza,* more than three years old (about 150ptas). Haro parties hard on June 24-29, culminating in the **Batalla del Vino** on June 29, when participants spray wine at innocent bystand-ers. The **Fiesta Mayor,** on and around September 8, is more sedate.

■ Pamplona (Iruña)

Long, long ago, Pamplona's *fiestas* in honor of its patron saint San Fermín were just another Spanish religious holiday. Known to locals as *los Sanfermines,* the week of July 6-14 is now as undiluted an expression of lunacy and joy as ever careened down a city's streets. Ever since Nobel-prize-winning author Ernest Hemingway brought the city to international attention in *The Sun Also Rises,* hordes of visitors from around the world have come to witness and experience the legendary *encierro* (running of the bulls). At the bullring, a huggable statue of Papa Hemingway welcomes *aficiona-dos* (fans)—mostly just rowdy blowhards—to Europe's premier festival: eight days of dancing, drinking, dashing, and otherwise feeding the wild beast within.

Although *los Sanfermines* is Pamplona's biggest draw, it is still a pleasant enough city the other 357 days of the year. Lush parks, a lovely Gothic cathedral, a massive citadel, and the winding streets of the *casco antiguo* entertain those who show up when 1000lb. horned beasts aren't running through the streets. Pamplona (pop. 180,000) is the capital of the province of Navarra, but its roots are Basque. Although the city was named after Pompey the Great by its Roman "founders," the area had actually been settled earlier by the Basques. Graffiti and posters remind visitors of the city's involvement with the several Basque Separatist movements.

ORIENTATION AND PRACTICAL INFORMATION

Almost everything of interest to visitors is in the **casco antiguo,** the northeast quarter of this provincial capital. **Plaza del Castillo,** marked by a bandstand, is Pamplona's center. From the **bus station,** turn left onto Av. Conde Oliveto. At the traffic circle on Pl. Príncipe de Viana, take the second left onto Av. San Ignacio, follow it to the end of pedestrian thoroughfare **Paseo Sarasate,** and bear right. From the **train station,** take bus #9 (95ptas); disembark at the last stop, cut across Po. Sarasate, then walk diago-nally left to Pl. Castillo. North of Pl. Castillo, the Baroque **Casa Consistorial** (a.k.a. Ayuntamiento) makes a handsome marker amid the swirl of medieval streets.

Although Pamplona is usually a very safe city, crime skyrockets during the *San Fer-mines,* when assaults and muggings do occur. Some come to the *fiesta* only to take advantage of awe-struck tourists. Do not roam alone at night, and take extreme care in the parks and shady streets of the *casco antiguo.* Enthused revelers who pass out in parks can often say good-bye to their wallets and money belts. Some stores close during the *San Fermines,* and many restaurants and bars close after the *fiestas* for a well-deserved rest.

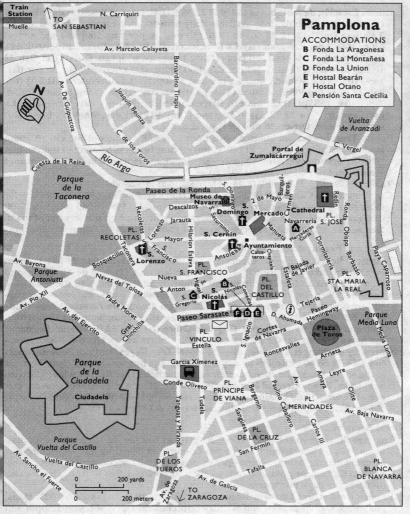

Pamplona

ACCOMMODATIONS
B Fonda La Aragonesa
C Fonda La Montañesa
D Fonda La Union
E Hostal Bearán
F Hostal Otano
A Pensión Santa Cecilia

Transportation

Flights: Aeropuerto de Noaín (tel. 948 31 71 82), 6km away, accessible only by taxi (about 1200ptas). To Madrid (7 per day) and Barcelona (30min., M-F 4 per day).

Trains: Estación RENFE, off Av. San Jorge, 20min. from the *casco antiguo* by bus #9 from Po. Sarasate (95ptas). Info (tel. 948 13 02 02) open daily 6am-10pm. Another more accessible **ticket/info office,** C. Estella, 8 (tel. 948 22 72 82), sits near the bus station. Exit the bus station and go around the right corner; the office is across the parking lot. Open M-F 9am-1:30pm and 4:30-7:30pm, Sa 9:30am-1pm. Pamplona is miserably connected by rail. Reservations are often mandatory on longer trains during *San Fermines;* it's much faster and easier to take the bus. To: Olite (40min., 1-4 per day, 370ptas); Vitoria-Gasteiz (1¼hr., 1-3 per day, 575ptas); Tudela (1½hr., 8-9 per day, 800-1300ptas); Zaragoza (2hr., 4-8 per day, 1220-1800ptas); San Sebastián (2 hr., 2 per day, 1400-1500ptas); Madrid (5hr., 2 per day, 4100ptas); Barcelona (6-8hr., 3 per day, 4100ptas).

Buses: Estación de Autobuses (tel. 948 22 38 54), C. Conde Oliveto at the corner of C. Yanguas y Miranda. Info available daily 6am-10pm. Nearly 20 companies. **La Tafallesa** (tel. 948 22 28 36) to Olite (50 min., 6 per day, 360ptas) and Roncal (2hr., M-Sa 2 per day, 880ptas). **La Ronclesa** (tel. 948 22 20 79) to San Sebastián (1 hr., 7-8 per day, 750ptas) and Jaca (1¾hr., 1 per day, 855ptas). **Conda** (tel. 948 22 10 26) to: Tudela (1½hr., 5-7 per day, 800-880ptas); Zaragoza (2-3hr., 6 per day, 1450-1650ptas); Madrid (5hr., 4-5 per day, 3140ptas). **La Burendesa (ALSA)** (tel. 948 22 17 66) to Vitoria-Gasteiz (1½hr., 6-13 per day, 835ptas) and Bilbao (2hr., 4-7 per day, 1535ptas). **Bilman** to Barcelona (5½hr., 3-4 per day, 2090ptas). **La Estellesa** (tel. 948 22 22 23) to Logroño (1hr., 4-12 per day, 900ptas). Buses also serve Burguete, Orbaiceta, and Ochagavía.

Public Transportation: Fourteen bus lines cover all corners of the city. A route guide is available at the tourist office. Bus #9 runs from Po. Sarasate to train station (20min., departs every 10-15min. 6:30am-10:30pm, 95ptas). During *San Fermines* some routes run night shifts (150ptas).

Taxis: (tel. 948 23 21 00 or 948 23 23 00). Stand at Pl. Castillo.

Car Rental: Nal-Car (tel. 948 22 35 69), in Hotel Tres Reyes. 6500ptas per day for more than 3 days. **Europcar,** Hotel Blanca Navarra, Av. Pío XII, 43 (tel. 948 17 60 02). Take bus #1, 2, or 4 and get off after the traffic circle on the way out of town. Min. age 21. 56,000ptas per week. Open M-F 9am-1pm and 4-7:30pm, Sa 9am-1pm.

Tourist and Financial Services

Tourist Office: C. Duque de Ahumada, 3 (tel. 948 22 07 41; fax 948 21 14 62). From Pl. Castillo, take Av. Carlos III 1 block, turn left on C. Duque de Ahumada, and cross C. Espoz y Mina. Fair **map** and minute-by-minute guides to the festivities. English spoken. Info about **currency exchange,** public baths, and buses to campsite are posted on a bulletin board outside. Open during *San Fermines* daily 10am-5pm; July-Aug. M-Sa 10am-2pm and 4-7pm, Su 10am-2pm; Sept.-June M-F 10am-2pm and 4-7pm, Sa 10am-2pm. **City Info Office** (tel. 948 42 01 00), in the rear of the Ayuntamiento, off the plaza by the market, offers a map. Open M-F 8am-3pm.

Currency Exchange: Reception desk at **Hotel Tres Reyes,** Jardines de la Taconera (tel. 948 22 66 00), changes money 24hr. From the bus station turn right, bear left at the second fork, and then bear left again; the hotel is to the left where the road next forks. **Banco Central Hispano,** Pl. Castillo, 21, and in Pl. Vinculo, on the corner of C. Estella and C. Alhondiga. Open May-Sept. M-F 8:30am-2:30pm; Oct.-Apr. M-F 8:30am-2:30pm, Sa 8:30am-1pm. Both have **ATMs**.

Local Services

Luggage Storage: At the **bus station.** 200ptas per bag per day, large packs 300ptas. Open M-Sa 6:15am-9:30pm, Su 6:30am-1:30pm and 2-9:30pm. Closes for *San Fermines,* when the Ayuntamiento opens storage around the corner at C. Garcia Jimenez and C. Yanguas y Miranda (open 24hr.). **RENFE** (tel. 948 13 02 02) has lockers (400ptas per day). Buy tokens at the ticket counter daily 7am-10pm.

English Bookstore: Librería Gómez, Pl. Castillo, 28 (tel. 948 22 67 02). Maps, guidebooks, pulp fiction, and Wordsworth classics. Open M-F 9am-1:30pm and 4:30-8pm, Sa 9am-1:30pm.

Youth Services: Departmento de Deporte Juventud, C. Arrieta, 25 (tel 948 42 78 78). ISIC and HI cards available. Open M-F 8:30am-2:30pm.

Laundromat: Lavomatique, C. Descalzos, 28 (tel. 948 22 19 22). From Pl. San Francisco follow C. Hilarión Eslava to the end, then turn right. Wash, dry, and soap for 900ptas. Open M-F 10am-1pm and 4-8:30pm; closed during *San Fermines.*

Public Toilets and Baths: Squat **toilet booths** are set up for *San Fermines.* Permanent bathrooms in the Jardines de Taconera let you sit. **Casa de Baño,** C. Hilarión Eslava, 2 (tel. 948 22 17 38), at the corner of Jarauta. Showers 110ptas, towel 40ptas, soap 40ptas. Open Tu-Sa 8am-8pm, Su 8am-2:30pm.

Swimming Pool: Piscinas de Aranzadi (tel. 948 22 30 02), 15min. from Pl. Castillo, on Vuelta de Aranzadi. M-Sa 300ptas, under 14 100ptas; Su 500ptas, under 14 100ptas. *San Fermines* 800ptas, under 14 250ptas. Open daily 10:30am-8:30pm.

Emergency and Communications

Emergency: call 112. **Police: National Police,** C. General Chinchilla, to the right on Av. Taconera with your back to the statue on Po. Sarasate. **Municipal Police,** C. Monasterio de Irache, 2 (tel. 092). English spoken.

24hr. Pharmacy: Check the *Diario de Navarra* listings or call 948 22 21 11.

Medical Services: Hospital de Navarra, C. Irunlarrea (tel. 948 42 21 00). The **Red Cross** sets up stands at the bus station and the *corrida* during *San Fermines.*

Internet Access: iturNet cibercafé, C. Iturrama, 1 (tel. 948 25 28 20), on the corner of C. Abejeras. Bus #2 stops on C. Iturrama. From the bus station, take a left on C. Yanguas y Miranda, then head across Pl. Fueros to C. Abejeras. 500ptas per hr. Open M-Sa 10am-2pm and 4:30-10pm.

Post Office: Po. Sarasate, 9 (tel. 948 22 12 63). Lista de Correos window #8. Open M-F 8:30am-8:30pm, Sa 9:30am-2pm; *San Fermines* M-Sa 8:30am-2pm. **Postal Code:** 31001.

ACCOMMODATIONS AND CAMPING

If there was a lucky convergence of stars on the day of your birth and you have truck-loads of cash, you *may* find a room during the first few days of *San Fermines.* For solo travelers, even these assets will probably not be enough. Diehard *sanferminis-tas* book their rooms for next year before going home. In most cases, you must reserve at least a month ahead and pay rates (up front) up to four times higher than those listed (anywhere from 4000-8000ptas per person in most budget *pensiones*). Arriving several days before the *fiestas* may help. Check the newspaper *Diario de Navarra* for **casas particulares.** Early in the week, people accost visitors at the train and bus stations, offering couches and floor space. Be wary—accommodations and prices vary tremendously, and you might find yourself blowing your money for a blink of sleep on a dirty floor in a bad part of town. Because of past scams, the tourist office will neither recommend nor aid in this effort. Many who can't find rooms sleep outside on the lawns of the Ciudadela, Pl. Fueros, and on the banks of the river. Vet-eran park-sleepers recommend extreme caution. If you can't leave your belongings at the *consigna* at the bus or train station (it fills fast), sleep on top of them (still not foolproof). Always sleep in groups. It's safer to nap during the day when it's warmer and brighter and stay up through the night. During those months when Pamplona manages to keep its street free of pesky bulls, finding a room is no problem. Accom-modations that define the word "budget"—in price *and* style—line **Calle San Nicolás** and **Calle San Gregorio** off Pl. Castillo. Be aware that most hostel owners fol-low separate price schedules for *temporada alta (San Fermines), temporada media* (summer), and *temporada baja* (rest of the year).

Pensión Santa Cecilia, C. Navarrería, 17 (tel. 948 22 22 30). Take C. Chapitela and make the first right on C. Mercaderes, then take a left at a 45° angle. The *hostal* is on your left. Comfort lies behind the impressive (and spooky) portal. Bright red trim in hallways and high-ceilinged rooms. *San Fermines* dorms 4000ptas. July-Aug.: singles 2500ptas; doubles 4000ptas; triples 5600ptas. Sept.-June: singles 2500; doubles 3700ptas; triples 5200ptas. Most credit cards accepted.

Fonda La Aragonesa, San Nicolás, 22 (tel. 948 22 34 28). Walk across the street to Hostal Bearán for reception desk. Simple rooms, shiny hallways, and aromatic bath-rooms. *San Fermines* doubles 9000ptas. July-Sept. doubles 3500ptas. Oct.-June: singles 2000ptas; doubles 3000ptas. Visa, MC, AmEx.

Hostal Otano, C. San Nicolás, 5 (tel. 948 22 50 95). Adequately comfortable rooms, all with sinks. Doubles with bath also have TV. Don't even try for *San Fermines*—they've had the same people for 15 years. Singles 1800ptas, with bath 3000ptas; doubles 4000ptas, with bath 5000ptas. Visa, MC, AmEx.

Hostal Bearán, C. San Nicolás, 25 (tel. 948 22 34 28). Squeaky-clean salmon-colored rooms with phone, TV, bath, and safebox. *San Fermines:* singles 13,000ptas; dou-bles 15,000ptas. July-Sept.: singles 5500ptas; doubles 6500ptas. Oct.-June: singles 4500ptas; doubles 5500ptas. Breakfast 450ptas. Visa, MC, AmEx.

LA RIOJA & NAVARRA

Fonda La Montañesa, C. San Gregorio, 2 (tel. 948 22 43 80). You can't beat the price. With several floors of beds and lots of turnover, it's definitely worth a try during the party. No winter heating. *San Fermines* dorms up to 4000ptas; the rest of the year dorms 1400-1500ptas.

Fonda La Union, C. San Nicolás, 13 (tel. 948 22 13 19), next to Restaurante San Nicolás. Proprietors have recently renovated their rooms and it shows, especially in the new bathrooms. *San Fermines* dorms 5000ptas; the rest of the year dorms 1500-2000ptas. Visa, MC, AmEx.

Camping: Camping Ezcaba (tel. 948 33 16 65), in Eusa, 7km outside Pamplona on the road to Irún. From Pl. Toros, La Montañesa bus runs to Eusa (4 per day, get off at the gasoline station, the last stop). Capacity for 714 campers, although it fills fast during the big bull week. 450ptas per person, per tent, and per car. Open June-Oct. No reservations accepted.

FOOD

While *San Fermines* draws street vendors selling everything from roast chicken to *churros,* the tiny neighborhoods of Pamplona advertise hearty *menús* throughout the entire year. Try side streets in the neighborhood of Pensión Santa Cecilia, the cathedral area above Pl. San Francisco, and C. Jarauta and C. Descalzos, near Po. Ronda. **Calle Navarrería,** near the cathedral, overflows with small bars and restaurants. More restaurants crank away on **Calles Estafeta, Mayor,** and **San Nicolás;** the last is longer on crowds and alcohol than solid food. Calles Navarrería and San Lorenzo and Po. Sarasate house *bocadillo* bars. During *fiestas,* cheap drinks and cheaper ideology can be found at *barracas políticas* (bars organized by political interest groups that don't expect any interest in their platforms) set up next to the amusement park on the west end of the Ciudadela. A fine Navarrese finish is the dessert liqueur *Patxaran (Pacharán).* The official soft drink of all Spanish northern *fiestas* is **calimocho,** a mixture of wine to keep you happy and Coca-Cola to keep you up. Many cafes and restaurants close for one to two weeks after *San Fermines.*

The **market,** C. Mercado, is to the right of Casa Consistorial's facade and down the stairs (open M-Sa 8am-2:30pm). For a **supermarket,** check out **Vendi** at the corner of C. Hilarión Eslava and C. Mayor (open M-F 9am-2pm and 5:30-7:30pm, Sa 9am-2pm; *San Fermines* M-Sa 9am-2pm; Visa, MC).

Bar-Restaurante Lanzale, C. San Lorenzo, 31 (tel. 948 22 10 71), between C. Mayor and C. Jarauta, above Pl. San Francisco. Pleasant, spacious dining room serves up a changing *menú* (1100ptas), often with tender pork ribs and delicious desserts. Open M-Sa for meals 1:30-3:30pm and 9-11pm. Bar open daily 10am-midnight.

Restaurante Sarasate, C. San Nicolás, 19-21 (tel. 948 22 57 27), above the seafood store. Healthful, all-vegetarian cuisine. Simply scrumptious. Lunchtime *menú* 1200ptas. Open M-Th 1:15-4pm and 8-11pm, F-Sa 1:15-4pm and 9-11pm.

Restaurante San Fermín, C. San Nicolás, 44-46 (tel. 948 22 21 91). Tranquil upstairs dining room. *The* place to celebrate your near brush with horned death or your consummate sanity in avoiding the whole thing altogether. Locals rate it as one of the best. Weekday *menú* 1600ptas. Open M-F 1-3:30pm and 9-11:30pm, Sa 1-3:30pm and 8:30-11:30pm.

Hong-Kong, C. San Gregorio, 38 (tel. 948 22 66 35). Ignore the Chinese pop music; the 4-course, 850ptas *menú* will win you over. Look for the red balcony. Open daily noon-4pm and 8pm-midnight.

Self-Service Estafeta, C. Estafeta, 57 (tel. 948 22 10 65). Service so quick you can stop, chow, and the bull *still* won't catch you. *Paella* (550ptas), roast half-chicken (500ptas), *menú* (1110ptas). Don't come here for atmosphere. Open *San Fermines* M-Sa 12:30pm-2am; in summer M-Sa 1-4pm. Visa, MC, AmEx.

SIGHTS

Pamplona's rich architectural legacy gives ample reason to visit, even beyond that mythical week. The recently restored late 14th-century **Gothic cathedral** (tel. 948 21 08 27) is at the end of C. Navarrería. *(Open M-F 10am-1:30pm and 4-7pm, Sa 10am-*

1:30pm. Tours at 10:30, 11:30am, 12:30, 5, and 6pm.) It houses an ornately sculpted alabaster mausoleum where Carlos III and his wife Queen Leonor are interred. Off the lovely cloister is a 5-chimneyed kitchen dating from 1335, one of four of its kind in all of Europe. Aside from the cathedral, dedicated church-goers can check out the Gothic 13th-century **Iglesia de San Cernín,** near the Ayuntamiento, and **Iglesia de San Nicolás,** in Pl. San Nicolás. For a peek at San Fermín himself, head to **Iglesia de San Lorenzo,** C. Mayor, 74. *(Open daily 8am-12:30pm and 6:30-8pm.)*

The pentagonal **Ciudadela,** built by Felipe II as part of the city's defense, now sprawls in a grassy park that hosts free exhibits and concerts in the summer. *(Open daily 7am-10pm; closed during San Fermines. Free.)* Its impressive walls even scared off Napoleon, who refused to launch a frontal attack and staged a trick snowball fight instead. When Spanish sentries joined in, the French entered the city through its gates. To get to the **walls** from the old quarter, pick up C. Redín at the far end of the cathedral plaza. A left turn follows the walls past the **Portal de Zumalacárregui** and along the Río Arga. Bear left through the gardens of **Parque de la Taconera**—where some random peacocks and assorted wildlife hang out—until reaching the Ciudadela.

Back in the *casco antiguo,* the **Museo de Navarra** (tel. 948 42 64 92), up C. Santo Domingo from Casa Consistorial, shelters beautifully preserved 4th- and 5th-century Roman mosaics, murals from all over the region, and a nice collection of 14th- to 20th-century paintings, including Goya's portrait of the Marqués de San Adrián. *(Open San Fermines Tu-Su 11am-2pm; year-round Tu-Sa 10am-2pm and 5-7pm, Su 11am-2pm. 300ptas, students 150ptas, Saturday afternoons and Sundays free.)*

ENTERTAINMENT

Throughout the year, **Plaza de Castillo** is the city's social heart, with people of all ages congregating in and around its bars and cafes. Hemingway's favorite was **Café-Bar Iruña,** the backdrop for much of *The Sun Also Rises.* It maintains a timeless feel, although its prices for outdoor dining are well into the 21st century *(café con leche* 225ptas; good *bocatas* 600ptas). From 5pm until 3am, the cafe morphs into an overdressed bingo palace; the bar, a couple of doors down, stays itself.

The young and restless booze up at bars in the *casco antiguo.* **Calle de Jarauta** is a nighttime favorite, as well as **Calle San Nicolas** and **Calle San Gregorio.** **Bodega La Ribera,** on C. Carmen, is a good place for cheap beers (175ptas) and foosball, where you can begin your evening with bacchanalian petulance. **Mesón de la Navarrería,** C. Navarrería, 15, draws an older but still hip crowd. Tranquil **Mesón del Caballo Blanco** serves its drinks from an outdoor patio overlooking the old city walls and surrounding countryside. Claustrophobes escape the cramped streets of San Gregorio and San Nicolás to bars in **Barrio San Juan,** beyond Hotel Tres Reyes on Av. Bayona; many draw a gay clientele. **Café Niza,** C. Duque de Ahemada, is also a gay hangout.

LOS SAN FERMINES (JULY 6-14)

> ¡Uno de enero, dos de febrero, tres de marzo, cuatro de abril,
> Cinco de mayo, seis de junio, siete de julio es San Fermín!
> ¡A Pamplona hemos de ir! Con una bota, con una bota,
> ¡A Pamplona hemos de ir! Con una bota y un calcetín.

Visitors from the world over crowd Pamplona for the *Fiestas de San Fermín*—known to many visitors as "The Running of the Bulls"—in search of Europe's greatest party. Pamplona orgiastically delivers, with an eight-day frenzy of parades, wine, bullfights, parties, dancing, fireworks, wine, rock concerts, and wine to topple even the most Dionysian ne'er-do-wells. "My gosh! I'm sleepy now," says Robert Cohn in *The Sun Also Rises.* "Doesn't this thing ever stop?" "Not for a week," comes the seasoned response. Pamplonese, uniformly clad in white garb with red sashes and bandanas, throw themselves into the merry-making with inspired abandon, displaying obscene levels of physical stamina and alcohol(ic) tolerance. Try to keep up at your own risk.

The mayor kicks off the festivities at noon on July 6, firing the first rocket, or *chupinzao,* from the Ayuntamiento's balcony. A barbaric howl explodes from the sea of expectant *sanferministas* in the plaza below, and within minutes the streets of the *casco antiguo* flood with improvised singing and dancing troupes. The *peñas,* taurine societies more concerned with beer than bullfighting, lead the brouhaha. At 5pm on the 6th and at 9am or 9:30am every other day, they are joined by the *Comparsa de Gigantes y Cabezudos,* a troupe of *gigantes* (giant wooden monarchs) and *zaldikos* (courtiers on horseback). *Kilikis* (swollen-headed buffoons) run around chasing little kids and hitting them with play clubs. These harlequinesque misfits, together with church and Ayuntamiento officials, escort San Fermín on his triumphant procession through the *casco antiguo.* The saint's 15th-century statue is brought from the Iglesia de San Lorenzo at 10am on the July 7, the actual day of *San Fermín.*

The Running of the Bulls

The running of the bulls, called the *encierro,* is the focal point of the *San Fermines.* The ritual dates back to the 14th century, when it served the practical function of getting the bulls from their corrals to the bullring. These days, the first *encierro* of the festival takes place at 8am on July 7 and is repeated at 8am every day for the following seven days. Hundreds of bleary-eyed, hung-over, hyper-adrenalized runners flee from very large bulls as bystanders cheer, provoke, and make mischief from barricades, windows, balconies, and doorways.

Rockets mark the bulls' progress on their 825m dash. Six steers accompany the six bulls—watch it, they have horns, too. Both the bulls and the mob are dangerous. Terrified runners, all convinced the bull is breathing on their tushes, flee for dear life and react without concern for their peers who might get trampled in the process. Experienced runners, many of whom view the event as an athletic art form with its own protocol, try to get as dangerously close to the bull as possible—without, of course, the bull getting dangerously close to them.

After cascading through a perilously narrow opening (where a large proportion of the injuries occur), the run pours into the bullring, amid scores of appreciative—and decidedly saner—spectators who sit cheering the runners. Hemingway had the right idea: don't run. Watch the *encierro* at the bullring. Music, waves, chanting, and dancing pump up the spectators until the headline entertainment arrives. Bullring spectators should arrive around 6:45am to experience the crowd heating up. Tickets for the Grada section of the ring are easily available before 7am (M-F 450ptas, Sa-Su 600ptas). You can watch for free too, but the free section is overcrowded, and it can be hard to see (or breathe). In the ring, one to three animals are released from their pens as runners scurry from the horny bulls. If you want to participate in the bullring excitement, you can line up by the Pl. de Toros before 7:30am and run in before the bulls are even in sight. Then you can "play" with the bulls in a mass of 350 people or so.

To watch one of the bullfights, you must wait in the line that forms at the bullring around 8pm every evening (tickets start at 2000ptas). As one bullfight ends, tickets go on sale for the next day. Try to avoid tickets in the *sol* (sun) section, as these seats fill with *peña* members who spend more time dousing each other with wine than watching—or allowing anyone else to watch—the fight.

Day and Nightlife

After the taurine track meet, the insanity spills into the streets, gathering steam until nightfall explodes with singing in the bars, dancing in the alleyways, spontaneous parades, and a no-holds-barred party in Pl. Castillo, southern Europe's biggest open-air dance floor. Be prepared with sturdy shoes (there's glass everywhere), a white t-shirt that will soon be soaked with wine, and a red *pañuelo* (bandana). Many English speakers congregate where C. Estafeta hits Pl. Toros, an outdoor consortium of local *discotecas.* A word to the wise: avoid the fountain-jumping (you'll know it when you see it). It is *not* a traditional part of the festivities (inebriated Americans, Aussies, and Kiwis came up with it), and several people on the giving and receiving end of this idiotic stunt have died. The truly inspired **carousing** takes place the first few days of *San Fermines.* After that, the crowds thin, and the atmosphere goes from dangerously

Before You Decide to Run...

Running with the bulls is a dangerous exercise. Every year, 10 to 12 people are severely gored, and many more are inadvertently crushed by fellow runners. On July 13, 1995, a 22-year-old American was killed. Inexperienced runners endanger not only themselves but also fellow sprinters. Although the Pamplonese are happy to share their party, they do not relish dying a bloody death because of a foreigner's stupidity. The tourist office dispenses a pamphlet that outlines the exact route of the three-minute run and offers tips for inexperienced runners. Runners must be at least 18. Those who run should follow some basic rules:

- Watch an *encierro* before you run—once on TV to get an overview of what you're in for, and once in person to feel the crush and hysteria.
- Do not stay up all night drinking and carousing. Inebriated foreigners have the highest rate of injury. Experienced runners get some sleep the night before and arrive at the course no later than 7am. Many locals recommend arriving at 6am. Access to the course closes at 7:30am.
- Stretch out before running.
- Give up on getting near the bulls and concentrate on getting to the bullring in one piece. Although some whack the bull with rolled newspapers, runners should never distract or touch the animals; anyone who does is likely to anger the bull and get the bejeezus kicked out of him or her by locals.
- Try not to cower in a doorway; people have been trapped and killed this way.
- Be particularly wary of isolated bulls—they seek company in the crowds.
- If you fall, curl into a fetal position, lock your hands behind your head, and **do not get up** until the clatter of hooves is well past you. STAY DOWN!

crazed to mildly insane. In between, the city eases the transition with concerts, outdoor dances, and a host of other performances. The end of the festivities culminates at midnight of July 14 with the singing of *Pobre de mí* (Poor Me): *"Pobre de mí, pobre de mí, que se han acabao* [finished] *las Fiestas de San Fermín."*

Nearby towns sponsor *encierros* as well: Tudela holds its festival during the week of July 24; Estella for a week from the Friday before the first Sunday in August; Tafalla during the week of August 15; and Sangüesa for a week beginning September 11. Many Pamplonese opt for these festivals instead, preferring not to partake in their own.

■ Olite

Olite (pop. 3000) was a city fit for kings in the early 15th century. Its proximity to Pamplona (35min.) and its Gothic, Baroque, and medieval architecture may make it fit for you too. The **Palacio Real,** former palace of the Navarrese kings, is Olite's crown jewel. (Open July-Aug. daily 10am-2pm and 4-8pm; Apr.-June and Sept. daily 10am-2pm and 4-7pm; Oct.-Mar. 10am-2pm and 3:30-5:30pm. 350ptas, students 250ptas, seniors and children 200ptas. Guided visits in Spanish every hour on weekends.) In the early 15th century, Carlos III made this sumptuous palace the focus of Navarrese court life. Although the 1937 restoration was far from subtle, the palace's spiral staircases, lookout perches, and abundant towers are still fun to explore. Sandwiched between the Palacio Real and the **Palacio Viejo** (now a *parador*) is the **Iglesia de Santa María,** noted for its 14th-century Gothic facade and belfry. **Iglesia de San Pedro** is fitted with an octagonal tower; for San Pedro, turn right on Rua Villavieja and follow it to its end. (Both open during mass, 10am and 8pm. Ask in the tourist office about guided visits.) Every August, the palace plays the backdrop for the **Festivales de Navarra,** a month-long shindig featuring concerts, theater, and dance. September 13-20 ushers in the **Fiesta de la Cruz,** a week of dancing and taurine torment.

Those with their own wheels can drive 20km from Olite up a winding road to the medieval hilltop town of **Ujué** (pop. 240), crowned by an 11th-century church with stunning views. From Olite you can also head to the Cistercian **Monasterio de la Oliva,** 34 km in the opposite direction.

PRACTICAL INFORMATION Trains (tel. 948 70 06 28) run to Pamplona (40min., 2-4 per day, 450ptas), Tudela, and other points on the Vitoria-Gasteiz-Zaragoza line. To get from the **RENFE station** to Pl. Carlos III, take C. Estación to Bar Orly, walk through the archway and follow Rua San Francisco past **Plaza Teobaldos** and through another arch to **Plaza Carlos III.** Do yourself a favor and take the **bus.** It's far more convenient and far less expensive. **Conda** (tel. 948 82 03 42) and **La Tafallesa** (tel. 948 70 09 79) run buses to Pamplona (35min., 6-12 per day, 345ptas) and Tudela (Conda only; 50min., 5-7 per day, 455ptas). La Tafallesa stops at Bar Orly; to reach Pl. Carlos III from here, follow the instructions from the train station. Conda stops at the Carretera; to reach Pl. Carlos III, follow C. El Portillo for a block. The staircase leading underground from the middle of the plaza goes to the **tourist office** (tel./fax 948 71 23 43; open Apr.-Sept. M-F 10am-2pm and 4-7pm, Sa-Su 10am-2pm; Oct.-Mar. daily 10am-2pm). In any **emergency,** call 112. The **post office** is on the far end of the plaza from the palace (tel. 948 74 05 82; open M-Sa 9-11:30am). The **postal code** is 31390.

ACCOMMODATIONS AND FOOD The luxurious air of the court lingers in many of Olite's restaurants and accommodations. One exception is the budget-minded **Pensión Cesareo Vidaurre,** Pl. Carlos III, 22, 1st fl. (tel. 948 74 05 97), to the right of the tourist office staircase with your back to the battlements. The nondescript entrance and teeny *camas* sign belie bright rooms upstairs (doubles 3500ptas). The second option is **Fonda Gambarte,** Rua Seco, 13, 2nd fl. (tel. 948 74 01 39), off Pl. Carlos III, which has basic doubles (3500ptas) and a downstairs **restaurant** (3-course *menú,* 1100ptas; open daily 1-3:30pm and 8:30-10:30pm). There are several **supermarkets** on C. Mayor, off Pl. Carlos III.

■ Tudela

A somewhat homely modern city with an attractive historic center, Tudela (pop. 30,000) offers enticing versions of standard regional attractions—ghostly medieval churches and elegant old mansions in a labyrinthine *casco antiguo.* A major Muslim center until Christian King Sancho the Strong outmuscled the Moors in 1114, Tudela hosted eminent Muslim and Jewish populations throughout the Middle Ages. Nowadays, solid transportation connections make Tudela a potential hub for exploring Navarra and nearby destinations in Aragón.

ORIENTATION AND PRACTICAL INFORMATION Old town and new meet in **Plaza de los Fueros,** erstwhile sight of bullfights. To get to Pl. Fueros from the combined **bus and train station,** cross the plaza up Cuesta de la Estación, make the second right onto Av. Zaragoza, go straight for five blocks, and then turn left onto C. Gaztambide-Carrera, which leads to the plaza. The **Casa del Reloj,** with its ornate clock tower, presides over the city's west end. Right (north) of the plaza when facing the clock is the *casco antiguo,* overlooked by the **Castillo de Sancho el Fuerte** and the **Monumento al Corazón de Jesús,** which crown a hill at the edge of town.

Two **RENFE** train lines (tel. 948 82 06 46) run through Tudela: one connects La Rioja to Zaragoza via Castejón de Ebro; the other connects Zaragoza to Vitoria-Gasteiz via Pamplona. Buses go to Pamplona (1hr., 4-6 per day, 800ptas) and Zaragoza (1hr., 4-6 per day, 500 ptas). Conda **buses** (tel. 948 82 03 42) run to: Pamplona (1½ hr., 6-7 per day, 800ptas); Olite (1hr., 5 per day, 475ptas); Tarazona (1hr., M-Sa 5 per day, 215ptas); and to Madrid, Soria, Zaragoza, and San Sebastián.

The **tourist office** (tel. 948 82 15 39), on Pl. Vieja alongside the cathedral, has a fax machine and a great map (open M-F 10am-3pm, Sa-Su 10am-2pm). To get there from Pl. Fueros, head sharply right when facing the clock tower onto C. Concarera. Cross Pl. San Jaime to the street in the far right corner, follow it around the corner, and look on your right. For **currency exchange,** Banco Central Hispano is across the street from Hostal Remigio on C. Gaztambide and has an **ATM** (open M-Sa 8:30am-2:30pm).

Luggage storage is in lockers at the station (400ptas per day; open 24hr. on the train station side). The **municipal police** (**emergency** tel. 091 or 092) are on C. Carcel Vieja. To find the **post office,** C. Juan Antonio Fernandez, 4 (tel. 948 82 04 47), take a left at the end of C. Eza D. Miguel, off Pl. Fueros. The **postal code** is 31500.

ACCOMMODATIONS AND FOOD Tudela does not abound with budget options. **Hostal Remigio,** C. Gaztambide, 4 (tel. 948 82 08 50), on the way from the train and bus station to Pl. Fueros, has sleek modern rooms, firm beds, and pristine bathrooms. (Singles 1850ptas, with bath 2750ptas; doubles 3700ptas, with bath 5000ptas. Higher rates July, Aug., and Semana Santa. Breakfast 425ptas, *menú* 1400ptas. Visa, MC, AmEx.) **Bar/Casa de Huéspedes Estrella,** C. Carnicerias, 14 (tel. 948 41 04 42), off C. Yanguas y Miranda from the northwest corner of Pl. Fueros, offers rooms overlooking a pleasant plaza (doubles 3000ptas). Ask in the bar about rooms (reception 9am-3pm and 6pm-midnight). Chow down at the Chinese restaurant **Gran Mundo,** Av. Zaragoza, 51 (tel. 948 82 05 19), one block past Cuesta de Estación. The lunchtime *menú* is 795ptas. Picnickers can shop at **Supermercado Agid,** Av. Pamplona, 10 (open M-Sa 9am-1:30pm and 5-8pm, Su 10am-2pm), or pick up fresh local produce at the **mercado** on C. Concarera, off the plaza (open M-F 8am-1:30pm and 5-8pm, Sa 8am-2pm).

SIGHTS AND ENTERTAINMENT Tudela's airy Gothic **cathedral,** built on the site of the town's old mosque, rises from Pl. Vieja in the *casco antiguo,* across from the tourist office. *(Cathedral open Tu-Sa 9am-1pm and 4-7pm, Su 9am-1pm. Admission to the cloister 100ptas.)* An amalgam of styles from different periods, the cathedral features a rose-filled Romanesque cloister, several 15th-century Gothic *retablos* (altarpieces), and a chilling Last Judgment tympanum over the west portal.

While the cathedral is the highlight, strolling through the *casco antiguo* can be a pleasure. Points-of-interest include the 12th-century **Iglesia de la Magdalena** to the northeast, such imposing mansions as the 16th-century **Palacio del Marqués de San Adrián** or the 18th-century **Palacio del Marqués de Huarte,** home to a Rococo carriage, and the lovely Romanesque portico of the **Iglesia de San Nicolás.**

Tudela's **nightlife** is lively and nomadic. Early in the evening, friends gather in bars and cafes between Pl. Fueros and the cathedral. Then it's on to **Calle San Marcial,** east of the plaza, and **Calle Aranaz y Vides,** north from the bus station toward the old town, where pits of revelry carry on into the wee hours.

■ Near Tudela: Bardenas Reales

The awesome desert **Bardenas Reales,** with textured hills and cliffs wrought by erosion, covers over 400 square km near the beginning of the Tudela-Pamplona road. The vistas are best contemplated from a mountain bike or car. To rent a bike, take the bus from Tudela to Pamplona and ask to be let off in the unremarkable, sun-blasted town of **Arguedas** (20min., 125ptas). There, **Ciclos Marton,** C. San Ignacio, 2 (tel. 948 83 15 77 or 948 83 00 85), has mountain bikes for full-day rental (2000ptas for first day, 1000ptas each additional day). Cyclists should remain on the official roads to prevent damage to themselves. Don't forget that Bardenas is a desert; call ahead about weather conditions as the heat can sometimes be prohibitive. The tourist office in Tudela provides tips and directions. We can recommend that you bring *agua.*

■ Estella

Suspended between the robust cities of Logroño and Pamplona, charming Estella (pop. 13,000) snuggles into a bend in the Río Ega. What it lacks in size and glamor, it makes up for in hospitality toward the faithful. With tell-tale walking sticks in hand, pilgrims traversing the Camino de Santiago have been descending upon Estella since the town's founding expressly for that purpose in 1090. A number of monuments attest to Estella's medieval dynamism.

ORIENTATION AND PRACTICAL INFORMATION Two streets form a cross through the heart of town, which in turn is bounded by the river. **Calle San Andrés/ Calle Baja Navarra** runs north-south from the bus station on Pl. Coronación to **Plaza de los Fueros. Paseo de la Inmaculada Concepción** runs east-west from C. Dr. Huarte to the **Puente (bridge) del Azucarero,** which spans the river and leads to the old town, where most sights and the tourist office await. To get to the *puente* from the bus station, go right and then follow the river road to the left.

All **buses** running from the station on Pl. Coronación belong to **La Estellesa** (tel. 948 55 01 27). Buses go to: Logroño (50min., 5-7 per day, 490ptas); Pamplona (1hr., 6-10 per day, 425-495ptas); San Sebastián (1½-2hr., 4 per day, 1195 ptas); and Zaragoza (2½hr., M-Sa 1 per day, 1595ptas). The **tourist office,** C. San Nicolás, 1 (tel./fax 948 55 40 11), is a straight shot from the bridge through Pl. San Martín, around the corner to the right. The staff has a map and info on the *camino* and surrounding areas. (Open Mar.-Sept. M-F 10am-2pm and 4-7pm, Sa-Su 10am-2pm; Oct.-Feb. daily 10am-2pm.) Dial 112 in all **emergencies.** The **police,** Po. Inmaculada, 1, answer at 948 55 08 13. The **post office** is at Po. Inmaculada, 5 (tel. 948 55 17 92; open for stamps and Lista de Correos M-F 8:30am-2:30pm, Sa 9:30am-1pm). The **postal code** is 31200.

ACCOMMODATIONS, CAMPING, AND FOOD Near Pamplona, Estella is a good place to catch some shut-eye during *San Fermines.* Reservations are advisable during its own August *encierro* (running of the bulls). **Pensión San Andrés,** Pl. Santiago, 50 (tel. 948 55 04 48), overlooks a pretty plaza. The first left off C. Baja Navarra after crossing Po. Inmaculada, down C. Mayor, leads you there. San Andrés adorns his tidy rooms with little refrigerators, TVs, and woven bedspreads. (July-Aug. and Semana Santa: doubles 3200ptas, with bath 5000ptas. Sept.-June: doubles 3000ptas, with bath 4000ptas. Breakfast 350ptas.) **Fonda Izarra,** C. Calderería, 20 (tel. 948 55 06 78), off Pl. Fueros, offers simpler rooms (doubles 4000ptas; Visa). **Camping Lizarra** (tel. 948 55 17 33; fax 948 55 47 55) is on C. Ordoiz, left from the tourist office and 1km downriver. The grounds have a supermarket, a pool, and mountain bike rentals. (675ptas plus I.V.A. per half *parcela,* with tent, car, and electricity; 495ptas per extra person.)

Estella is known throughout the region for its *gorrín asado* (roast piglet, also called *gorrín de Estella*); take it or leave it. Picnickers can stock up at **Supermarket Vendi,** C. Zapatería, at the corner of C. Navarrería. To get there, take the first right off C. Baja Navarra after Po. Inmaculada Concepción, then go straight three blocks. (Open M-F 9am-1:30pm and 4:30-8pm, Sa 9am-1:30pm.) **Restaurante Casanova,** C. Fray Wenceslao de Oñate, 7 (tel. 948 55 28 09), upstairs on the left as you enter Pl. Fueros, has overwhelming portions that are sure to slow any pilgrim's progress. The lunch and dinner *menú* are 1200ptas; entrees 500-1700ptas. (Open in summer daily 1-3:30pm and 8:30-11pm; in winter M 1-3:30pm, Tu-Su 1-3:30pm and 8:30-11pm.)

SIGHTS In the "modern" quarter, the 12th-century **Iglesia de San Miguel** commands a view of the town from the hilltop Pl. San Miguel. Its highlight is its ornately carved stone portal depicting St. Michael fighting dragons, weighing souls, and generally taking care of business. Up the stairs and opposite the tourist office, the **Iglesia de San Pedro de la Rúa** towers above **Calle de la Rúa,** the main street of the original mercantile center. The bulbous 12th- to 13th-century late Romanesque/early Gothic church has an unusual half-destroyed cloister. Left from the tourist office at the end of C. Rúa lurks the **Iglesia del Santo Sepulcro,** whose 14th-century facade features a monstrous Satan swallowing the damned by the mouthful. *(Outside of mass hours, the San Miguel and San Pedro churches can be visited only by taking tours in Spanish. 30min. tour of San Pedro 200ptas. 30min. tour of San Pedro, San Miguel, and the outside of Santo Sepulcro 400ptas.)*

Across from San Pedro and next to the tourist office, the oldest representation of Roland in the world jousts with Farragut the Moor on the columns of the 12th-century Romanesque **Palacio de los Reyes de Navarra,** now the **Museo Gustavo** (tel. 948 54 60 37). *(Open Tu-Sa 11am-1pm and 5-7pm, Su 11am-1pm. Free.)* Inside are the works of painter Gustavo de Maesta, who spent the last years of his life in Estella.

The week-long **Fiestas de la Virgen del Puy y San Andrés** kick off the Friday before the first Sunday in August. Estella has an *encierro* with baby bulls, smaller and less ferocious than Pamplona's. Kiddie entertainment, a fair, and Navarrese dancing and *gaitas* (bagpipes without the bags) round out the *fiestas*.

NAVARRESE PYRENEES

Navarra encompasses the most topographically diverse range of the Pyrenees. While truly forbidding peaks dominate the eastern Valle de Roncal, the mountain slopes to the west are diminished in ferocity and height, allowing easier access to the streams, waterfalls, and green meadows dotting the area. Mist and fog obscure visibility at high altitudes, creating either a dreamy atmosphere or slightly nerve-racking driving conditions, depending on your point of view. Most of the inhabitants settle into jobs with the cattle and logging industries.

Tourism is also a booming business. **El Camino de Santiago** is the celebrated cross-kingdom super-trek of intrepid pilgrims clambering over from France (see **Pilgrim's Progress,** p. 183). The most popular pilgrim route crosses the border at Roncesvalles and winds down through Pamplona on the way to Santiago de Compostela in Galicia. Many free and cheap **refugios** cater to certified modern-day pilgrims along the way. To join the fun, get the best available guide, the *Guía práctica del peregrino* (pilgrim's guide; in Castilian only), published by Ediciones Everest (2500ptas). We also highly recommend picking up a copy of the useful *Guía de alojamientos de turismo rurales* (free in any of Navarra's tourist offices), which lists *casas rurales*, beautiful rural houses that lodge travelers. As a rule, these homes are welcoming places to stay and great budget options, usually costing between 3200 and 4400ptas for a double. For reservations, call the multilingual tourist office (tel. 948 22 93 28).

Pamplona is the only sensible base for those depending on public transportation; you can head east toward Valle de Roncal (via Sangüesa), or north toward Roncesvalles. **Buses** are one-a-day affairs (if that) throughout most of the area.

■ Sangüesa

At first glance, Sangüesa (pop. 5000), set in the arid foothills 44km east of Pamplona, isn't much to look at. Yet Sangüesa's beautiful churches and streets demand a second chance. The town also acts as an entry point for some spectacular nearby sights—both natural and manmade—and is often a necessary stop-over for pilgrims.

Sangüesa earns its place on the Camino due to the **Iglesia de Santa María,** on C. Mayor by the bus stop. Its portal is a veritable triumph of Romanesque sculpture. The central relief depicts the Day of Judgment, with fanged devils casting the damned into the cavernous mouth of Lucifer. The woman nursing a toad on one breast and a snake on the other is a conventional iconographic rendering of Lust. Inside is a hairy Baroque Madonna whose human locks change every 10-15 years. St. James, made of Gothic stone, stands atop a large conch before the **Iglesia de Santiago.** (Churches open for mass only. Ask at the tourist office about guided visits or call 948 43 04 97. 250ptas for Santa María only, 400ptas for tour of all monuments.)

Sangüesa's lucky tourist office occupies the **Palacio de Ongay-Vallesantoro,** a Baroque palace with a facade inspired by the owner's visits to Mexico and Peru. A few doors down, a traditional **metalsmith,** at C. Alfonso el Batallador, 9, lets visitors into his forge. In July and August, the town hosts a series of **medieval dinners,** when hucking half-eaten bones is totally kosher.

PRACTICAL INFORMATION, ACCOMMODATIONS, AND FOOD Veloz Sangüesina **buses** (tel. 948 87 02 09) go to and from Pamplona (45 min., M-Sa 3 per day, Su 4 per day, 420ptas). La Tafallesa (tel. 948 22 28 86) heads to Javier and Yesa (M-Sa 1 per day). All buses deposit passengers on C. Mayor. For **taxis,** ring 948 87 02 22. The helpful, English-speaking **tourist office,** C. Alfonso el Batallador, 20 (tel./fax 948 87 03

29), has maps and lots of info on the surrounding area. (Open in summer M-F 10am-2pm and 4-7pm, Sa-Su 10am-2pm; in winter daily 10am-2pm.) From the bus stop, take the first right off C. Mayor. In **emergencies,** dial 088 or 112. For **medical services,** there's a **Centro de Salud** (tel. 948 87 03 38) on the road to Cantolagua. Call 092 for the **Guardia Civil.** The **post office,** Fermín de Lubián, 17 (tel. 948 87 04 27), is at the end of C. Mayor beyond Pl. Fueros. The **postal code** is 31400.

A pleasant place to snooze for a night is **Pensión Las Navas,** C. Alfonso el Batallador, 7 (tel. 948 87 00 77), where flowered bedspreads enliven clean, comfortable rooms, all with baths (singles 2000ptas; doubles 4000ptas; closed Sept. 18-Oct. 10). The **Albergue de Pereginos,** free and for pilgrims only, rests on C. Enrique Labrit. Ask at the tourist office for a guide to *casas particulares.* **Camping Cantolagua** (tel. 948 43 03 52) is located near the Ciudad Deportivo (400ptas per person, per car, and per tent. 7% I.V.A. not included). The town's **market,** Pl. Toros, bustles at the end of C. Alfonso el Ballatador away from C. Mayor (Fridays 9am-2pm). **Autoservicio Lozano Hermanos,** C. Mayor, 80, is the supermarket in town. **Restaurante Las Navas** (downstairs from the Pensión) has great **bocadillos** (375-500ptas).

■ Near Sangüesa: Gorges

Two fantastic gorges lie within 12km of Sangüesa. The **Foz de Lumbier** (Lumbier Gorge) is outside the little town of **Lumbier.** Fifty-meter walls tower on one side of this yawning gorge on the Río Irati. A path alongside leads through old railway tunnels. Rio Irati (tel. 948 22 24 70) runs **buses** to the town from Pamplona (1hr., M-F 3 per day, Sa 1 per day, 365-410ptas). A 12km ride from Lumbier brings you to **Iso** and the mouth of an even more impressive gorge, the 6km **Foz de Arbayún.** A lookout affords gorgeous views and glimpses of swooping **griffin vultures.** From Iso, a short path in the chasm leads along the Río Salazar, until it gets too narrow. No buses go directly to Iso. Ask the tourist office in Sangüesa for transportation information; if you have a car, look for the signs off N-240 in the direction of Pamplona.

■ Near Sangüesa: Castillo de Javier

Eight kilometers from Sangüesa by the small village of **Javier** is the restored **Castillo de Javier,** the birthplace of San Francisco Xavier (Javier). *(Open daily 9am-1pm and 4-7pm. Free, but donations requested. Occasional tours in Spanish.)* On the border between Navarra and Aragón, this picture-perfect castle has changed hands many times over the last millennium. Today it's safely in the Jesuits' possession. Its Chapel of the Holy Christ houses a 14th-century effigy that suffered a spontaneous blood-sweating fit at the moment of San Francisco Xavier's death. **La Tafallesa** (tel. 948 22 28 86) runs a bus from Pamplona to Javier (1hr., M-F at 5pm, Sa at 1:30pm, 500ptas), and on to nearby Yesa (510ptas); it also stops in Sangüesa, 45 minutes from Pamplona. Buses return Monday through Saturday at 8am.

▓ Monasterio de Leyre

Windswept and austere, the Monasterio de Leyre (50km from Pamplona) silently surveys the foothills of the Pyrenees and the fabricated lake, Lago de Yesa. It lies about one hour away from Pamplona, off the highway to Huesca. If you don't have your own wheels, it's a 5km uphill slog from Yesa. Here hang-gliders launch themselves off the hills where great wealth and power once presided. In the 12th century, medieval Navarrese kings took up residence in the **monasterio medieval** (tel. 948 88 40 11). *(Open daily Apr.-Oct. 10:30am-2pm and 4-7pm; Nov.-Mar. M-Sa 10:15am-1:30pm and 3:30-6:30pm, Su 10:15am-1:30pm and 4-7pm. 225ptas, children 50ptas. Guided tours when there are enough people. Mass with Gregorian chanting M-Sa 9am and Su at noon.)* Because monks still live at Leyre, you can enter neither this part nor the 20th-century **monasterio nuevo.** However, the dank, subterranean **cripta** eagerly welcomes the public. The architectural highlight of the monastic complex is the ghoulish 12th-century

Portal de la Iglesia. Outside the monastery is a path to the **Fuente de San Virila.** The fountain occupies the site where, according to legend, the abbot of San Virila fell into a 300-year trance induced by the singing of a nightingale.

Connected to the monastery, the **Hospedería de Leyre** (tel. 948 88 41 00; fax 948 88 41 37) offers comfortable rooms that, with cozy beds, TVs, and private bathrooms, make the monks' cells look like, well, monks' cells. (July-Aug. and Semana Santa singles 4400ptas; doubles 8600ptas; the rest of the year singles 4050ptas; doubles 7100ptas. Breakfast 700ptas, *menú* 1500ptas.) Cheaper shut-eye, a **supermarket,** and **banks** await at the bottom of the hill in Yesa.

■ Roncesvalles and Auritz-Burguete

The first stop in Spain on the Camino de Santiago, **Roncesvalles'** mist-enshrouded ten-odd buildings rest amid miles of thickly wooded mountains. This itty-bitty town (pop. 30), 48km from Pamplona, 20km from France, and eons from reality, lives off legends and the accompanying tourists. Charlemagne's favorite soldier Roland was supposedly slain just up the hill in AD 778, at the hands of the ambushing Basque-Navarrese, who were perturbed that Charlemagne had razed the walls of Pamplona. **Puerto Ibañeta** (1057m), less than 2km up the main road from the monastery, supposedly marks the spot where he breathed his final breath. The heavily restored **Capilla de Sancti Spiritus** stands over the remains of the bone heap (courtesy of dead soldiers and pilgrims), where Roland's tomb may be. The tiny 12th-century **Capilla de Santiago** is next door to the left. (They can only be visited by guided tours; see below.)

Inside the **Colegiata** (tel. 948 76 00 00), up the driveway from the *capilla,* tombs of King Sancho El Fuerte (the Strong) and his bride rest in solitary splendor, lit by the huge stained-glass windows of the **Capilla de San Agustín.** (*Capilla* and claustro open M-F 10:30am-1:30pm, Sa-Su 10am-2pm and 4-7pm. 225ptas; students, seniors, and pilgrims 150ptas.) In the decisive battle of the Navas de Tolosa, Sancho reputedly broke the chains protecting the Arab king Miramomolin with his own hands then promptly decapitated him. The heavy iron chains hanging from the walls of the chamber are represented in Navarra's flag. The monastery's lovely French Gothic **church,** endowed by the Sancho and consecrated in 1219, is its main attraction. (Open daily 8am-8pm. Free. Guided visits including other monuments 425ptas; students, seniors, and pilgrims 325ptas. Call 948 79 04 80 for more info.)

PRACTICAL INFORMATION AND ACCOMMODATIONS La Montañesa **buses** (tel. 948 22 15 84) run from Pamplona to Roncesvalles (1¼hr., M-F 6pm, Sa 4pm, 525ptas); the return bus leaves Roncevalles M-Sa at 7:10am. The bus stops in Burguete each way. A **tourist office** (tel. 948 76 01 93) in Roncesvalles, in the mill behind Casa Sabina Hostería, has maps and guides to the Camino de Santiago. (Open Apr.-Oct. M-Sa 10am-2pm and 3-6pm, Su 10am-2pm; Nov.-Mar. Sa 10am-2pm and 3-6pm, Su 10am-2pm. Check during the week—someone may be there.). For a **Banco Central Hispano,** a supermarket, and more eating options, head to nearby **Burguete** (2km south); there is hardly any food for sale in Roncesvalles.

The **monastery** in Roncesvalles has free lodging for official pilgrims—enter the door to the right as you face the monastery. The attached **Oficina de Peregrinos** (tel. 948 76 00 00) gives out credentials. **Albergue Juvenil Roncesvalles (HI)** (tel. 948 76 03 02; fax 948 76 03 62) is in an 18th-century hospital tucked to the right behind the monastery. (Members only. 1000ptas per person, with *pensión completa* 2250ptas—not always available; over 26 1400ptas, with *pensión completa* 2800ptas. Breakfast 315ptas. Call in winter, as the hostel sometimes closes.)

In nearby **Burguete,** accommodations are numerous and several *casas rurales* line the street. Those following the **Camino de Hemingway** will want to check out the **Hostal Burguete,** San Nikolas, 59 (tel. 948 76 00 05). The big boy slept here and did a little writing on his way back to Paris from *San Fermines.* By the looks of it, the place hasn't changed much—high, plump beds in spacious, old-fashioned rooms. (Singles 2800ptas; doubles with sink 4200ptas, with bath 5400ptas. Breakfast

400ptas, *menú del día* 1350ptas. Open Mar. 15-Dec. 15.) **Camping Urrobi** (tel. 948 76 02 00), 2½ kilometers downhill from Burguete in Espinal, has a grocery store and recreational facilities. (450ptas per person, per tent, and per car; open Apr.-Oct.)

■ Valle de Salazar: Ochagavía

On the banks of the Río Andena, **Ochagavía** (pop. 600) is that perfect picturesque mountain village urbanites dream about. Forty kilometers from Pamplona, the Valle de Salazar's biggest town spans both sides of a cheerful river. Ochagavía's cobbled streets and whitewashed houses lead to forested mountains that make it a great base for hiking, trout fishing, and cross-country skiing. The charming 12th-century **Hermita de Muskilda** is a 30-minute hike away; follow the stone path behind the church or the road to the left just outside of town if you've got wheels. From the *hermita* there are beautiful views of the valley. (July-Aug. open daily 11am-1pm and 4-7pm; Sept.-June Sa-Su 11am-1pm and 4-6pm, although schedule may vary.)

Hikers will find the climb up the Pico de Orhy (2021m) fairly easy. The trail leaves from the parking lot at Puerto de Larrau, 9km north of Ochagavía on the highway to France. The ascent from *el puerto* takes about one hour. Another good hike is along the Río Irati, through the **Selva de Irati** to **Orbaitzeta**. Leave your car at the Ermita de las Nieves, 24km from Ochagavía, and make the 20km hike to Orbaitzeta (6hr. one-way but one needn't make the whole hike). **Cross country skiers** can enjoy two circuit trails starting a little farther down the same highway.

Río Irati (tel. 948 22 14 70) runs **buses** to and from Pamplona (M-Sa 1 per day, 815ptas). Buses to Pamplona leave at 7am Monday to Saturday. The **tourist office** (tel./fax. 948 89 00 04), on the main road, is in the same building as a nature center. (Tourist office open Semana Santa-Oct. M-Sa 10am-2pm and 4:30-7:30pm, Su 10am-2pm; Nov.-Semana Santa Sa-Su 10:30am-2pm.) In **emergencies,** call 112. Several **ATMs** are located on the main road; the **pharmacy,** C. Urrutia, 31 (tel. 948 89 05 06), waits on the other side.

Hostal Orialde (tel. 948 89 00 27), across the river from the main road, has attractive, spacious rooms. (Singles 2500ptas; doubles 3000ptas, with bath 4500ptas. Breakfast 300ptas. 7% I.V.A. not included. *Menú* 1400ptas.) Ask at the tourist office or look for the "CR" signs advertising one of the town's 11 *casa rurales.* **Camping Osate** (tel. 948 89 01 84), at the entrance to town, provides a modern campsite on the river and rents **mountain bikes** (475ptas per person and per car, 425 per tent).

■ Valle de Roncal

Carved by the Río Esca, Valle de Roncal is a particularly handsome valley stretching from the French border. With its darling towns, inviting *casas rurales,* prime **hiking** and **cross-country skiing** grounds, and overall laid-back air, Valle de Roncal is a showcase of the best the Navarran Pyrenees have to offer.

■ Roncal

Smack in the center of the Valle de Roncal, the diminutive town of **Roncal** (pop. 300) puffs up with pride over its famed *queso Roncal,* a sharp cheese made from sheep's milk, and its own Julián Gayarre (1844-1889), a "world-renowned" tenor. **Casa Museo Julián Gayarre** (tel. 948 47 51 80), on C. Arana, is a museum in the singer's birth-house, showcasing his personal belongings and assorted memorabilia. (Open Apr.-Sept. Tu-Su 11:30am-1:30pm and 5-7pm; Oct.-Mar. Sa-Su 11:30am-1:30pm and 4-6pm. 200ptas.)

La Tafallesa (tel. 948 22 28 86) **buses** run from Pamplona (depart M-F 5pm, Sa 1pm), through Javier, and on to Roncal (2hr., 880ptas from Pamplona); buses also return to Pamplona and Javier from Roncal (depart M-Sa 7am). There is an extremely helpful **tourist office** (tel. 948 47 51 36) on Roncal's main road. Ask about nearby hiking and *casas rurales.* (Open July-Sept. M-Sa 10am-2pm and 4:30-7:30pm, Su 10am-

2pm; May-June and Oct.-Dec. Tu-Su 10am-2pm.) **Banco Central Hispano** is across the street (open M-F 8:30am-2:30pm). The **Guardia Civil** is at 948 47 50 05. In an **emergency,** call 122. A **pharmacy** is next door to the tourist office and a couple of **supermarkets** cluster by the bridge at the south end of town.

Try one of the splendid *casa rurales* for a night's rest. **Casa Villa Pepita,** Po. Julián Gayarre, 4 (tel. 948 47 51 33), south of the bridge on the main road, has rooms that you can't help but call adorable. (Singles 1650ptas; doubles 3300ptas, with bath 4400ptas. Breakfast 350ptas; meals 1300ptas.) If Pepita is full, the owner will gladly direct you to another *casa rural.*

■ Isaba and Environs

The more populous village of **Isaba** (pop. 500) straddles the highway 7km north of Roncal. The **tourist office** (tel. 948 89 32 51) is right off the main road. (Open in summer Tu-Th 10am-2pm and 5-8pm, F-Sa 10am-2pm and 4:30-8pm, Su 10am-2pm; in winter Tu-Su 10am-2pm.) **Phones** and **ATMs** huddle at the southern end of town. **Albergue Oxanea,** C. Bormapea, 47 (tel. 948 89 31 53), is left up the stone staircase, opposite the Centro de Salud. Wooden *literas* (bunks) fit eight and 14 to a room, and there's a TV/VCR room. (1000ptas per night, 900ptas with own sleeping bag. Hot showers included. Breakfast 300ptas. Other meals 1200ptas. 7% I.V.A. not included.) **Camping Asolaze** (tel. 948 89 30 34), 6km toward the French border, houses a restaurant and a store and offers *literas* (1000ptas per person, sheets 200ptas), in addition to regular plots of earth (475ptas per person, 450ptas per tent, 500ptas per car; doubles with bath 3900ptas). Eight kilometers north of Isaba, the earth opens up into the idyllic **Valle de Belagua. Refugio Angel Oloron** (tel./fax. 948 39 40 02) is open year-round and offers *literas* (950ptas), breakfast (300ptas), and other meals (1200ptas). The refuge is located at km 19 on the highway to France from Isaba, and the drive offers grade-A views. Check also in the guide to *Casas Rurales* (see p. 263) for local houses offering lodging.

A standard yet stunning hike goes from Isaba to Zuriza (6hr.). Shorter, but steeper, are the ascents from Collado Argibiela to **Punta Abizondo** (1676m) and **Peña Ezkaurre** (2050km). Ask the tourist office for routes of differing durations and difficulty. Ski trails run north of Isaba, at the **Estación de Ski Larra-Belagna** (tel. 948 22 43 94). The **Escuela de Esquí Valle del Roncal,** with offices in Hotel Isaba (tel. 948 89 30 00), offers lessons and skis in Isaba at 4200ptas per hour lesson for one or two people as well as group lessons. A village festival runs July 25 to 28 in Isaba.

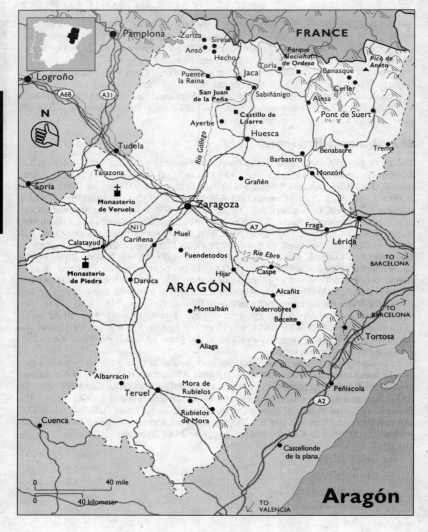

Aragón

Traveling south to north through Aragón can make it hard to fit the pieces together. In the south, a sun-baked assemblage of hardworking towns and flaxen plains, scattered with fine examples of ornate Mudéjar architecture (a Moorish-Christian mix), gives way to prosperous and industrious Zaragoza. Up north the stunning snow-capped peaks of the Pyrenees rise up, interspersed with tiny medieval towns and their remarkable Romanesque architecture.

The harsh terrain and climate coupled with the region's strategic location engendered a martial culture known among Spaniards for its obstinacy. Established as a kingdom in 1035 and united with enterprising Catalunya in 1137, Aragón forged a far-flung Mediterranean empire that brought Roussillon, Valencia, Murcia, the Balearic

Islánds, Naples, Sicily, and even the Duchy of Athens under its sway. Aragón retained the privileges of internal government even after its union with Castilla in 1469 and held them until Felipe II marched into Zaragoza in 1591 and brought the region to its knees. Economic decline followed political humiliation; as eyes turned to the new world, people (and capital) moved to the coast in search of riches. Today, however, Aragón is pretty much back on its feet economically, although much of the region is still relatively tourist-free. Only some areas of the rural Pyrenees and the **Parque Nacional Ordesa y Monte Perdido,** with its dramatic peaks and copious hiking and skiing opportunities, attract many visitors—and those mostly Spanish urbanites escaping the city heat during July and August.

Aragonese cuisine is as hearty as the people who make it. *Migas de pastor* (bread crumbs fried with ham) and lamb chops are ubiquitous; more surprising treats include *chilindrón* (lamb and chicken stewed with red peppers) and *melocotones al vino* (sweet native peaches steeped in wine). *Frutas de Aragón,* another specialty, are candied fruits dipped in semi-sweet chocolate. Cariña wines, produced in the south of Aragón, complement the local cuisine.

The *Guía de servicios turísticos de Aragón,* available at any tourist office in the kingdom, makes roaming easy, with information on accommodations (including *casas rurales, refugios,* and campgrounds) and tourist offices.

🖐 HIGHLIGHTS OF ARAGÓN

- Hiking and/or skiing among the jagged rock faces and snow-covered peaks of **Parque Nacional de Ordesa** (see p. 286).
- A summertime visit to the adorable little Pyrenean town of **Ansó** (see p. 285).
- The stunning hidden monastery of **San Juan de la Peña** (see p. 283), near Jaca.

■ Zaragoza

Whoever said God and mammon can't peacefully co-exist never visited Zaragoza (pop. 700,000). Firmly conscious of its rich historical and artistic heritages, yet a thoroughly modern city, Zaragoza successfully achieves harmony among its different selves. Augustus founded the city in 19 BC, naming it Caesaraugusta after himself, as a retirement colony for Roman veterans. Zaragoza gained everlasting fame some years later when the Virgin Mary dropped in for a visit; since then the city has been a pilgrimage site. Centuries later, industrial, not spiritual, vibes drove General Motors to set up shop here, cementing an already strong manufacturing sector. The city hums with prosperity, making Zaragoza a sample of urban Spain, blessed by a beloved patron saint, *Nuestra Señora del Pilar,* and the convenience of lower price tags.

ORIENTATION AND PRACTICAL INFORMATION

Bordered to the north by the Río Ebro, Zaragoza is laid out like a slightly damaged bicycle wheel. Five spokes radiate from the hub at **Plaza Basilio Paraíso.** Facing the center of the plaza with the IberCaja bank building at your back, the spokes going clockwise are: **Paseo de Sagasta; Gran Vía,** which turns into Po. Fernando el Católico; **Paseo de Pamplona,** which leads to Po. María Agustín and the train station; **Paseo de Independencia,** which ends at **Plaza de España** (the entrance to the *casco viejo,* or old quarter); and **Paseo de la Constitución.** To get to Pl. Paraíso from the **train station,** start upstairs, bear right down the ramp, and walk across Av. Anselmo Clavé. Head one block down C. General Mayandía and turn right onto Po. María Agustín. Go seven blocks; the street becomes Po. Pamplona ending at Pl. Paraíso.

The *casco viejo* lies at the end of Po. Independencia and stretches between Pl. España and **Plaza del Pilar,** which sits along the river. Several key museums and sights frame the Pl. Pilar, the most central being the grandiose Basílica de Nuestra Señora del Pilar. Its blue-and-yellow tiled domes make good landmarks.

To reach Pl. Pilar from Pl. Paraíso, walk down Po. Independencia to Pl. España and continue on to C. Don Jaime I (a bit to the right), which runs to the plaza. The user-

ARAGÓN

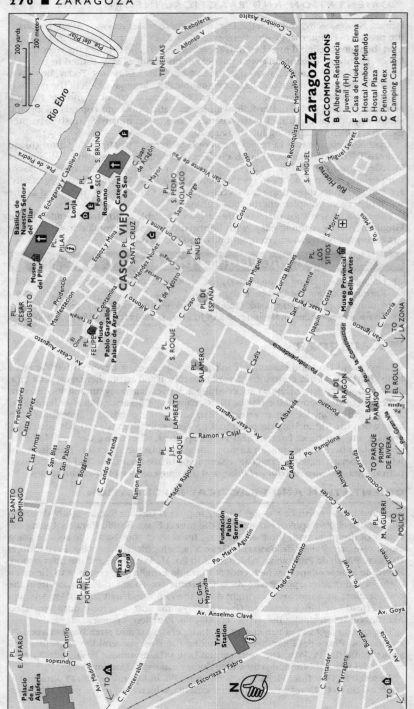

Zaragoza

ACCOMMODATIONS

- B Albergue-Residencia Juvenil (HI)
- F Casa de Huespedes Elena
- E Hostal Ambos Mundos
- D Hostal Plaza
- C Pension Rex
- A Camping Casablanca

Río Ebro

Pte. del Pilar

200 yards
200 meters

C. Rebolería
C. Alfonso V
C. Coimbra Asalto
C. Manuelo San...
C. Reconquista

PL. TENERIAS

Po. Echegaray y Caballero
Pte. de Piedra

PL. S. BRUNO
PL. LA SEO

Foro
Romano

C. Mayor
C. Juan de Aragón
C. San Vicente de Paul

Basílica de Nuestra Señora del Pilar

La Lonja

SEO Catedral de Seo

PL. PILAR
PILAR

Museo del Pilar

C. Coso
C. Coso
C. Miguel Servet

PL. S. PEDRO
S. NOLASCO
Jorge
C. San
PL. S. MIGUEL
Río Huerva

PL. CESAR AUGUSTO

Espoz y Mina
PL. SANTA CRUZ

CASCO VIEJO

C. Prudencio
C. Manifestacion

Museo Pablo Gargallo
Palacio de Argüillo

C. Don Jaime I
C. Mendez Nuñez
C. Liberdad
C. 4 de Agosto
C. Alfonso I

PL. SINUES

PL. LOS SITIOS
Museo Provincial de Bellas Artes

C. San Miguel
C. J. Zurita Balmes
C. Isaac Peral
C. Joaquin Costa
C. San Clemente

S. Moret
Po. la Mina

C. Vitoria
TO LA ZONA

Av. Cesar Augusto

C. Olmo
FELIPE II
C. El Temple

PL. S. ROQUE

C. Coso
PL. DE ESPAÑA

Po. Independencia

San Ignacio
TO EL ROLLO

C. Predicadores
Casta Alvarez
C. Las Armas
C. San Blas
C. San Pablo
C. Boggiero
C. Cando de Aranda

Ramon Pignatelli

PL. S. LAMBERTO
PL. SALAMERO

C. Cadiz
C. Albareda
Ponzano

PL. DE ARAGON
PL. BASILIO PARAISO
Po. en Construcción

Po. de Sagasta
TO EL ROLLO

PL. SANTO DOMINGO

PL. J.M. FORQUE

C. Ramon y Cajal
Av. Cesar Augusto

PL. CARMEN

Po. Pamplona

Cerrada
C. Doctor
TO PARQUE PRIMO DE RIVERA

Po. Gran Via

C. Madre Rapóls

Fundación Pablo Serrano

Po. Maria Agustin

Av. de H. Cortes
C. Aznaro

PL. M. AGUERRI
TO POLICE

PL. DEL PORTILLO

Plaza de Toros

C. Gral. Mayandia
C. Madre Sacramento

C. Carmen
C. Burgos
Av. Goya

PL. E. ALFARO
Palacio de la Aljaferia

C. Castillo
C. Diputados

C. Madrid
C. Fuenterrabia
TO A

Train Station

Av. Anselmo Clavé

C. Escoriaza y Fabro

TO B

C. Santander
C. Tarragona
C. Teruel
Po. Valencia

N

friendly public bus system as well as city map blow-ups at major intersections make touring easy. The narrow streets to either side of **Calle Conde de Aranda** may be unsafe at night and should be avoided by solo travelers.

Transportation

Airplanes: Airport info (tel. 976 71 23 00). Flights to major Spanish and European cities. **Iberia,** C. Bilbao, 11 (tel. 976 21 82 56; reservations 902 40 05 00). Open M-F 9:30am-2pm and 4-7pm, Sa 9:30am-1:30pm. **Ebrobus,** Pl. Aragón, 10 (tel. 976 32 40 09), off Pl. Paraíso at the beginning of Po. Independencia, shuttles between the airport and its terminal (30min., 5-7 per day, 5am-9pm, 200ptas). A taxi to the airport costs about 2000ptas.

Trains: Estación Portillo, Av. Anselmo Clavé (24hr. info tel. 976 28 02 02). Taxi to Pl. Pilar (500ptas) or bus #21 from Po. María Agustín. Info booth open 8am-9pm. The **RENFE** office, C. San Clemente, 13 (tel. 976 28 02 02), is helpful. From Pl. Paraíso, follow Po. Independencia 4 blocks, and then turn right. Open M-F 9am-1:30pm and 4:30-8pm, Sa 9:30am-1pm. To: Tudela (45min., 14-15 per day, 580ptas); Jaca (3hr., 3 per day, 1400ptas); Logroño (2¼hr., 4 per day, 1400ptas); Pamplona (2¼hr., 5 per day, 1400ptas); Teruel (3hr., 3 per day, 1400ptas); Madrid (3hr., 8 per day, 3100-3800ptas); Barcelona (4hr., 7 per day, 3100-3800ptas); San Sebastián (4hr., 2 per day, 2700ptas); Valencia (6hr., 2 per day, 2580ptas).

Buses: Various bus companies dot the city, each with private terminals.

Agreda Automóvil, Po. María Agustín, 7 (tel. 976 22 93 43). Bus #21 stops in front. From station, turn right and follow Po. María Agustín to Pl. Paraíso. Info available 7:30am-9pm. To: Madrid (3½hr., 15-18 per day, 1740ptas); Barcelona (3½hr., 15-18 per day, 1640ptas). **Second terminal** at Av. Valencia, 20 (tel. 976 55 45 81). Enter on C. Lérida (bus #38). To: Muel (30min., M-Sa 2 per day, 260ptas); Cariñena (45min., M-Sa 2 per day, 400ptas); Daroca (1½hr., 2-3 per day, 715ptas).

La Oscense, Po. María Agustín, 7 (tel. 976 22 93 43). Shares terminal with Agreda Automóvil. To Jaca (2¼hr., 4-6 per day, 1450ptas).

Therpasa, C. General Sueiro, 22 (tel. 976 22 57 23). From station, turn left onto C. General Sueiro and follow for 1½ blocks, then turn left onto C. San Ignacio; after 2 blocks, turn right into Pl. Paraíso. To Tarazona (1½hr., 4-5 per day, 665ptas) and Soria (2½hr., 3-5 per day, 1075ptas).

CONDA, Av. Navarra, 79 (tel. 976 33 33 72). To get to the center from this station, take a right and follow Av. Navarro, bearing left onto Av. Madrid. Cross the highway and railbed on the blue pedestrian bridge. After 2 blocks, turn right on Po. María Agustín and continue along Po. Pamplona until Pl. Paraíso. Or take bus #25 to Po. Pamplona. To: Tudela (1hr., 6 per day, 690ptas); Pamplona (2½hr., 8 per day, 1650ptas); San Sebastián (3¼hr., 4 per day, 2345ptas).

Grupo Autobús Jimenez, C. San Juan Pablo Bonet, 13 (tel. 976 27 61 79). To get to the center from this station, turn right and then take a left on Po. Sagasta. Pl. Paraíso sits 7 blocks away. To get to the station, take bus #33 from Pl. España; find road sign for C. San Juan Pablo Bonet after 2 stops on Po. Sagasta. To Logroño (3hr., 3-6 per day, 1400ptas) and Teruel (3hr., 3-4 per day, 1330ptas).

Public Transportation: Red **TUZSA** buses (tel. 976 41 39 00) cover the city (85ptas, 10-ride 550ptas, ticket available from any kiosk). Tourist office offers a free map of bus routes. Bus #21 is particularly useful, running from near the train station to Po. Pamplona, Pl. Paraíso, Pl. Aragón, Pl. España, Pl. Pilar, and then up C. San Vincente de Paúl. Bus #33 is more central, going through Po. Sagasta, Pl. Paraíso, Po. Independencia, and Pl. España.

Taxis: Near the train station. **Radio-Taxi Aragón** (tel. 976 38 38 38). **Radio-Taxi Zaragoza** (tel. 976 42 42 42). Train station to Pl. Pilar about 500ptas.

Car Rental: Avis, Po. Fernando El Católico, 9 (tel. 976 55 50 94). From Pl. Paraíso take Gran Vía, which becomes Po. Fernando El Católico. Open M-F 8am-1pm and 4-8pm, Sa 8am-12:45pm.

Tourist and Financial Services

Tourist Office: Main Branch, Pl. Pilar (tel. 972 20 12 00 or 902 22 12 12; fax 972 20 06 35), in the black glass cube across from the basilica. Multilingual staff to help the Spanish-impaired. Request the tourist map, the guide *Paseos del Color* (thematically organized walking tours), and the *...guía de TAPAS.* **Additional branch** at Torreón de la Zuda, Glorieta de Pío XII, in a tower at the crumbling Roman walls.

From the main tourist office, proceed left along the length of the plaza. Both open M-Sa 9:30am-1:30pm and 4:30-7:30pm, Su 10am-2pm. **Third branch** at train station. Open M-Sa 11am-2:30pm and 4:30-8pm.

Currency Exchange: Banks open 8:30am-2pm; some open afternoons in winter. Many luxury hotels will change currency in emergencies. Banks line Po. Independencia, and **ATMs** are everywhere. **Banco Central Hispano,** Pl. Aragón, 6, has good rates on traveler's checks. Other locations dot the city.

American Express: Viajes Turopa, Po. Sagasta, 47 (tel. 976 38 39 11; fax 976 25 42 44), 6 blocks from Pl. Paraíso; around the corner on C. de las Torres. Bus #33 from Pl. España stops nearby. Full services. Cardholder mail held. Better exchange rates than most banks. Open M-F 9am-1:30pm and 4-8pm, Sa 9:30am-1pm.

El Corte Inglés: Po. Sagasta, 3 (tel. 976 21 11 21), and Po. Independencia, 11 (tel. 976 23 86 44). **Currency Exchange** (no commission but poor rates), **supermarket,** telephones, and a free **map.** Open M-Sa 10am-9:30pm.

Local Services

Luggage Storage: At the **train station,** 400ptas. Open 24hr. At **Agreda Automóvil** bus station, Po. María Agustín, 7, for 200ptas. Open 8am-8pm. At the other Agreda Automóvil, Av. Valencia, 20, 100ptas per piece per 24hr. period. Open M-F 10am-2:30pm and 4:30-7:30pm. At **Therpasa** bus station (tel. 976 22 67 10), 100ptas. Open M-F 9am-1pm and 4:15-7:30pm, Sa 9am-12:45pm.

English Bookstore: Librería General, Po. Independencia, 22 (tel. 22 44 83). Large selection downstairs of cheap Wordsworth classics. Open June-Aug. M-F 9:30am-1:30pm and 5-9pm, Sa 10am-2pm; Sept.-May M-Sa 9:30am-1:30pm and 4:30-8:30pm. Also see **El Corte Inglés,** above.

Youth Services: CRIDJA, Franco y López, 4 (tel. 976 55 19 87), in the HI hostel. ISIC 700ptas. HI card 1800ptas. Open M-F 11am-2pm.

Women's Services: Casa de la Mujer, C. Don Juan de Aragón, 2 (tel. 976 39 11 16), offers judicial assistance and general info. Open Sept.-June M-Th 9am-2pm and 4:30-7:30pm, F 9am-2pm; July-Aug. M-F 9am-2pm. **24hr. hotline** at 970 26 25 52.

Laundromat: Lavandería Rossell, C. San Vicente de Paul, 27 (tel. 976 29 90 34). From Pl. España turn right on C. Coso, go 4 blocks, then head left 4½ blocks. Wash and dry 990ptas per load. Open M-F 8:30am-1:30pm and 5-8pm, Sa 8:30am-1:30pm.

Emergency and Communications

Emergency: tel. 091 or 092. **Police:** Domingo Miral, s/n (tel. 092). **Lost and Found:** tel. 976 55 91 76; weekdays only.

Medical Services: Hospital Miguel Servet, Po. Isabel La Católica, 1 (tel. 976 35 57 00). In **emergencies,** turn to **Ambulatorio Ramón y Cajal,** Po. María Agustín, 12 (tel. 976 43 41 11). **Ambulance:** tel. 976 35 85 00.

Internet Access: Pub Vía Sacra, Arzobispo Domenech, 12 (tel. 976 22 04 73). From Pl. Paraíso follow Gran Vía for 2 blocks, then make a left on Arzobispo Domenech. 500ptas for 30min., 800ptas for 1hr. Open daily 6pm-3am.

Post Office: Po. Independencia, 33 (tel. 976 22 26 50), 1 block from Pl. Aragón on the right. Open for stamps, **fax,** and Lista de Correos (downstairs at window 4) M-F 8:30am-8:30pm, Sa 10am-2pm. Another branch next to train station at C. Clavé. Open M-F 8:30am-8:30pm, Sa 9:30am-1pm. **Postal Code:** 50001.

ACCOMMODATIONS AND CAMPING

Hostales and *pensiones*—some on the seedy side—pepper the narrow streets of the *casco viejo,* especially within the rectangle bounded by **Calle Alfonso I, Calle Don Jaime I, Plaza de España,** and **Plaza del Pilar,** and in the area to the right of the train station exit. Be wary the week of October 12, when Zaragoza celebrates the *Fiesta de la Virgen del Pilar.* Make reservations as early as possible and expect to pay as much as double the rates listed below; or just party the night straight through. *Ferias* (trade shows) are held from February through April. The biggest is the agricultural machinery show, FIMA, usually in late April, when you may have to scour everything within a 100km radius to find a room.

Albergue-Residencia Juvenil Baltasar Gracián (HI), C. Franco y Lopez, 4 (tel. 976 55 15 04). Take bus #22 from the train station, or turn right out of the station onto Av. Clavé, take the 2nd right onto C. Burgos, and follow 6 blocks then turn right onto C. Franco y Lopez. Forty beds clad with sheets and blankets in sparkling rooms of 2, 4, and 8; the rest of the building is a college dormitory. Dorms 1025ptas, over 26 1425ptas. Must call ahead for reservations. No lockout. Midnight curfew.

Casa de Huéspedes Elena, C. San Vicente de Paúl, 30 (tel. 976 39 65 80), behind the Catedral de la Seo on Pl. Pilar and across the street from Lavandería Rossell. Elena treats you like a grandchild. Remarkably clean, big rooms with big furniture and sparkling bathrooms. Singles and doubles 2000ptas.

Hostal Ambos Mundos, Pl. Pilar, 16 (tel. 976 29 97 04; fax 976 29 97 02), at C. Don Jaime I. Comfortable, tidy rooms with bright bedspreads. Try to get a room with a balcony overlooking the plaza. All rooms have showers and sinks. Singles 2300ptas; doubles 4065ptas. Breakfast 350ptas; other meals 1200ptas.

Pensión Rex, C. Méndez Nuñez, 31 (tel. 976 39 26 33), at C. Don Jaime I. Spacious rooms, some with balconies, many with full-length mirrors, and all with big windows. Singles 1800ptas, with shower 2300ptas; doubles 3200ptas, with shower 4300ptas. 350ptas to shower in a clean common bathroom.

Hostal Plaza, Pl. Pilar, 14 (tel. 976 29 48 30 or 976 28 48 39; fax 976 39 94 06). Immaculate, yellow-and-green plaid wallpapered rooms on the pricier side. Some have terrific views of the basilica and Pl. Pilar. Singles 3500ptas, with shower 4500ptas; doubles with bath 5800ptas. All rooms have phones and TV.

Camping: Casablanca, Barrio Valdefierro (tel. 976 75 38 70), down Cra. Madrid. Bus #36 from Pl. Pilar or Pl. España to the suburb of Valdefierro. Ask the driver to let you know when you've arrived, as it's notoriously difficult to find. By car, take the road to Madrid to the Valdefierro Exit (km 316), and from there follow the signs. Good facilities, including a pool open in summer. July-Aug. 600ptas per person, per tent, and per car; Sept.-June 545ptas. Open Apr.-Oct. 15.

FOOD

The poor and the hungry strike it rich in Zaragoza's *casco viejo. Tapas* bars, inexpensive restaurants, and *bocadillo* factories crowd the area known as **El Tubo** (C. Mártires, Cinegio, 4 de Agosto, and Estébanes). Several *marisquerías* serve seafood *raciones* at good prices on C. Don Jaime I, near Pl. Pilar. The tourist office gives out ... *guía de TAPAS,* which lists specialties and *tapas* bars, many clustered around Pl. Santa Marta (to the right and behind the Catedral del Seo). The **market** thrives in the long green building on Av. César Augusto off Pl. Pilar. Fresh fruits and veggies and freshly butchered baby pigs and rabbits are available (open M-Sa 9am-2pm and 5-8pm). Zaragoza's oldest **bakery,** Fantoba, C. Don Jaime, 21 (tel. 976 29 85 24), tempts with scrumptious pastries and chocolate-dipped fruits (open M-Sa 10am-2pm and 5-9pm). **Supermarket** shoppers can refuel at **Galerías Primero,** C. San Jorge, the continuation of C. Merdeo Nuñez (open M-Sa 9am-2pm and 4:30-8:30pm), or at **El Corte Inglés's** well-stocked but pricey basement mega-mart (see **Orientation and Practical Information,** p. 269).

Bar Los Amigos, C. Mártires, 8, (tel. 976 39 25 14), off Pl. España. A snug hole in the wall with a massive selection of sandwiches at prices you can't beat (250-475ptas). Tantalizing platters of *tapas.* Open daily noon-3pm and 7-11pm.

Tasquilla de Pedro, C. Cinegio, 3 (tel. 976 39 06 58), in the heart of El Tubo. Cluttered bar serves a wide array of typical Aragonese *tapas* (125-150ptas), to the (loud) tunes of Spanish top 40. Open daily 10am-3pm.

Casa Pascualillo, C. Libertad, 5 (tel. 976 39 72 03). In El Tubo district, off Méndez Nuñez. Filling, homestyle meals in a lively atmosphere. *Menú del día* 875ptas. Stewed bull meat fresh from the ring *(toro de lidia)* 775ptas—a steal considering the extravagant butchering. Open Tu-Sa 10:30am-4pm and 8-11pm, Su 10:30am-4pm. Meals served 1-4pm and 8-11pm. Visa.

Restaurante Caball, C. Don Jaime I, 3 (tel. 976 29 85 81), has a varying *menú del día* for 950ptas. Friendly waiters and a comfortable setting. Open daily 7am-midnight. Meals served 1-4pm and 8pm-midnight. Visa, MC.

El Real, C. Alfonso I, 40, (tel. 976 29 59 29), on Pl. Pilar. The perfect place to watch promenading *Zaragosanos* on the plaza or join bleary-eyed partyers for a Sunday morning *café.* Tables in the plaza when the weather permits. Entrees start at 550ptas in the restaurant downstairs. Open Su-Th 7am-11pm, F-Sa 7am-1:30am. Meals served 1-4pm and 9pm-midnight.

La Zanahoria, C. Tarragona, 4 (tel. 976 35 87 94). From Pl. Paraíso take Gran Vía, turn right on Av. Goya, then take the first left after crossing Av. Teruel/Valencia. Yuppie vegetarians come for the excellent salads and quiches. *Menú* 1000ptas. *Platos combinados* 950ptas. Open daily 1:30-4 and 9-11:30pm. Call for reservations. Visa, MC.

SIGHTS

The **Plaza del Pilar,** a vast square surrounded by a unique combination of architectural styles, is the place to begin a tour of Zaragoza's sights. The **Basílica de Nuestra Señora del Pilar,** the patroness after whom millions of Spanish women are named, dominates the plaza. *(Open daily in summer 6am-9:30pm; in winter 6am-8:30pm. Free.)* Its massive Baroque structure (begun in 1681) defines the skyline with brightly colored tiled domes decorated with frescoes by Goya, González Velázquez, and Francisco Bayeau. Evidence of the miraculous abounds inside. Two bombs (on display) were dropped on the basilica during the Civil War but failed to explode, bearing witness to the divine intervention of the Virgin. The **Museo del Pilar** (tel. 976 39 74 97) exhibits the glittering *joyero de la Virgen* (Virgin's jewels) and original sketches of the ceiling frescoes. *(Open daily 9am-2pm and 4-7pm. 150ptas.)*

On the left as you exit the basilica is Zaragoza's town hall. Next to the town hall is the Renaissance building **La Lonja,** which hosts occasional art exhibits. *(Open M-Sa 10am-2pm and 5-9pm, Su 10am-2pm.)* In front of La Lonja is an outdoor **monument** where statues act out scenes from Francisco de Goya's paintings. On the other side of C. Don Jaime I, the large glass and marble cube houses the entrance to the **Foro Romano** (tel. 976 39 97 52), built from 1 BC-AD 1. *(Ruins open Tu-Sa 10am-2pm and 5-8pm, Su 10am-2pm. Visits begin on the hour. 400ptas, students 200ptas, free for over 65 and under 8.)* Excavated ruins lurk underground.

Following the Muslim conquest of the Iberian Peninsula in the 8th century, a crisis over succession smashed the kingdom into petty tributary states called *taifas.* The **Palacio de la Aljafería** (tel. 976 28 95 28), on C. Castillo, is the principle relic of Aragón's Moorish *taifa. (Buses #21 and 33 stop here, or head left on Coso from Pl. España—facing the casco viejo—to the pedestrian street that leads to the castle. Open Apr. 15-Oct. 15. Su-W 10am-2pm and 4:30-8pm, F 4:30-8pm; Oct. 16-Apr. 14 M-W 10am-2pm and 4-6:30pm, F 4-6:30pm, Su 10am-2pm. Free guided visits on the half hour every hour. Entrance free until May 17, 1999. After then admission is 300ptas, students and senior citizens 150ptas, under 12 free.)* Previous alterations and renovations have somewhat encumbered the building's original grace, but its awesome stone exterior and exquisite interior still impress. The ground floor has a distinctly Moorish flavor in contrast to the Gothic second floor. The fortified tower imprisoned *el trovador* in García Gutierrez's drama of the same name, the source of Verdi's opera *Il Trovatore.*

In addition to an extensive collection of medieval Aragonese paintings, the **Museo Provincial de Bellas Artes,** Pl. Los Sitios, 6 (tel. 976 22 21 81), hangs a selection of works by Goya, including a collection of his excellent drawings. *(Open Tu-Sa 9am-2pm, Su 10am-2pm; special exhibits 4-8pm. Free.)* From Pl. España, follow Po. Independencia about five blocks, turn left and go five more blocks on C. Joaquín Costa. Turn left at Pl. Sitios; the museum is on your right.

The **Museo Pablo Gargallo,** dedicated to one of the most innovative sculptors of the 1920s, houses a small but marvelous collection of his works in the graceful **Pala-**

cio de Arguillo, built in 1670. *(Open Tu-Sa 10am-2pm and 5-9pm, Su 10am-2pm. Free.)* Walking down C. Don Jaime I from Pl. España, turn left on C. Ménendez Nuñez. The museum is on the left in Pl. San Felipe, five blocks down.

The **Fundación Pablo Serrano,** Po. María Agustín, 26, honors another fascinating sculptor, Pablo Serrano (1908-85), and features various works of his in bronze. *(Museum open in summer M and W-Sa 10am-2pm and 6-9pm, Su 10am-2pm; in winter M and W-Sa 10am-2pm and 5-8pm, Su 10am-2pm. Free.)* Look for *Gran Pan Partido (Big Bread Parted)* and sculptural reinterpretations of works by Picasso, Velázquez, and Goya. Once a year the museum displays work by his wife, painter Juana Francés.

Those hungering for green should head for the shaded walks and fountains of the **Parque Primo de Rivera,** opposite the old quarter from Pl. Paraíso. On summer weekends exercise your mind, body, and soul with free outdoor classes in chess, aerobics, canoeing, and tai chi.

ENTERTAINMENT

Young Zaragozans rightfully brag that their city has *mucha marcha* (lots of action). The scene begins in *La Zona,* as it's known to locals, in the streets bounded by Po. Constitucion, C. Leon XIII, Po. de las Damas, and Camino de las Torres. Teeny-boppers and soldiers favor **Calle Dr. Cerrada,** off Po. Pamplona, while the older and more affluent patronize **Residencial Paraíso** and **Calles Dr. Casas, Bolonia,** and **La Paz.** Gulping beer from *litros* (about 400ptas) is the primary sport around **El Rollo,** the zone bounded by C. Moncasi, Bonet, and Maestro Marquina at the southern end of **Paseo Sagasta,** also popular with the *militares* and fans of techno. University students storm **Paseo Sagasta** and its offshoot, C. Zumalacárregui. Later on, herds of *casco viejo*-goers move in around midnight in the market area, on **Calles Predicadores, El Olmo, El Temple, Contamina,** and **Manifestación** around Pl. San Felipe. For late-night, or rather early-morning, dancing check out **La Casa del Loco,** Calle Mayor 16, and **Oasis** on C. Boggiero behind the market. **Club Nautico** (don't arrive before 4:30am), on the Río Ebro behind Pl. Pilar, and **KWM,** Fernando el Católico, 70, also go to the wee hours. Gay bars and discos are situated around the west side of the *casco viejo.* **Atuaire,** C. Contamina, 13, and **Sphing,** C. Ramón y Cajal, are long-standing favorites. **Club Morrissey,** off Gran Vía, four blocks from Pl. Paraíso away from the *casco viejo,* has live music. The **Teatro Principal,** C. Coso, 57 (tel. 976 29 60 90), hosts performances of all kinds (ticket booth open Sept. 15-June 15 daily noon-1:30pm and 5pm-showtime).

Flea markets occur all over town on Sunday mornings. **Mercadillo** occurs outside the Pl. de Toros. **El Rastro,** also on Wednesday mornings, shows up by the soccer stadium. An **antiques market** hides in Pl. San Bruno (behind the cathedral), paintings are displayed in Pl. Santa Cruz, and stamp collectors indulge in the Pl. San Francisco.

The city erupts for a week of unbridled hoopla around October 12 in honor of *La Virgen Santa del Pilar,* one of the few full-blown autumn *fiestas.* Although you may not find lodging, you might not need it. City patrons San Valero (Jan. 29) and San Jorge (Apr. 23) are also celebrated. The city tourist office distributes info on *fiestas.*

▓ Near Zaragoza

Ask at the Zaragoza tourist office for info on such excursions as the *Ruta del Vino* (wine route) and the *Ruta de Goya.* **Teruel** (see p. 278) and **Tarazona** (see p. 277) are good daytrips from Zaragoza. Fans of the Romanesque should inquire about visits to the **Cinco Villas** (five villages), particularly Sos del Rey Católico and Uncastillo.

■ Monasterio de Piedra

An oasis of waterfalls and trees springs out of the dry Aragón plain around the **Monasterio de Piedra** (tel. 976 84 90 11), about 110km southwest of Zaragoza, near Calatayud (open daily 9am-9pm). Founded in 1195 by an order of Cistercian monks from Tarragona and abandoned under government orders in 1835, the monks' quarters are now three-star lodgings. The 12th-century **Torre del Homenaje,** the only part of the existing building that hasn't been restored, still towers over the valley.

The main attraction is the surrounding park and the **Río Piedra,** which casts off waterfalls and lakes as it plunges down the valley. Follow the path leading through, under, and around this aquatic paradise (park open daily 9am-nightfall; 1000ptas for monastery and park). **Automóviles Zaragoza buses,** C. Almagro, 18 (tel. 976 21 93 20), leave from Zaragoza for the monastery once a day on Wednesday, Thursday, Saturday, and Sunday at 9am and return at 5pm (round-trip 2220ptas).

■ Ruta del Vino and Ruta de Goya

The scorched countryside south of Zaragoza is surprisingly fertile, its warm days and cool nights yielding prime grape harvests. To visitors, however, the mystique of these cherished vineyards is lost among the advanced wine-making machinery. Locals will graciously recommend local vintages, but if you envision taking tours through dusky commercial wineries, think again. Several *bodegas* offer wine for tasting and for purchase out of industrial warehouses. **Cariñena,** the self-titled "*bodega del Aragón,*" is the most important wine-producer in Aragón. During its fiestas to celebrate the grape harvest (Sept. 13-18), wine flows from the town fountain.

The little town of **Muel,** otherwise uninspired, is home to Goya frescoes in the **Ermita de la Virgen de la Fuente** (open daily 9am-8pm). Ágreda Automóvil (tel. 976 55 45 81) **buses** cover both Muel (35min., 260ptas) and Cariñena (45min., 400ptas; see **Zaragoza: Practical Information,** p. 269). **Fuendetodos** (pop. 120), Goya's birthplace, is difficult to reach, but is worth the trip for diehard fans. The humble home where Goya was born, **La Casa Natal** (tel. 976 14 38 30) and the **Museo del Grabado** are open Tuesday to Sunday 11am to 2pm and 4 to 7pm (300ptas for both). Call the town hall (tel. 976 14 38 01) for lodging and general tourist information. **Samar Buil buses,** C. Borao, 13 (tel. 976 43 43 04), run there (1½hr., 2 per day, 410ptas), and one return bus a day runs to Zaragoza on alternating mornings and afternoons.

■ Daroca

Daroca (pop. 2400) is an enchanting little town where burros and wagons occasionally wander the streets. Cut into a dramatic gorge, the town's burnt-sienna roofs match the surrounding cliffs. The ruins of Daroca's walls, 4km in circumference, were begun in the 9th century and were once punctuated with 114 towers. Dirt paths trace along the walls and reward hikers with a sentry's-eye view of the town and surrounding valleys. The town's main artery, **Calle Mayor,** runs uphill from **Puerta Baja** (lower gate) to the **Puerta Alta** (upper gate). Calle Arrabal is one approach to the wall; exit the Puerta Baja and turn right, then head up and around. Getting down from the walls on the other side requires ingenuity but can be done.

The main sight in town is the icon-filled museum of the **Colegiata de Santa María,** a 16th-century Renaissance church. (Church and museum open Tu-Sa 11am-1pm and 5:30-7:30pm, Su before mass at 11:30am and 6:30pm only. 300ptas. The tourist office arranges guided tours; call for more info.) To reach the church, take C. Juan de la Huerta from C. Mayor. Little Daroca puts on a good party during its week-long **Fiesta de Corpus Christi,** held every year in late May or early June. The town also hosts the annual **International Program for Ancient Music** during the first two weeks of August. Musicians from the world over gather to teach, learn, and give free concerts.

Buses to Zaragoza (1½hr., departs 8, 9am, and 4:30pm, 715ptas) and Teruel depart from in front of **Mesón Felix,** C. Mayor, near Puerta Baja. Buses arriving in Daroca, the last stop on the Agreda Automóvil bus line, halt at Puerta Baja. Daroca's **tourist office** is at Pl. España, 4 (tel. 976 80 01 29), opposite Colegiata de Santa María. From Puerta Alta, pursue the sights along C. Mayor for 4-5 blocks and hang a right on C. San Juan de la Huerta. (Open Tu-Sa 11am-2:30pm, Su 11:30am-2pm.) **Guardia Civil** (tel. 976 80

01 13) headquarters are on the highway next to the swimming pool. The **post office,** C. Mayor, 114 (tel. 976 80 02 11), lies near Puerta Baja (open M-F 8:30am-2pm, Sa 9:30am-1pm). The **postal code** is 50360.

Although Daroca probably works best as a side trip, sleepy travelers should try the comfortable **Pensión El Ruejo,** C. Mayor, 88 (tel. 976 80 09 62), complete with spotless modern rooms, heating, A/C, a disco, and a flowering courtyard. Inquire at the bar downstairs, after 9am (singles 2000ptas; doubles 3000ptas, with bath 4500ptas). The **restaurant** on the first floor serves a satisfying 1000pta *menú*. Picnickers can stock up at **%Día,** the supermarket on C. Mayor, or the town **market** in Pl. Joaquín Costa, off C. Mayor (open Th 9am-2pm).

■ Tarazona

Owing to its ubiquitous Arab-influenced architecture, Tarazona (pop. 10,400) has earned the name "The Mudéjar City," and several buildings typify Spain's ornate 16th-century brickwork. The residents of this lovely, little-touristed town all seem to know one another; they talk to each other from one rooftop to the next or stop to chat on the steep, winding streets of *El Cinto,* the medieval quarter. Although it's best to visit during the **Tarazona Foto** festival (mid-July to mid-August), the town makes a pleasant stopover just about anytime.

PRACTICAL INFORMATION Therpasa buses (tel. 976 64 11 00) operate from the station on Av. Navarra to Soria (1hr., 4-8 per day, 540ptas) and Zaragoza (1hr., 4-7 per day, 665ptas). **Conda** leaves from Parque de Estación; from Pl. San Francisco, it's up C. Carrera Zaragoza. For trips to Tudela (1hr., M-Sa 5 per day, Su 1 per day, 215ptas), buy tickets on the bus. The very helpful **tourist office,** C. Iglesias, 5 (tel. 976 64 00 74), sits alongside the cathedral. From the Therpasa bus station, turn right on Av. Navarra, and at the circular Pl. San Francisco follow the Soria/Zaragoza signs on C. Martínez until the tree-shaded Pl. Seo; turn left and go up the steps. (Open M-F 9am-1:30pm and 4:30-7pm, Sa-Su 10am-1pm and 4-7pm.) For **currency exchange** check out the Banco Central Hispano in Pl. San Francisco (open May-Sept. M-F 8:30am-2:30pm; Oct.-Apr. M-F 8:30am-2:30pm, Sa 8:30am-1pm). **Luggage storage** is available from the Therpasa bus station (open daily 7am-1pm and 2-10pm; free). The **Red Cross** (tel. 976 64 09 26) is outside town on Ctra. Zaragoza. In **medical emergencies** you can also turn to **Ambulatorio San Atilano,** Av. Paz, 29 (tel. 976 64 12 85). The **municipal police** are next to the library on Pl. San Francisco (tel. 976 64 16 91, **emergency** tel. 092). They provide maps when the tourist office is closed. The **post office** is at Pl. Seo (tel. 976 64 13 17), downhill from the cathedral (open M-F 8:30am-2:30pm, Sa 9:30am-1pm). The **postal code** is 50500.

ACCOMMODATIONS AND FOOD Options for lodging are scant, but **Hostal Palacete de los Arcedianos,** C. Marrodán, 16 (tel. 976 64 09 45 or 976 64 23 03), is perfectly adequate. To get there, start with your back to the bank in Pl. San Francisco and head right along the river on Po. Constitución. Take the second right onto C. Marrodán; enter through the arched doorway on the left under the Centro de Estudios sign. Comfortable rooms and tidy bathrooms lie off a stairway with a star-studded vaulted ceiling (singles 3000ptas; doubles 4500ptas).

Día, on the corner of C. Quiñones and C. Visconti, just off Pl. San Francisco, sells groceries (open M-Sa 9am-2pm and 5-8pm). **Hotel/Restaurante Ituri-Asso,** C. Virgen del Río, 3 (tel. 976 64 31 96), cooks up an inventive, tasty *menú del día* (1200ptas) featuring salad and rabbit with almonds. (Open M-F 1-4 and 9-11pm, Sa 1-4 and 9-11:30pm, Su 1-4pm. Visa, MC, AmEx.) **S'ha Feito...Taverna,** Pl. de Toros, 18, is a new bar made to look old, run by hip youngsters and serving traditional Aragonese *tapas* (open M-F noon-4pm and 6pm on, Sa-Su noon-close).

SIGHTS The splendid Gothic 13th- to 15th-century **cathedral** is undergoing painstaking restorations. Supposedly, the glorious towers, belfry, lantern, and plasterwork tracery in the inner cloister are particularly fine examples of *Mudéjar* work. The cloister may be open by the time you read this, but it'll take a return trip in 10 or 15 years to catch a glimpse of the interior. The quirky, octagonal **Plaza de Toros Vieja** was built in the 18th century to include private residences. To get there from the cathedral, follow signs to Soria/Zaragoza down C. Laureles then make the first right at the Olympia Gym and pass through the arch.

Tarazona was a seasonal residence of medieval Aragonese kings until the 15th century. Their Alcázar has since served as the **Palacio Episcopal.** Now the bishop's workplace, the palace lies across the bridge from the Pl. Toros Vieja; go left one block, and then up the zig-zagging stairs of the Recodos and Rúa Baja. Opposite the Palacio Episcopal, in the heart of El Cinto (the medieval quarter), rises the **Iglesia de Santa Magdalena,** with a graceful *Mudéjar* tower that hovers over the old town. The entrance is a left up Cuesta del Palacio from the Palacio Episcopal and the first left thereafter (open only for mass). **Murallas** (walls) surround the quarter's heart; go uphill from La Magdalena past the remarkable Renaissance facade of **Iglesia San Atilano** and continue past Pl. Puerto, then exit left. Your reward is a panoramic vista of the broad Valle del Moncayo and, on a clear day, the distant Aragonese Pyrenees.

During Tarazona's **fiestas** (Aug. 27-Sept. 1), crowds pelt each other and *el Cipotegato* with tomatoes (see **Ketchup made with Pain** below). Try to catch the **Tarazona Foto** festival (mid-July to mid-August) when many monuments are opened for a city-wide photography exhibition.

Sticks and Stones May Break My Bones But Fruit Will Never Hurt Me

When José Albercio describes the evolution of Tarazona's tastes by saying, *"antiguamente piedras y ahora tomates"* (in ancient times stones and now tomatoes), he is, fortunately, not talking about sandwich toppings, but pointing out a change in weaponry. During the Middle Ages, the **Moors** pelted town heretics with a barrage of bricks and stones. If the heretic lived, he was freed. Tarazonans continue the tradition during the Fiestas de Cipotegatos every August 27th with a more festive (and less disturbing) twist to the ceremony. They shower *el Cipotegato,* their damned citizen, with **plump, luscious** tomatoes—a thousand kilograms of them, supplied by local social clubs. Townspeople costume their scapegoat in a harlequinesque mask and colorfully quilted suit. He is then guided through the multitudes, wielding just a ball of yarn attached to a stick for protection while being showered with **fruit.** Eventually the whole shebang becomes a giant **food fight,** thus ushering in the Corpus Christi holidays.

■ Near Tarazona: Monasterio de Veruela

Travelers with cars can visit the enchanting walled monastery of Veruela (tel. 976 64 90 25), which slumbers in the Sierra de Moncayo, 15km south of Tarazona. Its golden stone walls guard a Romanesque-Gothic church and a transcendentally peaceful cloister. Nineteenth-century poet Gustavo Adolfo Bécquer sought the mountain air here and penned his *Cartas desde mi celda (Letters from My Cell)* within these walls. The Cistercian monastery participates in the **Tarazona Foto exhibitions.** *(Grounds open in summer Tu-Su 10am-2pm and 4-7pm; in winter 10am-1pm and 3-6pm. 200ptas.)* **Buses** on their way to Alcalá de Moncayo might stop at the monastery if you ask the driver before departure from Tarazona. Buses also run to Vera de Moncaya, 4km from the monastery. Ask at the tourist office in Tarazona for more transportation information.

■ Teruel

A sleepy town that still turns in en masse for the afternoon *siesta,* the provincial capital of Teruel practices traditional Spanish habits that belie its cosmopolitan history. From the 12th to the 15th centuries, Muslims, Jews, and Christians lived here in cultural collusion, as evidenced by the resulting Mudéjar architecture, a blend of characteristically Arab patterns with Gothic and Romanesque touches. An easy enough stopover between Valencia and Zaragoza, Teruel doesn't really reach its prime until July, when citizens celebrate the resilience of their dear *torico* (iron bull) in an 168-hour anarchic liquor fest.

Star-Crossed Lovers

The tombs of Diego de Marcilla and Isabel de Segura in the **Mausoleo de los Amantes,** next to Torre San Pedro, graphically explain why Teruel is called the *ciudad de los amantes* (city of lovers). To prove his worth to Isabel's affluent family, Diego left Teruel in search of fortune and fame, only to return five years later just in time to watch Isabel marry his rival. Diego's request for one last kiss was refused, and he promptly died. At the funeral, Isabel kissed the corpse and, overcome with grief, died herself. Life-size alabaster statues of the lovers reach out over their tombs to touch hands, but, in Grecian urn fashion, never do. For a spot-lighted peek at the lover's remains, duck down near their heads. From Pl. Torico, take the alleyway to the left of the purple *modernista* house. Stairs from there lead directly to the mausoleum. (Open daily 10am-2pm and 5-7:30pm. 50ptas.)

ARAGÓN

ORIENTATION AND PRACTICAL INFORMATION

Teruel's nonsensical layout can confound even the most finely tuned sense of direction. Maps from the tourist office are helpful, but street signs don't always exist and several major streets and *plazas* go by two names. The *casco histórico* perches on a hilltop, linked to modern Teruel by bridges. The center of the *casco* is **Plaza de Carlos Castell,** affectionately known as **Plaza del Torico** for its pillar crowned by a tiny iron bull. To reach Pl. Torico from the train station, take the staircase from the park and follow signs to the *centro histórico*. To reach Pl. Torico from the **train station,** take the *modernista* staircase from the park and follow signs to the *centro histórico*. The new **bus station** at the edge of town is only a few blocks form the *casco antiguo*. To get to Pl. Torico, head straight up C. Abadía.

Trains: Station, Camino de la Estación, 1 (tel. 978 61 02 02), down the stairs from Pl. Ovalo. To: Mora de Rubielos (45min., 3 per day); Rubielos de Mora (50min., 1 per day); Valencia (2¾hr., 3 per day, 2200ptas); Zaragoza (3hr., 4 per day, 1355ptas).
Buses: Companies work out of the new station (tel. 978 60 10 14), Ronda de Ambeles, at the edge of town, only a few blocks from the *casco antiguo*. **La Rápida** (tel. 978 60 20 04) rolls to Barcelona (5½-6½hr., 1-2 per day). **Samar** (tel. 978 60 34 50) runs to Valencia (2-3hr., 3-5 per day) and Madrid (5hr., 2-3 per day). **Magallón** (tel. 978 41 72 52) and **Jiménez** (tel. 978 60 10 40) go to Zaragoza (4 per day). **Autotransport Teruel** (tel. 978 60 15 90) sends buses to Albarracín (45min., 1 per day). **Furio** (tel. 964 60 01 00) drives to Mora de Rubielos (1hr.) and Rubielos de Mora (1½hr., 1 per day).
Tourist office: C. Tomás Nogues, 1 (tel. 978 60 22 79), at C. Comandante Fortea/del Pozo. From Pl. Torico, follow C. Ramón y Cajal/San Juan and take the first left; the office is 1 block away on the right. Open in summer Tu-Sa 9am-2pm and 5-8pm, Su 9am-2pm; in winter Tu-Sa 9am-2pm and 5-8pm.
Luggage storage: Lockers in the train station 400ptas. Open daily 6:30am-10:30pm. In the bus station, 250ptas per piece. Open M-Sa 9am-3pm and 4:45-6:30pm.
Emergency: call 091 or 092. **Municipal police:** tel. 978 60 21 78.
Post office: C. Yagüe de Salas, 17 (tel. 978 60 76 86). Lista de Correos and **fax** available. Open M-F 8:30am-8:30pm, Sa 9:30am-2pm. The **postal code** is 44001.

ACCOMMODATIONS AND FOOD

Lodgings are scarce during August and Semana Santa and impossible during *fiesta*-time in early July. Restaurant standards and prices are high. The *casco viejo* is the place to look. Teruel is famous for its salty, flavorful cured ham, *jamón de Teruel,* featured in *tapas* bars in Pl. Torico. For veggie diversion, there is a **market** on Pl. Domingo Gascón. From Pl. Torico, take C. Joaquín Costa/Tozal. (Open M-Sa 8am-1:30pm.) **Supermercado Muñoz** is at Pl. Castell/Torico, 23. (Open M-F 9:30am-2pm and 5-7:30pm, Sa 9:30-2pm.)

Hostal Aragón, C. Santa María, 4 (tel. 978 60 13 87). Head in the direction the Torico faces, and take the first left as you leave Pl. Torico. Attractive hotel-quality rooms at *hostal* prices. Ultra-firm beds. Singles 2000ptas, with bath 3000ptas; doubles 3200ptas, with bath 4900ptas; triples with bath 7000ptas.

Camping: The nearest campgrounds are in Albarracín, 37km away, and in Mora de Rubielos, 42km away (see **Near Teruel,** below).

Restaurante La Parrilla, C. Esteban, 2 (tel. 978 60 59 17), lies 2 blocks uphill from the tourist office. Magnificent 1200ptas *menú* grilled before you on a stone fireplace. Open M-Sa 11am-5pm and 8pm-midnight, Su 11am-5pm.

SIGHTS AND ENTERTAINMENT

Muslim artisans built the brick-and-glazed-tile **Torres Mudéjares** (Mudéjar Towers) between the 12th and 15th centuries, and then the Christian churches adapted the structure of the Almohad minarets to their own purposes. *(Open in summer daily 11am-2pm and 5-8pm; in winter Sa-Su 11am-2pm and 5-8pm. 300ptas includes optional guided tour.)* The more intricately designed of the three towers are the richly tiled 14th-century **Torre de San Martín,** in Pl. Pérez Prado ·near the post office, and the **Torre de San Salvador,** on C. del Salvador, built around 1277. In the latter, 123 skinny steps climb through several chambers to the panoramic belltower up top.

The alpha and omega of Teruel's Mudéjar monuments is the 13th-century **Catedral de Santa María de Mediavilla,** in Pl. Catedral. *(Open 11am-2pm and 5-8pm. Free.)* The magnificently decorated brick tower is a mere preface to the 14th-century stylized *artesonado mudéjar* (Mudéjar coffered ceiling) roofing the central nave. All roads left of Pl. Castell/Torico lead one block away to Pl. Catedral. Behind the cathedral, the ethnographic- and archaeology-oriented **Museo Provincial,** Pl. Fray Anselmo Polanco (tel. 978 64 74 00), is housed in the 16th-century porticoed Casa de la Comunidad. *(Open Tu-Sa 10am-2pm and 4-7pm, Su 10am-2pm. Free.)*

Teruel's Iron Calf

The drunken celebration of historical events is a Spanish tradition, and the folks of Teruel do it right. In the winter of 1937, one of the Spanish Civil War's most gruesome battles was fought on Teruel's Republican ground. With temperatures reaching below -20°C, General Franco levelled the city, outdueling his military academy classmate General Rojo. When the smoke cleared, only Teruel's chrome statue of a pint-sized *torico* (bull) remained—perched on its Doric pedestal and surveying the surrounding rubble.

Seven days of non-stop debauchery honor the *torico*'s resilience during the annual **Vaquillas del Angel,** beginning the week following the first Monday in July and culminating the second weekend in July. Saturday afternoon, a group of teenagers belonging to one *peña* (private social club) erects a human web around the diminutive *torico.* One lucky member dons the bull with a red bandana and smooches it silly. The bandana is removed the following night, after a raucous *encierro* (running of the bulls) while the *torico* is showered with red, yellow, and purple alcoholic concoctions. The celebration is certainly not as grandiose or renowned as Pamplona's (you won't find any ESPN2 camera crews), but Papa Hemingway would still be proud.

■ Near Teruel

Protected by ancient walls, medieval townships are suspended in Teruel's countryside amid acres of feral land. Getting to these mystical hamlets is less of an ordeal now that **Regionales** trains from Teruel, Valencia, and Zaragoza make the journey. Only one bus per day ventures from Teruel and returns the next morning. Unless you have a car (plan ahead as there are no car rentals in Teruel), you'll have to spend the night. The almighty *Guía de servicios turísticos,* available at any Aragonese tourist office, has information on accommodations in the area. Some folks hitch, although *Let's Go* does not recommend it. Traffic is heaviest between Teruel and Albarracín; hitchers post themselves with placards at the end of Camino de la Estación, the beginning of

ARAGÓN

the road to Zaragoza. For Mora de Rubielos and Rubielos de Mora, hitchers favor the end of the aqueduct bridge on the road to Valencia.

Thirty-five kilometers west of Teruel, **Albarracín,** once a powerful Islamic city, now lives mainly off the fading grandeur of its stone houses, small churches, and dispersed towers. The **tourist office,** Pl. Mayor, 1 (tel. 978 71 02 51), will direct you to tours of the *pinturas rupestres,* post-paleolithic shelter paintings dating from 5000 BC. (Open July-Sept. M-Sa 10am-2pm and 5-7:30pm, Su 10am-2pm. In summer free guided tours daily at 2:30 and 5:30pm; in the off-season, consult the **Ayuntamiento** at 978 71 02 51; open M-F 9am-3pm.) **Camping Ciudad de Albarracín** stakes out here (tel. 978 71 01 97; 375ptas per person, per tent, and per car).

Mora de Rubielos, 42km east of Teruel, has the largest and best-preserved 15th-century castle in the area. **Bus** is the best way to get there—Furio vehicles (tel. 964 60 01 00) roll right into town from Valencia and Teruel. **Trains** run to Mora de Rubielos from Valencia (3 per day), Zaragoza (3 per day), and Teruel (3 per day) but arrive at a station 14km away from Mora de Rubielos. In the summer, a **tourist office** sets up on C. Diputación (tel. 978 80 00 00). There's **camping** at El Morrón-Barrachinas (tel. 978 80 03 62; 600ptas per person, car and tent included; open July-Aug.).

Local connoisseurs insist the most *precioso* (exquisite) of the medieval towns around Teruel is **Rubielos de Mora,** 15km east of Mora de Rubielos. Its 600 souls live in an unrestored and unscathed architectural set-piece from medieval days, complete with two city gates and a 16th-century town hall (courtyard, dungeon, and all). The **tourist office** is in the Ayuntamiento building, Pl. Hispano América, 1 (tel. 978 80 40 96; open July-Aug. 10am-2pm and 5-7pm; Sept.-June M-F 10am-2pm). **Trains** run to Rubielos de Mora from Teruel and Valencia (1 per day from each).

ARAGONESE PYRENEES

Political geographers look at the Aragonese Pyrenees, consider the infrequency of invasions of Spain from the north, and say it all makes sense. Everyone else looks and can't say a word. Their jagged cliff faces, deep, wrenching gorges, icy snow-melt rivers, and alpine meadows have awed humans for centuries. Despite scanty train and bus transportation, the area draws both mountaineering veterans and casual walkers to its famous peaks. **Jaca,** the entry point, is fairly bland. To truly enjoy the area, explore the cobbled streets and meandering trails of outlying villages and valleys. The region's spectacular features crescendo at the magical **Parque Nacional de Ordesa.**

Hikers should be sure to get a hold of a detailed regional map. *Editorial Alpina* maps (600-900ptas at bookstores, many hotels, and other stores) are always excellent. Tourist offices can also recommend other maps that are good for a particular region. Local sports centers offer info and guides for everything from sweat-free strolls to heart-stopping rappels. In summer, the Aragonese Pyrenees are a **climber's fantasy.** In winter, **skiers** find their own brand of bliss. Five major resorts—Astún, Panticosa, Formigal, Cerler, and Candanchú—lie at their pole-tips. The pamphlets *Ski Aragón* and *El Turismo de Nieve en España,* free at tourist offices, give the lowdown on them all. **Huesca** and **Jaca** provide limited access through the area by bus, but the most efficient and enjoyable way to explore the valleys is by car. And although you usually have to be 21 to rent a car, some smaller companies in the area may be flexible. Even if you can't get your own wheels, Ordesa is definitely worth the hassle to get there.

■ Jaca

For centuries, pilgrims bound for Santiago would cross the Pyrenees into Spain, crash in Jaca (pop. 14,000) for the night, and be off by sunrise. They had the right idea. Although Jaca served a brief stint as capital of Aragón between 1035 until 1095, there is little to do here, outside of organizing transport and excursions into the Pyrenees and nearby ski resorts.

ORIENTATION AND PRACTICAL INFORMATION

If you arrive by bus, you'll be dropped at the edge of the city center onto **Avenida de la Jacetania,** which loops around downhill to become **Avenida de Oroel.** Avenida Oroel connects with **Avenida Regimiento de Galicia** at the bottom of the hill, which becomes **Avenida Primer Viernes de Mayo,** a broad street that runs back uphill to Av. Jacetania. Within this circle, the central artery is **Calle Mayor.** From the **bus station,** walk straight through the plaza to C. Zocotin and go straight for two blocks. The shuttle bus from the **train station** will drop you off at the **Ayuntamiento,** in the middle of C. Mayor, or at the intersection of C. Mayor and Av. Regimiento de Galicia.

Trains: Shuttle buses run from downtown to the train station roughly 30min. before each train leaves. They leave from the Ayuntamiento on C. Mayor or, if C. Mayor is closed, the taxi stop next to C. Mayor and the bus station. If you're walking to town from the station, take Av. Juan XXIII until its end, and take a left on C. Francia and continue straight for about 6 blocks as it becomes C. Primer Viernes; then make a left onto C. Mayor. **RENFE,** C. Estación, s/n (tel. 974 36 13 32). Ticket booth open 10am-noon and 5-7pm. To: Ayerbe (1½hr., 2 per day, 500ptas); Zaragoza (3hr., 2 per day, 1900ptas); Madrid (7hr., 1 per day, 4100ptas).

Buses: La Oscense (tel. 974 35 50 60). To: Sabiñánigo, where **Empresa Hudebus** (tel. 974 21 32 77) connects to Torla, near Ordesa and Aínsa (20min., 1-2 per day, 180ptas); Zaragoza (2hr., 1 per day, 1450ptas); Pamplona (2hr., 1per day, 855ptas). **Josefa Escartín** (tel. 974 36 05 08) runs 1 bus (departs M-Sa 6:30pm) to: Hecho (55min.); Siresa (1hr.); and Ansó (1½hr.). Tickets cost 400-500ptas.

Taxis: (tel. 974 36 28 48). Taxis line up at the intersection of C. Mayor, Av. Regimiento Galicia, and Av. Viernes de Mayo.

Car Rental: Europcar, in Huesca (tel. 974 23 10 36). Must be 21 and have had a license for at least a year. Additional charge for bringing the car to Jaca.

Tourist Office: Av. Regimiento Galicia, 2, local 1 (tel. 974 36 00 98), left off C. Mayor. English-speaking staff. Useful **map** and hiking advice. Open July-Aug. M-F 9am-2pm and 4:30-8pm, Sa 10am-1:30pm and 5-8pm, Su 10am-1:30pm; Sept.-June M-F 9am-1:30pm and 4:30-7pm, Sa 10am-1pm and 5-7pm.

Currency Exchange: Banks cluster on Av. Jacetania. Open daily 10am-1:30pm. **Banco Central Hispano** sits on C. Primer Viernes de Mayo at the corner of C. Mayor (open M-F 8:30am-2:30pm).

Ski Rental: Nieve Sport, Av. Francia, 33 (tel. 974 36 35 72).

Hiking, Climbing, and X-treme Sports: Alcorce, Av. Regimiento Galicia, 1 (tel./fax 974 36 39 72; email alcorce-pirineos@encomix.es), across from the tourist office. Organizes hiking, rock climbing, spelunking, and rafting trips. Guided hiking trips start at 3000ptas per day, per person; rafting at 5500ptas. Open M-Sa 10am-1:30pm and 5-8:30pm, later July to August.

Ski Conditions: Teléfono Blanco (tel. 976 20 11 12), or call resorts directly.

Emergency: call 091 or 092. **Police:** C. Mayor, 24 (tel. 092), in the Ayuntamiento.

24Hr. Pharmacy: Check listings in the local paper, *Pirineo Aragonés.*

Medical Services: Centro de Salud, Po. Constitución, 6 (tel. 974 36 07 95).

Post Office: C. Correos, 13 (tel. 974 36 00 85), at Av. Regimiento Galicia, across from the tourist office. Open M-F 8:30am-2:30pm, Sa 9:30am-1pm. Lista de Correos in the side entrance on Av. Regimiento Galicia. **Postal Code:** 22700.

ACCOMMODATIONS AND CAMPING

Jaca's *hostales* and *pensiones* cluster around C. Mayor and the cathedral. Lodgings are scarce only during the bi-annual Festival Folklórico in late July and early August. For Santiago-bound pilgrims, the **Albergue de Peregrinos** sits on C. Hospital.

Albergue Juvenil de Escuelas Pias (HI), Av. Perimetral, 6 (tel. 974 36 05 36). From C. Mayor, turn left onto C. Regimento de Galicia and left again on C. Perimetral. On the right side of the road, turn off on the driveway to the left of the modern metal sculpture. Rows of red-shuttered bungalows. Rooms with 2, 3, or 4 beds and sinks. Midnight curfew. 1300ptas per person, over 26 1750ptas. Nonmembers pay 400ptas more. Breakfast 250ptas.

Hostal Paris, Pl. San Pedro, 4 (tel. 974 36 10 20), by the cathedral. A left off Av. Jacetania as you face the *ciudadela*. Big-windowed rooms, with firm beds and winter heating. If nobody answers, ring on the 3rd floor to the left. July-Aug. singles 2300ptas, doubles 3600ptas. Sept.-June singles 2100ptas, doubles 3300ptas.

Habitaciones Martínez, C. Mayor, 53 (tel. 974 36 33 74), above a bar. Smells like cigarettes, but some rooms have balconies and you can't beat the price. Singles 1500ptas; doubles 3000ptas.

Camping: Peña Oroel (tel. 974 36 02 15), 3½km down the road to Sabiñánigo. Wooded grounds along a riverbank shelter, market, and swimming pool. 650ptas per person, per tent, per car. Open Semana Santa and mid-June to mid-Sept.

FOOD

Restaurants offering *menús* and *tapas* spin off **Calle Mayor;** those lining **Avenida Primer Viernes de Mayo** serve *bocadillos*, pizzas, and *platos combinados*. Jaca is know for its pastries and baked goods; pop into a bakery and try *corazones* (or *lazos*) *de Jaca*, a sugary pastry. Groceries are at **Supermercado ALDI,** C. Correos, 9, next to the post office (open M-Sa 9:30am-1:30pm and 5-8pm).

Restaurante Vegetariano El Arco, C. San Nicolas, 4, off the bus station plaza. Tasty vegetarian *menú* (1000ptas) changes daily—hopefully they'll have their stellar vegetable couscous. *Platos* 850ptas. Open M-Sa 1:30-3pm and 8:30-11pm.

Crepería El Bretón, C. Ramiro I, 10. French owner makes authentic dinner (*galettes* 400-1000ptas) and dessert crepes (300-700ptas), all served in a Frenchified room with lace curtains. Salads 650ptas. Open Tu-Sa 6pm-1am.

SIGHTS AND ENTERTAINMENT

The pentagonal fortress referred to as **La Ciudadela** (tel. 974 36 04 43) or Castillo de San Pedro sprawls out along Av. Primer Viernes de Mayo. *(Open July-Aug. daily 11am-12:30pm and 5-6:30pm; Sept.-June 11am-noon and 4-5pm. By tour only. 300ptas, under 15 100ptas.)* Begun by King Felipe II in 1595, the citadel originally served to protect Jaca from French Huguenot attacks. It last saw gunfire during the Civil War when the original canons were melted down for ammunition.

The Romanesque **cathedral** is modestly noteworthy and houses the **Museo Diocesno.** *(Tel./fax 974 35 63 78. Open daily 10am-1:30pm and 4-8pm. Free. Museum open daily May-Sept. 10am-2pm and 4-9pm; Oct.-Apr. Tu-Su 11am-1:30pm and 4-7pm. 300ptas.)* Started in 1063, it influenced most designs for churches along the Jacobean route.

Jaca's biggest **fiesta** (in honor of **Santa Orosia**) falls on June 23-29. During odd-numbered years in late July and early August, people from all over the world come with bells on their toes for the **Festival Folklórico de los Pirineos.** The rest of the year, look for excitement in the many **bars** along **Calle de Gil Berges,** off C. Mayor.

■ Near Jaca: Monasterio de San Juan de la Peña

Tel. 974 34 80 99. Open Mar. 16-July and Sept-Oct 15 Tu-Su 10am-1:30pm and 4-7pm. Aug. daily 10am-1:30pm and 4-8pm; Oct. 16-March 15 W-Su 11am-2:30pm; Free.

The spectacular Monasterio de San Juan de la Peña is difficult to reach—and meant to be. Determined hermits hid the original monastery in a canyon 22km from Jaca and maintained such extreme privacy that invading Moors never discovered it or the Holy Grail supposedly concealed here for three centuries. It's worth a visit, both for the 10th-century underground church carved directly into the rock and for the 12th-century cloister dwarfed by a massive boulder. The stunning carved capitals of the cloister's columns are among the best preserved around. Don't confuse the monastery with the boring 17th-century *monasterio nuevo* 1km uphill. **Viages Arán,** C. Mayor, 46 (tel. 974 35 54 80), schedules bus trips to San Juan July 15 through August, usually on Thursdays (1300ptas). For 5000ptas round trip, taxis (tel. 974 36 28 48) will make the journey, with a one-hour wait at the monastery.

■ Near Jaca: Castillo de Loarre

Same hours as San Juan de la Peña (see above). Free.

In the 11th century, King Sancho Ramírez built a marvelous castle to protect himself from Moorish attacks. Sharp cliffs at its rear and 400m of thick walls to the east make **El Castillo de Loarre** (5km from the town of Loarre) nearly impenetrable. The building's outer walls follow the turns and angles of the rock so closely that an attacker at night might have only seen the silhouette of the awesome stone monolith. A crypt opens to the right of the steep entrance staircase where the remains of Demetrius were stashed after the French saint died in Loarre. You can climb up to the battlements of both towers, but the only access designed for the larger of the two is a precarious footbridge. Be careful when climbing the wobbly steel rungs to the roof or descending into the dark and doorless *sótano* (basement). Incidentally, Loarre comes in first hands-down in the "Best View from a Toilet" competition.

Reaching the castle requires a little ingenuity. **La Oscence** (tel. 974 35 50 60) sends one **bus** (1hr., 1 per day M-Sa, departs at 7:15am, 665ptas) from Jaca to the town of Loarre, 5km from the castle; the return bus at 5pm stops only in Ayerbe, 7km away from Loarre. **Trains** go only to Ayerbe. From there, you can request a taxi or trek the two hours to the town of Loarre. You can **camp** in the lovely surrounding pine forest.

■ Valle de Hecho

The craggy Valle de Hecho and its picturesque hamlets are just 40km west of Jaca, the closest hiking area to the city. From early July to early August, villages in the valley host the **Simposio de Escultura y Pintura Moderna.** Artists come from far and wide, turning the surrounding hills into a huge open-air museum. Although near many skiing areas, the valley's peak season generally occurs during July and August; the rest of the year, it is decidedly tranquil. A **Josefa Escartin** bus (tel. 974 36 05 08) leaves Jaca Monday through Saturday at 6:30pm, stopping at Hecho (7:25pm) and Siresa (7:40pm), and continuing to Ansó (8:10pm). Every morning except Sunday the bus returns from Ansó (6am) via Siresa (6:30am) and Hecho (6:45am) on its way to Jaca.

■ Hecho (Echo)

Hecho (pop. 670) is the valley's geographical and administrative center, a title far too official to do justice to its peaceful atmosphere. Sculptures from the valley's modern art festival pleasantly clash with Hecho's traditional stone architecture. The **Compania de Guías Valle de Echo** (tel. 974 37 52 18; or ask at the bar next to Casa Blasquico), leads hiking trips (7900ptas for a 2-day trip to the Selva de Oza) and rents cross-country skis (2000ptas per day).

The **Ayuntamiento** provides information for tourists at tel. 974 37 53 29. A **bank** is on C. Traversia Muro, behind Pl. Fuente, where the **bus** stops. (Bank open M-F 8:30am-2pm.) A **post office** sits in a small square off C. Mayor (open M-F 8:30am-2:30pm, Sa 9:30am-1pm). **Supermercado Aldi,** on C. Mayor, stocks provisions (open M-F 8:30am-2:30pm and 4:30-8:30pm, Sa 9am-1:30pm). Ansó or nearby campgrounds provide better **accommodations** options. One good place in Hecho, though, is **Casa Blasquico,** Pl. Fuente, 1 (tel. 974 37 50 07), a white house with balconies facing the bus stop. The proprietor's cooking skills are formidable, as is her command of English and French. (Doubles 3500ptas, with bath 6000ptas; meals 1700ptas. Call ahead July-Aug.) **Camping Valle de Hecho** (tel./fax 974 37 53 61), at the entrance to Hecho on the Crta. Fuente la Reina, has new facilities in a lovely location. (500ptas per person, per car, per tent; 7% IVA not included.) *Literas* (1000ptas) are also available in the *albergue* on the same site. The knowledgeable staff can help organize excursions.

■ Siresa

Between Hecho and Siresa, a tranquil town just 2km up the road from Hecho, carved wood signs mark trails (none of which is particularly difficult) to Picoya, La Reclusa, Lenito, Fuente de la Cruz, and Ansó. While some trails are partly eroded, all offer spectacular views of the Pyrenees. From Siresa, the road weaves up the valley, passing by the river-rock formation known as **La Boca del Infierno** (The Mouth of Hell), where the river slips into a profound gorge.

Prepare yourself by acquiring the orange *Pirineo de Huesca: Mapa Excursionista de Los Pirineos: Valles de Ansó, Echo, y Aragües,* which is carried by area stores (550-700ptas). You can also ask at the campsite about further organized excursions. North of the site, the peaks along the French border beckon hikers—**Pic Rouge** (2177m), **Pic Lariste** (2168m), and **Pic Laraille** (2147m), each strenuous but feasible day-long climbs. Check the forecast before departure (tel. 976 23 43 36, in Spanish).

■ Valle de Ansó

A little farther from Jaca than Hecho and somewhat more rewarding than its larger neighbor, Ansó is one of the most appealing valleys in the Pyrenees. Like Hecho, this valley lives for July and August, when it receives the bulk of its visitors. The best treks take off from Zuriza, farther up the valley than the little town of Ansó.

■ Ansó

Tiny Ansó's (pop. 530) cobblestone streets and matching stone houses are peacefully removed from the rest of the world. Near inviting mountains and lakes, this welcoming little town is well worth a stop. The city relives its past during the **Fiesta del Traje**, the last Sunday in August, when residents don their traditional garb for a day. At the **Museo de Etnología**, inside the **Iglesia de San Pedro**, mannequins model customary dress next to spinning wheels and looms. (Open June to mid-Sept. daily M-F 10:30am-1:30pm and 3:30-8pm; mid-Sept. to June talk to the priest in the stone house in front of the church. 200ptas.)

The Josefa Escartín **bus** (tel. 974 36 05 08) that makes the rounds of these valleys from Jaca stops at C. Mayor; it leaves for Jaca again at 6am the next day (1½hr., M-Sa, 380ptas). For info, call the **Ayuntamiento** (tel. 974 37 00 21), on Pl. Mayor, or in July and August call the **tourist office** downstairs at tel. 974 37 02 25. A **bank, phones,** and a **supermarket** are on C. Mayor. In an **emergency**, call 974 37 00 04 for the **Guardia Civil** at the edge of town, and for **medical services** call 974 37 00 75. The **post office** is on Pl. Mayor. (Open M-F 9am-1pm, Sa 10am-noon.)

Those who spend the night are in for a treat. The friendly owners of **Posada Magoria,** C. Chapitel, 8 (tel. 974 37 00 49), have restored a traditional stone house with wide-planked wood floors and antique-filled rooms. They make their own yogurt, bake bread, and grow organic vegetables, then serve it all at family-style vegetarian meals. (2400ptas per person. Breakfast 700ptas, dinner 1800ptas. Call ahead for July and Aug.) Around the corner of the cobbled street (look for the sign) is the newer and more standard family-run **Posada Veral,** C. Cocorro, 6 (tel. 974 37 01 19; singles 1800ptas; doubles 3800ptas; *menú* 1500ptas for guests only; breakfast 375ptas).

■ Zuriza and Environs

Fifteen kilometers north of Ansó, **Camping Zuriza** (tel. 974 37 01 96 or 974 37 00 77) lies on a mountain stream 2km away from the Río Veral, suitable for fishing, rafting, or kayaking and set in a gorgeous valley. The site also provides a **supermarket** and **hostel.** (Campsite 450ptas per person and per car, tents 400ptas. *Hostal:* doubles 4000-4500ptas, with bath 5500-6000ptas; bunk in *literas* 900-1000ptas. Includes hot showers. Mountain bike and ski rental. Visa, MC.) From the campground, it's a day-hike (3½hr.) to the **Mesa de los Tres Reyes,** a series of peaks close to the borders of France, Navarra, and Aragón (ergo the three kings). From Zuriza, the **Fountain of Linza** lies north and east of the Collado de Linza, a break between two smaller peaks. There is one lean-to **refugio** 50m from Linza open to anyone (free), and a more substantial one, **Refugio Linza** (tel. 974 37 01 12), 5km from Zuriza on an unpaved road, with winter heating, hot showers (200ptas), and bunkbeds (1000ptas; reservations recommended). Hereabouts the terrain alternates between the shallow **Agujero de Solana** (Hole of Solana) and the steep summit of **Escoueste.** From Zuriza, you can also make the arduous trek to **Sima de San Martín,** on the French border. To enjoy the area without straining yourself, walk 2km south of Ansó to the fork in the road. Just above the tunnel toward Hecho, you can see the striking, weather-sculpted rock formation called **El Monje y la Monja** (The Monk and the Nun). Sweep all lurid thoughts from your mind and enjoy the view.

■ Parque Nacional de Ordesa

If there is a park that can reduce the world-weary, been-there-done-that traveler to stupefied monosyllables, Ordesa is Spain's version of it. Well-maintained trails cut across idyllic forests, jagged rock faces, snow-covered peaks, rushing rivers, and alpine meadows. Located just south of the French border, Ordesa contains the canyons of Ordesa, Añisclo, Escuaín, and Pineta. The entrance to Ordesa through the village of Torla is the most accessible; it has trails for hikers of all levels of experience, which accounts for the crowds in July and August.

PRACTICAL INFORMATION Although those without cars once had to ride a mail truck to get to Ordesa, regular bus service now exists. **La Oscense** (tel. 974 35 50 60) sends a bus from Jaca to Sabiñánigo (30min., M-Sa 10:15am and 6:15pm, Su 10:15am, 110ptas). Sabiñánigo is also easily accessible by train, as all trains on the Zaragoza-Huesca-Jaca line stop at its station. From there **Empresa Hudebus** (tel. 974 21 32 77) runs to Torla at 11am (55min., 1 per day, 355ptas), with an additional 6:15pm departure in July and August. A bus shuttles between Torla and Ordesa only during July and August (departs every 15min., round-trip 200ptas). Off season you'll have to either hike the 8km to the entrance or call a cab (tel. 974 48 62 43; 1500-2000ptas). To leave the area, catch the bus as it passes through Torla again at 3:30pm, on its way back to Sabiñánigo (arrives 4:30pm). Drivers should arrive to the park early in the day, as parking is limited.

The **visitor center** "El Parador" awaits beyond the Ordesa park entrance. They sell maps (400ptas) and give out lots of info about the park and various hikes. (Open daily July-Aug. 9am-1pm and 3:30-7pm; possibly open spring and fall.) Back in Torla, the indispensable *Editorial Alpina* guide is on sale at numerous stores (675ptas). Torla also has a **tourism hut,** on the highway at the entrance to town, that dispenses info on accommodations and such (sporadically open July-Aug.).

Supermercado Torla, on C. Francia, is near Refugio L'Atalaya. (Open daily 8:30am-2pm and 4-8:30pm, later in summer.) Across from Refugio L'Atalaya, **Compañia de Ordesa** (tel. 974 48 64 17) rents mountain bikes and organizes excursions. In an **emergency,** call the **Guardia Civil** (tel. 974 48 61 60) at the edge of town. The town's **post office** is on C. Francia at Pl. Ayuntamiento, behind a tiny door (open M-Sa 9-11am). The **postal code** is 22376.

ACCOMMODATIONS Within the park, many **refugios** (mountain huts, usually without facilities) allow overnight stays. The 120-bed **Refugio Góriz** (tel. 974 34 12 01), about a four-hour walk from the park's parking lot, has winter heating and meager hot showers (950ptas per person). The town of Torla has a greater range of accommodations, but it tends to fill up fast in July and August, so reserve ahead. Cobblestoned Calle Francia is the only road in Torla off the highway to the park—ascend it, and on your right after one block, under some wooden beams, you'll find the newly renovated **Refugio L'Atalaya**, C. Francia, 45 (tel. 974 48 60 22). Its 31 bunks go for 1000ptas per person (kitchen and dining area available for use; owner's own *menú* 1400ptas; breakfast 500ptas). The newer **Refugio Briet** (tel. 974 48 62 21), across the street, has similar facilities (1000ptas per person; *menú* 1400ptas), but its bunks are kindly dispersed through a few rooms. For less atmosphere and more luxury, there's a row of (accordingly) more expensive **hotels** along the highway, one of which is **Edelweiss Hotel**, Av. Ordesa, 1 (tel. 974 48 61 73; fax 974 48 63 72). (June 30-Sept. singles with shower 3300ptas, with full bath 4000ptas; doubles 5700ptas, with full bath 6700ptas.; 7% IVA not included. Prices drop considerably during the off season.)

Three **campgrounds** lie just outside Torla. Both **Camping Río Ara** (tel. 974 48 62 48) and **Camping San Anton** (tel. 974 48 60 63) are small and pretty (445ptas per person, per tent, and per car; open Apr.-Oct.). Midway between the two is the more upscale **Camping Ordesa** (tel. 974 48 61 46). (600ptas per person, 630ptas per tent and per car. IVA not included. 30% off in low season. Open Apr.-Oct.)

CIRCO DE SOASO AND OTHER HIKES If you have only a day to spend in Ordesa, the **Soaso Circle** is the most practical hike, especially for inexperienced mountaineers. Frequent signposts along the wide trail clearly mark the six-hour journey. The trail traverses forests, waterfalls, cliffs, and plateaus. Be forewarned that the trail gets slippery and rather dangerous when wet. Check weather forecasts before starting out, and remember that heavy snow can make the trail impassable in winter. Less intrepid types who want to cut the hike to about two hours may return to the parking lot rather than continue past the tiered Gradas de Soaso waterfall to **Refugio Góriz.** Whichever route you choose, try to arrive at the park early in the day during July and August because by noon the entire Soaso Circle can resemble Picadilly Circus.

If you prefer a private mountain hike to a multilingual parade, try the **Circo Cotatuero** or the **Circo Carriata.** Both are two- to three-hour hikes that can be combined into a single five-hour hike. More experienced hikers might attempt the **Torla-Gavarnie** trail, a six-hour haul (one-way) all the way to Gavarnie, France. The **Ordesa-Gavarnie** trail is longer; plan to spend at least 10 hours. An even more rugged climb begins at the Refugio Góriz and scales Monte Perdido (3355m; mountaineering equipment recommended). Count on three hours to get from the refugio to the peak. For any of these hikes, the *Editorial Alpina* topographical map is an absolute must. If your car can handle a very bumpy 4km road, take it through the delightful **Valle de Bujaruelo,** a left at the park entrance.

■ Near Parque Nacional de Ordesa: Aínsa (L'Ainsa)

A pleasant stopover about an hour away from Ordesa, Aínsa hides within its bland and modern new town a perfectly preserved and enchanting medieval quarter, where flowers spill over stone walls into the streets. A thousand years ago Aínsa was the capital of the Kingdom of Sobrarbe (incorporated into Aragón in the 11th century), and the ruins of its 11th-century **castle** on **Plaza Mayor** remind visitors of the fact. In 1181, priests consecrated the **Iglesia de Santa María,** across the plaza from the castle, where you can climb the tower for 100ptas (not for tall claustrophobes).

Buses run by **Compañía Hudebus** (tel. 974 21 32 77) travel from Sabiñánigo to Aínsa, stopping in Torla along the way (2hr., departs Sabiñánigo daily at 11am, 720ptas). Buses return to Torla and Sabiñanigo at 2:30pm. **Compañía Cortés** (tel. 974 31 15 52) sends a bus from Aínsa to Barbastro (departs at 7am daily), where you can connect to Benasque. The **tourist office,** Av. Pirenáica, 1 (tel. 974 50 07 67), at the highway crossroads, advises on transport, lodgings, and excursions. (Open July-Aug. daily 10am-2pm and 4:30-8:30pm; Sept.-June Tu-Sa 10am-2pm and 4:30-8:30pm, Su 10am-2pm.) Countless outdoor activities can be arranged with companies in town, although Aínsa is not as well situated as Torla or Benasque for hiking. The **postal code** is 2230.

Behind the church in the old town is **Casa Rural El Hospital,** C. Sta. Cruz, 3 (tel. 974 50 07 50), a darling place to stay the night. (Doubles with bath, TV, and A/C 4000-4500ptas). Other budget lodgings congregate just uphill from the bus station, and **Camping Aínsa,** Ctra. Aínsa-Campo, km 1.8 (tel. 974 50 02 60), is right outside of town (550ptas per person and per car, 525ptas per tent). **Casa Albás,** at the *castillo* end of Pl. Mayor, offers a succulent Aragonese *menú* (1500ptas; open 1:30-4pm and 8:30-11pm). The supermarket **Alimentación M. Cheliz,** on Av. Ordesa at the new town's main intersection, stocks numerous delights.

Far Trek

On your way to Berlin? A *Gran Recorrido* (Great Hike) trail will get you there—eventually. One of the most beautiful and rugged stretches of the pan-European *Gran Recorrido* network trudges east to west just below the French-Aragonese border. Strung together by old mountain roads, animal tracks, and forest paths, the Aragonese portion of **GR-11** passes by clear mountain lakes and under, over, and through snow-covered peaks (the highest being Mt. Aneto, at 3404m). Though some parts of GR-11 are pretty gentle, the full trek across Navarra requires hiking experience, especially early in the season when snow cover is extensive. The border-to-border route takes eight to ten days.

For detailed info on this and other GR trails (including some with cultural and historical motifs), consult tourist offices in the area or the Federación Aragonesa de Montañismo at C. Albareda, 7, Zaragoza 50004 (tel. 976 22 79 71), or pick up a detailed and trail-specific *Topoguía* guide. The extremely useful *Editorial Alpina,* widely available in the area, also has a good map of the route.

■ Valle de Benasque

The Valle de Benasque is a haven for no-nonsense hikers, climbers, and skiers. Countless trails wind through the surrounding peaks, and the area teems with *refugios,* allowing for longer expeditions. Soft-core strollers are often scared away by the valley's reputation for serious mountaineering—the area has the Pyrenees' highest peak—but everyone can enjoy the beautiful Río Esera gorge. With its many excursion companies and nearby trailheads, the town of **Benasque** (pop. 1000) offers an excellent albeit unattractive base for outdoor adventurers. As always, pick up a copy of *Editorial Alpina*'s excellent topographical map of the valley or *Editorial Pirineo* (both about 600ptas; available in any store in Benasque) before starting a hike.

PRACTICAL INFORMATION, ACCOMMODATIONS, AND FOOD La Alta Aragonesa (tel. 974 21 07 00) runs **buses** between Huesca and Benasque (3hr., 1-2 per day, 1275ptas). To find the **tourist office** (tel./fax 974 55 12 89) and volumes of hiking info, face the Hotel Aragüells at the main highway intersection and continue one block down the alley that angles to the right. (Open July-Aug. and Semana Santa daily 9:30am-1:30pm and 4:30-8pm; Sept.-June Tu-F 5-8pm, Sa 5-9pm, Su 9:30am-1:30pm, though hours may vary.) Take your pick from among oodles of **outdoor adventure companies.** Signs point to the **Guardia Civil** (tel. 974 55 10 08) from the main highway intersection. The **post office** (tel. 974 55 20 71) is in the Ayuntamiento building (open M-F 9am-noon, Sa 10am-noon, only for stamps). The **postal code** is 22440.

Fonda Barrabés, C. Mayor, 5 (tel. 974 55 16 54), a left from the bus stop and straight ahead 200m, is a cheap option. (Bunks 850-1000ptas; singles 1500ptas; doubles 3000ptas; restaurant downstairs). **Camping Aneto** (tel. 974 55 11 41), 3km out of town up the hill past the Cerler turnoff, has both summer and winter facilities (440ptas per person, tent, or car). **Supermarkets** are along Av. Tilos. **Restaurante-Crêperie Les Arkades** (tel. 974 55 12 02), hiding down a street between the post office and church, flips all kinds of crepes (ham and cheese 395ptas, honey and nuts 400ptas) and dishes out a four-course *menú* with roast quail (1400ptas; open daily 1-4pm and 8pm-midnight; creperie open Dec.-Apr. daily 5:30pm-midnight).

HIKES If you start early from Benasque, you can hike just over 8km down the valley road, cross the river on the camping area bridge, and climb up, up, and away, following the falls of the Río Cregueña. Four sweaty hours later you'll reach **Lago de Cregueña** (2657m), the largest and highest lake in the **Maladeta** massif.

To scale **Mount Aneto** (3404m), the highest of the Pyrenees, acquire some technical climbing skills and gear and then head out at about 5am with the experts from the **Refugio de la Renclusa** (tel. 974 55 21 06; open June 22-Sept. 24). To reach the *refugio,* take the main road north for about 15km until the paved road ends. From where it ends, it's a 45-minute hike. Many companies in Benasque also organize trips. If lugging heavy equipment up a mountain isn't your idea of fun, head downhill to the road and follow signs to **Forau de Aigualluts,** a lovely pond at the base of a waterfall (30min.). Another strenuous hike from the *refugio* leads to the peak of **Sacroux** (2675m). Although snow may prevent you from reaching the top and peering into France, the rush of the **Torrents de Gorgutes** and the sight of **Lago Gorgutes** make the four-hour climb worthwhile.

ARAGÓN

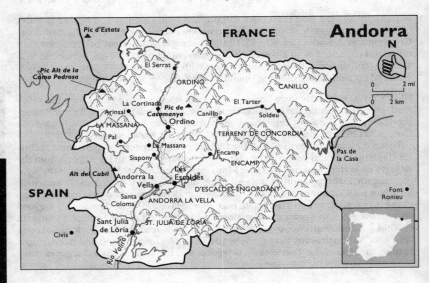

Andorra

This tiny Pyrenean country is an anomaly. The peace and serenity of stunning land-scapes compete for attention with the frantic atmosphere of duty-free shopping amid neon-lit towns. Pragmatists might say Andorra (pop. 65,000; 468sq. km) is the best of both worlds, but a purist might beg to differ. Known officially as Principat d'Andorra (Principality of Andorra), it is ruled by two co-princes—the French president and the Bishop of Urgell—and a popularly elected *Consell General* that represents the seven parishes and retains the bulk of the power.

According to legend, Charlemagne founded Andorra in 784 as a reward to the val-ley's inhabitants for having led his army during battle against the Moors. For the next 12 centuries, Andorra played the rope in a game of tug-o'-war between the Spanish Counts of Urgell, the Church of Urgell, and the French King. Not until 1990 did Andorra create a commission to draft a democratic constitution, adopted on March 14, 1993. Andorra today is far less progressive than other industrialized western Euro-pean nations. In the 1993 election, only the 10,000 native Andorrans (out of 65,000 total) were granted the vote, and women have had suffrage only since 1970.

Sandwiched between France and Spain, Andorra struggles to assert its identity. Its citizenry is comfortably trilingual, but Catalan, the official language, is spoken with pride. Other manifestations of cultural pride appear every summer when each of the seven parishes holds its own three-day jubilee. These spectacles start the third week-end of July and continue through mid-September. The national *festa* on December 8 honors Andorra's patron saint *Nostra Senyora de Meritxell* (Our Lady of Meritxell).

The country has no currency of its own. All establishments are required to accept both *pesetas* and *francs,* although *pesetas* are far more prevalent. The absence of a sales tax draws consumers from all over Europe. With Andorran towns spaced mere minutes apart on local bus routes, a single day can include wading through eight aisles of duty-free cheese, hiking through a pine-scented Pyrenean valley, and then languishing for several hours in a luxury spa.

■ Getting There

Planes and trains defer to automobiles and tour buses in Andorra, as the country has no airport and no train station. French and Spanish border police supposedly, if not always in practice, require a valid passport or an EU identity card to enter the country. All traffic from France must enter Andorra through the town of **Pas de la Casa;** the gateway town on the Spanish side is **La Seu d'Urgell. Andor-Inter/Samar** buses (in Madrid tel. 91 468 41 90; in Toulouse tel. 61 58 14 53; in Andorra tel. 82 62 89) run to Madrid (9hr.; Tu, Th, and Su; 4700ptas). **Alsina Graells** (tel. 82 65 67) runs to Barcelona (4hr., 6 per day, 2600ptas). Both arrive at and depart from **Estació d'Auto-busos** on C. Bonaventura Riberaygua. To get to the station from Pl. Princep Benlloch, follow Av. Meritxell past the tourist office to the other side of the river. Make an immediate right after crossing, an immediate left, then take the fourth right and go straight for four to five blocks (20min.). To go anywhere else in Spain, you must first go to La Seu d'Urgell on **La Hispano-Andorra** (tel. 82 13 72; 30min., 5-7 buses per day, 330ptas), which leave from in front of Pyrénées, Av. Meritxell, 11. From La Seu, **Alsina Graells buses** (tel. 82 65 67 in Andorra) continue to the rest of Spain via Puigcerdà (1hr., 2 per day, 560ptas) and Lérida (2½hr., 2 per day, 1600ptas).

■ Getting Around

Driving in Andorra la Vella is a nightmare. The main road turns into a parking lot as red-clad traffic officers gesticulate and blow whistles in a desperate attempt to keep traffic moving. Drivers will find a map totally useless; it's best to follow signs. Find one of the free parking lots in the city and desert the car. (All are free two consecutive days, but it is unclear whether anyone is really counting.) The first you'll see on the road from Spain is located at the intersection of C. Moll and C. Prat de la Creu, across from the Holiday Inn.

Efficient **intercity buses** connect villages along the three major highways that converge in Andorra la Vella. The entire country is navigable in an hour or two via public transportation; most towns are only 10 minutes away. Bus rides can cost 90 to 590ptas. All buses stop at each stop in the city, so don't worry about finding the right one, just pay attention to the direction sign in the front window. The tourist office has schedules, and bus stops are easy to find on the map and street.

■ Andorra la Vella

Andorra la Vella (Andorra the Old; pop. 20,000), the capital, is little more than a narrow, cluttered road flanked by shop after duty-free shop and sprinkled with American fast food chains. Anything but *vella,* the modern city disguises—actually, suffocates—its old quarter well, upstaging it with dozens of electronic and sporting goods stores. After doing a little shopping, you're best off escaping to the countryside.

ORIENTATION AND PRACTICAL INFORMATION

Avinguda Meritxell, the main artery, runs through the city beginning at Pl. Princep Benlloch in the heart of the tiny **barri antic** (old quarter) and continuing through the modern city's heart, across the **Riu Valira,** and becoming the main highway to parishes northeast of the capital. West of Pl. Princep Benlloch, to the right when facing the Eglésia de Sant'Esteve, Av. Meritxell becomes **Avinguida Princep Belloch.**

Taxis: (tel. 86 30 00). Flag one of these yellow-and-white puppies down.
Car Rental: Europcar, Av. Tarragona, 42 (tel. 82 00 91; fax 82 06 42), at the bus station. Must be over 21. Prices start at 4500ptas per day, 35ptas per km, or 18,500ptas for 3-day weekend (limit of 1000km). Open M-Sa 9am-7pm.
Tourist Office: (tel. 82 02 14; fax 82 58 23), on Av. Doctor Villanova. Multilingual staff has bucketloads of brochures—the *Sports Activities* and the *Hotels i Restaurants* guide are particularly useful. Open July-Sept. M-Sa 9am-1pm and 3-7pm; Oct.-

June M-Sa 10am-1pm and 3-7pm, Su 10am-1pm. To get here from the bus stop on Av. Princep Benlloch, continue east (away from Spain) just past the *plaça* on your left, then take C. Dr. Villanova, which curves down to the right. The office is on the left right before the hill. A **second office** (tel. 82 71 17) is on Pl. Rotunda where Av. Meritxell crosses the river. Open daily 9:30am-1pm and 4-8pm.

Currency Exchange: Banc Internacional, Av. Meritxell, 32 (tel. 88 44 89). 500ptas commission on all transactions. Open M-F 9am-1pm and 3-5pm, Sa 9am-1pm. They will exchange traveler's checks. **Pyrénées,** Av. Meritxell, 11, has long hours and no commission but worse rates. Open M-F 9:30am-8pm, Sa 9:30am-9pm, Su 9am-7pm.

American Express: Viatges Relax, C. Mossèn Tremosa, 2 (tel. 82 20 44; fax 82 70 55). From Pl. Princep Benlloch, take the first left off Av. Meritxell.

Weather and Ski Conditions: In Spanish (tel. 84 88 52) or French (tel. 84 88 53).

Emergency: call 116 or 110. **Police:** C. Prat de la Creu, 16 (tel. 82 12 22).

Late-Night Pharmacy: Each pharmacy has the "duty roster" posted on its door, listing which is open on a given night. Alternatively, call the police or check *7 Dies,* the free weekly paper available at the tourist office.

Hospital: Clinica Nostra Senyora de Meritxell, Av. Fiter I Rossell (tel. 87 10 00).

Internet Access: Bavaria, Pl. Rotunda (tel. 81 26 12), across from the tourist office. 600ptas per 30min., 1100ptas per hr. Open daily 8:30am-1am.

Post Offices: Both at the east end of town, on the other side of the river from Pl. Princep Benlloch. **Spanish Post Office,** Carrer Joan Maragall, 10 (tel. 82 20 57). Lista de Correos upstairs. Open M-F 8:30am-2:30pm, Sa 9:30am-1pm. **French Post Office,** *La Poste,* C. Pere d'Urg, 1 (tel. 82 04 08). Poste Restante. Open June-Sept. M-F 8:30am-2:30pm; Oct.-May M-F 9am-7pm, Sa 9am-noon.

Telephones: Purchase an STA *teletarjeta* (telecard) at the tourist office, any post office, or kiosk (500ptas min.). Collect calls are not available, and AT&T does not maintain an access network with Andorra. For **directory assistance** within Andorra, dial 111. Andorra's **telephone code** is 376.

> As of 1995, all of Andorra's phone numbers, formerly 5 digits, added an 8 in front to make 6 digits. You may still occasionally see 5-digit numbers listed. Just dial 8 before any of these, or you will be subjected to a confusing Catalan recording.

ACCOMMODATIONS, CAMPING, AND FOOD

It's as easy to find a place to drop as it is to find a place to shop—cheap pensions proliferate. Andorra's restaurants serve decent meals, but grocery shopping here can be a thrill. Check out one of the amazing three-story supermarkets in nearby Santa Coloma (you can't miss them) or the **Grans Magatzems Pyrénées,** Av. Meritxell, 11, the country's biggest department store, with an entire aisle dedicated to chocolate bars alone (open M-F 9:30am-8pm, Sa 9:30am-9pm, Su 9am-7pm).

Pensió La Rosa, Antic Carrer Major, 18 (tel. 82 18 10), just south of Av. Princep Benlloch. Friendly owners. Immaculate rooms in which blossoms of various species and colors compete for dominance over wallpaper and bed spreads. Singles 1700ptas; doubles 3000ptas. Breakfast 350ptas.

Hotel Costa, Av. Meritxell, 44 (tel. 82 14 39), above Restaurant Mati. Big rooms, some with views of the city (for what it's worth), are somehow both dingy and bright. Large communal lounges. Singles 1500ptas; doubles 3000ptas.

Camping: Camping Valira (tel. 82 23 84), located behind the **Estadi Comunal d'Andorra la Vella.** Shade, video games, hot showers, and an indoor pool. 525ptas per person, per tent and per car. Call ahead. 2½km down the road, **Camping Santa Coloma** (tel. 82 88 99) charges 500ptas per person, per tent, and per car, but has no video games.

Minim's Restaurant, Pl. Consòrcia, 5 (tel. 86 75 11), at the end of C. Mayor. Delivers French delights on a pretty *plaça. Menú* 1350ptas. Escargot 750ptas. *Platos combinados* 850ptas. Open Tu-Sa 11am-midnight, Su afternoons.

Restaurant Marti, Av. Meritxell, 44 (tel. 82 09 46). Good, cheap victuals. *Menú* (1100ptas) topped off with *crema catalana.* Open daily noon-4pm and 8-10pm.

SIGHTS AND ENTERTAINMENT

Although there is more to Andorra la Vella than shopping, there isn't *much* more. Sixteenth-century **Casa de la Vall** (House of the Valleys; tel. 82 91 29), home to Andorra's pocket-sized parliament, sits at the end of the stone alley winding west from Pl. Princep Benlloch and past the church. *(Open M-F 9am-1pm and 3-7pm. Guided visits only. Call or stop by to book a spot.)* Each of Andorra's seven parishes holds a key to the "seven-keyed" cupboard containing General Council documents.

The tourist office offers information and sells tickets for Andorra la Vella's annual **Festival Internacional de Música i Dansa,** showcasing an international array of ballet, jazz, and classical concerts (mid-Nov. to May). The city's annual festival colors the capital on the first Saturday, Sunday, and Monday in August. The tourist office's monthly pamphlet *Un mes a Andorra* lists cultural activities. *7 dies a Andorra* is a free weekly with useful phone numbers and entertainment info.

▓ Elsewhere in Andorra

"Elsewhere" in Andorra is where one ought to go. Escape the polluted air that drips over Andorra la Vella and follow other tourists' leads as they ski, bike, fish, climb, ride horses, or just bask in the serenity of the rural *parròquias* (parishes). For more information on hiking, see p. 294; for more information on skiing, see p. 294.

■ La Massana and Sispony

Mountain ventures shove off from the *parròquia* of **La Massana** (pop. 5000; elev. 1252m), directly north of Andorra La Vella and easily accessible by bus from the city (10min., departs every 30min., 110ptas). The town of La Massana (pop. 3000), the capital of the parish, is little more than an overdeveloped suburb of Andorra La Vella. The village *festa* is held August 15-17. The helpful **tourist office** in La Massana (tel. 83 56 93) is in a steep-roofed cabin by the bridge, just ahead of the bus stop. Get a copy of "Walking along La Massana" here for easy walking trips. (Open July-Aug. and Dec.-Apr. M-Sa 9am-1pm and 3-7pm, Su 9am-1pm and 3-6pm; May-June and Sept.-Nov. M-Sa 9am-1pm and 3-7pm, Su 9am-1pm.) The **Hotel Rossell** (tel. 83 50 92; fax 83 81 80), on C. Josep Rossell, has spacious rooms with yellow spreads and baths (singles 3000ptas; doubles 5000ptas). **Camping Santa Catarina** is on the uphill outskirts of La Massana, on the highway to Ordino (tel. 83 50 65). The grounds are low on facilities but cost only 375ptas per person and 300ptas per car and per tent (open June 25-Aug. 15). **Establiments Garralla** (tel. 83 50 49) sells groceries across the street from the bus stop (open M-Sa 9am-1pm and 4-8pm, Su 9am-1pm).

Just up the hill is the town of **Sispony,** home to the friendly **Alberg Borda Jovell** (tel. 83 65 20; fax 83 57 76), on Av. Jovell. To get here from La Massana's bus stop, go back toward Andorra la Vella (75m) and turn right at the main intersection. Follow the signs south for 1.3km until the *alberg,* a 700-year-old stone house, appears on the left (a bus goes up 4 times a day from La Massana). The renovated, all-wood interior has large bunk-bed-filled rooms with tiny windows and bathrooms with stand-up toilets. (1600ptas per person including breakfast. Sheets 600ptas. Call ahead in July and Aug. Midnight curfew. Visa, MC, AmEx.) If you're in the area July 10, stop by the town of **Anyós,** where as part of the **Festa Major,** the priest blesses all the cars in the churchyard. (4 buses per day from La Massana, 75ptas.)

■ Ordino

Ordino (pop. 3000), 5km northeast of La Massana, has yet to be converted into a strip mall and is conveniently located for hiking and skiing adventures. The least populated of Andorra's seven parishes, Ordino is distinguished by the presence of a **seignorial mansion** *(pairals),* the home of Andorran aristocrats, in this case the D'Areny i Plandolit family. They accrued a small fortune in the region's iron industry and their 17th-century home is now a **museum** (tel 83 69 08; open M-Sa 9:30am-1pm and 3-6:30pm,

Su 10am-2pm for guided visits; 300ptas). The **bus** from Andorra la Vella to La Massana continues on to Ordino (130ptas). Ordino's **tourist office,** C. Nou Desvio (tel. 83 69 63), supplies comprehensive brochures on hiking and skiing in the area (open M-Sa 9am-1pm and 3-7pm, Su 9am-noon). The stone-faced **Hotel Quim** (tel. 83 50 13), on the *plaça,* contains homey, comfortable rooms (doubles 4000ptas). **Restaurants** are easy to come by in this tourist town. Ordino's **Rose Festival** takes place on the first Sunday in July.

■ Canillo

The diminutive town of Canillo, in the center of the country, suffers from the same architectural short-sightedness as the rest of Andorra but is surrounded by particularly fine scenery and perhaps the principality's best skiing. The colossal **Palau de Gel D'Andorra** (Andorran ice palace; tel. 85 15 65) is an eclectic recreational facility almost as monumental as the mountains themselves. The palace's marvels, including a swimming pool, ice-skating rink ("ice disco" come night), and squash courts are accessible by individual tickets. In winter, you can swim outdoors in a heated pool while snow melts around its edges. (Palace open daily 10am-midnight. Each facility has its own hours. 650ptas for one of each or 1300ptas for all facilities in one day. 350ptas equipment rental.) At the edge of town on the road to Andorra La Vella, **Hotel Comerç** (tel. 85 10 20) has unmemorable rooms at memorable prices (singles 1450ptas; doubles 2900ptas). **Encamp** houses the **Museu Nacional de l'Automòbil** (tel. 83 22 66), with 80 antique cars, motorbikes, and bicycles all revved up and nowhere to go. (Open Tu-Sa 9:30am-1:30pm and 3-6pm, Su 10am-2pm. 300ptas, seniors and students 150ptas.) Slink toward **Escaldes-Engordany,** just outside Andorra la Vella, for the waterborn pleasures of the **Caldea Spa,** Parc de la Mola, 10 (tel. 80 09 99), if not to bathe, then to see what all the hype's about. Housed in a glass steeple, the "Centre Termolúdic" offers steam baths, hydro and human massages, tanning beds, and decadent dips in faux Roman baths. (Admission 2500ptas per 3hr., not including fees for each service. Open daily 10am-9pm.)

■ Hiking Trails

For almost any type of excursion the excellent tourist office brochure *Sports Activities* is essential, with suggested itineraries, potential routes, and bike rental locations. Andorra's countryside lends itself to **mountain biking,** with a panoply of clearly marked trails. One loop trail begins and ends in Andorra la Vella, passing through La Comella for an aerial view of lazy shoppers (11km). **Club Hipic L'Aldosa** (tel. 83 73 29), in La Massana, has **horses** and **ponies** available for excursions.

    Hiking aficionados will find a plethora of trails. The *Grandes-Randonnées* trails #7 and 11 traverse nearly all of the country. La Massana is home to Andorra's tallest peak, **Pic Alt de la Coma Pedrosa** (2946m). Ordino is another base for trails of varying difficulty levels: an easy four-hour hike tours the lakes of **Tristaina;** a very difficult eight-hour climb brings summit-oriented hikers to **Pic de Casamanya** (2740m), **Coll d' Arenas** (2539m), **Pic de l'Estanyó** (2915m), **Pic de la Cabaneta** (2863m), and **Pic de la Serrera** (2913m), on a route that can also be split up. Cabins and mountain refuges dot each trail. *Sports Activities* sketches out 52 itineraries ranging from 15-minute strolls to longer affairs and lists cabin and refuge locations within the principality. To do it all at once, try the **La Rabassa Sports and Nature Center** in the southwest corner of Andorra, in the parish of Sant Juliàde Lòria (tel. 84 34 52). In addition to *refugio*-style accommodations, it offers mountain biking, guided hikes, horseback riding, archery, and all sorts of field sports.

■ Skiing

And then it snows. Famed for its slopes, Andorra has **skiing** opportunities galore. The six outstanding resorts within its boundaries all rent equipment and attract the masses. **Pal** (tel. 83 62 36), 10km from La Massana, is a biggie. Four daily buses leave

Take a Hike

You're broke, out of shape, and there's a thickening layer of dirt, city exhaust, and last night's sangría on your forearms, enough so that you can now successfully etch your name with a fingernail in the grime. It's time to strap on your hiking boots and take a hike. The melted snow opens up a whole new country—one boasting glacial legacies, navigable peaks, rolling forests, wild meadows, and scenic vistas. Like most everything else in Andorra, few of the routes are far away, and most all can be tackled by even the least seasoned outdoors enthusiast. An extensive system of hiking trails traverses the tiny country, ranging from short and sweet to long and rewarding. Moreover, the sights en route vary greatly as well, from heavenly lakes to lookouts onto Andorra la Vella to humble mountain shacks. Mountain bike enthusiasts can revel in their very own trails that, although less numerous than the corps of hiking routes, nevertheless provide a fresh, natural perspective of Andorra. For more info, contact one of the country's tourist offices and obtain a comprehensive brochure.

for there from La Massana; the last bus returns at 5pm (250ptas each way). Nearby **Arinsal** (tel. 83 58 22) can be reached by 7 daily buses from La Massana; the last one returns at 7:45pm (150ptas). On the French border, **Pas de la Casa Grau Roig** boasts 600 hectares of skiable land, with 48 different trails for all levels of ability. The resort (tel. 85 69 92) provides 27 mechanical lifts, downhill instruction, two medical centers, and **night skiing. Soldeu-El Tarter** (tel. 85 11 51) clocks in with 840 hectares of skiable area, between Andorra la Vella and Pas de la Casa. **Free buses** transport skiers from their hotels in Canillo. Other smaller resorts are **La Rabassa** (tel. 84 34 52), with 15km of cross country runs, and **Ordino-Arcalis** (tel. 83 63 20). Andorra's tourist office publishes a winter edition of *Andorra: The Pyrenean Country,* a guide to all its ski resorts. **SKI Andorra** (tel. 86 43 89) or the tourist offices can answer questions.

ANDORRA

Barcelona

Like a prize fighter swaggering into the ring, Barcelona has stepped into the international spotlight and won the world's attention—and it knows it. After the suffocating years of Franco's regime, Barcelona, it seems, took only a moment to reclaim its role as the world's premier showcase of avant-garde architecture. Its triumphant return as host of the 1992 Summer Olympics showed the world once and for all that Barcelona was a uniquely forward-looking city. While southern Europe's other grand and tourist-reliant cities stagnate behind sandblasted facades, packaging antiquated glory, and Spain's coastal cities play the obsequious role for northern European vacationers looking to dabble in the simpler life, Barcelona has chosen instead to market its cocksure contemporaneity. Europe's fastest-growing tourist city enters the 21st century with a stylish, modern culture more northern European than Iberian.

Barcelonenses have long been the privileged class of Spain. During the Middle Ages, the city was the commercial fulcrum of a far-flung Mediterranean empire. The discovery of America and Sevilla's monopoly on that trade brought decline as commercial routes shifted from the Mediterranean. The Industrial Revolution's textile mills were the impetus behind Barcelona's *fin de siècle* return to greatness. During the *febre d'or* (gold fever, 1875-1885), the city's financial moguls geographically separated the aristocratic class from the proletariat. As the twentieth century approached, Josep Batllò, Antoni Amatller, and their compatriots commissioned architects like Montaner, Cadafalch, and the legendary Antoni Gaudí to build private residences in L'Eixample, a spacious, gridded "upper" Barcelona, higher in elevation and status than the tangled, plebeian Barri Gòtic (Gothic Quarter).

The result was Modernisme, an artistic movement that celebrated Catalunya's past and future, incorporating tradition and innovation in a brand new style. Soon brilliantly daring and heterogeneous buildings and parks studded the city scape and engaged in a grandiose battle for attention. Amid the graceful Gothic churches, wrought-iron balconies, and colonial-age grandeur of traditional European avenues, you will find not only Gaudí's flights of fancy, but also the city's latest architectural triumphs—the white-space-angles-and-glass Museum of Contemporary Art and the millennium-ready Maremagnum mall, jutting at a precarious angle into the water. While Paris, New York, and London have been described as noir cities, better captured in black and white, Barcelona must be seen in vibrant color.

🌐 HIGHLIGHTS OF BARCELONA

- The **Ruta del Modernisme** (see p. 316), but especially Gaudí's Parc Güell, Casa Milà, and Sagrada Familia Cathedral.
- Late-night **people-watching** at a sidewalk cafe on **Las Ramblas,** Barcelona's most famous street (see p. 316).
- Two of Barcelona's best museums—the **Museu Picasso** (see p. 323), celebrating the artist's early years, and the striking new **MACBA** (see p. 323).
- A walk among the eerie rock formations at the mountaintop monastery of **Montserrat** (see p. 331).

■ Arrivals and Departures

BY PLANE

All domestic and international flights land at **El Prat de Llobregat** airport (tel. 93 298 38 38), 12km southwest of Barcelona. The most convenient way to Plaça Catalunya (the center of town) or Estació-Sants is by **Aerobus** (40min., departs every 15min., 475ptas; from the airport to Pl. Catalunya M-F 6am-10:55pm and Sa-Su 6:30am-10:55pm; to the airport from Pl. Catalunya M-F 5:30am-10:20pm, Sa-Su 6am-10:20pm).

RENFE trains provide slightly cheaper transportation from the airport (20min., departs every 30min. 6:13am-10:13pm, M-Sa 305ptas, Su 350ptas). The most useful stops are **Estació Barcelona-Sants** and **Plaça de Catalunya.** Buy tickets at the red automatic machines. The walkway to the trains is accessible from inside the national terminal. Trains run to the airport from Pl. Catalunya (M-Sa 6:11am-10:13pm, Su 6:41am-10:13pm) and from Estació-Sants (M-Sa 5:46-10:13pm, Su 6:16-10:13pm). In Sants, buy tickets to the airport at the "Aeroport" window (open 5am-11pm); otherwise, get them from the ticket machines or the Recorridos Cercanías window.

The regular city **bus** offers the only inexpensive late-night service. Take bus EN from the airport to Pl. Espanya (departs every hr. daily 6:20am-2:40am), or to the airport from Pl. Espanya (departs every hr. daily 7am-3:15am). The stop at Pl. Espanya is on the corner of Gran Vía de les Corts Catalanes and Av. Reina María Cristina. A **taxi** ride between Barcelona and the airport costs 2000-3500ptas.

Three **national airlines** serve all domestic and major international destinations. **Iberia/Aviaco,** C. Diputació, 258 (tel. 93 401 33 81; reservations and info tel. 902 400 500), or Pl. Espanya (tel. 93 325 73 58), is the largest and has the most extensive coverage. Students can usually get a discount, except when fares are already reduced. **Air Europa** (24hr. reservation and info tel. 902 24 00 42) and **Spanair** (tel. 902 13 14 15; airport tel. 93 298 33 62), are both smaller and less established, but their standard fares are often cheaper.

All major **international airlines** also serve Barcelona. **British Airways,** Pg. Gràcia, 85, 3rd fl. (tel. 93 215 69 00), **Delta Airlines,** Pg. Gràcia, 15, 5th fl. (tel. 93 412 43 33), **TWA,** Consell de Cent, 360, 5th fl. (tel. 93 215 81 88), and most others have Barcelona offices. Iberia, TWA, and Delta all offer a direct New York to Barcelona flight.

BY TRAIN

Call **RENFE** for general train info or to purchase tickets up to 24 hours before departure (tel. 93 490 02 02, open daily 7:30am-10:30pm; international tel. 93 490 11 22). RENFE has service to: Valencia (4hr., 15 per day, 3500-4200ptas); Madrid (7hr., 6 per day, 5900-7000ptas); Sevilla (12hr., 4 per day, 6700-7700ptas); Milan (13hr., 1 per day); Montpellier (5hr., 2 per day, 5305ptas), with connections to Geneva and Paris; and other destinations. Student discounts are only sporadically available.

Trenes Euromed offers high-speed service along the Mediterranean coast. Trains leave from Sants for Valencia (3hr., 5 per day, 4600ptas) and Alicante (4¾hr., 2 per day, 6300ptas), with stops also at Tarragona and Castellón.

For other destinations, see the transportation section of the town you wish to reach for details.

Estació Barcelona-Sants (tel. 93 490 24 00), Pl. Països Catalans. M: Sants-Estació. For late arrivals, the N2 Nitbus shuttles to Pl. Catalunya (departs every 30min., 10pm-4am, 150ptas). To get to the N2, exit Sants to Pl. Joan Peiró, then walk down C. Sant Antoni to Pl. Sants. Cross C. Sants (which cuts through the plaza) to catch the bus. Sants is the main terminal for domestic and international traffic. **Currency exchange** 8am-10pm, **ATMs, pharmacy, tourist office.** Open daily 6:10am-11pm.
Estació França (tel. 93 490 02 02), Av. Marqués de L'Argentera. M: Barceloneta. A few domestic and international routes. All domestic trains leaving França pass through Sants. If in doubt, head to Sants. Open daily 7:30am-10pm.
Ferrocarrils de la Generalitat de Catalunya (FFCC) (tel. 93 205 15 15). Commuter trains with main stations at Pl. Catalunya (tel. 93 317 84 41) and Pl. Espanya (tel. 93 325 02 27). Service to Montserrat (from Espanya), and Terrassa (from Catalunya). Symbols resembling two interlocking "V"s mark connections with the Metro. The commuter line charges the same as the Metro until Tibidabo (T1 or T2 pass valid).

BY BUS

Most—but not all—buses arrive at the **Estació del Nord,** C. Ali-bei, 80 (tel. 93 265 65 08; info open daily 7am-9pm, station open 5:30am-1am). M: Arc de Triomf (exit to Nàpols). Buses offer a cheaper and sometimes more direct mode of travel than trains. For other destinations, see the transportation section of the town you wish to reach for details.

BARCELONA

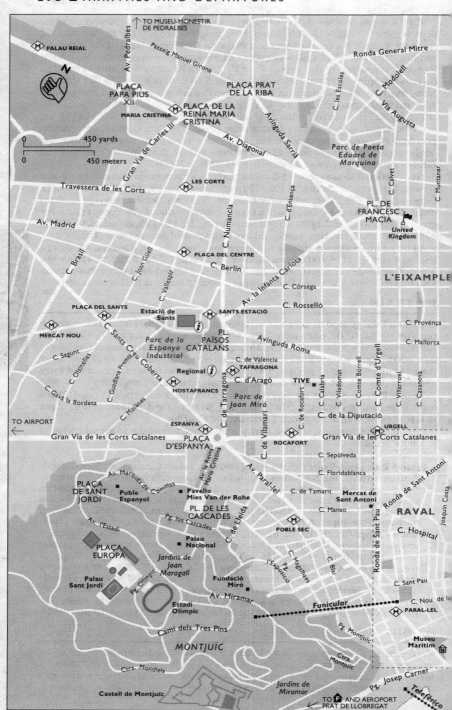

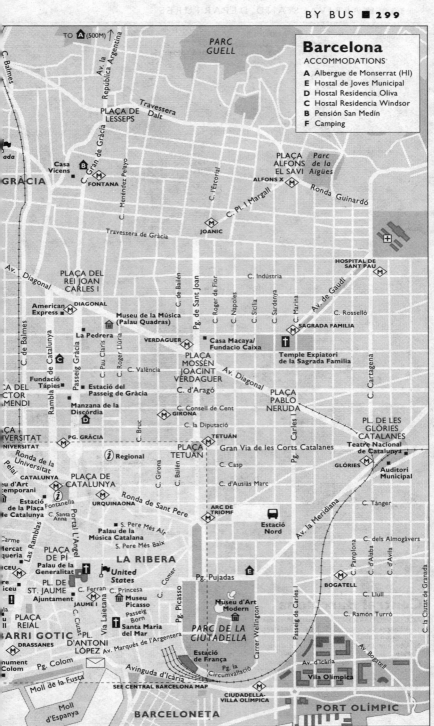

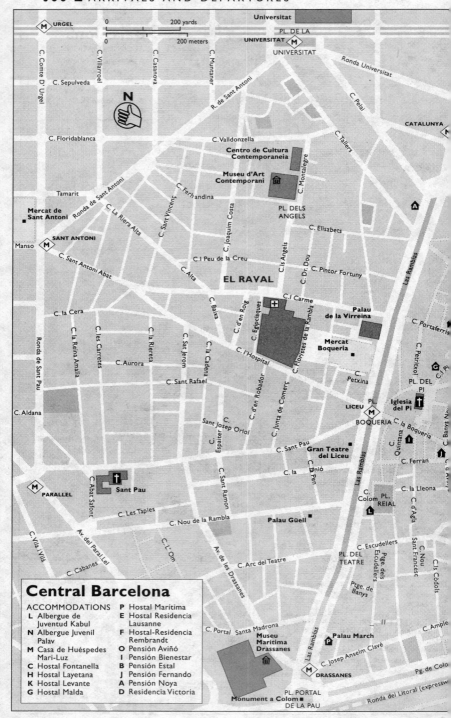

Central Barcelona

ACCOMMODATIONS
L	Albergue de Juventud Kabul	**P**	Hostal Marítima
N	Albergue Juvenil Palav	**E**	Hostal Residencia Lausanne
M	Casa de Huéspedes Mari-Luz	**F**	Hostal-Residencia Rembrandt
C	Hostal Fontanella	**O**	Pensión Aviñó
H	Hostal Layetana	**I**	Pensión Bienestar
K	Hostal Levante	**B**	Pensión Estal
G	Hostal Malda	**J**	Pensión Fernando
		A	Pensión Noya
		D	Residencia Victoria

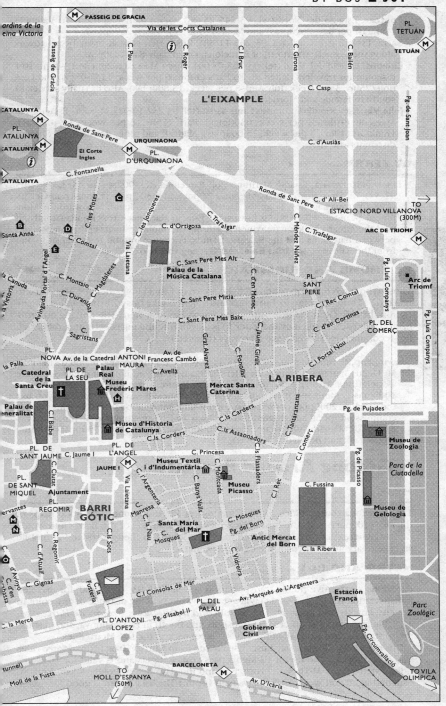

ardins de la
eina Victoria

PASSEIG DE GRACIA Ⓜ

Via de les Corts Catalanes

Passeig de Gràcia

C. Pau

C. Roger

C.I Bruc

C. Girona

C. Bailen

PL.
TETUÁN

TETUÁN Ⓜ

Pg. de Sant Joan

CATALUNYA

PL.
ATALUNYA Ⓜ

ATALUNYA Ⓜ

CATALUNYA

Ronda de Sant Pere

El Corte
Ingles

C. Fontanella

URQUINAONA

PL.
D'URQUINAONA

C. Casp

L'EIXAMPLE

C. d'Ausiàs

Ronda de Sant Pere

C. d'Alí-Bei

TO
ESTACIO NORD VILLANOVA
(300M)

ARC DE TRIOMF Ⓜ

Santa Anna

Ⓑ

C. les Motes

Ⓓ

C. Comtal

Ⓔ

C. Montsio

C. Duranlas

Avinguda Portal d'Angel

la Canuda

a Victoria

C. Magdalenes

Via Laietana

C. les Jonqueres

C. d'Ortigosa

C. Trafalgar

C. Sant Pere Mes Alt

Palau de la
Música Catalana

C. Sant Pere Mitia

C. Sant Pere Mes Baix

Méndez Núñez

C. d'en Monec

C. Trafalgar

PL.
SANT
PERE

C.I Rec Comtal

C. d'en Cortinas

PL. DEL
COMERÇ

Pg. Lluís Companys

Arc de
Triomf

Pg. Lluís Companys

C. Sagristans

PL.
NOVA Av. de la Catedral

ANTONI
MAURA

Av. de
Francesc Cambó

C. Avellà

Gral Alvarez

C. Jaume Giralt

C. Fonollar

C.I Portal Nou

C.I Rec Comtal

Pg. de Pujades

Catedral
de la
Santa Creu

la Palla

PL. DE
LA SEU

Palau
Real

Museu
Frederic Mares

Mercat Santa
Caterina

LA RIBERA

C. Tantarantana

C.I Comerç

Museu de
Zoologia

Palau de
eneralitat

C. Bisbe

Museu d'Historia
de Catalunya

C.Is Carders

C.I Corders

Pg. de Picasso

Parc de la
Ciutadella

PL. DE
SANT JAUME

C. Jaume I

PL. DE
L'ANGEL

C. Princesa

Museu Textil
i d'Indumentària

C.Is Assaonadors

C.I Rec

C. Fussina

Museu de
Gelologia

ervantes

PL.
DE SANT
MIQUEL

C. Ciutat

Ajuntament

JAUME I Ⓜ

PL.
REGOMIR

BARRI
GÓTIC

Ⓝ

C. Regomir

C. d'Atauf

C. Gignas

C. d'Avinyò

C.la Fustella

C. la Merče

C.I Consolat de Mar

Via Laietana

C. l'Argenteria

C. Manresa

C. la Nau

C.Is Sots

Santa María
del Mar

C.
Mosques

C. Montcada

C. Banys Vells

Museu
Picasso

C. Mosques

Pg. del Born

C. Vidreira

Antic Mercat
del Born

C. la Ribera

PL. DEL
PALAU

Pg. d'Isabel II

Av. Marquès de L'Argentera

Estación
França

Parc
Zoològic

PL. D'ANTONI
LOPEZ

Gobierno
Civil

Pg. de Circumvallació

TO VILA
OLIMPICA

tunnel)

Moll de la Fusta

TO
MOLL D'ESPANYA
(50M)

BARCELONETA Ⓜ

Av. D'Icària

Enatcar, Estació del Nord (tel. 93 245 25 28). Open daily 6am-1am. To Valencia (4hr., 10 per day, 2690ptas) and Madrid (8hr., 5 per day, 2690ptas).

Sarfa, Estació del Nord (tel. 93 265 11 58). Buses that stop at many beach towns along the Costa Brava, north of Barcelona. Open daily 8am-8:30pm.

Linebús, Estació del Nord (tel. 93 265 07 00). Open M-Sa 8am-2pm and 3-8pm. 10% discount for travelers under 26. To Paris (14hr., 6 per week, 11,750ptas) and London (25hr., 3 per week, July-Aug. 5 per week, 13,800ptas). Also has daily service to southern France and Morocco.

Julià Vía, Estación de Autobuses Sants Viriat (tel. 93 232 10 92). M: Sants-Estació. To: Marseille (10hr., 4 per week, 6300ptas); Paris (15hr., 6 per week, 11,400ptas); Frankfurt (19hr., 4 per week, 15,000ptas); Madrid; and other destinations. Student discounts available.

BY FERRY

Trasmediterránea, Estació Marítima-Moll Barcelona (tel. 902 45 46 45; fax 93 295 91 34). M: Drassanes. Open M-F 9am-1:30pm and 4:30-7pm, Sa 9am-1pm. Get tix from any travel agency. From the Metro, head down Las Ramblas toward the Monument a Colom, which points toward the Estació Marítima. Cross Ronda Litoral and pass the Aduana building on your left. During the summer, boats embark most days between Barcelona and the Balearic Islands. For more info on ferry transit to and from the Balearics, see **Islas Baleares: Getting there,** p. 367.

BY THUMB AND RIDESHARE

Those who hitch to France often take the Metro to Fabra i Puig, then Av. Meridiana to reach A-7. Those en route to Tarragona and Valencia take bus #7 from Rambla Catalunya on the side Gran Vía side. *Autopista* access lies near here. Hitchhiking on *autopistas* (toll roads, marked by the letter A) is illegal. Hitchhiking is permitted (although not recommended) on national highways (marked by N).

Barnastop, C. Sant Ramon, 29 (tel. 93 443 06 32), on the corner of Nou de Rambla. M: Liceu. Matches drivers with riders and can hook you up with other ride-share associations. Driver gets 3ptas per km in Spain, 4ptas per km outside Spain. 1000ptas commission paid to Barnastop for domestic travel the 1st time you use the service. 2000ptas commission for 1st-time international travel. 1pta per km commission for all subsequent travel. Open Tu-F 11am-2pm and 5-7pm, Sa noon-2pm. To: Madrid (3000ptas); Paris (7000ptas); Amsterdam (8500ptas); Rome (8000ptas); and Berlin (10,000ptas).

■ Getting Around Barcelona

MAPS

The Barcelona **tourist office** (in Pl. Catalunya or Pl. Sant Jaume) sells good maps of the city (100ptas) with the best enlargement of the streets of the Barri Gòtic you'll find anywhere. El Corte Inglés's free map, distributed in their stores and at mobile and stationary info centers, is the next best thing.

METRO AND BUS

Barcelona's extensive public transportation system (tel. 93 412 00 00; for disabled transportation tel. 93 412 44 44) will get you within walking distance of any point in the city quickly and cheaply. The useful *Guia d'Autobusos Urbans de Barcelona,* available free at tourist offices, the transport info booth in Pl. Catalunya, and in some metro stations, maps out all of the city's bus routes and the five Metro lines.

Bus rides cost 140ptas. Day buses usually run from 5am to 10 or 11pm. **Metro** rides also cost 140ptas. The useful T2 Metro pass costs 750ptas and is valid for 10 Metro rides. (Metro open M-Th 5am-11pm, F-Sa and the days before holidays 5am-1am, Su 6am-midnight, and weekday holidays 6am-11pm.) The T-DIA card is good for unlimited travel for a day on the bus and Metro (575ptas), but it can be hard to get your money's worth. Automatic vending machines and ticket windows sell Metro passes. T1s are available at ticket windows and *estancos* (tobacco stores). Hold on to your ticket or pass until you leave the Metro—riding without a receipt carries a hefty 5000ptas fine. Since both the regular bus system and metro close early, at night you'll have to ride the **Nitbus** (150ptas), which runs from 10pm to 4am, or use a taxi.

The clearly marked **Bus Turístic** makes for kick-back sight-seeing at a hefty price. It stops at 21 points of interest along two different routes; each circuit takes about two hours, but the full day pass (1700ptas, 2 consecutive days 2300ptas) allows you to get on and off either or both of the routes as often as you wish. The easiest place to hop on the bus is Pl. Catalunya, in front of El Corte Inglés. Tourist offices have a free pamphlet that displays the bus route and special discounts on sights accompanying the pass. Tickets can be purchased on the bus or at the Plaça de Catalunya tourist office. (Buses run March 28-Jan. 6 every 15min. 9am-9:30pm.)

TAXIS

Barcelona's taxis are everywhere. A Libre sign in the windshield or a lit green light on the roof means they are not occupied, while red means you're out of luck. Cabs can be summoned by phone (tel. 93 330 03 00 or 93 300 11 00; for disabled travelers tel. 93 358 11 11 or 93 357 77 55). The first six minutes or 1.9km cost 295ptas; then 101-120ptas per kilometer, depending on when you ride.

CAR RENTAL

Docar, C. Montnegre, 18 (24hr. tel. 93 322 90 08; fax 93 439 81 19). Free delivery and pickup. From 3000ptas per day, including insurance, plus 19ptas per km. Open M-F 9am-2pm and 4-8pm, Sa 9am-2pm.

Tot Car, C. Berlín, 97 (tel. 93 430 01 98, fax 93 419 22 94). Free delivery and pickup. 2500ptas per day, 21ptas per km. Insurance 1300ptas per day. Open M-F 8am-8pm, Sa 9am-1pm.

BICYCLE AND MOPED RENTAL

Vanguard Rent a Car, C. Londres, 31 (tel. 93 439 38 80; fax 93 410 82 71). Mopeds 3000ptas per day, weekend rate (F-M) 5300ptas, plus 1000ptas insurance. Helmet included. 7% IVA not included.

Biciclot, C. Sant Joan de Malta, 1 (tel. 93 307 74 75). M: Clot. Leave through exit Aragó-Meridiera, turn 180 degrees at the top of the steps; take 2nd right, then 2nd left (C. Verned), then 2nd right on to C. Sant Joan de Malta. 10-speeds 375ptas per hr., 1500ptas per day. Mountain bikes 600ptas per hr., 2100ptas per day. Multi-day and group rates available. Open M-F 9am-2pm and 5-8pm, Sa 10am-2pm.

ORIENTATION

Barcelona's layout is simple to grasp and best pictured by imagining yourself perched atop Columbus's head at the **Monument a Colom** (on **Passeig de Colom,** which runs parallel to the shore), viewing the city with the Mediterranean at your back. From the harbor, the city slopes gently upward toward the mountains. On most *avingudas* (avenues), keeping this fact in mind should help you re-orient yourself. From the Columbus monument, **Las Ramblas,** the city's most lively thoroughfare, proceeds away from the harbor. It runs directly to **Plaça de Catalunya,** the city's center, and is divided into five segments: Rambla de Santa Mónica, Rambla de Caputxins, Rambla de Sant Josep, Rambla de Estudis, and Rambla de Canaletas.

To the right (east) of Las Ramblas spans the **Barri Gòtic,** enclosed on the other side by **Vía Laietana. Carrer de Ferran** bisects the Barri Gòtic into northern and southern halves, beginning at Rambla de Caputxins and finishing at Vía Laietana, passing the **Plaça Reial** and **Plaça de Sant Jaume I,** site of the **Ajuntament.** Beyond Vía Laietana (farther east) lies the labyrinthine neighborhood **La Ribera,** which borders **Parc de la Ciutadella** and the **Estació de França train station.** Beyond Parc de la Ciutadella (eastward still) is the **Vila Olímpica,** with its twin towers (the tallest buildings in Barcelona) and a shiny assortment of malls, discos, and hotels.

On the west side (left, with your back to the sea) of Las Ramblas is **Barri Xinès** (Barrio Chino), now officially called **El Raval.** The southern half of El Raval composes Barcelona's shrinking red-light district. In the background (farther west) rises **Montjuïc,** a picturesque hill crammed with gardens, museums (including the Fundació Miró), the '92 Olympic grounds, castles, and other tourist attractions.

Directly behind you as you sit atop the Monument a Colom is the **Port Vell** (Old Port) development, where a wavy bridge leads across to the ultramodern shopping and entertainment complex **Moll d'Espanya** and **Maremagnum.**

L'Eixample, the gridded neighborhood created during *fin de siècle* urban expansion, fans outward from Pl. Catalunya toward the mountains. **Gran Vía de les Corts Catalanes** defines its lower edge and **Passeig de Gràcia,** the Eixample's commercial center, bisects the neighborhood. **Avinguda Diagonal** marks the oblique upper limit of the grid-planned neighborhoods, separating the Eixample from **Gràcia,** an older neighborhood in the foothills. The peak of **Tibidabo,** the northwest border of the city and the highest point in Barcelona, offers the most comprehensive view of the city.

Barcelona is fairly safe, even at night, but secure your valuables in your lap while sitting in an outdoor cafe, doing anything in the Plaça Reial, watching street shows on Las Ramblas, or wandering through the narrow streets of the Barri Gòtic. The deeper into El Raval you venture, the more unsafe it becomes. Pick-pocketers roam by day, and it can be spooky at night. Most areas with active nightlife (see p. 326) are well patrolled, well lit, and, for the most part, safe.

■ Practical Information

TOURIST AND FINANCIAL SERVICES

Tourist Info: For **free info** call 93 304 31 34 or 906 30 12 82. For **general city info** call 1010 (one-time 130ptas charge); on the Internet, head to http://www.bcn.es. **Turisme de Barcelona** (tel. 93 304 31 34 or 902 30 12 82), underneath Plaça Catalunya. M: Catalunya. Biggest and best city office. Provides multilingual advice and a slew of **maps,** pamphlets, transportation passes, and guides. Hotel info and **currency exchange** also available. Open daily 9am-9pm. **Branch office** nearby at Pl. Sant Jaume, 1. M: Jaume I. Open M-Sa 10am-8pm, Su 10am-2pm. **Mobile info offices** dot the city in the summer—there's one at Templo Sagrada Familia Mar.-June 10am-8pm. **Estació Central de Barcelona-Sants office,** Pl. Països Catalans (tel. 93 491 44 31). M: Sants-Estació. Open in summer daily 8am-8pm; in winter M-F 8am-8pm, Sa-Su 8am-2pm. For information on all of Catalunya, go to **Centre d'Informació Turística de Catalunya-Palau Robert,** Pg. de Gràcia, 107 (tel. 93 238 40 00; http:www.gencat.es/probert). M: Diagonal. Open M-Sa 10am-7pm. A **branch office** is at Aeroport El Prat de Llobregat (tel. 93 478 47 04), in the international terminal. Open M-Sa 9:30am-8:30pm and Su 9:30am-3pm. For information on cultural events, stop by **Palau de la Virreina,** Las Ramblas, 99 (tel. 93 301 77 75), between La Boqueria market and C. Carme M: Liceu. Open M-Sa 10am-2pm and 4-8pm. More cultural info and Barcelona's monthly cultural magazine in English, *Metropolitan,* is available across the street at **Centro de Informacion Cultural,** Las Ramblas, 118 (tel. 93 302 15 22, ext. 266). Open M-F 10am-2pm and 4-8pm, Sa 10am-2pm.

Budget Travel Offices: Wasteels, Pl. Catalunya-Estació RENFE (tel. 93 301 18 81; fax 93 301 18 53). M: Catalunya. In the Metro/RENFE terminal; enter the Metro in front of El Corte Inglés. Air and train discounts for students. Open M-F 8:30am-8:30pm, Sa 10am-1pm. Visa, MC. **Unlimited Student Travel,** C. Rocafort, 116-122 (tel. 93 483 83 78). M: Rocafort. 2 blocks from the Metro. A full-fledged travel agency. Expect a long wait during the summer. Open M-F 10am-8pm, Sa 10am-1:30pm. **Centre d'Informació Assesorament per a Joves,** C. Ferrán, 32 (tel. 93 402 78 01 or 93 402 78 00). More of a local student assistance office than a travel agency. No tickets for sale, but plenty of free advice and a bulletin board with youth events. Excellent library of travel guides. Open M-F 10am-2pm and 4-8pm.

Consulates: See **Spain: Essentials: Embassies and Consulates,** p. 41.

Currency Exchange: The good rates can be obtained at **banks.** As always, **ATMs** give the best rates, with no commission. General banking hours M-F 8:30am-2pm. **Banco Central Hispano,** Las Ramblas at C. Boqueria, is good for AmEx Traveler's Check exchange. **Banco de Espanya** (tel. 93 453 37 18), in Pl. Catalunya, and the **American Express office** (see below) charge no commission on traveler's checks. On Sundays you can change money at **Estació de Sants** (tel. 93 490 77 70) for no commission. Open daily 8am-10pm.

American Express: Pg. Gràcia, 101 (tel. 900 99 44 26; 24hr. tel. 91 572 03 03; fax 93 415 37 00; travel agency tel. 93 415 28 50). M: Diagonal. The entrance is around the corner on C. Rosselló. Mail held free for cardholders. Open M-F 9:30am-6pm, Sa 10am-noon. **ATM** outside. A **currency exchange** office (with so-so rates) is at Ramblas, 74. Open M-F 9am-8pm, Sa 10am-2pm and 3:15-7pm, Su 10am-2pm.

El Corte Inglés: Pl. Catalunya, 14 (tel. 93 302 12 12), Av. Diagonal, 471-473 (tel. 93 419 20 20), and Av. Diagonal, 617 (tel. 93 419 52 06). Department store behemoth. Gives out a good **map. English books,** haircutting, rooftop cafeteria, **supermarket, currency exchange** (at weak rates), and **telephones.** Open M-Sa 10am-9:30pm.

LOCAL SERVICES

Luggage Storage: Estació Sants. M: Sants-Estació. Small lockers 400ptas, large 600ptas. Open 5:30am-11:30pm. **Estació França.** M: Barceloneta. Small lockers 400ptas, large 600ptas. Open 6am-11:30pm. **Estació del Nord.** M: Arc de Triomf. Lockers 300-600ptas. Open 24hr.

Lost Property: Objetos Perdidos, C. Ciutat, 9 (tel. 93 402 31 61), on the ground floor of the Ajuntament, Pl. Sant Jaume. M: Jaume I. Open M-F 9am-2:30pm.

English Bookstores: LAIE, Av. Pau Claris, 85 (tel. 93 318 17 39), 1 block from the Gran Vía. M: Urquinaona or Pl. Catalunya. Open M-Sa 10am-9pm. **Librería Francesa,** Pg. Gràcia, 91 (tel. 93 215 14 17). M: Diagonal. Between C. Provença and C. Rosselló. Open M-F 9:30am-2:30pm and 4-8:30pm, Sa 9:30am-2pm and 5-8:30pm. **The Bookstore,** C. La Granja, 13 (tel. 93 237 95 19), in Gràcia off Travesera del Dalt. M: Lesseps. Best used bookstore around, run by an eccentric British expat. Trade-ins. Open M-Sa 11am-1:30pm and 2:30-7pm.

Library: Institut d'Estudis Norteamericans, Vía Augusta, 123 (tel. 93 209 27 11). Open Sept.-July M-F 11am-2pm and 4-7pm. **Biblioteca General,** C. Hospital, 56 (tel. 93 302 07 97), next to Hospital de Santa Creu, off Las Ramblas. Open M-F 9am-2pm and 3:30-8:30pm, Sa 9am-2pm. Closed for 3 weeks in Sept.

Foreign Periodicals: Try the newsstands along Las Ramblas and Pg. Gràcia.

Religious Services: Jewish services, Sinagoga de la Comunidad Judía, C. Avenir, 24 (tel. 93 200 85 13; fax 93 200 61 48). Services daily at 7:30am. **Muslim services,** Comunidad Musulmana, Mezquita Toarek Ben Ziad, C. Hospital, 91 (tel. 93 441 91 49). Open daily until 10pm.

Women's Services: Librería de Dones Prolég, C. Dagueria, 13 (tel. 93 319 24 25). M: Jaume I. Women's bookstore stocks a large feminist collection with new and used books in English, French, and German. Notice board and info on workshops and seminars. Open Sept.-July M 5-8pm, Tu-F 10am-2pm and 5-8pm, Sa 11am-2pm and 5-8pm; Aug. M-F 5-9pm.

Gay and Lesbian Services: Coordinadora Gay Lesbiana, C. Les Carolines, 13 (tel. 93 237 08 69; toll-free 900 601 601, available 6-10pm). **Cómplices,** C. Cervantes, 2 (tel. 93 412 72 83). M: Liceu. From C. Ferrán, take C. Avinyó, then 2nd left. A gay and lesbian bookstore with publications in English and Spanish and a map of gay and lesbian bars and discos. Open M-F 10:30am-8:30pm, Sa noon-8:30pm.

Laundromat: Tintoreria San Pablo, C. San Pau, 105 (tel. 93 329 42 49). M: Liceu. Wash, dry, and fold 1600ptas; do-it-yourself for 1200ptas. Open M-F 9am-1pm and 4-8pm. **Lava Super,** C. Carme 63. 1200ptas for full service or do-it-yourself.

EMERGENCY AND COMMUNICATIONS

Emergency: dial 092, 062, or 091.

Police: Las Ramblas, 43 (tel. 93 301 90 60), across from Pl. Reial and next to C. Nou de La Rambla. M: Liceu. Multilingual officers.

BARCELONA

Crisis Services: Oficina Permanente de Atención Social (24hr. toll-free tel. 900 30 90 30). **STD treatment:** Av. Drassanes, 17-21 (hotline tel. 93 441 29 97). **Association Ciutadana Anti-SIDA de Catalunya** (AIDS info), C. Tantarantana, 4 (tel. 93 317 05 05; open M-F 10am-2pm and 4-8pm).

Late-Night Pharmacy: Pharmacies open late on rotating basis. Check pharmacy windows for current listings.

Hospitals: Barcelona Centro Médico (BCM), Av. Diagonal, 612, 2nd floor, #14 (tel. 93 414 06 43; 24hr. tel. 939 30 34 64), coordinates referrals, especially for foreigners. **Hospital Clínic,** Villarroel, 170 (tel. 93 227 54 00). M: Hospital Clínic. Main entrance at intersection of C. Roselló and C. Casanova. **Hospital de la Santa Creu i Sant Pau** (tel. 93 291 90 00; emergency tel. 93 291 91 91), at intersection of C. Cartagena and C. Sant Antoni Moria Claret. M: Hospital de Sant Pau. **Médicos de Urgencia,** C. Pelai, 40 (tel. 93 412 12 12). M: Catalunya. Dial 061 for **ambulance.**

Internet Access: El Cafe de Internet, Gran Vía de les Corts Catalanes, 656 (tel. 93 412 19 15). M: Pg. Gracia. Trendy restaurant offers access for 600ptas per 30min., 800ptas per hr. with student ID. Live concerts, poetry readings, slide shows, and art exhibits as well. Open M-W 10am-midnight and Th-Sa 10am-2am. A younger crowd frequents **Café Interlight** (tel. 93 301 11 80), just off Corts Catalanes, on Pau Claris toward Diputaciò. M: Pg. Gracia. 500ptas per 30min., 800ptas per hr. Open M-Th 11am-11pm, F-Sa 11am-midnight, Su 5-10pm.

Post Office: Pl. Antoni López (tel. 93 318 38 31 or 902 19 71 97), at the end of Vía Laietana, portside. M: Jaume I or Barceloneta. **Fax** and Lista de Correos. Open M-F 8am-9pm, Sa 8am-2pm. A little shop in back of the post office building, across the street, wraps packages for mailing (about 300ptas). Open M-Sa 9am-2pm and 5-8pm. **Postal Code:** 08003.

Telephones: Get phone cards at tobacco stores or tourist offices. **Private phone service** (tel./fax 93 490 76 50) at Estació Sants. M: Sants-Estació; **faxes** received and sent (1st page 250ptas, each additional page 100ptas). Open M-Sa 9am-10:15pm. For general info on the Spanish phone system, see **Keeping in Touch,** p. 58.

■ Accommodations and Camping

Although *hostales* and *pensiones* abound, visitors without reservations end up scrambling in summer, when tourists flood every corner of the city. Most accommodations have some rooms with splendid balconies onto the street and others with windows onto stuffy interior patios. Ask for an exterior room if you value sunlight and breeze.

YOUTH HOSTELS

Barcelona's *albergues* offer lodging staples (bed, shower, bath) at the lowest prices. They are also the best places in town to meet fellow backpackers. *Let's Go* urges you to check out a room before signing your night away.

Albergue de Juventud Kabul, Pl. Reial, 17 (tel. 93 318 51 90; fax 93 301 40 34). M: Liceu. As you head to the port on Las Ramblas, turn left on Pl. Reial after C. Ferrán. Kabul is on the near right corner of the *plaça.* Renowned for its social atmosphere, helpful staff, and beer vending machines, Kabul has earned a spot in Eurail lore. Satellite TV, music, and a pool table create an almost raucous environment. Those looking for sobriety might consider lodging elsewhere. A mobile police unit keeps the area relatively safe, but still use caution around Pl. Reial at night. 130 beds. New kitchen. Dorms 1500ptas, key deposit 1000ptas. Shower heads are like elevated sink spouts. Free lockers; safe deposit boxes with key deposit. Sheets 200ptas. 4.5kg laundry 800ptas. Flexible 5-day max. stay. Multilingual receptionist (24hr.).

Albergue Juvenil Palau (HI), C. Palau, 6 (tel. 93 412 50 80). M: Jaume I. One block from Pl. Sant Jaume. From the *plaça,* take C. Ciutat to C. Templaris, then take the 2nd left. A small, tranquil refuge in the heart of the Barri Gòtic. Offers kitchen (open 7am-10pm) and dining salon where you can meet fellow backpackers, read a complimentary magazine, or watch the tube. 2-8 people per room. 40 beds. Dorms 1300ptas, breakfast included. Sheets 150ptas. Flexible 5-day max. stay.

Reception daily 7am-3am. Showers available 8-11am and 4-10pm. Curfew 3am. Same-day reservations with a night's deposit accepted.

Albergue Mare de Déu de Montserrat (HI), Pg. Mare de Déu del Coll, 41-51 (tel. 93 210 51 51; fax 210 07 98), beyond Parc Güell (way out there). Bus #25 or 28 from Pl. Catalunya stops across the street from the hostel, as does night bus N-4. Otherwise, from M: Vallcarca, walk up Av. República Argentina and across C. Viaducte de Vallcarca; signs point the way up the hill. This 180-bed government-sponsored villa has its own private woods and a hilltop view of Barcelona. HI members only. Dorms 1800ptas, over 25 2275ptas; breakfast included. Lunch and dinner 750ptas each. Sheets 350ptas. Flexible 3-day max. stay. Reception daily 7-10am and 2pm-midnight. Bedrooms closed 10am-2pm for cleaning. No showering 10am-2pm. Move-in 5pm. Midnight curfew, but doors open every 30min. from midnight-3am. Wheelchair accessible. Reservations accepted.

Hostal De Joves Municipal (HI), Pg. Pujades, 29 (tel./fax 93 300 31 04). M: Arc de Triomf. From Metro, exit to C. Nápols, walk toward Parc de la Ciutadella, and turn left on Pg. Pujades. Warm, skillful staff guides you through the city. Full kitchen, dining hall, hot showers, and 68 beds. 2- to 6-bed dorms 1500ptas, breakfast included. 5-day max. stay. Sheets 350ptas. Laundry (500ptas wash, 700ptas dry). Reception daily 8-10am and 3pm-midnight. Hostel closed 10am-3pm.

CIUTAT VELLA

B
A
R
C
E
L
O
N
A

The neighborhood **Barri Gòtic** spans eastward from **Las Ramblas,** and **El Raval** spans westward. The three zones, along with La Ribera to the east of the Barri Gòtic, are collectively known as the **Ciutat Vella** (old city). The entire zone offers a wealth of budget accommodations, but in July and August you *must* call ahead. Police patrol the area, but remember to watch your belongings on and near Las Ramblas. If you are in dire straits, check Las Ramblas or C. Boquería, but expect to pay more for less.

Lower Ciutat Vella

The following hostels are centrally located in the southern areas of El Raval and the Barri Gòtic, below C. Portaferrissa in the Barri Gòtic, and below C. Pintor Fortuny in El Raval. They are "lower" in elevation than the Upper Ciutat Vella, generally lower in price, and their interiors are usually, but not always, a bit lower in quality. Though atmospheric, these streets can be a little unnerving at night for solo travelers.

Hostal-Albergue Fernando, C. Ferrán, 31 (tel. 93 301 79 93). M: Liceu. One of the best deals in the Barri Gòtic. Recent renovations have completely transformed the appearance (but not the price) of this hostel. It sparkles with cleanliness. Groups share larger rooms, and many rooms have bunk beds. Dorms 1600ptas; doubles with bath 5000ptas; triples with bath 5500ptas.

Hostal Avinyo, C. Avinyó, 42 (tel. 93 318 79 45 or 93 301 75 70; fax 318 68 93). M: Drassanes. An unassuming entrance leads to clean, cheery rooms with either streetside balconies or windows onto a tranquil central courtyard. Recently renovated, and bathrooms are in good shape. Singles 1700ptas; doubles 2600-3000ptas, with shower 3300-3800ptas; triples 3900-4500ptas, with bath 4800-5700ptas; quads 5200-7600ptas. Prices vary according to length of stay and time of year. Visa, MC.

Pensión Francia, C. Rera Palau, 4 (tel. 93 319 03 76). M: Barceloneta. From Estació de França, cross the main avenue (Marquès de l'Argentera) and go left; C. Rera Palau is the 5th right, just one block toward the Colón Monument. From the Metro, head toward town, crossing Pl. Palau, then turn right on Marqués de l'Argentera, and C. Rera Palau is the 2nd left. A diamond in the rough, near Museu Picasso but a bit off Las Ramblas. Brand-new wooden furniture, and a mini-library of English books. They'll even lend you a TV. Singles 1600ptas; doubles 2700ptas, with shower 3300ptas, with bath 5000ptas; triples with shower 3900ptas; quads with shower 4500ptas. Breakfast 275ptas. Credit cards accepted. Keys for 24hr. entry.

Hostal Residencia Rembrandt, C. Portaferrisa, 23 (tel./fax 93 318 10 11). M: Liceu. As you walk up Las Ramblas (away from the ocean), Portaferrisa is on the right. Clean *hostal* with large windows, some looking onto one of 3 charming patios.

Theme rooms, from "little kid" to "faux ritzy." Singles 2700ptas; doubles 4000ptas, with shower 4500ptas, with bath 5000ptas; triples 7000ptas. Breakfast 350ptas.

Casa de Huéspedes Mari-Luz, C. Palau, 4 (tel. 93 317 34 63), 1 block from Pl. Sant Jaume. M: Jaume I or Liceu. Take C. Ciutat to C. Templaris, then take the 2nd left. After dark it is safer not to approach via C. Escudellers. Narrow hallways flanked by ultra-clean, barracks-style bedrooms for 4-5 inhabitants. Dorms 1500ptas. Laundry 800ptas per load. Good-sized lockers in rooms. Keys for 24hr. entry, and kitchen use with permission. Owner posts info on bike tours. Reservations accepted.

Hostal Malda, C. Pí, 5 (tel. 93 317 30 02). M: Liceu. Take C. Portaferrissa (on the right with your back to the sea) from Las Ramblas. C. Pí is your fourth right. *Hostal* is directly above the Cine Malda. Offers simple rooms and a dining room with travel library. Singles 1500ptas; doubles 2500ptas; triples 3500ptas.

Hotel Rey Don Jaime I, C. Jaume I, 11 (tel. 93 310 62 08). M: Jaume I. Every room has a bathroom and telephone, every bed a double mattress, and every luxury a price. Reception 24hr. with multilingual staff. Singles 4000ptas; doubles 5800ptas; triples 6900ptas. Visa, MC.

Hostal Layetana, Pl. Ramón Berenguer el Gran, 2 (tel. 93 319 20 12; fax 93 319 20 12). M: Jaume I. Less than a block from the Metro, on your left as you walk away from the ocean. Balconies open to contrasting scenes: the sectarian vista of the cathedral on one side and the vanity view of the fashionable plaza on the other. Luxurious living room with terrace. Singles 2400ptas; doubles 3800ptas, with bath 5400ptas. Exterior showers 200ptas each. Visa, MC.

Hostal La Terrassa, Junta de Comerç, 11 (tel. 93 302 51 74; fax 93 301 21 88). Descending Las Ramblas, turn right on C. Hospital, then turn left after Teatre Romea. M: Liceu. Lots of rooms. Social courtyard—a relative rarity among non-youth hostels. Singles 2200ptas, with shower 2800ptas; doubles 3500ptas, with shower 4300ptas; triples 4700ptas, with shower 5300ptas. Credit cards accepted.

Hostal Levante, Baixada de San Miguel, 2 (tel. 93 317 95 65l; fax 93 317 05 26; email hostallevante@mx3.rebestb.es). M: Liceu. Walk down C. Ferrán and turn right on C. Avinyó; Baixada de San Miguel is the first left. Shabby entrance, but rooms inside are up to par. Wooden interior, large windows, good ventilation, clean shared bathrooms, excellent TV lounge, and knowledgeable owner. Singles 2500ptas; doubles 4000ptas, with bath 5000ptas. Safe available 7am-10pm. Reception 24hr.

Hotel Call, Arco San Ramón del Call, 4 (tel. 93 302 11 23; fax 93 301 34 86). M: Liceu. From Las Ramblas, take C. Boqueria to its end, veering left onto C. Call; the *hostal* is on the first corner on the left up C. Call. Look for the neon Hotel sign. Good spot for the weary wayfarer craving hotel amenities—phone and bathroom in every room. Try for a room with a balcony. Singles 3200ptas; doubles 4400ptas; triples 5700ptas; quads 6400ptas. Visa, MC. Reception 24hr.

Hostal Marítima, Las Ramblas, 4 (tel. 93 302 31 52), down a tiny alley off the port end of Las Ramblas. M: Drassanes. Follow the signs to Museo de Cera, which is next door. Prime location, but a mix of street noise and intercom music can clutter the airways a bit. Comfortable rooms. Singles 2000ptas; doubles 3000ptas, with shower 4000ptas, with bath 4500ptas; triples 3900ptas, with shower 4500ptas, with bath 5000ptas. Washing machine 800ptas. Reception 24hr.

Hostal Residencia Romay, C. Avinyó, 58 (tel. 93 317 94 14). M: Drassanes. In a slightly seedy area. Heading toward the sea on Las Ramblas, turn left onto C. Josep Anselm Clavé; C. Avinyó lies on the left after the church. Enter through a midget-sized door and head up to the 3rd floor. Very basic rooms with pink windows onto a courtyard. Some baths without toilet seats. Singles 1500ptas, with shower 2000ptas; doubles with bath 3500ptas. Keys for 24hr. entry.

Pensión Bienestar, C. Quintana, 3 (tel. 93 318 72 83). M: Liceu. Two blocks from Las Ramblas, off C. Ferrán, with a quiet location on a pedestrian-only street. The 27 rooms may be dim and very simple, but high ceilings and freshly painted walls brighten them up. Basic foam mattresses in ramshackle beds. Central patio is practically a botanical garden. Singles 1800ptas; doubles 3000ptas; triples 5200ptas. Bathrooms vary from elephantine to claustrophobic. Hot water only 8am-midnight.

Hostal-Residencia Europa, C. Bouqería, 18 (tel. 93 318 76 20). M: Liceu. A popular spot only a few feet off Las Ramblas, in the heart of the old town. Very basic rooms in an excellent location. Lounge with TV and vending machine. Singles 1900ptas, with bath 2800ptas; doubles 3800ptas, with bath 4800ptas.

Upper Ciutat Vella

This subdivision mostly includes the area south of Pl. Catalunya, bounded by C. Fontanella to the north and C. Portaferrisa to the south. **Portal de L'Angel,** the better-behaved little brother of Las Ramblas, is a broad pedestrian avenue running through the middle, southward from Pl. Catalunya. A bit pricier than the hostels in the Lower Ciutat Vella, accommodations here are safer, more modern, and just a skip from Las Ramblas. The nearest Metro stop is Pl. Catalunya unless otherwise specified. Reservations are almost obligatory in July and August, and increasingly so in June.

⊛Pensión L'Isard, C. Tallers, 82 (tel. 93 302 51 83), near MACBA, the new contemporary art museum. M: Universitat. Take Pelai exit from the metro, go left at the end of the block, then immediately left at the pharmacy. Ultra-tidy rooms with balconies and new mattresses. Helpful multilingual staff. Singles 1900ptas; doubles 3700ptas, with bath 4700ptas; triples 4800ptas. Keys for 24hr. entry.

Hostal Fontanella, Vía Laietana, 71 (tel./fax 317 59 43). From Pl. Catalunya, go 3 blocks past El Corte Inglés and hang a right. Refined owner maintains decor with soft lights, floral bouquets, lace curtains, and logo-endowed towels. Hotel-quality beds and baths. Singles 2900ptas, with bath 3800ptas; doubles 4800ptas, with shower 5500ptas, with bath 6600ptas. Reservations with deposit. Visa, MC, AmEx.

Residencia Australia, Ronda Universitat, 11 (tel. 93 317 41 77). M: Universitat. María, the gregarious English-speaking owner, shows she cares with embroidered sheets and curtains, a spotless bathroom, and ceiling fans in rooms. Singles 2800ptas; doubles 4000ptas, with bath 4800ptas. Prices do not include 7% IVA.

Hostal Residencia Lausanne, Av. Portal de L'Angel, 24 (tel. 93 302 11 39). Restful *hostal* lives up to the building's imperial facade and entryway. Front balcony overlooks a shopping promenade and the rear terrace, a golden sanctuary—try for a room overlooking one or the other. Couches and chairs in many rooms, new wallpaper, renovated baths, and a TV lounge. Singles 2500ptas; doubles 3500ptas, with shower 5000ptas; triples with shower 6000ptas, with bath 7500ptas.

Hotel Toledano/Hostal Residencia Capitol, Las Ramblas, 138 (tel. 93 301 08 72; fax 412 31 42; email toledano@idgrup.ibernet.com). Near the top of Las Ramblas. This family owned, split-level hotel/*hostal* has been making tourists happy for 78 years. All rooms have cable TV and phones; some have balconies with a panoramic views. English-speaking owner. 4th floor *hostal:* singles 2900ptas; doubles 4600ptas, with shower 5200ptas; triples 5900ptas, with shower 6500ptas; quads 6800ptas, with shower 7400ptas. 5th floor hotel: singles 3600ptas, doubles 6900ptas, triples 8600ptas, quads 9600ptas. Add 7% IVA. Credit cards accepted. Reception 24hr.

Hostal Plaza, C. Fontanella, 18 (tel./fax 301 01 39). Calle Fontanella stems right out of Pl. Catalunya at El Corte Inglés. Texan couple welcomes traveling students. American art and 3-speed fans decorate 18 rooms and a plush lounge. Phone, fax, TV, the internet (access 600ptas per 30min.), kitchen. Room quality varies, but bathrooms are all new. Singles with shower 3500ptas, with bath 4000ptas; doubles with shower 5000ptas, with bath 6000ptas; triples with shower 7500ptas, with bath 9000ptas. 5kg laundry 1500ptas. Reception closed 2-5pm. Visa, MC, AmEx.

Pensión Nevada, Av. Portal de L'Angel, 16 (tel. 93 302 31 01), just past Hostal Residencia Lausanne. Great location. Your cozy bedroom away from home, complete with matching throw pillows, firm beds, comfortable chairs, and flowers on the balcony. Knick-knacks emulate Little Bo Peep's bedroom. TV in common room. Singles 3700ptas; doubles 5400ptas. No heat. Keys for 24hr. entry.

Pensión Estal, C. Santa Anna, 27 (tel. 93 302 26 18), near Pensión Santa Anna. Some of the tiny, very simple rooms offer views of Iglesia de Santa Anna. French-speaking owner takes great pride in his establishment, and happy customers attest to its merits. Singles 2500ptas; doubles 3500ptas, with bath 5000ptas.

Residencia Victoria, C. Comtal, 9 (tel. 93 317 45 97). From Pl. Catalunya, take the 1st left on Av. Portal de L'Angel. The offerings outside of the rooms—social lounge, outdoor terrace, kitchen, TV, washer for 300ptas—trump the rooms themselves, (very basic, with sinks). Singles 2500ptas; doubles 4500ptas. 7% IVA not included.

Pensión Santa Anna, C. Santa Anna, 23 (tel. 93 301 22 46). From the green line, take the Las Ramblas exit and then your 1st left onto C. Santa Anna heading toward the water. From the red line, take the Pg. Gràcia exit, descend Pg. Gràcia past El Corte Inglés (on your left), cross C. Fontanella onto Portal de L'Angel, and take the 1st right on C. Santa Anna. What this place lacks in size, ambience, and water temperature it makes up for with a friendly owner, clean bathrooms, and great eateries nearby. Singles 2500ptas; doubles 4500ptas, with bath 6000ptas; triples 6000ptas.

Pensión Arosa, Av. Portal de L'Angel, 14 (tel. 93 317 36 87), next to Pensión Nevada. The pinkest *pensión* in town. Rooms are airy and clean. Singles 2200ptas; doubles 4500 with shower; triples 6600ptas with shower. Visa, MC, AmEx.

Pensión Noya, Las Ramblas, 133 (tel. 93 301 48 31). Above the noisy restaurant Nuria. This tiny 10-room retreat welcomes backpackers with open arms but no winter heat and cramped bathrooms (hot water 8am-midnight). Singles 2000ptas.; doubles 4000ptas; triples 5200ptas.

Pensión Aris, C. Fontanella, 14 (tel. 93 318 10 17). Near Hostal Plaza. Huge, clean rooms furnished with little more than beds. Space-age windows shut out all sound. Singles 2500ptas; doubles 4000ptas, with bath 5000ptas; triples 5000ptas, with bath 6000ptas. Laundry 500-1000ptas. Open 24hr.

L'EIXAMPLE

The most beautiful *hostales* are found here along wide, safe *avingudas*. Most have colorfully tiled interiors and Modernista elevators styled with wood and steel. Rooms often have high ceilings, plenty of light, and small *balcones*.

◉Hostal Residencia Oliva, Pg. Gràcia, 32, 4th fl. (tel. 93 488 01 62 or 93 488 17 89), on the intersection of C. Diputació. M: Pg. Gràcia. The Aerobus drops you off in the lap of luxury. Some windows overlook the *manzana de discordia* (see p. 319), where you can watch Puig, Domènech, and Gaudí compete for aesthetic prominence. Posh woodwork distinguishes bureaus, bed frames, and mirrors. Color TVs in rooms. Funky elevator and catwalk over the central patio make leaving and returning an adventure in *Modernisme*. Some doubles are cramped. You'd be well advised to call ahead. Singles 3100ptas; doubles 5700ptas, with bath 6700ptas.

Hostal Residencia Palacios, Gran Vía de les Corts Catalanes, 629, 2nd fl. (tel./fax 93 301 37 92). M: Pg. Gràcia. An excellent choice, with well-furnished rooms. Singles 2700ptas, with shower 3500ptas, with bath 3750ptas; doubles 4000ptas, with shower 4950ptas, with bath 5250ptas. 7% IVA not included. Breakfast 350ptas. Laundry (wash and dry) 1000ptas. Credit cards accepted.

Hostal Residencia Windsor, Rambla Catalunya, 84 (tel. 93 215 11 98), near the intersection of C. Mallorca. M: Pg. Gràcia. Aristocratic *hostal* lives up to its name with crimson carpets, palatial quarters, and prices to match. Good location, though a bit far up into L'Eixample. Try to get a balcony room—the balconies are ornate and scenic. Singles 3500ptas, with bath 4300ptas; doubles 6000ptas, with bath 7100ptas. 7% IVA not included. Laundry 600ptas.

Hostal Girona, Girona, 24, 1st fl. (tel. 93 265 02 59). Located between C. Casp and C. Ausias Marc. M: Urquinaona. Carpeted hallways, large wooden doors, airy rooms with TVs, and affordable prices are Girona's comforts. It's on a tranquil tree-lined street and directly above a small university, so look forward to interaction with Catalan students. Singles 2500ptas; doubles 4500ptas, with shower 5500ptas, with full bath 6000ptas. Breakfast 200ptas.

GRÀCIA

In Gràcia, an area five to ten minutes on foot from M: Diagonal, locals outnumber travelers. Berlitz Spanish won't help in this quiet Catalan-dominated area. The accommodations listed here are small and well kept. Quaint neighborhood bars and *pastelerías* remain "undiscovered."

Pensión San Medín, C. Gran de Gràcia, 125 (tel. 93 217 30 68; fax 93 415 44 10). M: Fontana. You get a lot for your *peseta* here. Delicately embroidered curtains and paintings of fox hunts adorn this excellent family-run *pensión*. Each newly renovated room has fine furniture and a phone. Common room with TV. Singles 2500ptas, with bath 3500ptas; doubles 4500ptas, with bath 5800ptas. Visa, MC.

Hostal Bonavista, C. Bonavista, 21 (tel. 93 237 37 57). M: Diagonal. Walk toward the fountain at the end of Pg. Gràcia and make your first right; the *hostal* is just off the traffic circle. Well-kept rooms and a nice common *salón,* with a flashy TV. Singles 2200ptas; doubles 3300ptas, with bath 4300ptas. Showers 300ptas. Keys for entry 24hr. No reservations.

CAMPING

Although there is no camping in Barcelona, inter-city buses (200ptas) run to all the following locations in 20 to 45 minutes. Campsites are classified according to size and the number of services offered. For more information, contact the **Associació de Càmpings de Barcelona,** Gran Vía Corts Catalanes, 608 (tel. 93 412 59 55).

El Toro Bravo (tel. 93 637 34 62), 11km south of Barcelona, accessible by bus L95 and L94 (summer only) from Pl. Catalunya or Pl. Espanya. Laundry and supermarket. 650ptas per person, 463ptas per child, 700ptas per tent. 7% IVA not included. Reception daily 8am-1:30pm and 4:30-8pm. Open year-round. Visa, MC, AmEx.

Filipinas (tel. 93 658 28 95), 1km down the road from El Toro Bravo, accessible by bus L95. 630ptas per person, 463ptas per child, 700ptas per tent. Reception 24hr. Open year-round. Visa, MC, AmEx.

La Ballena Alegre (tel. 93 658 05 04), 1km from El Toro Bravo, 13km from Barcelona, accessible by buses L95 and L94 (summer only). 575ptas per person, 270ptas per child, 1375ptas per tent (without car). Reception 24hr. Open Feb.16-Dec. 14. Credit cards accepted.

Gavá, 15km south of Barcelona, has several campgrounds accessible by bus 95 from Pl. Universitat. **Albatros** (tel. 93 633 06 95) costs 520ptas per person, 380ptas per child, and 795ptas per tent. Reception daily 8am-midnight. Camping May-Sept. Services for the disabled. **Tortuga Ligera** (tel. 93 633 06 42) costs 518ptas per person, 378ptas per child, and 675ptas per tent. Reception daily 9am-10pm. Closed Dec. Both sites are near the Tortuga Ligera bus stop. **Tres Estrellas** (tel. 93 633 06 37) is one stop past Ballena Alegre. 588ptas per person, 470ptas per child, and 770ptas per tent. Reception 24hr. Open Mar.-Sept. Services for the disabled.

■ Food

In addition to numerous delectable *tapas* like *calamares picantes* (squid in spicy sauce), Barcelona offers such Catalan specialities as *merluza* (whitefish), *butifarra con judías blancas* (sausage with white beans), *berenjenas rellenas* (eggplant casserole), and *crema catalana* (similar to *crème brulée*). *Torrades* are a Catalan delight not to be missed, consisting of toasted bread rubbed with olive oil, garlic, and tomato.

For the cheapest meals, be on the lookout for 850 to 950ptas *menús* posted in the restaurants in the Barri Gòtic's side streets. Small, family-owned eateries a bit off the beaten track serve basic but satisfying dishes. Closer to the port, bars and cafes get more crowded and harried, whereas on Rbla. Catalunya leisurely *al fresco* meals are a good excuse for people-watching. Be aware that food options shrink drastically in August, when restauranteurs and bar owners close up shop and take their vacations. On Sundays year-round, most restaurants close down (Sunday is family day in Barcelona), and those few restaurants that do stay open attract flocks.

Consult the weekly *Guía del Ocio* (available at newsstands, 125ptas) for additional dining options. The *Guía* provides listings by specialty for hundreds of restaurants (many somewhat expensive) and also includes sections on *servicio a domicilio* (delivery), *para llevar* (take-out), *abiertos en domingo* (restaurants open Sundays), and *cenar de madrugada* (late-night dining).

BARCELONA

Groceries: La Boqueria, officially Mercat de Sant Josep, off Rbla. Sant Josep, 89, is Barcelona's best market, with fresh fish and produce in an all-steel modernist structure. Lowest prices around for fruit, cheese, and wine and enough spices to have precluded Columbus's notorious blunder. Open M-Sa 7am-8pm. **Supermarket Simago,** Las Ramblas, 113, stocks essentials. Open M-Sa 9am-9pm.

Fast Food, Spanish Style: PANS & Co., Rbla. Catalunya, 13 (tel. 93 412 45 67), near Gran Vía Corts Catalanes. Just one of many PANS franchises in Barcelona (others include an all-night branch at Maremagnum). It's decidedly mass-packaged, but prices are surprisingly low. *Bocadillos* (300-695ptas) and other deli-type food. Budget traveler's dream: *bocadillo* of the month, 195ptas. Hours vary by branch.

CIUTAT VELLA

El Raval

Students and workers congregate in the neighborhood west of Las Ramblas, in the type of eateries where Spaniards, Catalan or otherwise, feel most at home—a simple space, straightforward food, lots of people and noise, and unlimited bread and wine. **Calles Tallers** and **Sitges,** just one block off Rbla. Canaletes, overflow with inexpensive restaurants. Good Galician food is served off **Calle Lluna** and **Calle Joaquín Costa.** The shrinking red-light district begins roughly south of **Calle Hospital.**

Bar Restaurante Los Toreros, C. Xuclá, 3-5 (tel. 93 318 23 25), on a narrow alley between C. Fortuny and C. Carme, both off Las Ramblas. M: Catalunya. The floors, faded from red to brown, would no longer anger the bull, nor would the traditional Spanish food. Who could be angry when the 4-course *menú,* with excellent gazpacho, costs 875ptas (Sa 975ptas, Su with paella 1075ptas)? Popular *tapas* 250-600ptas. Open Tu-Sa 9am-midnight, Su 9am-5pm.

Restaurante Riera, C. Joaquín Costa, 30 (tel. 93 443 32 93). M: Liceu or Universitat. Off C. Carme coming from Liceu, or off Ronda de Sant Antoni coming from Universitat. The Riera family supplies a feast fit for a poor, hungry king. 3-course gorgefest plus dessert (750ptas) offered day and night. Or try the *merluza* 475ptas. Open Sept.-July Su-Th 1-4pm and 8-11:30pm, F 1-4pm.

Pla dels Angels, right across from MACBA (tel. 93 443 31 03). A delightful lunchtime *menú* (1300ptas) comes with a buffet selection of salads, pasta, a cheese course, and dessert (try the *miel y matá,* with sheep's cheese and honey). Eating outdoors brings less for more. Lasagna 800-875ptas. Open daily noon-4pm and 8-11:30pm.

Restaurante Pollo Rico, C. Sant Pau, 31 (tel. 93 441 31 84). Calle Sant Pau breaks directly off Las Ramblas one street down from C. Hospital. M: Liceu. Little ambiance, but you can take home your very own chicken (800ptas). Half chicken, fries, and bread 675ptas. Baked whole artichokes 150ptas. Afternoon *menú* 900ptas. Open Th-Tu 10am-midnight.

Bar Universitat de Barcelona, in a medieval courtyard inside the university, on Gran Via Corts Catalanes between Aribau and Balmes. M: Universitat. A lovely university student cafe with prices that you'll think at first are misprints. Don't order in English (how's your Catalan?), act nonchalant, and blend right in with the lively student crowd. Daily dish, like *fideua* (noodles with saffron and seafood, 100ptas when available), and a drink (beer 125ptas). *Bocadillos* 185ptas and up. Open daily, usually during daylight hours (depending seasonally on school sessions).

La Morera, Pl. Sant Augustí, 1 (tel. 93 318 75 55). M: Liceu. Take C. Hospital to Pl. Sant Augustí. A friendly establishment near La Boqueria that specializes in *comida del mercado* (fresh market food). Argentine and Catalan dishes 595-1000ptas. Afternoon *menú* 995ptas. Open M-Sa 1-3:30pm and 8:30-11:45pm.

Restaurante Garduña, C. Morera, 17-19 (tel. 93 302 43 23), inside the market La Boqueria. Simple restaurant serving fresh and well-priced daily produce. Typical Catalan fare in the midday *menú* (975ptas, weekends 1375ptas) and special of the day (1375ptas). *Bocadillos* 300-450ptas. Open M-Sa 1-4pm and 8pm-midnight.

Restaurante Can Lluís, C. Cera, 49 (tel. 93 441 11 87). M: San Antoni. Head down Ronda S. Pau from the metro; C. Cera will be the second side street on your left. A Barcelona mainstay for over 100 years, Can Lluís is a fine place to spend a little more for a memorable, authentic Catalan meal. The 3-course midday *menú* is good value at 950ptas; ordering a la carte by night brings more creative cuisine at higher prices. A bit out of the way, Can Lluís caters mainly to locals—the menu will put your Catalan skills to the test. Try the fried sardines or *caracoles* (sea snails). Open M-Sa 1:30-4pm and 8:30-11:30pm.

Restaurante Biocenter, C. Pintor Fortuny, 25 (tel. 93 301 45 83). M: Catalunya. Across the street from the store of the same name, off Las Ramblas. Bustling, serve-yourself vegetarian restaurant. *Menú* with unlimited soup and salad bar, vegetarian entree, and dessert 1500ptas. Open M-F 9am-noon and 1-5pm, Sa 1-5pm.

Raim D'or Can Maxim, C. Bonsuccés, 8 (tel. 93 302 02 34), off the right-hand side of Las Ramblas as you face the port. M: Catalunya. Hams hang in hoofed glory over the bar. Multilingual staff and menu, fresh fish from 475ptas, popular oily *torrades* (475-700ptas) and pizzas (650-925ptas). Midday *menú* 1000ptas. Open Oct.-Aug. M-Th 9am-5pm and 8pm-midnight, F-Sa 9am-5pm and 8pm-1am. Visa, MC, AmEx.

Barri Gòtic

The Barri Gòtic spans east of Las Ramblas and is confined by Pl. Catalunya to the north, Pg. Colom to the south, and Vía Laietana to the east. The interiors of corroding buildings are continually being disemboweled to furnish room for ever classier cafes and restaurants. *Barcelonenses* are proud of L'Eixample, but they cherish the Barri Gòtic, where one can find cheap, quality food in a familiar *barrio*.

Restaurante Bidasoa, C. Serra, 21 (tel. 93 318 10 63). M: Drassanes. Take 3rd left off C. Josep Anselm Clavé as you head from Las Ramblas. Locals greet the owner with hugs and kisses, and for good reason—40 years of practice have produced 43 permutations of soups, salads, and meat and fish items, all under 600ptas or so. Open Tu-Su noon-midnight, but no food 3:30-8pm. Closed Aug.

La Fonda, C. Escudellers, 10 (tel. 93 301 75 15). M: Drassanes or Liceu. Calle. Escudellers stems into Barri Gòtic from Las Ramblas between Liceu and Drassanes. Waiting in line outside is somewhat painful, only because large windows let you watch patrons inside savoring Catalan cuisine with fancy tablecloth-and-crystal presentation. Try to snag a chair on the balcony and watch the tastefully presented meals (deceptively cheap at 390-995ptas plus 7% IVA) whisk by. Elaborate desserts. Open daily 1-3:30pm and 8:30-11:30pm. Visa, MC, AmEx.

Els Quatre Gats, C. Montsió, 3 (tel. 93 302 41 40). M: Catalunya. From the metro, go down Av. Portal de L'Angel and take the 2nd left. Modernista-designed hangout of Picasso, who designed the famous menu (on display at Museu Picasso). Lunchtime *menú* (1500ptas)—you'd be better off sampling from their fine beerlist. (300-600ptas), accompanied by a *tapa* or two (150-550ptas). Entrees around 2000ptas. Live music 9pm-1am. Open M-Sa 8am-2am, Su 5pm-2am. Visa, MC, AmEx.

Can Conesa, C. Llibreteria, 1 (tel. 310 13 94), on the corner of Pl. Sant Jaume. Classic little nook distinguishes itself with ultra-low prices and crispy grilled *bocadillos* (250-425ptas). Speedy service and a young local crowd. Cheap pizza 290-390ptas. Open M-Sa 8am-9:30pm. Closed first half of Aug.

Les Quinze Nits, Pl. Reial, 6 (tel. 93 317 30 75). Streams of locals and foreigners alike wait in line every night to try this Catalan restaurant's contemporary and traditional dishes. Don't despair—the line moves quickly and it's surprisingly affordable. *Menú* 950ptas. Braised rabbit 690ptas, octopus with onions and mushrooms 690ptas. Entrees 500-1200ptas. Open daily 1-3:45pm and 8:30-11:30pm.

El Gran Café, Avinyó, 9 (tel. 93 318 79 86). Posh turn-of-the-century interior. Fine wine cellar, delicious paella (1350ptas per person) and French-Catalan dishes (800-1900ptas). Not cheap, but a Barcelona mainstay. At lunchtime, *menú rapido* 1200ptas. Open M-Sa 1-4pm and 9-11:30pm. Visa, MC, AmEx.

Restaurant Pitarra, C. Avinyó, 56 (tel. 93 301 16 47). M: Drassanes. Turn left down C. Clavé at the end of Las Ramblas and take the 3rd left after a church. In the former home of great Catalan poet-dramatist Pitarra, art lives on in epic dishes concocted by Queen Sofía's former chef Señor Marc. The veal with peppers is 995ptas deliciously spent. Paella 1300ptas. *Vino de la casa* 750ptas. Open M-Sa 1-4pm and 8:30-11pm. Visa, MC, AmEx.

El Gallo Kiriko, C. Avinyó, 19 (tel. 412 48 38). M: Liceu. Walk down C. Ferrán, and it's the 4th right. Fill up on big plates of Pakistani rice and couscous dishes in the back room, where, out of nowhere, a 4th-century stone wall takes you back to Barcelona's Roman origins. Most dishes under 500ptas, all under 750ptas. Several **vegetarian options.** 5% discount for ISIC holders. Open daily noon-1am. Visa, MC.

Restaurante Self Naturista, C. Santa Ana, 11-17 (tel. 93 318 23 88). M: Catalunya. Two blocks down Las Ramblas and to the left. Self-service **vegetarian cafeteria** feels like fast food. Desserts and salads spill over the counter. Variety of breads and veggie dishes, most under 660ptas; lunch *menú* 910ptas. Open M-Sa 11:30am-10pm.

Bar Restaurante Cervantes, C. Cervantes, 7 (tel. 93 317 33 84), 2 blocks down C. Avinyó off C. Ferran. M: Jaume I (L4). Bustling waitstaff feverishly weaves through a prattling administrative- and intellectual-looking lunchtime crowd. New artist is exhibited on the walls each month. Scrumptious chicken croquettes or a gigantic plate of macaroons (275ptas). Lunch *menú* 1000ptas. Open M-F 7:30am-8pm.

Bar Restaurant La Poste, Gignes, 23 (tel. 93 315 15 04). M: Drassanes. Appropriately right near the post office, this place is where the downtown crowd comes to gorge on the plentiful 900ptas *menú* (3 courses plus dessert, bread, and drink). A surprisingly elegant setting, with tablecloths and crystal, for such an of-the-people establishment. Open M-F noon-4:30pm and 8:30-11:30pm, Sa-Su noon-4:30pm.

Around Plaza del Pí

Some of the liveliest between-meal hangouts cluster around Església Santa María del Pí. Relax at the *terrazas* for drinks and ice cream. From Las Ramblas, enter Llano de la Boqueria and take a left at the Banco Central Hispano onto C. Cardenal Casanyes, leading into Pl. Pí. From El Corte Inglés, follow Portal de l'Angel down to the end, veer right onto Portaferrissa, and take the first left at C. Pí.

Irati, C. Cardenal Casanyes, 17 (tel. 93 302 30 84). An excellent Basque *tapas* bar that attracts droves of hungry *tapas*-seekers. Bartenders pour *sidra* (cider) with the bottle 3 ft. above the glass—to rid the cider of oxygen—and parade new platters of treats every 5min. Specialties include *anchoa rellena* (anchovies stuffed with ham and cheese) and *turutu* (fried chicken, bacon, ham, and cheese). All *tapas* 130ptas (they count your toothpicks when you're done). Credit cards accepted. Open Tu-Sa noon-midnight, Su noon-5pm, but *tapas* only noon-3pm and 7-11pm.

Osterhase, Pl. Pí, 5 (tel. 93 412 58 34). *Gelati* and drinks on the *terraza* by the church. Ice cream 225-600ptas. Open daily 8:30am-11pm.

Café de Ciutat Vella, Carrer del Pí, 5 (tel. 93 302 10 21). Mellow student hangout plays popular music, pleasingly low on the decibels. A variety of hot and cold coffee concoctions (110-475ptas). *Picardía* (coffee with condensed milk and whiskey) 250ptas. Pastries from 100ptas. Open M-F 8am-9pm, Sa 9am-9pm.

La Ribera

East of La Laietana and lower in altitude than the Barri Gòtic is La Ribera, home to the Museu Picasso and art galleries. Families of the fishing industry once settled around Esglesia Santa Maria del Mar, the religious sponsor of fisherman. Today, some of the city's greatest art showcases and food bargains are found in the recesses of La Ribera.

Nou Celler, C. Princesa, 16 (tel. 93 310 47 73). M: Jaume I. From the Metro, cross Vía Laietana from Pl. Angel. Calle Jaume becomes C. Princesa. Maintains a tavern atmosphere without touristy tackiness. Eclectic list of *platos de día* and authentic Catalan specialties. *Menú* 1000ptas. Sandwiches 250-400ptas. Open M-F 8am-midnight, Su 8am-4pm. Closed June 15-July 15. Credit cards accepted.

Lluna Plena, C. Montcada, 2 (tel. 93 310 54 29), same street as Museu Picasso. M: Jaume I. A bit of a splurge for dinner, but afternoon *menú* 1000ptas. Looks and smells like an old brick smokehouse. Assorted Catalan pâtés and *quesos* 700-900ptas. Open Tu-Sa 1-4pm and 8-11:30pm, Su 1-4pm. Closed Aug.

Nice-Café Milena, Vía Laietana, 6 (tel. 93 319 23 61), at the corner of Vía Laietana and C. Joan Hassan. M: Jaume I. Elegant restaurant with tiled bar and a varied menu. Moderately priced Catalan dishes. Midday *menú* is a deal at 850ptas, 1395ptas on weekends. Fresh paella and *arroces* 900-1200ptas. Pizzas 625-925ptas. Open daily 7:30am-11pm, sometimes until midnight or later.

La Habana Vieja, C. Baños Viejos 2 (tel. 93 319 10 97). Baños Viejos is parallel to C. Montcada. Feast on delicious Cuban cuisine in a small but mighty wooden-beamed house. *Arroz cubano* 500-800ptas; *carnes* 1300-1600ptas; *platanos fritos* 400-600ptas. Tempting papaya, guava, and coconut desserts. Open M-Sa 6pm-1am.

Peimong, C. Templarios 6-10 (tel. 93 318 28 73). From Pl. Sant Jaume, take C. Ciutat; C. Templaris is the 2nd right. In the mood for meat? Generous portions of hen, goat, veal, duck, and fish Peruvian-style, all under 750ptas. Vegetarians beware—you won't find anything here. Open Tu-Su 1-5pm and 8pm-midnight.

L'Eixample

When dining uptown, expect restaurants to be a bit more expensive. Cheaper *bocata* fare can be found in area *patisserías,* along with croissants and desserts.

ba-ba-reeba, Pg. Gràcia, 28 (tel. 93 301 43 02 or 93 302 21 29). M: Pg. Gràcia. Offers a wide selection of *tapas* and Catalonian *pa* (bread). Ba-ba is chi-chi, but not too expensive. So many *tapas,* so little time (most under 500ptas). Outdoor dining on the *passeig* available. Open daily 8am-2pm.

Comme-Bio, Gran Vía de les Corts Catalanes, 603 (tel. 93 301 03 76), just off Rambla Catalunya. M: Catalunya. Groceries in front, food and drink in back. The all-veggie menu is quite creative: specialties include spring rolls of spinach with Roquefort (950ptas) and *zumo de zanahorias* (carrot juice, 325ptas). Salads 550-995ptas. Pastas around 1200ptas and up. Pizzas 825-975ptas. You pay for all the TLC those veggies get. Open M-Sa 9am-midnight, Su noon-midnight. Credit cards accepted.

El Cafe de Internet, Gran Vía de les Corts Catalanes, 656. See **Practical Information,** p. 306.

GRÀCIA

You know you are in mellow Gràcia when you hear fellow diners speaking Catalan instead of Spanish, English, French, or German. The food is likewise authentic.

Taverna El Glop, C. Sant Lluís, 24 (tel. 93 213 70 58). Near the Joanic Metro stop off C. Escorial. This 2-story rustic tavern has become super-popular with the locals for its *chorizo* (Spanish sausage), cooked over an open flame. Carbo-load on gigantic *torradas.* Open Oct.-Aug. Tu-Su 1-4pm and 8pm-1am. If there's a long line (as there often is after 10pm), let the staff direct you to **Taverna El Nou Glop,** C. Montmary, 49 (tel. 93 219 70 59), for an equally gloppy experience. Open M 1-4pm and 8pm-1am, W-Sa 8pm-1am, Su 1-4pm.

El Tastavins, C. Ramon y Cajal (tel. 93 213 60 31), near Pl. Sol. M: Joanic. Admire work by local artists (and caricatures of the owners) while enjoying Catalan mainstays. Afternoon *menú* 850ptas. Open Tu-Sa 9:30am-5pm and 8:30pm-1am, Su 12:30-5pm.

Can Suñé, C. Mozart, 20 (tel. 93 218 54 86). M: Diagonal. Take C. Goya off C. Gran de Gràcia, then take the 2nd right. A petite, family-run restaurant with marble tables and ceiling fans. Neighbors gather to spin yarns and eat a different meal each day (including wine and dessert, available at night, too; M-Sa 875ptas, Su 975ptas). Fried calamares (700ptas). Open Tu-Su 1pm-midnight.

Xavi Petit, C. Bonavista, 2 (tel. 93 237 88 26), off C. Gran de Gràcia. M: Diagonal (L3, L5). Crêpes as a meal or just dessert start around 450-500ptas. Crêpe-less afternoon *menú* 950ptas. Open M-F 7am-midnight, Sa-Su 6pm-midnight.

■ Sights

Barcelona's Modernista treasures stand above all else—the Ruta del Modernisme passes are the best way to go (see below and **Marvelous Modernisme,** p. 319). In terms of neighborhoods, Las Ramblas, everyone's favorite street, and the lovely Barri Gòtic are the traditional tourist areas, but don't neglect other vibrant neighborhoods outside the Ciutat Vella. The wide avenues of L'Eixample, the Gaudí delights in Parc Güell, the panoramic city views from Montjuïc and Tibidabo, and the dramatic Port Olimpíc and harborside areas each have plenty to offer.

Ruta del Modernisme

Barcelona's hyper-organized tourism administration has designed a route that covers Modernista architecture all over the city. Although largely Gaudí-dominated, it features a few other prominent Modernista architects as well. **Ruta del Modernisme passes** (1530ptas, students 900ptas) are an excellent deal and allow privileged and economical access to Barcelona's architectural masterpieces. The pass, good for a month, allows one entrance to each of Casa Batlló, Casa Amatller, Casa Lleó Morera (inaccessible without pass), Palau Güell, Templo La Sagrada Familia, Casa Milà, Palau de la Música, Casa-Museu Gaudí, Fundació Antoni Tàpies, and the Museu d'Art Modern. Passes are sold in the **Palau Güell,** the first stop on the Modernista tour (see below), or at **Casa Lleó Morera** on Pg. Grácia (see p. 319). During the summer, the easiest—if least creative—way to take in the sights is to hop on the air-conditioned **Bus Turístic** (see p. 303). There is also a special four-hour Gaudí tour, given by the Centre Cultural Caixa Catalunya (tel. 93 484 89 09, fax 93 484 88 40) and running daily at 10am and 3pm. The tours start from **La Pedrera** (see p. 320), and tickets can be bought then and there (a hefty 5000ptas per person).

The best way to approach this macro-museum of Catalan architecture is with two handy pamphlet guides available free at the tourist office, *Discovering Modernist Art in Catalonia* and *Gaudí.* When you buy a pass, you will be furnished with a good map that indicates all 50 stops on the tour. Although there are many fascinating Modernista sights, the following thirteen rank, in our humble opinion, as highlights: **Palau Güell**; **Els Quatre Gats** (see **Food,** p. 313); **Palau de la Música Catalana** (see p. 318); **Casa Calvet** (if you can peek in); the three houses along the **Manzana de Discordia** (see p. 319); the amazing **Casa Milà (La Pedrera);** the enormous **Templo de la Sagrada Familia** (see p. 320); the fairytale **Parque Güell** and its **Casa Museo Gaudí** (see p. 321); **Casa Vicens** (see p. 321); and the **Museo de Arte Moderno (see Museums,** p. 324). Due partly to the fact that a number of these sights can only be seen by hour-long guided tours, visiting all of them together would be an exhausting day. It's better to spread it over two days; if you have even more time, though, you could spend an entire day just hanging out in the fabulous Parc Güell alone.

CIUTAT VELLA

Las Ramblas

The pedestrian-only median strip of Las Ramblas is a veritable urban carnival: street performers dance flamenco, fortune-tellers survey palms, human statues shift poses for a small fee, and tourists hoist their packs. The wide, tree-lined boulevard dubbed "Las Ramblas" actually comprises five distinct segments (**Canaletes, Estudis, Sant Josep, Capuxtins,** and **Santa Monica**). The boulevard begins at Pl. Catalunya and continues down to the towering **statue of Columbus.** A portward journey begins at the **Font de Canaletes** (more a pump than a fountain), where visitors who wish to return someday to Barcelona traditionally sample the water.

The upper part of Las Ramblas is dubbed "Rambla de las Flores" for the numerous flower vendors that inhabit it. Halfway down Las Ramblas toward the port, coming from Pl. Catalunya, **Joan Miró's pavement mosaic** brightens Pl. Boqueria. The opera house, **Gran Teatre del Liceu,** Las Ramblas, 61, lies a few feet away to the right, on the corner of C. Sant Pau. On opening night here in 1892, an anarchist launched two bombs into the crowd of aristocrats, killing 22 and wounding many. After executing five innocents for the crime, authorities finally found the real culprit, who cried, *"¡Viva la anarquía!"* before being hanged. The Teatre was one of Europe's leading stages, having nurtured the likes of José Carreras. Ravaged by a fire in its latest bout with disaster on January 31, 1994, the Teatre will hopefully reopen sometime in 1999 (see **Music,** p. 328). The outdoor tables at Cafe de l'Opera, across from the Teatre, is a prime spot for some serious people-watching (see **Entertainment,** p. 326).

At the far end of C. Sant Pau stands Barcelona's oldest Romanesque church, the 10th-century **Església de Sant Pau** (tel. 93 441 00 01), in stark contrast to its setting

---

Chris-Crossed Columbus

The majestic **Monument to Columbus** (Colom in Catalan) bridges Las Ramblas with Barcelona's busy port. When Renaixença enthusiasts "rediscovered" the region's role in the discovery of the Americas, they convinced themselves that Colom was Catalan. Today, the knowledge that Colom was actually Genoese and that Columbus proudly points toward Libya, not the Americas, detracts from statue's historical veracity. But contemporary and past nationalists agree that where Colom is pointing is not as important as where he is not pointing: Castile. (From Robert Hughes, *Barcelona*, 1992)

---

in the former red-light district, El Raval. *(Visiting hours M-F 5-8pm.)* The church is noted for its ornate cloister with lobed arches, dating from the 11th and 12th centuries.

Antoni Gaudí's **Palau Güell,** C. Nou de la Rambla, 3-5 (tel. 93 317 39 74), two streets down from Teatre Liceu, has reopened its doors. *(Open M-Sa 10am-2pm and 4-8pm. 300ptas, students 150ptas.)* It has the most spectacular Gaudí interior in Barcelona, mixing a haunted house aesthetic with Art Nouveau. The rooftop chimneys brightly display Gaudí's first use of the *trencadís,* the covering of surfaces with irregular shards of ceramic or glass. **Plaça Reial,** on the other side of Las Ramblas, is patrolled by police cars, but still crawls with pickpockets during the day and is worse at night.

At the port end of Las Ramblas, the **Monument a Colom,** Portal de la Pau (tel. 93 302 52 24), towers above the city. Spotlights turn the statue into a firebrand at night. *(Elevator to the top open daily June-Sept. 9am-8:30pm; Oct.-Mar. M-F 10am-1:30pm and 3:30-6:30pm, Sa-Su 10am-6:30pm; Apr.-May 10am-2pm and 3:30-7:30pm, Sa-Su 10am-7:30pm. 250ptas, children 150ptas.)* **Las Golondrinas** (tel. 93 442 31 06) ferries steam around Montjuïc to **Rompeolas** and **Port Vell** (30min., departs high-season daily every 20min. 11am-8:30pm; off-season M-F 11am, noon, and 1pm, Sa-Su every 30min., 11am-5pm, 500ptas). A longer excursion includes a tour of **Port Olímpic** (2hr., high-season 4 per day 11am-6pm; off-season 3 per day 11am-4:30pm; round-trip 1250ptas). Tourists sail from Portal de la Pau, in front of the Monument a Colom.

Barcelona's drive to refurbish its seafront has not only resulted in **Vila Olímpica,** but also in the amplification of **Port Vell,** the port complex and waterfront area by Pg. Colom. After moving the coastal road underground, the city opened **Moll de la Fusta,** a wide pedestrian zone that leads down to the docks past scenic, pricey restaurant-cafes and the **Museu de la Historia de Catalunya** (see **Museums,** p. 324). The wavy, modern bridge **Rambla de Mar** links Moll de la Fusta with the **Maremagnum** mall (see **Shopping,** p. 330). The cobblestone docks are ideal for an evening stroll.

Barri Gòtic

Carrer de la Pietat and **Carrer del Paradis** have preserved their medieval charm; meanwhile, the tourist economy has infused a liveliness—and livelihood—it would otherwise lack. The handsome **Plaça de Sant Jaume,** Barcelona's political center since Roman times, took its present form in 1823. It is dominated by two of Catalunya's most important buildings: the **Palau de la Generalitat** (seat of Catalunya's autonomous government) and the **Ajuntament,** the Spanish government's seat of power. *(Call 93 402 73 64 or 93 402 73 00 to visit. Open Sa-Su 10am-2pm. Free.)* Fittingly, the two proud buildings stare each other down across the *plaça.*

Past the Generalitat and up C. Bisbe is **Plaça de la Seu** and the jagged spires of the 14th-century Gothic **Església Catedral de la Santa Creu.** *(Cathedral open M-F 8am-1:30pm and 4-7:30pm, Sa-Su 8am-1:30pm and 5-7:30pm. Cloister open M-F 9am-1:15pm and 4-7pm, Sa-Su 9am-1:15pm and 5-7pm. Free. Elevator to the rooftop open M-F 9:30am-12:30pm and 4-6:30pm, Sa-Su 9:30am-12:30pm. 200ptas.)* The church was begun in 1298, but the facade was not completed until the 1880s, although you wouldn't know it from looking at it. It looks especially lovely at night when lit up. A guard will let you enter the cathedral's remarkable choral chamber *(coro)* for 125ptas. Barcelona's patron saint and Christian martyr Santa Euália naps below the altar in the church **crypt.** The cathedral's lovely **cloister** has magnolias growing in the middle and geese waddling around the periphery.

Palaces and museums congregate on the opposite side of the Església Catedral, on C. Comtes. The former home of the royal family, **Palau Reial** (Royal Palace), is the pearl of the *plaça*. Inside, the **Museu Frederic Marès** and the **Museu d'Historia de la Ciutat** hold court. The royal palace can be visited with admission to the history museum (see **Museums**, p. 324). Also in the Barri Gòtic is the lively **Plaça del Pi** and the picturesque old **Església del Pi**, just off Ramblas (follow Cardenal Casañas, which branches off from Las Ramblas at the same place as C. Boqueria does).

Barri de la Ribera

Felipe V demolished most of La Ribera to clear space for the Ciutadela in the 18th century. The remaining neighborhood has since evolved into the Ciutat Vella's bohemian nucleus. Ribera's ismithian streets converge at the foot of the 14th-century Gothic **Església Santa María del Mar's** (tel. 93 310 23 90) octagonal towers. *(Open M-Sa 9am-1:30pm and 4:30-8pm, Su 9am-2pm and 5-8:30pm.)* As its name suggests, the church once stood on the coastline of the Mediterranean, before Barceloneta's mud flats were solidified and used as foundation. **Carrer de Montcada,** beginning behind the church, exemplifies Barcelona's local reputation as *"la ciudad del diseño"* (the city of design). Museums, art galleries, art workshops, and Baroque palaces that once housed Barcelona's 16th-century bureaucrats pack its two blocks of narrow space. The **Museu Picasso** now stands in the stead of the Palau de Agüilar (see **Museums**, p. 323). **Galeria Maeght** (#26), one of several prestigious art galleries on the block, was once the manor of a medieval aristocrat (see **Art Galleries**, p. 324).

Modernista architect Lluís Domènech i Montaner designed the fabulous **Palau de la Música Catalana,** C. Sant Francesc de Paula, 2 (tel. 93 268 10 00), up Vía Laietana near the intersection of C. Ionqueres. *(For performance info, see **Music,** p. 328. Open M-F 10am-9pm. Closed Aug. 500ptas. Mandatory tours normally depart M-F 2 and 3pm, Sa every hr. 10am-1pm; more days in summer.)* The music hall is festooned with stained-glass cupolas, flowing marble reliefs, *preciosa* woodwork, and colorful ceramic mosaics.

PARC DE LA CIUTADELLA AND VILA OLÍMPICA

Barcelona's military resistance to the Bourbon monarchy in the early 18th century convinced Felipe V to quarantine Barcelona's influential citizens in the Ciutadella, a large citadel on what is now Pg. Picasso. The city razed the fortress in 1868 and replaced it with the peaceful promenades of **Parc de la Ciutadella.** Host of the 1888 Universal Exposition, the park now harbors several museums, well-labeled horticulture, the wacky **Cascada** fountains, a **pond,** and a zoo. *(Rowboat rental 10am-7pm. 250ptas per person per 30min.)* Buildings of note include Domènech i Montaner's Modernista **Castell dels Tres Dragons** (now **Museu de Zoología**) and Josep Amergós's **Hivernacle.** Expo '88 also inspired the small Arc de Triomf, just across Pg. Pujades from the park. Little Snowflake *(Copito de Nieve)*, the world's only albino gorilla behind bars, vegetates in the **Parc Zoològic** (tel. 93 221 25 06), on the south end of the park. *(Open daily in summer 9:30am-7:30pm; in winter 10am-5pm. 1400ptas.)* On Pl. Armes is the **Museu d'Art Modern** (see p. 324).

The **Vila Olímpica,** beyond the east side of the zoo, was built from the ground up (on top of what was once a poor neighborhood) to house 15,000 athletes and entertain millions of tourists for the 25th Summer Olympiad in 1992. Now a yuppie village, the area is home to several public parks, a shopping center, offices, and in-line skate rental. Toward the Mediterranean, **Port Olímpic** flaunts twin towers, a huge fish-inspired sculpture, a long pier, and waves of touristy and upscale bars and restaurants indoors and out. In the area called **Barceloneta,** beaches—not exactly Sitges-quality but decent for a day in the sun—stretch out from the port. Barcelona's quaint old fishing quarter stretches lazily along the waterfront, although pricey seafood restaurants are now moving into what many consider an up-and-coming neighborhood.

L'EIXAMPLE

The *Renaixença* of Catalan culture and the growth of Barcelona during the 19th century pushed the city past its medieval walls and into ordered modernity. Ildefons Cerdà, a Catalan architect, drew up a plan with a comprehensible aerial view: a geometric grid of squares, softened by the cropped corners of streets forming octagonal intersections. Cerdà's plan attempted to relieve the stress that had festered in the overcrowded Barri Gòtic. Wide avenues and diagonal corners were intended to ease traffic flow. The original plan also called for three-sided city blocks that facilitated air circulation and imitated Catalan country-side *massas* (neighborhoods). Unfortunately, virtually every block was immediately enclosed by a fourth wall, thus sullying the genius of Cerdà's original design. But the **Eixample** (pronounced uh-SHOMP-luh) did give rise to other, more fantastic designs (see **Marvelous Modernisme**).

Marvelous Modernisme

In the late 19th and early 20th centuries, Barcelona's flourishing bourgeoisie commissioned a new class of architects to build their houses, reshaping the face of the Eixample neighborhood with Modernista architecture that employed revolutionary shapes, materials, and spaces to reflect the signs and symbols of Catalunya. Antoni Gaudí's serpentine rooftops, warrior-like chimneys, and skeletal facades are perhaps the most famous examples of this new style, *Modernisme* (often described as a Catalan version of Art Nouveau). A staunch nationalist, Gaudí incorporated in his organic architecture a vast array of Catalan symbols and myths. Gaudí designed every feature of his buildings, down to the undulating furniture, colorful ceramic mosaics, and elaborate light fixtures that fill his boisterous buildings. Even his methods were unconventional; Gaudí designed the vault of the Colònia Güell by hanging sand bags from a wire model of the ceiling, the inversion of which was perfectly balanced against structural stress. Although most of Gaudí's creations seem fantastical upon first glance, many, such as the attic of La Pedrera, which regulates heat with its vaulted ceilings, are architectural breakthroughs that have since been imitated only by advanced computer technology. Fellow Modernista luminaries include **Luis Domènech i Montaner**, noted for his profusely decorated surfaces, and **Josep Puig i Cadafalch**, who developed an antiquarian style uniting local and foreign traditions. For info on the **Ruta del Modernisme** and the practicalities of visiting these architectural gems, see p. 316.

Manzana de la Discordia

A short walk from Pl. Catalunya, the odd-numbered side of Pg. Gràcia between Aragó and Consell de Cent is popularly known as **la manzana de la discordia** (block of discord), referring to the aesthetic competition of the buildings on the block. The block offers a little overview of the peak of the Modernista movement. The bottom two floors of the facade of **Casa Lleó i Morera,** by Domènech i Montaner, were destroyed to house a store, but the upper floors sprout flowers and winged monsters. You can buy the **Ruta del Modernisme pass** here and take a guided tour. Puig i Cadafalch opted for a geometric, Moorish-influenced pattern on the facade of **Casa Amatller** at #41. Gaudí's balconies ripple and tiles sparkle in blue-purple glory on **Casa Batlló,** #43. The rooftop is supposedly a scaly representation of Catalunya's patron Sant Jordi slaying a dragon (the chimney plays the lance). Although the central hallway and blue-tiled stairway are sometimes open to the public, only the privileged holders of the Ruta de Modernisme pass can enter the main apartment. **Fundació Antoni Tàpies,** designed by Domènech, is around the corner from *la manzana.* The **Museu de la Música** is nearby on Av. Diagonal, 373 (see **Museums,** p. 322), and **Fundació la Caxia** in **Casa Macaya** awaits down the street on Pg. Sant Joan. Macaya provides a rare opportunity to enter one of Puig i Cadafalch's most famous buildings.

Casa Milà (La Pedrera)

Many Modernisme buffs argue that the spectacular **Casa Milà** apartment building, popularly known as **La Pedrera** (Stone Quarry), Pg. Gràcia, 92 (tel. 93 484 59 95), is Gaudí's most refined works. *(Open daily 10am-8pm. One guided tour departs per day: M-F 6pm, Sa-Su 11am. 500ptas, students 300 ptas—or better, buy your Ruta del Modernisme multipass.)* The entrance to this undulating mass of granite is around the corner, on C. Provença. Note the intricate ironwork around the balconies and the irregularity of the front gate's egg-shaped window panes. The roof sprouts chimneys resembling armored soldiers, one of which is decorated with broken champagne bottles. Rooftop tours provide a closer look at these Prussian helmets, spiral chimneys inspired by the helmets worn in Wagner's operas. The winding brick attic (recently restored along with the rooftop in a multi-million-*peseta* project) has been transformed into the **Espai Gaudí,** a multimedia presentation of Gaudí's life and works.

Sagrada Familia

Only Gaudí's genius could draw thousands of tourists to a half-finished church. The architect himself estimated that the **Temple Expiadori de la Sagrada Familia** (tel. 93 455 02 47), on C. Marinara between C. Mallorca and C. Provença (M: Sagrada Familia), would take 200 years to complete. *(Open Sept. and Mar. 9am-7pm; Jan.-Feb. and Oct.-Dec. 9am-6pm; Apr.-Aug. 9am-8pm. Guided visits 4pm and 5:30pm. Admission to church and museum 800ptas. Elevator 200ptas.)* For 43 years, Gaudí obsessed over the Sagrada Familia, living in the complex for his last eleven until, in 1926, virtually forgotten by the public, he was run over by a trolley and died. Since then, construction has progressed erratically and with tremendous controversy. A furor has arisen over recent additions, such as sculptor Josep Subirach's Passion Facade on C. Sardenya (the first facade you see as you enter), which some argue doesn't flow with the structure. Of the church's three proposed facades, only the first (believe it or not, one of the smaller ones), the nativity facade, was finished under Gaudí. Elevators and a maze of vertiginous staircases lead to its towers and bridges. The **museum** displays a model of the completed structure and various artifacts relating to its construction.

MONTJUÏC

Throughout Barcelona's history, whoever controlled Montjuïc (hill of the Jews) ruled the city. Dozens of despotic rulers have modified the **fortress,** built atop the ancient Jewish cemetery; Franco made it one of his "interrogation" headquarters. Somewhere deep in the recesses of the structure, his *beneméritos* ("honorable ones," a.k.a. the Guardia Civil) shot Catalunya's former president, Lluís Companys, in 1941. Only in 1960 did Franco return the fortress to the city to be used for recreational purposes. This act was commemorated with a huge stone monument expressing Barcelona's thanks, a reminder of forced gratitude (it's visible from the castle battlements). Since reacquiring the mountain, Barcelona quickly made it an Olympically popular attraction. To get to **Parc de Montjuïc,** take the metro to Pl. Espanya (M: Espanya) and catch bus #61 either at Av. Reina María Cristina (flanked by two large brick towers) or along the way as it heads up the hill (departs every 10min.). The scenic outdoor escalators (installed for the Olympics) in front of the Palau Nacional.

Palau Nacional and Poble Espanyol

The newly reopened **Fonts Luminoses** (Illuminated Fountains), dominated by the huge central **Font Mágica** (Magic Fountain), are visible from Pl. Espanya up Av. Reina María Cristina. They are employed in an audio-visual show given every night at 10pm that illuminates the whole mountainside and the **Palau Nacional,** located directly behind the fountains. The palace was designed in the "international style" by German architect Pavelló Mies van der Rohe as his country's 1929 Expo pavilion. Now it houses the **Museu Nacional d'Art de Catalunya** (see p. 323), which has an exquisite Romanesque and Gothic art collection. Just below the hillside to the left when facing the palace lies the intriguing **Museums of Archaeology** (see p. 324). To your right when facing Palau Nacional, is **Poble Espanyol** (tel. 93 325 78 66), a "town" of replicas of famous buildings and sights from every region of Spain. *(Open Su 9am-midnight, M 9am-8pm, Tu-Th 9am-2am, F-Sa 9am-4am. 500ptas, 1900ptas per family, 1000ptas nightly.)* While this pseudo-town is great in theory, it boils down to an artificial village with a souvenir bazaar, several mediocre restaurants, and a few discos.

Olympic Area and Upper Montjuïc

In 1929, Barcelona inaugurated the **Estadi Olímpic de Montjuïc** (tel. 93 426 20 89) in its bid for the 1932 Olympic games. Over 50 years later, Catalan architects Federic Correa and Alfons Milà, who were also responsible for the overall design of the **Anella Olímpica** (Olympic Ring) esplanade, renovated the shell with the help of Italian architect Vittorio Gregotti. *(Open daily in summer 10am-8pm; in winter 10am-6pm. Free.)* Designed by Japanese architect Arata Isozaki, the **Palau d'Esports Sant Jordi** (tel. 93 426 20 89) is the most technologically sophisticated of the Olympic structures. *(You must call in advance to visit.)* You can also swim in the Olympic pools for a reasonable fee (see p. 330). The **Galeria Olímpica** (tel. 93 426 06 60), at the south end of the stadium, also evokes Olympic memories. *(Open July-Sept. Tu-Sa 10am-2pm and 4-8pm, Su 10am-2pm; Oct.-Mar. Tu-F 10am-1pm and 4-6pm, Su 10am-2pm; Apr.-June M-Sa 10am-2pm and 4-7pm, Su 10am-2pm. 390ptas, students 340ptas.)* About 100m down the road from the stadiums is the unique **Fundació Miró** (see **Museums,** p. 322).

Farther along Av. Miramar is the rightfully popular **Parc d'Atraccions** (amusement park; tel. 93 441 70 24). *(Open in summer Tu-F 5:30-11:15pm, Sa-Su 11:30am-11:15pm; 700ptas; in winter Sa-Su and holidays 11:30am-10pm; 2000ptas with unlimited rides, except Calle de Terror, which costs 700ptas.)* To get there from the Fundació Miró, walk down Av. Miramar and take the **teleferic** (cable car; tel. 93 443 08 59) halfway up (departs daily 11:30am-9:30pm; off-season Sa-Su 11am-2:45pm and 4-7:30pm; 400ptas, round-trip 600ptas). To get there from Barcelona, take the **funicular** (tel. 93 412 00 00) from Pl. Raquel Meller (M: Parallel) to Av. Miramar, where you can hop on the *teleferic.* (departs daily every 10min. 11am-10pm; off-season every 10min. 10:45am-8pm; 200ptas, round-trip 300ptas). Uphill, at the highest *teleferic* stop, the historically rich **Castell de Montjuïc** guards over the port with a large armaments display.

GRÀCIA

Located just beyond the Eixample (M: Fontana or Lesseps), lovely, little-visited Gràcia is more of a living, breathing neighborhood than most of the stops on Barcelona's tourist conga line. It charms as it confuses, with narrow alleys and numerous plazas. The **Torre del Reloj** (Clocktower), on popular **Plaça Rius i Taulet,** is an emblem of the Revolution of 1868. **Plaça del Diamant,** on nearby C. Astúries, was made famous by Mercè Rodoreda's eponymous novel. Gràcia's best is **Plaça del Sol,** to which local youths swarm each night. Cafes and bars skirt its edge, and the air is one of vitality and activism. Protest graffiti, signs, and banners touching on issues from Catalan independence to the Zapatista uprising in Chiapas fill the streets and plazas. Cruise the streets coming off **Gran de Gràcia,** as well as **Plaça del Sol,** for nighttime diversions. Gran de Gràcia eventually leads to **Plaça de Lesseps.**

Modernisme brushed Gràcia as well. One of Gaudí's youthful experiments, **Casa Vicens,** C. Carolines, 24-26, may remind you of the house that Hansel and Gretel stumbled upon. *(The interior is closed to the public, at least for now.)* The *casa* illustrates the colorful influence of Arabic architecture and a rigidness of angles that is uncharacteristic of Gaudí's later works.

PARC GÜELL

Like all Barcelona city parks, open May-Aug. 10am-9pm; Apr. and Sept. 10am-8pm; Mar. and Oct. 10am-7pm; Nov.-Feb. 10am-6pm. Free.

On a hill just north of the Gràcia district lies one of Barcelona's greatest treasures—perhaps the world's most enchanting public park. Gaudí intended Parc Güell (after Eusebi Güell, its commissioner; tel. 93 424 38 09) to be a garden city, its multicolored dwarfish houses and sparkling ceramic-mosaic stairways to house the city's elite.

When only two aristocrats signed on, it became a park instead. The park was designed entirely by Gaudí, and—in typical Gaudí fashion—not completed until after his death. The front entrance puts you face to face with a gaping, multicolored lizard. Some believe that the animal is a reference to the shield of the French city of Nîmes, which marks the northern limit of Old Catalunya. Two mosaic staircases flank the curious creature, leading to a towering Modernista Roman pavilion that Gaudí originally designed as an open-air market for the park's would-be but never-were residents. The top of the pavilion is decked out by the longest park bench in the world, a multi-colored, tile-shard, serpentine wonder. From here, sweeping paths, supported by columns meant to resemble palm trees, swerve through hedges and ascend to the park's summit, which commands tremendous views of the city. In the midst of the park awaits the **Casa-Museu Gaudí** (see **Museums,** p. 322)—but no sight could equal the park itself. One has to wonder whether the schoolchildren nonchalantly bouncing through during *siesta* think this is what all parks look like.

The easiest way to reach the park is by bus #24 from Pg. Gràcia, which lets you off at the upper park entrance. You can also take the Metro to Lesseps. From the Metro, follow the signs to the stop light where you cross Av. República Argentina; follow Pl. Lesseps signs up the slight incline until it becomes Travessera de Dalt; follow Dalt past Blockbuster and go left up C. Larrard (follow the signs). It's a fairly taxing uphill hike, but the views will reward your efforts. The entrance is on C. d'Olot.

SARRIÀ AND PEDRALBES

Northwesterly Sarrià is the domain of Barcelona's old money—residents still talk about "going down to Barcelona." The last *barri* to lose its independence, Sarrià merged with Barcelona in 1921. A walk through the peaceful streets reveals elegant mansions, manicured gardens, and exclusive Modernista private schools.

The **Monestir de Pedralbes,** Baixada del Monestir, 1 (tel. 93 280 14 34), at the end of Pg. Reina Elisenda, has a Catalan Gothic single-aisle church and 14th-century three-story cloister. The artistic highwater is in the **Capella Sant Miguel,** where murals by Ferrer Bassa depict Mary's seven joys, as well as some of her low moments. (*Open Tu-Su 10am-2pm. 300ptas, students 175ptas.*) The monastery has received a part of the Thyssen-Bornemisza collection, purchased by Spain in 1993.

TIBIDABO

The curious name comes from the smashing view this area commands over Barcelona, the Pyrenees, the Mediterranean, and even (on clear days) Mallorca. In St. Matthew's Gospel, the devil tempts Jesus, *"Haec omnia tibi dabo si cadens adoraberis me."* ("All this I will give to you if you fall prostrate and worship me.") The souvenir shop and telescopes tucked away in the spires of the huge **Temple del Sagrat Cor's** make its religious function an afterthought. (*Round-trip elevator ride 75ptas.*) Squeals peal from the neighboring **Parc d'Atraccions** (tel. 93 211 79 42). (*Open Tu-Su 11:30am-8pm. Unlimited use of 12 rides 1900ptas, no rides 700ptas.*) Riding the elevator up the nearby **Torre de Collserola** communications tower (560m above sea level) may be just as scary as the amusement park. (*500ptas.*)

The **Tibibús** runs from Pl. Catalunya to the Torre de Collserola (departs June 9-Sept. 9 every 30min. from 30min. before park opening until 30min. after closing; Sept. 10-June 8 Sa-Su and holidays every hr., 270ptas). An **FFCC train** and buses #17, 22, and 58 from Pl. Catalunya run to Av. Tibidabo (train round-trip 1900ptas including funicular and park entrance fee). To reach the mountaintop, either wait the 15 minutes for the **Tramvia Blau** (blue tram) or walk up Av. Tibidabo in almost the same time (departs daily June-Sept. 9:05am-9:35pm; Oct.-May Sa-Su 9:05am-9:35pm; M-F 135ptas, Sa-Su 225ptas; round-trip 350ptas, or use a T1 combined train pass). At the top of the street you have to take a funicular (departs every 30min. 7:15am until 30min. after the park closes, 300ptas).

A quick prowl around the area surrounding the train station reveals several recently constructed concrete parks. **Parc de l'Espanya Industrial,** a modern interpretation of Roman baths, sinks below its smoggy surroundings (directly right upon exiting the train station). **Parc de Joan Miró,** down a few blocks on C. Tarragona, replaced a former slaughterhouse. The erect yellow, red, blue, and gray sculpture capped by a banana, Miró's *Dona i ocell (Woman and Bird),* rises triumphantly out of a small pool.

■ Museums

> When I was a child, my mother said to me, 'If you become a soldier, you'll
> be a general. If you become a monk, you'll end up as the pope.' Instead, I
> became a painter and wound up as Picasso.
>
> —Pablo Picasso

Barcelona's museums, springing up seemingly daily, provide a rare opportunity to simultaneously explore the city's architectural feats and admire the works of accomplished Catalan artists. Barcelonans invest more in experimentation than preservation, a philosophy to which their museums attest. Most museums offer **free admission** the first Sunday of each month. While this section includes all major museums, consult *Guía del Ocio* and *Metropolitan* for more exhaustive listings.

Museu Picasso, C. Montcada, 15-19 (tel. 93 319 63 10). M: Jaume I. A comprehensive collection of Picasso's early and late works is scattered throughout the numerous rooms of the Gothic Palau Berenguer d'Aguilar. Although the museum offers little from Picasso's middle years, it boasts the world's best collection from his formative period in Galicia and Barcelona (where he began his Blue Period), and an outstanding display of lithographs and ceramics. Check out the perfect pencil sketches by Pablo the 11-year-old mack daddy. Picasso's Cubist interpretations of Velazquez's *Las Meninas* (which hangs in the Prado) fill 4 rooms. Open Tu-Sa 10am-8pm, Su 10am-3pm. 600ptas, students 300ptas, under 16 free.

Museu d'Art Contemporani (MACBA), Pl. dels Angels, 1 (tel. 93 412 08 10; http://www.macba.upf.es). M: Universitat or Catalunya. This gleaming white edifice, constructed by American architect Richard Meier, contrasts with the surrounding run-down Gothic neighborhood. The museum's gentle curves and large windows, however, are designed to complement, not challenge, the buildings in El Raval. Not to be missed, MACBA is a world-class museum and one of Barcelona's best. Eclectic and often interactive exhibitions focus on three-dimensional art, photography, video, and graphic work from the past 40 years. Excellent rotating exhibits. Open Tu-F noon-8pm, Sa 10am-8pm, Su 10am-3pm. 600ptas, students 300ptas.

Fundació Joan Miró, Parc de Montjuïc (tel. 93 329 19 08), Av. Miramar, 71-75, at Pl. Neptú. M: Espanya, then bus #61 from Pl. Espanya. Designed by Miró's friend Josep Luís Sert, the Fundació, tucked into the side of Montjuïc, links interior and exterior spaces with massive windows and outdoor patios (offering wide-angle views of the city). Sky lights illuminate an extensive collection of statues, paintings, and tapestries from Miró's career. The stunning *Barcelona Series* depicts Miró's personal reaction to the Spanish Civil War. Espai 13 displays experimental work by young artists. The Fundació also sponsors music recitals and film festivals. Open in summer M-W and F-Sa 10am-8pm, Th 10am-9:30pm, Su 10am-2:30pm; in winter M-W and F-Sa 11am-7pm, Th 11am-9:30pm, Su 10am-2:30pm. 700ptas, students 400ptas.

Museu Nacional d'Art de Catalunya (MNAC), Palau Nacional, Parc de Montjuïc (tel. 93 423 71 99). M: Espanya, then bus #61; or walk up Av. Reina M. Cristina and up the escalators. Besides housing the world's finest collection of Romanesque art, the museum also has Gothic altarpieces and paintings of Catalunya's medieval churches scavenged from museums around the world. Open Tu-W and F-Sa 10am-7pm, Th 10am-9pm, Su 10am-2:30pm. 800ptas, students 550ptas.

Fundació Antoni Tàpies, C. Aragó, 255 (tel. 93 487 03 15), around the corner from the *manzana de la discordia.* M: Pg. Gràcia, between Pg. Gràcia and Rbla. Catalunya. Tàpies' bizarre wire sculpture atop Domènech's red brick building rambunctiously announces this collection of contemporary art. The top floor is dedicated to the namesake Catalan artist. The other 2 floors feature special exhibits of other modern artists. Open Tu-Su 11am-8pm. 500ptas, students 300ptas.

Museu d'Art Modern (part of MNAC), Pl. Armes in the Parc de la Ciutadella (tel. 93 319 57 28). M: Cuitadella-Vila Olímpica. A potpourri of paintings and sculptures, mostly by 19th-century Catalan artists. Noteworthy works include *Plein Air* by Casas, *Els Primers Freds* by Blay Fabregas, Josep Llimona's *Desconsol,* and Isidre Nonell's paintings of Gypsy women. Also displays furniture designed by Gaudí. Open Tu-Sa 10am-7pm, Su 10am-2:30pm. 500ptas, students 250ptas.

Museu d'Historia de la Ciutat, Pl. del Rei, with entrance at C. Verguer (tel. 93 315 11 11). M: Jaume I, next to Pl. Rei. In the 6th century, Visigoths buried the Roman ruins to make room for their cemetery. Their buildings, in turn, became the foundations for medieval structures. Ruins of the Roman colony are in the basement— some well-preserved floor mosaics and villa walls with interesting inscriptions are all that remain. The upper floors of the museum boast the **Capella de Santa Agueda,** built to store the king's holy relics. Get a city map at the museum and join an ancient treasure hunt: find the Roman remains in other parts of the Ciutat Vella. Open July-Sept. Tu-Sa 10am-8pm, Su 10am-2pm; Oct.-June Tu-Sa 10am-2pm and 4-8pm, Su 10am-2pm. 500ptas, students 250ptas. Wednesday afternoons free.

Centre Cultural de la Fundació "la Caixa," Pg. Sant Joan, 108 (tel. 93 458 89 05). M: Verdaguer, between C. Provença and C. Mallorca. Stroll through Puig i Cadafalch's **Casa Macaya** as you admire the *fundació's* permanent modern art collection and temporary exhibits of contemporary artists and photographers. Open Tu-Sa 11am-8pm, Su 11am-3pm. 300ptas, students 175ptas, free Su.

Museu Arqueològic de Catalunya, Parc de Montjuïc, Pg. Santa Madrona, 39-41 (tel. 93 423 21 49). M: Espanya, then bus #55 or 61. Or take bus #55 from Pl. Catalunya. East of the Palau Nacional. Includes a collection of Carthaginian art from Ibiza. Several rooms are dedicated to relics from the excavation of the Greco-Roman city of Empúries (near Girona). Open Tu-Sa 9:30am-7pm, Su 10am-2:30pm. 200ptas, Su 500ptas with guided tour.

Museu d'Historia de Catalunya, Pl. Pau Vila, 3 (tel. 93 225 47 00). M: Barceloneta. This high-tech and hands-on museum guides you through Catalunya's Roman, Industrial, Civil War, and recent eras. Computer screens, original film clips, and music stations help narrate the region's tumultuous past. Open Tu-Th 10am-7pm, F-Sa 10am-8pm, Su 10am-2:30pm. 500ptas, students 250ptas.

Casa-Museu Gaudí, inside Parc Güell, C. Olot (tel. 93 284 64 46). Take bus #24 from Pl. Catalunya. Designed by Gaudí's associate Francesc Berenguer, Gaudí's former house now contains a small, eclectic *Modernisme* collection of designs, furniture, and portraits. Open Apr.-Sept. Su-F 10am-2pm and 4-7pm; Oct.-Mar. 10am-2pm and 4-6pm. 250ptas.

Museu de la Música, Casa Vidal-Quadras, Av. Diagonal, 373 (tel. 93 416 11 57). M: Diagonal. An exhibit of antique instruments housed in Puig i Cadafalch's Casa Baró de Quadras. Particularly good guitar collection. Open Tu-Su 10am-2pm, W 5-8pm. 300ptas. Wednesdays free.

Palau de la Virreina, Las Ramblas, 99 (tel. 93 301 77 75), on the corner of C. Carme. M: Liceu. Once a Peruvian viceroy's residence, this 18th-century palace displays temporary photographic, musical, and graphic exhibitions. It serves as the headquarters for tickets to the summer **Grec festival.** Open Tu-Sa 11am-9pm, Su 11am-3pm. 300ptas, students 150ptas.

Museu Frederic Marès, Pl. Sant Iu, 5-6 (tel. 93 310 58 00). M: Jaume I. Housed in the Palau Reial, on the opposite side of the cathedral. Founded in 1946 with an idiosyncratic personal collection of the sculptor Marès. The 1st floor houses an almost overwhelming collection of crucifixes and other biblical motifs. The 2nd and 3rd floors contain an eclectic collection of 15th- to 20th-century commonplace objects, such as canes, ashtrays, and pipes. Open Tu-Sa 10am-5pm, Su 10am-2am. 300ptas, students 150ptas. Wednesday afternoons free.

Centre de Cultura Contemporània de Barcelona (CCCB), Casa de Caritat, C. Montalegre, 5 (tel. 93 306 41 00). M: Catalunya or Universitat. Sparkles next to the MACBA. Investigates modern urban design and development, among other things. Temporary exhibits are only part of the brand-new CCCB. Also sponsors concerts, workshops, and lectures. Open Tu and Th-F 11am-2pm and 4-8pm, W and Sa 11am-8pm, Su 11am-7pm. Th-Tu 600ptas, students and W 400ptas.

L'Aquàrium de Barcelona, Moll d'Espanya del Port Vell, next to Maremagnum (tel. 93 221 74 74). M: Barceloneta. Barcelona's new aquarium is state of the art, featuring myriad tropical fish both and an 80m-long glass tunnel through a huge shark tank (watch yourself). Whopping 1400ptas per person. Open July-Aug. 9:30am-11pm; Sept.-June 9:30am-9pm. Admission up to 1hr. before closing.

ART GALLERIES AND CULTURAL CENTERS

One of the world's cutting edge cultural capitals, Barcelona showcases the latest artistic trends. Myriad private galleries display the works of budding artists, as well as more established masters. The *Guía del Ocio* (125ptas at local newsstands) is the best source for the latest exhibits and other info.

Galería Maeght (tel. 93 310 42 45), at Carrer de Montcada, 25, near the Museu de Picasso, is Catalunya's most prestigious gallery for contemporary artists. *(Open Tu-Sa 10am-2pm and 4-8pm.)* At C. Moncada, 14, is another popular gallery, **Fundación La Caixa's Sala Montcada** (tel. 93 207 74 75; open Tu-Sa 11am-8pm and Su 11am-3pm; free). **Galería Surrealista** (tel. 93 310 33 11), also on Moncada (#19), sells Dalí studies, paintings, and sculptures 1000 to 50,000,000ptas. *(Open daily 10am-2pm and 4-8pm.)*

A galaxy of avant-garde galleries brightens the single block of **Calle Consell de Cent,** between Rbla. Catalunya and C. Balmes. **Carles Taché,** #290 (tel. 93 487 88 36), and **René Metras,** #331 (tel. 93 487 58 74), face each other on Cent. *(Taché open Tu-Sa 10am-2pm and 4-8:30pm, closed Sa in July. René Metras open Tu-F 11am-1:30pm and 5-8:30pm.)* Around the corner lies **Joan Prats-Art Gràfic,** Balmes, 54 (tel. 93 488 13 98). *(Open Sept.-July Tu-Sa 10:30am-1:30pm and 5-8pm.)*

At the **Kiku Mistu Imaginary Cultural Center,** C. de Palau, 5 (tel. 93 318 25 08, http://www.mister.com; M: Liceu or Jaume 1), across the street from Hostel Mari-Luz, a number of hands-on exhibits have been designed to link the world of dreams and reality. You can fall asleep on the *cama de sueños* (bed of dreams), have a drink at the shattered "Ethylic Mirages" bar, or call home from the fur-line phone booth. *(Email access available. Open Tu-Sa 5-9pm. 1st entrance 200ptas.)*

The **Centre d'Art Santa Mònica,** Las Ramblas, 7 (tel. 93 301 77 75), features rotating exhibits which you can check out as you cruise by on Las Ramblas. *(Open M-Sa 11am-2pm and 5-8pm, Su 11am-3pm.)*

■ Entertainment

Nightlife in Barcelona begins with the 5pm stroll and winds down about fourteen hours later. *Ocio* (leisure) here ranges from sophisticated to debaucherous. After *siesta,* the masses roll into Las Ramblas to browse magic shows and periodical stands or stroll the portside *moll,* while youngsters mill around Portal l'Angel and Portaferrissa purveying the latest fashions. To recharge, the theater crowd makes conversation in cafes and *tapas* bars around Liceu, and foreign twenty-somethings order *copas* in Pl. Reial. Farther away from the Barri Gòtic, well-off adults can be found cruising L'Eixample, while bonafide Barcelonan students head for the bars and cafes in Gràcia. Barcelona's bar scene begins around 9pm; the discos start bumping around 2am.

For info on movies, concerts, cultural events, and bars, consult the weekly *Guía del Ocio* (http://www.guiadelociobcn.es), available at newsstands for 125ptas. The *Cine* section denotes subtitled films with *V.O. subtitulada;* other foreign films are dubbed, usually in Catalan. The *Tarde/Noche* section suggests bars and discos galore, while the Música section lists Barcelona's live music venues.

BARS AND DISCOS

After dinner, *bar-restaurantes* and *cervecerías* fill up. Later on, *bares-musicales* (small discos for socializing, not dancing) draw the pre-*discoteca* crowd. The hippest folks hit the dance floor around 2am and jam for at least four hours (some discos don't close until 9am). The more swish spots may discriminate on the basis of hair and dress style. Bouncers may also invent a cover charge for men to meet quotas.

What's popular changes from one day to the next—talk to locals to stay on top of things. Expect to pay around 400ptas for a beer and 700ptas and up for mixed drinks. Closing times are approximate—places don't shut down until people leave (or, more often, until the police decide they want to sleep).

Las Ramblas and Barri Gótic

Cookie-cutter *cervecerías* and *bar-restaurantes* can be found every five steps. If slabs of meat are swinging from the ceiling and there's *fútbol* piped into a little TV, you know you're in a local hang. Nightlife on and around Las Ramblas is people-packed and exciting, but not disco-oriented.

La Oveja Negra, Sitges, 5 (tel. 93 317 10 87). M: Catalunya. From Pl. Catalunya, down Las Ramblas and the first right at C. Tallers; C. Sitges is the first left. The most popular tavern in town, where locals fraternize over pitchers of beer and foosball. 0.5L beer 325ptas. *Sangría* 1000ptas for 1.5L. Open M-Th 9am-2:30am, F 9am-3:30am, Sa-Su 5pm-3:30am.

Schilling, C. Ferrán, 23 (tel. 93 317 67 87). M: Liceu. You'll have to push to find a seat in this chic, popular bar. Columns, chandeliers, and friendly service cry out "exclusive," but the crowd is surprisingly diverse. ½ liter beer 295ptas, glass of wine 200ptas. Mixed gay and straight. Open M-F 9am-2am, Sa-Su 11am-2am.

Xampanyet, C. Montcado, 15, off Pg. Born behind La Església Santa María del Mar, and just before the Museu Picasso. George Costanza look-alike Juan Carlos is the 3rd-generation proprietor. He and his father serve *cava* and anchovies in a colorful champagne bar. *Cavas* 110ptas and up, bottle 750ptas and up. Open Tu-Sa noon-4pm and 6:30-11:30pm, Su 6:30-11:30pm.

Bar Almirall, C. Joaquim Costa, 33, just up the street from Restaurante Riera (see **Food,** p. 312). A dim red cave with a decaying ceiling and weathered couches in back. They serve *absenta* (absinthe), the licorice-flavored liquor banned in France for its eerie effects on the minds of Impressionist painters. This is the oldest bar in Barcelona, and you won't find its name on neon-colored 2-for-1 fliers. Beer 250ptas. Open Su-Th 7pm-2am, F-Sa 7pm-3am.

Harlem Jazz Club, C. Comtesa de Sobradiel, 8 (tel. 93 310 07 55). M: Liceu. Between the Pl. Reial and Via Laietana. Jazz and a variety of other live music. A well-known spot. Open daily 10pm-4am (but doesn't hop 'til past midnight). Su-Th free, Sa 500ptas with drink.

L'Antiquari, C. Verquer, 13 (tel. 93 310 04 35), in Pl. Rei. M: Jaume I. A 3-floor bar housed in a former antique shop with a view of Barri Gòtic palaces. In this bar, "A" stands for anarchy (a *barcelonense* tradition). A chaotic mix of live samba, reggae, and Scottish folk. Small beer 275ptas. Mixed drinks 600ptas. Open Su-Th 10am-1am, F-Sa 10am-3am.

Cafe d l'Opera, Ramblas, 74 (tel. 93 317 75 85 or 93 302 41 80). M: Liceu. A Barcelona institution; a drink at this cafe was once a post-opera tradition for bourgeois *barcelonenses*. Today, it caters to all types. Beer 380ptas. 4-person *sangría* 1495ptas. *Bocadillos* 350-500ptas. Open daily 9am-3am.

Euskal Etxea, Placeta Montcada, 1-3 (tel. 93 310 21 85). Down the street from the Museu Picasso. This "Basque House" serves *tapas* at around 7:30pm and cheap wines (100ptas) in traditional low-ball Basque glasses. Open M-Sa 8am-5pm and 7-11:30pm, Su 7-11:30pm.

Cafe D'Estiu, Pl. de Sant Iu, 5-6, in the courtyard outside the Museu Marés. Tiny outdoor cafe offers a tranquil refuge from the Barri Gòtic's hustle and bustle. Sip tea (275ptas) beside a fish pond and orange trees. Open Tu-Su 10am-10pm.

Jamboree, Pl. Reial, 17 (tel. 93 301 75 64). M: Liceu or Drassanes. Plaça Reial lies just off Las Ramblas, via C. Colom. Turn right upon entering; it's toward the end on the right. Jazz, blues, be-bop, reggae, pop-funk, and jazz-funk. Concerts M-Sa 11pm-12:30am and dancing afterward. 1500-1800ptas, with drink. More spirited dancing upstairs. Very popular with locals. Free passes sometimes handed out on Ramblas.

Karma, Pl. Reial (tel. 93 302 56 80). Open later than most bars, Karma keeps it lively indoors and out Tu to Th nights. A thoroughly mixed crowd: late-teen to early-twenties, both foreign and local crowd.

Margarita Blue, Clave 6 (tel 93 317 71 76). M: Drassanes. Off Ramblas to the east, a block up from the waterfront. A Mexican-themed bar draws a lively 20 to 30-some-thing crowd swinging to jazz tunes under mellow blue neon. Open M-W 10am-1am, Th-F 10am-3am, Sa 7pm-3am, Su 7pm-1am.

Chistú Bar, Tallers 14. M: Catalunya. Tallers comes off the west side of Ramblas 2 blocks down from Pl. Catalunya. Long and narrow, smoky, and inexpensive, this bar-restaurant hops with a local crowd. Large beer 325ptas, bottle 200ptas. Open Su-Th 11am-1am, F-Sa 11am-3am.

Eixample

A mod crowd: leave your jeans, sneakers, and *Let's Go* at home—or face the fashion police. A slew of *bares-musicales,* disco bars, and other hybrids lie between Pg. Grà-cia and C. Aribau, and C. Rossell and C. València.

Velòdrom, C. Muntaner, 213 (tel. 93 430 60 22). M: Diagonal. Pre-party crowd. Stu-dents meet to drink in cushioned booths and shoot pool in a weather-worn hang-out. *Jarras* (mugs) of beer 275ptas. M-Sa 6pm-2am.

La Bodegueta, on the corner of Rbla. Catalunya and Provença, a block away from La Pedrera. M: Diagonal. In the hours before dinner, this wine bar hops with chic Bar-celonans (not tourists) sampling local wines and *cavas* with their cheese and pâté. Dress for success. Open M-Sa noon-1am.

Montjuïc

Lower Montjuïc is home to two epic "disco theme parks."

Poble Espanyol, Av. Marqués de Comillas (tel. 93 322 03 26). M: Pl. Espanya. The numbers are impressive: 12 restaurants, 15 bars, 3 *bares-musicales,* and a large *dis-coteca* called **Le Fou.** Touristy, but quite a show. Dancing starts at around 1:30am, and usually doesn't end until 9am. Open in summer nightly; in winter Th-Sa.

Firestiu, Pl. del Universo (tel. 93 410 89 17). M: Espanya. An incredibly popular open-air complex with a medley of bars, bungee-jumping, carnival games, and out-door dancing. Open June 5-Aug. 29 Th-Sa 10pm-4:30am. 1000ptas, includes one drink. Free before midnight.

Port Olímpic

Nestled next to Barcelona's *platjas,* the Olympic Village brims with glitzy restaurants that give way to throngs of dance fiends, from the merely light-of-foot to the crackpot *discotecarios.* Twenty or so *bares-musicales* occupy the strip, but many revelers choose to dance on the port itself. If you don't like the music, take five steps to the next scene (there's no cover anywhere). You'll do best if you follow your ears to the latest hotspot. Things begin at midnight and wind down at 6am. From the metro stop Ciutadella-Vila Olímpica (L4), walk down C. Marina toward the twin towers.

Maremagnum

At 1am the adults leave, the children go to bed, and the older kids boogie. There's a variety of venues for even the least mall-cultured, although prices tags are a bit higher.

Sub 34.3, on the middle floor of Maremagnum. Ride a submarine into the depths of the ocean, grind to American pop, and swill 800ptas drafts, all at once. The sub theme is all-pervasive and quite amusing. Open Su-Th 11pm-4am, F-Sa 11pm-5am.

Mojito Bar (tel. 93 225 80 14). The place for Caribbean music, merengue, and salsa. Free classes given on weekends. Open Su-Th midnight-4am, F-Sa midnight-5am.

Nayandei (tel. 93 225 80 10). Top floor of Maremagnum. Indoor/outdoor dance floor hops and rocks with tunes from the 60s and 70s. Open daily 9pm-5:30am.

Distrito Marítimo, Moll de la Fusta, Edicles, 1 (tel. 93 221 55 61). Techno with gay environment and outdoor terrace. Open F-Sa midnight-5am.

Elsewhere

Most of the biggest and baddest *discotecas* are outside of the Plaça Catalunya area.

Otto Zutz, C. Lincoln, 15 (tel. 93 238 07 22 or 93 238 07 73). M: FFCC Muntaner. Uptown near Pl. Molina where C. Balmes intersects Vía Augusta. 3 floors, 6 bars. Most lights, most dancing, most flash—yet to be matched by any other club. Live music F midnight-2am. The beautiful people don't show up 'til after 3am. Cover negotiable 2000ptas, includes one drink. Open Tu-Sa midnight-5am.

Zeleste, C. Almogàvers, 122 (tel. 93 309 12 04), a 15min. walk from Pg. Lluís Companys; or take the Nit Bus (11pm-4:30am). M: Llancuna. Located in an old warehouse, this dance club sometimes has rooftop terraces and live performances for a separate charge. Cover 1000ptas. The shindig freaks around 2:30am.

Fibra Óptica, C. Beethoven, 9 (tel. 93 202 00 69). M: Hospital Clinic. From the metro, walk up C. Comte Urgell, turn left at Diagonal; it's in Pl. Wagner, 1 block up on the right. A 20-something crowd hits this ultrapopular disco. Cover around 1800ptas, includes 1 drink. Open M-F midnight-5am, Sa-Su midnight-9:30am.

La Boîte, Av. Diagonal, 477 (tel. 93 419 59 50). M: Hospital Clinic. More emphasis on dance than decor. Live jazz, soul, and blues Tu, Th, and F. Big names sometimes come to perform in an intimate disco setting. Open daily 11pm-5:30am.

KGB, C. Alegre de Dalt, 55 (tel. 93 210 59 06). M: Joanic. C. Alegre de Dalt is the first left off C. Pi i Maragall from the Metro. Caters to those who like their rock and roll loud and hard. Live music at times. Open F-Su 10pm-5am.

Les Carpes del Cel, Castelldefels "Canal Olimpic," on Autovia A-16, Castelldefels Platja exit (tel. 93 634 34 04). Huge outdoor disco complex with 3 separate dancefloor tents, each pumping different music genres. 18 bars, plus other amusements. Cover 1000ptas includes 1 drink. Open June 19-Sept. 19 10:30pm-5am.

MUSIC

The **Gran Teatre del Liceu,** Ramblas, 61 (tel. 93 485 99 13; http://www.gt-liceu.es), founded in 1847, was one of the world's leading opera stages. Unfortunately, its interior was destroyed by a fire in 1994, but it will supposedly reopen in spring 1999. Many anticipated performances have been moved to the **Palau de la Música Catalana** and **Teatro Victòria** (see below). Museums and parks also host concerts and recitals (Parc Güell, Parc de la Ciutadella, Fundació de Joan Miró, Fundació la Caixa, and the Centre de Cultura Contemporània). Consult the Palau de la Virreina office at Las Ramblas, 99, or check local periodicals for specific listings.

Palau de la Música Catalana, C. San Francesc de Paula, 2 (tel. 93 268 10 00), off Vía Laietana near Pl. Urquinaona. Lluis Domènech i Montaner's fairytale *Modernisme* concert hall, illuminated by an inconceivably ornate stained-glass chandelier and tall stained glass windows. Concerts include all varieties of symphonic and choral music, plus performances relocated from the Teatre del Liceu. Tickets run 1000-3500ptas. Ask about free Tuesday night winter concerts and the Oct. music festival. Box office open M-F 10am-9pm, Sa 3-9pm, Su from 1hr. prior to the concert. Tours are offered daily, in rotating languages, at 2 and 3pm (check first). 300ptas, free with a *Ruta del Modernisme* pass.

Teatro Victòria, Av. Paral.lel, 67 (tel. 93 441 39 79). M: Paral.lel. Hosts many of the displaced Liceu performances.

Rock concerts are held in the main soccer stadium and in the sports palace. Get tickets in the booth on Gran Vía at C. Aribau, next to the university. Open daily 10:30am-1:30pm and 4-7:30pm.

THEATER

Barcelona offers many options for theater aficionados, although most performances are in Catalan (*Guía del Ocio* lists which language the performance is in). Tickets can be reserved by phone through **TelEntrada** (tel. 902 10 12 12), or in any branch of **Caixa Catalunya** bank (open M-F 8am-2pm).

The **Grec-Barcelona** summer festival (http://www.grecbcn.com) turns Barcelona into an international theater, music, and dance extravaganza from late June to mid-August. For info about the festival, ask at the tourist office or contact **Institut de Cultura de Barcelona (ICUB),** Palau de la Virreina, Ramblas 99 (tel. 93 301 77 75; open daily 10am-2pm and 4-8pm). Some of the major venues (such as the **Teatre Grec** and the **Convent de Sant Augusti**) are open-air theaters. Tickets can be purchased through **TelEntrada,** or perhaps more easily, at the Pl. Catalunya **tourist office** (tickets sold Tu, W, and F 6-10pm, Th and Sa 4-10pm, Su 3-7pm).

Teatre Nacional de Catalunya, Pl. dels Arts, 1 (tel. 93 306 57 31, info tel. 93 306 57 44), near the intersection of Av. Diagonal and Av. Meridiana. M: Monumental or Glòries i Marina. A brand-new, glass-enclosed classic revival temple by Ricard Bofill. Tickets 2500-3000ptas. Tours M 5pm and W noon; 200ptas.

Teatre de l'Eixample, C. Aragó, 140 (tel. 93 323 39 50 or 93 451 34 62). M: Urgell. This new facility showcases contemporary theater, foreign and domestic. Tickets 2000ptas; available W-M 11:30am-noon and after 5pm.

Teatre Lliure, C. Montseny, 47 (tel. 93 218 92 51). M: Fontana, in Gràcia. Innovative productions of contemporary theater. Tickets cost 1350-2200ptas. The season runs Oct.-June. Box office open T-Sa 5-8pm, Su and holidays 2hr. before the show.

Mercat de les Flors, C. Lleida, 59 (tel. 93 426 18 75). M: Pl. Espanya. Hosts dance and theater performances (3000ptas). Tickets available at Palau de la Virreina, Las Ramblas 99, Tu-Sa 11am-2pm and 4-7pm.

FILM

Most screens display the latest Hollywood productions, some subtitled (*versión original*), some dubbed. Many theaters have a bargain ticket day (usually Monday). **Filmoteca,** Av. Sarrià, 33 (tel. 93 410 75 90; M: Hospital Clínic), screens classic, cult, exotic, and otherwise exceptional films (both foreign and domestic, 400ptas). For more mainstream fare, try **Maremagnum, Moll d'Espanya** (tel. 93 405 22 22), which has 8 new screens (Tu-Su 725-750ptas, M 600ptas). **Casablanca,** Pg. Gràcia, 115 (tel. 93 218 43 45), has two screens (Su and Tu-Th 725ptas, F-Sa 750ptas, M 500ptas), and **Verdi,** C. Verdi, 32 (tel. 93 237 05 16), has four screens (Tu-Su 700ptas, F-Sa 750ptas, M 575ptas, students 550ptas). **Icaria-Yelmo,** C. Salvador Espira, 61 (tel. 93 221 75 85), in the Olympic Village, boasts 15 screens (750ptas, M 575ptas). **Maldà,** C. Pí, 5 (tel. 93 317 85 29), does double features (625-675ptas). **Méliès Cinemas,** Villarroel, 102 (tel. 93 451 00 51; M: Urgell), screens classics (Tu-Su 600ptas, M 400ptas).

The new **IMAX Port Vell** (tel. 93 225 11 11), on the Moll d'Espanya, features an IMAX screen, an Omnimax 30m in diameter, and 3-D projection. Get tickets at the door, through ServiCaixa automatic machines, or by phone (850-1500ptas).

FÚTBOL AND CORRIDAS

You may think that the lunatics running around covered head to toe in red and blue must have escaped from a nearby asylum. Chances are they are **F.C. Barcelona** fans. Grab some face paint and head to the 110,000-seat **Nou Camp** to join fearless locals going berserk over one of the finest pro *fútbol* teams on earth, the current home of Brazil's celebrated Rivaldo. To cheer on "Los Cules" firsthand, it would be wise to go to the stadium box office at C. Aristedes Maillol, 12-18, well before the match or call them at 93 496 36 00—demand for tickets is high. **R.C. Deportivo Espanyol,** a.k.a. *los periquitos* (parakeets), Barcelona's other (lesser) professional soccer team, spreads its wings at **Estadi Olímpic,** Pg. Olímpic, 17-19 (info tel. 93 424 88 00). You can also obtain tickets for both from Banca Catalana or by phoning TelEntrada.

Although the best *toreros* rarely venture out of Madrid, Sevilla, and Málaga, Barcelona's **Plaça de Toros** (tickets tel. 93 253 38 21), on Gran Vía at Pg. Carles I (M: Marina), is an excellent facility and a joy to look at, with Arabic influence and a Modernista twist. Buy tickets by phone, at local travel agencies or ServiCaixa ("la Caixa" banks; tel. 902 33 22 11). The box office also sells them before the start of the *corrida*. Bullfights usually take place from June to October on Sundays at 6:30 or 7pm.

POOLS AND BEACHES

Guía de l'esport, available free at the tourist offices, lists info (in Catalan) about swimming, cycling, tennis, squash, sailing, hiking, scuba diving, white-water rafting, and kayaking. Info is available over the phone (tel. 93 402 30 00, no English). Barcelona tends to ignore its beaches and focus more on the industrial utility of the oceanside, but there's plenty of sand. Nearby **Sitges** (see p. 333) is a popular daytrip.

Swimming Pools and Workout Facilities: Piscinas Bernat Picornell, Av. de l'Estadi, 30-40 (tel. 93 423 40 41). M: Espanya, then bus #61 up Montjuïc. Pretend you're Janet Evans—this is *the* Olympic pool. Open M-F 7am-midnight, Sa 7am-9pm, Su 7:30am-2:30pm. 1200ptas. **Club Sant Jordi,** C. París, 114 (tel. 93 410 92 61 or 93 419 66 94). M: Sants. Olympic-sized pool. Passes are available for other facilities including the sauna, weights, treadmills, and stairmaster. Bring your passport. Open M-F 7am-5pm, Sa 8am-6pm, Su and holidays 9am-2pm. Pool 500ptas per hr. **Frontó Colon,** Las Ramblas, 18 (tel. 302 32 95). M: Jaume I. Mediocre facilities but convenient location. Weights, minuscule indoor pool, and track. Open M-F 7:30am-10pm, Sa 9am-8pm, Su 9am-2pm.

Beaches: Several lie between Vila Olímpica and the sea, all are accessible from M: Ciutadella. The closest and most populous is **Platja Barceloneta,** off Pg. Marítim. **Castelldefels,** 20min. from Barcelona on the same train line as Sitges, is an enormous beach perfect for young children and hydrophobes—the water takes its time to get deep. The L93 bus leaves Barcelona's Pl. Espanya for Castelldefels (180ptas).

SHOPPING

There's a lot of style walking around Barcelona. Unfortunately, *Let's Go*ers don't always have the necessary funds. Barcelona's reputation as a fashion capital has led to outlandish prices in the elegant shops along **Passeig Gràcia** and **Rambla Catalunya**—but, hey, it's fun to look. Some of the stores on Portaferrissa and Av. Universitat are closer to range. Shoes, leather goods, and sometimes clothing can be cheaper than in the U.S.—the further from Ramblas, the better (try Gràcia).

Carrer Banys Nous, in the Barri Gòtic, off Pl. Pí. A narrow and picturesque antique-shop haven. Prices and quality vary widely. Painters gather in Pl. Pí to sell their work Sa 11am-8pm, Su 11am-2pm.

Carrer Pelai, between Pl. Catalunya and Pl. Universitat. Home to a Zara's store and other shops for chic-but-high value clothing and footwear.

Carrer Portaferrissa, between Las Ramblas and Av. Portal de l'Angel. Naf-Naf and Pull & Bear join other Generation X-geared clothing stores. Shoe stores galore and a maze of indoor malls. Swarming with youths M-F 5:30-8pm.

El Corte Inglés: See **Practical Information,** p. 304.

Maremagnum, the ultra-modern mall complex at **Port Vell,** has shops and restaurants like Steven Spielberg's submarine-themed Dive. Open generally daily 9am-9pm.

VIPS, Rbla. Catalunya, above Pl. Catalunya. A super-sized store, this late-night locale is crammed with books, records, food, alcohol, and a cafe. Open M-Th 8am-2am, F 8am-3am, Sa-Su 9am-3am.

SARDANAS AND FIESTAS

The **sardana,** Catalunya's regional dance, is one of Barcelona's most popular amusements. Teenagers and grandparents join hands to dance in a circle in celebration of Catalan unity in front of the cathedral, Pl. Sagrada Familia, or at Parc de la Ciutadella, near the fountains, on Sundays at noon. Dances are also held in Pl. Sant Jaume on Sundays at 6:30pm, at Parc de l'Espanya Industrial on Fridays at 7:30pm, in Pl. Catedral on Saturdays at 6:30pm and Sundays at noon, and in other locations throughout the city on Tuesdays, Thursdays, and Fridays. Consult papers for current info.

    Fiestas are abundant in Barcelona. Before Christmas, **Feria de Santa Llúcia** (info tel. 93 291 61 00) fills Pl. Catedral and the area around the Sagrada Familia with stalls and booths. **Carnaval** (info tel. 93 221 11 22) is celebrated wildly February 7 to 13, but many head to the even more raucous celebrations in Sitges and Vilanova i la Geltrù. Soon thereafter the **Festa de Sant Jordi** (St. George), April 23, celebrates with a feast for Catalunya's patron saint (and Barcelona's St. Valentine's Day). Men give women roses, and women give men books (how progressive). On May 11, the **Festa de Saint Ponç,** a traditional market of aromatic and medicinal herbs and honey, sets up in Carrer Hospital, close to Las Ramblas. Barcelona erupts on June 23, the night before **Día de Sant Joan.** Bonfires roar throughout the city, unsupervised children play with fireworks, and the fountains of Pl. Espanya and Palau Reial light up in anticipation of fireworks on Montjuïc. August 15-21, city folk jam at Gràcia's **Fiesta Mayor** (tel 93 291 66 00). Lights blaze in the plazas and streets, and rock bands play all night.

    On September 11, the **Fiesta Nacional de Catalunya,** you'll see traditional costumes, dancing, and Catalan flags hanging from balconies everywhere. The **Feria de Cuina i Vins de Catalunya** brings wine and *butifarra* (sausage) producers to the Rambla de Catalunya. For one week you can sample fine food and drink for a pittance. On September 24, during the **Festa de la Verge de la Mercè** (info tel. 93 301 77 75), fireworks light up the city while the traditional *correfocs* (wild parades of people dressed as devils) whirl pitchfork-shaped sparklers. Buckets of water are hurled at the demons from balconies overlooking fiery streets. The beginning of November marks the **Fiesta del Sant Çito,** when locals and tourists alike roll up their sleeves and party on Las Ramblas. Finally, from October through November, a **Festival Internacional de Jazz** (info tel. 93 318 53 37) swings the city's streets and clubs.

■ Near Barcelona: Montserrat

An hour northwest of Barcelona, the mountain of Montserrat, whose unmistakable serrated profile protrudes from the flat Río Llobregat Valley, makes an easy and popular daytrip. Sometime during the 9th century, a mountaineer wandering the crags had a blinding vision of the Virgin Mary. Once his story started attracting pilgrims to the mountain in droves, an opportunistic bishop-abbot named Oliba founded a monastery (1025) to worship the Virgin, who became the spiritual patroness of Catalunya. Nowadays 80 Benedictine monks tend the building, which mostly dates from the 19th century, although two wings of the old Gothic cloister survive. During the Catalan *Renaixança* in the early 20th century, politicians and artists, such as poets Joan Maragall and Jacint Verdaguer, turned to Montserrat as a source of Catalan legend and tradition. During Franco's regime, it was the site of resistance: Catalan Bibles were printed here covertly, and nationalist demonstrations were held on the mountain. The site still attracts devout worshipers today, as well as numerous everyday tourists, who come to check out the Virgin of Montserrat, her ornate basilica, her surprisingly good accompanying art museum, and perhaps most of all, the panoramic views of the mountain's awesome, anthropomorphic rock formations.

PRACTICAL INFORMATION RENFE **trains** (tel. 93 205 15 15) to Montserrat leave from M: Espanya in Barcelona (1hr., departs every hr. 6am-9pm, 1145ptas, 1785ptas same-day round-trip); be sure to get off at the Aeri de Montserrat stop, *not* Olesa de Montserrat. Trains leaving Barcelona on odd hours (destined for Manresa) go direct to

BARCELONA

Aeri de Montserrat; if you take an even-hour train (destined for Igualada), you must change at Martorell-Enllaç. On weekends, trains leave for Montserrat only on odd hours. The train stops at the base of the mountain, where you can take the heartstopping **Aeri cable car** up to the monastery (departs every 15min. 10am-1:45pm and 2:20-6:35pm, price included in train fares or 600ptas, 900ptas round-trip by itself). Trains heading from Montserrat back to Barcelona depart every hour, 6am-10pm, direct on odd hours, and weekends every other hour (direct only). Upon exiting the upper cable car station, turn left and walk up 100m to reach **Plaça Creu,** Montserrat's tourist-oriented commercial area.

For a **map,** a schedule of daily religious services, and help with mountain navigation, go to the **info booth** in **Plaça Creu** (tel. 93 835 02 51), a providential and multilingual source of advice. Not all is charity, however; the *Official Guide to Montserrat* sells for 875ptas (or 475ptas for the old one; booth open daily in summer 10am-7pm; in winter 9am-6pm). Other conveniences in Pl. Creu include **currency exchange** at poor rates (open June-Sept. M-F 9:15am-2pm, Oct.-May M-F 9:15am-2pm, Sa 9:15am-1:30pm) and a **post office** (open June-Sept. M-F 9am-12:45pm and 2-5:30pm, Sa 9-11:30am). La Caixa and the nearby Caiver Maresa have **ATMs.** For an **ambulance** or **mountain rescue team,** call 93 835 02 51 and say *ambulancia* or *socorro,* meaning emergency. The **Guardia Civil** is headquartered in the main square (tel. 93 835 02 51 ext. 3602).

ACCOMMODATIONS AND FOOD If you choose to spend the night, apartments for up to 10 people are available through **Administración de les Cel.les** (tel. 93 835 02 01; fax 93 835 06 59; open daily 9am-1pm and 2-6pm; after 6pm, they're at the Hotel Abat Cisneros reception), found in the far plaza. The office runs three *hostales* and a three-star hotel. **Abat Marcet,** the newest and nicest of the three hostels, has rooms to accommodate one to four people, and every room comes with private bath and a microwave (singles 3975-4250ptas; doubles 4225-4500ptas). Rooms at **Abat Oliba,** all with bath, accommodate two to seven people but are closed during the low season (doubles 3580-3900ptas; quads 5600ptas-6100ptas). **Hotel Monestir** is the oldest of the three and has shared baths. (Singles 2990-3290ptas, with bath 3985-4285ptas; doubles 5415-6015ptas, with bath 6980-7580ptas.) A shower-equipped **campground** (tel. 93 835 02 51, ext. 582) lies five minutes up the hill past the St. Joan funicular. (375ptas per person, 350ptas per tent. Office open 8am-2pm and 4-9pm. Closed in chilly winter.)

As food options are less than thrilling, the prudent beat a path to the *pastissería* and *autoservei* **supermarket,** on the right as you go up Pl. Creu, which carry baked goods and groceries to appreciate on the quiet mountain paths (open Su-F 9am-6:45pm, Sa 9am-7:45pm). The best palce to dine in town is the informal **Bar de la Plaça,** in the far plaza, serving up *bocadillos* (365-510ptas) and other treats. (Roast chicken 975ptas, hamburgers 445ptas. Open Su-F 9:30am-7:30pm, Sa 9:30am-8pm.) **Bar-Snack de Montserrat** is cafeteria-style with an open dining hall. (*Bocadillos* 410-445ptas; Apr.-Nov. Su-F 8:45am-6:45pm, Sa 8:45am-7:30pm. Platters from 950ptas; daily noon-4pm.) If you're spending the night and haven't had the foresight to buy groceries, the hotel's cafeteria will serve *bocadillos* (350-600ptas) until 10pm.

SIGHTS From Pl. Creu there are a number of options. Above Creu, the entrance to the **basilica** looks out onto Pl. Santa Noría. (*Open daily 7:30am-8:30pm. Mass 9, 11am, 12:15, and 7:30pm, Su 8, 9:30am, 12:15, 1:15, 5:30, and 7:30pm. Vespers daily 6:45pm. Choir daily 1pm.*) Right of the main chapel is a special route through the **side chapels** leading to the glimmering **La Moreneta,** the black Virgin, Montserrat's venerated icon of Mary and child. (*Route open daily 8-10:30pm, 12:15-6:30pm, and 7:30-8:30pm.*) Legend has it that St. Peter hid the figure, which was carved by St. Luke, in Montserrat's caves. Removed from Montserrat after the Napoleonic Wars and the Spanish Civil War, the solemn little figure is now showcased in an elaborate silver case. Rubbing the orb in Mary's outstretched hand brings good luck. Songs by the renowned Escalonia (a boys' choir) ring through the basilica daily, including ""Virolai," the anthem of Catalunya. (*Performances Aug.-June 1pm.*) Men, but not women, are allowed to tour the

monastery and **cloisters,** accompanied by a monk. *(Ask at the Basilica's office, left of the entrance, for details on arranging a walk-through.)*

Also in Pl. Santa María, the **Museo de Montserrat** exhibits a wide range of art, including several early and late Picassos—his *Sardana of Peace,* done just for Montserrat, is striking, as is his *Old Fisherman* oil, done when he was 14. *(Open daily 9:30am-7pm. 500ptas, students 300ptas.)* The museum's Impressionist paintings are its highlight, including works by Catalan artists such as Joaquim Mir and Ramón Casas, whose famous *Madeline Absinthe* is one of many evocative portraits. For a change of pace, take a peek at the mummified Egyptian woman.

WALKS A visit to Montserrat without a meditative walk along one of the ridges of what Maragall called "the mountain of a hundred peaks" would be a sin. Some of the most beautiful areas of the mountain are accessible only on foot. There are two ways to go: down or up. From Pl. Creu, the Santa Cova funicular descends to paths which wind along the sides of the mountain to ancient hermitages. *(Departs every 20min. 10am-1pm and 3:30-7pm, round-trip 350ptas.)* Take the **St. Joan funicular** up for more inspirational views of Montserrat. *(Departs every 20min. 10am-7pm, round-trip 875ptas.)* The dilapidated **St. Joan monastery** and **shrine** are only a 20-minute tromp from the highest station. But the real prize is **Sant Jerónim** (the area's highest peak at 1235m), with its mystical views of Montserrat's celebrated rock formations—enormous domes and serrated outcroppings resembling human forms, including "The Bewitched Friars" and "The Mummy." The hike is about two hours from Pl. Creu (or a 1hr. trek from the terminus of the St. Joan funicular). The paths are long and winding though not all that difficult—after all, they were made for guys wearing long brown robes. En route, make sure you take a sharp left when, after about 45 minutes, you come to the little old chapel—otherwise you're headed straight for a helicopter pad. On a clear day the spectacular views of Barcelona, the Balearic Islands, and the eastern Pyrenees will have you singing *hosannas* all the way.

■ Near Barcelona: Sitges

Forty kilometers south of Barcelona, the resort town of Sitges has earned considerable fame for its prime tanning grounds, lively cultural festivals, international gay community, and wired nightlife. Long considered a watered-down Eivissa (Ibiza City), Sitges has better beaches right downtown than the notorious Balearic hotspot, although it may be a bit less picturesque and flamboyant. On mainland Spain, however, you won't find much crazier beach-oriented nightlife than this. Sitges' boomtown status means famous visitors like pro soccer players and movie stars, as well as a budget accommodations market that can be quite a challenge.

PRACTICAL INFORMATION Cercanías Trains (tel. 93 490 02 02) link Sitges to Barcelona-Sants and M: Gràcia (40min., departs every 15min., M-F 305ptas, Sa-Su 350ptas), as well as Vilanova (7min., departs every 15min. until 11:45pm, M-F 150ptas, Sa-Su 170ptas). Cheap **car rental,** to access beaches between towns, is at **Car Office,** Oasis Local, 14 (tel. 93 811 12 12), at the corner of Vilafranca and Vilanova, up Carbonell from the train station. The **tourist office** awaits on Pg. Vilafranca (tel. 93 894 42 51; fax 93 894 43 05; email info@sitgestur.com), up near the train station. From the station, turn right on C. Salvador Mirabent Paretas, an uninviting highway, and go downhill until you see the big "i." It has a super map with a bounty of information on accommodations, services, and festivals. (Open daily July-Aug. 9am-9pm; mid-Sept. to June M-F 9am-2pm and 4-6:30pm, Sa 10am-1pm.) In an **emergency,** dial 062. The municipal **police,** Pl. Ajuntament, answer at 93 811 76 25. **Medical Assistance** is way uptown on C. Samuel Barrachina (tel. 93 894 64 26). **Internet access** and **fax** service are available at El Patí, C. Parellades, 38 (tel. 93 894 76 76; 500ptas per 30min.; open M-Sa 9am-2pm and 5-10pm, Su 10am-2pm). The **post office** (tel. 93 894 12 47) posts on Pl. Espanya (open M-F 8:30am-2:30pm, Sa 9:30am-1pm; no packages Sa). The **postal code** is 08870.

ACCOMMODATIONS AND FOOD Accommodations are expensive and extremely difficult to find in high season, so consider daytripping from Barcelona. If you plan to stay, reserve early or else. **Hostal Parelladas,** C. Parellades, 11 (tel. 93 894 08 01), one block from the beach, is dirt cheap for Sitges, with standard rooms, an airy terrace, and no surprises (singles 2500ptas; doubles with bath 5200ptas). **Casa Julián,** C. Carbonell, 2 (tel. 93 894 03 06), at the corner with C. Sant Francesc across from the tourist office, has cheap, clean shared-bath rooms, some with couches (singles 3000ptas, doubles 5350ptas; open June 20- Sept. 20). If you're caught without a place to stay, you might try neighboring Vilanova (see below), 7min. away on the RENFE train.

Chickens roasting on an open fire at **Restaurante La Oca,** C. Parellades, 41 (tel. 93 894 79 36), cause Pavlovian salivation. Try the succulent *half-pollo al ast* (roasted chicken, 730ptas), or grab a whole one to go for 850ptas (not including IVA; open daily 1pm-midnight). The baguette fast-food stop **Bocapà,** on C. Montroig, is cheaper, with a 495ptas meal. Add to the immense popularity of **Mont Roig Café,** on C. Montroig, 11-13, just off Parellades and join the throngs in the huge indoor patio sucking in coffee (130-200ptas), beer, and *bocadillos* (400-500ptas; open Su-F 9am-3am, Sa 9am-3:30am). At the spiritual bookstore-cafe **Hatuey,** C. Sant Francesc, 44 (tel. 93 894 52 09), in spite of its sneezy name, you can ponder the mural depicting man's evolution from primate to TV-headed yuppie while sipping *cola de caballo* (horse's tail infusion, 175ptas; open daily 7am-3am).

SIGHTS Plenty of soothing sand pacifies vacationing families and twenty-somethings with a *resaca* (hangover). The **beach** is a 10-minute walk from the train station via any street. In summer, the main beaches get crowded, but a quick walk brings you to quieter areas, on your right as you face the water.

Back in town, **Carrer Parellades** is the main tourist drag, with enough shopping, eating, and drinking to make you forget your Communist roots. Although beachgoers may consider cultural activities as frightening as rain, Sitges has some can't-miss beachside attractions—a perfect chance to let your burns cool a bit. Check out Morell's whimsical **Modernista clock tower** above Optica at Pl. Cap de la Vila, 2, at the intersection of Parellades and Sant Francesc. Behind **Església del Evangelista** on C. Fonollar, the **Museu Cau Ferrat** (tel. 93 894 03 64) hangs over the water's edge. *(All 4 museums open June 22-Sept. 10 Tu-Sa 9:30am-2pm and 4-9pm, Su 9:30am-2pm; Sept. 11-June 21 Tu-F 9:30am-2pm and 4-6pm, Sa 9:30am-2pm and 4-8pm, Su 9:30am-2pm. Combo entrance 800ptas, 1400ptas with the Palau, students half price; otherwise 500ptas per museum, students 250ptas.)* Once home to Catalan modernist Santiago Russinyol and a rendezvous point for young Catalan artists Picasso and Ramón Casas, the collection is a shrine to Modernista iron, glasswork, and painting. Next door, the **Museu Maricel del Mar** (tel. 93 894 03 64) has a selective collection of medieval painting and sculpture. The stately **Palau Maricel** (tel. 93 894 03 64), built in 1910 for American millionaire Charles Deering, rivals Richie Rich's playpad. The **Museu Romàntic,** C. Sant Gaudenci, 1 (tel. 93 894 29 69; take C. Bonaire from the waterfront), is a 19th-century bourgeois house filled with period pieces, like music boxes and 17th- to 19th-century dolls. *(8pm classical concerts on select days July-Aug.; 800ptas, including a glass of cava.)*

ENTERTAINMENT Late-night foolhardiness clusters around **Carrer Primer de Maig,** which runs directly from the beach, and its continuation, **Carrer Marques Montroig.** There's also action on **Carrer Bonaire.** The wild ones get radical at the "disco-beach" Atlántida, Sector Terramar (tel. 93 894 26 77), then shuffle their feet at **Pachá,** Pg. Sant Didac (in nearby Vallpineda; tel. 93 894 22 98). Buses run all night to the two discos from C. Primer de Maig (midnight to 4am). Other popular digs include **Ricky's** (tel. 93 894 96 81) and **Otto Zutz** (on Moll de Llevant, right on the port). **Road House,** on Primer de Maig, has salsa Saturday 11:30pm to 3am.

Sitges celebrates holidays with all-out style. During the **Festa de Corpus Christi** on June 6, townspeople collaborate to create intricate fresh-flower carpets. For *papier-mâché* dragons, devils, and giants dancing in the streets, visit during the **Festa Major,** held August 23 to 25, in honor of the town's patron saint Bartolomé. Nothing compares to the **Carnaval,** Sunday and Tuesday of the first week of Lent (Feb. 14 and 16, 1999), when Spaniards of every ilk and province crash the town for a frenzy of dancing, outrageous costumes, and vats of alcohol. On the first Sunday of March, a pistol shot starts the **Rallye de Coches de Epoca,** an antique car race from Barcelona to Sitges. June brings the **International Theater Festival** (1500-3500ptas per show), July and August the **International Jazz Festival** (1700ptas per concert), while the one-to-two-week **Festival Internacional de Cine Fantástico de Sitges** rolls around mid-October.

■ Near Sitges: Vilanova i la Geltrù

Catalunya's most important port after Barcelona and Tarragona, **Vilanova i la Geltrù** (45km south of Barcelona) is actually two cities blended into one. The industrial side does not overpower its well-groomed **beaches** (10min. from the train station), which is a good thing, since you'll want to spend all your time on the beach side of things. There's little to divert in the dusty uptown areas except a couple of older churches and stone facades. Far less frenzied than their neighbors in Sitges, Vilanovans are more likely to choose an evening of beach volleyball or soccer at the Gran Parc de Ribes over late-night madness—if it's clubbing you seek, head for Sitges.

Vilanova serves as an alternative place to stay if you can't find lodging in Sitges, but the last train from Sitges to Vilanova (7min., 130ptas) runs at 11:45pm, before the nightlife gets going. A taxi ride between the two towns will cost you around 1500ptas, or you can rent a scooter for about 2500-3000ptas per day, which will also give you access to more secluded beaches along the coast to the north and south.

PRACTICAL INFORMATION Cercanías Trains run to Sitges (7min., departs every 15min., M-F 150ptas, Sa-Su 170ptas); continuing to Barcelona (55min., M-F 305ptas, Sa-Su 350ptas); and Tarragona (10 per day). Many also continue to Port Aventura (10min., 5-7 per day, 130ptas) and Valencia (30min.-2hr., delay due to necessary connection on 3-8pm trains, 330ptas). **Mon Bus** (tel. 93 893 70 60) also connects Vilanova to Sitges, Vilafranca, and Barcelona. The **train station** doubles as the **bus station.**

To exit the station, turn left on C. Forn de Vidre (the perpendicular street with your back to the station), take your third left onto the thoroughfare Rambla de la Pau, head under the underpass, and follow the *rambla* all the way to the port. When you hit the waterside road, the **tourist office** (tel. 93 815 45 17), with an excellent **map** and lodgings advice, is about 50m to your right, in a small park called **Parc de Ribes Roges** (open July-Aug. M-F 10am-8pm, Sa 10am-2pm; Sept.-June 10am-2pm and sometimes 4-7pm, unpredictably). To get to the beach, either head right, past the tourist office toward **Platja de Ribes Roges,** or left to the smaller **Platja del Far.** Expect fine sands, good sun, and tons of company.

ACCOMMODATIONS AND FOOD If you decide to stay in town, the popular **Can Gatell,** C. Puigcerdà, 6-16 (tel. 93 893 01 17), near the waterfront, has clean rooms. With your back to the station, head down the leftward of the two parallel streets (C. Victor Balaguer), then take a right onto Rbla. Ventosa when Balaguer ends; hang a quick left at the sign. (Singles 3000ptas, with bath 4000ptas; doubles 5000ptas, with bath 6000ptas.) There's a **supermarket** right down the street from Can Gatell on Rbla. Ventosa; the *hostal's* four-course 1300ptas *menú* is also popular with locals.

Map labels (within image): FRANCE, Perpignan, Vall d'Aran, Beret, Baqueira, Parque Nacional de Aigüestortes, ANDORRA, Céret, Port-bou, Pont de Suert, La Seu d'Urgell, Puigcerdà, Port de la Selva, Cadaqués, CATALAN PYRENEES, Núria, Sant Joan de les Abadesses, Camprodon, Figueras, Llançà, Tremp, Ripoll, Olot, Besalú, Río Fluvià, L'Escala, Berga, Banyoles, Girona, Éger, Cardona, Vic, Río Ter, Tamariu, Palafrugell, S. Feliu de Guíxols, Palamós, Balaguer, Cervera, Río Cardoner, Manresa, Lérida, N II, Tàrrega, Sant Jerónim, Montserrat, Sabadell, A7 E15, Tossa de Mar, Lloret de Mar, Blanes, Calella, COSTA BRAVA, A2, Terrassa, Mataró, Río Segre, Monestir Poblet, Montblanc, Santes Creus, Badalona, Barcelona, Valls, Reus, Sitges, El Prat de Llobregat, Castelldefels, Móra d'Ebre, Cambrils de Mar, Tarragona, Vilanova i la Geltrú, TO GENOVA, Salou, MEDITERRANEAN SEA, TO MALLORCA, Tortosa, A7 E15, COSTA DORADA, N, TO ISLAS BALEARES, Catalunya

Catalunya (Cataluña)

Once in Catalunya, it is easy to understand the pride and nationalism of the *Catalanes*. The rocky Costa Brava, smooth Costa Daurada, tranquil, interior vineyards of Penèdes, and striking Pyrenees mountains, over all of which chic and cosmopolitan Barcelona rules, have kept the region physically and figuratively removed from Castilian Spain. *Catalanes* are proud, devoted to their land, and industrious, and have consequently become privileged denizens of the richest region in the country.

Colonized by the Greeks and the Carthaginians, Catalunya was later one of Rome's favored provinces, to which scattered ruins testify. Only briefly subdued by the Moors, Catalunya's counts achieved independence in 874 and gained recognition as sovereign princes in 987. After nabbing the throne of Aragón in 1137, Catalunya became linked to the rest of Spain, yet Catalan *usages* or *fueros* (legal codes) remained in effect. It took a Bourbon, King Felipe V, to suppress Catalunya as punishment for siding against him in the War of Spanish Succession (1702-1714). In the late 18th century, Catalunya's fortunes revived when the region developed into one of Europe's premier textile manufacturers and opened trade with the Americas. Nineteenth-century industrial expansion nourished a flowering of arts and sciences, an age known as the Catalan *Renaixença* (Renaissance).

The 20th century gave birth to the Modernist architectural movement and an all-star list of artists and architects, including Picasso, Miró, Dalí, and Antoni Gaudí. Home to staunch opponents of the Fascists during Spain's Civil War, Catalunya lost its

CATALUNYA

autonomy in 1939 when the Republicans lost to Nationalist powers. Franco suppressed Catalan language instruction (except in universities), and publication in the language was limited to special areas. Since Catalunya regained autonomy in 1977, Catalan media and arts have flourished. Today, Catalan is once again the region's official language, although Catalunya is almost entirely bilingual and still politically divided over the language issue. While some worry that the use of Catalan will discourage talented Spaniards from teaching or studying in Catalunya, effectively isolating the principality, others argue that extensive regional autonomy has generally led to progressive ends. Many Catalans will answer inquiring visitors in Catalan, even if asked in Castilian, and visible displays of Catalan spirit abound, including the "Freedom for Catalunya" graffiti left from the 1992 Olympics.

Lauded throughout Spain, Catalan cuisine boasts *pan con tomate,* bread smeared with olive oil, tomato, and garlic, and ali-oli, a garlic-and-olive oil sauce. Lovers exchange books and roses to honor the region's patron, St. George, on the Fiesta de Sant Jordi (April 23). On September 11, *catalanes* whoop it up for *Diada* (La Festa Nacional de Catalunya), a celebration of the region's political autonomy.

🔍 HIGHLIGHTS OF CATALUNYA

- The jumbled, medieval streets of historic, charming, and under-touristed **Girona.**
- Laid-back **Cadaqués's** rocky beaches and charming streets (see p. 346).
- **Teatre Museu Dalí,** Salvador Dalí's self-built monument (see p. 349).

■ Girona (Gerona)

If you've come to Spain to reflect on the ages, then Girona is for you. A world-class city waiting for the rest of the world to notice, Girona (pop. 72,500) displays layer upon layer of ethnic influences and epochal transitions, marked by stone alleyways twisting through the old Jewish Quarter. Images of medieval dwellings reflecting off Riu Onyor's glassy waters dreamily evoke Girona's past glory, when Christian, Arab, and Jewish communities settled along its shores in peaceful co-existence to capitalize, as the Romans did, on the city's favorable geography—as a gateway to Europe by land and to the Orient by sea. The renowned *cabalistas de Gerona* originated here, practicing mystical Judaism and later spreading the teachings of the Kaballah westward. Scholarly vivification continues to thrive today in Girona's university, and a student population brings life to tempting restaurants and cozy bars.

ORIENTATION AND PRACTICAL INFORMATION

Girona is the transportation hub of the Costa Brava. All trains on the Barcelona-Portbou-Cerbère line stop here and seven different lines send buses to the Costa Brava. Transportation to Ripoll and Olot is also easy by bus, making Girona a good jumping-off point for exploring the Catalan Pyrenees.

The **Riu Onyar** separates the new city from the old. The **Pont de Pedra** connects the two banks and leads directly into the old quarter by way of Carrers Ciutadans, Peralta, and Força, off of which branch the **cathedral** and **El Call,** the historic Jewish neighborhood. **RENFE** and **bus terminals** are situated off **Carrer de Barcelona,** in the modern neighborhood. To get to the old city from the stations, head straight out the station through the parking lot, turning left on C. Barcelona. Follow C. Barcelona for two blocks until it forks at the traffic island. Take the right fork via C. Santa Eugenia to the **Gran Vía de Jaume I,** and continue straight across at the Banco Central Hispano to get on **Carrer Nou,** which runs directly to the Pont de Pedra.

Transportation

Trains: RENFE (tel. 972 20 70 93), in Pl. Espanya. Info open daily 6:30am-10pm. To: Figueres (30min., 28 per day, 330-370ptas); Portbou (1hr., 19 per day, 500ptas); Barcelona (1¼hr., 26 per day, 880ptas); Valencia (5hr., 3 per day, 4600-5200ptas); Zaragoza (5-6hr., 2 per day, 3700-4700ptas); Madrid (9-10½hr., 3 per day, 5400-6500ptas). To Jaca, change in Zaragoza.

Buses: (tel. 972 21 23 19) around the corner from the train station. Info open daily 6am-10pm. **Sarfa** (tel. 972 20 17 96). To Tossa de Mar (1hr., July-Aug. 2 per day, Sept.-June 1 per day, 625ptas) and Palafrugell (1hr., 12 per day, 525ptas), for connections to Begur, Llafranc, Calella, and Tamariu. **Teisa** (tel. 972 20 48 68). To: Olot (1¼hr., 6-16 per day, 625-715ptas); Ripoll (2hr., 3 per day, 1080-1230ptas); St. Feliu (45min., 9-15 per day, 425-485ptas); Lerida (3½hr., 2-4 per day, 2120ptas). **Barcelona Bus** (tel. 972 20 24 32) express to Barcelona (1½hr., 3-4 per day, 1050ptas) and Figueres (50min., 3-4 per day, 435ptas).

Taxis: (tel. 972 20 33 77 or 972 22 10 20), at Pl. Independència and Pont de Pedra.

Car Rental: Most companies cluster around C. Barcelona, near the train station. Must be over 21 (for most) and have had a license for at least 1-2 years. **Hertz** (tel. 972 21 01 08), in the train station. Min. age 25. Rentals start at 5000ptas for one day with unlimited mileage. Open M-F 9am-1pm and 4-7:30pm, Sa 9:30am-noon.

Tourist, Financial, and Local Services

Tourist Office: Rambla Llibertat, 1 (tel. 972 22 65 75; fax 972 22 66 12), in a watermelon-red building directly on the left as you cross Pont de Pedra from the new town. Loads of info on the region and city. Open M-F 8am-8pm, Sa 8am-2pm and 4-8pm, Su 9am-2pm. The **train station branch** (tel. 972 21 62 96) is downstairs, on the left as you face away from the RENFE ticket counter. Nifty electronic info server with zoom-able info maps. Open July-Aug. M-F 8:30am-1:30pm.

Currency Exchange: Banco Central Hispano (with an **ATM**) is on the corner of C. Nou and Gran Vía de Jaume I, and in the old city on Pujada Pont de Pedra, just after crossing the bridge on the right. Both open M-F 8:30am-2:30pm, Sa 9:30am-1pm.

Luggage Storage: Lockers in train station (600ptas). Open daily 5:30am-11pm.

English Bookstore: Gerona Books, C. Carme, 63 (tel. 972 22 46 12). Rambla Llibertat runs into C. Carme as you walk with the river on your right. Some new and used pulp fiction and classics. Open M-F July 9am-2pm; Sept.-June 9am-1pm and 4-8pm.

Youth Services: Punt D'Informació Juvenil, Casa Cultura, Pl. L'Hospital (tel. 972 20 57 03). Walking from the train station, make a right on Gran Vía de Jaume I and a left on Pl. L'Hospital (1-2 blocks). Railpasses, buses, HI cards (500ptas), ISICs (700ptas). Does not handle flight reservations, but tons of travel info. Open July-Sept. 14 M-F 9am-2pm; Sept. 15-June 9am-2pm and 3:30-5:30pm.

Hipercor (El Corté Inglés's Not-So-Chic Cousin): (tel. 972 24 44 44). On C. Barcelona, take a right out of train station (15min.). Groceries, telephones, **currency exchange,** English books, *cafeteria*, and reliability. Open M-Sa 10am-10pm.

Emergency and Communications

Emergency: tel. 091 or 092. **Police: Policía Municipal,** C. Bacià, 4 (tel. 092). From Banco Central Hispano, turn right on the Gran Vía, then right on Bacià.

Hospitals: Hospital Municipal de Santa Caterina, Pl. Hospital, 5 (tel. 972 18 26 00). **Hospital Doctor Josep Trueta** (tel. 972 20 27 00), on the highway to France has an interpreter in summer.

Internet Access: Ciberxuxes, C. Carme, 55 (tel. 972 22 61 91), one block before the English bookstore. 300ptas for the first 30min., 500ptas for the first hr., 100ptas every additional 15min. Open daily July-Sept.; Oct.-June 8am-midnight.

Post Office: Av. Ramón Folch, 2 (tel. 972 20 32 36), at the beginning of Gran Vía de Jaume I. Turn right on Gran Vía coming from the old city. **Second office,** Ronda Ferrán Puig, 17 (tel. 972 21 07 71). Lista de Correos only. Both open M-F 8:30am-8:30pm, Sa 9:30am-2pm. **Postal Code:** 17070.

ACCOMMODATIONS

Rooms are most difficult to find in June and August. Most budget accommodations are sprinkled in and around the old quarter and are both reasonably priced and well kept. The tourist office has helpful listings.

Alberg-Residència Cerverí de Girona (HI), C. Ciutadans, 9 (tel. 972 21 81 21; fax 972 21 20 23). Prime location in the heart of the old quarter, on the street running left after Pont de Pedra. A college dorm during the year, it's ultra-modern inside. 8

beds are available Oct.-June; 103 beds July-Sept. Sleek sitting rooms with TV/VCR; rooms of 3 and 8 beds, with lockers. High-caliber staff, high-fashion sheets. Dorms 1700ptas, over 25 2275ptas. Breakfast included. Other meals 750-800ptas. Sheets 350ptas. Laundry 500ptas. Members only, but HI cards available. Make reservations at the Barcelona office (tel. 93 483 83 63) in Aug.

Pensió Viladomat, C. Ciutadans, 5 (tel. 972 20 31 76), next door to the HI. Clean rooms and bathrooms. Neat and well furnished with desks. Some rooms have balconies. Singles 2000ptas; doubles 4000ptas, with bath 6000ptas.

Pensió Pérez, Pl. Bell-lloc, 4 and **Pensió Borras,** Trav. Auriga, 6 (tel. 972 22 40 08). Keep straight after crossing Pont de Pedra into the old quarter onto C. Non del Teatre; Pl. Bell-lloc is on the right. To Pensión Borras from Pérez, take a right out the door and follow the street around the corner, making a left at its end. Energetic owner lets simple rooms with bright white walls. Singles 1600ptas, with bath 2000ptas; doubles 2800ptas, with bath 3200ptas; triples 4000ptas.

Hostal Residencia Bellmirall, C. Bellmirall, 3 (tel. 972 20 40 09). Go straight from the door on the right side of the cathedral (angle left) until the blue sign appears. Stone rooms are the delightful and creative project of 2 Gironese artists—a mix of the husband's oil paintings and the wife's colorful needlework. Singles 4540ptas, with bath 4800ptas; doubles 7200ptas, with bath 7800ptas. Breakfast included. Call ahead for reservations May-Sept.

FOOD

Considered home to the best in Catalunyan cuisine, Girona abounds with innovative specialties and exotic surf-and-turf combos. The city's restaurants are almost uniformly excellent and relatively inexpensive. Some of the best places huddle near the cathedral and along **Carrer Cort Reial.** Others, including several outdoor eateries, are found on **Plaça Independència** at the end of C. Santa Clara in the modern section of the city. Scores of cafes line **Rambla de la Llibertat.** In the old quarter, even more cater to university students. Girona's permanent **market** is in Pl. Clave and Rubalcaba, on the new side of the city near the river (open M-Sa 8am-1pm). In summer, the **second location** opens near the Polideportivo in Parc de la Deversa (open Tu and Sa 8am-1pm). One street north of C. Nou (off the Gran Vía) is supermarket **Valvi,** C. Sequia, 10 (tel. 972 21 45 16; open M-Sa 9am-1:30pm and 5-8:30pm).

Café Le Bistrot, Pujada Sant Domènec, 4 (tel. 972 21 88 03), a right off C. Ciutadans. Hipsters crowd marble tables outside to munch and people-watch. Lunchtime *menú* 1200ptas; abridged version 950ptas. Freshly made pizzas (475-675ptas) and crepes (425-600ptas). Open M-Th 1pm-midnight, F-Sa 1pm until late, Su 7pm-midnight. Kitchen closed 4-8pm. Closed some Mondays in winter.

Café la Torrada, C. Ciutadans, 18 (tel. 972 21 71 04), a block from the youth hostel. Student crowd chats over *torradas,* delectable toasts with toppings (575-1100ptas), and a wide selection of salads. Catalan only menu. Open in summer M-F 9am-11pm; in winter M-F 9am-11pm, Sa 7pm-midnight.

Crepes: La Crêperie Bretanne, C. Cort Reial, 4 (tel. 972 21 81 20). In a kitchen inside a small blue bus, French owners prepare extravagant crepes (300-700ptas) and delish *galletas* (brown flour crepes, 400-785ptas). Crayons provided for your inner artsy child. Open mid-July to Sept. daily 1-4pm and 8pm-midnight; Oct. to mid-July Tu-Su 1-4pm and 8pm-midnight. **Crepdequé?,** C. Ballesteries, 49, around the corner, sells simpler, cheaper crepes to go (200-350ptas). Open daily 6am-10pm.

L'Anfora, C. Força, 15 (tel. 972 20 50 10). Upstairs dining hall with wicker chairs and stone walls was once the secret site of Jewish religious ceremonies. Downstairs, large hunks of decidedly un-kosher ham hang over the bar. Multilingual lunch *menú* 1400ptas. Open in summer M-Sa noon-4pm and 7-11pm; in winter daily noon-4pm and 7-11pm. Visa, MC.

Granje Mora, C. Corte Reial, 18 (tel. 972 20 22 38). Jovial, down-to-earth owners have been a Gironan institution for 60 years. They offer all-natural *Orxata de Xufu* (*horchata* 225ptas) to die for and delicious sandwiches and ice-cream drinks.

Restaurant Vegetariano La Polenta, C. Corte Reial, 6 (tel. 972 20 93 74). Vegetarian fare with an international accent. Catalan rice dishes 575ptas, Italian pasta 650ptas, sushi 650ptas, and pita sandwiches 700ptas. Plenty of no-lacto choices. *Menú* (lunch only) 1100ptas. Open M and W-Sa 1-4pm and 8-11pm, Tu 1-4pm.

SIGHTS

A 30-day pass for the old city's 6 museums is available at museums or the tourist office (800ptas). The tourist office also leads guided tours of El Call (800ptas) July-Aug. Contact them for info.

The narrow, winding streets of the medieval old city, interspersed with steep stairways and low arches, reward wanderers; signs direct tourists on foot. Start your self-guided historical tour at the Pont de Pedra and turn left at the tourist office down tree-lined **Rambla de la Llibertat.** Continue on C. Argenteria, bearing right across C. Cort Reial. Up the flight of stairs, C. Força begins on the left.

El Call

El Call is the medieval Jewish neighborhood. ("Call" comes from *kahal,* meaning "community" in Hebrew.) For a history of El Call, see **Rebuilding Sepharad,** below. It begins at C. Sant Llorenç and is centered along C. Forçà. The entrance to the **Centre Bonastruc Ça Porta** (tel. 972 21 67 61) is off C. Sant Llorenç about halfway up the hill. *(Open June-Oct. M-Sa 10am-8pm, Su 10am-3pm; Nov.-May M-Sa 10am-6pm, Su 10am-2pm. Free.)* Probable site of the last synagogue in Girona, it now serves as a museum linking the baths, butcher shop, and synagogue, all of which surround a serene central patio. The center is named for Girona-born Rabbi Moshe ben Nahman (Nahmanides), most famed for his studies of Kabbalah, a mystical reading of the scriptures proposing to unlock certain mysteries and foretell the future.

Cathedral Complex

Cathedral and Tesoro open July-Aug. Tu-Su 10am-2pm and 4-7pm; Sept.-June Tu-Sa 10am-2pm and 4-7pm, Su 10am-2pm. Tesoro and cloister 400ptas.

Farther uphill on C. Forç and around the corner to the right, Girona's imposing Gothic **cathedral** rises up a record-breaking 90 steps (the largest Roccoco stairway in Europe) from its *plaça.* The northern **Torre de Charlemany** and the cloister are the only structures left standing from the 11th century. The more youthful part of the building dates from the 15th and 16th centuries. Inside, three customary naves have been compressed into one, producing the world's widest Gothic nave (22m).

A door on the left leads to the trapezoidal cloister and the **Tesoro Capitular** (tel. 972 21 44 26), holding some of Girona's most precious possessions, including the 10th-century *Libre de l'Apocalipsis* or *Beatus,* an illuminated commentary on the end of the world. The *tesoro's* (and possibly Girona's) most famous piece is the **Tapis de la Creació,** an 11th- to 12th-century tapestry depicting the creation cycle and covering the entire wall of Room IV.

Elsewhere

From the cathedral, with your back to the stairs, take a right on C. Ferran Catòlic to the **Banys Àrabs** (tel. 972 21 32 62). *(Open Apr.-Sept. M-Sa 10am-7pm, Su 10am-2pm; Oct.-Mar. daily 10am-2pm. 200ptas, students 100ptas.)* Inspired by Muslim bath houses, this graceful 12th-century building once contained saunas and baths of varying temperatures for soaking off medieval gunk. The **Museu Arqueològic** (tel. 972 20 26 32), left from the Banys Àrabs and through the gates of Pl. Jurats, is housed in the 11th- to 12th-century Romanesque **Monasterio de Sant Pere de Galligants,** the final resting place of medieval tombstones that once marked Jewish burial sites. *(Open in summer Tu-Sa 10:30am-1:30pm and 4-7pm, Su 10am-2pm; in winter Tu-Sa 10am-2pm and 4-6pm. 200ptas. Sundays free.)* On Pujada de la Catedral is the **Museu d'Art** (tel. 972 20 95 36), with a large collection including 12th-century Romanesque wood sculpture and remnants of the medieval stained-glass industry. *(Open July-Sept. Tu and Th-Sa 10am-7pm, W 10am-7pm and 8pm-midnight, Su 10am-2pm; Oct.-June Tu-Sa 10am-7pm, Su 10am-2pm.*

Rebuilding Sepharad

The Jews of Girona underwent severe discrimination, ostracism, and eventual expulsion. Despite it all, they contributed ineradicably to the city's culture as poets, scientists, astronomers, rabbis, philosophers, and ministers of the court. The *aljama* (Jewish quarter) in Girona, once populated by 300 people, became a leading center for the study of the **Kabbalah,** a mystical reading of the Torah in which number values are assigned to each Hebrew letter and numerical sums are interpreted to reveal spiritual meaning. Operating like a tiny, independent country within the city (they answered to the King, not the city government), El Call was protected by the crown of Catalunya in exchange for financial tribute. City officials of Girona, however, often passed oppressive measures asserting control over the Jews in the name of protecting the Christian quarters.

Until the 11th century, Christians and Jews basically coexisted peacefully, sometimes intermarrying. Predictably, though, this awkward balance between political independence and subjugation soon led to conflicts. Historical sources cite attacks and looting of the Jewish quarter in eight different years, the first in 1276 and the last in 1418. Eventually, almost every entrance to El Call had been blocked off, not to be reopened until August 4, 1492, when Ferdinand and Isabella expelled all Jews from Spain through enforced emigration, conversion, and the Inquisition's *autos-de-fé.* The complete reopening of the streets of El Call began only after Franco's death in 1975. In recent times, eight Spanish mayors have created a network called *Caminos de Sepharad,* an organization aimed at restoring the synagogues and Jewish quarters and fostering a broader understanding of the Sephardic legacy.

200ptas. Sundays free.) On the fourth floor, moody 19th-century landscape paintings hang alongside contemporary Catalan works.

Near the **University of Girona** is the start of the extremely beautiful **Passeig de la Muralla.** Railed steps lead up onto the walls of the city for a bird's eye view of old Girona. The walk ends two blocks to the left of the Pont de Pedra. The **Passeig Arqueològic,** partly lined with cypresses, pines, and flower beds, skirts the medieval wall on the east side of the river and overlooks the city.

In the **New City** and on a completely different note from the rest of Girona is the **Museu del Cinema,** Sèquia, 1 (tel./fax 972 41 27), one block north of C. Nou off C. Santa Clara, which runs along the river. The museum chronicles the invention of movies, from the rise of shadow theater to early special effects, in wacky interactive exhibits. *(Open Tu-Su 10am-8pm; Oct-May 10am-6pm. 400ptas, students 200ptas.)*

ENTERTAINMENT

The **Rambla** and **Plaça de Independencia** are the places to see and be seen—to chat, gossip, politic, flirt, and dance. Some summer Fridays inspire spontaneous *sardanas,* traditional Catalan dances resurrected in 19th-century Girona, involving 10 to 12 musicians serenading a ring of dancers. One musician plays a *tambón:* with one hand he pipes on a small flute, with the other he taps a tiny drum slung over his forearm.

After a *passeig* (walk) comes dinner, and after dinner, bar-hopping—the throngs move to the newer part of the city. Bars near Pl. Ferrán Catòlic draw big crowds, but during the summer, **Parc de la Devesa,** across the river from the old town and several blocks to the left, has all the cachet and often live music as well. Of Girona's four discos, the mightiest is **La Sala de Cel,** C. Pedret, 118 (tel. 972 21 26 64), off Pl. Sant Pere, in the north quarter of the city (open Sept.-July Th-Su; 2000ptas cover includes 2 drinks). Artsy folk mill around oh-so-cute bars and cafes in the old quarter. Enter on C. Ferreires Vellas, parallel to C. Ciutadans, to try the **Cafe del Lliberia,** C. Ciutadans, 15 (tel. 972 20 48 18), which caters to chic intellectuals (open M-Sa 8:30am-2am, Su noon-2am). Low tables and cozy nooks fill the unmarked **La Terra,** C. Ballesteries, 23 (tel. 972 21 57 64; open Su-W 5pm-1am, Th-Sa 5pm-2am).

During the second half of May, **flower exhibitions** spring up in the city, local monuments swim in blossoms, and the courtyards of Girona's fine old buildings open to the public. From July through September, the city hosts the **Festival de Noves Músiques,** a series of six concerts in La Mercè. The **concert hall** (tel. 972 22 33 05) is at Pujada de la Mercé, 12. In June and July, **concerts** take place in front of the cathedral, in the Jardins de la Devesa. From July through September, the Museu d'Art hosts lectures, movies, and concerts every Wednesday night at 10pm (free). Check with the tourist office for schedules and prices. The complete *sardana* guide, the *Guia d'Aplecs Sardanistes de les Comarques Gironines,* is available at the tourist office, along with a complete listing of observed holidays and festivals. Girona's two local holidays are the July 25 holiday for Sant Jaume and the October 29 holiday for the Fires de Sant Narcís. Like the rest of northern Spain, Girona lights up for the **Focs de Sant Joan** on June 24, an exuberant outdoor party featuring fireworks and campfires.

COSTA BRAVA

The Costa Brava's jagged cliffs cut into the Mediterranean Sea from Barcelona to the French border. Though savage by name, the coast is tamed in July and August by planeloads of Europeans dumped onto its once tranquil beaches (you'll make the most friends if you speak German). More solitary types should come in early June and late September when the water is still warm but less populated. Still, much of the Costa Brava has avoided the high-rises that plague the Costa del Sol, and in winter, the fierce winds of the *tramontana* sweep the coast, leaving behind tranquil, boarded-up beach towns. The rocky shores have traditionally enticed artists, like Chagall and Surrealist icon Salvador Dalí, a Costa Brava native. Dalí's house in Cadaqués and his museum in Figueres display the largest collections of his work in Europe.

Transportation on the Costa Brava is fickle, with frequent service during July and August, less service the rest of the tourist season (May-Oct.), and bare subsistence service in winter. **RENFE trains** stop at the southern tip of the coast at Blanes, Figueres, and again at Llançà and Portbou (near the French border). **Buses** are the preferred mode of transportation, often running along beautiful winding roads. Know that prices vary considerably according to season. Tossa de Mar is the crown of the southern Costa Brava and a base to explore the area. To the north, Figueres is linked to Cadaqués by bus and Portbou by rail. Palafrugell is an inland connection to central Costa Brava. Local tourist offices distribute maps of off-road sights, camping areas, and coastal trails.

▓ Portbou

Sitting on Catalunya's border with France, Portbou (pop. 1500) was a virtually non-existent fisherman's village when the Barcelona-Cerbère railroad showed up in 1872, bringing life, albeit an industrial one, to the town. As Europe indecisively marches toward economic unity, Portbou faces the threat of losing its customs economy and valuable jobs. Still, as border towns go, Portbou is not so bad; it has preserved its pleasant pebble beach and leafy trees lining its few streets.

PRACTICAL INFORMATION RENFE **trains** (tel. 972 39 00 99) go to Barcelona (2¾hr., 14 per day, 1220-2200ptas) via every town with a station in western Catalunya, including Figueres (30min., 19 per day, 295ptas), as well as north to Collioure, France. The friendly **tourist office** (tel. 972 39 02 84) sits beachside (open June 15-Sept. 15 M-Sa 9am-2pm and 3-8pm, Su 9am-1pm). **Banco Central Hispano,** C. Mercal, 13, on the street from the train station, **exchanges currency** and has an **ATM** (open M-F 8:30am-2:30pm, Sa in winter). There's **luggage storage** in lockers at the train station (600ptas). The Ajuntament, at the end of Pg. Sardanes at the end of the beach, houses the **police** (tel. 972 39 02 84). The **post office** is at Pg. Enric Granades, 10 (tel. 972 39 01 75; open M-F 8:30am-2:30pm, Sa 9:30am-1pm). The **postal code** is 17497.

ACCOMMODATIONS AND FOOD Hostal Juventus, Av. Barcelona, 3 (tel. 972 39 02 41), has simple rooms with sinks. The same owners run a *croissanterie* downstairs. From the train station, head straight down to the water, past beachside cafes on Passeig Sardana for one block, and take the last right. (Singles 1700ptas; doubles 3300ptas; triples 4800ptas.) Portbou's **market** (Tuesdays and Fridays) is located one block down from the train station on C. Mercat. One of the bigger **supermarkets** is on Rambla Catalunya behind the tourist office. Morbid, hungry types can eat cheaply from the same place where philosopher Walter Benjamin ate his last meal and then died upstairs. **Restaurant International,** C. Del Mar, 5, is left off C. Mercat as you exit the station (*menú* 900-1000ptas; open daily 12:30-4pm and 7:30-11pm). Restaurants by the waterfront offer typical tourist fare at unfortunate prices.

Walter Benjamin

Although Portbou may seem fairly insignificant on the cultural landscape, it *is* where the extremely influential literary and cultural critic Walter Benjamin died. Benjamin, a social theorist of the Frankfurt school and close friend of Bertold Brecht, left behind a legend that is posthumous but profound. A pessimist Marxist, he elucidated the relationship between literature and social structures. Of German-Jewish descent, Benjamin was fleeing the Nazis in 1940 when he arrived at the border town of Portbou. There he was detained and not permitted to enter Spain. He retired to the Pensión at Restaurante Internacional and killed himself by overdosing on morphine. Local lore, however, claims that Benjamin was murdered by the Nazis. The legend runs that Fascist camaraderie between Franco and the Nazis led Franco to permit the Gestapo to enter Portbou, where the secret police supposedly tracked down Benjamin and killed him. Regardless of the way he died, a lovely memorial to Benjamin sits above the town, right outside the cemetery where his grave lies.

■ Llançà (Llansà)

Fifteen kilometers south of the French border, Llançà (pop. 3900) is the northernmost resort of any magnitude on the Costa Brava, with many beaches and coves and few historical sights. It's pleasant rather than scintillating, but it's good enough to work on your tan. The main beach, **Platja del Port,** opens onto a protected harbor. The town center is home to the central *plaça,* **església,** and the 14th-century Romanesque **Torre de Llançà** (open July to mid-Sept. M-Sa 10am-1pm and 6-9pm, Su 10am-1pm.).

ORIENTATION AND PRACTICAL INFORMATION From the **train station,** cross the highway and continue on Av. Europa until the fork: right leads to the town center, left to the beach. The bus stops across from the tourist office, with the beach to the right and the town center to the left (follow C. Rafael Estela to **Plaça Major**). RENFE **trains** (tel. 972 38 02 55) run to: Portbou (15min., 18 per day, 145ptas); Figueres (30min., 22 per day, 165ptas); Girona (1hr., 22 per day, 395ptas); and Barcelona (2½hr., 22 per day, 1220ptas). **Sarfa** (tel. 972 38 08 55) runs **buses** to Port de la Selva (15min., 2-9 per day, 140ptas) and Figueres (25min., 3-5 per day, 300ptas). From July to August, Sarfa has service to Barcelona (2 per day, 1175ptas). Buy tickets on the bus. The English-speaking staff at the **tourist office,** Av. Europa, 37 (tel. 972 38 08 55; fax 972 38 12 58), on the road to the port, gives out info and a detailed but superfluous map (open July-Aug. M-Sa 9:30am-9pm, Su 10am-1pm; Sept.-June M-F 10am-1pm and 5-8pm, Sa 10am-1pm and 5-7pm, Su 10am-1pm). **Banks** hang around Pl. Major. In an **emergency** dial 091 or 092; the **local police** pick up at 972 38 13 13. The **post office,** C. Pablo Picasso, 10 (tel. 972 22 21 11), is next to the parking lot at the town entrance (open M-F 8:30am-2:30pm, Sa 9:30am-1pm). The **postal code** is 17490.

ACCOMMODATIONS AND FOOD Habitaciones Ca'n Pau, C. Puig d'Esquer, 4 (tel. 972 38 02 70), is comfortable and quiet, with a rooftop for hanging laundry and taking in the view. Take the second left as you enter town (C. Cabrafiga), and continue straight 2-3 blocks taking the first left after %Día supermarket, then left three blocks later on C. Deciana; turn right almost immediately on C. Puig d'Esquer. The hostal is on the corner on your right. (Singles 2000ptas; doubles 3500ptas; winter heating.) **Habitaciones Pacreu,** Av. Europa, 33 (tel. 972 38 03 37), next door to the tourist office, has cozy rooms with bathrooms off a plant-filled terrace (singles 2500ptas; doubles 3750ptas; open June-Aug.). **Camping L'Ombra,** Ctra. Portou, 13 (tel. 972 38 03 35), has 123 spaces 500m from the beach (July-Aug. 470-550ptas per person, 800-935ptas per site; Sept.-June 550ptas per person, site free).

Llançà's waterfront *menú*-suppliers serve up standard meals at standard prices, although cheaper places pepper the town. Pack your picnic basket at **Fàmila Supermercats** (tel. 972 38 07 52), a large supermarket on Av. Europa, on the right as you head toward the beach. (Open July-Aug. M-Sa 8am-9pm, Su 9am-9pm; Sept.-June M-F 9am-1:30pm and 4:30-8:30pm, Sa 9am-2pm and 4:30-9pm, Su 4:30-8:30pm.) **Restaurant Grill Pati Blanc,** C. Rafael Estela, 6 (tel. 972 38 08 00), on the way to Pl. Major, offers grilled fare on a shaded, white patio. The meats are succulent (grilled chicken, 550ptas), as are veggie dishes like *escalivada* (grilled and marinated red peppers, eggplant, and onions, 725ptas). (Open daily 1-4pm and 7:30pm-midnight.)

■ Near Llançà: Sant Pere de Rodes

Thirteen kilometers south of Llançà on the coast are the glorious ruins of the Benedictine **monastery,** Sant Pere de Rodes, built in the 10th and 11th centuries. On a clear day, Portbou is easily espied to the north and Cadaqués to the south. *(Open June-Sept. Tu-Su 10am-7pm; Oct.-May 10am-1:30pm and 3-5:30pm. 300ptas.)* Getting there may present something of a challenge. The tourist office at Llançà organizes **excursions.** *(Min. 4 people. 800ptas per half-day, 1000ptas per full day.)* If you choose to go it alone and lack a car, be prepared for some serious foot mileage. Committed **hikers** can take a strenuous trek from Llansà (2½-3hr.), with splendid views along the way. Alternatively, the **Sarfa bus** from Llançà to Port de la Selva (15min., 9 per day, 140ptas) stops on the road to the monastery. From there, make the far less arduous 1½-hour climb.

■ Figueres (Figueras)

In 1974 Salvador Dalí chose his native Figueres (pop. 37,000) as the site to build a magnificent museum for his works, instantly catapulting the city to international fame. Ever since, a multilingual parade of Surrealist fans has been filing past Dalí's melting clocks and erotic nightmares daily. Though a beachless sprawl, Figueres hides other quality museums and pleasant cafes, not to mention seven centuries of history. It also is a convenient base for visiting the often booked-solid Costa Brava.

ORIENTATION AND PRACTICAL INFORMATION

Roughly 20km inland, Figueres marks the center of the Costa Brava's breadbasket. Trains and buses arrive at **Plaça Estació** on the edge of town. Cross the plaza and bear left on **Carrer Sant Llàtzer,** walk several blocks to **Carrer Nou,** and take a right directly to Figueres's arboreal **Rambla.** To reach the **tourist office,** walk up the Rambla and continue on **Carrer Lasauca** straight out from the left corner. The big blue all-knowing **"i"** beckons across the rather treacherous intersection with **Ronda Frial.**

Trains: (tel. 972 20 70 93). To: Girona (30min., 22 per day, 320-350ptas); Portbou (30min., 15 per day, 245ptas); Barcelona (1½hr., 22 per day, 1085-1240ptas).
Buses: All lines leave from the Estació Autobuses (tel. 972 67 33 54), Pl. Estació.
Sarfa (tel. 972 67 42 98) runs to Cadaqués (1¼hr., July-Aug. 5 per day, Sept.-June 2-3 per day, 460ptas) and Llançà (4 per day, Sept.-June 1 per day, 285ptas). **Barce-**

Iona Bus (tel. 972 50 50 29) drives to Girona (1hr., 4-6 per day, 415ptas) and Barcelona (2¼hr., 4-6 per day, 1375ptas).

Taxis: (tel. 972 50 00 08). Taxis line up on the Rambla.

Car Rental: Europcar, Pl. Estació, 16 (tel. 972 67 34 34). Min. age 22. All-inclusive rental from 8900ptas per day.

Bike Rental: At the HI hostel (see below). 1300ptas per day.

Tourist Office: (tel. 972 50 31 55), on Pl. Sol. Has a good city **map** and list of accommodations and restaurants. Open July-Aug. M-Sa 9am-9pm, Su 9am-2pm and 4-6pm; Easter-June and Oct. M-F 8:30am-3pm and 4:30-8pm, Sa 9:30am-1:30pm and 3:30-6:30pm; Sept. and Nov.-Easter M-F 8:30am-3pm. 2 **branch offices** open in summer, one in front of the bus station (open July 15-Sept. 15 M-Sa 9:30am-1pm and 4-7pm), and the other in a yellow mobile home by the Dalí museum (open July 15-Sept. 15 M-Sa 10am-2:30pm and 4:30-7pm).

Currency Exchange: Banco Central Hispano, Rambla, 21, has an **ATM.** Open M-F 8:30am-2pm.

Luggage Storage: At the train station, large lockers 600ptas. Open daily 6am-10pm. At the bus station 300ptas.

Emergency: dial 088. **Police: Mossos d'Esquadra** (tel. 972 67 50 89), on C. Ter.

Internet Access: Cafè Virtual, Pl. del Sol, 10, 1st fl. (tel. 972 67 51 90), up the street from the supermarket. Look out for the rocket ship out front. 500ptas per 30min. 800ptas per hr. Open daily 3pm-midnight.

Post Office: C. Santa Llogaia, 60-62 (tel. 972 50 54 31). Open M-F 8:30am-2:30pm, Sa 9:30am-1pm. **Postal Code:** 17600.

ACCOMMODATIONS AND FOOD

Finding a place to sleep can be a surreal experience. Although the town is reorganizing to better accommodate the influx of tourists, Figueres hides its affordable hotels and *pensiones* in unlikely spots. Some cluster on **Carrer Jonquera,** but they necessitate trekking northeast from the Dalí museum; others are on C. Pep Ventura. Restaurants near the Dalí museum scoop overcooked *paella* to the masses; better choices surround the **Rambla.** The **mercado** is at Pl. del Gra and nearby Pl. Catalunya (open Tu, Th, and Sa 7am-1pm). Or, mass-buy at the mass-supermarket **MAXOR,** Pl. Sol, 5 (tel. 972 51 00 19; open July-Sept. M-F 8am-9pm, Sa 8am-9pm; Oct.-June M-Sa 8am-8:30pm; Visa, MC).

Alberg Tramuntana (HI), C. Anciet de Pagès, 2 (tel. 972 50 12 13; fax 972 67 38 08), 1 block behind the tourist office. Everything a backpacker with wanderlust could want—friendly hosts, fax service, VCR, library, board games, bike rentals, and laundry. Closed Oct. 15-30, mid-Jan. to mid-Feb., and in winter Sundays and Mondays. Members only, but HI cards for sale. May-Sept. dorms 1700ptas, over 26 2275ptas; Oct.-Apr. 1425ptas, over 26 1950ptas. Breakfast included. Sheets 350ptas. Laundry service 600ptas. Curfew midnight; in summer open for 10min. at 1 and 2am. Lockout M-F 10am-4pm, Sa-Su 10am-5pm. Reception daily 8-10am and 4pm-midnight. Reserve 1 month in advance through the Barcelona office (tel. 93 483 83 63) or call the hostel 2-3 days prior to arrival. Visa, MC, AmEx.

Pensión Mallol, C. Pep Ventura, 9 (tel. 972 50 22 83). Follow the Rambla toward the tourist office, turn right on Castell at its end, and take the second left. The friendly owner keeps large rooms with sinks and holds cleanliness sacred. Singles 1850ptas; doubles 3100ptas. Visa.

Restaurante La Torrada, La Rosa, 6 (tel. 972 50 95 66), left off the Rambla on C. Vilatant, then the 2nd right. Open W-M 1-3:30pm and 8pm-midnight. Closed July 1-14. Also, **La Torrada II,** C. Mestre Falla, 15 (972 67 58 26), up the street from the youth hostel. Open W-M 7am-3:30pm and 6pm-2am. The *menú* is delish and served with toasted bread, a tomato, and fresh garlic for a do-it-yourself *torrada* (900ptas). Tasty *bocadillos* and *torradas* available anytime at La Torrada II.

Restaurante La Pansa, C. l'Emporda, 8 (tel. 972 50 10 72). The back is across from the youth hostel. Comfortable restaurant, extremely popular with workmen on their lunchbreaks. *Menú* 1000ptas. Open Aug.-Sept. M-Sa 1-4pm and 8-10pm; Oct.-July daily 1-4pm and 8-10pm.

CATALUNYA

SIGHTS AND ENTERTAINMENT

Despite his reputation as a Fascist and self-promoting cad, Dalí's self-built theater/museum/monument-to-himself is undeniably a masterpiece. The **Teatre-Museu Dalí** (tel. 972 51 18 00; fax 972 50 16 66) is the second most popular museum in Spain. *(Open July 1-25 and Sept. daily 9am-7:15pm; July 26-Aug. daily 9am-7:15pm and 10pm-12:30am; Oct.-June Tu-Su 10:30am-5:15pm. July-Sept. 1000ptas, seniors and students 800ptas; Oct.-June 800ptas, seniors and students 600ptas.)* It's all here: Dalí's naughty cartoons, his own surprisingly low-key tomb, and a painting of Gala—his wife and muse—that when viewed through a telescope (10ptas) morphs into a portrait of Abraham Lincoln. A treasure trove of paintings, by other artists as well as Dalí, includes the remarkable *Self Portrait with a Slice of Bacon.* From the Rambla, take C. Girona from the end furthest from the tourist office, which goes past Pl. Ajuntament and becomes C. Jonquera. A flight of steps by a Dalí statue leads to the museum.

If you're feeling overwhelmed by crowds, head up the hill to the massive 18th-century **Castell de Sant Ferran,** the largest stone fortress in Europe (12,000 square meters; tel. 972 50 26 53). *(Open daily June 15-Sept. 10:30am-7pm; Oct.-June 14 Tu-Su 10:30am-2pm. 350ptas, includes audio tape.)* **Museu de l'Empordà,** Rambla, 2 (tel. 972 50 23 05), packs in a pleasingly random assortment of archaeological finds and paintings from the 19th-century Catalan *Renaixença.* *(Open July-Sept. Tu-Sa 10:30am-2pm and 3:30-7pm, Su 10am-2pm; Oct.-June M-Sa 11am-1pm and 3-7pm, Su 11am-1:30pm. 300ptas, seniors and students 150ptas, under 18 free. Free entry with ticket from Teatre-Museu Dalí.)*

In September, Figueres hosts classical and jazz music at the **Festival Internacional de Música de l'Empordà.** *(Tickets available at Caixa de Catalunya. Call 902 10 12 12 for info and tickets or get a brochure at the tourist office.)* From September 9-12, the area *bodegas* descend on Figueras for the **Mostra del Vi de L'Alt Empordà** and wine-tasting galore. Near May 3, the **Fires i Festes de la Santa Creu** sponsors cultural events, art and technology exhibitions, and parties. Merrymaking at the **Festa de Sant Pere,** held June 28-29, honors the town's patron saint.

■ Near Figueres: Cadaqués

This charming cluster of whitewashed houses facing a small bay has attracted artists, writers, and musicians ever since Dalí built his summer home here in the 30s. To preserve its facade, an affluent, pseudo-bohemian crowd of property owners and renters just say no to condos, big hotels, and trains. The rocky beaches attract their share of tourists, but Cadaqués (pop. 1800) preserves a pleasantly laid-back atmosphere.

ORIENTATION AND PRACTICAL INFORMATION The bus to Cadaqués halts at a shack by a miniature two-fisted Statue of Liberty. With your back to the Sarfa office, walk right and downhill along Av. Caritat Serinyana to the waterfront **Plaça Frederic Rahola.** Once there, a signboard map with indexed services and accommodations will orient you. Cadaqués has no train station. Sarfa **buses** (tel. 972 25 87 13) run to: Figueres (1hr., 3-5 per day, 460ptas); Girona (2hr., 1-2 per day, 865ptas); and Barcelona (2-5 per day, 2025ptas). Buses stop at the junction of Ctra. Port Lligat and Pg. Caritat Serinyana, which leads to the town center. **Escola de Vela Ones** (tel. 939 31 02 84; ask for Xavi) sets up shop on the beach directly in front of the tourist office and rents **mountain bikes** (900ptas per hr., 1900ptas per ½day and 2500ptas per full day), kayaks, and wind-surfing gear (open July-Sept. 15 daily 10am-8pm).

The staff at the **tourist office,** C. Cotxe, 2 (tel. 972 25 83 15; fax 972 15 95 42), off Pl. Frederic Rahola opposite the *passeig,* is helpful and gives out an adequate map. (Open July-Aug. M-Sa 10am-2pm and 4-9pm, Su 10am-1pm; Sept.-June M-Sa 10:30am-1pm and 4-8pm.) **Banco Central Hispano** is on C. Caritat Serinyana, 4 (open M-F 8:30am-2:30pm). In an **emergency,** contact the **local police** (tel. 972 15 93 43), Pl. Frederic Rahola, beside the promenade. For **medical assistance,** call 972 25 88 07. The **post office** is on Av. Rierassa off C. Caritat Serinyana (open M-F 8:30-11:30am, Sa 9am-11pm). The **postal code** is 17488.

ACCOMMODATIONS AND FOOD **Hostal Cristina,** C. Riera, s/n (tel. 972 25 81 38), right on the water, has bright, newly renovated rooms. (Mid-July to Aug. singles 2000ptas, with bath or terrace 3000ptas; doubles 4000ptas, with bath 6000ptas; Sept. to mid-July doubles with bath or terrace 5000ptas.) **Hostal Marina,** C. Riera de Sant Vicenç, 3 (tel. 972 25 81 99), has clean, airy rooms, some with balconies. (Singles 2200ptas, with bath 3500ptas; doubles 4000ptas, with bath 7000ptas. Breakfast 450ptas. Open Apr.-Dec. Visa, MC.) **Camping Cadaqués,** Ctra. Portlligat, 17 (tel. 972 25 81 26), is on the left on the way to Dalí's house; ask the bus driver to stop before you arrive in town. The campsite is 100m from the beach and has a pool, supermarket, and bungalows. (535ptas per person, 675ptas per tent, 535ptas per car. Open June-Sept. 15.) Cadaqués harbors the usual slew of overpriced, under-exciting tourist **restaurants** on the waterfront. Head into the back streets for more interesting options or pack a picnic at **Super Auvi,** Riera, s/n (tel. 972 25 86 33; open July15-Aug. M-Sa 8am-9pm, Su 8am-2pm; Sept.-July 14 M-Sa 8am-2pm and 4-9pm, Su 8am-2pm). Check out the family-run **Can Pelayo** (tel. 972 25 83 56), on C. Pruna, a right off waterfront Riba Pitxot. The fried fish, accompanied by crisp-fried eggplant, is yummy. (*Menú*, 1600ptas. Open Dec.-Oct. 14 daily 1-4pm and 7:30-11:30pm.)

SIGHTS AND ENTERTAINMENT The **Centre d'Art Perrot-Moore,** C. Vigilant, 1 (tel. 972 25 82 31), near the town center, houses a bizarre collection of Dalí fun, including an erotic fantasy room (no children permitted) and sketches done for a Disney version of Dante's *Divine Comedy*. *(Open July-Aug. daily 10:30am-1:30pm and 4:30-8:30pm; Apr.-June and Sept.-Oct. M-Sa 10:30am-1:30pm and 4-8pm, Su 10:30am-1:30pm. 800ptas, students and children 500ptas.)* Also check out the impressive Picassos, backdrops for a 1953 García Lorca play. The **Museu de Cadaqúes,** C. Monturiol, 15 (tel. 972 25 88 77), has changing exhibits, often on a Dalí theme. *(Open daily mid-June to Sept. 11am-1:30pm and 3-8pm. 800ptas, students and children 500ptas.)* A short walk away is **Casa-Museu Salvador Dalí,** Port Lligat (tel. 972 25 80 63), the home where Dalí and his wife Gala lived until Gala's death in 1982. *(Open daily June 15-Sept. 15 10:30am-9pm; Mar. 15-June 14 and Sept. 16-Nov. Tu-Su 10:30am-6pm. Multilingual tours depart every 10min.; ticket office closes 45min. before closing. 1200ptas, seniors, students, and children 700ptas.)* A pop-art miniature Alhambra, the building flaunts Dalí's favorite lip-shaped sofa and more stuffed snakes and swans than you bargained for. To get there, stay on the waterfront road past the bars and restaurants until C. Miranda appears on the left. Follow this road out of town and take a right onto Av. Salvador Dalí.

The **Festival Internacional de Música** (tel. 933 01 95 55) sponsors 10 concerts in late July and early August. *(Tickets around 2000ptas.)* Throughout the summer, locals dance *sardanas* outdoors (schedules listed on the *passeig* by the waterfront) and occasionally hop to live tunes. Those looking to catch some rays can try the rocky **Platja Gran,** near the town center, or **Sa Concha,** south of town (5min.).

■ Palafrugell and Around

Forty kilometers east of Girona, Palafrugell plays the trampoline for takeoffs to nearby beach towns **Callela, Llafranc,** and **Tamariu,** which cater to wealthy Europeans whose idea of budget accommodation is any hotel that doesn't leave mints on the pillow. To save some *pesetas,* stay in admittedly bland (and beachless) Palafrugell and daytrip to nearby beaches. Minuscule Tamariu is isolated from the other two beach towns, and is therefore likely to be least crowded. Callela is the largest and liveliest of the three, and is connected to Llafranc by one of several **Caminos de Ronda,** a series of small stone footpaths allowing exploration of the coast.

ORIENTATION AND PRACTICAL INFORMATION

Turn right from the Palafrugell Sarfa **bus station,** and walk down **Carrer Torres de Jonama** to **Carrer de Pi i Maragall.** Turn right and walk past the **Guardia Civil** and the **market** until you hit **Plaça Nova.** Back up C. Pi i Maragall to your left lies the center of the city and Pl. Esglesia. From the Sarfa station, buses dash the paltry 3km to

Llafranc and **Calella.** There are many stops in Calella—get off by the **inflatable beach balls.** Service to **Tamariu,** also by a Sarfa bus, is far less frequent and nonexistent in winter. Otherwise, spin away on moped or mountain bike, or take a pleasant, if lengthy, walk through the countryside (1hr. to each coastal town).

Buses: Sarfa, C. Torres Jonama, 67-79 (tel. 972 30 06 23). Prices rise weekends. To: Calella and Llafranc (in summer 11-24 per day, in winter 4-5 per day, 140ptas); Tamariu (in summer 3-4 per day, 140ptas); Sant Feliu (45min., 18 per day, 240-290ptas); Girona (1hr., 14 per day, 505-535ptas); Figueres (1½hr., 3-4 per day, 750-860ptas); Barcelona (2hr., 17 per day, 1500-1705ptas).

Taxis: Ràdio Taxi (tel. 972 61 00 00). 24hr. service throughout the area.

Bike Rental: Bicismarca, C. Barrisi Buixo, 55 (tel. 972 30 44 47). 500ptas per 2hr., 1200ptas per ½day, 1700ptas per full day.

Tourist Office: Can Rosés, Pl. L'Església (tel. 972 61 18 20; fax 972 61 17 56). First right off C. Cavallers walking away from Pl. Nova. The *Guía Municipal* is indispensable. A larger **branch** is at C. Carrilet, 2 (tel. 972 30 02 28; fax 972 61 12 61). From the bus station go left on C. Torres i Jonama, left again at the traffic circle, and walk about 200m. A profoundly inconvenient location, but loaded with info. Both open Apr.-Sept. M-Sa 10am-1pm and 5-8pm, Su 10am-1pm; Oct.-Mar. M-Sa 10am-1pm and 4-7pm, Su 10am-1pm; Carrilet branch open July-Aug. M-Sa 9am-9pm, Su 10am-1pm. **Branches** in **Llafranc,** C. Roger de Llúria (tel. 972 30 50 08) and **Calella,** Les Voltes, 6 (tel. 972 61 44 75). Both open July-Aug. daily 10am-1pm and 5-9pm; Apr.-Sept. M-Sa 10am-1pm and 5-8pm. Branch at **Tamariu,** C. Riera (tel. 972 62 01 93). Open June-Sept. M-Sa 10am-1pm and 5-8pm, Su 10am-1pm.

Currency Exchange: Banco Central Hispano, at the corner of C. Valls and Cavallers off Pl. Nova. Open in summer M-F 8:30am-2:30pm, in winter M-Sa 8:30am-2:30pm.

Luggage Storage: Sarfa bus station (200ptas per bag). Open daily 6:30am-8:30pm.

Emergency: tel. 091 or 092. **Municipal police:** Av. Josep Pla and C. Cervantes (tel. 972 61 31 01). Call them for 24hr. **pharmacy** info.

Medical services: Centro de Atención Primaria, C. d'Angel Guimerà, 6 (tel. 972 61 06 07). Open 24hr.

Post Office: C. Torres Jonama, 14 (tel. 972 30 06 07). Open for stamps and Lista de Correos M-F 8:30am-2:30pm, Sa 9:30am-1pm. **Postal Code:** 17200.

ACCOMMODATIONS AND FOOD

Accommodation prices are reasonable and room quality high in Palafrugell proper, but there are only three options. Be sure to call ahead on summer weekends. Restaurants near the beach are predictably expensive. For super beach daytrips, try shopping at **Super Stop,** C. Torres Jonama, 33. (Open July-Aug. M-Sa 8:30am-2pm and 5-9pm, Su 9am-2pm; Sept.-June M-Sa 8:30am-1:30pm and 5-8:30pm, Su 9am-2pm.)

Fonda L'Estrella, C. Quatres Cases, 13-17 (tel. 972 30 00 05), at the corner of C. La Caritat, a right off C. Torres Jonama. High-ceilinged, well-lit rooms with sinks off a Moorish courtyard bursting with plant life. Singles 2300ptas; doubles 4200ptas. Breakfast in the garden 475ptas. Parking 200ptas. Open May-Sept.

Residencia Familiar, C. Sant Sebastià, 29 (tel. 972 30 00 43). C. Quatres Cases crosses Pl. Nova and turns into C. Sant Sebastià. Halls à la Jackson Pollack, but rooms, with sinks, are clean. Singles 2000ptas; doubles 4000ptas (less for longer stays and off-season). Open Semana Santa-Oct.

Hostal Plaja, C. Sant Sebastià, 34 (tel. 972 30 05 26). Grand, frescoed foyer gives way to a broad courtyard surrounded by spiffy rooms, all with balconies, clothesline, new beds, and bathrooms. July-Aug.: singles 2800ptas, with breakfast 3200; doubles 5000ptas, with breakfast 6000ptas. Sept.-June: singles 2600ptas, with breakfast 3000ptas; doubles 4700ptas, with breakfast 5700ptas. Open Jan.-Oct. Visa, MC.

Camping: Camping Moby Dick, C. Costa Verda, 16 (tel. 972 61 43 07), on bus route off Av. Costa del Sol in Calella. No Pequod in sight, but near the water (5min.). Plenty of shade from abundant pine trees. Good showers. 530ptas per person, 540ptas per car and per tent. Cheaper in off season. Open Semana Santa-Oct. 15.

Restaurant el Rebost del Pernil, C. Mayor, 3 (tel. 972 61 06 95). A delicious option on the Palafrugell restaurant scene. Wide-ranging *menú del día* (M-F 1000ptas) features truly outstanding versions of Catalan classics like *exalivada* and *fideu*. Open in summer daily 1-4pm and 8pm-midnight; in winter closed Tu night.

Restaurant Bar L'Espasa, C. Fra Bernat Boil, 14 (tel. 972 61 50 32), on the seaside walk from Calella to Llafranc. Delicious food, great views. Specializes in seafood stews and *arroz negro* (black rice). *Menú* 1100ptas. Meals served daily 1-4pm and 8-11pm. Open June-Sept. Visa, MC.

SIGHTS AND ENTERTAINMENT

Palafrugell proudly boasts Spain's finest and only cork museum, the **Museu del Suro,** C. Tarongeta, 31 (tel. 972 30 39 98), with everything you wanted to know and more about cork. *(Open July-Aug. Tu-Sa 10am-1pm and 5-9pm, Su 10:30am-1:30pm; Sept-June Tu-Sa 5-8pm, Su 10:30am-1:30pm. 200ptas, seniors and students 100ptas. English explanations available.)* Palafrugell's Friday evening **passeig** ends up at the *plaça*, where young and old do the *sardana* at 10:30pm from July to August. Don't be afraid to join; all it takes is a little coordination and a truckload of chutzpah. For more familiar dancing, check out **Discoteca X qué** (pronounced *por qué*), 1km down the old road to Calella. The tourist office prints a monthly bulletin of upcoming events. The town's biggest party takes place July 18 to 20, when the dance-intensive **Festa Major** bursts into the streets. Calella honors Sant Pere on June 29, Tamariu celebrates on August 15, and Llafranc honors Santa Rose August 27 to 30. A 40-minute walk up the road from Llafranc, the **Ermita de San Sebastià** crowns the mountain of the same name (50m from the lighthouse) and surveys the entire Palafrugell valley, beaches, and sea.

Callela

The tourist office in Palafrugell provides maps of paths and trails that criss-cross the area and join the coastal towns, including the **Camino de Ronda** (incredible climbs near the coast from Callela to Llafranc, 1½hr.). **Poseidón Nemrod Club,** Port Pelegri (tel. 972 61 53 45) offers **scuba diving** courses and equipment. **Jardí Botànic de Cap Roig** (tel. 972 61 45 82), the botanical gardens in front of Hotel Garbí, offer an excellent view of the coast. *(Open daily in summer 9am-8pm; in winter 9am-6pm. 300ptas.)* Russian Colonel Nicolas Voevodsky built the seaside castle after fleeing the Bolshevik Revolution. He and his wife planted and pruned a splendid maze of paths and flower beds with their own hands. The first sign for the castle points to the right at the fork of Av. Costa Daurada and C. Consolat del Mar. The castle also hosts the **Festival de Jazz de la Costa Brava** through July and August. On Calella's waterfront, anglers spend the first Saturday in July crooning the old sea chanties of the **Cantada d'Habaneras,** scaring away most of the fish.

■ Near Palafrugell: L'Escala

L'Escala (pop. 6000, in summer 70,000), 45 bus-minutes north of Palafrugell, is mostly just a string of tacky souvenir shops. It's the beaches and ruins that make it worthwhile. Sandy expanses with room enough for you and your towel sprawl outside of town, toward and beyond the Roman ruins of **Empúries.**

PRACTICAL INFORMATION Sarfa **buses** (tel. 972 77 01 29) depart from Pl. Escoles across from the tourist office to: Palafrugell (35min., 4 per day, 345ptas); Figueres (55min., 4-5 per day, 415ptas); Girona (2hr., 2-3 per day, 530ptas). Buy tickets on the bus. **Taxis** (tel. 972 77 09 40) await at Pl. Escoles. The HI arranges **mountain bike rental** if you contact them in advance, otherwise **Cicles JK,** Av. Ave Maria, 9 (tel. 972 77 40 47), rents bikes (450ptas per hr., 1200ptas per 5hr., 1700ptas per day). The **tourist office,** Pl. Escoles, 1 (tel. 972 77 06 03; fax 972 77 33 85), has a decent map, info on tourist sites, and **fax** service (open July-Sept. M-Sa 9am-8:30pm, Su 10am-1pm; Oct.-June M-F 10am-1pm and 4-7pm). A **Banco Central Hispano** with **ATM** sits at C. Maranges, 16 (open in summer M-F 8:30am-2:30pm; in winter M-Sa 8:30am-2:30pm). The **municipal police,** C. Pintor Joan Massanet, 24 (tel. 972 77 48 18), are next to the to the tourist office. In **medical emergencies** call 908 09 43 33. The **post office** is also next to the tourist office (tel. 972 77 16 51; open M-F 8:30am-2:30pm, Sa 9:30am-1pm). The **postal code** is 17130.

ACCOMMODATIONS AND FOOD Although there are plenty of options, finding a room in L'Escala is taxing; many *pensiones* require summer guests to pay full board. The **Alberg de Juventut,** Les Coves, 41 (tel. 972 77 12 00), is 100m from the Empúries ruins and 30m from the beach in a grove of trees. Facing the tourist office, follow the road on the right toward the coast; follow signs or ask bus drivers on the way to town to stop near the ruins. The hostel has friendly owners, English books, TV, and lots of beds to a room. (Apr.-Sept. dorms 1700ptas, over 25 2225ptas. Oct.-Mar. dorms 1475ptas, over 25 1950ptas. Breakfast included. Lunch and dinner offered. HI members only; cards available at the hostel. Call Barcelona's youth office (tel. 93 483 83 63) for reservations 1 month in advance.) **Pensió Torrent,** Carrer Riera, 28 (tel. 972 77 02 78), has pleasing whitewashed rooms with bath and tiled floors (in summer doubles 3600ptas; in winter 3000ptas). From Pl. Escoles walk downhill one block on C. Pintor, turn left, and follow the street around the corner. The town **market** is held daily from 7:30am to 1:30pm in **Plaça Victor Català.** Fill your basket at **MAXOR,** Pl. Les Escoles Ronda Pedró, 2 (open M-Sa 8am-9pm, Su 9am-2pm). **Restaurante-Snack Galan,** C. Torre, 18 (tel. 972 77 30 54), serves up a nice flan. (*Menú* 1000ptas. Open in summer daily 1-4pm and 7-10:30pm; in winter W-M 1-4 pm and 7-10:30pm.)

■ Near L'Escala: Empúries

Just one kilometer north of L'Escala are the ruins of Empúries. In the 7th century BC, Greek traders landed on a small island on the northeast Iberian coast. As the settlement grew, it moved to the mainland and became the prosperous colony of Emporion (marketplace), falling into Roman hands four centuries later. Remnants of both Greek and Roman cities, including some gorgeous mosaic floors and a Visigothic early Christian basilica, fill Empúries's 40 hectares of **ruins.** Excavation of the ruins continues behind profits from the 1992 Olympic Games, whose torch formally entered Spain through this ancient Greek port city. The small but rich **Museu Monogràfic d'Empúries** (tel. 972 77 02 08) showcases a large collection of ceramics, Etruscan goodies, and phallic symbols. (*Grounds and museum open daily June-Sept. 10am-8pm; Oct.-May 10am-6pm. 400ptas, seniors and students free. Audiovisual program screened every 30min. from 10:30am until closing, 300ptas. Audio tape 600ptas.*) Explanatory signs through the ruins indicate the ancient urban plan without marring the aura of fountains, mosaics, and columns against a backdrop of cypress trees and the breezy Mediterranean. Half a kilometer north of the ruins starts the 47sq.km **Parc Natural deis Aiguamolls de l'Empordà,** a protected habitat with miles of marsh land, lakes, and animal and plant species (the unenviably named *fartet* fish, for example). Bird-watchers should purvey the skies during the morning and early evening from March to May and August to October. For more info, contact **El Cortalet** (tel. 972 25 42 22).

If you can't bear a 15-minute walk, take the little blue train, *Carrilet,* from **La Punta** in L'Escala (between the main beach and **Port d'en Perris**) to St. Martí d'Empúries (June 15-Sept. 15 departs every hr., 200ptas). Ask to get off at the ruins.

■ Near Palafrugell: Sant Feliu de Guíxols

A perilous but panoramic road twists 23km north from Tossa de Mar to Sant Feliu (pop. 18,000). Cork production was once Sant Feliu's main industry—today tourism takes center stage. The town sees its share of visitors, many towing small children along, but the scent of the sea still overpowers that of Coppertone. Sandy beaches and a number of reasonably priced pensions make it a fine place to soak up the rays.

ORIENTATION AND PRACTICAL INFORMATION Sarfa buses arrive at the **bus station** on Ctra. Gerona. The main *plaça,* **Plaça Mercat,** is right off Pg. Mar and Av. Juli

Garreta. A tree-lined promenade and pedestrian path, **Passeig del Mar,** runs parallel to the beach. If entering by sea, you'll disembark mid-beach in front of Passeig del Mar. **Teisa** buses stop and depart at Pl. Monestir across from the tourist office.

Sarfa, Ctra. Gerona, 35 (tel. 972 32 11 87), runs **buses;** prices rise on weekends. They have service to: Palafrugell, on the Girona line (45min., 18 per day, 255-290ptas); Tossa (1hr., 2 per day, 360ptas); and Barcelona (1½hr., 14 per day, 1280-1444ptas). **Teisa** (tel. 972 20 48 68), down the stairs from the bus stop on the left, sends buses to Girona from Pl. Monestir (45min., 8-13 per day, 485ptas). **Crucetours Ferry** (tel. 972 76 60 91) has a stand on the beach and sails July to August to: Tossa (45min., 5 per day, round-trip 1200ptas); Lloret (1¼hr., round-trip 1250ptas); and other beaches north and south. The **tourist office,** Pl. Monestir, 54 (tel. 972 82 00 51), up Av. Juli Garetta, has a good map and info about *pensiones.* (Open July-Sept. M-Sa 10am-2pm and 4-8pm, Su 10am-2pm; Oct.-June M-Sa 10am-1pm and 4-7pm, Su 10am-2pm.) **Banco Central Hispano** sits on Pg. Mar, 26-27. (Open in summer M-F 8:30am-2:30pm; in winter M-F 8:30am-2:30pm, Sa 9:30am-1pm.) **Luggage storage** is available at the Sarfa bus ticket window (200ptas per bag; open 6:30am-8:30pm). In **emergencies,** call 092. The **municipal police** (tel. 972 32 42 11), on C. Callao, are on the outskirts of town. The **post office** is at Ctra. Gerona, 15 (tel. 972 32 11 60; open M-F 8:30am-2:30pm, Sa 9:30am-1pm).

ACCOMMODATIONS AND FOOD Many hotel owners discount prices for stays of five days or more. Reservations are suggested for July and August. **Pensión Geis,** C. Especiers, 27 (tel. 972 32 06 79), is off Pl. Mercat. A cheerful owner keeps neat-as-a-pin rooms, all with blue-tiled bath and winter heating. (July-Aug. singles 2000ptas; doubles 4000ptas. Sept.-June singles 1900ptas; doubles 3800ptas. Breakfast 350ptas. Visa, MC.) At **Hostal Zürich,** Av. Juli Garreta, 43-45 (tel. 972 32 10 54), friendly, English-speaking owners rent huge, pleasant rooms with lots of light, some with balconies, some with TV. (Singles 3500ptas; doubles 5500ptas, with bath 6500ptas. Breakfast included.) Clean rooms with sinks and big windows reside 10 minutes from the beach at **Pension El Gas Vell,** C. Sta. Magdalena, 29 (tel. 972 32 10 24). Follow C. Especiers to its end and bear right, taking the first left on C. Mall. Carrer Sta. Magdalena is 5 blocks down. Ring the doorbell by the restaurant of the same name. (Singles 1750ptas; doubles 3500ptas, with bath 4500ptas; triples 5000ptas.)

The excellent **market** is in Pl. Mercat (open in summer daily 8am-2pm; in winter Tu-Su 8am-2pm). If you need a supermarket, head for **%Día** at the end of C. Concepción (open M-Sa 9am-1:30pm and 5-9pm, Su 10am-2pm). For lip-smacking *tapas,* check out **Bar El Gallo,** C. Especiers, 13 (tel. 972 82 23 44). Snack on grilled sardines (450ptas) or go for the *tapeo menú* (4000ptas for two), which tops off six different *tapas* with a dessert crepe. (Open daily 10am-3pm and 5:30-11pm.) **Nou Casino La Costancia,** Rambla Portalet, 2 (tel. 972 32 10 92), is a neo-Mudéjar cafe-bar and casino (beers from 150ptas; open daily June-Sept. 8am-1am; Oct.-May 9am-midnight).

SIGHTS AND ENTERTAINMENT Little remains to distinguish Sant Feliu from other mildly pretty Costa Brava towns, since most traces of its 1000-year history have been obliterated by successive invaders. Still, the **Monestir** church and monastery at Pl. Monestir is an architectural potpourri patched together from the remains of various buildings, including the **Torre de Fum,** which stands over Visigothic and Roman walls and houses a nice Romanesque crucifixion. *(Open daily 8-11am for mass. Free.)* Behind the tourist office is the vaguely interesting **Museu d'Història de la Ciutat** with changing exhibits, artifacts, and fun about cork. *(Open in summer Tu-Sa 11am-2pm and 6-9pm, Su 11am-2pm; in winter Tu-Sa 11am-2pm and 5-8pm, Su 11am-2pm. Free.)*

If you've come for the **beaches** (hardly a big "if"), you're in the right place. Sant Feliu's own beach is sandy and pleasant enough. It's a 20-minute walk to the **Platja de Sant Pol.** *(Crurisa buses go from Pl. Monestir and Pg. Mar. every 10min., July-Aug. depart every 30min., Sept.-June 6 per day, 100ptas.)* With no commercial docking, the cove has unmediated access to the sea. Next to Sant Pol, a 2km path scampers across the rocky hills, past picturesque coves and lagoons, to **La Conca,** another popular beach. In sum-

CATALUNYA

mer, Sant Feliuans **dance** *sardanas* one block from the beach in Pl. Espanya. *(July-Sept. Friday 10:15pm.)* Throughout July, August, and September, a wide range of music and theater performances take place all over Sant Feliu in the **Festival Internacional de la Porta Ferrada,** the oldest in Catalunya. Many events are free; get a schedule from the tourist office. Every June and July local songsters get together at restaurants throughout town for the **Mostro de Cançó de Taverna.** Groups of men compete over a few accordion-assisted ditties and then enjoy a meal of bluefish. Needless, to say, the wine flows freely.

■ Tossa de Mar

Once upon a time, falling in love in, and with, Tossa was easy. In 1934, French artist Marc Chagall commenced a forty-year love affair with this seaside village—deeming its sparkling waters "Blue Paradise." When *The Flying Dutchman* was filmed here in 1951, Ava Gardner fell hard for Spanish bullfighter-turned-actor Mario Cabrera, much to the chagrin of Frank Sinatra (a.k.a., "Old Blue Eyes"), her husband at the time. Nowadays, Tossa (pop. 3800) suffers from the usual tourist industry blemishes: souvenir shops specializing in tacky baubles and scads of cocoa-buttered visitors. That said, Tossa still has plenty to recommend it: beaches framed by reddened cliffs, small-town sincerity long since abandoned by the larger resort towns, and a sun-baked cluster of 12th- to 14th-century buildings that knot themselves inside a walled *vila vella*.

ORIENTATION AND PRACTICAL INFORMATION

Tossa is near the southern corner of the Costa Brava, about 40km north of Barcelona (90km of winding roads). Buses arrive at **Plaça de les Nacions Sense Estat,** at the corner of **Avinguda Pelegrí** and **Avinguda Ferrán Agulló;** the town slopes gently down from there to the waterfront (10min.). Walk away from the station on Av. Ferrán Agulló, turn right on **Avinguda Costa Brava,** and continue until your feet get wet. **Passeig del Mar,** at the end of Av. Costa Brava, curves along the **Platja Gran** (Tossa's main beach) to the foot of the old quarter.

Buses: Av. Pelegrí at Pl. Nacions Sense Estat. **Pujol i Pujol** (tel. 972 36 42 36) to: Lloret del Mar (20min.; departs in summer every 30min., in winter every hr.; 150ptas, Sa-Su 170ptas). **Sarfa** (tel. 972 34 09 03) to Girona (1hr., in summer 2 per day, in winter 1 per day, 615ptas) and Barcelona (1½hr., 12 per day, 1120ptas).

Ferries: Round-trip ferries are often more economical than the bus service. For a one-way trip, take the bus. **Crucetours** (tel. 972 36 23 05) runs from the main beach to St. Feliu (45min., July-Aug. 5 per day, 725ptas, round-trip 1200ptas). Check with the booth near the Vila Vella end of the Platja Gran for changes.

Car Rental: Europcar and **Avis** operate from the same storefront, Av. Costa Brava, 23 (tel. 972 34 28 29). One-day rentals start at 6700ptas. No age restriction.

Mountain Bike and Moped Rentals: Road Runner, Av. de la Palma, s/n (tel. 972 34 05 03). Bring passport and license (for moped). 1hr. mountain bike rental 600ptas. 2hr. moped rental 1950ptas. Open Apr.-Oct. daily 9:30am-9pm.

Tourist Office: Av. Pelegrí, 25 (tel. 972 34 01 08; fax 972 34 07 12), in the bus terminal building at the corner of Av. Ferrán Agulló and Av. Pelegrí. Handy, thoroughly indexed town map. English spoken. Open June 15-Sept. 15 M-Sa 9am-9pm, Su 10am-1pm; May and Oct. M-Sa 10am-1pm and 4-8pm; rest of year M-F 10am-1pm and 4-7pm, Sa 10am-1pm.

Currency Exchange: Banco Central Hispano, C. Ferran Aguilló. Open in summer M-F 8:30am-2:30pm; in winter M-Sa 8:30am-2:30pm.

Police: Municipal police, C. Església, 4 (tel. 972 34 01 35) in the Ajuntament. English spoken. They'll escort you to the **24hr. pharmacy.** Call them in an **emergency.**

Medical Services: Casa del Mar, Av. Catalunya (tel. 972 34 18 28). Primary health services and immediate attention. Nearest hospital is in Blanes.

Post Office: C. Maria Auxiliadora, s/n (tel. 972 34 04 57), down Av. Pelegrí from tourist office. Open M-F 8:30am-2:30pm, Sa 9:30am-1pm. **Postal Code:** 17320.

CATALUNYA

ACCOMMODATIONS AND CAMPING

Tossa lives seasonally—many *pensiones,* restaurants, and bars open only from May to October. In the summer, Tossa fills quickly. Make reservations, as some establishments are booked solid in July and August. The tourist office provides a list of travel agencies that help with reservations and aids room searches during this period. A signboard near the office lists and plots *pensiones* on a map. The **old quarter** hotels are the only ones worth considering.

Fonda/Can Lluna, C. Roqueta, 20 (tel. 972 34 03 65). Turn right off Pg. Mar onto C. Peixeteras, through C. Estalt until it ends, then go left and straight for the amazing budget find for which you have searched long and hard. Delightful family keeps immaculate rooms, all with private baths. July-Aug. 1900ptas per person; Sept.-June 1750ptas. Washing machine 500ptas. Breakfast included—eat on the rooftop terrace and take in the lovely view. Winter heating. In the high season, either show up in the morning or call 1-2 days prior to arrival. Open all year, but call first.

Pensión Moré, C. Sant Telmo, 9 (tel. 972 34 03 39). Downstairs, a dim and cozy sitting room. Upstairs, large rooms with basins and views of the old quarter. July-Aug. singles and doubles 3000ptas; Sept.-June 1300ptas per person. Open year-round.

Camping: Often costs as much as or more than *pensiones* for those not traveling in large groups. The tourist office has listings of nearby campgrounds. The closest is **Can Martí** (tel. 972 34 08 51; fax 972 34 24 61), at the end of Rambla Pau Casals, off Av. Ferrán Agulló, 15min. from the bus station. July-Aug.: 750ptas per person, 755ptas per tent, 500ptas per car. Sept.-June: 600ptas per person, 650ptas per tent, 400ptas per car. Open mid-May to mid-Sept.

FOOD

The old quarter also holds the best cuisine and ambience. Restaurants catering to tourist appetites serve up *menús* at reasonable prices on checked tablecloths. Most places specialize (though not exclusively) in local seafood. **Megatzems Palov,** C. Enric Granados, 4 (tel. 972 34 08 58), the first left after Club Nàutic along the beachside road, will delightedly debit your Visa or MC for your daily bread. (Open June-Aug. daily 8am-9:30pm; Sept.-May M-Sa 8am-2pm and 4:30-8:30pm, Su 8am-2pm.)

Restaurant Marina, C. Tarull, 6 (tel. 972 34 07 57). Faces the Església de Sant Vincenç—look for the striped awning and tables out front. Family from Fonda Lluna cooks up a *paella* as good as it gets. Popular *paella de verduras* (veggie paella) cooked up for animal-friendly folks (900ptas). *Menú* 950ptas. Ultra-yummy *crema catalana.* Open Semana Santa-Oct. daily 11am-11pm.

SIGHTS AND ENTERTAINMENT

Inside the walled fortress of the **Vila Vella,** a spiral of medieval alleys leads to tiny Pl. Pintor J. Roig y Soler, where the **Museu Municipal** (tel. 972 34 07 09) has a nifty collection of 20s and 30s art, including—because the artist had a pad here—one of the few Chagall paintings currently in Spain. *(Open June-Sept. Tu-Su 10am-7pm; Oct.-May Tu-Su 10am-1pm and 3-6pm. 200ptas.)* Tossa's Roman mosaics, dating from the 4th to the first century BC, and other artifacts from the nearby **Vila Romana** and the excavation site off Av. Pelegrí are displayed in the museum, originally a 12th-century palace. The Gothic **Església de Sant Vincenç** is in the center of the Vila Vella.

All of Tossa's **beaches** are lovely, although beware flying umbrellas. **Calas** (small bays) are accessible by foot and less crowded. **Hikers** pass through on the GR-92 but several shorter trails and **mountain bike** paths also criss-cross the area; gear up with the tourist office pamphlet. Several companies, like **Fonda Cristal** (tel. 972 34 22 99), send **glass-bottom boats** to nearby beaches and caves. *(1hr., 8 per day, 1000ptas per excursion.)* Tickets are available at booths on the Platja Gran. **Club Aire Libre** (tel. 972 34 12 77), on the highway to Lloret, organizes various excursions, including canoeing and kayaking (2000ptas), water skiing (4250ptas for 2 lessons), scuba diving (44,000ptas for 5-day certification course), sailing (1700ptas per hr.), and windsurfing (1600ptas per hr.).

Bars line the streets of the old quarter—just follow your ear. Many occasionally offer live music. **Bar La Pirata,** C. Portal, 32 (tel. 972 34 14 43), has outdoor tables overlooking the sea. *(Open Apr.-Oct. daily 10am-3am.)* **Snoopy's Bar,** C. Ignasi Meté, 6, inside the *vila vella,* is an English-style pub that packs them in like dogs for half-pints of Guinness (200ptas). *(Open daily 6pm-3am.)* For info about outdoor concerts and cultural festivals, contact the **Casa de Cultura,** Av. Pelegrí, 8 (tel. 972 34 09 05), in a historic red-roof building. *(Open M-F 4-6pm.)* Local festivals take place on January 20 to 21, when the townsfolk make a 42km pilgrimage from Tossa to Santa Coloma in honor of St. Sebastián. The **Festa Major d'Estiu** (Summer Fair) is held June 29 to July 2 in honor of St. Peter. Tossa's residents take to the hills on October 13 for a traditional picnic on **Aplec Sant Grau.** Reserve a room if you plan to come on these dates.

CATALAN PYRENEES

While the Costa Brava and Barcelona have attracted tourists in droves since the discovery of disposable income, the jagged green mountains, simple Romanesque churches, and tranquil towns of the Catalan Pyrenees draw a more select group— mostly hikers and high-brow skiers from the neighboring towns in Spain and France. Those who make their way away from the coast will discover the uncommon beauty in the *Parc Nacional d'Aigüestortes i Estany de Sant Maurici* and excellent outdoor adventure opportunities for fun in the sun or snow. Although Catalunya's Pyrenees are not as ostentatious as Aragón's, they still take their fair share of breaths away.

Besides Catalan and Spanish, inhabitants of the ancient Catalan villages are often fluent in French, while people in the Val d'Aran (the westernmost area of the Catalan Pyrenees) speak Aranese, a variant of the French Gascon dialect. For each Catalan *comarca* (district), the Department of Commerce and Tourism distributes pamphlets with info on local winter sports or scenic areas. **Skiers** will find the English-language guide *Snow in Catalonia* (free at tourist offices) especially useful. *Ski España* lists vital stats of all ski stations in Spain. Ask at tourist offices for the best maps of each region. For those coming from the east, **Ripoll** is the point of entry, while those coming from the west, south, and Barcelona enter through **Lérida** (Lleida), the town that provides the only public transportation (bus) to the lakes and trails of the national park.

Isn't It Romanesque?

Romanesque castles, churches, and monasteries fill the old medieval counties of the Pyrenees region. This style emerged after the breakup of the Carolingian Empire in the latter 10th century and dominated Europe until the end of the 13th century. Romanesque architecture mixed Roman building traditions (such as the vaulted roofs) with newer techniques (such as massive masonry to uphold barrel vaults) necessary for the grandiose edifices of an expanding society. The buildings are characterized by their rounded arched doors and windows, and modest (as compared to Gothic) heights. Benedictine monks and the Knights Templar hired builders to spread Romanesque influence far and wide, making it the first truly pan-European architectural style. The increasing popularity of the Camino de Santiago also contributed to the rapid diffusion of the style.

■ Val d'Aran

Some of the Catalan Pyrenees' most dazzling peaks cluster around the Val d'Aran, in the northwest corner of the province. Those peaks have proven to be sizeable barriers to outside infiltration—the Araneses have maintained not only a language distinct from both Catalan and French, but also unique festivals, music, and dances.

Though increasingly popular in summer, the Val d'Aran is best known as a chic ski resort—the royal family's favorite slopes are those of **Baquiera-Beret.** It's probably as good a place as any to have a chance encounter with the very eligible Prince Felipe and snag a ticket to royalty. Currently, there are about 80 alpine trails, as well as a few cross-country ones, winding down the surrounding peaks. Although budget accommodations have disappeared at the ski station itself, there is a youth hostel in the town of Salardú, **Albergue Era Garona** (tel. 973 64 52 71; reservation tel. 934 83 83 63), only a few kilometers away and accessible by high-season shuttle bus from Vielha. (Members only, although cards available. Dorms 1800ptas, over 25 2375ptas.; Sheets 350ptas. Breakfast included.) Vielha itself is only 12km away from Bacquiera-Beret, and the two are connected by a shuttle bus in the high season. Check at the tourist office for schedules. For skiing info and reservations, contact the **Oficeria de Baquiera-Beret** (tel. 973 64 44 55; fax 973 64 44 88) or the tourist office in Vielha (tel. 973 64 01 10).

■ Vielha

The biggest town in the valley (pop. 3700), Vielha suffers from the usual multi-story architectural blunders but seems cheerfully unaware of its errors as it welcomes hikers and skiers to its lively streets with every sort of service and amenity the outdoorsy might desire. An impressive 12th-century wood carving of the *Crist del Mig-Aran*, one of the few signs of the Vielha's rich past, hangs in the town church.

PRACTICAL INFORMATION, ACCOMMODATIONS, AND FOOD Alsina Graells (tel. 973 26 85 00) runs **buses** to Vielha from Lérida (3hr., 2 per day, 1500ptas) that continue on to Barcelona (5½hr., 3320ptas). **Taxis** answer at 973 64 01 95. The **tourist office,** C. Sarriulèra, 6 (tel. 973 64 01 10; fax 973 64 05 37), hangs one block upriver from the *plaça*. (Open July-Sept. 15 daily 9am-1pm and 4-8pm; Sept. 16-May M-Sa 10am-1pm and 4:30-7:30pm.) The multilingual staff handles spacey hikers, wanna-be skiers, and uptight Romanesque-seekers with equal aplomb. **ATMs** and **supermarkets** pepper Av. Castiéro, which intersects the river. **Guardia Civil** picks up at 973 64 00 05. In **emergencies,** dial 091 or 092. The **pharmacy** answers at 973 64 23 46. The **post office,** C. Sarviulèra, 2 (tel. 973 64 09 12), is by the tourist office. (Open M-F 8:30am-2:30pm, Sa 9am-1pm.) The **postal code** is 25530.

Several inexpensive *pensiones* cluster at the end of Camin Reiau, off Pg. Libertat, which intersects Av. Casteiro at Pl. Sant Antoni. The best of the bunch is **Casa Vicenta,** Camin Reiau, 3 (tel. 973 64 08 19), with sparkling rooms with bath. (Singles 3000ptas; doubles 5000ptas. Breakfast included.) **Pensión Busquets,** C. Mayor, 11 (tel. 973 64 02 38), has homey rooms in the old part of town. (Aug.-Sept. and Dec.-Mar. 2000ptas per person; Apr.-July and Oct.-Nov. 1800ptas.) **Bar-Restaurante Vidal,** C. Mayor, 6A, cooks a 1200ptas *menú*. (Open daily 1-4pm and 9-11:30pm.)

SWM seeking...

Tall, dark, handsome, rich beyond imagination, famous and friend of the famous, respected, powerful, and searching for life partner. Enjoys water sports (competed on the Olympic sailing team) and studied at Georgetown. Looking for that special someone—attractive, charismatic, and preferably of royal lineage—who shares interests and would like to raise a family.

His name is Felipe, the Prince of Asturias and heir to the Spanish throne. With his 30th birthday just behind him and his two older sisters recently married, all eyes are now on Felipe. Whom will he choose to hold his hand when he takes over one of the few remaining monarchies with any real power? The competition is fierce. Lovely ladies from fine families are stalking the streets of Madrid and the slopes of the Val d'Aran, but so far there are no front runners. You never know...cross your fingers and pack something nice—you might be the lucky gal to add your gene pool to the Bourbon dynasty.

SIGHTS AND ENTERTAINMENT The **Iglesia de San Miguel,** a simple 12th-century Romanesque church, houses the intricately carved 12th-century *Crist de Mijaran*. *(Open daily 11am-8pm.)* Vielha also has the **Museu de Val d'Aran** (tel. 973 64 18 15), on

C. Mayor, an ethnographic collection that sheds light on the arcane Aranese culture. *(Open Tu-F 5-8pm, Sa 10am-1pm and 5-8pm, Su 10am-1pm. 200ptas.)*

Vielha is a good base for all sorts of outdoor activities, as it hosts various outdoors companies offering guides. **Camins**, Av. Pas d'Arro, 5 (tel. 973 64 24 44; fax 973 64 24 97; email camins-guias.pirineo@Ird.servicom.es), has helpful staff that can answer questions. They organize treks into the Aigüestortes National Park and surrounding mountains (prices start at 2000ptas), lead rafting and horseback trips, and rent mountain bikes (1900ptas half day, 2500ptas full day). Ask about winter activities as well.

■ Parc Nacional d'Aigüestortes

The spectacular Parc Nacional d'Aigüestortes is Catalunya's only national park, tucked away in its northwestern corner in the province of Lleida (Lérida). On a sunny spring day, brilliant blue skies, snow-capped peaks, and green-and-yellow, wildflower-dusted meadows make for one helluva technicolor experience. A 2500m range divides the park into western and eastern halves, known respectively as the Estany de Sant Maurici and the Aigüestortes. The two halves are reached separately by motor vehicle—only a foot trail connects them. With over 10,000 hectares and 50 ice-cold mountain lakes, the park merits at least two days, and if you rely on public transport, it's hard to see much in fewer than three. Cars can go only as far as the park entrance, 1km outside Espot; when the lot fills there, you must park in Espot.

Don't rely on the freebie maps of the park from the info offices. They sell a better map (1000ptas, available in area stores as well) put out by the Generalitat de Catalunya, that is worth the extra cash. The red *Editorial Alpina* guides, one each for Montardo, Vall de Boí, and Sant Maurici, are also an option (600ptas, at bookstores). The park brochure published by the Generalitat de Catalunya, available at tourist offices, is likewise useful. For info on the park, contact the park tourist offices (in Espot tel. 973 62 40 36; in Vall de Boí tel. 973 69 61 89; general info tel. 973 69 40 00).

The park's four *refugios* (government-maintained dormitories; about 1000ptas per person) and *Casas de Pagés* (lodging in private homes usually including breakfast) are good **accommodation** options. For the telephone numbers of the nine *refugios* in the area, contact the park tourist offices (English spoken). The mountains are deceptively placid from afar, but the sometimes unpredictable weather can be dangerous, especially in winter. Listen to local advice: bring warm clothing even for July and August and be sure to check with the Espot or Boí park office before heading out.

■ Due East: Espot and Estany de Sant Maurici

The official gateway to the eastern half of the park is the quiet little town of **Espot**. Espot is actually a good 4.5km from the entrance proper, an arrangement that respects the tranquility of the park but disturbs that of the traveler. The only consolation is that the hike to the entrance is quite scenic. Unfortunately, the **Alsina Graells bus** (tel. 973 26 85 00 or 93 265 68 66) from Barcelona through Lérida—the only mass transit in the area—only comes within 7km from the *other* side of Espot, on Highway C-147 at the La Torrassa crossing (3hr., M-Sa 4:30pm, 1820ptas). A **jeep service** (tel. 973 62 41 05) taxis into the park from Espot and will even collect you from the bus stop if you call ahead (1000ptas to Espot per 7- to 8-person jeep). From Espot, jeeps run to Estany Sant Maurici (one-way 600ptas per person), a lake in the northeast section of the park, and to Amitges (round-trip 2000ptas), in the north of the park by the best and biggest **refugio** (tel. 93 315 23 11 or 973 25 01 09; open Feb. 13-28 and June 12-Sept. 26, plus additional weekends; schedule may vary—call ahead). Estany de Sant Maurici is the launch pad for most hikes; the two-hour hike from there to Amitges is one of the park's best. The **park info office** (tel. 973 62 40 36; in **medical emergencies** call 973 62 10 05), on the main road on the right as you enter town, provides good brochures and advice. (Open daily 9am-1pm and 3:30-6:45pm.)

CATALUNYA

A night's rest in Espot allows hikers to start early. **Supermarkets** sell picnic supplies. Many local residences take in travelers (inquire at the tourist office). **Residència Felip** (tel. 973 62 40 93), a *Casa de Pagés,* provides lovely rooms and breakfast (Sept.-June 2000ptas per person, Aug. 3000ptas). Cross the main bridge, follow the road two blocks, then turn left. **Càmping la Mola** (tel. 973 62 40 24) and **Càmping Sol i Neu** (tel. 973 62 40 01), both on the way to Espot, have good facilities and pools. (Both open June-Sept. and Semana Santa. 575ptas per person, per tent, and per car.)

■ Due West: Aigüestortes and Vall de Boí

The western half of the park's proximity to Lérida makes it more popular with casual strollers than the eastern half, hours away by car. To savor the park's two halves, take the main trail along the Riu de Sant Nicolau from Aigüestortes to the **Portarró de Espot,** the 2400m gateway between the two sides. Heading west, the descent to Estany de Sant Maurici is steep and covered in patches of snow at higher altitudes. This six- to eight-hour hike crosses the whole park, passing the **Estany Llong,** a llong llake indeed. Near its western tip lies the park's first *refugio,* also called **Estany Llong** (tel. 973 69 61 07; open mid-June to mid-Oct. and additional weekends; 725ptas per person, over 18 970ptas per person).

Entering the park from its west side isn't much easier than the eastern approach. When it's running (July-Sept.), the **Alsina Graells** (tel. 973 26 85 00 or 93 265 68 66) bus from Lérida drops explorers off in **Boí,** a community of 150 people, 7km from the park's entrance. **Taxis** (tel. 973 69 60 36) go from the town's *plaça* to the park (500ptas per person). The helpful **park info office** (tel. 973 69 61 89) is near the bus stop on the *plaça* (open daily 9am-1pm and 3:30-6:45pm).

Despite the nearby ski resort in **Taüll,** Boí maintains its pastoral feel. Low arches and cobblestone streets surround several family-run accommodations. The proprietor at **Casa Guasch** (tel. 973 69 60 42) lets simple rooms (1500ptas per person, 200ptas per person per day for kitchen access). Leave the plaza through the stone arch, turn right through the next arch, then bear left and turn left again where the street ends. Look for the entryway on the left. The family knows the mountains well and can give you pointers in Spanish or Catalan.

Pont de Suert, 17km south of Boí, offers most emergency services. The **Guardia Civil** can be reached at tel. 973 69 00 06. In an **emergency,** call 973 69 11 59.

■ Ripoll

Do doorways ever excite you? If not, it's best to bypass the sprawling industrial town of Ripoll (pop. 11,000). But if a good Romanesque portal carved with copious allegorical figures floats your boat, Ripoll may just be your town. Die-hard Romanesque fans may pass a night in Ripoll while visiting the **Monasterio de Santa María de Ripoll** and nearby **Sant Joan de las Abadesses,** although staying in Sant Joan is more pleasant.

PRACTICAL INFORMATION RENFE, Pl. Mova, 1 (tel. 972 70 06 44), runs **trains** to Ribes de Freser (20min., 9 per day, 165ptas); La Molina (50 min., 6 per day, 320ptas); Puigcerdà (1hr., 5 per day, 395ptas); and Barcelona (1½hr., 5-12 per day, 765ptas). The bus station next door sends **Teisa buses** (tel. 972 70 20 95) to: Girona, via Olot (4 per day, 900ptas); Sant Joan de las Abadesses (15 min., 7 per day, 230ptas); and Barcelona (1½hr., 1 per day, 1500ptas). To reach the monastery, take a left on C. Progrés from the train and bus stations, and then follow it until it merges with C. Estació. Take the first left after the "metal dancers" onto Pont d'Olot, cross the river, and continue straight on C. Bisbe Morgades to the Pl. Ayuntament and Pl. Abat Oliba. The **tourist office** (tel. 972 70 23 51), next to the monastery on Pl. Abat Oliba, gives out feeble maps. (Open June 12-Sept. 15 M-Sa 10am-1pm and 5-7pm, Su 10am-1pm; Sept.16-June 11 M-Sa 10am-noon and 4-6pm, Su 10am-2pm.) A **Banco Central Hispano** is on Pl. Sant Eudald, off Pl. Gran. In **emergencies,** call 088. The **police** (tel. 972 71 44 14) are at Pl. Ajuntament, 3. The **post office,** C. Sant Bartolomeu, 6 (tel. 70 07 60), at the corner of C. Progrés, shuffles letters (open M-F 8am-2:30pm, Sa 9:30am-1pm).

ACCOMMODATIONS AND FOOD For those who need a bed, the luxurious **Fonda La Paula,** C. Berenfuer, 4 (tel. 972 70 00 11), in the plaza alongside the tourist office, has big rooms with TVs and bathrooms. (Singles 3000ptas; doubles 4500ptas. 7% IVA not included.) Restaurants surround **Plaça Gran.** Follow C. Bisbe Morgades and take a right before the river on C. Mossen; the plaza is to the left. **Restaurante La Perla,** Pl. Gran, 4 (tel. 972 70 00 11), has a 1000ptas *menú* (open M-Sa 1-5pm and 8pm-midnight, Su 1-5pm). Stock up on groceries at **Supermercat Bonet,** C.Vinyes, 26 (tel. 972 70 03 74). (Open M-F 8:30am-2pm and 5-8:30pm, Sa 8:30am-5:30pm.) Follow C. Bisbe Morgades to the river and bear right on C.Vinyes.

SIGHTS Almost everyone who comes to Ripoll is here to see the incredibly intricate 11th-century portal of the **Monasterio de Santa Maria,** founded in 879 by Count Guifré el Pelú (a.k.a. Wilfred the Hairy) and once the most powerful monastery in Catalunya. Nicknamed the "Stone Bible," the curved doorway depicts survival scenes from the Old and New Testaments as well as a hierarchy of the cosmos and a handy 12-month calendar. Explanatory panels (in Catalan) decode the doorway, more or less. The **church** has been heavily restored, but adjoining it is a beautiful two-story Romanesque and Gothic **cloister.** *(Church open daily 8am-1pm and 3-8pm. Free. Cloister open daily 10am-1pm and 3-7pm. 100ptas.)* To the left of the church up a long spiral staircase is the bizarre **Museu Enogràfic de Ripoll** (tel. 972 70 31 44). Birds' nests, slightly worn 19th-century socks, a noisy working scale model of a Catalan forge—they're all here. *(Open Mar. 21-Sept. 20 Tu-Su 9:30am-1:30pm and 3:30-7pm; Sept. 21-Mar. 20 Tu-Su 9:30am-1pm and 3:30-6pm. 300ptas, students and seniors 200ptas.)*

■ Near Ripoll: Sant Joan de les Abadesses

Count Hairy was nothing if not an equal-opportunity employer. After founding Ripoll's first monastery, the Hirsute One went on to endow a convent 10km away, where he appointed his daughter Emma as the first abbess in 887. A town (pop. 3700) developed around the nuns, but not all authorities were so feminist-minded—their community was suppressed in the 11th century and it took 100 years before anyone moved into their old digs. The Augustinians who eventually took over turned the convent, appropriately, into a monastery, and dotted the town with other Romanesque buildings. The **monastery** includes a Romanesque **church,** containing the **Santíssim Misteri,** a 13th-century seven-piece polychromatic sculpture. *(Open daily Mar.-Oct. 10am-2pm and 4-6pm; May-Sept. 10am-2pm and 4-7pm; Nov-Feb M-F 10am-2pm and Sa-Su 10am-2pm and 4-6pm. 200ptas, includes a visit to the attached museum.)* The monastery may be reached by following the *rambla* to the circle at the end. The **tourist office,** Pl. l'Abadia, 9 (tel. 972 720 599), is next door to the monastery alongside a lovely 15th century cloister in the Palau de l'Abadia. *(Open M-F 9am-1pm and 4-7pm Sa-Su 10am-2pm and 4-7pm.)*

TEISA buses (tel. 972 70 20 95) connect Sant Joan de les Abadesses to Ripoll (15min., 5-7 per day, 230ptas), where trains go on to Barcelona. For **currency exchange, Banco Central Hispano** is on C. Comella, 4 (open M-F 8:30am-2:30pm).

Hostal Restaurant Nati, C. Perre Rovira, 3 (tel. 972 72 01 14), has simple rooms with TVs, sinks, and the standard saggy beds (2000ptas per person). Friendly **Restaurant La Ramba,** Rambla Count Guifré, 1 (tel. 972 02 94), has tables on the *rambla* and serves a *menú* for 1200ptas. (Meals served daily 1-4pm and 8-10pm.) Shop for your own grub at **Supermercado Super Avui** (tel. 972 72 02 67), on the corner of Av. Conte Guife and C. Comella (open M-Sa 9am-2pm and 5-9pm, Su 9am-2pm).

■ Núria

You should be forewarned that the ascent to Núria may take your breath away but that Núria itself will not. A small valley close to the French border, these mountains are inaccessible by train or car. For centuries, only the pious and unhappily infertile (see **Our Virgin of Fertility Drugs,** p. 360) made it through the high passes to the Santuario de Sant Gil. In 1931, however, the valley installed a second-hand cable car, the *Cremallera* (the Zipper), to prepare Núria as a major ski resort in the 1940s, 50s, and 60s. Unfortunately, as bigger mountains and longer slopes grew popular, the resort deteriorated, only to be revived as a Club Med-type destination with right-at-your-doorstep hiking and skiing. The bland modern complex sits aside a blatantly artificial "lake," unpleasantly incongruous with the idyllic valley and grazing cows. Somehow the masses of international family units who flock here don't seem to mind.

In summer, vacationers picnic along the shores of Núria's "lake," **ride horseback** along its trails, and use the valley as a base for **hiking** up to the snow-capped peaks of **Puigmal** (2913m; 4hr.) and **Eina.** Less ambitious trekkers can follow the path (2-3hr.) to neighboring **Queralbs,** which passes alongside waterfalls and gorges carpeted with wildflowers (the way back up to Núria from Queralbs is significantly more challenging than the way down). In winter, ten **ski trails** offer slopes ranging from *molt facil* (very easy) to *molt difficil* (very difficult or expert). The Cremallera zips from the Ribes de Freser stop on the Ripoll-Puigcerdà train line, scaling over 1000m through virgin mountain faces to which stubborn sheep, goats, and pine trees cling (45min., 6-11 per day depending on season, round-trip 2200ptas; closed Nov. 2- Dec. 3; call 972 73 20 20 for more info).

PRACTICAL INFORMATION, ACCOMMODATIONS, AND FOOD From Núria's station, a funicular (included in the price of Cremallera ticket) whisks passengers straight to **Alberg de Joventut Pic de l'Aliga** (tel. 972 73 20 48), the alternative route being an arduous 20-minute climb (dorms 1800ptas, over 25 2375ptas; breakfast included). For reservations, especially advisable July to August and (if there's snow) January to March, call the Barcelona office at tel. 93 483 83 63.

The **Bar Finistrelles,** downstairs from the souvenir store in the main complex, vends tortilla sandwiches (400ptas) and whole roast chicken with potatoes (975ptas). The complex also offers **ski rentals, ATMS, telephones, lockers** (300ptas), and—given the rising fertility here—a **condom vending machine.**

If you find the shiny artificiality of Núria a little spooky, escape to the more honest village of **Queralbs** (pop. 80 in winter, 500 in summer). If bare charm doesn't cut it, check out the sublime views from beside Queralbs's medieval rubble or the lovely 10th-century Romanesque church. There's one official *pensión* in town—**Hostal L'Avet,** C. Mayor, 21 (tel. 972 72 73 77; singles with bath 3000ptas, doubles with bath 4800ptas, 4800ptas per person with breakfast and dinner included). However, **Cans Constans** (tel. 972 72 70 13), right off the main road at the entrance to Queralbs, rents four-person apartments with fireplaces for 6000ptas per night. The **Cremallera** stops in Queralbs on its journey between Ribes and Núria.

■ Puigcerdà

A challenge for foreign tongues, Puigcerdà (pop. 7000; Pwee-chair-DAH) has a refreshingly "real" feel to it, especially compared with the more touristy towns that dot much of the Pyrenees. Although the town itself is nothing to write home about, it commands an undeniably beautiful valley view and serves as the best vantage point from which to explore the teeny region of Cerdanya. Hikers, bikers, and skiers alike will find plenty of diversion in the area. Incidentally, Puigcerdà sated its thirst for glory by appearing in the 1993 Guiness Book of World Records for the world's longest *butifarra* (sausage), a Freudian nightmare measuring 5200 meters.

CATALUNYA

Our Virgin of the Fertility Drugs

The Vall de Núria was just another remote mountain pass when recluse Gil of Nimes stumbled across it around the year 700 and envisioned it as the perfect place for his hermitage. With nothing better to do, the soon-to-be saint carved himself a nice statue of the Virgin and child. Almost 400 years later, that statue, along with Gil's bell and cooking pot, were discovered by a local shepherd, and the hermit's isolated sanctuary became a pilgrimage destination. In a twist of events on which it is perhaps best not to speculate, some daredevil pilgrim discovered her fertility increased if she put her head in the pot while ringing the bell. Ever since, barren women have been doing the same—one chime for each desired child. Visitors today can stick their own heads in the progeny-producing pot. Counterintuitively, the same procedure is purported to cure headaches.

ORIENTATION AND PRACTICAL INFORMATION

Puigcerdà's center sits squarely on a hill. **Plaça Ajuntament,** to the west, is nicknamed *el balcón de Cerdanya,* as it offers a commanding view of the valley and the decidedly less picturesque RENFE station at the foot of the western slope. Buses stop at the train station and then **Plaça Barcelona,** where it's best to get off.

To reach Pl. Ajuntament from the absolutely inconvenient **train station,** walk past the stairs in the station's *plaça* to the first real flight of stairs (between two buildings). Turn right at the top of the stairs, and then look for the next set on your left, just before a sign for C. Hostal del Sol. Climb these to the top and turn left on C. Raval de les Monges, where the final set of stairs winds up to the right. With your back to the wall, **Carrer Alfons I** runs straight out of the left-hand corner of the *plaça.* It will lead you after one block to **Carrer Major,** the principal commercial street. A left on C. Major will convey you to **Plaça Santa María.** Continuing straight across C. Major on C. Alfons I brings you to **Passeig 10 d'Abril,** while a right on C. Major leads to Pl. Cabrinetty. From Pl. Santa Maria with your back to the bell tower head out diagonally to the left to Pl. Barcelona, the other main square in town.

Trains: RENFE (tel. 972 88 01 65). To: La Molina (20min., 6 per day, 300ptas); Núria, via Ribes de Freser (6 per day, round-trip train and Cremallera-Núria 2500ptas); Ripoll (1¼hr., 6 per day, 395ptas); Barcelona (3hr., 6 per day, 1085ptas). To reach Jaca or Huesca, you must first go to Zaragoza via Barcelona, a full day of travel.

Buses: Alsina Graells (tel. 973 35 00 20). To: Llivia (10min., 1-4 per day, 100ptas); La Seu d'Urgell (1hr., 2-3 per day, 560ptas); Barcelona (3hr., 1-4 per day, 1650ptas); Lérida (3½hr., 1 per day, 2165ptas). From La Seu there is passage to Andorra. First bus departs Puigcerdà at 7:30am; the last returns from La Seu at 7pm. Buses depart in front of the train station and from Pl. Barcelona; purchase tickets on board. See schedule on the side of cigarette machine in Bar Estació, left of the station.

Taxis (tel. 972 88 00 11), Pl. Cabrinetty.

Bike Rental: Top-Bikes, Pl. d'Avenes, 21 (tel. 972 88 20 42), 800ptas per hr., 1500ptas per 4hr., 2500ptas per day. Visa, MC.

Tourist Office: C. Querol, 1 (tel./fax 972 88 05 42), a right turn off Pl. Ajuntament with your back to the view. Friendly English-speaking staff gives out a good map and lodging, entertainment, and daytrip listings. Open July-Sept. 15 M-Sa 9am-2pm and 3-8pm, Su 9am-2pm; Sept. 16-June Tu-F 10am-1pm and 4-7pm, Sa 10am-1:30pm and 4:30-8pm, Su 10am-2pm.

Currency Exchange: Banco Central Hispano, Pl. Cabrinetty. Open M-F 8:30am-2:30pm.

24Hr. Pharmacy: C. Alfons I, 16 (tel. 972 88 01 60). Pharmacy doors, the local paper *Reclam,* and police all list current 24hr. pharmacies.

Medical Services: Centre Hospitalari (tel. 972 88 01 50 or 972 88 01 54), in Pl. Santa María. English spoken.
Emergency: tel. 091 or 092. **Municipal Police:** Pl. Ajuntament, 1 (tel. 972 88 19 72).
Post Office: Av. Coronel Molera, 11 (tel. 972 88 08 14), off Pl. Barcelona on your left after 1½ block. Open M-F 8:30am-2:30pm, Sa 9:30am-1pm. **Postal Code:** 17520.

ACCOMMODATIONS AND FOOD

Since many visitors daytrip to Puigcerdà, rooms come easily, if not cheaply. Most cheaper *pensiones* hole up in the old town off Pl. Santa María. The neighborhood of **Calle Alfons I** is a cornucopia of bakeries, markets, and inexpensive restaurants. Pick up fresh bread at **Palau,** C. Alfons I, 9. The deli next door, **Gourmet Cerdà,** has your sandwich meat awaiting. (Both open Tu-Sa 9am-1pm and 4-8pm, Su 9am-2pm.) The **market** is at Pg. 10 d'Abril (Su 9am-2pm), and there's a **supermarket** diagonally across from the post office (open Tu-Sa 9am-1pm and 4:30-8:30pm, Su 10am-2pm).

Mare de Déu de les Neus (HI) (tel. 972 89 20 12; reservations tel. 93 48 383 63), in La Molina-Alp on Ctra. Font Canaleta, 500m from the RENFE station in La Molina. 20min. by car or 30min. by train from Puigcerdà, but only 4km from the slopes; in winter a bus goes up every 30min. Modern facilities in a beautiful locale. 154 beds. Members only, although HI cards available. Jan.-Nov. dorms 1700ptas, over 25 2275ptas; Dec. dorms 1800ptas, over 25 2375ptas. Call ahead in high season. Breakfast included. Sheets 350ptas. Visa, MC, AmEx.

Hostal Núria, Pl. Cabrinetty, 18 (tel. 972 88 17 56), a block downhill from Pl. Ajuntament. Huge rooms, all with equally huge bathrooms. Mattresses adhere to traditional Spanish guidelines for concavity. July-Aug. and Nov.-Apr. singles 3500ptas, doubles 5500ptas. The rest of the year: singles 3000ptas, doubles 5500ptas.

Pensió Campamar, C. Mayor, 37 (tel. 972 88 14 27). Clean and simple rooms with hardwood floors and sinks. Singles 2200ptas, doubles 4200ptas.

Camping: Camping Stel (tel./fax 972 88 23 61). Full-service camping 1km from Puigcerdà on the road to Llivia. Supermarket and pool. *Parcela* (includes tent and car) 1950ptas. 615ptas per person. Open June 19-Sept. 29 and weekends in winter.

Bar-Restaurant El Meson, Pl. Cabrinetty, 11 (tel. 972 88 19 28). Homestyle cooking. *Menú* 900ptas. *Bocadillos* available all day long. Open daily 1-3 and 8-10pm.

SIGHTS AND ENTERTAINMENT

Puigcerdà calls itself the capital of snow—you can **ski** in your country of choice (Spain, France, or Andorra) at one of 19 ski areas within a 50km radius. The closest one on the Spanish side is at **La Molina. Biking** throughout the area is also a popular option. The tourist office has a brochure with 17 potential routes mapped out.

Between runs and two-wheeled exploration, dash over to the **campanario,** the octagonal bell tower in Pl. Santa María. This 42m-high 12th-century tower is all that remains of the **Església de Santa María** and is an eerie reminder of the destruction wreaked by the 1936 Civil War. *(Open July-Sept. daily 11am-2pm and 4-8pm; Oct.-June weekends. Free.)* **Església de Sant Domènec,** on Pg. 10 d'Abril, is the largest church in Cerdanya. Its most interesting holdings are several Gothic paintings, probably by Guillem Manresa, that are considered to be among the best of their genre. On the outskirts of town, spanning the Riu Querol, is the **Pont de Sant Martí d'Aravó,** with a Romanesque base and a Gothic superstructure.

Spend an idyllic afternoon paddling around the **Estany** (lake) up Av. Pons i Guasch from Pl. Barcelona. Or sip a coffee on the shore, long a center of Puigcerdà social life—the 19th-century mansions surrounding it were summer houses for Cerdanyan elite. The **Festa de l'Estany** is held the third Sunday of August. In July and August, devotees gather for the *sardana* every Wednesday at 10pm. More concentrated dancing takes place during the **Festa Major** in the third weekend of July.

CATALUNYA

COSTA DAURADA (COSTA DORADA)

■ Tarragona

Tarragona's strategic position made the city a provincial Roman capital, when it was known as Tarraco, and an amphitheater and other remains of the Empire still pay homage to the port's imperial days. Today, tourists climb through these jagged remnants while natives retreat to the beach below. Catalunya's second most important port, Tarragona has earned an image as younger sibling of Spain's urban elites, but vestiges of its "august" past, not its fledgling cosmopolitan character, are still Tarragona's most compelling attractions.

ORIENTATION AND PRACTICAL INFORMATION

Most sights are clustered on a hill, surrounded by the remnants of Roman walls. At the foot of the hill, **Ramblas Vella** and **Ramblas Nova** (parallel to one another) are the main thoroughfares of the new city. Rambla Nova runs from **Passeig de les Palmeres** (which overlooks the sea) to **Plaça Imperial Tarraco,** the monstrous rotunda and house of the bus station. To reach the old quarter's center from the train station, take a right and walk 200m to the killer stairs parallel to the shore.

Trains: (tel. 977 24 02 02) on Pl. Pedrera on the waterfront. Info open daily 7am-9:45pm. To: Sitges (1hr., 14 per day); Barcelona (1¼hr., 30-40 per day); Valencia (3hr., 15 per day, 3100ptas); Zaragoza (3¼hr., 7-10 per day); Alicante (4½hr., 7 per day); Madrid.

Buses: (tel. 977 22 91 26) Pl. Imperial Tarraco. **Transportes Bacoma** (tel. 977 22 20 72) serves most destinations. To: Barcelona (1½hr., 10 per day); Valencia (3½hr., 9 per day); Alicante (6½hr., 6 per day). The train, however, is a better option.

Public Transportation: EMT Buses (tel. 977 54 94 80) runs lines all over Tarragona. Tourist offices have route info. Buses runs daily 7am-10:30pm, some routes until 11pm. 105ptas, 10-ride "bono" ticket 665ptas.

Taxi: Radio Taxi (tel. 977 22 14 14 or 977 23 60 64).

Tourist Office: C. Major, 39 (tel. 977 24 52 03; fax 977 24 55 07), below the cathedral steps. Crucial free maps and a guide to Tarragona's Roman ruins. Open June-Sept. M-F 9:30am-8:30pm, Sa 9:30am-2pm and 4-8:30pm, Su 10am-2pm; Oct.-May M-F 10am-2pm and 4:30-7pm, Sa-Su 10am-2pm. **Information booths,** Pl. Imperial Terraco, at the bottom of Rambla Vella. Open daily July-Oct. 10am-2pm and 4-8pm; Nov.-June 10am-2pm. **Generalitat de Catalunya,** C. Fortuny, 4 (tel. 977 23 34 15). Open M-F 9am-2pm and 4-6pm, Sa 9am-2pm.

Luggage Storage: 24hr. lockers at the train station (600ptas).

Emergency: call 1006, 091, or 092. **Police: Comisaría de Policía** (tel. 977 23 33 11), on Pl. Orleans. From Pl. Imperial Tarraco on the inland end of Rambla Nova, walk down Av. Pres. Lluis Companys, and take the 3rd left to the station.

Medical Assistance: Hospital de Sant Pau i Santa Tecla, Rambla Vella, 14 (tel. 977 25 99 00). **Hospital Joan XXIII** (tel. 977 29 58 00), on C. Dr. Mallafré Guasch. **Ambulance:** (tel. 977 22 22 22).

Internet Access: Café Internet, C. St. Pedro y Estuvas, 7. Off the street (called Santa Anna) branching off the middle of Pl. Rei. Take your first left and then look for the neon sign. 3 terminals. Open erratic hours.

Post Office: Pl. Corsini (tel. 977 24 01 49), below Rambla Nova off C. Canyelles. Open M-F 8:30am-8:30pm, Sa 8am-2pm. **Postal Code:** 43001.

ACCOMMODATIONS AND CAMPING

Tarragona is not famous for its cheap beds, but search in the area behind **Plaza Pedrera,** outside the train station or in Plaza Font, or peruse the tourist office's list.

CATALUNYA

Residencia Juvenil Sant Jordi (HI), C. Pres. Lluis Companys, 5 (tel. 977 24 01 95). Past Pl. Imperial Tarraco, Rambla Nova changes into C. Pres. Lluis Companys. Go left after leaving the train station, take the 1st right, and catch bus #2 in front of Bar Fa; it leaves you on C. Presidente Lluis Companys, 2 blocks from the bus station. Institutional dorm rooms. Facilities include TV, table tennis, lounge, and washing machine. June-Sept. dorms with a student card 1575ptas, under 26 1700ptas, over 26 2275ptas. Oct.-May dorms 200-300ptas less. Breakfast included. Add 1050-1325ptas for full board. Sheets 350ptas. Reception daily 7am-midnight. Doors close at midnight but open on the hour throughout the night. Reserve July-Aug.

Pensión Marsal, Pl. Font, 26 (tel. 977 22 40 69), in the heart of the historic town. Unassuming entrance through a cafe. Tidy rooms with private baths, nice beds, and fans. Singles 2300ptas; doubles 4600ptas. Breakfast included. Visa, MC, AmEx.

La Pilarica, C. Smith, 20 (tel. 977 24 09 60). From the train station, turn left and cross Pl. Pedrera to C. Barcelona, which becomes C. Sant Miguel. Turn left on C. Misericòrdia, and then take the 3rd right. Talkative owner offers mediocre rooms near the city's nightlife. All rooms with shared bath. 2140ptas per person.

Camping: Several sites line the road toward Barcelona (Vía Augusta or CN-340) along the beaches north of town. Take bus #9 from Pl. Imperial Tarraco, opposite the market (departs every 20min., 80ptas). The closest is **Tarraco** (tel. 977 23 99 89), at Platja ed l'Arrabassada. Well-maintained facilities; the beach is right there. 520ptas per person, per car; 375ptas per tent. Reception 24hr. Open Apr.-Sept.

FOOD

Ramblas Nova, Vella, and **Plaza Font** are full of daily *menús* (800-1200ptas) and greasy *platos combinados.* Tarragona's **indoor market,** next to Pl. Corsini by the post office, hawks food and wares (open M-Th 7am-2pm, F 7am-2pm and 5:30-8:30pm). For **groceries,** turn to **Simago,** C. Augusta at Comte de Rius, on a street parallel to and between Ramblas Nova and Vella (open M-Sa 9am-9pm).

La Teula, C. Merceria, 16, in the old city off Pl. Santiago Rusiñol. Salads (450-600ptas) and savory *Pan de payes* (country bread with meat or tortilla, 675-1000ptas). Afternoon *menú* 950ptas. Open Tu-Sa 11am-4:30pm and 6:30-11:30pm.

Restaurant El Caserón, Trinquet Nou, 4 (tel. 977 23 93 28), parallel to Rambla Vella (off Pl. Font). Ceiling fans cool stomach-stuffing, home-cooked meals. Family-run. *Menú* 1000ptas. Open M-Sa 1-3:30pm and 8:30-10:30pm, Su 1-3:30pm.

Arimany, Rbla. Nova, 43-45 (tel. 977 23 79 31). Has a few cheap *menús* despite its fancy atmosphere, and serves *bocadillos* (300-500ptas) all day long.

SIGHTS

Unless otherwise noted, all monuments and museums are open June-Sept. Tu-Su 10am-8pm; Oct.-May Tu-Su 10am-1:30pm and 4-5:30 or 6:30pm. The five Roman sights in Tarragona form a consortium. 475ptas, students free.

Tarraco's status as provincial capital (thanks to Augustus) transformed the small military enclosure into a glorious imperial port. Countless Roman ruins stand like statues amid 20th-century hustle and bustle. Below Passeig de les Palmeres, you can see the **Amfiteatre Romà** (tel. 977 24 25 79), where gladiators hurled each other and wild animals across the arena. Above the amphitheater, across Pg. Sant Antoni, sits the **Museu de la Romanitat** (tel. 977 24 19 52), which houses the **Pretori** and the **Circ Romans.** The Pretori was the governor's palace in the 1st century BC. Rumor has it that Pontius Pilate was born here. The Circ Romans, connected by vaults that both the Romans and Franco's troops used as dungeons, was once a chariot race track that extended across the old city. Most of it is buried today but some sections are still visible in the basements of restaurants and apartment buildings. To see the remaining fourth of the 2nd-century BC walls, stroll through the **Passeig Arquelògic** (tel. 977 24 57 96). *(Open July-Sept. until midnight.)* The walls originally stretched to the sea and fortified the entire city. The scattered **Fòrum Romà** lies near the post office on C. Lleida, clearly demonstrating how far the walls extended.

If too much Roman roamin' has left you parched, stop for a drink in the **Casa-Museu Castellarnau** (tel. 977 24 22 20). It housed 18th- and 19th-century *noblesa*, the *Vizcondas de Castellarnau* (Viscounts of Castellarnau). To get there, descend the steps in front of the cathedral and take the third right onto C. Cavellares.

Across Pl. Rei from the Pretori, the **Museo Nacional Arqueològic** (tel. 977 23 62 09) displays ancient utensils, statues, and mosaics, including a ravishing *Cap de Medusa (Head of Medusa)*. *(300ptas, students 150ptas.)* Cornered down narrow streets and lit by a huge rose window is a Romanesque-Gothic **cathedral,** on C. Major near Pl. Seu. *(Open in summer M-Sa 10am-7pm; in winter M-Sa 10am-12:30pm and 3-6pm. 300ptas, students 150ptas, includes admission to the Museu Necròpolis.)*

For a bit of the macabre, creep over to the **Museu i Necròpolis Paleocristians,** Av. Ramón y Cajal, 78 (tel. 977 21 11 75), at Pg. Independència on the edge of town. The huge early Christian burial site has yielded a rich variety of urns, tombs, and sarcophagi, the best of which are in the museum. *(300ptas, students 150ptas, includes admission to Museu Arqueològic.)* The **Pont del Diable** (Devil's Bridge) is a perfectly preserved Roman aqueduct. Take municipal bus #5 from the corner of C. Christòfor Colom and Av. Prat de la Riba (departs every 20min., 100ptas).

The hidden access to **Platja del Miracle,** the main **beach** in town (below everything else), is along Baixada del Miracle, starting off Pl. Arce Ochotorena, beyond the Roman theater. A more legitimate but inconvenient route is around the far side of the train station. A bit farther away are the larger beaches, **l'Arrabassada,** with dirt-like sand, and the windy **Llarga.** To find them, take bus #9 from Pl. Imperial Tarraco.

ENTERTAINMENT

Nightlife in Tarragona mimics that of Barcelona, but on a smaller scale. Between 5 to 9pm, **Rambla Nova** and **Rambla Vella** (and the area in between) are packed with strolling families. Around 9pm, the bars liven up. **Pau de Protectorat** is the most popular street. When these bars close around 2am, everyone heads to the new Port Esportiu, across the train tracks. Inaugurated by King Juan Carlos I last year, this strip of *bares-musicales* usually rocks until 4am.

July and August usher in the **Festivales de Tarragona** (tel. 977 24 47 95; for 24hr. tickets, call 902 33 22 11). The Auditori Camp de Mart near the cathedral holds rock, jazz, dance, and theater performances, as well as film screenings. A booth on Av. Catalunya at Portal del Roser sells tickets for the 10:30pm performances until 9pm for 500 to 2500ptas. Arrive one hour before the performance. On even-numbered years, the first Sunday in October brings the **Concurs de Castells,** which features tall stacks of people forming "human towers" and groups of acrobats. They appear amid dragons, beasts, and fireworks during the annual **Festa de Santa Tecla** on September 23.

■ Near Tarragona: Port Aventura Amusement Park

Tel. 902 20 22 20. Open daily Mar. 26-June 19 10am-8pm; June 20-Sept. 13 10am-midnight; Sept. 14-Jan. 11 10am-8pm. One-day admission 4100ptas, 2-day 6250ptas. Seniors and children 3100ptas for 1 day, 4850ptas for 2 days. Nighttime admission 2500ptas, seniors and children 1900ptas. Admission fee includes all rides and shows.

Catalan youth are all a-buzz over Port Aventura, Spain's latest and greatest theme park. Although veterans of Florida's Walt Disney World will find Port Aventura strangely familiar (despite the preponderance of Catalan and *castellano*-speakers), it makes for a refreshing break from museum and history-heavy itineraries. Spain's take on the Disney original is composed of five "lands" surrounding a lagoon, each representing regions of the world: the Mediterranean, Polynesia, China, Mexico, and the "Far West." While all that might be fine and good, the park's blockbuster attraction is undoubtedly its high speed entertainment provided by such bad-ass roller coasters as the **Dragon Khan,** which loops eight times and makes a sheer drop at 70mph. Other headliner rides include Stampida in the Far West, El Diablo in Mexico, and two different water rides guaranteed to wet your party wear. Although prices for food are predictably high, Mexico's **self-service cantina** (entrees 600-900ptas) won't break the bank and, set in an old colonial hacienda, ain't bad for ambiance either.

About half the **trains** on the Barcelona-Sitges-Tarragona-Tortosa line stop at Port Aventura (1½hr., 7 per day; heading south from Barcelona 9-11am, heading north towards Barcelona 5-9pm; 150ptas). A **taxi** from Tarragona costs 1900ptas (10min.).

CATALUNYA

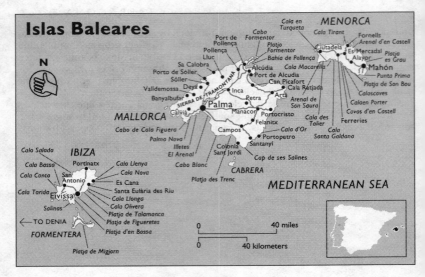

Islas Baleares

Islas Baleares

Dreaming, perhaps, of the vast fortunes to be made in the 20th-century tourist industry, nearly every culture with boats and colonists to spare has tried to conquer the Baleares. English imperialist efforts notwithstanding, the isles have been Spanish since the 13th century. Today's attractions are discos and beaches, drawing nearly two million of the hippest European bourgeois tourists to the islands each year.

Mallorca is home to Palma, the Balearic capital, and absorbs the bulk of invaders. Its museums, architecture, and nightlife compete with Eivissa (Ibiza City) as the Baleares's cultural hub. Mallorca is not short on natural beauty, albeit in the shadows of urbanization. To the west and north, Sierra de Tramontana's jagged limestone cliffs drop abruptly into the turquoise sea. Condominiums loom over lazy bays that scoop into the coastline, while olive orchards and orange groves shade its fertile interior. Ibiza, a counter-culture haven since the 1960s, plays the entertainment and style capital of the islands; its capital may just be the most radical scene on the planet. Ibiza's little neighbor, Formentera, is more peaceful, but unspoiled sands may quickly lose their charm as Brits, Italians, and Germans continue flocking to Spain. Wrapped in green fields and stone walls, Menorca leads a private life with empty white beaches, hidden coves, and mysterious Bronze Age megaliths. Each island maintains its own dialect as part of its distinctive culture—*ibsenco* in Ibiza, *menorquín* in Menorca, and *mallorquín* in Mallorca, all of which derive closely from Catalan.

Balearic island cuisine is relatively simple, but mayonnaise, a Menorcan innovation, puts the Baleares in the culinary hall of fame. Mallorca's *ensaimadas,* doughy, candied pastries smothered in powdered sugar, are famed throughout Spain. Not to be missed is *sopas mallorquinas,* a stocky vegetable soup ladled over brown bread.

Summers tend to be hot, dry, and crowded but fun. Winters, especially on the northern Mallorca and Menorca, are windy and chilly. Spring and autumn can be gorgeous, and easy times to find budget accommodations, but the beaches remain a bit cool and the nightlife doesn't heat up—especially on Mallorca and Menorca— until early July. Most information listings, opening hours, schedules, and prices in the Islas Baleares section of this book are for the summer months only. Off-season prices at hotels can drop by up to 50%, and opening hours are often cut drastically.

🎵 HIGHLIGHTS OF THE ISLAS BALEARES

- Need you ask? **Ibiza's** mad crazy nightlife (see p. 389).
- **Formentera's** sprawling expanses of empty sands (see p. 390).
- **Mahón,** the mysterious, quiet isle that makes a perfect place to get away from it all (see p. 377).

■ Getting There and Away

Flying is so fast and cheap (25min. from Barcelona) that it can often trump the ferry scene. Before hopping on a ferry, younger island-goers should consult **Iberia/Aviaco Airlines** (tel. 902 400 500; http://www.iberia.com) to inquire about youth discounts. **SOM** (Servicios de Ocio Marítimo; tel. 971 31 03 99; email ibizasom@ctv.es) collaborates with bus companies, ferry lines, and *discotecas* on packages to Ibiza specially designed for disco fiends seeking transportation and an all-night party, with no particular use for lodging.

BY PLANE

Charters are the cheapest and quickest means of round-trip travel. Most deals entail a week's stay in a hotel, but some companies (called *mayoristas*) sell fares for unoccupied seats on flights booked with full-package passengers. The leftover spots, called "seat only" deals, can be found in newspaper ads or through travel agencies (check TIVE and other budget travel havens in any Spanish city). Summer and Semana Santa prices more than double standard off-season (Oct.-May) fares.

Scheduled flights are easier to book, and flights from Spain won't break the bank. Frequent flights soar from Barcelona, Madrid, and Valencia as well as Düsseldorf, London, Frankfurt, Hamburg, and Paris. Foreign carriers provide service to the islands, but Iberia and Aviaco handle all flights from Spain. **Student fares** (must be 22 and under or 26 and under with ISIC) are available only for round-trip flights on Iberia and range from 17,000 to 20,000ptas between Barcelona and the islands (25min.) and 25,000 to 30,000ptas between Madrid and the islands (1hr.).

On **Iberia,** many daily flights connect each of the three islands to each other and to Madrid and Barcelona. From Valencia, Iberia goes to Palma de Mallorca (7 per day), Ibiza (1-2 per day), and Menorca (3 per week). Alicante and Bilbao have less frequent flights to the islands. Schedules and prices change often, so call the local Iberia office listed in the Practical Information section of each city or the 24hr. national reservation and info line (tel. 902 40 05 00). **Air Europa** (24hr. reservation and info tel. 902 24 00 42) is the new competitor, but its schedules can be unreliable. Air Europa flies between Barcelona and all three islands (2-6 per day) and to other cities. **SpanAir** (tel. 902 13 14 15; http://www.spainair.com) also flies to and from the islands.

Tickets are not hard to get a week or so before leaving except in August. If coming or going in late summer, you should try reserving tickets several months in advance.

BY BOAT

Ferry service is comparable in price to air service but longer in duration. On-board discos and small swimming pools on some boats help ease the longer passage. The best way to get tickets is to stop at a travel agency in Barcelona, Valencia, or on any of the islands; agents have more up-to-date information and charge no fee. You should reserve all tickets a few days in advance, but seats may be available up to an hour before departure. For all companies, call for low season information.

Trasmediterránea ships (tel. 902 45 46 45; http://www.trasmediterranea.com) leave from Barcelona, Estació Marítima Moll, Sant Bertrán (tel. 93 295 91 34), and Valencia, Estació Marítima, Pta. de Valencia (tel. 963 67 06 44). The following schedules and fares apply to departures from both the mainland and the islands: Barcelona-

ISLAS BALEARES

Palma (12-14 per week; fast 4¼hr., 8150ptas; slow 8hr., 6660ptas); Barcelona-Ibiza (9½hr., 6-7 per week, 6660ptas); Barcelona-Mahón (9hr. overnight, 2-6 per week, 6660ptas); Valencia-Palma (7-10 per week; fast 5¼hr., 8150ptas; slow 8½-12hr., 6660ptas); Valencia-Ibiza (5-6 per week; fast 3¼hr., 6950ptas; slow 6hr., 5725ptas); and Valencia-Mahón (16½hr. via Palma, 1 per week, 6660ptas).

Flebasa Lines (general tel. 902 160 180; Dénia tel. 96 578 40 11) is based on the mainland in Dénia, in the province of Alicante. The short trip between Dénia and Eivissa (3-4½hr., 1 per day) continues from Eivissa to Palma (4500ptas). Dénia lies on the FEVE rail line between Valencia to the north and Alicante to the south. In summer, ferry tickets can be combined with a bus connection from either of those cities or from Madrid, Albacete, or Benidorm for just 350ptas extra. **Pitra car ferries** (Dénia tel. 971 19 10 68) also depart from Estació Marítima in Dénia (tel. 96 642 31 20) and run to Formentera via Eivissa and to San Antonio de Portmany, Ibiza (4hr., 2 per day, 5475ptas, children 2738ptas, cars 15,050ptas). **Buquebus** (tel. 902 41 42 42 or 93 481 73 60; email reservas@buquebus.es) has just begun super-fast catamaran service between Barcelona and Palma (4hr., 2 per day, one-way 8150ptas, cars 18,560).

■ Getting Around

Flying is the most efficient way to island-hop. **Iberia** flies between Palma and Ibiza (20min., 3-4 per day, 7800ptas and up), between Palma and Mahón, Menorca (20min., 2-3 per day, 7800ptas and up), and between Menorca and Ibiza, with a long stopover in Palma (2-3 per day, 14,000ptas). **Air Europa** has better connections (at least on paper). Youth discounts are available on round-trip Iberia flights.

Ferries are also an option. **Trasmediterránea** ferries sail between Palma and Mahón (6½hr., 1 per week, 3330ptas) and between Palma and Ibiza (2-6 per week; fast 2½hr., 5210ptas; slow 4½hr., 3330ptas). There is no Mahón-Ibiza connection. **Trasmapi** (tel. 971 31 20 71), owned by Flebasa, links Ibiza and Formentera (fast ferry, 25min., 12 per day). **Umafisa Lines** (tel. 971 31 45 13) runs that route as well, but with car ferries (1hr., M-F 6 per day, Sa 5 per day, Su 4 per day, 1350ptas, children 675ptas; cars 6000ptas). Formentera-based **Inserco**, C. del Carmen, La Savina, Formentera (tel. 971 32 22 10), runs cheap Eivissa-Formentera boats (1hr., 6 per day, 8:15am-10pm, round-trip 2000ptas). **Balear de Ferrys** (tel. 971 22 91 24) connects Alcúdia, Mallorca and Ciutadella, Menorca (2½hr., 2 per day).

All three major islands have extensive **bus** systems. Mallorca has two narrow-gauge **train** systems, but they don't accept Eurailpasses. Intra-island travel is reasonably priced—bus fares between cities range from 200 to 700ptas each way. You might try self-operated transport for greater mobility and access to remote areas. A day's rental of a tiny standard-transmission **car** costs around 4500ptas including insurance, less on Mallorca. Vespa or **moped** rental costs around 2700ptas and **bicycle** rental 1000ptas.

MALLORCA

Mallorca, sought after since the days of the Romans, has always had appeal. Whether hosting the royal vacations of King Juan Carlos I or the scandalous honeymoon of Polish pianist Fréderic Chopin and French novelist George Sand, the island has long drawn visitors. These days, ever larger numbers of European package tourists have converged on the island, virtually suffocating the coastline.

There are reasons for such Mallorca lust. To the northwest, white sand beaches, frothy water, lemon groves, and olive trees adorn the jagged Sierra de Tramontana. To the east, expansive beaches sink into calm bays, while to the southeast, beauty is masked underground in a network of caves. Inland, windmills drawing water for almond and fig trees power a thriving agricultural economy, and many towns retain their unique history and culture. Although the coastline has long been doomed to prospectors, even jaded backpackers can sigh wistfully, if not alone, at the stunning expanses of sea, sand, and rock that sprawl across much of this island.

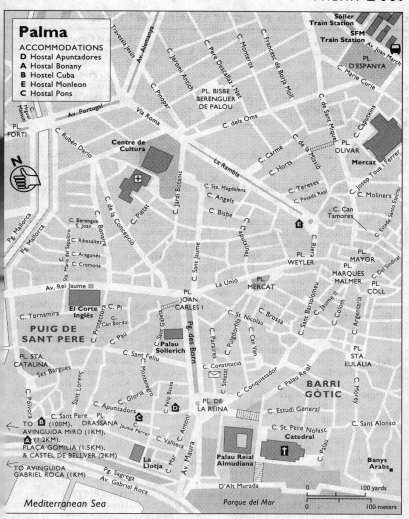

Palma

ACCOMMODATIONS
- **D** Hostal Apuntadores
- **A** Hostal Bonany
- **B** Hostel Cuba
- **E** Hostal Monleon
- **C** Hostal Pons

ISLAS BALEARES

■ Palma

The undisputed capital of the Balearics, Palma does not shy from conspicuous consumption. Streets bustle with shoppers buying leather accessories, designer clothes, and jewelry, and myriad restaurants along the port and in the old town cater to expensive taste. Even the city's namesake, palm trees, have gone commercial, picking up and moving to hotel lobbies where they've acquired plastic roots. Though flooded by *pesetas* and nearly every other currency, Palma pleasantly surprises with its well-preserved old quarter, colonial architecture, and a noticeable local flavor. Thanks to a large year-round population (pop. 323,000), Palma maintains the feel of a true metropolis—and has the swinging nightlife to show for it.

ORIENTATION AND PRACTICAL INFORMATION

To get to the town center from the airport, take bus #17 to **Plaça d'Espanya** (15min., departs every 30min., 290ptas). From the dock, walk out of the parking lot and turn right on Pg. Marítim then left onto Av. Antoni Maura, which leads to **Plaça de la Reina** and **Passeig des Born**. Passeig des Born leads away from the sea to **Plaça del Rei Joan Carles I,** the bustling old town center. **Avinguida Rei Jaume III,** the business artery, runs to the left. To the right, Carrer de la Unió leads (after some stairs) to the **Plaça Major,** the center of the pedestrian shopping district. Calle Sant Miquel connects Pl. Major to Pl. Espanya, where you can catch a bus.

Transportation

Flights: Aeroport Son San Juan (tel. 971 26 42 10) is 8km from downtown Palma. Bus #17 goes to and from Pl. Espanya. **Iberia** (tel. 971 75 71 51), **Air Europa,** foreign carriers, and a host of charter operators all offer service to Palma. For more info, see **Getting There and Away: By Plane,** p. 367, or **Getting Around,** p. 368.

Ferries: Trasmediterránea, Estación Marítim, 2 (tel. 971 70 06 11). Ferries dock at Moll Pelaires (south of the city). Bus #1 runs there along Pg. Marítim. Tickets sold M-F 9am-1pm and 5-7pm, Sa 9am-noon, or at travel agencies in town. **Flebasa** (tel. 971 40 53 60). See **By Boat,** p. 367, or **Getting Around,** p. 368.

Trains: Ferrocarril de Sóller, Pl. Espanya (tel. 971 75 20 51 or 971 75 20 28). To Sóller (6 per day, one-way 380ptas). Avoid the 10:40am "tourist train"—prices inflate to 735ptas (round-trip 1115ptas) for a 10min. stop in Mirador del Pujol d'en Banya. **Servicios Ferroviarios de Mallorca (SFM),** Pl. Espanya, 6 (tel. 971 75 22 45), goes to Inca (35min., departs about every hr., one-way 240ptas).

Buses: Most buses run out of the main terminal, **Estació Central D'Autobus,** Pl. Espanya (tel. 971 43 10 24). The tourist office has a complete schedule that orders the confusion, but the system is inefficient and restrictive. Major roads fan out from Palma like fingers, making travel to and from the capital relatively painless, but travel between most other areas is indirect and will probably route you through Palma. Check our write-up of the town you wish to visit for more detailed bus information. Buy tickets aboard or in Pl. Espanya kiosks. **Autocares Mallorca,** Pl. Espanya (tel. 971 54 56 96), serves Alcúdia (via Inca), Sóller, and other areas in northern Mallorca. **Autocares Aumasa,** Pl. Espanya (tel. 971 75 71 78), provides links to the eastern seaboard, including Manacor and Porto Cristo. **Bus Nord Balear,** C. Arxiduc Lluís Salvador, 1 (tel. 971 49 06 80), near Pl. Espanya, connects the west coast. **Autocares Villalonga,** Pl. Espanya (tel. 971 53 00 57), serves Pollença through Inca. **DarBus,** Pl. Espanya (tel. 971 75 06 22 or 971 20 07 58), serves towns in the southeast, including Sa Sapita, Es Trenc, and Colonia San Jordi. **Autocares Alorda** (tel. 971 50 15 03) serves Lluc, Consell, and Inca from Pl. Espanya. **Playa-Sol** (tel. 971 29 64 17) runs to nearby resort areas El Arenal, Magaluf, Andratx, and Palma Nova.

Public Transportation: Empresa Municipal de Transportes (EMT), Pl. Espanya (tel. 971 75 22 45). Plaza Espanya is the hub. Stops around town and as far as Palma Nova and Arenal. 175ptas, 10 tickets 1500ptas. Buy tickets aboard or in Pl. Espanya kiosks. Buses run approximately 6am-10pm. The airport bus, #17, runs until about 2am.

Taxis: (tel. 971 75 54 40, 971 40 14 14, or 971 72 80 81). Airport fare from the center of town is about 2000ptas—agree on the price before getting in.

Car Rental: Mascaro Crespi, Av. Joan Miró, 9 (tel. 971 73 61 03). 2000-3000ptas per day with insurance. Open M-Sa 8am-1pm and 3-7pm, Su 9am-1pm and 5-7pm. More reliable **Betacar/Europcar** (tel. 971 73 75 89) is on Paseo Marítimo, 19. 4000ptas per day with insurance. Open M-Sa 9am-1pm and 4-8pm, Su 9am-noon and 6-8pm.

Scooter Rental: RTR Bike Rental, Av. Joan Miró, 340 (tel. 971 40 25 85). Near Pl. Gomila. Mopeds 2150ptas per day. Open M-Sa 9am-8pm, Su 9am-1pm.

Tourist and Financial Services

Tourist Offices: Helpful multilingual staff at the **municipal branch,** C. Sant Dominic, 11 (tel. 971 72 40 90; email turisme@palma.es), hands out a monthly guide in Catalan, bus and train schedules, and a good map of the city. From Pl. Reina, take C.

ISLAS BALEARES

Conquistador until it turns into C. Sant Dominic; the office is at the bottom of a stairway, a level below the street above. Open M-F 9am-8pm, Sa 9am-1pm. An **info booth** sits in Pl. Espanya (open M-F 9am-8pm, Sa 9am-1pm). The **island tourist office,** Pl. Reina, 2 (tel. 971 71 22 16), offers info on other Balearic islands, a fine city map, bus and train schedules, hiking info, and lists of all sporting and cultural events on Mallorca. Open M-F 9am-1pm and 5-8pm, Sa 9am-1:30pm. **Branch office** at the airport has similar info. Open M-Sa 9am-2pm and 3-8pm, Su 9am-2pm.

Budget Travel: TIVE, C. Jerónim Antich, 5 (tel. 971 71 17 85), near Pl. Bisbe Berenguer de Palou and Pl. Espanya. ISIC cards, HI cards, Interrail tickets, and mainland flights. Not for inter-island travel and charters. Open M-F 8am-2pm.

Currency Exchange: Seek out 24hr. **ATMs** (all around the center of town) for the best rates. **Banco Central Hispano,** Pg. Born, 17, has good rates. Open May-Sept. M-F 8:30am-2:30pm, Oct.-Apr. M-F 8:30am-2:30pm, Sa 8:30am-1pm.

American Express: Av. Antonio Maura, 40 (tel. 971 72 23 44), downtown right next to C. Apuntadors, off Pl. Reina. Open M-F 9am-1pm and 2-8pm, Sa 10am-2pm.

El Corte Inglés: Av. Rei Jaume III, 15, or Av. Alexandre Rosselló, 12 (tel. 971 77 01 77). **Fax,** photocopies, phones, money exchange (poor rates), a supermarket, and a free **map** of town (at the info booth). Both branches open M-Sa 10am-10pm.

Local Services

Luggage Storage: SFM office, Pl. Espanya. Small locker 300ptas; big 500ptas. Lockers available M-F 7am-8pm, Sa-Su 7am-2pm.

English Bookstore: Book Inn, C. Horts, 20 (tel. 971 71 38 98), right off La Rambla. An impressive selection of literature. Children's books, too. Open M-F 10am-1:30pm and 5-8pm, Sa 10:30am-1:30pm. Hours change in August.

Women's Center: Centro Informació Drets de la Mujer, C. Portella, 11, 2nd fl. (tel. 971 72 25 51), near Parc de la Mar. Rape crisis assistance available. Open M-F 9am-2pm. 24hr. hotline (tel. 900 19 10 10).

Emergency and Communications

Emergency: tel. 092 or 091. **Police:** On Av. Sant Ferran (tel. 971 28 16 00).

24hr. Pharmacy: See listings in local paper, *Diario de Mallorca* (125ptas).

Medical Services: Recommended for foreigners are the **Clínica Juaneda,** Son Espanyolet, 55 (tel. 971 73 61 47 or 971 73 61 48), and **Femenía,** Camilo José Cela, 20 (tel. 971 45 23 23). The **Clínica Rotger,** Santiago Russinyol, 971 (tel. 971 72 02 00 or 971 71 66 00), is more central. All open 24hr.

Internet Access: La Red, Concepción 5 (tel. 971 71 35 74; http://www.laredcafe.com), next to the intersection with San Martí. 500ptas per 30min. Drinks served. Open M-F 3pm-1am, Sa 4pm-2am, Su 4pm-11pm.

Post Office: C. Constitució, 5 (tel. 971 72 18 67), one block off Pl. Reina. Parcels upstairs. Lista de Correos downstairs at window #3. Fax service. Open M-F 8:30am-8:30pm, Sa 9:30am-2pm. **Postal Code:** 07080.

ACCOMMODATIONS

Accommodations vary from the bed-stuffed-in-a-closet approach to the mini-villa. There aren't many of the latter—call in advance for any summer stay.

Hostal Cuba, C. San Magín, 1 (tel. 971 73 81 59), at C. Argentina. From the port, go left along Av. Gabriel Roca and turn right onto C. Argentina. Look for the "Restaurant Cuba" sign and the blue shutters on the left. Friendly and market-conscious owner always making improvements to keep ahead of the competition. Rooms are simple but clean; smart view of cathedral and port from balconies and rooftop terrace. Right on the edge of the town center. Singles 1500ptas; doubles 3000ptas, with full bath 3500ptas; triples 5000ptas.

Hostal Bonany, C. Almirante Cervera, 5 (tel. 971 73 79 24), in a wealthy residential neighborhood, 3km from the center toward the nearest beaches and 5min. from the nightlife. Take bus #3, 20, 21 or 22 from Pl. Espanya to Av. Joan Miró, walk up C. Camilio José Cela. Take the 1st right, then the 1st left. Spacious rooms with bath and balcony overlook the hostel's little pool and patio. Singles 2400ptas; doubles 4200ptas. Hearty breakfast 400ptas. Open Feb.-Nov.

ISLAS BALEARES

Hostal Apuntadores, C. Apuntadores, 8 (tel. 971 71 34 91; email apuntadores@jet.es), smack in the middle of things, less than a block from Pl. Reina. Rooms are clean yet uninspiring, but the rooftop lounge and crowded downstairs bar raise the quality of living (happy hour at the bar 6:30-8:30pm). Balconied rooms are less steamy than the interior ones. Singles 2000ptas; doubles 3500ptas, with shower 4000ptas. Opt for the shared bath over the communal showers. Breakfast 375ptas.

Hostal Pons, Carrer del Vi, 8 (tel. 971 72 26 58). From Pl. Reina, take C. Apuntadores until its end, then take a right on Pl. Vi. A back-street hostel, lesser known than the more visible spots but just as good. Ancient floors and only one bathroom are part of the charm. Quite a deal—singles 2000ptas; doubles 4000ptas.

Albergue Residencia de Estudiantes (HI), C. Costa Brava, 13 (tel. 971 26 08 92), in the beach town El Arenal. Take bus #15 from Pl. Espanya (every 8 min., 170ptas), and ask to get off at Hotel Acapulco. A pristine, palatial *pensión* on the beach but not near Palma. New furniture, showers, lounge with big-screen TV, and library. 1200ptas per person. HI card required. Curfew Su-Th midnight, F-Sa 3am. Reception daily 8am-3am. Sheets included. Breakfast 300ptas. Open only Jul.-Aug.

Hostal Monleon, La Rambla, 3 (tel. 971 71 53 17). An old, vaguely spooky building with tall ceilings. Some rooms somewhat dark but with big windows. Noises drift up from the street. Singles 2200ptas, with shower 2500ptas, with bath 2800ptas; doubles 4000ptas, with shower 4300ptas, with bath 4700ptas.

Camping: Platja Blava (tel. 971 53 78 63 or 971 86 00 02; fax 971 53 75 11) is located at km 8 on the highway between Alcúdia and C'an Picafort. Take Autocares Mallorca direct from Pl. Espanya (5 per day, 9am-7:30pm, 575ptas). 475-575ptas per person; 1300-1530ptas for a 6-by-6m plot. **Camping Sant Pere** (tel. 971 58 90 23), a 3rd-class site 2km outside Colònia de Sant Pere. To get here from Palma, hop on a C'an Picafort bus and take a connecting bus to Colònia de Sant Pere. 530ptas per person; 1185ptas per tent. Open Apr.-Sept.

FOOD

Menus come in German, French, Swedish, Hittite, English, Spanish, and *mallorquín,* but the best food is rarely as international. Mom-and-Pop operations serve tourists and locals along side streets, especially around **Passeig Born.** Two **markets** vie for customers. One is in Pl. Olivar off C. Padre Atanasio; the other is across town by Pl. Navegació in Es Jonquet (both open M-Sa 7am-3pm). For **groceries,** try **Servicio y Precios,** C. Felip Bauzà (tel. 971 72 78 11), near C. Apuntadores and Pl. Reina (open M-F 9am-2pm and 5:30-9pm, Sa 9am-2pm).

Merendero Minyones, C. Minyones, 4. A teeny booth on a small street one block from C. Constitució. From Pg. Born walk up C. Constitució then take your 1st left and 1st right. This is as cheap as they come. Take-out only—they'll wrap up sandwiches (155-210ptas) for the beach. Munch your *pa-amb-oli i tomate* (tomato and olive oil on bread, 115ptas) or *bocadillo de sobrasada* (bread with soft Mallorcan chorizo spread, 155ptas). Open M-F 7:30am-8:30pm, Sa 8am-2pm.

Celler Pagès, C. Felip Bauzà, 2 (tel. 971 72 60 36), at the end of C. Pintor Guillem Mesquida, off Pl. Reina. Disregard the exterior; a bourgeois Mallorcan crowd is all over the local cuisine. Bowl of spiced olives with every afternoon *menú* (1100ptas). Open M-F 1-4pm and 8:30-11pm, Sa 1-4pm.

C'an Joan de S'aigo, C. Sanç, 10 (tel. 971 71 07 59), near Pl. Coll. Red velvet curtains, a mini-garden, and marble tables deck out the city's oldest house. Enjoy the exquisite pastries and ice creams, including Mallorca's specialty *gelado de almendra* (almond ice cream, 180ptas). Not to be missed. Open W-M 8am-9:15pm.

Celler Sa Premsa, Pl. Bisbe Berenguer de Palou, 8 (tel. 971 72 35 29), between Via Roma and Pl. Espanya off Carrer OMS. Traditional *mallorquín* food on vegetable-laden platters served by superhumanly efficient waiters. *Menú del día* 1075ptas. *Sopas mallorquinas* 540ptas. Open M-Sa noon-4pm and 7:30-11:30pm.

Na Bauçano, Sta. Bárbara, 4 (tel. 971 72 18 86), off C. Brossa between Pl. Mercat and Pl. Cort. It's all natural, and it's all vegetarian—homemade breads with curried vegetables and delicious vegetable soups. Entertains a wide variety of foreigners. Afternoon *menú* 1200ptas. No smoking. Open M-W and Sa 1-4pm, Th-F 1-4pm and 8:30pm-midnight.

ISLAS BALEARES

Bar Bosch, Pl. Rei Joan Carles I, 6, next to McDonald's. Serving food into the wee hours, this Palma mainstay (since 1936) refreshes with tasty *tapas* (200-450ptas). Open daily 1pm-2am.

SIGHTS

Palma's architecture proudly displays Arabic, Christian, and Modernist influences that have passed through with the island's many conquerors. Two of the city's most important buildings share close quarters, just off Pl. Reina. **Palau Almudaina** (tel. 971 72 71 45) was built by the Moors and later controlled by *los Reyes Católicos* (Fernando and Isabel). *(Open Apr.-Sept. M-F 10am-6:30pm, Sa 10am-2pm; Oct.-Mar. M-F 10am-2pm and 4-6pm, Sa 10am-2pm. 400ptas, students 200ptas, Wednesdays EU members free.)* Guided tours, which pass through the museum, are given in numerous languages, except when King Juan Carlos I is tromping about the halls on business. Next door, one of the world's largest **cathedrals** (tel. 971 72 31 30) overlooks Palma and its bay. *(Cathedral and museum open M-F 10am-6pm, Sa 10am-2:30pm; Nov.-Mar. M-Sat. 10am-2pm. 400ptas.)* The laggard Gothic giant, dedicated to Palma's patron saint San Sebastián, was begun in the 1300s, finished in 1601, and then modified by Gaudí in modernist fashion in 1909. Now the interior and the ceiling ornamentation blend smoothly with the stately exterior. The tangle of tight streets full of wide-eyed tourists around the cathedral constitutes the **Barri Gòtic** (medieval quarter).

Due in no small part to its bourgeois clientele, Palma also hosts a multitude of art exhibits. **Colleccio March, Museo d'Art Espanyol Contemporani,** C. Sant Miquel, 11 (tel. 971 71 35 15), has one work each by dozens of different 20th-century Spanish artists, including Picasso, Dalí, Miró, Juan Gris, and Antoni Tàpies. The curator answers the questions of those befuddled patrons who thought art ended with Monet. *(Open M-F 10am-6:30pm, Sa 10am-1:30pm. 300ptas.)* The **Casal Solleric,** C. Sant Gaietà, 10 (tel. 971 77 20 92), opens contemporary art exhibits to the public. *(Open Tu-Sa 10:30am-1:45pm and 5-8:30pm, Su 10am-1:45pm. Free.)* **Fundacio "la Caixa,"** Pl. Weyler, 3 (tel. 971 72 01 11), hosts a permanent collection of paintings as well as other special exhibits in Domènech's modernist Gran Hotel. *(Open T-Sa 10am-9pm, Su 10am-2pm. Free.)* **Centre de Cultura "Sa Nostra,"** C. Concepción, 12 (tel. 971 72 52 10), features rotating contemporary exhibits and sponsors cultural events such as lectures, concerts, and movies. *(Open M-F 10:30am-9pm, Sa 10am-1pm. Exhibitions open M-F 10:30am-1:30pm and 5-9pm, Sa 10:30am-1:30pm. Free.)* Inaugurated in December 1992, **Fundació Pilar i Joan Miró,** C. Saridakis, 29 (tel. 971 70 14 20), is a collection of the works found in the Catalan artist's Palma studio at the time of his death. *(Open May 16-Sept. 14 Tu-Sa 10am-7pm, Su 10am-3pm; Sept. 15-May 15 Tu-Sa 11am-6pm, Su 10am-3pm. 675ptas.)* Buses #3, 21, and 22 whisk you from Pl. Espanyol to C. Joan Miró.

Overlooking the city and bay and set in a park, **Castell de Bellver** (tel. 971 73 06 57) served as summer residence for 14th-century royalty. For centuries thereafter it housed distinguished, albeit unwilling, prisoners. The castle contains a municipal museum of archaeological displays and several paintings. *(Buses #3, 21, and 22 can get you there from Pl. Espanyol. Castle, grounds, and museum open daily Apr.-Sept. 8am-9:20pm; Oct.-Mar. 8am-8pm. 250ptas, Su free but museum closed.)* Also outside of town is Palma's **Poble Espanyol** (Spanish Village), C. Poble Espanyol, 39 (tel. 971 73 70 75), a reproduction of its parent in Barcelona, with mini samples of Spanish architecture. *(Open daily 9am-8pm; Nov.-Mar. 9am-6pm. 800ptas.)* Bus #4 and 5 pass by along C. Andrea Doria.

Although better **beaches** speckle the island, decent ones (sand and snacks) are a mere bus ride from Palma. The huge beach at El Arenal (Platja de Palma, bus #15), 11km to the southeast (toward the airport), is expansive and well-sanded but tends to be over-touristed. **Aquacity** (tel. 971 44 00 51), a huge water park, resides next door. The equally crowded Palma Nova and Illetes beaches (buses #21 and 3, respectively) are 15km and 9km southwest. The tourist office (see above) distributes a list of over 40 nearby beaches, so take your pick—the smaller and lesser known, the better.

ENTERTAINMENT

The municipal tourist office keeps a comprehensive list of sporting activities, concerts, and exhibits. Every Friday, *El Día de Mundo* (125ptas) publishes an entertainment supplement with listings of bars and discos all over Mallorca. Look for *La Calle*, a monthly review of clubs and bars.

The *casa-antigua*-turned-bar **ABACO,** C. Sant Joan, 1 (tel. 971 71 59 11), in the Barri Gòtic near the waterfront, may be the most perfect place on Earth for a cocktail. Sip drinks in the midst of a dreamy 19th-century courtyard, with elegant wicker and marble furniture, cooing doves, a wide array of fresh fruit, flowers, and hundreds of dripping candles, all to the accompaniment of classical music. (Fruit shakes 1100ptas, potent cocktails 1900ptas and up. Wandering the chambers is prohibited. Open daily 9pm-3am; shower of rose petals every Friday at midnight.)

The streets around **La Llotja** flow with bar-hoppers. You can't help but dance to the Cuban rhythms at **La Bodeguita del Medio,** C. Vallseca, 18 (tel. 971 71 78 32), featuring Hemingway's favorite: *mojito* (500ptas), a drink with seltzer water, sugar, lemon juice, rum, and *hierbabuena* (open M-F 9pm-3:30am, Sa-Su 9pm-4am). Live jazz (Tu and Th midnight-3am) and salsa (W midnight-3am) give a lift to the calm and cool **Barcelona,** C. Apuntadores, 5 (tel. 971 71 35 57; open M-Sa 10pm-3am). Otherwise, try **Blues Ville** on Má Del Moro, 3, or **El Agua,** C. Jaime Ferrer, 6.

The rest of Palma's nightlife boogies near **El Terreno** and its beach, with a motherload of nightclubs centered on Pl. Gomilia and along C. Joan Miró. **Tito's Palace,** Pl. Gomilia, 1 (tel. 971 73 76 42), an indoor colosseum of mirrors and lights, overlooks the water (cover 1500-2000ptas; open 11am-6am). **Plato,** across the street at Pl. Gomilia, 2, keeps a lower, more local profile. **Sa Finestra,** Av. Joan Miró, 90, features live music every night after 11:30pm. The gay bar **Sombrero** is on C. Joan Miró, 26 (tel. 971 73 16 00; open nightly 9pm-3am). The divine **Baccus** (tel. 971 45 77 89), around the corner on C. Lluis Fábregas, 2, draws lively lesbian and gay hedonists (open until 3am). Word is that **Pachá** will found its own island by the year 2000; for now freak out at its Av. Gabriel Roca site (cover 2000-3000ptas and up, try for free tix at bars in town; open midnight-6am). **BCM** is supposedly the biggest nightclub in Europe. (Playa-Sol bus company sends its last bus at 8pm, but you can return on bus #10 at 6:45am. Taxi from Palma 1800ptas. Cover 2000-2500ptas. Open nightly 11pm-6am.)

Islanders use any and every occasion as an excuse to party. One of the more colorful bashes, **Día de Sant Joan** (June 24) involves a fireworks display the night before, accompanied by singing, dancing, and drinking in Parc del Mar.

▌West Coast

Mallorca's west coast is its pride and joy. Ten minutes out of Palma on the road to Valldemossa, your jaw will drop as whitewashed megaplexes give way to verdant rolling hills, sparse cliffs, and dramatic seascapes. The best way to explore is to choose a destination along the gorgeous coast then meander on foot. **Playa-Sol** (tel. 971 29 64 17) runs **buses** to the transport hub **Andratx,** 30km from Palma.

■ Valldemosa

Valldemossa's storybook colonial houses huddle against each other along the verdant slopes of the Sierra de Tramontana. Little in this tranquil, ancient village hints at the passion that shocked the townsfolk in the winter of 1838-39, when tubercular Frédéric Chopin and George Sand (her two children in tow) stayed in the picturesque and floral monastery called **Cartoixa Reial** (tel. 971 61 21 06), loudly flouting the monastic tradition of celibacy. Chopin memorabilia includes the piano upon which they played. Short piano recitals recapture the magic in the summer. (Every hr. during opening hours. Open Mar.-Sept. M-Sa 9:30am-1:20pm and 3-6:30pm, Su 10am-1pm; Nov.-Feb. M-Sa 9:30am-1pm and 3-5:30pm, Su 10am-1pm. 1100ptas, including visits to the Museu Municipal and the Palau del Rei Sancho.)

Hostal Ca'n Mario, C. Vetam, 8 (tel. 971 61 21 22; fax 971 61 60 29), offers great views of town (singles with shower 4000ptas; doubles with shower 6000ptas). Simple and cheap fare can be found at several cafe-bars around the main town square. The town goes to bed early, so don't expect anything in the way of nightlife—enjoy the peace and quiet. **Nord Balear buses** (tel. 971 49 06 80) to Valldemosa leave from Palma at C. Arxiduc Salvador, 1 (45min., 5 per day, 200ptas).

■ Deià

An artists' hangout, relatively unspoiled Deià affords sensational views of miles and miles of twisted olive trees. In the town center, picturesque houses and the occasional church line lantern-lit cobblestone squares. Local hotels are pricey and cater to the honeymoon set, so you'd be better off staying elsewhere; the best place to eat is in the small cafe-bars around the center. **Ca'n Quet** restaurant, on the winding Valldemosa-Deià road just before Deià, is expensive but might be the most romantic spot on the island for a meal (entrees 1500ptas and up). Deià is 10km north of Valldemosa on the **Nord Balear bus** route to Sóller (1½hr., 5 buses per day, 295ptas).

■ Sóller and Puerto de Sóller

Another 30km up the coast, cobblestoned **Sóller** basks in a mountain valley widening to a golden port. At the end of a train ride through the mountains, the town hums with tourists all day long. Every available plot of land is lined with citrus groves, and freshly squeezed OJ is a local specialty. In August, the Ajuntament hosts an international **Festival of Folk Dancing**, with dancers from all over Europe and Asia.

In Sóller, the **tourist office** on Pl. Constitució, 1 (tel. 971 63 02 00), supplies a map and list of the few accommodations (open M-Sa 9:30am-1:30pm; info posted in front of the church near the entrance if the office is closed). They can also suggest good hikes. For snacks, local patisseries specialize in *Coca Mallorquina,* a cold pizza-like snack (large costs about 250ptas). For **emergencies,** call 971 63 11 91 or 085. The **police** are at 971 63 02 03 or, in the port, 971 63 02 00. For **health concerns,** call the private **Clinic Balear,** Es Traves, 23 (tel. 971 63 44 11; 24-hr. mobile tel. 970 08 47 26), along the water and open 24hr.

From Sóller it is a pleasant half-hour walk down the valley to **Puerto de Sóller** and the beach, but a trolley also connects the two (departs every 30min., 115ptas). Puerto de Sóller absorbs the bulk of the tourists. A pebble-and-sand beach lines the small bay, where windsurfers zip back and forth. Numerous hotels lie on C. Marina along the water. **Hotel Miramar,** C. Marina, 12-14 (tel. 971 63 13 50), provides spotless rooms and full baths (singles 3950ptas; doubles 4900ptas; triples 7300ptas). There are two **grocery stores** up C. Jaume Torrens, and **restaurants** of all sorts and sizes file along the beach. Food tends toward the pricey, but the *paella* (1275ptas) is a godsend at **Restaurante Balear,** Santa Caterina d'Alexandria (tel. 971 63 15 24), a few feet off the fork with C. de la Marina (menú 900ptas; open F-W noon-3:30pm and 7-10pm; closed Jan.-Feb.).

Exploring the rest of the coves on the coast is easiest by **boat.** Tramontana and Barcos Azules (tel. 971 63 20 61), on the port near the last trolley stop, sail to **Sa Calobra,** most people's final destination (May-Oct. 15 3-5 per day, round-trip 1900ptas), and **Cala Deià** (June-Oct. 15, round-trip 1200ptas). Nord Balear **buses** link Puerto de Sóller to Palma's Pl. Espanya via Valldemosa (2hr., 5 per day, 450ptas). The old-fashioned Palma-Sóller **train,** run by Ferrocarril de Sóller, C. Castanyer, 7 (tel. 971 63 03 01, Palma tel. 971 75 20 51), is a highlight in itself. Bravehearts can ride in the wind between cars through olive orchards and scary tunnels (6 per day, one-way 380ptas).

■ Sa Calobra

An asphalt serpent, the road to Sa Calobra drops 1000m to the sea over 10 nail-biting hairpin kilometers, writhing back underneath itself in the process. The boat from Puerto de Sóller is easier on the nerves (see above). **Torrent de Pareis,** toward the bottom of the road, is a favorite Kodak moment. In Sa Calobra proper, two dark, ominous cliffs sandwich a smooth pebble beach bordering the crystalline sea. Despite its beauty, the cove is actually somewhat infested with tourists, restaurants, and gift shops. It may not be quite worth the trip down, but hey, getting there is half the fun.

■ Monestir de Lluc

Tucked away quietly in the mountains, the Monestir de Lluc is an inland enigma. Twenty kilometers from the coast in Escorca, Lluc is the home of the 700-year-old wood-carved *La Verge de Lluc (The Virgin)*. Behind the monastery, the **Via Crucis** winds around a hill over the valley's olive trees and jingling goats. Gaudí designed the path's stations of the cross. Monks, pilgrims, and a few guests stay at Lluc's **monastery** (tel. 971 51 70 25; true pilgrims stay for a donation—others pay 2700ptas for doubles with bath; quads with bath 3500ptas.).The monastery's store sells groceries, and its restaurant-bar pushes pricey food and drink. All in all, Lluc doesn't have much to see, yet some tourists mysteriously return day after day. To join them, take **Autocares Alorda** from Palma direct (1hr., M-Sa 2 per day, Su 1 per day, one-way 555ptas). You can also connect from Puerto Sóller and Alcúdia.

■ Northern Gulfs

Longer stretches of beaches, finer sand, and a nightmarish quantity of older tourists distinguish the north edge of Mallorca. Secluded coves are tough to come by, especially with the package tours wheeling in visitors from sunless lands. Buses from Palma run through Inca to more appealing spots.

■ Puerto de Pollença

Puerto de Pollença (Puerto Pollensa) features a stretch of fine white sand slightly less crowded than some parts of the island. The area hosts a **Music Festival** from July to September. A complete schedule of events and list of ticket vendors is available at the tourist office (tickets 1000-5000ptas).

Bike and **moped rentals** are at **Rent March,** C. Joan XXIII, 89. (Tel. 971 86 47 84. Open April-Oct. M-Sa 9am-1pm and 3-8pm, Su 9am-1pm and 6-7:30pm. Bikes 600ptas per day. Mopeds 2500ptas per day.) The **tourist office,** C. Formentor, 31 (tel. 971 86 54 67; email fundaciobocchoris@oninet.es), across from Hotel Daina, is helpful and can plan excursions (open May-Oct. M-F 9am-1pm and 4-7pm, Sa 9am-1pm). **Hostal Corro,** C. Joan XXIII, 68 (tel. 971 86 66 83, fax 971 86 50 05), has big, pristine rooms with sinks (doubles 4000ptas, triples 5000ptas, with bath 5500ptas). Autocares Mallorca **buses** connect Alcúdia and Pollença (every 15min.).

At the end of **Cabo Formentor,** 15km northeast of Puerto de Pollença, lookouts spy on spectacular seaside cliffs. Before the final twisting kilometer, the road drops to **Platja Formentor,** where a canopy of evergreens nearly sinks into the water. Here the sand is softer, the water calmer, and the crowds smaller than in Puerto de Pollença. **Autocares Villalonga,** San Isidro, 4 (tel. 971 53 00 57), sends **buses** from Palma (5 per day, 595ptas). All buses leave from the rotunda where the beach meets the pier. There's also a **boat** to Formentor from Puerto de Pollença, Estación Marítima (6 per day, round-trip 825ptas to Platja Formentor, 1600ptas to Cabo Formentor).

■ Puerto de Alcúdia

Hard-packed sand stretches around the small bay. Hotels, bars, and pizzerias outnumber the boats in the marina—Puerto de Alcúdia is far from undiscovered. Most people come here for the beach, but if you're looking for a bit more, Alcúdia proper preserves 14th-century ramparts around **Roman remains** dating back to 2 BC (15min. walk; buses depart every 15min. from C. dels Mariners). **Museu Pollentia** (tel. 971 54 70 04) documents the archaeological discoveries. (Open Apr.-Sept. M-Sa 10am-1:30pm and 5-7pm, Su 10:30am-1pm; Oct.-Mar. M-Sa 10am-1:30pm and 4-6pm, Su

ISLAS BALEARES

10:30-1pm. 200ptas.) For mindless fun, head to **Hidropark** (tel. 971 89 16 72), a water slide park accessible by bus (departs every 15min. from C. dels Mariners).

You can rent **bikes** from **Vanrell Bicicletas**, Av. Reina Sofía. For a **taxi,** call 971 89 21 87. The multilingual **tourist office** (tel. 971 89 26 15), near the waterfront at Av. Pere Mas Reus, at Ctra. Arta, has maps (open May-Oct. M-Sa 9:30am-7pm). The municipal **police** answer at 971 54 50 78.

Hostal Puerto, C. Teodoro Canet, 29 (tel. 971 54 54 47), on the road that leads up to Alcúdia, offers hotel-quality rooms with private baths (doubles with shower 3600ptas, with bath 4000ptas; open May-Oct.). **Alberg Victoria (HI),** Ctra. Cap Pinar, 4 (tel. 971 54 53 95), lolls 100m from an empty beach on the Bahía de Pollença. From the town center, signs lead east 4km to the *albergue* (1hr. walk or 1000pta taxi ride). Reserve at least six months in advance for July or August. (1000ptas, with breakfast 1500ptas, with 2 meals 1950ptas, with 3 meals 2530ptas. Members only.)

Autocares Mallorca **buses** (tel. 971 54 56 96) leave for Alcúdia (570ptas) and Puerto de Alcúdia (580ptas) from Pl. Espanya in Palma (1hr., M-Sa 15 per day, Su 5 per day). The bus from Alcúdia to Puerto de Pollença and onto Cabo Formentor leaves from C. dels Mariners. Bus service to the south goes only as far as C'an Picafort on **Aumasa** (tel. 971 55 07 30) and to the Cuevas Drach (see Southeast, below).

■ Southeast

The southeast interior is owned by the grandsons of Joan March, an infamous Spanish banker. On the coast, east of **Cap de Salinas,** Mallorca's southernmost point, is a scalloped fringe of bays and caves that are the newest hotel towns. To their credit, builders have aspired to some architectural integrity. A 1 to 2km walk is usually enough to put plenty of sand between you and the thickest crowds. West of Cap de Salinas and east of Cap Blanc sprawls one of Mallorca's best beaches, **Trenc.** To get to Trenc, take a **Dar Bus** from Pl. Espanya in Palma to Sa Rapita, Es Trenc, or Colonia San Jordi. Again, a 2km walk will take you away from clothes and crowds.

The **Cuevas del Drach,** near Porto Cristo, are among the most dramatic natural wonders in Mallorca's southeast. Only here can you float on an underground lake below menacing stalactites while listening to classical music. A **bus** runs from Port Alcúdia to the caves (M-Sa 3 per day, 770ptas). One must leave the caves, however, via Porto Cristo (9 per day; from Porto Cristo to Port Alcúdia 3 per day, 600ptas).

Dar Buses (tel. 971 75 06 22) leave Pl. Espanya in Palma for a number of other destinations in the southeast: **Santanyí,** an inland town whose Porta Murada (defensive wall) testifies to the piracy that once plagued the region; **Cala d'Or,** an inlet of pinewoods and massive boulders; **Porto Petro,** on the beach; and **Colonia Sant Jordi.** From Colonia Sant Jordi, a boat ventures to **Cabrera,** the largest island (30 sq. km) of a small archipelago. Dar Buses do not arrive early enough to catch the boat. For boat info, call **Excursiones a Cabrera** (tel. 971 64 90 34). Uninhabited except for a small military installation, Cabrera has a gruesome history. Eight thousand French prisoners-of-war died here during the Peninsular War in 1809 when the Spanish abandoned them with no food. A monument to the dead stands by the port. Nearby looms a 14th-century fortress used as a pirates' den. Adding to the carnage, large numbers also died in shipwrecks poking up from the ocean floor.

MENORCA

Menorca's raw beaches, rustic landscape, and well-preserved ancient monuments spark the diverse interests of ecologists, sun worshippers, and photographers, although prices here are generally higher and tourists fewer in comparison with the other Balearics. Since the island's incorporation into the Catalan kingdom in 1287, Menorca (pop. 69,000) has endured a succession of foreign invaders—Arab, Turkish, French, and British. After occupying the island for three separate stints during the 18th century, the dominant Brits have returned as tourists and restauranteurs.

In 1993, UNESCO (an arts and sciences agency of the UN) declared Menorca a 702-square-mile biosphere reserve. Since then, public administrators have directed their efforts at preserving the island's natural harbors, pristine southerly beaches, rocky northern coastline, and latticed network of farmlands. The act has also encouraged further protection, excavation, and study of Menorca's stone burial chambers, sepulchers, and homestead complexes, remnants of a mysterious Talayotic stone-age culture dating from 1400 BC. Some of these relics are even home to contemporary cave-dwellers who originally sought a communal lifestyle here in the 1960s.

Menorca's two main cities, Mahón in the east and Ciutadella in the west, serve as gateways to the island's real attractions. A small chapel caps Mont Toro, the island's highest peak. At the foot of the road leading to the chapel is Es Mercadal, a brilliantly white town and departure point for Fornells, close to numerous beaches.

■ Mahón (Maó)

Perched atop a steep bluff, Mahón's white-splashed houses overlook a well-trafficked harbor 5.5km long. The British occupied Menorca's verdant capital (pop. 23,300) for almost a century in the 1700s, leaving Georgian doors, brass knockers, and wooden shutters in their wake. Gin distilleries, British-style pubs, Anglo accents, and the city's early bedtime testify to a continuing influence, as do elite visitors who spend money almost as old as the island. Vacationers from the coasts of France, Italy, and Spain cruise in on mammoth yachts and leave the port in luxury sedans and private helicopters. If it is sun, surf, and sand you seek, plan to rent a scooter or a car or take a bus to the nearby beaches—there are none within easy walking distance.

ORIENTATION AND PRACTICAL INFORMATION

Between the **airport** and Mahón, you must take a taxi (7km, 1065ptas) unless it's Friday, curiously the only day the Aerobus runs (30min., departs every hr.). If you arrive by sea at the **ferry station,** walk to your left (with your back toward the water) about 150 yards, then turn right at the steps that cut through the serpentine **Costa de ses Voltes.** The steps top off between Pl. Conquesta and Pl. Espanya. From here, take Portal de Mar to Costa de Sa, which becomes Hannover and then Ses Moreres. Continue straight ahead to reach **Plaça de s'Esplanada.**

Mahón is a maze of narrow, one-way streets lined with whitewashed houses. Luckily for new arrivals, there are map kiosks with street indexes everywhere.

Transportation

Airplanes: Airport (tel. 971 15 70 00), 7km out of town (see **Orientation** above). Main office open daily 7:15am-midnight. **Aviaco/Iberia** (reservations tel. 971 36 56 73; info tel. 971 36 90 15). In summer advance booking is essential. Many travel agencies book charter flights. See **By Plane,** p. 367, or **Getting Around,** p. 368.

Ferries: Trasmediterránea, Nuevo Muelle Commercial (info tel. 971 36 60 50, reservations tel. 971 36 29 50), at Estació Marítima along Moll (Andén) de Ponent. Open M-F 8:30am-1pm and 5-7pm, Sa 8:30am-noon, Su 3-4:30pm. For fares and routes, see **By Boat,** p. 367, or **Getting Around,** p. 368.

Buses: Transportes Menorca (TMSA), C. Josep M. Quadrado, 7 (tel. 971 36 03 61), off Pl. s'Esplanada. To: Alaior (6 per day, 150ptas); Son Bou (5 per day, 250ptas); Es Mercadal (6 per day, 250ptas); Ferreries (10 per day, 300ptas); Ciutadella (55min., 6 per day, 550ptas); Platja Punta Prima (9 per day, 225ptas); and Es Castell (departs every 30min., 125ptas). Some depart from Pl. s'Esplanada, some from nearby C. Quadrado; check signs at the bus stop. Buy tickets at the TMSA office, except for Punta Prima and Castell, which you buy on the bus. **Autobuses Roca Triay** (tel. 971 37 66 21), has buses that depart from C. Vassallo, diagonally across from Pl. s'Esplanada. To Fornells (5 per day); Arenal d'en Castell (6 per day); Son Parc (6 per day); and Es Grau (6 per day). The tourist office and the *Menorca Diario Insular* (125ptas) have schedules with exact times. Buy Roca Triay tickets on the buses.

Taxis: Main stop at Pl. s'Esplanada (tel. 971 36 12 83), or **radio taxi** from anywhere on the island (tel. 971 36 71 11). Flat rates for all routes. To: Airport (1065ptas), Cala Mesquida (1270ptas), Cala'n Porter (1865ptas), Es Castell (800ptas).

Car Rental: English-speaking car rental at British **Jan Cars,** Pl. s'Esplanada (tel. 971 35 13 21, 24hr. tel. 971 37 71 57). 4500ptas per day; 13,000ptas for 3 days. Tourist office has list of all rental places on Menorca. **Gas stations** open 6am-10pm. Rotating 24hr. service listed in Menorca *Diario Insular.* Some gas stations have 24hr. automatic machines that accept 1000 and 3000ptas bills.

Bike and **Scooter Rental:** Scores of places, all with similar prices. For a bike, try **Just Bicicletas,** C. Infanta, 19 (tel. 971 36 47 51), run out of Hostal Orsi (1 day 800ptas plus IVA, 3 days 2000ptas). **Autos y Motos Valls,** Pl. Espanya, 13 (tel. 971 36 28 39 or 971 35 42 44), rents scooters (3000ptas per day). Open daily 9am-2pm and 5-8pm.

Tourist and Financial Services

Tourist Office: Pl. s'Esplanada, 40 (tel. 971 36 37 90; fax 971 36 74 15; http://www.menorca.com), across the plaza from the taxi stand. Pamphlets, bus schedules, and a fabulous free **map.** English spoken. Open M-F 8:30am-7:30pm, Sa 9am-2pm. Summer office at the **airport** (tel. 971 15 71 15) provides similar materials. Open May-Oct. daily 8:30am-11pm.

American Express: Viajes Iberia, C. Nou, 35 (tel. 971 36 28 48), two doors from Pl. Reial. No commission on traveler's checks. Cardholder mail held. Open M-F 9am-1:30pm and 4:30-8pm, Sa 9:30am-1pm.

Currency Exchange: Banks with 24hr. **ATMs** crowd along C. Hannover and C. Nou.

Emergency and Communications

Emergency: tel. 091, 092 or 112. **Police: Municipal,** Pl. Constitució (tel. 971 36 39 61). **Guardia Civil,** Ctra. Sant Lluís (tel. 971 36 32 97 or 062).

24-Hour Pharmacy: See listings in *Menorca Diario Insular,* or look in the window of Farmàcia Segui Chinchilla, Ses Moreres, 30.

Medical Assistance: Hospital at C. Barcelona, 3 (tel. 971 15 77 00), near the waterfront, 1 block inland from Pg. Marítim. English spoken. **Ambulance:** 061.

Internet Access: Nou Bar (see p. 381). A hefty 1500ptas per hr.

Post Office: C. Bonaire, 11-13 (tel. 971 36 38 92), at C. Esglésias. From Pl. s'Esplanada, take C. Moreres until it turns into C. Hanover, then take the 1st left. Open M-F 8:30am-8:30pm, Sa 9:30am-1:30pm. **Postal Code:** 07703.

ACCOMMODATIONS

Space is a problem only in August, but call a few days in advance. The tourist office keeps a complete listing of accommodations. Prices listed below are for high season.

Hostal La Isla, C. Santa Catalina, 4 (tel. 971 36 64 92), take C. Concepció from Pl. Miranda. This pleasant family-run bar-restaurant-hotel offers spanking clean rooms and friendly service. All rooms with private bath and powerful water pressure. The restaurant downstairs (see **Food,** below) offers a cheap and typical *menú.* Singles 2200ptas; doubles 4100ptas. Breakfast 300ptas.

Hostal-Residencia Jume, C. Concepció, 6 (tel. 971 36 32 66; fax 971 36 48 78), near Pl. Miranda. TV room downstairs, lounges on each floor, restaurant, and pool table. Nondescript rooms are in tip-top shape, all with full baths. Ask for a room overlooking the street rather than a steamy indoor-patio room. 2750ptas per person with breakfast, 3600ptas per person with dinner.

Hostal Orsi, C. Infanta, 19 (tel. 971 36 47 51). From Pl. s'Esplanada, take C. Moreres as it becomes C. Hannover. Turn right at Pl. Constitució and follow C. Nou through Pl. Reial. The warm Scottish and American owners are in the "They were *so* nice" Hosteling Hall of Fame. Complimentary continental breakfast and clean, sunlit rooms. Rooftop terrace with a view of the backyard gardens and church. Discounts on bicycle rentals. Singles 2500ptas; doubles 4300ptas, with shower 4900ptas; triples 6300ptas. Laundry 850ptas. Credit cards accepted.

FOOD

Bar-cafes around **Plazas Constitució, Reial,** and **s'Esplanada** serve filling *platos combinados* (450-850ptas) to rows and rows of sidewalk seating. The myriad restaurants on the port, spread along Moll de Llevant, have scenic views, but the prices at most will keep your wallet anchored in your pocket. A coffee can buy you a view, though.

Mahón-esa was invented in Mahón, and here mayonnaise lends its subtle overtones to a wide variety of edibles. Local favorites are *sobrasada* (soft chorizo spread), *crespells* (biscuits), and *rubiols* (turnovers filled with fish or vegetables). Also worthy are Menorcan stuffed eggplant and peppers, and *oliaigua,* a hearty vegetable soup.

A fresh fruit and vegetable **market** meets in the cloister of the church in Pl. Espanya (open M-Sa 9am-2pm). Get your **groceries** at **Miny Prix,** Calle J.A. Clavé and Av. Menorça (open M-Sa 8am-2pm and 5-8:30pm).

Mos i Glop, C. Alayor, 12 (tel. 971 36 64 57), off C. Hannover. Tucked away in a narrow alley, Glop is much more of a feast than its name—which means an alcoholic shot in Catalan—might intimate. Sample a number of fresh Menorcan dishes (stuffed eggplant 775ptas, stuffed peppers 800ptas, *oliaigua* 525ptas). Also serves the standard *bocadillos* (350ptas) and pizza. Multi-optioned Menorcan *menú* 925ptas. Open M-F 8am-midnight, Sa 8am-5pm. Credit cards accepted.

Restaurante La Isla, C. Santa Catalina, 4 (tel. 971 36 64 92), at the Hostal La Isla. There is no *a la carte* menu at this congenial little eating hole—just a 900ptas lunch or dinner *menú,* which changes daily, and a host of satisfied locals. Open daily for breakfast (275ptas) 7-10am, lunch 1-3pm, and dinner 8:30-10pm.

El Turronero, C. Nou, 22-26 (tel. 971 36 28 98), off Pl. Reial. An old-fashioned parlor that has been serving up home-made *turrón* (Spanish nougat) and ice cream for over 100 years. Double scoops 185ptas, bigger servings 260ptas. *Bocadillos* 275-300ptas. Stock up on Menorcan munchies in connected grocery store. Open M-F 9am-3pm and 4-10:30 or 11pm, Sa and Su 9am-2pm and 7-10pm.

Ristorante Pizzeria Roma, Ander de Levante, 295 (tel. 971 35 37 77), on the port. It's the next best thing to dining on your very own yacht. Authentic Italian pizzas (630-975ptas) and lasagna (945ptas). *Menú* 1250ptas. Fresh ingredients and speedy service that puts its overpriced port neighbors to shame. Expect a wait for terrace dining at night. Open F-W 12:30pm-midnight, Th 7pm-midnight.

SIGHTS AND ENTERTAINMENT

Església de Santa María la Major in Pl. Constitució, founded in 1287 and rebuilt in 1772, trembles to the 51 stops, 4 keyboards, and 3210 pipes of its disproportionately large organ, built by the Swiss Juan Kilburz in 1810. A **festival de música** in July and August showcases this immense instrument. Festival concerts are given Monday through Saturday at 11am; seat prices are minimal.

Up C. Sant Roc, **Arc de Sant Roc,** the last fragment of the medieval wall built to defend the city from marauding Catalan pirates, straddles the streets. A boat trip leaves from the harbor to the island beach **Illa d'en Colom,** 8km away, stopping at secluded beached coves. Shipmates serve up *paella* and *sangria.* Ships leave at 10am and return by 6pm. Buy tickets at the port, or at **Bar Rosales,** Moll de Ponent, 73 (tel. 971 36 70 07; tickets 3500ptas, children under 12 2000ptas).

The **Museo de Menorca,** C. Dr. Guàrdia (tel. 971 35 09 55), in an old Franciscan monastery that closed in 1835, has excavated items and displays on Menorcan history going back to Talayotic times in 1400 BC. *(Open Apr.-Sept. Tu-Sa 10am-2pm and 5-8pm, Su 10am-2pm; Oct.-Mar. Tu-Sa 10am-1pm and 4-6pm, Su 10am-2pm.)* From Pl. Bastió in the center of town, head down C. Rector Mort to its end, then left on C. Isabel II.

Free liquor samples (15 brews including Schnapps de rosas and herbal gin), are available at the **Xoriguer distillery** on the port. *(Open M-F 8am-7pm, Sa 9am-1pm.)* Behind the store, visitors watch their drinks bubble and froth in large copper vats.

From May to September, merchants sell shoes, clothes, souvenirs, and neon T-shirts in **mercadillos** held daily in at least one locale's main square. *(Tu and Sa Mahón; F and Sa Ciutadella; Th Alaior; Su Mercadal; Tu and F Ferrerias; M and W Es Castell.)*

ISLAS BALEARES

Mahón is not famed for its **nightlife,** and curtain hour is sometimes an unseemly midnight. A string of *bares-musicales* is on the left, a bit down **Costa d'els Generals** after you come down Costa de ses Voltes to the water. Dancing doesn't really get going until 1 or 2am on weekends, and weekdays are quiet except in August. The disputed champion is **Akelarre** (tel. 971 36 85 20), a dim and attractive two-floor bar right next to the castle; a straight and gay crowd frequents the dancier upstairs (open June-Oct. daily 7:30am-4am, Nov.-May daily 7pm-4am; live music W-Th 11pm-2am). Away from the port, **Discoteca Sí,** 16 Virgen de Gracia, turns on the strobe only after midnight, while **Nou Bar,** C. Nou, 1, serves drinks, including Guinness on tap (600ptas per pint; open daily noon-3pm and 7:30am-3am).

Mahón's **Verge del Carme** celebration, July 16, floats a colorful trimmed armada into the harbor. The **Festa de Nostra Senyora de Gràcia,** the city's celebration of its patron saint, swings out September 7-8. For a list of **beaches,** see p. 384.

■ Ciutadella (Ciudadela)

Ciutadella's blue and red townhouses sink calmly into serpentine streets. The colorful stucco architecture above meshes with dark, medieval cobblestone below in an unlikely but successful juxtaposition. Far more tranquil than eastern neighbor Mahón, Ciutadella (pop. 21,200) is out of reach for most budget travelers. But if you've reached Menorca, then a few extra bucks will be well spent effervescing in Ciutadella's uncrowded port. It lacks the glitz—but not the opulence—that has usurped most of Europe's Mediterranean coastline. If you stay in a hostel, pack up at the grocery store and then beach yourself; your budget will stay right on track.

ORIENTATION AND PRACTICAL INFORMATION

To get from the **bus station** to **Plaça de la Catedral** and the tourist office, head left half a block; then take a left on Camí de Maó, go straight through Pl. d'Alfons III, and continue along C. de Maó as it turns into Quadrado (Ses Voltes) after crossing Pl. Nova. To get from Pl. de la Catedral to **Plaça de s'Esplanada** (also called Pl. dels Pins), exit the plaza on C. Major d'es Born, with the cathedral behind you and to your right, cross P. d'es Born on its right side, and bear diagonally across to your left. The **port,** and its accompanying street, Marina, lie below the rest of the city; they can be reached via a gentle stone stairway just off the corner of Pl. d'es Born.

Buses: Transportes Menorca buses leave from C. Barcelona, 8 (tel. 971 38 03 93), and go to Mahón (6 per day, 550ptas). **Torres,** Poligona Industrial c/Sastres, 3 (tel. 971 38 64 61), offers daily service to surrounding beaches for less than 200ptas. To: Cala Blanca (14 per day); Sa Caleta and Santandria (14 per day); Cala Blanes, Los Delfines, and Cala Forcat (16 per day); Cala Bosch and Son Xoriguer (16 per day). Torres's ticket booth and bus departure point located at Pl. s'Esplanada.

Ferries: Balear de Ferrys (tel. 971 22 91 24) has just begun service between Ciutadella and Alcúdia, Mallorca (2½ hr., departs 11:30am and 8:30pm).

Taxis: (tel. 971 38 28 96). Pl. s'Esplanada/Pins is a prime hailing spot.

Bike/Moped Rental: Bicicletas Tolo, C. Sant Isidor, 28, 32-34 (tel. 971 38 15 76). Across the street from Hostal Oasis (see below). Bike 450ptas per day, 2550ptas per week. Mountain bike 600ptas per day, 3300ptas per week. Scooter 3400ptas for 2 days, 10,600ptas per week. Extensive bike supplies and repair services too. Open M-F 8:30am-1:30pm and 3:30-8pm, Sa 8:30am-1:30pm.

Tourist Office: The **main office,** Pl. Catedral (tel. 971 38 26 93; http://www.infotele-com.es/ciutadella), hands out maps, beach info, and a mega-guide to Menorca. Open M-F 9am-1:30pm and 6-8pm, Sa 9am-1pm.

Banks: La Caixa, C. dés Seminari, 5, and **Central Hispano,** Negicle, 7, exchange money and have 24hr. **ATMs.**

Emergency: call 091 or 092. **Police: Guardia Municipal,** Pl. des Born (tel. 971 38 07 87), in the Ajuntament.

Medical Emergencies tel. 971 48 01 11. **Ambulance:** call 061.

ISLAS BALEARES

24-Hour Pharmacy: Farmàcia Martí-Sureda, Pl. s'Esplanada, 20 (tel. 971 38 03 94), posts a list of night pharmacies in the window (as do all other pharmacies).
Medical Assistance: Clínica Menorca: tel. 971 48 05 05.
Internet Access: Pl. s'Esplanada, 37 (tel. 971 48 40 26). 500ptas for the first 30min. Open M-Th 10am-10pm, F-Sa 10am-4am, Su 3-10pm.
Post Office: Permanent office at Pl. des Born (tel. 971 38 00 81). Temporary office (during renovations) at C. Pio IV, 4-6. Lista de Correos. Open M-F 8:30am-2:30pm, Sa 9:30am-1pm. **Postal Code:** 07760.

ACCOMMODATIONS

Pensiones are packed (and pricey) during peak season (June 15-early Sept.).

Hotel Geminis, C. Josepa Rossinyol, 4 (tel. 971 38 58 96; fax 971 38 36 83). Take C. Sud off Av. Capital Negrete; turn left onto C. Rossinyol. Brand new renovations sparkle. Hotel-quality rooms with phones, shiny baths, fans, and TVs. A small, well-kept pool graces the outdoor terrace. Singles 4000ptas; doubles 7000ptas. Breakfast included at the cafe/restaurant downstairs. Reserve early for Aug.
Hostal Residencia Oasis, C. Sant Isidre, 33 (tel. 971 38 21 97). From Pl. s'Esplanada, take Negrete to the 3rd left (C. Purissima). Isidre is first street on right. Trudge through a tunnel to arrive at this centrally located floral paradise. Clean, breezy rooms have large wooden shutters. Breakfast is served in sunlit garden. Singles 3000ptas; doubles with bath 5500ptas. Keys for 24hr. entry. Breakfast included.
Pensió Bar Ses Persianes, Pl. Artruitx, 2 (tel. 971 38 14 45), off Av. Jaume I El Conqueridor, close to the city center. Bright white walls enclose smallish rooms. Air-conditioned bar below (also hotel reception) serves breakfast. Rooms are all doubles with shared bath; 1 person 3000ptas, 2 people 3500ptas. Only 8 rooms, so make reservations in August.

FOOD

Cruise pedestrian-packed C. Quadrado for *platos combinados* and *tapas.* Sandwich bars have infiltrated Pl. de s'Esplanada. Shop for staples at **Supermercado Diskont,** C. Purísima, 6 (tel. 971 38 15 69; open M-Sa 8am-1:30pm and 5-8pm).

Ca'n Magí, C. Quadrado (Ses Voltes), 24 (tel. 971 48 06 67). Smack in the center of town. Join a teeming mass of locals eating indoors and out. *Platos combinados* 550-1000ptas, BLT 275ptas. Open M-Sa 7am-11pm, Su 7-11pm.
La Guitarra, C. Dolores, 1 (tel. 971 38 13 55). Take St. Francesc off Born to Dolores. Golden oldies like rabbit in onion sauce and ox tongue with capers in a restaurant that challenges patrons to "try our meals the way we do them." 2-person *paella* 1400ptas per person. *Arroz brut,* a local specialty, 900ptas. *Menú* 950ptas. Open in summer M-Sa noon-3:30pm and 7-11:30pm. Credit cards accepted.
Hostal Ciutadella Cafeteria, S. Eloy, 10 (tel. 971 38 34 62), at Ses Parres. From Pl. Nova at the end of C. Quadrado, head down C. de Maó to Pl. d'Alfons III; take a right onto S. Eloy, and the Hostal is one block down on the right. A bit off the beaten path. The generous 900ptas *menú*—including wine and available at lunch or dinner—is this place's crowning glory. Open daily 8-10:30am, 1-4pm, and 8-10:30pm.

SIGHTS AND ENTERTAINMENT

For beach options, see **Beaches,** p. 384, and **Ciutadella: Orientation and Practical Information: Buses,** p. 381.
   A mind-stretching alternative is to investigate the Bronze Age remnants at Menorca's archaeological sites. **Naveta dels Tudons,** one of the oldest buildings in Europe (despite some cosmetic restoration), sits 4km from the city. These community tomb ruins are the island's best preserved. **Torre Trencada** and **Torre Llafuda** were rounded towers for overlooking the countryside. Both protect Stonehenge-esque *taulas,* formations that have stood for over 3000 years. Buses don't come near

these sights, so consider hiking (about 5km) along C. Camí Vell de Maó. Hitchers report luck along the route. Get a descriptive *Archeological Guide to Menorca* at the tourist office.

Ciutadella's 16th-century law requiring all citizens to shack up by midnight (still officially on the books) has generated a community of early-to-bedders. Two salsa clubs, however, spice things up: **Asere,** C. de Curinola, 25, one block off Pl. Nova (open F-Sa 8pm-midnight), and **El Mosquito,** C. de sa Muradeta, 16, near the stairs down to the port (open June-Aug. daily 11pm-4am, Sept.-May F-Sa 11pm-4am). From the first week in July to the end of August, Ciutadella hosts the **Festival de Música d'Estiu** in the Claustre del Seminari, featuring some of the world's top classical musicians. Tickets (1600-3500ptas) are sold at Foto Born, C. del Seminari (C. Bisbe Vila), 14 (tel. 971 38 17 54), and at the box office. In late June, locals burn gallons of midnight oil during the **Festival de Sant Joan.** Even veteran partiers of Palma and Ibiza join in Menorca's biggest fiesta. A week before the festivities, a man clad in a sheepskin carries a decorated lamb on his shoulders through the city. The main events include jousting. The **mercadillo** of artisanry passes through Pl. Born (F-Sa 9am-2pm).

Every Day Is Earth Day In Menorca

Earth-lovers rejoiced in 1993, when UNESCO declared Menorca's 701.84 sq. km a Biosphere Reserve. In light of relentless urbanization of Mallorca and Ibiza, where the only things sprouting are banks, airports, and beachside *bocadillo* stands, the new approach improves upon blindly conservationist quarantine measures by protecting the area's rich agricultural, archaeological, and cultural heritage in a way that also capitalizes on the island's natural resources. The plan is complemented by designated zones where industrial exploitation is prohibited (Natural Areas of Special Interest, or ANEI).

So what has all this ecological protection meant to the light-pocketed Let's Goer? So far, certain Menorcan coves have remained uncontaminated by tourist colonies, but the future may hold rising exclusivity on an already exclusive island—*hostales* will continue to either upgrade to hotels or fold. The budget traveler may be the newest endangered species on Menorca. For now, though, the island's sweetest pleasures remain unexploited and free of charge. For more info, call CIME in Mahón (tel. 971 34 71 35).

■ Northern Coast: Fornells

A small fishing village long known mostly for its lobster farms, Fornells has just begun to attract tourists. Windsurfers busily zip around Fornells' long, shallow port, while beach gurus make short excursions to **Cala Tirant** and **Binimella,** both a few kilometers west. Fornells also makes a calm base from which to explore coves and jagged cliffs by car or bike (buses' reach is very limited). Consider **renting a bike** for a full or half day (800ptas, 500ptas) from the multi-talented hostel-restaurant-bike rental establishment **S'Algaret,** Pl. S'Algaret, 7 (tel. 971 37 65 52).

Currency exchange is possible only at Sa Nostra, C. Gabriel Gelabert, 4, near the *plaça* (open June-Sept. M-F 8:15am-2:30pm). The **police** answer at tel. 971 37 52 51. For other services, go to **Es Mercadal,** 8km away. Accommodations here are few and pricey, but **Casa de Céspedes La Palma,** Pl. S'Algaret (tel. 971 37 66 34), provides tidy rooms with terraces (singles 1500ptas; doubles with bath 6000ptas; triples with bath 7000ptas). Lobster restaurants in town are prohibitively expensive. *Bocadillos* are an option at the numerous *bares* on Pl. S'Algaret. Or make up a meal at **Supermercado Spar,** C. Major, 24 (open M-Sa 8am-1:30pm and 4-8pm, Su 8am-noon).

Autobuses Roca Triay (tel. 971 37 66 21) sends buses to C. Vassallo in Mahón (30min., 5 per day), Arenal d'en Castell (departs 8:30am and 3:45pm), and Son Parc (departs 8:30am and 3:45pm) from the port. Buses also run from Platges de Fornells to Mahón (M-Sa 9:20am and noon). Service is cut in half Sundays and holidays.

■ Beaches

Some of the more popular (i.e. crowded) Menorcan beaches are accessible by bus from Mahón and Ciutadella. Even though many of the best require a vehicle and sometimes legwork, they are worth the extra hassle. Northern beaches are rocky but less crowded. Finer sands are hidden under hundreds of tourists on the southern coast. Virtually all bus rides to and from beaches take around half an hour and cost between 50 and 200ptas—there are no long or expensive trips on small, flat Menorca.

■ Near Mahón

Es Grau: A small bay about 8km north of Mahón, popular with Menorcan locals. A 35min. bike ride from Mahón takes you through part of Menorca's protected lands. Hike on the beach toward the small coves across the bay from the village. Roca Triay buses leave from C. Vasallo in Mahón (6 per day, 10:15am-6:15pm). Once at Es Grau, catch a boat out to the **Illa d'en Colom,** a tiny island with more beaches (tickets on sale at Bar C'an Bernat at the beach). Quiet until July.

Cap de Favàrtix: An area far more tranquil than the beaten-path beaches. From Mahón take a moped or car in the direction of Es Gran/Fornells, turn off the highway at Favàrtix (9km), pass through farmlands, and break off from the bushy-edged roadway through an open gate to sink your toes in your very own black sand cove.

Arenal d'en Castell: A sandy and touristy ring around calm water on Menorca's northern shore, behind a thin barrier of pine trees. Coastal ravines and cliffs are honeycombed with caves where prehistoric Menorcans lived. Autocares Fornells buses to Castell leave from C. Vasallo in Mahón (6 per day, 10:30am-7pm).

Calan Porter: Expansive and extremely touristy. Its huge bluffs shelter curving beaches beneath. Here the Covas d'en Xoroi, spooky prehistoric dwellings, gaze down on the sea. A disco inside a cave (starting at midnight; it's a bar by day) is hugely popular. It is connected to Mahón by TMSA bus (6 per day 9:30am-6pm).

Calascoves: A 30min. walk to the east (left facing the sea) from Porter, with tan bodies strewn across the rocks (no beach) and a string of prehistoric caves where modern-day hippies keep the dream alive and rent them.

Platges de Son Bou: A gorgeous, 3km-long string of beaches with crystal waters on the southern shore—but it's far from undiscovered. There is a 5th-century Christian **basilica** in the nearby settlement of Son Bou. Transportes Menorca buses leave from Mahón (5 per day, 8:50am-7pm).

■ Near Ciutadella

Cala Bosch: Jagged cliffs plummet into clear pale-blue water, a perfect backdrop for a refreshing dip in the Mediterranean. Accessible by Torres bus from Ciutadella (13-16 per day, 8:15am-10:30pm).

Son Xoriguer: Small, overdeveloped, and crowded, but a mere 20min. from Ciutadella (use the same bus as Cala Bosch).

North Shore: The stretch east of Cala Morell is home to some of the most outstanding and pristine beaches on the island. Platges d'Algaiarens may be the superstar of the series, also including Cala en Carabó, Penyal de l'Anticrist, Sa Falconera, and the beautiful Cala del Pilar Ets Alocs. Consult the tourist office's map of the island. Cars can go only up to a few km from these beaches; from there you must walk.

Cala Santa Galdana: A narrow beach 9km south of Ferrerias, Galdana is accessible by public transportation from Ferrerias (10 per day, 8:30am-7:40pm).

Cala Macarella: The 600ptas toll for private road to Macarella is well-spent. No tourist developments here, only crystal clear water in one of Menorca's least spoiled coves. *Naturistas* hang out on an even more secluded cove to the west (15min. walk). Access by bike, moped, or car off the country road to Sant Joan de Missa.

IBIZA

Perhaps nowhere on Earth does style trump substance more than on the island of Ibiza (pop. 84,000). Ibiza's style warriors arrive in droves to showcase themselves in the island's outrageous nightlife and to debauch in a sex- and substance-driven summertime culture. Only recently a hippie enclave, Ibiza's summer camp for disco fiends and high fashion victims evokes a sense of new-age decadence. Although a thriving gay community still lends credence to Ibiza's image as a center of tolerance, the island's high price tags preclude true diversity.

Since the Carthaginians retreated to Ibiza from the mainland in 656 BC, the island's list of conquerors reads like a "Who's Who of Ancient Western Civilization." The 1235 invasion by the Catalans, who brought Christianity and constructed the massive Renaissance walls that still fortify Eivissa (Ibiza City), was the last incursion prior to the hippie influx of the 1960s.

Beaches mitigate the summer heat with a warm Mediterranean surf and can be reached in minutes by bus. Formentera, a tiny, sparsely populated island annex of Ibiza and a convenient daytrip by ferry, fulfills the undiscovered-beauty quota, and there are even places of historical interest, like ancient castles, scattered around Ibiza. But undoubtedly the island's most alluring sight is its tourists, flaunting themselves before each other in a wondrous three-ring circus beginning anew every night.

■ Eivissa (Ibiza Town, Ibiza City)

Day and night, Eivissa (pop. 35,000) throbs to a techno beat. When the sun rises, revelers at the city's infamous *discotecas* crawl into bed and *sol*-seekers scurry to Eivissa's nearby beaches. In the daytime, while the sun blazes, the city is ghostly; only an occasional, faraway sample track hints at the high fashion and drag-queen revelry that wait quietly behind fluttering shutters. At sunset the show begins. Grab a front-row seat at one of the outdoor cafes to enjoy the action, as tourists and summertime residents parade the latest designs from Eivissa's swank boutiques.

ORIENTATION AND PRACTICAL INFORMATION

Three distinct sections comprise Eivissa. **Sa Penya,** the area in front of Estació Marítima, is mobbed with vendors, bars, and boutiques. Atop the hill behind Sa Penya, high stone walls circle **Dalt Vila,** the old city. **Sa Marina** and the commercial district occupy the gridded streets to the far right of the Estació (back to the water).

Buses to the **airport** (7km south of the city) run from Av. Isidor Macabich, 20 (30min., departs every hr., 7:30am-10:35pm, 125ptas), and return to town (30min., departs every hr., 7:30am-10:30pm, 125ptas). To get to the **waterfront,** walk down Av. Isidor Macabich, which becomes Av. Bartolomé Roselló and runs to the port.

The local paper *Diario de Ibiza* (125ptas) has an *Agenda* page that lists essential information: the bus schedule for the whole island; the ferry schedule; the schedule of all domestic flights to and from Ibiza for the day; water and weather forecasts; 24-hour pharmacies in the cities; 24-hour gas stations; and important phone numbers.

Transportation
Flights: Airport (tel. 971 80 90 00). Open for tickets and reservations M-F 9am-1:15pm and 4:30-7:45pm. Airport booth open 7am-11pm. **Iberia,** Pg. Vara de Rey, 15 (tel. 971 30 25 80), at the end of the street, has flights to Palma, Barcelona, Madrid, Valencia, and Alicante. **Air Europa** (tel. 971 80 91 91) and **Air Nostrum** (tel. 971 26 00 15) run some of the same routes. For routes and schedules, see **By Plane,** p. 367, or **Getting Around,** p. 368.
Ferries: Estació Marítima (tel. 971 31 16 50), at the end of Av. Bartolomé Roselló. **Trasmediterránea** (tel. 971 31 21 04) sells tickets at Estació Marítima and sends

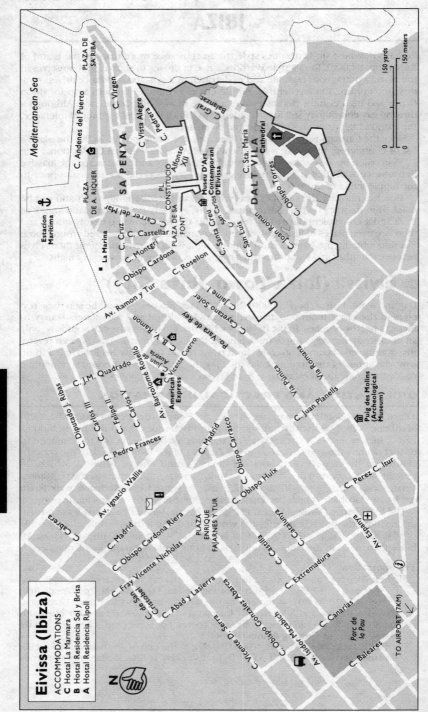

ISLAS BALEARES

Eivissa (Ibiza)

ACCOMMODATIONS
C Hostal La Marmara
B Hostal Residencia Sol y Brisa
A Hostal Residencia Ripoll

N

Mediterranean Sea

Estacion Maritima

PLAZA DE SA RIBA

PLAZA DE A. RIQUER

C. Andenes del Puerto

C. Virgen

C. Vista Alegre

C. Pedrera

C. Gral. Balanzat

SA PENYA

PLAZA DE A. MAR

C. Cruz

La Marina

Carrer del Mar

C. Castellar

C. Monegri

C. Obispo Cardona

Pl. CONSTITUCIO
Alfonso XII

PLAZA DE SA FONT

Museu D'Art Contemporani D'Eivissa

Santa Creu

C. san Carlos

C. Sta. Maria

C. San Luis

C. San Luis

DALT VILA

Cathedral

C. Obispo Torres

C. Joan Roman

C. Rosellon

Av. Ramon y Tur

Po Vara de Rey

C. Cayetano Soler

C. Jaime I

Av. B. V. Ramon

C. J.M. Quadrado

C. Juan de Austria

American Express

Av. Vicente Cuervo

B

A

Av. Bartolome Rosello

C. Dipuado J. Ribas

C. Carlos III

C. Felipe II

C. Carlos V

C. Pedro Frances

Av. Ignacio Wallis

C. Madrid

C. Madrid

C. Obispo Cardona Riera

PLAZA ENRIQUE FAJARNES Y TUR

C. Obispo Carrasco

C. Obispo Huix

C. Catalunya

Via Punica

Via Romana

C. Juan Planells

Puig des Molins (Archeological Museum)

C. Perez C. Itur

C. Castilla

C. Extremadura

Av. Espanya

C. Cabrera

C. Fray Vicente Nicholas

C. Vicente D. Serra

C. Cristofol Serra

C. Obispo Gonzalez Abarca

C. Abad y Lasierra

Av. Isidor Macabich

C. Canarias

Parc de la Pau

C. Baleares

TO AIRPORT (7KM)

150 yards

150 meters

ferries to Palma, Barcelona, and Valencia. **Flebasa Lines** (tel. 971 34 28 71) runs daily to and from Dénia, near Alicante; a connection in Eivissa continues to and from Palma. For rates, fares, and schedules, see **By Boat,** p. 367, or **Getting Around,** p.367. For transport to the island of Formentera, see **Formentera: Getting There and Away,** p. 390.

Buses: The two main bus stops are Av. Isidor Macabich, 42 and Av. Isidor Macabich, 20. For an exact schedule, check the tourist office or *El Diario*. Intercity buses are 200ptas or less and run from Av. Isidor Macabich, 42 (tel. 971 31 21 17) to: San Antonio (M-Sa departs every 15-30min., Su every 30min.); Santa Eulalia (M-F 9 per day, Sa-Su departs every hr., 8:30am-11:30pm). Buses to beaches (85-95ptas) leave from #20 (tel. 971 34 03 82) to: Salinas (departs every hr.); Platja d'en Bossa (departs every 30min.); Cap Martinet (M-Sa 11 per day); Cala Tarida (5 per day).

Taxis: call 971 30 70 00 or 971 30 66 02.

Car and Motorbike Rental: Most places have similar prices. **Casa Valentín,** Av. B.V. Ramón 19 (tel. 971 31 08 22), near Vía del Rey, the street parallel to and one block off Pg. Vara de Rey, rents mopeds (2500ptas), as does **Extra,** Av. Sta. Eulalia, 25, near the Formentera boats (1900ptas per day). **Panda** and **Marbella** cars rent for 5500ptas per day. Open M-Sa 9am-1pm and 5:30-8pm, Su 9am-noon and 5:30-8pm. Open M-Sa 8am-8pm, Su 8am-1:30pm and 5-8pm.

Tourist and Financial Services

Tourist Office: C. Antoni Riquer, 2 (tel. 971 30 19 00; http://www.ibizaonline.com), right on the water, across from where the huge Trasmediterránea ferries come in. Good maps, especially for hiking, and a complete bus schedule. Open M-F 9:30am-1:30pm and 5-7pm, Sa 10:30am-1pm. Also a **booth** at the airport arrivals terminal (tel. 971 80 91 18; fax 971 80 91 32). Open May-Oct. M-F 9am-2pm and 3-8pm.

Currency Exchange: La Caixa, Av. Isidor Macabich, offers good exchange rates for cash or traveler's checks. **American Express** services available at Viajes Iberia, C. Vicente Cuervo, 9 (tel. 971 31 11 11 or 971 30 43 64). Open Apr.-Oct. M-F 9am-1:30pm, Sa 9am-1pm; Nov.-Mar. M-F 9am-1pm and 4:30-8pm, Sa 9am-1pm.

Luggage Storage: Extra, Av. Sta. Eulalia, 25 (tel. 971 19 17 17). 700-1000ptas per 24hr. Open M-Sa 8am-1:30pm and 4-8:30pm, Su 8am-noon and 5:30-7:30pm.

Emergency and Communications

Emergency: call 091, 092, or 112. **Police:** C. Madrid (tel. 092), by the Post Office.

Medical Assistance: Hospital, Barrio Can Misses (tel. 971 39 70 00). Heading out of town on Av. Espanya, the hospital is on the left at the corner of C. Extremadura.

Internet Access: Samarkànda Ciber Cafe, Av. Ignacio Wallis, 19. 800ptas for 1hr., 1400ptas for 2hr. Or try **Eurocentro,** C. Juan de Austria, 22 (tel. 971 31 09 09; email eurocent@teleline.es), which offers similar services.

Post Office: C. Madrid, 23 (tel. 971 31 13 80), off Av. Isidor Macabich. Lista de Correos. Open M-F 8:30am-8:30pm, Sa 9:30am-2pm. **Postal Code:** 07800.

ACCOMMODATIONS AND CAMPING

Decent, cheap accommodations in town are rare, especially in the summer. "CH" *(casa de huespedes)* marks many doorways, but often the owner can only be reached by the phone number on the door. Prices skyrocket in July and August, and you must make reservations two to three weeks in advance. Eivissa has a relatively safe and up-all-night life-style, so owners offer keys for 24-hour entry.

Hostal Residencia Sol y Brisa, Av. B. V. Ramón, 15 (tel. 971 31 08 18; fax 971 30 30 32), parallel to Pg. Vara de Rey. Upstairs from Pizzeria da Franco (signs point the way to the pizzeria). Two verdant terraces. Singles 2200ptas; doubles 4000ptas. Off season: singles 1800ptas; doubles 3000ptas.

Hostal La Marina, C. Andenes del Puerto, 4 (tel. 971 31 01 72), conveniently across from Estació Marítima. Salty air floating through the window carries loud dance music from the bars next door. Annexed housing near the bus stop is quieter. Dimly lit rooms keep the temperature down. Singles 2000ptas; doubles 3300-3500ptas, with bath 5000-6500ptas; triples 4500-4800ptas. The 5000ptas 2-person apartment, down the street, with kitchen is an excellent deal.

ISLAS BALEARES

Hostal Residencia Ripoll, C. Vicente Cuervo, 14 (tel. 971 31 42 75). Huge windows in doubles and triples, fans in interior rooms—a breezy bargain. July-Sept. singles 2500ptas; doubles 4500ptas. Half price Apr.-June.

Camping: Es Cana (tel. 971 33 21 17). 500ptas per person; 600ptas per site; 450ptas extra for a tent. Bungalow 2250ptas. Open daily 9am-1pm and 4:30-9:30pm. **Cala Nova** (tel. 971 33 17 74). 475ptas per person; 450ptas per site; 850ptas extra for tent. Both are close to Santa Eulalia del Río.

FOOD

There is little supply of or demand for cheap eats. Full meals rarely cost less than 1200ptas in the port and downtown areas. **Sa Penya** and **Dalt Vila** proffer exquisite fare in elegant settings for no less than 1500ptas per person. Head into the residential, square-block areas of town for cheaper eats. Some Ibizan dishes worth hunting down are *sofrit pagès,* a deep-fried lamb and chicken dish; *flao,* a lush lemon- and mint-tinged cheesecake; and *graxonera,* cinnamon-dusted pudding made from eggs and bits of *ensaimada* (candied bread). The **market,** C. Extremadura and C. Canarias, sells a variety of food, meat, fruits, and vegetables (open M-Sa 7am-1pm). For a super-market, try **Comestibles Tony,** Carrer d'Enmig, 1 (open 8am-2pm and 5-11pm).

Comidas Bar San Juan, C. Montgrí, 8 (tel. 971 31 07 66), the 2nd right on the Puerto Moll walking from Pg. Vara de Rey. Tiny, popular family-run restaurant with a surprisingly cheap selection. *Paella* 350ptas, *chuletas de cordero* (lamb chops) 450ptas. Crowded weekend nights. Open M-Sa 1-3:15 and 8-10:15pm.

Restaurante Ca'n Costa, C. Cruz, 19 (tel. 971 31 08 65), down the street from Victoria. Rows of tables tucked away in a basement eatery. Meats 550-1200ptas, fishies 600-1400ptas, lunchtime *paella* 500ptas—all cooked in a wood-burning stove. Afternoon *menú* 900ptas. Open Feb.-Dec. M-Sa noon-3:30pm and 8pm-midnight.

Pizzeria da Franco e Romano, Av. B. V. Ramon, 15 (tel. 971 31 32 53), below Hostal Sol y Brisa; signs point the way. Owner promises "economy, happiness, and sympathy" at her popular, somewhat touristy pizzeria. Filling pasta and pizzas under 1000ptas. Afternoon *menú* 925ptas. Open W-M 12:30-4pm and 7:30pm-1am. Credit cards accepted.

Restaurante Victoria, C. Riambau, 1 (tel. 971 31 06 22), at the end of Pg. Vara de Rey. 50-year-old family eatery. *Sopas mallorquines* 400ptas. *Graxonera* 300ptas. *Platos* hover around 500-700ptas. Open M-Sa 1-4 and 8:30-11:30pm.

La Torre del Canónigo, C. Obisbo Torres, in Dalt Villa next to the cathedral. Fresh fruit concoctions and thirst-quenching drinks in a medieval tower. *Cava* (cheap champagne) breakfasts from 900ptas. Make your way toward the table on the mini-terrace. Open M-Sa 10am-8pm, Su 10am-2pm.

SIGHTS

Wrapped in 16th-century walls, **Dalt Vila** (High Town) hosts 20th-century urban bustle in the city's oldest buildings. Its twisty, sloping streets lead up to the 14th-century **cathedral,** which offers super views of the city and beyond. *(Open M-Sa 10am-1pm.)* Amid the antique action sits the **Museu D'Art Contemporani D'Eivissa,** C. Sa Carrosa (tel. 971 30 27 23), with a wide range of current art exhibitions. *(Open M-F 10am-1pm and 5-8pm, Sa 10am-1pm. 200ptas, students free.)*

The archaeological museum, **Puig des Molins,** is on Via Romana, which runs off the Portal Nou at the foot of the Dalt Vila. The museum displays Punic, Roman, and Iberian art, pottery, and metals. Adjoined to Puig is the 4th-century BC Punic-Roman **necropolis.** *(Both open M-Sa 10am-2pm and 5-8pm. 150ptas.)*

The power of the rising sun draws thousands of solar zombies to nearby tanning grounds. A 10-minute bike ride from the port reaches **Platja Figueredes,** a thin stretch of sand in the shadow of tourists and large hotels. Farther down, **Platja d'en Bossa** has one-foot waves that bring bottle caps and other plastic goods ashore. **Platja des Duros** is a small nook tucked in across the water from the cathedral, just before the lighthouse. **Platja de Talamanca** and **Platja de Ses Figures** have fine sand, plenty of snack-shops, and are 20 minutes away on bike. More private sands are in the northern part of the island and are accessible by car or scooters.

A Sign of the Times

Hippies who swarmed Ibiza during the 1960s and 70s knew it affectionately as "magic island." They organized communal societies in pre-historic lithic housing complexes, similar in design to adobe houses. They wore sandals, no skins, hated war, and loved peace. Those "hang-loose" hippies have since morphed into the disco-raving, self-marginalized generation of the 90s, the newest counterculture to adopt Ibiza as its home. The epochal change from war politics surrounding Vietnam to the peacetime post-cold war atmosphere may account for the island's facelift. Today's Ibizans are full of pomp: men masquerade as women and vamps stalk the portside walkways, vying for attention. From sundown to sun-up, spectators gawk from cafe patios at showboating passers-by, who promenade the sidewalks as if they were catwalks. The island's facelift is symbolized by a change in drugs of choice. Today's hardcore *disoteca*-lovers savor alcohol and synthetic treats like Ecstasy, whereas the hippies preferred herbal delights.

ENTERTAINMENT

The crowds return to Eivissa by nightfall, when even the clothing stores (open until 1am) dazzle with throbbing music and flashing lights. **Jazz** music and mellowness waft through the smoky air of **Arteca** on C. Bisbe Azara (open until 4am). **Calle Virgen** is the center of gay nightlife. **Capricios,** C. Virgen, has an outdoor terrace. **Bar Galerie,** C. Virgen, 64, and **Exis,** down the street, are a bit livelier. A great scene for people-watching is the **Dôme Bar,** Carrer d'Alfons XII, off C. Virgen. Above, **Incognito** and **Angelo's,** with mostly gay crowds, look down on the crazy fashion scene. The island's **discos** are world-famous and ever-changing. The best sources are regulars and the zillions of posters that plaster every store and restaurant. Generally, *discoteca*-goers pub-hop in Eivissa or San Antonio and jet off to clubs via bus or taxi (guess which is more chic) around 2am. PR reps sell discounted invitations to clubs outside the cafes by the seaport. If by the early evening you manage to befriend a bartender or manager in the old town, you may just end up with a free pass—they give out a certain number each night. The tourist office and hotels have the **Discobus** schedule—Bus D runs to and from all the major hotspots (midnight-6:30am, 225ptas). Virtually all discos have a mixed gay-and-straight crowd.

Privilege, Urbanización San Rafael (tel. 971 19 81 60), on the road to San Antonio (taxi 1500ptas). No purple rain, but this club—formerly known as **KU**—has everything else you can imagine. The mini village has double-digit bars, small garden terraces, and a stage set on a pool, where bizarre rock operas are performed during the night. Manumission parties (Monday nights) feature a live sex show. Cover 3500ptas (but can reach as high as 12,000ptas for select parties), including one drink. Open June-Sept. midnight-7am. Credit cards accepted.

Amnesia, on the road to San Antonio. Take the Discobus. This may be *the* most nuts disco scene ever. Cover 4000-5000ptas. Foam parties 2 or 3 nights a week.

Pachá, Pg. Perimitral (tel. 971 31 36 12), a 20min. walk from the port. The most famous club chain in Spain—and wildly popular some nights. A playful atmosphere with palm trees, terraces, and wax candle chandeliers. 3500-4000ptas cover includes one beverage. Open daily 11pm-7am, heats up at 1:30am or so.

El Divino (tel. 971 19 01 76), Puerto Ibiza Nueva, has welcomed supermodels Linda Evangelista and Karie Miller. This terraced club overlooks Ibiza Town and comes complete with performance stages for exotic dancers, strippers, and an S&M room. Have a drink at El Divino's Bar (on the port) and get a free pass to ride the disco shuttle boat—otherwise, it costs 150ptas one-way, and you can walk or taxi back to the old town. Cover 3000ptas. Open mid-June to mid-Sept. nightly 1:30-6am.

Space, Pl. de Bossa (tel. 971 31 40 78 or 971 39 67 93). The most happening spot on Ibiza for after-parties. Cap off your night with a morning in Space. Open daily 7am-noon, most popular Saturday through Tuesday mornings.

Discoteca Anfora, C. San Carlos, 7 (tel. 971 30 28 93), in the heart of Dalt Vila. Late-night partying for a gay crowd. Midnight-1am cover 500ptas, 1-6am 1000ptas (varies).

■ Near Evissa: Formentera

The tiny island of Formentera is Spain's best attempt at a Mediterranean island para-dise. Despite recent invasions by beach-hungry Germans and Italians, the 11-mile moat separating Formentera from Ibiza City has sufficed to deter complete besiege-ment. While Formentera is certainly a bourgeois vacation haven, at least for now it maintains decent square footage per person, a low clothing-to-skin ratio on its languid white beaches, and a pervading sense of hypnotic calm. Join Formentera's "save our island" spirit by renting a bike or hiking, although many find scooters efficient. The tourist office provides a comprehensive list of "Green Tours" for cyclists and hikers.

ORIENTATION AND PRACTICAL INFORMATION Atop the northern side of the island is its main port, **La Savina.** The main artery runs from the port (km 0) to the eastern tip, **Punta D'Esfar** (km 21). Basics and little else can be found in the island's "capital," **San Francisco,** which parts from the main artery at km 3.1. **Buses** run from La Savina to Es Pujols (8 per day), to Playa Illete (2 per day), to Playa Migjorn (6 per day), and to San Francisco (8 per day). **Taxis** from La Savina can be reached at 971 32 20 02. Your arrival at La Savina is avalanched by **car-scooter-bike rental booths** that line the dock (car 5000ptas per day; scooter 2500ptas; bike 900ptas). Main roads have lanes where scooters can putter along freely with bicycles. The **tourist office,** Edificio Servicios La Savina (tel. 971 32 20 57; fax 971 32 28 25; http://www.ifsys-tems.es/formentera; email ifsystems@ifsystems.es.), is at the port (open M-F 10am-2pm and 5-7pm, Su 10am-2pm). For the **cops,** dial 971 32 20 22 or 971 32 22 01; the **centro médico** is at 971 32 23 69.

FOOD AND ACCOMMODATIONS Cool air and the scent of pine trees mark the windy ascent through the mountainous regions of La Mola to Punta D'Esfar, which is marked by a lighthouse at the edge of a cliff. *Bocadillo*-eaters choose to enhance the moment with food from **Bar Es Puig.** Equally satiating is the *paella* (1300ptas) and vista from **El Mirador** (tel. 971 32 70 37; km 14.3; open daily 12:30-4pm and 7-11pm). From here, the narrow strip of the Formentera Island looks like the stem of a cham-pagne glass that widens out to the northern port, La Savina, and the southern tip, Cap de Barbaria. Others say it looks like a bull leering straight at the observer.

   Hostal La Savina (tel. 971 32 22 79), near the port on Av. Mediterránea, offers ceil-ing fans, brown-tiled balconies, private access to a lake, and a breakfast buffet (4500ptas for one person, 5700ptas for two). Up the road and across the street is the **Supermarket La Savina** (open M-Sa 8am-2pm and 4:30-9pm; Su 9:30am-1:30pm).

RISQUÉ BEACH SCENE To bask on Formentera's best beaches, take Av. Mediter-ránea from the port, go left at the sign pointing toward Es Pujols, and hop onto the dirt road at the sign marking **Verede de Ses Salines.** Paths to the right lead to **Platja de Llevant,** a long strip of strippers on fine sand. Farther up the peninsula, roads to the left lead to **Platja de Ses Illetes,** more popular and rocky swimming holes. While the entire peninsula provides ample privacy, walking to the end (which requires wading through two shallow pools where sand level dips), will assure you of absolute solitude, although you'll have to nestle between rocks to catch some rays. A tourist **boat** also runs to Ses Illetes and Espalmador from La Savina (outbound from La Savina 10:45, 11:45am, and 1:15pm, returning 4:15, 5:30, and 6:45pm, 1200ptas). To the south, **Platja de Migjorn** has fine beaches but more surf. The bus runs to **Cala Saona,** a small cove on the west coast.

GETTING THERE AND AWAY Four ferry lines at Estación Marítima in Eivissa pro-vide the best alternative to swimming from Eivissa: **Pitra car ferries** (tel. 971 32 30 07), **Trasmapi** (tel. 971 31 20 71 or 971 31 07 11), **Umafisa car ferries** (tel. 971 31 44 86; Formentera tel. 971 32 30 07), and Formentera-based **Inserco,** C. del Carmen, La Savina (tel. 971 32 22 10). For transport to and from Formentera from the mainland, see **Getting There and Away: By Boat,** p. 367. For transport from Evissa to Forment-era, see **Getting Around,** p. 368.

ISLAS BALEARES

■ Near Evissa: San Antonio de Portmany

Every summer rowdy British hooligans storm San Antonio's huge crescent beach, busy harbor, and boozing 'n' bruising night scene. Most of the biggest Eivissa clubs—Privilege and Amnesia among them—are actually on the Eivissa-San Antonio road, closer to San Antonio. Sand space at the beach dwindles toward noon, so many people relocate to beaches farther out. **Boats** leave from Pg. Ses Fonts, before it becomes Pg. Mar, going to **Cala Bassa** (600ptas), a sandy beach on a thin strip; **Cala Conta** (550ptas), a slightly rocky beach; and the island of **Formentera** (2900ptas). **Buses** leave from Pg. Mar before it intersects with C. Madrid. They serve **Cala Tarida** (150ptas), a protected inlet, as well as Cala Gració, Port des Turrent, and Santa Eulalia.

If you have wheels, explore **Cueva de Ses Fontanelles,** north of Platja Cala Salada, where faint prehistoric paintings cover the walls; or head north to **Cala Salada.** This tranquil cove (at the end of a windy road that wards off buses) offers an escape from San Antonio's over-populated beaches. It's also accessible on foot. Consult the tourist office for **hiking** excursions around San Antonio.

Those headed for the mainland can contact **Pitra car ferries** (tel. 971 19 10 68), which run to Dénia, near Alicante. The office in San Antonio de Portmany is on the **Muelle Comercial** (tel. 971 34 52 99). The **tourist booth** (tel. 971 34 33 63), at the beginning of Pg. Fonts, can help with local transport. (Open M-F 9:30am-8:30pm, Sa 9am-1pm, Su 9:30am-1pm; Nov.-Apr. M-Sa 9:30am-1pm.) In **medical emergencies,** get help on C. Cervantes (tel. 971 34 51 21), or call 091 or 092. The **municipal police** (tel. 971 34 08 30) are on Av. Portmany.

Rooms in San Antonio are good values but tough to come by—some may be booked years in advance. Ask the tourist office for a list. **Hostal Marí,** C. Progreso, 42 (tel./fax 971 34 19 74), offers bright, renovated rooms with full bath (July-Aug. 2750ptas per person; breakfast 250ptas; Visa). Or try **Hostal Nicolao,** C. Valencia, 9 (tel. 971 34 08 45), a few blocks inland, parallel to C. Progrés. Modern rooms have comfy beds, a terrace, and full bath (1500ptas per person, breakfast 250ptas). **Camping** is available at **Cala Bassa** (tel. 971 34 45 99), on the bay, 6km west of San Antonio (500ptas per person; 475ptas per tent; 500ptas for tent rental). **Cafes** line C. Balanzat, one street in from the waterfront, and **bars** prevail on C. Vara de Rey and Pg. Mar.

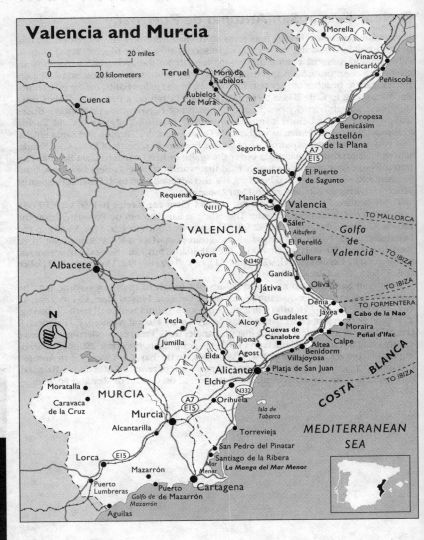

Valencia and Murcia

Valencia's rich soil has earned the region its nickname: "Huerta de España" (Spain's Orchard). Spring and autumn river floods transport soil down the alluvial plain, nurturing Valencia's famous orange and vegetable groves, while pre-medieval irrigation networks designed by the Moors continue to nourish Valencia's farmlands. Dunes, sandbars, jagged promontories, and lagoons mark the coast's grand bay, and lovely fountains and pools grace the cities' carefully landscaped public gardens.

Valencia's past is a tangle of power struggles between the Phoenicians, Carthaginians, Romans, Moors, and Visigoths. El Cid conquered the Moors here in the 11th century and ruled for five years. The last region to be sacked by Franco in 1939, Valencia regained its autonomy with the Bourbon monarchy's reinstitution in 1977. *Valenciá*, the regional language spoken sparingly in the north and inland, differs from Catalan as little as American English differs from British. Although Valencia's regionalism is not as intense as Catalunya's, the Generalitat's recent mandate that all students enroll in one course of *Valenciá* reflects the growing resurgence of regionalist sentiments.

Local fiestas amplify Valencia's enchantment with fire, water, and love to hyperbolic proportions. Whereas Spaniards in the south are infatuated with the valorous bull and the fiery looks of *sevillana* dancers, it is a curious fascination with fire that characterizes the *valencianos*. All festivals promote *fuegos artificiales* (fireworks), and every little town along the coast has its own celebration. From the reactionary art and furor invested in the effigies at Valencia's Las Fallas (March), to the artful displays in during San Juan (June), to the recklessly adrenaline filled Nit de l'Alba (August) in Elche, two common threads unite the celebrations: fire as a purifier and as a destructive force.

With Valencia to the north, the Mediterranean to the east, and Andalucía to the west, the unique cultural mosaic that is today's Murcia reflects an intricate past. The diverse physical appearance of *murcianos* dates to the intermarriages and interbreeding of fair-haired Visigoths with the Alfonso X El Sabio's *moreno* (dark hair and olive-skinned) troops from Castilian. The Murcian accent hybrids the Castilian lisp with a light Andalucían tongue that is reluctant to pronounce suffixes. Inland townspeople speak with a sexy, throaty delivery.

Four centuries ago, a bizarre wave of plagues, floods, and earthquakes wreaked havoc throughout Murcia. Ironically, the earthquakes uncovered a rich supply of minerals and natural springs. Thermal spas, pottery factories, and paprika mills pepper the lively coastal towns, and its orange and apricot orchards bolster Murcia's reputation as the "Huerta de Europa" (Europe's Orchard). Overlooked by most vacationers, this unjaded region is Spain at its casual, everyday best.

Paella (saffron rice with meat and/or fish), the pride of Spaniards everywhere, is a *levante* (east) coast matter-of-fact. First concocted in a huge *paellera* (paella pot) somewhere in the rice fields around Valencia, it is available in varying degrees of glory from Peñiscola to Cartagena.

> ### 🖐 HIGHLIGHTS OF VALENCIA AND MURCIA
>
> - Valencia's festival of **Las Fallas,** a pyromaniac's dream (see p. 399).
> - *Paella* (and hundreds of other rice-based specialties) straight from the source (see **Valencia: Food,** p. 397).
> - Whether it's *Las Fallas* or not, **Valencia** and the beachside resort of **Alicante** are both known for their nightlife—even in Spain (see p. 393 and 404).
> - The hilltop medieval fortress town of **Morella** (see p. 401).

■ Valencia (València)

Valencia is a stylish, cosmopolitan, and business-oriented nerve center, a striking contrast to its surrounding orchards and brown speckled mountain ranges. Fountainous parks and gardens soothe the city's congested environment, and soft-sanded beaches nearby complement its kinetic day and nightlife. Unique architectural surprises hide behind the crowded city center, but the presence of somewhat unfortunate neo-style buildings (e.g. the Ayuntamiento) discredits Valencia's bid for architectural fame.

Graffiti "correcting" Castilian road signs into *valenciá* reflects a recent surge in regionalism. Regionalist sentiments, however, are rarely seen or heard beyond a few spray-painted expressions, and the university students who invigorate Valencia during term-time still favor *castellano*.

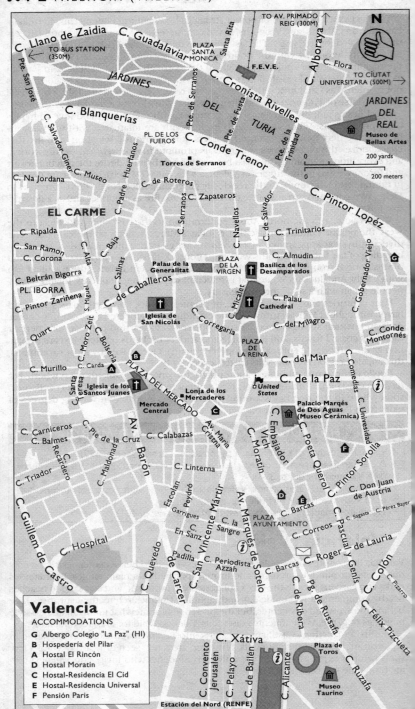

N

TO AV. PRIMADO REIG (300M)

C. Llano de Zaidia

Pte. San José

TO BUS STATION (350M)

C. Guadalaviar

Santa Rita

PLAZA SANTA MONICA

F.E.V.E.

C. Alboraya

C. Flora

TO CIUTAT UNIVERSITARA (500M)

JARDINES

Pte. de Serranos

C. Cronista Rivelles

DEL

Pte. de Fusta

TURIA

Pte. de la Trinidad

JARDINES DEL REAL

Museo de Bellas Artes

C. Blanquerías

PL. DE LOS FUEROS

C. Conde Trenor

Torres de Serranos

200 yards

200 meters

C. Salvador Giner

C. Na Jordana

C. Museo

C. Padre Huérfanos

C. de Roteros

C. Serranos

C. Zapateros

C. Navellos

C. de Salvador

C. Pintor Lopéz

EL CARME

C. Ripalda

C. San Ramon

C. Corona

C. Alta

C. Baja

C. Salinas

C. Trinitarios

C. Almudin

Gobernador Viejo

G

C. Beltrán Bigorra

PL. IBORRA

C. Pintor Zariñena

Palau de la Generalitat

PLAZA DE LA VIRGEN

Basílica de los Desamparados

C. de Caballeros

Micalet

C. Palau

Cathedral

Quart

C. Moro Zeit

C. Miguel S.

C. Bolsería

Iglesia de San Nicolás

C. Corregaría

C. del Milagro

C. Conde Montornés

C. Murillo

C. Carda

A

B

PLAZA DEL MERCADO

PLAZA DE LA REINA

C. del Mar

C. de la Paz

C. Comedias

C. Universidad

i

C. Santa Teresa

Iglesia de los Santos Juanes

Lonja de los Mercaderes

C

United States

Palacio Marqés de Dos Aguas (Museo Cerámica)

C. Carniceros

C. Balmes

C. Pie de la Cruz

Mercado Central

Av. María Cristina

Av. Barón

C. Calabazas

C. Embajador Vich

C. Moratin

C. Poeta Querol

C. Pintor Sorolla

F

C. Triador

C. Recaredo

C. Maldonado

C. Linterna

C. Don Juan de Austria

C. Hospital

Escolan

Peydró

Garrigues

C. San Vicente Mártir

C. la Sangre

Av. Marqués de Sotelo

D

E

C. Barcas

C. Sagasta

C. Pérez Bayer

C. Guillem de Castro

C. Quevedo

C. En Sanz

de Carcer

Padilla

C. Periodista Azzah

PLAZA AYUNTAMIENTO

i

C. Correos

C. Barcas

C. Pascual y Genís

C. Roger de Lauria

C. Colón

C. Pizarro

Valencia

ACCOMMODATIONS

G Albergo Colegio "La Paz" (HI)
B Hospedería del Pilar
A Hostal El Rincón
D Hostal Moratin
C Hostal-Residencia El Cid
E Hostal-Residencia Universal
F Pensión Paris

C. Convento Jerusalén

C. Pelayo

C. de Ballén

C. Xátiva

C. Alicante

i

Plaza de Toros

Museo Taurino

C. de Ribera

Pg. de Russafa

C. Félix Pizcueta

C. Ruzafa

Estación del Nord (RENFE)

VALENCIA & MURCIA

ORIENTATION AND PRACTICAL INFORMATION

Valencia is best approached by train, since **Estación del Nord** is close to the city's center. **Avenida Marquéz de Sotelo** runs from the train station to **Plaça del Ayuntamiento,** where the city tourist office is located. The avenue then splits into **Avenida María Cristina,** which leads to the central market, and **Carrer de Sant Vicent,** which leads to **Plaça de la Reina** and the cathedral. The *casco antiguo* (old quarter) hosts most everything of interest, except for the university area and beaches, and is nestled into a bend of the Río Turia. Valencia's geographical tangle and sprawl make unaided tours futile. Although few maps do it justice, the sporadically available tourist office map is best.

Transportation

Flights: The airport is 15km southwest of the city (tel. 96 370 95 00). Cercanías trains run between the airport and train station (32min.; departs M-F every 30min., 150ptas; departs Sa-Su every hr., 170ptas). Flights to all major domestic and some international destinations. **Iberia** office, C. La Paz, 14 (tel. 96 352 75 52; 24hr. info and reservation tel. 902 400 500). Open M-F 9am-2pm and 4-7pm.

Trains: Estación del Nord, C. Xàtiva, 24. Ticket windows open 7am-9pm. **RENFE** (24hr. tel. 96 352 02 02) to: Alicante (2hr., 6 per day, 2800ptas); Barcelona (4-6hr., 11 per day, 3200ptas); Madrid (5-7½hr., departs every 1½hr., 4400ptas); Sevilla (9hr., 2 per day, 5200ptas). **Cercanías** to Gandía and Játiva.

Buses: Estación Terminal d'Autobuses, Av. Menéndez Pidal, 13 (tel. 96 349 72 22), across the river, a 25min. walk northwest of the city center. Take municipal bus #8 (105ptas) from Pl. Ayuntamiento. **Auto Res** (tel. 96 349 22 30) sends 5 regular and 9 express buses per day to Madrid (4-5hr., 2845-3145ptas). **Bacoma** (tel. 96 347 96 08) runs to: Málaga (11hr., 5 per day, 5960ptas); Granada (5 per day, 4855ptas); Sevilla (12hr., 2 per day, 6080ptas). **Enatcar** (tel. 96 340 08 55) drives to Barcelona (4½hr., 8 per day 7am-8pm, 2900ptas). **Ubesa** (tel. 96 340 08 55) stops along the Costa Blanca on its way to Alicante (2¼-3hr., 9 per day, 1970ptas). **Eurolines** (tel. 96 349 68 55) has international service to the rest of Europe.

Ferries: Trasmediterránea, Estació Maritima (Valencia port tel. 96 367 06 44; general tel. 902 45 46 45). Take bus #4 from Pl. Ayuntamiento. Boats run to Menorca, Mallorca, and Eivissa (Ibiza). Buy tickets at any travel agency, or on the day of departure at the port office. Ask a travel agent about **Flebasa's** (Denia office tel. 96 578 40 11) Denia-Eivissa service. See **Islas Baleares: By Boat,** for details p. 367.

Public Transportation: EMT Buses (tel. 96 352 83 99). Bus **map** available at the tourist office and at the EMT office, C. En Sanz, 4. Open M-F 8am-2pm. Plaça Ayuntamiento is the hub. Bus #8 runs to the bus station; bus #19 (in summer also #20, 21, 22) heads to Las Arenas and Malvarrosa. Buy tickets aboard (110ptas) or a 10-ride ticket (695ptas) at a newsstand. Service stops at 10:30pm. Late-night buses run through Pl. Ayuntamiento (departs every 45min. 11pm-1:38am).

Taxis: (tel. 96 370 33 33 or 96 357 13 13).

Tourist and Financial Services

Tourist Office: Regional, Estación del Nord, C. Xàtiva, 24 (tel. 96 352 85 73), on the right of the train tracks (inside the station) as you disembark. Lots of pamphlets and maps. Open M-F 9am-6:30pm. Another regional **branch** with similar information is on C. Paz, 46-48 (tel. 96 398 64 22). Open M-F 10am-6pm, Sa 10am-2pm. **City,** Pl. Ayuntamiento, 1 (tel. 96 351 04 17; info tel. 010), has the only Ajuntament-sponsored info. Open M-F 8:30am-2:15pm and 4:15-6:15pm, Sa 9am-12:45pm.

Budget Travel: IVAJ, C. Hospital, 11 (tel. 96 386 97 00). From the train station, head left on C. Xàtiva, which becomes C. Guillem de Castro, and turn right on C. Hospital. Several travel handbooks in English. ISIC 700ptas. HI cards 1800ptas. Open in summer M-F 9am-2pm, in winter M-F 9am-2pm and 4:30-6:30pm.

Currency Exchange: Banco Central Hispano (tel. 96 159 85 00), across the street, offers decent exchange rates. 24hr. **ATMs** everywhere.

American Express: Duna Viajes, C. Cirilo Amorós, 88 (tel. 96 374 15 62; fax 96 334 57 00), next to Pl. América on the edge of Río Turia. No commission on AmEx traveler's checks. Accepts wired money. Mail held (1 year) and **fax** service for card-

VALENCIA & MURCIA

holders. Open in summer M-F 10am-2pm and 5-8:30pm, Sa 10am-2pm; in winter M-F 9:30am-1:30pm and 4:30-7:30pm.

El Corte Inglés: C. Pintor Sorolla, 26 (tel. 96 351 24 44). From Pl. Ayuntamiento, go down C. Barcas as it turns into a pedestrian walk; Corte's on the left. **Currency exchange,** free **map,** English books, **groceries.** Open daily 10am-9:30pm.

Local Services

Luggage Storage: At the bus station, lockers 200ptas and 400ptas. Or at the train station, lockers 300-600ptas. Open daily 7am-10pm.

English Bookstore: The English Book Centre, C. Pascual y Genis, 16 (tel. 96 351 92 88), off C. Barcas. Open M-F 10am-1:30pm and 4:30-8pm, Sa 10am-1:30pm.

Laundromat: Lavandería El Mercat, Pl. Mercado, 12 (tel. 96 391 20 10). Self-service wash and dry 950ptas. Open M-F 10am-2pm and 4:30-8:30pm, Sa 10am-2pm.

Emergency and Communications

Emergency: call 091 or 092; 085 for **ambulance. Police:** (tel. 96 362 10 12).

24-hour Pharmacy: Check listing in the local paper *Levante* (125ptas) or check the *farmacias de guardia* schedule posted outside any pharmacy.

Hospital: Hospital Clínico Universitario, Av. Blasco Ibañez, 17 (tel. 96 386 26 00), at the corner of C. Dr. Ferrer. Take bus #70 or 81 from Pl. Ayuntamiento. An English-speaking doctor is often on duty.

Internet Access: In El Corte Inglés and shopping center **Nuevo Centro.** Follow along the edge of the river north and cross the river at Puente de las Glorias Valencianas. Open daily 10am-9pm.

Post Office: Pl. Ayuntamiento, 24 (tel. 96 351 67 50). Open M-F 8:30am-8:30pm, Sa 9:30am-2pm. **Postal Code:** 46080.

ACCOMMODATIONS

The business of Valencia is business, not tourism—rooms are plentiful during the summer. During the papier-mâché orgy of Las Fallas (Mar. 12-19), reserve well in advance. Avoid the areas by the *barrio chino* (Red Light district) around Pl. Pilar. The best options cluster around **Plaza del Ayuntamiento** and **Plaza del Mercado,** a lively area at night. Last resort *hostales* cluster left of the train station off **Calle Xátvia.**

Alberg Colegio "La Paz" (HI), Av. Puerto, 69 (tel. 96 369 01 52), nearly halfway between the city and the port. Take bus #19 from Pl. Ayuntamiento (next to Citibank); it's the 3rd stop on Av. Puerto. Forbidding fortress safeguards a peaceful ambiance. 2-4 people and a bathroom in every room. HI membership required. Dorms 1100ptas, with full board 2500ptas; over 26 dorms 1600ptas, with full board 3000ptas. Breakfast included. Sheets 400ptas for 5 days. Lockout 10am-3pm. Curfew 1-2am. Reception daily 9am-2pm and 5pm-midnight. Open July-Sept. 15.

Near Plaza del Ayuntamiento

Hostal-Residencia Universal, C. Barcas, 5 (tel. 96 351 53 84), off the plaza. 3 floors of spacious rooms with balconies, ornate ceilings, and new sinks. Some rooms are quite a vertical hike. Singles 2000ptas; doubles 3000ptas, with shower 3600ptas; triples 4200ptas.

Pensión Paris, C. Salvá, 12 (tel. 96 352 67 66). From Pl. Ayuntamiento turn right at C. Barcas, left at C. Poeta Querol, and right onto C. Salvá. 13 spotless rooms with angelic white curtains and balconies. A bargain. Singles 2200ptas; doubles 3200ptas, with shower 3800ptas, with bath 4200ptas; triples 4700ptas.

Hostal-Residencia El Cid, C. Cerrajeros, 13 (tel. 96 392 23 23). Coming from the train station take the 2nd left off C. Vicente Mártir after passing Pl. Ayuntamiento (and before Pl. Reina). Spotless, homey rooms. Fans provided. Singles 1700ptas; doubles 2800ptas, with shower 3300ptas, with bath 3800ptas.

Hostal Moratin, C. Moratin, 15 (tel. 96 352 12 20), 1st street on the left off C. Barcas from Pl. Ayuntamiento. Well located with solid, clean rooms and a rooftop terrace. Bathrooms and walls sparkle like teeth on a toothpaste commercial. Singles are limited, but don't pay more for a double bed. Singles 2900ptas; doubles 4200ptas, with bath 5000ptas; triples with bath 7500ptas. Keys distributed.

Near Plaza Mercat

Hostal El Rincón, C. Carda, 11 (tel. 96 391 60 83). From Pl. Ayuntamiento, Pl. Mercado extends past the market building; its continuation is C. Carda. The 54-room hostel was once a medieval lodging for wayfarers. Most rooms are newly renovated (thank goodness) and spotless though a bit dark; rooms with private bath are nicer. Singles 1500ptas, with bath 2000ptas; doubles 2800ptas; with bath 3600ptas.

Hospedería del Pilar, Pl. Mercado, 19 (tel. 96 391 66 00). Past the market and Llonja, on the far right-hand side. Room size varies, but all have hot water and tiled bathrooms. Noisy and big. Singles 1600ptas, with bath 2140ptas; doubles 2995ptas, with bath 3850ptas; triples 3950ptas, with bath 4815ptas.

Pilgrim's Youth Hostel, Pl. Hombres del Mar, 28 (tel. 96 356 42 88; email direc tor@albergue.cybered.es). Take bus #19 from Pl. Ayuntamiento to the 3rd stop on C. Doctor Lluch. Walk between the tennis courts and the soccer field on your right along C. Pescadores, which leads to Pl. Hombres del Mar. Travelers should use caution when approaching the plaza at night. Two blocks from the beach, it offers modern comforts: A/C, free email, internet access 500ptas per 30min., TV, free laundry, and kitchen. Dorms 1000ptas, over 26 1500ptas, over 30 2000ptas. Prices reflect substantial *Let's Go* discount (show your book). Breakfast included. Call ahead. Visa, MC.

FOOD

The taste: meat-shellfish-lemon-saffron-rice-chicken. The connotations: unadulterated Spain. The birthplace: Valencia. The word: *paella*. Unbeknownst to most tourists, *paella* is just one of 200 Valencian rice specialties. Other local specialties include *arroz a banda* (rice and fish with garlic, onion, tomatoes, and saffron), *all i pebre* (eels fried in oil, paprika, and garlic), and *sepia con salsa verde* (cuttlefish with garlic and parsley). Another favorite dish is *horchata,* a sweet, milky drink pressed from locally grown *chufas* (earth almonds). Buckets of fresh fish, meat, and fruit are sold at the **Mercado Central,** on Pl. Mercado (open M-Th 7am-2pm, F 7am-2pm and 5-8:30pm, Sa 7am-3pm). For **groceries,** glide up to the 5th floor of **El Corte Inglés,** C. Pintor Sorolla, 26 (tel. 96 351 24 44; open M-Sa 10am-9:30pm).

Restaurante La Utielana, Pl. Picadero Dos Aguas, 3 (tel. 96 352 94 14). Take C. Barcelonina off the narrowly tapered end of Pl. Ayuntamiento, turn left at its end into and across Pl. Rodrigo Botet, make a right onto C. Procida, and duck into a little alley/plaza on the left called Pl. Picadero Dos Aguas (look for the Utielana sign). Ideal service, and not a plate on the menu over 825ptas. Choose from a super scoop of scrumptious seafood *paella* (a shocking 375ptas). Afternoon *menú* just 800ptas. A/C. Open Sept.-July M-F 1:15-4pm and 9-11pm, Sa 1:15-4pm.

La Lluna, C. Sant Ramón (tel. 96 392 21 46), in El Carme district. A veggie restaurant to moon over. A 4-course *menú* and whole-grain bread served only weekday afternoons (850ptas) under refreshing A/C. Juices 260ptas. Open M-Sa 1:30-4pm and 8:30-11:30pm.

La Pappardella, C. Bordadores, 5 (tel. 96 391 89 15). Facing the cathedral, look right. Sit among a lively, chic crowd and enjoy deliciously fresh pasta dishes (800-1100ptas), on the outdoor terrace. Nice inexpensive wine selection. Open W-M 2-4:30pm and 9pm-midnight.

Comidas Esma, C. Zurradore, 5 (tel. 96 391 63 52), off C. Correjería. A local working-class diner. Full meal with hefty bowls of homemade soup and freshly grilled *merluza* (hake). A la carte dishes at rock-bottom prices. Afternoon *menú* 800ptas. Open mid-Sept. to mid-Aug. M-F 1-4pm and 8:30-11pm, Sa 1-3pm.

SIGHTS

Touring Valencia on foot is complicated. Most of the sights line the Río Turia or cluster near Pl. Reina, which is linked to Pl. Ayuntamiento by C. San Vicente Mártir. EMT's cushy **Bus Turistic** (tel. 96 352 83 99) makes loops of the old town sights all day. *(1-day pass 600ptas.)* Valencia is on the cutting edge of contemporary art, and its **galleries** display Spain's freshest works. *(Contact the tourist office for exhibition schedules.)*

VALENCIA & MURCIA

The Arm That Left

In AD 1104, 800 years after San Vicente's martyrdom in Valencia, the Obispo de Valencia attempted to transport Valencia's patron saint's left arm to a holy resting spot in Vatican City. Despite the left arm's perseverance during the long journey, it never reached Rome because the Obispo died in Bari, Italy. Handily, San Vicente's forearm found a new right-hand man in Don Pedro Zampieri de Venezia, who returned the reddened limb to Valencia 800 years later in 1970.

The Aragonese began work on the **cathedral** (tel. 96 391 81 27), in Pl. Reina, shortly after the *Reconquista*. *(Open daily 7:30am-1pm and 4:30-8:30pm. Closes earlier in winter. Free.)* The three different entrances represent centuries of architectural styles, including Gothic, Baroque, and Romanesque. Seized by a fit of Romantic hyperbole (or perhaps "new math"), French novelist Victor Hugo counted 300 bell towers in the city from atop the **Micalet** (or Miguelete, the cathedral tower)—actually, there are only about a hundred. *(Tower open daily 10am-1pm and 4:30-7pm. 200ptas.)*

The **Museo de la Catedral** (tel. 96 391 81 27) squeezes a great many treasures into very little space. *(Open Mar.-Nov. M-F 10am-1pm and 4:30-7pm, Sa 10am-1pm; Dec.-Feb. M-Sa 10am-1pm. 200ptas.)* Check out the overwrought tabernacle made from 1200kg of gold, silver, platinum, emeralds, and sapphires; a Holy Grail; two Goyas; and the *Crucifijo de Marfil* (crucifix) statues depicting "man's passions." Behind the cathedral on Pl. Virgen, elliptical **Basílica Virgen de los Desamparados** houses a resplendent golden altar. *(Open daily 7am-2pm and 4-9pm. Free.)*

In Pl. Mercado, the old Lonja de la Seda (Silk Exchange; tel. 96 352 54 78), one of the foremost examples of Valencian Gothic architecture, testifies to Valencia's medieval prominence in the silk trade. *(Open Tu-F 9am-2pm and 4-8pm, Sa-Su 9am-1:30pm. Free.)* The 15th-century **Torres de Serranos,** from which boiling oil was dumped on invaders, guards the edge of the historic district in Pl. Fueros. *(Open Tu-F 9am-2pm and 4:15-8pm, Sa 9am-1:30pm. Free.)*

On C. Sant Pius V, next to the Jardines del Real, the compelling **Museu Provincial de Belles Artes** (tel. 96 360 57 93) displays superb 14th- to 16th-century Valencian primitives and works by later Spanish and foreign masters, including a Hieronymous Bosch triptych, El Greco's *San Juan Bautista*, Velázquez's self-portrait, Ribera's *Santa Teresa*, and a slew of Goyas. *(Open Oct.-July Tu-Sa 10am-2:15pm and 4-7:30pm, Su 10am-2:15pm; Aug. Tu-Su 10am-2:15pm. Free.)*

West across the old river, the **Instituto València de Arte Moderno (IVAM),** C. Guillem de Castro, 118 (tel. 96 386 30 00), has a permanent collection of abstract works by 20th-century sculptor Julio González and temporary exhibits of cutting-edge art and photography. *(Open Tu-Su 10am-7pm. 350ptas, students 175ptas.)*

For botanical diversion, the city maintains impressive **parks** on the outskirts of the historic district. Taxonomists marvel at the **Jardín Botánico,** C. Beato Gaspar Bono, 6 (tel. 96 391 16 57), on the western end of Río Turia. *(Open Tu-Su 10am-9pm. 50ptas.)* This university-maintained, open-air garden cultivates 43,000 plants of 300 precisely labeled species from around the world. One block farther, Valencia shows the world what should be done with dry riverbeds. A series of pillared public recreation areas mark the banks of the now diverted Río Turia, ending with hundreds of children climbing up a gigantic rendition of Jonathan Swift's Gulliver in Lilliput. *(Open daily 10am-2pm and 5-9pm.)* Moving past the Jardines del Real toward the sea, Santiago Calatrava's bridge is nicknamed the Peineta because it resembles headdresses worn by *falleras* (young women in Las Fallas).

Sand-seekers will find the **beaches** close to Valencia along the Levante coastal strip overcrowded. Most popular are **Las Arenas** and **Malvarrosa,** both on bus #19's route from Pl. Ayuntamiento (also #20, 21, and 22 in summer). Equally crowded but more attractive is **Salér,** a long, pine-bordered strand 14km from the city center. Cafeterias and snack bars line the shore, with shower and bathroom facilities nearby. Mediterráneo Urbano **buses** (tel. 96 349 72 22) make for Salér (on the way to El Perello) from the intersection of Gran Vía Germanias and C. Sueca, on the right side of the train station (25min., departs every 30min., 180ptas).

ENTERTAINMENT

Rest up during siesta, because Valencia's nightlife will keep you drinking and dancing until sunrise. Bars and pubs around the **El Carme** district, just beyond the market, start rolling around 11:30pm. Follow Pl. Mercado and C. Bolsería (bearing right) to Pl. Tossal, where outdoor terraces, upbeat music, and *agua de Valencia* (orange juice, champagne, and vodka) entertain the masses. **Bar Sant Jaume** and **Café Infanta,** both in Pl. Tossal, stay lively late into the night. **Plaza Cánovas del Castillo** and **Plaza de los Fueros** also buzz until the disco hour.

American students and expats frequent two Irish pubs in town. One is **Finnegan's** at Pl. Reina in front of, and to the right of, the cathedral. The other is **The Black Sheep,** Pl. Porta de la Mar, 6, in the plaza on the old-town side of the huge bridge that looks like the dorsal fin of a fish; Wednesday is student night (pints of Guinness and Kilkenny 350ptas). Both stay open until around 2am, when disco life begins.

Discos dominate the university area, particularly on **Avenida Blasco Ibáñez.** Young twenty-somethings begin dancing at the pubs off Av. Ibáñez at **Plaza Xúquer.** Walk around the Pl. Xúquer pubs to pick up discounted passes to the discos. Discos don't draw a crowd until 3am, at the earliest. Be warned: hot spots flash in and out. Local university students remain the best sources. Taxi drivers generally know *discotecas* by name. It's wise to tackle the labyrinth of the old city in groups; the dark areas in between the clusters can be dangerous. For info on activities in the city, consult the *Qué y Dónde* weekly magazine, available at newsstands (150ptas), or *Levante's* weekly entertainment supplement (usually Tuesdays), *La Cartelera* (125ptas).

Caballito de Mar, C. Eugenia Viñes, 22 (tel. 96 371 07 63), at Playa de Malvarrosa. The most popular disco in town. Remixing recent favorites and Spanish techno, it mimics a cruise ship with outdoor tables and a decorative pool on deck. Popular every day off the week after 2am, but only open June-Sept.

Distrito 10, C. General Elío, 10. Another hot spot, with mirrors, 3 floors of balconies, and a gigantic video screen. Open Sept.-July Th-Sa 6-9:30pm and midnight-7am, Su 6-9:30pm. Early session 500ptas, late 1500ptas.

Club Perdido, C. Sueca, 17, past the train station, a bit out of the way. Plays jazz.

Carnaby Club, C. Poeta Liern, 17. A lesbian favorite.

Movie selections are bountiful and varied. Ask at the tourist office for info on the **Mostra de València de Cine Mediterrani** and the **Independent Film Festival.** Vintage and foreign films, many in English, show at the **Filmoteca,** Pl. Ayuntamiento, 17 (tel. 96 352 23 30). Look in *Qué y Dónde* for films marked *V.O. subtitulaela* (in their original languages). The brand-new L'Hemisfèric, south along the riverbed bank off Autopista al Saler, houses an **IMAX theater** and **planetarium** (shows 850-1700ptas).

Valencia's Plaza de Toros, right next to the train station, stages **bullfights** three to four evenings a week from 7 to 11pm. For info and tickets, call 96 351 93 15.

During **Semana Santa,** the streets clog with lavishly attired monks riding platforms enacting Biblical scenes and children performing the miracle plays of St. Vincent Ferrer. The festival of **Corpus Christi** features *rocas,* intricate coaches that double as stages for religious plays. The **Fira de Juliol** (July Fair) brings fireworks, cultural events including concerts in the riverbank park, bullfights, and a *batalla de flors,* a violent skirmish in which girls on passing floats throw flowers at the crowd, which in turn flings them back.

Las Fallas

If you can choose any time of the year to come to Valencia, make it March 12 to 19, when Valencia's most illustrious event, **Las Fallas,** grips the city. Neighborhoods compete to build the most elaborate and satirical papier-mâché effigy; over 300 such *ninots* spring up in the streets. Parades, bullfights, fireworks, and street dancing enliven the annual excess. On the final day—*la nit del foc* (fire night)—all the *ninots* simultaneously burn in one last, clamorous release. The inferno exorcises social ills and brings luck for the agricultural season.

VALENCIA & MURCIA

■ Near Valencia: Sagunto (Sagunt)

Spaniards still puff with pride over the courage of this town's inhabitants. In the third century BC, residents of Phoenician-controlled Sagunto held out for eight months against Hannibal's besieging Carthaginians. Some sources say that on the brink of annihilation, Sagunto's women, children, and elderly threw themselves into a burning furnace; others insist that the residents chose starvation over defeat. Monuments reflect the influence of a rambling list of conquerors (six seizures, not including barbarian, Alan, Vandal, Visigoth, and Byzantine invasions in the 5th to 7th centuries). By 1874, Sagunto had learned the hard way that if you can't beat 'em, join 'em; it became the first town to recognize Alfonso XII's restoration of the Bourbon monarchy.

The old town peaks at the refurbished medieval **castle.** *(Open June-Sept. Tu-Sa 10am-8pm, Su 10am-2pm; Oct.-May Tu-Sa 10am-2pm and 4-6pm, Su 10am-2pm.)* Along the way there, heading into town, you'll pass the once-crumbling Teatre Roman, which has survived a controversial restoration process to become an impressive modern performance stage, built entirely on the still-visible skeleton of the Roman structure. On a different note, **beaches,** including the **Puerto de Sagunto,** which won an EU beach award, and Almarda, beckon by the port (4km away).

Frequent **RENFE trains** (tel. 96 266 07 28) from Valencia (on the C-6 Cercanías line) stop in Sagunto (30min., departs every 30min. 8am-9pm, 320ptas), as do Vallduxense **buses** (tel. 96 349 37 38; 30min., 275ptas). Take the bus if you're heading to the beaches and the train if you're heading to Sagunto proper. **Buses** to the beaches leave from Av. Santos Patronos next to the tourist office (departs every 20min., 100ptas). In summer, a number of nameless restaurants set up shop on the beach along Av. Mediterrani and Pg. Marítim. To get to Sagunto's town center from the **train station,** turn right at the exit; then turn left at the traffic lights onto the diagonal street (C. Vicent Fontelles), heading the wrong way down a one-way street to a small plaza. Here, turn left onto Cami Real, which runs directly to the center of town and to the **Ayuntamiento.** The **tourist office** (tel. 96 266 22 13), in Pl. Cronista Chabret, is nearby. (Open M-Sa 10am-2pm and 4-6pm, Su 10am-2pm.)

■ Near Valencia: Manises

The small town of Manises has made the province of Valencia famous for its colorful, hand-decorated ceramics. Tacky-souvenir-o-phobes will love the city's main square, where ceramics dealers push their wares. **CVT buses** (tel. 96 340 47 15) leave from Valencia's bus station (30min., departs almost every hr., 105ptas), but *Cercanías trains* from Valencia along the line to Riba-Roja de Turia are more frequent (20min., departs every 30min., 155ptas). Fine ceramics closer to Valencia are at the famous **Fábrica Lladró** workshop in Tavernes Blanques (take bus #16 from Pl. Ayuntamiento in Valencia; 105ptas).

■ Near Valencia: L'Albufera

The Albufera (tel. 96 162 01 01), Spain's largest lagoon, is 13km south of Valencia. Nature lovers flock to see fish and wild fowl frolicking in the water and rice fields lining the edges. Motorized boat tours weave around reeds and through the marsh while flying fish serenade cruisers. **Buses** (tel. 96 349 14 25), from the corner of Gran Via de Germanía and C. Sueca in Valencia (between the train station and Pl. Toros) stop here on the way to El Perello (40min., departs every 30min., 165ptas). To catch the return bus, cross the bridge on your right with your back to the lagoon.

■ Near Valencia: Cullera

The rapidly growing town of Cullera, south of Valencia, glories under the protective glare of its 13th-century **castle.** *(Both castle and santuari open daily in summer 9am-9pm; in winter 8am-6pm. Free.)* Those who complete the 15-minute zig-zag hike are rewarded with a 360-degree postcard view of the mountains, verdant rice paddies, a sea, a river, and a city. Attached to the castle, the 19th-century **Santuari de la Verge** displays sundry religious treasures "collected" by castle residents over the years.

Cullera lies on the **Cercanías train** line between Valencia and Gandía (35min., departs every hr., 320-375ptas). From the train station, take the bus into the city and ask the bus driver to let you off near Pl. Mercat (also Pl. de la Virgen). From the plaza go up the stairs in the back. Continue up C. Calvari at the top of the steps. This road narrows into a stone path that climbs to the castle. The bus also runs through town to the *faro* (lighthouse), and you can walk north to a seemingly endless strip of less-populated **beaches.**

■ Near Valencia: Morella

Morella is like a coveted cookie jar hidden above the kitchen cabinet—high up and hard to reach but full of delights once within your grasp. Surrounded by a ring of thick walls and guarded by the stoic remains of a majestic castle, Morella still looks like an impenetrable fortress in an otherwise empty, rolling green countryside. The **Castell de Morella** (tel. 964 17 31 28), perched atop a massive rock, dazzles even the most jaded castle-goers. *(Entrance to the castle is on C. Hospital, uphill from the basilica with two Gothic portals. Open daily in summer 10:30am-7:30pm, in winter 10:30am-6pm. 200ptas, students 100ptas.)* Celts, Romans, and Moors all chose Morella for its natural defenses. El Cid stormed the summit in 1084, while Don Blasco de Aragón took the town in the name of Jaume I in 1232. Various civil wars in the 19th century damaged the castle, but the craters only add to the castle's allure. A serpentine path scales the rock past 14th- to 19th-century dungeons, slithering up to the **Plaça de Arms.** The view from there spans a fertile countryside and an ancient Roman aqueduct.

In the Pl. Arciprestal, the Gothic **Basílica Santa María la Mayor's** dual portals display amusingly dopey statues. Inside, a ghostly, fair-skinned statue of Nuestra Señora de la Asunción, a windy stairwell, an overgrown organ, and a phasmantalogical gold altarpiece evoke images of Damien and The Omen. A five-minute walk from Puerta de San Miguel, remnants of the 13th-century Gothic **aqueduct,** with 16 towers and six gates, arch above the road. If possible, try visiting Morella during **Sexeni,** the town's most famous fiesta, celebrated every six years to honor the Virgen de Vallivana (not due to roll around again until August 2000). The rest of the time Morella charms with its unhurried daily life, uninterrupted by the sprinkling of tourists.

Autos Mediterráneo (tel. 964 22 00 54) runs **buses** to Morella from Pl. Fadrell in Castelló, infrequently and at inconvenient hours (2½hr.; from Castelló to Morella M-F 7:15am and 3:30pm, Sa 7:15am; from Morella to Castelló M-F 7:30am and 4pm, Sa 4pm; 1000ptas). Castelló is on the Cercanías-Valencia **train** line (1hr., departs every 30min., 470-535ptas). The **tourist office** (tel. 964 17 30 32) is at Puerta de San Miguel, uphill from the bus stop. (Open July-Aug. daily 10am-2pm and 4-7pm; Sept.-June Tu-Sa 10am-2pm and 4-6pm, Su 10am-2pm.) In **emergencies,** call the Guardia Civil (tel. 964 16 00 11).

If you're staying overnight, head to **Fonda Moreno,** C. San Nicolás, 12 (tel. 964 16 01 05), with ancient rooms and wood ceilings (doubles 2140ptas). Also inexpensive is **Hostal El Cid,** Puerta San Mateo, 3 (tel. 964 16 00 08), down from the bus stop, with balconies with a view (singles 1300ptas; doubles 2200ptas, with shower 3100ptas, with bath 3500ptas; breakfast 350ptas). Morella sports a unique cuisine that features *rufas* (truffles) dug up from the local turf. Specialties include *paté de trufas* (truffle pâté) and *cordero relleno trufado* (lamb with truffle stuffing). Eat in style at **Restaurante Casa Roque,** C. Segura Barreda, 8 (tel. 964 16 03 36), the best in town (*menú* 1500ptas; open Tu-Su).

■ Játiva (Xàtiva)

Once the second most populous city in the Valencian republic, Játiva, a town of palaces and churches, still retains traces of its opulent past. The birthplace of the Borgia Popes Calixtus III, and Alexander VI, and later home of the Baroque painter José Ribera, the town was once both prosperous and well-known. Unfortunately for Játiva, the last person of note to pass through was 18th-century Felipe V, who burned it to the ground. With an imposing, mountainous backdrop and land that lends itself to *huertas* (orchards) and vineyards, Játiva is now a small, pleasant city. Nonetheless, it snares few tourists and even loses its locals during the hot summer months.

ORIENTATION AND PRACTICAL INFORMATION 64km south of Valencia and 102km north of Alicante, inland Játvia is easily accessed by rail. **Alameda de Jaume I** divides the town into two: the old village, at the foot of the hill with the castles and ancient walls, and the modern village. To reach the old village and the tourist office from the train station in the modern village, go straight up **Baixada de L'Estació** (beginning at the Bar Bienvenidos) and turn left at its end.

RENFE **trains** chug from Av. Cavaller Ximén de Tovia (tel. 96 227 33 33) to: Gandía, via Silla (45min., departs every 30min., 370-430ptas); Valencia (1hr., departs every 30min., 370-430ptas); and Madrid. **Buses** stop at the corner of Av. Cavaller Ximén de Tovia and C. Don Carles Santhou, to the left and down from the train station. Cambipos (tel. 96 287 41 10) goes direct to Gandía (1¼hr., 1 per day, about 400ptas). Call the bus station in Valencia (tel. 96 349 72 22) for a schedule from there to Játiva. The **tourist office**, Av. Jaume 1, 50 (tel. 96 227 33 46), across from the Ajuntament, speaks English and shovels out pamphlets, a map, a restaurant guide. (Open June 15-Sept. 15 Tu-Sa 10am-2pm and 4:30-6pm, Su 10am-2pm; Sept. 15-June 15 Tu-F 9am-2pm and 4-6pm, Sa-Su 10am-2pm.) In an **emergency,** dial 091 and 092. The local **police** hold fort on Baixada del Carme at Al. Jaume I, 33. The **Hospital Lluis Alcanyis,** Ctra. Alzira (tel. 96 228 95 00; emergencies 96 228 95 21), is 2km from the town center. The **post office,** Av. Jaume I, 33 (tel. 96 227 51 68), is open for stamps and Lista de Correos (open M-F 8:30am-2:30pm, Sa 9:30am-1pm). The **postal code** is 46800.

ACCOMMODATIONS AND FOOD Call before coming if you plan to stay the night. **Margallonero,** Pl. Mercat, 42 (tel. 96 227 66 77), looks out on the city's active market plaza. To get there, go left on Al. Jaume I coming from the train station (like going to the tourist office), take the first right onto C. St. Francese, go straight up the ramp onto C. Alos, and take the first left at C. Botigues, which runs into Pl. Mercat. Margallonero proffers large, flowery rooms with sinks and shared bath at reasonable prices. (1400ptas per person.) Játiva's traditional desserts are unmistakably Arabic in origin, but its version of *paella, arroz al horno* (baked, slightly drier, and loaded with chick peas), is more famous. Blue- and white-tiled **Casa Floro,** Pl. Mercat, 46 (tel. 96 227 30 20), next door to the Margallonero, has A/C and a tasty four-course *menú* for 1300-1500ptas (open M-F 1-4pm, Sa 1-4pm and 9pm-midnight). Tuesdays and Fridays are **market** days on Pl. Mercat (open 8am-1pm). The Mercadona **supermarket** is on Av. Abu Masaif, just off Baixada de L'Estació (open M-Sa 9am-8:30pm).

SIGHTS AND ENTERTAINMENT The striking ramparts atop the hill in back of town lead to the awe-inspiring **castell,** a roughneck 2km climb made either on the tedious, winding pavement or on the steep dirt shortcut. *(Open Tu-Su 10:30am-7pm. 300ptas. Tuesdays free.)* The castle has two sections: the **castell machor** (larger), on the right as you come in, and the pre-Roman **castell chicotet** (smaller). The former, used from the 13th through the 16th centuries bears the scars of many a siege and earthquake. Its arched, stone **prison** has held some famous wrongdoers, including King Fernando el Católico and the Comte d'Urgell, would-be usurper of the Aragonese throne. Referred to in Verdi's *Il Trovatore,* this castle is where Comte spent his final years before being buried in its chapel.

Leaving the tourist office to the right, take the first right and ascend Portal de Lleo and C. Peris Urios to find **Colegiata de Santa María,** a giant church known as **La Seu.** *(Open daily 9:30am-1:30pm. Museum 100ptas.)* In front, the town's two popes scheme in bronze. Constructed from 1596 to 1920, the ornate *colegiata* operates as a religious museum—paintings and figurines lurk in nooks and crannies, and on the ceiling.

The **Museu Municipal l'Almodí,** in a 16th-century palace on C. Corretgeria, 46 (tel. 227 65 97), off Pl. Calixto III, holds four floors of Spanish paintings, including three

VALENCIA & MURCIA

Riberas. *(Open in summer Tu-F 10am-2:30pm and 4-6pm, Sa-Su 10am-2:30pm; in winter Tu-Su 10am-2pm. 75ptas.)* Here the townspeople avenged Felipe V's 1707 destruction of the town by hanging his portrait upside down. Thus it remains. From La Seu, cross the plaza where C. Corretgeria runs to the right of the 15th-century hospital.

■ Gandía

Centuries before the EU began blue-flagging the Mediterranean's best beaches, Gandía (pop. 53,000) had already attracted the refined and powerful Borjas family. Five centuries later, as an agribusiness and mercantile exchange nexus, Gandía still cashes in on sugar cane, oranges, silk, daffodils, and mulberries—but mostly on beach, condos, and more beach. The youth hostel here offers the most privileged (and economical) access to the great, languid Gandian *platja.*

ORIENTATION AND PRACTICAL INFORMATION

Everything you need is a stone's throw from the train station on **Marqués de Campo.** Everything you want is at the **beach,** 4km away.

Trains: RENFE (tel. 96 286 54 71) departs from Marqués de Campo to Valencia (1hr., departs every 30min., 480ptas) and Játiva, via Silla (370ptas). Trains also run from Valencia to Platja i Grau de Gandía, Gandía's beach (3-4 per day, 480ptas).
Buses: UBESA (tel. 96 296 50 66; in Valencia tel. 96 359 26 11) runs between Alicante and Valencia via Gandía. Buses arrive and leave from C. Magistrado Catalan, 3. Go right as you leave the train station, take a left at the statue onto C. D'Alfaro, then take the 1st right (C. Magistrado Catalá). To: Valencia (1¼hr., 9-12 per day, 700ptas); Alicante (3hr., 10-13 per day, 1170ptas); Barcelona (7-8hr., 1 per day, 3685ptas); other stops along the Costa Brava on the Valencia-Denia-Alicante line.
Auto Res, Marqués de Campo, 12 (tel. 96 287 10 64). Buses stop at the beach at Pg. Marítim en route to Madrid (5½hr., 7 per day, 3295ptas).
Tourist Office: Marqués de Campo (tel. 96 287 77 88), across from the train station. Detailed map. Open in summer M-F 10am-2pm and 4:30-7:30pm, Sa 10am-2pm; in winter M-F 10am-2pm and 4-7pm, Sa 10am-2pm. English spoken. A beach **branch** (tel. 96 284 24 07) is at Pg. Marítim on the water. Open Mar. 15-Oct. 15 M-Sa 10am-2pm and 5-8pm, Su 10am-1pm; Oct. 16-Mar. 14 Su 10am-1pm.
Luggage Storage: At the train station, with 300ptas token purchased at ticket windows. Lockers and ticket windows available 6am-10:30pm.
Bike/Windsurfer Rental: At the HI hostel in Platja de Piles (see below). Bikes 500ptas per day. Kayaks 700ptas per hr. Windsurfing lessons also offered.
Emergency: dial 091 or 092. **Police:** (tel. 96 287 88 00).
Hospital: C. Sant Pere and Pg. Germanies (tel. 96 295 92 00).
Post Office: Pl. Jaume I, 7 (tel. 96 287 10 91), a few blocks behind the Ajuntament. Open for stamps and Lista de Correos M-F 8:30am-2:30pm. **Postal Code:** 46700.

ACCOMMODATIONS AND FOOD

HI cardholders rejoice at Gandía's hostel, especially given the number of expensive *hostales* about. Make reservations in the summer, especially in August and on weekends, or go bedless. Gandía cooks up seafood specialities like *fideuà,* a shellfish dish with saffron, like paella but with noodles, and the invariably expensive but tempting *zarzuela,* an assorted seafood stew. Before hopping on the bus, stock up at **Supermarket Macedona,** C. Perú, across from the La Amistad stop (open M-Sa 9am-9pm).

Alberg Mar i Vent (HI), C. Doctor Fleming (tel. 96 283 17 48), in Platja de Piles, a town 10km south of Gandía. Take **La Amistad** bus (tel. 96 287 44 10), which departs from the right of the train station (105ptas; check Bar La Amistad, across from the bus stop, for exact times). Flattery cannot do justice to this hostel/beachfront resort. There's a weight room, pool table, outdoor patio, and basketball/soccer court. They rent bikes, kayaks, and windsurfers, while water laps at the front door; beach in front is relatively uncrowded. Dorms 800ptas, with breakfast

900ptas, with full board 1900ptas; over 26 300-500ptas extra. Sheets 300ptas for entire stay. Dishware, microwave, and fridges available until late at night. No alcohol. Washing machine and library. Silence after midnight. Curfew weeknights 2am, weekends 4am (otherwise enter at 7am). 3-day max. stay (flexible unless crowded). Open Feb. 15-Dec. 15.

Hotel Europa, C. Levante, 12-14 (tel. 96 284 07 50). From the tourist office, hop on the **La Marina** bus and ask to be let off at the C. Levante stop (105ptas). A regal hotel with elevator, solarium, and nice rooms. Singles with bath 3000ptas; doubles with shower 4000ptas, with bath 5000-5500ptas. Breakfast 350ptas.

Camping: The tourist office has directions to and details about the 3 campsites near the beach. The cheapest is **L'Alqueria** (tel. 96 284 04 70), on the La Marina bus route between Gandía and the beach (ask to be dropped off). 565ptas per person and 700ptas per tent. Open April-Sept.

Spinach, Av. del Mar, 33 (tel. 96 283 15 86), around the corner from the Playa de Piles bus stop. Fresh fruit shakes and sinful desserts. Tasty crepes like asparagus and ham (525ptas) will make your forearms bulge and your pipe toot. Open in summer daily noon-2am; in winter F-Su noon-2am.

Asador Josman, C. Ermita, 16 (tel. 96 284 05 30), 100m down the street from Hotel Europa; Levante becomes C. Ermita as it nears the highway. Whole chickens 800ptas; whole chicken with french fries for 4 people 1050ptas. Open in summer M-Sa 9am-3pm and 6:30-10pm, Su 9am-3pm; in winter F-Su 9am-3pm.

SIGHTS AND ENTERTAINMENT

There is not much here aside from the **beach,** but who cares? Wedged between the blue sea and the tiled Pg. Marítim, fine sands stretch for several km from the port to the condos. **La Marina buses,** Marqués de Campo, 14 (tel. 96 287 18 06), next to the tourist office and near the RENFE station, run along Pg. Marítim (departs every 12min., night service on weekends, 125ptas).

The pre-college crowd cashes in on the **discos.** The older duck into numerous **bars** lining C. Gutiérrez Más. Follow Marqués de Campo to the end, turn right on C. Magistrat Catala, and take the fifth right onto C. Gutiérrez Más. *Fiesta*-wise, Gandía has been honoring San Francisco, its patron saint, every September since 1310. The town also revs up for its version of *Las Fallas* between March 16 to 19.

■ Alicante (Alacant)

Sun-drenched Alicante (pop. 250,000) has somehow been chiseled into a gem, the most redeeming sort of resort town: it quietly charms as it dutifully entertains. Although a multifaceted nightlife energizes the city, Alicante's famous, mosaic-lined waterside Explanada is almost relaxing at sunset. Posh yachts ooze with wealth and pint-sized wooden fishing *lanchas* deck the bustling port, while the sizeable Playa Postiguet sprawls a few feet from the town's center, where lanky palms line the glossy avenues. High above the rows of sun-darkened bodies, the ancient *castillo,* spared by Franco when Alicante was the last Republican city to fall in the Civil War, guards the wicked tangle of streets in the cobblestoned *casco antiguo.*

ORIENTATION AND PRACTICAL INFORMATION

Avenida de la Estación runs straight out from the train station and becomes **Avenida Alfonso X el Sabio** after passing through **Plaza de los Luceros. Explanada d'Espanya** stretches along the waterfront between **Rambla Méndez Núñez** and **Avenida Federico Soto,** which reach back up to Av. Alfonso X El Sabio. Together these form a box of streets around which nearly all services cluster.

Transportation

Flights: Aeroport Internacional El Altet (tel. 96 691 90 00), 10km from town. **Alcoyana** (tel. 96 516 79 11) sends bus C-6 to the airport (departs every 40min. from Pl. Luceros and the airport, 105ptas). The tourist office has a schedule. **Iberia** (airport office tel. 96 691 91 00; 24hr. reservation and info tel. 902 400 500) flies to: Palma (3-4 per day); Barcelona (4 per day); Madrid (4-5 per day); Sevilla (3 per

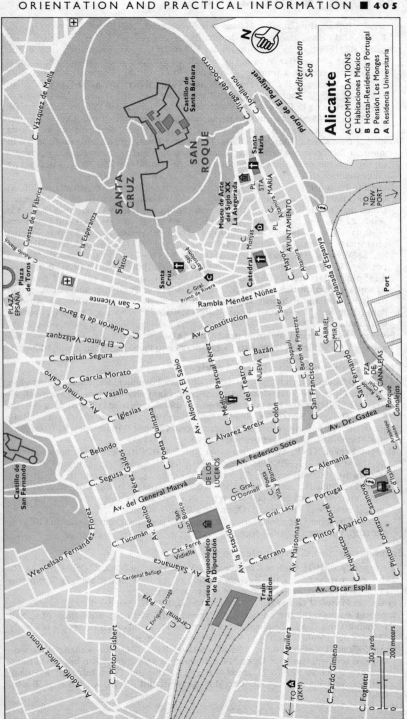

Alicante

ACCOMMODATIONS
C Habitaciones México
B Hostal-Residencia Portugal
D Pensión Les Monges
A Residencia Universitaria

Mediterranean Sea

Playa de El Postiguet

Castillo de Santa Bárbara

C. Virgen del Socorro
C. Jovellanos

SANTA CRUZ

SAN ROQUE

Santa María
PL. STA. MARÍA
C. Altamira

Museu de Arte del Siglo XX La Asegurada
C. Monjas
PL. AYUNTAMIENTO
C. Altamira
C. Mayor

TO NEW PORT

C. Vázquez de Mella
Cuesta de la Fábrica
C. de la Fábrica
C. la Esperanza
C. la Esperanza
Adolfo Blanch
C. Platos

Santa Cruz
C. San Bautista
C. Gral. Primo de Rivera

Catedral
C. Soler

Port

C. San Vicente
C. Calderón de la Barca
C. El Pintor Velázquez

Rambla Méndez Núñez

PLAZA EPSAÑA
Plaza de Toros

Av. Constitución

Esplanada d'Espanya

C. Capitán Segura
C. García Morato
Av. Carmelo Calvo
C. Vasallo
C. Iglesias

C. Alfonso X El Sablo
C. Poeta Quintana

C. Médico Pascual Pérez
C. Bazán
PL. NUEVA
C. del Teatro
C. Colón
C. Chapalí
C. Barón de Finestrat
PL. GABRIEL MIRÓ
C. San Francisco
C. San Fernando
PZA DE Av. CANALEJAS

C. Belando
C. Segusa
Pérez Galdós

C. Álvarez Sereix

Av. Federico Soto

C. Soler

Av. Dr. Gadea
Parque Canalejas
C. Arzobispo Loazes

Castillo de San Fernando

Wencelsão Fernandez Florez

PL. DE LOS LUCEROS

C. Gral. O'Donnell
C. Poeta Vila y Blanco

Av. del General Marvá

C. Tucumán
Av. Benito
C. San Juan Bosco

C. Gral. Lacy

C. Alemanía
C. Portugal
C. Pintor Aparicio
C. d'Italia
C. Arquecto Casanova

C. Pintor Lorenzo Casanova

C. Cat. Ferré Vidiella
Av. Salamanca
C. Cardenal Belluga

Museu Arqueológico de la Diputación

C. la Estación
C. Serrano
Av. Maisonnave

C. Enriqueta Ortega
C. Cardenal

Av. Aguilera

Train Station

Av. Oscar Esplá

C. Pintor Gisbert

Av. Adolfo Muñoz Alonso

TO A (2KM)

C. Pardo Gimeno
C. Fogletti

0   200 yards
0   200 meters

VALENCIA & MURCIA

week); Bilbao; the Canaries; Málaga. **Air Europa** (tel. 902 300 600) serves Oveido, Bilbao, and Palma, among other destinations.

Trains: RENFE, Estació Término (tel. 96 592 02 02), on Av. Salamanca, west of the city center and not far from El Corte Inglés. Info open daily 7am-midnight. Most destinations require a transfer. Direct to: Murcia (1½hr., departs every hr., 500-590ptas); Valencia (2hr., 2600ptas); Madrid (4hr., 9 per day, 3200-4700ptas); Barcelona (4½-6hr., 7 per day, includes 2 super-fast Euromed trains, 3600-4200ptas). **Ferrocarriles de la Generalitat Valenciana,** Est. Marina, Av. Villajoyosa, 2 (tel. 96 526 27 31), a 15min. walk down Explanada d'Espanya, away from Rambla Méndez Núñez; or bus G from the bus station and El Corte Inglés. Service along the Costa Blanca (see **Costa Blanca: Getting There and Away,** p. 409, for more info). In summer the **Trensnochador** (night train) runs all night to discos *("¡viva españá!")* on the beaches near Alicante (departs every hr., round-trip 150-700ptas depending on destination).

Buses: C. Portugal, 17 (tel. 96 513 07 00). To reach Explanada d'Espanya, turn left on Carrer d'Italia and take the third right on Av. Dr. Gadea, and then left at the waterfront. Buses A and G service the station (100ptas). **UBESA** (tel. 96 513 01 43) sends 22 buses per day to the Costa Blanca's Villajoyosa (335ptas) and Benidorm (430ptas). Also runs to: Calpe (630ptas); Jávea (855ptas); Altea (535ptas); Dénia (1015ptas); Valencia (1960ptas). **Mollá** (tel. 96 513 08 51) goes to Elche (M-F every hr., Sa-Su every 2hr., 5ptas). **Enatcar** (tel. 96 513 06 73) runs to: Granada (6hr., 6 per day, 3325ptas); Madrid (6½hr., 8 per day, 2895ptas); Málaga (8hr., 6 per day, 4435ptas); Barcelona (8hr., 8 per day, 4590ptas); Sevilla (10hr., 2 per day, 5740ptas). **Bilman Bus** (tel. 96 592 06 93) drives to Pamplona and San Sebastián (daily 8:35am and 8:20pm). **Linebús** to Brussels (daily 8am, 17500ptas); Amsterdam (daily 8am, 19500ptas); Paris (daily 11:30am, 15675ptas); Germany, Switzerland, and Italy.

Ferries: Flebasa lines leave from nearby **Dénia** (see p. 411).

Taxis: (tel. 96 525 25 11 or 96 510 16 11). Service to Platja Sant Joan about 1000ptas.

Tourist, Financial, and Local Services

Tourist Office: City, (tel. 96 520 03 77), on Playa Postiguet. Maps and info; English spoken. Open M-F 10am-8pm, Sa 10am-2pm. **Main city office** on C. Portugal, 17 (tel. 592 98 02), at the bus station. **Regional office,** Explanada d'Espanya, 2 (tel. 96 520 00 00; fax 96 520 02 43; email alicante.touristinfo@turisme.m400.gva.es). Info about the city and entire coast. English spoken. Open M-F 10am-8pm, Sa 10am-2pm and 3-8pm. Also an **airport branch** (tel. 96 528 50 11).

Budget Travel: TIVE, Av. Aguilera, 1 (tel. 96 590 07 70), near the train station off Av. Oscar Esplá. ISIC 700ptas. HI card 1800ptas. Open M-F 9am-1:30pm.

El Corte Inglés: Maisonnave, 53 (tel. 96 511 30 01). The mammoth department store. Free map. Currency exchange with no commission but bad rates, haircutting, cafeteria, restaurant, fax, and telephones. Its annex down the street has novels and guidebooks in English. Open M-Sa 10am-9:30pm.

Luggage Storage: At the bus station (200ptas per bag) and the train station (400ptas per bag). Open daily 8am-8:30pm.

Emergency and Communications

Emergency: dial 091. **Police: Comisaría,** C. Médico Pascual Pérez, 27 (tel. 96 514 22 22).

24hr. Pharmacy: Check the *Agenda* section of the local newspaper, *Información* (125ptas), or look in the window of any pharmacy.

Hospital: Hospital General, C. Maestro Alonzo, 109 (tel. 96 593 89 99).

Internet Access: On the corner of C. Gravina (the virtual continuation of C. San Fernando) and C. San Telmo, 1 block from the Pl. Ayuntamiento. Access is a hefty 250ptas per 15min. Open M-Sa 9am-1:30pm and 3-6pm.

Post Office: Pl. Gabriel Miró, 7 (tel. 96 521 99 84), off C. San Fernando. Lista de Correos services available. Open M-F 8am-9pm, Sa 9am-2pm. A 2nd **branch** at Bono Guarner, 2 (tel. 96 522 78 71), next to the RENFE Station. Open July-Sept. M-F 8am-2:30pm, Sa 9:30am-1pm; Oct.-June M-F 9am-2pm and 3-8pm, Sa 9am-2pm. **Postal Code:** 03000.

ACCOMMODATIONS AND CAMPING

Although there seem to be *pensiones* and *casas de huéspedes* on every corner, the number of clean rooms is considerably smaller. The tourist office keeps accommodations listings. Stay away from most places along C. San Fernando and around the Església de Santa María, and opt instead for the newer section of town. Good, cheap rooms require an early arrival or a reservation; in summer, the *hostales* below can be booked a week or more in advance. In winter, prices drop significantly.

Pensión Les Monges Palace, C. Monjas, 2 (tel. 96 521 50 46), behind the Ayuntamiento. In the center of the historic district a few blocks from the beach. A palace indeed: impeccable taste and charm have made this *pensión* a budget traveler's dream. Immaculate rooms are well decorated, and the newly constructed downstairs section features satellite-wired Trinitron TVs. A real Dalí hangs in the living room. The owner can direct you to the best restaurants and bars. A/C (600ptas per day), hair dryer, TV, and excellent mattress in each room. Singles 1700ptas, with sink 2000ptas, with shower 2300ptas, with bath 3000ptas; doubles: 3000ptas, with sink 3500ptas, with shower 3800ptas, with bath 4500ptas; triples with shower 5000ptas, with bath 5500ptas. Parking 800ptas per day. Winter heating. Visa, MC.

Residencia Universitaria (HI), Av. Orihuela, 59 (tel. 96 511 30 44). Take bus G (100ptas, make sure you're going the right way) to the last stop (the bus will stop for a while), directly behind the large *residencia*. Facilities are great, but the staff can be less than helpful. Hybrid college dormitory/one-star hotel—individual rooms, with private bath and A/C, cheap snack bar (wine 50ptas), big-screen TV, pool table, and foosball. Dorms 800ptas, with breakfast 900ptas, with 3 meals 1900ptas. Over 26 dorms 1100ptas, with breakfast 1400ptas, with 3 meals 2400ptas. HI members only. 3-day max. stay. Check-in before 10pm. Rooms scarce Sept.-June.

Habitaciones México, C. General Primo de Rivera, 10 (tel. 96 520 93 07; email mexrooms@lix.ctv.es), off the end of Av. Alfonso X El Sabio. Pristine rooms and a cozy TV-illuminated common room. Friendly owners organize a book swap and allow use of kitchen and free email. **Internet access** 800ptas per hr. Singles 1900ptas; doubles 3200ptas, with bath 3800ptas; triples 4500ptas. Laundry service 900ptas per load.

Hostal-Residencia Portugal, C. Portugal, 26 (tel. 96 592 92 44), across from the bus station. Friendly atmosphere nurtured by Ramón and his staff. The functional dining room/lounge has a color TV. Steamy interior rooms have fans. Singles 2200ptas; doubles 3700ptas, with bath 4400ptas. TV loan 400ptas.

Camping: Playa Mutxavista (tel. 96 565 45 26), 2nd class site near the beach. Take bus C-1. 530ptas per person and per tent. Open year-round.

FOOD

Most tourists refuel along the main pedestrian thoroughfare. Less traveled are the smaller, family-run, *bar-restaurantes* in the old city (between the cathedral and the castle steps). The most popular *terrazas* stuff **Calle San Francisco** with cheap *menús* and *tapas*. Locals and tourists devour *tapas* on the **Calle Mayor** and enjoy *churros* and coffee at Churrería Santa Faz, Miguel Soler, 14 (tel. 96 520 53 02), in front of the cathedral. A number of pricier restaurants line the new port. The **market** near Av. Alfonso X El Sabio sells picnic materials (open M-Sa 8am-2pm). For the real do-it-your-selfers, buy basics at **Supermarket Mercadona,** C. Alvarez Sereix, 5 (tel. 96 521 58 94), off Av. Federico Soto (open M-Th and Sa 9am-8pm, F 9am-8:30pm).

Capitol, C. Bazan, 45 (tel. 96 520 05 92), between Alfonso El Sabio and the Explanada. An appetizing 1150ptas *menú* (day and night) offers Spanish dishes in 4 courses. Open M-F 1-4:30pm and 8-11pm, Sa 1-4:30pm. Closed the first half of Aug.

La Taberna del Gormet, C. San Fernando, 10 (tel. 96 520 42 33). Head to this restaurant for some of the best *tapas* in town. Restaurant courses are pricey, but *tapas,* like *montaditos* (panini-like sandwiches with pate, tuna, or salmon, 150-

200ptas) and *croquetas de bacalao* (cod croquettes, 120ptas) are particularly delicious and reasonably priced at the lively bar. Open daily noon-midnight.

La Venta del Lobo, C. San Fernando, 48 (tel. 96 514 09 85), 2 blocks toward the center from Av. Dr. Gadea. A neighborhood grill ambitious enough to prepare specialties from all over Spain. Try *gazpacho andaluz* (370ptas) or *paella.* Four-course *menú* all-day 1075ptas. Open Tu-Sa 1-4pm and 8:30pm-midnight, Su 1-5pm.

Café Mediterraneo, C. Meca at C. San Fernando, 1½ blocks from the Explanada. A low-key, bustling, bright *café* that bursts with locals delighted by the 4-course *menú,* which includes *paella* and grilled tuna or salmon among its selections (975ptas). Open M-Sa 1-4 and 8-11pm, Su 1-4pm.

SIGHTS AND BEACHES

Complete with drawbridges, dark passageways, and hidden tunnels, **Castell de Santa Bárbara** (tel. 96 526 31 31) keeps silent guard over Alicante's bustling beach. *(Open daily Apr.-Sept. 10am-7:30pm; Oct.-Mar. 9am-6:30pm. Free.)* Built by the Carthaginians and recently reconstructed, the 200m-high fortress has a dry moat, dungeon, spooky ammunition storeroom, and an all-encompassing view of Alicante. A paved road from the old section of Alicante leads to the top; most people take the **elevator** from a hidden entrance on Av. Jovellanos, across the street from the beach and near the white crosswalk over the road. *(Elevator 400ptas.)* Bronze Age dowries and Roman statues from excavations throughout the province coexist inside the **Neoclassical Museu Arqueológic de la Diputación,** Av. Estación, 6 (tel. 96 512 13 00). *(Open M-F 10am-6pm. Free.)* Skipping ahead a few centuries, a crowd of Valencian modernist art pieces, along with a few Mirós, Picassos, Kandinskys, and Calders fraternize in the **Museu de Arte del Siglo XX La Asegurada** (tel. 96 514 07 68), at the east end of C. Mayor. *(Open Oct.-Apr. Tu-Sa 10am-1pm and 5-8pm, Su 10am-1pm; May.-Sept. Tu-Sa 10:30am-1:30pm and 6-9pm, Su 10:30am-1pm. Free.)*

Alicante's own **Playa de El Postiguet** attracts a disturbing number of patrons. Six-kilometer-long **Playa de San Juan** and **Playa del Mutxavista** are popular options, accessed by bus C-1 from Pl. Espanya and bus S from either Pl. Espanya or Pl. Mar (both depart every 15min., 105ptas) or the Alicante-Dénia train (20min., departs every hr., 105ptas). If crowds have soiled every inch, try Urbanova's **Platja de Saladar,** featuring a marked-off nudist area. Buses from the Alicante station run to Urbanova (20min., 5-7 per day, 100ptas). The regional tourist office also has a listing of *bandera azul* (blue flag) beaches (an award given by the European Union), accessible by the Alicante-Dénia rail line.

ENTERTAINMENT

Warm-weather nightlife centers on the **Platja de Sant Joan.** In July and August, **Ferrocarriles de la Generalitat Valenciana** runs special **Trensnochador** night trains from Est. Marina to several points along the beach (departs every hr. 9pm-7am, round-trip 100-700ptas depending on destination). Pick up a schedule, along with discounts on cover charges, at the tourist office. A **taxi** for up to four people from Alicante to Platja de Sant Joan costs about 1000ptas. A night **Buho-Bus** leaves from Pl. Ayuntamiento to San Juan (Friday and Saturday nights from 12:30 to 6:30am. **Voy Voy,** on Av. Niza at the "Discotecas" night train stop, has disco to go go both inside and out (beer from 350ptas; open nightly until 6am). *Bares-musicales* line side streets off the beach to the right of the same train stop. The **Copity** disco, on Av. Condomina, is a long walk or short taxi ride away from the "Condomina" night train stop. The "Disco Benidorm" stop (round-trip 650ptas), in package-tour crazy Benidorm, has hard-core *discotecas* like **Penélope, Pachá, KM,** and **Insomnia** (open nightly until 9am; cover from 1500ptas).

For those in search of parties closer to home, Alicante itself offers a number of popular discotecas and bars. In the old section of town, **El Barne,** students hop from one *bar-musical* to the next. Popular with both gay and straight dancers is **Celestial Copas** on C. San Pascual. **Rosé** on C. San Juan Bosco also attracts a gay crowd, while **Desdén** on C. Santo Tomás attracts an astronomical number of Americans. Closer to the water is **Buggatti** (tel. 96 521 06 46), on C. San Fernando (cover 1500ptas includes one drink, but women usually get in free; open nightly until 5:30am). On the Explanada, at Pl. Canelejas, a **petit Pachá** welcomes those who don't want to brave the bigger brother in Benidorm. Lined with late-night bars, *bares-musicales,* and a lively after-hours scene, the **new port** throbs with masses of tourists and sunglass vendors in the shadow of the posh yachts, providing some quality people-watching.

From June 20 to 24, the *casco antiguo* bursts with celebration for the **Festival de Sant Joan,** comprised of romping *fogueres* (symbolic or satiric effigies). The figures burn on the June 24, but the party continues with breathtaking nightly fireworks. On the last day, a marching band and parade of candy hurlers whet people's appetites for next year's festival. The **Verge del Remei** procession takes place on August 3; pilgrims trek to the monastery of Santa Faz the following Thursday. Alicante honors La Virgen del Demedio all summer with the **Fiestas del Verano,** including concerts and theatrical performances often held in the new open-air theater on the port; inquire at the tourist office for a schedule.

■ Near Alicante

Isla Tabarca (tel. 902 10 09 10), an island 15km south of Alicante, was once a prison. Today, it is a natural reserve and a great place for **SCUBA diving.** Cruceros Kon Tiki **boats** (tel. 96 521 63 96) leave for Tabarca from the Explanada d'Espanya (30min.; in summer 4 per day leave 10:30am-3:30pm, and return 2pm-7:30pm, in winter 1 per day; round-trip 1700ptas). **Cuevas de Canalobre** (tel. 96 569 92 50) are spectacular, stalagmited caves, 24km north of Alicante. The caves hang over the splendid coastline, above the tiny village of **Busot.** (Open daily June 21-Sept. 10:30am-9:50pm; Oct.-June 20 11am-6:50pm. 550ptas.) Get there on **Alcoyana bus** C-14 (tel. 96 513 01 04; 3 per day, 280ptas). **Jijona,** 37km north of Alicante, is home of the wondrous **Turrones El Lobo** (tel. 96 561 02 25), a nougat factory. Drool over free samples of the traditional honey and almond Spanish Christmas candy, *turrón,* that has made Jijona a household name. (Guided tours depart every 30min. Open daily 9:30am-1pm and 4-8pm.)

COSTA BLANCA

The "white coast" that extends from Dénia through Calpe, Alicante, and Elche down to Torrevieja, derives its name from the fine, white sand of its shores. A varied terrain of hills blanketed with cherry blossoms, craggy mountains, lush pine-layered hillsides, and natural lagoons envelop densely inhabited coastal burghs. Altea, Calpe, Dénia, and especially Jávea offer relief from the disco-droves that energize Alicante and Benidorm, but they too have their fare share of tourists. The rail line out of Alicante snakes through the mountains, hugging the coast and connecting most towns; UBESA buses go to almost all coastal towns.

■ Getting There and Away

UBESA (in Valencia tel. 96 340 08 55; in Gandía tel. 96 296 50 66; in Dénia tel. 96 643 50 45; in Calpe tel. 96 583 90 29; in Benidorm tel. 96 585 01 51; in Alicante tel. 96 513 01 43) runs **buses** every hour from 6:30am to 9pm between Alicante and Valencia. From **Valencia to Alicante,** buses run to: Gandía (1hr., 13 per day); Dénia (2hr., 8 per day); Javea (2hr., 6 per day); Calpe, Altea, and Benidorm (3-3½hr., 13 per day); Vila-Joiosa (4hr., 13 per day, 6:30am-6pm); and Alicante (4½hr., 13 per day, 6:30am-6pm). From **Alicante to Valencia** buses run to: Vila-Joiosa (30min., 16 per day); Benidorm (1hr., 16 per day); Altea (1¼hr., 16 per day); Calpe (1½hr., 16 per day); Javea (2½hr., 5 per day); and Dénia (2½hr., 11 per day). Only buses that leave by 6pm make it all the way to Valencia.

Ferrocarrils de la Generalitat Valenciana (in Alicante tel. 96 526 27 31), with its Alicante-Dénia line, competes with UBESA and offers similar prices and frequencies, but added stops at beaches near Alicante (San Juan, El Campello). Trains depart Alicante every hour on the hour from 6am to 9pm to: San Juan (15min.); El Campello (25min.); Vila-Joiosa (1hr.); Benidorm (1¼hr.); and Altea (1½hr.). Trains leaving at an even-numbered hour continue to Calpe (1¾hr.) and Dénia (2¼hr.). From Dénia and Calpe, trains return to Alicante every 2 hours (6:25am-7:25pm), while from Altea, Benidorm, Vila-Joiosa, El Campello, and San Juan trains depart every hour (6:24am-10:24pm). Railpasses are not valid on these trains. **Trensnochador,** the night train running out of Alicante, goes as far as Altea in the summer (departs every hr., 11pm-6am).

■ Altea

A whitewashed beach town clustered on a small hill, Altea makes for a relaxing and pleasant daytrip from Alicante. From the pebbled beach, narrow, stone streets and steps wind up to **Plaza de la Iglesia.** Shaded by the cobalt dome of the church of the **Virgen del Consuelo,** the square commands breathtaking views of the turquoise Mediterranean. An extended meal or drink here is reason enough to visit—the crooked streets lead to other squares that offer glimpses of the sea framed by bright white houses. Altea celebrates the **Fiestas de Moros y Cristianos** during the last week of September, when the city erupts with music, gunpowder, and dance.

For transportation to and from Altea, see **Getting There and Away,** p. 409. Both trains and buses stop at the foot of the hill and along the coast on C. La Mar (coming out of the station, head left to go toward the center). If arriving by bus from Alicante, get off at the 1st stop; if arriving from Valencia, get off at the 2nd stop. The **tourist office** is on C. Sant Pere, 9 (tel. 96 584 41 14; fax 96 584 42 13), parallel to C. La Mar (open M-F 10am-2pm and 5-8pm, Sa 10am-2pm). To get to the office from either the train station or the bus stop, walk 50m toward the sea to C. Sant Pere. In **emergencies,** dial 091. The **post office** (tel. 96 584 01 74) is on Av. Alt Rei en Jaume I, in the old town on the hill. The tourist office can direct visitors to lodgings and campsites should you wish to spend the night.

■ Calpe (Calp)

Stepping into Calpe is like stepping into a Dalí landscape mobbed with sun-seeking package vacationers. Sixty-two kilometers northeast of Alicante, the whitewashed town cowers beneath the **Peñó d'Ifach** (327m), a gargantuan, flat-topped rock protrusion whose precipitous face drops straight to the sea. If you decide to climb the surreal rock (round-trip 2hr.), wear sneakers, bring water, and scrap the excess baggage. It's not a bad hike, but do it during the day, since ghosts in goats' clothing are rumored to haunt the rock and butt unwary travelers over the cliff at full moon. Farther north hang the hard rock and caves of the easterly **Cabo de la Nao,** from which you can see Ibiza. Around the bend from the *cabo,* a castle and watchtower have protected the old fishing village of **Moraira** from freeloading pirates for centuries (buses run from Calpe).

Like Dalí, commercialized Calpe attracts hordes of *madrileños* and the European bourgeoisie. The main avenue, **Gabriel Miró,** descends to **Platja Arena-Bol,** which gets deep quickly (a plus), but has a rocky, floral bottom (a minus). **Platja Levante,** beyond the Peñó, and the cove of **Calalga** bear the flapping *bandera azúl.* A free **tourist train** (tel. 96 583 69 20), leaving from the train station, gives rides around the city (M-F 6pm). Leaving from the port, **boats** take tourists out on recreational rides.

For transportation info, see **Getting There and Away,** p. 409. UBESA **buses** stop 2km from the beach at C. Capitán Pérez Jorda. To get to town, head across the intersection (away from the bus's road), and curve downhill to the left on Av. Masnou. If you come in by train (not as convenient), take a municipal bus downhill past the bus station and to the beach (1 per hr., 90ptas)—otherwise it's an arduous walk.

VALENCIA & MURCIA

The **tourist office,** Av. Ejércitos Españoles, 62 (tel. 96 583 12 50), between the old town and the beach, has all the info you need on Costa Blanca beaches (open in summer M-Sa 9am-9pm, Su 10:30am-2pm; off-season hours vary). The **post office** (tel. 96 583 08 84), on C. 18 de Julio, lies in the old town (open M-Sa 8:30am-2:30pm, Sa 9:30am-1:30pm). Hang your hat at the bright and comfortable English-run **Pensión Céntrica,** Pl. Ifach (tel. 96 583 55 28). With your back to the water, take a right off Av. Gabriel Miró at the Banesto bank. TV lounge and carpeted floors are a refreshing welcome after a day in the sun. (1500ptas per person.) Deserving backpackers can try **Camping La Merced** (tel. 96 583 00 97), a 2nd-class site 400m from the beach (520ptas per person and per tent). The most reasonably-priced **restaurants** line the steep incline toward the older *pueblo.* Joints lining Av. Miró offer *bocadillos* for 300 to 450ptas.

■ Elche (Elx)

An oasis city surrounded by one of Europe's only palm forests, Elche, 23km from Alicante, is a tropical paradise. Locals, however, have no time to lounge—they're busy supplying Spain with their highly-regarded footwear. The **Dama de Elche,** Spain's finest example of pre-Roman sculpture, hails from here, although it rests at the Museo Arqueológico Nacional in Madrid (see **Museums,** p. 103). At the corner of Av. Ferrocarril and Po. Estación begins the **Parque Municipal,** where doves and palm trees glide and sway above subtropical flora and imitation arabic fountains. A mini-train tours the park and another baby palm forest across the street (departs every ½hr., 300ptas). Of the parks and public gardens that fill odd corners of the city, the most beautiful is the **Hort del Cura** (Orchard of the Priest), where magnificent trees shade colorful flower beds (open in summer 9am-9pm; in winter 9am-6pm; 300ptas).

Papal orders allow Elche to host from August 11 to 13 the **Misteri d'Elx,** a 14th-century religious musical once forbidden by the Council of Trent (tourist office has ticket info). The work includes the only interpretation of Mary's ascent to heaven. On August 13, the city shuts off its lights and sets the sky ablaze with 220 million *pesetas'* worth of Roman Candles to celebrate **Nit de L'Alba** (Night of the Dawn). During even numbered years, repeat performances occur on October 31 and November 1.

The train station is **Estación Parque,** at Av. Ferrocarril Estación. The **bus station** (tel. 96 545 58 58) is on Av. Llibertat, serving Alicante and the private, quietly rolling sand dunes of La Marina d'Elx (M-Sa 5 buses per day, 210ptas). For transportation details on getting to and from Elche, see **Getting There and Away,** p. 409. To get to the town center and tourist office from the bus and train stations on Av. Ferrocarril Este, go left leaving either station and left again on Po. Estación. The **tourist office** (tel. 96 545 27 47) sits on Pl. Parc, at the end of Po. Estación (open in summer M-F 9:30am-2:15pm and 4:15-7:45pm, Sa-Su 10:15am-1:15pm; in winter M 9am-2:30pm). The **police station** (tel. 96 542 25 00) is also in Parque Project. The **post office** (tel. 96 544 69 11) is in Parque Project.

■ Dénia

Halfway between Valencia and Alicante on the promontory that forms the Golfo de Valencia, Dénia (named by the Greeks for Diana, goddess of the hunt, the moon, and purity), is an upscale family resort, where only bright rowboats interrupt the smooth sweep of *platja.* Its harbor, however, serves as an important ferry connection to the Balearic Islands, and in the summer, the town goes nuts with its wild festivals.

PRACTICAL INFORMATION The **train station** (tel. 96 578 04 45) is on C. Calderón. The **UBESA bus station** is on Pl. Arxiduc Carles. Local buses leave from the tourist office to big sandy retreats (105ptas). To head Balearicward by sea, consult **Flebasa Lines** (tel. 96 578 40 11), Puerto de Dénia. Boats float to Ibiza, Palma, and back. **Pitra car ferries** (tel. 971 19 10 68) also depart from Estació Marítime in Dénia (tel. 96 642 31 20) to the islands. For full transportation info, see **Balearic Islands: Getting There and Away,** p. 367.

Most **tourist services,** including local buses, trains, ferries, the tourist office, and the post office, are clustered on **Calle Patricio Fernandez,** running straight to the port. Take a left out of the Enactean/UBESA bus office, walk out of the plaza and turn left onto C. Patricio Fernandez to reach the center of town. The **tourist office,** C. Glorieta Oculista Baigues, 9 (tel. 96 642 23 67), 30m inland from Estación Marítime, directs to beach and bed options (open July-Sept. M-F 9am-8pm, Sa 9am-2pm and 4-8pm, Su 10am-1pm and 4-8pm; Oct.-June M-F 9:30am-1:30pm and 4:30-7:30pm, Sa 10am-1pm). The **post office,** C. Patricio Ferrándiz, 38 (tel. 96 578 15 33), is west of the tourist office (open M-F 8:30am-2:30pm, Sa 9:30am-1pm).

ACCOMMODATIONS AND FOOD Dénia is a place for padded wallets (bring your own). The tourist office has a list of (expensive) accommodations; otherwise try **Hostal Comercio,** C. de la Vía, 43 (tel. 96 578 00 71), between the tourist office and the bus station. Its roomy rooms have TVs, phones, and baths tiled in brilliant blue. (Singles 3000ptas; doubles 5300ptas.) Among several campgrounds, **Camping Las Marinas,** C. Les Bovetes Nord, 4 (tel. 96 578 14 46), is a 3km bus ride (105ptas) from Platja Jorge Joan (500ptas per person and per tent; open Nov.-Sept.). Say *bocadillo* and get used to it, because they are the only budget meal in town. Restaurants hover around **Calle Marqués de Campo.**

SIGHTS AND ENTERTAINMENT An 18th-century **castle** (tel. 96 642 06 56) sprawls across the hill overlooking the marina (open June-Sept. 10am-1:30pm and 5-8:30pm; Oct.-May 10am-1pm and 3-6pm; 300ptas). A tourist train chugs to the castle from outside the tourist office (departs every 30min., 10am-1pm and 5-8pm, 500ptas includes ride and entrance to castle). Dénia holds a mini **Fallas festival** from March 16 to 19, burning effigies on the final midnight. During **Festa Major** (early July), locals prove they're just as ballsy as their fellow countrymen in Pamplona: bulls and fans dive simultaneously into a pool of water, a feat known as **Bous a la mar.** During the second week of July, the **Fiestas de la Santísima Sangre** (Holy Blood) feature street dances, concerts, mock battles, and wild fireworks over the harbor. The colorful parades and religious plays of the **Moros y Cristianos** celebration take place between August 14 and 16.

■ Jávea (Xàbia)

Jávea's wide, sheltered position offers tranquil waters that have yet to be ruined completely by kicking and screaming tourists—for now, the town still lives up to its nickname as the "Jewel of the Costa Blanca." Although a municipal bus runs (2km inland) to the port and then on to a larger beach, Jávea's hidden beauties—its coves, capes, and cliffs—are only accessible by bike, car, or foot. A number of secluded coves line the coast south of the port and **El Arenal.** The most populated beaches, **Playa La Granadella, Playa de Ambolo** (for nudies), and **Playa La Barraca,** are serene and accessible. Jávea's **Moros y Cristianos festival** erupts the second fortnight of July; fireworks jolt wide-eyed tourists roaming among costumed Moors and Christians.

Inconvenient **public transportation** to Jávea has spared the town from tourist havoc. UBESA buses stop at C. Príncipe de Asturias. To get to the port, walk up C. Príncipe de Asturias, which (after a couple bends), becomes Av. Alicante. The **municipal bus** to the port passes here (departs every 30min.-1hr. 8am-2pm and 4-10pm). If you don't feel like waiting, continue walking down Av. Alicante, which runs directly to the port (20min.). For complete transportation info on getting to and from Jávea, see **Getting There and Away,** p. 409. The regional **tourist office,** Pl. Almirante Bastarreche, 24 (tel. 96 579 07 36; fax 96 579 60 57), is at the port; **another office** lies on Playa Arenal (open M-F 9am-2pm and 5-9pm, Sa 10am-2pm and 5-9pm, Su 10am-2pm). The **municipal police,** Pl. Constitución, 6, respond at (tel. 96 579 00 81), while the **Civil Guard** answer at (tel. 96 579 10 85). For **medical emergencies,** call the Centro de Salud (tel. 96 579 58 11). To rent a **bike,** head to Jávea's Auda Marina Española, 13 (tel. 96 646 11 50), at the port.

Jávea's remote location may convince you to spend the night. If so, **Pensión La Favorita,** C. Magallanes, 4 (tel. 96 579 04 77), offers comfortable rooms near the port (singles 2800; doubles 4300-6400ptas). To get to the *pensión*, follow the signs near the tourist office. **Camping Jávea,** Ctra. Cabo de la Nao, km 1 (tel. 96 579 10 70), is a 2nd-class site between the town and the port. **Restaurants** with reasonable *menús* line C. Andrés Lambert, away from the port. Particularly appetizing is **La Yaya,** C. Andrés Lambert, 8 (tel. 96 646 09 20), offering a 1000ptas *menú* with delicious bread and *mantequilla con ajo* (garlic butter; open daily 11am-4pm and 6-11pm).

■ Murcia

Skirted by citrus orchards, quiet Murcia was unheeded until the 13th century when the Moors and then the Christians spontaneously declared it the region's capital. Today, Murcia thrives on university-infused energy when the temperatures are right (fall and spring), but dies in the roasting summer when everyone flees to the Mediterranean. The sightseer must have a high tolerance for oceans of 1960s-style apartment buildings to find Murcia's few islands of tranquility and architectural beauty. An abundance of beachward buses and frequent trains to Lorca may be Murcia's most appealing feature.

ORIENTATION AND PRACTICAL INFORMATION

To lazy travelers' dismay, most places of interest scatter around the town's periphery. The **Río Segura** divides the city, with sights and services in the northern half and the train station in the southern half, a marathon walk to town (the wise take bus #9 or 11). Major avenues spread out from **Plaza Circular. Gran Vía de Alfonso X El Sabio** runs toward the river, becoming C. Traperia. The cathedral is in **Plaza Cardenal Belluga,** at C. Traperia's end. The bus station is to the west of town (10min. walk).

Transportation

Flights: Aeropuerto San Javier (tel. 968 17 20 00). **Iberia** heads to Madrid and Barcelona. **British Airways** flies 4 times per week to London.

Trains: Estació del Carmen (RENFE tel. 968 25 21 54), on C. Industria. Ticket window open daily 6am-11pm. To: Lorca (1hr., 1 per hr., 515ptas); Alicante (1½hr., 9-17 per day, 515ptas); Valencia (3-4½hr., 3 per day, 1800-3000ptas); Madrid (4-5hr., 4 per day, 4900-5900ptas); Barcelona (7-10hr., 3 per day, 4600-6000ptas). **RENFE office,** is on C. Barrio Nuevo. Open M-F 9am-1pm and 4:30-7:30pm.

Buses: (tel. 968 29 22 11) C. San Andrés, behind the Museo Salzillo. Info window open daily 7am-10pm. To Elche (50min., 600ptas) and Lorca (1½hr., 800ptas). **Alsina Graells** (tel. 968 29 16 12); info window open M-F 8am-4pm and 6-10pm, Sa-Su 8-11:30am, 2-4pm and 8-10pm. To: Granada (4-5hr., 6 per day, 2430ptas); Sevilla (7-9hr., 3 per day, 4860ptas); Córdoba (9hr., 1 per day, 4135ptas). **La Albatarense/ Alsa** (tel. 968 29 16 23) goes to Valencia (3¾ hr., 3-7 per day, 1850ptas) and Alicante (9-17 per day, 600ptas). **Gimenez Garcia Hermanos** (tel. 968 29 19 11) services La Manga (6 per day, 655ptas). **Busmar** (tel. 968 25 00 88) runs to Lo Pagán and Santiago de La Ribera on the Mar Menor (1hr., departs every hr., 375ptas). **Enatcar** (tel. 968 29 41 26) drives to Madrid (12 per day, 3140ptas) and Barcelona (6 per day, 5255ptas).

Public Transportation: Municipal buses (tel. 968 25 00 88) cover the city and outskirts. Fare 100ptas. Route maps available at municipal tourist office. Bus #9 runs a circular route past the train and bus stations; bus #3 passes near the bus station.

Taxis: (tel. 968 29 77 00 or 968 24 88 00).

Tourist, Financial, and Local Services

Tourist Office: Regional: C. San Cristobal, 6 (tel. 968 36 61 00; fax 968 36 61 10), behind the casino. Enthusiastic staff is ready to unload truckloads of slick pamphlets on the city and province. Open Aug. M-F 9:30am-2:30pm; in rest of summer M-F 9:30am-2:30pm and 5:30-7:30pm, Sa 11am-1:30pm; in winter M-F 9am-2pm and 5-7pm, Sa 11am-1:30pm. **Municipal:** Palacio Almudí, C. Plano San Francisco, s/

n (tel. 968 21 98 01, ext. 23). From the train station take bus #9, from the bus station take bus #3 or 9. Smaller than the regional one, but friendly staff offers a map and sound advice. Open in summer M-F 9am-2:30pm; in winter M-F 9am-2:30pm and 5-7:30pm.

El Corte Inglés: Av. Libertad (tel. 968 29 80 50). The old standby gives away maps and has **currency exchange.** Also offers novels and guidebooks in English, haircutting, cafeteria, restaurant, and telephones. Open M-Sa 10am-9:30pm.

Budget Travel: TIVE, Conde Roche, s/n (tel. 968 21 32 61) offers discounted airline tickets, ISIC cards, and HI cards. Open M-F 9am-2pm, Sa 9am-noon.

Luggage Storage: At the bus station (300ptas per bag). Open 24hr. At the train station (300-600ptas per day). Open 6am-11pm.

Emergency and Communications

Emergency: dial 091 or 092. **Police:** C. Isaac Albéniz, 10 (tel. 968 26 66 00).

Late-Night Pharmacy: Check listings in *La Opinión de Murcia* (local paper, 125ptas) or postings outside any pharmacy.

Hospital: Hospital General Universitario, Av. Intendente, Jorge Palacios, 1 (tel. 968 25 69 00).

Post Office: Pl. Circular, 8a (tel. 968 24 12 43 or 902 197 197), where Av. Primo de Ribera connects to the plaza, in a modern building. Open M-F 8:30am-8:30pm, Sa 9:30am-2pm. **Postal Code:** 30001 for the center of town.

ACCOMMODATIONS AND FOOD

When Murcia steams up and empties out in summer, finding a room is a breeze, but winter competition is a bit stiffer. Prices are high year-round. **Plaça San Juan** is nothing but restaurants, while *mesones* fill **Plaça de Julián Romea.** Happily, all are pretty local in flavor due to the small number of tourists. Murcians end up with a vitamin surplus from veggies produced in the surrounding countryside. *Paella murciana* is vegetarian *paella.* Locals also nibble on *hueva de mujo* (millet roe). Sample the harvest at the **market** on C. Verónicas (open M-Sa 9am-1pm). **Simago,** Av. de la Libertad, challenges Corte Ingles' chi-chi grocery store across the street (open 9am-9pm).

Hostal Legazpi, Av. Miguel de Cervantes, 8 (tel. 968 29 30 81; fax 968 29 91 27). Take bus #9 from the train or bus station to the last Ronda Norte stop (near the Renault dealership), and turn the corner to the right. Ample rooms with TV and heavenly ceiling fans. A bit outside of the center. Singles 2000ptas, with bath 2800ptas; doubles 4000ptas, with bath 4400ptas; triples with bath 6300ptas. Garage 500ptas per day.

Hostal-Residencia Murcia, C. Vinadel, 6 (tel. 968 21 99 63), off Pl. Santa Isabel; bus #11 from the train station. TVs, phones, and decorations from Sonny and Cher's heyday embellish rooms being renovated this year. A/C should be running by late 1998. Singles 2500ptas, with bath 3500ptas; doubles 5000ptas, with bath 7000ptas.

Tío Sentao, C. La Manga, 12 (tel. 968 29 10 13), hidden off Pl. Agustinas, 1 block from the Convento de Agustinas. From the bus station, take a right on C. Dr. Jesús Quesada, a left at Pl. San Agustín, and then right on C. Sta. Cecilia. Turn right on C. Doctrinos, left on C. Baeza, and then left on C. La Manga. A warm, family restaurant serving authentic Murcian fare in a colorful *comedor. Morcilla* (fried sausage with onions) 50ptas, *menú* 1000ptas. Open daily 1-4pm and 7pm-midnight.

Mesón el Corral de José Luís, Pl. Santo Domingo, 23-24 (tel. 968 21 45 97). Chefs in the open kitchen toss together Murcian cuisine and bring it to outdoor customers taking in the sights of the town's main plaza. *Tapas* 150-600ptas. Afternoon *menú* 1150ptas. Open daily 11am-4pm and 8pm-midnight.

Cocina de Vives Comidas Para Llevar, C. Frenería y Meseguer, 7 (tel. 968 212 266), right behind the Ayuntamiento. Amazingly cheap fare. Specialty main courses, like meat-filled eggplant or rice with rabbit and snails vary by the day and run from 250-450ptas. Most take their food out, but there are tables and chairs, too. Open daily 1-4pm and 8-10pm.

SIGHTS AND ENTERTAINMENT

The palatial **Casino de Murcia** (Casino Cultural), C. Traperia, 18 (tel. 968 21 22 55), began as a social club for the town's 19th- and 20th-century bourgeoisie. *(Open daily 9:30am-9pm. 100ptas.)* Rooms inside were designed according to a particular theme. Mammoth, implausibly ornate chandeliers fill the **Versailles ballroom.** *(100ptas to illuminate chandeliers.)* The English billiard room offers a whiff of Pall Mall, while the Arabic patio and its multicolored, glass doors simulate the Alhambra. Look for the Oxfordian **library** with plush leather chairs and a gilt powder room. Next door to the casino, 400 years of procrastination made Murcia's **cathedral**, Pl. Cruz, 2 (tel. 968 21 63 44; buses #2 or 3), an odd confusion of architectural styles, including an oft-photographed Baroque facade, a Gothic entrance, and a Renaissance tower. *(Open daily in summer 10am-1pm and 6-8pm; in winter 10am-1pm and 5-7pm. Tower closed for renovations in 1998; call for an update.)*

The **Museo de Arqueología de Murcia,** Gran Vía Alfonso X El Sabio, 9 (tel. 968 23 46 02), one of the finest in Spain, chronicles provincial history from prehistoric times. *(Open July-Aug. M-F 10am-2pm; Sept.-June M-F 9am-2pm and 5-8pm, Sa 10am-1:30pm. 75ptas.)* The **Museo de Bellas Artes,** C. Obispo Frutos, 12 (tel. 968 23 93 46), near the university, boasts a fine collection of Iberian painting and sculpture. *(Open July-Aug. M-F 9am-2pm; Sept.-June M-F 9am-2pm and 5-8pm, Sa 10am-2pm.)* The **Museo Taurino** (tel. 968 28 59 76), within the Jardín del Salitre between Pl. Circular and the bus station, displays bullfighting memorabilia, matador costumes, and mounted bulls' heads that pay homage to particularly valorous beasts. *(Open M-F 10am-2pm and 5-8pm. Free.)* Of questionable taste is the enshrinement of José Manuel Calvo Benichon's shredded, bloody shirt, worn the day he was gored to death in Sevilla by his 598kg opponent.

On Thursday through Saturday nights, local university students (no school on Fridays) study the effects of alcohol at **bars** near C. Saavedra Fajardo (near the main campus). On the day before Easter the **Fiestas de Primavera** starts a week-long harvest celebration bringing jazz and theater to the already crowded streets.

Just outside of Murcia, the Río Espuña courses through rocky mountains dotted with the pines and sagebrush of the **Parque Natural Sierra Espuña** (highest elevation 1585m). The flowers explode into dazzling color in springtime, the best season to visit the park. Accommodations range from a campsite and a hostel to mountainside refuges. Ask about camping at the tourist office.

■ Near Murcia: Lorca

A stroll through Lorca, from its colorful, modern train station to its crumbling medieval castle, leads you through centuries of aesthetic and economic disparities. Medieval ghettos, Renaissance artistry, Baroque vainglory, post-Franco urban expansion, and contemporary elitism demarcate the town's small but distinct neighborhoods.

Battles between Romans and Visigoths and between Christians and Muslims left Lorca without an orange grove, much less a full-fledged *huerta* (orchard). Yet each conquering force left its own peculiar imprint on the **castillo** atop Lorca's central hill, a 15-minute walk from Pl. Espanya (always open and free). The Moors built the **Torre Espolón** shortly before the city fell to Alfonso el Sabio of Castilla, who in self-adulation ordered the construction of the **Torre Alfonsín.** The ruins of Lorca's first church, the **Ermita de San Clemente,** deteriorate at the castle's eastern edge. Once Granada fell in 1492, inhabitants left the fortresses and moved to the bottom of the slope, leaving in their wake three idyllic churches—**Santa María, San Juan,** and **San Pedro.** Starting anew, Lorcans erected six monasteries and the **Colegiata de San Particio.** Of the many well-preserved private residences, **Casa de Guevarra,** also a 16th-century pharmacy, has wreathed columns and intricate carvings (open M-F 11am-1pm and 5-7pm). Behind the train station are the opulent estates of **Las Alamedas,** with aromatic gardens and red clay paths, tucked away from the city center.

Trains (tel. 968 46 69 98) toot by Av. Estació, parallel to C. Juan Carlos I (round-trip to Murcia 525-560ptas). Next door, the **bus station** (tel. 968 46 92 70) sends Trapemusa buses to Murcia (departs every hr., 600ptas), Barcelona, Granada, Alicante,

Valencia, and points in Andalucía. The **tourist office** (tel. 968 46 61 57) in Casa de Guevarra on C. Lópes Gisbert, doles out a detailed map. To get there from the train station, take the pedestrian path on to C. Juan Carlos I, then left on C. E. García Navarro. (Open M-F 9:30am-1:30pm and 5:30-7:30pm, Sa 10am-1pm.) **Luggage storage** is available in the bus station (daily 6am-11pm, 400ptas). In an **emergency**, call 091 or 092. The **police** come running from C. Villascusa (tel. 968 44 33 98). The **post office** (tel. 968 46 77 75) is on C. Museo Valiente (open M-Sa 8am-3pm).

Accommodations are cheap in arid Lorca. Shining ceramic tiles and new wicker furniture are the siren calls of **Hostal del Carmen,** C. Rincón de los Valientes, 3 (tel. 968 46 64 59), off C. Nogalte (singles 1500ptas, with bath 2000ptas; doubles with bath 4000ptas). From the train or bus station, head across to C. Juan Carlos I, and head on C. Serrallo past a little plaza until you hit C. Nogalte. Take a left, and then the 3rd right on a dead-end street. **Pensión La Alberca,** Pl. Juan Moreno, 1 (tel. 968 40 65 16), across from the archaeological museum, is cheaper. The pink-and-white **Restaurante Rincón de los Valientes,** C. Rincón de los Valientes, 13 (tel. 968 44 12 63), concocts a 900 to 1000ptas homestyle *menú* (open Tu-Su 1:30-4pm and 8pm-midnight).

Valiant Visigoth Vixens

Lorca's proximity to Granada made the province an attractive stronghold during the Muslim invasion in the 8th century. When almost the entire peninsula had been conquered by the Moors, Lorca remained one of the few provinces under Christian Visigoth rule. Eager to solidify his kingdom, Muslim leader Abd al-Aziz attacked the dwindling Visigoth troops commanded by one Theodomir. Suffering serious casualties, the Christian troops were forced to flee to Orihuela. Supposing that his Christian nemesis' troops were near surrender, Abd launched yet another attack. His machinations, however, were thwarted by a large line of violent Visigoth warriors who bravely stood guard over Orihuela. Immediately canceling the attack, Abd agreed to a pact with the Christians; and for many years the province of Lorca survived as an important Christian nucleus in an otherwise Muslim world. What the Moor leader never learned, however, was that the brave Visigoth defenders were actually women disguised as warriors.

■ Near Lorca: Águilas

Tourists delight in the fortified medieval town of Águilas (tourist office tel. 968 41 33 03), 30 minutes from Lorca and one hour from Murcia by bus or along the Cercanías train line (5 per day). Its popularity owes much to its 35 **coves,** picturesque beaches, lush greenery, iron pier on the Bay of Hornillo, and **Tower of Cope** (on the wonderfully-named Cape of Cope).

■ La Manga del Mar Menor

A geographic fluke created the popular vacation spot known as La Manga (sleeve) of the Mar Menor. Centuries of marine deposits settled over a small ridge of volcanic origin and then solidified into a 19km strip of land separating the calm, tepid Mar Menor from the luxurious breaks of the Mediterranean. **Windsurfers** take advantage of the waveless Mar Menor, while beachlovers kick it in the white sands and crystal waters of the Mediterranean. The two seas are only a somersault apart, and despite the 1963 Law of Touristic Interest Centers that doomed La Manga to the architectural blasphemy of the Mediterranean coastline, the strip's 40km beach and lack of industry promotes a relaxing getaway.

Nightlife on La Manga is straightforward and crowded. From 1 to 5am, thousands of Eurokids storm hundreds of *bares-musicales* in Pl. Zoco Alcazaba (km 4), then hop onto nocturnal buses that run to **El Palmero,** a *discoteca* in an imitation castle just outside of La Manga. Keep an eye out for El Palmero invitations at Zoco.

VALENCIA & MURCIA

ORIENTATION AND PRACTICAL INFORMATION La Manga has one main road, **La Gran Vía,** that runs its length. Addresses are indicated by km point (km 0 is at the mainland pole), plazas, and *urbanizaciones* (tourist complexes). The first 3.75km of La Manga belongs to the municipality of Cartagena, and the rest to San Javier.

Local **buses** zip back and forth along La Manga (departs every 20min., after 10pm every hr., 120ptas or less, depending on destination). **Autobuses Gimenez Hermanos** (tel. 968 29 22 11) runs to and from Murcia (5-6 per day, 665ptas) and makes several stops along the strip. Longer distance voyages originate from a parking lot near Pl. Cavanna (km 2-3). **Autobuses Egea** (tel. 968 10 33 00) runs to Cartagena (18 per day, 260-330ptas); **Autocares Costa Azúl** (tel. 968 50 15 43) goes to and from Alicante (2½-3½hr., 1 per day, 930ptas); and **Autobuses Enatcar** (tel. 968 56 48 11) cruises to Madrid (3 per day); Bilbao (2 per day); and Pamplona/San Sebastián (2 per day). The Enatcar office is next to Bar La Parada, across from the bus stop (open M-Sa 9:30am-3:30pm and 5:30-11:15pm, Su noon-3:30pm and 8-11:15pm).

The **tourist office,** Gran Vía, Salida 2, km 0 (tel. 968 56 33 55), in Cartegna, has a map and accommodations list. **Another office,** Urbanización Castillo de Mar, Salida 45 (tel. 968 14 18 12), is in San Javier. Serma, C.B. (tel. 968 56 41 19), in Pl. Cavanna, **rents bikes** (1400ptas per day) and **scooters** (3000ptas per day; open daily 10am-2pm and 5-9pm). The **Escuela de Vela Pedruchillo,** km 8-9 (tel. 968 14 00 02), markets water sports equipment (open daily 10am-2pm and 4-8pm). The **police** respond at (tel. 968 57 08 80). For **medical emergencies** call 968 14 20 60. There's a **post office** in Pl. Bohemia (open M-F 8:30am-2:30pm).

ACCOMMODATIONS AND FOOD The closest thing to budget accommodations on La Manga is the **Albergue Juvenil Deportivo,** Urbanización Hawai V, km 8-9 (tel. 968 14 07 42), in the Grimanga Club. Bunk beds, locker room showers, and rambunctious summer campers are downers, but the front door opens on one of the nicest beaches in Spain, **Playa de Pedrucho.** (Dorms 1500ptas, *pensión completa* with 3 meals 2800ptas.) Also in Hawai V, the **Restaurante Philadelphia** (tel. 968 14 37 15) wheels out mountainous platters of Murcian dishes (open daily 9am-midnight).

VALENCIA & MURCIA

Andalucía

Andalucía derives its *duende* (spirit) from an intoxicating amalgam of cultures. The ancient kingdom of Tartessus—the same Tarshish mentioned in the Bible for their fabulous troves of silver—grew wealthy off the Sierra Nevada's rich ore deposits. The Greeks and Phoenicians established colonies and traded up and down the coast, and the Romans later cultivated wheat, olive oil, and wine from the fertile soil watered by the Guadalquivir. The Vandals flitted through the region on their way to North Africa leaving little more than a name—Vandalusia (House of the Vandals). The Moors provided a more enduring influence. Arriving in AD 711, they established a yet unbroken link to Africa and the Muslim world and bequeathed the region with far more than the flamenco music and gypsy ballads proverbially associated with southern Spain.

Under Moorish rule, which lasted until 1492, Sevilla and Granada reached the pinnacle of Islamic arts, and Córdoba matured into the most culturally influential Islamic city of the western caliphate. But, oddly enough, it is the Moors' toleration and openness for other cultures that created its most enduring 'iainfluences on Andalucía today. The Moors preserved, perfected, and blended Roman architectural techniques with their own, resulting in a setting that became distinctively and uniquely Andalucían. Cool patios, garden oases with fountains and fish ponds, and alternating red brick and white stone were its hallmarks. Two descendant peoples, the Mozarabs, or "Muslim-like" Christians, and later the Mudéjares, Moors conquered by Christians, made further architectural impacts, the former with horse-shoe arches and the latter with intricate wooden ceilings. More importantly, the mingling of Roman and Moorish influences helped spark the European Renaissance by merging the wisdom and science of Classical Greece with that of the Arab world.

However rich in history and culture, Andalucía has been one of the poorest regions of Spain, and many residents chose to flee rather than face a future of indigence. Fourteen percent of its population emigrated in the 1960s due to severe droughts and stagnant industrialization, arguably Europe's largest peacetime emigration of the 20th century. Despite Spain's recent economic boom, residents still complain that even with a university education, finding a good job is as probable as winning the ONCE national lottery. At the same time, Andalucíans retain an unshakable faith in (and perhaps grasp of) the good life, as long as good food, good drink, and spirited company continue to abound. The *festivales, ferias,* and *carnavales* of Andalucía—no matter how sober the religious theme—are world famous parties. Catholicism has never been this much fun.

👋 HIGHLIGHTS OF ANDALUCÍA

- **Sevilla's** beautiful streets, historic cathedral, quiet Alcázar, and amazing nightlife.
- Granada's legendary **Alhambra**, as well as its old Arab quarter, the gorgeous and fascinating **Albaícin** (see p. 457).
- **Córdoba's** unique and bizarre **Mezquita** (see p. 443), with its brilliant red-and-white horseshoe-arch colonnade and its tranquil Patio de los Naranjos.
- **Baeza,** a taste of quintessential Spain (p. 447).
- The desloate and beautiful beach, **Cabo de Gata** (p. 467).

■ Sevilla

The charm of Sevilla is infectious. Site of a small Roman acropolis founded by Julius Caesar, thriving seat of Moorish culture, focal point of the Spanish Renaissance, and guardian angel of traditional Andalusian culture, this city has never failed to spark the imagination of newcomers. Jean Cocteau included it with Venice and Peking in his trio of magical cities. Santa Teresa denounced it as the work of the devil. *Carmen, Don Giovanni,* and the *Barber of Seville* are only a few of the artistic works inspired

Andalucía

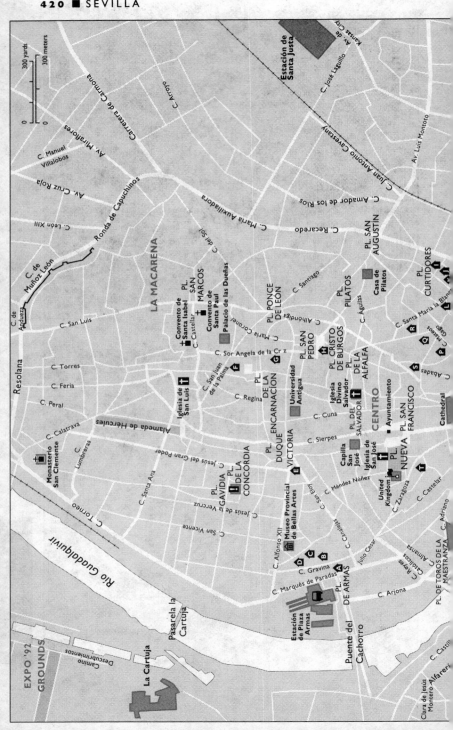

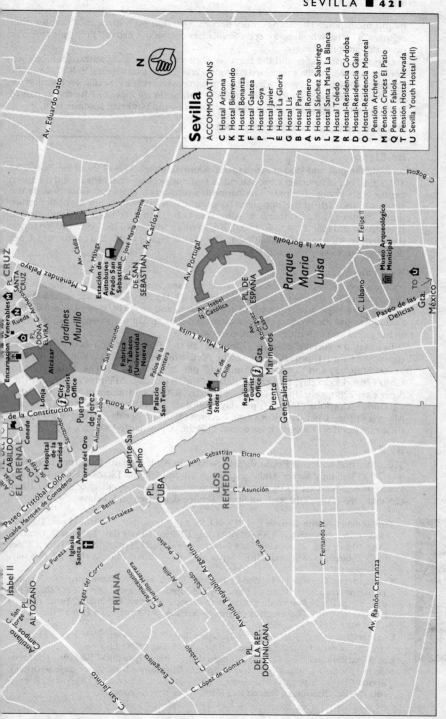

Sevilla

ACCOMMODATIONS

- **C** Hostal Arizona
- **K** Hostal Bienvenido
- **H** Hostal Bonanza
- **F** Hostal Galatea
- **P** Hostal Goya
- **J** Hostal Javier
- **E** Hostal La Gloria
- **G** Hostal Lis
- **B** Hostal Paris
- **A** Hostal Romero
- **S** Hostal Sánchez Sabariego
- **L** Hostal Santa Maria La Blanca
- **N** Hostal Toledo
- **R** Hostal-Residencia Córdoba
- **D** Hostal-Residencia Gala
- **O** Hostal-Residencia Monreal
- **I** Pensión Archeros
- **M** Pensión Cruces El Patio
- **Q** Pensión Fabiola
- **T** Pensión Hostal Nevada
- **U** Sevilla Youth Hostal (HI)

by this metropolis. The 16th-century maxim *"Qui non ha visto Sevilla non ha visto maravilla"* ("he who has not seen Sevilla has not seen a marvel") remains true five centuries after its coinage.

During Semana Santa and the Feria de Abril, two of the most extravagant celebrations in Europe, Sevilla's jasmined balconies and exotic parks spring to life. Matadors, flamenco dancers, and virgins lead the town in endless revelry. Sevilla's reputation for gaiety is rivaled only by its notoriety as *la sartenilla de España* (the frying pan of Spain)—not even the Guadalquivir River can quell the blistering summer heat.

ARRIVALS AND DEPARTURES

By Plane

All flights depart and land at **Aeropuerto San Pablo** (tel. 95 467 29 81 or 95 467 52 10), 12km out of town on Ctra. Madrid. A taxi ride between the airport and the town center costs about 2000ptas. **Los Amarillos** runs a bus (750ptas) from outside the Hotel Alfonso XIII in the Pta. Jerez (departs about every hr.). For flight departure times, call 95 441 52 01. **Iberia,** C. Almirante Lobo, 2 (tel. 95 422 89 01; nation-wide reservation and info tel. 902 400 500), has an office in front of the Torre de Oro (open daily 9am-1:30pm and 4:30-7:30pm). They book flights to Madrid (45min., 3-4 per day) and Barcelona (55min., 2-3 per day).

By Train

All train service is centralized in the modern **Estación Santa Justa,** Av. Kansas City (reservations tel. 95 454 02 02, info tel. 95 454 03 03). Services include an **info booth, a luggage storage,** a telephone office, a cafeteria, and an **ATM.** Buses C1 and C2 link Santa Justa and the Prado de San Sebastián bus station. They stop on Av. Kansas City, to the left as you exit the train station.

In town, the **RENFE office,** C. Zaragoza, 29 (tel. 95 422 26 93), is near Pl. Nueva (open M-F 9am-1:15pm and 4-7pm). The **AVE** whizzes to Madrid (2½hr., 17 per day, 7000-9500ptas) and Córdoba (45min., 17 per day, 2700ptas). The **Talgo** runs to: Cádiz (2hr., 13 per day, 1200ptas); Málaga (3hr., 3 per day, 2655ptas); Granada (4hr., 3 per day, 2280ptas); Huelva (1½hr., 3 per day, 980ptas); Antequera (2hr., 3 per day, 1400ptas); Córdoba (1½hr., 6 per day, 980ptas); Jaén (3hr., 1 per day, 2125ptas); Almería (12hr., 1 per day, 3680ptas); Cáceres (5½hr., 1 per day, 2120ptas); Valencia (8½hr., 4 per day, 5200ptas); Barcelona (12½hr., 6 per day, 6400ptas).

By Bus

The older bus station at **Prado de San Sebastián,** C. José María Osborne, 11 (tel. 95 441 71 11), mainly serves Andalucía. Buses C1 and C2 link Estación Santa Justa and Prado de San Sebastián. **Luggage storage** *(consigna)* is open daily 6:30am to 10pm (250ptas). As is usual throughout Spain, service decreases on Sundays.

Transportes Alsina Graells (tel. 95 441 88 11). Open daily 6:30am-11pm. To: Córdoba (2hr., 10 per day, 1200ptas); Málaga (2½hr., 10 per day, 1850ptas); Granada (3hr., 9 per day, 2400ptas); Jaén (4hr., 4 per day, 2120ptas); Nerja (4½hr., 1 per day, 2300ptas); Almería (7hr., 1 per day, 3780ptas); Murcia (8hr., 2 per day, 4630ptas).

Transportes Comes (tel. 95 441 68 58). Open M-Sa 6:30am-9pm, Su 7:15am-10:30pm. To: Cádiz (1½hr., 12 per day, 1300ptas); Jerez de la Frontera (2hr., 8 per day, 875ptas); El Puerto de Santa María (2hr., 2 per day, 1050ptas); Tarifa (3hr., 4 per day, 2020ptas); Algeciras (3½hr., 4 per day, 2100ptas); La Línea (4hr., 4 per day, 2500ptas).

Enatcar-Bacoma (tel. 95 441 46 60). Open daily 9:30am-9pm. To Valencia (10hr., 2 per day, 6080ptas) and Barcelona (16hr., 1 per day, 8820ptas).

Los Amarillos (tel. 95 441 52 01). Open daily 7:30am-2pm and 2:30-8pm. To: Arcos de la Frontera (2hr., 2 per day, 905ptas); Chipiona (2hr., 9 per day, 970ptas); Ronda (2½hr., 6 per day, 1235ptas); Marbella (3hr., 3 per day, 1820ptas); Fuengirola (3½hr., 2060ptas); Barcelona (16hr., 1 per day, 8820ptas).

The newer bus station at **Plaza de Armas** (tel. 95 490 80 40; open daily 8am-9:15pm), on the river bank, serves destinations beyond Andalucía, including Portugal and other European countries. Services include an **ATM,** cafeteria, photocopies, drugstore, **luggage storage** (30ptas for the first day, 85ptas each additional day), and lockers (300ptas). Buses C1, C2, C3, and C4 stop near here.

Socibus (tel. 95 490 11 60; fax 95 490 16 92). Open daily 8:30am-12:45am. To: Madrid (6hr. nonstop, 15 per day, 2715ptas) and Portugal (1 per day, various destinations including Lagos, from 2540ptas).

Damas (tel. 95 490 80 40). Open M-F 8am-1:30pm and 4:30-10:45pm, Sa-Su 10:30am-1:30pm and 8-10:45pm. To: Huelva (1¼hr., 26 per day, 875ptas); Badajoz (3½hr., 6 per day, 1690ptas); Lisbon (9hr., 2 per day, 4500ptas).

Alsa Internacional (tel. 95 490 78 00). On Th and Sa, 1 per day to: Toulouse (21hr., 12,600ptas); Lyon (28hr., 18,800ptas); Geneva (30hr., 18,000ptas); Zurich (31hr., 20,500ptas). July-Sept. 1000ptas more.

Cunisa (tel. 95 441 10 59 or 95 490 30 93). Open M-Th 6:30am-1pm and 2:30-5:15pm and 9-10pm, F 6:30am-10pm, Sa 9am-3:45pm, Su 9am-1:15pm and 4-10pm. To: Cáceres (4hr., 9 per day, 2250ptas); Salamanca (8hr., 6 per day, 3940ptas); Valladolid (9hr., 6 per day, 4850ptas).

GETTING AROUND SEVILLA

Public Transportation: The city bus network (tel. 95 441 1152) is extensive but worth mastering. Most lines run every 10min. (6am-11:15pm) and converge on Pl. Nueva, Pl. Encarnación, or in front of the cathedral on Av. Constitución. Limited **night service** departs from Pl. Nueva (departs every hr., midnight-2am). City **bus guides** stocked at any tourist office and at most tobacco shops *(estancos)* and kiosks. Fare 125ptas, 10-trip *bonobús* 550-600ptas. Particularly useful are buses C3 and C4, which circle the center, and #34, which hits the youth hostel, university, cathedral, and Pl. Nueva.

Taxis: Tele Taxi (tel. 95 462 22 22). **Radio Taxi** (tel. 95 458 00 00). Starting fare 350ptas, Sunday 25% surcharge.

Car Rental: Hertz, Av. República Argentina, 3 (tel. 95 427 88 87), and at the airport (tel. 95 451 47 20). From 10,000ptas a day. Min. age 23. Open M-F 9am-1:30pm and 4-7pm, Sa 9am-1pm

Moped Rental: You'll never be as cool as the locals, but if you insist try **Alkimoto,** C. Fernando Tiraolo, 5 (tel. 95 458 49 27), near Est. Sta. Justa. 4700ptas per day.

Bike Rental: El Ciclismo, Po. Catalina de Ribera, 2 (tel. 95 441 19 59), in Pta. Carne, at the north end of Jardines de Murillo. 1500ptas per day. Open M-F 10am-1:30pm and 6-8pm, Sa 10am-1pm.

Hitchhiking: Not recommended. Those who hitch toward Madrid and Córdoba take bus #70 out on Av. Kansas City by the train station. This road becomes the highway. Those heading to Granada and Málaga take bus #23 to Parque Amate and walk away from the park to the highway (about 20min.); to Cádiz they take bus #34 to Heliopolis and walk west to the bridge; for Huelva they take bus C1 to Chapina, crossing the bridge and walking straight ahead until reaching the highway.

ORIENTATION

Over the centuries Sevilla has incorporated a number of neighboring villages, now colorful *barrios* in their own right. The **Río Guadalquivir** flows roughly north-south through the city. Most of the city, including the alleyways of the old **Barrio de Santa Cruz,** is on the east bank. The historic and proud **Barrio de Triana** and modern, middle-class **Barrio de los Remedios** occupy the west bank. The **cathedral,** next to Barrio de Santa Cruz, is Sevilla's centerpiece. If you're disoriented, look for its conspicuous *giralda* (the minaret turned bell tower). **Avenida de la Constitución,** home of the tourist office, runs alongside the cathedral. **El Centro** (downtown), a busy commercial pedestrian zone, lies north of the cathedral starting where Av. Constitución hits **Plaza Nueva,** site of the Ayuntamiento. **Calle Sierpes** takes off from here and cuts northward through El Centro. Be aware that Sevilla still has a well-earned reputation as the Spanish capital of purse-snatchers, pickpockets, and car thieves. Violent crime is extremely rare, but be cautious.

To reach El Centro from **Estación Santa Justa,** catch bus #27 that heads to **Plaza de la Encarnación,** several blocks north of the cathedral. To get directly to Barrio Santa Cruz and the cathedral from either the train station or the bus station at **Prado de San Sebastián,** take bus C1 or C2. If you decide to sweat the walk from the train station to the cathedral (40min.), exit through the front door and turn right on C. José Laguillo, which is past the apartment buildings. When this road ends, turn left on C. María Aux-iliadora and continue 30 minutes as it turns into C. Recaredo and then C. Menéndez Pelayo. At C. San Fernando, turn right. After this long block, take a soft right at the Pta. Jerez onto Av. Constitución. The tourist office is on the right while the cathedral looms a few blocks up. To walk to the cathedral from the bus station at Prado de San Sebastián (15min.), walk straight ahead to C. Menéndez Pelayo. Take a left and imme-diate right on C. San Fernando, then a right at the Pta. Jerez onto Av. Constitución.

Buses C1, C2, C3, and C4 connect the newer bus station **Plaza de Armas** to Prado de San Sebastián and the center. To walk to El Centro from Pl. Armas (10min.), walk upstream (right when facing the river) three blocks and make a right onto C. Alfonso XII. To get to the cathedral (20min.), exit right onto C. Marques de Paradas, go right onto Po. Cristobal Colón along the river, and take your first left on to C. Adriano. This street leads to C. García Vinvesa, which ends at the cathedral.

PRACTICAL INFORMATION

Tourist and Financial Services

Tourist Offices: Junta de Andalucía, Av. Constitución, 21B (tel. 95 422 14 04; fax 95 422 97 53), 1 block south of the cathedral. Make this office your first stop in Sevilla. Gushing staff with excellent regional and city info. Superb city **map** (100ptas) with a detailed insert of the Barrio de Santa Cruz. English spoken. Perpetually swamped, but most crowded before and after *siesta.* Open M-F 9am-7pm, Sa 10am-2pm and 5-7pm, Su 10am-2pm. **Municipal,** Po. Delicias, 9 (tel. 95 423 44 65), by the Puente del Generalísimo. Open M-F 9am-6:30pm. **Info booths** in Estación Santa Justa and Pl. Nueva stock city maps and bus guides.

Currency Exchange: Banco Central Hispano, C. Sierpes, 55 (tel. 95 456 26 84), exchanges cash at good rates without commission. Open M-F 8:30am-2:30pm.

American Express: Pl. Nueva, 7 (tel. 95 421 16 17), changes cash and traveler's checks without commission, holds mail, and offers emergency services for card-members. Open M-F 9:30am-1:30pm and 4:30-7:30pm, Sa 10am-1pm.

El Corte Inglés: Pl. Duque de la Victoria, 7 (tel. 95 422 09 31 or 95 458 17 00). 6 other locations in Sevilla. Offers an excellent **map** (49ptas), **currency exchange,** guidebooks in English, CDs, haircutting, cafeteria, restaurant, **supermarket,** and **telephones.** Open M-Sa 10am-9:30pm.

Local Services

Luggage Storage: At Prado de San Sebastián bus station (250ptas), at Pl. Armas bus station (300ptas), and at Santa Justa train station (300-500ptas).

Lost Property: C. Almansa, 21 (tel. 95 421 50 64). Or contact the municipal police.

English Bookstore: Vertice, C. San Fernando, 33 (tel. 95 421 16 54; fax 95 422 56 54), near Pta. Jerez. Large and diverse collection of fine English-language literature. Open M-F 9:30am-2pm and 5-8:30pm, Sa 10am-1:30pm. Closed Saturdays in July.

VIPS: C. República Argentina, 25 (tel. 95 427 93 97), 3 blocks from Pl. Cuba. A mod-ern convenience store. International newspapers and non-perishable groceries. Holds a restaurant as well. Open Su-Th 8am-2am, F 8am-3am, Sa 9am-3am.

Women's Center: C. Alfonso XII, 52 (tel. 95 490 47 76 or 95 490 61 12). Info on feminist, gay, and lesbian organizations, plus legal and psychological services for rape victims. Employment listings for women. Open daily 9am-2pm.

Gay and Lesbian Services: COLEGA (Colectiva de Lesbianas y Gays de Andalucía), Cuesta del Rosario, 8 (tel. 95 456 33 66). Open Tu and Th 6-9pm.

Laundromat: Lavandería Robledo, C. F. Sánchez Bedoya, 18, a block west of the cathedral. 5kg wash and dry 950ptas. Open M-F 10am-2pm and 5-8pm.

Swimming Pool: Mar de Plata (tel. 95 445 40 85), on C. Pablo I in Triana. Take Av. República Argentina from Pl. Cuba past Pl. República Dominicana and make the next right (or take bus C1 or C2 to Pl. República and follow above directions). 450ptas, under 12 200ptas. Open Tu-F 2:30-4:30pm, Sa-Su 11am-8pm.

Emergency and Communications

Emergency: tel. 091 or 092. **Police:** Av. Paseo de las Delicias, 15 (tel. 95 461 54 50). **24Hr. Pharmacy:** 5-6 pharmacies open each night, all night, on a rotating basis. Check list posted at any pharmacy in the city.

Medical Assistance: Ambulatorio Esperanza Macarena (tel. 95 442 01 05). **Hospital Universitario Virgen Macarena,** Av. Dr. Fedriani (tel. 95 424 81 81). English spoken.

Internet Access: Cibercenter, C. Julio Cesar, 8 (tel. 95 422 88 99), off C. Reyes Católicos. Internet and email access. 250ptas per 15min. Open daily 9am-9pm.

Post Office: Av. Constitución, 32 (tel. 95 421 64 76), across from the cathedral. Open for stamps, Lista de Correos, and **faxes** M-F 8:30am-8:30pm, Sa 9:30am-2pm. **Postal Code:** 41080.

ACCOMMODATIONS AND CAMPING

During Semana Santa and the *Feria de Abril,* rooms vanish and prices soar. Make reservations months ahead if you value your footleather. At other times, call a day or two ahead. Tourist officials have lists of *casas particulares* that open on special occasions. Accommodations prices are often negotiable, so be sure to ask.

Sevilla Youth Hostel (HI), C. Isaac Peral, 2 (tel. 95 461 31 50; fax 95 461 31 58). Take bus #34 from Prado de San Sebastían. To connect to the Prado from the train station take C2 or #27, or from Pl. Armas take C1, C2, C3, or C4. Bus #34 stops behind the hostel just after Po. Delicias. Bright, white, and disinfected. Up to 4 per room. Many private baths. Dorms 1300ptas, over 26 1800ptas. Non-members pay 300ptas a night for 6 nights to become members. Wheelchair accessible.

Barrio de Santa Cruz

The narrow streets east of the cathedral around **Calle Santa María la Blanca** are full of cheap *hostales.* Room quality varies little. The *barrio* is overwhelmingly touristed, but its narrow streets and fragrant, shady plazas are all within a few minutes' walk from the cathedral, river, Alcázar, and El Centro.

🏵**Hostal Sánchez Sabariego,** C. Corral del Rey, 23 (tel. 95 421 44 70), on the continuation of C. Argote de Molina, northeast of the cathedral. Follow signs to Hostel Sierpes. Friendly little hostel with antique furniture and painstakingly decorated, spacious rooms. All rooms have bath. A/C upstairs. Singles 3000ptas; doubles 5000-7000ptas. You get your own key. Prices are somewhat negotiable.

🏵**Hostal-Residencia Córdoba,** C. Farnesio, 12 (tel. 95 422 74 98), off C. Fabiola. Immaculate, family-run joint with spacious rooms and a beautiful indoor patio. Every room has A/C. Singles 2800-3800ptas; doubles 4500-7000ptas, with bath 5500-8000ptas. Front door closes 3-6:30am.

Hostal Toledo, C. Santa Teresa, 15 (tel. 95 421 53 35), off C. Ximénez de Enciso. Just west of Jardines de Murillo. Quiet, comfortable hostel, with private baths. Singles 2675-3200ptas, depending on bath size; doubles 5350ptas. Curfew 1am.

Hostal Santa María La Blanca, C. Sta. María la Blanca, 28 (tel. 95 442 11 74). Great bargain for the district. Hallways decorated with cheap paintings of bullfights and provocative *gitanas.* Fan in each room. Singles 1500ptas, with bath 2000ptas; doubles 3000ptas, with bath 4000ptas; triples 4500ptas, with bath 6000ptas.

Hostal Goya, C. Mateos Gago, 31 (tel. 95 421 11 70), off the cathedral. Ample rooms cooled by fans. Lounge area. Doubles with shower 6000ptas, with bath 6300ptas; triples with shower 7840ptas, with bath 8820ptas.

Hostal Bienvenido, C. Archeros, 14 (tel. 95 441 36 55). English-speaking owner welcomes you to simple rooms. Spacious doubles with balconies, small singles with big windows. Firm beds. 3rd floor is oven-like July-Aug. Guests mingle on the terrace. Singles 1800-2000ptas; doubles 3000-3600; triples 4500-5400ptas.

Hostal-Residencia Monreal, C. Rodrigo Caro, 8 (tel. 95 421 41 66). From the fountain in front of the cathedral, walk uphill on C. Mateos Gago to the 1st block on your right. A large, hotel-style place with unremarkable yet clean rooms with tiled floors, A/C, and little sinks. Singles 2500ptas; doubles 4000ptas, with shower 6000ptas; triples 5600ptas, with shower 9300ptas.

Pensión Fabiola, C. Fabiola, 16 (tel. 95 421 83 46). Basic rooms surround a plant-filled patio. Huge rooms on top floor can accommodate entire groups of backpackers. Beds are a bit floppy. Singles 2500ptas; doubles 4000ptas, with bath 6000ptas; triples 5500ptas.

Pensión Archeros, C. Archeros, 23 (tel. 95 441 84 65). Relaxed, friendly owner oversees pleasant rooms facing a wide-open, fern-laden patio. Singles 2000ptas; doubles 3500ptas, with shower 4500ptas.

Pensión Cruces El Patio, Pl. Cruces, 10 (tel. 95 422 96 33). Dim interior rooms, some with bunkbeds. Colorful patio is home to parakeets and one hairy dog. Singles 2000ptas; doubles 3500ptas, with bath 4000ptas.

Hostal Javier, C. Archeros, 16 (tel. 95 441 23 25). Well-furnished rooms with fans are comfortable. Singles 2500-3000ptas; doubles 3500-5000ptas; triples 6500ptas.

El Centro

The *casco viejo* in El Centro, a mess of narrow, winding streets radiating from the Pl. Encarnación, is as charming as it is disorienting.

Hostal Galatea, C. San Juan de la Palma, 4 (tel. 95 456 35 64; fax 95 456 35 17). From the west end of Pl. Encarnación, take C. Regina, then turn right. Spic 'n' span rooms with fans could accommodate a posse. Colorful bar/patio and tiled roof terrace. Some rooms have TV. Singles 3100ptas; doubles 4900ptas, with shower 5600ptas. Recently renovated. Cheaper in winter. Visa, MC.

Hostal La Gloria, C. San Eloy, 58 (tel. 95 422 26 73), on a lively pedestrian shopping street. Striking exterior with ornate wood trim. Flawlessly tiled floors. A/C upstairs. Beds a little droopy. Singles 2000ptas, with bath 2500ptas; doubles 3500ptas.

Hostal Lis, C. Escarpín, 10 (tel. 95 421 30 88), on an alley just east of Pl. Encarnación. Eye-popping entry and patio with psychedelic Sevillian tiles. Large rooms, all with showers. Singles 1500-2000ptas; doubles 4000ptas; triples 5000ptas.

Near Plaza de Armas

Most *hostales* on the quiet backstreets around the Pl. Armas bus station are on C. Gravina, parallel to C. Marqués de las Paradas and two blocks inland. Upstairs rooms can feel like attics; downstairs rooms often have high, adorned ceilings.

Hostal Paris, C. San Pedro Mártir, 14 (tel. 95 422 98 61 or 95 421 96 45; fax 95 421 96 45), off C. Gravina. Brand new, clean, and classy. Bath, A/C, phone, and TV. If you're looking for comforts, this place is one of the best values in town. Singles 3500ptas; doubles 5000-6000ptas. Ask about student discounts. Visa, MC, AmEx.

Hostal Arizona, Pedro del Toro, 14 (tel. 95 421 60 42), off C. Gravina. Clean, attractive rooms, some with lounge chairs, balconies, and huge wardrobes. Fans cool rooms. Singles 1500ptas; doubles 3000ptas, with bath 3500ptas. Visa, MC.

Hostal Romero, C. Gravina, 21 (tel. 95 421 13 53). Potted plants, antique furniture, and hanging brass pots embellish the inner courtyard. Mattresses are a bit smooshy. Singles 1600ptas; doubles 3000ptas; triples 3900ptas.

Hostal Residencia Gala, C. Gravina, 52 (tel. 95 421 45 03). Friendly owner. Clean bathrooms. Some rooms are windowless, but the A/C rocks. Singles 2000ptas, with bath 2500ptas; doubles 3000ptas, with bath 3500ptas.

Elsewhere

Pensión Hostal Nevada, C. Gamazo, 28 (tel. 95 422 53 40), centrally located in El Arenal. From Pl. Nueva, take C. Barcelona and turn right on C. Gamazo, a street lined with pubs. Naturally cool courtyard. Sleek leather sofas and large collection of *abanicos* (fans). Dim, tapestry-laden rooms. Singles 2200-2500, with bath 3000-3500ptas; doubles 4000-4500ptas, with bath 5000-6000ptas.

Camping Sevilla, Ctra. Madrid-Cádiz, km 534 (tel. 95 451 43 79), 12km out of town near the airport. From Est. Prado de San Sebastián, take bus #70, which stops 800m away at Parque Alcosa. A happy medium between metropolis and outback. Grassy sites, hot showers, supermarket, and swimming pool. 460ptas per person, per car, per tent. Children 375ptas.

Club de Campo, Av. Libertad, 13, Ctra. Sevilla-Dos Hermanas (tel. 95 472 02 50), 8km out of town. Los Amarillos' buses leave from C. Infante Carlos de Borbón, at the back of the Auditorium in the Prado de San Sebastián, directly to Dos Hermanas (departs about every 45min., 140ptas). Grassy site, swimming pool. 485ptas per person and per car, 475ptas per tent. Children 395ptas.

FOOD

Sevillians offset the merciless midday sun by keeping their cuisine light. The town claims to be the birthplace of *tapas;* true or not, locals prepare and devour them with a vengeance. Favorites include *tortilla, caracoles* (snails), and *cocido andaluz* (a thick soup of garbanzo beans). *Sangría* offers another popular relief against the lethargy of hot afternoons, as does *tinto de verano,* a cold blend of red wine and lemon soda. No beverage, however, rivals the passion for *la cerveza* (beer). Defying the need for hydration and sobriety, locals imbibe Sevilla's own Cruzcampo, a light, smooth pilsner, whether in *tubos* (tube-like glasses) or *litrones* (liter bottles). The label's beer-bellied, feather-capped logo, Gamrinus, is a regional icon.

Popular venues for *el tapeo* (*tapas*-bar hopping) hide out in Barrio Triana, but avoid places on C. Betis that overlook the river—they are expensive. **Barrio Santa Cruz** and **El Arenal** around the bullring are also reliable feeding grounds. Sevilla's bountiful markets offer chances for home cooking. **Mercado del Arenal,** near the bullring on C. Pastor y Leandro, between C. Almansa and C. Arenal, has fresh produce, *toro de lidia* (fresh bull meat from next door), and screaming vendors. Merchants also hawk excellent fresh produce, fish, meat, and baked goods at **Mercadillo de la Encarnación.** (Both markets open M-Sa 9am-2pm.) Buy renowned jams, pastries, and candies from convent kitchens or the stores in **Plaza Cabildo** off Av. Constitución. For a supermarket, try **%Día,** C. San Juan de Ávila, on Pl. Gavídia, around the corner from El Corte Inglés (open M-F 9:30am-2pm and 6:30-9pm, Sa 9am-1pm).

Near the Cathedral

Restaurants next to the cathedral cater exclusively to tourists. Beware the unexceptional, omnipresent *menús* featuring *gazpacho* and *paella* for about 1000ptas. Food and prices improve in the back street establishments between the cathedral and the river in El Arenal, and along side streets in the Barrio Santa Cruz.

Restaurante-Bar El Baratillo/Casa Chari, C. Pavia, 12 (tel. 95 422 96 51), on a tiny street off C. Dos de Mayo. Friendly owner patiently explains Spanish cuisine to confused foreigners while presenting tasty samples of her cooking in a room plastered with early 1980s posters and images of Christ. Call or ask in advance for the tour-de-force: homemade *paella* and drinks (2500ptas for 2). Rock-bottom prices. *Menú* 500ptas. Meals served M-F 8am-10pm, Sa noon-5pm.

Bodega Santa Cruz, C. Rodrigo Caro, 1 (tel. 95 421 32 46). Take C. Mateos Gago from the fountain in front of the cathedral; it's on the 1st corner on your right. Casual and crowded, with locals coming in at all hours to sample varied and tasty *tapas* (175-200ptas) and wash them down with *cañas de cerveza* (125ptas). Megawatt A/C. Particularly busy on weekend nights. Open daily 8am-midnight.

Texas Lone Star Saloon, C. Placentines, 25 (tel. 95 421 03 34). The Tex-Mex cuisine is surprisingly delicious. Feast on the *chile relleno:* peppers stuffed with cheese, fried, and drenched in salsa, lettuce, and tomato (875ptas). A collection of American beers. Open daily 1pm-2am, later on weekends.

San Marco Pizzería, C. Mesón de Moro, 4 (tel. 95 421 43 90 or 95 456 43 90), off C. Mateos Gago. Housed in a huge, atmospheric, 12th-century, Moorish bath house.

ANDALUCÍA

Thin-crust pizzas drowned in chunky toppings (650-975ptas) are beautiful, but don't go if you're starving. Pastas around 775ptas. Always packed with tourists; try dining upstairs. Open Tu-Su 1:15-3:30pm and 8:15pm-12:30am. Visa, MC.

Modesto, C. Cano y Cueto, 5 (tel. 95 441 18 16), next to the Jardines Murillo. Come here if you don't mind spending the big bucks for the best seafood in Sevilla (1200-4000ptas). The oysters are succulent, the service impeccable. Open nightly 8pm-2am, always packed. Visa, MC, AmEx.

Casa Diego, Pl. Curtidores, 7 (tel. 95 441 58 83), 1 block up from C. Sta. María la Blanca along C. Cano y Cueto. Their renowned *brochetas de pescado y carne* (fish and beef skewers 900ptas) have speared tourists and locals alike for the last 30 years. *Menú* 1000ptas. Open M-F 1-4pm and 8:30-11:30pm, Sa 1-4pm. Visa, MC.

Pizzería Renato, C. Pavia, 17 (tel. 95 421 00 77), on the corner of C. Dos de Mayo. Pizzas 480-750ptas, lasagna 750ptas, pasta 450-750ptas. Open Su-Tu and Th-F 1-4pm and 8-11:45pm, Sa 8pm-midnight. Visa, MC, AmEx.

Bar Caceres, C. San José, 24. The closest thing to a buffet-style breakfast in Spain. An impressive spread of cheeses, jams, and countless other condiments. *Desayuno de la Casa* (orange juice, coffee, ham, eggs, *tostado*) 600ptas. Open daily 7am-9pm.

El Centro

Just beyond the usual tourist coops, this area belongs to professionals and shoppers by day, and to young people on their *paseo* by night.

Jalea Real, Sor Ángela de la Cruz, 37 (tel. 95 421 61 03). From Pl. Encarnación, head 150m east on C. Laraña, then left immediately before Iglesia de San Pedro. The Shangri-La of vegetarian restaurants—so recondite, so rewarding. Hip management dishes out interesting salads and homemade desserts. Delectable spinach crepe 675ptas. Lunch *menú* 1250ptas. No alcohol served. Open July-Aug. M-F 1:30-5pm and 8:30-11:30pm, Sa 8:30-11:30pm, Sept.-June M-Sa 1:30-5pm and 8:30-11:30pm.

Bodega Sierpes, C. Azofaifo, 9 (tel. 95 421 30 44), off C. Sierpes in a quiet alley. Specializes in cheap, enormous portions of chicken eaten outside in a modest *terraza*. *Gazpacho* in a glass 150ptas. Half-chicken, bread, salad, and beverage 775ptas. Meals served W-M 11am-midnight.

Bodegón Alfonso XII, C. Alfonso XII, 33 (tel. 95 421 12 51), near the Museo de Bellas Artes. Dark-stone walls with columns and arches. Fleet waiters sprint the dizzying circuit from kitchen to counter to you. Breakfast with eggs and ham, coffee (or beer!) about 425ptas. *Menú del día* 800ptas. Open M-Sa 8am-10:30pm.

Rincón San Eloy, C. San Eloy, 24 (tel. 95 421 80 79). Waiters can barely be heard above the din of the crowd. Airy courtyard, old wine barrels, massive beer taps, and bullfight posters. *Tapas* 200ptas. *Raciones* 900ptas. *Menú* with wine or beer 900ptas. Open M-Sa noon-4:30pm and 7pm-midnight.

Bar El Camborio, C. Baños, 3 (tel. 95 421 75 34), directly off Pl. Gavidia. Standard Sevillian decorative triumvirate: the bullfighting wall, the flamenco wall, and the Semana Santa wall. A boisterous local crowd. *Menú del día* 800ptas noon-4pm. Whopping *platos combinados* from 450ptas. *Tinto de verano* 150ptas. A/C. Open M-Sa 8:15am-10:30pm, later in winter.

Barrio de Triana and Barrio de los Remedios

This old maritime *barrio*, on the far side of the Guadalquivir, was once a separate village. Avoid overpriced C. Betis and plunge instead down side streets to find *freidurías* (fish-fry vendors) and *bar-restaurantes* by day, *tapas* bars by night.

Casa Cuesta, C. Castilla, 3-5 (tel. 95 433 33 37), north of the Puente Isabel II, 1 block inland. Locals speak highly of the beautiful dining room and exceptional food. A bit expensive, but worth it. *Pescado* 900-1700ptas. *Cola de toro* (bull's tail) 1700ptas. Open for lunch and dinner; especially popular on weekends.

La Ortiga, C. Procurador, 19 (tel. 95 433 7418), off C. Castilla. An ecological organization operates this pleasant health food *tapas* bar/patio. *Tapas ecológicas* include pitas stuffed with cheese, lettuce, tomato, corn, and salsa (225ptas), all organically produced. Beer available. Open M-Sa in summer from 8pm; in winter from 5pm.

Café-Bar Jerusalem, C. Salado, 6, at C. Virgen de las Huertas. Kick-back bar with an international crowd and inventive *tapas*. Chicken, lamb, or pork and cheese *shaw-*

erma called a *bocadillo hebreo* (bread, lettuce, roast pork, holland cheese, Hebrew spices) ain't kosher but sure is tasty (400-625ptas). Open daily 8pm-3am.

Freiduría Santana, C. Pureza, 61 (tel. 95 433 20 40), parallel to C. Betis, a block from the river. Fresh, greaseless fried fish. Free samples ease the wait. Eat *sevillano* style at a nearby bar serving icy *cerveza. Calamares* and *gambas* (shrimp) 1600ptas per kg. *Variado* (mix) 1200ptas per kg. Open Sept.-July Tu-Su 7pm-midnight.

Casa Manolo, C. San Jorge, 16 (tel. 95 433 47 92), north of Puente Isabel II. Waiters in bolo ties serve all sorts of cheap seafood *tapas* (200ptas). *Pescado frito variado* (assorted fried fish) 1200ptas. *Menú* 1600ptas. Open Tu-Su noon-midnight; in winter 9am-midnight. Visa.

SIGHTS

Sevilla spills over with sights, from the famous and not-to-be-missed Alcázar and cathedral to the winding streets and plazas of its *casco viejo* and El Barrio de Santa Cruz. Important museum collections are sprinkled throughout the city.

The Cathedral

Tel. 95 421 49 71. Cathedral complex and Giralda open M-Sa 10:30am-6pm, Su 2-7pm. Tickets sold until 1hr. before closing. 700ptas, seniors and students 200ptas, under 12 free. Sundays free.

In 1401, Christians razed an Almohad mosque to clear space for a massive cathedral. All that remains of the former mosque is the famed minaret **La Giralda.** The tower and its twins in Marrakesh and Rabat are the oldest and largest surviving Almohad minarets (its lower walls are 2.5m thick). In 1565, a Renaissance belfry and a bronze orchestra of 25 bells were added. A well-preserved stone ramp, built for horseback ascent, leads to the top.

The *reconquistadores* demonstrated their religious fervor by constructing a church so great that, in their own words, "those who come after us will take us for madmen." It took more than a century to build the world's fourth-largest cathedral and the largest Gothic edifice ever built. The inside of the structure is disorienting; the sights listed here are in counter-clockwise order.

In the middle of the cathedral, the **main chapel** and its altar stand face to face with the dark wooden choir made of recycled mahogany from a 19th-century Austrian railway. The **retablo mayor** (altarpiece), one of the largest in the world, is a golden wall of intricately wrought figurines, depicting 36 biblical scenes. The floor mirror reflects a distorted version of yourself and the ornate dome above. By encircling the choir, you will approach the **Sepulcro de Cristóbal Colón** (Columbus' tomb). The black and gold coffin-bearers represent the eternally grateful kings of Castilla, León, Aragón, and Navarra. Most likely, the man who stumbled upon the Americas on his way to China does not actually lie inside—there is considerable mystery surrounding the whereabouts of his remains.

Farther on and to the right stands the cathedral's most precious museum, the **Sacristía Mayor,** which holds works by Riberas and Murillos and a glittering Corpus Christi icon, **la Custodia processional.** A small, disembodied head of John the Baptist eyes visitors who enter the giftshop and overlooks two keys presented to the city of Sevilla by Jewish leaders after King Fernando III ousted the Muslims in 1248. The neighboring **Sacristía de los Cálices** (or **de Los Pintores**) maintains a collection of minor canvases by masters Zurbarán and Goya. In the corner of the edifice are the impressive **Sala de Las Columnas** and the perfectly oval **cabildo,** or chapter house. Outside the cathedral proper, on the north end, the elegant **Patio de Los Naranjos** (orange trees) evokes the bygone days of the Arab Caliphate.

Alcazar and Surroundings

Alcázar tel. 95 450 23 23. Open Tu-Sa 9:30am-7pm, Su 9:30am-5pm. 600ptas, seniors, students, and under 12 free. Consider renting an audio guide (available in several languages), which gives helpful anecdotes, information, and a clearly marked route through the buildings and garden. Audio guide 400ptas.

The imposing 9th-century walls of the **Alcázar**, the oldest palace still serving European royalty, face the cathedral's south side. The walls and several interior spaces,

ANDALUCÍA

including the **Patio del Yeso** and the exquisitely carved **Patio de las Muñecas,** remain from the Moorish era. The latter patio displays handfans and a bed where Queen Isabel purportedly laid her Catholic head. One of the most exceptional Christian additions is the **Patio de las Doncellas** (Maids' Court). Court life in the Alcázar revolved around this colonnaded quadrangle, encircled by foliated archways adorned with glistening tilework and coffered ceilings. The theme of overwhelmingly kaleidoscopic detail carries over into the adjacent chambers. The astonishing golden-domed **Salón de los Embajadores** is allegedly the site where Fernando and Isabel welcomed Columbus back from America. Nearby, the **Corte de las Muñecas** contains the private quarters of the palace, decorated with the building's most exquisite carvings. Verdant gardens stretch from the residential quarters in all directions.

Between the cathedral and the Alcázar stands the 16th-century **Casa Lonja,** built by Felipe II as a *Casa de Contratación* (commercial exchange) for trade with the Americas. In 1785, Carlos III converted the building into the **Archivo General de las Indias** (Archive of the Indies; tel. 95 421 12 34), a collection of over 44,000 documents relating to the discovery and conquest of the New World, including the "official" history of the conquest. *(Exhibits open M-F 10am-1pm. Free. Full access to documents is restricted to scholars.)* Offended by a number of unflattering interpretations of Spanish-American colonial history written by Englishmen, Carlos III commissioned philosopher Juan Bautista Muñoz to write the definitive version. Highlights include the wildly inaccurate *Mapa Mundi* of Juan de la Costa and letters from Columbus to Fernando and Isabel, as well as a 1590 letter from Cervantes (pre-*Don Quijote*), asking for employment in America.

Barrio de Santa Cruz

The tourist office has a detailed inset map (on the main map) of the winding alleys, wrought-iron *cancelas* (gates), and courtyards of the Barrio de Santa Cruz. King Fernando III forced Jews in flight from Toledo to live in this former ghetto. Haloed with geraniums, jasmine, and ivy, every street corner in the *barrio* echoes with a legend. On **Calle Susona,** a glazed skull above a door recalls the beautiful Susona, a Jew who fell in love with a Christian knight. When Susona learned that her father and friends planned to kill several inquisitors, including her knight, she warned her lover. A bloody reprisal was unleashed on the Jewish ghetto, during which Susona's entire family was slaughtered. She requested that her skull be placed above her doorway in atonement for her betrayal, and the actual skull purportedly remained until the 18th century. Calle Susona leads to **Plaza Doña Elvira,** where Sevillian Lope de Rueda's works, precursors to the drama of Spain's Golden Age, were staged. A turn down C. Gloria leads to Pl. Venerables, site of the 17th-century **Hospital de los Venerables** (tel. 95 456 26 96), a hospital-church adorned with art from the Sevillian school, including Leal and Montañés. *(Open daily for guided visits 10am-2pm and 4-8pm. 600ptas, students 300ptas.)*

Calle Lope de Rueda, off C. Ximénez de Enciso, is graced with two noble mansions, beyond which lies the charming and fragrant **Plaza de Santa Cruz.** South of the plaza is the **Jardines de Murillo,** a shady expanse of shrubbery and benches. **Convento de San José,** C. Santa Teresa (off Pl. Santa Cruz), cherishes a cloak of Santa Teresa de Ávila and her portrait. *(Open daily 9-11am.)* The church in Pl. Santa Cruz houses the grave of artist Murillo, who died in what is now known as the **Casa Murillo** (tel. 95 422 12 72) after falling from a scaffold while painting ceiling frescoes in Cádiz's Iglesia de los Capuchinos. *(Open M-F 8am-3pm and 4-8pm. Free.)* The house has information on Murillo's life and paintings. **Iglesia de Santa María la Blanca,** on the street of the same name, was built in 1391 on the foundation of a synagogue. *(Open M-Sa 10-11am and 6:30-8pm, Su 9:30am-2pm and 6:30-8pm.)* It features red marble columns, Baroque plasterwork, and a *Last Supper* by Murillo.

The Barrio de Santa Cruz is also home to several excellent **art galleries.** Plaça Alianza, the small square at the end of C. Rodrigo Caro, houses the bullfighting-oriented **Estudio de John Fulton.** *(Open M-Sa 11am-2pm and 4:30-7:30pm, Su 11am-2pm.)* Fulton is an accomplished expatriate artist and the first bullfighter from the U.S. ever to fight in Mexico City's ring. Some pieces are reputedly painted in bull's blood.

Sierpes and the Aristocratic Quarter

In Pl. San Francisco stands the **Ayuntamiento** (tel. 95 459 01 45), with 16th-century Gothic and Renaissance interior halls, a richly decorated domed ceiling, and a Plateresque facade. *(Often displays art exhibitions; check tourist office for information. Open to public Tu-Th 5:30-7:30pm, Sa 11am-1pm.)* Originating from the plaza, **Calle de Sierpes** cuts through the Aristocratic Quarter. At the beginning of this pedestrian street lined with shoe stores, fan shops, and chic boutiques, a plaque marks the spot where the royal prison loomed. Some scholars believe Cervantes began writing *Don Quijote* there.

Iglesia del Salvador, fronted by a Montañés sculpture, occupies the square of the same name, one block inland from Sierpes. This 17th-century church was built on the foundations of the city's main mosque, from which the courtyard and the belfry's base come. As grandiose as a cathedral, it is adorned with outstanding baroque *retablos* (altarpieces), sculptures, and paintings, including Montañés's *Jesús de la Pasión.* *(Open daily 6:30-9pm.)* **Plaza del Salvador** fills up around noon with professionals and students taking their first well-earned *cerveza* break of the day.

A few blocks southeast of Pl. Salvador on C. Mármoles stand the excavated ruins of an old Roman temple. The remaining columns rise 15m from below street level and offer a glimpse of the literal depth of Sevilla's history. In the early 1600s, several of the massive columns were carried through the narrow streets across town to the Alameda de Hércules as part of an urbanization project that aimed at reclaiming an area that was once a lake. A few blocks east of Pl. Salvador, in Pl. Pilatos, the **Casa de Pilatos** (tel. 95 422 52 98) houses Roman antiquities, Renaissance and baroque paintings, several courtyards, and a pond. *(Open daily 9am-7pm. 1000ptas.)* Use the bell pull if the gate is closed during visiting hours. The interesting **Iglesia de la Anunciación,** in Pl. Encarnación, features a pantheon honoring illustrious *sevillanos,* including poet Gustavo Adolfo Bécquer. *(Open daily 9am-1pm.)*

El Arenal and Triana

Immortalized by Siglo de Oro writers Lope de Vega, Quevedo, and Cervantes, **El Arenal** and **Triana** (across the river) were Sevilla's chaotic 16th- and 17th-century mariner's quarters. The **Museo Provincial de Bellas Artes,** Pl. Museo, 9 (tel. 95 422 07 90), contains Spain's finest collection of works by Sevilla School painters, most notably Murillo, Leal, and Zurbarán, as well as aliens El Greco and Dutch master Jan Breughel. *(Open Tu 3-8pm, W-Sa 9am-8pm, Su 9am-3pm. 250ptas, E.U. members and students free.)* The museum building itself is a work of art—take time to sit in its shady gardens. To reach the museum, walk toward the river along C. Alfonso XII. The 12-sided **Torre del Oro** (Gold Tower), built by the Almohads in 1200, overlooks the river from Po. Cristóbal Colón. A glaze of golden tile once sheathed its squat frame; today, a tiny yellow dome is the only reminder of its original splendor. Climb to the top to visit the **Museo Náutico** (tel. 95 422 24 19), with engravings and drawings of Sevilla's port in its heyday. *(Open Sept.-July Tu-F 10am-2pm, Sa-Su 11am-2pm. 100ptas. Tuesdays free.)* On the far bank of the river, the Torre del Oro was connected to the **Torre de la Plata** (silver tower) by underwater chains meant to protect the city from river-borne trespassers. The river was later diverted to its present course (the Alameda de Hércules area was also drained), exposing El Arenal (the sandbank). The Torre de la Plata has been absorbed by a bank building, but one side lies in a cul-de-sac near the corner of C. Santander and C. Temprado.

The inviting riverside esplanade **Paseo de Marqués de Contadero** stretches along the banks of the Guadalquivir from the base of the Torre del Oro. Bridge-heavy boat tours of Sevilla leave from in front of the tower (1hr., 700ptas). The tiled boardwalk leads to **Plaza de Toros de la Real Maestranza** (tel. 95 422 45 77), a veritable temple of bullfighting. Home to one of the two great schools of *tauromaquia* (the other is in Ronda), the plaza fills to capacity for the 13 *corridas* of the *Feria de Abril* and for weekly fights. See **La Corrida,** p. 436, for ticket and other information.

Behind the Teatro de la Maestranza on C. Temprado perches the **Hospital de la Caridad** (tel. 95 422 32 32), a 17th-century complex of arcaded courtyards. *(Open M-Sa 9am-1:30pm and 3:30-6:30pm, Su 9am-1pm. 400ptas.)* Its randy founder, Don Miguel de Marañe, is believed to be the model for legendary Sevillian Don Juan. He allegedly converted to a life of piety and charity after stumbling out of an orgy into a funeral cortège that he was told was his own. Inside, the **Iglesia de San Jorge's** walls display paintings and frescoes by Valdés Leal and Murillo. Murillo supposedly couldn't refrain from holding his nose when he saw Leal's morbid *Finis Gloria Mundi*, which depicts corpses of a peasant, a bishop, and a king, putrefying beneath a stylized depiction of Justice and the Seven Deadly Sins. Don Miguel is buried in the crypt.

On the revertant just before the Puente de Isabel II is Eduardo Chillida's sculpture entitled **Monumento a la Tolerancia** (Monument to Tolerance). The abstract figure has its back turned to the ruins of the Castillo de la Inquisición (Castle of the Inquisition), and its arms are outstretched to embrace. Across the river is the former potters', tilemakers', and gypsies' quarter **Triana,** now gentrified but still preserving a cultural autonomy from Sevilla. **Pottery** studios and stores line both C. Alfarería (ceramics street) and C. Antillano Campos; #6 on the latter street has Sevilla's oldest kilns. Off C. Correa, two blocks inland from the river midway between Puente de Isabel II and Puente de San Telmo, stands the **Iglesia de Santa Ana** and its **Capilla de los Marineros,** Sevilla's oldest church and the focal point of the exuberant fiestas that take over the *barrio* in July. *(Open M and W 7:30-8:30pm.)* The terraced riverside promenade **Calle Betis** is an ideal spot to view Sevilla's monumental profile.

La Macarena

Macarena is the name of both a Sevillian virgin and a popular rumba (not the one you're thinking of) that advises women to give their bodies *"alegría y cosas buenas"* (happiness and good things). The quarter, northwest of El Centro, is traversed by the *ruta de los conventos*. The founder of **Convento de Santa Inés,** as legend has it, was pursued so insistently by King Pedro el Cruel that she disfigured her face with boiling oil so he would leave her alone. So much for the happy advice of the rumba. Cooking liquids are used more productively today—the cloistered nuns sell patented puff pastries and coffee cakes through the courtyard's revolving window. The convent lies on C. María Coronel. **Convento de Santa Paula** (tel. 95 453 63 30) includes a church with Gothic, Mudéjar, and Renaissance elements, a magnificent coffered ceiling, and sculptures by Montañés. *(Open Tu-Su 10:30am-12:30pm and 4:30-6:30pm.)* The **museo** inside has a *St. Jerome* by Ribera. Nuns here peddle scrumptious homemade marmalades and angel-hair pastry.

Opposite the belfry of the Iglesia de San Marcos rises **Iglesia de Santa Isabel,** featuring an altarpiece by Montañés. Nearby on C. San Luís stands the exuberantly Baroque **Iglesia de San Luis,** crowned by octagonal glazed-tile domes. *(Open W-Th 9am-2pm, F-Sa 9am-2pm and 5-8pm.)* The site of the church was the endpoint of a 12-step prayer route based on the ascent to Golgotha. More recently, it has been immortalized by the Cruzcampo beer logo.

A stretch of **murallas,** restored since their 12th-century nativity, runs between the Pta. Macarena and Pta. Córdoba on the Ronda de Capuchinos ring road. Flanking the west end of the walls, the **Basílica Macarena** (tel. 95 437 01 95) houses the venerated image of *La Virgen de la Macarena,* which is hauled around town during Semana Santa processions. A **treasury** glitters with the virgin's jewels and other finery. *(Basílica open daily 9:30am-1pm and 5-9pm. Free. Treasury open daily 9:30am-1pm and 5-8pm. 300ptas.)* Toward the river, in Pl. San Lorenzo, is **Iglesia de San Lorenzo y Jesús del Gran Poder** (tel. 95 438 45 58), with Montañés's remarkably lifelike sculpture *El Cristo del Gran Poder. (Open daily 8am-1:45pm and 6-9pm, F 7:30-10pm. Free.)* Worshipers kiss Jesus' ankle through an opening in the bulletproof glass. Semana Santa culminates in a procession honoring his statue.

For the secularly oriented, C. San Luis, near Iglesia de San Luis, is home to the **Centro Andaluz de Teatro** (tel. 95 490 14 93), an independent theater workshop that has produced some of Spain's best contemporary actors. Calle Dueñas leads to another great mansion, **Palacio de las Dueñas,** birthplace of 20th-century poet Antonio Machado. A large garden beyond the *murallas* and the Basilica Macarena leads to the **Hospital de las Cinco Llagas,** a spectacular Renaissance building recently

ANDALUCÍA

primped to host the present-day Andalucían parliament. Toward the river is the **Alameda de Hércules,** a leafy promenade patrolled by prostitutes and other shady types at night and site of the tremendous Sunday morning *Rastro* (flea market).

Elsewhere

In 1929, Sevilla made elaborate plans for an Ibero-American world fair. When Wall Street crashed, so did the fair, but the event bequeathed the lovely landscapes of the **Parque de María Luisa,** framed by Av. Borbolla and the river. *(Open daily 8am-10pm.)* Innumerable courtyards, turquoise-tiled benches, and tailored tropical gardens send many visitors off to *siesta*-land. On the park's northeast edge, the twin spires of **Plaza de España** poke above the city skyline. The plaza is the perfect setting for a high bourgeois Sunday afternoon outing, evoking images of horse-drawn carriages, top hats, puffy dresses, bottles of wine beside the fountain, and **boat rides** along the narrow moat. *(300ptas per hr.)* Mosaics depicting every provincial capital in Spain line the decaying colonnade. The balconies above offer a beautiful bird's-eye view. Nearby, on C. San Fernando, stands the 18th-century **Antigua Fábrica de Tabacos** (Old Tobacco Factory), setting of Bizet's *Carmen* and now part of the University.

Sevilla's **Museo Arqueológico** (tel. 95 423 24 01), inside the park at Pl. América, shows off a small collection of pre-Roman and Roman artifacts excavated in the surrounding provinces. *(Open Tu 3-8pm, W-Sa 9am-8pm, Su 9am-2:30pm. 250ptas, E.U. members free.)* About a block toward the river down Palos de la Frontera is the 17th-century **Palacio de San Telmo,** built as a sailor training school. Saint Telmo, patron saint of sailors, hovers over the door amid a maelstrom of marine monsters. Across the river and north of Triana, one can visit the **Centro Andaluz de Arte Contemporáneo** (tel. 95 448 06 11), in the Cartuja district. This large complex holds the collection of the former Modern Art Museum and such 20th-century star painters as Joan Miró. *(Open Tu-Sa 10am-9pm, Su 10am-3pm. 300ptas, E.U. members free. Tuesdays free. Guided visits at 11am, noon, 6, and 7pm.)* Nearby, one can also visit the old grounds of **EXPO '92,** now mostly used its dance floors.

ENTERTAINMENT

The tourist office distributes *El Giraldillo,* a free monthly entertainment magazine with complete listings on music, art exhibits, theater, dance, fairs, and film.

Movies, Theater, and Musical Performances

Cine Avenida, C. Marqués de las Paradas, 15 (tel. 95 422 15 48), and **Cine Cristina,** Puerto de Jerez, 1 (tel. 95 422 66 80), both show predominantly foreign (i.e. American) films dubbed in Spanish. **Corona Center,** Pagés del Corro, s/n (tel. 95 427 80 64), in the mall between C. Salado and C. Paraíso in Barrio de Triana, screens subtitled films, often in English. (Most theaters around 600-700ptas, W half price, Th two for one. Morning matinees W, Sa, and Su.) For info on all three cinemas call or check under "Cinema" in *El Giraldillo.*

The venerable **Teatro Lope de Vega** (tel. 95 423 45 46), near Parque María Luisa, has long been the city's leading stage. Ask about scheduled events at the tourist office, or check the bulletin board in the university lobby on C. San Fernando. If you can't make it to a show, at least stop by for a drink at **Casino,** the popular *terraza* outside. In Pl. San Antonio de Padua, **Sala La Herrería** and **Sala La Imperdible** put on more avant-garde productions (both can be reached at tel. 95 438 82 19).

The **Teatro de la Maestranza** (tel. 95 422 33 44), on the river next to the Pl. Toros, is a splendid concert hall accommodating both orchestral performances and opera. (Purchase tickets at the box office in front of the theater daily 10am-2pm and 6-9pm.) On spring and summer evenings, neighborhood fairs are often accompanied by free **open-air concerts** in Barrios de Santa Cruz and Triana.

Nightlife

Sevilla's reputation for gaiety is tried and true. A typical Sevillian sampling of *marcha* (revelry) begins with visits to several bars for *tapas* and *copas,* followed by dancing at

ANDALUCÍA

Sevilla's Cup of Tea

Got a few hours to kill before hitting Sevilla's thunderous nightlife? Bastions of Sevillian culture, the following local watering holes help ease the transition from daytime sight-seeing to nighttime swinging.

Two blocks inland from Pl. Encarnación, **El Rinconcillo,** C. Gerona, 40-42 (tel. 95 422 31 83), founded in 1670, is Sevilla's oldest tavern. Look behind the hanging hams for the plaque/anagram. Cheap *tapas* and *cervezas* enhance the timeless flavor. Around the corner on C. San Felipe, **Cervecería El Tremendo,** a popular lunchtime and after-work meeting place, claims to use a unique keg siphon treated with salt. It's the same beer as anywhere else, but regulars swear it's the best in Sevilla. When they come to Sevilla, Peruvian author Mario Vargas Llosa and Argentine president Carlos Menem hang at **Café Bar Las Teresas,** C. Santa Teresa, 2 (tel. 95 421 30 69), in the Barrio Sta. Cruz, down C. Méson del Moro from C. Mateos Gago. Ask the bartenders about Sevilla's two *fútbol* teams (Sevilla and Betis), and they'll fight all night. At **Casa Morales,** C. Garcia de Vinuesa, 11, one block from Catedral, sit around a huge barrel and sample regional wines, *finos, manzanillos,* brandies, and other sherries (from 100ptas per glass). To be *muy sevillano,* buy fried fish across the street and eat it here.

nightclubs, and culminating in an early morning breakfast of *churros con chocolate.* Most clubs don't expect business until well after midnight; the real fun often starts after 3am. Women and foreigners, especially Americans, are sometimes admitted to discos free of charge. Ask bartenders or patrons at bars Capote, Alfonso, Líbano, or Chile (see below) to recommend hot spots.

Popular bars year-round cluster **Plaza Alfalfa** and **Plaza Salvador** in El Centro, **Calle Mateos Gago** near the cathedral, **Calle Adriano** by the bullring, and **Calle Betis** across the river in Triana. Summer crowds sweep towards the river in hopes of a pleasant breeze—even on "slow" nights, *terrazas* will stay open until 4am.

Several bars popular with exchange students line C. Betis. **Alambique, Mú Dáquí,** and **Big Ben** huddle together near Puente Isabel II. Farther down C. Betis, **Lo nuestro** swings until the wee hours with nightly performances of *sevillanas* and *rumbas.* On the other bank and downstream on Po. Delicias, near Parque María Luisa, **Alfonso, Libano,** and **Chile** are popular *chiringuitos* (beach bars). Upstream, there's always a crowd at **Bar Capote,** Po. Cristóbal Colón, beside Puente Isabel II (beer 200ptas; open M-Th until 4am, F-Sa even later with live music; DJs W-Th).

Dancing during the summer also requires outdoor settings. A number of sandy dance floors open up in **Puerta Triana,** upstream from Triana on the old Expo '92 grounds. There is usually no cover (crowds build around 3am). **El Simpecao,** in the same area, devotes itself entirely to dancing *sevillanas.* Some of these dance floors may be closed or renamed after summer 1999 due to the city's plans to open a new sports center in the area. A few kilometers out of town on Ctra. San Juan de Aznalfarache (the road towards Huelva), **La Recua** asks a hefty cover charge in return for an open-air dance floor crowded with *gente guapa* (beautiful people).

In winter time, bar-hoppers stick to El Centro around Pl. Alfalfa and Pl. Salvador. The most popular disco is ultra-chic **Catedral,** Ctra. Rosario off Pl. Salvador (expect a cover charge). Other popular spots congregate on **Avenida de la Raza,** parallel to the river off Puente de las Delicias. Two such clubs, **Hipódromo** and **Aduana,** admit ladies for free; guys pay 1000ptas, one drink included. **Bestiario,** C. Zaragoza, 13, is known as a late-night bar, and the last stop before an early morning *churros.*

Over the past several years, the **gay scene** in Sevilla has become more distinct from the general nightlife; places that used to host mixed gay and straight crowds now cater more exclusively to one group or the other. Nevertheless, the scene is thriving. Across the street from Puente Isabel II and Bar Capote, **Isbiliyya,** Po. Colón, 2, and **To Ca Me,** C. Reyes Católicos, 25, host a mostly gay crowd until 4am. Both have outdoor tables; the latter has a video jukebox and blue neon lights. **Itaca,** on C. Amor de Dios, in El Centro, is the liveliest gay disco in town (open Su-Th until 5am, F-Sa even later; shows W 1am; knock on the door to be let in). **Poseidon,** C. Marqués Paradas, is another option.

Sevillanas

When in Sevilla, do as the *Sevillanos* do. *Sevillanas* is the widely popular folk form of flamenco. While elegant flamenco dancers must study technique for years, just about any putz can perform *sevillanas*. All that it requires is that you openly embrace both the city and its residents—*sevillanas* is the people's dance. In little bars in Sevilla, you will often witness yuppie couples, chic young women, and teethless old men all taking the dance floor side-by-side as soon as the guitar and its mournful song begin to play. A partner dance, the *sevillanas* consists of four segments that together act out a courting ritual. The basic step is easy to pick up; ask sweetly to get an impromptu lesson, and before you know it, you'll be twisting your wrists like a native.

During the *Feria de Abril* the whole world takes to the streets, stomping their feet, flipping their skirts, and holding their heads high as they turn and sashay. If for some reason you don't manage to catch any live, check out Carlos Saura's movie *Sevillanas* for a showcase of variations on the dance.

Around 12:30am a number of hipper (and more expensive) joints start getting lively. The ambience at the bars listed here is nothing less than artistic:

Abades, C. Abades, 13 (tel. 95 422 56 22), off C. Mateos Gago. Notorious for its free-loving during Franco, this 18th-century mansion has hosted the likes of Plácido Domingo, princes, and *infantas*. Abades has since quieted down although the chic file in during winter and trickle in at other times to sip divinely multi-liquored *agua de sevilla* (500ptas)—order first, ask ingredients later. Sit back in a plush wicker chair, listen to Mozart's *Requiem*, and forget you're slumming through Spain on the cheap. Open nightly in summer until 2am; in winter until 4am.

Garlochí, C. Boteros, 26, a few blocks inland (east) from Pl. Alfalfa and Pl. Salvador. A Baroque den of cherubs, chandeliers, and brass-framed mirrors. House specialty is *Sangre de Cristo* (pomegranate liqueur, champagne, and whiskey served in a cut-glass goblet, 600ptas). Beer 300ptas. Open Su-Th until 3am, F-Sa even later.

Antigüedades, C. Argote de Molina, just north of the cathedral. A new decorative theme every few weeks (such as lifelike plastic insects, lizards, and frogs arranged on the wall by ecosystem). Outdoor tables host a mixed-age, international crowd. Beer 200ptas, mixed drinks 600ptas. Open Su-Th until 3am, F-Sa until 4am.

Flamenco and Other Live Music

The lightning-quick stomping and footwork of Andalucía's flamenco dancers will dazzle your eyes, while the wailing *cantaores* will overwhelm your ears. In Sevilla, the art of flamenco has evolved into something distinct, called *las sevillanas*, a dance of partners performing matador-like passes and turns, which locals have memorized as if it were law (see *Sevillanas*). Unfortunately, professional flamenco rarely comes cheap (unless you catch the *Feria de Abril*, when dancers take over the city). The flashiest show in town, catering exclusively to tourists, is on the west edge of Barrio Sta. Cruz, at **Los Gallos,** Pl. Sta. Cruz, 11 (tel. 95 421 69 81; fax 95 422 85 22; http://www.infor.es/gallos). The cover starts at 3000ptas and includes one drink. Shows run nightly at 9 and 11:30pm. Arrive early to get a good seat (and a ticket). Stores and *hostales* in Barrio Sta. Cruz sell advanced tickets. Half the passion of a *sevillana* comes from the rowdy, hand-clapping audience—an ambience that clueless foreigners cannot provide. High up in the Triana, **Casa Anselma,** C. Pagés del Corro, 49 (no sign), quakes with floor-stomping and guitar strumming nightly as patrons take turns dancing and singing. (No cover. *Copas* 600ptas. Music nightly 12:30-3am. Follow C. San Jacinto from the bridge and take the 3rd right.) **El Tamboril,** Pl. Sta. Cruz, is slightly upscale with a pink interior and padded benches, but often hosts *sevillanas* and *rumbas* after midnight without a cover. **La Carbonería,** C. Levies, 18 (tel. 95 421 44 60), a few blocks up from C. Santa María la Blanca, was established 30 years ago to support artists and musicians censored during Franco's dictatorship, and has free live music nightly. Camarón de la Isla occasionally used to play here. Current acts may not be as prestigious but are at least inventive. Flamenco and sometimes rock, jazz, or a combination of the above are performed next to cutting-edge art exhibits.

El Fútbol

Sevilla has two wildly popular pro teams within its city limits. The pride of the Guadalquivir is **Betis,** which plays in Estadio Benito Villamarín (tel. 95 461 03 40), downstream on Av. Palmera. Team **Sevilla** has suffered from coaching changes and recently was demoted to second division, leaving followers humiliated. Sevilla plays in the Estadio Sámche Pizjuán (tel. 95 453 53 53), east of Av. Menéndez Pelayo on Av. Eduardo Dato. Tickets can be purchased at the respective stadiums, but price and availability range wildly depending on the quality of the match-up. Fan(atic)s have been known to camp out at least one week ahead. Even if you can't make it to the stands, you'll likely know who's won judging by the colors worn by the fans in the streets (Betis wears green and white, Sevilla white and red). Sevilla's fans are so dedicated—even *madrileños* will readily laud Ultra Sur, a hard-core fan club—that all international battles fought on Spanish turf are held in Sevilla.

La Corrida (The Bullfight)

The cheapest place to buy bullfight tickets is at the ring on Po. Marqués de Contadero. For a good *cartel* (line-up), however, one of the booths on C. Sierpes, C. Velázquez, or Pl. Toros might be the only source of advance tickets. **Ticket prices,** depending on the quality of both your seat and the *matador,* can run from 3000ptas for a *grada de sol* (nosebleed seat in the sun) to 13,000ptas for a *barrera de sombra* (front-row seat in the shade). Buying a ticket from a scalper usually adds 20% to the ticket price. *Corridas de toros* (bullfights) or *novilladas* (cut-rate fights with young bulls and novice bullfighters) are held on the 13 days around the *Feria de Abril* and into May, nearly every Sunday in June, often during Corpus Christi in June and early July, and again during the Feria de San Miguel near the end of September. During most of July and August, they occur on occasional Thursdays. You'll know when a top-notch *matador* is scheduled to fight: hours before the big event, the ring is surrounded by throngs of female devotees who don their most seductive dresses and alluring lipstick in hopes of catching the eye of the stud. Some of the most popular Sevillian bullfighters include the aging Curro Romero and Emilio Muñoz, a.k.a. "El Espártaco" (Spartacus). For current info and **ticket sales,** call 95 422 35 06. The stadium is open to visitors on non-bullfight days from 10:30am to 2pm and 4 to 6pm, on bullfight days from 10am to 3pm (tours every 30min., 400ptas).

Festivals

Sevilla swells with tourists during the *fiestas.* The world-famous **Semana Santa** lasts from Palm Sunday to Good Friday (April 2). Penitents in hooded cassocks guide bejeweled floats lit by hundreds of candles through the streets. Book your room well in advance, and expect to pay triple the ordinary price. The tourist office issues a helpful booklet with advice on how to stay awake through the week's festivities. Two or three weeks after Semana Santa, the city rewards itself for its Lenten piety with the six-day **Feria de Abril** (April Fair). Begun as part of a 19th-century popular revolt against foreign influence, circuses, bullfights, and flamenco shows roar into the night in a showcase of local customs. The fairgrounds are on the southern end of Barrio Los Remedios. A spectacular array of flowers and lanterns festoon over 1000 kiosks, tents, and pavilions. Don't even dream of sleeping.

The **Romería del Rocío** (May 23) takes place 50 days after Easter on Pentecost and involves the veneration of the Blanca Paloma (white dove) by candle-light parades and traditional dance. The festival culminates with a pilgrimage from Sevilla to the nearby village of **Rocío,** 80km away. Hundreds of Sevillians participate in the two-day trek, accepting food from strangers and camping by the road at night. In the best Spanish fashion, the Romería is half religious penitence, half party. Singing and dancing break out around campfires and *sevillanas* ring until sunrise.

ANDALUCÍA

■ Near Sevilla: Itálica

A mere 9km northwest of Sevilla, the village of **Santiponce** (pop. 6200) shelters the ruins of **Itálica,** the first important Roman settlement in Iberia. Itálica, itself born in 206 BC, was the birthplace of emperors Trajan (AD 53) and Hadrian (AD 76). The city walls and Nova Urbs were constructed between AD 300 and 400, otherwise known as the *apogeo* (apogee). In the following centuries, Itálica's power declined, and by the 5th century Sevilla had usurped the region's seat of power. Archaeological excavations began in the 18th century and continue today. The **anfiteatro** (tel. 95 599 73 76), among Spain's largest, seats 25,000. It used to stage fights between gladiators and lions, but, more mellow nowadays, it hosts occasional classical theater performances instead. *(Open Tu-Sa 9am-8pm, Su 9am-3pm. 250ptas, E.U. citizens free.)* Some buildings and streets have preserved **suelos de mosaicos** (mosaic floors). For schedules and info on the annual **Festival Internacional de Itálica,** which brings dance, classical music, and theater to Itálica in July and August, check Sevilla's *El Giraldillo.* To get there, take Empresa Casal's **bus** (tel. 95 441 06 58) toward Santiponce from C. Marqués de las Paradas, 33, across from the Pl. Armas bus station. Tell the driver you're going to Itálica *(30min., departs every 30min., 125ptas.)*

■ Near Sevilla: Carmona

Thirty-three kilometers east of Sevilla, ancient Carmona (pop. 25,000) dominates a tall hill overlooking the gold and green countryside. Once a thriving Arab stronghold, it was later the favorite 14th-century retreat of Pedro el Cruel. Mudéjar palaces mingle with Christian Renaissance mansions in a network of streets partially enclosed by fortified walls. The **Puerta de Sevilla,** a horseshoe-shaped passageway with both Roman and Arab elements, and the Baroque **Puerta de Córdoba,** on the opposite end of town, once linked Carmona to both the east and west and still delineate the boundaries of the *barrio antiguo.* The **Alcázar de la Puerta de Sevilla** (tel. 95 419 09 55), adjacent to the **Puerta,** originally served (unsuccessfully) as a Carthaginian fortification against Roman attack. During the reign of Augustus, the structure was expanded to nearly its current size. *(Open M-Sa 10am-6pm, Su 10am-3pm. 200ptas, students 150ptas, seniors and under 12 100ptas. Guided visits M-Sa 11am, noon, 1, 4, and 5pm.)* Opulent Baroque mansions dot the streets uphill past the Alcázar, while the **Alcázar del Rey Don Pedro,** an Almohad fortress, guards the eastern edge of town. In Pl. Marqués de las Torres looms the late Gothic **Iglesia de Santa María** (tel. 95 414 13 30), built over an old mosque. The splendid **Patio de los Naranjos** remains from Moorish days. *(Mass daily 9am-noon and 6:30-9pm.)* Even older, a Visigothic liturgical calendar graces one of the church's columns. Nearby, several convents sell their infamous *dulces.*

Just west of town lie the ruins of the **Necrópolis Romana** (tel. 95 414 08 11). Highlights include the **Tumba de Servilia** and **Tumba del Elefante,** where depictions of Mother Nature and Eastern divinities are trumped by the presence of a curious, pagan-looking stone elephant. Next door, the **Museo Arqueológico** (tel. 95 414 08 11) displays remains from over a thousand tombs that were unearthed at the necropolis. *(Necropolis and museum open in summer Tu-F 9am-2pm, Sa 10am-2pm; in winter Tu-F 10am-2pm and 4-6pm, Sa-Su 10am-2pm. 250ptas, E.U. citizens free.)*

Carmona is a convenient, one-hour **bus** ride from Sevilla (M-F 20 per day, Sa 10 per day, Su 7 per day, 295ptas). In Sevilla, buses depart from Prado de San Sebastián. In Carmona, buses leave from C. Jorge Bonsor, off C. Sevilla. The **tourist office** (tel. 95 419 09 55; fax 95 419 00 80) is located at the Puerta de Sevilla/Alcázar entrance, down C. San Pedro from the bus stop (open M-Sa 10am-6pm, Su 10am-3pm). The **police,** Pl. San Fernando, take calls at tel. 95 414 00 08. For **medical assistance,** on C. Paseo de La Feria, dial 95 414 00 97. The **post office** (tel. 95 414 15 62) is on C. Primm (open M-F 8:30am-2:30pm, Sa 9:30am-1pm). The **postal code** is 41410.

Carmona's few accommodations are generally cheaper than Sevilla's. Take a gamble at **Casa Carmelo,** C. San Pedro, 15 (tel. 95 414 05 72), a vintage 19th-century casino turned *pensión,* toward the Alcázar from the bus stop (singles 1500-1750ptas; doubles 3000-3500ptas, with bath 4000ptas). **Restaurante San Fernando,** C. Sacremento, 3 (tel. 95 414 35 56), comes highly recommended (open Tu-Sa 1:30-4pm and 9pm-midnight, Su 1:30-4pm).

■ Near Sevilla: Osuna

Julius Caesar founded Osuna (pop. 17,000), naming it after the *osos* (bears) that once lumbered about the land. Now, there is little to remind one of Osuna's distant past. The peaceful stone mansions lining the streets are instead testimony to Osuna's more recent days as a cushy ducal seat. The **Colegiata de Santa María de la Asunción** (tel. 95 481 04 44), the large church atop the hill, is one of many works of art commissioned by the Dukes of Osuna. *(Open Tu-Su 10am-1:30pm and 3:30-6:30pm. 300ptas.)* Goya's portrait of the family—his most assiduous patrons—now hangs in the Museo del Prado in Madrid, but the Colegiata contains an impressive array of paintings (including five Riberas) and religious artifacts. Facing the church's entrance is the **Monasterio de la Encarnación** (tel. 95 481 11 21). *(Open Tu-Su 10am-1:30pm and 3:30-6:30pm. 250ptas.)* A resident nun will show you room upon room of polychromed wooden sculptures and silver crucifixes. Must-sees are the 18th-century statue of *Cristo de la Misericordia* in the adjoining Baroque church and the Sevillian *azulejos* in the patio. In the town proper, **Calle San Pedro** is decked out in palatial facades.

  Trains stop at the small, desolate station on Av. Estación (tel. 95 481 03 08), a 15-minute walk from the town center. To reach Pl. Mayor from the train station, walk up Av. Estación, curving right on C. Mancilla. At Pl. Salitre, turn left on C. Carmen and then right on C. Sevilla, which leads into the plaza. Trains run to Sevilla (1¼hr., 4 per day, 660ptas) and Bobadilla (30min.), RENFE's hub for other Andalucía destinations. **Empresa Dipasa/Linesur** (tel. 95 481 01 46) runs buses to Sevilla (1½hr., 5-10 per day, 830ptas). **Alsina Graells** (tel. 95 481 01 46) connects to: Antequera (1hr., 5 per day, 750ptas); Málaga (2½hr., 2 per day, 1525ptas); and Granada (3½hr., 3 per day, 1905ptas). The **bus** station (tel. 95 481 01 46), on Av. Constitución, is a 10-minute walk from the center. To get to Pl. Mayor from the bus station, walk downhill on C. Santa Ana past tiny Pl. Santa Rita; continue on Av. Arjona until you hit the plaza.

  You can pick up a **map** at the **Casa de la Cultura,** C. Sevilla, 22 (tel. 95 481 16 17), a left off Pl. Mayor. The **municipal police** (tel. 95 481 00 50) are on Pl. Mayor; in an **emergency,** dial 091 or 092. For **medical assistance,** call Hospital Nuestra Señora de la Merced (tel. 95 481 09 00). The **postal code** is 41640.

  There are precious few hostel options in Osuna. **Hostal Caballo Blanco,** C. Granada, 1 (tel. 95 481 01 84), furnishes comfy, cream-colored rooms with bath and A/C (singles 3000ptas; doubles 4900ptas). Osuna hides a number of old-time *tapas* bars. **Casa Curro** in Pl. Salitre (take C. Sevilla from Pl. Mayor two blocks and turn left on C. Carmen), has a fantastic *cerveza con tapa* deal (135ptas)—two will fill you up. The **Pardillo supermarket** is on C. Carrera (open M-Sa 9am-2pm and 5:30-9:20pm).

■ Córdoba

A Spaniard well-versed in regional subtleties made the following distinction between Córdoba and her more flamboyant Andalucían sister to the west: "Sevilla is a young girl, gay, laughing, provoking—but Córdoba…Córdoba is a dear old lady." Córdoba (pop. 350,000) does indeed cloak itself in quiet dignity, its refinement befitting a town whose natives have always been known less for joviality than for breadth of mind. In Roman times, playwright and philosopher Seneca settled here, while under Islamic rule (711-1263) Córdoba reemerged as an intellectual and political center, producing Maimonides, the premier medieval-Jewish philosopher, and becoming the seat of the western Caliphate. During Spain's Golden Age of literature in the 16th and 17th centuries, luminaries such as poet Luís de Góngora resided here. The historical and cultural melange left a unique architectural legacy that attracts hordes of tourists every year. Nowhere else in Spain are the remnants of ancient Islamic, Jewish, and Catholic civilizations so visibly intermixed. Springtime brings roaring festivals to these ancient facades, but in the summer, monuments and tourists bake.

ANDALUCÍA

ORIENTATION AND PRACTICAL INFORMATION

Córdoba is split in two: a modern and commercial northern half extending from the train station on **Avenida de América** down to **Plaza de las Tendillas,** the center of the city; and a medieval maze, the **Judería** (old Jewish quarter), in the south. This tangle of beautiful and disorienting streets extends from Pl. Tendillas to the banks of the **Río Guadalquivir,** winding past the **Mezquita** and **Alcázar.**

Transportation

Trains: Av. América (tel. 957 49 02 02 or 957 40 02 02). Trains run to: Sevilla (AVE: 45min., 15 per day, 2300-2700ptas; regular: 1¼hr., 12 per day, 890-2100ptas); Antequera (1½hr., 4 per day, 1500ptas); Madrid (AVE: 2hr., 15 per day, 5900-7000ptas; regular: 2-6hr., 11 per day, 3500-5800); Málaga (AVE: 2¼hr., 4 per day, 2200ptas; regular: 3hr., 11 per day, 1535-2200ptas); Cádiz (AVE: 2½hr., 2 per day, 3700ptas; regular: 3hr., 4 per day, 1960-4000ptas); Granada, via Bobadilla (3hr., 8 per day, 2015-2610ptas); Algeciras (5hr., 4 per day, 2400-3270ptas); Barcelona (11hr., 4 per day, 6200-9200ptas). For international tickets, contact **RENFE,** Ronda de los Tejares, 10 (tel. 957 47 58 84).

Buses: The main station, C. Diego Serrano, 14, is 1 block south of Av. Medina Azahara. To reach the town center, exit left, make an immediate left, then go right onto Av. Medina Azahara. When you reach the park, Av. Republica Argentina will be directly in front of you. From there, follow the Córdoba map. **Alsina Graells Sur** (tel. 957 23 64 74) covers most of Andalucía. To: Sevilla (2hr., 11 per day, 1200ptas); Jaén (2hr., 6 per day, 920ptas); Antequera (2½hr., 3 per day, 1075ptas); Granada (3hr., 8 per day, 1765ptas); Málaga (3-3½hr., 6 per day, 1500ptas); Marbella (4hr., 2 per day, 2085ptas); Cádiz via Los Amarillos or Comes Sur (4-5hr., 5 per day, 2120ptas); Algeciras (5hr., 3 per day, 2805ptas); Almería (5hr., 1 per day, 2995ptas). **Bacoma** (tel. 957 45 65 14) to: Valencia, Murcia, and Barcelona (1 per day, from 7625ptas). **Socibus** (tel. 902 22 92 92) provides exceptionally cheap service to Madrid (4½hr. 7 per day, 1540ptas), departing from Camino de los Sastres in front of Hotel Melia. Intra-provincial buses depart from Av. República and Po. Victoria: **Autocares Priego** (tel. 957 29 01 58) runs anywhere in the Sierra Cordobesa; **Empresa Carrera** (tel. 957 23 14 01) functions in the Campiña Cordobesa; **Empresa Ramírez** (tel. 957 41 01 00) runs buses to nearby towns and camping sites. Hopefully, all of this confusion will subside around the year 2000 with the construction of a new, centralized bus station beside the train station.

Taxis: In Pl. Tendillas. **Radio Taxi** (tel. 957 47 02 91) charges a minimum of 385ptas.

Car Rental: Hertz (tel. 957 40 20 60), in the train station. Must be at least 25. Cheapest car 7800ptas per day. Open M-F 8:30am-9pm, Sa 9am-1pm and 3:30-7pm, Su 9am-1pm.

Tourist, Financial, and Local Services

Tourist Offices: Junta de Andalucía, C. Torrijos, 10 (tel. 957 47 12 35; fax 957 49 17 78), on the west side of the Mezquita. From the train station, take bus #3 (from Av. América, about 750m to the left of the station) along the river to Puerta del Puente, the stone arch on the right. Office is 1 block up C. Torrijos. Abundant info on Córdoba and all of Andalucía. Gregarious English-speaking staff with good free **map** of the monument section. Open in summer M-Sa 9:30am-8pm; in winter M-Sa 9:30am-6pm. Less crowded and less useful, the **Oficina Municipal de Turismo y Congresos,** Pl. Judá Leví (tel./fax 957 20 05 22), next to the youth hostel, gives out maps. Open June-Sept. M-Sa 8:30am-2:30pm; Oct.-May M-Sa 9am-2pm and 4:30-6:30pm.

Currency Exchange: Banco Central Hispano (tel. 957 47 42 67), Pl. Tendillas, charges no commission. Open in summer M-F 8:30am-2:30pm; in winter M-F 8:30am-2:30pm, Sa 9am-1pm. Banks and **ATMs** dot Pl. Tendillas.

El Corte Inglés: (tel. 47 02 67). Superstore on the corner of Av. Ronda de los Tejares and Av. Gran Capitán. **Supermarket** (5th fl.) and a thorough **map** with traffic directions (575 ptas). Open M-Sa 10am-9:30pm.

Luggage Storage: Lockers at the train and main bus stations (300-600ptas). Open 24hr.

ANDALUCÍA

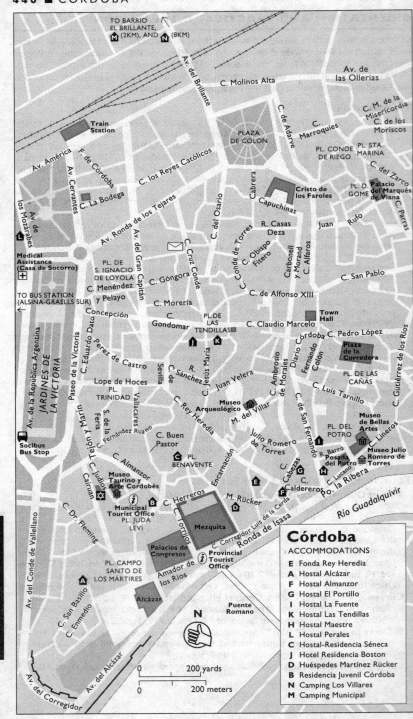

TO BARRIO
EL BRILLANTE,
M (2KM), AND N (8KM)

Av. del Brillante

C. Molinos Alta

Av. de
las Ollerias

Train
Station

PLAZA
DE COLON

C. de Adarve

C.
Marroquies

C. M. de la
Misericordia

C. de los
Moriscos

PL. CONDE
DE RIEGO

PL. STA.
MARINA

C. del Zarco

Av. América

F. de Córdoba

Av. Cervantes

La Bodega

C. los Reyes Católicos

Av. Ronda de los Tejares

Av. del Gran Capitán

Cabrera

Capuchinas

Cristo de
los Faroles

PL. D.
GOME

Palacio
del Marqués
de Viana

C. del Osario

R. Casas
Deza

Juan

Rufo

C. Patras

Av. de
los Mozárabes

Medical
Assistance
(Casa de Socorro)

PL. DE
S. IGNACIO
DE LOYOLA

C. Menéndez
y Pelayo

C. Góngora

C. Cruz Conde

C. Morería

C. Conde de Torres

C. Obispo
Fitero

Carbonell
y Morand

C. Alfaros

C. San Pablo

C. de Alfonso XIII

TO BUS STATION
(ALSINA-GRAELLS SUR)

Concepción

C. Eduardo Dato

Perez de Castro

C.
Gondomar

PL. DE
LAS
TENDILLAS

C. Claudio Marcelo

Town
Hall

Diario Córdoba

Fernando
Colón

C. Pedro López

Plaza
de la
Corredera

C. Gutiérrez de los Ríos

Av. de la República Argentina

JARDINES
DE LA
VICTORIA

Paseo de la Victoria

Lope de Hoces

PL.
TRINIDAD

Vallacares

R.
Sánchez

C. de Jesús María

Sevilla

Juan Velera

C. Ambrosio
de Morales

PL. DE LAS
CAÑAS

C. Luis Tarnillo

Socibus
Bus Stop

S. de la
Feria

K. León

C. Fernández Ruano

C. Rey Heredia

C. Buen
Pastor

C. Almanzor

Encarnación

M. del Villar

Museo
Arqueológico

Julio Romero
de Torres

C. de San Fernando

PL. DEL
POTRO

Museo
de Bellas
Artes

C. Lineros

Museo Julio
Romero de
Torres

C. Teijón

C. Judios

Cairuan

Museo
Taurino y
Arte Cordobés

i

B

PL. JUDA
LEVÍ

Municipal
Tourist
Office

C. Herreros

M. Rücker

C. Calabazas

C. Cabezas

C. Calderereos

C. Lucano

Pº. la Ribera

R. Barro
Posada
del Potro

C. Dr. Fleming

PL.
BENAVENTE

C

E

D

F

G

H

Mezquita

C. Torrijos

C. Corregidor Luis de la Cerda

Ronda de Isasa

Río Guadalquivir

C. San Basilio

C. Enmedio

Av. del Conde de Vallellano

PL. CAMPO
SANTO DE
LOS MÁRTIRES

Palacios de
Congresos

Amador de
los Ríos

i

Provincial
Tourist
Office

Alcázar

A

N

Puente
Romano

Av. del Alcázar

Av. del Corregidor

0   200 yards
0   200 meters

Córdoba

ACCOMMODATIONS

- E Fonda Rey Heredia
- A Hostal Alcázar
- F Hostal Almanzor
- G Hostal El Portillo
- I Hostal La Fuente
- K Hostal Las Tendillas
- H Hostal Maestre
- L Hostal Perales
- C Hostal-Residencia Séneca
- J Hotel Residencia Boston
- D Huéspedes Martínez Rücker
- B Residencia Juvenil Córdoba
- N Camping Los Villares
- M Camping Municipal

ANDALUCÍA

Emergency and Communications

Emergency: tel. 091 or 092. **Police:** Av. de Medina Azarah, by the main bus station.

Medical Assistance: Red Cross Hospital (tel. 957 29 34 11), Po. Victoria. English spoken. **Hospital de Reina Sofía** (tel. 957 21 70 00). English spoken. **Ambulance:** 061.

24Hr. Pharmacy: On a rotating basis. Refer to the list posted outside the pharmacy in Pl. Tendillas or to the local newspaper.

Internet Access: El Navegante Café Internet, C. Llanos del Pretorio, 1 (tel. 957 49 75 36), off Av. de America, near the train station. Email and World Wide Web access in a bar with a nautical theme. 250ptas per 15min., 350ptas per 30min., 600ptas per hr. Open daily 8am-3:30pm and 8pm-3am.

Post Office: C. Cruz Conde, 15 (tel. 957 47 81 02), just north of Pl. Tendillas. Open for stamps and Lista de Correos M-F 8:30am-8:30pm, Sa 9:30am-2pm. **Postal Code:** 14070.

ACCOMMODATIONS AND CAMPING

Córdoba is especially crowded during Semana Santa and May through September, so call ahead to make reservations.

Residencia Juvenil Córdoba (HI) (tel. 957 29 01 66; fax 957 29 05 00), Pl. Juda Leví, next to the municipal tourist office and a 2min. walk from the Mezquita. Huge, recently renovated, modern, and antiseptic. Rooms are doubles with private baths, or quads with shared bath. 1300ptas per person, over 26 1800ptas. 300ptas extra per day for nonmembers for 6-night stay to gain membership. Wheelchair accessible. A/C. Check-out 10am. Check-in 1pm. No curfew. Reservations recommended.

In and Around the Judería

The Judería's whitewashed walls, narrow, twisting streets, and proximity to major sights make it the most pleasing and convenient area to make home. Those without Ariadne's thread should procure a map. At night the area becomes desolate and a little spooky, so be cautious if walking alone.

Hotel/Hostal Maestre, C. Romero Barros, 16 (reservations tel. 957 47 24 10; tel./fax 957 47 53 95). From the Mezquita, follow the river east to Pl. Potro, walk uphill and take a left (10min.). A recently renovated complex, with an intimate, patio-lined *hostal* and a modern hotel with elevator, as well as spacious apartments for 3-5 people (with kitchens). All rooms with private bath, some with TV. In *hostal:* singles 2000-2500ptas; doubles 4000-4500ptas, with A/C 5000ptas. In hotel: doubles 5000-6000ptas with TV, phone, A/C; apartments 7000-8000ptas. Parking 850ptas. 10% discount for *Let's Go* readers Oct. 20-Mar. 20. Visa, MC, AmEx.

☜Huéspedes Martínez Rücker, Martínez Rücker, 14 (tel. 957 47 25 62), just east of the Mezquita. The gregarious young owner moonlights as an antique collector, and the comfortable patio is his gallery. All rooms have fans. Singles 1500ptas; doubles 3000-3500ptas. 1500ptas per person for up to 5 people in a room.

Hostal-Residencia Séneca, C. Conde y Luque, 7 (tel./fax 957 47 32 34), 2 blocks north of the Mezquita; follow C. Céspedes. Impeccably maintained by a vivacious English- and French-speaking owner. All rooms have fans. Patio. Singles 2000ptas; doubles 3600ptas, with bath 4600ptas. Breakfast 450ptas. 1000ptas extra for A/C.

Hostal La Fuente, C. San Fernando, 51 (tel. 957 48 78 27 or 957 48 14 78; fax 957 48 78 27), off C. Corregidor Luis de la Cerda. Friendly owners watch over immaculate rooms, all with bath, some with TV. Beautiful patio. Singles 3000ptas; doubles 4000-5000ptas; 1800ptas per person for large groups. Breakfast 300ptas. Parking 700ptas. Visa, MC, AmEx.

Hostal Almanzor, C. Corregidor Luis de la Cerda, 10 (tel./fax 957 48 54 00), at the end of C. Rey Heredía close to the river, 3 blocks from the Mezquita. Spotless rooms with balconies and flowing white drapes. All singles have king-sized bed. All rooms have TV; some have A/C. Singles 1500-2500ptas, with bath 2000-3000ptas; doubles with bath 3000-4000ptas. Reception 24hr. Free parking. Visa, MC.

Fonda Rey Heredia, C. Rey Heredia, 26 (tel. 957 47 41 82), on a long, narrow street parallel to the northeastern corner of the Mezquita. Tiled rooms with fans and high ceilings. Clean and modern common bathrooms. Singles 1500ptas; doubles 3000ptas; triples 4000ptas. Usually closed Nov.-Semana Santa, but call to check.

Hostal Alcázar, C. San Basilio, 2 (tel. 957 20 25 61), on a tiny alley off the Jardines Santo Mártires, 2 blocks uphill from the Alcázar. The kind of place that makes you want to powder your nose—dainty furnishings and floral motif. Rooms with fans. Singles 2000ptas; doubles 3000ptas, with bath 4300ptas. Generous 300ptas breakfast for *Let's Go* readers. Reservations would be wise. Visa, MC, AmEx.

Hostal El Portillo, C. Cabezas, 2 (tel. 957 47 20 91), off C. Caldereros, the continuation of C. Rey Heredía near the river. Another quaint patio. Fans in all rooms. A few singles 1200ptas; doubles 2500-3000ptas; triples 3500-4000ptas.

Around Plaza de las Tendillas and the New City

Just five minutes north of the Judería, rooms in this busy area offer a glimpse of bustling, modern Córdoba. In the afternoons, locals gather on its *terrazas* bordering the plaza for conversation and overpriced drinks. From RENFE, take bus #3; from the main bus station, bus #7. For the truly exhausted, try a hostel near RENFE or the bus station, on the west side of Av. República Argentina.

Hotel Residencia Boston, C. Málaga, 2 (tel. 957 47 41 76; fax 957 47 85 23), on Pl. Tendillas. Good value for great amenities: A/C, TV, phones, and baths. Full-time concierge. Singles with small bath 3200-3800ptas; doubles with bath 5300-6300ptas; triples 6300-7300ptas. Breakfast 400ptas. Visa, MC, AmEx.

Hostal Las Tendillas, C. Jesús y María, 1 (tel. 957 47 30 29), on Pl. Tendillas. Respectable rooms and bathrooms. Deafening plaza revelry below. Refrigerator in the hall. Unusually enormous singles 1900ptas; doubles 3300ptas; triples 4000ptas.

Hostal Perales, Av. Mozárabes, 15 (tel. 957 23 03 25), a half block from the train station and around the corner from all bus stations. Look for the yellow sign. Smallish rooms on a loud street. Singles 1800ptas; doubles 3000-3600ptas.

Camping

Camping Municipal, Av. Brillante (tel. 957 28 21 65). From the train station, turn left on Av. América, left at Av. Brillante, then walk about 2km uphill. Or take bus #10 or 11 from Av. Cervantes near the station to the campsite. Public pool. 560ptas per person, per tent, and per car, children under 10 400ptas.

Camping Los Villares, Carretera Vecinal Córdoba-Obejo (a.k.a. Carretera de Los Villares; tel. 957 33 01 45). Inaccessible by public transportation, but the best option if the Municipal is full. Drive past Camping Municipal and follow signs for 8km. 300ptas per car, 375ptas per tent and per person, children 275ptas.

FOOD

The famed Mezquita attracts nearly as many high-priced eateries as tourists to eat in them, but a five-minute walk in any direction but south yields local specialties at reasonable prices. **Calle Doctor Fleming,** demarcating the west side of the Judería, is sprinkled with little *mesones* dispatching *platos combinados* for a moderate 600ptas. Students and student-priced eateries cluster farther west in **Barrio Cruz Conde,** around Av. Menéndez Pidal.

The roster of regional specialties includes gazpacho, *salmorejo* (a gazpacho-like cream soup topped with hard-boiled eggs and pieces of ham), and *rabo de toro* (bull's tail simmered in tomato sauce). Nearby towns of Montilla and Moriles produce superb sherries for about 150ptas per glass: a light, dry *fino;* a darker *amontillado;* a sweet *oloroso;* and a creamy *Pedro Ximénez.* Teetotalers favor the delicious and refreshing *horchata de almendra* (a bitter almond drink), and the similar *horchata de chufa,* as sweet as liquid *turrón.* Ice-cold *granizados* (slushies) work wonders on hot days. **Supermarket Simago,** C. Jesús María, lies half a block south of Pl. Tendillas (open M-Sa 9am-9pm). For a mind-boggling selection but higher prices, try the fifth floor of **El Corte Inglés** (see **Practical Information,** p. 439).

ANDALUCÍA

◉**Sociedad de Plateros,** C. San Francisco, 6 (tel. 957 47 00 42), between C. San Fernando and the top end of Pl. Potro. Casual atmosphere and good food and drink have made this place popular since 1872. Wide selection of *tapas* 150-200ptas. *Raciones* and *media raciones* 300-600ptas. Fresh fish daily. Bar open Tu-Su 8am-4pm and 7pm-2am; meals served 1-4pm and 8pm-midnight. Visa, MC.

Bodega Guzmán, C. Judíos, 7 (tel. 957 29 60 09), half a block north of the synagogue. A wine cellar decorated with barrels, bullfighting posters, and mosaics. Frequented by retired men who sit for hours, talking and drinking house wines. *This is Andalucía.* Beer 130ptas, half-carafe of wine 85-135ptas. Reasonably priced *tapas* and *raciones.* Open F-W 11:15am-3:30pm and 8pm-midnight.

Taberna Salinas, C. Tundidores, 3 (tel. 957 48 01 35), down cobbled stairs from the Ayuntamiento. Waiters dash around the indoor fountain with traditional *cordobés* cooking. Superb *salmorejo* and eye-popping spinach-garbanzo mash. *Raciones* 600-700ptas. Beer 125ptas. Open M-Sa noon-4pm and 8pm-midnight.

Taberna San Miguel, Pl. San Miguel, 1 (tel. 957 47 83 28), 1 block north of Pl. Tendillas. Another classic *tapas* joint with bullfighting decor, always packed during lunchtime. Ask for their card, a name-tag which reads, "I am partying. If you find me somewhere, please return me to the following address..." *Tapas* 230-275ptas, *raciones* 750-1500ptas. Open Sept.-July M-Sa noon-4pm and 8pm-midnight.

Mesón San Basilio, C. San Basilio, 19 (tel. 957 29 70 07), west of the Alcázar. The breezy patio is so relaxing that the simulated bird chirping almost sounds authentic. Scrumptious *revuelto de ajetes, salmón, y gambas* (scrambled eggs with green beans, salmon, and shrimp; 850ptas). *Menú* (1000ptas) served M-F. Open daily in summer 12:30-4pm and 8pm-midnight; in winter noon-4pm and 7-11:30pm.

El Pincantón, C. F. Ruano, 19, one block east of the top of C. Judíos. The selection in this little room includes nothing above 300ptas, making it a perennial favorite among young locals. Specializes in *salsas picantes* with names like *mala leche* (sour milk, sour person, or anger, depending on the context). Huge *bocadillos* 150-250ptas. Beer 100ptas. Open daily 10am-2pm and 8pm-midnight.

Halal, C. Rey Heredia, 28 (tel. 957 48 32 35). With a mosque upstairs, there's no alcohol served downstairs in the cushioned den or peaceful patio. Instead, the thirsty huddle around freshly made *batidos* (shakes) of fruit or nuts (275-300ptas). Tea 200-250ptas. Open in summer Tu-Su 6-11pm; in winter Th-Su 4pm-midnight.

Oh Mamma Mia, C. Reyes Católicos, 5 (tel. 957 47 00 52), off Av. del Gran Capitán. Kids may overrun this popular chain restaurant, but it maintains high standards; every pizza is a work of art. Pictures of Leonardo da Vinci and other great Italians grace the walls. Pizzas 595-740ptas. Pastas 595-840ptas. Open Su-Th 1:30-4pm and 9pm-midnight, F-Sa 1:30-4pm and 9pm-12:30am. Visa, MC.

Restaurante Jaluar, C. Corregidor Luis de la Cerda, s/n (tel. 957 48 29 76), off C. Rey Heredia. Flexible staff cooks whatever you desire, including veggie dishes. *Menú* 1000-1500ptas. Breakfast 500ptas. Free *tapas* with beer. Open daily 7am-late.

SIGHTS

La Mezquita

Tel. 957 47 05 12. Open in summer M-Sa 10am-7pm, Su 2-7pm; in winter M-Sa 10am-5:30pm, Su 2-5:30pm. 750ptas, ages 8-11 375 ptas. Same ticket valid for Museo Diocesano de Bellas Artes. Last ticket sold 30min. before closing. Free during mass M-F 8:30-10am, Su 9:30am-1:30pm. Patio always open to public.

Built in AD 784 on the site of a Visigoth basilica during Sultan Abderramán's reign, Córdoba's **Mezquita** was intended to surpass all other mosques in grandeur. Over the next two centuries, the architectural masterpiece was enlarged to cover an area equivalent to several city blocks, making it the largest mosque in the Islamic world at the time. The 14th-century Mudéjar door, **La Puerta del Perdón,** opens to the northwest. Visitors enter through the **Patio de los Naranjos,** an arcaded courtyard featuring carefully spaced orange trees, palm trees, and fountains. Inside, 850 pink and blue marble, alabaster, and stone columns—no two the same height—support hundreds of red-and-white striped two-tiered arches. At the far end of the Mezquita lies the **Capilla Villaviciosa,** where Caliphal vaulting, greatly influential in later Spanish architecture, appears for the first time. In the center, the **Mihrab** was the naturally lit central dome where the Muslims guarded the Quran. Its prayer arch faces Mecca. The intricate gold, pink, and blue marble Byzantine mosaics shimmering across its arches were given by the Emperor Constantine VII to the *cordobés* caliphs. His gift is estimated to weigh close to 35 tons.

The Christians converted the Mezquita into a church when they conquered Córdoba in 1236. The **Capilla Mayor** (High Chapel) was enlarged in 1384, but in 1523, Bishop Alonso Manrique, an ally of Carlos V, proposed plans for a full-blown Renaissance cathedral that would rise out of the center of the mosque. The town rallied violently against this idea, promising a swift, painful death for any worker who helped tear down the Mezquita. Nevertheless, the Christians soon erected the towering **Crucero** and **Coro** (transept and choir dome), combining all major Renaissance styles of the epoch. Even Carlos V lamented the befoulment of the Mezquita, griping "You have destroyed something unique to create something commonplace."

In and around the Judería

*A combined ticket for the Alcázar, the Museo Taurino y de Arte Cordobés, and the Museo Julio Romero (see **Elsewhere,** below) is available for purchase at all three locations. 1050ptas, students 525ptas. Individually, each sight costs 425ptas and is free on Fridays.*

Just west of the Mezquita along the river lies the **Alcázar** (tel. 957 42 01 51), constructed for the Catholic Monarchs in 1328 during the *Reconquista.* Between 1492 and 1821 it served as a headquarters for the Inquisition. Its walls enclose a manicured hedge garden with flower beds, terraced goldfish ponds, multiple fountains, and palm trees. Inside, the **museum** displays first-century Roman mosaics and a 3rd-century Roman marble sarcophagus. *(Open May-Sept. Tu-Sa 10am-2pm and 6-8pm, Su 9:30am-3pm; Oct.-Apr. Tu-Sa 10am-2pm and 4:30-6:30pm, Su 9:30am-3pm. Illuminated gardens open 8pm-midnight.)*

Tucked away downhill from the Moorish arch, the **Sinagoga,** C. Judíos, 20 (tel. 957 20 29 28), is a solemn reminder of the 1492 expulsion of the Jews. *(Open Tu-Sa 10am-2pm and 3:30-5:30pm, Su 10:30am-1pm. 50ptas, E.U. citizens free.)* It is one of Spain's few remaining Jewish temples, decorated with Mozàrabe patterns and Hebrew inscriptions from the psalms. The statue of **Maimonides** in Pl. Tiberiades was used as the model for the New Israeli Shekel. Half a block down C. Judíos to the left is **El Zoco,** a beautiful courtyard with leather, ceramics, and silversmith workshops. *(Open M-Sa 10am-2pm and 5-8pm, Su 10am-2pm.)*

The **Museo Taurino y de Arte Cordobés** (tel. 957 20 10 56), Pl. Maimonides, recounts lore of *la lidia* (bullfighting), with galleries full of heads of bulls that killed matadors and shrines to legendary Cordoban *toreros.* *(Open May-Sept. Tu-Sa 10am-2pm and 6-8pm, Su 9:30am-3pm; Oct.-Apr. M-Sa 10am-2pm and 5-7pm, Su 9:30am-3pm. Last entrance 30min. before closing.)* Across from the Mezquita, the **Museo Diocesano de Bellas Artes** (tel. 957 47 93 75), C. Torrijos, in a splendid 17th-century palace, displays the works of 13th- to 18th-century local artists. *(Open May-Sept. M-F 9:30am-3pm, Sa 9:30am-1:30pm; Oct.-Apr. M-F 9:30am-1:30pm and 3:30-5:30pm, Sa 9:30am-1:30pm. 150ptas. Free with entrance to Mezquita.)*

Townspeople take great pride in their traditional **patios,** many dating from Roman times. These open-air courtyards—tranquil pockets of orange and lemon trees, flowers, and fountains—flourish in the old quarter. Among the streets of exceptional beauty are **Calleja del Indiano,** off C. Fernández Ruano at Pl. Angel Torres, and the aptly named **Calleja de Flores** (flowers), off C. Blanco Belmonte.

Elsewhere

The **Museo de Bellas Artes** (tel. 957 47 33 45), Pl. Potro, 5-10 minutes east of the Mezquita, now occupies the building that was once King Fernando and Queen Isabel's Charity Hospital. *(Open Tu 3-8pm, W-Sa 9am-8pm, Su 9am-3pm. Last entrance 20min. before closing. 250ptas, E.U. citizens free.)* Its small collection displays works by Cordoban artists. Check out the varied sculptures on the ground floor. Housed in the same building, the **Museo Julio Romero de Torres** (tel. 957 49 19 09) exhibits the

Romero's sensual portraits of Córdoban women. *(Open May-Sept. Tu-Sa 10am-2pm and 6-8pm, Su 9:30am-3pm; Oct.-Apr. Tu-Sa 10am-2pm and 5-7pm, Su 9:30am-3pm. Last entrance 30min. before closing.)* Facing the museums is the **Posada del Potro,** a 14th-century inn mentioned in *Don Quijote* that now contains the collection of *guadameciles* formerly held in the Museo Taurino. The **Museo Arqueológico** (tel. 957 47 40 11), Pl. Paez, is several blocks northeast of the Mezquita. *(Open Tu 3-8pm, W-Sa 9am-8pm, Su 9am-3pm. 250ptas, E.U. citizens free.)* Housed in a Renaissance mansion, the museum contains a chronological exhibit of tools, ceramics, statues, coins, jewelry, and sarcophagi. Especially impressive are the Roman mosaics.

Those who share the city's passion for gardens can find bliss in the **Palacio del Marqués de Viana,** Pl. Don Gome, 2 (tel. 957 48 01 34), a 20-minute walk northeast of the Mezquita. *(Open June 16-Oct. 1 M-Tu and Th-Su 9am-2pm; Oct. 2-May 31 M-Tu and Th-Sa 10am-1pm and 4-6pm, Su 10am-2pm; closed June 1-15. Patio only 200ptas. Guided tours of mansion every hr. 500ptas, children 200ptas.)* The elegant 14th-century mansion displays 14 quintessentially Cordoban patios complete with sprawling gardens and majestic fountains. West of the Palacio del Marqués de Viana in Pl. Capuchinos (a.k.a. Pl. Dolores) is the **Cristo de los Faroles** (Christ of the Lanterns), one of the most famous religious shrines in Spain and frequently the site of all-night vigils.

ENTERTAINMENT

Pick up a free copy of *La Guía de Ocio,* a monthly guide to cultural events, at the tourist office. Unfortunately, cheap **flamenco** isn't easy to come by in Córdoba. Hordes of tourists flock to the **Tablao Cardenal,** C. Torrijos, 10 (tel. 957 48 33 20), facing the Mezquita, where big names flaunt their hips with intense proximity to the audience. *(Reserve seats in the tourist office, the tablao, or your hostal. Shows Tu-Sa 10:30pm. 2800ptas, includes 1 drink.)* For classical or traditional music, the **Palacio de Viana** (tel. 957 48 01 34) has free chamber music concerts on Fridays at 8:30pm during the summer. The city's open-air theater hosts concerts and festivals, including the irregularly scheduled **International Guitar Festival** (tel. 957 48 02 37) in June or July. For **info** and tickets stop by F.P.M. Gran Teatro, Av. Gran Capitán, 3 (tickets 400-1800ptas).

From the first weekend of June till the heat subsides, the **Brillante barrio,** uphill from and north of Av. America, is the place to be—the Sierra is cool, the beer is cold, and the prices fall to near zero. Bus #10 goes there from RENFE until about 11pm; a cab costs 500-900ptas. Around 4am, Cordoban youth climb even higher into the mountains to reach **Kachao,** a huge disco and *terraza* that hops past dawn. It is a few kilometers outside the city along Ctra. Santa María de Trassierra. The disco's name occasionally changes, so ask around (no cover and the bouncers may look kindly upon foreigners). The city has tried to divert revelers to the **Recinto Ferial** (a.k.a. **El Arenal).** The sandy fairground along the river is most efficiently accessible from the Mezquita by crossing the Puente Romano, cutting across the peninsula, and taking Puente del Arenal to the other bank. The *terraza* and discos here are sometimes lively, but usually flooded by *cordobeses* shouldering coolers and cook-out equipment. In the winter, students lounge around the bars and lawns of barrio **Ciudad Jardín,** the area south of RENFE between the Plaza de Toros and Po. Victoria. Pubs around **Plaza de las Tendillas** are also a safe bet.

Of Córdoba's festivals, floats and parades, **Semana Santa,** in early April, is the most extravagant. May, however, is a never-ending party. During the **Festival de los Patios,** in the first two weeks of May, the city erupts with classical music concerts, flamenco dances, and a city-wide decorated patio contest (don't forget to ask the owners of your hostel how theirs ranked). Late May brings the week-long **Feria de Nuestra Señora de la Salud** (commonly known as *La Feria),* for which thousands of Cordoban women don colorful, traditional apparel. A carnival, dozens of stands, lively dancing, and non-stop drinking keep spirits blithe for the entire week. In early September, Córdoba celebrates its patroness with the **Feria de Nuestra Señora de la Fuensanta.** The **Concurso Nacional de Arte Flamenco** (National Flamenco Contest) is held every third year during May. The next one will be in 2001.

ANDALUCÍA

■ Near Córdoba: Medina Azahara

Built in the **Sierra Morena** by Abderramán III for his favorite wife, Azahara, this 10th-century medina (tel. 957 32 91 30) was considered one of the greatest palaces of its time. *(Open May-Sept. Tu-Sa 10am-2pm and 6-8:30pm; Oct.-Apr. Tu-Sa 10am-2pm and 4-6:30pm, Su 10am-2pm. 250ptas, E.U. citizens free.)* It was divided into three terraces: one for the palace (alcázar), another for the servants' living quarters, and a third for an enclosed garden replete with an almond grove. After moving from Granada, Azahara missed the Sierra Nevada, so the white-blossoming almond groves were planted to replace her beloved snow. The site, long thought to be mythical, was discovered in the mid-19th century and excavated in the early-20th century. Today, it is one of Spain's most impressive archaeological finds. The **Salón de Abd al-Rahman III,** also known as the *salón rico,* on the lower terraces, is being restored to its original intricate and geometrical beauty.

Reaching Medina Azahara takes some effort if you go without a tour group. The **O-1 bus** (info tel. 957 25 57 00, or see the list in the tourist office) leaves from Av. República Argentina in Córdoba for Cruce Medina Azahara, stopping 3km from the site (departs about every hr., 100ptas). From the bus stop, it's about a 35-minute walk (mostly uphill), and the path ain't shady. A taxi costs about 800ptas one way. **Córdoba Visión** (tel. 957 23 17 34; fax 957 23 73 94) offers transportation and a guided visit to the sight in English, Spanish, and French (2hr., May-Sept. Tu-Sa 10:30am and 6pm, Su 10:30am; Oct.-Apr. Tu-Sa 10:30am and 4pm, Su 10:30am; 2150ptas).

■ Near Córdoba: Almodóvar del Río

Thirteen kilometers from Córdoba on the rail to Sevilla, the impenetrable **castle** at **Almodóvar del Río** crowns a solitary, rocky mount commanding a tremendous view of the countryside and the village's downward spiral of whitewashed houses. On the second Sunday in May, the town celebrates the **Romería de la Virgen de Fátima** with a parade from C. Cuatro Caminos to C. Fuen Real Bajo. **RENFE trains** run here to from Córdoba (15-20min., 5 per day, last train returns 4pm, 225ptas).

■ Jaén

The hills near Jaén are streaked with olive trees and wheat fields. Unfortunately, Jaén proper offers barely a glimpse of them amid its steep and narrow streets, crowded with people and cars. This bustling olive capital of Spain possesses little in the way of unique sights or tourist resources, but it may be a necessary stopover. Úbeda and Baeza, two considerably more appealing destinations, lie only an hour away.

ORIENTATION AND PRACTICAL INFORMATION Jaén centers around **Plaza de la Constitución,** roaring with autos and mopeds. **Calle Bernabé Soriano** leads uphill from the plaza to the cathedral and old section of town. **Calle Roldán y Marín** and **Calle Virgen** head downhill and become **Paseo de la Estación** and **Avenida de Madrid,** respectively. To reach the town center from the bus station, exit where the buses arrive and follow Av. Madrid uphill to Pl. Constitución (5min.). From the train station, follow Po. Estación, which turns into C. Roldán y Marín, into the main square. It's a 25-minute walk that can be cut short by the #1 bus along Po. Estación (85ptas).

Trains (tel. 953 27 02 02) leave from Po. Estación at the bottom of the slope and go to: Madrid (4-5hr., 3 per day, 2950ptas); Sevilla (3hr., 1 per day, 2170ptas); and Córdoba (1½hr., 1 per day, 1200ptas). **Buses,** Pl. Coca de la Piñera (tel. 953 25 50 14), are the best means of transport within Andalucía. They head to: Úbeda (30min., 12 per day, 535ptas); Baeza (1hr., 12 per day, 445ptas); Cazorla (2hr., 2 per day, 920ptas); Granada (1½hr., 14 per day, 900ptas); and Málaga (3hr., 3 per day, 2010ptas). The **tourist office,** C. Arquitecto Berges, 1 (tel./fax 953 22 27 37), is off C. Roldán y Marín, on the left when heading downhill. They offer info on sights and accommodations, and have a free **map** (open M-F 9am-7pm, Sa 9am-1pm). There's a **Banco Central Hispano** in Pl. Constitución (open M-F 8:30am-2:30pm). Call 091 or 092 in an **emergency**. The **police** answer at (tel. 953 21 91 05).

ACCOMMODATIONS AND FOOD Quality budget beds are scarce in Jaén. At the **Hostal La Española,** C. Bernardo López, 9 (tel. 953 23 02 54), vines canopy the dining room and a vertiginously slanting staircase spirals its way upwards. Everything exudes antiquity and, unfortunately, so do the saggy beds. To get there, follow the street across from the cathedral's side entrance and take a left onto the alley Bernardo López. (Singles 1600ptas; doubles 3500ptas, with bath 4000ptas.) More mainstream is **Pensión Carlos V,** Av. Madrid, 4 (tel. 953 22 20 91), downhill from Pl. Constitución (singles 2500ptas; doubles 3700ptas). **Calle Nueva,** a pedestrian street down C. Roldán y Marín, offers several palatable **restaurant** options. **Yucatán,** C. Bernabé Soriano, 1 (tel. 953 24 17 28), has tasty hot and cold *bocadillos,* burgers (300-350ptas), and *platos combinados* (900-1000ptas), served indoors or out (open daily 8am-2am). **Supermarket Simago,** sits off Pl. Constitución on C. San Clement (open 9am-9pm).

SIGHTS Construction of the Renaissance **Catedral de Santa María,** uphill from Pl. Constitución on C. Bernabé Soriano, began in 1492. *(Open daily 8:30am-1pm and 5-8pm. Free.)* The **Museo de la Catedral** displays sculptures by Martínez Montañés and canvases by Alonso Cano. *(Open Sa-Su 11am-1pm. 100ptas.)* Jaén's most imposing and least accessible sight is the **Castillo de Santa Catalina** (tel. 953 21 91 16), a 3km climb from the center of town. *(Open Th-Tu 10:30am-1:30pm. Free.)* From the cathedral, take C. Maestra, which leads to C. Madre de Dios, which continues to C. San Lorenzo. Take a left when you reach Cra. Circunvalación, which becomes Cra. Neveral and leads to the castle. This former Arab fortress now houses a four-star hotel. If you don't feel like walking, a cab ride to the *castillo* from the bus station costs about 900ptas.

The Renaissance **Palacio de Villadompardo** (tel. 953 23 62 92), in Pl. Santa Luisa Marillac, contains Arab baths inside. *(Open Tu-F 9am-8pm, Sa-Su 9:30am-2:30pm. Free.)* The recently restored 11th-century baths, though not as elaborate as those in Granada, are Spain's largest. Follow C. Maestra from the cathedral to C. Martínez Molina.

The centuries-old **Peña Flamenca Jaén,** C. Maestra, 11 (tel. 953 23 17 10), uphill from the cathedral, serves up drinks and flamenco, indoors and out. **Del Posito,** a cafe bar tucked in a plaza below Yucatán, has the hippest outdoor tables in town.

■ Baeza

To visit tiny Baeza, which sits on a ridge overlooking the olive-tree covered valley of the Guadalquivir River, is to lose oneself amid twisty medieval streets. A former Moorish capital and the first Andalusian town to fall during the *Reconquista,* Baeza flaunts its Renaissance heyday with exceptionally well-preserved monuments on nearly every street. Thanks perhaps to the limited lodging options, the town remains uncorrupted, and those who spend the day here will satisfy their quest for quintessential Spain. Poet and one-time resident Antonio Machado expected to long for Baeza's charm long after his death: *"Campo de Baeza, soñaré contigo cuando no te vea…"* (Countryside of Baeza, I shall dream of you when I see you no more).

ORIENTATION AND PRACTICAL INFORMATION The center of town is the **Plaza de España,** which leads downhill to the long **Plaza de la Constitución.** Facing Pl. Constitución from Pl. España, the **Barrio Monumental** is uphill to the left. To get to the center of town from the bus station, follow C. Julio Burrel to C. San Pablo (on the right), which leads to Pl. España and Pl. Constitución. **Trains** leave **Estación Linares-Baeza** (tel. 953 65 02 02), 13km from town on the road to Madrid, for Madrid (5 per day, 2500ptas) and Málaga (3 per day, 2900ptas). The **bus station** (tel. 953 74 04 68), at the top of Av. Alcalde Puche Pardo, which becomes C. Julio Barrel, offers service to: Úbeda (15min., 15 per day, 100ptas); Jaén (1hr., 11 per day, 445ptas); Granada (2-

ANDALUCÍA

3hr., 7 per day, 1320ptas); Málaga (4hr., 1 per day, 2425ptas); Cazorla (1½hr., 2 per day, 495ptas). To transfer to Almería take the bus to Granada. The **tourist office,** Pl. Pópulo, s/n (tel. 953 74 04 44), offers free maps of Baeza and info on tours of Andalucía (open M-F 9am-2pm, Sa 10am-12:30pm). In an **emergency,** dial 092. The **police** are on C. Cardenal Benavides, 5 (tel. 953 74 06 59). A **pharmacy** (tel. 953 74 06 81) is on C. San Pablo, 19 (open M-F 9:30am-2pm and 6-9pm, weekend hours vary). The **hospital,** Centro de Salud Comarcal (tel. 953 74 09 17) is on Av. Alcalde Puche Pardo. **Internet Access** is available for 250ptas per hour at **Speed Informática,** Pl. Constitución, 2 (tel. 953 74 70 75). The **post office** (tel. 953 74 08 39) is at C. Julio Burell, 19 (open M-F 8:30am-2:30pm). The **postal code** is 23440.

ACCOMMODATIONS AND FOOD Hostels are scarce, so call ahead for a room. **Hostal el Patio,** C. Romanones, 13 (tel. 953 74 02 00), has a delightful lounge replete with plants and a mini-zoo (singles 1500ptas; with shower 2000ptas; doubles 3000ptas, 3500ptas). **Hostal Residencia Comercio,** C. San Pablo, 21 (tel. 953 74 01 00), furnishes large, attractive rooms with showers or baths and *fin de siècle* antiques (singles 1500ptas; doubles 3300ptas; 100-300ptas more during the summer).

A plethora of bars, *cafeterías,* and *pastelerías* line Pl. Constitución and neighboring streets. **Café Las Vegas,** on the plaza's southwest corner on Portales Tundidores, has choice *bocadillos* (300ptas) and *platos combinados* (under 800ptas). **Helados los Valencianos,** C. Gaspar Becerra, 10 (tel. 953 74 15 05), might make the best ice cream in Spain. Their stand in the plaza sells cones (50-200ptas) and cool lemon and coffee *granizados* (250ptas).

SIGHTS A stroll through the **Barrio Monumental** yields a sight on every corner. If you follow C. Romanones up the stairs next to the tourist office, before it opens on to the Pl. Santa Cruz, the **Antigua Universidad** (founded in 1595) stands on your left. Ask someone to let you into the courtyard, where Antonio Machado had a day job teaching French (open daily 9:30am-1:30pm). Across from it survives the **Palacio de Jabalquinto,** featuring a gracefully decaying courtyard punctuated with ancient stonework and orange trees (open daily 11am-1pm and 4-6pm). To the right of the Antigua Universidad looms the Romanesque **Iglesia de Santa Cruz,** Baeza's oldest church (13th century), with its frescoes of La Virgen, Santa Catalina, and the martyr San Sebastián (open M-F 11am-1pm, Su noon-2pm). Adjacent to the *palacio,* the **seminario's** facade bears the names of some egotistical graduates and a caricature of an unpopular professor, rumored to be painted in bull's blood. The *seminario* now houses the **Universidad Internacional de Andalucía Sede Antonio Machado** (tel. 953 74 27 75; fax 953 74 29 75; email machado@uniaam.uia.es), which teaches students from Spain and beyond during the summer. Across the Pl. Santa María from the seminary looms the **Santa Iglesia Catedral,** housing *La Custodia de Baeza,* Spain's second-most important (to Toledo's) Corpus Christi icon (open daily 10:30am-1pm and 4-7pm). Farther uphill, the barrio fades into a modern residential neighborhood; on its edge is a terrific view of the Guadalquivir valley as olive trees converge in the distance. West of the plaza, on C. Cardenal de Benarides, the **Ayuntamiento** sports magnificent Plateresque windows.

■ Úbeda

Fifteen minutes from Baeza and two hours from Granada and Córdoba, the cobbled streets of Úbeda's monumental district dip between ivied medieval walls and old churches and palaces. A stop on the crucial 16th-century trade route linking Castilla to Andalucía, the town fattened on American gold shipped up from Sevilla. The *barrio antiguo,* surrounded by friendly, newer neighborhoods, remains one of the best-preserved gems of Spanish Renaissance architecture.

ORIENTATION AND PRACTICAL INFORMATION The town is centered around **Plaza de Andalucía.** The **barrio antiguo** stretches downhill from Pl. Andalucía along C. Doctor Quesada (which leads to **Calle Real**) and surrounding streets. To reach Pl.

Andalucía from the **bus station,** go right when you exit the front of the station. Walk a block downhill, and take a left on **Avenida Cristo Rey,** which turns into **Calle Obispo Cobos** and then into **Calle Mesones,** and leads to Pl. Andalucía (5min.). From the bus station, walk one block left (uphill) and take a right at C. Huelva to reach its continuation, **Calle Ramón y Cajal.** After a six-way intersection, Av. Ramon y Cajal is packed with hostels and restaurants.

There's **no train service** to Úbeda. The nearest station is **Estación Linares-Baeza** (tel. 953 65 02 02), 40 minutes northwest by bus. **Buses** leave from C. San José, 6 (tel. 953 75 21 57). **Alsina Graells** travels to: Baeza (15min., 15 per day, 100ptas); Estación Linares-Baeza (30min., 8 per day, 255ptas); Jaén (1hr., 12 per day, 535ptas); Cazorla (1hr., 4 per day, 425ptas); Granada (2-3hr., 7 per day, 1400ptas). **Bacoma** goes to Córdoba (2½hr., 3 per day, 1305ptas) and Sevilla (5hr., 3 per day, 2555ptas).

The **tourist office** in the **Centro Cultural Hospital de Santiago,** C. Obispo Cobos, s/n (tel./fax 953 75 08 97), on the way from the bus station to Pl. Andalucía, offers books, brochures, and a map with English translations (open M-F 9am-2:30pm, Sa 11am-1:30pm). A **second office** across the walkway also provides information and a helpful map, in Spanish only (open M-F 8am-3pm and 4-10pm, Sa-Su 11am-3pm and 6-10pm). Change money at **Banco Central Hispano,** C. San Fernando, 28 (tel. 953 75 04 43), uphill from Pl. Andalucía. (Open May-Sept. M-F 8:30am-2:30pm; Oct.-Apr. M-F 8:30am-2:30pm, Sa 8:30am-1pm.) **Luggage storage** at the bus station costs 300ptas. For **emergencies** call 091 or 092. Contact **police** at 953 75 00 23. Two **pharmacies** face each other in Pl. Andalucía, at Pl. Andalucía, 5 (tel. 953 75 00 57), and C. Rastro, 1 (tel. 953 75 01 51). (Both pharmacies open M-F 9:30am-1:45pm and 5:30-8:30pm; call for weekend hours.) The **hospital** (Centro de Salud; tel. 953 75 11 03) is on C. Explanada, off Av. Ramón y Cajal. The **post office,** C. Trinidad, 4 (tel. 953 75 00 31) is along the Hospital de Santiago. The **postal code** is 23400.

ACCOMMODATIONS AND FOOD Úbeda's best bargain is the **Hostal Castillo,** Av. Ramón y Cajal, 20 (tel. 953 75 04 30 or 953 75 12 18), with comfy singles upstairs and a popular bar and affordable restaurant downstairs. (Singles 2000ptas, with bath 2300ptas; doubles 3000ptas, with bath 4300ptas; triples from 6400ptas. Prices jump 300-400ptas June-Oct. and during Semana Santa.) The ritzier **Hostal Victoria,** C. Alaminos, 5, 2nd fl. (tel. 953 75 29 52), features glistening private bathrooms, color TVs, and A/C. From the bus station, walk down C. Mesones past Hospital de Santiago and turn right on C. Alaminos. (Singles 2300ptas; doubles 4300ptas. Prices jump 300-400ptas June-Oct. and during Semana Santa.) Similarly, the **Hostal Sevilla,** Av. Ramón y Cajal, 7 (tel. 953 75 06 12), has private baths, A/C, and TVs. (Singles 2300ptas; doubles 3500ptas—but bargain for cheaper rooms. TVs 400-700ptas extra.)

Úbeda's roster of regional cooking includes *andrajos* (soups with pasta, meat, and spices) and *pipirrana* (a hot or cold soup of tomato, green pepper, onion, egg, and tuna). C. Rastro leading from Pl. Andalucía has many *terrazas* with combination platters under 1000ptas and entrees for around 600ptas. **Restaurante Castille-Victoria,** conveniently located inside Hostal Castillo at Av. Ramon y Cajal, 20, serves up a great *menú* for 1000ptas. **Helados los Valencianos,** C. Obispo, 1, and Av. Ramón y Cajal, 18 (next to Hostal Castillo), serves delicious *granizados* for 200-300ptas and ice cream cones for 100-300ptas (open daily 9am-midnight). The **market** is down C. San Fernando from Pl. Andalucía (open M-Sa 7am-2:30pm).

SIGHTS A walk through historic Úbeda should begin with the **Hospital de Santiago** (tel. 953 75 08 42). *(Museum open M-F 8am-3pm and 3:30-10pm, Sa 8am-3pm. 225ptas, children and seniors 75ptas.)* The building, a worthy sight in its own right, lists current cultural events, houses a modern art museum, and holds concerts. From Pl. Andalucía, C. Real leads downhill to C. Juan Montilla, which brings you to **Plaza de Vázquez de Molina,** the center of historic Úbeda. Two stone lions at the head of a garden-lined pathway guard the **Palacio de las Cadenas,** now the Ayuntamiento. Across the pathway is the Gothic **Colegiata de Santa María de los Reales Alcázares,** its side chapels embellished by wrought-iron grilles. A Renaissance church, the **Sacra**

Capilla del Salvador, originally designed as part of a palace commissioned by Carlos V, sits across the far end of the plaza. *(Open M-F 6-7pm. Free.)* One can usually peek in during mass, but it is better to view during visiting hours. Uphill from the Pl. Vásquez de Molina along C. Juan Ruíz Gonzales is **Plaza 1 de Mayo,** in front of **Iglesia de San Pablo.** The **Museo Arqueológico,** uphill from the church on C. Cervantes, 6 (tel. 953 75 37 02), displays a narrative of Úbeda's history through prehistoric, Roman, Moorish, and Castillian times. *(Open Sa 10am-2pm and 4-7pm, Su 10am-2pm. 250ptas, E.U. citizens free with passport.)* A walk all the way downhill leads to a stunning view of the olive-laden **Guadalquivir valley** and the ruins of the **muralla,** an old Moorish wall.

■ Cazorla

Nestled between foreboding cliffs and two ancient castles, Cazorla is one northern Andalucían *pueblecito blanco* (whitewashed village) that should not be missed. A hike through the mountainous town itself provides exceptional views of the Guadalquivir valley. Most tourists pass through on their way to the **Parque Natural de las Sierras de Cazorla, Segura, y las Villas,** one of the largest national parks in Europe (1hr. away). The national park's 210,000 hectares of protected mountains and waterways offer some of the choicest hiking, mountain biking, and horseback riding in Andalucía, inferior only to the Sierra Nevada and the Alpujarras.

ORIENTATION AND PRACTICAL INFORMATION Facing the peaks, walk down **Calle de Dr. Muñoz** (to the right) to reach **Plaza de Corredera** (5min.). Farther downhill is **Plaza de Santa María** and the **barrio antiguo.** A bus (tel. 953 75 21 57)with stops in Granada, Jaén, and Úbeda arrives in the bare **Plaza de la Constitución** twice a day and departs three times daily for **Alsina Graells** in Úbeda. Call for the current schedule. The helpful **tourist office,** C. Paseo del Santo Cristo, 17 (tel. 953 71 01 02; fax 953 72 00 60), up a garden-lined walkway from Pl. Constitución away from Pl. Corredera, has free maps and brochures. (Open May-Sept. M-F 10:30am-2:30pm; Oct.-Apr. M-F 10:30am-2:30pm, Sa 8:30am-1pm.) In an **emergency** call 091 or 092. The **police** are on Pl. Corredera (tel. 953 72 01 81). The nearest **hospital** is the Centro de Salud, Av. Ximenez de Rada, 1 (tel. 953 72 10 61 or 953 72 20 00), a few kilometers away. The **post office,** C. Mariano Extremera, 2 (tel. 953 72 02 61), sits uphill on the left from Pl. Corredera. The **postal code** is 23470.

ACCOMMODATIONS AND FOOD From the far end of Pl. Corredera, walk uphill on C. Carmen to reach the **Albuerge Juvenil Cazorla (HI),** Pl. Mauricio Martinez, 6 (tel. 953 72 03 29; fax 953 72 02 03). This spankin' clean hostel has a TV lounge, outdoor patios, a heaven-sent pool (open July-Aug.), an English-speaking staff, and spacious rooms for one to six people. (HI members 1300ptas, over 26 1800ptas; nonmembers add 300ptas. Prices discounted 500-700ptas Sept. 15-June 15. Sheets provided.) **Hostal Betis,** Pl. Corredera, 19 (tel. 953 72 05 40), has firm beds and rooms with valley-side views (singles with bath 1300ptas; doubles 2500ptas, with bath 2700ptas). Open-air bar-restaurants serving such traditional platters as *rin-ran* (a cold soup of potatoes, red peppers, olives, and fish) ornament Pl. Corredora and Pl. Santa María. Set in a 16th-century house on Pl. Santa María, **La Cueva** (tel. 953 72 12 25) cooks veggies in its ancient hearth as well as crispy roast rabbit (midday *menú* 1000ptas, entrees around 800ptas). For the sweet toothed, **Fran's Café Bar,** C. Muñoz, 28 (tel. 953 72 06 15), has scrumptious pastries (around 100ptas; open daily 9am-10pm). The **market** is at Pl. Mercado, downstairs from C. Dr. Muñoz (open M-F 9am-noon). A **supermarket** sits in Pl. Corredera (open M-F 9am-noon and 6-9pm, Sa 9am-noon).

SIGHTS AND ENTERTAINMENT There are many opportunities for scenic strolls around town. The **Castillo de la Yedra,** started by the Romans, provides a pretty vista of Cazorla from its solitary peaks and houses an art museum (open Tu-Sa 9am-3pm). A flood in 1694 and wartime fires left their mark on the unfortunate **Ruinas de la Iglesia de Santa María,** in the plaza of the same name.

ANDALUCÍA

For longer excursions, stop by **Quercus,** C. Juan Domingo, 2 (tel. 953 72 01 15; fax 953 71 00 68), where a private concessionary tour operator can tell you all you need to know about the **Parque Natural de las Sierras de Cazorla, Segura, y las Villas.** *(Open daily 10am-2pm and 5-9pm, holidays 10am-2pm and 6-9pm. 375 ptas.)* The tour operators speak English and have good maps. Inquire about **camping** options—alas, no free sites or back country camping. **Bus** service to the park is subject to change. *(1hr. Currently 5:45am and 3pm during the school year, 6:30am and 2:40pm during the summer. 400ptas.)* The Carecesa bus departs from Pl. Constitución and goes to the **Torre del Vinagre Visitor Center,** near the trailhead of the popular **Sendero Cerrada de Elias/ Río Borosa,** a 4km or 12km (take your pick) trail up a river canyon carved with natural pools. On getting off the bus, follow the sign to the kiosk. **Horses** (about 1400ptas per hr., with groups of 4 or more) and **mountain bikes** (1200ptas per ½-day, 2000ptas per full-day) are available. Bring drinking water. The last bus back to Cazorla leaves Torre del Vinagre at 4:30pm.

■ Granada

When Moorish ruler Boabdil fled Granada, the last Muslim stronghold in Spain, his mother berated him for casting a longing look back at the Alhambra: "Weep like a woman for what you could not defend like a man." The Alhambra, a spectacular palace-fortress complex that is Spain's most famous tourist destination, continues today to inspire melancholy in those who must depart from its timeless beauty. The saying holds true: *"Si has muerto sin ver la Alhambra no has vivido"* (If you have died without seeing the Alhambra, you have not lived).

After it was conquered by invading Muslim armies in 711, Granada blossomed into one of Europe's wealthiest, most refined cities. As Christian armies turned back the tide of Muslim conquest during the 13th century, Granada became the last Muslim outpost on the peninsula, surrounded on all fronts by a unified Christian kingdom. Despite its threatening neighbors, in the 13th and 14th centuries the Moorish kingdom, largely relocated to Granada, celebrated an era of peace and enlightenment.

In the latter decades of the 15th century, however, Granada was continuously besieged by Fernando and Isabel's troops, while ruling Sultan Moulay Abdul Hassan, obsessing over one of his concubines, ignored his civic duties. When Queen Aïcha caught on, she drummed up local support, had her husband deposed, and thrust her young son Boabdil on the throne. Fernando and Isabel capitalized on the disarray by capturing Boabdil and the Alhambra on the momentous night of January 1, 1492.

Although the Christians torched all the mosques and the lower city, Granada's Arab essence lingers to this day. The Albaícin, an enchanting maze of Moorish houses and twisting alleys, is Spain's best-preserved Arab settlement and the only part of the Muslim city that survived the Reconquista intact. University of Granada students make their mark as well—look for plenty of eating, drinking and dancing, as they can party with vigor.

ORIENTATION AND PRACTICAL INFORMATION

The geographic center of Granada is the small **Plaza de Isabel la Católica,** the intersection of the city's two main arteries, **Calle de los Reyes Católicos** and **Gran Vía de Colón.** Two short blocks uphill on C. Reyes Católicos sits **Plaza Nueva,** framed by Renaissance buildings, hotels, and restaurants. Downhill, also along C. Reyes Católicos, lie **Plaza del Carmen,** site of the **Ayuntamiento,** and **Puerta Real,** the six-way intersection of C. Reyes Católicos, C. Recogidos, C. Mesones, C. Acera de Darro, C. Angel Gavinet, and C. Acero del Casino. The **Alhambra** commands the steep hill up from Pl. Nueva. To get there, take **Calle Cuesta de Gomérez,** off Pl. Nueva, and be prepared to pant (25min. uphill; no unauthorized cars from 9am-9pm). You can also take the cheap, quick **Alhambra-Neptuno microbus** (departs every 15min., 120ptas) from Pl. Isabel la Católica or Pl. Nueva. Atop the hill across from the Alhambra sprawls the **Albaícin,** or Arab quarter.

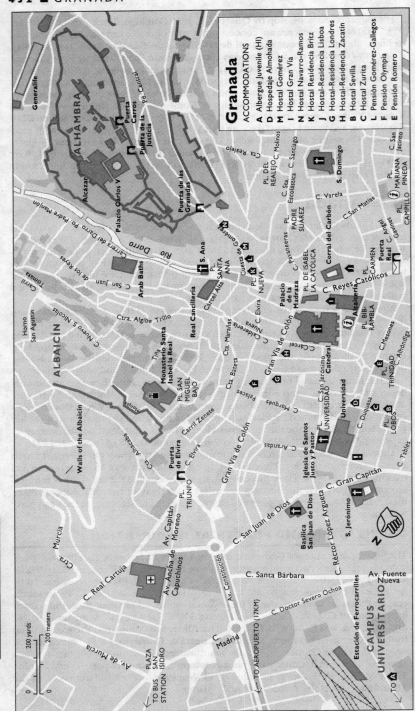

ANDALUCÍA

Granada

ACCOMMODATIONS

A Albergue Juvenil (HI)
D Hospedaje Almohada
M Hostal Gomérez
I Hostal Gran Vía
N Hostal Navarro-Ramos
K Hostal Residencia Britz
J Hostal-Residencia Lisboa
G Hostal-Residencia Londres
H Hostal-Residencia Zacatín
B Hostal Sevilla
C Hostal Zurita
L Pensión Gomérez-Gallegos
F Pensión Olympia
E Pensión Romero

To reach **Calle Gran Vía** from **RENFE**, walk 3 blocks up Av. Andaluces to Av. Constitución, and take bus #3, 4, 5, 6, 9, or 11. From the bus station, take bus #3 (120ptas). **Plaza de la Trinidad** sits at the end of C. Mesones from Pta. Real. On Gran Vía de Colón, you'll find the **catedral**, and next to it the **Alcaicería**, an old Arab silk market now specializing in souvenirs. Municipal **buses** (see **Public Transportation**, below) cover practically the entire city. Since the Alhambra and Albaicín hills are near both each other and the center, the best way to explore is on foot. If you are alone when night falls, stick to major streets in the Albaicín, and avoid paths higher up on the neighboring **Sacromonte.**

Transportation

Flights: Airport (tel. 958 24 52 00), 17km west of the city. **Salidas** bus (tel. 958 13 13 09) runs from C. Gran Vía, in front of the cathedral (5 per day, 4 on Su, 425ptas). **Taxi** to the airport are about 2000ptas. **Iberia** (tel. 958 22 75 92) to Madrid (45min., 2-3 per day) and Barcelona (1¼hr., 2-3 per day). Open M-F 9am-1:45pm and 4-7pm.

Trains: RENFE Station, Av. Andaluces (tel. 958 27 12 72). From Pl. Isabel la Católica, follow Gran Vía de Colón to the end, and then bear left on Av. Constitución; or take bus #3, 4, 5, 6, 9, or 11 from C. Gran Vía to the stop marked Constitución 3 (ask the driver). Turn left on Av. Andaluces; RENFE is at the end of the street. To: Madrid (5hr., 4 per day, 3200ptas); Barcelona (12-13hr., 2 per day, 6400ptas); Sevilla (4-5hr., 4 per day, 2575ptas); Antequera (2hr., 3 per day, 970ptas); Algeciras (5-7hr., 3 per day, 2375ptas); Almería (3hr., 3 per day, 1710ptas); Cádiz (7hr., 3 per day, 2000ptas); Ronda (3-4hr., 3 per day, 1510-1710ptas).

Buses: All major bus routes originate from the new bus station on the outskirts of Granada on the Ctra. de Madrid, near C. Arzobispo Pedro de Castro.

Alsina Graells (tel. 958 18 50 10) goes to: Algeciras (5hr., 2 per day, 2485ptas); Almería (2¼hr., 10 per day, 1610ptas); Antequera (2hr., 5 per day, 895ptas); Cádiz (4hr., 2 per day, 3700ptas); Córdoba (3hr., 9 per day, 1780ptas); Jaén (1½hr., 15 per day, 900ptas); La Línea (4hr., 2 per day, 2390ptas); Madrid (5hr., 10 per day, one-way 1945ptas, round-trip 3540ptas); Málaga (2hr., 15 per day, 1165ptas); Sevilla (3hr., 8 per day, 2400ptas).

Bacoma (tel. 958 15 75 57) goes to: Alicante (6hr., 5 per day, 3335ptas); Barcelona (14hr., 3 per day, 7830ptas); Valencia (8hr., 4 per day, 4855ptas).

Autocares Bonal (tel. 958 27 31 00) sends one bus per day to Veleta from Palacio de Congresos. Follow Acera del Darro from Pta. Real across the river to Po. Violón, or take bus #1 on C. Gran Vía towards Pl. Isabel la Católica to the last stop. Tickets are sold daily 8:30-9am at Ventorillo Bar across from the *palacio*. Bus departs from the bar at 9am, returns from Veleta at 5:30pm (45min., round-trip 700ptas).

Public Transportation: (tel. 958 81 37 11). The buses you will grow to love are: "Bus Alhambra" from Pl. Nueva; #10 from the bus station to the youth hostel, Camino de Ronda, C. Recogidas, and Acera del Darro; and #3 from the bus station to Av. Constitución, C. Gran Vía, and Pl. Isabel la Católica All buses 120ptas, *bonobus* book of 15 tickets 1000ptas. Handy **free map** available from the tourist office.

Taxis: (tel. 958 28 06 54 or 958 15 14 61). Taxis abound at Pl. Nueva and Trinidad.

Car Rental: Atasa, Pl. Cuchilleros, 1 (tel. 958 22 40 04; fax 958 22 77 95). Cheapest car 46,000ptas per week with unlimited mileage and insurance. Prices rise with shorter rentals. Must be at least 20 and have had a license for at least one year.

Tourist and Financial Services

Tourist Office: Oficina Provincial, Pl. Mariana Pineda, 10 (tel. 958 22 66 88; fax 958 22 89 16; email turismo@mail.valnet.es; http://www.dipgra.es). From Pta. Real turn right onto C. Angel Ganivet, then take a right 2 blocks later to reach the plaza. Possibly the most helpful tourist office in Andalucía. The multilingual staff gives out free maps, posters, and brochures. Open M-F 9:30am-7pm, Sa 10am-2pm. **Junta de Andalucía,** C. Mariana Pineda (tel. 958 22 10 22; fax 958 22 39 27). From Pta. Real, take C. Reyes Católicos to Pl. Carmen. Calle Mariana Pineda is the first street on the left. More prominently signposted on C. Reyes Católicos, this office is also helpful. Free city maps, Andalucían hotel guide (800ptas) and brochures on hiking, hunting, and golf (400ptas). Open M-Sa 9am-7pm, Su 10am-2pm.

Currency Exchange: Banco Central Hispano, Gran Vía de Colón, 3 (tel. 958 21 73 00), off Pl. Isabel la Católica, exchanges money and AmEx traveler's checks without commission. Open May-Sept. M-F 9am-2pm; Oct.-Apr. M-Sa 9am-2pm.

American Express: C. Reyes Católicos, 31 (tel. 958 22 45 12), between Pl. Isabel la Católica and Pta. Real. Exchanges money, cashes checks for members, and holds mail. Open M-F 9:30am-1:30pm and 2-8pm, Sa 10am-2pm and 3-7pm, Su 9am-2pm.

Local Services

Luggage Storage: At the train and bus stations (400ptas). Open daily 4-9pm.

El Corte Inglés: (tel. 958 22 32 40), C. Geril. Follow Acera del Casino from Pta. Real onto the tree-lined road. This Spanish superstore stocks everything including a thorough map (475ptas). Open M-Sa 10am-10pm.

Foreign Language Bookstore: Librería Flash, Pl. Trinidad (tel. 958 52 11 90), has a modest selection (including guidebooks) in several languages. Open M-F 10am-2pm and 5-9pm, Sa 10am-2pm.

Laundry: C. La Paz, 19. From Pl. Trinidad, take C. Alhóndiga, turn right on C. La Paz and walk 2 blocks. Wash 400ptas per load; dry 100ptas per 15min. Open M-F 9:30am-2pm and 4:30-8:30pm, Sa 9am-2pm.

Swimming Pool: Piscina Neptuno (tel. 958 25 88 21), next to flamenco club Jardines Neptuno and near the intersection of C. Recogidas and Camino de Ronda. M-Sa 600ptas, Su 800ptas, children 400ptas. Open June-Sept. daily 11am-7:30pm.

Emergency and Communications

Emergency: call 091 or 092. **Police:** C. Duquesa, 21 (tel. 958 24 81 00). English spoken. **Guardia Civil:** Av. Puliana Pol. Almanjayar (tel. 958 25 11 00).

Pharmacy: Farmacia Gran Vía, Gran Vía de Colón, 6 (tel 958 22 29 90). Open M-F 9:30am-2pm and 5-8:30pm. For late-night pharmacies, check listings in any local paper or signs posted in pharmacies.

Medical Assistance: Clínica de San Cecilio, C. Doctor Oloriz, 16 (tel. 958 28 02 00 or 958 27 02 00), on the road to Jaén.

Internet Access: Net, C. Santa Ecolástica, 13 (tel. 958 22 69 19), up C. Pavaneras from Pl. Isabel la Católica. Fast connections, email, worldwide web, and drinks. 400ptas per hr. English spoken. Open M-Sa 9am-11pm, Su 4-11pm.

Post Office: Pta. Real (tel. 958 22 48 35; fax 958 22 36 41), on the corner of Acera de Darro and C. Angel Ganinet. Lista de Correos. Open M-F 8:30am-8:30pm, Sa 9:30am-2pm. **Wires money** M-F 8:30am-2:30pm. **Faxes** sent and received. **Postal Code:** 18009.

ACCOMMODATIONS AND CAMPING

Granada has more cheap accommodations than shoe stores. Finding lodgings is a problem only during Semana Santa, when you must call ahead.

HI Hostels

Albergue Juvenil Granada (HI), Ramón y Cajal, 2 (tel. 958 27 26 38 or 958 28 43 06; fax 958 28 52 85). From the bus station, take bus #10 (from C. Gran Vía) or RENFE #11 and ask the driver to stop at "El Estadio de la Juventud." It's the peach building across the field on the left. Rooms are spacious with comfortable beds. All rooms are doubles with baths or triples. Dorms 1300ptas, over 26 1600ptas, non-HI guests pay an extra 300ptas per night for 6 nights to join. Sheets provided, towels 175ptas. 24hr. reception. No curfew. Limited wheelchair access.

Along Cuesta de Gomérez

Hostales line **Cuesta de Gomérez,** the street leading uphill to the Alhambra and to the right of Pl. Nueva. Crashing in this area is wise for those planning to spend serious time at the Alhambra complex.

Hostal Residencia Britz, Cuesta de Gomérez, 1 (tel. 958 22 36 52), on the corner of Pl. Nueva. Large rooms with luxurious beds and green-tiled bathrooms. Soda machine in the lobby says *"Gracias";* management is even friendlier. Singles 2300ptas; doubles 3500ptas, with bath 5000ptas. 6% discount for *Let's Go* readers if you pay in cash, are courteous, and show them the book. Prices expected to rise by summer 1999. Use the washing machine for 600ptas. 24hr. reception. Visa, MC.

Hostal Gomérez, Cuesta de Gomérez, 10 (tel. 958 22 44 37). Clean rooms with firm beds. Amiable, multilingual owner will wash and dry clothing for 1000ptas per load. Singles 1500ptas; doubles 2500ptas; triple 3500ptas. Offers a 100-200ptas discount to *Let's Go*ers during the off season. Will assist guests planning longer stays.

Pensión Gomérez-Gallegos, Cuesta de Gomérez, 2, 3rd fl. (tel. 958 22 63 98). Small hostel with large rooms, some balconies, and numerous plants. Singles 1600ptas; doubles 2800ptas; triples 4200ptas. One clean and roomy shared bath. Ask about discounts on longer stays. Expect prices to rise 100ptas by summer 1999.

Hostal Navarro-Ramos, Cuesta de Gomérez, 21 (tel. 958 25 05 55). Quarters are comfortable and cool in the evening. Small balconies in some rooms are ideal for spying on the Alhambra-bound passersby below. Singles 1500ptas; doubles 2400ptas, with bath 3800ptas; triples with bath 5100ptas. Shower 150ptas.

Near the Cathedral/University

The area alongside boutique-saturated C. Mesones and C. Alhóndiga is nearest to the cathedral, the Alcaicería, Pta. Real, and Pl. Isabel la Católica. Hostels cluster around Pl. Trinidad, a cozy palm- and orange-tree-laden square (at the end of C. Mesones from Pta. Real). Many *pensiones* around C. Mesones cater to students during the academic year but free up during the summer. The ones listed below are open year-round.

Hospedaje Almohada, C. Postigo de Zarate, 4 (tel. 958 20 74 46). Walk 1 block from Pl. Trinidad along C. Duquesa; it's to your right at the top of C. Málaga (no sign). A successful experiment in communal living: guests enjoy socializing in the sky-lit courtyard, the living room, and the kitchen. Singles 1800ptas; doubles 3500ptas. Longer stays are common and encouraged (33,000-36,000ptas per month). Laundry 500ptas per load.

Hostal-Residencia Lisboa, Pl. Carmen, 29 (tel. 958 22 14 13 or 958 22 14 14; fax 958 22 14 87). Take C. Reyes Católicos from Pl. Isabel la Católica; Pl. Carmen is on the left. Same owner as Hostal Britz, same friendly atmosphere. Rooms are well furnished, with phones and fans. Singles 2600ptas, with bath 3900ptas; doubles 3900ptas, with bath 5400ptas; triples 5200ptas, with bath 7200ptas. Visa, MC.

Hostal Residencia Zacatín, C. Ermita, 11 (tel. 958 22 11 55). Enter through the Alcaicería from C. Reyes Católicos (C. Ermita is on the left). Rooms are amply sized and baths are immense. Some rooms have balconies, but interior rooms are more tranquil. Singles 1600ptas, with bath 2400ptas; doubles 2800ptas, with shower 3300ptas, with bath 4000ptas.

Hostal Zurita, Pl. Trinidad, 7 (tel. 958 27 50 20). Beautiful rooms, high-quality beds, and 24hr. hot water. Double-paned balconies keep out noise. Singles 1875ptas; doubles 3750ptas, with bath 4500ptas; triples 5000ptas, with bath 5500ptas.

Hostal Sevilla, C. Fábrica Vieja, 18 (tel. 958 27 85 13). From Pta. Real follow C. Alhóndiga into C. Fábrica Vieja, past Pl. Trinidad. Spotless and well-furnished with friendly staff. Singles 2000ptas, with bath 2700ptas; doubles 3000ptas, with bath 4200ptas; triples 4500ptas.

Pensión Romero, C. Sillería de Mesones, 1 (tel. 958 26 60 79), off Pl. Trinidad with a big sign. Bright, little rooms, but not much peace from the plaza below. Singles 1600ptas; doubles 2800ptas.

Along Gran Vía de Colón

Hostels are sprinkled along Gran Vía de Colón and its side streets, the main thoroughfare linking Pl. Isabel la Católica with Av. Constitución. In all cases, rooms with balconies over the street are much noisier than those that open onto an inner patio.

Residencia Universitaria Antares, Cetti Meriém, 10 (tel. 958 22 83 13), on the corner of with C. Elvira, 1 block from the Gran Vía. A spotless and cheap little guesthouse in a great location, a block from Pl. Nueva and the cathedral. All rooms have balconies and sinks, and there are plenty of shared bathrooms. Singles 1500ptas; doubles 3000ptas; triple (only one) 4500ptas.

Hostal Gran Vía, Gran Vía de Colón, 17 (tel. 958 27 92 12), about 4 blocks from Pl. Isabel la Católica. Clean, bright rooms. Singles with shower 2500ptas; doubles 3000ptas, with shower 3500ptas, with bath 4000ptas; triples with bath 5000ptas.

Hostal-Residencia Londres, Gran Vía de Colón, 29 (tel. 958 27 80 34), a bit farther down than Hostal Gran Vía. Pretty rooms and a big patio with views of the Alhambra, Albaicín, and hundreds of Granadan rooftops. Large shared bathrooms, one for every 2 bedrooms. Singles 2000ptas; doubles 3000ptas; 1500ptas per additional person. Local students get first dibs Oct.-June, so call ahead.

Pensión Olympia, Alvaro de Bazán, 6 (tel. 958 27 82 38). From Pl. Isabel, walk down C. Gran Vía 6 blocks and make a right. Same owner as Hostal Gran Vía, but this place is a cheaper version. Communal bathrooms. Singles 2000ptas; doubles 3000ptas.

Camping

Buses serve five campgrounds within 5km of Granada. Check the departure schedules at the tourist office, and ask bus drivers to alert you to your stop.

Sierra Nevada, Av. Madrid, 107 (tel. 958 15 00 62). Take bus #3 or 10. Lots of shady trees, modern facilities, and free hot showers. If the town fair is here, stay elsewhere or forget about REM sleep. 560ptas per person, per tent, and per vehicle. Children under 10 460ptas. There is also a hotel on the grounds. Open Mar.-Oct.

María Eugenia, Ctra. Nacional, 342 (tel. 958 20 06 06), at km 436 on the road to Málaga. Take Santa Fé or Chauchina bus from the train station (departs every 30min.). 425ptas per person, per tent, and per car. Children 325ptas. Open Mar.-Oct.

Los Alamos (tel. 958 20 84 79), next door to María Eugenia. 1300ptas per person, per tent, and per car. Children 300ptas. Showers 50ptas. Open Apr.-Sept.

FOOD

Granada offers a welcome variety of ethnic restaurants to emancipate your tastebuds from the fried-fish-and-pig-products doldrums. Cheap and tasty Middle Eastern cuisine can be found in and around the **Albaicín,** a fabulous place for a meal. Near **Plaza Nueva** and **Plaza Trinidad,** the usual fare of *menús* awaits. Menus are multilingual and prices steeper near **Plaza Trinidad.** Picnickers can gather fresh fruit and vegetables at the market on C. San Augustín. Get **groceries** at **Supermercado T. Mariscal,** C. Genil, next to El Corte Inglés. (Open M-F 9:30am-2pm and 5-9pm, Sa 9:30am-2pm.)

Try one of Granada's holistic *platos típicos* (typical fare)—they eat the *whole* cow. *Tortilla sacromonte* (an omelette with calf's brains, bull testicles, ham, shrimp, and veggies), *sesos a la romana* (batter-fried calf's brains), and *rabo de toro* (bull's tail) are common. Granada also hosts dozens of cafes, called *churrerías,* named for the classic *chocolate con churros,* a snack of thin, sugar-coated pastries with a cup of thick hot chocolate for dipping.

Near Plaza Nueva

Consider an evening of restaurant-hopping—the places around Pl. Nueva make great stops on a *ruta de tapas* (*tapas* route). Order your favorite drink and wait for the *tapas* to arrive (free in Granada), or try the house specialties for 300-1000ptas.

La Nueva Bodega, C. Cetti Meriem, 9 (tel. 958 22 59 34), on a small side street off C. Elvira out of Pl. Nueva. Sit-down area and bar separated by a wrought-iron partition. Winding staircase leads up to a fancier *comedor.* Popular with locals and tourists. *Menús* 825-1400ptas. *Bocadillos* around 300ptas. Open daily noon-midnight.

Bodega Mancha, C. Joaquin Costa, 8, and **Bodega Castañeda,** C. Elvira, 5, both located in the alleyways around C. Elvira leading from Pl. Nueva. *Bocadillos* and *tapas* (under 300ptas) are the major fare preferred in these dens of Dionysus, the area's two *bodegas* (wine bars). The salty pork aroma might make you drowsier than the wine and sherry *de barril* (3 or 4 varieties of each, straight from the bar-

ANDALUCÍA

rel, 125-200ptas). And do as the sign says: "*Pidau Sangría*" (ask for sangría). Both open M-F noon-4pm and 6pm-1am, Sa-Su noon-4pm and 6pm-3am.

Restaurante Boabdil (tel. 958 22 81 36), serves lunch and dinner in a little outdoor nook on C. Elvira leading from Pl. Nueva. *Platos combinados* (725ptas) include staples like paella and macaroni and cheese as well as dessert. Open F-W 1-5pm and 8pm-midnight, Th 8pm-midnight. Visa, MC.

Restaurante Alcaicería, C. Oficios, 6 (tel. 958 22 43 41), in the Alcaicería, between the cathedral and C. Reyes Católicos. Eat outdoors in a corner of the souvenir market. Owner recommends the *rabo de toro,* and of course some *vino tinto. Menús* 1500ptas. Open daily noon-11:30pm. Visa, MC.

The Albaicín

Wander the romantic, winding streets of the Albaicín and you will discover a number of economical bars and restaurants on the slopes above Pl. Nueva. **C. Calderería Nueva,** off C. Elvira leading from the plaza, is crammed with teahouses and cafes.

⊛**Naturi Albaicín,** C. Calderería Nueva, 10 (tel. 958 22 06 27). Excellent vegetarian cuisine from an owner who has written the book on "healthy living." Tasty options include *berenjenas rellenas* (stuffed eggplant), quiche, and *kefir* (yogurt drink). *Menú* 950-1150ptas. Open Sa-Th 1-4pm and 7-11pm, F 7-11pm.

Las Cuevas, Placeta de San Gregorio, 30, on the top of Caldrería Nueva, near El 22 disco. A delightful selection of local meat and vegetarian dishes served at outdoor tables. Quite a setting. *Paella* 800ptas per person. Open daily noon-4pm and 8pm-midnight or so.

El Ladrillo II, C. Panaderos (tel. 958 29 26 51), off Cuesta del Chapiz near the Iglesia El Salvador, high on the Albaicín. Consume immense rations of delicious, fresh seafood to the sound of *sevillanas.* Thunderous evening hangout. The restaurant's other location on Pta. Fátima has a *terraza.* Open daily 12:30pm-1:30am.

Los Chirimías (tel. 958 22 68 82), on Po. Padre Manjón up C. del Darro from Pl. Nueva, has a breezy *terraza* along the Darro River, surveyed by the towering Alhambra. Pizzas range between 550 and 775ptas and the *plato del día* costs a mere 600ptas. Open daily 12:30pm-2am.

Medina-Zahara, C. Calderería Nueva, 2 (tel. 958 22 15 41). This Mediterranean takeout joint slices lamb kebab before your very eyes and makes delicious samosas (275-325ptas) and falafel (325ptas).

Elsewhere

Restaurante Chino Estrella Oriental, C. Alvaro de Bazán, 9 (tel. 958 22 34 67), 5 blocks down Gran Vía de Colón from Pl. Isabel la Católica. A bright-red Pagoda facade welcomes all to cheap, tasty *menús* (695ptas). No fortune cookies and a curious amount of ham, but the meal does conclude with a refreshing Chinese liqueur. Delivery with order of 1500ptas or more. Open daily 12:30-4:30pm and 8pm-12:30am. Visa, MC.

SIGHTS

> Alms, lady, alms! For there
> is nothing crueler in life
> than to be blind in Granada.
> —Francisco de Icaza, inscribed in the Torre de la Pólvora

The Alhambra Complex

Open Apr.-Sept. M-Sa 9am-8pm, Su 9am-6pm; Oct.-Mar. M-Sa 9am-5:45pm. 750ptas, free for handicapped and children under 8. **Night-time visits:** open in summer T, Th, and Sa 10pm-midnight; in winter Sa 8-10pm. 750ptas. **Entry limited** to 8400 visitors per day in summer, 6800 in winter, so get there early.

Behind a simple red facade lies the **Alhambra** (tel. 958 22 09 12; fax 958 21 05 84). The name, from the Arabic for "red," may refer more to the nickname of the founder of this fortress-complex, al Ahmar, than to the color of the walls, which originally

ANDALUCÍA

gleamed white. Enter the Alhambra through Pta. de Granada, off Cuesta de Gomérez, and climb to the well-marked main entrance; alternatively, take the Alhambra bus from Pl. Nueva (120ptas). Night-time visits of the illuminated complex are also available (see above). Enter the Palace of the Nazarites (Alcázar) during the time specified on your ticket, but stay as long as desired.

The Alcazaba

Against the silvery backdrop of the Sierra Nevada, the Christians drove the first Nazarite King Alhamar from the Albaicín to this more strategic hill. Here he built a fortress called the Alcazaba, the oldest section of today's Alhambra.

In the Alcazaba, the **Torre de la Vela** (watchtower) provides the finest view of Granada and the Sierra Nevada. The tower's bells were rung to warn of impending danger and to coordinate the Moorish irrigation system. Napoleon stationed his troops here, but before leaving he blew up enough of the place to ruin the citadel's utility as a military outpost. Exit through the **Puerta del Vino** (wine gate), where inhabitants of the Alhambra once bought tax-free wine (alas, no more).

The Alcázar

Follow signs to the *Palacio Nazaries* to see the Alcázar (Royal Palace), which was built for the great Moorish rulers Yusuf I (1333-1354) and Muhammed V (1354-1391). An unexplained force allegedly murdered Yusuf I in an isolated basement chamber of the Alcázar, so his son Muhammed V was left to complete the palace.

The entrance leads into the **Mexuar,** a great pillared council chamber. The Mexuar opens onto the **Patio del Cuarto Dorado** (Patio of the Gilded Hall). Off the far side of the patio, foliated horseshoe archways of successively diminishing width open onto the **Cuarto Dorado** (Gilded Hall), decorated by Carlos V. Its opulent wooden ceiling is inlaid with ivory and mother-of-pearl.

Next is the **Patio de los Arrayanes** (Courtyard of Myrtles), an expanse of emerald water filled with goldfish and bubbling fountains at both ends. Stand at the top of the patio for a glimpse of the 14th-century **Fachada de Serallo,** the palace's elaborately carved facade. The long and slender **Sala de la Barca** (Boat Gallery), with an inverted boat-hull ceiling, flanks the courtyard.

In the elaborate **Sala de los Embajadores** (Hall of Ambassadors) adjoining the Sala de la Barca to the north, King Fernando and Christopher Columbus discussed the (misguided) route to India. Every surface of this magnificent square hall is intricately wrought with inscriptions and ornamental patterns. The dome, carved of over 8000 pieces of wood and inlaid cedar, depicts the seven skies of paradise mentioned in the Quran (the ceiling style is called *mozárabe*).

From the Patio de los Arrayanes, once a harem and center of the Sultan's domestic life, the Sala de los Mocárabes leads to the **Patio de los Leones** (Courtyard of the Lions), the most photographed sanctum of the palace. The grandeur continues: a symmetrical arcade of horseshoe arches and white marble columns borders the courtyard, and a fountain supported by 12 marble lions tinkles in the middle.

Moving counter-clockwise in the courtyard, next comes the **Sala de los Abencerrajes.** Sultan Abul Hassan piled the heads of the sons of his first wife here (16 of them) so that Boabdil, son of his second wife, could inherit the throne. The rust-colored stains in the basin are said to mark the indelible traces of the butchering. Untainted, the intricate ceiling, perhaps the most beautiful in the complex, dazzles irreverently.

At the far end of the courtyard from the Patio de Los Leones, the **Sala de los Reyes** (Hall of Kings) is covered by eroded, but still spectacular, wall-paintings on leather surfaces, plus another amazing ceiling. On the remaining side of the courtyard, the resplendent **Sala de las Dos Hermanas** (Chamber of the Two Sisters) was named for twin marble slabs embedded in its floor. Its staggering honeycomb dome (Mozárabe style) is made of thousands of tiny cells. From here a secluded portico, **Mirador de Daraxa** (Eyes of the Sultana), overlooks the Jardines de Daraxa.

Passing the room where American author Washington Irving resided in 1829, a balustraded courtyard leads to the 14th-century **Baños Reales** (Royal Baths), the center

ANDALUCÍA

of court social life. Light shining through star-shaped holes in the ceiling was once refracted through steam, creating indoor rainbows (currently closed during summer months for conservation studies).

Towers and Gardens

Just outside the east wall of the Alcázar in the **Jardines del Partal,** lily-studded pools flow beside terraces of roses. The **Torre de las Damas** (Ladies' Tower) soars above it all, as one tower after another traverses the area between the Alcazaba and El Generalife, one for captives, one for princesses, etc. The beautiful floral gardens also merit a visit.

El Generalife

Over a bridge, across the **Callejón de los Cipreses** and the shady **Callejón de las Adelfas,** are the vibrant blossoms, towering cypresses, and streaming waterways of El Generalife, the sultan's vacation retreat. Arab engineers changed the Darro's flow by 18km and employed dams and channels to prepare the soil for Aben Walid Ismail's design of El Generalife in 1318. Over the centuries, the estate passed through private hands until it was repatriated in 1931. The two buildings of El Generalife, the **Palacio** and the **Sala Regia,** connect across the **Patio de la Acequia** (Courtyard of the Irrigation Channel), embellished with a narrow pool fed by fountains forming an aquatic archway. Honeysuckle vines scale the back wall, and shady benches invite long rests.

Palacio de Carlos V

After the *Reconquista* drove the Moors from Spain, Fernando and Isabel restored the Alcázar. Little did they know that two generations later omnipotent Emperor Carlos V would demolish part of it to make way for his **Palacio de Carlos V,** a Renaissance masterpiece by Pedro Machuca (disciple of Michelangelo).

Although the building is glaringly incongruous amid all the Moorish splendor, experts have somehow agreed that the *palacio* is one of the most beautiful Renaissance buildings in Spain. A square building with a circular inner courtyard wrapped in two stories of Doric colonnades, it is Machuca's only surviving effort. Inside, the **Museo de La Alhambra** (tel. 958 22 62 79) contains the only original furnishings remaining from the Alhambra. *(Open Tu-Sa 9am-2:30pm, ask about exhibits with extended hours. 250ptas, free for E.U. citizens.)* Upstairs, the **Museo de Bellas Artes** (tel. 958 22 48 43) displays mostly religious sculpture and paintings of the Granada School from the 16th century to the present. *(Open in summer Tu 2:30-6pm, W-Sa 9am-6pm; in winter Tu 2:30-7:45pm, W-Sa 9am-7:45pm, Su 9am-2pm.)*

The Cathedral Quarter

Downhill from the Alhambra's Arab splendor is splendor of the Christian kind—the **Capilla Real** (Royal Chapel; tel. 958 22 92 39), Fernando and Isabel's private chapel. During their prosperous reign, they funneled almost a quarter of the royal income into the chapel's construction (which lasted from 1504 to 1521) to produce their proper burial place. Their efforts did not go unrewarded; intricate Gothic carvings, and meticulously rendered statues (St. Peter and St. Paul among them), as well as **La Reja,** the gilded iron grill of Master Bartolomé, now mark the resting place of the legendary couple. Behind La Reja, one of the finest iron grills in all of Spain, rest the elaborate, almost lifelike marble figures of the royals themselves. Fernando and Isabel's feet face visitors as they enter; beside them sleeps their daughter Juana la Loca (the Mad) and her husband Felipe el Hermoso (the Fair). To the horror of the rest of the royal family, Juana insisted on keeping the body of her husband with her for an unpleasantly long time after he died. Friends had a hard time convincing the insanely jealous wife that Felipe was actually dead. The lead caskets, where all four monarchs were (finally) laid to rest, lie in the crypt directly below the marble statues, accessible by a small stairway on the left. The smaller, fifth coffin belongs to the hastily buried child-king of Portugal, Miguel, whose death allowed Carlos V to ascend the throne.

Next door in the **sacristy,** Isabel's private **art collection,** the highlight of the chapel, favors Flemish and German artists of the 15th century, including Memling,

ANDALUCÍA

Bouts, and Roger van der Weyden. *(Open Apr.-Sept. M-Sa 10:30am-1pm and 4-7pm; Oct.-Mar. M-Sa 10:30am-1pm and 3:30-6:30pm, Su 11am-1pm. 300ptas.)* The glittering **royal jewels**—the queen's golden crown and scepter and the king's sword—shine in the middle of the sacristy. Some original clothing and letters are also on display.

The adjacent **cathedral** (tel. 958 22 29 59) was built by *los Reyes* upon the foundation of the major Arab mosque. *(Open daily Apr.-Sept. 10am-1:30pm and 4-7pm; Oct.-Mar. 10am-1:30pm and 3:30-6:30pm. Closed Sunday mornings. 300ptas.)* The first purely Renaissance cathedral in Spain, its massive Corinthian pillars support an astonishingly high vaulted nave. Admission is also good for the cathedral's **tesoro** and **museo.**

At the end of C. San Juan de Dios, the 16th-century **Hospital Real** is divided into four tiled courtyards. *(Open M-F 9am-2pm. Free.)* Above the landing of the main staircase, the Mudéjar-coffered ceiling echoes those of the Alhambra. Nearby rise the twin spires of **Basílica de San Juan de Dios,** a Baroque temple. *(Open for mass.)* The 14th-century **Monasterio de San Jerónimo** (tel. 958 27 93 37) is around the corner; badly damaged by Napoleon's troops, it has been restored admirably. *(Open daily Apr.-Sept. 10am-1:30pm and 4-7pm; Oct.-Mar. 10am-1:30pm and 3-6:30pm. 300ptas.)*

The Albaicín

The Albaicín is a gorgeous and fascinating old Arab quarter where the Moors built their first fortress. After the *Reconquista*, a small Moorish population clung to the neighborhood on this hill until their expulsion in the 17th century. The abundance of Middle Eastern cuisine and the recent construction of a mosque near Pl. San Nicolas attest to a continued Arab influence in Granada. Be cautious here at night.

The best way to explore this maze is to proceed along Carrera del Darro off Pl. Nueva, climb the Cuesta del Chapiz on the left, then wander aimlessly through Muslim ramparts, cisterns, and gates. On Pl. Nueva, the 16th-century **Real Cancillería** (or Audiencia), with the beautiful arcaded patio and stalactite ceiling, was the Christians' Ayuntamiento. Farther uphill are the 11th-century **Arab baths,** C. Darro, 31 (tel. 958 22 23 39). *(Open Tu-Sa 10am-2pm. Free.)* Behind the Plateresque facade of Casa Castril, the **Museo Arqueológico,** C. Darro, 41 (tel. 958 22 56 40), showcases funerary urns, coins, Classical sculpture, Carthaginian alabaster vases, Muslim lamps, and ceramics. *(Open Tu 3-8pm, W-Sa 9am-8pm, Su 9am-2:30pm. 250ptas, free for E.U. members.)*

Cármenes—traditional whitewashed Arab villas with luxurious walled gardens—characterize the neighborhood. Bus #12 travels from beside the cathedral to C. Pagés at the top of the Albaicín. There is also another **Alhambra bus** that departs from Pl. Nueva and weaves its way to the top. From here, walk down C. Agua through the **Puerta Arabe,** an old gate to the city at Pl. Larga. The terrace adjacent to **Iglesia de San Nicolás** affords the city's best view of the Alhambra, especially in winter when glistening snow adorns the Sierra Nevada behind it. To the west of San Nicolás, **Monasterio de Santa Isabel la Real,** founded by Queen Isabel in 1501, has exceptional coffered ceilings and a Plateresque Gothic facade.

ENTERTAINMENT

Entertainment listings are near the back of the daily paper, the *Ideal* (120ptas), under *Cine y Espectáculos;* the Friday supplement lists more bars, concerts, and special events. The *Guía del Ocio,* sold at newsstands (100ptas), lists the clubs, pubs, and cafes. The tourist office distributes a monthly cultural guide (*Cultura en Granada*).

Flamenco and Jazz

For **flamenco,** the most authentic performances are advertised on posters around town and change monthly. Tourists and locals alike flock to **Los Jardines Neptuno,** C. Arabial (tel. 958 52 25 33), near the Neptuno shopping center at the base of C. Recogidas. Rows and rows of plastic chairs sit in this huge, enclosed theater. (Cover 3500ptas, includes one drink). A more smoky, intimate setting awaits at **Eshavira,** C. Postigo de la Cuna (tel. 958 20 32 62), in an alley off C. Azacayes, between C. Elvira and C. Gran Vía. This joint is *the* place to go for flamenco, jazz, or a fusion of the two. Photos of Nat King Cole and other jazz greats plaster the walls. There is one drink minimum. Call ahead for the music schedule.

Pubs, Bars, and Clubs

Pubs and bars spread across several neighborhoods, genres, and energy levels. The most boisterous crowd belongs to **Calle Pedro Antonio de Alarcón** running from Pl. Albert Einstein to C. Perogidas. Here, on Thursday, Friday, and Saturday nights, rowdy university students and high school groupies flood the many pubs, disco bars, and late-night pizza joints. **Iguazu** on C. Socrates off C. Pedro Antonio de Alarcon offers a merengue or salsa beat. Also along C. Pedro Antonio de Alarcon, the daring cram into **Bar-Rama,** nicknamed **"Chupitos"** for the shot-sized concoctions they serve—some with such appetizing names as *"Aborto de gallona"* (chicken abortion) and *"Vomito Lagarto"* (lizard vomit). Farther down the street, bars become strip-tease clubs and the street gets progressively darker. Closer to Pl. Nueva, at the top of Calderería Nueva, a young throng of vacationers with beer bottles lounge on the steps of Pta. San Gregorio outside **El 22.** If you are looking for a bit more class and have a bit more cash, try **Hannigan and Sons** (tel. 958 22 48 26), C. Cetti Meriem between C. Elvira and Gran Vía de Colon. The Irish bartender pours a succulent Guinness (500ptas) in a jovial atmosphere. (Open daily 4:30pm-late.)

Teatotalers can lounge the night away in the candle-lit pillowed dens of **Jardín de los Sueños,** on C. Calderería Nueva, while sipping exotic *infusions* for 250ptas. Higher up, in the Albaicín, patrons of the refined **Casa de Yanguas** casually sip beer (200ptas) amid contemporary art in fountained Moorish patios. Follow Cuesta del Chapiz to its end near C. San Buenaventura (open daily 8pm-3am). **Babylon,** Placeta Sillería, 5, off C. Reyes Católicos before Pl. Nueva, pumps Reggae, hip-hop, and funk, and moonlights as a speakeasy for foreign students. *Tapas* and *terrazas* attract friendly folks to **Campo del Principa,** up C. Pavaneras from Pl. Isabel la Católica, off Pl. del Realejo. The twenty- to thirty-something crowd dresses elegantly for **Cine/ Disco Granada 10,** C. Cárcel Baja, 14 (tel. 958 22 40 01), 3 blocks from Pl. Isabel la Católica along Gran Vía de Colon. They turn off the projector at midnight and bop to Eurohouse; it gets really hopping at 2am. (Cover 700-1000ptas, includes one drink.)

Theaters, Concerts and Festivals

The **Aliatar,** C. Recogidas (tel. 958 26 19 84), near Pta. Real, is a conventional movie theater showing mostly American films (dubbed in Spanish), along with an occasional Spanish one (Th-Tu 500ptas, W 300ptas).

A number of festivals sweep the city during the summer. Granada's **Corpus Christi** celebrations, processions, and bullfights are well known (they happen in May or June). **Espárrago Rock** now cultivates performances by contemporary Spanish musicians as well as foreign big-name bands, usually in March. Every May, avant-garde theater groups from around the world make a pilgrimage to Granada for the **International Theater Festival** (tel. 958 22 93 44 or 958 22 43 84). The **Festival Internacional de Música y Danza** (mid-June to early July) sponsors open-air performances of classical music and ballet in the Alhambra's Palacio de Carlos V. Seats run 1000-6000ptas. Granada also hosts the new **Auditorio Manuel de Falla** (tel. 958 22 21 88), one of Spain's premier concert halls. Performances at the **Cuevas Gitanas de Sacromonte** (Gypsy caves) are not as appealing as they may sound. Once home to a thriving Gypsy community, the hill is now essentially a snare for tourists.

■ Near Granada: La Cartuja and Fuente Vaqueros

On the outskirts of Granada stands **La Cartuja** (tel. 958 16 19 32), a 16th-century Carthusian monastery and pinnacle of Baroque artistry in Granada. *(Open Apr.-Sept. M-Sa 10am-1pm and 4-8pm, Su 10am-noon; Oct.-Mar. M-Sa 10am-1pm and 3:30-6pm, Su 10am-noon. 300ptas.)* Marble with rich brown tones and swirling forms (a stone unique to nearby Lanjarón) marks the sacristy of Saint Bruno. To reach the monastery, take bus #8 from the front of the cathedral.

Author of *Bodas de sangre (Blood Wedding)* and *Romancero Gitano (Gypsy Ballads),* poet and playwright Federico García Lorca was born outside the tiny town of **Fuente Vaqueros** and was shot by right-wing forces near Granada at the outbreak of the Civil War. For Lorca fans, Fuente Vaqueros is a must-see. Walk through the restored **Casa-Museo** (tel. 958 51 64 53), Lorca's house-turned-museum, to see everything from the piano where the master played to the very bed in which he was born. *(Open Oct.-Mar. Tu-Sa 10am-1pm and 4-7pm; Apr.-Sept. Tu-Sa 10am-1pm and 5-8pm. 200ptas. Tours given every hour.)* Upstairs in the *granero* gaze upon first-edition photos of Lorca with the painter Salvador Dalí and original costumes from performances of his plays around the world. Buses run hourly from the train station (25min., 160ptas). From the bus stop, turn right on Paseo del Prado and follow signs to Casa-Museo, which is left on C. Poetra García Lorca.

■ Near Granada: Sierra Nevada

The peaks of Mulhacén (3481m) and Veleta (3470m), the highest in Spain, sparkle with snow and buzz with tourists for most of the year. Ski season runs from December to April. During the summer, tourists hike, parasail, and take jeep tours.

Before you go, check road and snow conditions (tel. 958 24 91 19; English spoken) and hotel vacancies. Bring warm clothes. If you plan to hike extensively, head to **Librería Flash** in Granada for their indispensable **map** of the Sierra for 800ptas (see **Granada: Practical Information: Foreign Language Bookstores,** p. 454).

■ Veleta And Prado Llano

Near the foot of Granada's Alhambra, the highest road in Europe begins its ascent to one of its highest peaks, **Veleta.** The road begins as a run-of-the-mill *camino* through the arid countryside then scales the daunting face of the Sierra. Due to snow, cars can cruise to the very top of Veleta only in August and September.

Veleta has 39 slopes and 61km of skiing area, with a vertical drop of 1300m. Lift tickets cost 2325ptas in *temporada alta* (winter), 2025ptas in *temporada baja* (off-peak season). **Rent skis** in the Gondola Building and in Pl. Prado Llano (full equipment 2500ptas per day). This ski resort is the southernmost in Europe—wear sunscreen or suffer DNA mutations. The cheapest accommodation is the **Albergue Universitario** (tel. 958 48 03 05), Peñones de San Francisco (1300ptas per person, over 26 1600ptas; reserve early in winter; open year-round).

The Autocares Bonal **bus** (tel. 958 27 31 00) from Granada to Veleta is a bargain (departs 9am, round-trip 700ptas). Buy tickets in the bar El Ventorrillo (see **Granada,** p. 451). The bus runs to the resort community of **Prado Llano** (19km from the peak), stopping at a **cabina-restaurante,** but you may be able to coax the driver to go to the top (for 200ptas) if conditions allow it. The hike to the top is steep, treacherous, and takes about three hours—bring water and wear sunscreen. Call **Cetursa** (tel. 958 24 91 11) for info on other activities.

▓ La Alpujarra

La Alpujarra's secluded white villages huddle along the southern slopes of the Sierra Nevada. Although its roads are now paved and the towns well traveled, a medieval Berber influence is still evident in the region's architecture. Low-slung houses rendered from earth and slate prevail only here and in Morocco's Atlas Mountains. After the fall of Granada, the Berbers were exiled to La Alpujarra, where Christian-Muslim conflicts resumed. In a gory battle at Bananco de la Sangre, Christian blood is said to have trickled uphill to avoid contamination with the plasma of the heathens below. Finally, in 1610, John of Austria ousted the Moors from La Alpujarra and ended their reign on the peninsula. On the heels of the Muslims, settlers from Galicia and Asturias brought Celtic and Visigothic traditions found nowhere else in Andalucía. The legacy of Moorish defiance lives on and peaks during Trevélez's **Fiestas de Moros y Cristianos,** a dramatization of the Moorish-Christian conflict, usually held in early June.

Although tourists have recently discovered the beauty of these settlements and the surrounding region's numerous hiking trails, the Alpujarras remain among Spain's poorest areas. Until the 1950s, travel was possible only by foot or mule, and the area still suffers from severe drought, unemployment, and low literacy rates. Nevertheless, the region's slow-paced life-style and hospitality make for a refreshing visit.

Alsina Graells **buses** zoom from Granada to many of the elevated towns, including Lanjarón, Órgiva, Pampaneira, Capileira, Bubión, and Trevélez. Often, bus drivers will stop to let travelers off at intermediate points. A different bus running to Almería serves Ugíjar and the eastern villages (each line has 2-3 departures daily). Plan for a night in the mountains since the single return buses to Granada and Almería leave early the next morning. Although these buses are the only forms of public transportation between the villages, travel **on foot** is a tradition of the Alpujarras. The locals, aware of the transportation problem, often sympathize with **hitchers.**

■ Lanjarón

Lanjarón (pop. 4300) is Spain's version of Evian, France. Famed throughout the country for mineral water that's sucked down by the gallon, Lanjarón once attracted Spaniards in droves after mineral water was said to have medicinal value. Many said it cured kidney ailments and rheumatism. A mere 45km daytrip from Granada, Lanjarón nevertheless abounds with accommodations. **Hostal Dólar,** Av. Andalucía, 5 (tel. 958 77 01 83), offers bright and clean rooms (singles 1500ptas, with bath 1700ptas; doubles 3000ptas, with bath 3200ptas). Drivers should turn left just before Órgiva to reach the hotel. Lanjarón is a nice stopover on the **bus** ride to Ugíjar; travelers can disembark to wander past flower-filled houses and drink from delicious public water fountains (marked *agua potable*).

Holy Water, Batman!

The water-endowed ecstasy in Lanjarón explodes the third week of June, during the **Fiestas del Agua y del Jamón** in honor of San Juan. While the rest of Spain celebrates with bonfires and fireworks, Lanjarón celebrates with water. From midnight to 1am water is dumped from balconies and spewed from squirt bottles while throngs of soaked youngsters parade through town chanting *"mucha agua, mucha agua, eh, eh, olé!"* Fire hoses, plastic buckets, bedpans, and plastic cups are all acceptable instruments for aquatic assault, but the unwitting tenderfoot who dares splash murky puddles will be sternly scolded.

■ Pampaneira

As the road winds in serpentine curves up to Pampaneira, the lowest of the high Alpujarran villages (1059m), the landscape quickly becomes harsh. Pampaneira is the first in a trio of hamlets overlooking the **Poqueira Gorge,** a huge ravine cut by the Río Poqueira that trickles down from Mulhacén. Tourists and handmade crafts abound. For more info on the region's natural wonders, visit **Nevadensis** (tel. 958 76 31 27; fax 958 76 33 01) in Pampaneira's main square. A local organization associated with the Parque Natural de La Sierra Nevada, they arrange for rural accommodations, horseback riding, and other services. (Open Su-Tu 10am-3pm, W-Sa 10am-2pm and 4-6pm.) **Hostal Pampaneira** (tel. 958 76 30 02), just off the highway in front of the bus stop, provides large rooms with polished chestnut furniture, all with bath (singles 2000ptas; doubles 3000ptas; triples 4000ptas). Stock up at the **supermarket** three blocks uphill from the hostel (open daily 9am-2pm and 5-8pm).

■ Bubión

Bubión, a steep 3km hike from Pampaneira, beams with Berber architecture, village charm, and three contemporary art galleries. For info, check out **Rustic Blue,** Barrio La Ermita, s/n (tel. 958 76 33 81; fax 958 76 31 34), the closest thing to a tourist office in the Alpujarras. The helpful staff organizes excursions, cooking lessons with Irish mountaineer/chef Conor Clifford, and lodging. (Open M-F 10am-2pm and 5-8pm, Sa

ANDALUCÍA

Buddhism in Bubión

Bubión has a distinctly Buddhist slant. It was the birthplace of Osel, the Spanish reincarnation of the Tibetan lama Yeshe, one of the first lamas born in the West. Visitors from around the world (among them the Dalai Lama himself) come to meditate at the Buddhist retreat **Osel-Ling** (clear light), high in the mountains above Bubión. Osel is now in India, but his retreat is currently organizing courses in Buddhist studies and opens its *sala de meditación* to the public from 3 to 6pm (free). For more information, call Osel-Ling (tel. 958 34 31 34).

10:30am-1:30pm. English spoken.) **Las Terrazas,** Pta. del Sol (tel. 958 76 30 34), has spotless rooms with terra-cotta tiled floors, Alpujarran woven bedspreads, and baths (singles 2500ptas; doubles 4000ptas). Locals rave about the portions at **Restaurante La Artesa,** on the main road in front of the bus stop. (*Menú* 1100ptas, *menú alpujarreño* 1300ptas. Open daily 1:30-4pm and 8-11pm.) See **Buddhism in Bubión** for info on Bubión's spiritual heritage.

■ Capileira

Capileira (1436m) is perched atop the Poqueira Gorge and makes a good base for exploring the neighboring villages and the back side of the Sierra Nevada. Cobblestone alleys wind up the slope while peaks loom above and the valley plummets below. The road through Capileira continues up the mountainside, and by June the road may be clear enough for travelers to make the two-hour climb to **Mulhacén,** Spain's highest peak. Proceed with extreme caution when approaching the summit—the wind is gusty, the snow is slippery, and the drop to the other side is unforgiving. The area above 2700m may become a national park with limited private access. To reach the trail, follow the Sierra Nevada signs. A fork appears after 20km. Go right to Mulhacén.

Hiking around Capileira is pleasant if undramatic—*tómalo tranquilo* (take it easy) as the locals do and saunter from the whitewashed village to the verdant gorge. Descend the stairs to the left of Fonda El Tilo and follow the dirt road to the bridge. Catch glimpses of traditional Alpujarran homes, built with flat, gray stone and deep rounded windows to blend with the landscape. More ambitious hikers should consult Nevadensis or **Rustic Blue** (see **Pampaneira,** p. 463) for further suggestions.

Enjoy the vista from your bedroom window at **Mesón-Hostal Poqueira,** C. Dr. Castillo, 6 (tel. 958 76 30 48). Rooms are pleasant and fresh, with baths and central heating. (Singles 2000ptas; doubles 3000ptas; triples 4000ptas. Ask about apartments with kitchen and TV for 4-6 people.) Scrumptious and filling 1200ptas *menú* served at the attached restaurant (open Tu-Su). **Supermercado Rubies,** downhill from the bus station, supplies provisions (open M-Sa 9am-2pm and 5-9pm, Su 9am-2pm).

■ Trevélez

Rural isolation characterizes Trevélez, continental Spain's highest community (1476m). Aside from its Alpujarran charms, the town is best known for its cured ham, whose special qualities will probably elude all but the true *jamón* connoisseur. Steep roads weave in and out of three distinct *barrios* (upper, middle, lower) amid the sounds of rushing water carefully channeled down thousand-year-old Moorish irrigation systems. In fact, some Moors were spared from the Inquisition because the Christians could not operate the channels without them.

Trevélez is a logical base for the ascent to **Mulhacén.** Every August, throngs of locals climb to pay homage to the **Virgen de las Nieves** (Virgin of the Snow), whose shrine is at the peak. Those summit-bound should head north on the trail leaving the upper village; avoid the lower trail that follows the swampy Río Trevélez. You have three options: continue past the Cresta de los Postreros for a good 5½ hours and you will reach the Cañada de Siete Lagunas (the largest lake should be directly in front of

ANDALUCÍA

you); go right to see a famous cave-refuge. To reach Mulhacén, go up the ridge south of the refuge. It is *not* advisable to hike Mulhacén the same day you visit the lake.

Despite numerous signs near the bus stop advertising nearby *camas* (beds), the steep walk to **Hostal Fernando** (tel. 958 85 85 65) is well worth it. The hostal is on C. Pista, almost 1km uphill on the left side of town from the bus stop. The friendly management keeps spacious, attractive rooms with unbeatable views of the mountains from the terrace. (Singles 2000ptas; doubles 3000ptas.) They also rent apartments by the day for two people (4000ptas) and for four people (6000ptas). A great restaurant is **La Fragua**, C. Carcel (tel. 958 85 85 73), which overlooks the town and valley from the second-floor (*plato alpujarreño* 750ptas).

■ Yegen and Ugíjar

In the villages of the Eastern Alpujarras, donkeys—and increasingly tourists—are everywhere. On a mountaintop outside Berchules sits tiny **Yegen,** whose only monument is a plaque marking the house where British Hispanophile and Bloomsbury affiliate **Gerald Brenan** lived (and Virginia Woolf visited) in the 1920s and 30s. Brenan immortalized the name of Yegen and the customs and traditions of La Alpujarra in *South from Granada,* his autobiographical account of life in the region. Just around the corner, **Bar Nuevo La Fuente**, C. Real, 38 (tel. 958 85 10 67), offers inexpensive accommodations with private baths (1400ptas per person). Twelve kilometers southeast of Yegen is **Ugíjar,** a larger agricultural village where Odysseus stopped one day to patch up his ships. You too can stop for a day at **Pensión Vidaña**, Ctra. Almería (tel. 958 76 70 10), which has bright rooms, some with enormous balconies, and all with A/C and heat. (Singles 1700ptas; doubles 3200ptas. All with bath. Visa, MC.) The reasonably priced restaurant downstairs won the Washington, D.C. Golden Cock medal for best Alpujarran cuisine. A **supermarket** awaits shoppers down the street from Vidaña (open daily 9am-2:30pm and 5:30-9pm). Ugíjar is accessible by bus from Almería (2 hr., 2-3 per day) and from Órgiva and Lanjarón (2hr., 1-2 per day).

COSTA DEL SOL

The coast has sold its soul to the Devil, and now he's starting to collect. Artifice covers its once-natural charms as chic promenades and hotels seal off small towns from the shoreline. The former Phoenician, Greek, Roman, and Arab ports cater to an international clientele with wads of money and attitude. The Costa del Sol officially extends from Tarifa in the southwest to Cabo de Gata east of Almería; postindustrial Málaga is in the middle. To the northeast, the hills dip straight into the ocean, where there is well-preserved scenery but rocky beaches. To the southeast, the Costa is more built up and water washes almost entirely against concrete. Despite modernity's influence, nothing can take away from the coast's major attraction: eight months of spring and four months of summer. Sun-freaks swarm everywhere in July and August. Make reservations or be ready to search for a room. Prices double in high season. Some sleep on the beaches—not a wise option for solo travelers and women. Alternatively, ask around for *casas particulares.* June is the best time to visit, when summer weather has come to town but most vacationers haven't. **Trains** go as far as Málaga and Fuengirola; private **bus lines** offer connections along the coast itself. Railpasses are not valid, but prices are reasonable.

■ Almería

Once one of the poorer cities in Andalucía, Almería is a seaside oasis undergoing a boom. It came out of the Franco era in a slump with the rest of Andalucía, but a population of migrant professionals have led a resurgence. The newest Almeríans swear by the city's year-round temperate climate and sparkling beaches, and they hope to

ANDALUCÍA

promote Almería by hosting the eagerly awaited Mediterranean Games in 2005. A huge Moorish fortress still presides over the city, but travelers most appreciate Almería for the miles of soft sand stretching along the Mediterranean toward Cabo de Gata, the eastern edge of the Costa del Sol.

ORIENTATION AND PRACTICAL INFORMATION The city revolves around **Puerta de Purchena,** a six-way intersection with a fountain, just down C. Tiendas from the old town. To reach the Pta. Purchena from the **bus station** in Pl. Estación (20min.), follow Av. Estación out of Pl. Barcelona, turn right onto Av. Federico García Lorca, and then go left. **Rambla de Obispo Orbera** leads into Pta. Purchena. The **train station** is in Pl. Barcelona, across from the bus station.

The **airport** (tel. 950 22 41 14), 9km out of town, has daily flights to Madrid and Barcelona. **Trains,** Pl. Estación, 6 (tel. 950 25 11 35), run to: Granada (3hr., 3 per day, 1710ptas); Málaga (7hr., 3 per day, 3500ptas); Sevilla (7-10hr., 3 per day, 4105ptas); Madrid (7hr., 2 per day, 3900ptas). Across the way, **buses** leave from Pl. Barcelona (tel. 950 21 00 29) to: Granada (2hr., 5 per day, 1285ptas); Málaga (3½hr., 8 per day, 1915ptas); Córdoba (6hr., 1 per day, 3000ptas); Sevilla (5½hr., 3 per day, 3780ptas); Madrid (8hr., 3 per day, 3020ptas); Mojácar (1½hr., 5 per day, 820ptas); Murcia (3hr., 5 per day, 2125ptas); Alicante (5hr., 4 per day, 2540ptas); Barcelona (14hr., 3 per day, 7045ptas). There's a **RENFE** office (tel. 950 23 18 22) on C. Alcalde Muñoz, a block from Pta. Purchena. Call 950 21 00 00 or 950 25 11 11 for a **taxi.**

The **tourist office,** Parque Nicolás Salmerón, s/n (tel. 950 27 43 55), distributes information on the city and province as well as a map (open M-F 9am-7pm, Sa 9am-2pm). Follow Po. de Almería out of Pta. Purchena toward the port, and turn right onto Parque de Salmerón. **Viajes Alysol,** Po. Almería, 32 (tel. 950 23 76 22), offers **AmEx** and **Iberia** services (open M-F 9:30am-1:30pm and 5-8:30pm, Sa 9:30am-1:30pm). **Banco Central Hispano,** Po. Almería, 18 (tel. 950 23 43 43), offers **currency exchange** (open in summer M-F 8:30am-2:30pm; in winter M-F 8:30am-2:30pm, Sa 8:30am-1pm). **Luggage storage** is available at the train station for 400ptas. The **police** can be reached at tel. 950 22 37 04. In an **emergency,** dial 061. For a **pharmacy,** go to Po. Almería, 19 (open M-F 9:30am-1:30pm and 5-8:30pm, Sa 10am-1pm). **Hospital Torre Cardenas** answers at tel. 950 21 21 19. There's an **internet cafe,** Heladería La India II, C. Granada, 304 (tel. 950 27 48 61), 15 minutes from the center of town (300ptas per hr. daily 8am-3pm; 600ptas per hr. daily 3pm-2am). The **post office** (tel. 950 23 72 07) is in Pl. Juan Cassinello, down Po. Almería (open M-F 8:30am-8:30pm, Sa 9:30am-2pm). The **postal code** is 14070.

ACCOMMODATIONS AND FOOD The tourist office provides a list of accommodations, most of which cluster around **Puerta de Purchena.** There's an **albergue juvenil** (tel. 950 26 97 88), predictably far outside the town center (30min. walk) on C. Isla Fuerteventura. Well-located, bright, and attractive, **Hostal Bristol,** Pl. San Sebastián, 8 (tel./fax 950 23 15 95), beside the church in Pta. Purchena, provides a TV and full bath in every room. (Singles 2700ptas; doubles 4500ptas. Call a week in advance July-Aug. Visa, MC.) Many cafes line the Po. Almería. With ham chandeliers and over 70 types of *tapas,* **Casa Puga,** C. Jovellanos, 7 (tel. 950 23 15 30), in the old quarter, packs them in (open M-Sa 11am-4pm and 8pm-midnight). **Augusto Cesare,** Parque Nicolás Salmerón, 17 (tel. 950 27 16 16), located along the water and down the street from the tourist office, has over 30 varieties of pizza, only two of which are meat-free (950-1200pta; open daily noon-4pm and 7:30pm-1am). For groceries, browse the aisles of supermarket **Simago,** Po. de Almería (open M-Sa 9am-9pm).

SIGHTS AND ENTERTAINMENT Built in 995 by order of Abderramán III of Córdoba, the **Alcazaba** (tel. 950 27 16 17), a magnificent 14-acre Moorish fortress, spans two ridges overlooking the city and the sea. *(Open daily 9:30am-2pm and 4:30-7:30pm. 250ptas, free with E.U. passport.)* From Pl. Carmen next to Pta. de Purchena, follow C. Antonio Vico. The **cathedral** (tel. 950 23 48 48), in the old town, looks like a fortress due to repeated raids by Berber pirates. *(Open M-F 10am-5pm, Sa 10am-1pm. 300ptas.)*

In general, **la marcha** (nightlife) congregates in the small streets behind the post office. An especially die-hard crowd gathers in pubs **Endanza** and **Venue,** both on C. San Pedro off C. Padre Luque. **Georgia Jazz Club,** Padre Luque, 17 (tel. 950 25 76 84), near the post office and Po. Almería, has live music most nights, as does Venue. **Taberna Torreluz,** in Pl. Flores, draws hot-blooded *fútbol* fans to their outdoor TV. At **Carpa,** a few miles east along the coastal road to Cabo de Gata, a half-dozen tented bars and competing bass lines rock the beach deep into the night. Buses stop running around 11pm, but a taxi will go there for about 700ptas.

■ Near Almería: Cabo de Gata

Thirty kilometers east of urban Almería lies pristine **Parque Natural de Cabo de Gata-Níjar,** a 60km stretch of protected coast and inland environs. The near-desolate peninsula juxtaposes tropical and barren climates: flamingos flock to the area's salt marshes, while a desert and mountains farther inland have set the scene for a number of flicks, including *Let's Go*'s favorite spaghetti western, *The Good, the Bad, and the Ugly.* Contact **Grupo J. 126** (tel. 950 38 02 99) for tourist information and guided tours of the park. Long, sandy shores await in the refreshingly low-key fishing town of **San Miguel de Cabo de Gata** (often called simply **Cabo de Gata**). Farther south, the little resort of **San José,** which may just boast the nicest beach on the Spanish Mediterranean coast, attracts more visitors and serves as a base for exploring the park. **Autocares Becerra** (tel. 950 22 44 03) sends buses from Almería to San Miguel de Cabo de Gata (1hr., 2-4 per day, 275ptas) and San José (1-2 per day), although the area is really more rewarding if explored by car.

■ Mojácar

The houses of Mojácar rest on a hill, flanked by mountains of scorched earth and an expanse of turquoise-blue Mediterranean. This small resort community thrives in July and August, when hordes of international visitors join an already large contingent of expatriates who have wisely made Mojácar their home. Do not despair—the abundance of souvenir shops and non-*hispano hablantes* (Spanish speakers) have not diluted Mojácar's dramatic views.

PRACTICAL INFORMATION From the bus stop, follow the highway uphill for about 20 minutes; it eventually leads into Pl. Nueva, the town center. **Buses** leave for Almería (1½hr., 4 per day, Su 3 per day, 820ptas). The **tourist office** (tel./fax 950 47 51 62) is in Pl. Nueva (open M-F 9:30am-2pm and 5:30-7pm, Sa 10am-1pm). The only reliable **ATM** in the pueblo can be found just below Pl. Nueva, at C. Glorieta, 3. Summon the **police** by calling 950 47 20 00 or 908 05 52 66. The **postal code** is 04638.

ACCOMMODATIONS AND FOOD Finding a bed in small but confusing Mojácar can be difficult. To reach turn-of-the-century **Pensión Torreón,** C. Jazmín, 4 (tel. 950 47 52 59), from Pl. Nueva, follow C. Indalo, and take the second right on C. Enmedio, a left downhill along C. Unión, and a right at the end of this hill toward the *pensión*. Its five elegant bedrooms sit behind a breathtaking seaview terrace. The owner can chat with you over breakfast about the mystery surrounding Walt Disney, who was supposedly born here. (Dorms 600ptas; singles available in winter 4000ptas; doubles 6000ptas.) To reach the intimate but pricey **Hostal Luna,** C. Estación Nueva, 11 (tel. 950 47 80 32), walk up three flights of stairs from Pl. Nueva, continue straight ahead, and turn left at the ceramics shop past the church. The hike leads to friendly management, spotless rooms, and a rooftop dining terrace with priceless views. (Singles 5000-6000ptas; doubles 6000ptas. Breakfast included. Visa.)

Mojácar doesn't have a large selection of cheap eateries, but you'll find more variety and better value in the old or new town than at the *playa* or Pl. Nueva. **L'arlecchino** (tel. 950 47 80 37), in the aptly named Pl. Flores through the Moorish arch on C. Puntica, serves Italian, Spanish, and vegetarian dishes on the *terraza* or on roof-top *comedor* (*menú* 800ptas; open daily noon-4pm and 7pm-midnight).

ANDALUCÍA

It's a Small World After All

Residents of Mojácar each have their own version of the mystery surrounding Walt Disney, supposedly their most famous citizen. Rumor has it that Disney (born José Girao in 1901) was the product of an affair between a maid and the owner of Pensión Torreón. After the death of his father, Disney and his mother emigrated to California to avoid vicious rumors. When his mother died, the farming Disney clan adopted José, renaming him Walt. Evidence of Disney's birth in Mojácar mysteriously disappeared, perhaps looted from the town hall during the Spanish Civil War. Some Mojácan villagers, however, argue that the legendary Indalo Man explains Disney's ties to Mojácar. A crude, cartoonesque figure, first drawn on nearby cave walls in Mojácar around 2500 BC, the Indalo Man holds a rainbow to ward off bad luck and natural disaster. Proud residents of Mojácar link Disney's success with cartoons to his native town's history of animation.

BEACH AND OTHER ENTERTAINMENT Mojácar's winding streets and breathtaking *miradores* (plazas with picture-perfect views) make it well-suited to romantic strolls and rosy daydreams. **Buses** run every hour between the *pueblo* and *playa* and along the shore (in summer 9:45am-1:45pm and 3:45-9:45pm; in winter 10am-1pm and 5-10pm; 100ptas). In the village, buses leave from the stop below Pl. Nueva. To reach the village from the beach, get on at one of the stops along Av. Mediterránea.

Mojácar pulses with nightlife. Visit **Lapu Lapu,** on C. Horno and **Sahara,** a cafe/disc...o...asis, under the Moorish Arch near Restaurante L'arlecchino. **Budú Pub,** C. Estación Nueva, has a soaring rooftop terrace that may be the most romantic spot in Mojácar. Along the shore, pubs turn into loud *chiringuitos* (beach bars) until 5 or 6am in the summer. Go by car if you can, because buses stop running at 11pm, taxis disappear at sundown, and walking the highway is a poorly lit, dangerous alternative. Among the most popular pubs is **Pachá,** on Po. Mediterráneo, where palm trees shade the bar. The infamous **Tuareg,** on the road to Carboneras, has the highest decibel levels in town. For a midnight dip, the pool at **Master Disco** (tel. 950 46 81 33), on the highway midway between the *playa* and *pueblo,* is open until 5am. A huge inflatable creature dressed in mauve greets revelers at the entrance. Expats run more laid-back watering holes—the **Time and Place,** in Pl. Flores, serves soothing cocktails, while Gordon pours Guinness and cultivates an intellectual atmosphere at **La Sartén** (familiarly known as Gordon's), on C. Estación Nueva, behind the church. Keeping its promise as a *bar de copas* (night caps), **El Lord Azul,** C. Fronton, 1, plays blues and classic rock for an international crowd well into every night.

■ Almuñécar

In the 4th century BC, a booming fish-salting industry brought prosperity to this Phoenician port town. The Romans took over 100 years later, constructing temples and an aqueduct, and calling the town **Sexi.** You may, too. Although the sands are somewhat rocky, seemingly endless boardwalks entice visitors, and exotic birds and mangoes thrive in the sultry tropical environment.

PRACTICAL INFORMATION Buses run from the station (tel. 950 63 01 40) at the corner of Av. Fenicia and Av. Juan Carlos I to: Málaga (1½hr., 7 per day, 745ptas); Granada (1½hr., 7 per day, 830ptas); Madrid (7hr., 1 per day, 2300ptas); Nerja (30min., 8 per day, 295ptas). The **tourist office** (tel. 958 63 11 25; email ofitur@almu-necar-ctropical.org) provides info and a free map in a hideous mauve mansion on Av. Europa, off Av. Costa del Sol. From the bus station, exit right and follow Carrera de la Concepción through the rotary to Av. Costa del Sol; turn left onto Av. Europa and walk past the park (with its own mauve buildings). The office is on the right (open M-Sa 10am-2pm and 5-8pm). The bus station has **luggage storage** (300ptas). In an **emergency,** dial 091 or 092. The **police** (tel. 958 83 86 14) are in Pl. Constitución at the Ayuntamiento, up C. Puerta de Velez from Av. Europa. **Centro de Salud** (tel. 958 63 20 63), on Ctra. Málaga, provides medical assistance. The **postal code** is 18690.

ACCOMMODATIONS AND FOOD Several convenient and reasonably priced *hostales* are on **Avenida Europa.** Situated near the tourist office and the beach along Av. Europa, **Hotel Goya** (tel. 958 63 05 50 or 958 63 11 92; fax 958 63 11 92) has large, pristine rooms with bath, TV, phone, and heating. TV lounges and a restaurant complete this luxury *hostal.* (Singles 2000-3500ptas; doubles 3000-6000ptas: Visa, MC.) **Residencia Tropical** (tel. 958 63 34 58), on Av. Europa a half-block from the beach, has a bar and spotless, well-furnished rooms with bathrooms (singles 2300-3200ptas; doubles 3300-5200ptas; Visa, MC).

Plenty of restaurants line **Paseo Puerta del Mar** and **Paseo San Cristóbal,** the place to savor the day's catch on a beach-front terrace. Locals frequent **Bar Avenida Lute y Jesús,** Av. Europa, 24 (tel. 958 63 42 76), also on Av. Europa. They specialize in *fritura de pescado* (fried fish 650-1000ptas; *menú* 800ptas; open daily 8am-1:30am). Several heavenly **heladerías** (ice cream shops) dot the shore.

SIGHTS AND ENTERTAINMENT Alumñécar's historical protagonists, the Phoenicians, Romans, and Moors, fought over this subtropical paradise, and each left a distinguishable mark. Built by the Moors, **Castillo de San Miguel** rests atop a massive hill at the front of Pl. Puerte del Mar. The interior may still be closed due to the construction of a museum depicting the city's history. Inquire at the tourist office. The 1900-year-old, 8km-long **acueducto,** 3km up the Río Seco from the tourist office, watered the ancient Roman town—parts of it are still in use. Almuñécar is also home to nearly 100 different species of birds, which nest in the **Parque Ornitológico Loro Sexi,** beside El Castillo de San Miguel, 100m from the beach. *(Open in summer 11am-2pm and 5-9pm; in winter 10am-2pm and 4-6pm. In summer 309ptas, children and elders 206ptas; in winter 412ptas, seniors and children 258ptas.)* Nearby, uphill from the tourist office, **Parque El Majuelo's** has 400 varieties of imported plants that shade enticing benches and great views of Roman ruins. *(Free.)*

Located on the **Costa Tropical,** Almuñécar is a beach-lover's haven. The two main beaches are separated by the jutting **Peñón del Santo. Puerta del Mar** is on the left when facing the water, **San Cristóbal** on the right. Most streets from the bus station terminate at the beach. The easiest way is via Av. Europa (signs point to Playa San Cristóbal). Walk far beyond Po. Pta del Mar, past Apartamentos Las Goudolas, to beautiful **Playa de Velilla.** Buses to Málaga go through **La Herradura,** a suburb/beach frequented by windsurfers and scuba divers. The largest **nude beach** on the Costa Tropical is **Playa Cantarrijan.** Even after taking the bus to La Herradura, you will still need a car or taxi to reach the beach.

▌Nerja

Renowned for its pristine beaches and remarkable nearby caves, Nerja offers the best and worst of a coastal resort town. Flip-flopped English-speakers crowding Nerja's **Balcón de Europa** compete for the Costa del Sol's most stunning ocean view.

PRACTICAL INFORMATION The **bus station,** C. San Miguel, 3 (tel. 95 252 15 04), sends buses to: Málaga (1½hr., 12 per day, 450ptas); Almuñécar (30min., 6 per day, 295ptas); Almería (4hr., 5 per day, 1455ptas); Granada (2¼hr., 2 per day, 1065ptas); Sevilla (4hr., 3 per day, 2320-2695ptas); Marbella (change in Málaga). The multilingual **tourist office,** Pta. del Mar, 2 (tel. 95 252 15 31), beside the Balcón de Europa, gives out a free map of central Nerja and sells a more detailed version (100ptas; open M-F 10am-2pm and 5-8pm, Sa 10am-1pm). An **ATM** is on C. Pintada, on the way to the beach. In an **emergency,** dial 091 or 092. **Police** headquarters (tel. 95 252 15 45) are on C. Virgen del Pilar. The **post office** (tel. 95 252 17 49) sorts mail at C. Almirante Ferrándiz, 6 (open M-F 8:30am-2:30pm, Sa 9:30am-1pm). The **postal code** is 29780.

ACCOMMODATIONS AND FOOD The cheapest place in town, **Hostal Residencia Mena,** C. El Barrio, 15 (tel. 95 252 05 41), is conveniently located off the Balcón de Europa (follow signs from the bus station to the Balcón) and has bare rooms with very small balconies and a shady garden (singles 1300-2000ptas; doubles 2500-

470 ■ COSTA DEL SOL

The area around Mojácar has a sordid legacy. In the 1960s, as Spain was debating whether to join NATO, a USAF B-52 bomber carrying five hydrogen bombs blew up over the village of Palomares, 20km north of Mojácar, during an in-flight refueling mishap. Locals looked on as U.S. personnel in radiation suits combed the town in search of the bombs. Four were recovered and identified; the fifth supposedly emerged wrapped in a plastic tarp and without a serial number (Spanish Greenpeace still doubts that it was ever found). Much of Spain and Europe boycotted the area's produce (mostly tomatoes), as anti-NATO sentiment reached new heights. To downplay the accident, the U.S. Ambassador and Franco's Minister of the Interior staged a seaside photo-op, swimming in the water before a dozen CIA agents. The U.S. then built a health clinic in the town. Palomares has since prospered with copious harvests of tomatoes, leeks, and melons, but some locals still blame defects and illnesses on the mysterious fifth bomb.

3000ptas, with bath 3000-4000ptas). It's worth breaking a sweat for **Hostal Estrella del Mar,** C. Bellavista, 5 (tel. 95 52 04 61). From the bus station walk up the *carretera,* turn right toward "El Parador," and go left on C. General Asensio Cabanillas; C. Bella Vista is the third street on the right. Its spacious rooms have baths and terraces, most with ocean views (singles 2900-3700ptas; doubles 3700-4600ptas).

Overpriced restaurants near and along the Balcón de Europa tempt passers-by with views but offer stingy portions. For do-it-yourself cooking, there is a **market** two blocks up C. San Miguel (open daily 8am-2pm). On Playa de Burriana, **Merendero Montemar** serves fresh fish, English breakfasts (350ptas), and *paella* with salad, bread and a drink (1000ptas). In the heart of town, on C. Pintada, **Coconuts** has reasonably priced international dishes served on a tropical patio, as well as two-for-one happy hour drinks (daily 8-10pm). For tea and crumpets, head to one of the many **coffeehouses** on C. Puerta del Mar or C. Almirante Ferrándiz (near the tourist office).

SIGHTS To get to the Balcón de Europa, a promenade that looks out over Playa de la Caletilla, follow the highway uphill from the bus stop to C. Pintada, which leads downhill to the *balcón.* Below the cliff are nifty caves, best explored from the path **Paseo de los Carabineros** (off the stairs to the right of the tourist office). The walkway winds along the rocky shore to the east, past **Playa de Calahonda, Playa Carabeo,** and **Playa Burriana.** Nerja's long **beaches,** mostly gravel and coarse sand, sink into brilliant turquoise water. To reach the sprawling **Playa de la Torrecilla** from the *balcón,* cut through town westward to the Playa de la Torrecilla apartments; follow the shoreline from there (15min.) Much closer but more crowded is **Playa del Salón,** accessible through an alley off the *balcón,* to the right of Restaurante Marisal.

■ Near Nerja: Caves

The most impressive attractions near Nerja are the spectacular caves. **Cueva de Nerja,** just 5km east of Nerja, has piped-in music and photographers who try to sell you your own picture in a cave-shaped frame. (*Open daily July-Aug. 10am-2pm and 4-8pm; Sept.-June 10am-2pm and 4-6:30pm. 650ptas, ages 6-12 350ptas.*) The caverns consist of large chambers filled with rock formations formed over millions of years by calcium deposits and sea-borne erosion. One cave is used as an amphitheater for music and ballet performances at the spectacular **Festival Cueva de Nerja,** held every July. Intrepid spelunkers have just discovered a new section of caves, reportedly four times as large as the ones already known. **Buses** to the caves run to and from Nerja (departs every hr., 95ptas). Call the tourist office (tel. 95 252 95 20) for more info. **Maro** is a speck of a village near the caves, with paths to nearly empty, rocky beaches and coves. The Nerja tourist office has pamphlets suggesting local hikes.

Málaga

Once celebrated by Hans Christian Anderson and Rubén Darío, Málaga (pop. 531,140) has since lost some of its gleam. Dinginess and an infamy for petty thievery are especially hard to endure with the Costa del Sol's resort towns just down the road. Yet Málaga, the second-largest city in Andalucía, is a critical transportation hub for all of the province, and its residents are some of the liveliest, most genial people you are likely to meet in a city overrun by beach-bound tourists.

ORIENTATION AND PRACTICAL INFORMATION

To reach the town center from the **bus station** (25min.), exit right onto C. Perchel, walk straight through the big intersection with Av. Aurora, take a right on Av. Andalucía, and cross the bridge, **Puente Tetuán.** From here, the palm tree and flower shop-lined **Alameda Principal** leads into **Plaza de la Marina.** For public transportation, walk one block on C. Roger de Flor to the train station.

From the **train station,** you can walk a block up **Explanada de la Estación,** turn left toward the bus station, and follow the directions above, or take the C-1 local train (**Centro-Almeda**) to Puente Tetuán (135ptas). Even better, bus #3 goes directly to Pl. Marina (115ptas). At both stations, always watch out for lightning-quick pickpockets.

From Pl. Marina, **Calle de Molina Lario** leads to the cathedral and the old town. **Calle de Marqués de Larios** connects Pl. Marina to **Plaza de la Constitución.** Also from Pl. Marina, **Paseo del Parque** leads past the Alcazaba. Farther on, the seaside promenade **Paseo Marítimo** stretches toward the lively beachfront district **El Pedregalejo** (accessible via bus #11 or a 40min. walk).

Transportation

Flights: (tel. 95 213 61 28 or 95 213 61 66). From the airport, **bus #19** (departs every 30min., 200ptas) runs from the City Bus sign and stops at the bus station and the corner of C. Molina Lario and Postigo de los Abades behind the cathedral. **RENFE's** train to the airport is cheaper (135ptas) and quicker (12min.). In town, **Iberia** is at C. Molina Larios, 13 (tel. 95 213 61 47; 24hr. reservations tel. 902 400 500).

Trains: Estación de Málaga, Explanada de la Estación (tel. 95 236 02 02). Take bus #3 at Po. Parque or #4 at Pl. Marina to the station. Tickets and reservations also at the less-crowded **RENFE** office, C. Strachan, 4 (tel. 95 221 31 22), off C. Molina Lario. To: Fuengirola (30min., departs every 30min., 305ptas); Torremolinos (20min., departs every 30min., 150ptas); Linares-Baeza (4hr., 5 per day, 2900ptas); Córdoba (2½hr., 12 per day, 2100ptas); Sevilla (3hr., 3 per day, 1800ptas); Barcelona (13hr., 3 per day, 6700ptas); Madrid (4hr., 5 per day, 8000ptas).

Buses: Po. Tilos, s/n (tel. 95 235 00 61), 1 block from RENFE station along C. Roger de Flor. To: Algeciras (3hr., 11 per day, 1250ptas); Fuengirola (30min., departs every 40min., 290ptas); Marbella (1½hr., 1 per hr., 575ptas); Torremolinos (20min., departs every 15min., 125ptas); Nerja (1hr., 1 per hr., 450ptas); Madrid (7hr., 8 per day, 2800ptas); Murcia (7hr., 6 per day, 3800ptas); Alicante (8hr., 6 per day, 4500ptas); Granada (2hr., departs every hr., 1200ptas); Córdoba (3hr., 5 per day, 1500ptas); Sevilla (3hr., 10 per day, 2200ptas); Antequera (1hr., departs every 1½hr., 525ptas); Ronda (3hr., 4 per day, 1110ptas); La Línea (3hr., 5 per day, 1300ptas); Cádiz (5hr., 4 per day, 2515ptas); Gibraltar (3hr., 1 per day, 1650ptas).

Taxis: Radio-Taxi (tel. 95 232 79 50 or 95 232 80 62). From the town center to El Pedregalejo, 850-950ptas. From the town center to the airport, 1300ptas.

Tourist, Financial, and Local Services

Tourist Offices: Municipal, Av. Cervantes, 1 (tel. 95 260 44 10; fax 95 221 41 20), a little gray house along Po. Parque offering **free maps** and city info. Also has a kiosk in front of the post office on Av. Andalucía. Open M-F 8:15am-2:45pm and 4:30-7pm, Sa 9:30am-1:30pm. **Junta de Andalucía,** Pasaje de Chinitas, 4 (tel. 95 221 34 45), off Pl. Constitución at the corner with C. Nicasio. Enter the alley through the arch and take the 1st right. Brochures on the Costa del Sol and a map. Open in summer M-F 9am-7pm, Sa-Su 9am-1pm; in winter M-F 9am-2pm, Sa 9am-1pm.

Budget Travel: TIVE, C. Huéscar, 2 (tel. 95 227 84 13), off C. Hilera, which runs behind El Corte Inglés. Books international plane, train, and bus tickets. ISIC 700ptas. HI card 1800ptas. Open M-F 9am-2pm. Reservations until 1pm.

Luggage Storage: Lockers at the train station (open daily 7am-10:45pm) and bus station (open daily 6:30am-11pm). Both 300ptas per day.

El Corte Inglés, Av. Andalucía, 4-6 (tel. 95 230 00 00), across from the post office. City **map** (495ptas). **Currency exchange** with no commission. **Supermarket, telephones, laundry service,** health and beauty aids, a few English language books, and clothes. Open in summer M-Sa 10am-10pm; in winter 10am-9:30pm.

Emergency and Communications

Emergency: dial 091 or 092. **Police:** tel. 95 231 71 00.

Pharmacy: Farmacia y Laboratorio Laza, C. Molina Lario, 2 (tel. 95 222 75 97). Open M-F 9:30am-1:30pm and 5-8:30pm, Sa 10:30am-1:30pm.

Medical Services: Assistance: tel. 95 230 30 34. **Women's Services: Ayuda a la Mujer** (tel. 95 230 40 00 or 95 261 42 07).

Internet Access: Cibercafé Málaga, Av. Andalucía, 11 (tel. 95 204 03 03). 250ptas for 15min. Student discounts. Open M-F 8am-11pm, Sa-Su 4-11pm.

Post Office: Av. Andalucía, 1 (tel. 95 235 90 08). A tall building just over the Puente Tetuán. Open for stamps and Lista de Correos M-F 8:30am-8:30pm, Sa 9:30am-2pm. **Postal Code:** 29080.

ACCOMMODATIONS

Most budget establishments are downtown, between Pl. Marina and Pl. Constitución. In general, rooms are somewhat run-down. Try bargaining if prices seem unreasonable (above 2000ptas for a single, 3700ptas for a double). Excluding Semana Santa and late June to August, the market is usually slow. Be wary of the following neighborhoods after dark: **Alameda de Colón, El Perchel** (toward the river from the train and bus stations), **Cruz del Molinillo** (near the market), and **La Esperanza/Santo Domingo** (up the river from El Corte Inglés).

Hostal La Palma, C. Martínez, 7 (tel. 95 222 67 72), off C. Marqués de Larios. Grandfather-type watches over clean, albeit noisy, old rooms. Renovations in 1999 should add another floor of rooms with bathrooms. Singles 2000-2500ptas; doubles 3500ptas; triples 3300ptas; quads 4400ptas.

Pensión Córdoba, C. Bolsa, 11 (tel. 95 221 44 69), off C. Molina Lario. Decently sized interior rooms with antique furniture. Spotless common bathrooms. Singles 1500ptas; doubles 2700ptas; triples 4500ptas.

Hostal Residencia Avenida, C. Alameda Principal, 5 (tel. 95 221 77 28 or 95 221 77 29). Bare-bones rooms in centrally located, loud neighborhood. Singles 1500ptas with bath 2500ptas; doubles 2900ptas, with bath 3850ptas; triples 4000ptas.

FOOD

Along the **Paseo Marítimo** in **El Pedregalejo,** beachfront restaurants specialize in fresh seafood (40min. walk or bus #11 from Pl. La Marina; 115ptas). For land-bound creatures, try eateries around **Calle Granada** leading out of **Plaza de la Constitución.** Pick up fresh produce at the **market** on C. Afaranzas (open daily 8am-2pm). There's also a supermarket in the basement of **El Corte Inglés** (see **Tourist, Financial, and Local Services,** p. 471). Catch some sardines roasted over an open flame (usually in old rowboats) on the beach. Wash your meal down with either *malagueño* or *moscatel,* Málaga's own sweet wines.

Restaurante El Tintero II, Po. Marítimo, El Pedregal, 99 (tel. 95 220 44 64). The farthest restaurant east on the waterfront. Waiters stroll by with pitchers of beer and seafood platters while roving flamenco guitarists entertain diners. Loud, family style establishment. 650ptas per plate. Open daily 11am-5pm and 7:30pm-1am.

La Cancela, C. Jose Denis Belgrano, 5 (tel. 95 222 31 25; fax 95 222 31 50), off C. Granada. The 4-page, single-spaced, 2-column menu of this family-run restaurant accommodates vegetarians, finicky eaters, and just about everyone else. *Menú* 1425ptas (on the *terraza* 1525ptas). Open 1-4:30pm and 8-11:30pm,W 1-4:30pm. Visa, MC, AmEx.

SIGHTS

With 10 major towers inside concentric walls, the **Alcazaba** is Málaga's most impressive sight. *(Open W-M 9:30am-8pm.)* Guarding the east end of Po. Parque, this 11th-century structure was originally built as a fortified palace for Moorish kings. The attached **Museo Arqueológico** (tel. 95 221 60 05) has a good collection of neolithic pottery. *(Closed for renovations in '98—inquire at the tourist office.)* Shifty types prowl around here at night, so think twice about evening strolls.

The **cathedral,** C. Molina Lario, s/n (tel. 95 221 59 17), is a pastiche of Gothic, Renaissance, and Baroque styles and has organs dating from 1781. *(Open M-Sa 10am-12:45pm and 4-6:45pm. 200ptas.)* The cathedral's second tower, under construction between the 16th and 19th centuries, was never completed, hence its nickname *La Manquita* (One-Armed Lady). **Castillo Gibralfaro,** built by the Phoenicians and the site of an Arab lighthouse, offers sweeping views of Málaga and the Mediterranean—although exploring the grounds alone may put you at risk for muggings. *(Open daily 9:30am-8pm.)* Buses to Castillo (quite an uphill hike) leave hourly from plaza below.

The **Museo de Bellas Artes,** C. San Agustín, 8 (tel. 95 221 83 82), in the old palace of the Counts of Buenavista, has been undergoing renovations and is scheduled to be combined with a new museum devoted to Pablo Picasso in 1999. *(Check with the tourist office for more info.)* Meanwhile, diehards can visit **Picasso's birthplace** (tel. 95 221 50 05), in Pl. Merced. *(Open M-Sa 10am-2pm and 6-9pm, Su 10am-2pm. Free.)* It now houses the **Picasso Foundation,** which organizes a series of exhibitions, concerts, and lectures every October and at other times during the year. According to local officials, even though Picasso high-tailed it out of Málaga when he was quite young, he always "felt himself to be a true *malagueño.*"

ENTERTAINMENT

In summer, young *malagueños* crowd the boardwalk bars in **El Pedregalejo** (bus #11). A slightly older, more foreign crowd drinks *copas* on **Calle de Bolivia,** parallel to and a few blocks up from the beach. Check out bar **Donde Bolivia 41,** C. Bolivia, 97, to mellow out among shrubbery, pillows, and a pool table. The **Nocturno 1 bus** takes over the Pedragalejo line daily from 12:45 to 5:45am (departs every hr.).

On weekends throughout the year, crowds invade the bars in the area between C. Comedias and C. Granada, which leads out of Pl. Constitución. **O'Neill's,** C. Luis de Velazquez, 3 (tel. 95 260 14 60), has dark wooden decor, pints of Guinness (500ptas), Celtic music, and friendly bartenders imported from the Emerald Isle. **Casa Nostra,** C. Lezcano, 5, hosts live blues performances once a week.

As for festivals, Málaga's **Semana Santa** celebrations are (nearly) as grandiose as those in rival city Sevilla, and the **Feria de Agosto**—complete with bullfights, flamenco, concerts, and a *moraga* (sardine bake on the beach)—is among the most spectacular *fiestas* in all of Andalucía. Available at newsstands, the *Guía del Ocio* (200ptas) lists special events, singles bars, and gay and lesbian entertainment.

■ Near Málaga: Garganta del Chorro

The **Garganta del Chorro** (a.k.a. El Chorro, 50km northwest of Málaga) is one of Spain's premier geological wonders. El Chorro's rocky terrain rises to 1190m, while below, the Río Guadalhorce splits the landscape in two. An exhilarating walk leads to the gorge, but the route is both difficult to find and dangerous. Those who generally avoid walking through functioning train tunnels will be scared stiff. If you're still game, talk to the bartender at El Chorro's train station for directions. While closer to Ronda and Antequera by car, the gorge is accessible by public transportation only via the Córdoba-Málaga rail line. **RENFE** runs trains to El Chorro from Málaga (one hr., 1 per day at 1:45pm, 400ptas), but it's another few kilometers to the actual walkway.

ANDALUCÍA

■ Near Málaga: Torremolinos

On the coast less than 30 minutes from Málaga by train or bus, Torremolinos swells in the summer with tourists who are shamelessly, gluttonously, and almost embarrassingly on vacation. Bare-chested bathers mill in and out of McDonald's and KFC, while the slightly more attired drool in front of beckoning store windows. Even its ancient tower (the *torre* in Torremolinos) has an outcropping of souvenir shops. At night, snoop along Av. Palma de Mallorca, or join the hordes farther west at **La Carihuela,** a sandy expanse dotted with *freidurías* and *heladerías,* whose see-and-be-seen attitude makes it *the* place to be when the sun goes down.

Calle San Miguel, a bustling pedestrian street, is a shopper's heaven—if you're in the market for Lladró figurines, Mallorca pearls, or Louis Vuitton handbags. As it curves down to the beach, C. San Miguel becomes **Cuesta del Tajo,** laden with souvenir stands. Following Cuesta del Tajo to the shore, **Playa Bajondillo** is to the left, and **Playa Carihuela,** loaded with bars and restaurants, is on **Paseo Marítimo,** to the right. When exiting the **train station,** walk through the alleyway on the right to reach the main thoroughfare, **Avenida Palma de Mallorca;** turn right and C. San Miguel will be on your right. From the **bus station,** exit to the right and follow C. Hoyo to **Plaza Costa del Sol** and Av. Palma de Mallorca; C. San Miguel is on your left.

Portillo Buses (tel. 95 238 24 19) and **C-1 local trains** (tel. 95 238 57 64) depart frequently to Málaga, Fuengirola, and other destinations. The **tourist office** (tel. 95 237 11 59) is on Pl. Pablo Ruiz Picasso uphill from Av. Palma de Mallorca along Av. Isabel Manoja. The staff speaks English and French. (Open daily 9am-2pm.) **Luggage storage** is available at the bus station daily from 7am to 9pm (300ptas). In an **emergency,** call 091, 092, or, in a medical emergency, 061. The **police** answer at 95 238 99 99 or 95 238 14 22. Mail tacky postcards at the **post office** (tel. 95 238 45 18), on Av. Palma de Mallorca (open M-F 8:30am-2:30pm and 9:30pm-1am). The **postal code** is 29620.

Hostels tend to get lost amid towering hotels and apartment complexes; some huddle on Cuesta de Tajo and on streets off Pl. Costa del Sol. Visitors face evil price surges in August. **Hostal La Palmera,** Av. Palma de Mallorca, 37 (tel. 95 237 65 09), a few doors down from the post office (enter around the corner), has friendly owners who rent airy rooms with big closets. A TV and bar loiter in the reception room. (Singles 2500-3000ptas; doubles 3500-4000ptas; triples 4500-5000ptas. Breakfast 350ptas. Reservations suggested.) **Hostal Residencia Guillot,** C. Rio Mundo, 4 (tel. 95 238 01 44), offers cheap, quiet, dim rooms with shared baths. Follow C. Cruz from Pl. Costa del Sol, make a right onto Pasaje Pizarro, and a left onto tiny Rio Mundo.Singles 2000-2800ptas; doubles 3300-3800ptas.)

■ Near Málaga: Fuengirola

At the end of RENFE's Málaga C-1 line and easily accessible by bus from both Málaga and Marbella, Fuengirola's crowded beaches and chalk-hued villas are an extension of Torremolinos's but without a retail sector to exhaust the weary and *peseta*-less.

Since temperatures on the coast can be as much as 15°F cooler than they are a mere three blocks inland, visitors chill (relatively) in bars along **Paseo Marítimo** and on the beach in **Los Boliches,** a neighborhood several kilometers toward Málaga.

Trains leave to Málaga (40min., 305ptas) from the **RENFE** station (tel. 95 247 85 40) on Av. Jesús Santos Reino. To get to **Los Boliches,** get off one stop early. The **bus station** (tel. 95 247 50 66), on C. Alfonso XIII, runs buses to: Málaga (45min., departs every 30min., 290ptas); Marbella (30min., departs every 30min., 280ptas); Algeciras (2hr., 11 per day, 990ptas); and Ronda (2hr., 5 per day, 815ptas).

The **tourist office,** Av. Jesús Santo Reino, 6 (tel. 95 246 74 57), speaks English and provides a free map. (Open in summer M-F 9:30am-2pm and 5-8pm, Sa 10am-1pm; off-season M-F 9:30am-2pm and 4-7pm, Sa 10am-1pm.) **ATMs** abound. **Medical assistance** answers 24 hours a day at 95 246 86 53. The **local police** (tel. 95 247 31 57) are at C. Alfonso XII, 1. The **post office** (tel. 95 247 43 84) is on C. Paoiz y Velarde, near Pl. Chinorros (open M-F 8am-3pm, Sa 9am-1pm). The **postal code** is 29640.

Fuengirola's reputation as a tourist trap for jet-setters is outdated—the British middle-class and the tattoo crew have taken over. Reasonable *pensiones* and *hostales* abound between Pl. Constitución and the beach, and in Los Boliches. **Hostal Costabella,** Av. Boliches, 98 (tel. 95 247 46 31), is only one block up from the beach, and one block seaward from RENFE's Los Boliches stop. Some rooms have beach views; all have glistening private baths. (Singles 2000-3500ptas; doubles 3000-4700ptas.) **Hostal Amigo,** Av. Los Boliches, 71 (tel. 95 247 03 33), has plain interior rooms (singles 1800-3700; doubles 2500-4500). **Food** can be found on Calles de Hambre, south of Pl. Constitución. The local **market,** across the street from the Fuengirola RENFE stop, is reportedly the greatest thing since *churros con chocolate* (open Tu 9am-2pm). Supermarket **Cayetano** is at Av. Ramón y Cajal, 45 (open M-F 9am-2:30pm and 5-9:30pm, Sa 9am-9:30pm; Visa, MC).

When the sun sinks, hit the bars on Po. Marítimo and **Calle Miguel de Cervantes** and **Calle Oviedo.** The **Bowling Palmeras** (tel. 95 246 06 41), on Av. Martínez Catena, which leads up from the port (behind Hotel Las Palmeras), has a sauna, jacuzzi, gym, roller skating, bowling alley, and more (open M-Sa until 2am, Su until 1am).

Marbella

Glamorous Marbella (pop. 100,000), the jewel of the Costa del Sol, relieves the flashy and famous of their *pesetas* quickly, efficiently, and in many different languages. Amazingly, though, it's entirely possible to steal away from the city with a budgeted good time. The city's controversial mayor has "cleaned up" the "marginal" elements (drug dealers, prostitutes, fellow politicians, etc.). Now the greatest crime is skipping out on Marbella's raging nightlife.

ORIENTATION AND PRACTICAL INFORMATION

Marbella glitzes 56km south of Málaga. It can be reached only by bus. The brand new **bus station** surveys the sea from atop **Avenida Trapiche.** To reach the main strip, exit and walk left, make the first right onto Av. Trapiche, and follow any downhill route to the perpendicular **Avenida Ramón y Cajal,** which becomes **Avenida Ricardo Soriano** on the way to **Puerto Bonús. Calle Peral** curves up from Av. Ramón y Cajal and around the **casco antiguo** (old section).

Buses: Av. Trapiche, s/n (tel. 95 276 44 00). To: Málaga (1½hr., departs every 30min., 570ptas); Fuengirola (30min., departs every 35min., 280ptas); San Pedro de Alcántara (20min., 7 per day, 125ptas); Estepona (1hr., departs every 35min., 255ptas); Granada (4½hr., 4 per day, 1735ptas); Ronda (1½hr., 4 per day, 585ptas); Sevilla (4hr., 3 per day, 1820ptas); Cádiz (4hr., 4 per day, 1985ptas); Madrid (7½hr., 10 per day, 3085ptas); Barcelona (16hr., 4 per day, 8325ptas); Algeciras (1½hr., 9 per day, 760ptas); La Línea (1½hr., 4 per day, 695ptas).
Taxis: Out and about, or call 95 277 44 88.
Tourist Office: C. Glorieta de la Fontanilla (tel. 95 277 14 42), fronting the shore. Provides free maps and historical information. English spoken. **Another office** (tel. 95 282 35 50) doles out info from Pl. Naranjos. Both open in summer M-F 9am-9pm; in winter M-F 10am-8pm, Sa 10am-2pm.
Currency Exchange: Banco Central Hispano, Av. Ramón y Cajal, 9 (tel. 95 277 08 92). Good exchange rates. Open June-Sept. M-F 8:30am-2:30pm; Oct.-May M-F 8:30am-2:30pm, Sa 8:30am-1pm. **ATMs** abound, especially near the *casco antiguo.*
American Express: Av. Duque de Ahumada, s/n (tel. 95 282 14 94; fax 95 286 22 92), off Po. Marítimo. Open M-F 9:30am-2pm and 4:30-8pm, Sa 10am-1pm.
Luggage Storage: At the bus station (400ptas). Open 6:30am-11:30pm.
Emergency: call 091 or 092. **Police:** Pl. Los Naranjos, 1 (tel. 95 282 24 94).
Hospital: Comarcal, CN-340, km187 (tel. 95 286 27 48).
Pharmacy: Farmacia Espejo, Pl. Naranjos, 4, near C. Estación. Check listings in window for 24-hr. pharmacies. Open M-F 9:30am-2pm and 5-9pm, Sa 10am-2pm.

ANDALUCÍA

Internet Access: Stop N' Go, C. Sierra Blanca (tel. 95 286 09 99), off C. Ricardo Sori
ano. 500ptas every 30min. Open M-F 10am-2pm and 5:30-9pm, Sa 10am-2pm.

Post Office: C. Jacinto Benavente, 26 (tel. 95 277 28 98). On the street parallel to
and uphill from C. Ricardo Soriano. Open M-F 8:30am-2:30pm, Sa 9:30am-1pm.
Postal Code: 29600.

ACCOMMODATIONS AND CAMPING

If you are reservationless, especially from mid-July through August, arrive early and
pray. The area in the *casco antiguo* around Pl. Naranjos (also known as Orange
Square) is loaded with quick-filling little *hostales*. Several cheap guest houses line
Calle Ancha, Calle San Francisco, Calle Aduar, and **Calle de los Caballeros,** all of
which are uphill off C. Peral and C. Huerta Chica and inland from C. Ramón y Cajal.
Bartenders often know *casas particulares;* **The Tavern,** on C. Peral, can offer advice
in English.

🌎**Hostal del Pilar,** C. Mesoncillo, 4 (tel. 95 282 99 36; email hostal@marbella
scene.com), off C. Peral, an extension of C. Huerta Chica, or from the bus station
off C. San Francisco. Run by a Scottish woman and two multilingual Spaniards who
like to party with the young, international clientele. Bar downstairs is a great place
to start the evening. Mattresses on the roof (if warm) from 1000ptas. Dorm
1500ptas. Breakfast 600ptas. Guests get keys to the front door and to rooms.

Albergue Juvenil (HI), C. Trapiche, 2 (tel. 95 277 14 91; fax 95 286 32 27). Just
downhill from the bus station and only slightly removed from the action. It has
sterile feel, but facilities include a TV room, basketball court, and pool. Dorms 800
1300ptas, over 26 1100-1800ptas. Tents outside cost 700ptas per person. Non
members pay an extra 300ptas per night for 6 nights to become members. Full
board available. Wheelchair accessible.

El Castillo, Pl. San Bernabé, 2 (tel. 95 277 17 39), a few blocks uphill from Pl. Naran
jos in the old town. Medieval decor and sunny, comfortable rooms with private
bathrooms. Singles 1700-2600ptas; doubles 3000-4500ptas. Visa.

Pensión Aduar, C. Aduar, 7 (tel. 95 277 35 78). The beautiful courtyard, overflowing
with flowers and songbirds, gives a sunny glow to well-kept rooms. Balconies
upstairs. Singles 1700-2300ptas; doubles 2800-3400ptas. No curfew.

Camping Marbella Playa (tel. 95 277 83 91), 2km east on N-340. Along the Marbella
Fuengirola bus line. Ask the bus driver to stop at the campground. 520ptas per per
son; 860ptas per tent. Open year-round.

FOOD

The municipal **market** is on Av. Mercado, uphill from C. Peral (open M-Sa 8am
2pm). A **24-hour minimarket** beckons through the night on the corner of C. Pablo
Casals and Av. Fontanilla, which intersects with Av. Ricardo Soriano. **Terrazas** fill Pl.
Naranjos but are not particularly budget-friendly—some even charge for bread. Res
taurants farther uphill may be less picturesque but more satisfying for the wallet.

🌎**Restaurante La Paloma,** C. Ortiz de Molinillo, 1 (tel. 95 277 72 47), off Pl. Naranjos.
Friendly, flirty waitstaff "always has time for you," even amid the bustle of locals
who reserve tables days in advance. Specialties include *paella* for two (2750ptas).
Open daily 7-11:30pm. Visa, AmEx, Diners Club, Eurocard.

Restaurante Salvia, C. San Lazaro, 3, 1st fl., off Pl. Victoria. Marbella's only macrobi
otic vegetarian restaurant. Fresh, wholesome entrees around 800ptas. Assorted sal
ads, pastas and soups. Visa.

Bar El Gallo, C. Lobatas, 44 (tel. 95 282 79 98). Loud TV and louder locals won't distract
you from cheap, delicious food. *Ensalada mixta* 325ptas. The most expensive dish is
San Jacobo (pork stuffed with ham and swiss cheese, served with fries; 475ptas).
Open daily 9am-midnight.

La Famiglia, C. Cruz, 5, off Pl. Puente Ronda. A cozy setting with large portions. Piz
zas from 750ptas. *Rigatoni alla siciliana* (with eggplant; garlic, and tomato
950ptas. Open M-Sa 7:30-11:30pm.

SIGHTS

Although most come to Marbella for its 320 days of sunshine per year, no visit to the city would be complete without a stroll through the **casco antiguo,** a maze of cobbled alleyways and ancient whitewashed facades (and more than a few boutiques). The thick walls of an Arab fortress seal off the neighborhood, and houses with carefully tended courtyards huddle against its crumbling remains. The **Museo del Grabado Español Contemporáneo,** C. Hospital Bazán, in a restored hospital for the poor, is a treasure-trove of engravings by Miró, Picasso, Dalí, Goya, and contemporary artists. *(Open M-F 10:15am-2pm and 5:30-8:30pm. 300ptas.)* To the northeast is the small **Parque Arroyo de la Represa,** site of the **Museo del Bonsai** (tel. 95 286 29 26), the (self-proclaimed) "best in the world" collection of mini arboreal art. *(Open daily 10am-1:30pm and 4-7:30pm. 400ptas, botanists and under 12 200ptas.)*

With 22km of **beach,** Marbella offers a variety of sizzling settings, from below its chic promenade to **Playa de las Chapas,** 10km east via the Fuengirola bus. The sand is generally gritty and scorching (wear sandals), but the human landscape is scenic, to say the least. Because of the towering mountains nearby, Marbella's winter temperatures tend to be 5-8°F warmer than Málaga's, and beach season goes on and on for at least 10 months on the year.

City buses along Av. Richard Soriano (destination San Pedro, 125ptas) bring you to chic and trendy **Puerto Banús.** Buffered by imposing white yachts and row upon row of boutiques and fancy restaurants, *this* is where it's at. The port has been frequented by the likes of Sean Connery, King Fahd of Saudi Arabia (who built a huge palace modeled on the White House), and even Princess Diana, who once dined here. All the while, throngs of Euro-chicks search the marina for rich prospects. If star-gazing proves futile, gawk at the toys of the rich (Ferraris, Rolls Royces, yachts galore) or kick back at **Sinatra Bar** for a front row seat, and drink it all in. The Moroccan coast is visible on exceptionally clear days.

ENTERTAINMENT

Marbella's **nightlife** is unrivaled, swearing by the maxim, "All work and no play makes Juan a dull boy." Beaches don't fill up until three in the afternoon because people are just waking up—the night is still young at four in the morning, and in the summer, that's not just on weekends. In the *casco antiguo,* action brews at the many bars as well as some English pubs along C. Peral. A mellower ambience suffuses the **Townhouse Bar,** C. Alamo, on an alley off C. Nueva, which leads downhill from Pl. Naranjos (opens daily at 10pm). A young international crowd socializes in **Kashmir,** C. Rafina, 8, off C. Aduar. Its smoky lounges upstairs might remind Amsterdam natives of home. (Opens daily at 10pm.)

On the way to the beach, **Bar Incognito,** Av. Miguel Cano, 15, serves divine, fruit-garnished cocktails at half-price during Happy Hour (300ptas; daily 9-11pm). Later in the evening (i.e. early in the morning), the city's entire young population swarms to the **Puerto Deportivo** ("The Port"), an amusement park of disco-bars and clubs. **Loco's** plays any kind of music as long as it's jarringly loud and equally crazy (beer 300ptas). Attracting a (barely) older crowd is **Arturo's Bar,** Local 42-43 (tel. 95 282 03 11), a rustic, backwoods, American-style place, complete with bear-skin rugs and antlers on the walls. A British guitarist strums favorites, from dueling banjos to Queen. Try **La Rebotica,** next door to Locos, for a frat-party atmosphere and lots of beer.

The most sophisticated dance clubs are in **Puerto Banús.** Buses run there on the hour all night along Av. Ricardo Soriano (destination San Pedro, 125ptas). Be prepared to pay 2000ptas cover charges (women usually *gratis*), sometimes 1000ptas for water, and have your attire snootily scrutinized. **La Comedia,** Pl. Comedia in Banús, plays disco until dawn (1000ptas cover includes 2 drinks; women free).

As for festivals, the **Feria y Fiesta de San Bernabé** (mid-June) is the big event of the year, commemorating the patron saint of Marbella with fireworks and concerts.

ANDALUCÍA

■ Antequera

Antequera's whitewashed houses and church towers bask below an old Moorish fortress at the crossroads of Andalucía; few sunsets rival those from atop this *alcazaba*. The Romans named Antequera, but older civilizations preceded them—*dólmenes* (funerary chambers built from rock slabs, the oldest of their kind in Europe) lie on the outskirts of town. To add to Antequera's allure, the Sierra del Torcal, a Mars-like wasteland of eroded rock, looms to the south, within easy striking distance. Wise travelers will kick back here for a few days of inland visual splendor.

ORIENTATION AND PRACTICAL INFORMATION

It's a 10-minute hike up a shadeless hill (Av. Estación) to the town center from the train station. From the top, continue straight past the market, turn right on **Calle Encarnación,** and go past the Museo Municipal to reach **Plaza San Sebastián.** The **bus station** perches atop a neighboring hill. To reach Pl. San Sebastián from the bus station, walk downhill (to the right as you exit) to the bullring, then turn left onto **Alameda de Andalucía.** At the fork, follow **Calle Infante Don Fernando** (the right branch) to the plaza. C. Encarnación connects Pl. San Sebastián to **Calle Calzada.** Calle Calzada leads uphill to **Plaza San Francisco** and the market. If your pack weighs a ton, arrive by bus and leave by train to take advantage of the downhill walks. Otherwise, a cab from the center to the train or bus station costs 500ptas.

Trains: Av. Estación (tel. 95 284 32 26). To: Granada (2hr., 3 per day, 750-865ptas); Málaga (1½hr., 3 per day, 615ptas); Sevilla (2½hr., 3 per day, 1100-1370ptas); Algeciras (4hr., 3 per day, 1520ptas); Bobadilla (15min., 3 per day, 160-180ptas); Ronda (1½hr., 3 per day, 710ptas). Connections in Bobadilla (tel. 95 272 02 24).

Buses: Po. García del Olmo (tel. 95 270 35 73), near the Parador Nacional. To: Málaga (45min., 3 per day, 465ptas); Almería (5hr., 2 per day, 2325ptas); Córdoba (2¼hr., 2 per day, 1075ptas); Granada (1hr., 5 per day, 895ptas); Jaén (3hr., 1 per day, 1425ptas); Murcia (5½hr., 2 per day, 3275ptas); Sevilla (2¼hr., 4 per day, 1435ptas); Madrid (change in Granada).

Taxis: (tel. 95 284 10 76, 95 284 10 08, or 95 270 26 27).

Tourist Office: Pl. San Sebastián, 7 (tel./fax 95 270 25 05). Super helpful staff supplies free maps, transportation schedules, and free multilingual info on Antequera and nearby cities. Open in summer M-Sa 10am-2pm and 5-8pm; in winter M-Sa 9:30am-1:30pm and 4-7pm, Su 10am-2pm.

Banks: Banco Central Hispano: C. Infante Fernando, 51 (tel. 95 284 04 61), changes currency and AmEx traveler's checks without commission. Open in summer M-F 8:30am-2:30pm; in winter M-Sa 8:30am-2:30pm. **ATMs** line C. Infante Don Fernando.

Emergency: dial 091 or 092.

Police: Municipal, Av. Legión (tel. 95 270 81 04).

Pharmacy: C. Encarnación, near C. Calzada. Open M-F 9:30am-1:30pm and 5-8:30pm, Sa 10am-1:30pm.

Hospital: Hospital General Básico, C. Infante Don Fernando, 67 (tel. 95 284 44 11).

Post Office: C. Nájera (tel. 95 284 20 83). Stamps and Lista de Correos. Open M-F 8am-2pm, Sa 9:30am-1pm. **Postal Code:** 29200.

ACCOMMODATIONS AND FOOD

Food and lodging in Antequera are generally cheap and splendid. Most establishments lie near **Calle Infante Don Fernando,** between the Museo Municipal and the **market,** Pl. San Francisco (open daily 8am-3pm). Try a nibble of the town's renowned *queso de cabra* (goat cheese). Ten-aisle **Supermercado Multimas** is on C. Calzada, 18 (open M-F 9:30am-1:45pm and 5:30-9pm, Sa 9:30am-9pm).

Pensión Toril, C. Toril, 3-5 (tel./fax 95 284 31 84), off Pl. San Francisco. Grandfatherly owner offers clean, bright rooms, and free parking. Guests gather on patios to chat and play cards. Singles 1200ptas, with bath 2000ptas; doubles 2400ptas,

ANDALUCÍA

with bath 3000ptas. But before sleep, feast downstairs—*menú* 800ptas, whopping *platos combinados* 500ptas, and generous drinks 100ptas. Meals served daily 1-4pm and 7:30-9:30pm.

Pensión Madrona, C. Calzada, 25 (tel. 95 284 00 14). Walk through Bar Madrona to the *pensión*. Newly renovated with A/C and heating in every room. Hand-made quilts abound in this cozy and family-run *pensión*. Singles 1600ptas, with bath 2600ptas; doubles with bath 3600ptas. Restaurant/bar downstairs offers a worth-it *menú* (850ptas).

Hotel Colón, C. Infante Don Fernando, 29 (tel. 95 284 00 10; fax 95 284 11 64). Spotless, classy joint with wood floors, un-upholstered furniture, and a labyrinth of rooms and hallways. Ritzy section has full baths, A/C, and TVs. Singles 2000-2500ptas; doubles 3600-4800ptas. Older *pensión* wing has shared baths, 1000-2000ptas per person. Laundry service. Visa, MC, AmEx. Wheelchair accessible.

La Rinconda, C. San Agustín, 1 (tel. 95 284 13 45), on a narrow street off C. Infante Don Fernando. Pizza, pasta, and veggie options from 850ptas. Typical meat dishes including *chuletitas de cordero*. Lunch daily from 12:30pm, dinner from 7:30pm.

Manolo Bar, C. Calzada, 14 (tel. 95 284 10 15), downhill from the market. Filled with Wild West paraphernalia and good-humored patrons. Ultra-cheap *tapas* (100ptas) may cost more if the staff finds you impolite. Open Tu-Th 4:30-11:30pm, F-Sa 4:30pm-3am.

La Espuela (tel./fax 95 270 26 76), in Pl. Toros. The only restaurant in the world *inside* a bullring. Not surprisingly, prize-winning kitchen's specialty is *rabo de toro* (bull's tail). *Menú* 1700ptas, worth it if you have the money. Open daily noon-5pm and 5:30-11:30pm. Visa, MC.

SIGHTS

Antequera's three ancient **Cuevas de Dólmenes** are the oldest in Europe. *(Open Tu-F 10am-2pm and 3-5:30pm, Sa-Su 10am-2pm.)* Giant rock slabs form the antechamber (storeroom for the dead's possessions) and burial chamber. Hefty ancients lugged the mammoth 200-ton roof of the **Cueva de Menga** (2500 BC) over five miles to the burial site. The four figures engraved on the chamber walls typify Mediterranean Stone Age art. The elongated **Cueva de Viera** (2000 BC), discovered in 1905, is also oversized—and dark. Bring a flashlight. Small, flat stones cement the circular interior walls and domed ceiling of **Cueva de Romeral** (1800 BC).

To reach the Cuevas de Menga and Viera, follow the signs toward Granada from the town center (20min.) and watch for a small sign on C. Granada just past the gas station. To reach Cueva de Romeral from the other *cuevas,* continue on the highway to Granada for another 3km. Just past Almacenes Gómez, one of the last warehouses after the flowered intersection, a gravel road cuts left and bumps into a narrow path bordered by tall fir trees. Take this path across the train tracks to reach the cave.

Back in town, all that remains of the **Alcazaba** are its two towers, the wall between them, and well-trimmed hedges. The view of the city below is tremendous. Next to it, the towering **Colegiata de Santa María** is considered the first church in Andalucía to incorporate Renaissance style. *(Both open Tu-Su 10am-2pm. Free.)* From the plaza in front of the church, one can spot the massive **Peña de los enamorados** (Lovers' Rock), which looks exactly like the Sphinx lying down (tilt your head sideways). Legend has it that a Christian man and his Moorish girlfriend leaped from the rock's face to their deaths rather than be separated by invading soldiers. Downhill, the **Museo Municipal** (tel. 95 270 40 21) manages to exhibit avant-garde 1970s paintings by native son Cristóbal Toral alongside dozens of Roman artifacts, including the graceful **Efebo,** a rare bronze statue of a Roman pageboy; the postcards don't do him justice. *(Open Tu-F 10am-1:30pm, Sa 10am-1pm, Su 11am-1pm. 200ptas.)*

■ Near Antequera: Sierra de Torcal

A garden of wind-sculpted boulders, the Sierra de Torcal glows like the surface of a barren and distant planet. The central peak of **El Torcal** (1369m) spans most of the horizon, but the smaller clumps of eroded rocks are even more extraordinary.

Several trails circle the summit. The green arrow path takes about 45 minutes and is 1.5km long; the red arrow path takes over two hours and is 4.5km long. All but the green path require a guided tour; call the **Centro de Información** (tel. 95 203 13 89) for more details. *(Open M-Su 10am-2pm and 4-6pm.)* Each path begins and ends 13km from Antequera at the *refugio* (lodge) at the mountain base. Two-thirds of the 13km can be covered by **bus**; ask the driver to let you off at the turnoff for El Torcal (repeat: *"¿Usted me puede dejar en el cruce para El Torcal?"*) Buses leave from Antequera (M-F at 1 and 7pm, 170ptas); the return bus leaves from the turnoff (M-F at 4:15pm). Call **Casado buses** (tel. 95 284 19 57) for details. An easier, pricier way to go is by taxi to the *refugio* (round-trip 2700ptas). The driver will wait for an hour, giving you time to catch the sunset. Contact tourist office for more information.

■ Ronda

Ronda's history runs even deeper than the spectacular 100m gorge dividing it. Referred to as Arunda ("surrounded by mountains") by Pliny, Ptolemy, and pfriends, the town was a pivotal commercial center under the Romans. In Moorish times, the Machiavellian Al Mutadid ibn Abbad annexed the town for Sevilla by asphyxiating the ruling lord in his bath. This century, Ronda has attracted forlorn artistic types—German poet Rainer Maria Rilke wrote his *Spanish Elegies* here, and Orson Welles had his ashes buried on a bull farm outside of town.

Only an hour and a half from the resorts of the Costa del Sol, Ronda (pop. 38,000) draws streams of daytrippers to its numerous Moorish monuments, yet it manages to preserve a greater degree of authenticity than its more crowded neighbors. A welcome diversion on its own rights, it also makes a convenient base for exploring the *pueblos blancos* to the south.

ORIENTATION AND PRACTICAL INFORMATION

The **Puente Nuevo** (new bridge), in addition to Roman and Moorish bridges, connect the city's old and new areas. On the new side of the city, **Carrera Espinel** (the main street, including the pedestrian-only walkway known as **Calle la Bola**) runs perpendicular to **Calle Virgen de la Paz**. The **train** and **bus stations** rumble in the new city three blocks away from each other on **Avenida de Andalucía**. To reach the tourist office and the town center from the train station, turn right on Av. Andalucía and follow it through the **Plaza de Merced** past the bus station (it becomes C. San José) until it ends. Take a left on C. Jerez, and follow it past the lush **Alameda del Tajo** (city park) and **Plaza Toros** (C. Jerez turns into C. Virgen de la Paz at Pl. Merced), to **Plaza de España** and the new bridge. Cra. Espinel intersects C. Virgen de la Paz between the bullring and Pl. España. From the bus station, turn right and follow the directions above (10min.).

Trains: Station, Av. Alférez Provisional (tel. 95 287 16 73), near Av. Andalucía. **Ticket office** C. Infantes, 20 (tel. 95 287 16 62). Open M-F 10am-2pm and 6-8:30pm. To Algeciras (2hr., 5 per day, 880ptas). Change at Bobadilla for: Málaga (2hr., 5 per day, 1200ptas); Granada (3hr., 3 per day, 1500ptas); Sevilla (3hr., 2 per day, 1600-1800ptas).

Buses: Pl. Concepción García Redondo, 2 (tel. 95 218 70 61 or 95 287 22 62), near Av. Andalucía. To: Málaga (2½hr., 10 per day, 1110ptas); Cádiz (4hr., 3 per day, 1585ptas); Marbella (1½hr., 5 per day, 585ptas); Fuengirola (2hr., 5 per day, 815ptas); Torremolinos (1½hr., 5 per day, 965ptas); Sevilla (5 per day, 1235ptas).

Taxis: (tel. 95 287 23 16). From the train station to the town center about 350ptas.

Tourist Office: Pl. España, 1 (tel. 95 287 12 72). Staff has info on Andalucía and helpful map of Ronda. Open M-F 9am-2pm and 4-7pm, Sa-Su 10am-3pm.

Currency Exchange: Banco Central Hispano , Cra. Espinel, 17, near C. Los Remedios. Exchanges cash without commission at good rates. Open June-Sept. M-F 8:30am-2:30pm; Oct.-May M-F 8:30am-2:30pm, Sa 9am-1:30pm. **ATMs** along Cra. Espinel.

Luggage Storage: At the bus station for 300-400ptas per day. Open daily 8am-10pm.

Emergency: tel. 091, 092, or 061. **Police:** Pl. Duquesa de Parcent (tel. 95 287 13 69).
Pharmacies: Along C. Espinel and in Pl. de España.
Medical Services: Emergency Clinic: Notfall, C. Espinillo (tel. 95 287 58 52).
Internet Access: Zaidín Cervecería, C. Pozo, 11 (tel. 95 287 93 77), off Pl. Merced.,
  in a loud, lively bar. 500ptas per 30min., 700ptas per hour. Open daily noon-2pm
  and 4-9pm; closing hours flexible.
Post Office: C. Virgen de la Paz, 20 (tel. 95 287 25 57), across from Pl. Toros. Open
  for Lista de Correos M-F 8:30am-2:30pm, Sa 9:30am-1pm. **Postal Code:** 29400.

ACCOMMODATIONS AND FOOD

Most beds are bunched in the new city near the bus station, along the streets perpendicular to **Carrera Espinel**—try **Calle la Naranja** and **Calle Lorenzo Borrego.** Expect
room shortages during the Feria de Ronda in September. Restaurants and cafes line
the streets around Pl. España and those heading toward Cra. Espinel.

Pensión Virgen del Rocio, C. Nueva, 18 (tel. 95 287 74 25), off Pl. España. Spacious,
  attractive rooms with baths. TV salon for guests. Singles 2200-3500ptas; doubles
  3500-5000ptas. Breakfast 250ptas. Parking 1400ptas per day. Visa, MC.
Hostal Aguilar, C. La Naranja, 28 (tel. 95 287 19 94), off Av. Andalucía. Sparkling
  clean rooms. Older wing (without private bath): singles 1500ptas; doubles
  2500ptas. New wing (with private bath, TV, and telephone): singles 3000ptas; doubles 5000ptas. Laundry service available.
Restaurante Flores, C. Virgen de la Paz, 9 (tel. 95 287 10 40), behind the tourist
  office. Tent-shaded outdoor tables afford a perfect view of befuddled tourists.
  Menú 1300ptas. Open daily 11am-4:30pm and 7:30-11pm. Visa.
Restaurante Peking, C. Los Remedios, 14 (tel. 95 87 65 37). Fu dogs, red tablecloths, lanterns, and New Age music with a Spanish culinary slant. *Menú* 675ptas.
  Open daily noon-4:30pm and 7:30pm-midnight. Visa, MC.

A Lot of Bull

Bullfighting *aficionados* charge over to Ronda's **Plaza de Toros** (tel. 95 287 41
32), Spain's oldest bullring (est. 1785) and cradle of the modern *corrida*. The
Museo Taurino inside tells the story of local hero Pedro Romero, the first matador to brave the beasts *a pie* (on foot), and to use the *muleta* (red cape). *(Open
daily June-Sept. 10am-8pm; Oct.-May 10am-6pm. 300ptas.)* Romero killed his first bull
at age 17 in 1771, the start of a glorious career: "From 1781-1799, it can be said
that I killed in each year 200 bulls, whose sum totals 5600 bulls, yet I am per-
suaded that there may have been more." The museum displays heads of bulls,
legendary for their ferocity, and bloodied matador shirts, including the shirt of
Francisco Rivera ("Paquirri"), who was gored to death in 1984. Elaborate *trajes
de luces,* the traditional costume of the bullfighter, are kept behind glass cases.
An exhibit on 20th-century bullfighting showcases photos of Orson Welles,
Ernest Hemingway, and their giddy fans. In early September, the Plaza de Toros
hosts *corridas goyescas* (bullfights in traditional costumes) as part of the **Feria
de Ronda.**

SIGHTS

Ronda's precipitous gorge, carved by the Río Guadalevín, dips 100m below the
Puente Nuevo, across from Pl. España. During the Civil War, political prisoners were
cast into the canyon's depths from the bridge's midpoint. Two other structures
bridge the unsettling gap: the innovative **Puente Viejo** was rebuilt in 1616 over an
earlier Arab bridge, and the **Puente San Miguel** (a.k.a. **Puente Árabe**) is a prime
Andalucían hybrid with a Roman base and Arab arches. Puente Nuevo affords a spectacular view.

  To see the old city, cross Puente Nuevo and turn left. A colonnaded walkway leads
to the **Casa del Rey Moro** (House of the Moorish King), C. Cuesta de Santo Domingo,
17, which, notwithstanding its name and Moorish facade, dates from the 18th cen-

tury. *(Open daily 10am-7pm. 500ptas.)* From the gardens in back, 365 steep zig-zagging steps descend to *la mina* (the mine), a spring that once pumped in the town's water supply. Four hundred Christian prisoners were once employed in the arduous task of drawing water. Across the street, behind a forged iron balcony and a stone facade portraying four Peruvian Incas, stands the 18th-century **Palacio del Marqués de Salvatierra** (tel. 95 287 12 06). *(Open M-W and F-Sa 11am-2pm and 4-7pm, Th and Su 11am-2pm. 300ptas.)* With spectacular antiques and gardens, it has belonged to the same family since 1485.

To the left, C. Marqués de Salvatierra leads to the **Iglesia de Santa María la Mayor** (tel. 95 287 22 46), a large 16th-century church hall crowned by a Renaissance belfry, in the heart of Ronda's old city. *(Open daily 10am-8pm. 200ptas, groups 150ptas per person.)* The small arch just inside the entrance and the Quranic verses behind the sacristy are the only vestiges of the mosque that was once here. A faint sign announces *"Julius Divo, Municipe,"* revealing the church's original incarnation as a church consecrated for Caesar.

Facing the east stands the **Minarete de San Sebastián,** part of a former mosque converted into a church after 1485, when Ronda was reconquered by the Christians. On the other side of the church lies the **Palacio de Mondragón** (tel. 95 287 84 50), once owned by Don Fernando Valenzuela, one of Carlos III's ministers. *(Open M-F 10am-7pm, Sa-Su 10am-3pm. 200ptas, groups 100ptas per person, under 14 and handicapped free.)* Its Baroque facade, bracketed by two Mudéjar towers, hides 15th-century Arab mosaics and cultural displays about ancient life in Ronda.

Nightlife in Ronda congregates in pubs and *discotecas* along Calle Jerez and the streets behind Pl. del Socorro, including C. Pozo. **Disco-Bar Niágara** C. Jerez, 17 (tel. 929 84 41 82), blasts its music in an aquatic, green-blue atmosphere. *(Open daily 4pm until late.)* **Zaidín Cervecería**, C. Pozo, 11 (tel. 95 287 93 77), is packed until late with a young crowd playing pool. For a more tranquil evening, head to **Tetería Al-Zahra**, C. Las Tiendas, 19 (tel. 95 287 16 98). The Islamic decor, floor pillows, and arched entryways invite long stays. Patrons sip over 100 types of teas from all over the world. *(Open daily 4pm until late. Teas 200-250ptas.)*

■ Near Ronda: Cuevas de la Pileta

Twenty-two kilometers west of Ronda along the road to Sevilla are the **Cuevas de la Pileta** (tel. 95 216 73 43 or 95 216 72 02), a subterranean museum of bones, stalactites, stalagmites, and paleolithic paintings. *(Open daily 10am-1pm and 4-6pm. Tour lasts 1¼hr. Groups of 1-4 800ptas per person, groups of 5-11 700ptas per person, groups of 12-25 600ptas per person.)* Over 22,000 years ago, inhabitants colored the walls with enormous paintings of signs, human figures, and animals. Among the most notable are the *Yegua preñada* (pregnant mare) and *Pez* (fish). In order to preserve the climate of the cave, only 25 people are admitted at a time for guided tours by petroleum lamps. Wear comfortable shoes and dress warmly. Upon arrival at the caves, climb to the mouth to see if the guide is inside. If no one is around, walk to the farm below and rouse the owner, who'll make appropriate arrangements.

By **car,** take highway C-339 north (Ctra. Sevilla heading out of the new city). The turnoff to **Benaoján** and the caves is about 13km out of town, in front of an abandoned restaurant. Don't leave valuables in your car during the tour. Alternatively, take the **Los Amarillo bus** to Benaoján (22min., 8:30am and 1pm, returns to Ronda 9am and 1pm, 195ptas). The approach through the Serranía de Ronda is stupendous as you wind through small Montajaque. Plan your return trip ahead of time, as there are no accommodations nearby.

■ Near Ronda: Setenil de las Bodegas

A mere 16km from Ronda, the village of **Setenil de las Bodegas** sits on a mountain laden with caves first inhabited ages ago. Later residents built facades and then freestanding houses branching off the grottoes; long rows of chalk-white houses remain strategically built into the hillsides. The village stretches along a dramatic gorge cut by

MCI Spoken Here

Worldwide Calling Made Simple

For more information or to apply for a Card call: **1-800-955-0925**

Outside the U.S., call MCI collect (reverse charge) at: **1-916-567-5151**

International Calling As Easy As Possible.

Calling Card

MCI

123 456 7890 1234
J.D. SMITH

WorldPhone

The MCI Card with WorldPhone Service is designed specifically to keep you in touch with the people that matter the most to you.

The MCI Card with WorldPhone Service....

- Provides access to the US and other countries worldwide.

- Gives you customer service 24 hours a day

- Connects you to operators who speak your language

- Provides you with MCI's low rates and no sign-up fees

For more information or to apply for a Card call:
1-800-955-0925

Outside the U.S., call MCI collect (reverse charge) at:
1-916-567-5151

© 1998, MCI Telecommunications Corporation. MCI, its logo, as well as the names of MCI's other products and services referred to herein are proprietary marks of MCI Communications Corporation.

Pick Up the Phone,
Pick Up the Miles.

Please cut out and save this reference guide for convenient U.S. and worldwide calling with the MCI Card with WorldPhone Service.

ou earn
requent flyer
niles when you
ravel interna-
onally, why not
vhen you call
nternationally?
allers can earn
requent flyer
niles if they
gn up with
ne of MCI's
irline partners:

American
Airlines

Continental
Airlines

Delta Airlines

Hawaiian
Airlines

Midwest
Express Airlines

Northwest
Airlines

Southwest
Airlines

United Airlines

USAirways

Your MCI Worldphone Access Numbers

MCI

COUNTRY		WORLDPHONE TOLL-FREE ACCESS #
#Singapore		8000-112-112
#Slovak Republic (CC)		0421-00112
#Slovenia		080-8808
#South Africa (CC)		0800-99-0011
#Spain (CC)		900-99-0014
#Sri Lanka	(Outside of Colombo, dial 01 first)	440100
#St. Lucia ÷		1-800-888-8000
#St. Vincent		1-800-888-8000
#Sweden (CC) ♦		020-795-922
#Switzerland (CC) ♦		0800-89-0222
#Syria		0800
#Taiwan (CC) ♦		0080-13-4567
#Thailand ★		001-999-1-2001
#Trinidad & Tobago ÷		1-800-888-8000
#Turkey (CC) ♦		00-8001-1177
#Turks and Caicos ÷		1-800-888-8000
#Ukraine (CC) ÷		8♥10-013
#United Arab Emirates ♦		800-111
#United Kingdom (CC) To call using BT ■		0800-89-0222
To call using C&W ■		0500-89-0222
#United States (CC)		1-800-888-8000
#Uruguay		000-412
#U.S. Virgin Islands (CC)		1-800-888-8000
#Vatican City (CC)		172-1022
#Venezuela (CC) ÷ ♦		800-1114-0
Vietnam ●		1201-1022
Yemen		008-00-102

Automation available from most locations.
(CC) Country-to-country calling available to/from most
     international locations.
÷ Limited availability.
▶ Wait for second dial tone.
◀ When calling from public phones, use phones marked
     LADATEL.
■ International communications carrier.
✦ Not available from public pay phones.
♦ Public phones may require deposit of coin or phone card
     for dial tone.
● Local service fee in U.S. currency required to complete call.
▲ Regulation does not permit intra-Japan calls.
❖ Available from most major cities.

And, it's simple to call home.

1. Dial the WorldPhone toll-free access number of the country you're calling from (listed inside).

2. Follow the voice instructions in your language of choice or hold for a WorldPhone operator.
   • Enter or give the operator your MCI Card number or call collect.

3. Enter or give the WorldPhone operator your home number.

4. Share your adventures with your family!

The MCI Card with WorldPhone Service... The easy way to call when traveling worldwide.

MCI — Calling Card
123 456 7890 1234
J.D. SMITH
WorldPhone

For more information or to apply for a Card call: 1-800-955-0925

Outside the U.S., call MCI collect (reverse charge) at: 1-916-567-5151

Please cut out and save this reference guide for convenient U.S. and worldwide calling with the MCI Card with WorldPhone Service.

COUNTRY	WORLDPHONE TOLL-FREE ACCESS #
American Samoa	633-2MCI (633-2624)
#Antigua	1-800-888-8000
(available from public card phones only)	#2
#Argentina (CC)	0800-5-1002
#Aruba ÷	800-888-8
#Australia (CC) ◆	
To call using OPTUS ■	1-800-551-111
To call using TELSTRA ■	1-800-881-100
#Austria (CC) ◆	022-903-012
#Bahamas	1-800-888-8000
#Bahrain	800-002
#Barbados	1-800-888-8000
#Belarus (CC) From Brest, Vitebsk, Grodno, Minsk	8-800-103
From Gomel and Mogilev	8-10-800-103
#Belgium (CC) ◆	0800-10012
#Belize From Hotels	815
From Payphones	557
#Bermuda ÷	1-800-888-8000
#Bolivia (CC) ◆	0-800-2222
#Brazil (CC)	000-8012
#British Virgin Islands ÷	1-800-888-8000
#Brunei	800-011
#Bulgaria	00800-0001
#Canada (CC)	1-800-888-8000
#Cayman Islands	1-800-888-8000
#Chile (CC) To call using CTC ■	800-207-300
To call using ENTEL ■	800-360-180
#China ✆ For a Mandarin-speaking Operator	108-12
#Colombia (CC) ◆ Collect Access in Spanish	980-16-0001
	980-16-1000
#Costa Rica ✆	0800-012-2222
#Cote D'Ivoire	1001
#Croatia (CC) ★	0800-22-0112
#Cyprus ◆	080-90000
#Czech Republic (CC) ◆	00-42-000112
#Denmark (CC) ◆	8001-0022
#Dominica	1-800-888-8000
#Dominican Republic	1-800-888-8000
Collect Access	1-800-888-8000
Collect Access in Spanish	
#Ecuador (CQ) ÷	999-170
#Egypt (CC) ÷ (Outside of Cairo, dial 02 first)	355-5770
El Salvador	800-1767

COUNTRY	WORLDPHONE TOLL-FREE ACCESS #
#Federated States of Micronesia	624
#Fiji	004-890-1002
#Finland (CC) ◆	08001-102-80
#France (CC) ◆	0800-99-0019
#French Antilles (CC) (includes Martinique, Guadeloupe)	0800-99-0019
#French Guiana (CC)	0-800-99-0019
#Gabon	00-005
#Gambia ◆	00-1-99
#Germany (CC)	0-800-888-8000
#Greece (CC) ◆	00-800-1211
#Grenada ÷	1-800-888-8000
#Guam (CC)	1-800-888-8000
#Guatemala (CC) ◆	99-99-189
Guyana	177
#Haiti ÷	193
Collect Access in French/Creole	194
#Honduras ÷	8000-122
#Hong Kong (CC)	800-96-1121
#Hungary (CC) ◆	00▼800-01411
#Iceland (CC) ◆	800-9002
#India (CC) ◆	000-127
Collect Access	000-126
#Indonesia (CC)	001-801-11
#Iran ÷	(SPECIAL PHONES ONLY)
#Ireland (CC)	1-800-55-1001
#Israel (CC)	1-800-940-2727
#Italy (CC) ◆	172-1022
#Jamaica ÷	1-800-888-8000
#Japan (CC) ◆ To call using KDD ■ (From Special Hotels only)	00539-121▼ *2
To call using IDC ■	0066-55-121
(From public phones) To call using ITJ ■	0044-11-121
#Jordan	18-800-001
#Kazakhstan (CC)	8-800-131
#Kenya ◆ To call using KT ■	08001 / 009-14
#Korea (CC) To call using DACOM ■	00309-12
To call using ONSE ■	00369-12
Phone Booths÷	Press red button, 03, then *
Military Bases	550-2255
#Kuwait	800-MCI (800-624)

COUNTRY	WORLDPHONE TOLL-FREE ACCESS #
Lebanon Collect Access	600-MCI (600-624)
#Liechtenstein (CC) ◆	0800-89-0222
#Luxembourg (CC)	0800-0112
#Macao	0800-131
#Macedonia (CC)	99800-4266
#Malaysia (CC) ◆	1-800-80-0012
#Malta	0800-89-0120
#Marshall Islands	1-800-888-8000
#Mexico Avantel	01-800-021-8000
Telmex ▲	001-800-674-7000
Collect Access in Spanish	01-800-021-1000
	01-800-674-6000
#Monaco (CC) ◆	800-90-019
#Montserrat	1-800-888-8000
#Morocco	00-211-0012
#Netherlands (CC) ◆	0800-022-9122
#Netherlands Antilles (CC) ÷	001-800-888-8200
#New Zealand (CC)	000-912
#Nicaragua (CC)	166
(Outside of Managua, dial 02 first) From any public payphone ◆	*2
#Norway (CC) ◆	800-19912
Pakistan	00-800-12-001
#Panama	108
Military Bases	2810-108
#Papua New Guinea (CC)	05-07-19740
#Paraguay ÷	00-812-800
#Peru	0-800-500-10
#Philippines (CC) ◆ To call using PLDT ■	105-14
Collect Access via PLDT in Filipino	1026-14
To call using PHILCOM ■	105-15
Collect Access via ICT in Filipino	1237-77
To call using PHILCOM in Filipino	00-800-11-0-1234
#Poland (CC) ÷	00-800-111-21-22
#Portugal (CC) ÷	05-017-1234
#Puerto Rico (CC)	1-800-888-8000
#Qatar ◆	0800-012-77
#Romania (CC) ÷	01-800-1800
#Russia (CC) ◆ ÷ To call using ROSTELCOM ■	747-3322
(For Russian speaking operator)	747-3320
To call using SOVINTEL ■	960-2222
#Saipan (CC) ÷	950-1022
#San Marino (CC) ◆	172-1022
#Saudi Arabia (CC) ÷	1-800-11

FOLD

STUDENT TRAVEL
This ain't your parents travel agency.

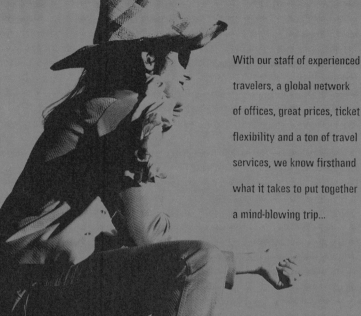

With our staff of experienced travelers, a global network of offices, great prices, ticket flexibility and a ton of travel services, we know firsthand what it takes to put together a mind-blowing trip...

...just remember to thank mom for packing your suitcase.

STA TRAVEL
We've been there.

800-777-0112
OR CONTACT YOUR NEAREST STA TRAVEL OFFICE

CST #1017560-60

AUSTIN	CAMBRIDGE	MADISON	ORLANDO	SEATTLE
BATON ROUGE	CHICAGO	MIAMI	PHILADELPHIA	TAMPA
BERKELEY	GAINESVILLE	MINNEAPOLIS	SAN FRANCISCO	WASHINGTON DC
BOSTON	LOS ANGELES	NEW YORK	SANTA MONICA	WESTWOOD

BOOK YOUR TICKET ONLINE

If you're stuck for cash on your travels, don't panic. Millions of people trust Western Union to transfer money in minutes to 153 countries and over 45,000 locations worldwide. Our record of safety and reliability is second to none. So when you need money in a hurry, call Western Union.

WESTERN UNION | MONEY TRANSFER®

The fastest way to send money worldwide.®

Austria 0660 8066* or (0222) 892 0380 Canada 1 800 235 0000* Czech Republic (02) 2422 2954 or (02) 2422 952
France (01) 4354 4612, (04) 5064 7175 or (01) 4335 6060 Germany 0180 522 5822* or (0681) 933 3328 Gree
(01) 927 1010 Ireland 1 800 395 395* Italy 167 22 00 55*, 167 464 464*, (79) 232281 or (45) 8068589 Netherlands 06 056
or (31) 70 379 1903 Poland 0 800 20224* Russia (095) 119 8250 Spain 900 633 633*, (95) 205 0219 or (91) 559 02
Sweden 020 741 742* or (08) 585 92626 Switzerland 0512 22 33 58 UK 0800 833 833* USA 1 800 325 600
*Toll-free telephone n

the Río Guadalporcún, and riverside streets or *cuevas* burrow under the gorge's cliff walls, creating long, covered passageways: **Cuevas Sombra, Cuevas del Sol,** and **Cuevas de Cabrerizos.** The 15th-century **Iglesia de la Encarnación,** atop the biggest rock, opens to views of the village below.

The **tourist office** (tel. 95 613 42 61) is on C. Villa. They can help plan several scenic walks around town and offer a useful, free **map.** (Open Tu-Su 11am-2pm and 4-7pm.) Follow signs uphill from the bus stop. From Ronda, Setenil is accessible by **Sierra de las Nienes/Ferrori Coín bus** (M-F 5 per day, Sa 3 per day, 170ptas) and **train** (13min., 1:30pm and 3:20pm, 200ptas; one stop in the direction of Bobadilla). By **car,** take Ronda's Ctra. Sevilla to C-339 North. For Olvera and Setenil, take the turn for El Gastor or the longer route via the dramatic outcropping of the village of Zahara.

■ Gibraltar

Anglophiles and homesick Brits get jolly well excited over Gibraltar's fish 'n' chips, pints of bitter, and changing of the guard. Called "Gib" by locals, this colony takes its Britishness seriously; citizens switch in and out of the Queen's English and Andalusian Spanish. The tumultuous history of the Rock leaves unresolved tensions to this day—residents look up to Britain and down on mainland Spain, and there's a massive British military presence.

The ancients considered the Rock of Gibraltar one of the Pillars of Hercules, marking the very end of the world. Supernatural connections aside, it remains one of history's most contested landmarks. After numerous squabbles between Moors and Spaniards, English troops stormed Gibraltar's shores during the War of the Spanish Succession, and the Treaty of Utrecht (1713) solidified Britain's hold on the enclave, now one of the last outposts of Britain's empire.

A 1969 vote showed that Gibraltar's populace overwhelmingly favored its British ties (12,138 to 44). Franco sealed off the border and forbade any contact between Spain and Gibraltar in that same year. After a decade of negotiations and 16 years of isolation, the border re-opened at midnight, on February 4, 1985. Tourists and residents now cross with ease, but Gibraltar remains culturally detached from Spain.

Despite the peninsula's history and refreshingly heterogeneous population, Gibraltar makes an interesting daytrip, at best—stand atop the imposing Rock, practice your neglected English, stock up on duty-free liquor and tobacco (cigarettes are 90 pence a pack), and then scurry back to the more picturesque Spanish coast.

ORIENTATION AND PRACTICAL INFORMATION

Gibraltar is regarded as a foreign destination from Spain; most buses terminate in bordering **La Línea.** From the bus station, walk directly toward the Rock; the border is five minutes away. After bypassing the line of sweating motorists, Spanish customs, and Gibraltar's passport control, catch bus #9 (40 pence or 100ptas), or walk across the airport tarmac (look both ways) and along the highway into town (20min.). Stay left on Av. Winston Churchill when the road forks with Corral Lane. Gibraltar's **Main Street,** a commercial strip lined with most services, begins at the far end of a square/parking lot past the Burger King on the left.

> Although **pesetas** are accepted everywhere (except in pay phones), the **pound sterling (£)** is the preferred method of payment in Gibraltar. Merchants sometimes charge a higher price in *pesetas* than in the pound's exchange equivalent. Change is often given in English currency rather than Spanish. **1£ = 260 ptas.**

Transportation
Airport: (tel. 73 026). **British Airways** (tel. 792 00) offers daily flights to Heathrow, Gatwick, and Manchester airports, as well as to destinations in Africa.
Buses: From the closest Spanish town, La Línea, to: Algeciras (40min., departs every 30min., 220ptas); Cádiz (3hr., 5 per day, 1440ptas); Sevilla (6hr., 3 per day, 2500ptas);

ANDALUCÍA

Ronda (2½hr., 1 per day, 990ptas); Marbella (1¾hr., 4 per day, 695ptas); Málaga (3¼hr., 4 per day, 1225); Granada (5-6hr., 2 per day, 2390ptas).

Ferries: Tourafrica Int. Ltd. (tel. 776 66; fax 767 54). Departures to Tangier (M and W 8:15am, F 6:30pm; return ferries Tu 3pm, F 9am, Su 4pm). One-way ticket £18, children under 12 £9, car £40; round-trip £30, children £15, car £80.

Taxis: Call 700 52 or 700 27.

Tourist, Financial, and Local Services

Tourist Office: (tel. 749 50; fax 749 43; email gib1@gibnet.gi), Duke of Kent House, Cathedral Square, across the park from Gibraltar Museum. Free street map of Gibraltar. Open M-F 9am-5:30pm. **Info Center,** Main St., The Piazza (tel. 749 82). Open M-F 9:30am-6pm, Sa 10am-2pm.

Currency Exchange: (see box above). Rates improve steadily as one proceeds along Main St. Booths charge no commission. Banks close daily at 3:30pm, reopening only on Friday 4:30-6pm. **Gib Exchange Center, Ltd.,** John Mackintosh Sq., 6A (tel. 735 17). Open M-F 9am-1pm and 3-7pm, Sa 10am-6pm.

American Express: Bland Travel (tel. 770 12), in Irish Town. It holds mail and sells traveler's checks, but doesn't cash them. Open M-F 9am-6pm.

Luggage Storage: Lockers at the bus station (400ptas). Open daily 7am-10pm.

English-Language Bookstore: The Gibraltar Bookshop, 300 Main St. (tel. 718 94). Choice of superior classics. Open M-F 10am-6:30pm, Sa 11:30am-2:30pm.

English-Language Periodicals: Everywhere, silly. **Sacarelo News Agency,** 96 Main St. (tel. 787 23), is the best. Open M-F 9am-7pm, Sa 9am-2:30pm, Su 11am-3pm.

Emergency and Communications

Emergency: call 199. **Police:** 120 Irish Town St. (tel. 725 00).

Hospital: St. Bernard's Hospital (tel. 797 00), on Hospital Hill.

Post Office: 104 Main St. (tel. 756 62). Possibly the world's easiest Poste Restante address (not one number unless your name is "Two"): Name, Poste Restante, Gibraltar (Main Post Office). Sells Gibraltar stamp sets for collectors. Open in summer M-F 8:45am-2:15pm, Sa 10am-1pm; in winter M-F 9am-4:30pm, Sa 10am-1pm.

Telephones: Red booths and pay phones don't accept *pesetas.* More expensive but without the hassle of coins is **Gibraltar Telecommunications International Ltd.,** 60 Main St. (tel. 756 87). **Faxes** also sent. Open M-F 9am-5pm.

Telephone Code: From Britain, (00) 350. From the U.S., (011) 350. From Spain, 9567. From Cádiz province 7. From Gibraltar, the USA Direct code is 88 00.

ACCOMMODATIONS AND FOOD

The few affordable accommodations in the area are often full, especially from July to September, and camping is illegal. If worse comes to worst, crash in La Línea, a 20-minute trudge across the border. International restaurants are easier to find—Chinese, English, French, Indian, Spanish, and Italian cuisines are available—but you may choke on the price. There's always the **supermarket**—Safeway, no less, in the Europort commercial complex (open M-Sa 8am-8pm).

Queen's Hotel, 1 Boyd St. (tel. 740 00; fax 400 30). Through Southport Gate, bear right and enter around the back. Comfortable, well-furnished rooms have phones; some also have TVs. Huge bar/lounge. Special rates for *Let's Go* readers. Singles £18, with bath £24; twin-bed double £28, with bath £40; triples with bath £45. Breakfast included. Laundry services. Free parking. Visa, MC, AmEx.

Emile Youth Hostel Gibraltar (tel. 511 06), on Line Wall Rd. across from the square at the beginning of Main St. Cramped bunkbeds, but clean communal bathrooms. Get intimate with your showermate behind a shared curtain. £10 per person includes continental breakfast. Lock-out 10:30am-4:30pm and curfew 11:30pm, but the owner is friendly and flexible.

Toc H Hostel, Line Wall Rd. (tel. 734 31). Walk toward the Rock on Main St., right just before the arch at Southport Gate, then left in front of the Hambros Bank. A maze of plants, cats, and itinerants. Dorms £5. Warm showers only during the day.

Smith's Fish and Chips, 295 Main St. (tel. 742 54). Run by a cheerful bloke who dishes out hearty servings of fish 'n' chips from £3, plus some vegetarian options, such as veggie burgers and curry. Open M-F 11am-6pm, Sa noon-3pm.

Maharaja Indian Restaurant (tel. 752 33), on Tuckey's Ln., off Main St. Filling meat dishes starting from £4.50, vegetarian entrees from £2.90. Open daily noon-3pm and 7-11:15pm. Visa.

The Leanse, 7 Bomb House Lane (tel./fax 417 51), off Main St., near Marks and Spencer. Kosher and international cuisine served in a cozy setting. Entrees £6-10. Open Su-Th 11:30am-3pm and 7:30pm-midnight, F 11:30am-3:30 pm.

SIGHTS

The northern tip of the massif known as **Top of the Rock** provides a truly remarkable view of Iberia and the Straits of Gibraltar. **Cable cars** carry visitors up from the south end of Main St., making a stop at Apes' Den. *(Cars depart every 10min. M-Sa 9:30am-5:45pm. £3.65, round-trip £4.90. You can buy a one-way ticket and walk down (1hr.). Tickets sold until 5:15pm. Ticket includes admission to St. Michael's Cave and Apes' Den.)* On the Upper Rock a **Nature Reserve** awaits. *(Tickets £5, in your own car £1.50. Price includes admission to the Moorish Castle, St. Michael's Cave, the Apes' Den, the Great Siege Tunnels, and "Gibraltar: A City Under Siege." Moorish Castle open daily 9:30am-7pm.)*

The ruins of a Moorish wall descend along the road from the cable car station to the south, where the spooky chambers of **St. Michael's Cave** were cut into the rock. The deep cavern metamorphosed into a hospital during the 1942 bombardments. Now it's an auditorium with the requisite colored lights and piped-in easy listening music. The first Neanderthal skull ever found was excavated from St. Michael's. Take a U-turn down old Queen's Rd. to **Apes' Den,** where a colony of Barbary *macaques* (monkeys) cavort amusingly on the sides of rocks, the tops of taxis, and tourists' heads. These tailless monkeys have inhabited the rock since before the Moorish invasion. The British believe they'll control the peninsula only as long as these animals survive. When the ape population nearly went extinct in 1944, Churchill ordered reinforcements from North Africa, so now the monkeys can be tormented by baby-talking, picture-snapping visitors for years to come. At the northern tip of the Rock facing Spain are the **Great Siege Tunnels,** built into the cliffside in the 1770s to defend against a Spanish assault. The views from the turrets are spectacular, and a talking mannequin bellows, "Halt! Who goes there?" in a full-bodied British accent.

At the southern tip of Gibraltar, **Europa Point** commands a seemingly endless view of the straits, guarded by three machine guns and a lighthouse. *(To get there, take bus #3 or 1B from Line Wall Rd., just off Main St., all the way to the end. Departs every 15min., 40 pence.)* On a clear day you can see Morocco.

ENTERTAINMENT

Main St. hosts throngs of lively **pubs.** Early evening busybodies people-watch from the **Angry Friar,** 287 Main St. (tel. 715 70), also known as **The Convent.** Don't miss having your photo taken with the fist-shaking monk. A pint of lager, ale, or bitter goes for £1.60 to 1.80. (Open daily 9:30am-midnight. Food served 10am-3pm.) As evening wears into night, pub-hoppers slide down to the **Horseshoe Bar,** 193 Main St. (tel. 774 44; open Su-Th 9:30am-midnight, F-Sa 9:30am-1am). **Bourbon Street,** 150 Main St. (tel. 437 63), has cajun cookin', a pool table, darts, and live music nightly (open M-Th 11am-midnight, F-Sa 11am-1am, Su 5:30pm-midnight).

■ Algeciras

Few visitors to Algeciras venture beyond the seedy, noisy port area. Moroccan migrant workers, young Spanish army recruits, and European and American tourists, all in transit between North Africa and Spain, traffic the area day and night. But hidden in the city proper is the city's calmer, more attractive old neighborhood, a pleasant refuge from the chaotic port. So while most visitors to Algeciras are in short transit between Morocco and Europe, less harried travelers can spend a reasonably pleasant first or last night in Spain and perhaps saunter off to Gibraltar for the day.

ANDALUCÍA

ORIENTATION AND PRACTICAL INFORMATION

Stretching along the coast, **Avenida de la Marina,** which turns into Av. Virgen del Carmen north of the port, is lined with travel agencies, banks, and hotels. **Calle Juan de la Cierva** runs perpendicular to the coast from the port, becoming **Calle San Bernardo** as it nears the **train** and **bus stations.** To reach the **tourist office** from either one, follow C. San Bernardo/C. Juan de la Cierva along the abandoned tracks toward the port, past a parking lot on your left. From the **port,** take a left onto Av. Virgen del Carmen, then a quick right onto C. Juan de la Cierva; the office is on the left. All services necessary for transit to Morocco cluster around the port, accessible by a single driveway. Be wary of imposters who peddle ferry tickets.

Transportation

Trains: RENFE (tel. 956 63 02 02), on Ctra. Cádiz, way down C. Juan de la Cierva and its connecting street. To: Granada (5½hr., 3 per day, 2325-2520ptas). Also to Bobadilla (1395ptas) with connections to: Málaga (5½hr., 3 per day, 2015ptas); Sevilla (6hr., 3 per day, 2625-2935ptas); Madrid (6hr., 3 per day, 4500ptas).

Buses: Empresa Portillo, Av. Virgen del Carmen, 15 (tel. 956 65 10 55). To: Marbella (1½hr., 10 per day, 760ptas); Málaga (3hr., 11 per day, 1290ptas); Granada (5hr., 2 per day, 2455ptas); Córdoba (6hr., 2 per day, 2805ptas). **Linesur La Valenciana,** Viajes Koudubia, C. Juan de la Cierva, 5 (tel. 956 60 34 00). To Jerez de la Frontera (2hr., 6 per day, 1060ptas) and Sevilla (3½hr., 6 per day, 1930ptas). **Transportes Generales Comes,** C. San Bernardo, 1 (tel. 956 65 34 56), adjoining Hotel Octavio. To: Tarifa (30min., 10 per day, 215ptas); La Línea, for Gibraltar (45min., departs every 30min., 220ptas); Cádiz (2½hr., 10 per day, 1225ptas); Sevilla (3½hr., 5 per day, 2100ptas). **Empresa Bacoma,** Av. Marina, 8 (tel. 956 65 22 00). To Barcelona (19½hr., 4 per day, 10,000ptas).

Ferries: Tickets, surprisingly, are the same price in any of the dozens of travel agencies in town or in the port terminal. It is recommended that you purchase tickets at the port, not the train station. Allow 30min. to clear customs and board, 90min. with a car. In summer **departures** to: Tangier (normal ferry: 2½hr., departs every hr., 3200ptas per person, 1600ptas per child under 12, 9900ptas per car, 3000ptas per motorcycle, 20% discount with Eurail pass; hydrofoil service: 1hr., 3 per day, 3900ptas) and Ceuta (*buque ferry:* 1½hr., 5-6 per day, 9-10 during high demand, 1884ptas per person, 8665ptas per car, 1870ptas per motorcycle; *embarcaciones rápidas:* 35min., 25 per day, 3002ptas, children under 12 1505ptas). Limited service in winter, no service in bad weather.

Taxis: (tel. 956 65 55 12 or 956 65 55 51).

Tourist, Financial, and Local Services

Tourist Office: C. Juan de la Cierva (tel. 956 57 26 36; fax 956 57 04 75). It's the tube-shaped, pink-and-red building. Sells **maps** (100ptas), plus some brochures. Also has a message board. Open M-F 9am-2pm.

Currency Exchange: To buy **pesetas** there are plenty of banks along Av. Virgen del Carmen, directly in front of the port, many with ATMs. **Banco Central Hispano,** Av. Virgen del Carmen, 9-11, changes traveler's checks without commission. Open M-F 8:30am-2pm. Travel agencies offer poor rates. For a daytrip to Tangiers, buying **dirhams** may not be necessary (many places accept *pesetas*), and you will not be able to convert back to *pesetas*. Convert at the train station or in Morocco.

Luggage Storage: At Empresa Portillo **bus** terminal lockers 400ptas per day. Open daily 7:40am-9:50pm. At **RENFE** 400ptas per day. Open daily 5:30am-10:30pm.

Camping Gear: Adventura Sport, Ventura Morón, 5 (tel. 956 66 92 34), off Pl. Alta. Handy place to grab goods for those headed to Morocco. Hiking boots, tents, sleeping bags, etc. Open M-F 10am-1:30pm and 5:30-9pm, Sa 10:30am-2pm.

Emergency and Communications

Emergency: call 091 or 092. **Police: Municipal,** C. Ruiz Zorilla (tel. 956 66 01 55).

Pharmacy: C. Cayetano del Toro (tel. 956 65 27 57), at C. Tarifa. Open M-F 9am-1:30pm and 5-8:30pm. 24hr. pharmacies *(de guardia)* listed on windowpane.

Hospital: Residencia Sanitaria (tel. 956 60 57 22).

ANDALUCÍA

Post Office: C. Ruiz Zorilla (tel. 956 66 31 76). From the train station, turn left on the street to Málaga; it becomes C. Ruiz Zorilla. Open for Lista de Correos M-F 9am-8pm, Sa 9am-1:30pm. There's a more convenient **branch** on C. José Antonio, 4 (tel. 956 66 36 48). Open M-F 9am-2pm, Sa 9am-1pm. **Postal Code:** 11080.

ACCOMMODATIONS AND FOOD

Lots of convenient *casas de huéspedes* and *hostales* bunch around **Calle José Santacana,** parallel to Av. Marina and one block inland following the train tracks, and **Calle Duque de Almodóvar,** two blocks farther from the water. Consider asking for a back room—wanna-be mods cruise the narrow streets on Vespas at ungodly hours. This neighborhood is also notoriously squalid, and should only be considered as a last resort. The beach in Algeciras is not the place to camp. Police patrol the waterfront, and when they don't, unsavories do. Walk a couple more blocks into town for a more pleasant area. Many pleasant outdoor cafes and *heladerías* line nearby **Calle Regino Martinez,** the main *paseo*. Welcome yourself back from Morocco with *pollo asado* (baked chicken)—or relish your last taste of it—on your way south along Av. Virgen del Carmen, near the port, and on C. Juan de la Cierva. A **supermarket** sells food on the corner of C. Santacana and C. Maroto (open daily 9am-2pm and 5-8pm). The place for fresh fruits, veggies, and seafood (including squirmy snails) is the outdoor **market** at Pl. Palma, one block in from Av. Virgen del Carmen (open M-Sa 8:30am-2pm).

Hostal Rif, C. Rafael de Muro, 11 (tel. 956 65 49 53). Follow C. Santacana into the small market square, bear left around the large kiosk and continue up C. Rafael del Muro for 1 block. In a restored 18th-century building with a palm-studded inner courtyard, Rif is quiet, cool, and spotless. Helpful management dispenses info on forays into Morocco. Dorms 1200ptas. Clean communal showers with hot water.

Hostal Residencia Versalles, C. Moutero Rios, 12 (tel 956 65 42 11), off C. Cayetano del Toro. Decently sized rooms aren't too noisy; all with phones, some with TVs (200ptas extra). Singles with shower 1900ptas, with bath 2500ptas; doubles with shower 3000ptas, with bath 3500ptas.

Hostal Residencia González, C. José Santacana, 7 (tel. 956 65 28 43). A decent bargain close to the port. Roomy quarters with wood furnishings. Singles 1500ptas, with bath 1750ptas; doubles 3000ptas, with bath 3500ptas.

La Alegría, C. José Santacana, 6 (tel. 956 66 65 09). Enthusiasts can indulge in whopping portions of homestyle, ham-free Moroccan cooking. Savory chicken *tahini* with bread and legumes 700ptas. Also *para llevar* (to go). Open daily 7am-11pm.

Casa Blanca, C. Juan de la Cierva, 1 (tel. 956 60 31 21), the big green building near the tourist office. No-nonsense eatery frequented by port employees. *Tortillas* (400-500ptas) make a substantial meal. *Menú* 900ptas. Open Su-F noon-11pm.

La Buganvilla, C. Garcia de la Torre. From the Banesto bank corner of Pl. Alta, head down C. Joaquin Costa and take an immediate left down an alley to an unmarked entrance at its end. Mellow *tapas* bar draws a young crowd to this idyllic locale. Delicious *tapas* from 100ptas. Open M-Sa 11am-4pm and 7pm-1am.

SIGHTS

Plaza Alta, crowned by a handsome blue- and gold-tiled fountain, is a "must-see"; just about everything else, though, is a "don't bother." From the plaza, a pleasant, flower-filled park lies down C. Alfonso XI and to the left on Av. Blas Infantes. **Gibraltar** and The Rock lie 45 minutes and less than 500ptas away (see the listings under **Buses, Transportes Generales Comes).**

■ Tarifa

When the wind picks up in Tarifa (pop. 15,000), the southernmost city in continental Europe, one can easily understand why the city is known, even to locals, as the Hawaii of Spain. Shelter-seeking residents and tourists leave miles of white sandy beaches desolate, but for the intrepid, the gnarly, the few—the windsurfers. You'll see more stickered vans and Quicksilver attire here, on the western edge of the Costa del Sol, than since your last trip to Venice Beach, California. In Tarifa, even the Spaniards wear shorts and sandals.

ORIENTATION AND PRACTICAL INFORMATION Transportes Generales Comes buses roll from in front of the office on Batalla del Salado, 19 (tel. 956 68 40 38; window open M-F 7:15-11:15am and 4-8pm, Sa-Su 3-8pm). Buses run to: Algeciras (30min., 10 per day, 215ptas); Cádiz (2¼hr., 8 per day, 1000ptas), with a stop in Vejer (1hr., 460ptas); and Sevilla (4hr., 4 per day, 2020ptas). **Ferries** leave from the port to Tangier (1hr.; Sa-Th 9:30am, F 9am; 2500ptas, children 1250ptas, 5000ptas per car, 2500ptas per motorcycle). There is one return trip per day (see **Tangier, Orientation and Practical Information,** p. 656). The helpful **tourist office** (tel. 956 68 09 93; fax 956 68 04 31), on Po. Alameda, packs a basic plan of the city, a list of hostels, and bus schedules into one nifty brochure (200ptas). From the bus station, exit toward the castle-shaped arch, follow C. Batalla del Salado for 2½ blocks, turn right on Av. Andalucía and then left onto the tree-lined Alameda. The tourist office is the small glass building under the stairwell. (Open in summer daily 10:30am-2pm and 6-9pm; in winter M-F 10am-2pm and 5-7pm.) A **Banco Central Hispano** and an **ATM** are at C. Batalla del Salado, 17, next to the bus stop (open M-F 8:30am-2pm). Dial 091 or 092 in an **emergency,** or call the **police** (tel. 956 68 41 86), on Pl. Santa María. In a **medical emergency,** dial the Centro de Salud (tel. 956 68 15 15). The **post office,** C. Colonel Moscardó, 9 (tel. 956 68 42 37), is near Pl. San Maleo and the church (open M-F 8:30am-2:30pm, Sa 9:30am-1pm). The **postal code** is 11380.

ACCOMMODATIONS AND FOOD Affordable rooms line the main strip, **Batalla del Salado.** If you visit in August, call ahead or arrive early. Comfortable and clean **Hostal Villanueva,** Av. Andalucía, 11 (tel. 956 68 41 49), features a rooftop terrace with an ocean view and friendly, multilingual management (singles 1800-2500ptas; doubles 3500-4000ptas). The dining room downstairs serves specialty *paella* (open Tu-Su 1:30-4pm and 8:30-11:30pm). Uphill, where Av. Andalucía becomes C. Amador de los Ríos, **Hostal El Asturian** (tel. 956 68 06 19) keeps brightly tiled rooms, all with full bath. (Singles 2500ptas; doubles 4000ptas; triples 6000ptas; quads 8000ptas. Prices rise slightly in summer.) Ask for the deluxe quad that was once part of an Arab castle. Sample the Asturian *sidra* in the lively restaurant downstairs (open daily 1-4pm and 8pm-2am). A number of official **campgrounds** lurk a few kilometers to the west on the beach (400-500ptas per person), although unofficial camping does indeed occur.

Eateries cluster in the streets through the arch and downhill in the old town. **Café-Bar Central** (tel. 956 68 05 90), on C. Sancho IV El Bravo, has one of the few *terrazas* in town buffered by enough buildings so as not to blow away. It serves a wide variety of meat- or vegetable-filled *bocadillos* (400-500ptas) and specialty drinks. (Open daily 9am-2am.) Up the street, **Ali-Baba,** C. Sancho IV El Bravo, 8, serves falafel (350ptas) and kebab (400ptas) to go (open daily 1:30-4pm and 7pm-1am).

SIGHTS At the eastern end of town, next to the port, stand the ruins of the **Castillo de Guzmán el Bueno.** *(Open daily 10am-2pm and 5-7pm. 200ptas, students 100ptas.)* In the 13th century, the Moors kidnapped Guzmán's son and threatened to kill him if Guzmán didn't relinquish the castle. Guzmán did not surrender, even after they brutally sliced his son's throat in front of his eyes. Those with something more tranquil in mind can head 200m south to **Playa Lances** for 5km of the finest white sand on the coast. Bathers should be aware of high winds and a strong undertow. **Tarifa Spin Out Surfbase** (tel. 956 23 63 52), 9km up the road toward Cádiz, rents windsurfing boards and instructs all levels.

■ Cádiz

Located in the southwestern recesses of the Iberian Peninsula, today's Cádiz (pop. 160,000) is far removed from the rest of continental Europe. The Phoenicians landed here in 1100 BC, making Cádiz the gateway to West Africa. From the 16th century to the 18th, the Spanish colonial sea trade transformed the port into one of the wealthiest in Europe. It was also the capital of a new political discussion surrounding the exciting problem of how to manage an empire that had extended to exotic lands.

Ever since New World fervor subsided, liberal politics have been a hallmark of Cadisian life. The city's decisive resistance to Napoleon in 1808 helped preserve the Spanish nation. They subsequently designed the Constitución de Cádiz (1812), an assertion of democratic ideals that inspired a wave of Latin American nationalism but sadly proved ineffectual in its own land. Cadisian liberalism was thwarted again during the Civil War when it fell early and hard to Franco's Nationalist army. As fitting retaliation, Cádiz rekindles its immortal spirit once a year, celebrating its extravagant *Carnaval,* the only festival of its size and kind not suppressed by the Generalísimo. Perhaps Spain's most dazzling party, *Carnaval* makes Cádiz an imperative destination on February itineraries. During the rest of the year, Cádiz offers a little of everything for visitors—not only a large urban center but also the nearby golden sand beaches of the Costa de Luz that put their pebble-strewn eastern neighbors to shame.

ORIENTATION AND PRACTICAL INFORMATION

To reach **Plaza de San Juan de Dios** (the town center) from the **Comes bus station,** walk along Av. Puerto for about five minutes, keeping the port to your left; the plaza lies to the right just after a park. From the **Los Amarillos bus stop,** walk inland about 100m. From the **train station,** walk past the fountain, keeping the port to your right, for about two blocks; Pl. San Juan de Dios is the first plaza on the left. The tangled *casco viejo* is pretty disorienting—a map is necessary.

Transportation

Trains: RENFE (tel. 956 25 43 01), on Pl. Sevilla, off Av. Puerto. To: Pto. de Sta. María (30min., 35 per day, 370ptas); Jerez (40min., 20-35 per day, 435ptas); Sevilla (2hr., 12 per day, 1240ptas); Córdoba (5hr., 10-12 per day, 2325-3700ptas); Madrid (5hr., 2 per day, 8500-9300ptas); Granada (6hr., 3 per day, 3525ptas); Valencia (10-14hr., 1 per day, 5800ptas).

Buses: Transportes Generales Comes, Pl. Hispanidad, 1 (tel. 956 22 42 71). To: Pto. de Sta. María (30min., departs every 30min., 190ptas); Jerez de la Frontera (1hr., 16 per day, 350ptas); Rota (1¼hr., 11 per day, 450ptas); Arcos de la Frontera (1½hr., 3 per day, 670ptas); Vejer de la Frontera (1½hr., 9 per day, 550ptas); Sevilla (2hr., 12 per day, 1300ptas); Algeciras (3hr., 10 per day, 1225ptas); La Línea (3hr., 5 per day, 1440ptas); Málaga (4hr., 3 per day, 2515ptas); Córdoba (5hr., 1 per day, 2185ptas); Granada (7hr., 2 per day, 4010ptas). **Transportes Los Amarillos** (tel. 956 28 58 52) leaves from beside the port, off Pl. San Juan de Dios, across from Po. Canalejas. Purchase tickets on the bus. To: Pto. de Sta. María (30min., 9 per day, 175ptas); Sanlúcar (1½hr., 9 per day, 375ptas); Chipiona (2hr., 9 per day, 460ptas); Arcos (2hr., 3 per day, 770ptas). Both companies reduce service on weekends.

Ferry: El Vapor (tel. 956 87 02 70) leaves from the port next to the Comes station. To Pto. de Sta. María (45min., 5 per day, 250ptas).

Municipal Buses (tel. 956 26 28 06). Pick up a map/schedule and *bonobus* (discount packet) at the kiosk across from the Comes bus station. Most lines run through Pl. España. Beach bums' favorite bus #1 (Cortadura) runs along the shore.

Taxis: (tel. 956 22 10 06, 956 28 69 69, or 956 21 21 21).

Tourist, Financial and Local Services

Tourist Office: Municipal, Pl. San Juan de Dios, 11 (tel. 956 24 10 01), in the mauve Pozos de Miranda building at the end of the plaza. Bright yellow "i" marks the spot. Useful free **map.** English spoken. Open M-F 9am-2pm and 5-8pm. **Junta de Andalucía,** C. Calderón de la Barca, 1 (tel. 956 21 13 13). From the Comes bus sta-

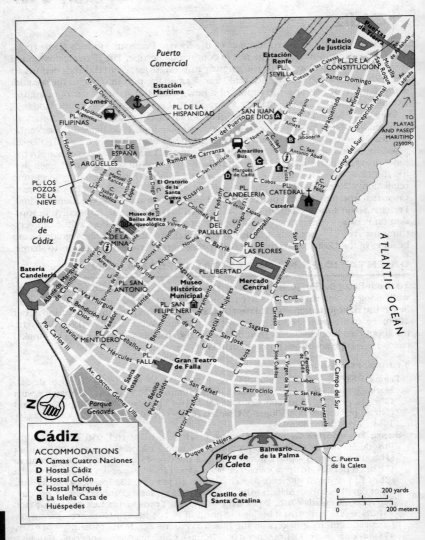

Cádiz

ACCOMMODATIONS
A Camas Cuatro Naciones
D Hostal Cádiz
E Hostal Colón
C Hostal Marqués
B La Isleña Casa de
  Huéspedes

tion, cross over to Pl. España and walk uphill on C. Antonio López. Office is across Pl. Mina, on the corner of C. Calderón de la Barca and C. Zorrilla. Good regional and transport info. Free map. Open M and Sa 9am-2pm, Tu-F 9am-7pm.

Currency Exchange: Banco Central Hispano, C. Ancha, 29 (tel. 956 22 66 22). No commission on cash exchanges or AmEx traveler's checks. Open M-F 8:30am-2pm.

Luggage Storage: Lockers at train station (400ptas). Open daily 8am-11pm.

Emergency and Communications

Emergency: dial 092. **Police: Municipal:** (tel. 092) in Campo del Sur, in the new city. **Medical Assistance: Ambulatorio Vargas Ponce,** Pl. Mendizábal (tel. 956 27 45 53). **Internet Access: Cibercentro Café Internet,** Pl. Glorieta Ing. La Cierva, 1 (tel./fax 956 28 24 59), across from McDonald's and in front of Playa Victoria. Internet and

ANDALUCÍA

email access. 250ptas per 15min., 400ptas per 30min., 750ptas per hr. Open M-Sa 11am-1:30pm and 6-11pm.
Post Office: (tel. 956 21 39 45) in Pl. Flores, next to the market. Open M-F 8:30am-8:30pm, Sa 9:30am-2pm. **Postal Code:** 11080.

ACCOMMODATIONS

Most *hostales* huddle around the harbor, in **Plaza San Juan de Dios,** and just behind it on **Calle Marqués de Cádiz.** Others scatter throughout the old town. Singles and private bathrooms are scarce but individual rooms are sometimes negotiable in the off season. Call months in advance to find a room during February's *Carnaval.*

Hostal Colón, C. Marqués de Cádiz, 6 (tel. 956 28 53 51), off Pl. San Juan de Dios. Spotless rooms with sinks and colorful tiles. All rooms have balconies, but the best view is from the terrace: the cathedral among hundreds of TV antennas. 2 window-less singles 2000ptas; doubles 3400ptas; triples 4200-4800ptas.

Hostal Marqués, C. Marqués de Cádiz, 1 (tel. 956 28 58 54). Newly renovated 18th-century rooms with firm mattresses surrounding a resonant interior courtyard. Most have balconies except for one unloved single. Singles 1800ptas; doubles 2800-3300ptas, with bath 4500ptas; triples 3900-4500ptas.

Hostal Cádiz, C. Feduchy, 20 (tel. 956 28 58 01), near Pl. Candelaria. Clean, comfy rooms—almost all triples. Mix of plastic and wood furniture. Ask the amicable owner for tips on cheap eateries and hip nightlife. Dorms 1500ptas, with shower 2000ptas. Laundry available. You get a key to the front door.

Camas Cuatro Naciones, C. Plocia, 3 (tel. 956 25 55 39), in a corner of Pl. San Juan de Dios. Clean rooms with no frills decorating. Rooms facing the street get a lot of sunshine. Singles 1500ptas; doubles 3000ptas; triples 4000ptas.

La Isleña Casa de Huéspedes, Pl. San Juan de Dios, 12, 2nd fl. (tel. 956 28 70 64). Small and family run with simple, floral rooms, some with huge white balconies overlooking the main square. Singles 1300-1500ptas; doubles 2400-3000ptas.

FOOD

Once you leave Pl. San Juan de Dios, finding eateries can be a trying experience. But seek and thou shalt find a rewarding culinary experience. Try the cafes and *helad-erías* around **Plaza Flores** (also called Pl. Topete), near the post office and the municipal **market.** If you absolutely detest seafood, head to **Supermarket Simago,** next to the municipal market, off Pl. Flores (open M-Sa 9am-9pm).

Bar Pájaro Pinto, Pl. Tío de la Tiza, 12, among similar *terrazas* hidden off C. Rosa on the way down to Playa Caleta; follow C. Rosa to C. Martínez Campos and turn left down a small dead-end street. Enormous *raciones* of the day's catch (700-1000ptas). Open daily June-Sept. 8:30pm-2am.

Freiduría Sopranis, C. Sopranis, 2 (tel. 956 25 64 31), off Pl. San Juan de Dios. Every imaginable type of seafood 1200-2200ptas per kg (feeds 4). Try fresh *gambas* (shrimp), *salmonetes* (mullet), *sardinas* (sardines), or *calamares* (calamari). Open daily 11am-4pm and 7pm-midnight. Take-out only.

Bar-Restaurante Pasaje Andaluz, Pl. San Juan de Dios, 9 (tel. 956 28 52 54). Out-door metal tables with plastic covers hardly spell "Ritz," but this casual place has a solid *menú* (850-1000ptas). Open in summer daily 1-4:30pm and 8pm-midnight; in winter Sa-Th 1-4:30pm and 8pm-midnight.

SIGHTS AND ENTERTAINMENT

Most sights lie in the old town within walking distance of one another. Thanks to a Fine Arts/Provincial Archaeological Museum fusion, Murillo, Rubens, and Zurbarán live in unholy union with some Phoenician sarcophagi in the **Museo de Cádiz** (tel. 956 21 22 81), Pl. Mina. *(Open for guided tours Tu 9am-2:30pm; for general public Tu 2:30-8pm, W-Sa 9am-8pm, Su 9:30am-2:30pm. Free.)* Follow C. Zorrilla inland five blocks to the **Museo de las Cortes de Cádiz,** C. Santa Inés, 9 (tel. 956 22 17 88), which flaunts an enormous, painstakingly wrought 18th-century ivory-and-mahogany model of the city upstairs. *(Open in summer Tu-F 9am-1pm and 5-7pm, Sa-Su 9am-1pm; in winter Tu-F 9am-1pm and 4-7pm, Sa-Su 9am-1pm. Free.)* From Pl. Mina, C. Tinte leads downhill to C. Rosario, and the art of Goya, Cavallini, and Camarone at **El Oratorio de la Santa Cueva** (tel. 956 28 76 76), currently under construction.

Continue down C. Rosario and turn right on C. Manzanares to reach the gold-domed 18th-century **cathedral** (tel. 956 28 61 54), considered the last great cathedral built by colonial riches. *(Open Tu-Sa 10am-1pm. 500ptas, children 200ptas. Cathedral mass Su noon. Free.)* Its treasury bulges with opulent valuables—the *Custodia del Millón* is said to be set with a million precious stones.

Cádiz's **seaside paseo** runs along the Atlantic and the bay of Pto. de Santa María and is accessible via the Muralla de San Carlos off Pl. España. Stupendous views of ships leaving the harbor recall the golden age of yore. Inland, infinite rows of antennae rising from the rooftops recall 1950. Exotic trees, fanciful hedges, and a few chattering monkeys enliven the adjacent **Parque Genovés.**

Since Cádiz was built on a long peninsula surrounded on three sides by the Atlantic, the exhaust-spewing ships on one coast don't profane the extensive line of pristine **beaches** on the other. **Playa de la Caleta,** the easiest beach to reach, is nestled between two castles in the *casco antiguo.* Other sands skirt the new part of town, serviced by bus #1 (towards Cortadura), which leaves from Pl. España (115ptas). The first beach beyond the rocks is the unremarkable 400m **Playa de Santa María del Mar.** Next to it, **Playa de la Victoria,** stretching 2500m, has earned the E.U.'s *bandera azul* (blue flag) for cleanliness, and has by far the most visitors. A more natural landscape, with fewer hotels and straw mats, belongs to **Playa de Cortadura** (5000m), where the coveted *bandera azul* also flaps proudly. Take bus #1 until it almost reaches the highway, when the bus will reverse its route. The boardwalk ends here and sunbather density falls steadily the farther one walks.

ENTERTAINMENT

After midnight in summer, anyone and everyone finds fresh air (and refreshments) by the beach. **Paseo Marítimo,** the main drag along Playa Victoria, has some of Cádiz's best bars, discos, cafes, and *terrazas.* **La Jarra** (tel. 956 26 57 74), on C. José G. Agullo, is one such hotspot, blaring *música española* and American hard rock favorites. Another choice locale for bar-hoppers and disco-maniacs is **Punta de San Felipe,** reached by walking north along the sea from Pl. España, just beyond the Comes station; most of its real action kicks off at 4 or 5am. Look for signs on the boardwalk advertising theme parties. In **El Centro,** try the area around **Plaza Mina,** which is liveliest on weekends in winter. **Calle de Manuel Rances,** nearby off C. Antonio López, features some of the hippest bars.

Carnaval insanity is legendary. The gray of winter gives way to dazzling color, from February 11 to 21, when the city hosts one of the most raucous *carnavales* in the world. Costumed dancers, street singers, ebullient residents, and folks from all over take to the streets in a week-long frenzy that makes New Orleans's Mardi Gras look like Thursday night bingo.

■ Near Cádiz: El Puerto de Santa María

Across the bay from Cádiz and a 12-minute train ride from Jerez, low-key and beach-centered El Puerto de Santa María (pop. 75,000) is one of three cities (along with Jerez and Sanlúcar) that form the renowned "sherry triangle." Here, wine reigns next to God, and in a final concession to vice, El Puerto boasts the only functioning casino in western Andalucía.

PRACTICAL INFORMATION El Puerto's bus stop is in front of Pl. Toros, but many buses passing through drop off and pick up passengers at the train station; ask at the tourist office for specific times and departure points. **Buses** connect El Puerto to:

Jerez (30min., 18 per day, 150ptas); Rota (30min., 8 per day, 325ptas); Cádiz (40min., 41 per day, 190ptas); and Sanlúcar and Chipiona (10 per day, 215-275ptas). Service is reduced on weekends. **Trains** (tel. 956 54 25 85) depart to: Jerez (12min., 20 per day, 150ptas); Cádiz (30min., 35 per day, 350ptas); and Sevilla (2hr., 17 per day, 1050ptas). An El Vapor **ferry** (tel. 956 87 02 70) links El Puerto with Cádiz, departing from the port near the tourist office (45min., 5 per day, 250ptas). The **tourist office,** C. Guadalete, 1 (tel. 956 54 24 13; fax 956 54 22 46), is off Av. Bajamar near the port. From the train station, take a left on Ctra. Madrid, then a right onto C. Pozas Dulces. Follow it along the water; the tourist office is on the right. From the bus stop in front of Pl. Toros, follow C. Santa Lucía into Pl. España, turn right on C. Palacios, and continue to the end; turn left and the tourist office will be on the right. (Open daily in summer 10am-2pm and 6-8pm; in winter 10am-2pm and 5:30-7:30pm.) In **emergencies,** call 091 or 092. The **municipal police** (tel. 956 54 18 63) can be alerted at Ronda de las Dunas. In a **medical emergency,** call 956 54 33 02 or 956 87 11 11. The **post office,** Pl. Polvorista, 3 (tel. 956 85 53 22), does it all (open M-F 8:30am-8:30pm, Sa 9am-2pm). The **postal code** is 11500.

ACCOMMODATIONS AND FOOD Unless you really feel like gambling, El Puerto de Santa María makes the most sense as a daytrip. The family-run **Pensión Santamaría,** C. Nevería/C. Pedro Muñoz Seca (*not* C. Dr. Muñoz Seca), 38 (tel. 956 85 36 31), keeps clean rooms surrounding a relaxing patio (singles 1500-1750ptas; doubles 3000ptas, with bath 4000ptas; triples with bath 5000-6000ptas). From the tourist office, head up C. Palacios toward Pl. España and take the fourth left. **Camping Playa Las Dunas,** Po. Marítimo La Puntilla (tel. 956 87 22 10), is a 20-minute walk along the shore from the tourist office or a painless local bus ride (#26). A *cafetería,* supermarket, and clean showers await. (555ptas per adult and per tent, 455 ptas per child, 455ptas per car.) The campground lounges in a pine forest across the street from **Playa de la Puntilla,** a beach with views of Cádiz's industrial harbor on the other side of the bay. Avoid overpriced restaurants near the water. Instead, try **La Tortillería,** C. Palacios, 4, a bar famous for its inventive omelette sandwiches for 200ptas (open Tu-Th and Su 8:30pm-1am, F-Sa 8:30pm-2am). For international food, Italian **Restaurante Pasta Gansa,** on C. Puerto Escondido, off C. Ribera del Rio, has pasta dishes (700-900ptas), while **Restaurant Hong Kong** (tel. 956 85 7204 for delivery), across from the ferry dock, has a four-course Chinese *menú* (525ptas; Visa, MC, AmEx).

SIGHTS AND ENTERTAINMENT El Puerto's history as an embarking point for exploration and conquest has resulted in a few noteworthy monuments. Columbus's second voyage to the New World was launched here, and as business in the Americas developed, prominent families emptied their coffers to build structures that are now open to the public. Before the boom in the 13th century, Alfonso X El Sabio constructed the **Castillo de San Marcos.** (*Open Tu, Th, and Sa 11am-1:30pm. Guided tours every 30min. Free.*) Visitors can survey the city from the castle's tower. **Iglesia Mayor Prioral** has a Baroque front topped with a one-armed nude and two sidekicks. (*Open daily 10am-noon and 7:30-8:30pm. Free.*) Two of El Puerto's *bodegas* sponsor tours, but both require reservations. **Bodega Terry** (tel. 956 48 30 00) has standard tours. (*Tours Sept.-July M-F 9:30, 11am, and 12:30pm; Aug. M-Tu and Th 11am. 325ptas.*) **Bodega Osborne** (tel. 956 85 52 11), original sponsors of those gigantic black bull billboards that fill the countryside (see p. 150), has an hysterical promotional film in addition to the basics. (*Open M-F 10:30am-1pm. 300ptas.*) The **Fundación de Rafael Alberti,** C. Santo Domingo, 25 (tel. 956 85 07 11), displays the poet's books, correspondence, and personal belongings. (*Open in summer M-F 10:30am-2:30pm; in winter Tu-Su 11am-2:30pm. 300ptas, seniors and students 150ptas.*) El Puerto de Santa María has three beaches for summer sun worshippers: **Playa La Puntilla** (accessible by city bus #8 or 26), **Playa Santa Catalina-Fuentebravía** (bus #35), and **Playa Valdelgrana** (also bus #35). The latter two lie west of the city and are less populated than Pl. Puntilla.

ANDALUCÍA

▓ Vejer de la Frontera

Before coming to Spain, you may have dreamt of a majestic white town crowning a hill, where friendly locals invite you into their ancient homes hemmed by narrow, cobbled alleys. Vejer de la Frontera (pop. 13,000) is as close as it gets. Although women no longer venture out cloaked in *cobijados* (long, black garb that covers the face), the town hasn't lost its Arab mystique. Without the distraction of textbook monuments and must-see sights, beautiful Vejer invites you to sit back and soak it up.

ORIENTATION AND PRACTICAL INFORMATION Getting to Vejer can be a pain. While some buses stop at the end of **Avenida de Los Remedios,** which leads uphill into La Plazuela (10min.), many just leave you by the highway at **La Barca de Vejer.** Ask at the restaurant whether you can catch one of the infrequent buses to town, or take one of the numerous taxis waiting by the bus stop (700ptas to take you up the hill). The alternative, a steep 20-minute uphill walk, can be arduous with a backpack. If you do make the trek, climb the cobbled track to the left of the restaurant. When you reach the top, keep walking straight; all roads lead to quiet **Plaza de España,** not to be confused with **La Plazuela,** which is a tiny intersection across town inhabited by the market, the **tourist office,** and many bars.

For **bus** info, either visit the tourist office or call the **Comes** office in Cádiz (tel. 956 22 42 71). Buses run from Av. Remediosto to Cádiz (1½hr., 7 per day, 550ptas) and Sevilla via Jerez (3½hr., 2 per day, 1640ptas). For other destinations, descend the hill to **La Barca de Vejer,** with service to: Tarifa (1hr., 3 per day, 500ptas); Cádiz (1½hr., 7 per day, 550ptas); Algeciras (2hr., 8 per day, 1225ptas); La Línea (2¼hr., 4 per day, 1300 ptas); Sevilla (3½hr., 3 per day, 1940ptas); and Málaga (4hr., 3 per day, 2515ptas). Visit the **tourist office,** C. Marqués de Tamarón, 10 (tel. 956 45 01 91), off the Plazuela, to receive maps, info, and occasionally, *tortas vejeriegas* (cookie samples; open in summer M-F 10:30am-2pm and 6-9pm, Sa 10:30am-2pm; in winter M-F 9am-2:30pm and 5-9:30pm). **Banco Central Hispano** sits at C. Juan Bueno, 5, off La Plazuela (open M-F 8:30am-2:30pm). In a **medical emergency,** call the Centro de Salud (tel. 956 44 76 25) or visit them on Av. Andalucía. Call the **police** at 956 45 04 00. The **post office** (tel. 956 45 02 38) is on C. Juan Bueno, 22 (open M-F 8:30am-2:30pm, Sa 9am-1pm). The **postal code** is 11150.

ACCOMMODATIONS AND FOOD The best accommodations in Vejer are in its two **casas particulares** (private houses) on C. San Filmo, up a stone staircase from Av. Los Remedios. The friendly Sra. Rosa Romero owns **Casa Los Cántaros,** C. San Filmo, 14 (tel. 956 44 75 92), a beautifully restored Andalucían home with a grape-vined patio. The spotless suites have sitting rooms, antique furniture, and private bathrooms, and you can use the kitchen (doubles 2500-3000ptas). Señora Luisa Doncel keeps tidy little rooms with common bathrooms in **Calle San Filmo, 12** (tel. 956 45 02 46). If Doña Luisa is not at room #12, try #16. (Singles 1500ptas; doubles 2500-3000ptas.) Where you stay may depend on which woman you meet first.

The cheapest eats are *tapas* or *raciones* at the bars around the Plazuela. At **Bar El Cura,** Po. Cobijadas, 1 (tel. 956 45 07 76), at the very bottom of C. Juan Bueno, locals place bets on who can make the solemn owner laugh (or at least crack a smile). A cup of *fino* (dry sherry) costs a mere 50ptas. (Open daily 7am-3pm and 5:30pm-late.) For a sit-down meal, try **La Posada,** Av. Los Remedios, 19 (tel. 956 45 01 11), a few buildings uphill from the bus stop. Inside is a bar and an ornate dining room with a 1200ptas *menú del día.* (Open daily 1:30-4pm and 8pm-midnight. Visa, MC, AmEx.)

SIGHTS AND ENTERTAINMENT To enjoy Vejer properly, simply wander along the labyrinthine streets and cliffside *paseos,* stopping frequently for drinks and *tapas.* As for monuments, the **Castillo Moro,** down C. Ramon y Cajal from the church, offers the usual assortment of battlements and crenelated walls, plus a blinding view of the glowing white houses. (*Open daily July-Aug. 11am-2pm and 5-10pm; Sept.-June 10am-2pm. Patio open at all hours. A boy scout troop leads the way around the ramparts.*) The **Iglesia del**

Divino Salvador, behind the tourist office, is a choice blend of Romanesque, Mudéjar, and Gothic styles. *(Open daily 10:30am-1:30pm and 7-9pm.)*

Ten kilometers from Vejer on the road to Los Caños lies **El Palmar,** 7km of fine white sand and clear water easily accessible by car. Many beach-goers hitch rides at the bend of **Los Remedios** or catch the bus to **Conil de la Frontera** and walk southeast along the beach for three or four kilometers. For quasi-info on the town and outdoor activities, like bike rentals, consult **Magnum Bike and Surf Shop** (tel. 956 44 75 75) on Av. Los Remedios. *(Bikes from 1000ptas per day, surf boards from 2000ptas per day. Open M-F 10:30am-2pm and 6-9:30pm, Sa 10:30am-2pm. Visa, MC, AmEx.)*

The old quarter hops at night. Leave another little piece of your heart at **Bar Janis Joplin** on C. Marqués de Tamarón, with plush wicker chairs, an amazing view, and me and Bobby McGee. *(Open nightly 9:30pm-late.)* Across the street, **La Bodeguita** is another favorite spot. *(Open in summer M-F 9:30am-3:30pm and 8pm-late, Sa 10am-3:30pm and 8pm-late, Su noon-3pm and 8pm-late; in winter daily 9:30am-late.)* Students jam the underground **Pub Sótano,** on C. Altozano. Several other popular pubs lie downhill from the Plazuela on **Calle Sagasta** and **Calle Santísimo.** From July to August, everyone dances among the thatched huts of **Discoteca Bekkeh** in Parque de Los Remedios, behind the bus stop. Stupendous terrace views make **Café-Bar El Arriate,** C. Corredera, 55 (tel. 956 44 71 70 or 956 45 1305), a good place for a *copa* and *tapas* anytime. For local wine sampling year-round, try **Bodegas Gallardo** (tel. 956 45 10 80), down in La Barca.

The village throws brilliant *fiestas.* As soon as the **Corpus Christi** revelry ends in June, Vejer starts anew with the **Candelas de San Juan** (June 23), climaxing with the midnight release of the *toro de fuego* (bull of fire) at midnight. A local (obviously with a death wish) dressed in an iron bull costume charges the crowd as a bevy of attached firecrackers fly off his body in all directions. The town demonstrates its taurine creativity again during the delirious **Semana Santa** celebrations, when a *toro embolao* (sheathed bull), with wooden balls affixed to the tips of his horns, is set loose through the narrow streets of Vejer on the Sunday of the Resurrection. The good-natured **Feria de Primavera** (2 weeks after Semana Santa, in April) is a bit tamer, with people dancing *sevillanas* and downing cupfuls of *fino* till sunrise.

■ Jerez de la Frontera

Though unremarkable in appearance, Jerez de la Frontera (pop. 200,000) is the cradle of three staples of Andalucían culture: flamenco, Carthusian horses, and above all, *vino de jerez,* also known as sherry. Visit *bodegas* (wine cellars) to sample grape-based liqueurs, then recover in time to hear live flamenco in the evening. Jerez also makes a good departure point for several popular tourist circuits: the *ruta de los pueblos blancos* (route of the white villages), the *ruta del toro* (bulls), the *ruta de la costa* (coast), and, of course, the *ruta del vino* (wine).

ORIENTATION AND PRACTICAL INFORMATION

The labyrinthine, *bodega*-studded streets of Jerez are almost impossible to navigate without a highly detailed map. Get one free from the tourist office or buy one from any bookstore or newsstand (around 500ptas). To reach the town center from the **bus station,** exit away from the restrooms and walk left. Calle Cartuja becomes C. Medina, which beelines for **Plaza Romero Martínez** (the city's commercial center), and *Teatro Villamarta.* From here, walk left on C. Cerrón, which leads to C. Santa María and C. Lencería, heading into **Plaza del Arenal.** From the **train station,** exit to the right and take C. Cartuja to the bus station, then follow the directions above.

Transportation
Flights: (tel. 956 15 00 00). Airport is 7km from town on Ctra. Jerez-Sevilla. A taxi to the airport runs 1800ptas. **Iberia,** Av. Albaro Domecq (tel. 956 18 43 94). **British Airways** (tel. 956 15 00 93).

Trains: Pl. Estación (tel. 956 34 23 19), at the end of C. Medina after it becomes C. Cartuja. **RENFE,** C. Larga, 34 (tel. 956 33 48 13). To: Cádiz (45min., 11 per day, 365ptas); Sevilla (1½hr., 11 per day, 735ptas); Madrid (4½hr., 4 per day, 7600-8800ptas); Barcelona (13½-14½hr., 4 per day, 9700ptas).

Buses: Station (tel. 956 34 52 07) on C. Cartuja, at the corner of Madre de Dios, 2 blocks from the train station at end of C. Medina. **Transportes Generales Comes** (tel. 956 34 21 74) to: Puerto de Sta. María (30min., 4-6 per day, 150ptas); Cádiz (1hr., 18 per day, 350ptas); Vejer (2hr., 1 per day, 790ptas); Ronda (2¾hr., 3 per day, 1255ptas). **Los Amarillos** (tel. 956 34 78 44) to Arcos (45min., 18 per day, 295ptas) and Córdoba (4hr., 1 per day, 1850ptas). **Linesur** (tel. 956 34 10 63) to: Sanlúcar de Barrameda (30min., departs every hr., 215ptas); Chipiona (1hr., departs every hr., 295ptas); Sevilla (1½hr., 7 per day, 870ptas); Algeciras (2hr., 8 per day, 1425ptas). **Sevibus** (tel. 956 30 50 05) to Madrid (5hr., 6 per day, 2920ptas). Fewer on weekends.

City buses: Each of the 12 lines runs every 15min., most passing through Pl. Arenal and by the bus station (100ptas). Info office (tel. 956 34 34 46) in Pl. Arenal.

Taxis: (tel. 956 34 48 60).

Car Rental: Hertz (tel. 956 15 00 38), at the airport. Starting price 9500ptas per day. Min. age 25. Open M-F 7:30am-9pm, Sa 7:30am-2:30pm and 3-7pm, Su 9:30-11:30am and 3:30-9pm.

Tourist, Financial, and Local Services

Tourist Office: C. Larga, 39 (tel. 956 33 11 50; fax 956 33 17 31). From Pl. Arenal, take C. Lencería to C. Larga. Friendly and English-speaking staff doles out highly technical info on brandy and sherry production, *bodegas* tours, and the royal equestrian school. Free maps. Open in summer M-F 8am-2pm and 5-8pm, Sa 10am-2pm; in winter M-F 8am-3pm and 4-7pm, Su 10am-2pm and 5-7pm.

Currency Exchange: Banco Central Hispano, C. Medina, 36. Good rates and no commission on traveler's checks. Open M-F 8:30am-2:30pm.

Luggage Storage: Next to the Sevibus office at the bus station (60ptas per day).

Emergency and Communications

Emergency: dial 091 or 092. **Police:** (tel. 956 33 03 46).

Medical Assistance: Ambulatorio de la Seguridad Social (tel. 956 34 84 68), on C. José Luis Díaz.

Internet Access: Cybersur, C. Divina Pastora, 48 (tel 956 32 87 90). Internet, email, and online chat services. Open daily 10am-2pm and 5:30-9pm.

Post Office: Main Office, C. Cerón, 2 (tel. 956 34 22 95; fax 956 32 14 10), off Pl. Romero Martínez. Open for stamps and Lista de Correos M-F 8:30am-8:30pm, Sa 9:30am-1:30pm. **Postal Code:** 11480.

ACCOMMODATIONS AND FOOD

Finding a bed to crash in is as easy as finding a cork to sniff. Look along **Calle Medina,** near the bus station, and **Calle Arcos,** which intersects C. Medina at Pl. Romero Martínez. The area may not be interesting to look at, but is only a short walk from the fountains and *terrazas* of C. Larga. *Tapas*-hoppers bounce in, out, and all about **Plaza del Arenal** and northeast on Av. Alcalde Álvaro Domecq around **Plaza Caballo.** Supermarket **Cobreros** sells victuals on the second floor of the Centro Comercial, on C. Larga, next door to McDonald's (open daily 9am-2pm and 5:30-9:30pm).

Albergue Juvenil (HI), Av. Carrero Blanco, 30 (tel. 956 14 39 01; fax 956 14 32 63), in an ugly suburb, a 25min. walk or 10min. bus ride from downtown (bus L-8 from the bus station, bus L-1 from Pl. Arenal). Clean and modern, with spacious doubles, a pool, tennis and basketball courts, mini-soccer field, library, TV and video room, and a rooftop terrace. Dorms 800-1300ptas, over 26 1100-1800ptas. Non-members pay an extra 300ptas per night for 6 nights to become members. Call ahead to make sure there's room.

Hostal San Andrés, C. Morenos, 12 (tel. 956 34 09 83; fax 956 34 31 96). Take C. Fontana (off C. Medina) for 1 block, and turn left; C. Morenos is the first right. Two

ANDALUCÍA

beautiful patios, one with stained glass, the other with hanging grapes. Singles 1600-2500ptas; doubles 2500-4500ptas.

Hostal Sanvi, C. Morenos, 10 (tel. 956 34 56 24). Generic hotel rooms at hostel prices. Sparkling baths. Singles 1500-1800ptas; doubles 2500ptas, with bath 3000ptas. They "almost never" charge higher prices—just during festivals.

Casa Pepa, Pl. Madre de Dios, 14 (tel. 956 32 49 06), around the corner from the bus station. A local meeting place and landmark. Locals keep coming back for scrumptious *menús* (775ptas), *platos combinados* (450-700ptas), and *tapas* (150-200ptas). Open daily 9:30am-5pm and 8pm-midnight.

Restaurante Los Girasoles, C. Diego de Fernández Herrera, 2 (tel. 956 33 41 00), off Pl. de las Angustras. Macrobiotic foods of all types, homebaked bread, and many vegetarian options. Delicious *ensalada "Los Girasoles"* (sunflower salad; 700ptas). Open M-W 9am-midnight, Th-Sa 9am-1am.

Dolce Vita (tel. 956 33 34 61), C. Divina Pastora, around the corner from the equestrian school. Not classy, but cheap and filling. Big pasta portions start at 620ptas, burgers at 250ptas. Pizza delivery. Open M-Th 8pm-1am, F-Su 8pm-3am

SHERRY BODEGAS

Most people come to Jerez for the *jerez*. Multilingual tour guides distill the sherry-making process for you, and then let you sample for free. The best time to visit is early September during the harvest; avoid August when many *bodegas* close down. *Bodegas* are plotted on any map and the tourist office can help find the right one for you. Group reservations for hour-long tours must be made at least one week in advance; reservations for individuals may be required. *Bodegas* open during specific hours, and most conduct tours in English. Call ahead for exact times.

Williams and Humbert, Ltd., Nuño de Cañas, 1 (tel. 956 34 65 39; fax 956 34 51 91). One of the prettiest, with gardens and a stable of prize-winning Carthusian horses. Tours M-F 1:30pm. 300ptas. Reservations required.

Harveys of Bristol, C. Arcos, 53 (tel. 956 15 10 02; fax 956 15 10 08). Live crocodiles. Tours M-F noon. 300ptas.

B. Domecq, C. San Idelfonso, 3 (tel. 956 15 15 00; fax 956 33 86 74). The oldest in town. Overrun with house cats. Tours M-F 9am and 1pm. 325ptas. Reservations required.

González Byass, C. Manuel María González, s/n (tel. 956 35 70 00; fax 956 35 70 46). Tours M-F 10, 11am, noon, 1, 5, 6, 7pm (Th tour 1:30 instead of 1pm), Sa 10, 11am, noon, 1pm. The largest tour with scenic gardens and trained mice that sometimes climb miniature ladders propped against wine glasses and sip the juice. 400ptas. Reservations required on Saturdays.

OTHER SIGHTS AND ENTERTAINMENT

Jerez's love for wine is closely followed by its passion for horses. During the last week of April or the first week of May, the **Real Escuela Andaluza de Arte Equestre** (Royal Andalusian School of Equestrian Art; reservations tel. 956 30 77 98; fax 956 30 99 54), on Av. Duque de Abrantes, sponsors a **Feria del Caballo** (Horse Fair) with shows, carriage competitions, and races of Jerez-bred Carthusian horses. Otherwise, shows held every Thursday in July and August at noon feature a troupe of horses dancing in choreographed sequences. *(1500-2400ptas, children 600-960ptas.)* Dress rehearsals are almost as impressive. *(M-W and F 11am-1pm. 450ptas.)*

For more standard sights, just west of Pl. Arenal on the Alameda Vieja is the Moorish **Mezquita** (tel. 956 33 73 06), an 11th-century mosque. *(Open in summer M-Sa 10am-2pm; in winter M-F 10am-2pm and 4-6pm. Free.)* Almohad **baños árabes** (Arab baths) lie within, while the **Torre Octagonal** rises above. Inside, the **Cámara Oscura** offers exhibits on Jerez as well as startling views of the city. Near the Mezquita is the imposing Baroque **cathedral** (tel. 956 34 84 82), with a Mudéjar belfry, built on the site of an Arab mosque. *(Open daily in summer 10am-8pm; in winter 10am-6pm. 200ptas, students, children, and seniors 100ptas.)*

ANDALUCÍA

Mother Nature and Family

Bust out your binoculars—the 60,000 acre **Parque Nacional Coto de Doñana** on the Río Guadalquivir delta is home to flamingos, vultures, and thousands more feathered favorites, along with geese (and mongeese), wild boars, and lynx. Despite a huge mining spill on a tributary of the Guadalquivir River in April of 1998, one that threatened to be one of Spain's biggest ecological disasters, the park has done surprisingly well, and tourist visits to the park have continued relatively unaffected. If ornithological delights don't entice you, the salt marshes, sand dunes, wooded areas, and relaxing beach might. Nature purists beware, though, lest you stumble upon the lair of the dreaded species *turgrupus touristicus*—the park neighbors Matalascañas (30km toward Huelva), a settlement with a concrete shopping center and hotel complex.

Access to most of the park is restricted and backcountry hiking and camping are prohibited. The western end of the park is accessible from Huelva and Matalascañas. Also, boat tours on **S.S. Real Fernando** (tel. 956 36 38 13; fax 956 36 21 96) depart from Sanlúcar (4hr., May to mid-Sept. Tu-Su 9:30am and 5pm; mid-Sept. to Apr. Tu-Su 10am). Call to make reservations or visit the kiosk by the dock on Av. Bajo de Guía. Those more interested in sand than life on the wild side can take the round-trip launch across the bay (8am-8pm, 400ptas) to one of the few *chiringuito* (refreshment stand)-free beaches in Spain. To get a taste of Doñana without leaving Sanlúcar, check out the **Visitor Center** (tel. 956 36 07 15), on Av. Bajo de Guía near the boat kiosk (open M-F 9am-3pm, Sa-Su 10am-2:30pm), or **Fábrica de Hielo** (tel. 956 36 16 35), another visitor information center on Av. Bajode Gura (open daily 10am-2:30pm and 4-7pm).

Flamenco dancing and music reputedly originated in Jerez. If you're only a bit lucky, you'll catch a free, spontaneous show. Rare footage and concert appearances of Spain's most highly regarded flamenco singers, dancers, and guitarists, is available for viewing at the **Centro Andaluz de Flamenco** (tel. 956 34 92 65; fax 956 32 11 27), in Palacio Pemartín, on Pl. San Juan. *(Open M-F 9am-2pm. Audio-visuals every 30min. Free.)* Most *peñas* and *tablaos* (clubs and bars that host flamenco) hide in the old town, a maze of narrow streets west of C. Larga and south of C. Porvera and C. Ancha in the old town. Most only perform for large groups, and require reservations in advance. Ask for details about big shows in the tourist office or at the Centro Andaluz de Flamenco. A bit secluded but worth the trek, **El Lagá de Tío Parrilla**, Pl. Mercado, s/n (tel./fax 956 33 83 34), is the only *tablao* that hosts open shows frequently. *(Shows M-Sa 10:30pm. Cover 1200-1500ptas, includes 1 drink.)*

For more conventional **nightlife**, try the triangle formed by **Calle Santo Domingo, Calle Salvatierra,** and **Avenida Méjico,** several blocks north of C. Larga. This area thunders on weekends, as does **Plaza de Canterbury,** a mini-mall of bars and *terrazas* located on C. Paul at C. Santo Domingo. **Cancún,** C. Parjarete, 18 (tel. 956 33 17 22), a huge, trendy *bar musical* off C. Zaragoza (a block from Pl. Canterbury), features Caribbean themes, but the usual techno-pop blasts from the speakers. *(Couples, ladies, and "members" only. Free.)*

Autumn is festival season, when Jerez showcases its best equine and flamenco traditions. The **Fiesta de la Bulería** in September celebrates the latter. During late September and early October, Jerez toasts the pagan roots of religious festivals with the **Fiestas de la Vendimia,** a celebration of the season's harvest. In September, the **Festival de Teatro, Música, y Baile** celebrates flamenco dancing. Altogether, these festivals are known as the **Fiestas de Otoño,** occurring from September 10 until October 13. The largest **horse parade** in the world, with races in Pl. Arenal, is the highlight of the month-long celebration. *(Ask for details at the tourist office.)*

■ Near Jerez de la Frontera: Sanlúcar de Barrameda

Sanlúcar de Barrameda (pop. 60,000) sits at the mouth of the Río Guadalquivir, offering access to the **Parque Nacional Coto de Doñana** and some of Spain's most pristine beaches. Home to a handful of sherry *bodegas* and a few palaces, Sanlúcar is a mix of a traditional Spain and a European seaside resort. Its industrial outskirts are a bit of an eyesore, but fret not—alongside superbly fine sand, small-town charm still glitters under the sun.

PRACTICAL INFORMATION Los Amarillos (tel. 956 38 50 60), on Pl. Salle at the end of C. San Juan, runs **buses** to: Chipiona (30min., departs every hr., 95ptas); Cádiz (1hr., 10 per day, 375ptas); and Sevilla (2hr., 13 per day, 885ptas). **Linesur La Valenciana** (tel. 956 34 10 63) is two blocks toward the beach from Pl. Cabildo, by the tourist office and Bar La Jaula. Buses run to Chipiona (30min., departs every hour, 95ptas) and Jerez de la Frontera (45min., departs every hour, 215ptas). Buy tickets on the bus. For **taxis,** call 956 36 11 02 or 956 36 00 04.

The **tourist office** (tel. 956 36 61 10; fax 956 36 61 32), on Calzada del Ejército, which runs perpendicular to the beach, provides info on the city and the Parque Nacional de Doñana (open in summer M-F 10am-2pm and 6-8pm, Sa and Su 10am-1pm; in winter M-F 10am-2pm and 6-8pm, Sa 10am-1pm). Dial 091 or 092 in any **emergency. Police** stand guard at Av. Constitución, s/n (tel. 956 38 80 11). In a **medical emergency,** call Ambulatorio de la S.S., Calzada del Ejército, s/n (tel. 956 36 71 65). The **post office,** Av. Cerro Falón, s/n (tel. 956 36 09 37), sits three blocks northeast of the tourist office toward the beach (open M-F 8:30am-2:30pm, Sa 9am-1pm). The **postal code** is 11540.

ACCOMMODATIONS AND FOOD Few true bargains exist; it may be worth inquiring at doorway signs reading *"se alquilan habitaciones"* (for rent). **Hostal La Blanca Paloma,** Pl. San Roque, 15 (tel. 956 36 36 44), keeps spacious, clean rooms, a few with balconies (singles 1500-2000ptas; doubles 3000-4000ptas; prices do not include 7% IVA). **Pensión La Bohemia,** C. Don Claudio, 1 (tel. 956 36 95 99), just off C. Santo Domingo, offers beige bedspreads, cold showers, and no frills simplicity after a day at the beach (singles 2000ptas, with bath 2500ptas; doubles 4000ptas, with bath 4500-5000ptas). Sanlúcar is famous for its *langostinos* (king prawns). For a sit-down meal, head for the side streets off **Calle San Juan.** *Terrazas* fill **Plaza San Roque** and **Plaza Cabildo,** its tree-lined neighbor. **Bar-Restaurante El Cura,** C. Amargura, 2 (tel. 956 36 29 94), between the two plazas, serves up divinely ordained *paella* (500ptas) in a family atmosphere (open daily 7:30am-3am).

SIGHTS AND ENTERTAINMENT Most of the sights in town are best accessed via the tourist office—get to know it and love it. Two impressive palaces compete with the enormous 14th-century **Iglesia de Nuestra Señora de la O** (tel. 956 36 05 55), in Pl. Paz, for the attention of sun-struck tourists. *(Open 15min. before and after mass. Mass M-Sa 8pm, Su noon and 8pm. Free.)* The **Palacio Medina Sidonia** (tel. 956 36 01 61) was inhabited until recently. *(Call in order to arrange group visiting time. Free.)* The 19th-century **Palacio Infantes de Orleans** (tel. 956 38 80 00) now houses the Ayuntamiento. *(Open for guided visits Th-Tu. 100ptas.)* Several **bodegas** tower over Sanlúcar's small streets. Groups can arrange to go to Cigarrera, Barbadillo, or Pedro Romerao through the tourist office. *(Tours M, Th 12:30pm, Sa noon. 200ptas.)* The tourist office also organizes cheap tours around town to see both the monuments and *bodegas. (200-350ptas per person. Inquire for more info.)* Numerous **festivals** testify to Sanlúcar's fondness for merrymaking. The **Feria de la Manzanilla** (last week in May) involves the most alcohol, but **Corpus Christi,** in June, explodes with the biggest fanfare. In August, **Carreras de Caballos** (horse races) thunder along the beach, and the **Festival de la Exaltación del Río Guadalquivir** (end of August) enlivens the streets with poetry readings, a flamenco competition, popular dances, and bullfights.

ANDALUCÍA

■ Near Jerez de la Frontera: Chipiona

A quiet seaside village for nine months of the year, Chipiona (pop. 15,000) takes a summer somersault into domestic tourism. Spanish families turn Chipiona into one big cozy picnic, especially on weekends. The tradition began in the 19th century, when Chipiona's extremely salty and mineral-filled sea (the scent pervades the air) was reputed to have curative powers. A recuperative hospital was even opened along the beach to nurse ailing patients back to health; the hospital closed about 30 years ago. **Iglesia de Nuestra Señora de la O,** constructed in 1640, stands in the gorgeous Pl. Juan Carlos I, Chipiona's shadiest, most fragrant spot (open daily 7-8:30pm).

ORIENTATION AND PRACTICAL INFORMATION Los Amarillos buses (tel. 956 37 02 92), on Av. Regla at the top of C. Peral, run to: Sanlúcar (30min., 14 per day, 95ptas); Cádiz (1½hr., 8 per day, 460ptas); and Sevilla (2hr., 9 per day, 970ptas). **Linesur La Valenciana** buses (tel. 956 37 12 83) roll to Jerez de la Frontera (1hr., departs every hr., 275ptas) from Pl. San Sebastián. Follow C. Larga to reach the perpendicular C. Isaac Peral.

The **tourist office,** Plaza de Andalucía, s/n (tel. 956 37 28 28), dispenses a free map and beach information. To get there, follow C. Larga off C. Peral. (Open M-F 10am-1:30pm and 7-9pm, Sa 11am-1pm.) **Emergency** telephone numbers are 091 and 092. For the **local police** (tel. 956 37 10 88), go to C. Camacho Baños. The **post office,** C. Padre Lerchundi, 15 (tel. 956 37 14 19), is near Pl. Pío XII (open M-F 8:30am-2:30pm, Sa 9:30am-1pm). The **postal code** is 11550.

ACCOMMODATIONS AND FOOD The oligopoly of hostels in Chipiona has conspired against budget travelers. Consider sleeping in Jerez and commuting to the beach. One luxurious option is **Hostal Gran Capitán,** C. Fray Baldomero, 3 (tel. 956 37 09 29; fax 956 37 43 35), off C. Isaac Peral, sporting a charming patio and large rooms with baths and TVs (singles 2500-3500ptas; doubles 4000-5200ptas). The municipal **campground,** El Pinar de Chipiona (tel. 956 37 23 21), on Ctra. Rota at 3km, resides 800m from the beach, with a pool and supermarket (545ptas per person or per tent, 475ptas per car; electricity 450ptas). **Calle Isaac Peral** and the small streets stemming from it are dotted with bars, *heladerías,* and restaurants specializing in non-Spanish cuisine. Eateries also line Po. Cruz del Mar (at the end of C. Isaac Peral) and the area around Pl. Juan Carlos I and Pl. Pío XII. In the latter, try the scrumptious *pan montadito* (mini sandwiches on hot bread, 200ptas) at **El Rincón de Jabugo.** The **mercado,** C. Victor Pradera, is to your left as you exit Los Amarillos bus station (open M-Sa 9am-2pm).

■ Arcos de la Frontera

The road to Arcos de la Frontera (pop. 28,000) snakes through sunflower fields and sherry vineyards. The Spanish novelist Azorín best captures the town: "Imagine a long, narrow ridge, undulating; place on it little white houses, clustered among others more ancient; imagine that both sides of the mountain have been cut away, dropping downward sheer and straight; and at the foot of this wall a slow, silent river, its murky waters licking the yellowish stone, then going on its destructive course through the fields...and when you have imagined all this, you will have but a pale image of Arcos." The premier *pueblo blanco* on the *ruta de los pueblos blancos* (route of the white villages), with Roman ruins and castles at every turn, Arcos itself is in essence a historic monument.

ORIENTATION AND PRACTICAL INFORMATION

Arcos perches about 30km east of Jerez on the road toward Antequera. To reach the town center from the **bus station,** exit left, turn left, and then continue uphill along C. Muñoz Vásquez. Walk for about 20 minutes; the street eventually turns into **Calle Debajo del Corral,** which becomes **Calle de Corredera,** which then turns into

ANDALUCÍA

Cuesta de Belén and **Calle de Dean Espinosa** (also known as Callejón de las Monjas) as it reaches the old quarter. The **tourist office** is one block to the right in the magnificent **Plaza de Cabildo**. Mini-buses run every 30 minutes from the bus station to C. Corredera (100ptas); a taxi there costs 500ptas.

Buses: C. Corregidores. **Transportes Generales Comes** (tel. 956 70 20 15) to: Jerez (7 per day, 280ptas); Cádiz (1½hr., 6 per day, 670ptas); Ronda (1¾hr., 4 per day, 950ptas); Costa del Sol (3-4hr., 1 per day, 1535-2060ptas, depending on destination). **Los Amarillos** (tel. 956 70 02 57) to Jerez de la Frontera (15min., departs every 30min., 295ptas) and Sevilla (2hr., 2 per day, 905ptas). Fewer on weekends.

Taxis: (tel. 956 70 13 55 or 956 70 00 66).

Tourist Office: (tel. 956 70 22 64; fax 956 70 09 00), on Pl. Cabildo. General info and detailed free map of the old city. Hard-to-read 100ptas **map** of the whole town. Open in summer M-Sa 10am-2pm and 5-8pm, Su 11am-2pm; in winter M-Sa 9am-2pm and 5-7pm. They also offer informative tours of the old city and traditional patios. 400ptas, children free. Tours M-Sa 10:30am, noon, 5, and 6:30pm, Su noon.

Emergency: dial 091 or 092. **Police:** (tel. 956 70 16 52), on C. Nueva. **Guardia Civil:** tel. 956 70 00 52.

Medical Emergency: tel. 956 70 04 98.

Post Office: (tel. 956 70 15 60), on Pl. Boliches, parallel to C. Corredera. Open M-F 8:30am-2:30pm, Sa 9:30am-1pm. **Postal Code:** 11630.

ACCOMMODATIONS AND FOOD

Arcos has only a few budget hostels; call ahead during Semana Santa and in the summer to be safe. Restaurants huddle at the bottom end of C. Corredera, while *tapas* heaven is perched uphill in the old quarter.

Hostal Callejón de las Monjas, C. Dean Espinosa, 4 (a.k.a. Callejón de las Monjas; tel. 956 70 23 02), in the old quarter behind Iglesia de Santa María. Roomy, with fans or A/C; some with TV. The upstairs room has its own terrace. Singles 3500-4500ptas; doubles 3500ptas, with bath 4500ptas. Visa.

Bar-Restaurant-Hostal San Marcos, C. Marqués de Torresoto, 6 (tel. 956 70 07 21), past C. Dean Espinosa and Pl. Cabildo. Friendly young owner and his family run this new establishment crowned with a scenic rooftop terrace. Clean rooms, private baths. Singles 3000ptas; doubles 4000ptas. Home-cooked *menú* 900ptas.

Los Faraones, C. Debajo del Corral, 8 (tel. 956 70 06 12), downhill from C. Corredera. An Egyptian-Spanish couple serves Arab cuisine along with some Spanish staples. Extensive **vegetarian** menu includes couscous and yummy baklava (100ptas). *Menú del día* 800ptas. Huge *bocadillo de falafel* 400ptas (ask for it since it is not on the menu). Belly dancing for groups; arrange in advance. A/C. Open M 8am-5:30pm, Tu-Su 8am-5:30pm and 8pm-12:30am.

Bar Típico Alcaraván, C. Nueva, 1 (tel. 956 70 33 97). Take C. Nueva down from Pl. Cabildo. In a beautiful cave carved into a mountain 900 years ago. Popular nighttime hangout. *Tapas* from 250ptas. Open Tu-Su 11am-3pm and 8pm-1am.

SIGHTS

The most beautiful sights might just be the winding white alleys, Roman ruins, and hanging flowers of the old quarter, or the view from **Plaza Cabildo.** The plazas earned the nickname *Balcón de Coño* because the view's so startling that people exclaim, *"¡Coño!"* (damn or wow). In this square stands the **Iglesia de Santa María,** a mix of Baroque, Renaissance, and Gothic styles, built in 1553. Its most impressive attribute is the well-preserved wall painting from the 14th century. A symbol of the Inquisition is still etched into the ground near the church's left side. The late Gothic **Iglesia de San Pedro** was built on the site of an old Arab fortress in the northern edge of the old quarter. Some Murillos, Zurbaráns, Riberas, and Pachecos decorate the interior. *(Both churches open daily 10am-1pm and 4-7pm. 150ptas.)*

An artificial **lake** laps at Arcos's feet, its gentle waters beckoning over-heated travelers to take a dip, especially at Porto Alegre, a beach-like strip of the lake. Urban buses descend to **Mesón de la Molinera,** the beach (4 per day, more in summer, 100ptas). The incongruous **Mississippi Paddle Boat** (tel. 956 70 80 02) cruises around the lake on weekends at 5pm. *(250ptas.)* For further information on water sports at the lake, call the **Oficina de Deportes** (tel. 956 70 30 11).

Bornos, a hillside hamlet 11km to the northeast, is the next town along the *ruta de los pueblos blancos.* **Buses** for Bornos are run by both Comes and Los Amarillos from the bus station (20min., 12 per day, 145ptas). To swim in its freshwater lake, walk across town (15min.) and climb down the hill.

Festivals in Arcos are highly spirited. A favorite is the **Toro de Aleluya,** held on the last Sunday of Semana Santa. Two bulls run rampant through the steep, cobbled streets as residents drink and dance the flamenco.

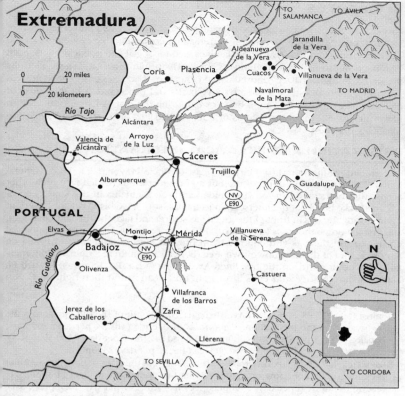

Extremadura

The aptly named Extremadura is a land of harsh beauty and cruel extremes. Arid plains bake under intense summer sun, relieved by scattered patches of glowing sunflowers. These lands hardened New World conquistadors such as Hernán Cortés and Francisco Pizarro, and although Cortés and Pizarro never returned home, they patterned the cities they founded after Extremaduran plazas.

Extremeños continue to struggle in one of the more economically depressed regions of Spain. Even the tourist industry is undernourished; although brochures and street maps are more readily available than they once were, offices are often understaffed or unexpectedly closed. Tourists are a rare breed in the smaller towns of Extremadura—the Roman ruins of Mérida attract most of the region's visitors.

Traditional Extremaduran cuisine comes from the wild. Tempting specialties include rabbit, partridge, lizard with green sauce, wild pigeon with herbs, and *faisán a la Alcántara* (pheasant with a truffle and port wine sauce). *Extremeño* soups are also scrumptious. *Cocido* (chick pea stew) warms in winter, while the many varieties of gazpacho (including an unusual white one) cool in the summer.

🐌 HIGHLIGHTS OF EXTREMADURA

- The awesome **Roman ruins** at Mérida (see p. 508).
- The glowing whitewashed walls of the **pueblos blancos** (see p. 511).

■ Cáceres

Founded by Romans in 34 BC, the thriving provincial capital and university town of Cáceres (pop. 80,000) is the closest Extremadura comes to a big city. Between the 14th and 16th centuries, rival noble families vied for social and political status, each building a miniature palace to glorify its image. The resulting old city is a wonderfully preserved jumble of palaces, museums, and churches. Cáceres's newer areas are less interesting, although they boast attractive parks and plazas plus a healthy dose of nightlife. The city makes a good base for exploring the rest of Extremadura. From here you can enter Portugal by bus or train via Badajoz, or by train via Valença de Alcántara, due west.

ORIENTATION AND PRACTICAL INFORMATION

The **ciudad monumental** (old city) lies east of **Plaza Mayor** (a.k.a. Plaza General Mola). The plaza is 3km north of the **bus** and **train stations,** which face each other across the intersection of Av. Hispanidad and Av. Alemania in the south end of Cáceres. Take bus #1 at the intersection to the last stop, Pl. Obispo Galarza. Go right upon exiting the bus in front of the green gas station and take the first left, first right, and first left down the steps to Pl. Mayor. Bus #2 stops on Av. Hispanidad, around the corner to the right as you emerge from the bus station, and runs to **Plaza de América,** hub of the new downtown area (80ptas). From there, "Ciudad Monumental" signs point north up the tree-lined Av. España (a.k.a. Po. Canovas) toward Pl. Mayor. When the *avenida* ends, bear right on C. San Antón then right on C. San Pedro.

Trains: (tel. 927 23 37 61), on Av. Alemania, 3km south of the old city across the highway from the bus station. *Regionales* to: Mérida (1hr., 4 per day, 500ptas); Badajoz (2hr., 3 per day, 980-1800ptas); Madrid (4½hr., 5 per day, 2300-3925ptas); Lisbon (6hr., 1 per day, 4475ptas); Sevilla (4hr., 1 per day, 2300ptas).

Buses: (tel. 927 23 25 50), on Ctra. Sevilla, across from the train station 3km south of the old city. Info window open M-F 7:30am-11:30pm, Sa-Su 8:30am-11:30pm. To: Madrid (4-5hr., 7-8 per day, 2390ptas); Sevilla (4hr., 5-7 per day, 2250ptas); Salamanca (4hr., 3-6 per day, 1695ptas); Badajoz (1½hr., 2 per day, 825-1085ptas); Mérida (1hr., 2-3 per day, 675ptas); Trujillo (45min., 6-10 per day, 385ptas); Valencia de Alcántara (2½hr., 2 per day, 940ptas); Valladolid (5½hr., 3-4 per day, 2670ptas). Fewer buses on weekends.

Taxis: Stands at Pl. Mayor and bus and train stations. **Radio Taxi** (tel. 927 23 23 23).

Car Rental: Hertz, Av. Virgen de Guadalupe, 3 (tel. 927 22 43 45).

Tourist Office: Pl. Mayor, 10 (tel. 927 24 63 47), on the east side of the plaza to the right of the steps. No English spoken. Open in summer M-F 9am-2pm and 5-7:30pm, Sa-Su 9:15am-2pm; in winter M-F 9am-2pm and 4-6:30pm, Sa-Su 9:15am-2pm. The **Patronato de Tourismo,** in Casa de Carva (tel. 927 25 55 97), within the old city, has good maps of the monuments (same hours).

Currency Exchange: Banks line Av. España and the streets leading to Pl. Mayor.

Luggage Storage: At the train station (400ptas per day) and bus station (75ptas per item per day).

Emergency: dial 091. **Police: Municipal** (tel. 927 24 84 24), C. General Margallo.

Late-Night Pharmacy: Four lie in Pl. Mayor, all with the *farmacias de guardia* (late-night pharmacies) list posted in window.

Hospital: Hospital Provincial (tel. 927 25 68 00).

Post Office: C. Miguel Primo de Rivera (tel. 927 22 50 71), off Av. España on the left from Pl. América (look for the *Caja Postal Argentaria* sign). Open for stamps and Lista de Correos M-F 8:30am-8:30pm, Sa 9:30am-2pm. **Postal Code:** 10071.

ACCOMMODATIONS

Hostales and *pensiones* line Pl. Mayor and are scattered throughout the new city. Call ahead for stays on summer weekends.

Pensión Carretero, Pl. Mayor, 22 (tel. 927 24 74 82), opposite the tourist office. High ceilings and low beds. TV Lounge. Singles 2000ptas, with sink 2500ptas; doubles 3000ptas; triples 4500ptas; quads 6000ptas. No winter heating. Visa, MC.

Hostal Residencia Almonte, C. Gil Cordero, 6 (tel. 927 24 09 25), 15min. south of Pl. Mayor, off Pl. América. A 90-room monster with luxuries in every room: full bath, TV, phone, fluffy towel, and firm bed. The fan even oscillates! Parking garage. Singles 2700ptas; doubles 4200ptas; triples 5250ptas.

Pensión Marquez, Gabriel y Galán, 2 (tel. 927 24 99 60), off Pl. Mayor, opposite the Ayuntamiento. Cheap and central, Marquez has colorful bed spreads and slanted walls. Singles 1500ptas; doubles 2500ptas, with TV 3000ptas. No winter heating.

Camping: Ciudad de Cáceres, Ctra. Nacional, 630, km 549.6 (tel. 972 23 04 03 or 972 23 01 30). First-class site just outside of Cáceres. 450ptas per person, per tent, and per car. Children 425ptas.

FOOD

Like any Pl. Mayor worthy of the name, the one in Cáceres is full of restaurants and cafes with *terrazas* ready to wine and dine the populace with cheap *bocadillos, raciones* (300-600ptas), and *menús* (900-1200ptas). For **groceries,** there's always **Super Spar,** C. Parras, 4, at the junction of C. San Antón and C. San Pedro (open M-F 9:30am-2pm and 6-8:30pm, Sa 9:30am-2pm).

El Toro, C. General Ezponda (tel. 972 22 90 34), just off Pl. Mayor. Yuppified Spanish cuisine in an attractive pastel setting, complete with cow brands on the wall. Salads 350-500ptas. Entrees 500-2000ptas. *Menú* 1200 or 1800ptas. Open Tu-Su.

Pizza Queen, Pl. Mayor, 6 (tel. 927 24 85 31), near the tourist office. Escape the touristy cafes for some cheap grub. Pasta 470-500ptas. Pizza slices from 195ptas. Open Su-Th 1-4pm and 7pm-1am, F-Sa 1-4pm and 7pm-4am.

SIGHTS AND ENTERTAINMENT

The golden, stork-filled **barrio antiguo** is one of the most heterogeneous architectural ensembles in Europe. Roman, Arabic, Gothic, Renaissance, and even Native American influences (via the conquistadors) have left their mark. The main attraction is the *barrio* as a whole; most edifices unfortunately don't open their doors to tourists.

From Pl. Mayor, the Almohad western wall leads into the old city. A jumble of mansions crowds the inside of the walls, each emblazoned with a different family crest. The most famous is the 16th-century **Casa del Sol,** the residence of the Solis family, whose crest has become something of an emblem for the city. It sits on the corner of C. Monja next to the Iglesia de San Mateo. The easily insulted aristocracy usually resolved their disputes through violence, prompting the monarchs to remove all battlements and spires from local lords' houses as punishment. Due to Don Golfín's loyalty to the ruling family, his **Casa y Torre de las Cigueñas** (House and Tower of Storks) was the only one allowed to keep its battlements. Storks nest on its spires every spring. The **Palacio de los Golfines de Arriba** is a Golfín-owned palace near C. Olmos and C. Adarros de Santa Ana. Here, on October 26, 1936, Francisco Franco was proclaimed head of the Spanish state and Generalissimo of its armies. The **Casa de Toledo-Moctezuma,** built by the grandson of the Aztec princess Isabel Moctezuma (Tecuixpo Istlaxochitl), is to the left as you enter the Arco de Estrella.

In front of Arco de la Estrella, **Plaza de Santa María** lies between stone buildings. A statue of San Pedro de Alcántara, one of Extremadura's two patron saints, eyes the plaza from an outside corner pedestal of **Catedral de Santa María.** *(Open daily for mass.*

Free.) His big toes shine because locals rub or kiss them for good luck. The cathedral itself, built between 1229 and 1547, is Romanesque and Gothic, with a Renaissance ceiling. The *retablo mayor* (altarpiece) is in Plateresque style, constructed with pine and cedarwood. Cáceres's nobility is buried beneath the cathedral floor; you can see some of the same crests on the palaces nearby.

Inside the Casa de las Veletas (House of Weathervanes), **Museo de Cáceres** (Museo Arqueológico Provincial; tel. 927 24 72 34) exhibits Celtiberian stone animals, Roman and Visigothic tombstones, an El Greco, and crafts. *(Open Tu-Sa 9am-2:30pm, Su 10:15am-2:30pm. 200ptas, students free.)* The main attraction is the 11th-century Arab *aljibe* (cistern), which supplied Cáceres with water until 1935 and is now a wishing well. Nearby **Convento de San Pablo** is late Gothic eye-candy for architecture buffs.

For **entertainment,** revelers crowd the **Plaza Mayor** and its environs, or stroll along **Avenida de España.** Calle Pizarro is dotted with live-music bars. Later at night, the party moves to the area called **La Madrila** in the new city, near Pl. Albatros.

■ Near Cáceres: Trujillo

Rising high on a granite hill, Trujillo (pop. 10,000) is known as the "Cradle of Conquistadors." Over 600 explorers and plunderers of the New World, including Francisco Pizarro, hailed from here. Romans, Arabs, Spaniards, and Jews thundered through Trujillo in bygone centuries, but the most impressive monuments within the medieval walls date from the 15th and 16th centuries, when wealthy explorers and their families constructed sumptuous residences. Twentieth-century Trujillo residents take pride in the well-preserved beauty of their churches, palace, and castle.

ORIENTATION AND PRACTICAL INFORMATION Trujillo offers access to many nearby cities and towns by **bus,** including Cáceres (45min., 6-10 per day, 385ptas), but there is no train station. The bus station (tel. 927 32 12 02) is on the road to Badajoz at the foot of the hill (look for the **AutoRes** sign). To get to the **Plaza Mayor** (15min.), turn left as you exit the station (up C. Marqués de Albayda). Go up C. Pardos, past the Convento de la Encarnación and the small Pl. Aragón; continue onto C. Romanos and turn right at the end onto C. Parra then left onto C. Carnicería. The **tourist office** (tel. 927 32 26 77) sits across the plaza and posts info in its windows when closed. (Open in summer M-F 9am-2pm and 5-7:30pm; in winter 9am-2pm and 4-6:30pm.) The gift shop three doors down has free maps. **Currency exchange** can be done at **Banco Central Hispano** in the Pl. Mayor. In an **emergency,** dial 091. In **medical emergencies** call 927 32 20 16. The municipal **police** (tel. 927 32 01 08 or 908 70 65 17) sit on Pl. Mayor. The **post office** (tel. 927 32 05 33) shuffles papers on Po. Ruiz de Mendoza; you'll see it as you walk from the station to Pl. Mayor (open M-F 9am-2:30pm, Sa 9:30am-1pm). The **postal code** is 10200.

ACCOMMODATIONS AND FOOD A maze of spacious rooms await at the **Casa Roque,** C. Domingo de Ramos, 30 (tel. 927 32 23 13), off Pl. Mayor to the right of the church. Guests enjoy access to a kitchen, TV lounge, and a patio (watch your head). If no one answers the door, ask at the gift shop three doors to the left of the tourist office. (Singles 2000ptas; doubles 3000ptas, with bath 3500ptas.) **Pensión Boni,** C. Domingo de Ramos, 7 (tel. 927 32 16 04), up the street from the Casa Roque, is also comfortable. (Singles 2000ptas; doubles 3000ptas, with bath 3500ptas; luxury triple with full bath and A/C 5500ptas.)

For a delicious repast, head to **Mesón-Restaurante La Troya,** Pl. Mayor, 8-12 (tel. 927 32 13 64), decorated like a typical Spanish house. The three-course *menú* is 1800ptas. (Open daily 1-4:30pm and 9-11:30pm.) **Nuria's,** Pl. Mayor, 27 (tel. 972 32 09 07), across the plaza, is less expensive, with *bocadillos* for 325-650ptas and *platos combinados* for 700-1100ptas (open daily 1-4pm and 8pm-2am).

Will Work for Booty

Sedate Trujillo probably won't strike you as the sort of town to inspire overseas exploration. For starters, it's landlocked—not the best training ground for budding seafarers. And, considering its small size, you would think much more than water would have to be added for Trujillo to breed so many skilled and adventurous sailors. Economic hardship, however, can be quite a motivating factor. An impoverished region, Extremadura sent a startlingly high percentage of its young men to the New World to make their fortunes. These hardy souls were more often than not sons of impoverished nobility or unemployed soldiers and sailors looking for work after the end of the Reconquista and wars in Italy. Few could resist the fabled allure of New World riches and the chance to make a name for themselves in such a status-conscious society.

Besides the daunting Pizarro (conqueror of the Incas in Peru), tiny Trujillo was the birthplace of a long list of other conquistadors. García de Paredes named Ciudad Trujillo in Venezuela in honor of his hometown; homeboy Orellana "discovered" the Amazon River; Nuflo de Chaves founded Santa Cruz in Bolivia; Francisco de Casas was among the first Spaniards to colonize modern Mexico…and the list goes on. These explorers' legacies, complemented by the town's intriguing architecture and layout, now attract the world to Trujillo—instead of the other way around.

SIGHTS Unlike Cáceres, Trujillo offers plenty of elbow room. The **Plaza Mayor** inspired the plaza built in Cuzco, Perú, after Francisco Pizarro defeated the Incas. Palaces, arched passageways, and one wide flight of steps surround a stone-paved space and central fountain. The **Estatua de Pizarro,** the gift of an American admirer of Pizarro, was erected in 1927 to honor the town's most famous native son. At night the eerie blue-checkered clock tower hovers over the fountain and statue.

Festooned with stork nests, **Iglesia de San Martín** dominates the northeastern corner of the plaza, while a baroque organ dominates the church's interior. *(Evening and Sunday mass not open to the public.)* The church has several historic tombs, but contrary to local lore, Francisco de Orellana, the first European to explore the Amazon, does not rest here. Conquistador graves in Spain are few, and Orellana, like most Spanish explorers, died abroad. Across the street, the seven chimneys of the **Palacio de los Duques de San Carlos** reputedly symbolize the religions conquered by Spaniards in the New World. *(Open daily 10am-1pm and 4:30-6:30pm. 100ptas donation requested.)*

Uphill from the Iglesia de San Martín stands the **Casa-Museo de Pizarro.** *(Open daily 11am-2pm and 4-8pm. 250ptas, seniors and students 100ptas.)* The bottom floor is a reproduction of the living quarters of a 15th-century *hidalgo* (nobleman), and the top floor displays the life and times of Francisco Pizarro. At the top of Trujillo's gentle 517m hill are the spectacular ruins of a 10th-century Arab **castillo.** *(Open daily dawn to dusk. Free.)* Battlements and ramparts offer a view of the unspoiled landscape—the air is thick with swallows, storks, and buzzards. You may also encounter a passel of burros, used as living lawnmowers. Inside the walls lie remnants of the castle's *aljibe* (cistern) and the entrance to the lower-level dungeons. The **Museo de la Coria** (follow the wall down to the left of the *castillo*) explores the historical relationship between Extremadura and Latin America. *(Open Sa-Su 11:30am-2pm. Free.)*

West on C. Ballesteros is the Gothic **Iglesia de Santa María.** *(Open daily 10:30am-2pm and 5-8pm; Su mass 11am. 50ptas.)* Pizarro is said to have been christened at a stone fountain here. According to legend, the giant soldier Diego García de Paredes (known as the "Extremaduran Samson") picked up the fountain at age 11 and carried it to his mother; the giant was buried here after he twisted his ankle and fell to his death. The church's 27-panel Gothic *retablo* at the high altar was painted by master Fernando Gallego. Downhill from Iglesia Santa María lies a reservoir, once used by both the Romans and the Moors as a public bath, watering trough, and reservoir.

■ Near Cáceres: Guadalupe

Two hours east of Trujillo and a four-hour bus ride southwest of Madrid, Guadalupe rests on a mountainside in the Sierra de Guadalupe. Despite the inconvenient location, pilgrims have been coming to Guadalupe since the Miracle of 1300, when the Virgin Mary appeared before a cowherd who was poised to kill and skin one of his cows. She sent him to fetch the local priests, explaining that an image of the holy mother was buried in the ground under the cow's body. This icon had, according to the story, been a gift of Pope Gregory the Great to St. Isidore of Sevilla and had been lost for centuries. In the end the cow was revived, the cowherd fled, the icon was found, and Guadalupe was on the map.

In 1340 at the Battle of Salado, Alfonso XI invoked the Virgin's aid and defeated a superior Muslim army. In gratitude to Mary he commissioned the sumptuous **Real Monasterio de Santa María de Guadalupe.** Later, it became customary to grant licenses for foreign expeditions on the premises. Columbus finalized his contract with Fernando and Isabel here and in the New World he named the present-day island of Turugueira Guadalupe. The Friars moved into the monastery early this century, now home to an ornate Gothic and Mudéjar **cloister,** a **museum** of ecclesiastical finery, a **tesoro** (the monastery received so many donations of precious metals and jewelry that they had to melt them together to save space), and a unique series by the painter Zurbarán. *(Monastery open daily in summer 9:30am-1pm and 3:30-6:30pm; in winter 3:30-6:30pm. 300ptas.)* The icon of the Virgin is the centerpiece. It's made of wood, blackened with age, and cloaked in gold and silver robes. The monastery's **basilica** hulks over Pl. Mayor. The *retablo* was designed by El Greco's son.

Buses run to Cáceres (Empresa Mirat; tel. 927 23 25 50), Madrid (M-F 1 per day; Empresa La Sepulvedana; tel. 927 530 48 00), and Trujillo (M-F 1 per day), but schedules force an overnight stay in Guadalupe. The **tourist office** in the plaza posts info on the door (open Tu-Su 10am-2pm and 5-7pm). **Plaza Mayor** is the place to find a room; you'll have difficulty only during Semana Santa. **Mesón Típico Isabel,** Pl. Santa María Guadalupe, 13 (tel. 927 36 71 26), offers modern rooms with private baths (singles 3000ptas; doubles 4000ptas). The bar serves a toothsome *caldereta* (lamb stew 350ptas; open daily 8:30am-4pm and 11pm-1am). At dreamy **Hostal Cerezo,** Gregorio López, 12 (tel 927 36 73 79), all rooms have baths, and many have nice views. (Singles 2800ptas; doubles 4300ptas; triples 5400ptas. 7% IVA not included. Visa.)

▓ Mérida

If you like Roman ruins, then you'll love Mérida (pop. 60,000), the town with the most ruins in Spain. As a reward for services rendered, Caesar Augustus gave a group of veteran legionnaires a new city in Lusitania, a nation comprising Portugal and part of Spain. The veterans chose a lovely spot surrounded by several hills on the banks of the Río Guadiana and called their new home "Augusta Emerita." Not content to rest on their laurels and itching to gossip with fellow patricians in Sevilla and Salamanca, soldiers built the largest bridge in Lusitania. The nostalgic crew adorned their "little Rome" with baths, aqueducts, temples, a hippodrome, an arena, and a famous amphitheater. Mérida's ruins and world-class Museo Romano merit at least a day's visit. In July and August, the spectacular *Festival de Teatro Clásico* presents some of Europe's finest classical and modern theater and dance, performed among the ruins.

ORIENTATION AND PRACTICAL INFORMATION

Deep in the heart of Extremadura, Mérida is 73km south of Cáceres and 59km east of Badajoz. **Plaza de España,** the town center, is two blocks up from the Puente Romano. From the **bus station,** cross the suspension bridge **(Puente de Lusitania)** in front of the station (it's fun!) and turn right on Av. Guadiana. Walk along the river until you reach the Puente Romano, then turn left on C. Puente, which leads straight into Pl. España (20min.). From the **train station,** walk down C. Cardero, which curves left out of the station, and its continuation, C. Camilo José Cela. Bear right onto C. Felix Valverde Lillo, and follow it to Pl. España (5-10min.).

Trains: (tel. 924 31 81 09), C. Cardero. Info open daily 7am-11pm. To: Cáceres (1hr., 4 per day, 500-1000ptas); Badajoz (1hr., 7 per day, 395-1100ptas); Zafra (1hr., 2 per day, 500ptas); Madrid (4hr., 5 per day, 2840-4000ptas); Sevilla (4½hr., 1 per day, 1825ptas). For trains to Lisbon, transfer in Cáceres (2 per day, 2900ptas).

Buses: (tel. 924 37 14 04), Av. Libertad, in the "Polígono Nueva Ciudad." To: Cáceres (1hr., 2 per day, 675ptas); Badajoz (1hr., 5-10 per day, 610ptas); Zafra (1¼hr., 6-8 per day, 600ptas); Sevilla (3hr., 8-12 per day, 1575-1695ptas); Salamanca (5hr., 4 per day, 2320ptas); Madrid (5½hr., 3 per day, 2720-3725ptas); Valladolid (6hr., 8-10 per day, 3230ptas); Burgos (9hr., 1 per day, 4130ptas); Barcelona (12hr., 1-2 per day, 6420ptas); San Sebastián (13hr., 1 per day, 5840ptas).

Taxis: Teletaxi (24hr. tel. 924 31 57 56). **Radiotaxi** (tel. 924 37 11 11).

Car Rental: Avis (tel. 924 37 33 11 or 909 26 32 32), at the bus station. Mid-sized car 9685ptas per day, 51,565ptas per week. IVA and insurance included.

Tourist Office: (tel. 924 31 53 53), on C. P.M. Plano, across the street from the Museo Romano. From Pl. España, the town center, head up C. Santa Eulalia, which becomes a pedestrian shopping street, then bear right on C. J. Ramon Melida at the little circle with the statue. The tourist office is at the end of the street to the right (10-15min.). Friendly, multilingual staff doles out small maps, theater schedules, and lists of accommodations. Open in summer M-F 9am-1:45pm and 5-7:15pm, Sa-Su 9:15am-1:45pm; in winter M-F 9am-1:45pm and 4-6pm, Sa-Su 9:15am-1:45pm. Get theater tickets at the **Caja Rural de Extremadura,** C. Felix Valerde Lillo, 17 (tel. 924 30 38 24; email festivalmerida@cajarural.com), or at the theater.

Luggage Storage: The bus (100ptas per day) or train station (400ptas per day).

Emergency: call 092 or 091. **Police:** Ayuntamiento, Pl. España, 1 (tel. 924 38 01 00), or at the Comisaría, C. Almendialejo, 48. Police station expected to move in 1999.

Medical Services: Residencia Sanitaria de la Seguridad Social Centralita (tel. 924 38 10 00). **Emergency:** tel. 924 38 10 18.

Post Office: (tel. 924 31 24 58), Pl. Constitución. Follow signs to the *parador;* the office is directly opposite. Open for Lista de Correos M-F 8:30am-8:30pm, Sa 9:30am-1pm. **Postal Code:** 06800.

ACCOMMODATIONS

Mérida attracts many camera-toting tourists; good ol' free market competition makes pleasant, centrally-located budget accommodations easy to come by.

Pensión El Arco, C. Cervantes, 16 (tel. 924 31 83 21 or 924 30 32 70), follow C. Santa Eulalia up from Pl. España; C. Cervantes is on the left. Only 200m from the train station. The gregarious owner of this spotless *pensión* collects mementos from guests; the best is the gallery of signed glossies from kings and queens. Spacious rooms, modern baths, and a free map. Singles 1800ptas; doubles 3000ptas.

Hostal Nueva España, Av. Extremadura, 6 (tel. 924 31 33 56 or 924 31 32 11), a block from the train station, at the end of C. Cardero. A Roman legion could fit in the closets. All rooms with private baths. Singles 2600ptas; doubles 4600ptas; triples 6000ptas (negotiable). Prices drop off-season.

Hostal-Residencia Senero, C. Holguín, 12 (tel. 924 31 72 07), off the winding street to the left of Hotel Emperatriz (on Pl. España). Spanish-tile interior. Clean and comfortable with space-saving baths and some balconies. Rooms overlooking the patio can get a bit hot and stuffy. Singles 2000ptas, with bath 2500ptas; doubles 4000ptas; triples 5100ptas. Cheaper in the off season.

FOOD

Meals and *tapas*—but few budget deals—can be found around **Plaza de España** and **Calle Juan Ramón Melida.** The **market** is on C. San Francisco, in between C. Lillo and Sta. Eulalia (open M-Sa 8am-2pm). The cheapest option is **groceries.** Try **%Día** (open M-F 9:30am-2:30pm and 6-9:30pm, Sa 9:30am-3pm) or **Supervol** (open M-F 9:30am-2:15pm and 6-9pm, Sa 9:30am-2pm) on C. Camilo J. Cela.

Casa Benito, C. San Francisco, 3 (tel. 924 31 55 00), to the left of the market. Admire photos, prints, and posters while sipping a *caña* (beer, 100ptas). *Menú* 1000ptas. Kitchen open daily 1-4pm and 9-11pm; bar open daily and nightly.

Bar-Restaurante Briz, C. Félix Valverde Lillo, 5 (tel. 924 31 93 07). Typical Extremaduran fare. Hefty *menú* (1350ptas) specializing in *callos* (tripe). Frogs 1200ptas.

La Peña (tel. 924 31 10 62), C. San Juan de Dios. Coming up from Pl. Mayor it's the first left after Cafeteria Lusi. African theme-bar with loud jazz or flamenco on the radio and beer for 125ptas. Open daily 1pm-3am. Visa.

Cafeteria Lusi (tel. 924 31 31 11), on a little plaza just behind Pl. España on the Hotel Emperatriz side. The *menú* (990ptas) is uninspired, but it's a popular spot in the evening for people-watching and *tapas*-consuming. Also does well in the breakfast department: *café con leche* or *churros con chocolate* (250ptas).

SIGHTS

Roman Ruins

Roman edifices fall apart beautifully. The road from Cáceres affords the best view of the **Acueducto de los Milagros.** Farther up the river are the **Acueducto de San Lázaro's** three remaining pillars. Over the wide, shallow Río Guadiana, the **Puente Romano,** one of the Romans' largest bridges, is still the main entrance into town.

Mérida's acclaimed **Museo Nacional de Arte Romano** (tel. 924 31 16 90), designed by Rafael Moneo, is an elegant museum with all the Romemorabilia you could ask for: statues, dioramas, coins, remains of wall paintings, and little Roman whistles. *(Open in summer Tu-Sa 10am-2pm and 5-7pm, Su and holidays 10am-2pm; in winter Tu-Sa 10am-2pm and 4-6pm, Su and holidays 10am-2pm. 400ptas, students 200ptas. Saturday afternoons and Sundays free.)* A Roman road passes under and through the museum, and a tour of the **cripta** offers a glimpse of what was Augusta Emerita. To get to the *museo,* follow C. Santa Eulalia from Pl. España and bear right up C. Juan Ramón Melida.

You can buy a **combined ticket** to visit the Teatro Romano, the Anfiteatro Romano, the Casa del Mitreo, the Casa del Anfiteatro, and Alcazaba. *(All open daily in summer 9am-8:30pm; in winter schedules subject to change. Combined ticket 750ptas, E.U. students 375ptas, Saturday afternoons and Sunday mornings free.)* The **Teatro Romano,** a gift from Agrippa to the city, in a park across the street from the museum, was used for political gatherings and as a theater. The audience (seating 6000) faces a *scaenaefrons,* an incredible marble colonnade built upstage. The notion that conquered Greece took captive her own fierce conqueror (Rome) is never more apparent than in the theater—the building could easily be Greek. **Teatro Clásico** performances (tel. 924 31 25 30; staffed daily noon-2pm and 7:30-11:30pm) take place here. *(Performances July-Aug. 10:45pm. Tickets 700-3500ptas.)* The more widely popular entertainment occurred next door in the 16,000-seat **Anfiteatro Romano.** *(Separate admission 600ptas.)* Inaugurated in 8 BC, the *anfiteatro* was used for man-to-man gladiator combat, combat between animals, and (everyone's favorite) contests between men and wild animals. Northeast of the theater complex is the **Circo Romano,** or hippodrome. Take Av. Extremadura through the underpass to the other side of the train tracks. The all-time best Lusitania racer, Diocles, got his start here only to finish in Rome with 1462 victories. Once filled with crazed spectators (capacity 30,000) cheering their favorite charioteers, the arena now resembles a quiet public park.

Casa del Mitreo (down Po. Alvarez with Teatro Romano on left and right on Via Ensarele) and **Casa del Anfiteatro** (to the left of the Anfiteatro) are ruins of Roman Residences. Here, among the solitary columns, you can find some of the world's finest Roman mosaics, including the Casa del Mitreo's **Mosaico Cosmólogico,** depicting the ancient Romans' conception of the world and the forces of nature.

Other Ruins

Down the banks of the Guadiana and near the elegant *terrazas* of Pl. España is the **Alcazaba,** a Moorish fortress built to guard the Roman bridge. The resourceful Moors built it with materials discarded by the Romans and Visigoths. The cistern is filled with river water, but not much else remains—go for a view of the river and Puente Romano. At the end of C. Rambla Mártir Santa Eulalia (from Pl. España, take C. Santa Eulalia and bear left onto the *rambla*) stand the **museo, basílica,** and **iglesia,** all commemorating the martyr Santa Eulalia. *(Museum and basilica open daily in summer 10am-1:45pm and 5-6:45pm; in winter 4-5:45pm. They are part of the combined ticket, see above. Church open during services daily 8:30am and 8pm. Free.)* During the course of repairs to the church in 1990 (which was originally constructed in the 6th century, turned over to the Arabs in 875, and rebuilt in 1230 during the *Reconquista*), ruins and remains built willy-nilly atop one another were discovered: Roman houses dating from the 3rd to 1st centuries BC, a 4th-century necropolis, and a basilica dedicated to Santa Eulalia. You can visit this fascinating mix of leftovers from centuries past, plus a little museum that explains their provenance.

■ Near Mérida: Los Pueblos Blancos

Named for their glowing whitewashed walls, the *pueblos blancos* are a series of tranquil towns in southern Extremadura that warrant a visit from Mérida or Badajoz.

Known as "little Sevilla" for its gaiety and magical beauty, **Zafra** is full of lovely white buildings with iron balconies and delicate tilework. It is home to stunning 17th- and 18th-century mansions, such as the **Casa de los Marqueses de Solanda,** a Renaissance Alcázar (now a *parador de turismo*), and charming plazas. Exiting the bus station, walk down the dusty road straight ahead to get to the town center. Call 924 55 39 07 to confirm bus schedules to Sevilla and Cáceres. Zafra has a **train station** (tel. 924 55 02 15), but it's a hike from town.

Picturesque **Llerena** was an important seat of the Inquisition, the center of the military Orden de Santiago, and a 14th-century frontier town. Now home to a beautiful Pl. Mayor, Llerna is a textbook example of Mudéjar architecture. Buses run from Zafra (1¼hr., 4 per day, 510ptas) and Mérida during the week.

The area around **Jerez de los Caballeros** is regarded as a mysterious prehistoric settlement. Roman inscriptions, funerary stelaes, and mosaics remain from later eras, as does the decorated brick and painted stucco of the 13th-century Knights Templar Castillo Fortaleza. The knights were later put to death in their own church towers. Buses run to and from Zafra (4 per day, 400ptas) and Mérida (1 per day, 950ptas).

Olivenza, founded by the Portuguese Knights Templar, is still rich in the Portuguese Manueline style. Buses run from Badajoz (8 per day, 215ptas).

▓ Badajoz

Badajoz is often a necessary stop en route to or from Portugal. The border is 6km to the west, and Elvas, Portugal, lies 11km beyond. Reputedly very beautiful in the 11th century, the city (pop. 120,000) has suffered from increasing urbanization. Badajoz resisted Franco in one of the Civil War's bloodiest battles but is still recovering from neglect and industrial pollution. For what it's worth, the nightlife is the region's best.

ORIENTATION AND PRACTICAL INFORMATION

Plaza España is the heart of the old town, across the unsightly Guadiana River from the train station. From Pl. España, C. Juan de Rivera leads to **Plaza Libertad** (5min.) and the tourist office. Between Pl. España and Pl. Libertad is **Plaza San Francisco** (next to the bigger **Plaza Minayo**), with the post office, a supermarket, restaurants, and *terrazas*. To get from the train station to the center of town, follow Av. Carolina Coronado straight to the Puente de Palmas, cross the bridge, and go straight on C. Prim and its continuation. Turn left on C. Juan de Rivera for Pl. España, right for Pl.

Libertad (35min.). To Pl. España from the **bus station,** turn left, take a quick right, and then left on C. Damión Tellez Lafuente. It becomes C. Fernando Cazadilla, passes through Pl. Constitución, becoming first Av. Europa and then C. Pedro de Valdivia, and runs uphill to the plaza (20min.).

Flights: Aeropuerto de Badajoz (tel. 924 21 04 00), Carretera Madrid-Lisboa, 10km outside the city. Small national airport services Palma de Mallorca and Tenerife, with **AirEuropa** and **Futuro** terminals.

Trains: (tel. 924 27 11 70), Av. Carolina Coronado. Info open daily 6am-9pm. To: Madrid (5hr., 2 per day, 4100ptas); Barcelona (2 per day, 8100ptas); Mérida (1½hr., 5-7 per day, 395-1000ptas); Cáceres (2½hr., 3 per day, 820-1600ptas); Lisbon (5½hr., 2 per day, 2530ptas); Zafra (1-2 per day via Mérida, 895ptas).

Buses: C. José Rebollo López, 2 (tel. 924 25 86 61). Info open daily 7:45am-9pm. To: Zafra (1hr., 5-8 per day, 745ptas); Mérida (1½hr., 4 per day, 610ptas); Cáceres (1½hr., 2 per day, 1000ptas); Madrid (4hr., 8 per day, 3200ptas); Sevilla (4½hr., 4 per day, 1670ptas, round-trip 2965ptas); Salamanca (5½hr., 2 per day, 2900ptas); Lisbon (6hr., 4-6 per day, 3000ptas).

Public Transportation: Buses (90ptas). Bus #1 (departs every 30min.) runs from train station to Pl. Libertad; buses #4, 6a, and 6b run between the bus station, Pl. Libertad, and the train station.

Taxis: At bus and train stations and Pl. España. **Radio-Taxi** (24hr. tel. 924 24 31 01).

Tourist Office: Pl. Libertad, 3 (tel. 924 22 27 63). City maps and glossy brochures. Staff helps with lodgings. Open M-F 9am-2pm and 5-7:30pm, Sa-Su 9am-2pm.

Luggage Storage: In the bus station (50ptas per item) and train station (400ptas).

Emergency: call 091. **Police:** (tel. 924 23 02 53), Av. Ramón y Cajal.

Hospital: Hospital Provincial, Pl. Minayo, 2 (tel. 924 22 47 43).

Post Office: (tel. 924 22 02 04), Po. San Francisco. Main entrance on Pl. San Francisco. Open for stamps and Lista de Correos M-F 8:30am-8:30pm, Sa 9am-2pm. **Postal Code:** 06001.

ACCOMMODATIONS AND FOOD

Most *hostales* are near **Plaza España.** For cafes and restaurants, check around **Plazas España, Libertad,** and especially **San Francisco. Simago,** next to the post office on Pl. San Francisco, is a grocery store (open M-Sa 9am-8:30pm; Visa).

Hostal Niza II, C. Arco-Agüero, 45 (tel. 924 22 38 81). Big solid beds, large rooms, and lofty ceilings. In the heart of the open-air party described below in **Sights and Entertainment;** on weekends, try an interior room and/or pillow over the head to block out revelry. Singles 1640ptas; doubles 3000ptas; triples 4500ptas. Visa, MC.

Hostal Victoria, C. Luís de Camoes, 3 (tel. 924 27 16 62), a 2min. walk down the boulevard from the train station, on a quiet street to your left. Small, modern rooms with A/C (when the powers that be turn it on) and phones. Lounge and doubles have TV. Singles 1928ptas, with shower 2500ptas; doubles with bath 4280ptas.

Café Bar La Ría, Pl. España, 7 (tel. 924 22 20 05). A popular hangout, central and cheap. Tasty and large entree (425-1600ptas). *Menú* 980ptas. Intimate *comedor* (dining room). A/C. Open W-M 8am-1am.

El Tronco, C. Muñoz Torrero, 16 (tel. 924 22 20 76), off Pl. España. Yellow on the outside, white stucco on the inside (Bananarama?). Typical Extremaduran fare (tasty *menú* for 850ptas). Open W-M.

SIGHTS AND ENTERTAINMENT

Badajoz recently inaugurated its **Museo Extremeño e Iberoamericano de Arte Contemporáneo** (tel. 924 26 03 84), a cylindrical-architectural wonder. *(Open in summer Tu-Su 10:30am-1:30pm and 6-9pm; in winter Tu-Su 10:30am-1:30pm and 5-8pm. Free.)* Its five floors exhibit recent works from Spain, Portugal, and Latin America, including a few controversial creations like Marta María Pérez Bravo's photograph of a woman's breasts as a communion offering. The museum also sponsors free cultural events.

While the newer parts of Badajoz tend to be loud and concrete, the old city is pleasant, especially in the older neighborhoods around **Plaza de España.** Visit the 13th-century **cathedral** in the Plaza, or stroll through nearby **Plaza de San Francisco.** The neighborhood gets progressively more run down as you walk farther uphill from the two plazas. The ruins of the **Alcazaba** are at the top. *(Open Tu-Su 10am-3pm. 200ptas, E.U. citizens, students, and under 21 free.)* To get there follow the road leading uphill, parallel to the highway, from the Puerta de Palma; the road runs into C. San Antón, which leads to the right to the main entrance. Nearby is the **Torre del Apéndiz,** nicknamed Torre de Espantaperros ("to shoo away Christian dogs"), which served as the Alcazaba's watchtower. At the top sits the simple and informative **Museo Arqueológico Provincial** (tel. 924 22 23 14); its prehistoric collection is a marvel.

Nightlife spills out from the bars and fills several blocks of the *centro;* the fun-lovers come from kilometers around, even Portugal, to partake. The tourist office has a *"tapas* route" listed in its *Guía de Servicios.* **Calle de San Blas,** off Pl. Mayor, is wriggling with teens passing around *minis* (large glasses) of *cerveza* or *sidra* (325ptas). **Calle de Zurbarán,** off Pl. Mayor, is wall-to-wall with 20-somethings.

Islas Canarias

From the snowy peak of Mount Teide to the fiery volcanic spectacle of Timanfaya, the Canary Islands have enchanted humanity since the time of the ancient Egyptians. Homer and Herodotus referred to their gardens of great beauty, and the lost civilization of Atlantis was said to have left behind these seven islands when it sank into the ocean. Now it is the Canaries' perfect weather (a spring-like 20-24°C year-round) that attracts the attention of millions of Europeans with a do-or-die sense of beach urgency. But beyond perfect beaches, it is the spectacular geographical contrasts that lend the Canaries their magic. Lush, fertile valleys climb into snow-covered mountain tops, golden dunes fall into the clear, blue ocean water, and molten rock fades into pale green hillsides. With advance planning, traveling to the Fortunate Isles, as the Canaries are so called, does not have to be prohibitively expensive. The only difficult part is ensuring you end up where you intended to be, as several regions, islands, and cities bear remarkably similar names.

The Canary Islands were once inhabited by Guanches—light-skinned cave dwellers who practiced a complicated death ritual that included mummification. How these Stone Age peoples, unfamiliar with the art of navigation, ever reached the islands remains a mystery. One theory considers the Guanches to be descendants of people who came over from Egypt during the time of the pharaohs. Using clubs and sheer valor, the Guanches delayed Spanish conquest of the islands for nearly a century. Even today, remnants of Guanche culture still remain: *Lucha canaria* (Canarian wrestling), *gofio* (a grain staple used in many local dishes), and place names such as Tenerife, Timanfaya, and Doramas.

After the Spanish conquest in the 15th century, the economy of the islands boomed with both sugar and wine production. As the Spaniards set their eyes beyond the horizon to the New World, the Canary Islands served as an important base for their colonization of the Americas. Their role as a bridge between Old and New Worlds has engendered in the Canaries a cultural mix that is most pronounced in the people themselves. Canarios watch Spanish television and eat Spanish food, but their spoken Spanish resembles that of Cuba and Puerto Rico. Nowadays, a booming tourism industry and approximately seven million annual visitors (mostly northern European tourists) only add to the cultural confusion of these alluring isles.

🌐 HIGHLIGHTS OF ISLAS CANARIAS

- The Saharan sand dunes of **Maspalomas** (see p. 522).
- **El Teide National Park,** the highest mountain in all of Spain (see p. 526).
- **Garajonay National Park** (see p. 528), the world's last living example of a laurisilva forest and an UNESCO World Heritage Site.

■ Getting There and Away

As long as you plan ahead, getting to and from the Canary Islands does not have to be particularly expensive. Located off the southern coast of Morocco, the Canaries make for a long haul by boat (2 days) but a relatively quick flight (2½-3½hr.). Direct flights from Portugal, Morocco, the U.S., and northern Europe are available. **Iberia/Aviaco** (24hr. reservation and info tel. 902 400 500; http://www.iberia.com) has frequent flights from Madrid, Barcelona, and elsewhere in Spain to the islands of Gran Canaria, Tenerife, and Lanzarote. A standard round-trip ticket costs between 70,000 and 80,000ptas (about US$450-$550), but youth and other discounts of up to 50% are often available (ask about the *Fin de Semana* and *Estrella* options). **Air Europa** (24hr. reservation and info tel. 902 24 00 42) flies from Madrid and Barcelona to Gran Canaria, Tenerife, and Lanzarote

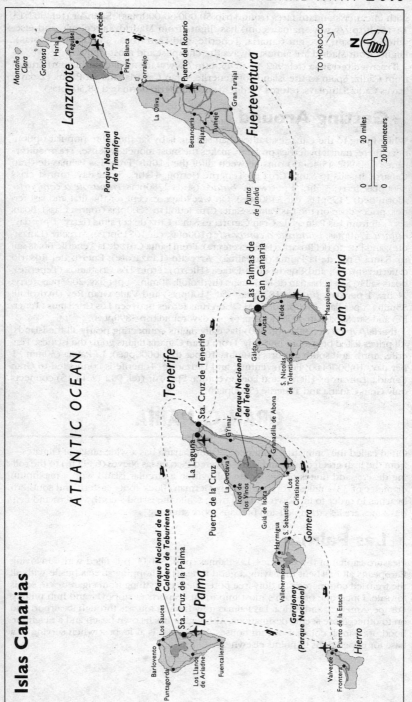

Islas Canarias

ATLANTIC OCEAN

TO MOROCCO

Montaña Clara
Graciosa
Haria
Teguise
Arrecife
Lanzarote
Parque Nacional de Timanfaya
Playa Blanca
Corralejo
Puerto del Rosario
La Oliva
Gran Tarajal
Betancuria
Pájara
Tuineje
Fuerteventura
Punta de Jandía

Las Palmas de Gran Canaria
Gran Canaria
Teide
Maspalomas
Gáldar
Arucas
S. Nicolás de Tolentino

Tenerife
Sta. Cruz de Tenerife
Parque Nacional del Teide
La Laguna
G Ymar
Puerto de la Cruz
La Orotava
Icod de los Vinos
Granadilla de Abona
Guía de Isora
Los Cristianos

La Palma
Parque Nacional de la Caldera de Taburiente
Sta. Cruz de la Palma
Barlovento
Los Sauces
Puntagorda
Los Llanos de Aridane
Fuencaliente

Gomera
Hermigua
S. Sebastián
Vallehermoso
Garajonay (Parque Nacional)

Hierro
Valverde
Frontera
Puerto de la Estaca

20 miles
20 kilometers

with cheaper standard fares (round-trip 50,000-60,000ptas). **SpanAir** (tel. 902 13 14 15; http://www.spainair.com) has flights from Madrid, Barcelona, and elsewhere in Spain to Gran Canaria, Tenerife, and Lanzarote (35,000-50,000ptas). Flights from Madrid are almost always the cheapest and most frequent.

Trasmediterránea (tel. 902 45 46 45; http://www.trasmediterranea.com) cruises from Cádiz, Spain to the islands of Tenerife, Gran Canaria, and La Palma (2 days, leaves Cádiz Saturdays, returns Wednesdays, round-trip dorm bed 58,500ptas).

■ Getting Around

While flying to the Canaries, rather than sailing, is by far the more popular option, once there, transit by ferries probably makes the most monetary sense. **Trasmediterránea** (tel. 902 45 46 45) runs between all of the islands. From Las Palmas de Gran Canaria, it sails to Santa Cruz de Tenerife (jetfoil: 1¼hr., 5 per day, tourist class 5800ptas; ferry: 3½hr., 4 per week, *butaca* (seat) 2780ptas, *camarote a compartir* (dorm bed) 3195ptas, car 3480ptas). On weekdays, except for the first and last ferries, prices drop on the Las Palmas-Santa Cruz jetfoil to 3600ptas (tourist class). Boats also sail from Las Palmas de Gran Canaria to Santa Cruz de la Palma (ferry: 1 per day, *butaca* 4740ptas, *camarote a compartir* 6100ptas, car 10815ptas); Arrecife (Lanzarote); and Puerto del Rosario (Fuerteventura). From Santa Cruz de la Tenerife boats sail to: Santa Cruz de la Palma (La Palma); Arrecife (Lanzarote); Puerto del Rosario (Fuerteventura); and Puerto de la Estaca (Hierro). From Los Cristianos (Tenerife), boats sail to San Sebastián de la Gomera (hydrofoil: 40min., 4 per day, 2023ptas; ferry: 1½hr., 1 per day, *butaca* 1873ptas, car 3100ptas) and Valle Gran Rey (hydrofoil: 55min., 3 per day, 4500ptas). **Fred Olson** runs ferries between Los Cristianos (Tenerife) and San Sebastián de la Gomera (4 per day, round-trip 3890ptas).

Iberia/Aviaco (tel. 902 400 500) has daily flights connecting nearly all the islands. All prices listed below are one way. From Gran Canaria flights go to the islands: Tenerife, north and south airports (30min., 10 per day, 6000ptas); La Palma (30min., 1 per day, 10,000ptas); Fuerteventura; and Lanzarote. Tenerife is connected to Gran Canaria, Lanzarote, Hierro, and Fuerteventura. **SpanAir** (tel. 902 13 14 15) connects only Gran Canaria and Tenerife (5000ptas).

GRAN CANARIA

Often called the "miniature continent," Gran Canaria has a wide range of climates—from the lush green center and snow-covered Pico de las Nieves (6395 ft.) to the rolling desert sand dunes of the south—all within a circular island with a maximum diameter of 33½ miles. Tourists (mostly German) flock to its eastern and southern beaches in order to lie down and roll over, while the island's northwestern and central zones are less trampled and perhaps more stunning.

■ Las Palmas

Pleasure capital of the Canaries, Las Palmas (pop. 350,000) is filled with fun-loving Europeans all hell-bent on having a good time. The shopping streets bustle with all the frenzied commerce of a duty-free port where everything from cigarettes to sex is for sale. Once one of Spain's most important seaports, a stopover and hub uniting Europe, America, and Africa, Las Palmas now funnels tourists through its airport and on to other, more scenic destinations. Although it has its own beach and a neighborhood of Spanish colonial dream houses, Las Palmas is at its best when serving as a base for expeditions to points elsewhere.

ISLAS CANARIAS

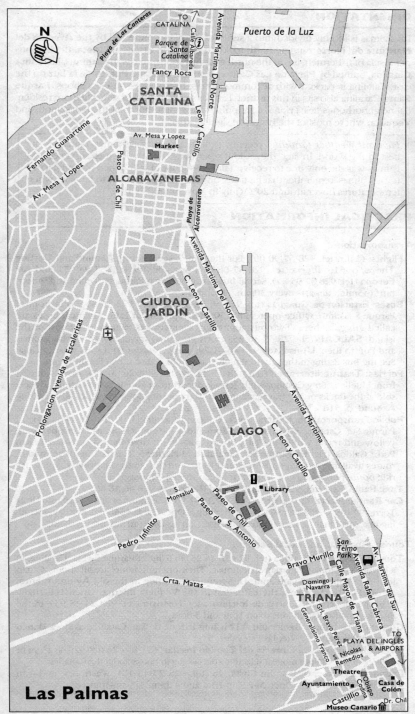

Las Palmas

ORIENTATION

Las Palmas is loosely divided into a series of districts, connected by the **Avenida del Marítima del Norte** running north to south along the east coast. **Isleta,** the bulbous peninsula of fishermen, lies at the north end. Just south, across the isthmus, lies **Santa Catalina,** framed by **Playa de Las Canteras** on the west and **Puerto de la Luz** on the east; Catalina is packed with accommodations, bars, discos, and sex shops. **Parque Santa Catalina** also sits in this district. Farther south through a series of more residential neighborhoods lies **Triana,** a shopping district and home of the bus station, and **Vequeta,** where most of the historical sights gather.

> *Pleasant Weather Rankings* recently proclaimed that Las Palmas' climate is the best in the world. In fact, they said it's perfect—of the 600 cities surveyed, Las Palmas was the only one to receive a flawless score of 100. When planning a trip to Las Palmas, remember that high season runs from December to January, when temperatures hover around 20°C (July to November 23-24°C).

PRACTICAL INFORMATION

Transportation

Flights: (24hr. tel. 928 57 90 00). For flight info, see **Getting Around** and **Getting There,** p. 516. **Iberia** (tel. 928 37 08 77), **Spanair** (tel. 928 57 94 07), and **Air Europa** (tel. 928 57 95 84). Saccai **buses** run between Parque S. Telmo and the airport (45min., departs every 30min., 230ptas).

Buses: Estacion de Guaguas (tel. 928 36 83 35; info tel. 928 36 86 35) in front of Parque S. Telmo. Office open M-F 6:30am-8:30pm. As in Latin America, buses are called *guaguas* here. Two bus companies connect Las Palmas to the rest of the island. **SALCAI** (tel. 928 37 36 25; green *guaguas*) travels south to Maspalomas and Puerto Rico. **Utinsa** (tel. 928 36 01 79; orange *guaguas*) travels west to Guia. See the bus listing in the city to which you would like to travel for more info.

Ferries: Trasmediterránea (tel. 928 47 44 39; fax 928 26 30 77). Ferries depart from Muelle León y Castillo, while Jetfoils depart from Muelle Santa Catlina. Tickets sold at the docks or any travel agency. For ferry destinations and times, see **Getting Around,** p. 516.

Public Transportation: Central office, C. León y Castillo, 330 (tel. 928 44 64 99), off Parque Sta. Catalina. Open M-F 8am-2pm and 4-7:30pm. **Guaguas Municipales** are yellow and travel within the city. Bus #1 runs 24hr. from Puerto de la Luz-Teatro Perez Galdós, passing Parque Sta. Catalina and Parque S. Telmo. Complete **map** of routes available at *guagua* offices and tourist offices. Individual ride 125ptas. 10-ride *bono,* purchased at *estancos* (tobacco shops) 745ptas.

Taxi: Radio Taxi (tel. 928 46 22 12). **Taxi Radio** (tel. 928 46 56 66).

Car Rental: Hertz, at the airport (tel. 928 57 95 77), another at C. Bernardo de la Torre, 94 (tel. 928 22 64 97), in the new city. Opel Corsa 4650ptas per day, including tax, insurance, and unlimited mileage. Can be taken to any other island.

Tourist, Financial, and Local Services

Tourist Offices: Main office (tel. 928 26 46 23) in front of Parque de Sta. Catalina, in a beautiful colonial Canarian-style house. Their opening hours are all about "Canaries time." Open M-F 9am-2pm. Less-frequented office in the **old Ayuntamiento,** across Pl. Sta. Ana from the cathedral in the Vequeta district. Open M-F 10am-5:30pm. Or try the **Centro de Iniciaturas y Turismo** (tel. 928 24 35 93), in the Pueblo Canario. Open M-F 10am-1pm and 5-8pm.

Currency Exchange: Banks and **ATMs** hug Parque de Sta. Catalina, as does **Banco Central Hispano,** C. Nicolás Estévelez, 5.

English Bookstore: La Librería del Cabildo Insular, C. Cano, 24 (tel. 928 38 15 94 or 928 38 15 39), offers a modest selection specializing in books about the Canaries.

Laundry: Lavesec, C. Joaquín Costa, 46 (tel. 928 27 46 17). Wash, dry, and iron 1000ptas (up to 7kg). Open M-F 9am-1pm and 4-8pm, Sa 9am-3pm.

Emergency and Communications

Emergency: call 091 or 092. **Police: Policía Municipal** (tel. 928 26 05 51), Parque Sta. Catalina. **Policía Nacional,** C. Dr. Miguel Rosa, 25 (tel. 928 26 16 71).

Hospitals: Hospital Insular, Pl. Dr. Pasteur, s/n (tel. 928 44 40 00). **Nuestra Señora del Pino,** Angel Guinerá, 93 (tel. 928 44 10 00). **Ambulance:** (tel. 928 24 50 23).

Post Office: Main Office, Av. Primero de Mayo, 62 (tel. 928 36 13 20). Open M-F 8:30am-8:30pm, Sa 9:30am-2:30pm. **Branch Office,** C. Nicolás Estevanez. Open M-F 8:30am-7:30pm, Sa 9:30am-1pm. **Postal Code:** 35007.

ACCOMMODATIONS

There are more beds for visitors to Gran Canaria than there are residents of Las Palmas, but apparently that's not enough. It is very difficult to find a place to stay without advance notice and nearly impossible during high season (Dec.-Feb., especially during *Carnaval*). All the same, Las Palmas probably has the cheapest accommodations on the island.

Unless you're traveling alone, renting an **apartment** is the most economical way to spend time on the island. Some require a minimum stay of five to seven days. Apartments are rated on "keys" (1-4). Most one- and two-key apartments in Las Palmas do not require reservations more than a week in advance. Two beds, a bathroom, a kitchen, and some furniture are standard in all apartments. Las Palmas' plentiful **two-key apartments** cost from 4000 to 7500ptas per night depending on length of stay and proximity to the beach. There's almost always a complex somewhere with room available, but unlike hostels, the owners don't necessarily wait around to see if a new client is going to pop in, so call ahead (*days* ahead). **One-key apartments** are harder to come by, and their owners are more elusive, but they're *cheap* (2500ptas per night). Because it's a sizeable city, **pensiones** (with no stay requirements) can be found in Las Palmas, but their owners make little effort to impress anybody—even these fill up quickly year-round. Calling a day or two in advance is a good idea.

Hotel Madrid, Pl. Cairasco, 4 (tel. 928 36 06 64; fax 928 38 21 76), in the Triana-Vegueta district, inland from C. Mayor. Entrance through the cafe on the plaza. No sand, but beautiful location and scrumptious rooms verging on luxury. Large TV lounge downstairs. Franco stayed in Room 3 the night before the Civil War began. Singles 3500ptas, with bath; doubles 4500ptas, with bath 5500ptas.

Apartments

Apartamentos Teide (one key), C. Luis Morote, 42 (tel. M-Sa 928 27 23 12 or 928 27 23 08). White and simple rooms with pink and simpler beds. Clean. 2 blocks from Playa Las Canteras. For stays less than 15 days, doubles 2500ptas per night; over 15 days doubles 2000ptas per night. 1-week min. stay.

Apartamentos Bajamar, Venezuela, 34 (tel. 928 37 62 54). In less demand as it's a bit off the main beach activity. Big, bright, comfortable rooms are well furnished. For stays less than 1 week, singles 2600ptas per night; doubles 3400ptas per night. Over a week singles 2000ptas per night; doubles 2300ptas per night. 5-day min. stay.

Hostels, Pensiones, and Camping

Pensión Plaza, Luis Morote, 16 (tel. 928 26 52 12). Red building facing Parque Sta. Catalina. This place is mellow, but the Parque gets rambunctious at night. Cool, simple, and comfortable rooms. Singles 1700ptas, with bath 2200 ptas; doubles 2700ptas, with bath 3200ptas. Reception 24hr.

Pensión Viera, Pedro Castillo, 9 (tel. 928 26 96 01). Intersects the isthmus, connecting beach to port. The *pensión* is a block from Las Canteras. Nothing glamorous, but rooms are ample and all have baths and a new paint job. Singles with bath 1800ptas; doubles with bath 2500ptas.

Pensión Pacífico, Sargento Llagas, 10 (tel. 928 26 51 65). One block from the beach, directly west of Parque Sta. Catalina. Rooms are small, some don't have windows, and the neighbors and neighborhood are noisy. But friendly and funny owners and low prices may ease your pain. Singles 1500ptas, with bath 1800ptas; doubles 2200ptas, with bath 2500ptas. Call ahead, but keep your promise.

Albergue Juvenil "San Fernando" (HI), Av. Juventud, s/n, Sta. María de Guía (tel. 928 55 06 85 or 928 55 08 27; fax 928 88 27 28). About 45min. outside Las Palmas by Utinsa bus #102 or 105 (285ptas); ask the driver to let you know when you get to Guía, as there is no sign. From the stop, walk back up the road toward Las Palmas and turn right on C. Marques del Muni. When the street forks left, go straight over the bridge with the green railing. Hostel is on the left, across from a swimming pool (200ptas). 2 foosball tables, a bar, and a cafeteria. Bright bunk beds 400ptas per night. Breakfast 250ptas. Lunch and dinner 800ptas each. Not many rooms available for travelers (most taken by groups, for whom most of the amenities are reserved).

Camping: Camping Guantánamo (tel. 928 56 02 07), in Mogán (a port town in the south) on Playa Tauro. 3rd-class site near a eucalyptus forest and a hunting zone. Over 750 campers. 350ptas per person, 400ptas per large tent, 345ptas per car.

FOOD

The range of food eaten in Las Palmas is matched only by the range of clothing (from topless to *saris*). You might end up downing Indian *tapas* in an Irish pub swinging to Moroccan pop music. Typical Canarian fare is itself a mixture of Guanche, Spanish, and Latin American tastes, including *papas arrugadas* ("wrinkled" potatoes encrusted with salt), *gofio* (a flour-like staple), and *potaje* (stew). The *plátanos* (bananas) of the Canaries are supposedly the best in the world, and the fish is fantastic, usually served with *mojo verde* (green sauce). The local wine is *Malvasia* (Malmsey), but it's hard to find. **Cruz Mayor,** a supermarket, has a branch on C. Nicolás Estévenez, 38, in the New City, and C. Pérez Galdós, 17, in the Triana district (both open M-Sa 8:30am-8:30pm). **Mercado de Vegueta,** C. Mendizábal, sells a glorious assortment of fresh fruit.

El Herreño, C. Mendizábal, 5 (tel. 928 31 05 13), just beyond the market in Vegueta. Canarian cuisine in a Canarian structure. Very popular. Pork specialties (800ptas). Delicious maritime *menús* (575-1100 ptas). Meals served daily until 1am.

Bar Amigo Camilo, El Confital, on the coast north of Las Canteras, at the end of C. Alonso Ojedo. Skip the beach and head straight for the ocean—this bar hides a hair's breadth away from the blue Atlantic. Fresh fish 2000-2800ptas per kg. *Papas arrugadas* 300ptas. *Menú* 1000ptas. Open M-Sa 1-5pm and 8-11pm, Su 1-5pm.

Hipócrates, C. Colón, 4 (tel. 928 22 64 15), across from Casa-Museo Colón in Vegueta. Vegetarian dining by candlelight. Restaurant has temporary exhibitions; the bathroom is a mystical experience.

La Strada, C. Tomás Miller, 58 (tel. 928 27 33 51). Aggressive self-service smorgasbord. All the so-so food you can stomach before paying the cashier 1250ptas. Open daily noon-4pm and 6-11pm. Grill open daily 7:30pm.

SIGHTS

The historical neighborhood, where Juan Retón and the conquering Spanish set up camp in the 15th century, is **Vegueta,** overlooking the **Guiniguada Ravine.** Even after the infiltration of Spanish mainland/mainstream culture in the 14th century, the islands retained a distinctive style, most visibly in the colonial architecture that lines the streets of Vegueta. **Calle Mayor de Triana,** a pedestrian shopping mall, offers up a wild assortment of edifices, from the typical old to the modern interpretation of it.

Catedral de Santa Ana, C. Espiritu Santo, 20 (tel. 928 31 49 89), is a 16th-century Gothic structure, with a Neoclassical facade by the Canaries' favorite sculptor, José Lujan Pérez (1765-1815). The three central naves are the same height, with a majestic dome towering above the crypt. Part of the cathedral is the **Museo Diocesano del Arte Sacro,** with more Lujan Perez works and a view into the Cathedral's Capilla de Nuestra Señora de Los Dolores, where the "incorruptible" body of Bishop Buenaventura Codina lies. The Vatican is checking him out for potential sainthood. *(Cathedral and museum open M-F 9am-1:30pm and 4-6:30pm, Sa 9am-2pm. 300ptas for both.)*

The **Pueblo Canario** (Canarian Village) is a whitewashed and wood-ridden wonder built specifically for tourists. It sits in Dorames Park, halfway between Parque de S. Telmo and Parque de Sta. Catalina. Designed in 1937 by the locally adored painter Néstor Martín-Fernández de la Torre, the first Canarian painter to receive international recognition, and built by his brother, Miguel, it's practically a historical sight by now—as an exhibit on tourist fanaticism. Outdoor performances of traditional Canarian music and traditional costumes take place biweekly (Th 5pm, Su 11:45am). At one end is the **Museo Néstor** (tel. 928 24 51 25), a stunning museum full of works by Néstor, whose name conjures up mythical thoughts among those familiar with his beautifully pudgy figures. *(Open M-Tu and Th-F 10am-1pm and 4-7pm, Sa 10am-noon, Su 10:30am-1:30pm. 150ptas.)* His vivacious *Poema del Atlántico* (Poem of the Atlantic; 1913-22) is a series of 8 paintings considered to be his most important work, and the intertwining bodies of *Poema de la Tierra* (Poem of the Earth) led to its censoring in the 1950s.

Other Museums

Museo Canario, C. Dr. Chil, 33 (tel. 928 31 56 00), past the cathedral, off C. Obispo Codina. Houses an important collection of artifacts from the early Guanche islanders and does its best to give a sense of how these people lived. Upstairs things get macabre, with 4 mummies and shelves of aboriginal skulls. The shapely *taras* (jugs used in ritual) are said to represent woman. Open M-F 10am-5pm, Sa-Su 10am-2pm. 400ptas, students 100ptas.

Casa de Colón, C. Colón, 2 (tel. 928 31 12 55). Everything you ever wanted to know about Columbus and then some. Fifteenth-century governor's house where Columbus supposedly stopped to fix a broken rudder before setting out to sea in 1492. The doorway and interior courtyard are original, while most everything else is a reconstruction, albeit a nice one. Open M-F 9am-5pm, Sa 9am-1pm. Free.

Casa-Museo Pérez Galdós, C. Cano, 6 (tel. 928 36 6 9 75). This typical 19th-century Canary-style house with double patio and plain front, where the "Spanish Balzac," Pérez Galdós, grew up. Furnished with astounding items from Galdós's Madrid residence, the house is evidence of a life well lived. Sorolla's famous 1894 portrait of the author hangs in the study. Open M-F 9am-1pm and 4-8pm, Sa 9am-1pm. Guided tours offered in the morning. Free.

Centro Atlántico de Arte Moderno, C. Los Balones, 9 (tel. 928 31 18 24). Behind the cathedral. Free museum with rotating exhibitions of all sorts of contemporary artists. Open Sept.-July Tu-Sa 10am-9pm, Su 10am-2pm.

Beaches

Playa de Las Canteras, one of the most famous beaches in European lore, is over 3km long, most of which is wave-free, the waters calmed by *la barra,* a mammoth barrier reef 200m out from shore. The area is nicknamed "the world's largest swimming pool." For waves and black sand, head to the less-pleasant south end of the beach.

ENTERTAINMENT

Faced with the difficult task of pleasing half of the world all at once, Las Palmas has unfortunately chosen karaoke as the *lingua franca* of the masses. Clubs are used primarily by tourists and thin out in the late spring and early summer months (low season)—most are located on and to the west of **Calle de Fernando Guanarteme** and **Calle de Secretario Artiles.** Packed by 2am, most don't empty out until 5am. Take advantage of year-round outdoor terraces on **Plaza de España** and along **Paseo de Canteras.** The latter are most attractive and popular at twilight, when the beach winds are still blowing bodies about.

Solo travelers should be careful late at night. Muggings are rare, but that's because everybody brings a buddy. Bring a friend or make one.

Cuasquías, C. San Pedro, 2 (tel. 928 37 00 46), on a small street off C. Juan de Quesada (in Vegueta-Triana). Wide range of live music (Tu-F at 12:30am, Sa at 1:30am) or classic favorites. Young crowd. Beer 350ptas. No cover.

La Cava, Av. Primero de Mayo, 57 (tel. 928 38 22 72). Take C. Bravo Murillo from Parque de San Telmo, turn left on Primero de Mayo. Less beer than Cuasquías and more posters of Malcom X and Cree Indians. Politically active students perk up their ears to theatrical and musical performances and the occasional presentation by Amnesty International. Beer 125-200ptas. Cover free-500ptas. Open Su-Th 9:30pm-1am, F-Sa 9:30pm-3:30am. Live performances F-Sa.

Donosti, C. Nicolás Estévanez at Po.Canteras. Large student playground with beach-front *terraza*. Part of the "Bermuda Triangle" pedestrian-only nighttime hubbub.

Las Palmas has over 70 **festivals** each year. During **Carnaval** (Feb. 7-16, 1999) the Canaries lose whatever small portion of sanity they might have had. Crazier still is the number of tourists who go to watch—this is the definition of high season.

■ Playa de Maspalomas and Playa del Inglés

Located on the southern tip of Gran Canaria, the famed Playa del Inglés and the sur-rounding shores are probably the best beaches in the Canaries. Huge swathes of per-fect sands, kilometers of pristine dunes untouched by development, and every commodity, food, and activity imaginable lie along these beautiful 17km of shoreline. Even the weather is better, as the sun often shines here while clouds obscure the rest of the island. Unfortunately, this is not just our little secret: planeloads full of Euro-pean tourists crowd the beaches, many of whom remember when talkies first got col-orized. Well connected to Las Palmas and with fewer accommodation options, Playa del Inglés and the surrounding areas may be easier as a daytrip from Las Palmas.

The Playa del Inglés—located next to the town center—is the center of activity, and people. Although most come for the sun and sand, a quick stroll of the beach should reveal people offering nearly every water-related activity conceivable: from **parasailing,** to **surfing** (the current world-champion lives 5min. away in San Agustín), to **jet-skiing,** to **scuba-diving,** to **deep-sea fishing.** The list of not-so-free activities is endless. If you can't find what your heart desires on the beach (highly unlikely), pick up the very helpful *Nautical Guide of Gran Canaria* at the tourist office or any travel agency. To the west of Playa del Inglés lie the sand dunes, a protected area off-limits to development; for the most part miraculously desolate, the dunes also hide a few **nudist beaches** (look for posted signs...or naked flesh). Farther west, another flawless beach, **Playa de Maspalomas,** bordered by dunes, is a little less crowded. Beyond, on the western coast, lie the rockier **Playa de la Mujer** and **Playa de las Mel-oneras.**

Getting to the beaches is easy. From the Estación de Guaguas in Las Palmas, **bus** #30 stops at Playa del Inglés before reaching Playa de Maspalomas (1hr., departs every 20-30min., 615ptas). Bus #50 runs directly to Maspalomas (50min., departs every hr., 615ptas). Both buses have a weekend round-trip ticket price discount (650ptas). Available at the bus station is the handy, and free, *Discover Gran Canaria by Bus* brochure, with a **map** on the back. The **tourist office** (tel. 928 77 15 50), near Playa del Inglés, on Av. España at C. Estados Unidos, has standard info (open M-F 9am-9pm). It lies next to the **Centro Commercial Jumbo,** a rather hideous outdoor mall hosting duty-free shops, bars, and nightclubs.

For cheap **hotels** on the beach, dialing up **Astor Travel** (tel. 928 76 53 25; fax 928 76 52 74; email astor@canari.step.es; http://www.step.es/astor-travel), in the Jumbo center, is probably your best bet. They should be able to find you a decent deal through a consolidator, especially in the low season.

■ The Interior: Arucas and Teror

As hard as it is to believe, Gran Canaria is not totally overrun by Euro-tourists. Just a few kilometers inland from the coast nary a word of English or German is spoken. Utinsa **buses** #205, 210, and 235 run from the bus station in Las Palmas to Arucas (30min., departs every 30min., 190-230ptas). Buses also run to most cities in the north of the island, including Teror (bus #215, departs every hr., 130ptas).

Arucas is a delightful mountain town with a stunning neo-Gothic church and a genuine, relaxed atmosphere—a perfect daytrip from Las Palmas for those who can tear themselves away from the beach. Overlooking a set of gardens, the **Church of San Juan Bautista** is a magnificent structure almost wholly constructed by local stonemasons and artisans; construction began in 1909 and wasn't completed until 1977. (Open daily 9am-1pm and 4-7pm. Free.) The square next to the church, Plaza de San Juan, once the commercial center of the city, now hosts a few cafes.

A **tourist office** (tel. 928 60 58 16) offers a map and other info (open daily). To get there go north up the hill from the bus station until the park, then head left (east) until reaching Plaza de la Constitución. The local **police** can be found at C. Alcalde Suárez Franche, 39 (tel. 928 60 40 54). There is one (and only one) place to stay in Arucas. A little *albergue* called **La Granja Escuela Anatol,** C. Ruz de Pineda, 5 (tel./fax 928 60 55 44), provides a home for scholars—and you, too, if you reserve in advance (3000ptas per person).

The quintessential Gran Canarian town, **Teror** is tucked away in the mountains and dominated by its church, the center of the town's social and religious life. The church was built to mark the spot where 17th-century conquistador Don Juan de Frias saw a vision of the Virgin Mary. In the plaza facing the entrance, there is a small museum, the **Casa de los Patronos de la Virgen,** a supposedly representative structure of 17th-century homes. Utinsa **bus** #215 connects Teror to Las Palmas (40min., departs every 30min., 510ptas) and Aruca (130ptas).

TENERIFE

Deriving its name from the aboriginal Guanche (*tener* means "snow," *ife* means "high mountain"), Tenerife boasts just that—the tallest mountain in all of Spain, El Teide, at 3718m. Rumored to be the site of hell by those funny 14th-century people, Tenerife is to modern eyes about as far from hell as possible, with a dramatic, jagged coastline in the north, smooth black sand beaches in the south, and a unique flora and fauna, all centered around its omnipresent and incongruous snow-capped peak. All this makes Tenerife, the largest island in the archipelago, the near equal of Gran Canaria and its raucous population center of Las Palmas. Although you will find no fewer tourists on Tenerife than Gran Canaria, the two islands do contrast in an appreciable way—stay on Gran Canaria for the nightlife, but come to Tenerife for the scenery.

■ Santa Cruz de Tenerife

Before the Spanish Civil War, the government had a policy of promoting troublesome officers to out-of-the-way provinces. Making Franco the General-in-Chief of the Canaries was the most graphic example of that policy's abject inadequacy. The site of the opening shots of the Spanish Civil War, the bustling port of Santa Cruz (pop. 250,000) is today dominated by the freighter ships pulling into its harbor and an enormous cross in the Plaza de España, a memorial to the war dead. Today such political activism is all but gone, replaced by a self-consciously pleasant city even more laid-back than Las Palmas.

ORIENTATION AND PRACTICAL INFORMATION

Most of the Santa Cruz's waterfront is taken up by the **port,** with the jetfoil and ferry docks at the northern end, and the water lies along the eastern side. **Plaza de España** sits on the waterfront, south of the jetfoil and ferry terminals.

Flights: See **Getting Around** and **Getting There,** p. 516, for info on flights to, from, and around the islands. There are two airports on Tenerife. **Los Rodeos** (tel. 922 25 23 50) is the northern airport a few kilometers west of Santa Cruz. From Los Rodeos, bus #102 runs to Santa Cruz (departs about every 30min., 230ptas). **Reina Sofia** (tel. 922 77 00 50) is in the south. From Reina Sofia, bus #341 heads to Santa

Cruz (departs about every hr., 230ptas). **Iberia** (tel. 922 281 112), **Spanair** (tel. 922 63 58 13), **Air Europa** (tel. 922 75 92 94).

Buses: TITAS (tel. 922 21 81 22) serves all major towns in the island from the Estación de Guaguas, Av. 3 de Mayo, 47, down C. Jose Antonio Rivera from Pl. España.

Ferries: Trasmediterránea (tel. 922 24 30 11). See **Getting Around,** p. 516, for info on ferry and jetfoil trips.

Car Rental: Car rental agencies in Santa Cruz are sprinkled throughout Santa Cruz. **Autos ADA,** C. Emilo Calzada, 10 (tel. 922 27 49 53; fax 922 24 27 56). Cheapest car is 4000ptas per day including insurance and taxes. Open M-F 8am-1pm and 4-7pm, Sa 8am-2pm and 4-6pm, Su 9am-noon.

Tourist Office: (tel. 922 60 55 92), located in a kiosk in the Pl. España. Lots of brochures, pamphlets, maps, and stuff, little for free. Open daily 8am-3pm. Maps also available at any news kiosk.

Currency Exchange: Banks and **ATM** machines are scattered around the Pl. España.

Police: Av. del Tres de Mayo, 72 (tel. 922 60 60 92).

Pharmacies: Scattered around Pl. España and Pl. de la Candelaria. Check the window of any of these pharmacies to see whose turn it is to be *"en guardia,"* or stay open late.

Hospital: At the corner of C. Ramon y Cajal and C. Gralo Galcerán.

Post Office: Pl. de España. Open M-Sa mornings. **Postal Code:** 38002.

ACCOMMODATIONS

As elsewhere in the Canaries, cheap accommodations are hard to find; what does exist fills up fast, so reserve in advance. Unlike the rest of the Canaries (or Spain for that matter), those traveling in pairs may actually find it cheaper to get two singles.

Hotel Oceano, C. Castillo, 6 (tel. 922 27 08 00 or 922 27 08 04). Large rooms with marble floors, mini-bars, TVs, and telephones. Singles 3500ptas; one-bed doubles 7000ptas, two-bed doubles 9500ptas. Breakfast included. If full, ask them to contact one of their sister hotels for you—**Hotel Atlántico** (tel. 922 24 63 75; fax 922 24 63 78) or **Hotel El Dorado** (tel. 922 24 31 84; fax 922 24 32 59).

Hotel Horizonte, C Sta. Rosa de Lima, 11 (tel. 922 27 19 36). Bright curtains, flowered bed spreads, and flame-retardant tile flooring reminiscent of a third-grade classroom. Singles 2600ptas; doubles 5200ptas. All rooms with bath.

Hotel Anago, Imeldo Serís, 19 (tel. 922 24 50 90). Bright white walls and TV. Singles 4494ptas; doubles 7268ptas.

Hotel Pelinor, Bethencourt Alfonso, 8 (tel. 922 24 68 75; fax 922 28 05 20), verges on plush. Singles from 5400ptas; doubles 7500ptas.

FOOD

Cafes, restaurants, and bars crowd the **Plaza de España** and nearby *calles.* **Avenida de Francisco,** hugging the port, has a series of good restaurants with *terrazas* for people-watching. Most restaurants in Santa Cruz are open daily from 11am to midnight. The **Mercado de Nosotra Señora de África** is a giant meat and produce market open most mornings. It's also across the river bed and a long block inland from the Museo de la Naturaleza y el Hombre (see **Sights,** below).

Bocata World Co., C. Villa Iba Herbas, 1. Features tasty sandwiches in long rolls (360-475ptas) and some vegetarian sandwiches.

Restaurante Dagigi, Av. de Francisco, 43. A charming Italian eatery overlooking the port. Pasta dishes start at around 600ptas, pizza at 750ptas.

Mr. Smile, on Pl. de la Candelaria, fries up great burgers for 250ptas. You can also get the usual sandwiches and *tapas.* Outdoor seating.

Viva Maria, C. Suares Guerra, 20. Reminiscent of the classic American diner, serving burgers and sandwiches (from 215ptas) and shakes (from 195ptas).

SIGHTS AND ENTERTAINMENT

The **Museo de la Naturaleza y el Hombre** (tel. 922 20 93 20), on C. San Sebastián, across from the river bed, devotes itself to the physical and human history of the Canaries. *(Open Tu-Su 10am-8pm. 400ptas, students 100ptas.)* Among other exhibits, it accomplishes the impressive task of making a big rock collection interesting. The **Museo de Belles Artes,** C. Hervas Villalba, near Pl. España, is Santa Cruz's art museum. *(400ptas, students 100ptas.)*

Santa Cruz is graced by two churches: The **Iglesia de la Conception,** three blocks south of Pl. de España, is a 16th-century creation, while the **Iglesia de San Francisco,** a block inland on C. Hervas Villalba, dates from the 17th century. The **Parque Garcia Sanabria,** in the city's northwest corner, doubles as an impressive botanical garden, with plants from around the world, and an open-air sculpture museum with avant-garde sculptures by Pablo Serrano, Rafael Soto, and Gustavo Torner, among others.

As on Gran Canaria, few come to Santa Cruz for the sights. The black sand of the **Almáciga, Benijo,** and **Las Gaviotas beaches,** as well as the golden sand of the **Las Teresitas,** an artificial beach, lie nearby and can be accessed by frequent buses departing from the central bus station.

Bars and **clubs** line the commercial areas of the city, but Santa Cruz is much calmer than Las Palmas. Bars and *terrazas* line **Calle José Antonio Rivera** along the waterfront. Two discos to the north of Pl. España, **Nocturna Anaga,** Av. de Anaga, 37, and **Tosca,** Av. de Anaga, 41, spin vinyl until the wee hours of the night.

The best time to visit Santa Cruz, like the rest of the Canaries, is during **Carnaval,** the week before Lent. This is when the city explodes in a shock of color, sound, and motion that rivals the best that even Rio de Janerio has to offer.

■ Playa de las Américas and Los Cristianos

The man-made Playa de las Américas and the gray-sand beaches of Los Cristianos, on the southern tip of Tenerife, are the most-touristed beaches on the Canary Islands. Developed into full-fledged tourist destinations in the 1960s and 70s, the towns probably have more five-star hotels than residents, but they do feature better dining and nightlife than the other beach towns. Luckily, they also play the jumping-off point for ferries to the smaller, far more *tranquilo* island of Gomera. Beyond their own more than respectable beaches, Las Américas and Los Cristianos can serve as a base for exploring other shores in the south, including **Playa del Médano,** one of the best Tenerife has to offer and a windsurfing hotspot.

Bus #111 runs between Santa Cruz and Las Américas and Los Cristianos (1hr., departs every 30min., 610ptas) and bus #487 runs to and from the southern airport (25min., departs every hr., 330ptas). Each town has its own bus station. If you are just going for the beach, you probably want to get off in Las Américas. From the stop, the beach is due west. Los Cristianos's beach is similarly easy to find from the stop on Av. los Cristianos; just head straight south. The **police** (tel. 922 79 31 21) are between Las Américas and Los Cristianos, in Los Morritos. The **Salud Medical Clinic** (tel. 922 79 12 53) is on C. Republica Dominica at Av. Litoral.

Finding an affordable place to stay is more difficult than in northern Santa Cruz. There are two reasonably priced hotels in Los Cristianos. **Hotel Silvia,** C. del Valle Menéndez (tel. 922 79 25 64; fax 922 79 79 20) is right across form the cultural center (singles 4705ptas; doubles 5225ptas). A block down from the Silvia is **Hotel Andrea's,** C. Antigua Gerard Franco (tel. 922 79 00 24; fax 922 79 42 76; May-Sept. singles 3700ptas; doubles 5700ptas; Oct.-Apr. singles 4200ptas; doubles 7250ptas). The **port** in Los Cristianos is also where the Trasmediterránea (tel. 922 79 61 78) and Fred Olson **ferries** run to Gomera (see **Getting Around,** p. 516). In both towns, but especially in Las Américas, hundreds of **mini-malls** hawk beach clothes and duty-free luxury items alongside restaurants, bars, and occasional discos.

■ Puerto de la Cruz

The largest town on the northern coast, Puerto de la Cruz has for years been a get-away spot for older British and Irish tourists. All this attention from Anglos makes the town a bit pricy, but Puerto de la Cruz is a necessary transfer point to visit El Teide by bus. **Bus** #101 connects Santa Cruz and Puerto de la Cruz (departs every 30min., 350ptas); the bus station is on the west side of the city, three blocks inland. The **tourist office** lies in Plaza Iglesia, on C. Quintana. Further north is the Parque Marítimo Municipal, and to the west and east along the coast are beaches.

Budget accommodations in Puerto de la Cruz depend on luck and timing. The **Hotel Chimsoy,** 14 Av. de Bethercourt (tel. 922 38 35 52; fax 922 38 28 40) has a pool and exercise room (high season singles 6300ptas, doubles 8500ptas; low season singles 4300ptas; doubles 5300ptas; tax not included, but breakfast is). Otherwise, contact Olga Mendes Nunes at **Promociones Luso-Canarias,** C. Cologan, 3 (tel./fax 922 37 17 87), about renting an apartment (from 4800ptas per night).

■ El Teide National Park

Towering 3178m over Tenerife, Spain's highest peak presides over a vast, unspoiled wilderness. Teide itself forms the northern ridge of a much larger ancient volcano that exploded cataclysmically millions of years ago. The result is El Teide and **Las Cañadas,** the sandy plateaus surrounding the mountain that support some of the most vibrant wildflowers on earth, many unique to the park.

The park is accessible by **bus** from Puerto de La Cruz. Bus #342 departs from the station at 9:15am and leaves El Teide at 4pm (90min., 700ptas). Consider renting a **car** and driving, as it provides more flexibility and allows one to explore the wildly different but equally beautiful views of the eastern (from El Puerto de la Cruz) and western (from Los Cristianos) access roads. Bus #342 stops at the **visitors' center,** which offers free brochures and maps of the park (open daily 9:15am-4pm).

Once in the park, you will have ample opportunity to ponder "our miserly insignificance," as the Spanish park service puts it, as you gaze across the eerie and enchanting volcanic landscape. Nine free guided **hikes** depart daily, and there are eight non-guided, sign-posted trails. A **cable car** climbs the final 1000m up to El Teide's peak (open daily 9am-5pm; 2100ptas, children 1000ptas).

Note that the 2km of earth between you and sea level exacerbate the normal strains of hiking; be sure to bring plenty of water. In the winter, the park is usually coated in a shimmering white coat of snow and hiking is restricted. **Camping** without a permit is forbidden.

GOMERA

According to many, the verdant island of Gomera, with its lush terraced hillsides, is the most blessed of the Canaries. Fortunately lacking an airport, Gomera's relative isolation and small, stony beaches keep the droves of tourists at bay. Nowhere on the island do the choruses of German, English, and French-speakers drown out those of the birds. The island's main town, San Sebastián, is refreshingly provincial and refreshingly cheap, but the crown jewel is the spectacular Garajonay National Park, an anachronistic refuge for species that died out elsewhere millions of years ago. The well marked walking paths (ranging from 0.5km—10km) make hiking accessible while managing to protect the park.

■ San Sebastián de Gomera

Before lifting his anchor and heading off to find the mythical Middle Passage to India, Christopher Columbus last touched dry land here. He drew water from the well, prayed at the church, and spent a night or two before embarking on the voyage that changed human history. Having resisted the temptation to cash in on Columbus kitsch, San Sebastián remains a charming provincial town and affordable base from which to explore the island.

ORIENTATION AND PRACTICAL INFORMATION

Navigating San Sebastián is a breeze. One road runs along the entire coast, intersected midway by **Calle del Medio,** the town's main drag, at the **Plaza las Americas.**

Buses: Three lines originate in the port and branch out across the island. Line 1 goes to Valle Gran Rey; Line 2 to Playa de Santiago and Alajero; Line 3 to Hermigua, Agulo, and Vallehermoso. All leave at 11am, 2, 5:30, and 9:30pm.

Ferries: Two companies ply San Sebastián's harbor. **Trasmediterránea** (tel. 920 87 13 24 or 920 80 59 68) and **Fred Olson.** See **Getting Around,** p. 516, for details.

Car Rental: Available in the port terminal or at Pl. las Americas. **Sport Moto,** C. Republica de Panama, 3 (tel. 920 87 15 31), rents **motorcycles** (5000ptas per day), **scooters** (3500ptas per day), and **mountain bikes** (2000ptas per day).

Tourist Office: C. Medio, 4 (tel. 920 14 01 47; fax 920 14 01 51), right behind Pl. las Americas. Extraordinarily helpful, they'll can help you find a countryside house to rent for a few days. Info about the entire island and the park. Inside is the well Columbus used before leaving for the New World. Have a sip—maybe you'll get lucky. Open M-Sa 9am-1:30pm and 3:30-6pm, Su 10am-1pm.

Currency Exchange: Banks and **ATMs** line Pl. las Americas, among them the Banco Santander. Open M-F 8:30am-2pm, Sa 8:30am-1pm.

Police: call 922 87 03 20.

Hospital: Nuestra Sta. de Guadalupe (tel. 920 14 02 02), 1 block west of Via Ronda.

Post Office: C. Medio, 60. Open M-F 8:30am-2:30pm. **Postal Code:** 38800.

ACCOMMODATIONS

San Sebastián's budget accommodations are more budget and more accommodating than elsewhere in the Canaries. Walk up C. Medio and a treasure trove of pensions and apartments will reveal itself.

Hostal el Pajar, C. Medio, 23 (tel. 920 87 02 07). Nestled in a 250-year-old house, the rooms are spacious, clean, and high-ceilinged. Restaurant below swaps tasty sandwiches (200ptas) and cheap beer (150ptas) for currency. Singles 2000ptas; doubles 3000ptas. Ask for the room with the terrace.

Pension Colon, C. Medio (tel. 920 87 00 20; fax 920 87 02 35). Rooms nestled in a cozy old house with wood-beam architecture. Singles 2600ptas; doubles 3800ptas; triples 4800ptas.

Hotel Villa Gomera, C. Ruiz de Padron, 68 (tel. 920 87 00 20; fax 920 87 02 35). Run by owners of the Colon. Singles 4200ptas; doubles 5500ptas; triples 6500ptas.

Apartamentos San Sebastián, C. Medio, 20 (tel. 920 87 13 54), can arrange nicely furnished apartments for as little as one night. For stays under 2 weeks 4500ptas per night; over 2 weeks 4000ptas per night.

FOOD

Restaurants, like everything else, are clustered around Pl. las Americas and C. del Medio. Sandwich shops, an ice-cream stand, and a few bars inhabit the region.

Bar-Restaurant Cubano, C. Virgen de Guadalupe, 2, specializes in seafood. Get adventurous in your eating and try the eel (750ptas) or squid (950ptas). Meat dishes served as well. Open daily 11am-midnight.

Oasis Pizzeria, a block east of Pl. las Americas. It may not take you back to that *trattoria* in Firenze, but it's still good. Serves salads (400ptas), pasta (600ptas), *tortillas* (300ptas), and pizzas (800ptas). Open daily noon-4pm and 6pm-midnight.

Kiosk Ramón, on the waterfront by the beach, serves *tapas*, drinks, and sandwiches (250ptas). Open daily 11am-midnight.

SIGHTS

San Sebastián is not a Christopher Colombus theme park, but his former presence is quite unmissable. On C. Medio is the **Iglesia de la Asunción,** where Colombus prayed before he left, and **Casa de Colón,** C. Medio, 50, which hosts a small exhibit on his life. *(Open M-F 9m-noon and 4-8pm. Free.)*

No Canarian city would be complete without a **beach.** San Sebastian's gets noticeably better as it stretches past the port. The tourist office has lots of info about **diving, boating,** and **fishing** excursions from the port.

■ Near San Sebastián: Garajonay National Park

Garajonay National Park provides dozens of **hikes** (marked and un-marked) through the voluptuous forest that has left even jaded UN bureaucrats so breathless that they declared it an "area of outstanding beauty." The forest is the last remaining example in the world of a **laurisilva forest;** once covering the Mediterranean basin, these forests died out elsewhere millions of years ago during the Terciary Era. Hundreds of plant species are thus unique to Gomera's forest. The forest's fauna acts like a giant sponge, preventing water from descending the mountain. As a result, the forest is green and lush year-round, while semi-desert conditions prevail closer to the shore.

For anything but a brief visit, it is best to preface a visit to the park with either a trip to the **Tourist Information office** in San Sebastián; the **Visitors Center** (tel. 920 80 09 93; open Tu-Su 9:30am-4:30pm), located 9km off the main road to Las Rosaba; or the **Park Service,** Carretera General de Sur, 20 (tel. 920 80 09 93), in San Sebastián. Any of these offices can help with camping applications or make the reservations required for the free guided tours on Wednesdays and Saturdays. **La Laguna Grande,** about half-way through the park, has restrooms, a small info center, and a restaurant.

■ Near San Sebastián: Valle Gran Rey

Although this idyllic Canarian town seems even farther removed from the rest of the Canaries, it is just over 25km away as the crow flies. But, because it is 80km away by road, and because reaching Valle Gran Rey takes well over 90 minutes by car and more by bus, its beaches remain uncrowded, the food local, and the people oh-so-chill. The best way to reach Valle Gran Rey from San Sebastián is by one of Trasmediterránea's (tel. 922 80 59 68) four daily **hyrdofoils** (2130ptas), although **bus** line #1 also runs here (4 per day).

This undiscovered charm, however, comes at a price as accommodations are relatively expensive. Two pensions are in Vueltas, along the south end by the beach: **Candelaria** (tel. 920 80 54 02) and **Las Vueltas** (tel. 920 80 52 16). Apartments are also available, but most are upscale. Contact the tourist office in San Sebastián for help locating a deal.

PORTUGAL

US $1 = 179.00 escudos ($)
CDN $1 = 116.32$
UK £1 = 299.10$
IR £1 = 256.51$
AUS $1 = 105.06$
NZ $1 = 90.05$
SAR 1 = 28.76$
SP 1pta = 1.20$
MOR 1dh = 18.76$
EURO $1 = 202.21$

100$ = US $0.56
100$ = CDN $0.86
100$ = UK £0.33
100$ = IR £0.39
100$ = AUS $0.95
100$ = NZ $1.11
100$ = SAR 3.49
100$ = SP 83.01ptas
100$ = MOR 5.33dh
100$ = EURO $0.49

ESSENTIALS

■ Getting There and Around

Portugal is easily accessible by plane from the U.S., Europe, and Spain. In Spain, long-distance trains run from Madrid (see p. 73) to Lisbon, while buses run from Sevilla (see p. 418) to Lagos. Closer to the border, trains run from Huelva (easily accessible from Sevilla, see p. 418) to Portugal, as they do from Cáceres (see p. 504). Trains and buses run from Badajoz (see p. 511), only 6km from the border, to Elvas and elsewhere. Ciudad Rodrigo (see p. 157) lies only 21km from the border, while buses run from Zamora (see p. 159) to Bragança. In the north, trains run from Vigo (see p. 185) to Porto, while from Túy (see p. 188), you can walk across to Valença do Minho.

BY PLANE

Most major international airlines serve Lisbon; some serve Porto, Faro, and the Madeiras. **TAP Air Portugal** (info and reservation tel. in U.S. and Canada (800) 221 7370; in U.K. (171) 828 2092; in Lisbon tel. (1) 841 69 90; for schedules, reservations, and a worldwide list of offices http://www.TAP-AirPortugal.pt) is Portugal's national airline, serving all domestic locations and most major international cities. **Portugália** (for schedules and a list of offices http://www.pga.pt) is a smaller Portuguese airline that flies between Porto, Faro, Lisbon, all major Spanish cities, and other Western European destinations. Their offices include Lisbon (tel. (1) 842 55 00) and Manchester (tel. (161) 489 50 40).

BY TRAIN

Caminhos de Ferro Portugueses is Portugal's national railway, but for long distance travel, aside from the Braga-Porto-Coimbra-Lisbon line, the bus is better. Local trains or commuter rails (e.g., in Lisbon), however, may be faster and cheaper than buses along the same route. Most trains have first- and second-class cabins, except for local and suburban routes. When you arrive in town, go to the station ticket booth to check the departure schedule; trains often run at irregular hours, and posted schedules *(horarios)* are not always accurate.

Unless you own a Eurailpass, the return on round-trip tickets must be used before 3am the following day. Anyone riding without a ticket is tagged over 3500$. Children under four travel free; ages four to 11 pay half-price. **Youth discounts** are only available to Portuguese citizens.

PORTUGAL

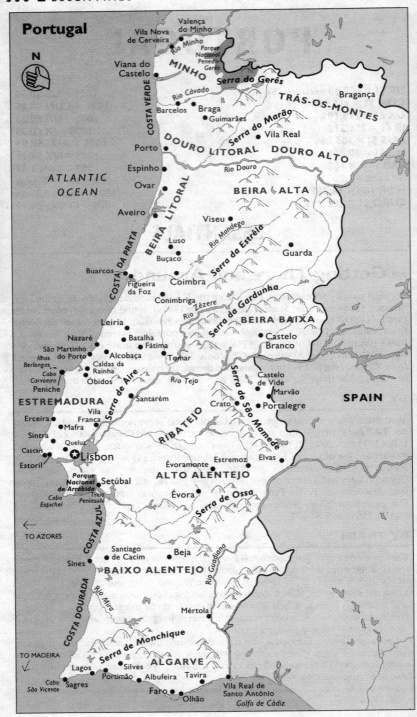

Portugal

N

ATLANTIC OCEAN

SPAIN

Valença do Minho
Vila Nova de Cerveira
Rio Minho
Parque Nacional Peneda-Gerês
Viana do Castelo
MINHO
Serra do Gerês
Bragança
TRÁS-OS-MONTES
Rio Cávado
COSTA VERDE
Barcelos
Braga
Guimarães
Serra do Marão
Vila Real
Porto
DOURO LITORAL
DOURO ALTO
Espinho
Rio Douro
Ovar
BEIRA ALTA
Aveiro
BEIRA LITORAL
Viseu
Rio Mondego
COSTA DA PRATA
Luso
Buçaco
Serra da Estrêla
Guarda
Buarcos
Figueira da Foz
Coimbra
Conimbriga
Rio Zêzere
Serra da Gardunha
BEIRA BAIXA
Leiria
Nazaré
Batalha
Fátima
Castelo Branco
São Martinho do Porto
Ilhas Berlengas
Alcobaça
Caldas da Rainha
Tomar
Cabo Carvoeiro
Peniche
Óbidos
Serra de Aire
Rio Tejo
Serra de São Mamede
Castelo de Vide
Marvão
ESTREMADURA
Santarém
Crato
Portalegre
Erceira
Vila Franca
Mafra
Queluz
RIBATEJO
Sintra
Cascais
Estoril
Lisbon
Évoramonte
Estremoz
Elvas
Parque Nacional de Arrábida
Setúbal
ALTO ALENTEJO
Cabo Espichel
Traía Peninsula
Évora
Serra de Ossa
COSTA AZUL
TO AZORES
Santiago de Cacím
Beja
Sines
BAIXO ALENTEJO
Rio Guadiana
COSTA DOURADA
Rio Mira
Mértola
TO MADEIRA
Serra de Monchique
Cabo São Vicente
Sagres
Lagos
Silves
Portimão
Albufeira
Tavira
Faro
Olhão
ALGARVE
Vila Real de Santo António
Golfo de Cádiz

BY BUS

Buses run frequently, are cheap, and link almost every town. **Rodoviária** (national info tel. (1) 354 57 75), the national bus company, has recently been privatized. Each company name corresponds to a particular region of the country, such as Rodoviária Alentejo or Minho e Douro (the above address is for Rodoviária da Estremadura), with notable exceptions such as EVA in the Algarve. Generally Rodoviária is still known by its old name. Private regional companies also operate, among them **Cabanelas, AVIC,** and **Mafrense.** Express coach service *(expressos)* between major cities is especially good, and the inexpensive city buses may run to nearby villages. Many cities offer several options. Schedules *(horarios)* are usually printed and posted; double check with the ticket vendor to make sure they are accurate.

BY CAR

Portugal has traditionally had the highest per capita automobile accident rate in Western Europe. The new highway system (IP) is quite good. Off the main arteries, the narrow, twisting roads prove difficult to negotiate. The locals' testy reputation is well deserved. Speed limits are effectively ignored, recklessness common, and lighting and road surfaces often inadequate. Buses and trucks are the safer option. Moreover, parking space in cities borders on nonexistent. **Gas** comes in super (97 octane), normal (92 octane), and unleaded. Gas prices may be high by North American standards, so factor this in prior to embarking roadward.

Portugal's national automobile association is the **Automóvel Clube de Portugal (ACP),** R. Rosa Araújo, 49A (tel. (1) 711 23 60). They provide **breakdown** and **towing service** (M-F 8am-11pm, Sa-Su 9am-10pm) and **first aid** (24hr.).

■ Accommodations

YOUTH HOSTELS

Movijovem, Av. Duque de Ávila, 137, 1050 Lisbon (tel. (1) 355 90 81 or 355 90 87; fax 352 14 66), the Portuguese Hostelling International affiliate, looks over the country's HI hostels. All bookings may be made through here. A cheap bed in a *pousada de juventude* (not to be confused with plush *pousadas*), costs 1100-2500$ per night and slightly less in the off season (breakfast and sheets included). Lunch or dinner usually costs 1000 to 1500$, snacks around 250$. Rates may be higher for guests 26 or older. Though often the cheapest option, hostels may lie some distance from the town center. Check-in hours are 9am to noon and 6pm to midnight; some have lockouts 10:30am to 6pm, and early curfews might cramp club-hoppers' style. The maximum stay at one hostel is eight nights unless you get special permission.

To stay in an HI hostel an **HI card** (3000$) is essentially mandatory. And although they're sold at Movijovem's Lisbon office, it is more convenient to get one before leaving home. To reserve a bed in the high season, obtain an **International Booking Voucher** from Movijovem (or your country's HI affiliate) and send it from home to the desired hostel four to eight weeks in advance. In the off season (Oct.-Apr.), double-check to see if the hostel is open. Large groups should reserve through Movijovem at least 30 days in advance. For more info, see **Hosteling Prep,** p. 11.

PENSÕES AND HOTELS

Pensões, also called **residencias,** will likely be your mainstay. They're far cheaper than hotels and only slightly more expensive (and much more common) than crowded youth hostels. All are rated on a five-star scale and are required to visibly post their category and legal price limits. (If you don't see it, ask!) During high season, most pensões do not take resevations, but for those that do, booking a week ahead is advisable. **Hotels** in Portugal tend to be pricey. A quality establishment typically includes showers and breakfast in the bill, and most rooms without bath or shower have a sink. Many will force you out by noon. When business is weak, try bargaining down in advance—the "official price" is merely the maximum allowed.

ALTERNATIVE ACCOMMODATIONS

Quartos are rooms in private residences, similar to *casas particulares* in Spain. These rooms may be your only option in less touristed, smaller towns (particularly in the south), or the cheapest one in bigger locales. The tourist office can usually help you find a *quarto*. When all else fails, feel free to ask at bars and restaurants for names and addresses, but you should try to verify the quality of the rooms.

Pousadas defy standard hotel rationale (and, unfortunately, rates) as castles, palaces, or monasteries converted into a luxurious, government-run hotels: *parador nacionales* are Spain's equivalent. "Historical" *pousadas* play up local craft, custom, and cuisine and may cost as much as expensive hotels. Most require reservations. Priced less extravagantly are *regional pousadas,* situated in national parks and reserves. For info, contact ENATUR, Av. Santa Joana Princesa, 10-A, 1749 Lisbon (tel. (1) 844 20 00; fax 844 20 58).

CAMPING

In **Portugal,** locals regard camping as a social activity more than anything else. Over 150 official campgrounds *(parques de campismo)* feature gobs of amenities and comforts. Most have a supermarket and cafes, and many are beach-accessible or near rivers or pools. Given the facilities' quality and popularity, happy campers arrive early; urban and coastal parks may require reservations. Police have been cracking down on illegal camping, so don't try it—especially near official campgrounds. Big tourist offices stock the free *Portugal: Camping and Caravan Sites,* a handy guide to official campgrounds. Otherwise, write the **Federação Portuguesa de Campismo e Caravanismo,** Av. 5 de Outubro, 15-3, 950 Lisbon (tel. (1) 842 84 80; open 9:30am-12:30pm and 1:30-6:30pm).

■ Tipping and Bargaining

As in Spain, a small tip is customary. Some restaurants include a 10% service charge; if they don't, round up and leave the change. Don't worry, big tips aren't the norm: 150-200$ after a dinner for two is generally fine. Others deserve your gratitude as well: tip porters 100-150$ and taxi drivers 15% of the meter fare. Bargaining is not customary in commercial establishments or pensões, but hone your skills at the local *mercado* (market).

■ Keeping in Touch

Most useful communication information (including **international access codes, calling card numbers, country codes, operator** and **directory assistance,** and **emergency numbers**) is listed on the **inside back cover.**

Telecom Portugal is Portugal's national telephone company. Phone offices exist in most cities, but like in Spain, there is little need to use them as all services are available in phone booths, located on the street and in post offices. Coin-operated phones are essentially non-existent in Portugal; you'll need phone cards.

The country uses both the **Credifone** and Telecom Portugal systems. Credifone uses magnetic cards sold at drugstores, post offices, and locations posted on phone booths. For both Credifone and its counterpart, Telecom Portugal, the basic unit for all calls (and the price for local ones) is 18$. The Telecom phone cards, using "patch" (not strip) cards, are most common in Lisbon and Porto and increasingly elsewhere. Credifone cards, with magnetic strips, are most useful outside these two hubs. While Telecom is gaining ground, travelers should tote both cards. Private calls from bars and cafes cost whatever the proprietor decides, typically 30-40$; a posted sign usually indicates the rates. Remember that the initial zero (0) in **city codes** is dialed only when dialing from another area within Portugal; from outside of Portugal the number is omitted. Local calls do not require dialing any portion of the city code.

Calling cards probably remain the best method of making international calls (see p. 50 for more details). The numbers to access major calling card services (including AT&T, MCI, Canada Direct, BT Direct, Ireland Direct, Australia Direct, New Zealand Direct, and South Africa Direct) are listed on the inside back cover.

Collect calls *(pago no destino)* are charged at person to person *(chamada pessoa à pessoa)* rates and are cheaper than calling from hotels; dial 18 01 23 for operators.

Air mail *(via aerea)* takes 6 to 10 business days to reach the U.S. or Canada. People in Europe should expect a shorter wait; Australia, New Zealand, and South Africa a longer one. **Surface mail** *(superficie)*, for packages only, takes up to two months. **Registered** or **blue mail** takes five to eight business days (for roughly three times the price of air mail). **EMS** or **Express Mail** will probably get there in three to four days, for more than double the blue mail price. **Stamps** are available at post offices *(correios)* and automatic (surprisingly efficient) stamp machines outside all post offices and in central locations around cities. Also at post offices, **fax** machines are available for public use at roughly 2500$ for the first page; 1700$ for each additional page.

Email is both faster and more reliable than the standard mail system. Cybercafes are relatively frequent in large Portuguese cities and are listed in the Practical Information section of our city descriptions and in the index, under Internet access. For information on how to obtain a free email account, see p. 51.

LIFE AND TIMES

From the 14th century until 1750 Portugal was one of the wealthiest nations in the world, and just 30 years ago it still rivaled other nations in the reach of its colonies. Today, while much of the prosperity has perished, the pride has not. Its collective diligence, coupled with new-found political and economic stability, once again has Portugal on the road to progress. Portugal's cultural revival was at the center of Expo 1998, an international cultural celebration held in Lisbon the summer of that year.

■ History and Politics

Early History

A variety of people inhabited the Iberian Peninsula around the first millennium BC. The first clearly identifiable immigrants were the **Celts,** who began to settle in northern Portugal and Galicia in the 9th and 8th centuries BC. The Celts established small agricultural and herding societies throughout the countryside. Around the same time, **Phoenicians** founded several fishing villages along the Algarve and ventured as far north as modern-day Lisbon, while **Greeks** from Asia Minor settled along the south and west coasts. The **Carthaginians** followed them, working chiefly on the west coast. Julius Caesar led a 15,000-man **Roman** force over the Sierras in the second century BC, paving the way for an Iberian *Pax Romana;* the "Latinization" of Portugal's language, law, roads, architecture, customs; and, most significantly, Christianity.

Swabians and Arabian Knights

As the Roman Empire declined in the 3rd and 4th centuries, the effects were felt on the Iberian peninsula. The Visigoths, a migrating Germanic people, slowly began to infiltrate and eventually take over the empire. The Church became the largest landholder in Europe, and monasteries and clerical schools became centers of learning and spiritual importance. The Visigoth monarchy collapsed in AD 712, and the Muslims took over. Most of the peninsula became known as *Al-Andalus* (land of the Vandals). Many Christians willingly converted to Islam, and those who chose not to convert were treated relatively well. Muslim society reached its height during the 9th and 10th centuries AD. After nearly four centuries of rule, the Muslims had left their mark on Portugal. Along with Muslim agricultural advances and architectural landmarks, the religion of Islam is a big part of Portuguese culture, and Arab traditions like ceremonial dance continue to characterize Portugal's broad cultural spectrum.

The Christian Reconquest

The reunification of Castilla and León by Fernando I in 1037 provided a strong base for the Christian effort to reclaim territory. Groups like the Knights Templars travelled to the continent to battle Muslim forces. In 1135 Alfonso I refused to join other northern Spanish provinces and established the house of Burgundy in Portuguese territory. The papacy officially recognized the title of King of Portugal in 1179.

By 1249, the Christian Reconquest defeated the last remnants of Muslim power with a campaign in the Algarve. Along with the change in political rule came sweeping cultural reforms. The Christian kings, headlined by **Dom Dinis** (1279-1325), promoted use of the vernacular, established Portugal's first university in 1290, and solidified its current borders in 1297. By the middle of the 14th century Portugal could claim to be the first unified nation-state in Europe.

The Age of Discovery

The reign of **João I** (1384-1433) ushered in a time of unity and prosperity never before seen in Portugal. João increased the power of the crown and in so doing established a strong base for future Portuguese expansion and economic success.

The 15th century was one of the greatest periods in the history of maritime travel and advances. Portugal established itself as a world leader in maritime science and exploration. Portuguese adventurers captured the Moroccan city of Ceuta in 1415, discovered the Madeiras Islands in 1419, happened upon the uninhabited Azores in 1427, and began to exploit the African coast for slaves and riches. **Henry the Navigator** organized seafaring adventures and those who followed.

Bartolomeu Dias changed the world forever when he rounded Africa's Cape of Good Hope in 1488. Dias opened the route to the East and paved the way for Portuguese entrance into the spice trade and empire in the east. In the meantime, **Christopher Columbus** begged the crown to patronize his trip east to the Indies, only to be turned down because Portuguese experts concluded his calculations were clearly wrong. Portugal's **Vasco da Gama** led the first European naval expedition to India in 1498, and thereafter Portugal added to its empire numerous colonies along the East African and Indian coasts. Two years later **Pedro Alvares Cabral** happened upon Brazil. Portuguese traders, colonists, and missionaries, often using oppressive tactics, boasted claims all around the globe. Portugal's explorers may not have been motivated by the most admirable of ambitions, but nostalgic relics of Portugal's global muscle endure to the present day: Portuguese surnames persevere in places where lonely sailors took lovers, and Catholic churches survive where missionaries passed.

Portugal's monarchy reached its peak with **Manuel I The Fortunate** (1495-1521) on the throne. Known to foreigners as "the King of Gold," Manuel controlled a spectacular commercial empire. However, signs of future decline were already becoming evident, and it did not take long before competition from the other commercial powers began taking its toll.

The Houses of Habsburg and Bragança

In 1581 **Habsburg King of Spain Philip II** forcibly affirmed his quasi-legitimate claim to the Portuguese throne, and the Iberian peninsula was now ruled by one monarch. For 60 years the Habsburg family dragged Portugal into several ill-fated wars, including the Spanish-Portuguese Armada's crushing loss to England in 1588. Inattentive King Philip did not even visit Portugal until 1619—his priorities were elsewhere. By the end of Habsburg rule, Portugal had lost a substantial part of its once vast empire.

In 1640, while Phillip IV was forced to deal with rebels, the **House of Bragança** engineered a nationalist rebellion. After a brief struggle they assumed control. The Bragança dynasty went to great lengths to reestablish ties with England. **João V** (1706-1750), often referred to as an "enlightened despot," used Brazilian gold to finance massive projects, such as the construction of fabulous buildings and palaces.

The Earthquake of 1755

One event in Portuguese history more than any other shook the annals of Western Civilization. The momentous **Earthquake of 1755** devastated Lisbon, killing 60,000 people. Such an impact, combined with the fact that it occurred on All Saint's Day (Nov. 1), shook Europeans' faith in God. The earthquake is said to have caused candles to flicker as far away as Ireland. Despite the massive amount of damage, dictatorial minister **Marquês de Pombal** was able to rebuild Lisbon, while instituting national economic reform.

Napoleon's Conquest and Its Aftermath

Napoleon took control of France in 1801, and had grand designs on much of Europe. Napoleon's army met little resistance when they invaded Portugal in 1807. Rather than risk death, the Portuguese royal family fled to **Brazil. Dom João VI** returned to Lisbon in 1821, only to face an extremely unstable political climate. Brazil declared its independence with a bloodless revolution only a year after João's return. While this meant a huge loss in revenue, the results were tempered by the fact that João's son **Pedro** became Brazil's first ruler. Today, Portugal and Brazil remain closely linked culturally, linguistically, and politically.

More problems developed with João's death in 1826. The **Constitution of 1822** had provided political guidance and improved the overall situation, but the constitution was handily suspended when chaos reverberated through Portugal following João's death. Absolutists halted the marriage of Pedro's seven-year-old daughter Maria da Glória and her uncle Miguel, adding fuel to the **War of the Brothers** (1823-1834). Eight gory years later, with Miguel in exile, **Maria II** (1834-1854) ascended to the throne at a mere 15-years-old. During the next 75 years, politics increasingly pitted liberals against conservatives and progressives against monarchists.

> ## If Gilligan Were Ever So Lucky
>
> Paradise on earth? Start with water, water, everywhere. Add some volcanic eruptions, for solidity's sake. Mix in hearty, friendly, and pleasingly relaxed inhabitants. Pepper it with astounding beauty, alluring beaches, and extract pollution, persecution, and stress. Voilá!—you have Portugal's Atlantic islands, the Azores and Madeiras, considered by many to be the world's most beautiful, serene locales. While beyond the *Let's Go* budget, these isles are integral to Portugal.
>
> The **Madeiras,** consisting of three islands—Madeira, along with Porto Santo and Desertas—rise abruptly from the ocean off Africa's northwestern coast. Discovered uninhabited in 1419 by Portuguese seamen, the Madeiras became an essential stopover for budding explorers. Its climate, colorful fauna, tropical fruits, and luxurious hotels make it a strong contender as the ideal vacation spot.
>
> Less commercial but no less awe-inspiring, the **Azores** lay alone in the Atlantic, thousands of miles from land. Immortalized in *Moby Dick* and all its visitors hearts, its nine islands boast rolling hills, lush fauna, cavernous lakes, glimmering seas, and friendly inhabitants. Tranquil and tempting, the Azores will leave 6- to 76-year-olds musing (as one brochure claims), "Is this God's home?"

From the "First Republic" to Salazar

At the turn of the 20th century, Portugal was trying to recover from the political discord of the 19th century. On October 5, 1910, 20-year-old King **Manuel II** fled to England. The new government, known as the **"First Republic,"** granted universal male suffrage and diminished the influence of the Catholic Church. Workers were given the right to strike, and merit, rather than birth-right, became the primary qualification for civil service advancement. However, the expulsion of the Jesuits and other religious orders sparked world-wide disapproval; governmental conflicts with worker's movements heightened tensions at home. The weak republic wobbled along until it fell in a 1926 military coup. The military-backed rule of **Antonio Carmona** ended with his death in 1951. Antonio Salazar succeeded to the dictatorial throne. **António de Oliveira Salazar** was the son of a village bailiff. Unrest after the 1926 coup paved the way for this economist to become Prime Minister in 1932. Salazar's *Estado Novo* (New State) granted suffrage to women, but did little else to end the country's authoritarian tradition. While Portugal's international economic standing improved, the regime laid the cost of progress squarely on the shoulders of the working class and the peasantry, as well as on the colonized peoples of Africa. A terrifying secret police (PIDE) crushed all opposition to Salazar's rule, and African rebellions were quelled in bloody battles that crippled the nation's economy.

And furthermore...

A slightly more liberal **Marcelo Caetano** dragged on the increasingly unpopular African wars after Salazar's death in 1970. On April 25, 1974, a left-wing military coalition overthrew Caetano in a quick coup. The **Captain's Revolution** sent Portuguese dancing into the streets and splashing graffiti on government buildings; today every town in Portugal has its own Rua 25 de Abril. The Marxist-dominated armed forces established a variety of civil and political liberties and withdrew Portuguese claims on African colonies by 1975.

The socialist government nationalized several industries and expropriated large estates in the face of substantial opposition. The country's first elections in 1978 put the more conservative Social Democrats into power under the charismatic Prime Minister **Mario Soares.** A severe economic crisis exploded; foreign debt, inflation, and unemployment skyrocketed. Soares instituted "100 measures in 100 days" to shock Portugal into economic shape. Austerity measures to stimulate industrial growth cut back on worker protections. The landmark year 1986 brought Portugal into the European Economic Community, ending a traditional isolation from more affluent northern Europe. Soares won new elections to become the nation's first civilian president in 60 years. Forced to step down because of Constitutional limitations, Soares was replaced by the former Socialist mayor of Lisbon, **Jorge Sampaio,** who defeated former prime minister and PSD head Silva. Although the PSD's force as a party has diminished, the Socialists remain a minority government, holding 112 of 230 parliamentary seats.

Current Events

Portugal has valiantly striven to catch up economically with the rest of Western Europe and seems to be succeeding. With one of the strongest economies in the E.U., stronger even than Spain's, and an inflation rate of under 2%, Portugal seems to be thriving on the eve of its entrance into the European Monetary Union. An infusion of E.U. funds over the past several years has not hurt the economy either, and new roads, railways, hospitals, schools, port and airport facilities, and sewage and waste disposal systems, among other things, are everywhere. Expo '98, one of the most grandiose projects, unfortunately turned out to be a disappointment, with attendance falling below the expected levels. A more serious worry is that of being gradually engulfed by neighboring Spain, with 30 million more residents and a far larger economy.

At the same time, despite Portugal's ongoing modernization, some things seem destined never to change—such as the pristine beaches along the Atlantic seaboard, the plush landscape in the north, the fine wines of Porto, and the hard-earned character and age-old traditions that evolved over the course of Portugal's rich history.

■ The Arts

PAINTING AND SCULPTURE

The Age of Discovery (15th-16th centuries) was an era of vast cultural exchange with Renaissance Europe and beyond. Flemish masters such as **Jan van Eyck** brought their talent to Portugal; likewise, many Portuguese artists polished their skills in Antwerp. King Manuel's favorite, High Renaissance artist **Jorge Afonso,** created realistic portrayals of human anatomy. Afonso's best works hang at the Conventos de Cristo in Tomar and da Madre de Deus in Lisbon. In the late 15th century, the talented **Nuno Gonçalves** led a revival of the primitivist school.

PORTUGAL

The Baroque Period boasted even more diverse artistic representation. Wood-carving became extremely popular in Portugal during the period. **Joachim Machado** carved elaborate crèches in the early 1700s. On canvas, portraiture was head and shoulders above other genres. The prolific19th-century artist **Domingos António de Sequeira** depicted historical, religious, and allegorical subjects using a technique that would later inspire French Impressionists. In another artistic tilt, Porto's **António Soares dos Reis** brought Romantic sensibility to sculpture in the 1800s.

Cubism, expressionism and futurism trickled into Portugal despite Salazar-inspired censorship. More recently, **Maria Helena Vieira da Silva** has won international recognition for her abstract works, and the master **Carlos Botelho** has become world-renowned for his wonderful vignettes of Lisbon life.

ARCHITECTURE

Few Moorish structures survived the Christian Reconquista, but Moorish influence persisted even in later examples. Colorful **azulejos** grace many walls, ceilings, and thresholds. Carved in fabulous relief by the pre-Reconquista Moors, these ornate tiles later took on flat, glazed Italian and Northern European designs. Ironically enough, this Arabic concept gained its greatest fame in Catholic churches, the palaces of Christian kings, and post-17th-century Portuguese urban architecture.

Portugal's signature **Manueline** style celebrates the exploration and imperial expansion which surfaced under King Manuel the Fortunate. This hybrid style boils down to late and extravagant Gothic, but also reflects aspects of Islamic heritage along with influences from Italy, Flanders, and the Spanish Plateresque. Manueline works routinely feature a sprinkle of marine motifs. The amalgam of styles found its most elaborate expression in the church and tower at **Belém,** built to honor Vasco da Gama. Close seconds are the **Mosteiro dos Jerónimos** in Lisbon and the **Abadia de Santa Maria de Vitória** in Batalha.

LITERATURE

Portugal's literary achievements, mostly lyric poetry or realist fiction, can be traced back to the 12th century, when the lyrical aspects of Portuguese were solidified by poet-king **Dinis I.** Dinis made Portuguese the region's official language (one of the first "official" non-Latin Romance vernaculars). Portuguese poetry blossomed in the Age of Discovery, notably in the letters of **Francisco de Sá de Miranda** (1481-1558) and the musical lyrics of **Antonio Ferreira** (1528-1569). Renaissance-era writer **Luís de Camões** celebrated Vasco de Gama's sea voyages to India in Portugal's greatest epic, *Os Lusíadas* (*The Lusiads,* 1572), modeled on the *Aenid.*

Classics of Portuguese prose were often related to the sea. An explorer himself, **João de Barros** penned a history of Portuguese in Goa in *Décadas*. **Gil Vicente,** court poet to Manuel I and considered Portugal's equivalent to Shakespeare in style and importance, wrote simultaneously light and heavy dramas about peasants, nature, and religion. The witty realism of Vicente's *Barcas* trilogy (1617-1619) influenced contemporaries Shakespeare and Cervantes, and earned him a distinguished place in Spanish literary ranks. Spanish hegemony, intermittent warfare, and imperial decline conspired to make the literature of the 17th and 18th centuries somewhat less triumphant than that of past eras. Still, **João Baptista de Almeida Garrett** and historian **Alexandre Herculano,** who were both exiled because of their liberal political views, sought to integrate Portuguese literature with the Romantic school of fiction they encountered while in exile. A lyric poet, dramatist, politician, revolutionary, frequent exile, and legendary lover, Garrett is credited with reviving drama in Portugal. His most famous play is *Frei Luís de Sousa* (*Brother Luís de Sousa,* 1843).

Portuguese literature shifted from romantic to the realist when political thinkers dominated the rise of the literary intelligentsia, the **Generation of 1870.** The most visible figure to influence this shift in the late 19th century was novelist and life-long diplomat (residing almost always outside Iberia) **José Maria Eça de Queiroz.** He conceived a distinctly Portuguese social realism, documenting 19th century Portuguese society, sometimes critical of its bourgeois elements. His best works were *O Crime do Padre Amaro* (*The Sin of Father Amaro*) and *Os Maias* (*The Maias*).

Fernando Pessoa was Portugal's most famed and creative writer of the late 19th and 20th centuries. Pessoa (literally, "person") wrote in English as well as Portuguese, developing four distinct styles under four pseudonyms: Pessoa, Alberto Caeiro, Ricardo Reis, and Alvaro de Campos. Ever the multiple personality, he introduced free verse to Portuguese poetry and his overall impact rivals T.S. Eliot's on English literature. His semi-autobiography, *Livro do Desassossego* (*The Book of Disgust*) is his only prose work, posthumously compiled and today seen as a classic in modernism. Other influential writers of the 20th century are **Aquilino Ribeiro,** author of *O Homem que Matou o Diabo* (*The Man Who Killed the Devil*), and **José Maria Ferreira de Castro,** widely known for his realist fiction, such as *A Selva* (*The Jungle*).

Contemporary writers, like **Miguel Torga,** have gained international fame for their wonderfully satirical novels. The work of **José Saramago,** probably Portugal's most important living fiction writer, has achieved new acclaim in the post-Salazar era; he is perhaps best known for *Ricardo Reis,* the story of a doctor who returns to Portugal during Salazar's reign and confronts the past. Another work, *The Stone Raft,* explores the literal and figurative separation of Iberia from the rest of Europe.

The end of Salazar's reign brought literary liberation; repression, once the condition, is now the topic. Female writers, long discouraged or censored, have come out of the woodwork with a vengeance. In **Novas Cartas Portuguesas** (*New Portuguese Letters*), the "Three Marias" (the authors) expose the maltreatment of women in a male-dominated society, based on 17th century work of the same nature. Though condemned as obscene in 1972, post-1974 Portugal opened its mind and pages to the cause of women's rights. Other acclaimed post-Salazar authors include António Lobo Antunes, who has achieved the status of Saramago but with a dramatically different style of prose known for its scattered form and psychoanalytic themes. José Cardoso Pires' novel *balada da Praia dos Cães* (*Ballad of Dog's Beach*) is a mystery-thriller based on an actual political assassination that occurred during the Salazar era, thus documenting the work of the secret police during the dictatorship.

MUSIC

The **fado,** according to one brochure, "causes the chords of the Portuguese soul to vibrate melancholically or passionately." Named after fate, *fado* is a musical tradition unique to Portugal, identified with a sense of *saudade* (yearning or longing) and characterized by tragic, romantic lyrics and mournful melodies. These solo ballads, accompanied by the acoustic *guitarra* (a flat-backed guitar, like a mandolin, essential to the sound of authentic *fado* music), appeal to the romantic side of Portuguese culture, consuming and enriching the soul. *Fado* centers are in Lisbon and Coimbra and each area offers a slightly different approach. Amália Rodrigues is the most famous *fadista* (*fado* singer); she has been singing *fado* ballads since the 1940s and has helped spread *fado* beyond Portugal. Argentina Santos is also a contemporary *fadista* and continues the tradition of running her own *fado* house, the now famous Parreirinha de Alfama in Lisbon. *Fadistas* wear a black shawl in memory of the first great *fadista,* Maria Severa.

Apart from its folk tradition, the music of Portugal has yet to achieve international fame (Yanni fans need not worry). Portuguese opera peaked with **António José da Silva,** victim of the 1739 Inquisition. The Renaissance in Portugal led to the development of pieces geared for solo instrumentalists and vocals. Italian **Domenico Scarlatti,** brought to Lisbon by João V, composed brilliant keyboard-geared pieces. His preeminent Portuguese contemporary, Coimbra's **Carlos Seixas,** thrilled 18th-century Lisbon with his genius and contributed to the development of the sonata form. **Domingos Bomtempo** (1775-1842) introduced symphonic innovations from abroad and helped establish the first Sociedade Filarmónica, modeled after the London Philharmonic, in Lisbon 822.

Although the French invasion, Civil War, and decreased patronage somewhat stifled Portuguese music, folk music and dancing is still quite popular in rural areas, and a modern revival in classical music has occurred in the latter half of this century, led by Joly Braga Santo. The Calouste Gulbenkian Foundation in Lisbon has kept Portuguese music alive, sponsoring a symphony orchestra since 1962, hosting popular local folk singers (Fausto and Sérgio Godinho), ballets, opera, and an International Jazz Festival every summer. The Teatro Nacional de São Carlos also has its own orchestra and ballet company. These orchestras have all spawned a group of young composers, including Filipe Pires, A. Vitorino de Almeida and Jorge Peixinho, who have begun to make their mark in international competition.

You Say Fado, I Say Fado

If the blues have a hold on your heart, then *fado* is sure to capture your soul. The melodies and lyrics of *fado* drip with the wrenching pain and passion of life and love. Although the origins of *fado* may have come from the African slave songs, *fado* did not ingrain itself in Portuguese culture until the life of legendary *fadista,* **Maria Severa.** Although she led a short life (1810-1836), Severa achieved mythical status because of her ability to move people with lyrics that expressed her own real-life dramas. She lived in Lisbon as the mistress of the famed noble bull-fighter Conde de Vimioso. Severa's life and early death (due to excessive gastronomic consumption) were a turning point in the history of *fado*, providing the basis for the first Portuguese sound movie in 1931 and spawning many other poems, novels, and *fado* lyrics. *Fado* houses, including A Severa in Lisbon, are the best places to enjoy a special *fado* moment and to celebrate for yourself the legend that Severa left behind. In addition to Lisbon, Coimbra is also home to many *fado* houses, though Coimbra *fado* differs significantly from the more urban, working-class inspired Lisbon *fado;* Coimbra *fado* has slower, more intellectual lyrics about romance and beautiful women and is often sung by male students from Coimbra's universities.

Language

Thanks to the Romans who colonized Iberia in the late third century BC, practiced Latinites will find Portuguese an easy conquest. This softer sister of Spanish is among the purest Romance languages, although pronunciation is relatively complex. Portugal's diversity duly evidences itself in its language. A close listener will catch echoes of Italian, French, Spanish, Arabic, and even English and Slavic. Portugal's global escapades also spurred its language's spread. Today, Portuguese (the world's fifth-most-spoken language) binds over 200 million people worldwide, most of them in Portugal, Brazil, Mozambique, and Angola. Prospective students of the language should note the handful of significant differences between Brazilian and continental Portuguese, mainly in pronunciation and usage.

Some may be heartened to know that English, Spanish, and French are widely spoken throughout Portugal, especially in tourist-oriented locales. In addition, look to the *Let's Go* glossary in the back of this book for terms (or their Castilian cousins) used recurrently in the text (see **Food Terms,** p. 717).

Food and Drink

TYPICAL FARE

Locals season their dishes with olive oil, garlic, herbs, and sea salt but relatively few spices. Seafood lovers will gleefully encounter a tantalizing selection of fish: *chocos grelhados* (grilled cuttlefish), *linguado grelhado* (grilled sole), and swordfish, to name a few. Probe the exotic *polvo* (boiled or grilled octopus), *mexilhões* (mussels), and *lulas grelhadas* (grilled squid). Pork, chicken, and beef appear on menus relentlessly, and often together. The comprehensive winter staple is *cozida à portuguesa* (boiled beef, pork, sausage, and vegetables). True connoisseurs add a drop of *piri-piri*

PORTUGAL

(mega-hot) sauce on the side. An expensive delicacy is freshly roasted *cabrito* (baby goat). No matter what you order, leave room for *batatas* (potatoes), prepared count less ways—including *batatas fritas* (french fries)—which accompany each meal.

On the lighter side, **sopas** (soups) give cheap satisfaction to an empty stomach Common soups are *caldo de ovos* (bean soup with hard-boiled eggs), *caldo de ver dura* (vegetable soup), and the tasty *caldo verde* (a potato and kale mixture with slice of sausage and olive oil). **Sandes** (sandwiches) such as the *bifana* or *prego n pão* (meat sandwich) may be no more than a hunk of beef or turkey on a roll. Cows goats, and ewes please the palate by providing raw material for Portugal's renowned **queijos** (cheeses).

Portugal's favorite **dessert** is *pudim,* or *flan,* a rich, caramel custard similar t crême bruleé. Simple rice puddings are age-old staples. For the sweet tooth in all o us, the almond groves of the Algarve produce their own version of marzipan. Fo something different, try *pêras* (pears) drenched in sweet port wine and served with sprinkling of raisins and filberts on top. Most common are countless varieties of inex pensive, high-quality **sorvete** (ice cream)—look for vendors posting the colorful ubiquitous "Olá" sign. *Pastelarías* (bakeries) are a social center in most towns, an tasty **pastries** make for a cheap (80-180$) breakfast.

DINING HOURS AND RESTAURANTS

Portuguese eat their hearty midday meal—*almoço* (lunch)—between 12 and 2 pn and *jantar* (dinner) between 9 and midnight. Both meals entail at least three courses There are no greasy lumberjack breakfasts to be found in Portugal—have a pastry (80 180$) from a *pastelaría* (bakery) and coffee from a café for your *pequeno almoç* (breakfast). If you happen to get the munchies between 4 and 7pm, snack- or café bars sell **sandes** (sandwiches) and sweet succulent cakes flavored with cinnamon.

A full meal costs 1000-2000$, depending on the restaurant's location and quality **Meia dose** (half portions) cost more than half-price but are often more than ade quate—a full portion may satisfy two. The ubiquitous **prato do dia** (special of the day) and **menu** (*ementa* in Portuguese) of appetizer, bread, entree, and dessert wil stifle the loudest stomach growls. The **ementa turística** (tourist menu) is usually rip-off aimed at foreigners (and inevitably the most expensive option). Standard pre meal bread, butter, cheese, and pâté may be dished without your asking, but these pre-meal munchies are not free (300-500$ per person).

Outdoor food stalls are the best way to eat on the cheap. **Vegetarians** should hit up the **mercado municipal** (an open-air market found in almost every town) before noon for the best produce. Groceries can be bought at the **supermercado** (supermar ket) or **loja de conveniência** (convenience store).

DRINKS

The quality and low cost of Portuguese *vinho* (wine) is truly astounding. The pinna cle, **vinho do porto** (port), pressed (by feet) from the red grapes of the Douro Valley and fermented with a touch of brandy, is a dessert in itself. Chilled, white port make a snappy aperitif, while the ruby or tawny port is a pleasing digestif. A cool heatin process gives **Madeira** wines their unique "cooked" flavor. Try the dry Sercial and Verdelho before the main course, and the sweeter Bual and Malmsey after.

Sparkling *vinho verde* (green wine, referring to its youth, not its color) comes in red and white versions. The red may be a might strong for the faux connoisseur but the white is brash and delicious by most anybody's standards. The Adega Coopera tives of Ponte de Lima, Monção, and Amarante produce the best of this type. Excel lent local table wines include Colares, Dão, Borba, Bairrada, Bucelas, and Periquita. I you can't decide, experiment with the **vinho de casa** (house wine); either the *tint* (red) or the *branco* (white) is a reliable standby. Tangy **sangría** comes filled with fresh orange slices and makes even a budget meal festive at a minimal expense (usu ally around 500$ for a half-pitcher).

Bottled Sagres or Super Bock are excellent beers. If you do not ask for it *fresco* (cool) it may come *natural* (room temperature). A tall, slim glass of draft beer is a **fino** or an **imperial,** while a larger stein is a **caneca.** To sober and/or wake up, gulp a **bica** (cup of black espresso), a **galão** (coffee with milk, served in a glass), or a **café com leite** (coffee with milk, served in a cup).

■ Sports

Futebol (soccer to Yanks) is the sport of choice for youngsters, professionals, and fans alike. The country has shown signs of making it big—at the 1996 European Championships, the national team ousted Denmark en route to the semifinals—but has fallen short at crucial moments, such as the World Cup '98 qualification matches. The quality of the national league, however, remains high, and games create a crazed fervor throughout Portugal. Lisbon's club, **Benfica,** features some of the very finest players in the world. Native Portuguese have also made names for themselves off the pitch, specifically in long-distance running, where marathon-queen **Rosa Mota** dominated her event for a number of years.

For recreation diverging from jogging and pick-up soccer games, Portuguese often return to the sea. **Windsurfers, body-surfers,** and **surfers** make waves along the wavy north coast, while **snorklers** and **scuba divers** set out on mini-explorations in the south and west.

■ Prose to Peruse

Fiction: Portuguese and Foreign with Portuguese Flavoring

For the scoop on Portuguese classics in most every genre, check out **Literature** (p. 537). Most of the more famous works have been translated into English; for more options, consult your librarian. For English literature with a Portuguese twist, check out *Sonnets from the Portuguese* by Elizabeth Barrett Browning, featuring some of the world's most timeless, beautiful poetry. Lord Byron in *Selected Letters and Journals* discusses honestly the few days he spent in Portugal. Also, Herman Melville's *Moby Dick* dives into whales, "Cap'ns," and the Azores.

History and Culture

There is no dearth of information on Portuguese history and culture for the inquisitive and intellectual traveler. Packing one of these works in your suitcase will help make the cities and towns of Portugal that much more meaningful and memorable. A good place to start may be *Roads to Today's Portugal: Essays on Contemporary Portuguese Literature, Art, and Culture* (1983) by Elanea Brown. Among the best history texts available is A. H. de Oliveira Marques' *History of Portugal* (1972). For more of a focus on contemporary history, in *Portugal: Fifty Years,* António de Figueiredo studies Salazar's dictatorship from the 1926 military coup to the 1974 revolution. A more academic account of Salazar is *Fascism and Resistance in Portugal*, by Dan L. Raby.

Lisbon (Lisboa)

Over 400 years ago, Lisbon was the center of the world's richest and farthest-reaching empire. Although the glorious Age of Discovery is part of the distant past, and modern problems such as traffic, smog, and urban decay assail Lisbon, the city retains a certain imperial grandeur. *Lisboetas* carefully preserve their traditions along with a relaxed urban atmosphere. The city continually renovates its historic monuments and meticulously maintains its black and white mosaic sidewalks, pastel facades, and cobbled, medieval alleys. Vintage streetcars weave between buses, motorcycles, cars, and pedestrians down broad avenues and narrow lanes.

Many nations claim to have settled Lisbon, with one legend crediting Odysseus as its founder. Officially, Lisbon is thought to have been inhabited over 3000 years ago by Phoenicians, Greeks, and Carthaginians in turn, until the Romans arrived in 205 BC. Under Julius Caesar's reign, Lisbon became the most important city in Lusitania, although it was not made the capital of the kingdom of Portugal until 1255. City and empire reached their apex toward the end of the 15th century when Portuguese navigators pioneered explorations of Asia, Africa, and South America. A huge earthquake on November 1, 1755, touched off the nation's fall from glory—close to one-fifth of the population died in the catastrophe, and two-thirds of Lisbon was reduced to a pile of smoldering rubble. Under the authoritarian leadership of Prime Minister Marquês de Pombal, the city quickly recovered as magnificent new squares, palaces, and churches were speedily built along the Cartesian guidelines of style and architecture in the heyday of the Enlightenment. Another wave of construction in the late 19th century extended the city to the north and west.

Lisbon has seen more than its share of changes over the course of the 20th century as well. During World War II, Lisbon's neutrality and Atlantic connections made the city a rendezvous for spies on both sides. In 1974, when Mozambique and Angola won independence, hundreds of thousands of refugees converged upon the Portuguese capital. Immigration, combined with reactionary liberalism in response to the demise of Salazar's dictatorship, have all combined to give the city a cosmopolitan air. Today, Portuguese of African, Asian, and European origin mix freely on the streets. In 1998 the World Expo descended upon Lisbon, providing the impetus for massive construction projects and a citywide facelift while helping to renew Lisbon's claim to the forefront of European culture.

🖐 HIGHLIGHTS OF LISBON AND AROUND

- Wandering through Lisbon's **Alfama district** (see p. 555).
- The magnificent palaces and castles at **Sintra,** less than an hour outside of Lisbon (see p. 562).
- The extravagent monastery complex at nearby **Belém** (see p. 556).
- **Estoril** (see p. 560) and **Cascais** (see p. 561), two nearby seaside resorts.

▮ Orientation

According to legend, Lisbon, like Rome, was built on seven hills, even though your calves might tell you there are many more. Navigating the maze of Lisbon's roller-coaster streets requires patience and stairmaster training. The three main *bairros* (neighborhoods) of the city center are the Baixa (low district, resting in the valley), the Bairro Alto (high district), and the Alfama.

The **Baixa,** Lisbon's old business center, sits in the center of town, sandwiched between the other two districts. Its grid of small, mostly pedestrian streets begins at the **Rossio** (also called the **Praça Dom Pedro IV**) and ends at the **Praça do Comércio,** on the **Rio Tejo** (otherwise known as the **Tagus River**). The **Praça dos Restauradores,** where buses from the airport stop, lies just above the Baixa. From Pr. Restauradores, the tree-lined **Avenida da Liberdade** runs uphill to the new business district centered around **Praça do Marquês de Pombal.** Boxy 60s-style buildings add color to the broad avenues radiating from the *praça*.

From the west side of the Baixa, the **Ascensor de Santa Justa**—an elegant historic outdoor elevator—lifts you up to the Bairro Alto's upscale shopping district, the **Chiado,** traversed by the fashionable **Rua do Carmo** and **Rua Garrett.** The **Bairro Alto** is a mix of narrow streets, tropical parks, and Baroque churches. Young Portuguese come here to party—activity on the street doesn't change between 2pm and 2am.

To the east of the Baixa, the **Alfama,** Lisbon's famous medieval *bairro* comprising the Moorish quarter, is the oldest district of the city, stacking tiny whitewashed houses along a labyrinth of narrow alleys and stairways beneath the **Castelo de São Jorge.** Expect to get lost. Without a detailed map expect to get doubly lost. The twisting streets change names about every three steps, and streets that share a name may not actually be the same street. There are *travessas* (side streets), *ruas* (streets), *calçadinhas* (walkways), and *escadinhas* (stairways). The tourist office's map is free, but does not list all the streets. A street-indexed *GeoBloco* **Planta Turística de Lisboa** or the *Poseidon* **Planta de Lisboa** (with Sintra, Cascais, and Estoril on the back) are worth the money (both sold in Estação Rossio and most magazine stands for 1000$).

■ Arrivals and Departures

BY PLANE

All flights land at **Aeroporto de Lisboa** (tel. 840 20 60 or 849 63 50) on the northern outskirts of the city. Walk out of the airport terminal and turn right, following the road around the curve to the bus stop, where you can take bus #44 or 45 (20min., 150$) to the **Praça dos Restauradores;** the bus lets you off directly in front of the tourist office. Or, take the express AeroBus or bus #91 (15min., departs every 20min., 430$) to the same location; it leaves directly from the airport exit. A taxi ride from the airport downtown will cost about 1300$, plus a 300$ luggage fee.

Major airlines have offices at Pr. Marquês de Pombal and along Av. Liberdade. Call for the current rates, as prices almost always fluctuate.

TAP Air Portugal, Pr. Marquês de Pombal, 3 (reservation and info tel. 841 69 90). Open M-F 9am-6pm. To Faro, Funchal (Madeira), Porto, Paris, London, Madrid, and Barcelona.

Iberia, R. Rosa Araújo, 2 (tel. 355 81 19).

Portugália Airlines, Av. Almirante Gago Coutinho, 88 (tel. 848 66 93), serves major domestic destinations. Airport office (tel. 842 55 00).

BY TRAIN

Train service into and out of Lisbon is potentially confusing because there are four main stations, each serving different destinations. For info about Portugal's national railway system, **Caminhos de Ferro Portuguêses,** call 888 40 25. Be aware that in Portuguese trains are called *comboios* (by oxen).

Estação Rossio, between Pr. Restauradores and Pr. Dom Pedro IV, takes you to points west. Open daily 8am-11pm. Schedules and assistance available from an info office on the ground level (open daily 10am-1pm and 2-7pm). Luggage storage available here, but not at any other station (500$ for 48hr.). English spoken. To Sintra via Queluz (45min., departs every 10min., 185$).

Estação Santa Apolónia, Av. Infante D. Henrique, east of the Alfama on the banks of the Rio Tejo, runs the international, northern, and eastern lines. The international terminal, with **currency exchange** and an info desk (English spoken) is located off the right side of the main platform. To reach downtown from the station, take bus #9, 39, or 46 to Pr. Restauradores and Estação Rossio. To: Aveiro (1680$); Braga (2500$); Bragança (2710$); Coimbra (1300$); Elvas (1600$); Mirandela (3000$); Madrid (8200$); and Paris (24,000$).

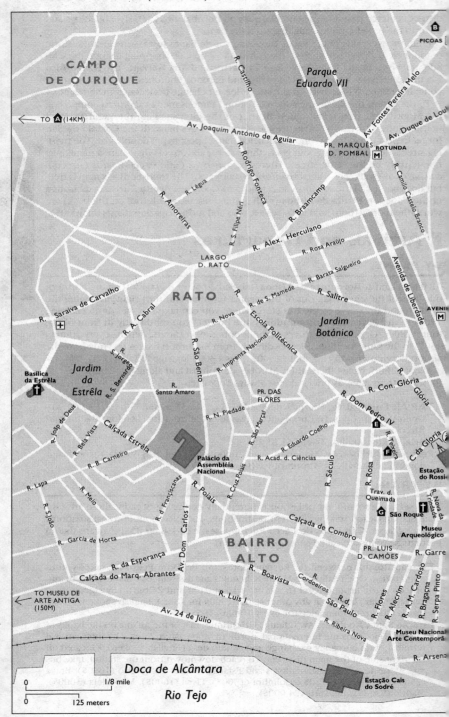

CAMPO DE OURIQUE

Parque Eduardo VII

PICOAS

R. Castilho

← TO Ⓐ (14KM)

Av. Joaquim António de Aguiar

Av. Fontes Pereira Melo

Av. Duque de Loul

PR. MARQUÊS D. POMBAL   ROTUNDA Ⓜ

R. Rodrigo Fonseca

R. Braamcamp

R. Camilo Castelo Branco

R. Légua

R. Amoreiras

R.S. Filipe Néri

R. Alex. Herculano

R. Rosa Araújo

LARGO D. RATO

R. Barata Salgueiro

Avenida de Liberdade

R. Saraiva de Carvalho

RATO

R. de S. Mamede

R. Salitre

AVENI Ⓜ

R. A. Cabral

R. Nova

Escola Politécnica

Jardim Botánico

R. São Bento

R. Imprensa Nacional

R. Con. Glória

R. Glória

Basílica da Estrêla

Jardim da Estrêla

R. S. Jorge

R. S. Bernardo

R. Santo Amaro

PR. DAS FLORES

R. Dom Pedro IV

Estação do Rossi

R. João de Deus

R. Bela Vista

Calçada Estrêla

R. N. Piedade

R. São Marçal

R. Eduardo Coelho

R. Teixeira

C.ᵃ da Glória

R. B. Carneiro

Palácio da Assembléia Nacional

R. Acad. d. Ciências

R. Século

R. Rosa

R. Lapa

R. Melo

R. d. Franciscanas

R. Poiais

R. Cruz Poiais

Trav. d. Queimada

São Roque

R. S.João

R. Garcia de Horta

Calçada de Combro

Museu Arqueológico

R. da Esperança

BAIRRO ALTO

PR. LUIS D. CAMÕES

R. Garre

Calçada do Marq. Abrantes

R. Boavista

R. Cordoeiros

R. Flores

R. Alecrim

R.A.M. Cardoso

R. Bragança

R. Serpa Pinto

TO MUSEU DE ARTE ANTIGA (150M)

R. Luis I

R.d. São Paulo

R. Ribeira Nova

Av. Dom Carlos I

Av. 24 de Júlio

Museu Nacional Arte Contemporã

R. Arsena

Doca de Alcântara

Rio Tejo

Estação Cais do Sodré

0   1/8 mile

0   125 meters

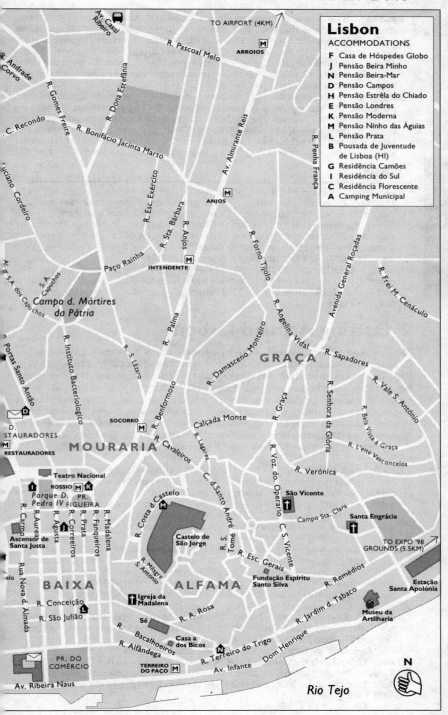

Lisbon
ACCOMMODATIONS
- **F** Casa de Hóspedes Globo
- **J** Pensão Beira Minho
- **N** Pensão Beira-Mar
- **D** Pensão Campos
- **H** Pensão Estrêla do Chiado
- **E** Pensão Londres
- **K** Pensão Moderna
- **M** Pensão Ninho das Águias
- **L** Pensão Prata
- **B** Pousada de Juventude de Lisboa (HI)
- **G** Residência Camões
- **I** Residência do Sul
- **C** Residência Florescente
- **A** Camping Municipal

Estação Cais do Sodré, just beyond the south end of R. Alecrim, east of Pr. Comér-cio, on the banks of the Tejo. Take bus #1, 44, or 45 to Pr. Restauradores or bus #28 to Estação Santa Apolónia. Trains to the Mastery in Belém (10min., departs every 15min., 110$); the youth hostel in Oeiras (20min., departs every 15min., 150$); Estoril and Cascais (30min., departs every 15min., 180$). Consult the video monitors above each platform. Some trains are expresses that go directly to Estoril/Cascais without stopping.

Estação Barreiro, across the Rio Tejo from Lisbon proper, serves southern lines like the Costa Azul and the Algarve. Station accessible by ferries from the Terreiro do Paço dock off Pr. Comércio. Be sure to distinguish the Estação from adjacent ferry docks. Ferries leave approximately every 30min. and take 30min. to reach the other side; ferry ticket included in the price of connecting train ticket. Trains to: Setúbal (1½hr., departs every hr., 290$); Lagos (5½hr., departs every 2 hr., 1700$).

BY BUS

Rodoviária da Estremadura, Av. Casal Ribeiro, 18 (info tel. 54 54 35; terminal tel. 55 77 15). From the metro stop "Saldanha," walk into the Pr. Duque de Saldanha. Av. Casal Ribeiro is the 2nd street on the left; the bus station is 2 blocks down on the left. English spoken. To: Évora (3½hr., 15 per day, 1350$); Coimbra (2½hr., 16 per day, 1350$); Peniche (2hr., 11 per day, 950$); Portalegre (4hr., 4 per day, 1500$); Lagos (5hr., 10 per day, 2200$); Porto (4hr., 15 per day, 1900$); Braga (5hr., 6 per day, 2100$); Tavira (5hr., 5 per day, 2200$); Vila Real St. Antonio (6hr., 6 per day, 2300$).

Caima, R. Bacalhoeiros, 16 (tel. 887 50 61 or 886 63 69), off the Pr. Comércio, runs comfortable express buses with movies and A/C to the Algarve and Porto. Fastest way to the Algarve from Lisbon. To: Porto (4hr., 6 per day, 2000$); Lagos (5hr., 6 per day, 2400$).

■ Getting Around Lisbon

Lisbon has an efficient system of buses, subways, trams, funiculars, and trains. Use them to full advantage—no suburb in or out of the city (even the beach) takes longer than 45 minutes to reach. If you don't speak Portuguese, however, taxi drivers and bus and train ticket booths may try to rip you off by charging an exorbitant fare or not returning your change. Make sure you know in advance what the fare should be, or else don't hand the ticket salesman more than 200$ for a local trip. If you are badly cheated and have a receipt or bill, consider writing or calling the **Departamento de Reclamações (Department of Complaints),** AMTRAL, R. Dr. António Cândido 8 R/C, 1097 Lisbon (tel. 356 38 31; fax 356 38 35), to see justice triumph (perhaps).

City Buses: CARRIS (tel. 363 93 43 or 363 20 44) runs the buses, subways, trains, and funiculars in Lisbon. 150$ within the city. If you plan to stay for any length of time, consider investing in a *bilhete de assinatura turístico* (tourist pass), good for unlimited travel on CARRIS transports. 7-, 4-, and 1-day passes available (2265$; 1600$; 430$). Passes sold in CARRIS booths located in most network train stations and the busier metro stations (e.g. Restauradores). Open daily 8am-8pm. You must show a passport to buy a tourist pass.

Subway: the **Metro** (tel. 355 84 57) follows Av. Liberdade then branches into lines covering the modern business district. A red "M" marks Metro stops (*Let's Go* indicates a metro stop by writing an "M" followed by the name of the stop). Tickets 70$ at window or from vending machines. Book of 10 tickets 550$. Tourist passes for 4, 7, or 30 days (1600$, 2265$, 3600$). Always keep your eyes peeled for pickpockets. Trains run daily 6am-1am.

Trams: Everywhere. These offer beautiful views of the harbor and older neighborhoods. Many date back to before WWI. Line #28 is great for sight-seeing in the Alfama and Mouraria (stops in Pr. Comércio, 150$).

Funiculars: Link the lower city with the hilly residential area (60-180$).

Taxis: Rádio Táxis de Lisboa (tel. 815 50 61), **Autocoope** (tel. 793 27 56), and **Teletáxi** (tel. 815 20 16). 24hr. service. Taxis swarm like pigeons along Av. Liberdade throughout the Baixa and cruise the streets elsewhere in the city. Flat rate of 300$ for luggage.

Lisbon Metro

A Gaivota
B Girassol
C Caravela
D Oriente

PORTUGAL

Car Rental: Pick up cars at the airport or in one of several locations downtown. Contact the central reservation numbers for pickup locations. **Budget,** Av. Visconte Valmar, 36BIC (tel. 796 10 28; fax 797 13 77); **Hertz,** Qto. Francelha Baixio (tel. 941 55 41; fax 941 60 68); **Avis,** Av. Praia da Vitória, 12C (tel. 346 26 76). See **By Car,** p. 45, for toll-free numbers to get rates and other info from home. If you're confining your visit to Lisbon, a car is uneccessary. You won't want to be a part of the hair-raising traffic—Portugal continually has the highest accident rate in Western Europe—and it's dangerous enough being a pedestrian.

■ Practical Information

Tourist and Financial Services

Tourist Office: Municipal, R. Jardin do Regidor, 50 (tel. 343 36 72), on the right side of Pr. Restauradores. Service specific to Lisbon. For all of Portugal, check **Palácio da Foz** (tel. 346 63 07 or 346 33 14), at Pr. Restauradores. M: Restauradores. English spoken. Bus schedules, *pensão* listings, and free map. Open daily 9am-8pm. Another office at the **Aeroporto de Lisboa** (tel. 849 36 89), right as you exit the baggage claim area. English spoken. Open daily 6am-2am.

Budget Travel: Movijovem, Av. Duque d'Avila, 37 (tel. 13 88 20), will make reservations at youth hostels for you throughout the country.

Embassies: see **Embassies and Consulates,** p. 41.

Currency Exchange: Banks are open M-F 8:30-11:45am and 1-2:45pm. For a relatively low commission and decent rates, try **Cota Cámbio,** R. Áurea, 283, 1 block off Pr. Dom Pedro IV in the Baixa. The **Banco Fonsecas and Burnay** branch in the international terminal at Estação Santa Apolónia charges a high commission. Open 24hr. The main post office, most banks, and travel agencies also change money. Ask first—fees can be exorbitant (1000$ or more). **ATMs,** which offer the best exchange rates, line the streets of the Baixa and are sprinkled through the rest of the city. Nifty **automatic exchange machines** can be found throughout the Baixa, although their high fees more than negate the convenience.

American Express: Top Tours, Av. Duque de Loulé, 108 (tel. 315 58 85). M: Rotunda. Exit toward R. Rodrigo Sampaio and walk up Av. Liberdade toward the Marquês de Pombal statue, then hang a right. This sole (and often crowded) Top Tours office handles all AmEx functions. Traveler's checks sold and cashed. Mail held. English spoken. Open M-F 9:30am-1pm and 2:30-6:30pm.

PORTUGAL

Local Services

Luggage Storage: Only at **Estação Rossio.** Lockers 450-600$ (depending on size) for 48hr. period. Open daily 6am-2am.

English Bookstore: Livraria Britânica, R. Luis Fernandes, 14-16 (tel. 342 84 72), across from the British Institute in the Bairro Alto. Good collection of classics and popular novels. Open M-F 9:30am-7pm. Visa, MC, AmEx. **Livraria Bertrand,** R. Garrett, 73 (tel. 342 19 41). Stock up on best-sellers, magazines, international maps, language books, and travel guides. Open M-F 9am-7pm, Sa 9am-1pm.

Library: Biblioteca Municipal Central, Palácio Galveias (tel. 797 38 62). M: Campo Pequeno. Open M-F 9am-7pm, Su 11am-5pm.

Shopping Center: Amoreiras Shopping Center de Lisboa (tel. 69 25 58), on Av. Duarte Pacheco. Take bus #11 from Restauradores. 383 shops including a humongous **Pão de Açúcar** supermarket, English bookstores, and a 10-screen **cinema.** Another option is **Colombo,** in front of Benefica stadium. M: Colégio Militar. Over 500 shops and a 10-screen cinema.

Laundromat: Lavatax, R. Francisco Sanches, 65A (tel. 812 33 92). M: Arroios. Self-service or wash, dry, and fold 1100$ per 5kg load. Open M-F 9am-1pm and 3-7pm, Sa 9am-noon.

Emergency and Communications

Police: R. Capelo, 3 (tel. 346 61 41 or 347 56 38). English spoken. **Fire:** (tel. 342 22 22). **Emergency:** Dial 112 from anywhere in Portugal.

Late-Night Pharmacy: Call 118. Pharmacies throughout the city stay open all night on a rotating basis for emergencies only. The address of the next night service is posted on the door of every pharmacy.

Crisis Lines: Drug Abuse: Centro das Taipas (tel. 342 85 85).

Medical Services: British Hospital, R. Saraiva de Carvalho, 49 (tel. 395 50 67; for appointments tel. 397 63 29). **Cruz Vermelha Portuguesa,** R. Duarte Galvão, 54 (emergency tel. 788 30 03; **ambulance** tel. 942 11 11). **AIDS Info: Abraço** (tel. 342 59 29).

Internet Access: Ciber Chiado, Largo do Picadeiro, 10 (tel. 346 67 22). Open M-F 11am-6pm and 8pm-midnight, Sa 8pm-midnight. Email access 900$ per hr.

Post Office: Marked by red Correios signs. Lisbon's main post office is in the Pr. Comércio (tel. 346 32 31) and provides all services including **telephone, fax,** *Posta Restante,* and international express mail (EMS). Open M-F 8:30am-6:30pm. Branch in **Praça dos Restauradores** provides the same services with longer hours and a central location. Open daily 9am-6pm. **Postal Code:** 1100 for central Lisbon.

Telephones: Portugal Telecom, Pr. Dom Pedro IV, 68 has pay phones and booths for international calls. M: Rossio. Pay the cashier after your call or use a phone card. Visa. **Phone cards** come in 50 units (875$) or 120 units (2100$) and can be purchased here or at neighborhood book stores and stationers. Local calls consume at least 1 unit. Office open daily 8am-11pm. **Telephone Code:** 01.

■ Accommodations and Camping

A price ceiling supposedly restricts how much *pensões* can charge for particular types of rooms, so if the fee seems padded request the printed price list. During low- or mid-season prices generally drop depending on room availability and the whim of the *pensão* owner—try bargaining the price down. Many establishments have rooms with only double beds and charge per person. Expect to pay from 3000 to 5000$ for a single and 5000 to 9000$ for a double, depending on amenities and location. If you're dissatisfied, ask the owner for a *livro de reclamações,* in which you can write your comments so the tourist bureau will see them.

Most hotels are in the center of town on **Avenida da Liberdade,** while many convenient budget *pensões* are in the **Baixa** along the **Rossio** and on **Ruas da Prata, dos Correeiros,** and **do Ouro.** Lodgings near the Castelo de São Jorge or in the Bairro Alto are quieter and closer to the sights and hence more expensive. If central accommodations are full, head east to the *pensões* along **Avenida Almirante Reis.** Be especially cautious around the docks and the area near Cais de Sodné, as well as after dark in the Bairro Alto, the Alfama, and the Baixa; many streets are isolated and poorly lit.

Pousada de Juventude de Lisboa (HI), R. Andrade Corvo, 46 (tel. 353 26 96; fax 353 75 41). M: Picoas. Exit the metro station facing south, turn right, and walk one block. This huge, ultra-clean youth haven has abandoned some of the typical HI restrictions—there is no curfew or lockout—but is typical in its inconvenient location. English spoken. In summer dorms 3000$; doubles with bath 6000$. In winter dorms 1900$; doubles 4800$. Breakfast included. Lockers 250$. Reception daily 8am-midnight. Check out by 10:30am. Disabled access. HI card required.

Pousada de Juventude de Catalazete (HI), Estrada Marginal (tel. 443 06 38), in the nearby coastal town of **Oeiras.** Take a train from Estação Cais do Sodré to Oeiras (20min., 155$). Exit through the train station underpass from the side of the train coming *from* Lisbon. Cross the street and follow signs to Lisbon and Cascais. The street curves through a residential district. At the intersection across from a bus stop (no street signs), make a left and go downhill along R. Filipa de Lencastre. At the underpass, go straight and follow HI signs to the INATEL complex. The hike will reward you with beautiful ocean views from the patio and quiet rooms. June-Sept. dorms 2000$; doubles with bath 4400$. Cheaper off-season. Breakfast included. Lunch and dinner each 900$. Reception daily 8am-midnight. Curfew midnight. Reservations recommended. HI card required.

BAIXA

Dozens of *pensões* surround the three connected *praças*, **Praça dos Restauradores, Praça Dom Pedro IV,** and **Praça da Figueira,** that form the heart of downtown Lisbon. This area is the most practical area to stay in, making a good base for visiting sights in and around the city. Although most *pensões* have fewer than 12 rooms, finding a vacancy shouldn't be a problem. For a good night's sleep, look for a *pensão* along the pedestrian-only streets of the Baixa. Some *casas de hospedes* may be brothels; though occasionally located beneath hostels, they are not desirable lodgings.

Pensão Campos, R. Jardim do Regedor, 24, 3rd fl. (tel. 346 28 64), between Pr. Restauradores and R. Portas de Santo Antão. Comfortable rooms with phones and well-scoured baths, overlooking a pedestrian street north of the Rossio. Cool multilingual owner. An elevator whisks you up to the *pensão*'s 12 rooms. Singles 3000$; doubles with shower 5500$; triples 6000$. Laundry 300$.

Pensão Moderna, R. Correeiros, 205, 4th fl. (tel. 346 08 18), one block off the south side of Pr. Figueira. A friendly family tends comfortable and clean if rather noisy apartment-style rooms. All 10 rooms are antique-filled and have large windows and balconies. Great location. Singles 3500$; doubles 6000$; triples 8000$.

Residencial Florescente, R. Portas de Santo Antão, 99 (tel. 342 66 09; fax 342 77 33), one block from Pr. Restauradores. Basically, a hotel without room service. The 72 impeccable, spacious rooms with phone and TV are luxurious by budget standards. Windowed (and better furnished) rooms have an incredible view of Pr. Figueira. Doubles with shower 7000$, with full bath, 10,000$; triples 7000$, with bath 14000$; large room with full bath and A/C 12,000$. Visa, AmEx, MC.

Pensão Beira Minho, Pr. Figueira, 6, 2nd fl. (tel. 346 18 46), beside the Rossio at the north end of the *praça,* through a flower shop. Twenty-eight plain, well-lit rooms with phones. Some have a veranda looking onto the square. Singles 3000$, with bath 5000$; doubles 5000-8000$. Breakfast included.

Residência do Sul, Pr. Dom Pedro IV, 59, 2nd fl. (tel. 342 25 11), through the souvenir shop. Somewhat dark but otherwise excellent rooms. Those opposite the square are quieter. English spoken. Singles with shower 4000$, with full bath 4500$; doubles 5500$; triples with shower 7000$. Prices drop off season.

Pensão Prata, R. Prata, 71, 3rd fl. (tel. 346 89 08), two blocks from Pr. Comércio. The entrance to a busy cafe obscures the staircase. Twelve clean, peaceful rooms with tiny baths. English-speaking owner very knowledgeable of Lisbon hotspots. Doubles 4000$, with shower 5000$, with bath 7000$. Discounts for singles. Prices drop 500-1000$ in the off season.

PORTUGAL

IN AND AROUND THE BAIRRO ALTO

The Bairro Alto is quieter than the Baixa and has a community feel that the town center lacks, but the uphill hike is inconvenient and daunting for luggage-bearers. Blessed (and financially prudent) are those who persevere; unto them shall be bestowed ample rooms of great value, enhanced by antiques and views of the castle. Most of Lisbon's nightlife is to be found here, but be cautious if you're out alone late.

⊛**Casa de Hóspedes Globo,** R. Teixeira, 37 (tel. 346 22 79), on a small street across from the Parque São Pedro de Alcântara at the top of the funicular. Safe and convenient location. From the entrance to the park, cross the street to Tr. Cara and make a right onto R. Teixeira. Recent renovations have refurbished spacious rooms with sturdy furniture, cheerful bedspreads, and partitioned *lavabos* (bathrooms). English, French, Spanish, and German spoken. Singles 2500$, with bath 4500$; doubles 5000-6000$. Prices drop 1000$ off season. Reservations recommended.

Pensão Estrêla do Chiado, R. Garrett, 29, 4th fl. (tel. 342 61 10). The 95-stair climb would tire Sisyphus, but the 12 spotless rooms, hot water, and large well-furnished singles entice. 3 rooms with verandas have views of the castle. The common bathrooms have undergone recent renovations. Singles 3000$, with shower 4000$; doubles 5000$, with shower 5500$.

Pensão Londres, R. Dom Pedro IV, 53, 2nd fl.(tel. 346 22 03; fax 346 56 82). Take the funicular next door to the tourist office in Pr. Restauradores and turn right at the last stop. Walk 3 blocks up from R. Dom Pedro V. The *pensão* is on a hilltop street corner; take the elevator to the 39 spacious, well-lit rooms (all with phones) overlooking the old town. Singles with shower 6700$; doubles 5800-6200$, with shower 7200-8600$; triples 12,000$. Prices drop 1000-2000$ in winter. Breakfast included. Visa, MC, Eurocheques accepted.

Residencial Camões, Tr. Poço da Cidade, 38, 1st fl. (tel. 347 75 10; fax 346 40 48), off R. Misericórdia. A pristine set of rooms in the heart of the Bairro Alto party district. English spoken. Doubles 5000-8000$, with bath 9000$. Prices drop 500-1000$ Oct.-June. Breakfast included. Reservations essential in summer.

ALFAMA

Staying in the Alfama grants flowering balconies and amazing views. It also means steep streets, a long walk to drop your pack in the *pensão,* and potential danger at night, when tourists no longer venture to the *castelo.* Yet rooms are cheap and surprisingly comfy, and the Alfama's narrow side streets and friendly *praças* are well worth exploring.

⊛**Pensão Ninho das Águias,** R. Costa do Castelo, 74 (tel. 886 70 08), down the street from the Teatro Taborda (behind the castle). Spectacular views of Lisbon are worth the long hike and additional staircase. Canary-filled garden looks out over the old city and the Tagus. Cheerful rooms with phones are in high demand—make reservations in advance. Singles 5000$; doubles 7000$, with bath 8000$.

Pensão Beira-Mar, Largo Terreiro do Trigo, 16, 4th fl. (tel. 886 99 33; or call the owner, who speaks only Spanish, at tel. 09 31 64 63 09). In a small square off Av. Infante Dom Henrique (the road parallel the Tejo) between Estação Santa Apolónia and the ferry station. Clean, spacious rooms, most with cheerfully mismatched bedclothes, some with water views. Some rooms recently renovated, some may still be under construction. Dorms 6000$, with bath 6500$; triples 8000$. Laundry 3000$ per load. Reservations recommended.

CAMPING

Although camping is popular in Portugal, campers are often prime targets for thieves. Info on all campgrounds in Portugal is available from the tourist office in the free booklet *Portugal: Camping and Caravan Sites.* There are 30 campgrounds within a 45-minute radius of the capital, although there is only one in Lisbon proper.

Parque de Campismo Municipal de Lisboa (tel. 760 20 61; fax 760 74 74), on the road to Benfica. Take bus #43 from the Rossio to the Parque Florestal Monsanto. Lisbon's municipal campground has a pool and supermarket. In summer 420$ per person; about 355$ per tent (depending on size); 275$ per car. In winter, 135$ per person; 110$ per tent; 110$ per car. Reception daily 9am-9pm.

■ Food

Lisbon has some of the least expensive restaurants and best wine of any European capital. A full dinner costs about 1800$ per person, and the *prato do dia* (special of the day) is often a great deal, allowing you to finish it off with a sinfully cheap Portuguese pastry. Any good restaurant, regardless of location, will be feeding as many locals as tourists; the odd toddler running among tables is a good sign of authenticity. In Lisbon, the closer you are to the industrial waterfront, the cheaper the restaurant. The south end of the Baixa, near the port and the area bordering the Alfama, are particularly inexpensive. If you are searching for a bargain, avoid restaurants with menus translated into a Babel of different languages (a tourist trap). Lisbon reels with seafood specialties such as *amêjoas à bulhão pato* (steamed clams), *creme de mariscos* (seafood chowder with tomatoes), and a local classic, *bacalhau cozido com grão e batatas* (cod with chick-peas and boiled potatoes).

SUPERMARKETS

Supermercado Celeiro, Rua 1 de Dezembro, 65, 2 blocks down the street from Estação Rossio. Centrally located, this medium-sized market stocks a wide variety of fruit, meat, and processed foods, as well as fresh bread and pastries. Open M-F 8:30am-8pm, Sa 8:30am-7pm.

Mercado Ribeira, a vast market complex inside a warehouse on Av. 24 de Julho outside the Estação Cais do Sodré, can be reached by bus #40. Go early for the freshest selection. Open M-Sa sunrise-2pm.

Supermercado Pão de Açucar, Amoreiras Shopping Center de Lisboa, Av. Duarte Pacheco. Take bus #11 from Restauradores or Pr. da Figueira.

BAIXA

Although the Baixa is home to some of Lisbon's most tourist-oriented restaurants, some very decent food can be had here for reasonable prices. Bargain eateries line **Rua Correeiros** (parallel to R. Prata) and neighboring streets. One block from Pr. Restauradores on **R. Portas de Santo Antão,** several superb seafood restaurants stack the day's catch in their windows. The small streets north of Pr. Figueira are all packed with eateries. Many of the Baixa's restaurants are not open on Sundays and close around 10pm on weekdays.

Restaurante João do Grão, R. dos Correeiros, 222 (tel. 342 47 57), with a yellow sign out front, is one of Lisbon's most highly recommended eateries. Try the house special, *bacalhau com grão-de-bico* (cod with chick-peas, 1400$) while watching a soccer game on TV. House wine a winner at 295$. Entrees from 850$.

Restaurante Bonjardim, Tr. de Santo Antão, 11 (tel. 342 43 89), off Pr. Restauradores. The self-proclaimed *rei dos frangos* (king of chicken) rules the roost with delicious roast chicken (1100$). Entrees 950-2800$. Open daily noon-11pm. Visa.

Hua Ta Li, R. dos Bacalhoeiros, 109-115A (tel. 887 91 70), near the Pr. Comércio. Great vegetarian options. Try the noodles with vegetables (710$) and seafood salad (750$). *Menú* 1400$. Open daily noon-3:30pm and 6:30-11pm.

Churrascaria Gáucha, R. dos Bacalhoeiros, 26 C-D (tel. 887 06 09), one block north of the riverside near the Pr. Comércio. This large, popular grill serves South American-style *churrasco* dishes like the bean-based *feijoada* (stewed with various meats, 1200$). Open M-Sa 2pm-2am. Visa, MC, AmEx.

Celeiro, R. 1 de Dezembro, 65, take the first right off the Estação Rossio, go 2 blocks. A macrobiotic restaurant accompanied by a health food supermarket, Celeiro will sate the strictest herbivore. Cafeteria-style salads, souffles, and sandwiches. Entrees 200-570$. Open M-F 8:30am-8pm, Sa 8:30am-7pm.

Abracadabra, Pr. Dom Pedro IV, 64, next to Estação Rossio. Popular high school hangout features pizza and burgers—Portuguese style. Open daily 7am-11pm.

Confeitaria Nacional, Praça Figueira 18-B. Succumb to the mirror-and-gold decor of this famous *pastelaría* (established 1820). Delicious sweets of every possible Portuguese kind, rich in almond pastes and sweetened egg filling. Try the almond-encrusted *austríaca* ($120). Open M-Sa 10am-5pm.

It's Good to Be King

If Portugal were ever to become a monarchy again, there is a man waiting in the shadows of history, ready at a moment's notice to dedicate his life to the Portuguese people. This man is Dom Duarte of Portugal, direct descendant of the royal crown. To meet him on the street in his home of Sintra (right near his ancestor's castle), you would not recognize his royal heritage. A Bavarian-looking man with whiskers and a round tummy, he has a jovial disposition, a degree in engineering, and a great love for his people. This love manifests itself in his amiability to one and all, commoners and aristocrats alike. In 1995 Dom Duarte's popularity soared when he chose to marry a Isabella, a beautiful young noble woman, 22 years is junior and from Spain, no less. Gone, however, are the days when the marriage of a Portuguese monarch to a Spaniard of any ilk is forbidden. The wedding, one of the most grand and regal of the decade, was cheerfully applauded across the nation—just about everyone watched the ceremony live on television. The match turned out to be a good one, producing Alfonso, an adorable blond baby named after the Portugal's first king. The light of Duarte and Isabella's lives, Alfonso, a courageous and daring boy with a majestic character, is said to have inherited his ancestor's best traits—the throne, and Portugal, await his arrival.

BAIRRO ALTO

Definitely the place to be at dinner time, the Bairro has its share of glamorous restaurants. It also has far more small and medium-sized eateries than the Baixa. Many inexpensive local haunts line **Calçada do Combro,** the neighborhood's main westward artery. **Rua Misericórdia's** side streets offer cheaper restaurants for quiet dinners among locals. The area around **Praça Dom Pedro V** is also peppered with small culinary diamonds in the rough.

Cervejaria da Trindade, R. Nova Trindade, 20C (tel. 342 35 06), 2 blocks down a side street that begins in the square in front of the Igreja do São Roque and parallels R. Misericórdia. Regal imagery on shiny *azulejos* in an elegant, but noisy, atmosphere, which is part restaurant, part beer hall. Popular with tourists. Entrees range from 950-2500$, budget finds are the *sugestões do chefe* (chef's suggestions) such as *bacalhau com natas* (1250$). Open daily noon-2am. Visa, MC, AmEx.

Restaurante Tascardoso, R. Século, 244 (tel. 342 75 78), off R. Dom Pedro V. Small restaurant with hearty food. Walls inscribed with such food-for-thought proverbs as "He who talks much says little." Mouth-watering pastries 150-350$. Entrees like *açorda de gambas* (prawn puff souffle) 900-1100$. *Vinho de casa* 650$ for a half-bottle. Open daily 8am-midnight. Visa, MC, AmEx.

Café Brasil, R. São Pedro de Alcântara, 51 (tel. 346 94 76), across the street from the park of the same name. Hot, cheap food in an airy local watering hole. Meat and fish dishes 640-900$. The *pra-to do dia* is a bargain at 650$. Open M-Sa 7am-10pm.

A Pérola do Bonjardim, R. Cruz dos Poiais, 95A (tel. 60 84 80), off R. Poiais, a continuation of Calçada do Combro. Stucco and tile family restaurant tucked away in a neighborhood of pastel colored buildings. Wonderful garlic aroma. *Pratos do dia* (830-1300$) and delectable entrees (500-1500$). Open M-Sa 7am-midnight.

ALFAMA

The winding streets of the Alfama conceal a number of tiny, unpretentious restaurants often packed with neighbors and friends of the owner. Lively chatter echoes through the damp, narrow alleys. Watch the clock—the labyrinthine Alfama grows dangerously dark after nightfall.

Restaurante Arco do Castelo, R. Chão de Feira, 25 (tel. 887 65 95), across from the gate to the Castelo de São Jorge. For a hearty, spicy meal, try one of their specialties from Goa, Portugal's former colony in India. Curry in a hurry (from 1100$). Open daily noon-midnight.

Malmequer Bemmequer, R. de São Miguel, 23-25 (tel. 887 65 35). Follow Av. Infante D. Henrique (the river road) east to Terreiro do Trigo. Take next left and climb the stairs to R. de São Miguel. The name means "He loves me not, he loves me well." The friendly cruise-ship-trained owner loves everyone and serves delicious seafood and meat dishes. Entrees from 1000$. Open daily noon-3:30pm and 7-10:30pm.

■ Sights

BAIXA

Although the Baixa features no museums and few historical sites, lively atmosphere and grandiose *praças* make it a living monument in its own right. The best place to embark upon your tour of Lisbon's Enlightenment-era center is from its heart—the **Rossio.** Let your eyes traverse the city's main square, also known as the **Praça Dom Pedro IV,** before your feet do. Once a cattle market with a public execution stage, bullfighting arena, and carnival ground, the *praça* is now the domain of drink-sipping tourists and heart-stopping traffic that whizzes around the statue of Dom Pedro IV in its center. A statue of Gil Vicente, Portugal's first great dramatist (see **Literature,** p. 537) peers down from the top of the columnal **Teatro Nacional de Dona Maria II** at the north end of the *praça.* Adjoining the Rossio is the elegant **Praça Figueira.**

The grid of pedestrian streets south of the Rossio caters to ice-cream eaters and window shoppers. After the calamitous earthquake of 1755, the Marquês de Pombal designed the streets to serve as a conduit for goods from the ports on the Rio Tejo to the city center. At the very height of Enlightenment urban planning, each street was designated for a specific trade; *sapateiros* (shoemakers), *correeiros* (couriers), and *bacalhoeiros* (cod merchants) each had their own avenue. Two centuries later, the streets of the Baixa retain these names as well as the bustling commercial nature they evoke—the Baixa is one of the most crowded areas of town in the daytime. Pedestrians wander about on the wide mosaic sidewalks, cars drag race down the Marquês's stately avenues, and visitors swarm upscale shops along side streets. From the streets of the Baixa, all roads lead to the **Praça do Comércio** on the banks of the Tejo. Also known as the **Terreiro do Paço,** Pr. Comércio lies before the towering statue of Dom João I, cast from 9400 pounds of bronze in 1755. The *praça* now serves as the headquarters of several Portuguese government ministries, while its center has been relegated to less dignified use as a fairgrounds.

Winding your way back up through the Rossio brings you to the **Praça dos Restauradores,** which commemorates the 1640 restoration of Portugal's independence from Spain with an obelisk and a bronze sculpture of the Spirit of Independence. Here begins **Avenida da Liberdade,** Lisbon's most imposing boulevard and one of the city's most elegant promenades, modeled after the wide boulevards of 19th-century Paris. This shady mile-long thoroughfare ends at **Praça do Marquês do Pombal,** from where an imposing 18th-century statue of the *Marquês* overlooks the city.

BAIRRO ALTO

Although it's just as easy to get from the Baixa to the Bairro Alto by walking, the classic way is to take the **Ascensor de Santa Justa,** a historic elevator built in 1902 inside a Gothic wrought-iron tower. *(Runs M-F 7am-11pm, Sa-Su 9am-11pm. 75$ each way.)* Tourists ride to admire the view from the upper levels, while many locals use the elevator as transportation into the hilly Bairro Alto. From the upper terrace, the narrow **walkway** connecting the Baixa to the Bairro Alto leads under a huge flying buttress to the 14th-century **Igreja do Carmo.** *(Walkway open daily until only 6pm.)* The 1755 earthquake left the church roofless but not without its dramatic Gothic arches. The ramshackle **Museu Arqueológico** (tel. 346 04 73), on the adjacent **Largo do Carmo,** includes Dom Fernando I's tomb. *(Open in summer M-Sa 10am-6pm; in winter M-Sa 10am-1pm and 2-5pm. 300$.)*

To reach R. Garret and the heart of the chic **Chiado** neighborhood, turn left as you exit the elevator and walk one block. In the *Bairro* (the hip name for Chiado), Portuguese intellectuals mix with rebellious teens and idealistic university students. It's the only place in Lisbon that never sleeps, yet there is as much to see here during the day as there is to do at night. To reach the **Museo do Chiado,** R. Serpa Pinto, 4 (tel. 343 21 48), go right on R. Garrett and then left onto R. Serpa Pinto and walk two blocks. *(Open Tu 2-6pm, W-Su 10am-6pm. 400$, ages 14-25, seniors, and teachers 200$. Free Sundays and holidays 10am-2pm.)* An educational (and aesthetic) experience awaits, courtesy of Portugal's most famous post-1850 painters and sculptors. En route to the museum you'll pass Lisbon's opera center, the **Teatro Nacional de São Carlos,** R. Serpa Pinto, 9, in a small square to the right. For tickets, call 346 59 14.

Turning right just before the Pr. Camões will put you on **Rua da Misericórdia,** where you'll find many of Lisbon's liveliest bars and *casas de fado* (see **Music,** p. 538). Uphill on R. Misericórdia is **Igreja de São Roque,** Largo Trinidade Coelho (tel. 346 03 61), dedicated to the saint who is believed to have saved the Bairro Alto from the devastation of the great quake. Inside the church, the **Capela de São João Baptista** (fourth from the left), ablaze with precious gems and metals, caused a stir upon its installation in 1747. It took three different ships to deliver the chapel to Lisbon after it was built in Rome from agate, lapis lazuli, alabaster, and mosaic tiles. Next door, the small but worthwhile **Museu de São Roque** (tel. 346 03 61), with its own share of gold and silver, features European religious art from the 16th to 18th centuries. *(Open Tu-Su 10am-5pm. 175$, students and seniors free. Free on Sundays.)*

The mercifully shady **Parque de São Pedro de Alcântara**—perfect for picnics—is on your right off R. São Pedro de Alcântara (the continuation of R. Misericórdia). The **Castelo de São Jorge** in the Alfama stares back from the cliff opposite the park, and the city of Lisbon twinkles at your toes. A mosaic points out the landmarks included in this vista. Continue uphill along R. Dom Pedro V and you'll hit the majestic **Parque Príncipe Real,** which connects to Lisbon's extensive **Jardim Botánico.**

For a more neighborhood flavor, walk through Pr. Camões and take R. Loreto, which turns into Calçada do Combro. At the base of the hill, the right fork becomes the Travessa do Convento de Jesús, where flowered balconies and hanging laundry frame the **Igreja das Mercês,** a handsome, 18th-century Travertine building. Its small *praça* overlooks the Neoclassical **Palácio da Assembléia Nacional** (House of Parliament). Back down the hill toward the small square, the left fork leads to R. Poiais de São Bento, which turns into Calçada da Estrêla and leads to more churches, such as the ornate **Basílica da Estrêla,** Pr. da Estrêla (tel. 346 04 73). *(Open daily 9am-1pm and 3-8pm. Free.)* Built in 1796, the basilica's exquisitely shaped dome, poised behind a pair of tall belfries, steals the sky. Half-mad Maria I, desiring a male heir, made fervent religious vows promising God anything and everything if she were granted a son. When a baby boy was finally born, she built this church. Ask the sacristan to show you the gigantic 10th-century *presépio* (manger scene).

Across from the church, wide asphalt paths of the **Jardim da Estrêla** wind through flocks of pigeons and lush flora. Park walkways are popular for Sunday strolls, as the benches fill with smoochers. Behind the park tropical plants, cypress trees, and odd

PORTUGAL

> ## A Camões Cameo
>
> **Praça de Camões,** right in the center of the Bairro Alto (off R. Garrett) is marked by a monument to Luís de Camões, Portugal's famed 16th-century poet. Camões, whose *Lusíadas* chronicled his nation's discoveries in lyric verse, is considered the Portuguese Shakespeare. This stud had so many affairs with ladies of the court that he fled to North Africa to escape their vengeful husbands. He died a pauper somewhere in Asia, and to Portugal's chagrin his body was never recovered.

gravestones mark the **Cemitério dos Inglêses** (English Cemetery). Its musty, Victorian chapel dates from 1885. A 30-minute walk down Av. Infante Santo leads to Portugal's national museum, the **Museu Nacional de Arte Antiga,** R. Janelas Verdes, Jardim 9 Abril (tel. 396 41 51). *(Open Tu 2-6pm, W-Su 10am-6pm. 500$, students 250$.)* A representative survey of European painting ranges from Gothic primitives to 18th-century French masterpieces. Buses #40 and 60 stop to the right of the museum exit and head back to the Baixa.

ALFAMA

The **Alfama,** Lisbon's medieval quarter, was the lone neighborhood to survive the famous 1755 earthquake intact. This *bairro* slopes in tiers from the **Castelo de São Jorge,** facing the Rio Tejo. Between the Alfama and the Baixa is the quarter known as the **Mouraria** (Moorish quarter), established, ironically, after Dom Afonso Henriques and the Crusaders expelled the Moors in 1147. Portuguese grandmothers gossiping and boys playing soccer on the hill are fun to watch, but watch out for muggers—especially at night. Visit by day and without handbags, cameras, or snatchables.

While the maze of streets in the Alfama can be entered by following any of the small uphill streets a few blocks east of the Baixa, the least confusing way to see the neighborhood is by climbing up R. Madalena, which begins two blocks away from the nearest corner of the Pr. Comércio. Hang a right when you see the **Igreja da Madalena** in the Largo da Madalena on your right. Take the R. Santo António da Sé and follow the tram tracks to the cleverly designed and richly ornamented **Igreja de Santo António da Sé** (tel. 886 91 45), built in 1812 over the saint's alleged birthplace. *(Open daily 7:30am-7:30pm. Mass held daily 11am, 5, and 7pm.)* The construction was funded with money collected by the city's children, who fashioned miniature altars bearing images of the saint to place on doorsteps—a custom re-enacted annually on June 13, the saint's feast day and Lisbon's largest holiday. In the square beyond the church is the stolid 12th-century cathedral known as the **Sé.** *(Open M-Sa 9am-5pm. Treasury open 10am-5pm.)* Although the interior of the Sé is unremarkable, its sheer antiquity and relic-filled treasury make it an intriguing visit. As a sign outside reads, "The Sé is so old that no one really knows how old it is."

From the cathedral, follow the yellow signs for a winding uphill walk to the **Castelo de São Jorge,** which offers spectacular views of Lisbon and the ocean. *(Open daily Apr.-Sept. 9am-9pm; Oct.-Mar. 9am-7pm. Free.)* Built in the 5th century by the Visigoths and enlarged by the 9th-century Moors, this castle was the primary lap of luxury for the royal family from the 14th to 16th centuries. The castle is a must-see; wander around the ruins and soak in the view of the cityscape below, or explore the ponds and gawk at the exotic bird population of the castle gardens. Nooks for sitting, relaxing, and enjoying the vista as well as plenty of stands selling well-merited *frescos,* ice cream, and *churros* await after the long climb up the hill.

On the way up to the castle, turn right onto Largo das Portas do Sol to reach the **Museu das Artes Decorativas,** Largo das Portas do Sol, 2 (tel. 346 04 73). *(Open Tu and Th 10am-8pm, W and F-Su 10am-5pm. 500$, over 65 or under 12 250$.)* Rooms filled with impressive furnishings and decorations convey a sense of 18th-century palatial luxury. The museum also features a tea room and bookstore with Portuguese art books in English.

On the far side of the castle, follow the main tram tracks along Tr. São Tomé (which changes names, winds uphill, and veers left as it goes along) to the **Igreja de São Vicente de Fora,** built between 1582 and 1627 and dedicated to Lisbon's patron saint. *(Open Tu-Su 9am-noon and 3-5pm. Free.)* Ask to see the deathly still *sacristia,* with fabulous 18th-century walls inlaid with Sintra marble. The **Igreja de Santa Engrácia** is farther down toward the coast. *(Open Tu-Su 10am-5pm.)* Walk along R. São Vicente and keep right as the road branches. This church took almost 300 years to complete (1682-1966), giving rise to the famous Portuguese expression, "Endless like the building of Santa Engrácia." At the **Feira da Ladra** (flea market) that takes place in the church's backyard, the cries of merchants hawking used goods are drowned out by the din of a lively social scene. *(Open Tu and Sa 6am-5pm.)* From the Baixa, take bus #12 or tram #28 from the bottom of R. dos Correeiros (150$).

Continuing down the hill will put you on Av. Infanta Dom Henrique, which runs parallel to the Tejo. The avenue leads to the Estação Santa Apolónia. From outside the station, take #13 bus for 10 minutes to **Convento da Madre de Deus.** *(Open W-Su 10am-6pm, Tu 2-6pm. 350$, students 180$.)* This 16th-century convent complex houses the **Museu Nacional do Azulejo,** R. da Madre de Deus, 4 (tel. 814 77 47), devoted to the classic Portuguese art of the *azulejo* tile, first introduced by the Moors (see **Architecture,** p. 537). The Baroque interior of the church, reached through a fine Manueline doorway, is an explosion of oil paintings, *azulejos,* and gilded wood. The rapturous excess continues in the choir and the **Capela de Santo António,** where bright *azulejos* and paintings intoxicate the eye.

BELÉM

Belém is more of a suburb than a neighborhood of Lisbon, but its high concentration of monuments and museums makes it an important stop in any comprehensive tour of the capital. Belém is imperial glory at the service of culture; here, the opulence and extravagance of the Portuguese empire is showcased in a number of well-maintained museums and historical sites. To visit Belém is to understand *saudade,* the "nostalgic yearning" expressed musically in *fado.*

To get to Belém, take tram #15 from Pr. do Comércio (20min., 150$) or the train from Estação Cais do Sodré (10min., departs every 15min., 110$). From the train station, cross over the tracks, cross the street, and go left. From the bus station, follow the avenue straight ahead. All museums are free before 2pm on Sunday.

The **Mosteiro dos Jerónimos** (tel. 362 00 34) rises from the banks of the Tejo behind a lush garden. *(Open Tu-Su 10am-5pm. 400$, students 200$; Oct.-May 250$. Free Su 10am-2pm and for students on holidays. Cloisters open Tu-Su 10am-5pm. Free.)* Established by King Dom Manuel I in 1502 to give thanks for the success of Vasco da Gama's voyage to India, the monastery stands as Portugal's most refined celebration of the Age of Discovery and showcases Portugal's native Manueline style, combining Gothic forms with early Renaissance details. The main door of the church, to the right of the main monastery entrance, is a sculpted anachronism; Henry the Navigator mingles with the Twelve Apostles under carved canopies on both sides of the central column. The symbolic tombs of Luís de Camões and navigator Vasco da Gama lie in two opposing transepts. Inside the monastery the octagonal cloisters of the courtyard drip with overdone stone carvings, a contrast to the simplicity of the rose gardens in the center.

At the far left end of the monastery complex is the **Museu da Marinha** (tel. 362 00 10). *(Open Tu-Su 10am-6pm. 400$, students 200$. Free Su 10am-2pm.)* This intriguing ship museum will bind you to its moorings—the Portuguese definitely know their ships. Globes from the mid-17th century show the boundaries of the continents with incredible accuracy.

Contemporary art buffs will bask in the glow of the gigantic, luminous **Centro Cultural de Belém** (tel. 361 24 00; http://www.fdescccb.pt). *(Open daily 11am-8pm.)* With four pavilions regularly holding world-class exhibitions, several art galleries, and a huge auditorium for concerts and performances, the center provides city-slick entertainment amid a slew of imperial landmarks.

Views from on High

Two towers, both evocative of Portugal's past sea-faring greatness but built centuries apart, share magnificent, panoramic views of Belém and the Rio Tejo. The **Torre de Belém** (tel. 362 00 34), built under Manuel I from 1515-1520 as a harbor fortress, rises from the north bank of the Tejo and is surrounded by the ocean on three sides. A 10-minute walk (heading away from Lisbon) along the coast from the Mosteiro dos Jerónimos leads to this Manueline symbol of Portuguese grandeur. *(Open Tu-Su 10am-5pm. 400$; Oct.-May 250$, students 200$.)*

Also along the river is the **Padrão dos Descobrimentos** (tel. 301 62 28), built in 1960 to honor Prince Henry the Navigator. The view here is similar to that at the tower, but instead of the historic stairs of the Torre an elevator transports visitors 70m up to a small terrace with great views. The Padrão also hosts temporary exhibits and films. *(Open Tu-Su 9:30am-6:45pm. 320$, students 160$.)*

Back toward the center of Belém is another nugget of the kings' former wealth, the **Museu Nacional dos Coches,** Pr. Afonso de Albuquerque (tel. 363 80 22), located across from the train station. *(Open Tu-Su 10am-5:30pm. 450$, seniors, teachers, and students 14-25 300$.)* The museum is the retirement home of 54 lavish carriages, ranging from late 18th-century models to the gilded Baroque coach that bore Queen Elizabeth II in this century. The **Palácio Nacional da Ajuda** (tel. 363 70 95), on Largo da Ajuda, is a short bus ride away to the hills overlooking Belém. *(Open Tu and Th-Su 10am-5pm. 250$, students free. Free Su 10am-2pm.)* Constructed in 1802, the 54 chambers make a rather telling display of decadence. Take bus #14, 32, 42, or 60 from in front of the Museu Nacional dos Coches. Alternatively, tram #18 (Ajuda) stops behind the palace.

■ Entertainment

The *Agenda Cultural* and *Lisboa em,* free at kiosks in the Rossio and on R. Portas de Santo Antão as well as the tourist office contains info on concerts, movies, plays, and bullfights, along with lists of museums, gardens, and libraries.

BARS AND CLUBS

Tap into the Bairro Alto's **Rua Norte, Rua Diário Notícias,** and **Rua da Atalaia**—but not before midnight—and choose your scene with care: smoking or non, punk or family style. With so many small clubs jammed into three or four short blocks, club-hopping means just crossing the street. Blaze your own trail. Most clubs don't charge a cover fee, but expect to pay about 350$ for a draft beer and 700$ for mixed drinks.

Portas Largas, R. da Atalaia, 105. A good ol' fashioned drinking establishment. Imbibe wisdom with your beer; signs say, "If you drink to forget, pay before you drink." Scrawl on the walls and hang with locals. Open daily 10am-2:30am.

Solar do Vinho do Porto, R. São Pedro de Alcântara, 45 (tel. 347 57 07). Not a club and not a bar, but something close enough—port-tasting in a sedate and mature setting. Glasses 130-2800$. Open M-F 10am-11:30pm, Sa 11am-10:30pm.

Pé Sujo, Largo de St. Martinho, 6-7 (tel. 886 56 29), in the Alfama. Live Brazilian music nightly 11:30pm-2am. Try the killer Brazilian drink *caipirinha* (made from sugarcane alcohol, 700$), or if you're truly brave, down a *caipirosca* (with lime and vodka, 700$). Open Tu-Su 10pm-2am.

Bar Artis, R. Diário Notícias, 95-97 (tel. 342 47 95). Sip beer with a cosmopolitan crowd under sultry red lights. Newspapers are on hand to peruse at this intimate but intense watering hole. Open Tu-Su 10pm-2am.

Termas D'Atalaia Bar, R. da Atalaia, 108 (tel. 342 47 74). One of the best, featuring drinks such as *orgasmo* and *sangue dos deuses* (blood of the gods, 600$). The quirky decor features a waterfall flowing down the front window and matchbox cars racing on the ceiling. Open M-Sa 10pm-3:30am.

Memorial, R. Gustavo de Matos Sequeira, 42A (tel. 396 88 91), one block south of R. Escola Politécnica in the Bairro Alto. This gay and lesbian disco-bar is far-out—in all senses. The lights and Europop blast from 10pm, but the fun starts after midnight. The 1000$ cover charge (except M and Th) includes 2 beers or 1 mixed drink. Male and female strippers on Thursdays. Open Tu-Su 10pm-4am.

Frágil, R. da Atalaia, 126/8 (tel. 346 95 78), on the corner of R. da Atalaia and Tr. Queimada. Mostly dance music rocks a mixed gay and straight crowd of beautiful people. As the night goes on, they groove outside in the streets. Beer 600$, but hard liquor could empty your wallet. Open M-Sa 10:30pm-3:30am.

Os Três Pastorinhos, R. da Baroca, 111-113 (tel. 346 43 01). Pop, soul, and disco merge. Kaleidoscopic multimedia effects send the hard-partying (mostly student) crowd into a dancing frenzy. Open Tu-Su 11pm-4am.

CAFES

The **Pastelaria Suíça** (tel. 342 80 92), on the south corner of Pr. Dom Pedro IV in the Baixa, is a boisterous gathering place that stays packed with people until midnight. In the stylin' Chiado neighborhood in the Bairro Alto, the 19th-century cafe **A Brasileira,** R. Garrett, 120-122 (tel. 360 95 41), has the best after-dinner scene in a wonderful *fin de siècle* atmosphere. Look for the bust of poet Fernando Pessoa outside. Eça de Queiroz, another famous Portuguese literary figure who once patronized this coffeehouse, is long gone, but members of the new intelligentsia take his place nightly. Gold and green woodwork and silver sconces further color the scene (coffee 180-300$, alcoholic drinks about 600$; open daily 8am-2am).

FADO

Lisbon's trademark is the heart-wrenching *fado,* an expressive art that combines elements of singing and narrative poetry (see **Music,** p. 538). *Fadistas,* cloaked in black dress and shawls, perform sensational tales of lost loves and faded glory. Their melancholy wailing is expressive of *saudade,* an emotion of nostalgia and yearning; listeners are supposed to feel the "knife turning in their hearts." On weekends, book in advance by calling the venues. The Bairro Alto, with many *fado* joints off **Rua Misericórdia** and on side streets radiating from the Museu de São Roque, is the best part of the city for top-quality *fado.*

Adega Machado, R. do Norte, 91 (tel. 346 00 95 or 342 87 13). Frequented by as many Portuguese as tourists. Dinner served (4600-6000$). Cover (with 2 drinks) 2500$. Open June-Oct. daily 8pm-3am; Nov.-May. Tu-Su 8pm-3am.

O Faia, R. Baroca, 54 (tel. 342 19 23). Typical Portuguese regional food combined with *fado* and folk dancing. Cover charge 2500$. Open M-Sa 8pm-2am.

Sr. Vinho, R. Meio à Lapa, 18 (tel. 397 26 81 or 397 74 56), in nearby Madregoa. Minimum food and drink charge 2500$, but with appetizers at 1200-2800$ it won't entirely deplete your wallet. Open M-Sa 8:30pm-2:30am.

THEATER AND CONCERTS

The **Teatro Nacional de Dona Maria II** (tel. 347 22 26), at Pr. Dom Pedro IV, stages performances of classical Portuguese and foreign plays (tickets 700-2000$, 50% student discount). At Lisbon's largest theater, the **Teatro Nacional de São Carlos,** R. Serpa Pinto, 9 (tel. 346 84 08), near the Museo do Chiado in the Bairro Alto, opera reigns from late September through mid-June (open daily 1-7pm). The **Fundação Calouste Gulbenkian,** Av. Berna, 24 (tel. 793 51 31), also sponsors classical and jazz concerts year-round. When the pop heavies come to town (Garbage, Whitney Houston, The Verve), they play at the **Coliseu dos Recreios,** R. Porta de Sto. Antão, 92 (tel. 346 16 77), which is easily accessible by metro (M: Restauradores).

Outside the city, the **Centro Cultural de Belém,** Pr. do Império (tel. 361 24 00), across from the Mosteiro dos Jerónimos, hosts a wide variety of performances ranging from classical music concerts to modern dance recitals. Take the train from Estação Cais do Sodré (15min., departs every 20min., 110$); bus #27, 28, 29, 43, 49, or 51 (150$); or tram #15, 16, or 17 (150$). **Tickets** for major events are available

The Many Lives of the Portuguese Feiras

While most nightlife in Lisbon revolves around the bars and *casas de fado,* those seeking more active revelry in June won't be disappointed. Open-air *feiras* (fairs)—smorgasbords of eating, drinking, live music, and dancing—abound. There's a lively one called *Oreal* at **Campo das Cebolas,** near the waterfront in the Alfama (open June M-F 10pm-1am, Sa-Su 10pm-3am). Don't miss the *feira* in the **Praça Camões** in the Bairro Alto (take the Elevador da Glória, or walk up R. Garrett), which goes until 3am every night in June. After savoring *farturas* (Portuguese doughnuts, 190$) and Sagres beer (200$), pick up your feet and join in the traditional Portuguese dancing. On the night of June 12, the streets become a mega-dance floor for the huge **Festa de Santo António**—banners are strung between streetlights and confetti falls like snow.

More commercial *feiras* combine shopping and cultural involvement. The open-air markets come in many varieties, and bargaining is the name of the game. Bookworms burrow for three glorious weeks in the **Feira do Livro** (in the Baixa from late May to early June). In June, the Alcântara holds the **Feira Internacional de Lisboa,** while in July and August the **Feira de Mar de Cascais** and the **Feira de Artesania de Estoril** take place near the casino.

Year-round *feiras* include the **Feira de Oeiras** (Antiques) on the fourth Sunday of every month, and the **Feira de Carcanelos** for clothes (Th 8am-2pm). Packrats should catch the **Feira da Ladra** (flea market), held at Campo de Santa Clara (Tu and Sa 7am-3pm). Take bus #12 or tram #28.

from box offices or the **Agência de Bilhetes dos Espectáculos Públicos (ABEP)** kiosk across from the Pr. Restauradores tourist office.

OTHER FUN THINGS TO DO

Portuguese **bullfights** (differing from the Spanish variety in that the bull is not killed) take place most Thursday nights from the end of June to the end of September at the **Praça de Touros de Lisboa** (tel. 793 24 42), at Campo Pequeno from 10am to 2am. Take bus #44, 45, 83, or 1, or get off at Metro stop "Campo Grande."

To refresh your sea legs, try a two-hour **cruise** on the Tejo. The boat leaves from the Estação Fluvial Terreiro Paço (tel. 887 50 58), off the Pr. Comércio. The boats run from April to October and leave at 3pm.

If sports are your thing, catch a *futebol* (soccer) match. Lisbon has two professional teams featuring some of the world's finest players: **Benfica** (tel. 726 03 21), at the Stadium of Light (M: Colégio Militar Luz), and **Sporting** (tel. 759 94 59), at Alvalade Stadium (M: Campo Grande). Check the APEB kiosk in Pr. Restauradores or the sports newspaper *A Bola.*

If all else fails, try the **movie theater** (tel. 242 25 23), at the corner of Av. Liberdade and Av. dos Condes, directly across the square from the Pr. Restauradores tourist office. Huge 10-screen cinemas are also located in the **Oreiras** and **Colombo** shopping centers. American movies (almost exclusively) are shown with Portuguese subtitles (550$, matinees 400$).

AROUND LISBON

The province of Estremadura envelops Lisbon with sultry beaches, serene fields, and shady mountainsides, while the flat expanses of the Ribatejo sidle up to the capital city from the south. The towns listed here all lie within these two provinces but are close enough to the city (about an hour's travel or less) so as to be relaxing and rewarding daytrips. Even those on the strictest of itineraries, however, will want more than a day in order to do a few of these destinations justice.

Within thirty minutes of Lisbon lie the elegant seaside resorts Estoril and Cascais; Queluz and Mafra, scenic and easily accessible, are also rightfully popular trips. With

PORTUGAL

fairytale castles and beautiful streets, Sintra, farther to the north, demands a longer stay. Nearby Ericeira, a hip seaside resort popular with cosmopolitan youth, lures the sight-weary and fun-loving to its attractive beaches and awesome surf. To the south of Lisbon, noisy and commercial Setúbal provides a surprisingly good base to see some of Portugal's most beautiful and rural coastline. Neighboring Sesimbra is a picturesque and refreshingly traditional town.

■ Queluz

The reason to visit the residential suburb of Queluz, 14km west of Lisbon and about that far south of Sintra, is the amazing **Palácio Nacional de Queluz.** (Open June-Sept. 10am-1pm and 2-5:30pm; Oct.-May 10am-1pm and 2-5pm. 400$, seniors, students, and children under 14 200$. Admission to garden 50$.) Portuguese architect Mateus Vicente de Oliveira and French sculptor Jean-Baptiste Robillan collaborated to create this pink-and-white Rococo wedding cake of a palace. Built by order of Dom Pedro III in the late 18th century, the building and furnishings are clearly French-inspired; the well-ordered, albeit slightly overgrown, garden replete with ornate fountains creates the feel of a miniature Versailles. Highlights include the **Sala dos Embaixadores,** with its gilded thrones and Chinese vases, and the purely Portuguese *azulejo*-lined canal in the garden. Of historical interest is the **Quarto Don Quixote** where Dom Pedro I, first emperor of Brazil, took his first and last breaths.

The fastest way to get to Queluz is by **train.** Take the Sintra line from Estação Rossio and get off at the Queluz-Belas (not the Queluz-Massomá) stop (20min., departs every 15min., 120$). To reach the palace, turn left from the station, walk down Av. da República, and follow the signs; it's a 10-minute walk downhill.

■ Estoril

With its bustling casino, stately villas, and beautiful beaches, Estoril enjoys a reputation of luxury. Luckily, the greatest luxuries can be savored at little to no cost: Estoril's best assets are natural. The **Praia Estoril Tamariz** beach greets your arrival, while the palm-studded **Parque do Estoril** blooms across the street.

Those bored of beach scenes can walk through the park to the **Casino Estoril** (tel. 468 45 21), if not to spend money, then to gawk at the gaming palace. (Open daily 3pm-3am. No beachwear, no shorts. Must be at least 18 for the slots and 21 for the game room. Foreigners must show passport.) Don't be fooled by the drab 1970s exterior: the casino houses sparkling game rooms and a glitzy music hall. A **music festival** descends upon Estoril from mid-July to mid-August, bringing both classical and jazz performances.

PRACTICAL INFORMATION A **train** from Lisbon's Estação do Sodré runs to Estoril (30min., departs approximately every 20min., 180$) before reaching Cascais, a pleasant 20 minute seaside stroll along the promenade. **Bus** #41B to Sintra departs from a stop next to the train station (45min., departs every hr., 300$). At the **tourist office** (tel. 466 38 13; fax 467 22 80), on Arcada do Parque opposite the tunnel from the train station, multilingual attendants offer detailed maps and events schedules for the entire **Costa do Estoril,** including Cascais (open M-Sa 9am-7pm, Su 10am-6pm). **Police** (tel. 466 38 13; fax 467 22 80) are on Av. Biarritz. In an **emergency** dial 112.

ACCOMMODATIONS AND FOOD If you get lucky at the casino (or are stranded with no way back to Lisbon), cash in some chips and head over to the recently renovated **Residencial São Cristóvão,** Av. Marginal, 7079 (tel./fax 468 09 13). Facing the park, turn right off the train platform; about one block up the hill on your right you'll find bright, airy rooms. (Doubles 8000-10,000$, with shower 10,000-12,000$. Continental breakfast and private parking included.) Farther from the beach is **Residencial Smart,** R. Maestro Lacerda, 6 (tel. 468 21 64). Follow Av. Marginal uphill past the Paris Hotel to the corner of Av. Bombeiros Voluntários and make a left. Walk three blocks uphill to R. Maestro Lacerda and follow the street three blocks until you see the *pensão* on the left. It has 13 spacious doubles overlooking a flower garden. (Doubles with shower 5000-7000$, with bath 7000-9000$. Breakfast and parking included.) The best options for budget meals are the cafeteria-like stands and **bars** along the beach. For a sit-down (read: pricey) meal, try the restaurants in the **Arcados do Parque** lining the park. Consider saving your appetite: a greater selection and better seafood await in Cascais.

■ Cascais

The favorite resort of celebrities, heads of state, and wealthy *Lisboêtas* on summer weekends, Cascais flaunts four renowned beaches—all no more than a few steps from town. Yet despite the tourist deluge, Cascais still manages to retain vestiges of its more humble fishing village days.

Several historic sites and parks invite wandering. To reach the overgrown municipal garden, **Parque de Gandainha,** walk away from Cascais along the coast for 10 minutes on Av. Dom Carlos, which turns into Av. Rei Humberto de Itália (open Tu-Su 9am-6pm). About 1km farther outside of Cascais (a 20 min. walk along Av. Rei Humberto de Itália) lies the **Boca do Inferno** (Mouth of Hell), a huge cleft carved in the rock by the incessant Atlantic surf. This ominous sight is often swamped with tourists, but the surrounding rocky turf sprinkled with red sand makes a nice perch for sitting and marveling at the sea in peace.

PRACTICAL INFORMATION A **train** from Lisbon's Estação do Sodré heads to Cascais (30min., departs approximately every 20min., 180$) after passing through Estoril, a pleasant 20 minute seaside stroll along the promenade from Cascais. Stagecoach **buses** leave from outside the train station. Bus #403 services Sintra (1 hr., 11 per day, 700$) and #415 runs to Praia do Guincho (20min., departs every hr., 300$). Tickets may be purchased in a booth outside the station or on board the bus.

If you reach Cascais by foot from Estoril, you can get to the tourist office by taking a right at the fork in the promenade and following the train tracks up to the station on the **Largo do Estação.** From the front of the train station, cross the square and take a right at the McDonald's onto Av. Valbom. The **tourist office,** Av. dos Combatentes, 25 (tel. 486 82 04), on the site of an archeological dig, has a small sign across the street from where Av. Valbom ends. The English-speaking staff will make calls to find you a budget *quarto* in a private home. (Rooms from 5000$. Open daily June-Sept. 15 9am-8pm; Sept. 16-May 9am-7pm.) **Police** (tel. 486 11 27) are on R. Afonso Sanches. In an **emergency** dial 112. A small pedestrian **shopping district** sits near the beach (left off Av. Combatentes heading from the tourist office toward the water).

ACCOMMODATION AND FOOD Cascais is at best a daytrip, but if you get hooked or are too sunburned to move, your best bet is to ask at the tourist office for a reliable *quarto.* Alternatively, bed down at **Residencial Parsi,** R. Afonso Sanches, 8 (tel. 484 57 44), off the beachfront Pr. 5 do Outubro. You'll pay the price for these rooms, all with TV and some with stunning views of the *praça* and the ocean. (Doubles with shower 7000-9000$. Breakfast included. Credit cards accepted.) A cheaper option is camping in Orbitur's **Parque de Campismo do Guincho** (tel. 487 10 14), in the nearby town of Areia, near the Praia do Guincho.

The cafes along Av. dos Combatentes offer deliciously fresh seafood, but dinner here may be quite pricey (seafood 1000-2700$). Perhaps the least expensive (and most adventurous) **food** option is to hike out to the Boca do Inferno, assemble a meal at one of the various food stands, and have a picnic on the rocks (sandwich, fruit, and drink for 650$). Alternatively, indulge your hummus cravings at **Joshua's Shoarma Grill,** R. Visconde da Luz, 19 (tel. 484 30 64), a half block uphill to the right from the tourist office's back door. An upbeat Middle Eastern joint, they have falafel (420$) and other delicacies. (Open M-F noon-4pm and 6pm-2am, Sa-Su 1pm-2am.)

PORTUGAL

PORTUGAL

Wet, Wild, and Wooly on the Estremadura Coast

With the country's sun, wind, and waves, no wonder rumors abound that **Baywatch** will move to Portugal in 2010. Dark-haired goddesses may easily fill the shoes of bronzed blond bombshells, as *Baywatch* is one of the most popular shows on Portuguese TV (broadcast weekly in English). Surfing is now the "in" thing to do, and lifeguarding and other watersports have become almost as fashionable among the younger crowds. Relive your own TV fantasies on the famed beaches of **Praia Grande, Ribeira d'Ilhas, Praia D'Abano,** and **Praia de Guincho.**

West of Cascais, the Praia do Guincho, considered to be one of the best and daunting windsurfing beaches in the world, lives up to its reputation by hosting the annual world windsurfing championships. Buses to Praia do Guincho leave from the train station in Cascais (see below). Two km west of Praia do Guincho lies the beautiful and more tranquil **Praia do Abano.**

Another wonder of the coast, for those who would rather leave the surfing gear at home, is the spectacular **Cabo da Roca** outside Cascais. The westernmost point on the European continent, Cabo da Roca offers unparalleled views of the Atlantic smashing against the jagged bluffs of the Estremadura coast. Hold onto your hats, as it can get mighty windy. Cabo da Roca can be reached by a 3km hike (1hr.) or by bus #403 from Cascais to Sintra (30min., 11 per day, 300$).

■ Sintra

In the epic poem *Childe Harold,* British Romantic poet Lord Byron called Sintra a "glorious Eden." His adulation made Sintra (pop. 20,000) a chic destination for 19th-century European aristocrats and ladies. These days, proletarians and aristocrats alike flock to Sintra's fairytale castles and romantic mountain panoramas. Its *vila velha* is an amalgam of flowering gardens and villas, crowned by three castles: the **Paço Real,** the **Palácio Nacional da Pena,** and the **Castelo dos Mouros.** Each evokes a different era—ranging from the 8th-century Moorish occupation to the reign of 19th-century Prince Ferdinand—for a surreal mixture of history and fantasy not to be missed.

ORIENTATION AND PRACTICAL INFORMATION

Sintra, 30km northwest of Lisbon and 15km north of Estoril, is connected by train to Lisbon's Estação Rossio (45min., departs every 15min., 180$). The town is split into two parts: a modern section around the train station, where most budget accommodations and banks are located, and **Sintra-Vila,** where the historic sights perch on the mountainside. To get to the old town, take a left out of the train station and a right down the small hill at the next intersection (15min.). At the bottom of the hill, take a left at the fountain in front of the castle-like **Câmara Municipal** (tel. 923 40 21), and follow the road around the curve past the **Parque da Liberdade.** Go up the hill, and you will be staring at the **Praça da República.** The **Palácio Nacional** is the large white building on your right. Theft is common in this heavily touristed area; consider stowing your gear in **lockers** at Lisbon's Estação Rossio before you come (450$, open daily 8:30am-11:30pm).

Trains: Estação de Caminhos de Ferro, Av. Dr. Miguel Bombarda (tel. 923 26 05). To Lisbon's Estação Rossio (40min., departs every 15min., 180$). There is no direct service to Estoril or Cascais and no locker service available.

Buses: Rodoviária, Av. Dr. Miguel Bombarda (tel. 921 03 81), across the street from the train station. Open daily 7am-8pm. To Cascais and Cabo da Roca (1 hr., 9 per day, 550$) and Estoril (40min., 13 per day, 320$). Green-and-white **Mafrense** buses depart 1 block to the right as you exit the train station. To Mafra (45min., 11 per day, 350$) and Ericeira (1hr., departs every 2 hr., 350$), with connections to points north.

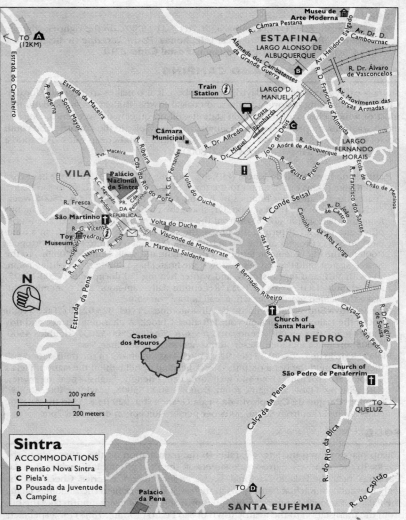

Tourist Office: A small branch (tel. 924 16 23) is located at the train station. Open M-Sa 9am-6pm. **Main office,** Sintra-Vila, Pr. República, 23 (tel. 923 11 57; fax 923 51 76). From the Pr. República with the palace on your right, walk straight ahead 1 block; the tourist office is beyond the palace in a columned marble building. English-speaking staff provides a map and list of accommodations. They can also help you find a *quarto* (3500-8000$). Upstairs is the **regional museum;** check out exhibits while waiting (free). Open daily June-Sept. 9am-8pm; Oct.-May 9am-7pm.

Currency Exchange: Banco Totta e Açores, Sintra-Vila, R. Padarias, 4 (tel. 924 19 19), on a side street off the main *praça.* Has an **ATM.** Open M-F 8:30am-noon and 1-3pm. ATMs beside the train station at **Banco Nacional Ultramarinho** (tel. 923 31 00).

Police: R. João de Deus (tel. 923 07 61), behind the train station. **Emergency:** Call 112.

Medical Services: Centro de Saúde, Largo Dr. Gregório Almeida (tel. 923 34 00).

Telephone code: 01.
Post Office: Sintra-Vila, Pr. República, 26 (tel. 924 15 90), on the right en route to the tourist office. Small, with local **telephones,** *Posta Restante* (indicate Sintra-Vila). Open M-F 9am-noon and 2:30-6pm. **Postal Code:** 2710.

ACCOMMODATIONS AND CAMPING

Sintra is easily accessible as a daytrip from Lisbon; it also makes an ideal base for day-trips to surrounding historical sights and coastal towns. Budget accommodations—most of which cluster near the train station—fill up quickly on weekends. Unfortunately, *pensões* are pricier here than almost anywhere else in the country. The youth hostel has a beautiful location (albeit way, way uphill) and cheap rates. The tourist office can provide a list of *quartos* (3500-8000$).

Pousada da Juventude de Sintra (HI), Sta. Eufémia (tel./fax 924 12 10), a hard-core uphill hike (2km) out of Sintra to the town of Sta. Eufémia, adjacent to São Pedro. Spare yourself and your buddies by hailing a taxi (1100$ weekdays, 1500$ weekends) in front of the train station. Or, shave the climb to 15min. by taking the bus from the train station (180$) or from the bus-stop in the old town (exit the tourist office and take a left turn in the *praça;* the stop is on the left across from a fountain). At São Pedro, get off the bus across from the Banco Crédito Predial Português (look for the big blue neon letters). Take a right and walk 1km (15-20min.) to the hostel. Seated amid flowering meadows, the hostel has a dining room, sitting room, TV with VCR and tapes, stereo, and winter heating. 50 dorm beds (1200-1400$) and 3 family-sized rooms (2700$). Reception daily 9am-noon and 6pm-midnight. Make the schlep worth your while: call before you come.

Pensão Nova Sintra, Largo Afonso de Albuquerque, 25 (tel. 923 02 20). Take a right out of the train station; it's on your left after 1 block. A charming terrace and tidy rooms grace this recently renovated *pensão.* Singles 2500-3200$; doubles 4500-5500$. Breakfast included. Reservations necessary in summer. Visa.

Piela's, R. João de Deus, 70-72 (tel. 924 16 91). Make a left out of the train station and then left around the bend onto the street heading uphill behind the station. Piela's 5 rooms are spacious, clean and well furnished. Friendly, English-speaking owner. Cafe with pool table and game room. Doubles 5000-7500$; in winter 4000-6000$.

Camping: Parque de Campismo da Praia Grande (tel. 929 05 81), on the Atlantic coast about 12km from Sintra. 300$ per person. Reception daily until 7pm.

FOOD

Cheap places crowd the street parallel to the train station on the other side of the tracks. In the old town, narrow side streets off the Pr. da República such as **Rue das Padárias,** near the Palácio Nacional, host a wider range of eateries. Check out the daily **mercado municipal** (8am-1pm) in the small square behind the buildings facing the Palácio Nacional. On the second and fourth Sundays of every month, take the bus from the train station to the nearby town of São Pedro (15min., 180$) for a spectacular **regional market.**

Casa da Piriquita, R. Padarias, 1 (tel. 923 06 26), up a small side street off the República. Inspiring bakery, snack bar, and candy counter flanked by a marble-floored coffee and tea room. Sintra's tiny pastries with cheese and cinnamon or egg filling (120-200$ each) are a welcome snack. Open Th-Tu 9am-10:30pm.

Adega dos Caves, R. da Pendoa, 2-10, Largo da Vila Velha de Sintra (tel./fax 923 08 48), along an *escadinha* (stair alley) across the Palácio Nacional. Steer clear of the pricey "tourist menu" and savor house specialties like *bacalhav à caves* (cod, 1200$). Visit the snack bar next door for drinks and fast food. After 9pm on Thursdays and Sundays, chill in the basement bar to the sound of live Portuguese folk music. Restaurant open daily 8am-10pm. Major credit cards accepted.

Bristol Restaurante, R. Visconce de Monserrate, 20 (tel. 923 34 38). Lively atmosphere, directly in front of you as you come up the hill toward Pr. República. Great deal for filling soups (260$) or omelettes (825$) for lunch. Fish or meat dishes from 1050$ for dinner. Open Tu-Su 9am-midnight.

SIGHTS

The road from the train station ambles and twists up the mountainside past the **Câmara Municipal** and its lush gardens and past the **Parque da Liberdade** on the left, until it reaches the old city and the **Palácio Nacional de Sintra** (tel. 923 00 85), also known as Paço Real or Palácio da Vila, in the Pr. República. *(Palace open Th-Tu 10am-1pm and 2-5pm. 400$, with student ID 200$.)* Once the summer residence of Moorish sultans and their harems, the Paço Real and its complex gardens were built in two stages, beginning in the early 15th century under Dom João I. A century later, Dom Manuel I created the best collection of *azulejos* in the world and contributed to a unique mix of Moorish, Gothic, and Manueline styles. The Palácio's more than 20 rooms run the gamut from the *azulejo*-covered **Sala dos Árabes** (Hall of the Arabs) to the gilded **Capela** (Chapel). Two rooms not to miss are the **Sala dos Cisnes** (Hall of Swans) and the **Sala das Pêgas** (Hall of Magpies) which, according to legend, acquired its name when Dom João I's wife caught him kissing one of the ladies of the court. Although he claimed that it was merely a gesture of friendship, the court ladies ("magpies," according to the king) made it a subject of scandalous gossip.

The **3km ascent** to the Palácio Nacional da Pena and the Castelo dos Mouros (crowning one of the highest peaks in the Sintra range) begins at the Palácio Nacional. The steep, strenuous hike uphill takes about 90 minutes. If you do walk, be sure to leave Sintra-Vila by about 1pm to have time to visit all the sights up top, and don't forget to bring a full water bottle. Take the road that begins to the left of the tourist office and follow the blue signs up the mountain. Beware the *escadinha* (stairs alley) shortcut; you might get lost. If pressed for time (or energy), take a taxi directly from the modern side of town (they swarm outside the train station, and occasionally appear elsewhere; one-way 1200$ weekdays, 1400$ weekends and holidays). A shuttle runs from the tourist office to the Castelo dos Mouros (15-20min., departs every 45min., round-trip 500$). From the gate, walk 10 minutes uphill to see the Palácio Nacional da Pena. Although *Let's Go* does not recommend it, some travelers choose to hitchhike up the road. Hit the Palácio first—it's mostly downhill from there.

The fantastic **Palácio Nacional da Pena** was built in the 1840s by Prince Ferdinand of Bavaria, the husband of Queen Maria II, on the site of a 16th-century monastery. *(Open in summer Tu-Su 10am-6pm; in winter Tu-Su 2-4:30pm. 600$, students 400$, off-season 200$.)* Nostalgic for his country, the prince rebuilt and embellished the ruined monastery with the assistance of a Prussian engineer, combining the aesthetic heritages of both Germany and Portugal. The result is a Bavarian castle embellished with Arabic minarets, Russian onion domes, Gothic turrets, Manueline windows, and a Renaissance dome. Interior highlights—decked in *chinoiserie* and other regalia of Romantic Orientalism—include the chapel, the fully furnished kitchen, and Her Majesty's toilet, done entirely in *azulejo* (not to mention the stunning views from the Queen's patio).

Signs point from the Palácio Nacional da Pena to the ruins of the **Castelo dos Mouros,** perched on the boulder-studded peaks towering over Sintra. *(Open daily 10am-7pm. Free.)* Stroll along the walls of the 16th-century fortress and clamber up its turrets for splendid views of the entire Serra da Sintra, the coast, Lisbon, and the Tejo.

The winding **peões** (pedestrian paths) will bring you down to São Pedro, where you can take a bus back down or walk. Kilometers of well-kept paths run through a eucalyptus forest and the strollable **Parque da Pena.** Keep your eyes open for the **cruz alta** (stone cross) and the **Igreja de São Pedro.**

The **Sintra Museu de Arte Moderna,** located past the train station in the more modern Sintra, houses contemporary works by Andy Warhol, Morris Louis, and Gerhard Richters (among others) in a cheerful *Belle Époque* building. *(Open W-Su 10am-6pm, Tu 2-6pm. 600$, students 300$, children under 10 free.)* The **Anjos Teixeira Museum-House** (tel. 923 61 23) can be reached by walking 100m downhill from the Pr. República and turning left into the park at the teeny sign. *(Open Tu-F 9:30am-1pm and 2-6pm, Sa-Su 2-6pm.)* The museum displays sculptures by one of Portugal's most revered artists, Master Anjos Teixeira. His son, sculptor Pedro Anjos Teixeira, lives and works in the precinct and greets visitors in person.

The towns surrounding Sintra may be worth visiting depending on your interest. Quaint **Mafra** offers a unique and remarkable palace, meriting an afternoon stop or daytrip from either Lisbon or Sintra. **Ericeira,** an up-and-coming seaside resort for the young and cosmopolitan crowd, is easy to reach from Sintra and may be worth a more extended stay. There are few sights to see, but great seafood, surf, and dancing make for a change of pace from the usual tourist agenda.

■ Near Sintra: Mafra

The sleepy, otherwise unremarkable town of Mafra (north of Sintra) is home to one of Portugal's most impressive sights and one of Europe's largest historical buildings, the **Palácio Nacional de Mafra.** *(Open W-M 10am-1pm and 2-5pm. Closed on national holidays. 300$, students free.)* Built by Dom João V in thanks for the birth of his first child, the massive castle incorporates a cathedral-size church, monastery, library, and palace. The monstrous 2000-room building, designed by architect Johann Friedrich Ludwig, took 50,000 workers 13 years (1713-1726) to complete. This Herculean task gave rise to a style of sculpture known as the Mafra School.

The exterior of the magnificent Baroque **igreja** (tel. 81 18 88) is undergoing restoration, although parts already completed gleam in their recaptured glory. Most renowned for its bell towers—two of the finest in Europe with 217 tons of bronze bells—the church also has an ornate and noteworthy dome. It was lifted from Bernini's unexpected plan for St. Peter's in Rome. The richly decorated interior—with bas-reliefs and statues of Carrara marble—is one of Portugal's gems.

To access the building's seemingly interminable corridors and extravagant living quarters, go through the door to the right of the church exit. Although most of the original 16th-century furniture was taken by Dom João V to Brazil, the **palace** nevertheless makes a fascinating visit, if only to hear the guides' fabulous free tour. *(45min. tours in Portuguese and English. Ask at the reception desk.)* Of particular interest are the **Sala dos Trofeus** (Trophy Room), furnished with stag antlers, skins, chandeliers, and chairs, and the **biblioteca** (library), with 38,000 volumes printed in the 16th, 17th, and 18th centuries, displayed on 290 feet of Rococo shelves.

Green and white Mafrense **buses** stop in the square in front of the palace. They serve Lisbon's Largo Martim Moniz in the Mouraria off Pr. Figueira. The **train** goes to Sintra (1hr., 1 per hr., 350$). If you plan on taking the train to Mafra from Lisbon's Estação Sta. Apolónia (1½hr., 1 per hr., 510$), be prepared for a two-hour walk to Mafra; the station is way out in the countryside where **cabs** are few and far between.

To reach the **tourist office** (tel. 81 20 23), on Av. 25 de Abril, take a right off the main steps of the palace and bear left—look for the blue Turismo sign. The office is on your right in a beige stucco building with a fountain, opposite the main bus station. The friendly staff distributes info on accommodations in surrounding areas (Mafra has only one hotel), like the popular town of Ericeira (see below). They will also **store luggage** while you visit the palace. (Open M-F 9:30am-7:30pm, Sa-Su 9:30am-1pm and 2:30-7:30pm.) For **police,** call 521 24. The **telephone code** is 061.

■ Ericeira

The little town of Ericeira (pop. 5000) pales in comparison to its beach. Known for its world-famous surfing waves just to the north, Ericeira has recently become the favorite hangout of young Lisbonites looking for a good time. With its sandy coves, fishing harbor, and whitewashed houses outlined in blue, Ericeira may very well merit a visit, especially for those less than thrilled by the Algarve's meager surf.

If basking in the town's warm atmosphere or the bright sun of **Praia do Sol** or **Praia do Norte** just doesn't do it for you, then take a stroll down the Largo da Feria toward Rébamar. Soon you'll hit the unmistakable **Praia da Ribeira d'Ilhas,** with its rolling surf, dramatic tides, and stunning sand dunes and rock formations. The world surfing championships were held here in 1994, and surfers still flock here from around the world to test the waters. **Ultimar,** R. 5 de Outubro, 37A (tel. 623 71) rents boards for 1200-2000$ per day.

PRACTICAL INFORMATION Buses leaving from the station head for Mafra (30min., depart every 45min., 300$) and Sintra (50min., departs every hr., 350$), as well as points north. Check at the tourist office for schedules of northern routes. To get to the tourist office from the bus station, cross the road and (while facing uphill) turn into the nearest sidestreet. Heading downhill and to the left on it or any of a number of streets parallel to it inevitably leads to the small pedestrian **Praça de República.** The **tourist office** (tel. 631 22) rests just a little farther down at R. Eduardo Burnay, 5. The attendant there will provide you with a map and accommodations list. (Open July.-Aug. daily 9am-midnight; Sept.-June 9am-8pm.) Dial 112 in an **emergency;** the **police** (tel. 635 33) are at R. 5 de Outubro. Look for the **hospital** (tel. 86 45 08) above town on R. Prudéncio Franco da Trindade. The **telephone code** is 061.

ACCOMMODATIONS AND FOOD If you choose to stay and party at one of the friendly bars or discos along the main drag—try the **Ferro Velho,** R. Dr. Eduardo Burnay, 7C—you'll most likely want a bed to wobble home to. A welcoming owner, two friendly cocker spaniels, and bright, clean rooms with TVs greet guests at the brand-new **Hotel Vilazul,** Calçada da Balcia, 10 (tel. 86 00 00). (Singles 6000$; doubles 8000$. Breakfast included. Credit cards accepted.) The **Residencial Pescador Fortunato,** R. Eduardo Burnay, 7 (tel. 86 28 29), offers smaller rooms but with views of the ocean. (Doubles 6000$. Breakfast included. Credit cards accepted.)

For a quick meal, try one of Ericeira's **pastry shops,** which serve some of the region's delicious specialties as well as sandwiches, drinks, and fruit. *Areias* and *queques* (100$) are especially yummy at **Pão de Nosa Vila,** Pr. da República, 12 (open W-M 7am-8pm). **Restaurante O Barco,** R. Capitão João Lopes (tel. 86 27 59), just down from Pr. de República and overlooking Praia Ribeira, dishes up spicy seafood. O Barco is justifiably famous for its *caldareda,* a tomato-based shellfish stew typical of Ericeira (1800$).

■ Setúbal

Setúbal's factories have created a noisy commercial center, surrounded on one side by no-nonsense sugar cane and cork tree plantations and on the other by a bustling port. Industry doesn't net tourists, most of whom head straight for the Algarve, but wait—don't turn the page yet. Some of the brightest *azulejo*-covered alleys in Portugal and the lapping waters of the largely rural Costa Azul beckon. Setúbal can serve as a base for daytrips to the beaches of Tróia and Figueirinha, the mountainous Serra da Arrábida, and the protected estuaries of the Rio Tejo.

ORIENTATION AND PRACTICAL INFORMATION

Setúbal's main drag is **Avenida Luisa Todi,** a loud boulevard with a nice park and cafes down its middle, parallel to the **Rio Sado.** North of Av. Todi lies a dense pedestrian district of shops and restaurants centered around **Praça du Bocage.** Going north out of Pr. Bocage takes you to another major thoroughfare, **Avenida do 5 de Outubro.** Several blocks farther east is the bus station and a few blocks farther is the **Praça do Quebedo,** where the tourist office sits. North of Pr. Quebedo along Av. Portela is the train station, in Pr. Brasil.

Trains: Estação de Setúbal, Pr. Brasil (tel. 52 68 45). To: Lisbon (1½hr., 31 per day, 300$); Évora (2hr., 13 per day, 850$); and Faro (4hr., 4 per day, 1350$).

Buses: Rodoviária do Alentejo, Av. 5 de Outubro, 44 (tel. 52 50 51). From the city tourist office, walk against traffic and turn left. To: Lisbon (1hr., departs every 30min., 550$); Évora (2½hr., 5 per day, 820$); Faro (4hr., 7 per day, 1700$); Porto (6hr., 6 per day, 1910$); and Vila Nova de Milfontes (3hr., 6 per day, 1190$).

Ferries: Transado, Doca do Comércio (tel. 201 52), off Av. Todi at the east end of the waterfront. Trips run back-and-forth from Setúbal to Tróia (15min., 4am-2pm, 130$, children 80$, cars with driver 500$).

Taxis: tel. 333 34, 314 13, 523 55, or 522 090.

PORTUGAL

Tourist Office: Posto de Turismo Municipal (tel. 53 42 22), off Pr. Quebedo. Out of the bus station, take a left onto Av. 5 de Outubro; take your first right and the office is on your left. Out of the train station, take your first left onto Av. da Portela, which will lead into Pr. Quebedo. Open M-F 9am-12:30pm and 2-5:30pm. **Tourist Office for the Costa Azul,** Tr. Frei Gaspar, 10 (tel. 52 42 84), off Av. Todi. Open Tu-F 9am-7pm, M and Sa 9am-12:30pm and 2-7pm, Su 9am-12:30pm.

Currency exchange: Banks line Av. Todi. For after-hours banking, visit **Agência de Câmbios Central,** Av. Todi, 226 (tel. 53 43 36). Open M-Sa 9am-7:30pm.

Emergency: Dial 112. **Police:** (tel. 52 20 22), on Av. Todi at Av. 22 de Dezembro.

Medical Services: Hospital (tel. 52 28 22), on R. Camilo Castelo Branco.

Telephone code: 065.

Post office: (tel. 52 27 78), on Av. Mariano de Carvalho at Av. 22 de Dezembro. *Posta Restante* and **telephones** open M-F 8:30am-6pm. Branch office in Pr. Bocage (tel 52 55 55). No *Posta Restante.* Open M-F 9am-12:30pm and 2-6pm. **Postal code** 2900.

ACCOMMODATIONS AND CAMPING

Summer prices are higher, but finding space for the night is no problem. Many *pensãos* line Av. Todi.

Centro de Juventude de Setúbal (tel. 53 27 78 or 53 28 35), on Largo José Afonso. Heading left on the river side of Av. Todi, hang a right on Rodos Trabalhadores do Mar and make your first right; the hostel is on the corner. Spic 'n' span rooms in a new government-sponsored youth center. Dorms 1200$; doubles with bath 3200$. For reservations call 4pm-midnight.

Pensão Bom Regresso, Pr. Bocaga, 49 (tel. 52 98 12). 4 well-furnished doubles in an excellent location, all with TV and views onto the *Praça.* Doubles with common bath 2000-3000$. No reservations. Cash only.

Residencial Setúbalense: R. Major Afonso Pala, 17 (tel. 52 57 90). Call it downright luxurious: 24 bright rooms with TV, private bath, and balconies. You get a lot for your wad of *escudos.* Room service and bar. Singles 5000-7000$; doubles 6000-8000$. Breakfast included. Credit cards accepted.

Camping: Get-away-from-it-all types should escape to one of the many campsites in the Parque Natural da Arrábida or one of the smaller locations near Setúbal in Azeitão or Sesimbra. Inquire at the tourist office for locations and rates. If you must stay in Setúbal proper, try **Toca do Pai Lopes** (tel. 52 24 75), on R. Praia da Saúde at the west end of Av. Todi on the road to Outão. On the beach. Reception daily June-Aug. 8am-10pm; Sept.-May 9am-9pm. June-Aug. 250$ per person and per car 200$ per tent; Sept.-May: 180$ per person and per car; 130$ per tent. Free hot showers.

FOOD

Hit the jackpot in the old town, especially off **R. A. Castelões** (turn off Pr. Bocage by the post office). **Groceries** and fresh baked goods are at **Pingo Doce,** Av. Todi, 149 (tel. 52 61 05; open daily 8am-9pm). Next door, on the corner of R. Ocidental do Mercado and Av. Todi, the **Mercado Municipal** hawks groceries at open stands. Setúbal's standard restaurants are located along Av. Todi across from the Doca do Comércio.

Jardim de Inverno, R. Alvaro Luz, 48-50 (tel. 393 73), off R. A. Castelões. Green walls, lights, and garden brighten up this dirt cheap *cafeteira-restaurante-bar Menú* 900$. Ask about holiday festival specials—São João in late June brings fried pork, salad, fries, and *sangriá* for 600$. Open M-F 8am-11:30pm, Sa-Su 8am-3pm.

Casa de Santiago, Av. Todi, 92 (tel. 216 88). What do all locals order when they dine at the self-proclaimed king of *choco frito?* You guessed it. Devour their generous half-portion of the *choco frito* (fried cuttlefish) for 800$.

SIGHTS AND ENTERTAINMENT

The most impressive sight in town is not really in town—the 16th-century **Castelo de São Filipe** perches on the top of a hill, a more than 30-minute walk up. Take Av. Todi to its western end, turn right, continue to the crossroads, and then ascend R. Estrada do Castelo about 600m. To the west of town (follow R. Bocage west from the *praça*), crumbling old houses are tiled with over 100 different kinds of *azulejos,* some covered with melted glass, others protruding from the wall. Back in town, the **Igreja de Jesús,** begun in the 15th century as part of a larger monastic complex, resides at Pr. Miguel Bombarda at the western end of Av. 5 de Outubro. Maritime decorations and faux-rope pillars mark the beginnings of the Manueline style.

For city-slicker entertainment, check out the **Forum Municipal Luisa Todi,** Av. Todi, 61-62 (tel. 52 21 27), which shows both independent and popular movies and community-produced plays. *(Both office open daily 11am-10pm on show days, 11am-7pm on off days. Tickets 300$).* The **Feira do Cinema** brings screening of European and American independent films during the first two weeks of June. In the last week of July and first week of August, **Feira de Santiago** is an industrial and agricultural extravaganza, accompanied by amusement parks, bullfighting, and folk dancing.

FUN IN THE SUN

The most worthwhile sights around Setúbal, however, are the natural ones. Get out of town to experience the fabulous **beaches** of peninsular **Tróia,** a 15-minute ferry ride away (140$, children 80$, cars with driver 500$). To the west of Setúbal is a large nature preserve, the **Parque Natural da Arrábida,** which includes a variety of nature trails (ask the tourist office for a copy of *A Walking Guide to Arrábida and Sado*) and the fabulously pristine **Praia da Figueirinha.** Outdoor adventurers (hopefully on generous grants from National Geographic) can contact **Safari Azul,** R. Cidade de Leira, 3, 5th fl. (tel. 55 24 47), for somewhat pricey mountain biking, hiking, canoeing, and other **nature adventure trips.**

■ Near Setúbal: Sesimbra

Nestled between unspoiled hillsides and the calm sea of *Costa Azul,* Sesimbra is a refreshingly traditional town where everyone seems to know each other. Despite recent influxes of beach-flocking tourists, it is still anchored to its roots as a fishing village. Sesimbra also pleases the less aquatically inclined—a steep 30-minute hike above town to the **Moorish castle** rewards the hardy with a Kodachrome view of the ocean and surrounding mountains. To reach the castle from the town center, take R. Gen. Humberto Delgado and follow the signs out of town.

Heavy traffic in the summer may lead you to take a **ferry** from Lisbon to Cacilhas (110$) from the Pr. Comércio station and catch a bus to Sesimbra (450$). Regular Rodoviária **buses** leave for Sesimbra from Lisbon's Pr. de Espanha (1hr., 540$). Covos e Filhos (tel. 22 30 72) buses leave from the main bus station for Lisbon (1hr., 8 per day, 540$) and Setúbal (45min., 9 per day, 410$). Buses for closer destinations also leave from the corner of Av. 5 de Outubro and Av. Alexandro Mercularo, a block west of the main bus station in Setúbal.

Maps, regional info, and accommodations info await at the **tourist office,** Largo da Morinha, 27 (tel. 223 57 43). (Open daily May-Aug. 9am-8pm; Oct.-Apr. 9am-12:30pm and 2-5:30pm. English spoken.) The **police** (tel. 223 02 69) are on Largo Gago Coutinino. Dial 112 in an **emergency.** The **telephone code** is (0)1. **Postal code** is 2970.

Inexpensive accommodations may be difficult to find, particularly in summer. The best option is to check with the tourist office for private rooms. Otherwise, **Residencial Chic,** Trav. Xavier da Silva, 2-6 (tel. 223 31 10), offers four breezy doubles with a common bath (singles 3500$; doubles 6000$; breakfast included). Across from Chic

PORTUGAL

are the 12 rooms (all with shower) of the **Garcia family,** R. Cándido dos Reis, 2 (tel. 273 32 27), which are well furnished and comfortable but a bit dark (singles 3000$; doubles 6000-9000$; triples 10,000$). For excellent seafood, follow the local fishermen to **Restaurante A Sesimbrense,** R. Jorge Nunes, 19 (tel. 223 01 48). People drive from kilometers around for their exquisite *caldeira à pescador* (fisherman's stew, 1500$). Entrees go for around 1000-1500$. (Open W-M 9am-3pm and 7-10pm.)

Algarve

⟨⟨⟩⟩ HIGHLIGHTS OF THE ALGARVE

- **Praia da Rocha,** arguably the most amazing beach on the Algarve (p. 576).
- Hopping resort town **Albufeira,** with its own spectacular beach (see p. 576).
- Quiet town, excellent beaches, peaceful people—**Tavira** (p. 581).
- **Lagos's nightlife**—it doesn't get much nuttier than this (see p. 572).

A freak of nature; a desert on the sea; an inexhaustible vacationland where happy campers from all over the world bask in the *sol*—behold the Algarve. Nearly 3000 hours of sunshine per year have transformed this one-time fishermen's backwater into one of Europe's favorite destinations for sun-filled fun and relaxation. Tourist resorts are mobbed in July and August, packing the bars and discos from the 10pm sunset until the all-too-early sunrise.

That said, not all is excess in the Algarve. In the off season, the resorts of the Algarve become pleasantly de-populated. The sun eases down a bit, presiding over tranquil grotto beaches lining the base of rugged cliffs and rocky islets. Salema, Burgau, and Sagres, to the west of Lagos, offer isolated beaches and steep cliffs, and the region between Olhão and the border remains understated. The west coast of the Algarve was recently declared a protected natural park, and flamingo wetlands float along Portugal's eastern border, near the town of Tavira.

Reaching more remote beaches is a snap. EVA has extensive bus services with convenient schedules and low fares. The train costs less than the bus but only connects major coastal cities, and in some towns the station is a hike from the center. Leave your car at home—the roads here are plagued by constant road work and legendary traffic jams—but rent a bike or a moped at your hub town; there is no better way to explore nearby beaches. In this region, reasonably priced private *quartos* are generally the best alternative to expensive *pensões. The Algarve News* (125$) runs articles on trendy clubs, local festivals, and special events. Topless bathing is the fashion here, but bottomless is restricted to numerous nude beaches, sequestered in nooks between cliffs, but easy to find with a little effort.

The Algarve's cuisine includes *sardinhas assadas* (grilled sardines), often accompanied by *caldeirada,* a chowder of fish, shellfish, potatoes, and tomatoes perked up with onion and garlic. Native figs and almonds are combined in all manners to tempt those with a sweet tooth, so save space for a *sobremesa* (dessert). To wash it all down, try *amêndoa amarga* (almond liqueur) or *medronho* (firewater) made from the mini strawberries of arbutus trees. Wines such as the young *vinho verde* are inexpensive and make a wonderful complement to any meal.

Lagos

ACCOMMODATIONS
- **C** Pousada de Juventude
- **B** Residencia Caravela
- **A** Residencia Rubi Mar
- **D** Campsites

571

■ Lagos

For many, many moons, swarms of Europeans, Australians, and North Americans have sojourned here to worship the almighty Sun, god of Lagos. Lately, however, the *sol* is in danger of being dethroned by the porcelain god—to date, 20 bars and discos stay open until the wee hours. As the town's countless international expats will attest, Lagos (pop. 22,000) is a black hole: come for two days and you'll stay a month. Although there isn't much more than beaches and bars, it is a very contented place. Whether you're soaking in the view from the cliffs, soaking in the sun on the beach, or soaking yourself in drinks at the bars, you'll be happy, too.

ORIENTATION AND PRACTICAL INFORMATION

Running the length of the river, **Avenida dos Descobrimentos** carries traffic in and out of Lagos. From the **train station,** go straight around the pink building, across the river, and hang a left. Out of the **bus station,** turn right onto the *avenida.* Follow it to **Rua das Portas de Portugal,** the gateway leading into **Praça Gil Eanes,** the center of the old town. Most restaurants, accommodations, and services hover about this *praça* (also known as the "statue square") and the adjoining **Rua 25 de Abril** and the parallel **Rua Cândido dos Reis.**

Transportation

Trains: (tel. 76 29 87). On the east side across the river from the bus station. To: Vila Real de Santo António, via Faro (3hr., 5 per day, 1100$); Beja (4hr., 2 per day 1200$); Évora (6hr., 2 per day, 1740$); Lisbon (6½hr., 3 per day, 2000$).

Buses: The **EVA** bus station (tel. 76 29 44), off Av. Descobrimentos, is on the east edge of town. To: Portimão (*expressos:* 30min., 10 per day, 335-450$; *regular:* 16 per day, 350$); Sagres (1hr., 4 per day, 445$); Faro (2½hr., 2 per day, 670$); Lisbon (*expressos:* 5hr., 4 per day, 2650$; *regular:* 8 per day, 2000-2500$).

Taxis: dial 76 24 69 or 76 30 48.

Car Rental: Marina Rent A Car, Av. Descobrimentos, 43 (tel. 76 47 89; fax 76 77 98). Must be at least 21 to rent. Including tax and insurance, cars start at 8700$ per day in summer; 6500$ in winter. **Hertz-Portuguesa,** Rossio de S. João Ed. Panorama, 3 (tel. 76 00 08), behind the bus station. Must be 21 or over to rent. Cars start at 10,000$ (including tax and insurance) per day in summer; less in winter. Cheaper though shadier deals can be found all over town.

Bike/Moped Rental: Motolagos, R. São José, 17 (tel. 76 03 65), on Pr. d'Armas, and a booth on R. 25 de Abril. Must be 16 or over to rent. Mountain bikes 500$ per hr. 1700$ per day. Motorbikes from 2000$ per day. Longer rentals for less. The youth hostel rents mountain bikes for 1000$ per day.

Tourist, Financial, and Local Services

Tourist Office: R. Marquês de Pombal (tel. 76 30 31). Take the side street R. Lima Leitão, which begins in the Pr. Gil Eanes. Take the 1st right—the door is on the side of the building. A 20min. walk from the train station, 15min. from the bus station. Brochures, maps, and transport info available, as well as a list of *quartos.* English spoken. Open daily 9:30am-12:30pm and 2-5:30pm.

Currency Exchange: ATMs and **automatic currency machines** can be found at the numerous banks on Pr. Gil Eanes and R. Portas de Portugal. Commission-free currency exchange is available at the youth hostel.

English Bookstore: Loja do Livro, R. Dr. Joaquim Telo, 3 (tel. 76 73 47). Best-sellers, pulp romances, and travel guides. Open M-F 10am-1pm and 3-7pm.

Laundromat: Lavandaria Miele, Av. Descobrimentos, 27 (tel. 63 969). 5kg wash and dry 1000$. Open M-F 9am-1pm and 3-7pm, Sa 9am-1pm.

Scuba Diving: Blue Ocean Diving Center, Quantro Estrados (tel. 78 27 18). Medical license required for experienced divers. Lessons in English, French, German, Portuguese. Half day 5000$; full day 7000$.

Emergency and Communications
Emergency: dial 112. **Police:** (tel. 76 26 30), R. General Alberto Silva.
Medical Services: Hospital (tel. 76 30 34), R. Castelo dos Governadores, next to Igreja Santa María. **Ambulance:** (24hr. tel. 76 01 81 or 76 43 00).
Post Office: (tel. 76 30 67), R. Portas de Portugal, between Pr. Gil Eanes and the river. Open M-F 9am-6pm. For Posta Restante, label all letters "Estação Portas de Portugal" or they may arrive at the **branch office. Postal Code:** 8600.
Telephone Code: (0)82.

ACCOMMODATIONS AND CAMPING

In the summertime, *pensões* (and the youth hostel) fill up quickly and cost a bundle. Reserve rooms over a week in advance. Rooms in *casas particulares* sometimes include kitchen access and can be the greatest deals in town at around 1000$ per person in winter and 2000 to 3000$ per person in summer. Try haggling with owners waiting at the train and bus stations and the tourist office, and (if possible) shop before you decide, as room quality varies greatly.

Pousada de Juventude de Lagos (HI), R. Lançarote de Freitas, 50 (tel./fax 76 19 70), from the train and bus stations, head into town on Av. República and turn right up R. Portas de Portugal. Head into Pr. Gil Eanes and turn right up R. Garrett into Pr. Luis de Camões, then take a left onto R. Cândido dos Reis. At the bottom of the hill, take a right onto R. Lançarote de Freitas; the hostel is on the right in front of the big green BP sign. Damn cool place with friendly staff and fun people who congregate in the central courtyard and TV room/bar. Barracks-style rooms 2000$. Doubles with bath 4700$. Oct.-June 16 rooms 1400$; doubles with bath 3550$. Breakfast included (take-out available). Fully equipped kitchen. Free valuables storage. Laundry 340$ per kg. Money exchange commission-free. Reception daily 9am-1am. Check-out noon. No curfew. Summer reservations not guaranteed; if the hostel is full when you get there, the attendant will help you find a room or *pensão* nearby.

Residencial Rubi Mar, R. Barroca, 70 (tel. 76 31 65, ask for David; fax 76 77 49), off Pr. Gil Eanes. Run by 2 friendly expats from London. Centrally located, quiet and comfortable—a good deal if you can grab one of their 8 rooms. Doubles 6000$, with bath 7000$; quads 8000-10,000$. Breakfast included and served in the room.

Residencial Caravela, R. 25 de Abril, 8 (tel. 76 33 61). Small but well-located rooms surrounding a courtyard. Singles 4000$; doubles 5500$, with bath 6000$. Prices lower in winter. Breakfast included.

Residencial Gil Vicente, R. Gil Vicente, 26, 2nd fl. (tel. 76 29 82), on the block behind the youth hostel. Clean, very quiet location. Rooms somewhat stuffy but with beautiful high ceilings. Rarely full—knock on their door if the youth hostel rejects you. Singles 2500$; doubles 3500$. Showers 80$.

Camping: Camping is *the* way most Europeans experience the Algarve; as a result, sites are crowded and expensive. On a beach 1.5km west of Praia da Luz and 6km outside Lagos, Orbitur's peaceful **Camping Valverde** (tel. 78 92 11) costs 700$ per person, 600-900$ per tent, 590$ per car. Free showers. Jam-packed **Parque de Campismo do Imulagos** (tel. 76 00 31) is frustratingly far away but linked to Lagos by a free shuttle bus serving the train and bus stations. 900$ per adult, under 10 230$, 450-640$ per tent, 430$ per car. Reception daily 8am-10pm. **Camping Trindade,** just outside town (follow Av. Descobrimentos toward Sagres), charges 400$ per person with tent, 800$ without tent.

FOOD

Tourists are treated to multilingual menus in and around **Praça Gil Eanes** and **Rua 25 de Abril.** Mexican, British, German, Chinese, and American food is everywhere, but a budget Portuguese meal is nearly impossible to find. The cheapest option is probably the **open market** (mornings only), Av. Descobrimentos, five minutes from the town center, or **Supermercado São Toque,** R. Portas de Portugal, opposite the post office (open July-Sept. daily 9am-5pm; Oct.-June M-F 9am-8pm, Sa 9am-2pm).

PORTUGAL

Casa Rosa, R. do Ferrador, 22. A Lagos standby, for better or for worse. Enjoy cheap all-you-can-eat specials with backpacker hordes. Monday and Wednesday are spaghetti and garlic bread day (850$). Happy Hour 10-11pm. Famous 199 meal menu includes 52 vegetarian dishes. Open daily 9am-2pm and 7pm-3am.

Restaurante Piri Piri, R. Lima Leitão, 15 (tel. 76 38 03). Locals and tourists of all ages mix here to enjoy any of 91 titillating *piri piri* (hot spice) dishes. Prices from 850-1500$. Open daily noon-midnight.

Mullin's, R. Cândido dos Reis, 86 (tel. 76 12 81). A Lagos hot spot. Servers dance to the tables with huge portions of spicy food. The crowd quivers with a carnal pulse, or perhaps in reaction to burned mouths. Chicken *piri-piri* smothered in hot sauce 1200$. Entrees 1000-2200$. After dinner, the place transforms into a happening bar. Restaurant open daily noon-10pm; bar open nightly until 2am.

Hasan's Döner Kebab, R. Silva Lopes, 27 (tel. 76 46 82), a continuation of R. 25 de Abril. Perfect for that post-beach snack. Huge falafel sandwiches only 550$. Open daily noon-10pm.

SIGHTS

Although sunbathing and round-the-clock partying have long erased memories of Lagos's more rugged (and sea-faring) past, most of Lagos is still surrounded by a nearly-intact 16th-century city wall. The **Fortaleza da Porta da Bandeira,** a 17th-century fortress holding maritime exhibitions, overlooks the Marina. *(Open Tu-Sa 10am-1pm and 2-6pm, Su 10am-1pm. Free.)* Also on the waterfront is the old **Mercado de Escravos** (slave market)—legend has it that in 1441 the first sale of African slaves on Portuguese ground took place here. Today, the waterfront and marina host more pleasant forms of commercialism: jet-ski rentals, scuba diving tours, sailboat trips, and motorboat tours of the rock formations and grottoes off the coast.

Lagos's beaches are seductive any way that you look at them. Flat, smooth, sunbathing sands (crowded during the summer, pristine in the off season) can be found at the 4km-long **Meia Praia,** across the river from town. For beautiful cliffs that hide less-crowded beaches as well as caves that are perfect to swim in and around, follow Av. Descobrimentos twenty minutes southwest to **Praia de Pinhão.** Five minutes farther lies **Praia Dona Ana,** whose sculpted cliffs and grottoes appear on at least half of all Algarve postcards. For other picturesque (and less populated) stretches, continue west to the **Praia do Camilo** and the grotto-speckled cliffs of **Ponta da Piedade.**

ENTERTAINMENT

Now that you've tanned your hide, what are you waiting for? Flaunt it. The streets of Lagos pick up as soon as the sun dips down, and by midnight the walls start to shake. The area between Pr. Gil Eanes and Pr. Luis de Camões is filled with cafes. The area around R. Marreiros Netto, south of Pr. Gil Eanes, forms the center of nightlife—bars and clubs runneth over until well past 5am. Everyone has a personal favorite, but club-hopping is more a profession than a pastime. South of Pr. Gil Eanes, **Joe's Garage (Garagem de José),** opposite Mullin's restaurant at R. 1° de Maio, 78, is packed from the late-evening Happy Hour to the early-morning tabletop dancing. **Tribes and Vibes,** R. Marreiros Netto, 52, is a Tex-Mex theme bar, cafe, and dance club. A wooden Indian welcomes you into the 70s-chic dance floor. (Open nightly 4pm-4am.) **Bad Moon Rising,** R. Marreiros Neto, 50, jams to grunge and indie rock from 8pm-4am, with a lively scam scene on the side. Stop by **Shots in the Dark,** R. 1° de Maio, 16, to hang out with a younger international backpacking crowd. Another hot watering hole is the **Calypso Bar,** R. 1° de Maio, 22. **Rosko's,** R. Cândido dos Reis, 79, is a mellower Irish bar for all crowds.

Close to the water, bars scatter along R. 25 de Abril and its extension, R. Silva Lopes. **Sins,** on R. Silva Lopes, has a friendly frat party atmosphere, with beer funneling and the infamous nine deadly sins (nine shots, 4000$). Across the street, **Stones** plays Pearl Jam, U2, and Hendrix in a packed, two-story setting. Farther on, the crowd shuttles between **Eddie's** and **Bon Vivant.**

On the way up to the youth hostel along R. Lançarote de Freitas, the **Phoenix Club** (off a side street; look for the black sign on the left) plays house and dance music until 4am but occasionally charges a cover (1000$) for crowd-control. A hopping gay bar, **The Last Resort,** along R. Lançarote de Freitas, has live entertainment every Thursday night. Up the street half a block, the British pub **Taverna Velha (The Old Tavern)** hosts jolly "happy hours" from 11pm to midnight with televised soccer matches. When the game craving strikes, play the hustler at **Taco d'Ouro,** R. Ferreiros, 25, where there are billiards, darts, pinball, and a river of beer daily from 1pm to 2am.

■ Near Lagos: Sagres

Marooned atop a bleak, scrub-desert plateau in the barren southwest corner of Europe, Sagres and its cape were known for centuries as the end of the world. The windswept, rugged scenery of the cape is as barren as the moon, until plunging dramatically off all three sides into the Atlantic. Here outward-looking Prince Henry founded his school of navigation, inspiring and training the likes of Magellan and Columbus. Sagres's dramatic, desolate location, and (relative) lack of recreation discourages tour groups and upscale travelers, instead catering mainly to travelers whose hearts are set on seeing the geography and history of Sagres's majestic cape.

PRACTICAL INFORMATION Rodoviária **buses** (tel. 76 29 44) run from Lagos (1hr., 4 per day, 445$; check the schedule at the Sagres bus stop to avoid getting stranded). The privately run **tourist office,** called Turinfo (tel. 62 00 03), in the central square Pr. Republica, is located to your right off the main road where the bus stops. The energetic, English-speaking staff recommends accommodations, **rents bikes** (2000$ per day, 1200$ per half-day), hands out bus and train schedules, gives info on **jeep tours** of nearby natural preserve (including lunch, 6500$), and provides **SCUBA** advice. They will even wash your clothes—seriously. (Open daily 10am-7pm.) For a **taxi** call 645 01. In an **emergency,** call 112. The **post office** is on R. Correio (open M-F 9am-12:30pm and 2:30-6pm). The **postal code** is 8650. The **telephone code** is (0)82.

ACCOMMODATIONS AND FOOD Finding a room in Sagres is not a problem: windows everywhere display multilingual signs for rooms, many in boarding houses with guest kitchens. Prices range from 3000-5000$ for singles and doubles to 4000-6500$ for triples. Follow the main road toward the traffic circle and take a left after the supermarket to reach **Atalaia Apartamentos** (tel. 646 81). These beautiful, fully furnished apartments and rooms above a grocery store are an exceptional value (apartments for two July-Oct. 7500$; Apr.-June 6500$; Nov.-Mar. 5500$). Open-air **camping** is strictly not allowed, so sleep peacefully at the **guarded ground** (tel. 643 51; fax 644 45), near town, just off E.N. 268 (July-Aug. 450$ per person, 625$ per tent, 350$ per car; considerably cheaper Sept.-June; open year-round).

The **market** is off R. Comandante Matoso; turn left at R. do Correio off the main street (open M-Sa 10am-8pm). Several restaurants serve up tasty meals on Sagres's main drag. **Restaurante-Bar Atlántico** (tel. 76 42 36) serves Portuguese cuisine, including heaping portions of *amêijoas ao natural* (plain clams, 900$). **O Dromedário Bistro,** R. Comandante Matoso (tel. 642 19), whips up fruit shakes (280-500$) and innovative pizzas (670-1140$) in a bar atmosphere (closes nightly 4am).

SIGHTS AND ENTERTAINMENT Near the town lurks the **Fortaleza,** the outpost where Prince Henry stroked his beard and formulated his plan to map the world. *(Free.)* Vasco da Gama, Magellan, Columbus, Diaz, and Cabral apprenticed here in Henry's **school of navigation.** The pentagonal 15th-century fortress and the surrounding area yield vertigo-inducing views of the cliffs and sea.

Six kilometers farther west, lies the desolate **Cabo de São Vicente,** which features the second most powerful lighthouse in Europe, a towering structure that overlooks the southwest tip of the continent and shines over 60 miles out to sea. Unfortunately, no buses connect the cape with Sagres. To reach the cape, rent a bike (see below) or brave the winds and take the hour-long cliffside walk past the **Fortaleza do Beliche,** one of several fortresses perched atop the cliffs. *(No fixed hours. Get permission to climb up from the gatekeeper, who disappears noon-2pm but is usually there 8am-9pm.)*

Several **beaches** fringe the peninsula, most notably **Mareta,** located at the bottom of the road from the center of town. Rock formations jut far out into the ocean on both sides of this sandy crescent. Not as picturesque or intimate as the coves of nearby **Salema** and **Luz** (see below), this beach is nevertheless popular for its length and isolation. West of town, **Praia de Martinhal** is the longest beach and has **windsurfing** that's just great.

Although Sagres may seem dead on arrival, if you hang around till nightfall, you may pick up a pulse. At night, the young set crowds the lively restaurant-bar **Rosa dos Ventos** (tel. 644 80), in Pr. República. *(Open daily 10am-2am.)* Get ready to rumble at **The Last Chance Saloon,** which blasts English dance tunes and overlooks the beach *(small bar open daily 5, hopping 11pm, closes 4am).*

■ Near Lagos: Luz, Burgau, and Salema

These three towns on the way to Sagres make perfect stopovers or daytrips from Lagos. Less "discovered" than their larger neighbor, they offer a quieter alternative to crowded Lagos, and a character markedly more charming than that of windswept Sagres. All three towns feature good beaches (although Salema is perhaps the least developed), and all three are accessible by the **bus** from Lagos to Sagres. To reach Luz, get off at Espiche, the nearest stop, 1.5km away (12 buses per day; to Espiche 10min., 80$; to Burgau 20 min., 180$; to Salema 40 min., 220$).

Excellent **camping** is found at the comfortable **Quinta dos Carrigos** (tel. 082 643 51) in Salema (650$ per person, 850$ per tent, 600$ per car). Deliciously fresh fruits, cheeses, and olives are sold by local farmers each morning at the main square in Salema, but decent bars and **restaurants** line the beachfront in all three towns.

■ Near Lagos: Praia da Rocha

A short jaunt from Lagos or Portimão, this grand beach is perhaps the very best the Algarve has to offer. Crowded by as many locals as tourists, it offers vast spans of sand, surfable waves, rocky red cliffs, and plenty of secluded coves. Praia da Rocha is also a town, as the towering resort hotels behind the beach will suggest, but that's not why anyone comes. Charm and history are practically nonexistent here, but the beachfront makes up in liveliness for its lack of cultural appeal.

To reach Praia da Rocha from Lagos, you must first take a **bus** to Portimão (*expressos:* 30min., 10 per day, 335-450$; *regular:* 16 per day, 350$). Switch at the station to the Praia da Rocha bus (10min., departs every 15min.). The **tourist office** (tel. 42 22 90), located at the end of R. Tomás Cabreina, offers maps and lists of accommodations and restaurants (open daily May-Sept. 9:30am-8pm; Oct.-Apr. M-F 9:30am-12:30pm and 2-6pm, Sa-Su 9:30am-12:30pm). In an **emergency,** call 112.

Ask at the tourist office for private *quartos:* they are your best bet for a good deal, at about 3000$ for singles, 4000-6000$ for doubles. **Pensáo Residencial Solar Penguin,** (tel. 42 43 08) R. António Feu, is a bit more expensive but has bright, airy doubles, some with sea views (7000-9000$; all with private bath; breakfast included). Down the cliff from the *pensáo,* its restaurant serves salads, seafood, and creative crêpes (900$) from its friendly terrace perch overlooking the sea.

▓ Albufeira

Those who come to Albufeira (pop. 20,000), the largest seaside resort in the Algarve, are hell-bent on having a good time. Sun, surf, and *cerveja* keep the English, German, and Scandinavian crowd satisfied; nary a Portuguese roams the cobblestone streets. It may appear that there is little "authentic" Portuguese culture here, but Albufeira is still strongly rooted in its origins as a fishing village, as a stroll through the old town or along the east edge of the beach will reveal. For those too jaded to care, the nightlife is jumping from dusk till dawn, and 12 beaches watch over the glassy blue surf.

PRACTICAL INFORMATION EVA buses connect the **train station** (tel. 57 16 16), 6km inland, to the town center (depart every hr., 180$). Albufeira lies on the Lagos-Vila Real de Santo António line and goes to: Faro (45min., 300$); Lagos (1½hr., 480$); Olhão (1½hr., 360$); Tavira (2hr., 550$); Vila Real de Santo António (690$); and Lisbon (3½hr., 3 per day, 1910$). The EVA **bus station** (tel. 58 97 55), on Av. Liberdade, is at the entrance of town. Walk downhill to reach the center. Buses head to: Faro (1hr., departs every hr., 570$); Portimão (1hr., 7 per day, 700$); Lagos (1½hr., 7 per day, 850$); Tavira (2hr., 750$); and Vila Real de Santo António (2½hr., 750$).

The **tourist office,** R. 5 de Outubro, 8 (tel. 58 52 79), has maps, a list of *quartos*, plus tons of brochures on stuff to do, including fishing trips, scuba diving, and day trips (open daily 9:30am-7pm). From the bus station, turn right and walk downhill into the main square, then onto the street at the other side of the square to the right. Go straight one block and take a left. A booth run by **Portela** (tel. 57 11 55) hands out tourist info in front of the train station (open M-Sa 9am-7pm). Call a **taxi** at (tel. 58 71 51). In an **emergency,** dial 112. The **police** (tel. 51 54 20) are in the *Caliços* zone, near the Mercado Municipal. The **Centro de Saúde** (Health Clinic) is at (tel. 58 75 50). The **post office** (tel. 58 66 01) is next to the tourist office at R. 5 de Outubro (open M-F 9am-6pm). The **postal code** is 8200. The **telephone code** is (0)89.

ACCOMMODATIONS AND FOOD Many places are booked solid from late June through mid-September, and truly cheap housing is scarce. Ask for *quartos* at the tourist office or at any restaurant or bar. Chances are, however, that you will be accosted by room renters upon stepping off the train or bus. Closest to the bus station is the comfortable **Residencial Capri,** Av. Liberdade, 83 (tel. 512 691), where bright, spacious doubles, all with bath, overlook the avenue (singles 5000$; doubles 5500-8000$). The modern **Pensão Albufeirense,** Av. Liberdade, 18 (tel. 51 20 79), one block downhill from the bus station, has comfortable rooms and a TV lounge (singles 3500$; doubles 5000$; triples 6500$; open May-Sept.). Weary campers can succumb to the ritz and glitz of the four-star rated **Parque de Campismo de Albufeira** (tel. 58 98 70; fax 58 76 33), a few kilometers outside town on the road to Ferreiras. The *parque* is more like a shopping mall than a campground, with four swimming pools, three restaurants, tennis courts, a supermarket, and a hefty price tag (850$ per person, per car, per tent). Open-air camping is illegal and not tolerated.

Unlike rooms, there is no shortage of cheap and varied eats. Locals recommend **Tasca do Viegas,** R. Cais Herculano, 2 (tel. 51 40 87), near the fisherman's beach. Meat and fish dishes start at 800$ (open daily 11am-11pm). A few blocks uphill from the central square is **Restaurante Manjar,** R. M.F.A., 17 (tel. 51 40 37), where you can *manjar* (eat) 'til your stomach's content (open daily noon-midnight). For something spicy, try **Minar Indian Tandoori Cuisine,** Trav. Cais Herculano (tel. 51 31 96), near the fisherman's beach, with great veggie options (most dishes 1100-1500; open M-Sa noon-3pm and 6-11:30pm, Su 6-11:30pm).

SIGHTS AND ENTERTAINMENT The last holdout of the Moors in southern Portugal, Albufeira preserves its graceful Moorish architectural heritage in its old quarters. Tiny minarets pierce the small Byzantine dome of the **Santana** chapel, an exquisite filigree doorway heralds the **São Sebastião** church, an ancient Gothic portal fronts the **Misericórdia,** and a barrel-vaulted interior receives worshippers into the **Matiz.**

Albufeira's spectacular slate of **beaches** ranges from the popular **Galé** and **São Rafael** west of town, to the centrally located **Baleeira, Inatel,** and **Oura,** to the very chic **Falésia** 10km east of town. Many small and relatively uncrowded beaches lie scattered among the main *praias*—it pays to explore. In town, the fisherman's beach is lined with boats that venture out to sea every day.

After a day at the beach, you could…go to a bar. Bars and restaurants line all the streets, and clubs blast everything from salsa to techno to *fado* as soon as the sun sets, continuing until it rises. One prime spot is **Fastnet Bar,** R. Cândido dos Reis, 5 (tel. 58 91 16), packed with beer-gobbling Northern Europeans. Down the street is **Classic Bar,** R. Cândido dos Reis, 10 (tel. 51 20 73), which covers its floor with sand every night so that the Grecian decor won't disorient you. The hottest clubs in town, **Disco**

Silvia's (tel. 58 85 74), and **Qué Pasa?** (tel. 51 33 06), face off on R. São Gonçalo de Lagos, each jam-packed with a hot (and sweaty) student crowd. For more **mellow nightlife,** head east along the coast into the old town. At **Café Latino,** on R. Latino Coelho, salsa tunes complement a stunning seaside view. There's nothing strange about nearby **Café Bizzaro,** R. Dr. Frutuoso Silva, 30, a cool, down-to-earth cafe-bar.

■ Faro

Although many northern Europeans begin their holidays in Faro, the Algarve's capital and largest city, few bother to stay long enough to fathom its charm and color. Faro is less packed than the rest of the Algarve. The city has two characters that live side by side: a modern, commercial one, visible in a chic shopping district and slick marina; and a quiet historical one, behind the walls of the perfectly preserved **old town.** If you're looking for sun, you'll find it on the calm beaches of the estuary's islands.

ORIENTATION AND PRACTICAL INFORMATION

Faro's ritzy center hugs the **Doca de Recreio,** a marina lined with small vacation yachts and bordered by the **Jardim Manuel Bívar.** The main road into town, **Avenida da República,** runs past the train station and bus depot along the harbor, spilling into a delta of smaller streets at the **Praça Dr. Francisco Gomes,** which borders the dock and garden. **Ruas Dr. Francisco Gomes** and **de Santo António** are the major pedestrian thoroughfares off Pr. Gomes. The old town begins at the **Avio da Vila,** a stone arch on the far side of the garden, next door to the tourist office.

Transportation

Flights: The international **airport** (tel. 81 85 82), 5km west of the city, has a police station, bank, post office, car rental companies, and tourism booth. Open daily 10am-midnight. Buses #14 and 16 run from the street opposite the bus station to the airport (20min., departs every 20min., 150$). A taxi costs 1200$-1450$. **TAP Air Portugal** (tel. 80 02 00), R. Dr. Francisco Gomes. Open M-F 9am-5:30pm.

Trains: (tel. 80 17 26), Largo da Estação. To: Albufeira (1hr., 6 per day, 300$); Vila Real de Santo António (1½hr., 13 per day, 460$); Lagos (2½hr., 8 per day, 680$); Beja (3hr., 2 per day, 1700$); Lisbon (5hr., 6 per day, 2060$). Be sure to consult the official schedule as departure times are often bunched together.

Buses: EVA (tel. 89 97 00), on Av. República. To: Olhão (20min., 15 per day, 175$); Albufeira (1hr., 4 per day, 570$); Albufeira (1hr., 14 per day, 530$); Vila Real de Santo António (1hr., 3-9 per day, 590$); Tavira (1hr., 3 per day, 300$); Lagos (2½hr., 2 per day, 950$); Beja (3hr., 2 per day, 1300$). **Caima** (tel. 81 29 80), across the street, provides express long-distance bus service. To: Lisbon (4½hr., departs every hr., 2300$); Porto (8½hr., departs every hr., 3000$); Braga (10hr., departs every hr., 3050$). International routes are run by **Intersul** (tel. 89 97 70), to Sevilla (2600$), with connecting buses to France and Germany.

Taxis: Rotaxi (tel. 82 22 89). Taxis congregate near Jardim Manuel Bívar (by the tourist office) and at the bus and train stations.

Tourist, Financial, and Local Services

Tourist Office: R. Misericórdia, 8 (tel. 80 36 04), conveniently located at the entrance to the old town. From the bus or train station, turn right down Av. República along the harbor, and turn left past the garden. Helps find accommodations. English spoken. Open in summer daily 9:30am-7pm; in winter M-F 9:30am-7pm, Sa-Su 9:30am-5:30pm.

Currency Exchange: A small office, **Agência de Câmbios de Vilamoura-Faro,** is just off Pr. Gomes on Av. República. No commission. Open M-F 9am-6:30pm, Sa 9am-2pm. **ATMs** are located all around the city.

English Bookstore: Livraria Bertrand, R. Dr. Francisco Gomes, 27 (tel. 281 47), in the pedestrian area. Decent selection of classics, trash, and textbooks. Open M-Sa 9am-10pm, Su 5-9pm.

Laundromat: Sólimpa, R. Batista Lopes, 30 (tel. 82 29 81), up R. Primeiro de Maio, to the *praça*. 350$ per kilo. Open M-F 9am-1pm and 3-7pm, Sa 9am-1pm.

Emergency and Communications

Emergency: call 112. **Police:** (tel. 82 20 22), R. Polícia da Segurança Pública.
Hospital: R. Leão Pinedo (tel. 80 34 11), north of town.
Post Office: Largo do Carmo (tel. 80 30 08), across from the Igreja de Nossa Senhora do Carmo. Open for Posta Restante M-F 9am-12:30pm and 2-6pm, Sa 9am-12:30pm.
Postal Code: 8000.
Telephone Code: (0)89.

ACCOMMODATIONS

Rooms are pretty available here, even during high season. Resort to the tourist office's top 20 list of *pensões* if in need. Lodgings bite the heels of the bus and train stations. For something cheap and cheerful, try to scrape up a *quarto;* virtually all of the low-end budget *pensões* are pretty sorry.

Pensão Residencial Oceano, R. Ivens, 21, 2nd fl. (tel. 82 33 49). From the marina-side of Pr. Gomes, head up R. 1° de Maio and you'll see the sign 1 block up on the right. If you don't mind the funerary supply store next door, the doubles—somewhat spare, but tidy and comfortable—make a great bargain. Attractive *azulejos* in the halls and baths. All rooms have bath and telephone. Singles 6000$; doubles 7000$; triples 8500$. 500-1000$ discount in winter.

Residencial Madalena, R. Conselheiro Bívar, 109 (tel. 80 58 06; fax 80 58 07), just off Pr. Gomes. Centrally located with pleasant, neat rooms, all with full bath, telephone, fan, and heater. Friendly, English-speaking reception. TV room and small bar. In summer singles 5500$; doubles 5000$, with bath 7000$. In winter singles 3000$; doubles 4500$. Traveler's checks accepted.

Pensão-Residencial Central, Largo Terreiro Do Bispo, 12 (tel. 80 72 91), located near the pedestrian area. Clean, bright, comfortable rooms, some with terraces giving onto the square. All with bath. Singles 4000$; doubles 7000$.

Casa de Hóspedes Adelaide, R. Cruz das Mestras, 7-9 (tel. 80 23 83; fax 82 68 70). Ten rough but basically clean rooms, good for big groups. Singles 3000$; doubles 4000$; quads 5000$. Private bath 500$ more. 500$ discount in winter.

Pausada de Juventude, R. da Polícia de Segurança Pública (tel. 80 19 70). Rather inconveniently located and lacks significant amenities, but at 1200$ per night, is a true budget option.

FOOD

Almonds and figs are native to the Algarve and local bakeries whip them up into delicious marzipan and fig desserts. Faro has some of the Algarve's chattiest cafes, many along **Rua Conselheiro Bívar,** off Pr. Gomes. At the **market,** Pr. Dr. Francisco Sá Carneiro, locals barter fresh seafood (open M-F 9am-1pm). Live the high life on **Rua Santo António,** a pedestrian district where costly *marisqueiras* (seafood restaurants) and credit cards reign, or shop at **Supermercado Minipreço,** Largo Terreiro do Bispo, 8-10 (tel. 80 32 92; open M-Sa 9am-10pm, Su 9am-1pm).

Restaurante Dois Irmãos, Largo Terreiro do Bispo, 13 (tel. 80 39 12). Go up R. 1° de Maio into the small square (it's on your right). Half portions of *lombos de porco* (pork chops) and *arroz de lingueirão* (sole-food with rice), around 700$ each. Groove to Portuguese hits. Open daily 11am-4pm and 6-11pm.

Restaurante Fim do Mundo, R. Vasco da Gama, 53 (tel. 262 99), down the street from Dois Irmãos. It's the end of the world, and you'll feel fine with chicken and fries (*meia dose,* 650$) or a fish omelette (850$). Take-out, too. Open M noon-3pm, W-Su noon-3pm and 5-10pm.

Pastelaria Chantilly, R. Vasco da Gama, 63A (tel. 207 80), next to Fim do Mundo. You can indulge in delicious marzipan sweets (130$ each) and other homemade pastries. Open M-Sa 8am-midnight.

PORTUGAL

SIGHTS AND ENTERTAINMENT

Faro's old city is a jewel—untouristed and deeply traditional, with ornate churches, museums, and shops selling authentic and typical handicrafts. Next to the tourist office, the 18th-century **Arco da Vila** pierces the old city wall. A narrow road leads through an Arab portico to the Renaissance **sé** that stands in a deserted square. *(Open M-F 10am-noon and 2-5pm.)* The cathedral's understated Renaissance interior is interrupted by the **Capela do Rosário,** decorated with 17th-century *azulejos,* a red Chinoiserie organ, and sculptures of two Nubians bearing lamps. Under the cathedral, a site once sacred to Romans, Visigoths, and Moors, lie traces of Neolithic civilization. Behind the church, **Museu Arqueológico e Lapidar** (tel. 82 20 42) flashes assorted royal memorabilia, from diamond-studded hairpins to silver spurs and swords. *(Open M-F 9am-noon and 2-5pm. 110$.)* The striking **cloister** is an ideal spot to relax with a book from the municipal library, housed in the same building.

Across from the old city and facing the huge and dusty Largo de São Francisco (the town fairgrounds) stands the mighty **Igreja de São Francisco,** with its hulking facade and delicate interior. *(Open M-F 10am-noon and 3-5pm.)* The city's **Museu de Etnografia Regional,** Pr. da Liberdade, 2 (tel. 80 60 02), introduces the folk life of the Algarve, with heartbreaking photos of the once tranquil, pristine fishing villages of Lagos, Albufeira, and Faro. *(Open M-F 9:30am-6pm. 300$.)* Deep in the city center, step into **Igreja de Nossa Senhora do Carmo** to inspect the **Capela dos Ossos,** a wall-to-wall macabre bonanza of crusty bones and fleshless monk skulls borrowed from the adjacent cemetery. *(Open daily 10am-1pm and 3-5pm. Church free, chapel 120$.)*

Near the marina and next to the hulking Hotel Eva, the **Museu da Marinha** (tel. 80 36 01) flaunts three notable, and interesting, boat models. One features the boat that took Vasco da Gama's on his epic journey to India in 1497, another the boat used by a group of imperialists on their ride up the Congo River in 1492, and the third a boat that outclassed the Turkish navy in 1717, highlighting a distant era when the Algarve was on the cutting edge of technology. *(Open M-F 9am-noon and 2-5pm. 120$.)*

Sidewalk **cafes** crowd the pedestrian walkways off the garden in the center of town. Several **bars** populated by young crowds liven the R. Conselheiro Bívar and its side streets. Faro's rock-free **beach** hides on an islet off the coast. Take bus #16 from the stop in front of the tourist office (departs every hr., 150$).

▓ Olhão and Islands

Olhão, eight kilometers or two train stops east of Faro, prefers fish to tourists. Yet beyond this no-frills town, gorgeous beaches spread over the neighboring islands, all easily accessible by ferry from Olhão's town dock. **Ilha da Armona,** the easternmost island, hosts a lively summer community that crowds around the ferry dock but leaves miles of oceanfront virtually deserted. Ferries run to Ilha da Armona regularly year-round (15min., in summer 10 per day, off-season 3 per day, round-trip 280$). Another ferry heads to **Ilha da Culatra,** which boasts two beach communities accessible by the same ferry (30-45min., departs every 2hr., off-season 3 per day, round-trip 300$). In summer, a ferry also runs from Faro. **Culatra,** the first stop, is known for its hospitality and fine bars while **Farol** has the more beautiful and less crowded beaches. Unfortunately, camping is discouraged on the islands.

PRACTICAL INFORMATION The **bus station** for Olhão is on R. General Humberto Delgado, one block west of Av. República (open daily 7am-7pm). Buses run to Faro (20min., departs every 30min., 175$ in advance, 240$ on bus) and Tavira (1hr., departs every hr., 310$). The **train station** is one block north of the bus station on Av. Combatentes da Grande Guerra. Trains run to Faro (30 min., 5 per day, 180$) and Tavira (1hr., 4 per day, 330$). To reach the **port,** take any of the small side streets off R. Comércio and weave your way to Av. 5 de Octubro, parallel to the shore.

The **tourist office** (tel. 71 39 36) is on Largo Sebastião Martins Mestre, an offshoot of R. Comércio. From the train station, head straight down R. 1° de Maio and left on

A Slug in the Face

Escargot? Well, not exactly...One of Portugal's favorite snack foods is the lowly *caracol* (snail). Unlike their escargot counterparts, *caracóis* are eaten in massive portions, boiled in shells with just a bit of salt and perhaps a sprig of fresh oregano. No forks here—pile a heap of the little creepies on your plate and skewer them with a toothpick. True connoisseurs use a needle-like spine carved out of palm leaves. If the dainty method doesn't suit you, crack the shell between your teeth. You might see folks prodding along the roadside in search of a snack, feel free to join in the fun. Alternatively, save your energy (the little fellas are surprisingly quick) and enjoy your *caracóis* at restaurants or cafes all over the country.

R. General Humberto Delgado. Go right at the intersection with Av. República, and straight into R. Comércio. The office is around the bend on the left. Its English-speaking staff has maps, ferry schedules, and free **luggage storage** during the day. (Open M-F 9am-12:30pm and 2-5:30pm, Sa 9:30am-noon.) In an **emergency**, dial 112. The **post office** is on Av. República, 17 (tel. 71 20 13; open daily M-F 8:30am-6pm). The **postal code** is 8700. The **telephone code** is (0)89.

ACCOMMODATIONS AND FOOD Cheerful, tiled rooms with baths surrounding a plant-filled courtyard can be found off a dusty sidestreet at **Pensão Bela Vista**, R. Teófilo Braga, 65-67 (tel. 70 25 38). Exiting the tourist office, make a left, then the first left; R. Teófilo Braga is the first right. (Singles 2500$, with bath 3500$; doubles: 3500$, with bath 5000$. 500$ discount in winter.) Four blocks uphill from the tourist office, left on R. 18 de Junho and a left 4 blocks farther, **Residencial Boémia**, R. Cerca, 20 (tel. 71 45 13), sits pretty with bright, clean rooms, all with bath and A/C (in summer: singles 4500$; doubles 5500$; in winter: singles 3500$; doubles 4500$; Visa, MC, AmEx). Olhão's highly recommended year-round campground is the **Parque de Campismo dos Bancários do Sul e Ilhas** (tel. 70 54 02; fax 70 54 05). It's off the highway outside of town and can be accessed via nine buses per day (620$ per person, 50$ per tent and per car; showers included).

Supermercado São Nicolau, R. General Humberto Delgado, 62, lies up the block from the bus station (supermarket open M-Sa 9am-9pm). For fish and fruit, try the **mercado,** adjacent to the city gardens along the river in two red brick buildings (open M-Sa 7am-2pm). The day's catch is grilled every evening at the many eateries that line the port on Av. 5 de Octubro. At **Casa de Pasto O Bote,** Av. 5 de Octubro, 122 (tel. 72 11 83), pick out your silvery meal from the trays of fresh fish, and watch it being charcoal-grilled right next to you (entrees from 750-1350$; open M-Sa 10am-3pm and 7-11pm).

■ Tavira

Farmers on motor scooters reputedly tease police by riding over the Roman pedestrian bridge—that's about as raucous as Tavira gets. If you're looking to relax for a while in one of Algarve's loveliest communities, that's just fine. White houses and palm trees fringe the river banks, and festive Baroque churches bring glory to the hills above. The easy-going fishing port doesn't sweat it over the recent influx of backpackers. In mid-afternoon, fisherfolk sit in small riverfront warehouses repairing nets alongside their beached craft.

PRACTICAL INFORMATION EVA **buses** (tel. 32 25 46) leave from the *praça* for Vila Real de Santo António (40min., 375$) and Faro (1hr., 10 per day, 405$, *expressos* 500$). **Trains** (tel. 32 23 54) leave for Vila Real de Santo António (30min., departs every hr., 270$) and Faro (1hr., departs every hr., 300$).

The **tourist office,** R. Galeria, 9 (tel. 32 25 11), is off Pr. República, up the steps on the near left corner coming into town from the train station. It's on your right if you are coming into town from the bus station. The English-speaking staff doles out maps and recommends accommodations. (Open in summer daily 9:30am-7pm; in off season M-F 9:30am-7pm, Sa-Su 9:30am-12:30pm and 2-5:30pm.) For a **taxi,** call 815 44. **Bikes and scooters** can be rented from Loris Rent, R. Damião Augusto de Vasconcelos, 4 (tel. 32 52 03), across the way from the tourist office. In an **emergency,** dial 112. Contact the **police** at (tel. 220 22). The **health center** answers at (tel. 320 10 00). The **post office,** R. da Liberdade, 64, one block uphill from Pr. República, has basic services and Posta Restante (open M-F 8:30am-6pm). The **postal code** is 8800. The **telephone code** is (0)81.

ACCOMMODATIONS AND FOOD No worries—there are *pensões* and *quartos* for all. To find the riverfront **Pensão Residencial Lagôas Bica,** R. Almirante Cândido dos Reis, 24 (tel. 222 52), from Pr. República, cross the pedestrian bridge and continue straight down R. A. Cabreira; turn right and go down one block. You'll find well-furnished rooms, an outdoor patio and rooftop picnic area, a sitting room, washing facilities, and a fridge for guest use. The kind owner speaks English. (Singles 2500$; doubles 3500-4000$, with bath 5000$. 500$ cheaper in winter.) Back on the other side of the river, expansionist **Pensão Residencial Castelo** is busy taking over the block and beyond with an ultra-modern, brand-new annex featuring bright, spacious rooms and savagely beautiful apartments. (Singles 4000$; doubles 4500$, with bath 6000$; apartments around 12,000$, 6-person max. stay.) **Ilha de Tavira campground** (tel. 323 505), with its entourage of snack bars and restaurants, sprawls on the beach of the island 2km from Pr. República (340$ per person, 510$ per tent; showers 100$; reception 24hr.; open Feb.-Sept.).

Nice cafes and restaurants lie on Pr. República and opposite the garden on R. José Pires Padinha. **Churrasqueira "O Manel,"** R. Almirante dos Reis, 6 (tel. 233 43), across the river from Pr. República, has a reasonably priced sit-down restaurant as well as a take-out counter, and serves up *febres na brasa* (pork chops) and *entrecostos* (baby back ribs, 700$). Take your food to the park and chow down. (Open W-M 4pm-midnight.) Also facing the square across the river is **Restaurante Ponto de Encontro,** Pr. Dr. A. Padiuha, 39 (tel. 23 730), where you can binge outdoors on specialties like *peixe con molho de amêndoa* (fish with almond sauce, 1400$).

SIGHTS Most of Tavira's sights are planted along the side streets leading off of **Praça República.** Steps off the *praça* lead past the tourist office to the **Igreja da Misericórdia,** whose superb Renaissance doorway glowers with faces sprouting from twisting vines and candelabra. Just beyond, the remains of the city's **Castelo Mouro** (Moorish Castle) enclose the church **Santa Maria do Castelo** as well as a handsome garden brimming with fuchsias, chrysanthemums, and bougainvillea. *(Church open daily 9am-8pm.)* The seven-arched pedestrian-only **Ponte Romana** footbridge leads to fragrant and floral **Praça 5 de Outubro.** At one end of the square is the imposing **Igreja do Carmo.** Its elaborately decorated chancel resembles a 19th-century opera set, as false perspectives give the illusion of windows and niches supported by columns.

Local **beaches,** including **Pedras do Rei,** are accessible year-round. To reach Tavira's excellent beach on **Ilha da Tavira,** an island 2km away, take the Tavira-Quatro Águas bus from Pr. República to the ferry (10min., 13 per day, round-trip 100$).

■ Vila Real de Santo António

Located at the east end of the Algarve and the mouth of the Rio Guadiana, the Vila Real is a transfer point. Before the construction of the highway bridge between Portugal and Spain in 1992, the town got a lot more tourist traffic, as marooned Spain-bound travelers frequently spent the night. Most tourists now bypass the quiet city.

The **Pousada de Juventude (HI),** R. D. Sousa Martins, 40 (tel./fax 445 65), is a white building on the fifth street into the grid from the river (2 blocks to the left of R. Teófilo Braga, the main pedestrian street). Living room, bar, and washing facilities complement decent quarters. (In summer: dorms 1600$; doubles with bath 3500$. In winter: dorms 1200$; doubles with bath 2700$. Breakfast included. Reception daily 9:30am-midnight. Lockout noon-6pm, but dropoff all day.) **Restaurante Snack-**

Bar El Conde (tel. 419 70), in the main square on the corner of R. Teófilo Braga, cooks up excellent seafood from 700$ (open daily noon-midnight).

Trains service Lagos (4½hr., 4 per day, 900$) and Faro (2½hr., 11 per day, 500$). For trains to Spain, cross the river by the cute **ferry** to Ayamonte (ferries run daily 8am-7pm; 150$ per person, 430$ per car). From Ayamonte, you can take a **bus** in the main square direct to Sevilla or Huelva (departs to Huelva every hr., 540ptas). Buses from Vila Real to the rest of the Algarve are more expensive, more reliable, and faster than trains. They zip to: Faro (1½hr., 5 per day, 750$), Tavira (2hr., 450$); Lagos (4hr., 8 per day, 1100$); and Lisbon (7½hr., 4 per day, 2200$). The last bus leaves at 6:30pm for Faro. Buses leave from the esplanade. Direct buses to Sevilla (3hr., 1 per day) help you avoid the hassle of train-ferry-bus-train transfers.

PORTUGAL

Alentejo

Alentejo (*além do Tejo,* beyond the Tagus) covers almost one-third of Portugal, but with a population barely over half a million it remains the least populated and least touristed region. Its plains, stretching to the horizons and punctuated only by olive and cork-oak trees, possess a beauty unlike any other in the country. Endless wheat fields—light green in spring and burnt gold in summer—and the vineyards covering the rolling hills of the Alentejo's northern half make the region a vast granary, though severe droughts have restricted its agricultural capacity. Évora, Elvas, and other medieval towns preserve their relatively pristine state in the Alentejo Alto, while Beja remains the only major town on the seemingly endless Alentejo Baixo plain. The Alentejo is at its best in the spring: if you come in summer, be prepared for temperatures that soar above 40°C (100°F) daily.

🖐 HIGHLIGHTS OF THE ALENTEJO

- The heart-stopping views across the plain from enchanting **Marvão's 13th-century castle** (see p. 589)
- The "museum city" of **Évora,** but especially its fabulous **cathedral**—perhaps Portugal's finest (see p. 584)
- The friendly, animated little town of **Elvas** (see p. 587)

◼ Évora

From a rolling plain of corktree groves and sunflower fields, Évora (pop. 45,000) rises like a megalith on a hill. Considered Portugal's foremost showpiece of medieval architecture, the picture-perfect town boasts a Roman temple, twisting streets that wind past Moorish arches, and a 16th-century university, all of which prompted the United Nations to grant Évora World Heritage status. Elegant marble-floored shops flash their wares in the windows, students chat on the streets, and a steady but not overwhelming trickle of tourists flows from Lisbon and the Algarve.

ORIENTATION AND PRACTICAL INFORMATION

Évora is accessible by train from most major cities, including Lisbon, but buses remain more convenient. No direct bus connects the **train station** to the center of town. To avoid hiking 1.5km up R. Dr. Baronha, hail a taxi (400$), or flag down bus #6 (100$), which halts at the tracks two blocks over. Near the edge of town, R. Dr. Baronha turns into **Rua República,** which leads to **Praça do Giraldo,** the main square with most of the monuments and lodgings. From the **bus station,** simply proceed uphill past the grand **Igreja de São Francisco** to the *praça.*

Trains: (tel. 221 25). On the Lisbon-Faro route. To get to the station from the main *praça,* walk down R. República until it turns into R. Dr. Baronha; the station is at the end of the road. To: Estremoz (1½hr., 3 per day, 420$); Beja (2hr., 4 per day, 650$); Lisbon (3hr., 6 per day, 810$); Faro (6hr., 2 per day, 1430$). Also runs to Setúbal, Elvas, and Portalegre.

Buses: R. República (tel. 221 21), 5min. downhill from Praça Giraldo, opposite and down 1 block from Igreja de São Francisco. Much more convenient than trains. To: Beja (1½hr., 6 per day, 940$); Elvas (1½hr., 1 per day, 900$); Setúbal (2½hr., 6 per day, 900$); Lisbon (3hr., 5 per day, 1120$); Faro (5hr., 3 per day, 1470$); Vila Real de Santo António (6½hr., 2 per day, 1820$); Porto (7hr., 6 per day, 2300$).

Taxis: (tel. 734 734). Taxis hang out 24hr. in Pr. Giraldo.

Tourist Office: Pr. Giraldo, 73 (tel. 226 71), on the left if you're facing the Igreja Santa Antão. Helpful, multilingual staff compensates for the illegible map by calling around until you have a room. Open Apr.-Sept. M-F 9am-7pm, Sa-Su 9am-12:30pm and 2-5:30pm; Oct.-Mar. daily 9am-12:30pm and 2-5:30pm.

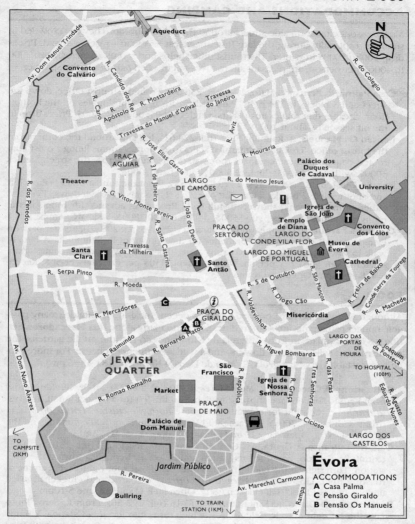

Évora

ACCOMMODATIONS

A Casa Palma
C Pensão Giraldo
B Pensão Os Manueis

PORTUGAL

Currency Exchange: Automatic 24hr. exchange machine outside the tourist office.
Luggage Storage: Try the tourist office.
Laundromat: Lavandaria Lavévora, Largo D'Alvaro Velho, 6 (tel. 238 83), off R. Miguel Bombarda. 370$ per kg. Open M-F 9am-1pm and 3-7pm.
Bookstore: Papeleria Nazareth, Pr. Giraldo, 46 (tel. 222 21). Small English and French sections. Inexpensive classics. Open M-F 9am-1pm and 3-5pm, Sa 9am-1pm.
Emergency: dial 112. **Police:** (tel. 220 22), on R. Francisco Soares Lusitano.
Hospital: (tel. 250 01), Largo Senhor da Pobreza, close to the city wall and the inter-section with R. D. Augusto Eduardo Nunes.
Internet Access: Ciber Évora, R. Fria, 7. Open daily 10:30am-10pm.
Post Office: R. Olivença (tel. 264 39). From the Pr. Giraldo, walk up R. João de Deus, keeping right. Pass under the aqueduct and make an immediate right uphill. Open for mail, Posta Restante, and **fax** M-F 8:30am-6:30pm. **Postal Code:** 7000.
Telephone Code: (0)66.

ACCOMMODATIONS AND CAMPING

Most *pensões* cluster on side streets around **Praça do Giraldo.** They are crowded in summer, especially during the late June mega-fest São João—reserve ahead. Prices drop 500 to 1000$ in winter. The tourist office helps find rooms. *Quartos,* from 2000 to 4000$ per person, are pleasant alternatives to crowded *pensões* in the summer.

🖐**Casa Palma,** R. Bernando Mato, 29-A (tel. 235 60). From the tourist office, down the street and 3 blocks to the right. Pink bedspreads in bright doubles on the bottom floor; cheaper dim singles lie upstairs. Singles 4000$; doubles 5500$. Prices drop in the off season by about 1000$.

Pensão Os Manueis, R. Raimundo, 35 (tel. 228 61), left and around the corner from the tourist office. Trek up the marbled stairs to 27 homey rooms lining a noisy sunroofed courtyard; more compact rooms pack the annex across the street. Singles 3000$, with bath 6500$; doubles 5000$, with bath 7000$.

Pensão Giraldo, R. Mercadores, 27 (tel. 258 33). From the tourist office, take a left and another left 2 blocks later. The *pensão*'s 24 rooms have windows, TVs, and either an in-room sink, shower, or full bath. Reserve in advance for rooms in the renovated annex. Singles 3900-5500$; doubles 4800-7800$. Visa, MC, AmEx.

Orbitur's Parque de Campismo de Évora (tel. 251 90; fax 298 30), a 3-star park on Estrada das Alcáçovas, which branches off the bottom of R. Raimundo. A 20min. walk to town; only 1 bus per day runs along this route. Washing machines and a small market. 500$ per person, 400$ per tent, 430$ per car. Shower 50$. Reception 8am-10pm. Open year-round.

FOOD

Although you may be hard pressed to find a decent meal in Pr. Giraldo, many passable budget restaurants are scattered nearby, particularly along **Rua Mercadores.** Setting up in the square in front of Igreja de São Francisco and the public gardens, the **public market** sells produce, flowers, and a wild assortment of cheese. For more processed feastables, try **Maxigrula,** R. João de Deus, 130 (open M-Sa 9am-7pm).

Restaurante A Choupana, R. Mercadores, 16-20 (tel. 244 27), off Pr. Giraldo, across from Pensão Giraldo (see above). Snack bar on the left for a budget lunch, and *restaurante* on the right for elegant Portuguese *nouvelle cuisine. Trutas do Minho* (trout with bacon, 700$). Entrees 900-1300$. Half-portions 600$. Sundries on the table cost extra. Open daily 10am-2pm and 7-10pm. Visa, MC, AmEx.

Café-Restaurante A Gruta, Av. General Humberto Delgado, 2 (tel. 281 86). After exiting Pr. Giraldo, pass the bus station and follow R. República toward the train station. Turn right at the end of the park; the cafe is on your right. Sweet aroma of roasting fowl. Lip-smacking *frango no churrasco* (barbecued chicken) buried under a heap of fries. Half-chicken 680$. Open Su-F 11am-3pm and 5-10pm.

Restaurante O Garfo, R. Santa Catarina, 13-15 (tel. 292 56). From R. Serpa Pinto take the 1st right onto R. Caldeireiros, which turns into R. Santa Catarina. Yummy entrees (950-1400$). *Gaspacho à alentejana com peixe frito* (gazpacho with fried fish, 1100$). Open daily 11am-midnight. Visa, MC, AmEx.

SIGHTS AND ENTERTAINMENT

Streets brimming with monuments and architectural riches earned Évora its UN status and nickname of "museum city." Starting from the Praça Giraldo, the fortress-like 1553 **Igreja Santo Antão** conceals massive columns and no-frill vaults. Off to the east side of the *praça,* R. 5 de Outubro leads to the colossal 12th-century **cathedral.** The 12 Apostles adorning the doorway are masterpieces of medieval Portuguese sculpture, while the **cloister** is designed in ponderous 14th-century Romanesque style and staircases spiral to its roof. The **Museu de Arte Sacra,** in a gallery above the nave, houses the cathedral's treasury and 13th-century ivory *Virgem do paraíso. (Open Tu-Su 9am-noon and 2-5pm. Cloister and museum 350$, cathedral free.)*

The Heart of Art in Portugal

A stroll around Évora brings you back to the time when the city was Portugal's cultural center. As early as the 13th century, a renowned school of sculpture was located here. Around 1400, the monk and painter Brother Carlos, along with a number of Portuguese and Flemish artists, inaugurated a first-class art school in the city. The artistic euphoria peaked during the reign of Dom João III (1521-1557), when a corps of Portugal's finest writers—including Gil Vicente, Garcia and André Rezende, Jerónimo Osório, Aires Barbosa, Dom Francisco de Melo, Clenardo, Vaseu and Jean Petit, not to mention the king himself—flourished in Évora. Visitors can imagine the days before Évora was a museum city, when it was *the* city in Portugal for urbanity and the arts.

Since the discovery of Roman, Visigoth, and Moorish ruins under its floor, archaeologists replaced engineers who sought to expand the basement of the nearby **Museu de Évora.** *(Open Tu-Su 10am-noon and 2-5pm. 250$, seniors and under 25 125$, under 14 free.)* The museum's collection (ranging from Roman tombs to a 17th-century Virgin Mary) has vied for attention with the fascinating (and on-going) digging.

Évora's most famous monument, the 2nd-century **Roman temple,** is across from the museum. After the temple served for centuries as a slaughterhouse, only a platform and 14 Corinthian columns remain today. Warning: climbing up into the temple is a no-no.

The town's best-kept secret, the **Igreja de São João Evangelista** (1485), faces the temple. *(Open Tu-Su 10am-noon and 2-5pm. 250$.)* The church is owned by the Cadaval family, who reside in their ancestors' ducal palace next door. The interior is covered with dazzling *azulejos,* but you must ask to see the church's hidden chambers.

Another standby is the **Igreja Real de São Francisco,** in its own square downhill from Pr. Giraldo. The church's real show-stopper is the perverse **Capela de Ossos** (Chapel of Bones). *(Church and chapel open M-Sa 8:30am-1pm and 2:30-6pm, Su 10-11:30am and 2:30-6pm. Chapel closed during mass. 50$, photography permit 100$.)* Above the door an irreverent sign taunts visitors: "*Nós ossos que aqui estamos, pelos vossos esperamos*" ("We bones lie here awaiting yours"). Three Franciscan monks ransacked local cemeteries for the remains of 5000 people in order to construct this chapel. Enormous femurs and baby tibias neatly panel every inch of wall, while rows of skulls and an occasional pelvis line the capitals and ceiling vaults. The three innovative founders grimace from stone sarcophagi to the right of the altar. Just south of the church lies the **Jardim Público.** To the northeast lies the **Igreja Conventual de Nossa Senhora das Mercês.** *(Open Tu-Su 10am-noon and 2-5pm. 150$.)* The church's multicolored tile interior is a museum of decorative arts. The **Jewish quarter** inhabited the neighboring side streets, whose whitewashed houses and connecting arches have changed little since the 13th century.

Although most of Évora turns in with the sun, **Xeque-Mate,** R. Valdevinos, 21 (second right off R. 5 de Outubro from the *praça),* and **Discoteca Slide,** R. Serpa Pinto, 135, blare music until 2am. Only couples and single women need apply at either locale. (Cover 1000$ at both, includes two beers.) The liveliest it ever gets in Évora is during the **Feira de São João,** seven nights, all night, starting on the last Friday in June. The entire town turns out for carnival rides, local dance troupes, and a circus.

■ Elvas

Elvas is dead, you say? No, the town is just keeping a low profile. Perched on the crown of a steep hill rising out of arid fields 15km from the Spanish border, Elvas is the perfect place for a taste of small-town Alentejo life. Although many come here mainly because it is a necessary stopover to or from nearby Badajoz, Spain, it merits the trip for its own sake. Quiet Elvas combines all things lovable in a Portuguese town: lively streets, friendly people, good food, few tourists, ruins, and great views.

PORTUGAL

PORTUGAL

PRACTICAL INFORMATION The **train station** (tel. 62 28 16), in the town of Fontainhas, 3km north of the city, connects to Pr. República by bus (M-F 6 per day, Sa 3 per day, Su 2 per day, 90$). Trains roll to Badajoz, Spain (15min., 3 per day, 450$) and Évora (3hr., 1 per day, 960$). Buses run from the **station** (tel. 62 87 50) on Pr. República to: the Spanish border at Caia (20min., 2 per day, 220$); Évora (2hr., 4 per day, 820$); Lisbon (4hr., 4 per day, 1400$). *Espresso* to Faro (5½hr., 1 per day, 2100$) passes through Beja, Évora, and Albufeira. **Taxis** answer at 62 22 87. The **tourist office** (tel. 62 22 36), in Pr. Rebública, resides next to the bus station (open daily 9am-7pm; off-season M-F 9am-6pm, Sa-Su 9am-12:30pm and 2-5:30pm). **Luggage storage** is available at the bus station (110$). In an **emergency**, dial 112. The **police** (tel. 62 26 13) are a block behind the tourist office. To reach the **hospital** call 62 22 25. The **post office** (tel. 62 26 96), on R. Cadeia one block behind the tourist office, has Posta Restante services (open M-F 8:30am-6:30pm, Sa 9am-12:30pm).

ACCOMMODATIONS AND FOOD The few *pensões* in Elvas are boarding houses for semi-permanent residents. Renting a room in a private home may be the only recourse. Try to bargain the price of a single down to 2500$ and a double down to 4000$. Be very cautious when accepting a room from people who solicit at the bus station, and confirm the price and available amenities—especially hot water—in advance. **António Mocissoe Garcia Coelho,** R. Aires Varela, 5 (tel. 62 21 26), rents *quartos.* Take the first left below the bus station, and then the first right off R. João d'Olivença. (June-Sept. singles 2500$; doubles 4500$. Oct.-May singles 1500$; doubles 3500$.) Campers may try **Campismo Varche** (tel. 62 89 97), a secluded orchard 4km from Elvas (500$ per person; hot showers 250$; electricity 300$; laundry 650$). Take buses to Évora, Lisbon, or Estremoz; they stop in Varche.

Every Monday fresh produce is sold at an outdoor **market** immediately outside town behind the aqueduct. Many stores and restaurants line **Rua da Cadeia** and the two streets perpendicular to it, **Rua da Carreira** and **do Alcamim,** just south of the *praça.* If all else fails, get **groceries** at the Loja de Convêniencia, R. Cadeia, 40, the first right going downhill on the street to the right of the tourist office (open daily 8am-11pm). For good food in a neighborhood joint, sidle over to **Canal 7,** R. Sapateiros, 16 (tel. 62 35 93), on the right side of Pr. República (open daily noon-3pm and 7-9:30pm). For Italian eats, **Rica Pizza,** R. do Escorregadio, 8 (tel. 62 47 73), off R. Carrieira, serves pizza (from 850$) and pasta (from 900$; open M-Sa noon-10pm).

SIGHTS Elvas's main spectacle, the **Aqueduto da Amoreira,** emerges from a hill at the entrance to the city. Begun in 1529 and finished almost a century later, the colossal structure is Europe's largest aqueduct. You can soak in the view from the **castelo** above Pr. República—rows of olive trees stretch to the horizon in every direction. To the right of the entrance, a stairwell veiled by plants leads up to the castle walls. Upon request, an attendant will unlock the museum upstairs and show you around.

At Pr. República, **Igreja de Nossa Senhora da Assunção** dominates the mosaic-covered main square. *(All churches open daily June-Sept. 10am-1pm and 3-7pm; Oct.-May 10am-1pm and 2:30-6pm.)* Abstract *azulejos* and a beautifully ribbed ceiling give splendor to the church's interior, which was rebuilt in a Manueline style. Behind the cathedral and uphill to the right is the **Igreja de Nossa Senhora da Consolação,** also known as **Freiras.** Its octagonal interior has beautiful geometric tiles. In the three-sided *praça* stands the 16th-century **pelourinho,** an octagonal pillory culminating in a pyramid.

▓ Castelo de Vide

Castelo de Vide (pop. 4500) is a town like few others in Portugal. Barely touched by the hands of modern development, it has maintained an age-old charm rooted in its picture-perfect whitewashed houses, cobblestone streets, and flowering fountains.

The **medieval quarter** is Castelo de Vide's unique attraction. Located just below its castle, the old town consists of a series of impossibly steep and narrow cobblestone alleys overflowing with potted plants, roses, sunflowers, and bougainvillea overhead.

Up above, the **castelo,** completed in 1280, offers stunning views of the foothills of the surrounding **Senna de Sllamede.** The town center, surrounding the two main *praças,* has a 19th-century feel thanks to Castelo's popularity as a spa resort at the turn of the century. Although tourists come here mainly for the old quarter and castle views, the **spa** water here is said to be quite salubrious—but don't get undressed yet, as the **termas** (thermal springs) are closed indefinitely.

Ask for schedules of connecting **buses** to and from Portalegre (30min., 5 per day, 150$), from which connections to larger cities are more frequent. The bus stops behind the tourist office. The **train station** lies 4km out of town. Express trains run to Lisbon and Madrid. **Taxis** (tel. 912 710) cost around 650$ to go to the train station. The **tourist office** (tel. 913 61), in the wide space in R. Bartolomeu, offers maps and brochures on local sights, helps find accommodations, and **stores luggage** temporarily (open daily June-Sept. 9am-12:30pm and 2-5:30pm). In an **emergency,** call 112. **Police** (tel. 90 13 14) are on Av. Anamenha. The **telephone code** is (0)45.

If you decide to stay at Castelo de Vide, you will have no trouble finding a room, but it might be difficult to locate a truly cheap one. Your best bet is **Casa de Hóspedes Cantinho Particular,** R. Miguel Bombarda, 9 (tel. 911 51), where simple but comfortable and clean doubles are about 5500$ per night (breakfast included). A **restaurant** downstairs serves filling regional foods (850-1200$) in a jovial atmosphere.

■ Marvão

The walled city of Marvão (pop. 1000) is an unreal relic of a distant past. Lost as much in time as in the enveloping fog that descends nightly, the town sits perched atop a craggy mountain overlooking the **Parque Natural de São Mamede.** This national park covers over 31,000 hectares and surrounds Marvão with verdant hillsides and flowering meadows. In contrast, almost all of the whitewashed houses of this haunting town still lie within the 17th-century walls. Marvão is as calm and deserted as they come, receiving a small but continuous trickle of daytrippers, mostly from nearby Spain (10km away), that have yet to perturb the peace.

The virtually impenetrable 13th-century **Castelo,** located at the west end of town, sits on top of the rocky ridge, guarding this town that has only been seized once in its 700-year lifetime. Previous to its construction, however, Marvão passed through quite a few different owners, including the Romans, Visigoths, and Moors. Remnants of these early days await at the **Museo Municipal,** just before the castle in the **Igreja de Santa Maria** (open daily 9am-12:30pm and 2-5:30pm; 150$).

Buses run to and from Portalegre (50min., 2 per day, 250$) and Castelo de Vide (25min., 3 per day, 150$). Ask at the *turismo* about express buses to Lisbon (you must buy a ticket one day in advance) and to the **train station** (9km north), where service to Lisbon and Madrid is available. If you arrive by bus, you will be dropped just outside the town wall. Enter through one of the gates and proceed up R. Cima until you see the pillory in Pr. Pelourinho (also a parking area). **Taxis** (tel. 932 33) are a valid option between Marvão and Castelo de Vide. From Pr. Pelourinho, R. Espíritu Santo leads toward the Castelo and the **turismo** (tel. 931 04), where the attendant doles out maps and info. In an **emergency**, call 112. The **telephone code** is (0)45.

If you spend the night in Marvão, your best budget option is to ask at the *turismo* for a list of private accommodations. **Casa da Caldeira,** R. Cima, 21 (tel. 33 11 70), has small but comfortable rooms with negotiable prices (about 4000$ for a double). Several **bar-restaurants** serve regional meals throughout the day on R. Cima.

■ Beja

Tucked amid the vast, monotonous wheat fields of the southern Alentejo, Beja is a town of beautiful architecture but truly scorching temperatures. Its name, pronounced like the Portuguese word for "kiss" (beija), is a corruption of its original name, Pax Julia, given to Beja by the Romans in 48 BC to commemorate the peace

PORTUGAL

Nekkid? What you mean nekkid?

Proverbially speaking, the Alentejo is the land that knows no shade...or at least, so they (the humans) say. The sheep, however, know better. To avoid the blazing sun beating mercilessly down on the Alentejan plains, they retreat en masse into the few square meters of shadow provided by the mushroom-like trees that dot the landscape. If you look closely, you will notice that there is something unique about these trees (besides the clumps of fuzzy livestock cowering beneath them), something very shocking, indeed. Unabashedly stripped to the bone, they flaunt their unprotected under-layers to all. These *quercus subers*, otherwise known as cork oaks, have unusually thick bark (actually the cambium, outer layers composed of dead phloem cells) that is shaved off meticulously by hand once every nine years to obtain cork. The harvest of the area yields 160,000 tons of cork per year, which amounts to 60% of the world's output, and quite a lot of nekkidness.

---

with the Lusitanians. Beja's name is highly appropriate, however, for this town is steamy in more ways than one. The 17th-century affair of a nun and her French Lieutenant boyfriend (unveiled at the Museu Rainha Dona Leonor) prompted a tell-all account, *Five Love Letters of a Portuguese Nun,* published in Paris in 1669, that vaulted the town forever into the annals of sexual impropriety. Besides being a summer-time oven and a prime getaway destination for romantic exploits, Beja is also a haven of traditional food, music, and handicrafts.

ORIENTATION AND PRACTICAL INFORMATION Ruas de Mértola and de Capitão João Francisco de Sousa brand the center of town. The streets are unmarked and confusing, especially in the town center. **Trains** run from the station (tel. 32 50 56), about 1km outside of town, to: Évora (1hr., 6per day, 690$); Lisbon (3hr., 3 per day, 1200$); and Faro (5½hr., 2 per day, 1100$). Those with heavy bags might want to take a **taxi** (tel. 224 74) to the town center (470$) rather than walk uphill for 30 minutes. The **bus station** (tel. 32 40 44) is on R. Cidade de São Paulo, at the roundabout on the corner of Av. Brasil. Buses motor to: Real de la Frontera, Spain (1½hr., 1 per day, 1000$); Évora (2hr., 4 per day, 730$); Lisbon (3hr., 4 per day, 1200$); Faro (3½hr., 4 per day, 1300$); and most of the rest of the Algarve. From the bus station to the center and the tourist office, walk straight out of the terminal and through the traffic circle (past the statue). After one block, turn right, go past the post office on the left, and continue up the curving street. At the intersection, take a left on R. Capitão J. F. de Sousa (with a small pedestrian square).

The **tourist office,** R. Capitão J. F. de Sousa, 25 (tel. 236 93), has an English-speaking staff that hands out decent maps and helps find accommodations (open in summer M-F 10am-8pm, Sa 10am-6pm; in winter M-Sa 10am-6pm). **Luggage storage** is on the way out of the bus station (160$ per day). The town's **swimming pool** (tel. 236 26), on Av. Brasil near the bus station, is excellent (pool and adjacent park 200$; open Sa-Th 10am-9pm). In case of an **emergency,** call 112. The **police** (tel. 32 20 22) lie on R. D. Nuno Álvares Pereira, one block downhill and a few meters to the left from the tourist office. To reach the **hospital,** call Dr. António F. C. Lima at 32 02 00. The **post office** (tel. 238 50), on Largo do Correio, is down the street from the beginning of R. Capitão de Sousa (open for Posta Restante M-F 8:30am-6:30pm). The **postal code** is 7800; the **telephone code** is (0)84.

ACCOMMODATIONS AND FOOD Most rooms and *pensões* lie within a few blocks of the tourist office and the central pedestrian street. **Residência Bejense,** R. Capitão J. F. de Sousa, 57 (tel. 32 50 01), down the street from the tourist office, features beautiful rooms with tile floors, ruffled bedspreads, TVs, phones, and private baths. (Singles 5500$; doubles 7000$. Breakfast included. A/C. Visa, MC, AmEx.) **Pensão Tomás,** R. Alexandre Herculano, 7 (tel. 32 46 13; fax 32 07 96), is uphill, past the post office and the 3rd right after Pousada São Francisco into a small square. Clean rooms with baths, phones, and fans await. (Singles 4000$; doubles 5000$. Prices drop in winter.) **Camping: Parque Municipal** (tel. 243 28), at the end of Av. Vasco da

Gama, lies past the stadium on the southwest side of town. Out of the bus terminal, go straight one block and take a left. The campsite is small, shady, and clean. (320$ per person, 220$ per tent and per car. Free showers. Town swimming pool nearby.)

Beja is one of the best places to taste authentic (and affordable) Portuguese cuisine, although most restaurants keep limited hours (noon-2pm and 7-10pm). The local specialty is *migas de pão*, a sausage and bacon soup thickened with bread. The municipal **market** sets up in a building one block up and one block to the right from the bus station (open M-Sa 6am-1:30pm). For **groceries**, go to Urbeja, SA, Largo de São João, 15, a block uphill from the museum. (Open in summer M-F 8am-8pm, Sa 8am-1pm; in winter M-Sa 8am-8pm.) **Restaurante Tomás,** R. Alexandre Herculano, 7 (tel. 32 46 13), beneath the *pensão,* is an award-winning restaurant offering rich soup and regional fish and meat dishes (900-1500$; open daily noon-4pm and 7-11pm). **Restaurante Alentejano** (tel. 238 49), Largo dos Duques de Beja, down the steps near the museum, serves unpretentious regional cuisine with great meat options at affordable prices (around 900$; open Sa-Th noon-3pm and 7-10pm).

SIGHTS AND ENTERTAINMENT The town's historical sites are scattered about, but the outstanding **Museu Rainha Dona Leonor** makes an excellent starting point. *(Open Tu-Su 9:45am-1pm and 2-5:15pm. 100$. Sundays free. Ticket also good for the Museu Visigótico behind the castelo.)* Walk past the tourist office and into the *praça*; the museum is on your right. Built on the site of Sister Mariana Alcoforado's famed indiscretion with a French officer, the museum features a replica of the cell window through which the lovers exchanged secret passionate vows. Inside, the gilded church's 18th-century *azulejo* panels depict the lives of Mary and St. John the Baptist. Nearby are fine *intaglio* marble altars and panels of *talha dourada* (gilded carvings). The *azulejos* and Persian-style ceiling make the chapter house look like a mini mosque.

One block downhill from the convent is the 13th-century, adobe-like **Igreja de Santa María,** transformed into a mosque during the Moorish invasion and back into a church when the city reverted to Portuguese control. A miniature bull on its corner column symbolizes the city's spirit. From here, R. Aresta Branco leads past handsome old houses to the city's massive **castelo,** built around 1300 on the remnants of a Roman fortress. *(Open Apr.-Sept. Tu-Su 10am-1pm and 2-6pm; Oct.-Mar. 9am-noon and 1-4pm.)* It still flaunts an enormous crenellated marble keep, vaulted chambers, stones covered with cryptic symbols, and walls covered with ivy. The castle's **Torre de Menagem** provides an impressive view of the vast Alentejan plains (100$).

Ribatejo and Estremadura

These two provinces enveloping Lisbon and continuing north of it offer some of Portugal's finest destinations. From the fantastically ornate monastery at Batalha, to the huge and mysterious Knights Templar complex above Tomar, to Óbidos, a completely walled medieval city—history and sights are packed into towns that manage to retain a taste of quintessential Portugal. A few industrial blemishes have emerged in these, two of Portugal's wealthiest provinces, but grace and charm are happily the rule rather than the exception.

Jagged cliffs and whitewashed fishing villages line Estremadura's Costa de Prata (Silver Coast), with beaches to rival even the Algarve. Throngs of tourists and summer residents populate the seafront Nazaré and Peniche, but smaller, less touristed towns, with nearly equally fantastic beaches, pepper the coast, while the rugged and beautiful Ilhas Berlingas lie offshore. Nearby, the fertile region of the Ribatejo (banks of the Tejo) is perhaps the gentlest and greenest you will come across in Portugal. Known as the "Heart of Portugal," it is famous for the rich pasturing found here at the meeting place of the arid Alentejan plain and Estremaduran wetlands. Its character is closely tied to the Tagus river and to two other renowned inhabitants of the area: the horse and the bull. Every summer, festivals showcasing beautiful Arabian ponies and crowd-drawing bullfights pay homage to these noble creatures. Although accommodations can sometimes be expensive in the smaller towns, camping is available, and both regions are connected by a reliable transportation network.

■ Santarém

Santarém presides over Ribatejo from atop a rocky mound that overlooks the calm Rio Tejo and the soft green pastures below. The town's name derives from the unhappy story of Santa Iria, a nun who was accused of lapse of virtue and cast into the river. When she washed up in Santarém, an autopsy was done on her body and she was pronounced innocent. As one of the three ruling cities of the ancient Roman province of Lusitania, Santarém enjoyed a prosperity that has persisted up to the present. Once a flourishing medieval center, it is the capital of the Portuguese Gothic style but boasts a mind-boggling range of styles in its many appealing churches.

ORIENTATION AND PRACTICAL INFORMATION

The core of Santarém is formed by the densely packed streets between **Praça Sá da Bandeira** and the park **Portas do Sol**, below which flows the Rio Tejo. **Rua Capelo Ivêns,** which begins at the *praça*, plays host to the tourist office and many *pensões*.

Trains: Station (tel. 231 80 or 33 31 80) is 2km outside town with bus service to and from the bus station (10min., departs every 30min., 150$). Otherwise take a taxi (350-400$)—the walk is steep and dangerous (20min.). To: Lisbon (1hr., departs almost every hr., 520$); Tomar (1hr., departs every 2hr., 370$); Portalegre, via Entroncamento (3hr., 3 per day, 920$); Faro, via Lisbon (4hr., 6 per day, 1800$); Porto (4hr., 6 per day, 1300$).

Buses: (tel. 33 32 00; fax 33 30 54), on Rodoviária Tejo, Av. Brasil, a convenient location. To: Lisbon (*expressos:* 1hr., 5 per day, 1450$; *regular:* 1½hr., departs every hr., 1000$); Nazaré (1½hr., 1 per day, 720$); Tomar, via Torres Novas (1½hr., 2 per day, 750$); Caldas da Rainha (1½hr., 4 per day, 600$); Coimbra (2hr., 4 per day, 1100$); Porto (3hr., 4 per day, 1000$); Faro (7hr., 3 per day, 2000$).

Taxis: Scaltaxis has a stand across from the bus station.

Tourist Office: R. Capelo Ivêns, 6 (tel. 33 33 18). Cross the park, walk past the church, and go right onto R. Capelo Ivêns. **Maps** and info on festivals, accommodations, and transportation schedules. English spoken. Open M 9am-12:30pm and 2-6pm, Tu-F 9am-7pm, Sa-Su 10am-12:30pm and 2:30-5:30pm.

Currency Exchange: Banco Nacional Ultramarino (tel. 33 00 07), at R. Dr. Texeira Guedes and R. Capelo Ivêns. 1000$ commission. Open M-F 8:30am-3pm.

Luggage Storage: Bus station (100$ per day). Train station (250$ per day).

Emergency: dial 112. **Police:** (tel. 220 22). Follow the signs from the bus station onto Pr. Sá da Bandeira.

Hospital: (tel. 37 05 78), on Av. Bernardo Santareno. From Pr. Sá da Bandeira, walk up R. Cidade da Covilhã, which becomes R. Alexandre Herculano. English spoken.

Post Office: (tel. 280 11 or 25 00 77). On the corner of Largo Cândido and R. Dr. Texeira Guedes. Open M-F 8:30am-6:30pm, Sa 9am-12:30pm. **Postal Code:** 2000.

Telephone Code: (0)43.

PORTUGAL

ACCOMMODATIONS, CAMPING, AND FOOD

You stay, you pay. During the Ribatejo Fair (10 days starting the first Friday in June), prices increase 10-40%. The tourist office can help find a room (3000-3500$) in a private house (room prices around 2000$ during the rest of the year). Eateries cluster along and between the parallel **Rua Capelo Ivêns** and **Rua Serpa Pinto.** The **municipal market,** in the colorful pagoda-thing on Largo Infante Santo near the Jardim da República, supplies fresh produce and vegetables (open M-Sa 8am-2pm). **Minipreço Supermarket,** R. Pedro Canavarro, 31, is on the street leading from the bus station to R. Capelo Ivêns (open M-Sa 9am-8pm). **Pastelaria Venezia,** R. Capelo Ivêns, 99 (tel. 223 12), has delicious pastries and croissants.

Residencial Abidis, R. Guilherme de Azevedo, 4 (tel. 220 17 or 220 18), around the corner from the tourist office. Although the hallways are a bit dreary, the residencial has 27 recently renovated rooms, all with TV, high ceilings, large windows, and walnut furnishings. Singles 3500$, with bath 5000$; doubles 4500$, with bath 6000-7000$. Breakfast included.

Residencial Muralha, R. Pedro Canavarro, 12 (tel. 223 99), next to the city's medieval wall. Basic room with phones. Singles 3000$, with bath 4500$; doubles 6500-8000$. Prices vary with the season. Breakfast 500$.

Pensão do José (a.k.a. **Pensão da Dona Arminda**), Trav. Froes, 14 and 18 (tel. 230 88). Go left exiting the tourist office and then take the first right. Small rooms, plastic flowers. Singles 2000$; doubles 3000$, with shower 3500$.

Pastelaria Abidis, R. Guilherme de Azevedo, 22 (tel. 222 50), next to the Residencial Abidis. Food is fast, fabulous, filling, and dirt cheap. Open daily 8am-7:30pm.

Casa d'Avó, R. Serpa Pinto, 62 (tel. 269 16). Home-cooked food served on petite tables surrounded by cast-iron garden chairs. Quiche, salad, and daily fish and meat specials. Entrees 350-750$. Open M-Sa 9:30am-7pm.

SIGHTS AND ENTERTAINMENT

Santarém's streets are littered with churches, each displaying a different style or character. The austere facade of the **Igreja do Seminário dos Jesuítas** dominates Pr. Sá da Bandeira, Santarém's main square. *(If the church is closed, enter the door to the right of the main entrance and ask Sr. Domingos to unlock it.)* Stone friezes carved like ropes separate each of its three stories, and Latin mottos from the Bible embellish every lintel and doorway. Left of the church, the former Colégio dos Jesuitas conceals two enormous palm trees that have outgrown their tiny **cloister.**

A statue of the Marquês da Bandeira embellishes the center of the *praça.* Stand back-to-back with him, and the street to the left, R. Serpa Pinto, leads to the wonderful **Praça Visconde de Serra Pilar,** formerly Pr. Velha. Centuries ago, Christians, Moors, and Jews gathered for social and business affairs here. The 12th-century **Igreja de Marvilha,** off the *praça,* has a 16th-century Manueline portal and a 17th-century *azulejo* interior. The early Gothic purity of nearby **Igreja da Graça** contrasts sharply with Marvilha's overflowing exuberance. Within Graça's chapel lies Pedro Alvares Cabral, the explorer who discovered Brazil and one of the few *conquistadores* to live long enough to return to his homeland.

Off R. São Martinho stands the medieval **Torre das Cabaças** (Tower of the Gourds), so-called because of the eight earthen bowls installed in the 16th-century to amplify the bell's ring. Across the street, the **Museu Arqueológico de São João do Alporão,** in a former 13th-century church, exhibits the elaborate Gothic "tomb" of Dom Duarte de Meneses, who died defended Santarém in a supposedly impossible battle between 500 Portuguese and 10,000 Moors. *(Open June-Sept. Tu-Su 10am-12:30pm and 2-6pm; Oct.-May Tu-Su 9am-12:30pm and 2-5:30pm. Free.)* Enclosed in a glass case is all that remains of Dom Duarte: a tooth. It would be a shame to quit Av. 5 de Outubro before it ends at the **Portas Do Sol,** a paradise of flowers, gardens, and fountains surrounded by old Moorish walls.

Ready to imbibe? Join the throng at **Bar Boaviela,** Pr. Município (tel. 229 72), for food, drink, and live music on Fridays (open daily until 2am) or **Município Cervejão,** Av. António Maria Baptista, 10 (tel. 264 33), crammed with beer and cocktails (open M-Sa until 2am). Or simply wait for a festival. The largest festival is the **Feira Nacional de Agricultura** (a.k.a. **Feira do Ribatejo**), a national agricultural exhibition. People come for the 10-day bullfighting and horse-racing orgy (starting the first Friday in June). Smack your lips at the **Festival e Seminário Nacional de Gastronomia** (the last 10 days of October), when each region of Portugal has a day to prepare a typical feast and entertainment.

Santarém Goes Goth

Santarém has oft been proclaimed the capital of Gothic architecture in Portugal, and as you can't help but notice the moment you begin to wander its narrow streets, the title is well merited. Every hundred meters or so lies yet another example of Santarém's unique version of the Gothic style, which flourished here in the 13th and 14th centuries. Elegance, clarity, and simplicity differentiate Santarém's Gothic from the almost excessive elaborateness of the later High Gothic. In Santarém's numerous *igrejas* and chapels, light overwhelms, pouring in through intricate *rosettas* (such as the one in the Igreja de Grega, which—amazingly—was carved out of a single stone), and pure, naked arches reach to the sky.

■ Caldas da Rainha

The town takes its name, "Baths of the Queen," from Queen Leonor, who soaked in its thermal springs after selling her jewels to finance this, the world's first thermal hospital. Victims of rheumatism, respiratory ailments, and skin afflictions still come here to be cured. This destination may not be the most ideal for healthy travelers, but Caldas's beautiful park, great pottery, and delicious pastries make it a short and sweet stopover en route to Óbidos.

PRACTICAL INFORMATION The **train station** (tel. 236 93) is on the northwest edge of town on Largo da Estação. From Av. 25 de Abril, take Av. 1 de Maio to reach the tourist office. Trains connect to Lisbon (12 per day, 2¼hr., 850$). The **bus station** (tel. 83 10 67), on R. Heróis da Grande Guerra, services: Óbidos (20min., 13 per day, 145$); Peniche (45min., 6 per day, 600$); Lisbon (1½hr., 8 per day, 900$); Porto (4hr., 9 per day, 1500$). To reach the tourist office, take a left out of the bus station; it's two blocks down on the right. **Taxis** (24hr. tel. 83 10 98 or 83 24 55) run all day. The **tourist office** (tel. 83 10 03; fax 34 51 1) is in Pr. 25 de Abril. Ask nicely for temporary **luggage storage.** (Open M-F 9am-7pm, Sa-Su 10am-1pm and 3-7pm.) In an **emergency,** call 112. The **hospital** (tel. 83 03 01) is on the first street to the right after the **police station** (tel. 83 20 22), which is at Frei de São Paulo, just off Pr. República. The **telephone code** is (0)62.

ACCOMMODATIONS AND FOOD The rooms at **Pensão Residencial Portugal,** R. Almirante Cândido dos Reis, 30 (tel. 342 80), are dim but comfortable, all with shower, TV, and telephone. (Singles 4000$; doubles 5000-7000$; breakfast included.) **Pensão Residencial Central,** Largo Dr. José Barbosa, 22 (tel. 83 19 14; fax 84 32 82), behind the Pr. da República, has more upscale rooms with TVs, bath, and phones. (July-Aug. singles 4000$, with bath 5000$; doubles 6500$, with bath 9000$. Rooms considerably lower in the off season; try bargaining. Breakfast included. Visa, MC, AmEx.) **Orbitur** (tel. 83 23 67) runs a **campground** just a 15-minute walk from the bus station in Parque Dom Carlos I. From the Thermal Hospital, continue on R. Camões, and turn left on Av. Visconde de Sacavém. (450$ per person, 550-720$ per tent, 420$ per car. Free hot showers. Reception daily 8am-10pm. Open year-round.)

Caldas is the fruit capital of Portugal. Even if you don't want any produce, visit the large and colorful **Mercado da Fruta,** Pr. República, where frenzied local vendors and shoppers haggle each morning (open daily 6am-2pm). The town's sweets—including *cavacas* (frosted bowl-shaped pastries) and *trouxas de ovos* (sweetened egg yolks)—are famed throughout the country. **Pastelarias** line Av. Liberdade and Av. Duarte Pacheco; many also serve decent *pratos do dia* at good prices (600-900$). Restaurants are sprinkled through town. **Restaurante Portugal** (tel. 342 80), on R. Almirante Cândido dos Reis, serves moderately priced local fare.

SIGHTS Although you can bathe at the historic **Hospital Rainha Dona Leonor** (tel. 83 03 01), it primarily serves as a hospital. *(Open M-F 8:15-11:45am and 3:15-4:30pm, Sa 8:45-10:45am. June-Oct. 550$; Nov.-May 490$.)* To reach the complex, follow the signs from Pr. República. For non-aquatic relaxation, head to the immaculately landscaped **Parque Dom Carlos I** by following R. Camões on Largo Rainha Dona Leonor. The park has mercifully shady walking paths with a wonderful 19th-century feel, a duck pond, and tennis courts. The prestige of Caldas's **pottery** is unrivaled, and most art museums throughout Portugal shelve at least a few pieces from the town. The park's **Museu de Cerâmica** traces the history and manufacturing process of Caldas clay. *(Open Tu-Su 10am-noon and 2-5pm. Free.)*

■ Óbidos

Walking through Óbidos's formidable stone gate is like stepping into the Middle Ages. The tiny village sits atop a hill dominated by a 12th-century fortress (now a luxury *pousada*). Tourism seems to have reinforced, not diminished, the town's commitment to historical authenticity. Narrow streets and stunning views have made Óbidos a romantic get-away destination since 1282, when Queen Isabel so admired Óbidos's beauty that King Dinis gave it to her as a wedding present. For centuries, in fact, Óbidos was considered the personal property of the Portuguese queen.

PRACTICAL INFORMATION Óbidos is an easy **train** ride from Lisbon's Estação Rossio. Take a commuter train to Cacém, then change trains for Óbidos (3hr., 8 per day, 600$). The train station is 10 minutes outside town to the north. Climb the stairs across from the station to head toward the town center. Buy tickets aboard the train. Frequent **buses** connect to Caldas da Rainha (20min., 6 per day, 180$) and to Peniche (40min., M-Sa 8 per day, Su 5 per day, 375$). Buses stop down a few stairs from the main gate, under the shelter for Caldas de Rainha. No bus schedules are posted at the stop, so inquire at the tourist office. The **tourist office** (tel. 95 92 31), not to be confused with the regional tourism bureau along the same street, is on R. Direita. Through the main gate to the town, take the high road to the left and follow it 200m. The English-speaking staff has extensive bus info and will **store luggage.** (Open daily 9:30am-1pm and 2-6pm.) In an **emergency,** dial 112, or for **police,** dial 95 91 49. The nearest **hospital** is in Caldas da Rainha (tel. 83 21 33), 6km away. The **post office** (tel. 95 91 99), nearby in Pr. Santa Maria, has **fax** and Posta Restante (open M-F 9am-12:30pm and 2:30-6pm). The **postal code** is 2510. The **telephone code** is (0)62.

PORTUGAL

Cherries on Top

Óbidos's castle has occupied its strategic position atop a steep hill since the Moorish occupation in the Middle Ages. From the height of the formidable walls you'll see why Portugal's first king, Dom Afonso Henriques, was thwarted in several attempts to capture the town. But on January 11, 1148, forces at the main gate diverted the guards' attention, while men disguised as cherry trees tiptoed to the castle. Noticing the advancing trees, an astute Moorish princess asked her father if trees walked. The distracted king paid her no heed, and by the time he realized what was happening, Afonso's men had broken through the castle door. To walk with the trees, follow R. Direita from the entrance at Porta da Vila to the back of the town, under the arch, and to the stairs. Arboreal attire is optional.

ACCOMMODATIONS AND FOOD There's no real reason to stay overnight; Óbidos is more a showpiece than a city. But if you enjoy the timeless feel of Portugal's castletowns, it only gets better with nightfall. Silence, stars, and a mesmerizing view of the distant lights of Caldas and Peniche on either side of the walls create a romantic atmosphere. **Agostinho Pereira,** R. Direita, 40 (tel. 95 91 88), rents four homey rooms. Some of these have window seats, prime for enjoying the view of the nearby *igreja*. A pleasant lounge with TV and small bar, washing machine, and kitchen can be shared by all. (Singles 3500$, doubles 4000-4500$, triples 5000$. Try to reserve ahead.) "Typical" **restaurants** (with tourist prices) and several reasonable mini-market **groceries** flesh out R. Direita. Eat light and save your *escudos* for Óbidos's signature *ginja* (wild cherry liqueur), even sweeter and more syrupy than the national norm. Stores along R. Direita sell gulp-sized bottles for 200$.

SIGHTS The **castelo** on the coast, built as a fortress in the 12th century, gradually lost its strategic importance as the ocean receded 7km. Although the castle itself opens only to *pousada* guests (28,000$ per night), its walls are open to all. You can walk the circular route or cozy up in a nook. The old castle's walls surround the entire city. The only *igreja* worth seeing is the 17th-century *azulejo* bonanza **Igreja de Santa Maria** (to the right of the post office in the central *praça*), built on the foundations of a Visigoth church and later used as a mosque. *(Open June-Sept. 9:30am-12:30pm and 2:30-7pm; Oct.-May 9:30am-12:30pm and 2:30-5:30pm. Free.)* Nun Josefa de Óbidos's vivid canvases mark the right of the main altar. The church was the site of the 1444 wedding of 10-year-old King Afonso V to his 8-year-old cousin, Isabel.

■ Peniche

Many travelers overlook Peniche, a seaport town 24km west of Óbidos en route to the Ilhas Berlengas. What they miss is a lively port city that is close to good beaches and hiking trails. Harboring Portugal's second largest fishing fleet, this rugged peninsular city is so obsessed with seafood that they dedicated a festival to the sardine. Its fishy odor lingers throughout the streets, for better or for worse.

ORIENTATION AND PRACTICAL INFORMATION

Peniche's town center fits neatly into the square tip of its isthmus. The **fortaleza** (fortress) and **Campo da República** are on the coast side, **Avenida do Mar** is on the river, and **Largo Bispo Mariana** bounds the city proper.

Buses: (tel. 78 21 33), R. Estado Português da India, on an isthmus outside the town walls. Express and regular service to: Caldas (1hr., 6 per day, 405$); Nazaré (1½hr., 6 per day, 900$); Santarém (1½hr., 3 per day, 780$); Alcobaça (1¾hr., 2 per day, 950$); Leiria (2hr., 6 per day, 1200$); Lisbon (2½hr., 11 per day, 950$).

Taxis: tel. 78 26 87.

Tourist Office: (tel. 78 95 71), R. Alexandre Herculano. From the bus station, cross the river (on Ponte Velha). Turn left on R. Herculano and walk alongside the public

garden, following signs to the office. English-speaking staff assists with accommodations and provides info on trips to the islands. Open daily June-Sept. 9am-8pm;
Oct.-May 9am-1pm and 2-5pm.

Currency Exchange: Try the main *praça*. **União de Bancos,** Av. Mar, 56 (tel. 78 10
75), on the way to the *fortaleza*. 1000$ commission. Open M-F 8:30am-3pm.

Luggage Storage: In the bus station (100$ per day).

Emergency: tel. 112. **Police:** (tel. 78 95 55), on R. Marquês de Pombal.

Hospital: (tel. 78 17 00), on R. Gen. Humberto Delgado.

Post Office: (tel. 78 70 11), R. Arquitecto Paulino Montez. From the tourist office,
turn right on R. Herculano, left on Arquitecto Paulino Montez, and walk 3 blocks.
Posta Restante and **fax.** Open M-F 9am-6pm. **Postal Code:** 2520.

Telephone Code: (0)62.

ACCOMMODATIONS AND CAMPING

Pensões fill quickly in July and August; try to arrive early in the day. Look for signs on
Av. Mar. Hostesses roam the streets promoting **beds** in their homes, but you should
insist on seeing the place and inquire about hot water and other amenities. The
rooms may be good budget options. You should pay around 1500 to 2000$ for a sin-
gle and 2500 to 3000$ for a double. Bargain—there are many of them and few of you.

Residência Mira Mar, Av. Mar, 40-44 (tel. 78 16 66), above a yummy seafood restaurant of the same name, near the beach. Pink shag rug, oak furniture, great views.
Rooms have TV and private bath. Singles 4000$; doubles with bath 5000-6000$.

Hospedaria Marítimo, R. José Estevão, 109 (tel. 78 28 50), off the square in front of
the fortress. Newly decorated rooms with bright pine furnishings and new carpets.
Some rooms have a TV; all have baths. Singles 3000$; doubles 4000$.

Hospedaria Cristal, R. Marechal Gomes Freitas de Andrade, 14-16 (tel. 78 27 24), 3
blocks in from Pr. Jacob Pereira. Plain rooms do the job. Private baths more appealing than common ones. Singles 3000$; doubles with bath 6000$; triples 7000$.

Camping: Municipal Campground (tel. 78 95 29; fax 78 96 96), 1.5km outside of
town, along the bus route to Caldas da Rainha and Lourinhã. 10 buses per day
speed to the campground (ask tourist office or check at the bus station for times).
Otherwise, it's a 40min. walk out of town across the Ponte Velha; once across, turn
right, then left at the T in the road. Go straight ahead a long, long time until the
Mobil station, behind which you can collapse in *campismo* comfort. Fronts a
beach. Small market. 520$ per person, per tent, per car. Open year-round.

FOOD

Eat some of the freshest seafood in Europe here, or don't eat at all. The real stuff sizzles in whale-sized portions on outdoor grills all along **Avenida Mar.** Peniche's
sardinhas (sardines) are said to be exceptional in a land of aficionados. Try the seafood *espetadas* (skewered aquatic treats served with a tub of melted butter). The outdoor cafes on **Praça Jacob Rodrigues Pereira** are lively, particularly on Sundays,
when the rest of town is virtually comatose. The **market,** R. António da Conceição
Bento, has fresh produce (open Tu-Su 6am-2pm).

Restaurante Beiramar, Av. Mar, 106-108 (tel. 78 24 79). Delectable grilled fare
served on wood tables in a stone-walled room. The *cataplana de peixe* lands Nir-
vanic stewed fish right at your table (1200$). The 2nd floor boasts some cherry bal-
cony tables. *Sardinhas grelhadas* (800$). Open daily 10am-11pm.

Restaurante Canhoto, Valadim, 23 (tel. 78 45 12), on the street connecting the
tourist office to Av. Mar, is a local tavern-type joint with a tasty *sopa de peixe* (fish
soup 200$). Entrees 800-1750$. Open daily noon-midnight.

Restaurante Mira Mar, Av. Mar, 40-44 (tel. 78 16 09). Surrounded by similar seafood
joints, but Mira Mar has remarkable *lulas* (squid). Mouth-watering squid kebabs
capped with pepper and lemon on a huge plate of fries for 1200$.

PORTUGAL

SIGHTS AND ENTERTAINMENT

Salazar, Portugal's longtime dictator, chose Peniche's formidable 16th-century **for- taleza** for one of his four high-security political prisons. Its high walls and bastions later became a camp for Angolan refugees. It now houses the **Museu de Peniche** (tel. 78 18 48), highlighted by a fascinating anti-Fascist Resistance exhibition. *(Open in sum- mer Tu-Su 10am-12:30pm and 2-7pm; in winter Tu-Su 10am-noon and 2-5pm. 100$, under 15 free.)* Photos, accompanied by text, trace the dictatorship and underground resistance from the seizure of power in 1926 to the coup that toppled the regime on April 25, 1974. The fortress is tough to miss at the far end of R. José Estevão, near the dock where boats leave for the Berlengas.

For sun and surf, head to any of the town's three **beaches.** The beautiful **Praia de Peniche de Cima,** along the north crescent, has the warmest water but gets windy. It merges with another beach at **Baleal,** a small fishing village popular with tourists. The southern **Praia do Molho Leste** is colder but safer and a good escape from the wind. Beyond it is the crowded **Praia da Consolação.** The strange humidity at this beach supposedly cures bone diseases, but its unfortunate side effect is trapping the stench of nearby sewers on windless days. The only other beach with similar recuperative properties is in Japan. Don't swallow the bones at the **Festa da Sardinha,** a massive sardine-devouring, wine-chugging party at the fishing port every Friday and Saturday night in July. Festivities acquire a less fishy (but no less sober) tint in the first Saturday of August, when boats—decked in wreaths of flags and flowers—file into the harbor in the procession that launches the two-day **Festa de Nossa Senhora da Boa Via- gem,** celebrating the protector of sailors and fisherman.

The Peninsula

To truly savor the ocean air, hike around the peninsula (8km). Start at **Papôa,** just north of Peniche, and stroll out to the tip, where orange cliffs rise from a swirling blue sea. Nearby lie the ruins of an old fortress, **Forte da Luz. Cabo Carvoeiro,** the most popular and dramatic of Peniche's natural sights, and its **farol** (lighthouse) punc- tuate the extreme west end of the peninsula. Nearby is a convenient snack bar where you can watch the waves crashing below as you relish *ginja* (cherry liqueur of Óbi- dos). The **Nau dos Corvos** (Crow's Ship), an odd rock formation and a popular bird roost, promises a seagull's-eye perspective.

■ Near Peniche: Ilhas Berlengas

The rugged, terrifyingly beautiful Ilhas Berlengas (Berlenga Islands) lie in the Atlantic Ocean, 12km northwest of Peniche. One minuscule main island, numerous reefs, and isolated rocks form an archipelago that's home to thousands of screeching seagulls, wild black rabbits, and a very small fishing community. Deep gorges, natural tunnels, and rocky caves ravage the main island. Although the island is fringed with several protected beaches, the only one accessible by foot lies in a small cove by the landing dock. For beach-goers willing to brave the cold, dips in the calm water bring instant respite from the heat. For hikers, the tiring trek to the island's highest point yields a gorgeous view of the 17th-century **Forte de São João Batista,** now a hostel.

From Peniche's public dock, the Berlenga **ferry** zips to the island (1hr., July-Aug. 9am, 11, and 5pm; returns 10am, 4, and 6pm; June-July and Sept. 10am; returns 6pm). In late July and August the ferry gets so crowded that you may have to line up at 7am; at other times, one hour in advance will suffice. A same-day round-trip ticket (2500$) for the 9am ferry means you'll return at 4pm; if you go at 11am, you return at 6pm unless there is space on the other boat. To stay overnight, buy a 1500$ one-way ticket for the 5pm boat and pay return fare on board a 10am return boat. Crossing can be rough—vomit bags given to all passengers are too frequently appreciated. Alterna- tively, cruise around in a **private motorboat.** Turpesca, docked at R. Marechal Gomes Freire de Andrade, 90 (tel. 78 99 60), in Peniche, tours underwater caves and other wonders in and around Peniche (prices from 2500$ with 5-person min.).

Pick one of three options for an overnight stay: the hostel, the campground, or the expensive *pensão*. While the community-run **hostel** (tel. 78 25 50), in the old fortress looks spectacular, it lacks facilities. Bring a sleeping bag and flashlight: the 30-minute walk from the boat landing to the hostel is lit only by periodic flashes from the lighthouse. The hostel has a kitchen, and the canteen and snack bar stock basic food. (Spartan doubles 2000$. Reception M-F 12:30-1:30pm, or call M-F 10am-noon (0936) 87 66 05. Reservations required. Open June-Sept. 21.) The island has a small, barren **campground** on a series of rocky terraces above the ferry landing. Be prepared to be shat upon by scores of seagulls. (Seven years of good luck may not be worth it miles away from your own tub.) Make the required reservations in person at the tourist office in Peniche. (2- or 3-person tent 1500$ per night; 4-person tent 2000$. 7-day max. stay. Open June-Sept. 20.) The nice **pensão** above **Pavilhão Mar e Sol** (tel. 75 03 31), the main restaurant on the island, will drain your *escudos* (doubles 10,000-12,000$; breakfast included).

■ Nazaré

It's hard to tell where authenticity stops and tourism starts in Nazaré. Fishermen clad in traditional garb go barefoot and women typically don seven petticoats, thick shawls, and large gold earrings. The day's catch dries in the hot sun while locals string their nets along the shoreline esplanade. This "traditional" lifestyle has, however, become the basis of Nazaré's most thriving business, tourism. In one of the most touristed beach towns in Portugal, entrepreneurial natives sell everything from seashell necklaces to fishing nets to dried fruit. But if Nazaré is part theater, at least it puts on a good show—and everyone gets front row seats on the glorious beach. Drop your anchor elsewhere at the end of July and August, when prices double and bathers jostle with each other for tiny spots on the sand.

ORIENTATION AND PRACTICAL INFORMATION

Practically all the action in Nazaré, including the beach scene, nightlife, and most restaurants, is located in the so-called **new town** along the beach. Its two main squares, **Praça Sousa Oliveira** and **Praça Dr. Manuel de Arriaga,** are near the cliffside, away from the fishing port. Either the cliffside funicular or a winding road takes you up to the **Sítio,** the old town, which preserves a sense of calm and tradition less prevalent in the crowded resort below. To get to the tourist office from the bus station, go toward the beach and right onto **Avenida República.** The office is a 10-minute walk along the beach, between the two major *praças.*

Buses: (tel. 55 11 72), on Av. Vieira Guimarães, perpendicular to Av. República. More convenient than taking the train (12km away). To: Alcobaça (30min., 15 per day, 200$); Caldas da Rainha (1¼hr., 20 per day, 600$); Leiria (1¼hr., 12 per day, 750$); Tomar (1½hr., 3 per day, 740$); Peniche (1½hr., 6 per day, 850$); Fátima (1½hr., 6 per day, 900$); Lisbon (2hr., 8 per day, 1050$); Coimbra (2hr., 6 per day, 1100$); Porto (3½hr., 9 per day, 1400$).

Taxi: (tel. 55 31 25 or 55 13 63).

Car Rental: M&M Travel Agencies, Av. de República, 28 (tel. 56 18 88). Renting a car is the easiest way to visit Alcobaça, Fátima, and Batalha without camping out in the bus station. Open M-F 9am-12:30pm and 2-7pm.

Tourist Office: (tel. 56 11 94), beachside on Av. República. **Maps,** transportation schedules, and the scoop on entertainment. Open daily July-Aug. 10am-10pm; Oct.-June 15 9:30am-12:30pm and 2-6pm.

Currency Exchange: Banco Fonsecas & Burnay (tel. 56 12 89), Av. Vieira Guimarães, has an **ATM** (Visa, AmEx). Open M-F 8am-3pm.

Luggage Storage: In the bus station (100$ per bag per day).

Emergency: Dial 115. **Police:** (tel. 55 12 68), 1 block from the bus station at Av. Vieira Guimarães and R. Sub-Vila.

Hospital: Hospital da Confraria da Nossa Senhora de Nazaré (tel. 56 11 16), in the Sítio district on the cliffs above the town center.

PORTUGAL

Post Office: Av. Independência Nacional, 2 (tel. 56 16 04). From Pr. Souza Oliveira walk up R. Mouzinho de Albuquerque, which veers to the right. It's 1 block past Pensão Central. Posta Restante. Open M-F 9am-12:30pm and 2:30-6pm. **Postal Code:** 2450.

Telephone Code: (0)62

ACCOMMODATIONS AND FOOD

By stepping off the bus, you unwittingly signal a phalanx of room-renters to stampede; once you've made it past them, you'll encounter insistent old ladies on most every street corner offering rooms. Be sure to check that they are authorized by the tourist office (they should have a card with the words *autorizado D.6. Turismo*). Bargain down to 2000$ for singles and 3000$ for doubles, but insist on seeing your quarters before settling the deal. For rooms in *pensões,* look above the restaurants on **Praça Dr. Manuel de Arriaga** and **Praça Sousa Oliveira.** For fruit and veggies, check the **market** across from the bus station (open in summer daily 8am-1pm; in winter Tu-Su 8am-1pm). Fish are everywhere. **Supermarkets** line R. Sub-Vila, parallel to Av. República and Pr. Dr. Manuel de Arriaga.

Casa de Hóspedes, R. Mouzinho de Albuquerque, 6A, 3rd fl. (tel. 55 15 41), on the beach side of Hotel Mare. Modern, carpeted rooms with baths, close to the beach. July 15-Sept. doubles 6500$, with bath 7000$. May-July 14 and Oct. doubles 3000$, with bath 4000$. Reservations recommended. Open May-Oct.

Pensão Leonardo, Pr. Dr. Manuel de Arriaga, 25-28 (tel. 55 12 59), above a restaurant of the same name, between Restaurant Mar Alto and Pensão Europa on a square parallel to the beach. Basic rooms, shared bathrooms. Sept.-July singles 2500$; doubles 3800$, with bath 4500$. Aug. singles 3000$, doubles 4-5000$, with bath 5-6000$. Reservations recommended. Visa, MC, AmEx.

Camping: Vale Paraíso, Estrada Nacional, 242 (tel. 56 18 00; fax 56 19 00), has swimming pools, a restaurant-bar, a supermarket, and, when working, internet access. To get there, take the bus to Alcobaça or Leiria (15min., 8 per day, 7am-7pm). 370-595$ per person, 305-650$ per tent, 305-490$ per car. Prices vary seasonally. Free showers. Laundry. Pool access 150$ in summer. Reception daily 8am-10pm. Open year-round.

A Tasquinha, R. Adrião Batalha, 54 (tel. 55 19 45), several blocks off Av. República, 1 block left off Pr. Dr. Manuel Arriaga. Locals jostle for a seat at the family-style picnic tables. Perhaps the only restaurant in Nazaré with a Portuguese-only menu (this is a good thing). *Sardinhas* 600$. Open daily noon-midnight. Visa, MC, AmEx.

Charcutaria O Frango Assado, Pr. Dr. Manuel de Arriaga, 20 (tel. 55 18 42). Facing the beach, at the far end of the square. For under 450$ get a half-chicken with *piri-piri* (a tabasco-esque sauce). Take-out only. Open daily 9am-1pm and 3-8pm.

Restaurante Riba Mar, Av. República (tel. 55 11 58), at the south corner of Pr. Dr. Manuel Arriaga. A reasonable "traditional" menu, with entrees from 800-1800$, hides behind the international facade. Open daily noon-midnight. Visa, MC, AmEx.

Cliff Hangers

One-hundred twenty meters above the sea, the tiny, whitewashed **Ermida da Memória** (Memorial Chapel) stands in a corner of the square diagonally opposite Sítio's church. The chapel, perched on the edge of the precipice, was built in 1182 by the lucky nobleman Dom Fuas Roupinho. Out on a hunting expedition, Dom Fuas was chasing a deer that just kept runnin' until it fell off the cliff. Dom Fuas slammed on the brakes and his horse stopped with two legs on *terra firme* and two over the side. In a split second, Our Lady of Nazaré appeared and pulled the horse (and Dom Fuas) to safety. Out of this event, the little chapel and the town of Nazaré was born.

SIGHTS AND ENTERTAINMENT

Why are you staring at that church? Go to the **beach!** If you've been there and done that, take the **funicular** (departs every 15min. until 1am, 90$) runs up from R. Elevador off Av. República to modest **Sítio,** a clifftop area of Nazaré and a perfect evening excursion. Its uneven cobbled streets and weathered buildings were all there before tourism was invented. Around 7:30pm, fishing boats return to the **port** beyond the far left end (facing the ocean) of the beach; head over to watch fishermen at work and eavesdrop as local restaurateurs spiritedly bid for the most promising catches.

Cafes in Pr. Souza Oliveira teem with people until 1am. For lively Brazilian and Portuguese tunes, imbibe with locals at **Bar A Ilha,** on R. Mouzinho Albuquerque (open nightly 7pm-about 3am). During the summer, look out for late-night gatherings of folk music on the beach. Every Thursday and Friday at 10pm from July 15 to August 1, a local group performs *fado* and **traditional dances** called *viras* at the **Casino,** a festival hall on R. Rui Rosa (500$).

■ Near Nazaré: São Martinho do Porto

The result of countless ages of surf smashing against, and finally through, the coastal cliffs, the bay of São Martinho is nearly enclosed on all sides. The town lies clustered at the base of the inlet, while the windless, swimmer-friendly **beach** sweeps 3km along and around the bay, forming an almost perfect circle. Hidden from the sea by the formidable cliffs and from the land by the hills behind it, São Martinho do Porto remains relatively undiscovered (except perhaps in August). With its red-roofed houses crowding down a palm-studded hillside to a small and colorful fishing harbor, São Martinho has an almost Mediterranean charm that makes an ideal escape from the crowded beach towns of Peniche and Nazaré.

Trains connect São Martinho to Nazaré (20min.), and other points north and south (schedules posted in the São Martinho tourist office), but buses run more frequently to Nazaré (20min., departs almost every hr., 180$). The bus stops on Av. 25 de Abril on the main road leading into town. The **tourist office** (tel. 98 91 10), at the northern end of Av. 25 de Abril, provides a list of private rooms (open M-F 9am-1pm and 3-7pm, Sa-Su 9am-1pm and 3-6pm). In an **emergency,** dial 115. The **telephone code** is (0)62.

In all probability you will accosted in the street by one of the local **room-renters,** with whom you should bargain (prices vary between 2000 and 5000$). **Pensão Carvalho,** R. Miguel Bombarda, 6 (tel. 98 96 05), is pricier but has bright, comfortable doubles with private bath (7000-10,000$; breakfast included). Restaurants, cafes, and lively bars line the southern side of the beachfront on Av. 25 de Abril.

■ Leiria

Capital of the surrounding district and an important transport hub, noisy Leiria (pop. 103,000) fans out from a fertile valley, 22km from the coast. An impressive ancient castle peers over this prosperous and industrial city, gazing upon countless shops and a shady park. While Leiria itself may not be the most exciting destination in Portugal, it makes a practical base for exploring the region nearby. Buses heading away from Leiria run frequently enough to satisfy both culture vultures (aching to get to the surrounding historic towns) and beach leeches (minds and bodies firmly set on the gorgeous beaches of the Costa da Prata).

ORIENTATION AND PRACTICAL INFORMATION

Most commerce bustles about the sight-packed path from the tourist office to the *castelo,* so don't expect to wander far.

Buses: (tel. 81 15 07) leave from just off Pr. Paulo VI, next to the town garden and close to the tourist office, and are the easiest way to get to and from Leiria. Buses run to: Batalha (15min., 9 per day, 190$); Nazaré (15min., 8 per day, 750$); Fátima (1hr., 13 per day, 600-720$); Santarém (1hr., 4 per day, 105$); Coimbra (1hr., 8 per day, 800$); Tomar (1hr., 2 per day, 850$); Figueira da Foz (1½hr., 4 per day, 800$); Lisbon (2hr., 11 per day, 1100$); Porto (3½hr., 8 per day, 1300$).

Trains: The train station (tel. 88 20 27) is 3km outside town. Buses run between the station and the tourist office (10min., departs every hr., 100$). Service to Figueira (1¼hr., 7 per day, 410$) and Lisbon (3½hr., 12 per day,1100$).

Tourist office: (tel. 81 47 48 or 82 37 73), across the park facing the bus station. Schedules for beach-going buses and maps. English-speaking staff allows temporary **luggage storage.** Open May-Sept. M-F 9am-1pm and 3-7pm, Sa-Su 10am-1pm and 3-7pm; Oct.-Apr. M-F 9am-1pm and 3-7pm, Sa-Su 10am-1pm and 3-7pm.

Taxi: tel. 81 59 00 or 80 17 59.

Hospital: (tel. 812 215), on R. Olhalvas along road to Fátima.

Emergencies: call 112. **Police:** Largo Artilharia, 4 (tel. 81 37 99).

Post office: (tel. 81 28 09), on Av. Combatentes da Grande Guerra 3 blocks from the youth hostel. Label Posta Restante mail "Estação Santana." Open M-F 8:30am-6:30pm, Sa 9am-12:30pm. **Postal code:** 2400.

Telephone code: (0)44.

ACCOMMODATIONS AND FOOD

Accommodations in Leiria will not take your breath away. Cheap rooms are hard to find and most *pensões* have seen better days. Shop for fruit and vegetables at the **market** in Largo da Feira, located on the far side of the castle from the bus station (open Tu and Sa 9am-1pm). **Supermercado Ulmar,** Av. Heróis de Angola, 56, has American and Portuguese foodstuffs (open M-Sa 8am-8pm, Su 10am-1pm and 3-6pm).

Pousada de Juventude (HI), Largo Cândido dos Reis, 7D (tel. 318 68). From the bus station walk to the cathedral, then exit Largo da Sé (next to Largo Cónego Maia) on R. Barão de Viamonte, a narrow street lined with shops. Largo Cândido dos Reis is about 6 blocks straight ahead. Clean and comfortable rooms. High-season dorms 1300$; off-season 1100$. Breakfast included. Kitchen, laundry facilities available. Flexible lockout noon-6pm. Reception daily 9am-noon and 6pm-midnight.

Residencial Dom Dinis, Travessa de Tomar, 2 (tel. 81 53 42). Turn left after exiting the tourist office, cross the bridge over Rio Lis, walk 2 blocks, and turn left again. 18 cozy, modern rooms with baths, telephones, and satellite TV. Singles 3500$; doubles 5500$; triples 6500$. Breakfast included. Visa, MC.

Camping: Praia do Pedrógão (tel. 69 54 03), 10km from Leiria. The grounds are nestled in the pines 100m from the beach. Has a mini-*mercado,* restaurant, and snack bar. 250$ per person, per tent, per car. Hot shower 120$. International camping ID card required. Open Apr.-Oct.

Restaurante Aquário, Mouzinho de Albuquerque, 17 (tel. 247 20). Superior regional specialties at pretty reasonable prices. Entrees 850-1450$. Open F-W noon-3pm and 7-10pm.

SIGHTS AND ENTERTAINMENT

From the main square, follow the signs past the austere **sé** (cathedral) to the city's most significant monument, the **castelo.** *(Castle open daily 9am-6:30pm. 130$.)* This granite fort, built by the first king of Portugal, Dom Afonso Henriques, after he snatched the town from the Moors, dramatically presides atop the crest of a volcanic hill overlooking the north edge of town. Left to crumble for hundreds of years, the castle retains only the **torre de menagem** (homage tower) and the **sala dos namorados** (lovers' hall). The terrace opens onto a panoramic view of town and the river. Nearby sits the roofless shell of the 14th-century **Igreja da Nossa Senhora da Penha.**

Nearby **beaches,** including **Vieira, Pedrógã,** and **São Pedro de Moel,** are all easily accessible via hourly buses departing from the tourist office.

Bars along Largo Cândido dos Reis near the youth hostel come alive after 10pm and have weekly drink specials. The **Teatro José Lúcio da Silva** (tel. 82 36 00), on the corner of Av. Heróis de Angola behind the bus station, features films (often American) and performances. *(Ticket office open daily 7-10pm. Tourist office has schedules.)*

Batalha

The *only* reason to visit Batalha (pop. 14,000) is the gigantic **Mosteiro de Santa Maria da Vitória,** which rivals Belém's Mosteiro dos Jerónimos in monastic splendor. Built by Dom João I in 1385 to commemorate his victory against the Spanish, the complex of cloisters and chapels remains one of Portugal's greatest monuments. To get to the *mosteiro,* enter through the church.

PRACTICAL INFORMATION, ACCOMMODATIONS, AND FOOD The **bus** stop is a concrete structure across from Pensão Vitória on Largo da Misericórdia. Inquire at the tourist office for info or call the bus station in Leiria (tel. 811 507). Buses run to: Leiria (20min., 7 per day, 180$); Fátima (40min., 3 per day, 250$); Alcobaça (45min., 12 per day, 350$); Nazaré, change at Alcobaça (1hr., 5 per day, 470$); Tomar (1½hr., 4 per day, 470$); and Lisbon (2hr., 5 per day, 2100$). The **tourist office** (tel. 76 51 80), on Pr. Mouzinho de Albuquerque along R. Nossa Senhora do Caminho, across from the unfinished chapels of the *mosteiro,* has **maps** and bus info. (Open M-F 10am-1pm and 3-7pm, Sa-Su 10am-1pm and 3-6pm; Oct.-Apr. M-F 10am-1pm and 3-6pm, Sa-Su 10am-1pm and 3-5pm.) In an **emergency,** dial 112. For **police,** call 961 34. The **post office** (tel. 961 11) is on Largo Papa Paulo VI, near the freeway entrance (open M-F 9am-12:30pm and 2:30-6pm). The **postal code** is 2440. The **telephone code** is (0)44.

Batalha is devoid of cheap beds or even a campground and is best as a daytrip. If marooned here, sleep at **Pensão Vitória** (tel. 966 78), on Largo da Misericórdia in front of the bus stop. Its three simple, dim rooms are bare and monastic (3000$ per room). The **restaurant** below does wonders with *pudim* (pudding) and is a handy place to wait for the bus. Several inexpensive *churrasquería* (barbecue houses) and cafes line the squares flanking the monastery.

SIGHTS Granted UN World Heritage status, the **monastery complex** is flamboyantly spectacular. *(Open daily 9am-5pm. 400$, under 25 200$. Church entrance free.)* The church **facade** soars upward in a heavy Gothic and Manueline style, opulently decorated and topped off by dozens of spires. Napoleon's troops turned the nave into a brothel, but none of that goes on today. The **Capela do Fundador,** immediately to the right of the church, shelters the elaborate sarcophagi of Dom João I, his English-born queen Philippa of Lancaster, and their son Henry the Navigator. The rest of the complex is accessible via a door in the north wall of the church. Enter through the broad Gothic arches of the **Claustro de Dom João I,** the delicate columns of which initiated the Manueline style. Adjacent to the cloister lies the **Tomb of the Unknown Soldier.** Through the **Claustro de Dom Afonso V,** out the door and to the right are the impressive **Capelas Imperfeitas** (Imperfect Chapels), with massive buttresses designed to support a large dome. The project was dropped when Manuel I ordered his workers to build the monastery in Belém instead.

Near Batalha

Nature is at its most psychedelic in a spectacular series of underground *grutas* (caves) in Estremadura's natural park between Batalha and Fátima. The vast labyrinth of minuscule stalagmite and stalactite formations is but a short bus-ride (1km) away from Batalha at **Mira de Aire.** About 15km farther, the **Grutas de Santo António** and Alvados are a bit more difficult to reach, but equally impressive. Take a **bus** to Alto de Alvados (from Leiria 1hr., 4 per day, 400$). Most of the caves have been "enhanced" with background music and strategically placed colored spotlights. The tourist offices in both Batalha and Fátima have info on how to reach the caves.

■ Fátima

Fátima used to be a sheep pasture; now it's a Roman Catholic religious center. Come only if you're interested in pilgrimages, and be prepared for total immersion in holy fervor. Only Lourdes rivals this site in popularity with Christian pilgrims. The miracles believed to have occurred here are modern-day phenomena, well documented and witnessed by thousands. The plaza in front of the church, larger than St. Peter's square in the Vatican, floods with pilgrims on the 12th and 13th of each month.

ORIENTATION AND PRACTICAL INFORMATION

Activity in Fátima focuses in and around the basilica complex in the town center **Avenida Dr. José Alves Correia da Silva,** running just south of the hubbub, contains the bus station and tourist office. A right turn and 10-minute walk from the bus station leads to the tourist office at the plaza leading to the basilica.

Trains: Station (tel. 461 22) is 20km out of town on Chão de Maçãs. To: Coimbra (1hr., 3 per day, 900$); Santarém, via Entroncamento (1½hr., 2 per day, 1100$) Lisbon, via Entroncamento (2hr., 2 per day, 1150$). Buses run between the train and bus stations (45min., 6 per day, 340$).

Buses: (tel. 53 16 11), on Av. Dr. José Alves Correia da Silva. On bus schedule Fátima is often referred to as **Cova da Ivia**—forget and you'll risk confusion. To Batalha (45min., 3 per day, 240$); Leiria (1hr., 15 per day, 600$); Santarém (1hr., per day, 850$); Tomar (1¼hr., 2 per day, 650$); Nazaré (1½hr., 4 per day, 900$) Lisbon (2½hr., 8 per day, 1100$); Porto (3½hr., 7 per day, 1350$).

Taxis: tel. 53 21 16 or 53 16 22.

Tourist Office: Av. Dr. José Alves Correia da Silva (tel. 53 11 39), left as you exit the bus station. Open May-Sept. M-F 9am-7pm, Sa-Su 10am-1pm and 3-7pm; Oct.-Apr M-F 9am-6pm, Sa-Su 10am-1pm and 3-6pm. Temporary **luggage storage.**

Currency Exchange: União de Bancos Portugueses, R. Francisco Marto, 139 (tel 53 39 68). Open daily 8:30am-3pm.

Emergency: tel. 115. **Police:** Av. Dr. José Alves Correia de Silva (tel. 53 11 05), near Rotunda de Sta. Teresa de Ourém.

Hospital: tel. 53 18 36.

Post Office: R. Cónego Formagião (tel. 53 18 10). Open June-Sept. M-F 8:30am-6pm Sa 3-8pm, Su 9am-noon; Oct.-May M-F 8:30am-6pm. **Postal Code:** 2495.

Telephone Code: (0)49.

ACCOMMODATIONS AND FOOD

Scores of *pensões* and *hotéis* inundate both sides of the basilica complex. Credit cards are almost universally accepted, and lodging prices vary little. The town fills most during the grand pilgrimages on the 12th and 13th of each month and both *pensão* and hotel prices tend to increase 500 to 2000$ during these days. Ruas **Francisco Marto, Santa Isabela,** and **Jacinta Marto** have similar, touristy restaurants.

Pensão Doña Maria, R. Av. Dr. José Alves Coneia da Silva, 122 (tel. 53 12 12) between the bus station and tourist office. Friendly, doting owner. Rooms 3500 5000$, all with bath, some with balcony. Breakfast included.

Pensão A Paragem (tel. 53 15 58). Upstairs in the bus station. The cheapest beds in town. Clean, pleasant, and ideal if you miss the last bus out of town. Try to get an early start in the morning—by 7:30am, diesel fumes begin to penetrate the room All rooms with bath; doubles have TVs. Singles 2500$; doubles 4500$; triple 5000$. Breakfast included.

Adega Funda, R. Francisco Marto, 103 (tel. 53 13 72). Take a break from prayer in this large wood dining room. Hefty traditional Portuguese dishes like *bacalhau churrasco* (barbecued cod, 1200$). Open daily 11am-3pm and 6-10pm.

Snack Bar A Lovca (tel. 53 16 21), R. Jacinta Marto in the Pope John Paul II building Yep, it's one crazy snack bar. Lighter food, including omelettes (650-800$) an *pratos do dia* (750$). Open daily 11am-midnight.

PORTUGAL

Mary and the Three Shepherds

On May 13, 1917, Mary appeared before three shepherd children—Lucía, Francisco, and Jacinta—to issue a call for peace in the middle of WWI. The children remained steadfast in their belief that the Virgin had spoken to them, despite the skepticism of clergy and attacks from the press as word of the vision spread through Portugal. Bigger crowds flocked to the site as Our Lady of Fátima returned to speak to the children on the 13th of each month, promising a miracle for her final appearance in October. On that morning, 70,000 people gathered under a torrential rain storm. At noon, the sun reportedly spun around in a furious light spectacle, appearing to sink to the earth. When the light returned to normal, no evidence remained of the morning's rain. Convinced by the "fiery signature of God," the townspeople built a chapel at the site to honor Mary.

SIGHTS

The legendary sanctuary is set in parks shaded by tall leafy trees that block out the surrounding commercial area, where religious memorabilia is sold for sacreligious prices. At the end of the plaza rises the super-cool **Basílica do Rosário** (erected in 1928), featuring a crystal cruciform beacon perched atop the tower's seven-ton bronze crown. *(Open daily 7am-8pm.)* Many of the devout approach the basilica on their knees across the length of the plaza. But beware; you must do so in style. A dress code is enforced for both sexes—no shorts, bathing suits, sleeveless tops, or other "inappropriate" clothing is allowed. Sheltered beneath a metal and glass canopy, the 1919 **Capelinha das Aparições** (Little Chapel of the Apparitions) holds masses in six languages all mornings and some evenings, beside the same **oak tree** under which the children spoke to the virgin. Surounding the basilica are various museums commemorating the miracle. To the right facing the basilica (three blocks off), the **Museu de Arte Sacra e Etnologia,** R. Francisco Marto, 52 (tel. 53 29 15), exhibits Catholic icons from various centuries. *(Open Apr.-Oct. Tu-Su 10am-6pm; Nov.-Mar. noon-5pm. 400$, seniors and students 200$.)* To the left of the basilica, through the park, and in the complex beneath the Hotel Fátima, the **Museu-Vivo Aparições,** R. Jacinta Marto (tel. 53 28 58), uses light, sound (in various languages), and special effects to re-create the apparition. *(Open daily May-Oct. 9am-8pm; Nov.-Apr. 9am-6pm. 450$.)*

■ Tomar

For centuries the arcane Knights Templar—part monks, part warriors—plotted crusades in this small town straddling the Rio Nabão. A celebrated convent-fortress, perched high above the old town, long served as the Knights' powerful and mysterious headquarters. Known as the Convento de Cristo, the complex beautifully combines architectural styles from the 12th to 17th centuries. Despite its quasi-mythical past, Tomar now rests quietly in the shade of the eucalyptus and sycamore trees that line the banks of the Rio Nabão and the surrounding hillside. Even their shade, though, is hardly enough during the blistering summer heat.

ORIENTATION AND PRACTICAL INFORMATION

The **Rio Nabão** divides Tomar, and almost everything—the train, bus stations, accommodations, and sights—lies on the west bank. The lush **Parque Mouchão** straddles the two banks, while the antique (albeit fully functional) **Ponte Velha** (old bridge) connects the two. The bus and train stations border the Várzea Grande, a vast wasteland. Four blocks north, Av. Dr. Cândido Madureira hems the south edge of the old city, with R. Everaro and Av. Marquês de Tomar on the river border and R. Dr. Sousa on the castle side. Rustic **Rua Serpa Pinto** cuts across town from river to castle and connects the Ponte Velha to the main square, **Praça da República.**

Trains: (tel. 31 28 15), on Av. Combatentes da Grande Guerra, at the southern edge of town. Tomar is the north terminus of a minor line, so most destinations require a transfer at Entrocamento; you can buy the transfer here. To: Lisbon (2hr., 12 per day, 870$); Coimbra (2½hr., 9 per day, 850$); Porto (4½hr., 5 per day, 1390$).

Buses: Rodoviaria Tejo (tel. 31 27 38), on Av. Combatentes Grande Guerra by the train station. To: Fátima (30min., 3 per day, 430$); Leiria (1hr., 3 per day, 580$); Santarém (1hr., 2 per day, 450$); Lisbon (2hr., 5 per day., 1200$); Coimbra (2½hr., 2 per day, 1150$); Porto (4hr., 1 per day, 1400$); Lagos (11hr., 1 per day, 2300$).

Taxis: (tel. 31 37 16 or 31 23 73). Taxis idle at R. Arcos.

Tourist Office: (tel. 32 24 27) on Av. Dr. Cândido Madureira, facing Parque Mata Nacional. From the bus or train station, go through the small square onto Av. General Bernardo Raria. Continue 4 blocks and go left onto Av. Dr. Cândido Madureira; the office is at the end of the street. Map, accommodations list, and temporary **luggage storage**. Ask kindly. Open M-F 9:30am-6pm, Sa-Su 10am-1pm and 3-6pm.

Currency Exchange: União dos Bancos, R. Serpa Pinto, 20, has an **ATM.**

Emergency: call 112. **Police:** R. Dr. Sousa (tel. 31 34 44).

Hospital: (tel. 32 11 00), on Av. Cândido Madureira.

Post Office: (tel. 32 23 54). On Av. Marquês de Tomar, across from Parque Mouchão. Open M-F 9am-noon and 2-5pm. **Postal Code:** 2300.

Telephone Code: (0)49.

ACCOMMODATIONS AND FOOD

Finding a place to stay is never a problem, except during the Festival dos Tabuleiros, which takes place once every four years. Tomar is a buyer's market—practice bargaining. It is also a fantastic place for **picnics.** A section of the lush Parque Mouchão is set aside just for that. The **market,** on the corner of Av. Norton de Matos and R. Santa Iria across the river, provides all the fixings (M-Th and Sa 8am-2pm). Friday is the big day, when the market gears up from 8am to 5pm. Several inexpensive **mini-markets** line the side streets between the tourist office and Pr. República.

Residencial União, R. Serpa Pinto, 94 (tel. 32 31 61; fax 32 12 99), halfway between Pr. República and the bridge. Look for the oversized *azulejo* panels outside. 28 bright, plush rooms with wood furniture and white-tiled baths. Well-stocked bar on the ground floor. All rooms with shower or full bath, telephone, and TV. Singles 3500-4500; doubles 6000-6500; triples 7500$. Prices lower in winter. Breakfast included. Reserve several days ahead July-Aug.

Residencial Luz, R. Serpa Pinto, 144 (tel. 31 23 17), down the street from União. Cozy, clean rooms with phones. Swank TV rooms with leather couches. Singles with shower 3000$, with bath 3500$; doubles 4500$, with bath 5400$; huge 4- to 6-person rooms with bath 2000$ per person. Oct.-May 20% off. Breakfast 300$.

Camping: Parque Municipal de Campismo (tel. 32 26 07; fax 32 10 26), on the river, conveniently across Ponte Velha near the stadium and swimming pool. Exit off E.N. 110 on the east end of the Nabão bridge. Thickly forested campground with a pool. 420$ per person, 200$ per tent, 280$ per car. Showers free. Reception daily in summer 8am-8pm; in winter 9am-5pm.

Restaurante Estrêla do Céu, Pr. República, 21 (tel. 32 31 38). Ex-Sheraton chef serves up innovative dishes in a relaxing rustic decor. *Lombinhos à corredoura* (veal with orange, red pepper, and carrots; 1450$) is featured, but the daily lunch specials are the real bargain at 450$. Open Tu-Su 11am-midnight.

Restaurante Bela Vista, R. Fonte do Choupo, 6 (tel. 31 28 70), across the Ponte Velha on your left. Dine on the riverside patio under a grape arbor with a handsome view of the park. Diverse meat and fish entrees, all with fries 700-1900$. Open M noon-3pm, W-Su noon-3pm and 7-9:30pm.

Pizzeria Bella Itaia (tel. 32 29 96), on Av. Marques de Tomar. Pizzas with very Portuguese toppings or good ol' Italian pasta dishes (850-1600$) in this friendly, family joint. Open Tu-Su noon-3pm and 7-11pm.

PORTUGAL

Judaism in Portugal

Tomar's **Museu Luso-Hebraico**, R. Dr. Joaquim Jaquinto, 73 (tel. 32 26 02, ext. 319), in the 15th-century Sinagoga do Arco, is Portugal's most significant reminder of its once vibrant Jewish community. Jews worshipped here for only a few decades before the convert-or-leave ultimatum of 1496. Since then the building has served as a prison, Christian chapel, hayloft, and grocery warehouse before becoming a national monument. In 1923, Samuel Schwartz purchased the synagogue, devoted himself to its restoration, and in 1939 donated it to the state. The government awarded Schwartz and his wife Portuguese citizenship, assuring them sanctuary during WWII. The museum keeps a collection of old tombstones, inscriptions, and donated pieces from around the world. A recent excavation of the adjacent building unearthed a sacred purification bath *(mikvah)*, used only briefly by the Jews for ritual purposes. Services are still held at the site on selected Saturdays. (Open Th-Tu 9:30am-12:30pm and 2-6pm.)

SIGHTS AND ENTERTAINMENT

It's worth trekking in from the far corners of the earth to explore the mysterious **Convento de Cristo** grounds (tel. 31 34 81). *(Open daily 9:30am-12:30pm and 2-5:30pm. 400$, seniors and students 200$.)* Walk out of the tourist office door and take your second right; bear left at the fork. Pedestrians can take the steeper dirt path a bit after the fork on the left or follow the cars up the paved road. The first structure was built by the Knights Templar in 1160, but various cloisters, convents, and structures were built in successive centuries. An ornate octagonal canopy protects the high altar of the **Templo dos Templares,** modeled after the Holy Sepulchre in Jerusalem. The Knights supposedly attended mass, each under one of the arches, in the saddle. A 16th-century courtyard is encrusted with the rich seafaring symbolism of the Manueline style: seaweed, coral, anchors, rope, and even artichokes, which mariners ate to prevent scurvy. Below stands the **Janelo do Capítula** (chapter window), an exuberant tribute to the Golden Age of Discoveries.

One of Europe's masterpieces of Renaissance architecture, the **Claustro dos Felipes** honors King Felipe II of Castile, who was crowned here as Felipe I of Portugal during Iberia's unification (1580-1640). Tucked behind the Palladian main cloister and the nave is the **Claustro Santa Bárbara,** where grotesque gargoyle rainspouts writhe in pain as they cough up a fountain. On the northeast side of the church is the Gothic **Claustro do Cemitério.** Elsewhere, pyromaniacs love the **Museu dos Fósforos** (match museum; tel. 32 26 02), which exhibits Europe's largest matchbox collection. *(Open Su-F 2-5pm. Free.)* It's in the Convento de São Francisco, just across from the train and bus stations. Nature freaks can take a hike on the trails leading away from the **Parque da Mata Nacional dos Sete Montes,** across from the tourist office.

O Covil dos Templários II, Av. Dr. Cândido Madureira, 94 (tel. 32 10 27), shows movies nightly. *(Open nightly 8pm-2am.)* For a week in either June or July, handicrafts, folklore, *fado,* and theater storm the city during the **Feira Nacional de Artesanato.** The big deal around here is really the **Festa dos Tabuleiros.** Unfortunately, this massive cultural celebration, involving the laborious construction of three-foot-tall decorative hats for women using cardboard, colored paper, and bread, takes place only once every four years; fortunately, 1999's the year. Women and hats parade through town for days, as well as children, bulls, and horses in finery. If you miss the party, view some of the costumes donned by mannequins at the tourist office.

The Three Beiras

Exquisite beaches and plush greenery make the three Beira regions perfect for getting acquainted with traditional Portuguese life. Fertile and well-watered by frequent rain, the soil in this region yields some of Portugal's best farmland, resulting in a countryside dotted with red-roofed farmhouses and corn, sunflower, and wheat fields shining under a mild sun. The **Beira Litoral** encompasses the unspoiled Costa da Prata (Silver Coast) beginning at the resort town of Figueira da Foz and passing through up-and-coming Aveiro on the way to Porto. Coimbra, a bustling university city, overlooks the region from its perch above the celebrated Rio Mondego. Unlike the progressive towns of the Beira Litoral to the west, the mountainous **Beira Alta** (high edge) and the **Beira Baixa** (low edge) have been slow to develop. These impoverished and at times snow-covered (a rarity for Portugal) provinces continue to cling tightly to tradition. Throughout the Beiras, farmers cultivate grapes along the mountainsides, while silvery almond trees cloud the horizon. As if this image is not ideal enough, rice fields spill down the valleys and wildflowers scatter across the roads.

■ Coimbra

Camouflage in Coimbra is easy—students and tourists shouldering backpacks blend harmoniously in and around town and at the renowned University of Coimbra. Established as the university's permanent home in 1537, Coimbra remained the country's only university city until the beginning of this century. The charm of the city and its people have long since blotted out Coimbra's infamous roles as center of the Inquisition and as educator of former economics professor Antònio Salazar, the notorious dictator of Portugal. Crew races, rowdy cafeteria halls, and swinging bars place Coimbra slightly on the wild side from September through May, but its youthful energy, diversity, and collection of medieval buildings welcome visitors year-round.

ORIENTATION AND PRACTICAL INFORMATION

Coimbra's steep streets rise in tiers above **Rio Mondego.** There are three centers of activity in town, all on the same side of the river. The most central is the **lower town** (site of the **tourist office** and Coimbra-A train station), within the triangle formed by the river, **Largo da Portagem,** the square across from the Santa Clara bridge, and **Praça 8 de Maio.** Coimbra's ancient **university district** is atop the steep hill overlooking the lower town. On the other side of the university, **Praça da República** plays host to cafes, a shopping district, and the youth hostel. Coimbra has two **train stations:** Coimbra-A and Coimbra-B.

Transportation

Trains: (tel. 82 46 32, 83 49 98, or 83 41 27). **Estação Coimbra-A** is 2 blocks from the lower town center; **Estação Coimbra-B** is 3km northwest of town. Trains from cities outside the region stop in Coimbra-B only. Regional trains stop first at Coimbra-B, then at Coimbra-A; regional trains departing leave in the reverse order. Bus #5 and the Figueira de Foz train connects the 2 stations (5min., 190$). To: Aveiro (45min., 15 per day, 470$); Figueira da Foz (1hr., 1 per hr., 280$); Viseu (2½hr., 4 per day, 720$); Porto (3hr., 13 per day, 900$); Lisbon (3hr., 15 per day, 1300$); Paris (22hr., 1 per day, 23,000$). In general, buses are quicker and more reliable than trains, but also more expensive.

Buses: (tel. 48 40 45), Av. Fernão Magalhães, on the university side of the river about a 10min. walk out of town, past Coimbra-A. Catch regional buses at the series of stops along the river, across the street from Largo Portagem. To: Condeixa (30min.,

PORTUGAL

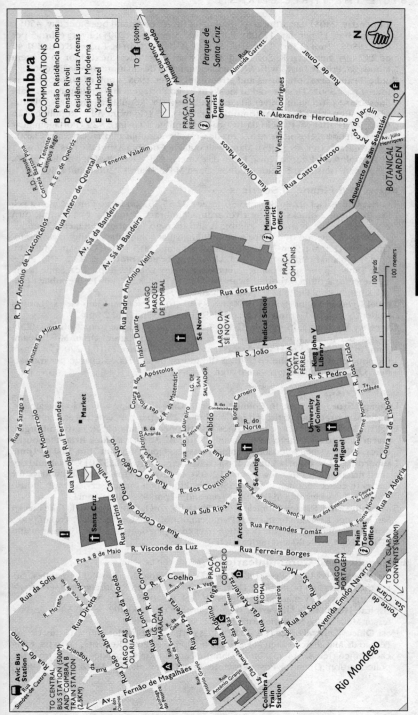

Coimbra

ACCOMMODATIONS

- B Pensão Residência Domus
- D Pensão Rivoli
- A Residência Lusa Atenas
- C Residência Moderna
- E Youth Hostel
- F Camping

PORTUGAL

14 per day, 240$); Luso/Buçaco (45min., on the Viseir-bound bus 5 per day, 450$); Lisbon (3hr., 15 per day, 1250$); Porto (6hr., 5 per day, 1200$); Évora (6hr., 5 per day, 1850$); Faro (12hr., 4 per day, 2800$). **AVIC,** R. João de Ruão, 18 (tel. 201 41 or 237 69), between R. Sofia and Av. Fernão Magalhães, next door to Viagem Mondego. Private buses with A/C and amenities to destinations across Europe.

Public Transportation: Buses and street cars. Fares 190$, book of 10 600$, 3-day tourist pass 850$. Tickets sold in kiosks at Largo Portagem and Pr. República. Main lines are #1 (Portagem-Universidade-Estádio); #2 (Pr. República-Fornos); #3 (Portagem-Pr. República-Santo António dos Olivais); #5 (Coimbra A-Pr. República-São José); #7 (Portagem-Palácio da Justiça-Pr. República-Tovim); #29 (Portagem-near the youth hostel-Hospital); #46 (Cruz de Celas-Pr. República-Portagem-Santa Clara).

Taxis: Politaxis (tel. 48 40 45). Many wait outside Coimbra-A and the bus station.

Car Rental: Avis, Estação Nova, Largo das Ameias (tel. 83 47 86; fax (02) 80 45 95). Coimbra-A, outside the platform door. Open M-F 8:30am-12:30pm and 2:30-7pm.

Tourist and Financial Services

Tourist Office: (tel. 82 86 86 or 83 30 19; fax 82 55 76), off Largo Portagem, in a yellow building 2 blocks up the river from Coimbra-A. From the bus station, turn right, follow the avenue to Coimbra-A and then go to Largo Portagem (15min.). Travel pros provide free **maps** and multilingual accommodation and daytrip info. Open July-Oct. M-F 9am-7pm, Sa-Su 9am-1pm and 2:30-5:30pm; Oct.-Apr. M-F 9am-6pm, Sa-Su and holidays 10am-1pm. **University branch office** (tel. 83 25 91), in Pr. Dom Dinis, up the stairs connecting the university with Pr. República. Same hours as the central office. Another **branch office** (tel. 83 32 02) in Pr. República provides handy info. Open M-F 10am-1pm and 2:30-6pm.

Travel Agency: Tagus (tel. 83 49 99; fax 83 49 16), R. Padre António Vieira. Handles student/youth budget travel. Open M-F 9:30am-12:30pm and 2-6pm.

Currency Exchange: Montepio Geral, C. Estrela, behind the tourist office. 1000$ charge per transaction above 10,000$; otherwise no charge. Open M-F 8:30am-3pm. In a pinch, go to **Hotel Astória,** Av. Emídio Navarro, 21 (tel. 220 55), across the square and down the river from the tourist office. 1000$ charge per transaction. Open 24hr. Bank rates are better.

Local Services

Luggage Storage: None in Coimbra-A or B. **Café Cristal,** Av. Fernão Magalhães, across the street and to the left of Coimbra-A. 250$ per bag. Open M-Sa 1-4pm.

English Bookstores: Three good ones line the pedestrian-only R. Ferreira Borges. **Livraria Bertrand,** Largo da Portagem, 9 (tel. 82 30 14), a block from the tourist office, offers a small selection of English classics. Open M-F 9am-7pm, Sa 9am-1pm.

Laundromat: Lavandaria Lucira, R. Sá da Bandeira, 86 (tel. 82 57 01). Wash and dry a full machine load in a few hours (1200$), or drop it off and wait a few days for Lucira to collect enough clothes (250$ per kg). Open for self-service wash, house wash, and dry cleaning M-F 8:30am-1pm and 3-7pm, Sa 8:30am-1pm.

Swimming Pool: Piscina Municipal (tel. 70 16 05), on R. Dom Manuel I. Take bus #5 São José or #1 Estádio from Largo Portagem outside the tourist office. Trio of pools near the stadium are terrific but often packed. Open daily July-Aug. 10am-1pm and 2-7pm. 160$, over 60 and under 6 free.

Emergency and Communications

Emergency: tel. 112. **Police:** (tel. 82 20 22), R. Olímpio Nicolau Rui Fernandes, facing the market and post office. There is a special division for foreigners *(Serviço de Estrangeiros),* R. Venâncio Rodrigues, 25 (tel. 82 40 45).

Hospital: Hospital da Universidade de Coimbra (tel. 400 400 or 400 500), Pr. Professor Mota Pinto. Near the Cruz de Celas stop on line #29.

Post Office: Central office (tel. 82 81 81) is in the pink powder-puff structure on Av. Fernão de Magalhães. Open M-F 8:30am-6:30pm. For Posta Restante, go to the **Mercado office** (tel. 82 43 56), on R. Olímpio Nicolau Rui Fernandes, across from the police station. Open for Posta Restante, **telephones,** and **fax** M-F 8:30am-6:30pm,

Sa 9am-12:30pm. **Branch office** (tel. 82 72 64), at Pr. República, is open M-F 9am-12:30pm and 2:30-6pm. The **university post office** (tel. 83 43 05), downhill from the large stairs, has the same hours as the Pr. República branch. **Postal Code:** 3000 for central Coimbra.
Telephone Code: (0)39.

ACCOMMODATIONS AND CAMPING

Decent *pensãos* (most on side streets of **Avenida Fernão Magalhães**) start at 3500$ for doubles; pay less and pay the consequences. Fortunately, an excellent youth hostel awaits those bearing the magic HI card and willing to walk about 20 minutes from the river (uphill; take a taxi).

Pousada de Juventude de Coimbra (HI), R. Henrique Seco, 14 (tel./fax 82 29 55). From either Coimbra-A or Largo Portagem, walk 20min. uphill along R. Olímpio Nicolau Rui Fernandes to Pr. República, then up R. Lourenço Azevedo (to the left of the park). Take the 2nd right; the hostel is on the right. Alternatively, take bus #7, 8, 29, or 46 to Pr. República and walk the rest of the way. This recently renovated hostel is clean, bright, and welcoming, albeit quite a walk from the main town center. Consistently hot and high-pressure showers, TV room, kitchen, laundry (1000$ per machine), and parrots make this hostel a cozy place. English-speaking manager. In summer dorms 1500$; doubles 4000$, with bath 5000$. In winter dorms 1300$; doubles 3600$. Breakfast included. Reception daily 9-10:30am and 6pm-midnight. Lockout all other times, but bag drop-off (a godsend in hilly Coimbra) all day.

Residência Moderna, R. Adelino Veiga, 49 (tel. 82 54 13). Welcoming management will usher you into bright comfortable rooms (many with terrace) in this charming *pensão* on a tiny pedestrian street. All with private bath, phone, A/C, and cable TV. Singles 3500-4500$; doubles 5500-6500$. Breakfast included.

Pensão Residencial Domus, R. Adelino Veiga, 62 (tel. 82 85 84). Across the street from the Moderna, this equally comfortable pensão lines up to the competition. Slightly dark, but clean and well-equipped rooms all with private bath, phone, A/C, and cable TV. Double 5500-6500$; triples 7100$. Breakfast included.

Residência Lusa Atenas, Av. Fernão Magalhães, 68 (tel. 82 64 12; fax 82 01 33), on the main avenue between Coimbra-A and the bus station, next to Pensão Avis (look for their neon sign). Phone, A/C, and cable TV in ritzy rooms. Singles 3500$, with bath 4000$; doubles 6000$, with bath 6500$; triples 7000-7500$. Breakfast included.

Pensão Rivoli, Pr. Comércio, 27 (tel. 82 55 50), in a mercifully quiet pedestrian plaza a block downhill (and closer to the river) from busy R. Ferreira Borges, the pedestrian street of Largo Portagem. Well-furnished rooms are comfortably worn. Singles 2200$; doubles 5000$, with shower 5500$; triples with shower 7000$.

Camping: Municipal Campground (tel. 70 14 97), corralled in the recreation complex with the swimming pool and surrounded by noisy avenues. The entrance is at the arch off Pr. 25 de Abril; take the same buses as for the pool (see **Swimming Pool**, p. 610). 231$ per person, 163-174$ per tent, and 294$ per car. Showers free. Reception daily Apr.-Sept. 9am-10pm; Oct.-Mar. 9am-6pm.

FOOD

The best cuisine in Coimbra lies in the area around **Rua Direita,** running west off Pr. 8 de Maio, on the side streets to the west of **Praça Comércio** and **Largo da Portagem,** and near the university district around **Praça República.** Restaurants in these areas serve up steamy portions of *arroz de lampreia* (rice cooked with chunks of lamprey meat—it does not taste like chicken). Don't tell anyone, but you can probably get the best budget meal deal in the entire country at the **UC Cantina,** the university's student cafeteria, located on the right side of R. Oliveiro Matos, about half a block downhill from the base of the steps leading from the university to Pr. República. A mere 270$

buys an entire meal (soup, salad, dessert, and beverage). An international student ID is (theoretically) mandatory. The cantina also has a small bakery (rolls 10$; open daily). Or grab a raw meal at the **mercado** in the huge green warehouse on the right just past the post office, uphill on R. Olímpico Nicolau Rui Fernandes (open daily 8am-1pm). **Supermercado Minipreço,** R. António Granjo, 6C, is in the lower town center; turn left leaving Coimbra-A, and take another left (open M-Sa 9am-8pm).

Café Santa Cruz (tel. 83 36 17). From the tourist office, walk down R. Ferreira Borges until you hit Pr. 8 de Maio. Formerly part of the cathedral (it still has a vaulted ceiling and stained-glass windows); it's the most famous cafe in Coimbra and remains a popular place to tank up on coffee (90$ for a *bica*) or grab a sandwich (around 400$). Open daily 7am-2am.

Restaurante Esplendoroso, R. Sota, 29 (tel. 83 57 11), up a side-street across from Coimbra-A. Splendid Chinese food and prompt service in a relaxing atmosphere. The real steals are the weekday-only lunch *combinados,* which include an egg roll, entree, and rice for around 800$. The flaming *gelado frita com rum* (fried ice cream in rum, 390$) is quite a treat. Open daily noon-3pm and 7-11pm. Visa, MC.

Churrasqueria do Mondego, R. Sargento Mor, 25 (tel. 82 33 55), off R. Sota, 1 block west of Largo Portagem. Great place for a meal among friends and friendly (mostly male) students. Unceremonious service at the counter. Their *frango no churrasco* (barbecued half-chicken, 350$) is classic—watch them cook it over the huge flaming grill. The *ementa turística* translates to a full meal for 750$. Open daily noon-3pm and 6-10:30pm.

Restaurante Democrática, Trav. Rua Nova, 5-7 (tel. 82 37 84), on a tiny lane off R. Sofia (1st full left after city hall). Popular with the young, local crowd for very democratic prices. For something different try *espetadas de porco à Africana* (pork kebabs African-style, 880$). Entrees 850-1200$. Open M-Sa noon-3pm and 7pm-midnight. Visa.

Arco Iris, Av. Fernão de Nagalhães, 22 (tel. 83 33 04). The smell of freshly baked breads of all kinds will lure you into this amazing *"boutique de pão,"* where not only bread but also mini-pizza (350$), countless varieties of sandwiches, and savory coffee abound. Take away or sit down for a warm meal. Open daily 8am-8pm.

SIGHTS

Fortunate perhaps only for those with Olympic-sized quads, the best way to take in Coimbra's old town sights is to climb from the river up to the university—and what a climb it is. Begin the ascent at the ancient **Arco de Almedina,** a remnant of the Moorish town wall, one block uphill from Largo Portagem, next to the Banco Pinto e Sotto Mayor on R. Ferreira Borges. The gate leads to a stepped street aptly named R. Quebra-Costas (Back-Breaker Street). Up a narrow stone stairway looms the hulking 12th-century Romanesque **Sé Velha** (Old Cathedral). *(Open daily 9:30am-12:30pm and 2-5:30pm. Cloisters 100$.)* Take a breather in the cool, dark interior, or get there around noon to follow the guide around the principal tombs and friezes while Gregorian chants echo in the background. Don't miss the cool, peaceful cloister upstairs from the cathedral's main nave. Jump ahead in time a few centuries and follow the signs to nearby **Sé Nova** (New Cathedral), built for the Jesuits in the late 16th century by a succession of builders. *(Open daily 9am-noon and 2-6:30pm. Mass Tu-Sa 6pm, Su 11am and 7pm. Free.)* The architectural competition awarded the cathedral with an ever-more elaborate exterior. Unfortunately, similar attention was not lavished on the interior.

From the new cathedral, it is but a few glorious blocks uphill to the 16th-century **University of Coimbra** campus. Although many of the buildings were built in functional-yet-ugly 1950s concrete style, the venerable law school gets an A in architecture. Enter the center of the old university through the **Porta Férrea** (Iron Gate), off R. São Pedro. These buildings were Portugal's de facto royal palace when Coimbra was the capital of the kingdom. The staircase at the right leads up to the **Sala dos Capelos,** where portraits of Portugal's kings (six born in Coimbra) hang below a beautiful 17th-century ceiling.

(Open daily 10am-noon and 2-5pm. Free.) The **university chapel** and mind-boggling, entirely gilded 18th-century **university library** lie past the Baroque clock tower. Press the buzzer by the library door to enter three golden halls with 300,000 works from the 12th through 19th centuries. *(Open daily 9:30am-noon and 2-5pm. 300$, teachers and students with ID free.)* For some green, walk downhill from the university alongside the **Aque-ducto de São Sebastião** to admire the sculpture and fountains of the **Jardim Botânico.** Another option is to descend the large staircase and pass through Pr. República into the lush **Santa Cruz Park** and its beautiful moss-covered fountain.

Back in the lower town, the **Igreja de Santa Cruz** (Church of the Holy Cross), on Pr. 8 de Maio at the far end of R. Ferreira Borges, is a 12th-century church of somber beauty, with a splendid, barrel-vaulted **sacristía** (sacristy) and ornate **túmulos reals** (tombs) where the first two kings of Portugal rest. *(Church open daily 9am-noon and 3-6pm.)* Crossing the bridge in front of Largo Portagem to the other side of the river, you will find the 14th-century **Convento de Santa Clara-a-Velha.** Since the convent was built on top of a swamp, it sinks a little deeper each year; today it is more than half underground. The convent was abandoned in 1687, but, thankfully, was reno-vated last year to reveal the ancient church founded in 1330 by Queen Isabel, wife of Dom Dinis. The Queen's Gothic tomb was moved uphill to the **Convento de Santa Clara-a-Nova** (1649-1677) when Coimbra's citizenry realized what was going down. Here, the queen's tomb and a later, solid silver tomb rest amid panels telling the story of her life. *(Open daily 8:30am-12:30pm and 2-6:30pm. Free.)* If you have any energy left, consider mingling with the minors at **Portugal dos Pequenitos,** between the new convent and the river bridge, featuring scaled-down reproductions of famous castles and monuments from across Portugal. *(Open M-Sa 10am-5pm. 500$, children 200$.)*

ENTERTAINMENT

Nightlife gets highest honors in Coimbra. After dinner, upend a few bottles with the "in" crowd at outdoor cafes around **Praça República,** which buzzes from midnight to 4am. Around the corner and uphill is the hot (in all senses of the word) disco **Via Lat-ina,** R. Almeida Garrett, 1 (tel. 330 34), near the Santa Cruz garden. Around the cor-ner downhill from Via Latina is **Teatro Académico de Gil Vicente,** which hosts university plays and concerts on most nights around 9 or 10pm. For jazz, try **Dixie Bar,** R. Joaquim António d'Aguiar, 6 (tel. 321 92), one block uphill from the main tourist office, to hear jam sessions until 3am. To absorb the most unrestrained **fado** singers, go from dinner to **Diligência Bar,** R. Nova, 30 (tel. 276 67), off R. Sofia, where *fado* is heard from 10pm to 2am. You can find free-form *fado* in the wee hours at **Bar 1910,** above a gymnasium on R. Simões Castro (open until 4am; beer about 200$). Dance and house music shake the walls of **E.T.C.,** Av. Afonso Hen-rigues, 43 (tel. 40 40 47), until 2am. These listings do not even dent the club scene; blaze your own trail.

Students rampage day and night in Coimbra's famous and distinctive week-long festival, the **Queima das Fitas** (Burning of the Ribbons) in the first or second week of May. The festivities begin when graduating students burn the narrow ribbons they received as first-years and get wide, ornamental ones in return. The carousing contin-ues with midnight *serenatas* (groups of black-clad, serenading youth), wandering musical ensembles, parades, concerts, and folk dancing. Live choral music echoes in festooned streets during the **Festas da Rainha Santa,** held the first week of July in even-numbered years. The firework-punctuated **Feira Popular** in the second week of July offers carnival-type rides and games across the river from the tourist office and traditional Portuguese dancing exhibitions in Pr. Comércio at the Camára Municipa.

PORTUGAL

■ Near Coimbra: Conímbriga

Ten kilometers south of Coimbra, Conímbriga boasts the largest Roman settlement in Portugal. Ongoing excavations of the **ruins** reveal more of the site each year. (Open daily in summer 9am-1pm and 2-8pm; in winter 9am-1pm and 2-6pm. Tu-Su 400$, seniors and students 200$, Sunday mornings free until 1pm. Price includes entrance to the Museu Monográfico de Conímbriga.) Outside the 4th-century town wall lies a luxurious villa, several small shops and houses, and baths complete with sauna and furnace room. Even more amazing are the elaborate and well-preserved mosaics under the shelter of a dark, glass canopy. The nearby **Museu Monográfico de Conímbriga** (tel. 94 11 77) displays artifacts unearthed in the area (open March 15-Sept. Tu-Su 10am-1pm and 2-6pm).

Buses departing from the stop in front of Coimbra-A will drop you off near the ruins; inquire at the Coimbra tourist office for schedules. Buses also run from Coimbra and to sleepy **Condeixa,** 2km away from Conímbriga. The tourism bureau in the Condeixa Town Hall (tel. 94 11 14) also carries info on the ruins. Coimbra to Condeixa buses run surprisingly regularly (30min., departs M-F every hr., Sa-Su 3 per day, 320$), with the last bus returning to Coimbra at 7:45pm. It is a seemingly endless (30min.) walk through Condeixa and the olive groves surrounding it up the road to Conímbriga.

■ Buçaco Forest and Luso

Buçaco (also spelled Bussaco), home to Portugal's most revered forest, has for centuries drawn wanderers in search of a pristine escape from the city. In the 6th century, Benedictine monks settled in the Buçaco Forest, established a monastery, and remained in control until the 1834 disestablishment of all religious orders. The forest owes its fame, however, to the Carmelite monks who arrived here nearly 400 years ago. Selecting the forest for their *desertos* (isolated dwellings for penitence), Carmelites periodically planted trees and plants brought from around the world by missionaries. Today, the fruits of their labor are inspiring.

Dom Manuel II's exuberant **Palácio de Buçaco,** adjoining the old Carmelite **convent,** is a flamboyant display of neo-Manueline architecture. The *azulejos* adorning the outer walls depict scenes from *Os Lusíadas,* the great Portuguese epic about the Age of Discovery (see **Portuguese Literature,** p. 537). The palace is now a luxury hotel *(pousada)* with a doting staff that can provide maps of the forest.

In the forest itself, landmarks include the **Fonte Fria** (Cold Fountain), with water rippling down the entrance steps; the **Vale dos Fetos** (Fern Valley) below; and the **Porta de Reina** (Queen's Gate). Robust walkers trek one hour along the Via Sacra to a sweeping panorama of the countryside from the **Cruz Alta** viewpoint. The little 17th-century **chapels** represent stations of the cross.

Bus service from Coimbra to Buçaco continues on to Viseu (1hr., M-F 5 per day, Sa-Su 3 per day, 440$). Buses leave from Buçaco's station on Av. Fernão de Magalhães, a 15-minute walk from downtown (last bus returns to Coimbra M-F 6:15pm, Sa-Su 4:20pm). Schedules change frequently—confirm departing times at the tourist office.

Luso, a 4km walk downhill from Buçaco, is home to the **Fonte de São João,** the source of all that bottled water you have been gulping in Portugal. Be sure to get directions or a map from the hotel/palace in Buçaco before attempting the long stroll to this tiny town, made famous by a crisp, cold **spring** that spouts water for free public consumption. **Buses** back to Coimbra leave from a couple blocks above the tourist office, across from the natural springs (M-F 5 per day, Sa-Su 3 per day; last bus returns to Coimbra 6:55pm). The staff at Luso's **tourist office** (tel. 93 91 33), on R. Emídio Navarro in the center of town, stacks lists of *pensões,* supplies a map, and is a fountain of knowledge about the area. (Open July-Aug. 12 M-F 10am-8pm, Sa-Su 10am-12:30pm and 2:30-8pm; Aug. 13-June M-F 9am-noon and 3-6pm, Sa-Su 9am-12:30pm and 2:30-5pm.) The **telephone code** is (0)31.

■ Between Coimbra and Porto: Ovar

Ovar, a sleepy, *azulejo*-fronted town hemmed in by two parts *pinheiro* (pine forest) and one part isolated beach, is perfect for a relaxing stopover on the way to Porto. The town's new HI youth hostel is a veritable nirvana, and the nearby **Praia do Furadouro** is charming, quiet, and virtually untouristed. The tiny town, as peaceful and authentic as they come, lies along the railroad tracks about 4km from the coast.

Conveniently, **buses** to the beach and youth hostel stop right in front of the train station and just past the tourist office, to the right of the garden (departs in summer every 15min., in winter every 30min., last bus 7pm, 120$ to the beach, 90$ to the hostel). The **train station** on Largo Serpa Pinto has service to: Aveiro (30min., departs every hr., 250$); Porto (45min., 250$); Coimbra (1hr., 700$); and Lisbon (3½hr., 1750$). The **tourist office** (tel. 57 22 15), on R. Elias Garcia, has maps and transportation information. From the train station head straight ahead (take the right fork), through the traffic circle in Pr. São Cristóvão and follow Av. do Bom Reitor to Régua R. Dr. Manuel Avala, which turns into R. Elias Garcia. (Open daily May-Sept. 9:30am-12:30pm and 2-5:30pm; Nov.-Apr. 10am-12:30pm and 2-5:30pm.) The **police** (tel. 57 29 99) are on R. José Estêvão. The **postal code** is 3880. The **telephone code** is (0)56.

If you are an HI member, put your feet up at the brand-new **Pousada de Juventude de Ovar (HI),** Av. Dom Manuel I (Estrada Nacional 327) (tel. 59 18 32). Take the bus to the beach (see above), get off at the stop right before the traffic circle 2km outside of town, turn right (follow the signs to Porto), and walk for about 10 minutes. You will see the sign for the hostel on the right. Pristine rooms, a relaxed bar with billiards and satellite TV, and home-cooked meals (lunch or dinner 900$) make this modern hostel a prime rest stop. **Bike rental** and **horseback riding** are also available. (In summer dorms 1700$; doubles with bath 4200$. In winter dorms 1400$; doubles with bath 3550$. Reception daily 9am-midnight. Call ahead in high season.) There is **camping** on **Praia do Furadouro** (tel. 59 14 71), 4km from the city center, with amenities including a restaurant, mini-mart, sports fields, and a hairdresser. (470$ per person, 305$ per tent and per car. Lower prices in the off season. Reception daily 8am-10pm. Open Feb.-Nov.) For food, shop at the **Mercado Municipal** (open M-Sa 9am-1pm); there are also a series of **food stalls** just off the Estrada nacional by the youth hostel.

■ Figueira da Foz

Figueira da Foz's best feature is undoubtedly its beach, a 3 sq. km Sahara-like expanse. Even when packed, it appears to have ample room for sunbathing and perfectly good (albeit chilly) sea-bathing. Figueira is also one of the biggest party towns in Portugal, a place where pleasure-seekers that don't mind the proliferation of ugly concrete buildings come to celebrate the sun and the neon sign. At night, tanned couples and rowdy youths crowd the numerous bars and discos and press their luck at the infamous casino. For all those who seek a bit of relaxation, the little fishing town of Buarcos, on the northern end of the beach, replaces mindless entertainment with a badly needed breath of serenity.

ORIENTATION AND PRACTICAL INFORMATION

Packed with hotels, beachfront **Avenida 25 de Abril** is the busy lifeline that distinguishes town from beach; after the fortress, it turns into **Rua 5 de Outubro** and leads toward the train station. Four blocks inland and parallel to the avenue, **Rua Bernardo Lopes** harbors semi-affordable *pensões* and restaurants. Much of the action in Figueira centers in the casino-cinema disco complex on this street.

PORTUGAL

Trains: (tel. 283 16), Largo da Estação, near the bridge. Trains are the easiest way to reach Coimbra and Porto. The station is an easy walk to the tourist office and beach (25min.). With the river to the left, Av. Saraiva de Carvalho becomes R. 5 de Outubro at the fountain and then curves into Av. 25 de Abril. To: Porto (3hr., 8 per day, 1120$); Lisbon (3½hr., 7 per day, 1400$); Coimbra (1hr., 13 per day, 280$).

Buses: Terminal Rodoviário (tel. 230 95), 15min. from the tourist office. Facing the church, turn right onto R. Dr. Santos Rocha. Walk about 10min. toward the waterfront and turn right onto R. 5 de Outubro, which curves into Av. 25 de Abril. To: Leiria (1½hr., 8 per day, 610$); Alcobaça (1½hr., 3 per day, 900$); Fátima (1½hr., 3 per day, 1000$); Coimbra (2hr., 6 per day, 645$); Aveiro (2hr., 4 per day, 950$); Lisbon (3½hr., 4 per day, 1350$); Faro (12hr., 1 per day, 2700$).

Taxis: (tel. 235 00, 237 88, or 232 18), at the bus or train stations. 24hr. service.

Tourist Office: (tel. 226 10; fax 285 49), Av. 25 de Abril, next to the Aparthotel Atlântico at the very end of the airport terminal complex. Useful map. English spoken. **Luggage storage** available. Open June-Sept. daily 9am-11pm; Oct.-May M-F 9am-12:30pm and 2-5:30pm.

Currency Exchange: Banco Crédito Predial Português (tel. 284 58), on R. João de Lemos, a small street between R. Dr. António Dinis and R. Cândido dos Reis. 750$ commission for cash exchange; no charge for traveler's checks. Open daily 8:30am-3pm. Major hotels near the tourist office exchange when banks are closed.

Emergency: dial 112. **Police:** (tel. 220 22), R. Joaquim Carvalho, near the bus station and the park.

Hospital: Hospital Distrital (tel. 200 00), in Gala, across the river.

Post Office: Main office, Passeio Infante Dom Henrique, 41 (tel. 241 01), off R. 5 de Outubro. Open for Posta Restante and **telephones** M-F 8:30am-6:30pm, Sa 9am-12:30pm. More convenient **branch** at R. Miguel Bombarda, 76 (tel. 230 10). Open for stamps and **telephones** M-F 9am-12:30pm and 2:30-6pm. **Postal Code:** 3080.

Telephone Code: (0)33.

ACCOMMODATIONS AND FOOD

Scour **Rua Bernardo Lopes** and neighboring streets for reasonable *pensões*. Proprietors may demand inordinate prices for rooms (especially in summer). Budget rooms are often questionable and feature dirty carpeting. Arrive early in the day to assure vacancies; many managers will not reserve rooms by phone in high season. Restaurants are more expensive than the Portuguese norm in Figueira, but hope (and good food) lies around **Rua Bernardo Lopes.** The truly lazy frequent any of the numerous eateries right on the beach. A local **market** sets up beside the municipal garden on R. 5 de Outubro (open in summer M-Sa 7am-7pm; in winter Su-F 8am-5pm, Sa 8am-1pm). For imported foods, check out **Supermercado Ovo,** on the corner of R. A. Dinis and R. B. Lopes (open M-F 9am-1pm and 3-7pm).

Pensão Central, R. Bernardo Lopes, 36 (tel. 223 08), is centrally located, next to Supermarket Ovo, down the street from the casino complex and all the action. High ceilings and huge rooms, comfortable and well furnished. All 15 rooms have TV and bath. Singles 4500$; doubles 6000$; triples 7000$. Winter discount. Breakfast included for singles. Credit cards accepted.

Pensão Residencial Bela Figueira, R. Miguel Bombarda, 13 (tel. 227 28; fax 299 60), 2 blocks from the tourist office and above an Indian restaurant. 12 simply furnished rooms all with phones, some with TVs. In summer singles 4500-6200$; doubles 5000-6950$; triples 5000-7500$. In winter singles 2500-4200$; doubles 3000-4950$; triples 3000-5500$.

Camping: Parque Municipal de Campismo da Figueira da Foz Municipal (tel. 327 42 or 330 33), on Estrada de Buarcos. With the beach on your left, walk up Av. 25 de Abril and turn right at the roundabout on R. Alexandre Herculano, then turn left at Parque Santa Catarina going up R. Joaquim Sotto-Mayor past Palácio Sotto-Mayor. Or take a taxi from bus or train station (500$). Excellent site complete with an Olympic-size pool, tennis courts, market, and **currency exchange.** 400$ per person, under 10 free, 300$ per tent and per car. Showers 100$. Reception daily June-

Sept. 8am-8pm; Oct.-May 8am-7pm. Silence reigns midnight-7am. June-Sept. each party must have a minimum of 2 people. Open year-round.

Restaurante Rancho, R. Miguel Bombarda, 40-44 (tel. 220 19), 2 blocks from the tourist office. Packed with locals at lunchtime. Hefty, delicious entrees (650-1100$) such as *chocos grelhados* (grilled cuttlefish, 650$). The *ementa turística* is a great deal (3 courses 1100$). Open M-Sa 11am-10pm.

Restaurante Bela Figueira, R. Miguel Bombardo, 13 (tel. 227 28), beneath the *pensão* of the same name. Tasty Indian food, including vegetable curry with *roti* (1000$) and chicken biryani (1200$). Several good vegetarian options are available, as is a less expensive menu with traditional Portuguese food. Entrees around 850$. Open daily noon-midnight. Credit cards accepted.

SIGHTS AND ENTERTAINMENT

In Figueira, the entertainment *is* the sight (and vice versa). If you get tired of lounging on the beach, head next door to Buarcos where remnants of a fishing village provide a colorful ambiance. The **Museu Municipal do Doutor Santos Rocha** (tel. 245 09), in Parque Abadias, re-awakens your intellect with everything from ancient coins to the fashions of Portuguese nobility. *(Open Tu-Su 9am-12:30pm and 2-5pm. Free.)* **Casa do Paço,** Largo Prof. Vitar Guerra, 4 (tel. 221 59), is decorated with 6888 Delft tiles that fortuitously washed ashore after a shipwreck. *(Open M-F 9:30am-12:30pm and 2-5pm. Free.)* The modest exterior of the **Palácio Sotto Mayor** (tel. 221 21), R. Joaquim Sotto Mayor, belies the shameless extravagance inside. *(Open Tu-Su 2-6pm. 150$.)* Lavish green marble columns line the main hallway, and gold leaf covers the ceiling.

Most people, however, do not come to Figueira for the culture, where hard-core partying is the name of the game. Nightlife takes off between 10pm and 2am, depending on the disco or bar, and continues all night. Joints line **Avenida 25 de Abril,** next to and above the tourist office. A student crowd gathers at **Bergantim** (tel. 238 85), R. Dr. António Lopes Guimarães, inland from the train station. Do the disco thing at **CC Café** (tel. 34 18 88), just off the water at the end of the ramp. A happening crowd can be found at **Bar 31,** a block away from the beach on R. Cândido dos Reis. Most popular of all is the **casino** complex on R. Bernardo Lopes (tel. 220 41) that includes a **nightclub** (cover charge 1500$), **cinema** (500$), and **arcade.** *(Casino open daily July-Aug. 4pm-4am; Sept.-June 3pm-3am.)* Entry to the slot machines and bingo is free. You must be over 18 and show proper ID if you wish to gamble. There is also a show, usually a pseudo-Las Vegas revue, at night. Figueira's standard party mode shifts from high gear to warp speed during the **Festa de São João** (June 6-July 9), featuring free public concerts every night. Around 5am, a huge rowdy procession heads for the beach at nearby Buarcos where all involved take a *banho santo* (holy bath). The **Festival de Cinema da Figueira da Foz** screens international flicks in September.

■ Aveiro

The old center of Aveiro is graced with a network of charming canals, along which traditional *gonalas*—polished, seaweed- and sea salt-laden fishing boats reminiscent of Venice's gondolas—drift out to sea. This maritime town boasts an amalgam of historical anecdotes, and houses the convent where canonized princess Santa Joana spent her days (see p. 619), but is most renowned for its numerous swimmable beaches. Prices may seem unjustifiably high here—rebel by camping at scenic São Jacinto.

ORIENTATION AND PRACTICAL INFORMATION

Aveiro is split by the *canal central* and a parallel street, **Avenida Dr. Lourenço Peixinho,** running from the train station to **Praça Humberto Delgado** (a *praça* that is

PORTUGAL

really no more than a few bridges spanning the canals). The fishermen's quarter of **Beira Mar** lies north of the *canal central*. The port to the south is the residential district and contains all of Aveiro's historical monuments.

To reach the **tourist office** from the **train station,** walk up Av. Dr. Lourenço Peixinho (the left-most street) until you reach the bridge; the office is on the right-hand side in the next block. You can also hop on a bus (departs every 15min., 150$) from the station. Trains are the most convenient means of travel in and out of Aveiro and the Rota da Luz region.

Trains: Largo Estação (tel. 244 85), at the end of Av. Dr. Lourenço Peixinho. To: Águeda (8 per day); Porto (30min., 21 per day, 330$); Coimbra (1hr., 21 per day, 460$); Braga (1½hr., 3 per day, 860$); Lisbon (5hr., 21 per day, 1600$).

Buses: Since the nearest Rodoviária station is 19km away in Águeda, trains are more convenient for long-distance travel. Eight buses per day go from the train station to Águeda (230$). **AVIC-Mondego,** R. Comandante Rocha Cunha, 55 (tel. 237 47), runs from the train station to the Águeda station and then to Praia da Mira (45min., 5 per day, 400$) and Figueira da Foz (2½hr., 6 per day, 650$). For buses to Fortalezada Barra, see **Ferries** (below).

Ferries: All ferries leave from Forte da Barra; buses go from the railway station to Forte da Barra (30min., 12 per day 7am-6pm, 220$). Boats sail to São Jacinto (May 2-Sept. 20 2 per day); reserve early via **Trans Ria** (tel. 33 10 95), on Av. Marginal in São Jacinto.

Taxis: (tel. 229 43 or 237 66). Taxis congregate around the train station and at the end of R. João Mendonça.

Tourist Office: R. João Mendonça, 8 (tel. 236 80 or 207 60; fax 283 26), in an old-style building off Pr. Humberto Delgado, on the street to the right of the canal as you are facing the ocean. Cheerful English-speaking staff doles out maps and lodging advice. If you have the time (and desire), watch a video about local fishermen. Free daytime **luggage storage.** Open June 16-Sept. 14 M-F 9am-8pm, Sa 9am-8pm, Su 9am-7pm; Sept. 15-June 15 M-F 9am-7pm, Sa 9am-1pm and 2:30-5:30pm.

Currency Exchange: Hotel Pomba Branca, R. Luís Gomes de Carvalho, 23 (tel. 225 29), 1st right on Av. Dr. Lourenço Peixinho from the train station. 24hr. service at bank rates. **ATM** at **Banco Fonsecas e Burnay,** R. Coimbra, 2 (tel. 231 31), across from the tourist office; more ATMs lie between the train station and tourist office.

Laundromat: Lavandaria União, Av. Dr. Lourenço Peixinho, 292 (tel. 235 56), near the train station. 500$ per kg. Open M-F 9am-1pm and 1:30-7pm.

Emergency: (tel. 112). **Police:** (tel. 220 22 or 211 37), Pr. Marquês de Pombal.

Hospital: Av. Dr. Artur Ravara (tel. 221 33), near the park across the canal.

Post Office: Estação Vera Cruz, Pr. Marquês de Pombal (tel. 271 00). Cross the main bridge and walk up R. Coimbra past the town hall. Open for Posta Restante, **fax,** and **telephones** M-F 8:30am-6:30pm, Sa 9am-12:30pm. A **branch office,** Av. Dr. Lourenço Peixinho, 169 (tel. 274 84), has similar services and is centrally located (2 blocks from the train station). Open M-F 8:30am-6:30pm. **Postal Code:** 3800.

Telephone Code: (0)34.

ACCOMMODATIONS AND CAMPING

The *pensões* lining Av. Dr. Lourenço Peixinho and the streets around Pr. Marquês de Pombal in the old city are more expensive than average but almost always have vacancies. The tourist office can assist in finding a place to stay.

Residencial Santa Joana, Av. Dr. Lourenço Peixinho, 227 (tel. 286 04), a block from the train station on the left. 5 floors stack spacious, no-frills, and reasonably priced rooms in a transport-friendly location. Naturally cool in summer. All rooms feature phone, TV, and private bath. Singles 3500$; doubles 5500$.

Residencial Estrêla, R. José Estêvão, 4 (tel. 238 18), in an elegant building overlooking Pr. Humberto Delgado. Grand stairway illuminated by an oval skylight. Lordly rooms are on the 1st floor; servant-type quarters higher up. Friendly, English-speaking owner. All rooms with TV. Singles 4000$, with bath 4500$; doubles 5500$,

PORTUGAL

with bath 6000$; triples 8000$. Prices drop by about 1000$ in winter. Breakfast included.

Pensão Ferro, R. dos Marnotos, 30 (tel. 222 14). From the tourist office turn right, then take the 2nd street on the right. 35 rooms featuring high ceilings, windows (request them), and clean common baths make this airy, pastel-colored *pensão* a soothing place to stay. Singles 3000$; doubles 4500$.

Camping: Orbitur São Jacinto (tel. 482 84; fax 481 22), on the beach northwest of Aveiro. Take the bus from the Canal Central stop to Forte da Barra (10min., 220$), then hop on the boat to São Jacinto (10min., 135$). Hike 5km or take a bus (150$) to the campsite. Sometimes crowded. 570$ per person and per tent, 480$ per car. Reception open daily Jan. 16-Nov. 15. 8am-10pm.

The Heart of the Matter

There's love, and there's *love*. Exhibit number one in the latter category is Dom Pedro I. While a prince, he fell head over heels for Inês de Castro, the daughter of a Spanish nobleman and lady-in-waiting to his first wife. Pedro's father, Afonso IV, objected to the romance, fearing such an alliance would open the Portuguese throne to Spanish domination. Pedro and Inês fled to Bragança where the couple secretly wed. Soon thereafter the disgruntled Afonso had Inês killed. Upon rising to the throne two years later, Pedro promptly—and personally—ripped out the hearts of the men who had slit his young wife's throat and proceeded to eat the broken *corações*. Henceforth, the hardy king became known as Pedro the Cruel. In a disheartening ceremony, he had Inês's body exhumed, dressed her meticulously in royal robes, set her on the throne, and officially deemed her his queen. She was eventually reinterred in an exquisitely carved tomb in the king's favorite monastery, the Mosteiro de Santa Maria de Alcobaça. The king would later join her, both figuratively and literally, in a tomb directly opposite hers. The inscription on their elaborately carved tombs, *"Até ao fim do mundo"* (until the end of the world), attests to Pedro's intention that the couple finally reunite—face to face—at the moment of resurrection.

PORTUGAL

FOOD

Seafood restaurants are common, but prices will make you want to catch your own fish. Cast around for cheaper gruel off **Avenida Dr. Lourenço Peixinho** and **Rua José Estêvão.** Aveiro's specialty is a dessert pastry called *ovos moles* (sweetened egg yolks), available at most cafes in town. For normal egg yolks, patronize **Supermercado Mini Preço,** Av. Dr. Lourenço Peixinho, 132.

Restaurante Salimar, R. Combatentes da Grande Guerra, 6, 2nd fl. (tel. 251 08), across the river and a block uphill from the tourist office. Fragrant *bacalhau no churrasco* (barbecued cod, 1200$) is served amid nautical decor. Their specialty is a bubbling, orange-red broth swimming with rice and seafood called *arroz de marisco* (1100$; for 2 people 2000$). Open daily 8am-midnight.

Sonatura Restaurante Self-Service Naturista, R. Clube dos Galitos, 6 (tel. 244 74), directly across the canal from the tourist office. **Vegetarian**-macrobiotic-dietetic-food-store-restaurant serves up 2 daily menus (700$) that include soup, organic bread, and an entree. Watch for their miso soup specials, made with delectable Aveiro seaweed. Open M-F 10am-10pm, Sa 10am-3pm.

Restaurante Zico, R. José Estêvão, 52 (tel. 296 49), off Pr. Humberto Delgado. Very popular with the locals. Pork on *prego de porco* (pork steak with fries, 650$) or try *omelete de camarão* (shrimp omelette, 950$). Entrees 950-1500$. Save room for the calorie-ridden desserts. Open M-Sa 8am-2am.

SIGHTS AND ENTERTAINMENT

Aveiro is known for its beautiful *azulejo* facades and its great beaches. Don't miss the former because you are spending too much time on the latter. Simple but strikingly blue *azulejos* coolly make up the walls of the **Igreja da Misericórdia** in Pr. da

República, across the canal and a block uphill from the tourist office. In the same square, the regal **Paça do Concelho** (town hall) flaunts its French design, complete with bell tower. The real thriller of the compact old town is the **Museu de Aveiro** (1458), R. Sta. Joana Princesa (tel. 232 97). *(Open Tu-Su 10am-12:30pm and 2-5pm. 250$, seniors and students 125$.)* The museum is in a convent, covered by flamboyant gilded woodwork in the interior, where King Afonso and the Infanta Joana, who at 18 wished to become a nun despite her father's objections, had a royal battle in 1472. She won and continued to live in the convent, caring for the sick and poor of Aveiro until tuberculosis carried her away when she was barely 30. Beneath *azulejo* panels depicting the story of her life is Sta. Joana's Renaissance tomb, supported by the heads of four angels and one of the most famous works of art in Portugal. The chapel beyond showcases the bewildering excesses similar to Baroque woodcarving; its *coro alto* (high chorus) is lined with lacquered panels reminiscent of *chinoiserie*.

Don't spend all your time *azulejo*-gawking. Neighboring **beach** towns and their beautiful sand dunes, like **Dunas de São Jacinto** (approx. 10km away), merit daytrips and are easily accessible by ferry (see **Ferries,** p. 618). At night, tap into the watering holes lining **Rua Canal de São Rogue,** or strut your stuff with the beautiful people at neighboring **Salpoente, Estrondo Bar,** and **Urgência.** The bars around **Largo Praça de Peixe,** in the old city, and the bars in the shopping center/entertainment complex, Av. Dr. Lourenço Peixinho, 146, are also definite possibilities. For four weeks starting in mid-July, the city shakes for the **Festa da Ria.** As part of the festivities, dancers groove on a floating stage in the middle of the *canal central*.

Douro and Minho

Although their landscapes and shared Celtic past invite comparison with neighboring Galicia in Spain, the Douro and Minho regions of northern Portugal are more populated, wealthier, and developing far faster than much of Galicia. The women's traditional local costume, which includes layer upon layer of gold necklaces encrusted with charms, attests to the area's mineral wealth and is indicative of the region's prosperous history. To add legacy to this affluence, the Kingdom of Portugal originated here in 1143 when Alfonso Henriques defeated the Moors in Guimarães. But neither wealth nor history impinge on the spectacular greenery, making the Douro and Minho a haven for nature lovers. Hundreds of trellised vineyards that grow grapes for *porto* and *vinho verde* wines beckon connoisseurs, while houses tiled in brilliant *azulejos* draw visitors to charming, quiet streets.

The region's mild coastal climate is too cool to attract the beach crowd until July, and only a few ambitious travelers ever make it past Porto and the Douro Valley to the greens and blues of the Alto Minho, which hugs the border with Spain. Happily untouristed, the cities of Vila Nova de Cerveira, Braga, Viana do Castelo, and Guimarães are truly memorable for the few who do make it there.

■ Porto (Oporto)

There's an old Portuguese proverb that says, "Coimbra sings, Braga prays, Lisbon sings, and Porto works." All that work has paid off: Porto is now one of Portugal's most sophisticated and modern cities. Although today it is a bustling center for all types of business, the source of its greatest fame can be sniffed in the bouquet of its *vinho do Porto*—port wine. Developed by English merchants in the early 18th century, the port wine industry is at the origin of the city's successful economy. Magnificently situated on a dramatic gorge cut by the Douro River, 6km from the sea, Portugal's second-largest city often seems more frenetic than Lisbon, even though its energy is framed within an elegance reminiscent of Paris or Prague. Granite church towers pierce the skyline, closely packed orange-tiled houses huddle along the river, and three of Europe's most graceful bridges (one credited to Gustave Eiffel of Eiffel Tower fame) span the gorge above.

Porto's history is the stuff from which nationalism is made. When native son Henry the Navigator geared to conquer Ceuta (a soon-to-be Christian base in Africa), Porto residents slaughtered their cattle, gave all the meat to the Portuguese fleet, and kept only the entrails for themselves. The tasty dish *tripas à moda do Porto* commemorates this culinary self-sacrifice; to this day, the people of Porto are known as *tripeiros* (tripe-eaters), although the fetid bouquet of that particular delicacy belies the absolutely savory scent of their gloried wine. Whatever the smell, capture it and follow your nose to Porto, a graceful city well worth a visit.

ORIENTATION AND PRACTICAL INFORMATION

Get ready to…get lost. Constant traffic and a chaotic maze of one-way streets fluster even the most well-oriented of travelers; find your location on the map ASAP. At the very heart of the city is the hillside **Praça da Liberdade,** home to the townhall. One of Porto's two train stations, **Estação São Bento,** lies right in the middle of town, just off the bottom of Pr. Liberdade. The other, **Estação de Campanhã,** is 2km east of the city. The **Ribeira** district is a few blocks to the south, directly across the bridge from **Vila Nova de Gaia,** where 80-odd port wine lodges contentedly ferment.

Transportation

Flights: Aeroporto Francisco de Sá Carneiro (tel. 941 32 60 or 941 32 70). Take bus #44 or 56 from Pr. Lisbon (departs every 20min.). **TAP Air Portugal,** Pr. Mouzinho de Albuquerque, 105 (tel. 948 22 91). To Lisbon and Madrid.

PORTUGAL

Trains: Estação de Campanhã (tel. 57 41 61). Porto's main station east of the center, through which all trains pass. Frequent connections to Estação São Bento (5min., 120$). To: Aveiro (1½hr., 21 per day, 370$); Viana do Castelo (2hr., 11 per day, 650$); Braga, via Nine (2hr., 11 per day, 450$); Coimbra (2½hr., 12 per day, 910$); Lisbon (4½hr., 5 per day, 1950$); Madrid, via Entroncamento (12-13hr., 2 per day, 9100$); Paris (28hr., 1 per day, 24,000$). **Estação de São Bento** (tel. 200 10 54), centrally located 1 block off Pr. Liberdade, is the terminus for trains with mostly local and nearby regional routes. If your train stops at Campanhã, it is usually best to take a connecting train to São Bento. Buses also run to Pr. Liberdade and beyond (departs every 30min., 170$). There is a handy info office at Estação São Bento, open as long as trains are running. Minimal English, but fluent French.

Buses: There is no central bus station; over 20 different companies each with their own garage. Some of the largest are: **Garagem Atlântico,** R. Alexandre Herculano, 366 (tel. 200 69 54). To: Coimbra (1½hr., 10 per day, 1200$); Viseu (2hr., 2 per day, 950$); Lisbon (5½hr., 5 per day, 1900$). **Auto Viação do Minho,** Pr. D. Filipa de Lencastre (tel. 200 61 21), 1 block from Av. Aliados. To Braga (2hr., departs every 30min., 600$) and Viana do Castelo (2hr., 12 per day, 650$). **Rodoviária Nacional** (tel. 200 31 52), R. Alexandre Herculano, also runs to Braga and Viana do Castelo. **Rodonorte** (tel. 200 56 27), R. Atenou Comercial do Porto, a.k.a. Trav. Passos Manuel, 1 block from R. Sá da Bandeira. To Vila Real (4hr., 6 per day, 1100$). **Internorte,** Pr. Galiza, 96 (tel. 69 32 20 or 48 75). To Spain, France, Belgium, Switzerland, Germany, and Luxembourg.

Public Transportation: A *Passe Turístico* discount pass is available for Porto's trolleys and buses. 4-day pass 1600$, 7-day 2150$. Single trip ticket purchased on the bus 160$, one-day unlimited ticket 350$. Tickets can be purchased at a small kiosk on the corner, half a block downhill and across the street from Estação de São Bento (discount single trip only 80$). You can pre-purchase tickets for half price.

Taxis: Raditáxis, R. Alegria, 1802 (tel. 52.80 61). 24hr.

Tourist and Financial Services

Tourist Office: R. Clube dos Fenianos, 25, just off the top of Pr. Liberdade. Robotically efficient multilingual staff doles out maps and specialized brochures. Open July-Sept. M-F 9am-7pm, Sa 9am-4pm; Su 10am-1pm; Oct.-June M-F 9:30am-5:30pm, Sa 9am-4pm. **Branch office,** Pr. Dom João I, 25 (tel. 31 75 14), at R. Bonjardim. Open M-F 9am-7pm, Sa 9am-2pm, Su 10am-2pm. There also are 24hr. multilingual **computer info stands** in the main shopping centers and the larger squares; one sits in front of the McDonald's in Pr. Liberdade.

Currency Exchange: ATMs line Pr. Liberdade, and are omnipresent throughout the city. Most banks on Pr. Liberdade offer currency exchange, and some have automatic currency exchange machines outside. Open M-F 8:30am-3pm.

American Express: Top Tours, R. Alferes Malheiro, 96 (tel. 208 27 85). Facing the town hall at the top of Pr. Liberdade, take the street to the left of the building and turn left after 2 blocks. Open M-F 9am-12:30pm and 2:30-6:30pm.

Local Services

Luggage Storage: Free in **tourist office** during the day. At **Estação de São Bento** in lockers to the right as you enter the platform (400-900 per 48hr.).

Laundromat: Lavanderia Penguin, Av. Boavista (tel. 69 50 32), in shopping center Brasília. One block past the youth hostel. Self-service (a rarity). 1500$ per 5.5kg load. Open M-Sa 10am-11pm.

Public Showers and Toilets: Pr. Liberdade (in the middle of the garden in the traffic island), Pr. Batalha, and Largo do Viriato. Open 24hr. Coin-operated toilets throughout the city.

English Bookstore: Livraria Británico, R. José Falcão, 184 (tel. 32 39 30). Decent choice of paperbacks: trendy, intellectual, classic, and trashy; plus hardcovers and magazines. Open M-F 9am-7pm, Sa 9:30am-1pm. **Livraria Diário de Notícias,** R. Sá de Bandeira, 5, across from Estação São Bento. Smaller selection of books. Maps. Open M-F 9am-7pm, Sa 9am-1pm.

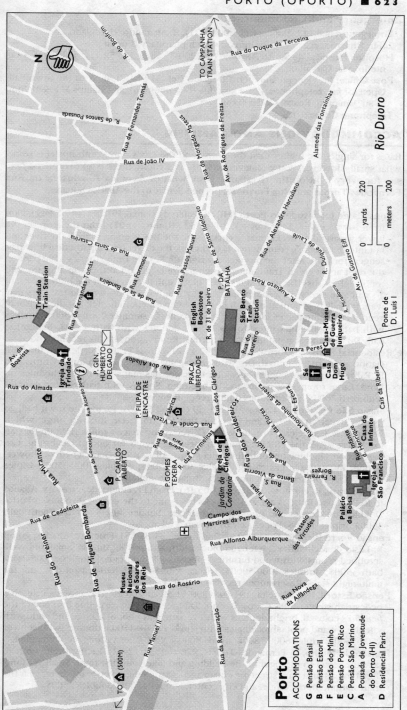

PORTUGAL

Rio Duoro

TO CAMPANHA
TRAIN STATION

Rua do Duque da Terceina

R. do Bonfim

Rua de Fernandes Tomás

R. de Santos Pousada

Rua de Morgado Mata

Av. de Rodrigues de Freitas

Alameda das Fontainhas

Rua de João IV

Rua de Passo Manuel

R. de Santo Ildefonso

Rua de Santa Catarina

Rua de Fernandes Tomás

Rua de Sá da Bandeira

Rua Formosa

P. DA
BATALHA

Rua de Alexandre Herculano

R. Augusto Rosa

Parque de Laulé

R. Dulho

Av. de Gustavo Eiff

R. Miragaia

220 yards
200 meters

Trindade
Train Station

English
Bookstore

São Bento
Train Station

Casa-Museu
de Guerra
Junqueiro

Vimara Peres

Ponte de
D. Luís I

R. de 31 de Janeiro

Rua do
Loureiro

Igreja da
Trindade

P. GEN.
HUMBERTO
DELGADO

Av. da
Boavista

Rua do Almada

Av. dos Aliados

PRAÇA
LIBERDADE

Rua dos Clérigos

Sé

Casa
Dom
Hugo

Rua Mouzinho da Silveira

Cais da Ribeira

Rua do Almada

Rua Ricardo José

P. FILIPA DE
LENCASTRE

Rua Conde de Vizela

Rua da Fábrica

Rua das Flores

R. da Vitória

Rua da Conceição

P. CARLOS
ALBERTO

Rua do

R. das Carmelitas

Galeria de Paris

Igreja de
Cordoaria Clérigos

Jardim de
Cordoaria

Rua de São Bento da Vitória

Rua dos Caldeireiros

Rua da Esteira

Casa do
Infante

Rua Infante D. Henrique

Rua Mirante

Rua de Cedofeita

P. GOMES
TEIXEIRA

Rua S. Bento da Vitória

R. Ferreira Borges

Igreja de
São Francisco

Rua do Breiner

Rua de Miguel Bombarda

Campo dos
Martires da Patria

Passeio
das Virtudes

Palácio
da Bolsa

Rua das Taipas

Rua Alfonso Alburquerque

Museu Nacional
de Soares
dos Reis

Rua do Rosário

Rua Nova
da Alfândega

TO A (500M)

Rua Manuel II

Rua da Restauração

Porto

ACCOMMODATIONS

G Pensão Brasil
B Pensão Estoril
F Pensão do Minho
E Pensão Porto Rico
C Pensão São Marino
A Pousada de Joventude
   do Porto (HI)
D Residencial Paris

Emergency and Communications

Emergency: dial 112. **Police:** (tel. 200 68 21), R. Alexandre Herculano.

24Hr. Pharmacy: call 118 for info on which pharmacy is open.

Hospital: Hospital de Santo António (tel. 200 73 54 or 200 52 41), on R. Prof. Vicente José de Carvalho.

Post Office: Pr. General Humberto Delgado (tel. 31 98 77), next to the town hall. Open for **fax, telephones,** Posta Restante (60$ per item), and stamps M-F 8am-9pm, Sa-Su 9am-6pm. **Postal Code:** 4000.

Telephone Code: (0)2.

ACCOMMODATIONS AND CAMPING

Rates for singles are higher than the norm, and the city's only youth hostel is somewhat small. However, you will never go without a room; there is an overpriced *pensão* for every light on the riverbank. Look west of **Avenida Aliados,** or on **Rua Fernandes Tomás** and **Rua Formosa,** perpendicular to the Aliados Square.

Pousada de Juventude do Porto (HI), R. Paulo da Gama, 551 (tel. 617 72 47), 2km from town center. Take bus #3, 20, or 52 (10min., 160$) from the stop on the lower west end of Pr. Liberdade (make sure the bus is going toward the river and not into the square). From here it is tricky; ask the driver or sympathetic fellow passengers for help. After the bus makes a right on R. Júlio Dinis (there's a big park on the right and a green Tranquilidade sign in front), get off at the stop after the 2nd traffic light. Cross the street and walk 1 block uphill; turn left at the billboard on to a small side street. In a somewhat sketchy neighborhood—women travelers may want to walk in groups at night. It is not the newest youth hostel, but the Carlsberg vending machine makes for a lively social scene. In summer dorms 1800$; doubles with bath 5000$. In winter dorms 1750$; doubles with bath 4500$. Reception daily 9-11am and 6pm-midnight. No curfew. Reservations highly recommended.

Residencial Paris, R. Fábrica, 27-9 (tel. 32 14 21). Cross Pr. Liberdade from the train station and turn left onto R. Dr. Artur de Magalhães Basto, which quickly turns into R. Fábrica. Friendly English-speaking manager has maps and train schedules on hand. Large rooms, TV room, and lush garden. Singles with bath 5000$; doubles with bath 7000$. Reservations highly recommended.

Pensão São Marino, Pr. Carlos Alberto, 59 (tel. 32 54 99). Facing the town hall, go up the street on the left and take the first left on R. Dr. Ricardo Jorge, which becomes R. Conceição; turn left on R. Oliveiras and make a quick right on Pr. Carlos Alberto. Ask the efficient, English-speaking owner for one of the bright, carpeted rooms looking out onto the quiet *praça*. All 14 rooms have a bath or shower, phone, TV, and winter heating. Singles 3000-4500$; doubles 4000-6500$; triples 4500-7000$. Off-season discount 500$. Breakfast included.

Pensão Brasil, R. Formosa, 178 (tel. 31 05 16). From Pr. Liberdade, cross Av. Aliados to R. Formosa; Brasil is about 3½ blocks up. Some of the cheapest rooms in Porto. Doubles are cleaner and brighter than singles. Singles 2000$; doubles with bath 3500$; triples 4500$. Prices vary by season. Call ahead.

Pensão Porto Rico, R. Almada, 237, 2nd fl. (tel. 31 87 85). From Av. Aliados, go up R. Elísio de Melo; after 2 left-hand blocks turn right on R. Almada. Small but well-scrubbed rooms with wood furniture, phones, TV, and radio. Singles 2500$, with bath 3500$; doubles 4000-5000$; triples 4500$-6000$. Off-season discount for multi-night stays. Reservations recommended. Visa, MC.

Pensão Estoril, R. Cedofeita, 193 (tel. 200 51 52 or 200 27 51), above a cafe on a pedestrian street off Pr. Cados Alberto. Sail the sea-green carpeting into one of the *pensão*'s colossal, bright doubles with TV, bath, and phone. Lounge and patio with satellite TV and pool table. Singles with shower 4000-4500$; doubles with shower 4500-5500$; triples 6000-7800$; quads 8000$. Visa. Reservations recommended.

Pensão do Minho, R. Fernandes Tomás, 926 (tel. 31 12 72). Facing the town hall, take the street to the right of the building and take your first right. Small yet functional rooms on a loud street are cheap and exactly where you want them: near the train station, tourist office, and city center. Singles 2500$; doubles 3500$.

PORTUGAL

Fine Wine, Port Gratis

Entertainment of an alcoholic nature might be one of the first things to go when money gets tight on the backpacker's trail. But in Porto, never fear—there is an abundant supply of fine port wines available for consumption at any one of 80-odd port wine lodges. And the best part is that it's all completely *gratuito* (free).

As you will learn while waiting impatiently for the tours to terminate and the toasting to begin, port was discovered when some enterprising English wine dealers added a strong brandy to cheap Portuguese wine to prevent it from souring en route to England. Nowadays, wine from grapes grown in the Douro Valley 100km west of Porto is mixed with 170 proof brandy (sorry, that stuff is *not* for sale) and aged in barrels to yield port that takes different forms: vintage, white, ruby, and tawny. The lodges are all across the river in Vila Nova da Gaia—be sure to cross the lower level of the large bridge. A good starter is **Sandeman,** with costumed guides and high quality port. **Cálem,** next door, has a less stilted tour, and the port is almost as good. At **Ferreira,** down the road from Sandeman, you will learn about the illustrious *senhora* who built the Ferreira empire in the late 19th century—1996 was the *saudade*-filled 100th anniversary of her death. Last, but certainly not least, **Taylor's** wins the highly unscientific *Let's Go* poll for best port in Porto. Ask for your wine on their terrace, which has a great view of Porto and the River Douro.

Camping: Prelada (tel. 81 26 16), on R. Monte dos Burgos, Quinta da Prelada, 5km from the beach. Take bus #6 from Pr. Liberdade. 550$ per person, 475$ per tent, and 475$ per car. **Salgueiros** (tel. 781 05 00), near Praia de Salgueiros in Vila Nova de Gaia, is less accessible, less equipped, and less expensive, but closer to the surf. 200$ per person and per tent, 100$ per car. Open May-Sept.

FOOD

Eating out costs more in Porto than in any other Portuguese city. Head for the *mercado* if you are on a tight budget. Pick up fresh olives and produce at one of the outdoor food and handicraft **markets** that line Cais de Ribeira (open daily 8am-8pm), or at the **Mercado de Bolhão,** on the corner of R. Formosa and R. Sá de Bandeira (open M-F 8am-6pm, Sa 7am-1pm). Doling out a few hundred more *escudos,* however, will land some tasty dishes on your table—this is *the* place to feast on *bacalhau* (cod). Expensive restaurants border the river in the Ribeira district, particularly on **Cais da Ribeira, Rua Reboleira,** and **Rua de Cima do Muro.** You will find budget fare in rowdier surroundings near **Praça Batalha** on **Ruas Cimo de Vila** and **do Cativo.** Cheaper eateries lie around the **Hospital de Santo António** and **Praça Gomes Teixeira,** a few blocks west of Pr. Liberdade. Adventurous gourmets savor the city's specialty, *tripas à moda do Porto* (tripe and beans).

Restaurante O Gancho, Largo do Terreiro, 11-12 (tel. 31 49 19), across from Boa Nova. Typical Portuguese *comida* as well as lighter food such as omelettes served in a plain indoor bar/dining room over an outdoor esplanade. Entrees 850-1200$. Open daily noon-3pm and 7-11pm.

Restaurante Boa Nova, Muro dos Bacalhoeiros, 115 (tel. 200 60 86), in the row of houses overlooking the riverside walk, next door to the house where the inventor/namesake of the cod dish *à Gomes de Sá* was born (read the plaque yourself). Wine served from huge, wooden barrels. *Carapaus fritos* (fried whitefish, 850$). Open M-Sa noon-3pm and 7:30-10:30pm.

Majestic Cafe, R. Santa Catarina, 112 (tel. 200 38 87). Touts itself as "the joy of the city of Porto"—not far from the truth. A bit pricey, but why not treat yourself to the classy servers and mirrored walls complete with molded cupids? Tea sandwiches (600-900) and entrees, or *cafe* (200$). Some of the fanciest (and sweetest) pastries in town (90-200$). Open daily 8am-midnight.

Churrasqueira Moura, R. Almada, 219 (tel. 200 56 36), on a street parallel to Av. Aliados. Dirt-cheap meals of solid food to satisfy the grumpiest stomachs. Half-portions around 850$; full portions less than 1300$. Open M-Sa 9am-10pm.

Restaurante China Pekim, R. Santo Ildefonso, 118 (tel. 200 16 80), on the corner with R. Sta. Catarina. Decidedly overdone setting, with waterfall and all. Chicken entrees 650-750$. Vegetarian options. Open daily noon-3pm and 6-11pm.

SIGHTS

Your very first brush with Porto's rich stock of fine artwork may be in, of all places, the **Estação de São Bento,** home to a celebrated collection of *azulejos,* including iron and glass trains decorated with the beautiful tiles. Outside the station and at the top of adjacent **Praça da Liberdade,** the formidable *Belle Epoque* **Prefeitura** (City Hall) is a monument to Porto's late 19th-century greatness. Fortified on the hilltop slightly south of the train station is Porto's pride and joy, the Romanesque **sé** (tel. 31 90 28), situated in one of the city's oldest residential districts. *(Open daily 9am-12:30pm and 2:30-6pm. Cloister 200$.)* It was built in the 12th and 13th centuries, and the Gothic, *azulejo*-covered cloister was added in the 14th century. The **Capela do Santíssimo Sacramento,** to the left of the high altar, shines with solid silver and plated gold. During the Napoleonic invasion, crafty townspeople whitewashed the altar to protect it from vandalism. Climb the staircase to the **Renaissance chapter house** for a splendid view of the old quarter.

Up R. Clérigos from Pr. Liberdade rises the 82m **Torre dos Clérigos** (Tower of Clerics), adjoined to the **Igreja dos Clérigos.** *(Tower open daily 10:30am-noon and 2-5pm. Tower 130$, church free.)* Built in the mid-18th century, the tower's granite bell tower (the city's most prominent landmark) glimmers like a grand processional candle. Mount the 200 steps for spectacular views of Porto and the Rio Douro Valley.

Cash acquires cachet at the **Palácio da Bolsa** (Stock Exchange), R. Ferreira Borges (tel. 208 45 66), the epitome of 19th-century elegance. *(Open Apr.-Oct. Tu-F 2-8pm, Sa-Su 10am-8pm; Nov.-Mar. Tu-Su 2-7pm. Multilingual tours depart every 30min. 700$, students 550$, main courtyard—thankfully—free.)* The ornate courtyard ceiling is just the beginning of the palace's opulence. It took a zealous artisan three years to carve the exquisite wooden table in the portrait room; the ornate **Sala Árabe** (Arabic Room) took 18 years to decorate. Modeled after Granada's Alhambra, its gold and silver walls are covered with plaques bearing the oddly juxtaposed inscriptions "Glory to Allah" and "Glory to Queen Maria II." To get to the Bolsa, turn left out of the *sé* and follow the winding streets straight ahead to Travessa da Banharia and Largo de Santo Domingos; the Bolsa is downhill on the right. From the train station, follow R. Mouzinho da Silveira to the square; signs point the way. Next door to the Bolsa, the Gothic **Igreja de São Francisco** (tel. 200 84 41) glitters with one of the most elaborately gilded wooden interiors in Portugal. *(Open Apr.-Oct. M-F 9am-6pm, Su 9am-5pm; Nov.-Mar. M-Sa 9am-5pm. 500$, seniors and students 250$.)* Under the floor, thousands of human bones have been cleaned and stored in preparation for Judgment Day.

A 10-minute walk west (away from the center) on R. Dom Manuel II, past the churches and a forested park and en route to the youth hostel, stands the 18th-century **Museu Nacional de Soares dos Reis** (tel. 208 19 56), a former royal residence. *(Open Tu-Su 10am-5pm. 230$, seniors and students 165$.)* It houses an exhaustive collection of 19th-century Portuguese paintings and sculptures, highlighting Soares dos Reis, sometimes called Portugal's Michelangelo.

For modern art in a lovely setting, visit the **Fundação Casa de Serralves (Museu de Arte Moderna),** west of the town center on the way to the beach. *(Museum open Tu-F 2-8pm, Sa-Su 10am-8pm. Park closes at sundown. 300$, seniors and students 150$. Thursdays free.)* The museum rotates temporary exhibits of contemporary Portuguese art and architectural design. Ask to see an English video on the artists—all descriptions in the museum are in Portuguese. The building crowns an impressive 44 acres of sculpted gardens, fountains, and even old farmland tumbling down toward the Douro River. Bus #78 leaves for the museum from Pr. Dom João I—ask the driver for the museum stop (30min.; return buses run until midnight, 160$). Another beautiful **park** lies outside the Palácio de Cristàl (glass building), near the hospital. *(Park open daily until dark.)* Geese, swans, ducks, peacocks, the best-kept garden in Portugal, and fountains welcome those in search of a good reading spot.

Porto's rocky **beach,** in the ritzy Foz district in the west end of the city, is a popular destination despite higher-than-normal levels of pollution. To get there, jump on bus #78 from Pr. Liberdade (160$ each way) and jump off wherever it suits you. At the bottom of the hill on R. Alfândega, past a marvelous quay filled with shops and restaurants, skirts the **Ribeira.** To see more of this riverside esplanade, take trolley #1 (160$) from the Igreja de São Francisco; trolleys go along the river to the Foz do Douro, Porto's beach community.

ENTERTAINMENT

The place to party on weekend nights is the tirelessly fun **Ribeira,** where bars vibrate with the rhythms of Brazilian and Latin tunes. **Praça da Ribeira, Mura dos Bacalhoeiros,** and **Rua Alfândega** harbor most of the bars and pubs. Try **Pub O Muro,** M. dos Bacalhoeiros, 87-88 (tel. 38 34 26), right above the riverside near the bridge going to the port wine houses. **Discoteca Swing,** on R. Júlio Dinis near the youth hostel, is reputed to have swinging action for a mixed gay-straight crowd (cover about 1000$). The "beautiful people" party in the Foz beach district—try discos **Industria, Twins,** and **Dona Urraca.** The riverside **Nova Alfândega** plays host to concerts, especially in summer—Beck, Prodigy, and the Smashing Pumpkins have recently played here.

English-language movies are shown in at least three cinemas in the town center alone; try **Cinema Passos Manuel,** R. Passos Manuel, 141 (tel. 200 51 96), with shows daily from 2 to 9:30pm (tickets M 400$, Tu-Su 600$), or **Cinema Praça da Batalha** (tel. 202 24 07). Live **concerts** and **theater** performances are held on sultry summer nights at the Claustros do Mosteiro de São Bento da Vitória (tel. 31 21 32). The historic **Teatro Nacional São João** (tel. 200 34 49), Pr. Batalha, frequently hosts international drama troupes. Consult the bulletins at the tourist office for upcoming events.

But we digress—back to your (probable) main focus of interest. You can enjoy the warm glow of Port wine and its Douro cousins by embarking on a "wine connoisseurship" **cruise** (a fancy booze-cruise) down the Douro River. Grab a few pamphlets at the tourist office, or head straight for the docks.

■ Near Porto: Amarante

Amarante (pop. 4900) is food for the soul. Mass tourism has yet to rear its ugly head in this emerald green valley sprinkled with whitewashed houses. Amarante's two halves greet each other across the lazy Rio Tamega, both lined with shady weeping willows. For a good dose of history, cross the **Ponte de São Gonçalo,** once a Portuguese stronghold against Napoleonic troops, into **Praça da República.** The lacy facade of Amarante's *pièce de résistance,* the Romanesque **Igreja de São Gonçalo,** hides the resting place of Amarante's patron saint, São Gonçalo, whose tomb is in the gilded chapel beside the altar. In the same complex are the **municipal library** and the well-curated **Museu Amadeo S. Cardoso** (open Tu-Su 10am-12:30pm and 2-5:30pm; closed holidays; 200$). The trek up R. 5 de Outubro offers a view of the ghostly remains of the **Solar dos Magalhães,** a sordid but hauntingly beautiful reminder of Napoleon's pyromaniacal legacy.

Rodonorte **buses** (tel. 32 32 34) zip to: Vila Real (45min., 10 per day, 700$); Guimarães (1hr., 3 per day, 485$); Porto (1½hr., 4 per day, 700$); and Bragança (2½hr., 5 per day, 1400$). To get to the **tourist office** (tel. 43 23 59), follow Av. Alexandre Herculano toward the river, then hang a left on R. 31 de Janeiro. Cross the bridge onto Pr. de República; the office is in the same building as the museum entrance on Alameda Teixeira de Pascoaes. The staff hands out slick maps and brochures. For **currency exchange,** Banco Mello, past Igreja São Gonçalo on R. 5 de Outobro, has automatic cash dispensers. The **hospital** (tel. 43 76 31) is north of town on Av. General Vitorino Laranjeira. The **postal code** is 4600. The **telephone code** is (0)55.

Accommodations are scarce and expensive in Amarante, best visited as a daytrip from Guimarães, Braga, or Porto. If you do spend the night, try the three-star **Pensão Restaurante Sena** (tel. 49 17 25), on S. Gens. Rooms are spacious and well lit. Prices vary according to season and demand is invariably high, so call ahead. (Singles 3000-4000$; doubles 4000-6000$.) Alternatively, pitch your tent at the new **campground** just outside town on riverside R. Pedro Alvellos. After exploring the town's sights, pick a riverside terrace, drink in the sun, and gorge on Amarante's culinary delights: sweets, sweets, and more sweets. Delicious regional *ovos moles* (egg pastries) and traditional cakes proliferate, particularly during the festival of São Gonçalo.

■ Braga

Well-heeled Braga (pop. 160,000)—once the seat of the Archbishop of Spain—is considered by some the most pious, by others the most fanatic, and by all the most conservative city in Portugal. Not surprisingly, the 1926 coup that paved Salazar's path to power was launched from here. Yet in spite of Braga's austere reputation and large number of (primarily Gothic) churches, hedonism—manifested in bars and discos—marches cheerfully onward. During Holy Week, a procession crosses the flower-carpeted streets; at night, somber devotion caves into fireworks and dancing. Lively pedestrian thoroughfares and fairytale plazas make Braga akin to a miniature Lisbon. It is also a sensible base for exploring the natural wonders of northern Portugal.

ORIENTATION AND PRACTICAL INFORMATION

Braga's focal point is the **Praça da República**, a spirited square filled with cafes, bordered by gardens, and crowned with a fountain. The **Avenida da Liberdade** emanates from the square. **Rua do Souto**, a pedestrian thoroughfare lined with deluxe stores, runs from the tourist office's corner at the *praça*. R. Souto becomes **Rua Dom Diogo de Sousa** and then **Rua Andrade de Corvo,** which leads straight to the **train station.** To get to Pr. República from the **bus station,** head downhill on the street to the left as you exit the bus station (10-15min.).

Trains: (tel. 26 21 66), on Largo Estação. Most trips are more inconvenient than the bus, requiring a change of train at Nine, 20min. to the west. To: Porto (1½hr., 14 per day, 520$); Viana do Castelo (2hr., 10 per day, 490$); Vila Nova de Cerveira (3hr., 9 per day, 710$); Valença (3hr., 8 per day, 820$, with 3 daily connections to Vigo, Spain); Coimbra (4hr., 12 per day, 1150$). Express **Inter-Cidades** runs to Porto and on to Lisbon (3 per day).

Buses: (tel. 68 31 33 or 68 32 28), Central de Camionagem, a few blocks north of the city center. **Rodoviária** runs to: Porto (1½hr., departs every 45min., 640$); Guimarães (1hr., departs every 30min., 360$); Campo do Gerês, a.k.a. São João do Campo (1½hr., 5 per day, 520$); Coimbra (3hr., 4 per day, 1450$); Lisbon (8½hr., 7 per day, 2200$); Faro (12-15hr., 7 per day, 3100$).

Taxis: (tel. 61 40 28). To the youth hostel from the train station 650$.

Tourist Office: Av. Central, 1 (tel. 26 25 50), on Pr. República. Maps and plenty of info on rustic excursions. Train schedules and bus info available. Temporary **luggage storage.** English spoken. Open July-Sept. M-F 9am-7pm, Sa-Su 9am-12:30pm and 2-5pm; Oct.-June M-F 9am-7pm, Sa 9am-12:30pm and 2-5pm.

Budget Travel: Tagus Youth Travel, Pr. Município, 7 (tel. 21 51 44; fax 21 51 94). Student flights and other services. Open M-F 9am-6pm. Visa, MC, AmEx.

Currency Exchange: Banco Borges e Irmão, on Pr. República, across from the tourist office. Open M-F 8:30am-3pm. **ATMs** are common.

Emergency: dial 112. **Police:** R. dos Falcões, 12 (tel. 20 04 20), on Largo de Santiago.

Hospital: Hospital São Marcos, Largo Carlos Amarante (tel. 601 30 00).

Telephones: In the post office and kiosk in Pr. República. **Telephone Code:** 053.

Internet Access: Restaurante Buondi, Pr. Município, 72 (tel. 21 83 93). 3 email stations. 600$ per hr. Open daily 8am-midnight.

PORTUGAL

PORTUGAL

Braga

ACCOMMODATIONS
A Residencia Grande Avenida
B Residencial Inácio Filho
D Youth Hostel
C Camping

Rua Ulisses Taxa

Rua Bernardo Sequeira

Rua de S. Domingos

Rua Dr. de Matos

Rua de S. Vítor

Rua de Restauração

Avenida 31 de Janeiro

LARGO DA SENHORA A BRANCA

Rua de Santa Margarida

Rua de Camões

Rua de Sardoal

Avenida 25 de Abril

Rua do Raio

Rua Constantino João Dr. Domingos Soares

Av. Artur

Rua Gabriel Pereira do Castro

Rua S. Vicente

PRAÇA MOUSINHO DE ALBUQUERQUE

Rua de S. André

Rua S. Gonçalo

Avenida dos Combatentes

Avenida dos Combatentes

Avenida da Liberdade

PRAÇA ALEXANDRE HERCULANO

Rua do Carvalhal

Rua dos Chãos

LARGO DE S. FRANCISCO

PRAÇA DA REPÚBLICA

L BARIO DE S. MARTINHO

Casa Dos Crivos

L. CARLOS AMARANTE

Avenida General Norton de Matos

PRAÇA DA GALIZA

Tr. do Carmo

Rua do Carmo

Rua Dos Capelistas

Torre de Menagem

Rua do Castelo

Rua do Souto

LARGO DE SANTA CRUZ

Estação Rodoviária

Avenida V. Nespereira

Rua San Antonio

Jardim de Santa Barbara

Rua Era de Querós

LARGO DO PAÇO

Rua Justino Cruz

Rua Franc Sanches

LARGO DE SÃO JOÃO DE SOUTO

Museu Medina e Museu Pio XII

Rua Abade Loureira

PRAÇA CONDE DE AGROLONGO

Rua de Misericórdia

Sé

Rua do Leita

Rua S. João

Rua do Forno

LARGO DE S. PAULO SANTIAGO

Market

PRAÇA DO COMÉRCIO

Rua Alf Ferreira

PRAÇA MUNICIPAL Town Hall

Rua do Cabido

Rua do Farto

Rua Gualdim Pais

Rua Santiago

Rua dos Chages

Museu dos Biscainos

Torres E Almeida

A. Diego de Sousa

PRAÇA VELHA

Rua D. Paio Mendes

Rua D. Frei Caetano Brandão

Sede do Parque Nacional Peneda-Gerês

Rua de S. Martinho

Avenida António Macedo

Rua da Boavista

LARGO DA PORTA NOVA

Rua Dos Biscainhos

Campo dos Hortos

Avenida S. Miguel-o-Anjo

CAMPO DAS CARVALHEIRAS

Rua da Cruz de Pedra

Rua Andrade

Rua Corvo

Praceta Padre Diamantino Martins

LARGO DA ESTAÇÃO

Estação Dos Caminhos de Ferro (train station)

Rua do Caires

Rua Tenenta Coronel Dias Pereira

Rua da Boavista

200 yards
200 meters

Post Office: (tel. 61 77 20) on Av. Liberdade, 2 blocks south of the tourist office. For Posta Restante, indicate "Estação Avenida" in address. Open for **telephones, fax,** and other services M-F 8:30am-6pm, Sa 9am-12:30pm. **Postal Code:** 4700.

ACCOMMODATIONS

Braga resounds with *pensões*, although few are truly budget. The cheapest cluster around the **Hospital de São Marcos,** the more expensive around **Avenida Central.**

Pusada de Juventude de Braga (HI), R. Santa Margarida, 6 (tel./fax 61 61 63). From the tourist office, walk down Av. Central until the park ends, then turn left on Largo Senhora Branca. A 35min. walk from the train station, 15min. walk from the bus station. Relaxing, although rooms are a bit cramped. Gargantuan windows open out onto a forested hill. June-Sept.: dorms 1500$; doubles 3700$. Oct.-May: dorms 1300$; doubles 3200$. Breakfast included. Reception daily 9am-noon and 6pm-midnight. Reservations recommended July-Aug.

Residência Grande Avenida, Av. Liberdade, 738, 2nd fl. (tel. 60 90 20), around the corner from the tourist office. Elevator whisks you up to 21 rooms with elegant mirrors and plush furniture, all with TV, phone, and winter heating. Boasts a Victorian sitting room. In summer: singles 3500$, with bath 4500$; doubles 5000$, with bath 6000$. In winter: singles 3000$, with bath 4000$; doubles 4500$, with bath 5500$. Breakfast included. Reserve ahead June-Aug. Visa, MC, AmEx.

Residencial Inácio Filho, R. Francisco Sanches, 42 (tel. 26 38 49). From the *praça,* walk down R. Souto 1 block; it's off the 1st perpendicular pedestrian street to the left. Hallways cluttered with cool antiques connect 8 well-kept, prim rooms prime for relaxing. Doubles 4400$, with bath 5000$.

Camping: Parque da Ponte (tel. 733 55), 2km down Av. Liberdade from the center, next to the stadium and the municipal pool. Buses stop every 30min. Market and laundry facilities. 340$ per person, 260$ per tent, 280$ per car.

FOOD

Braga has many cafes and several superb restaurants, but little in between. A colorful **market** sets up in Pr. Comércio, two blocks from the bus station (open M-Sa 7am-3pm). Numerous restaurants in this *praça* serve the Minho's typically heavy dishes. For groceries, stop and shop at **Supermercado Mini Preço,** on R. São Victor a long block away from the youth hostel (open M-Sa 9am-8pm). For fast food and a mall atmosphere, hit **BragaShopping,** a commercial center facing the *praça.*

Churrasqueira da Sé, Dom Paio Mendes, 25. This "cathedral barbecue" serves pork chops, barbecued chicken, veal, and omelettes fit for His Excellence and laymen alike. Half-portions (630-890$) easily fill up one person. The *prato do dia,* a real bargain, won't disappoint (500$). Open daily 11am-11pm.

Cafe Vianna, Pr. República, 87 (tel. 26 23 36), behind the fountain (which makes a cool pattern). A snappy, pink marble cafe. Full breakfasts (300-750$), light lunches, and dinner (sandwiches and *pratos combinados* 375-1050$). At night it turns into a popular hangout, sometimes with live music. Open daily 8am-2am.

Grupo Jolima, Av. Liberdade, 779, under the flamingo-pink archway a block from the tourist office. Food court pushes tasty pizza (325$ per slice), breads (60$ per buttered roll), and traditional Portuguese barbecue (600$). Open daily 7am-2am.

SIGHTS

Braga's **sé,** Portugal's oldest cathedral, is a granite structure that has undergone a series of renovations since its inception in the 11th and 12th centuries. *(Cathedral and treasury open daily in summer 8:30am-6:30pm; in winter 8:30am-5:30pm. Free. Treasury 300$.)* Guided tours in Portuguese of its treasury, choir, and chapels run most any time during opening hours. The treasury showcases the archdiocese's most precious paintings and relics. On display is the *Cruzeiro do Brasil,* a plain iron cross from Pedro Álvares Cabral's ship when it ran into Brazil in 1500. The real treats are the *cofres cranianos* (brain boxes), one with the 6th-century cortex of São Martinho Dume, Braga's first bishop. The choir has an organ with 2424 fully functional pipes. Off a

Renaissance cloister lie the cathedral's two historic chapels. The most notable, **Capela dos Reis** (Kings' Chapel), guards the 12th-century stone sarcophagi of Dom Afonso Henriques' parents. The mummified remains of a 14th-century archbishop have a more heart-stopping effect. The street behind the chapel leads to a square flanked by the 17th-century **Capela de Nossa Senhora da Conceição** and the picturesque **Casa dos Coimbras**. *(Chapel open M-F 10am-1pm and 3-7pm. Free.)* The chapel has an interior covered with *azulejos,* which tell the story of Adam and Eve.

The Rococo facade of **Igreja de Santa Cruz** gleams beside the monumental **Hospital de São Marcos** on Largo Carlos Amarante. In a very different spirit sits the **Casa dos Crivos** (House of Screens) on R. São Marcos, with Moorish latticed windows.

Nearby, the **Jardim de Santa Bárbara**, on R. Eça de Queiros, lies under archaic, free-standing arches. Around the corner in Pr. Município, **Câmara Municipal** (City Hall), and **Biblioteca Municipal** eye each other above a graceful fountain.

Braga's most famous landmark, **Igreja do Bom Jesús,** is actually 5km out of town on a hillside carpeted in greenery. Built to re-create Jerusalem in Braga, this 18th-century *igreja* was to provide Christians with a pilgrimage site other than Palestine. Take the long walk (20min.) up the granite-paved pathway that forks into two zig-zagging 565-step stairways. Don't waste your money on the water-powered funicular (100$), or take it only on the way up—you'll miss the **staircase** depicting, among other things, the five senses (the "smell" fountain sprouts water through a boy's nose) and the saga of Christ's crucifixion (The Stations of the Cross). The church and some incredibly tacky cafes are at the top. **Buses** labeled "#02 Bom Jesús" depart at 10 and 40 minutes past the hour (185$) from Braga's stop on Largo Carlos Amarante (in front of Hospital de São Marcos) or from the stop on Av. Liberdade (in front of Farmacià Cristal). Buses drop you off at the bottom of the stairway and the funicular.

■ Near Braga: Excursions

Parque Nacional de Peneda Gerês: Nature first! An unspoiled expanse of mountains, lakes, vegetation, and wildlife, Parque Nacional de Peneda Gerês lies in the Vale do Alto, 43km north of Braga. Hiking routes between the main village of Gerês and the lookout point of Pedra Bela twist past glistening waterfalls and natural pools. Stop by the **information office** in Braga, Quinta das Parretas (tel. 053 600 34 80; fax 053 61 31 69), on Av. Antonio Macedo north of the train station, for maps and info on accommodations and trails (open M-F 9am-noon and 2-5:30pm). The youth hostel, **Pousada de Juventude de Vilardinho das Furnas (HI)** (tel./fax 053 35 13 39) is in the village of Campo do Gerês (a.k.a. São João do Campo) and borders the park. (Dorms 1600$; doubles 3400$, with bath 4200$. Off-season dorms 1300$; doubles 2700$, with bath 3500$. Breakfast included). Rodoviária Nacional **buses** (1½hr., 5 per day, 520$) connect Braga with Campo do Gerês.

Citânia de Briteiros: Nine kilometers from Bom Jesus, stone house foundations and huts speckle the hills in Portugal's best-preserved collection of **Celtic ruins** (open Tu-Su 9am-noon and 2-5pm; 200$). **Bus #12** (to Pedraiva) leaves from the Braga tourist office (1hr., 4 per day, 370$). Get off at Lageosa and walk 2km up the road.

Mosteiro de Tibães: In an unspoiled forest, this beautiful and peaceful 11th-century Benedictine monastery has suffered from centuries of neglect. Stone tombs rattle eerily underfoot in the weathered cloister. Adjoining the cloister, however, is an exceptionally preserved **church** (open Tu-Su 9am-noon and 2-7pm; tour free). A city **bus** labeled "Sarrido" heads 6km from Braga to the monastery. Buses leave from Pr. Conde de Agrolongo, one block west up R. Capelistas from Pr. República. The stop is in front of the "Arca-Lar" store, which also posts a schedule (45min., departs every 2hr., 230$).

Near Braga: Guimarães

While some claim modernization and big-time shopping (i.e. McDonald's, Pizza Hut, and Benetton) have dulled its luster, Guimarães' castle-dominated center still emanates a certain rustic *eu não sei que* that attracts an endless barrage of history buffs and atmosphere seekers. In 1143, Dom Afonso Henriques, the first King of Portugal, defeated the Moors here, thereafter making the town the golden nugget of his kingdom. Since then, Guimarães has been known as the "cradle of the nation," as the huge *Aqui nasceu Portugal* (Here Portugal was born) sign will testify.

PRACTICAL INFORMATION The **train station** (tel. 41 23 51), a 10-minute walk south of the tourist office down Av. Afonso Henriques, services Porto only (2hr., departs every hr., 15 per day, 500$). The **bus station** (tel. 41 26 46) is located in the immense Guimarães shopping complex. To get there, follow Av. Londres (on the bank), then turn right at the intersection. **Rodoviária** dispatches buses to Braga (45min., departs every 30min., 360$) and Porto (1hr., 3 per day, 750$). **AMI** (tel. 41 26 46) travels locally to São Trocato and Madre de Deus (10-20min., 20 per day, 90$). **Rodonorte** runs to Vila Real via Amarante (1hr., 4 per day, 500$). A **taxi** (tel. 52 25 22) from the town center up to the Penha Shrine costs around 1200$.

The **tourist office** (tel. 41 24 50), on Alameda de São Dámaso, faces Pr. Toural. From the bus station, take the busy commercial road to the right, walk uphill, and make a right at the fork; the tourist office is on the corner ahead. **Maps,** but not the regional guide, are free. (Supposedly open M-F 9:30am-12:30pm and 2-6:30pm). An electronic sign outside displays opening hours for all sights. A **branch office,** Pr. Santiago, 37 (tel. 51 51 23, ext. 184), conveniently located in the old city, has the same info (open daily 9am-6pm; off-season 9am-12:30pm and 2-5:30pm). Free short-term **luggage storage** at the tourist office and—if you ask nicely—the bus station. In **emergencies,** dial 112. The **police station** (tel. 51 33 34) is at Alameda Alfredo Pimenta. Contact the **hospital,** on R. dos Cutileiros, near Matadouros, at 053 51 26 12. The **post office** (tel. 41 65 11) is on R. de Santo António (open M-F 8:30am-6pm, Sa 9am-12:30pm). The **postal code** is 4800. The **telephone code** is 053.

ACCOMMODATIONS AND FOOD A scarcity of budget accommodations makes Guimarães perhaps best as a daytrip from Braga or Porto. For angelic sleep, try the **Casa de Retiros**, R. Francisco Agra, 163 (tel. 51 15 15; fax 51 15 17), run by the Redentorista religious order. From the tourist office, head through Pr. Toural and straight up R. Santo Antônio; R. Francisco Agra curves left at the traffic circle. The pristine bedrooms come with full bath, radio, phone, heating, and crucifix. The 11:30pm curfew is not negotiable, and unmarried couples had best introduce themselves as *Senhor* and *Senhora*. (Singles 3000$; doubles 5000$. Breakfast included.) **Camping** is 6km outside of town at **Parque de Campismo Municipal da Penha** (tel. 51 59 12). Take the road to Fafe, following the signs to Penha, or hop on the bus to Penha (15min., departs from the shopping complex, 220$). The campsite is open year-round with free showers, swimming pool, bar, and supermarket. (280$ per person, under 10 250$, 250$ per tent and per car. Reception open daily 8am-7pm. Open May-Oct.) **Groceries** vegetate at **Hipermercado Guimarães** (tel. 421 22 00), in the huge, air-conditioned shopping center, deemed "Most Welcoming Sight After Waiting in Communist Bread Lines" (open daily 9am-9pm).

SIGHTS Guimarães predates Portugal itself by a few centuries. Galician countess Mumadona founded a Benedictine monastery here in the 10th century and supervised the construction of the **castelo**. *(Open daily 9am-5:30pm. Free, tower 100$.)* The castle, a grand granite structure perched on a rocky hill near the town center, is one of Portugal's foremost national symbols.

The castle protected its inhabitants from the Normans and the Moors, but it was still a bit stuffy. To have a place to let loose or get recluse, the Dukes of Bragança built the versatile, palatial manor next door, the **Palácia dos Duques de Bragança.** *(Open daily 9am-5:15pm. 400$, seniors and students 200$, under 14 and Thursdays free. Mandatory tour is available in various languages.)* After its construction, the elegant 15th-century palace, modeled after the manor houses of northern Europe, became the talk of European nobility. A **museum** inside includes furniture, silverware, crockery, tapestries, and weapons once used at the palace. In the banquet hall, tables that once seated 15th-century nobles now serve presidents of Portugal at their brouhahas. At dinnertime, at least a quarter of the 39 fireplaces burn in an attempt to heat the building.

The **Museu de Alberto Sampaio,** in the Renaissance cloister of the **Igreja Cole-giada de Nossa Senhora da Oliveira,** is in the center of town. *(Church open daily 9am-noon and 3-6pm. Museum open in summer Tu-Su 10am-12:30pm and 2-5:30pm; in winter Tu-Su 10am-12:30pm and 2-5:30pm. Both free.)* The church entrance faces an arched medi-eval square and outdoor temple. The museum, on Largo da Oliveira, displays late Gothic and Renaissance art. The 15th-century Gothic **Capela de São Brax** holds the granite tomb of Dona Constança de Noronha, the first duchess of Bragrança. *(Open Tu-Su 10am-12:30pm and 2-5pm. 200$, seniors and students 100$, Sunday morning free.)* The courtyard *oliveira* (olive tree) symbolizes the patron saint of Guimarães.

▓ Viana do Castelo

Viana do Castelo (pop. 20,000) is an elegant and immaculate beach town, though not a full-fledged resort—rampant commercialism has yet to rear its ugly head in this beautiful stop-over between Porto and Galicia. Viana boasts some intriguing architec-ture, including an exceptional main plaza and a bridge designed by Gustave Eiffel, as well as a superb beach just a ferry ride away. Even when the city beach fills in July and August, empty and enticing expanses of sand can still be found north of town.

ORIENTATION AND PRACTICAL INFORMATION

Avenida dos Combatentes da Grande Guerra, the main drag along the Rio Lima, glitters from the train station south to the port. The old town stretches east of the ave-nue, while the fortress and sea lie to the west.

> **Trains:** (tel. 82 22 96 or 82 12 15), at the north end of Av. Combatentes, under Santa Luzia hill. From the bus station, go left on Av. 28 de Setembro through a pedestrian underpass (15min.), or take the bus (110$). To: Caminha (30min., 7 per day, 230$); Vila Nova de Cerveira (1hr., 5 per day, 300$); Barcelos (1hr., 13 per day, 300$); Porto (2½hr., 7 per day, 720$); Vigo, Spain (2½hr., 3 per day, 1595$).
>
> **Buses: Rodoviária** (tel. 250 47). Except for *expressos* that leave from Av. Combat-entes (the tourist office has schedules), buses depart from **Central de Camiona-gem,** on the east edge of town. To Braga (1½hr., 8 per day, 570$). **AVIC** (tel. 82 97 05) and **Auto-Viação do Minho** (tel. 82 88 34) lie on Av. Combatentes da Grande Guerra. To Porto (1½hr., 5 per day, 900$) and Lisbon (6hr., 3 per day, 2200$).
>
> **Taxi: Táxis de Viana** (tel. 82 23 22 or 82 20 61).
>
> **Tourist Office:** Pr. Erva (tel. 82 26 20; fax 82 78 73), one block east of Av. Combat-entes. From the train station, take the fourth left at the sharp corner, then a quick right into the dead-end. Maps and lists of lodgings. English spoken. Open M-Sa 9am-12:30pm and 2:30-6pm, Su 9:30am-12:30pm. A handy **info desk** at the train station has similar info. Open M-Sa 9am-12:30pm and 2-5:30pm, Su 2-5:30pm.
>
> **Currency Exchange:** 24hr. **ATM** at Montepio Geral, Av. Combatentes da Grande Guerra, 332 (tel. 82 88 97), near the train station. Open M-F 8:30am-3pm.
>
> **Emergency:** dial 112. **Police:** (tel. 82 20 22), on R. Aveiro.
>
> **Hospital:** Av. Abril, 25 (tel. 82 90 81).
>
> **Internet Access:** Due to be open to the public at the public library and **Instituto de Juventude** (tel. 810 88 00), off Pr. Erva on R. do Poço.
>
> **Post Office:** (tel. 82 27 11), Av. Combatentes, across from the train station. Open M-F 8:30am-6:30pm, Sa 9am-12:30pm. **Postal Code:** 4900.
>
> **Telephone Code:** 058.

ACCOMMODATIONS AND CAMPING

Except in mid-August, accommodations in Viana are easy to find, though not particu-larly cheap. *Quartos* are the best option. Small, informal *pensões* (usually above fam-ily restaurants) are slightly cheaper but far worse in quality. Check the tourist office's list of accommodations or hunt on side streets off Av. Combatentes.

PORTUGAL

Pensão Guerreiro, R. Grande, 14 (tel. 82 20 99), corner of Av. Combatentes. Bright rooms with high ceilings, old-fashioned wallpaper, and big windows. Ask for a view of the port. Singles 1500$; doubles 3000$; triples 4000$.

Residencial Viana Mar, Av. Combatentes, 215 (tel./fax 82 89 62), off Pr. República. Large, luxurious rooms furnished with phones. Rooms with bath also come with TV. Singles 2500$, with bath 4000$; doubles 3500$, with bath 6500$; triples with bath 7500$. Prices drop 500$ in winter. Breakfast included. Visa, MC, AmEx.

Residencial Magalhães, R. Manuel Espregueira, 62 (tel. 82 32 93). From the tourist office, turn left onto Pr. República, then left again. Cross Av. Combatentes onto R. Manuel Espregueira; *residencial* is on the right. A homey, old-school establishment. All rooms with bath. English spoken. Singles 4000-6500$; doubles 5000-7500$; triples 6000-9500$. Prices drop 500-1500$ in winter. Breakfast included.

Camping: Two campsites are found near the Praia do Cabedelo, Viana's (ocean) beach across the Rio Lima. Hop a "Cabedelo" bus (100$) from the bus station or behind the train station near the funicular stop. Or take the ferry (100$) and hike 1km from the 1st boat stop; signs point the way. **INATEL** (tel. 32 20 42), off Av. Trabalhadores. 500$ per person. Showers 100$. Tents for rent. Open Jan. 16-Dec. 15. **Orbitur** (tel. 32 21 67) is closer to the beach, better equipped, more expensive. 600$ per person, per tent, and per car. Free showers. Open Jan. 16-Nov. 15.

FOOD

Bloodthirsty diners drool over the local specialty *arroz de sarabulho,* rice cooked in blood and served with sausages and potatoes. A less sanguine substitute is *arroz de marisco,* rice cooked with different kinds of shellfish. Most budget restaurants lie on the small streets off **Avenida Combatentes.** The large municipal **market** sets up in Pr. Dona Maria II, several blocks east of Av. Combatentes (open M-Sa 8am-3pm). For **groceries,** hit Brito's Auto Serviço, R. Manjovos, 31 (tel. 231 51). From the train station walk down Av. Combatentes and take the fifth side street on the right (open daily 8:30am-12:30pm and 2:30-8pm).

Restaurante Arcada, R. Grande, 34 (tel. 82 36 43). Relatively untouristed and popular with local families. Entrees 800-1000$. Open M-F 9am-10pm.

Restaurante O Vasco, R. Grande, 21 (tel. 246 65), on the side street across from Pensão Guerreiro. A clinically white interior with cheap, tasty specialties such as *polvo cozido* (boiled octopus 975$) and *rojões à moda do Minho* (mixed roast meat 975$). Entrees 950-1500$. Open daily 11:30am-11pm.

Restaurante Dolce Vita, R. Poço, 44 (tel. 058 248 60), across the square from the tourist office. Wonderful Italian cuisine. Pizza 730-950$. Portuguese dishes 1150-1700$. Open daily noon-11pm; off-season noon-3pm and 7-10:30pm. Visa, MC.

SIGHTS

Even in a country famed for its charming squares, Viana's **Praça da República** is remarkable. Its centerpiece is a 16th-century fountain encrusted with sculpture and crowned with a sphere bearing a Cross of the Order of Christ. The small **Paço do Concelho** (1502), formerly the town hall, seals the square to the east. Diagonally across the plaza, granite caryatids support the playful and flowery facade of the **Igreja da Misericórdia** (1598, rebuilt in 1714). An intriguing *azulejo* interior lies within.

For great views of the harbor and ocean, visit **Castelo de São Tiago da Barra.** From the train station, take the second right off Av. Combatentes (R. Gen. Luis do Rego) and go five blocks. The walls of the *castelo,* built in 1589 by Spain's Felipe I, rise to the left. Inside is a regional **tourist office** (tel. 82 02 71).

More vistas await at the cliff-like **Colina de Santa Luzia,** north of the city, crowned by an early 20th-century neo-Byzantine church and magnificent Celtic ruins. To reach the hilltop, head 200m behind the train station and take the long stairway (drenched with blood, sweat, and tears) or the **funicular** (departs daily 9am-7pm every hr. in the morning, every 30min. in the afternoon, 100$.)

Beach connoisseurs will find plenty to be happy about in Viana. Avoid the beach on Rio Lima, prowling ground of some ferocious insects, and head directly for **Praia**

do **Cabedelo** via the **ferry** behind the parking lot at the end of Av. Combatentes (departs daily every 30min. July-Sept. 8:45am-midnight; May-June and Oct.-Dec. 8:45am-10pm; Jan.-Apr. 8:45am-5pm. 120$ per ride, 30$ per piece of luggage.) Those in search of a pristine beach experience abandon Viana altogether and head north to some of the cleanest, least crowded, and best beaches in Portugal. **Vila Praia de Âncora,** 16km north of Viana, is the largest and most popular. **Moledo** and **Caminha,** farther north, are equally gorgeous. The **coastal rail line** stops at all three frequently. Vila Praia de Ancora has two rail stops, the main Âncora and the Âncora-Praia stations, just a few blocks from the beach. Moledo and Caminha have two and four local stops, respectively, but these trains let you off 1-2km from the sand. Some trains do not stop at every station; check the schedule to make sure the train services your beach of choice (7 per day, Âncora-Praia 160$; Moledo 200$; Caminha 230$). **Buses** leave for Caminha from the bakery on Av. 5 de Outubro, near the port (35min., 8 per day, 255$). Viana is the best place to spend the night—plan your return trip ahead.

Alto Minho

The Alto Minho, set apart from Spain only by the crystal clear Rio Minho, could have inspired Henry David Thoreau to pen a second *Walden*. Rocky mountains rise between unspoiled small towns and wildflowers spring from riverbanks, broken only by cottage gardens of cabbage, corn, and grapes. Intrepid travelers jump the train at stops between towns and get permission from farmers to camp in their fields.

Caminha

> One day Jesus and Peter were passing through these parts...
> St. Peter: My Lord, what should this place be called?
> Jesus: Caminha, Caminha (keep walking) we're in a hurry.

While everyone else keeps on walking, you can be the only tourist to slip off the train into Caminha and enjoy the hypnotically green hills, wide beaches, and peaceful medieval square. The village is slightly larger than its cousin five stops down the line, Vila Nova de Cerveira. The latter has a youth hostel, Caminha has a **beach.** Put on your bathing suit, turn left on the riverside road, and keep going along the river about 1.5km to bask under the sun and on breezy days, get whipped by the wind. The zealous will hop on the bus (10min.) or trek 3km to the wide, pristine **Praia de Moledo,** where the Rio Minho rushes into the Atlantic.

Caminha makes a good **daytrip** from Viana do Castelo or Vila Nova de Cerveira; as accommodations are generally expensive and difficult to come by, it's best to sleep elsewhere. The **train station** (tel. (058) 92 29 25), on Av. Saraira de Carvalho, has trains rolling to: Vila Nova de Cerveira (10min., 6 per day, 120$); Viana do Castelo (30min., 8 per day, 230$); and Porto (2-3hr., 8 per day, 900$). **AVIC buses** leave from the shopping center by the riverside road and head to Porto (2hr., 820$) and Lisbon (6hr., 3 per day, 2100$). The **tourist office** (tel. (058) 92 19 52) is on R. Ricardo Joaquim Sousa. From the train station, walk straight ahead down Av. Manuel Xavier to the square/traffic circle, go down Tr. São João (diagonally to the right), and take the second left (open M-Sa 9:30am-12:30pm and 2:30-6pm).

Vila Nova de Cerveira

Linked by ferry to Spain, a scant 100m away (close enough to hear Galicians partying at night), Vila Nova de Cerveira (pop. 11,000) is a sleepy town with lush mountain scenery, a historic town center, and, most importantly, a great youth hostel. The only thing to see in the town itself is the 14th-century **castle,** now the luxurious **Pousada Dom Dinis,** open for walks atop walls offering great views of the countryside. From Cerveira, jet to the handsome beaches of Âncora, Moledo, and Caminha, and to the even smaller towns of Valença do Minho and Ponte de Lima in the interior.

Bambi Thumps Spain

Vila Nova de Cerveira gets its name from the old Portuguese-Galician word for deer, an animal that turned out to be Cerveira's unlikely war hero. Back in the days before Spain and Portugal were E.U. buddies, the Rio Minho frontier hosted countless skirmishes. When the Spanish occupied the town, fleet-footed locals ran into the hills surrounding Vila Nova and tied torches to the horns of all the deer they could catch. When the Spaniards saw the hills filled with the torches of what they presumed to be a massive army, they gave up and fled. To this day, Vila de Cerveira rests quietly under the gaze of a huge metal deer sculpture, visible on the summit of the mountain behind town.

Hardy travelers can hike up the winding road, through heath and rocky outcrop (4km), to the **Veado** (deer) statue, offering a 360° view. From the main road just pas town to the east, turn right and begin climbing at the sign reading *Lovelhe (Igreja)*.

PRACTICAL INFORMATION The **train** station (tel. 79 62 65), off the highway 0.5km east of town, has service to: Valença do Minho (25min., 8 per day, 160$, 3 daily con nections to Vigo and Redondela, Spain); Vila Praia de Âncora (45min., 8 per day 200$); Viana do Castelo (1hr., 8 per day, 300$); and Porto (2½hr., 8 per day, 900$) Three **bus** companies ride the same route as the train—upstream to Valença an down the coast to Porto. **Turilis** buses leave from the Turilis travel agency (tel. 79 5 50), in the semicircular building to the left of the train station. **AVIC** and **A.V. Minh** depart from Cafe A Forja, Av. 25 de Abril (tel. 79 53 11), between the hostel and th town center, to: Valença do Minho (15min., 12-15 per day, 205$); Porto (2¼hr., 5 pe day, 950-1000$); and Lisbon (6hr., 5 per day, 2300$).

Vila Nova's **tourist office,** Pr. Muntápio (tel. 79 55 18), is on R. Antônio Douro, diag onally across from Igreja de São Roque. From the train station, turn left and it's th first yellow building on the right. (Open M-Sa 9:30am-12:30pm and 2-6pm. Tempo rary **luggage storage.**) The **police** (tel. 79 51 13) are at R. do Forte; dial 112 in emer **gencies.** Next to the bank on Pr. Alto Minho is the **post office** (tel. 79 51 11; open M F 9am-12:30pm and 2-5:30pm). The **postal code** is 4920; the **telephone code** is 051

ACCOMMODATIONS AND FOOD The **Pousada de Juventude de Vila Nova (HI** Largo 16 de Fevereiro, 21 (tel./fax 79 61 13), is to the left from the train station, the right at the fork, then left again at the Fonseca Porto mini-market (15min., signs lea the way). Guests enjoy large rooms, a grassy patio, TV with VCR, and a kitche Though there's usually plenty of space, the hostel hosts a summer camp and fills t the brim with Portuguese tots. (Dorms 1500$; doubles 3200$, with bath 3700$; of season: dorms 1200$; doubles 2700$, with bath 3200$. Breakfast included. Englis spoken. Reception 9am-noon and 6pm-midnight. Call ahead.) The nearest **camp ground** (tel. 72 74 72) digs in 4km southwest in **Vilar de Mouros** (550$ per perso 500$ per tent, 450$ per car). Eats are expensive—there is a seven-restaurant mono oly. At **Cafe-Restaurante A Forja,** upstairs on R. 25 de Abril, 63, you can feast on si ful *arroz de mariscos* (huge half portions 600$; open Tu-Su 8am-midnight).

■ Valença do Minho

Within easy reach of Vila Nova, **Valença do Minho** salutes Spanish **Túy** (Tui) from th entrance to northern Portugal. A 17th-century **fortaleza** (fortress) protects the city historic section. Its stone arches and cannon portal frame stunning views of rolli hills and the Rio Minho. The historically rich center of Valença has sadly fallen victi to unheard-of levels of commercial tackiness. Walk through town on the *pousad* side; the impressive stone walls yield spectacular views of both Spain and Portugal. road winds 4km up to the breathtaking summit of **Monte do Faro,** overseeing th coastline, the Vale do Minho, and the Galician mountains.

Valença is a stop on the Porto-Vigo **train** line with connections to: Viana (7 per da 420$); Vila Nova de Cerveira (15min., 7 per day, 160$); Porto (4hr., 7 per day, 980$

and Vigo (2 per day, 1465$). From Redondela (1 stop before Vigo; 1260$), you can connect to Spanish RENFE trains to points north. The **tourist office** (tel. (051) 233 24) is on Av. Espanha in a log-cabin-like building; exiting the train station, turn right on main drag (open daily 9am-12:30pm and 2:30-6pm).

Pensão Rio Minho (tel. (051) 223 31) has spacious, tidy rooms next to the train station (singles 4000$; doubles 5500$; prices drop in off-season). Dine in the less expensive new town. **Restaurante Cristina,** in the *centro comercial* next to the Lara Hotel, serves a hearty *cabrito assado no forno* (oven-roasted kid—as in goat, 1100$) and a *prato do dia* for 750$ (open daily 8am-midnight).

PORTUGAL

Trás-Os-Montes

The country's roughest, rainiest, and most isolated region, Trás-Os-Montes (Behind the Mountains) is light years off the beaten path. Dom Sancho I practically begged people to settle here after he incorporated it into Portugal in the 11th century, and Jews chose this remote spot to hide during the Inquisition. Today, charm, beauty, and tranquility are the region's biggest draws.

Getting to Trás-Os-Montes is less than half the fun. Train service is slow and rickety (where it exists at all), and roads tend to be twisty and treacherous. Soaking up the beautiful landscape is more than (the other) half of the fun; hikers delight in the isolation of unspoiled natural reserves in the Parque Natural de Alvão (accessible from Vila Real) and the Serra de Montesinho (north of Bragança). Brimming with splendid mountain views, this region is one of the last outposts of the traditional Portuguese stone house, complete with hand-cut hay piled into two-story conical stacks. The gastronomic specialities devoured in these houses hint at the region's rusticity: *cozido à Portuguesa* is made from sausages, other pig parts, carrots, and turnips. Visitors might want to consume lots of bread and *feijoada à Transmontana* (bean stew) and then burn it off with some serious hikes. A word to the wise—extremes of temperature make summertime hiking a hot affair.

∎ Bragança

Built on rough ground, Bragança (pop. 40,000), the capital of Trás-Os-Montes, is a proud and steadfast wilderness outpost. While most visitors come for the clean air and blue skies, Bragança's impeccably preserved medieval old town surrounding the *castelo* draws its share of gazers as well. The days when Bragança was the key to the frontier, marked by a massive 13th-century castle, live on in the imaginations of visitors. From its foothold on a terraced hilltop that grows hay and ubiquitous olives, Bragança is an excellent base for exploring the starkly beautiful terrain of the **Parque Natural de Montesinho,** which extends north and into Spain.

ORIENTATION AND PRACTICAL INFORMATION

Inter-city buses let you out on the modern square fronted by the cafe-lined **Avenida João da Cruz.** Downward-sloping **Rua Almirante Reis** leads to budget *pensões* and the **Praça da Sé** at the heart of the old town. To reach the **fortress,** situated on a hill west of Pr. Sé, take **Rua Combatentes da Grande Guerra** from Pr. Sé, walk uphill, and enter through the opening in the stone walls.

Trains: No train service. The Portuguese rail system does, however, organize a somewhat awkward (4 connections required) combination bus-train route between Porto and Bragança. Eurail passes can be used to pay for this combo. You can pick up a train in **Mirandela,** the nearest station (get there by bus).

Buses: Three competing agencies offer expresses to Porto and Lisbon. **Rodonorte** (tel. 30 01 83) leaves from Av. João da Cruz to Porto (5hr., 5 per day, 1440$), including stops at Mirandela and Vila Real, and to Lisbon (8hr., 3 per day, 2680$). **San-Vitur Travel Agency,** Av. João da Cruz, 36 (tel. 33 18 26), sells tickets and has schedules. *Expressos* leave from the Rodonorte stop. To: Vila Real (2hr., 3 per day, 1250$); Porto (5hr., 3 per day, 1400$); Coimbra (6hr., 4 per day, 1700$); Lisbon (8hr., 4 per day, 2400$); Amarante and Guimarães (2½hr., 13 per day, 1400$). **Internorte** runs to Zamora, Spain (2½hr., 1 per day, 2050$) and Braga (5hr., 2 per day, 1600$). Office open erratically, though always pre-departure. **Public Transportation:** From the **Caixa Geral de Depósitos** on the corner of Av. João da Cruz, yellow and blue line #7 STUB buses forge 4km northward to the campground (10min., M-F 3 per day, 120$). The tourist office has schedules.

Taxis: (tel. 32 21 38). Cabs congregate across from the post office and old train station. A ride to the campground costs about 700$.

Tourist Office: Av. Cidade de Zamora (tel. 33 10 78; fax 33 19 13), northeast of the center. From Pr. Sé take R. Abílio Beça and turn left on R. Marquez de Pombal, which leads to Av. Cidade de Zamora; the office is 1 block down on the lefthand corner. **Maps,** free daytime **luggage storage,** and help finding accommodations. English spoken. Open M-Sa 10am-12:30pm and 2-8pm, Su 10am-1pm.

Currency Exchange: Banco Nacional Ultramarino, Av. João da Cruz, 2-6 (tel. 33 16 45), next to the post office has **ATMs.** Open M-F 8:30am-3pm.

Emergency: dial 112. **Police:** (tel. 330 24 20), behind the town hall.

Hospital: Hospital Distrital de Bragança (tel. 33 12 33), Av. Abade de Baçal, before the stadium on the road to Chaves.

Post Office: (tel. 33 14 72), at the end of Av. João da Cruz. Open for Posta Restante, **fax,** and **telephones** M-F 9am-5pm. **Postal Code:** 5300.

Telephone Code: 073.

ACCOMMODATIONS AND FOOD

Plenty of cheap *pensões* cluster about **Praça da Sé** and up **Rua Almirante Reis.** The few restaurants are generally pricey and mediocre, but not always. Try hunting around Pr. Sé and **Avenida João da Cruz.** Cafes in front of the bus stop all prepare inexpensive *pratos combinados.* The region is celebrated for *presunto* (cured ham) and *salsichão* (sausages), for sale at **Supermercado Bem Servir,** R. Abílio Beça, 120, below Pr. Sé (open M-Sa 9am-1pm and 2-7pm).

◉**Pensão Poças,** R. Combatentes da Grande Guerra, 206 (tel. 33 11 75). Large and airy yet spartan rooms are kept spotless by the same family that monopolizes the block with **Restaurant Poças** next door and the **Charcutaria Poças** across the street. Singles 2000$, with bath 2500$; doubles with bath 4000$.

Pensão Rucha, R. Almirante Reis, 42 (tel. 33 16 72), on the street connecting Pr. Sé to Av. João da Cruz. The sign is *inside* the doors. Clean, old-school lodgings run by an old-school couple. Singles 2000$; doubles 4000$.

Camping: Parque de Campismo Municipal do Sabor (tel. 268 20), 6km from town on the edge of the Montesinho park (see **Public Transportation,** above). 200$ per person and per car, 150$ per tent. Electricity 100$. Open May-Sept. **Parque de Campismo Cêpo Verde** (tel. 993 71), on the road to Vinhais, 8km from town. Swimming pool. 500$ per person. 350$ per tent and per car. Open year-round.

Restaurante Poças, R. Combatentes da Grande Guerra, 200 (tel. 33 14 28), off Pr. Sé to the east, next to the eponymous *pensão.* Classic grub in a no-frills setting crowded with locals and tourists alike. *Costeleta de vitela grelhada* (grilled steak 1000$). Most entrees 900-1500$. Open daily 8am-midnight.

SIGHTS AND ENTERTAINMENT

High above Bragança sits the handsome old town with a brooding **castelo** as its centerpiece. The castle's **Museu Militar** (tel. 223 78) displays it all—from medieval swords to a World War I machine gun nest to African art collected by Portuguese soldiers. *(Open daily 9-11:45am and 2-4:45pm. 200$, free Sunday mornings.)* The venerable **pelourinho** (pillory) in the square in back of the castle bears the coat of arms of the House of Bragança. At the base of the whipping post is a prehistoric granite pig—in the Iron Age people were bound to the pig as a punishment. The **Domus Municipalis,** behind the church on the other side of the square from the castle, had cisterns in the 13th century and later became the municipal meeting house. If closed, the *senhora* across the street at #46 has the key; be sure to tip her.

On the 3rd, 12th, and 21st of each month, **feiras** (fairs) rollick near the hospital, 2km out of town—the place for clothes, *queijo* (cheese), food, and a heckuva good time (take a taxi from the town center for about 400$).

■ Near Bragança: Parque Natural de Montesinho

One of the largest protected areas of Portugal, the **Parque Natural de Montesinho** is a 290 sq. mi. testament to the possibilities for harmony between man and nature.

PORTUGAL

Some 9000 inhabitants, divided among 92 villages, continue to live much as they have since the fall of the Visigothic empire. Rich with tradition, these villages preserve ages-old communal customs and still enact ancient rituals—such as the December 25th "Youth Men's Rite," when young men, honoring Saturn, adorn themselves with shaggy suits and painted masks and skip throughout their villages.

Trekking on the old mountain paths linking the villages affords ample opportunity to mingle with the park's flora (oak, chestnut, pine, and cherry trees) and less frequently sighted fauna (the endangered Iberian wolf, royal eagle, and black stork, among others). The **information office,** Bo. Salvador Nunes Teixeira, lote 5 (tel. 38 14 44; fax 38 11 79), in Bragança, downhill from the tourist office, the first left (on a *paved* street) and the first left again, is a necessary first stop. The staff provides tons of useful maps, brochures, and advice. As trails are unmarked, they offer military maps and help plan hikes. (Open M-F 9am-12:30pm and 2-5:30pm.) There is no free **camping** in the park, but the information office does rent **Casas Abrigos** (traditional houses) for reasonable prices (doubles 5000-7500$; quads 10,000$; 23-person rooms 50,000$).

■ Vila Real

Vila Real (pop. 10,000) teeters over the edge of the gorges of the Corgo and Cabril Rivers in the foothills of the Serra do Marão. The charming and untouristed old town center is surrounded by new boroughs reaching into the hills, a main street swooning with the heady scent of rosebuds, and a few hopping cafes. Having flourished as the principal commercial center for the southern farms and villages of Trás-Os-Montes, Vila Real is a good point of departure for excursions into the fertile fields and rocky slopes of the **Serra do Alvão** and **Serra do Marão.**

ORIENTATION AND PRACTICAL INFORMATION

A hundred kilometers east of Porto, Vila Real's old neighborhood is centered around **Avenida Carvalho Araújo,** a broad tree-lined avenue that streams downhill from the bus station to the Câmara Municipal. All the action—cafes, shops, and *pensões*—is in this area. The **bus** lets you off at Rodonorte Station on **Rua Don Pedro de Castro;** head right after exiting the station to hit the main drag.

Trains: Av. 5 de Outubro (tel. 32 21 93). To Vila Real's center, walk up Av. 5 de Outubro over the iron bridge onto R. Miguel Bombarda and turn left on R. Roque da Silveira. Continue to bear left until Av. Primeiro de Maio. Trains take longer than buses and require transfers at Régua. To Porto, via Régua (4½hr., 5 per day, 980$).

Buses: Rodonorte, R. D. Pedro de Castro (tel. 32 32 34), on the square directly uphill from the tourist office. To: Guimarães via Amarante (3hr., 2-5 per day, 930$); Bragança (4hr., 4 per day, 1290$); Porto (2hr., 3 per day, 900$); Lisbon (7½hr., 4 per day, 2420$). **Rodoviária do Norte,** R. Gonçalo Cristóvão, 16 (tel. 37 12 34), out of the Ruicar Travel Agency, near Rodonorte uphill on the right. To: Viseu (2½hr., 2 per day, 1150$); Coimbra (4½hr., 2 per day, 1350$); Lisbon (7½hr., 2 per day, 2100$); Bragança (4hr., 3 per day, 1250$); Braga (4½hr., 5 per day, 1000$).

Taxis: (24hr. tel. 32 12 96). They queue along Av. Carvalho Araújo.

Tourist Office: Av. Carvalho Araújo, 94 (tel. 32 28 19; fax 32 17 12), to the right and downhill from the bus stations. Info about Parque Natural do Alvão and other excursions. Some transportation schedules available. Temporary **luggage storage.** Some English spoken. Open June-Sept. M-F 9:30am-7pm, Sa 9:30am-12:30pm and 2-6pm, Su 10am-1pm and 2:30-5pm; Oct.-May M-Sa 9:30am-12:30pm and 2-5pm.

Currency Exchange: Realvitur, Largo do Pioledo, 2 (tel. 32 18 00), 4 blocks uphill from the tourist office and to the right. Open M-F 9am-7pm, Sa 9am-1pm. **ATM,** Av. Carvalho Araújo, 84, at Banco Pinto and Sotto Mayor, next to the tourist office.

Luggage Storage: Free at the tourist office and Rodonorte station, upon request.

Emergency: dial 112. **Police:** (tel. 32 20 22), Largo Condes de Amarante.

Hospital: Distrital de Vila Real (tel. 34 10 41), in Lordelo, north of the town center.

Post Office: Av. Carvalho Araújo (tel. 059 32 20 06), up from the tourist office. Posta Restante, **telephones,** and **fax.** Open M-F 9am-6:30pm. **Postal Code:** 5000. **Telephone Code:** 059.

ACCOMMODATIONS AND FOOD

Accommodations cluster in the town center. Several cafes along **Avenida Carvalho Araújo** advertise rooms upstairs. Restaurants around **Avenidas António de Azevedo** and **Primeiro de Maio** cook up affordable meals, as do many cafes on the main drag. For **groceries,** hit **Mercado da Praça,** R. D. Maria das Chaves, 75 (open M-F 9am-1pm and 3-7pm, Sa 9am-1pm).

Residencial da Sé, Trav. São Domingos, 19-23 (tel. 32 45 75). As you descend Av. Carvalho Araújo, it's down a sleepy side street to the right next to the cathedral. Great, clean, bright rooms, all with bath and TV. Request one with windows. Singles 3500-4000$; doubles 6000$. Breakfast included. Visa, MC, AmEx.

Pensão Mondego and **Residencial São Domingos,** Trav. São Domingos, 33 (tel./fax 32 30 97 or 32 30 39), down from Residencial da Sé. Bright, carpeted rooms, all equipped with TV, phone, and bath. Singles 3000$; doubles 6000$. Prices are lower for larger groups and drop in the off season. No winter heating.

Camping: Parque de Campismo Municipal de Vila Real (tel. 32 47 24), on R. Dr. Manuel Cardona, just northeast of town on a bluff above the Corgo River. Get on Av. Marginal and follow the signs. 480$ per person, under 10 230$; 305$ per tent and per car. Free showers. Free swimming in the river or the pool complex. Reception open daily in summer 8am-11pm; in winter 8am-12:30pm and 2-6pm. .

Restaurante Nova Pompeia, R. Carvalho Araújo, 82 (tel. 728 76), next to the tourist office above a popular cafe of the same name. Low prices, middling environs, high A/C. *Prato do dia* around 750$. Excellent combination meals fill you up for 500-1100$. Open M-Sa 8am-11pm. Major credit cards accepted.

Restaurante Museu dos Presuntos, Av. Cidade de Orense, 43 (tel. 32 60 17), at R. D. Afonso III and R. Morgado de Mateus. Walk uphill from the tourist office, take the right fork, and turn left on R. Morgado de Mateus. Savor one of the house's myriad *presunto* (ham) combinations and chase it down with the region's spunky wine. Entrees 950-1500$. Open M-Sa noon-3pm and 7-10pm.

SIGHTS AND ENTERTAINMENT

Most of Vila Real's sights lie outside of the city proper, but camera-toters still dote on three churches in town. The stodgy 15th-century **sé,** its simple interior divided by thick, arched columns, looms at the lower end of Av. Carvalho Araújo. Two blocks east of the cathedral, **Capela Nova** (New Chapel) blushes behind a floral facade. At the end of R. Combatentes da Grande Guerra, **Igreja de São Pedro** resounds with 17th-century *azulejos.* A superabundance of cafes are the brunt of the town's entertainment. Locals rendezvous at the ensemble of cafes on Largo do Proledo. **Copos e Rezas, Billiards Bar,** and **Ritmin** are lively draws within steps of each other.

■ Near Vila Real

While transportation for backpackers without wheels can be a pain, only a scarce few will regret a visit to the village of **Mateus,** 3km east of Vila Real, world-renowned for its rosé wine. The **Sogrape Winery,** on the main road from Vila Real, 200m from the turn-off for the Palácio Mateus, has a terrific free tour of the wine-processing center, which includes complementary and unlimited tasting. *(Open daily June-Sept. 9am-noon and 2-4pm; Oct.-May 9am-noon and 2-5pm.)*

Up the road from the Sogrape Winery glitters the Baroque **Palácio de Mateus** (tel. 059 32 31 21), featured on the label of every bottle of Mateus rosé wine. *(Open daily in summer 9am-noon and 1-7pm; in winter 9am-12:30pm and 2-6pm. Last tour begins 1hr. before closing. Admission to mansion and gardens 1000$, to gardens alone 650$.)* The palace boasts a beautiful garden and features an original 1817 edition of Luís de Camões's *Os Lusía-*

PORTUGAL

das, Portugal's famous literary epic. In the somewhat macabre 18th-century chapel, the 250-year-old remains of a Spanish soldier recline fully dressed in a glass case.

To get to Mateus, take the **Rodonorte bus** (see **Buses,** p. 640) from Vila Real to the nearby town of Abambres (10min., 7 per day, 170$). Buses depart from the Câmara Municipal in Vila Real in the morning and from the Cabanelas bus station in the afternoon. Ask the driver to let you off at Mateus; walk from Mateus to Abambres to catch the return bus to Vila Real. Many people **walk** from Vila Real to Mateus; the road loops, so follow signs south from Vila Real's train station or north from the main highway out of town. A **taxi** costs around 850$.

Using Vila Real as a base, hardy souls explore the **Parque Natural do Alvão,** a protected area reaching to the heights of the mountainous Serra country north of Vila Real. The tourist office can provide maps and suggestions of places to visit. Even better, visit the park's **information office,** Pr. do Tronco, 17 (tel. 059 759 37). From the tourist office, head uphill and take the right fork on R. Dr. Margarida Chaves. Keep straight past Pr. Diogo Cão and then curve left on Cruz das Almas. The office is on the corner with R. Stuart Carvalhais. (Open M-F 9am-noon and 2-6pm.) The outskirts of Lamas de Ôlo hosts mysterious granite dwellings and the spectacular **Rio Ôlo gorge.** The bus from Vila Real to Dornelas passes through the village.

MOROCCO المغرب

US$1 = 9.55 dirhams (dh)	1dh = US $0.10
CDN$1 = 6.23dh	1dh = CDN $0.16
UK£1 = 16.03dh	1dh = UK £0.06
IR£1 = 13.81dh	1dh = IR£0.07
AUS$1 = 5.65dh	1dh = AUS $0.18
NZ$1 = 4.80dh	1dh = NZ $0.21
SAR1 = 1.54dh	1dh = SA R0.65
SP 1ptas = 0.06dh	1dh = SP 15.42ptas
POR 1$ = 0.05dh	1dh = POR 18.62$
EURO 1= 10.86dh	1dh = EURO .09

ESSENTIALS

Just two hours from Spain across the Straits of Gibraltar, Morocco offers an enticing medley of sights, sounds, and smells. Despite its proximity to Europe, Morocco is no more "European" than is any other Arab country and provides an excellent introduction to the Arab World. Morocco is blessed with a huge variety of climates and cultures in a relatively compact area (though short distances do not necessarily imply ease of travel). Many visitors who are limited to visiting, say, the four imperial cities (Fez, Meknes, Rabat, and Marrakesh), can hardly believe that they haven't crossed any international borders during their trip, so contrasting are the local atmospheres.

Budget travelers, once over the shock at the expense of arriving here, especially appreciate Moroccan prices. You may not be able to do Morocco on $5 per day, but at the same time you'd have a hard time spending $10. Do be warned that any Western-looking person is a target for the omni-present hustlers (called faux guides in the local argot) and some are amazingly persistent, aggressive, and even insulting.

All traveler's in Morocco face a different set of **health** issues than in Iberia. It is not generally advisable to drink tap water (or drinks with ice in them), street vendors may sell aged or otherwise bad food, and if you plan to visit more rural areas, a typhoid fever vaccination is recommended. For more info, see **Health,** p. 20. **Women travelers** will probably have extra difficulties traveling through Morocco without a male companion At the very least, women should never travel alone. Everyone, but especially women, should dress conservatively, both to avoid potential problems and as a sign of respect for Moroccan culture. For more information see **Specific Concerns: Women Travelers,** p. 29.

🏛 HIGHLIGHTS OF MOROCCO

- The imperial city of **Fez** (see p. 671), with its 9000-street medina, Attarine Souq (spice market), and exquisite Bou Inania Madrassa (seminary).
- The imperial city of **Marrakesh** (see p. 697), but especially its otherworldly bazaar, **Djemâa el-Fna.**
- The third imperial city, **Meknes** (see p. 665), its **Jamaï Museum,** and its spectacular **madrassa.**
- The **Chellah** in **Rabat** (see p. 685), one of the most peaceful spots in Morocco.
- The Roman ruins of **Volubilis** (see p. 669), North Africa's best-preserved Roman site.
- The new, high-tech **Hassan II mosque** (see p. 689) in Casablanca.

■ Getting There and Around

Although just across the Straits of Gibraltar and occasionally visible from Spain, Morocco can sometimes be a bit frustrating to reach. Whatever hassles it may involve, however, the trip is far more than worth it, and the transportation network between southern Spain and northern Morocco is frequent and reliable enough to allow one to "do" Morocco (or at least Ceuta or Tangiers) as a daytrip. The easiest way to Morocco is through Algeciras (see p. 485), which itself is well connected to the rest of Spain by train and bus. From Algeciras ferries depart all day long to both Ceuta (see p. 662) and Tangiers (see p. 656). Tangiers is also accessible from Gibraltar (3 ferries per week; see p. 483) and Tarifa (1 ferry daily; see p. 488), but both are a bit inconvenient to reach from within Spain.

Once in Morocco, navigating Morocco's byzantine streets can be made easier by knowing that the chief intersection of every city in Morocco, *villes nouvelles* (new city) only, is that of rue Hassan II and rue Mohammed V.

BY PLANE

Royal Air Maroc (in Casablanca tel. (2) 31 41 41; in U.S. tel. (800) 344-6726; in U.K. tel. (0171) 439 43 61), the national carrier of Morocco, flies to most major cities in Europe, including Madrid and Lisbon. Domestically, a network of flights radiates from the Mohammed V Airport outside Casablanca. Flights fly daily to Marrakesh, Agadir, Tangier, Fez, and less regularly to Ouarzazate.

If you hope to see a lot of Morocco in a short time, flying can be both a convenient and affordable option; you don't have to commit to a flight until the day before and the price of the ticket always remains the same, whether you but it 3 months, 3 weeks, or 3 days beforehand. Royal Air Maroc (RAM) and its competitor, Regional Airlines, fly to all major cities domestically. RAM offers the best deals for students and the under-25 crowd, while Regional Airlines has more convenient times.

BY TRAIN

Where possible, trains are the best way to travel. They are faster than buses, more comfortable, and fairly reliable and prompt. Second class tickets on trains are slightly more expensive than corresponding CTM bus fares; first class tickets cost around 20% more than second class tickets.

The main line runs from Tangier via Rabat and Casablanca to Marrakesh. A spur connects Fez, Meknes, and points east with the main line at Sidi Kasem, near Meknes. There is one nightly couchette train between Fez and Marrakesh. Air-conditioning (usually) and "non-smoking" cars are available. Tickets bought on board cost at least 10% more and may cause you all kinds of trouble with the conductor. No student fares are available. Be wary of old schedules that show times for the Atlantic coast spur south of Casa; it has been out of service for a couple of years now. InterRail (see p. 43) *is* valid in Morocco, although Eurorail is not. Fare so low, however, that Inter-Rail is not really worth using in Morocco.

BY BUS

In Morocco, wherever you want to go, whenever you want to go, there is a bus waiting to take you. They're not all that fast, and they're not all that comfy, but they're extremely cheap and reach nearly every corner of the country. **CTM (Compagnie de Transports du Maroc),** the state-owned bus line, has the fastest, most luxurious, and generally most epensive buses (all things being relative). In many cities the CTM has its own station separate from other lines and reservations are usually unnecessary. The second largest company is **SATAS,** focused primarily in southwest Morocco. While equal to CTM in speed and reliability, the buses are slightly less comfortable. Several dozen other private companies operate as well. Still other private companies, called **cars publiques** (a.k.a. souq buses), have far more departures and are generally slower, less comfortable, and cheaper. In the bus stations, each bus company has its own info window, so you must window-hop for destinations and schedules.

The **baggage check** at CTM bus depots is usually safe. Your bags, however, may not be accepted for storage if you don't have padlocks on the zippers. Private bus companies also have baggage checkrooms; they're generally trustworthy and accept any kind of bag.

BY TAXI

Two separate hordes of taxis prowl Moroccan streets: intra-urban *petits taxis* and inter-urban *grands taxis,* both dirt cheap by European standards. Petits taxis, small Renaults or Fiats that each can hold a strict maximum of three passengers, are all painted in one color depending on the municipality (red in Fez, blue in Meknes, etc.) and can't leave the city or take you to the airport. Make sure the driver turns the meter on; they are required to do so by law. If the driver won't turn it on, take another cab; at the very least, agree on the price before you go (around 25% of what the driver asks is probably a fair price). There is a 50% surcharge after 8pm. Don't be surprised is the driver stops for other passengers or picks you up with other passengers in the car, but if you are picked up after the meter has been started, note the beginning price.

Grands Taxis, typically beige or dark blue Mercedes sedans, travel anywhere in the country but are the most expensive way to travel. Unlike their *petit* cousins, they don't usually cruise for passengers, instead congregating at a central area in town. They hold up to six passengers (four in the back, two in the front), but it can be wise to buy two spaces for some extra room. A taxi won't go until it is filled with passengers going in the same direction. Ask other passengers what they are paying to avoid being ripped off. *Grands Taxis* will take you anywhere in the country, but are the most expensive way to travel. They usually congregate in a central area in a city.

BY CAR

There are two reasons to rent a car in Morocco: you are traveling in a large group, or you wish to travel to areas underserved by Morocco's public transportation system. Otherwise, don't. Moroccan roads can be very dangerous; reckless passing and maneuvers, excessive speed, bad roads, and poorly equipped vehicles are all par for the course. For more general information and advice on renting cars, see p. 645.

Hertz, Avis, and **Europcar** all rent cars; expect to pay about 400dh per day for an economy car once taxes and insurance is factored in. Large local firms such as **Afric Car, Moroloc,** and **Locoto** offer cars for considerably less money but are also less reliable. Both international and local firms are easy to find in all major cities.

Once in your car, you face a myriad of complications, the most serious being police **security checks.** Virtually any trip you take will take you through at least one, and usually many more, checkpoints. Expect to be pulled over and to be required to produce your passport and other relevant papers. One tactic if pulled over is to immediately ask for directions, either in French or Arabic. You also may be stopped for **traffic violations,** real or not. The fine is payable on the spot in dirhams and may be negotiable; asking for a receipt could be construed as provocative. Whatever you do, do not travel with drugs (which are illegal anyways) in your car.

Routes goudronées (principal roads), marked "P," are paved and connect most cities. **Pistes** (secondary roads), designated "S," are less smooth. If travelling in the **desert,** be sure to bring at least 10 liters of bottled water for each person and for the radiator on the trip. Move rapidly over sand; if you start to bog down, put the car in low gear and put the pedal to the metal. If you come to a stop in soft sand, push rather than sink. **Gas** is about 10dh per liter.

Driving in Morocco without the **Michelin map** of Morocco all but ensures that you will get lost. Fortunately it is available both abroad and in Morocco. Even with the map, you still should inquire if specific roads are passable. One place to make inquiries is the automobile association, the **Touring Club du Maroc,** 3 Ave. de F.A.R., Casablanca (tel. (2) 20 30 64).

MOROCCO

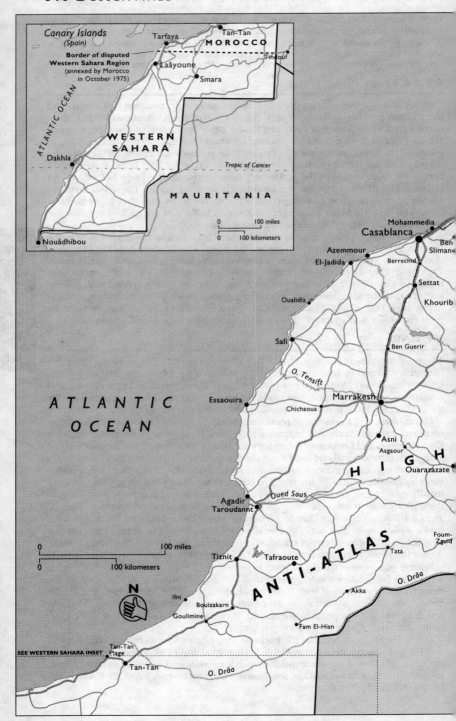

HUSTLERS AND FAUX GUIDES

Moroccans are generally extremely hospitable and friendly toward travelers. Unfortunately, it is often hard to distinguish between this genuine hospitality and the invitations from hustlers, who bear most of the responsibility for Morocco's extraordinarily low tourist return rate (between 10 and 20 per cent by some counts, even lower by others). Faux guides, loitering around attractions and city gates, usually have two motives: getting a cut of whatever you buy from local merchants (added to the cost of your purchase) or extorting money out of you to leave you alone. You may at times seem under siege, subtle threats are part of many hustlers' rhetoric, but rest assured that they pose almost no physical danger if you just keep your cool and repeat either "Non, merci" or "La shukran" enough times. Hustling is illegal and cops will help if you ask. If you want a guide, go to the tourist office and hire an official guide there for 120dh half day, 150dh full day. They generally know their stuff and will keep hustlers off you.

■ Accommodations

YOUTH HOSTELS

The **Federation Royale des Auberges de Jeunesse (FRMAJ)** is the Moroccan Hosteling International (HI) affiliate. Beds cost 20-40dh per night, and there is a surcharge for non-members everywhere but in Casablanca. Some hostels sell HI memberships on the spot. Call ahead for reservations as beds can be scarce. To reserve beds in high season, get an International Booking Voucher from FRMAJ (or your nearby HI affiliate) and send it to the hostel four to eight weeks in advance. A sleepsack is sometimes mandatory and always preferred, while lockouts and curfews are rare. For info like hostel addresses, write to FRMAJ, Parc de la Ligue Arabe, B.P. 15998, Casa-Principale, Casablanca 21000 (tel. (2) 47 09 52; fax 47 20 24). For info on your national youth hostel association and other general information see **Accomodations,** p. 11.

HOTELS

Although there is an official star-system for rating hotels in Morocco, the number of stars reflects little other than price. Hotels that are not part of the system are not necessarily worse—their standards vary greatly—but usually cheaper. Rooms can vary widely even within a particular hotel, so ask to see another room if you don't like the first offering. Or find another hotel, often next door. Cheap hotels in Morocco are really cheap—as little as 40dh per night. Listings are generally divided between medina and ville nouvelle establishments. Medina hotels are usually cheaper than their *ville nouvelle* counterparts, but less comfortable and with significantly fewer amenities. Hot showers, when available, may cost extra (usually less than 10dh). Cold showers are typically free.

CAMPING

Camping is popular and cheap (about 10dh per person), especially in the desert, mountains, and beaches. Like hotels, conditions vary widely. Use caution if camping unofficially, especially on the beaches, as theft is a problem.

■ Keeping in Touch

Most useful communication information (including **international access codes, calling card numbers, country codes, operator** and **directory assistance,** and **emergency numbers**) is listed on the **inside back cover.**

Morocco has recently invested hundreds of millions of dollars into modernizing their telephone system, resulting in markedly improved services. Pay phones accept either coins (2dh will cover most local calls) or, more often, Moroccan phone cards. The rates for the two types of phones are the same.

Phone cards, available at post offices, are in generally too large a denomination to be practical. Entrepreneurial Moroccans hang around phone banks (found near all post offices) and let you use their phone cards. You pay them only for the units used—typically 2dh per unit, a rate not much worse than doing it yourself. To use the card, insert and dial 00. Once the dial tone turns into a catchy tune, dial the number. **Phone offices** *(teleboutiques)* are located in most cities. To make a collect call, ask the desk attendant at the local telephone office to place a call *en P.C.V.* ("ahn PAY-SAY-VAY"). Write down your name and the country, state, city, and telephone number you want to call. Collect calls can also be made from payphones; simply dial 12 and ask to call *en P.C.V.* Remember that the initial zero (0) in **city codes** is dialed only when dialing from another area within Morocco; from outside of Morocco the number is omitted. Local calls do not require dialing any portion of the city code.

The best way to make international calls is probably a calling card; see p. 50 for more details. Numbers for major international calling cards (AT&T, MCI, Canada Direct, BT Direct, Ireland Direct, Australia Direct, New Zealand Direct, and South Africa Direct), are listed on the back cover.

Air mail *(par avion)* can take from 7 to 31 to an infinite number of days to reach the U.S. and Canada (about 10dh for a slim letter, postcards 4-7dh). Less reliable **surface mail** *(par terre)* takes up to two months. **Express mail** *(recommande* or *exprès postaux)*, slightly faster than regular air mail, is the most reliable way to send a letter or parcel. Post offices, shops, and some *tabacs* sell postcards and **stamps.** Faxes, email, phone calls, and jaunts to Spain are more reliable communication options.

LIFE AND TIMES

Morocco has carved its identity out of a host of disparate influences. At the crossroads of Africa, Europe, and the Near East, Morocco is also the Far West of the Arab world. It is both an ancient civilization descended from nomadic tribes and a modern nation that has struggled against imperial powers for its sovereignty. The distinct richness of Moroccan culture, arts, and food testifies to these influences.

■ History and Politics

Pre-Islamic

Morocco is a cultural as well as commercial crossroads. Berbers native to the mountains and plateaus met up with the Phoenician and Carthaginian colonists on the North African coast by 500 BC. The Romans who followed left behind economic prosperity and a few ruins. After Titus's destruction of the temple in Jerusalem in the third century BC, Jews trickled into Moroccan cities. The Vandals established control over the area until AD 683, when the Islamic army of **Uqua Ibn Nabir** swept in to convert the pagans, found Qu'ranic schools, and make Arabic the dominant language. The many southern Africans in the country share a common history; Arab slave traders kidnapped their ancestors from Mali, Guinea, the Sudan, and Senegal. Gold, spices, aphrodisiac rhinoceros horn, salt, ebony, ivory and, of course, camels made Morocco a wealthy link in the commercial chain between Africa and Europe.

The Rise and Fall of Islam

Berber princess and prophetess Kahina killed herself at the news of the Arab conquest in 702, and by the end of the 8th century the Moors had converted most of the Berber rebels to Islam. **Idris (I) Ibn Abdallah,** a distant relation to **Muhammed the Prophet,** fled Baghdad in 789 to found the Kingdom of Fès near the old Roman settlement of Volubilis. Centered in Spain, the Moorish empire displaced the Idrisian dynasty, but by the 11th century **Almoravids** from the Western Sahara had quashed Spanish-Muslim control and established their own kingdom in Marrakech.

MOROCCO

A golden age of **Merinid** and **Wattasid** rule (1244-1554) promoted a cultural and intellectual boom and tied Morocco to Spain. As Muslim influence in Christian Iberia waned, however, the Spanish turned aggressive. A second wave of Jewish immigrants fled to Morocco during the Spanish Inquisition of 1492, during which Queen Isabel and King Fernando forced them to choose between conversion or death. The Wattasids formed an army of refugees and converted or mercenary Christians to battle the conquering Spanish and Portuguese, but by the early 1500s, the Iberians had established control over Moroccan ports and a number of inland territories.

The European Contenders

The **Saadis** drove out the foreign influences and reunited Morocco. Under **Ahmed el Mansour**—a.k.a. Ahmed the Gilded—Morocco expanded its trade in slaves and gold in Timbuctoo and parts of the Sudan. When the **Alawite dynasty** overthrew the Saadis in 1659, they took over Marrakech and the area around Fès, controlled by religious mystics known as **marrabouts.** The Alawite dynasty rules to this day. But battling European rulers conspired to disintegrate Moroccan unity. England copped Tangier in 1662 as part of a settlement with a war-weary Spain; France slowly invaded northern Africa, winning a major battle at Isly in 1844.

France's major stroke of luck came with the death of Sultan Hassan of Rabat in 1893. His 13-year-old son **Abdul Aziz,** an expert at bicycle polo and a famous playboy, ascended the throne. The French encroached massively upon Moroccan territories, eventually occupying Casablanca. By 1912, the French had exiled the ruling vizier, Abd el-Hafid, and secured an official protectorate in the **Treaty of Fès.** The equivalent **Treaty of Algericas** gave the Spanish the same rights.

Struggle for Independence

In 1921, **Abd el Krim,** now considered the founder of modern Morocco, began to organize a rebel army against the Spanish in the Rif Country. The troops of Major Francisco Franco (future General and Spanish dictator), with aid from Marshall Pétain's French army, forced the rebels to surrender by 1926.

Sultan Muhammed V ignited the nationalist movement with the founding of the Independence Party in 1944. The French deported nationalist leaders and exiled Muhammed without so much as a suitcase in 1952. The ensuing popular unrest combined with the revolt in Algeria forced the French to abandon their hard line. Mohammed returned to the throne on November 18, 1955, and signed a treaty of independence for French Morocco on March 2, 1956. The independence of most of Spanish Morocco followed one month later.

Muhammed V's successor, King Hassan II, came to the throne in 1961 and introduced a constitution favoring pro-monarchists, only to be vehemently protested by opposition party UNFP. In 1963, ten of UNFP's leaders, including **Ben Barka,** were implicated in a plot to overthrow the monarchy and sentenced to death. In 1965, King Hassan declared a national **state of emergency,** snagging direct control of executive *and* legislative powers. Hassan's 1970 constitution ended the emergency and restored limited parliamentary government, but two abortive military coups and governmental divisions delayed democratic parliamentary elections until 1977.

Modern Morocco

Today Morocco is nominally a **constitutional monarchy:** though assisted by a parliament and a Chamber of Representatives, the king can dissolve parliament and easily manipulate the country's political parties. Hassan has pledged to "improve the balance between legislative and executive powers," but Morocco's human rights abuses, alleviated only in part by a 1991 initiative, have failed to foster political freedom. Censorship meticulously stamps out opposition from such groups as trade union activists and university radicals. A drought further sapped monarchist support, but after sluggish industrial growth, riots, and the drain of civil war in Western Sahara on national resources, Morocco began recovery in the 90s. The North Africa-wide Islamist movement has kept Morocco on paranoid toes, though King Hassan's regime is stable in comparison to neighboring countries. Morocco's relations with neighbors are strained, particularly with Algeria, where illegal arms shuttling resulted in the closing of the Morocco-Algeria border in 1994. Southern Europe, also aligned against Islamist infiltration, has been taking a greater interest in Morocco, for one advocating tighter border controls.

Current Events

A U.N. sponsored referendum is to be held on the status of Western Sahara in December 1998, but it now looks increasingly unlikely to take place—neither the Polisario Front nor the Moroccans wish to risk losing the vote and both are finding it easy to stall the U.N. brokered deal. Determining who receives a vote has become a contentious and byzantine process of geneaological research—each potential voter is being vetted by having tribal elders quiz them on their family tree. The Polisario Front wants voting restricted to those listed in a 1974 Spanish census from which the Moroccan government claims tribes were omitted. Polisario agrees tribes were skipped, but denies they number as many as 65,000, the Moroccan claim. To complicate matters, hundreds of thousands of Moroccans have been recently lured to the Western Sahara through tax breaks, subsidies, and public works projects. Sorting out these jumbled masses and deciding the status of the omitted has proven exceedingly difficult. Seven years after the original referendum was scheduled the issue still looks unlikely to be settled any time soon.

Morocco's economy continues to languish, partly due its dependence on IMF and World Bank loans, which plunge the economy into increasing dependence on Western funding, and exacerbate social inequalities. On the political front, King Hassan II has ushered in a set of political reforms that have given a center-life coalition a small, but nonetheless significant, amount of power. Mr. el Youssoufi, the leader of the opposition party (USFP), is optimistic about the new political scene, and expects to carry out massive reforms in educational, health-related, and social sectors.

■ Language

Morocco is a paradise for polyglots. Classical Arabic (al-Fusha) is the official language of the country, but it is now an almost exclusively a written language and is rarely spoken. A Moroccan Arabic dialect, Darija, is the language of the people, although almost everybody you meet will speak at least some French and will expect you to as well. In certain northern towns, Spanish fills the linguistic role of French. Many Moroccans speak English and German, but don't count on it.

In this book, city names appear first in English, then in Arabic. A massive shift from European street names is underway, so some of the streets mentioned in this book may go by a different title (listed in both French and Arabic when necessary and possible). *Rues* and *calles* may revolt and become *zankats, derbs,* or *sharias.*

■ Religion

There is much more uniformity of religion than language. **Islam** is the state religion (the king is also "commander of the faithful"), and less than 1% of the population is not Muslim. The Islamic calendar began in 622, the year Muhammad began ruling the Islamic polity. Muslims believe Muhammed was the last Prophet in a line including Noah, Abraham, Moses, and Jesus. He received God's (Allah's) words from the angel Gabriel; these words are recited to the people in the Qu'ran, the holy scripture of Islam. There are five pillars of Islam: profession of monotheistic faith, prayer, almsgiving, pilgrimage to Mecca, and fasting during the holy month of Ramadan. Muhammad led the polity until his death in 632, during which time his words and deeds were recorded in *hadiths* (reports) that comprise the *Sunna,* or exemplary practice of Muhammed. Since the Prophet failed to plan ahead, his death provoked a "who rules?" crisis, spurring the Sunni and Shia division; the former believed his successor

MOROCCO

MOROCCO

All About Ramadan

During **Ramadan**, Islam's holy month, Muslims abstain from food, drink, cigarettes, and sex from sunup to sundown (around 4:30am to 8:30pm) to cultivate spiritual well-being, compassion, and charity. Ramadan after dark is another story: sirens prompt adherents to chug *harira*, streets burst with music, and the feasting and religious services begin. The **Night of Power,** on the 27th day, honors the passing of the Qur'an from God to Muhammad. When the moon comes out, the king officially ends Ramadan, and **Aid el-Saghir,** celebrated with enormous breakfasts and gifts to children, marks the end of the daylight fast.

City services operate through the holy month for the most part, but restaurants and cafes catering to locals close during the day. Ramadan is slightly earlier each year (calculated using the Islamic *(hijri)* lunar calendar), so over 30 years it makes a full cycle. Ramadan falls between Dec. 20, 1998 and Jan. 19, 1999.

Non-Muslims should be especially respectful during Ramadan; watch where and when you eat, drink, and smoke. In rural areas, where locals are not accustomed to tourists, a lack of sensitivity may draw outright hostility. All but the fancier tourist establishments close from dawn to dusk. But in large cities such as Tangier and Rabat, many restaurants stay open all day during Ramadan.

---

should be chosen among a community of men, the latter insisted pure spiritual leaders (Imams) should succeed. Most Moroccans are Sunni Muslims.

Local Islamic holidays akin to Catholic saint days are **moussems.** These last several days and feature group pilgrimages to local shrines, street bazaars, and agricultural fairs. Rowdier *moussems* treat observers to music-and-dance events that may include charging cavalcades of costumed, armed equestrians. Most fall in summer; exact dates vary with the Islamic calendar and the decisions of local governments.

■ The Arts

ART AND ARCHITECTURE

Diverse architectural forms define Moroccan landscapes and cityscapes. Intense hot and cold combined with Berber austerity and Islamic privacy give **Berber architecture** an enclosed and stark nature. *Kasbah,* the monumental houses of Berber potentates, feature central courtyards, dark and narrow passageways, animal shelters, simple high slope-walled towers, thick walls, and plain facades. *Ksour* (plural of *ksar*), or fortified Berber villages densely pack "apartments." Both are made with *pisé* or packed earth, and are fast turning to ruins, unable to withstand wind and sand storms.

In the 10th century, Fez residents built the first Moroccan **mosques** (sometimes called *djemmas*), al-Andalus and the Kairaouine. Any place Muslims pray is a mosque, or *masjid* ("place of prostration"). The *qibla* wall contains the prayer niche *(mihrab)* and indicates the direction of Mecca. There are two basic designs for mosques: Arab style, based on Muhammad's house with a pillared cloister around a courtyard, and Persian style with a vaulted arch (an *iwan*) on each side. Non-Muslims may not enter Moroccan mosques, but tourists can gawk through doorways of famous ones. Out of respect, visitors should stay away during services. Attached to most mosques, Qu'ranic schools or **medersas** have classrooms, libraries, and a prayer hall around a central courtyard and fountain. Most Merinid and Saadien mosques display secular and/or devotional artistry.

Islam's opposition to idolatry spurred incredibly ingenious geometric and calligraphic decorations. Colorful patterns swirl across tiles, woodwork, stone, and ceramic. In less doctrinaire times, Almoravid artists slipped in designs that vaguely resemble leaves and flowers. **Calligraphy,** particularly elegant renderings and illuminations of the Qur'an, became another outlet for creativity as well as religious devotion. Merinids, following the strict Almohads, relaxed the formalism to include floral and geometric strains, manifest in curved nd straight-edged *zallij* (mosaic tiles).

Sultans reserved their most dazzling designs for **imperial palaces,** with long, symmetrical series of reception and dwelling rooms studded with decorative gates, hidden gardens, and tiny pools and fountains. The diversity of styles is truly incredible.

CRAFTS

Of Moroccan handicrafts, **carpets** are the most popular with tourists. For centuries, Moroccan women have made rug-weaving their occupation. The central motif of knotted Arabian-style rugs is a kaleidoscope of rich blues, reds, greens, and yellows, enclosed by an intricate border. Berber *kellim* carpets (often used as wall-hangings or bedspreads) are cheaper. Woven rather than knotted with wool, each is stunningly embroidered with "silk." Despite many mass-produced textiles, most Moroccans continue to dress in handmade clothing. Fès has been center of a renowned **leather** industry since the 15th century, when the Moors returned from Spain. High-quality Moroccan leather, a multimillion dollar export, can be inexpensive locally. Moroccan **pottery** dates back 1000 years, but, like leather work, the craft prospered in the 15th century. A medley of color splashes the white background of traditional Andalusian-inspired enameled pottery. Saharan and Berber **terra cotta** ware and roof tiles are also common. Especially in the South, distinctive and chunky **silver jewelry** often comes inlaid with colorful stones or plastic. Silver has long been valued by Berber women who couldn't afford gold. Craftsmen work wonders with **wood.** Boxes, chess sets, and desk paraphernalia—all splendidly inlaid—are available.

Souks (markets) display all of these handicrafts in abundance and widely varying quality. *Souks* target tourists for the sale of craftwork. Bargaining is big; the best policy is to gauge the personal worth of an item and stick to that price. It's unlikely you'll get a great deal by Moroccan standards, but the value ratio is still excellent in Western terms. Don't enter the store without an intent to buy. There's no obligation, but Moroccan merchants skillfully create needs previously nonexistent. When you walk in, act blasé. Declare that you've done your shopping already and/or claim student status. Walking out the door (with the faintest hint of reluctance) is very effective. Above all, never let a price escape your lips unless you intend to pay it.

■ Food and Drink

Moroccan chefs lavish aromatic and colorful spices on their dishes—pepper, ginger, cumin, saffron, honey, and sugar are culinary staples. The cuisine, climate, and unfamiliar microbes can combine to make gastrointestinal problems likely. Many travelers take every precaution and still end up running to the bathroom on an hourly basis. Bottled mineral water (Sidi Ali) is always recommended. A policy of peeling all fruit and cooking all vegetables can be helpful; the truly cautious avoid salads and raw vegetables on *kefta* sandwiches.

TYPICAL FARE

A dish of the North African staple, **couscous,** contains semolina grain, a cumin or saffron sauce, and whatever fish, meat, or vegetables the cook feels like throwing in. **Tajine,** the other common Moroccan main course (and the term for the ceramic bowl in which it's served), refers to a wide variety of stews with fish, chicken, or lamb mixed with potatoes, olives, prunes, nuts, and other vegetables. *Brochettes* (hamburger sandwiches), soups, and honey-soaked pastries are also on every street corner.

MEALS AND RESTAURANTS

The restaurant scene in Morocco consists mainly of tourist-oriented restaurants, replete with dancing and music, and small locally patronized restaurants, generally in the medina. A complete meal includes a choice of entree (*tajine*, couscous, or perhaps a third option), salad or *harira*, a side of vegetables, and yogurt or an orange for dessert. Lunchtime spans from noon to 2pm, dinner between 7 and 9pm. Still, many restaurants serve at any time. If a service charge isn't automatically included, a 10% **tip** will suffice. Even more informal than the *brochetteries*, marketers hawk everything from *harira* to fresh potato chips to *brochettes* (roasted skewered beef, lamb, or brain). Almost every Moroccan main course includes meat; *couscous aux legumes* probably has the least meat. For vegetarians, the best bet is to cook with produce from the market. Less expensive *tajine* is made with *kefta* (delicately seasoned ground meatballs) often served on a baguette sub-style, as is *Merguez*, a spicy beef or lamb sausage.

Gourmands and cheapskates alike swear by **harira**, a spicy chickpea-based soup with or without meat stock. **Poulet** (chicken) can be had either *rôti* (roasted on a spit with olives) or *limon* (with lemon). Pricier and harder-to-find specialties include **mechoui**, whole lamb spitted over an open fire, or **pastilla**, a pastiche of squab, almonds, eggs, butter, cinnamon, and sugar under a pastry shell. For a lighter treat, slurp sweet natural yogurt with mounds of peaches, nectarines, or strawberries, or try an oily Moroccan salad with finely chopped tomatoes, cucumbers, and onions. Snackers munch briny olives (about 1dh per scoop), roasted almonds, and cactus buds (on the streets 1dh a bud). Oranges are the cheapest, sweetest, most eminently peelable fruit in the country.

DRINKS

Drink plenty of **purified water**—only purified water. Send back any bottle that isn't completely sealed—it's most likely tap water. Water-sellers, with their red costumes and cymbals, earn more money posing for tourists' pictures than selling anything. Despite Islam's prohibition of alcohol, French, Spanish, and local **wines** can be bought in most supermarkets and some restaurants (but not in the medina). Moroccan wines tend to be heavy; go with the *gris* (try *Oustalet* or *Gris de Boulaouane*) rather than the *rouge*. Watery local **beer**, called Stork or Flag, goes for 12-15dh. Entirely male Moroccan **bars** major in heavy drinking, making them intimidating to most tourists. **Orange juice** (2-4dh) is always fresh and widely available. Other fruit juices blend whole fruit with milk. Make sure the juice is not diluted with tap water. **Tea**, the national drink, was introduced by the English in the 18th century. The ritual of preparing it with fresh mint sprigs and loads of sugar penetrates most Moroccan's daily routine (4-6dh per pot).

■ Sports

Moroccans are deeply passionate about soccer, with intense rivalries between competing clubs. Their national team was undefeated in qualifying matches for the World Cup; once in the cup, they were on the verge of advancing to the second round before being edged out by Norway. Basketball runs a distant second in popularity.

Participatory sports abound. Skiing is possible most winters in Ifrane (late Dec.-early March), hiking everywhere, water sports on the Atlantic coast, and biking nationwide. Karate and kick-boxing are also widely popular. Women, long restricted by Moroccan society, are increasingly—if somewhat controversially—partaking in various sports, mainly low-contact endeavors.

MOROCCO

■ Prose to Peruse

Edith Wharton's *In Morocco* (1925) is a collection of episondic descriptions of Rabat Salé, Fez, and Meknes. Walter Harris's *Morocco That Was,* a turn-of-the-century journalist's diary, features a wry account of a Brit's kidnapping by the international bandit Raissouli. *The Voices of Marrakech* by Bulgarian Nobel Prize recipient Elias Canetti eloquently records a European Jew's encounter with Moroccan Jews. *The House of Si Abd Allah,* edited by noted scholar Henry Munson, is an oral history of a Moroccan family which provides insight into the country's social history. Paul Bowles, an American who settled in Tangier, sets much of his fiction in Morocco. *The Spider's House* is a numbingly gorgeous introduction to the country and to Bowles, a semi-cult figure in Morocco. Albert Camus's classics *The Stranger* and *The Plague,* both set in neighboring Algeria, offer a vision of expatriate life under the Maghreb's sun.

Among the few Moroccan works available in English, *Love With a Few Hairs,* *M'hashish,* and *The Lemon* are Muhammad Mrabet's bits of contemporary Moroccan life. Historian Youssef Necrouf's *The Battle of Three Kings* is an entertaining account of medieval violence and intrigue under the Saadian dynasty.

MOROCCO

THE MEDITERRANEAN COAST

Northern Morocco comprises the ports and beaches of the Mediterranean Coast and the jagged Rif Mountains. This region is most easily accessible from Europe and is a likely point of entry into the country. It may not be "real Morocco," due to its proximity to Europe and the prevalence of prostitution (in Tangier) and cannabis farms (in the Rif mountains), but it still affords a taste of the Arab world.

■ Tangier طَنجَة

For travelers adventuring out of the European playground for the first time, disembarking in Tangier (pop. 554,000) can be a distressing experience. Upon arrival at the port, any number of guides—do not trust any of them, they are hustlers—aggressively coax vacationers into following their misleading lead. Since the concentration of guides greatly diminishes as one moves away from the port, they become little more than a small nuisance if the visitor approaches this situation with the proper attitude and preparation (see **Hustlers and Guides,** p. 648, and **Orientation and Practical Information,** below).

Once one has passed the hustlers, Tangier's peculiar, mongrel charm reveals itself. For centuries the region bounced from one imperial power to the next (Phoenicians, Romans, Portuguese, British, and Spaniards among them), culminating in 1923 with the declaration of Tangier as an "international zone," in which the city was loosely governed by eight European states and the U.S. During this period, the regime placed emphasis on ego rather than law and order, and Tangier consequently attracted an impressive assortment of bored heiresses, drug users, spies, pedophiles, currency speculators, Beat Generation poets, and mixtures thereof. Although Moroccan independence shortly ended Tangier's status as a free port and closed 100 brothels in 1960, vestiges of the epoch remain. The Anglican Church has Mass, the Café de Paris—*the* cafe of WWII secret agents—churns out lattes, hashish flows from the Rif, a gay community is visible, and hard currency circulates on the black market. The medina ("old town") looms, overlooking the town, the Mediterranean, and the European continent beyond. Tangier is unlike anywhere else in Morocco, and its aura of contemporary romance amid urban squalor endures.

ORIENTATION AND PRACTICAL INFORMATION

Relative to other Moroccan cities, Tangier is navigable. Guides are entirely unnecessary, so know your initial destination before arriving and don't listen to badgering guides who insist that your hotel has gone out of business or that you *must* visit the medina and drink tea. From the ferry terminal, you can take a blue *petit taxi* or walk to the center of town. If you take a **taxi**—this is advisable—either agree on the fare in advance (about 5dh to the center of town) or make sure the driver uses the meter. If you **walk,** leave the ferry terminal along the main road running through the port compound; it will lead you through the large double arches onto the **avenue d'Espagne.** On the right is a **CTM bus station;** on the left is a white **train station.**

The sprawling **ville nouvelle** ("new town") surrounds the port in all directions. The town's central road is the **boulevard Pasteur.** To find this road, follow av. d'Espagne running parallel to the beach and take a right on the narrow rue Ibn Zohr. Turn left onto the paved street after the steps and then turn right after two short blocks, bringing you to the intersection of bd. Pasteur and bd. Mohammed V. Turn right onto bd. Pasteur toward **place de France,** the heart of Tangier's ville nouvelle. A right turn at pl. France onto rue de la Liberté and a short walk down a winding hill leads to the **Grand Socco,** which is the largest square and sits outside the west wall of the **medina.** The **Petit Socco** can be reached by crossing the Grand Socco and entering the medina on rue as-Siaghin, which runs through the medina.

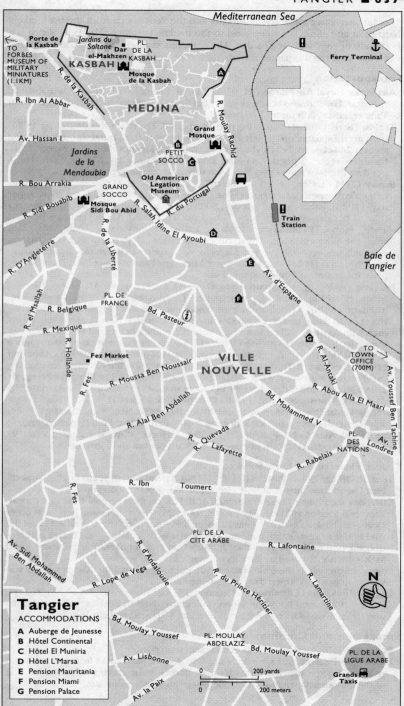

Mediterranean Sea

Ferry Terminal

Porte de la Kasbah

TO FORBES MUSEUM OF MILITARY MINIATURES (1.1KM)

Jardins du Soltane el-Makhzen

Dar

PL. DE LA KASBAH

KASBAH

Mosque de la Kasbah

R. de la Kasbah

R. Ibn Al Abbar

MEDINA

R. Moulay Rachid

Av. Hassan I

Jardins de la Mendoubia

Grand Mosque

PETIT SOCCO

R. Bou Arrakia

GRAND SOCCO

Mosque Sidi Bou Abid

Old American Legation Museum

R. Sidi Bouabib

R. Salah Idine El Ayoubi

R. du Portugal

R. D'Angleterre

R. de la Liberté

Train Station

Baie de Tangier

R. el Maallah

R. Belgique

PL. DE FRANCE

Bd. Pasteur

Av. d'Espagne

R. Mexique

R. Hollande

Fez Market

VILLE NOUVELLE

R. Fes

R. Moussa Ben Noussair

R. Al-Antaki

TO TOWN OFFICE (700M)

Av. Youssef Ben Tachine

R. Alal Ben Abdallah

Bd. Mohammed V

R. Abou Alla El Maari

R. Quevada

Lafayette

PL. DES NATIONS

Av. Londres

R. Rabelais

R. Ibn

Toumert

R. Fes

Av. Sidi Mohammed Ben Abdallah

R. d'Andalousie

PL. DE LA CITE ARABE

R. Lafontaine

R. Lope de Vega

R. du Prince Héritier

R. Lamartine

N

Bd. Moulay Youssef

PL. MOULAY ABDELAZIZ

Bd. Moulay Youssef

PL. DE LA LIGUE ARABE

Av. Lisbonne

Grands Taxis

Av. la Paix

0   200 yards
0   200 meters

MOROCCO

Tangier

ACCOMMODATIONS

A Auberge de Jeunesse
B Hôtel Continental
C Hôtel El Muniria
D Hôtel L'Marsa
E Pension Mauritania
F Pension Miami
G Pension Palace

For an alternative route to the medina and the Petit Socco from the port, take a sharp right and climb the steep road to the medina entrance. The Petit Socco is a short walk up av. Mokhtar Ahardan. The main **bus station** lies about 2km from the port. Following rue d'Espagne, turn right onto av. Beethoven.

Transportation

Airplanes: Royal Air Maroc (tel. 93 55 01), pl. France. To Marrakesh, Casablanca, Gibraltar, London, and destinations within Spain. A taxi to the **airport,** 16km from Tangier, costs 70dh for up to 6 people.

Trains: There is one **station** in the port compound. The **main station** (tel. 93 45 70) is on av. d'Espagne, on the left after exiting the port compound through the large arches. 2nd-class to: Fez (5½hr., 3 per day, 93dh); Meknes (5hr., 3 per day, 77dh); Casablanca (6hr., 3 per day, 114dh); Rabat (5½hr., 3 per day, 87dh); Asilah (1hr.,1 per day, 13dh—it leaves you 2km from town, so the bus is preferable).

Buses: CTM Station, av. d'Espagne (tel. 93 24 15 or 93 11 72), next to the port entrance. Buses to: Marrakesh (10hr., 1 per day, 165dh); Casablanca (6hr., 6 per day, 110dh); Rabat (5hr., 6 per day, 80dh); Larache (2½hr., 3 per day, 29dh); Fez (6hr., 4 per day, 85dh); Meknes (5hr., 4 per day, 70dh); Asilah (1½hr., 3 per day, 15dh). **Non-CTM buses** leave from rue Yacoub el-Mansor at pl. Ligue Arabe, 2km from the port entrance. These buses offer more departures at lower prices, although you get what you pay for in terms of speed and comfort. A *petit taxi* to the terminal costs 12dh. Ask blue-coated personnel about ticket info. The standard price for luggage is 5dh—don't give more.

Ferries: Try **Voyages Hispamaroc** (tel. 93 31 13; fax 94 40 31) on bd. Pasteur, below Hôtel Rembrandt. English spoken. Open daily 8am-12:30pm and 3-7pm. Alternatively, buy a ticket at the port. You'll need a boarding pass (available at any ticket desk) and a customs form (ask uniformed agents). Near the terminal, pushy men with ID cards will try to arrange your ticket and obtain (and fill out) your customs card for 10dh. Do it yourself instead. To: Algeciras (2½hr., 8 per day, Class B 2960ptas or 210dh); Tarifa (2hr., departs Sa-Th 3pm, F 7pm, 210dh); Gibraltar (2½hr., 3 per week Tu, F, and Su, 250dh). To reach the ferry companies directly, call **Trasmediterránea,** 31 av. de la Résistance (tel. 93 48 83); **Limadet Ferry,** av. Prince Moulay Abdallah (tel. 93 39 14); **Comanau,** 43 rue Abou Ala El Maari (tel. 93 26 49); or **Transtour,** 4 rue El Jabha Ouatania (tel. 93 40 04).

Grands Taxis: Quick transport to nearby locations (Tetouan, Ceuta, Asilah). Prices subject to bargaining, but a fair price is 20dh when taxis are full (6 passengers).

Car Rental: Avis, 54 bd. Pasteur (tel. 93 30 31). **Hertz,** 36 av. Mohammed V (tel. 93 33 22). Both charge 250dh per day plus 2.50dh per km and a 20% tax.

Tourist, Financial, and Local Services

Tourist Office: 29 bd. Pasteur (tel. 94 80 50). Friendly staff, some English spoken. Free tourist brochures, but little else. Open M-F 8:20am-noon and 2:30-6pm.

Currency Exchange: There is a branch of **BMCE** on most ferries. Its main office in Tangier is located at 21 bd. Pasteur (tel. 93 11 25). No commission here or at other Moroccan banks. Open M-F 9am-12:45pm and 3-6:45pm. There is an **ATM** on the street. Many hotels change money, some at a hefty commission. Travel agencies near the port must change money at official rates. Major banks line bd. Pasteur and Mohammed V. Say *non* to hustlers offering exchange service.

Luggage Storage: At the **train station** (5dh per bag). Open 24hr. Also at the **bus station** (5dh per bag). Open daily 4am-midnight.

English Bookstore: Librairie des Colonnes, 54 bd. Pasteur (tel. 93 69 55), near pl. France. Novels and books on Moroccan culture, English classics, and popular fiction (from 50dh). Open M-F 9:30am-1pm and 4-7pm, Sa 9:30am-1pm.

Emergency and Communications

Police: (tel. 19), located at the port and main train station.

Late-Night Pharmacy: 22 rue de Fez (tel. 93 26 19), two blocks from bd. Pasteur at pl. France. They dispense through tiny windows in the green wall on the left side of the entrance. Open M-F 1-4pm and 8pm-9am, S5a-Su 8pm-9am.

MOROCCO

Medical Assistance: Red Cross, 6 rue El Monoui Dahbi (tel. 93 11 99), runs a 24-hr. English-speaking medical service. **Ambulance:** (tel. 93 33 00).

Post Office: 33 bd. Mohammed V (tel. 93 25 18 or 93 21 25), the downhill continuation of bd. Pasteur. Poste Restante and telephones. Open M-Th 8:30am-6:30pm, Sa 8:30am-12:15pm.

Telephones: 33 bd. Mohammed V, to the right and around the corner from the post office. Open 24hr. **Telephone Code:** (0)9.

ACCOMMODATIONS

Those unphased by Tangier's frenzy can find plenty of hotels in the medina and stay close to the action. Those who wish to distance themselves from hustlers will prefer the ville nouvelle. There is a broad range of quality and prices, although the two don't always correspond.

Medina

The most convenient hotels cluster near **rue Mokhtar Ahardan,** formerly rue des Postes, off the Petit Socco. From the Grand Socco (see **Orientation,** above), take the first right down rue as-Siaghin to the Petit Socco. Rue Mokhtar Ahardan begins at the end of the Petit Socco closest to the port. At night parts of the medina can be unsafe.

Hôtel Continental, 36 Dar Baroud (tel. 93 10 24; fax 93 11 43). From the Petit Socco, take rue Jemaa el Kebir (ex-rue de la Marine) downhill toward the port to the Continental's blue gate. Veer left at the raised overlook. Swarming with English chaps, this is a truly grand hotel, former home of princes, artists, and writers. The grand piano and bird cage in the lobby have aged better than the mattresses, and showers are hot only in the morning, but the Art Deco rooms ooze character. Singles 180dh; doubles 210dh. Free breakfasts. Try to reserve ahead.

Pension Mauritania, rue as-Saghin (tel. 93 46 77) at the Petit Socco. Follow directions to the Petit Socco (see above). Enter right off the Socco. A bit of a backpacker's mecca. Shared toilets, free cold showers, and sufficiently clean rooms. Singles start at around 60dh; doubles 100dh.

Pension Palace, 2 rue Mokhtar Ahardan (tel. 93 61 28). Downhill, on the alley exiting the Petit Socco to the right. Sanitary, if teeny-tiny, rooms. Clean communal bathrooms. The establishment boasts an impressive courtyard featured, along with the Hôtel Continental, in Bertolucci's film adaptation of *The Sheltering Sky.* Singles 55dh; doubles 90dh, with bath 120dh.

Ville Nouvelle

Hotels line av. d'Espagne as it heads away from the port. The best values, though, lie a few blocks uphill toward bd. Pasteur and bd. Mohammed V.

Auberge de Jeunesse (HI), 8 rue el-Antaki (tel. 94 61 27), down av. d'Espagne away from the port and half a block up the road to the right after Hôtel Marco Polo. Visitors rave about the warden Mohssine, a friendly and reliable source of info. New, firm dormitory beds, but no lockers. HI members 35dh; non-members 45dh. Hot showers 5dh. Office open M-Sa 8-10am, noon-3pm, and 6-10:30pm, Su 8-10am and 6pm-midnight; closes at 10:30pm in winter.

Hôtel El Muniria (Tanger Inn), rue Magellan (tel. 93 53 37). Take the 1st right after Hôtel Biarritz on av. d'Espagne, walking away from the medina, and follow as it winds uphill. William Burroughs wrote *Naked Lunch* in room #9 (now the owner's room). Jack Kerouac and Allen Ginsberg stayed in room #4. Beat Generation aside, this establishment is a great deal for Tangier, with spacious rooms, hot showers, towels, and the relaxed, ex-pat-frequented Tanger Inn bar next door. Singles 120dh; doubles 140dh.

Pension Miami, 126 rue Salah Eddine el-Ayoubi (tel. 93 29 00), off av. d'Espagne. Frayed turquoise and magenta rooms, handsomely carved ceilings, and a balcony cluster on each floor. Basic communal bathroom. Singles 50dh; doubles 80dh. Hot showers 10dh.

MOROCCO

Hôtel L'Marsa, 92 av. d'Espagne (tel. 93 23 39), away from the port but right on the main drag; you can't miss its restaurant (see **Food** below), which juts out onto the sidewalk. Very clean rooms cost little considering their location. Singles 80dh; doubles 160dh. Hot showers 7dh.

FOOD

Medina

The medina dining experience begins at the **Grand Socco,** where you can stall-hop feasting upon Moroccan treats, including some foods only available elsewhere during Ramadan. On the southwest corner sprawls a huge vegetable and meat **market.** Head from the Grand Socco in the direction of the Petit Socco and you will find inexpensive local eateries *bizaf* (Moroccan Arabic for "galore"). Those listed here are more established, more expensive, and less local.

Africa Restaurant, 83 rue Salah Eddine el-Ayoubi (tel. 93 54 36), just off av. d'Espagne near Pension Miami. The name would indicate a sure-fire tourist trap, but the food and prices do not. Lip-smacking soup precedes delicious lamb couscous (30dh). Big 4-course *menu du jour* 45dh. Open daily 9am-12:30am.

Restaurant Hammadi, 2 rue de la Kasbah (tel. 93 45 14), the continuation of rue d'Italie just outside the medina walls. The only Moroccans here are waiters and serenading Andalusian musicians. Despite the touristy veneer, the food is excellent. Avoid lunch, when tour groups fill every seat. Specialties are *tajine* (40dh) and couscous (45dh). Beer and wine served. Open M-Su noon-3pm and 8pm-1am.

Ville Nouvelle

International cuisine can be found throughout the ville nouvelle—more a product of enterprising Moroccans than a vestige of Tangier's international status. For hot sandwiches, try the storefronts off bd. Pasteur. The restaurants along av. d'Espagne tout unspectacular *menus touristiques* for 50dh or more. You're better off starting at pl. de France, Tangier's heart, and scouting from there.

L'Marsa, 92 av. d'Espagne (tel. 93 19 28). Popular restaurant and cafe with outdoor dining, Italian menu, and *tajine* squeezed in. Praiseworthy pizzas (30-35dh) and 10 flavors of Italian ice cream (10-20dh). Open daily 6am-midnight.

Emma's BBC Bar, along the beach across from Hôtel Miramar. Beach club, catering to paunchy holidaying Brits, serves burgers and curry dishes. Has Morocco's only full English breakfast (45dh). 19% tax. Open daily 8am-2am.

La Pagode, 3 rue al-Boussiri. Take a left off av. du Prince Hertier, 3 blocks south of pl. de France, to find excellent but somewhat pricey Chinese food with wine.

SIGHTS

In and Near the Medina

While a guide is unneeded, it is dangerous to wander off the medina's main streets or on the beaches at night. Try to limit nighttime exploration to the ville nouvelle.

The medina's commercial center is the **Grand Socco.** This busy square and traffic circle is cluttered with fruit vendors, parsley stands, and kebab and fish stalls. In the colorful **Fez Market**—uphill on rue de la Liberté, across pl. de France, and two blocks down rue de Fez on the right—local merchants cater to Tangier's European community. Berbers from the Rif ride into the Dradeb district (west of the Grand Socco along rue Bou Arrakia and northwest on rue de la Montagne) on Thursdays and Sundays to vend pottery, parsley, olives, mountain mint, and fresh fruit. Opposite rue de la Liberté where rue Bou Arrakia joins the Grand Socco (through the door marked #50), a cache of 17th- and 18th-century bronze cannons hide in the **Jardins de la Mendoubia.**

To reach the **Kasbah** (fort), enter the next large gate to the right of gate #50. (*Open M-Sa 8am-2pm; off-season M-Sa 8:30am-noon and 2:30-6pm. 5dh.*) Veer left, then follow

Gold(trigger)finger

The **Forbes Museum of Military Miniatures** (tel. 93 36 06), set in the late American tycoon's old Tangier pad on rue Shakespeare, contains the world's largest collection of toy soldiers—115,000 of them. *(Open F-W 10am-5pm. Free.)* Tiny figures endearingly disembowel each other in meticulous re-creations of historic battles, complete with dramatic lighting and sound effects. Believe it or not, it's just plain cool. As are the gardens behind the museum, the setting of the James Bond movie *Never Say Never Again.* They offer a spectacular view of the ocean. To get here from the Kasbah, at the top of rue de la Kasbah turn left onto rue de la Corse. Bear right at the fork onto H. Assad Ibn Farrat and continue straight ahead past a hospital on the right until you reach the white mansion.

rue d'Italie north from the Grand Socco through **Bab Fahs,** the Moorish gateway, and up steep rue de la Kasbah. This street ends at the horseshoe-shaped **porte de la Kasbah,** guarded by industrious hustlers. Rue Riad Sultan runs from the main portal alongside the **Jardins du Soltane,** where artisans weave carpets. Rue Riad Sultan continues to **place de la Kasbah,** a sunny courtyard and adjacent promontory offering a view of the Atlantic and Spain. With your back to the water, walk straight ahead toward the far right corner of the plaza, where just around the corner to the right the sharp **Mosque de la Kasbah** rears its octagonal minaret.

Near the mosque is the main entrance to the **Dar el-Makhzen** (tel. 93 20 97), an opulent palace with handwoven tapestries, inlaid ceilings, and foliated archways, once home to the ruling pasha of Tangier. *(Open W-M 8:30am-noon and 3:30-7:30pm. Free.)* The palace's **Museum of Moroccan Art** is not the country's best, but it does have some intriguing exhibits of ceramics, carpets, silver jewelry, weapons, and Andalusian musical instruments.

An interesting museum, especially but not exclusively for homesick Yanks, is the **Old American Legation,** 8 rue America (tel. 93 53 17), south of pl. de la Kasbah in the far corner of the medina—look for the yellow archway emblazoned with the U.S. seal. *(Open M-F 10am-1pm and 3-5pm. Free, but donations are appreciated and needed.)* The first property acquired overseas by the U.S. in 1820, it was the budding nation's first ambassadorial residence. Among other documents relating to Tangier's international past, the museum displays correspondence between George Washington and his "great and magnanimous friend," Sultan Moulay ben Abdallah. An ever-changing selection of art ranges from strikingly inaccurate 16th-century maps to photographs of the 1943 Casablanca conference. The charming curators deliver excellent tours, even amid restoration efforts.

Avenue d'Espagne runs along Tangier's expansive **beach.** Stick to the main portions frequented by tourists—the deserted areas are prime locations for muggings.

Ville Nouvelle

The **Galerie Delacroix,** run by the French Cultural Center, resides on rue de la Liberté heading toward the medina. *(Open Tu-Su 11am-1pm and 4-8pm. Free.)* The collection displays works by Moroccans as well as foreign artists inspired by their experience here.

The tea-and-crumpet crowd should head down the rue Amengnedu Sud, where aging British expatriates convene at **St. Andrew's Church,** designed by the British to look like a mosque (take a left as you enter the Grand Socco from rue de la Liberté and then a quick left onto rue Amengnedu Sud). The Lord's Prayer is carved on the chancel arch in decorative Arabic. Surrounding gardens and benches offer respite from the medina. Caretaker of 32 years, Mustapha, leads informal **tours.** *(Tours available daily 9:30am-12:30pm and 2:30-6pm. A tip of a few dirham is appreciated. Sunday communion 8:30am, morning service 11am.)* The city's most recent monumental construction is the towering **New Mosque,** an ochre and white structure on **place el-Koweit,** southwest of the Grand Socco along rue Sidi Bouabib.

MOROCCO

ENTERTAINMENT

Place de France has hosted Tangier's social activity since the city's heyday. The most popular evening activity is sipping mint tea and people-watching from a **cafe** on bd. Pasteur. The **Café de Paris** (on the left coming from the Grand Socco), slightly more elegant than its neighbors, hosted countless *rendez-vous* between secret agents during WWII. Also consider downing some tea at **Café Central,** off the Petit Socco, a favorite of William S. Burroughs.

The best place for a quiet drink with little hassle is the **Tanger Inn,** similar to a pub, playing early 80s pop in the background. Those in search of alcohol or peace can try the relaxed **Negresco,** 20 rue Mexique (tel. 93 80 97), with free nuts and olives. Attached to the Hôtel El Muniria (see **Accommodations,** p. 659), it's the city's longest-running bar and regularly attracts resident ex-pats and backpackers. (Beer 18dh, mixed drinks 30-35dh. Open daily 10am-midnight.) Boisterous and seedy affairs run their shady course at many of the discos along **rue el-Moutanabi,** parallel to bd. Pasteur near pl. de France. Bear in mind that Moroccan discos are not safe for solo travelers but can be fun for groups.

■ Ceuta سبتة

Some opt to enter Morocco through Ceuta, a Spanish sovereign enclave, in order to avoid some of the stress of Tangier; Ceuta, however, is less convenient for train travel to the Atlantic coast or Marrakesh. By catching an early ferry, Ceuta-goers can power through to Tetouan or Chefchaouen for their first night. Just a 90-minute ferry ride from Algeciras, Ceuta has an unusual history largely hidden from the traveler by the huge presence of the military and duty-free shopping in town.

Public **buses** and **taxis** ply the route between downtown Ceuta, a couple blocks from the port, and the border crossing into Morocco, 3km away. Bus #47 runs from Pl. Constitución and costs 100ptas. Taxis will run around 400ptas. Once at the Moroccan border, you must cross on foot and find a **grand taxi** to Tetouan (15dh).

Heading both to and from Spain, there are 8 **ferry** departures daily (90min., 1885ptas), with more during the high season. There are also 8 **fast-ferry** departures (35min., 3100ptas). It is always safer to buy your tickets at the port itself. There is a small **tourist office** on the way out of the port as well as a larger one in town that can help with places to stay or transportation details.

■ Near Ceuta: Tetouan تطوان

Odds are that most travelers in Tetouan either just crossed into Morocco via Ceuta or are leaving via Ceuta. For new arrivals, Tetouan can be very intimidating (see **Hustlers and Guides,** p. 648). For those coming from deep in Morocco, Tetouan's drug dealers and other louts will be nothing new. Brush them off to soak up the large, whitewashed medina—considered by some to be one of Morocco's best, if not *the* best—and the engaging Hispanic architecture in this former capital of the Spanish protectorate. Exploration, however, should be limited to the day, as the Tetouan medina can be dangerous at night.

PRACTICAL INFORMATION The ville nouvelle centers around **place Moulay el-Mehdi,** with the medina to the east (a few blocks down the pedestrian street) and the **bus station** a couple of blocks southeast along **rue Achra Mai. CTM buses** run to: Casablanca (3 per day, 120dh); Rabat (3 per day, 100dh); Chefchaouen (1½hr., 4 per day, 25dh); Fez (5hr., 2 per day, 60dh); and Tangier (1½hr., 2 per day, 15dh). **Private companies** have more departures at lower prices. **Grand taxis** to Ceuta leave from in front of the bus station (15dh). Taxis to Chefchaouen (25dh) run from a stand several blocks away; walk from pl. Moulay el-Mehdi away from the bus station along rue Achra Mai and bear left onto rue al-Jazeer; the stand is a few blocks away. Or take a **petit taxi** for 9dh. The **tourist office** is a half block down C. Mohammed II toward the medina on the left. The friendly officials have a **map** to photocopy and **guides** for hire. (Open M-F 8:30am-noon and 2:30-6:30pm.) The **post office** and the adjacent **telephone** office are on pl. Moulay el-Mehdi, as are banks with **ATMs** and **currency exchange.** As always, dial 19 for the **police.**

ACCOMMODATIONS AND FOOD To get to **Hotel Trébol,** 3 bd. Yacoub el-Mansour al Mouahidi, exit the bus station from the lower level and walk a few steps uphill to the right; it's the first left. The hotel is convenient and clean, with a definite Spanish feel to the balconied rooms. (Singles 45dh; doubles 70dh.) **Pension Iberia,** pl. Moulay el-Mehdi, 3rd fl., has clean, breezy rooms and a capable manager (singles 50dh; doubles 70dh). **Restaurants** are cheaper and more Moroccan in the medina, more spiffy and Spanish in the new town, clustered along bd. Mohammed V.

■ Chefchaouen (Chaouen)شَفشَاون

A whitewashed town on a hillside high in the Rif Mountains, Chefchaouen is no longer the complete escape from hustlers it once was, but its relaxed, hippie-hangout atmosphere and cooler mountain air still refresh. This historically Hispanic-dominated town makes a good place to spend your first few days in Morocco coming from Ceuta or your last night before heading to Spain.

ORIENTATION AND PRACTICAL INFORMATION

From the **bus station,** head up the steep hill, taking a right after several blocks onto the only big road you'll hit. Follow this road to tree-filled, circular **place Mohammed V.** It's about a 20-minute walk to the center of town or a few dirhams for a cab. Cross the plaza and continue east on **avenue Hassan II,** the ville nouvelle's main road. Hassan II terminates at the small but busy **Bab al-Ain,** the main entrance gate into the medina. Passing through Bab al-Ain and following the main, twisting street will bring you to **place Uta el-Hammam,** the large plaza at the heart of the medina.

Buses: The bus station is downhill from town but easy to find. Buses heading south fill up, so get tickets early. **CTM:** 7am bus to Casablanca (90dh) and on to Rabat (65dh); 1 and 3pm buses to Fez (46-52dh); 4 afternoon departures to Tetouan (16-18dh); and 1 bus to Tangier (3pm, 33dh). Private companies have buses to Tangier and Tetouan all day long and about 5 buses to Fez every day.

Grands Taxis: Probably the easiest way to get to Tetouan (24dh). They leave a block downhill from pl. Mohammed V. Also to Ceuta (35dh).

Tourist Office: Both the ONMT and Syndicat d'Initiative are non-existent here, but they are unnecessary anyway.

Currency Exchange: BMCE is on av. Hassan II. **Banque Populaire** is just outside Bab al-Ain. Both are open for exchange M-F 8:15am-2:15pm.

Police and Emergency: Call 19.

Medical Services: Hospital Mohammed V, a block west from pl. Mohammed V.

Post Office: Av. Hassan II. Open M-F 8:30am-12:15pm and 2:30-6:30pm.

Telephones: In and around the post office. Same hours as post office.

ACCOMMODATIONS AND FOOD

Chefchaouen has a slew of colorful budget hotels, both in and out of the medina. In the medina, head up from Bab el-Ain; hotels are clustered all along this street and around **place Uta el-Hammam.** Outside, follow av. Hassan II toward Hotel Rif and beyond. Restaurants and cafes are ubiquitous—even inescapable. Find outdoor seating in pl. Uta el-Hammam and classier joints along **avenue Hassan II.**

Hotel Rif (tel. 98 69 82), just outside the medina walls. Follow av. Hassan II to the right around the medina; it's on your left after a few blocks. This classy hotel has clean, comfy rooms, a large salon with satellite TV, and several terraces decorated in a style drawing from 16th-century Morocco and 1970s Americana. Singles 70dh, with shower 90dh; doubles 100dh, with bath 120dh.

MOROCCO

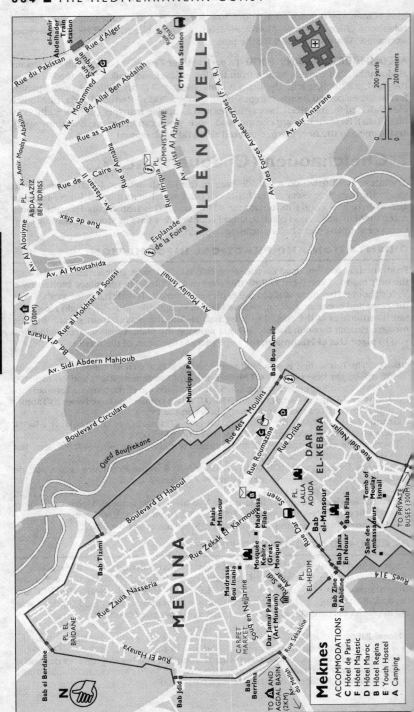

VILLE NOUVELLE

et-Amir Abdelhader Train Station

Rue d'Alger

Rue du Pakistan

Rue de Ghazza

CTM Bus Station

Rue Mohammed de V

Bd. Allal Ben Abdallah

Av. Amir Mouley Abdallah

Av. Mohammed V

Rue as Saadiyne

Rue d'Annaba

Rue Allal Ben Abdallah

PL. ADMINISTRATIVE

Av. Idriss Al Azhar

Av. des Forces Armées Royales (F. A. R.)

Av. Bir Anzarane

PL. ABDALAZIZ BEN IDRISS

Rue de II Caire

Av. Hassan II

Rue d'Annaba

PL. IFRIQUIA

Av. Al Aloulyne

Rue de Sfax

Esplanade de la Foire

Av. Al Moutahida

Rue al Mokhtar as Soussi

Av. Moulay Ismail

TO E (500M)

Bd. d'Ankara

Av. Sidi Abdern Mahjoub

Bab Bou Ameir

200 yards

200 meters

Municipal Pool

Boulevard Circulare

Oued Boufrekane

Rue des Moulins

Rue Roumazine

Rue Driba

Bab Bou Ameir

DAR EL-KEBIRA

Rue Sidi Nejari

Boulevard El Haboul

Smen

Karmoussa

Palais Mansour

Rue Zekak

Madrassa Filale

Rue Daf

Bab el-Mansour

PL. LALLA AOUDA

Tomb of Moulay Ismail

Bab Filala

Salle des Ambassadeurs

TO PRIVATE BUSES (300M)

MEDINA

Bab Tizimi

Rue Zauia Nasseria

Madrassa Bou Inania

Mosquée Kebira (Great Mosque)

Souq en Nejjarine

Rue Sidi Amar

Dar Jama' Palais (Art Museum)

Rue Sekakine

CARPET MARKET

PL. EL-HEDIM

Bab Zine el Abidine

Bab Jama En Nouar

Rues. 314

Rue El Hanaya

PL. EL BRIDANE

Bab el Berdaine

Bab Berrima

TO ▲ AND AGDAL BASIN (2KM)

Rue Mellah du

Bab Jdid

N

Meknes

ACCOMMODATIONS
C Hôtel de Paris
F Hôtel Majestic
D Hôtel Maroc
B Hôtel Regina
E Youth Hostel
A Camping

Hotel Abie Khanda (tel. 98 68 79), through Bab al-Ain on the right. Small bright pastel rooms, a nice terrace, and a pool table. Dorms 40dh.

Hotel Madrid (tel. 98 74 98), along av. Hassan II south of the medina. A newish, if characterless, hotel. Heat in the oft-chilly winter. Singles 120dh; doubles 180dh.

Hotel Bab El-Ain (tel. 98 69 35), on the right just inside its namesake gate. Clean and bare. Singles 26dh, with shower 51dh; doubles 62dh, with bath 102dh.

Chez Aziz, just outside Bab el-Ain, serves tasty sandwiches at low prices. Shrimp 15dh, *kefta* (a Moroccan hamburger) 10dh.

Bar-Restaurant Om Rabih, on the right along av. Hassan II toward Hotel Rif (see above). Inexpensive Moroccan all-stars (*tajine* 25dh), seafood (shrimp 30dh), and wine and beer. Open M-Sa 11:30am-2:30pm and 6-10pm.

SIGHTS AND ENTERTAINMENT

Chefchaouen's steep **medina** is one of Morocco's best and brightest. Entering through Bab al-Ain, walk uphill and east toward **place Uta al-Hammam,** the center of the medina. The 15th-century structure there, the **Tower of Homage,** belongs to the **kasbah,** built in the 17th century by the famous Moroccan rogue Moulay Ismail. *(Open daily 9am-1pm and 3-6:30pm. 10dh.)* Inside is a small **crafts museum,** a nice garden, and a little scholarly institute. Back in the square, opportunities abound for shopping and extended tea-sipping sessions. The minaret visible from the square, with the rare octagonal form, soars above the 16th-century **Grand Mosque.**

Chefchaouen's **souq** operates Mondays and Thursdays in the square beside the Hotel Magou (down the stairs from av. Hassan II). Berbers descend from all over the Rif to sell fresh veggies and not-so-fresh clothes. More appealing than this admittedly second-rate souq are **hiking** possibilities in the region. Following the **Ouad Laou River** upstream into the hills for just a few kilometers yields spectacular results. Ask at your hotel (or the Hotel Rif) about more organized hikes and guides.

THE MIDDLE ATLAS الأَطلَس المُتَوَسِّط

The cities and towns nestled among the peaks of the Middle Atlas mountains form Morocco's heartland. Home to the imperial cities of Fez and Meknes, the nation's agricultural breadbasket, the stellar Roman ruins of Volubilis, and the spiritual center of Moulay Idriss, the Middle Atlas region holds the key to Morocco's historical heart.

■ Meknes مكناس

Meknes lies amid a gray-green agricultural checkerboard, an hour west of Fez and three hours east of Rabat. Named for the Berber tribe Meknassa, this decidedly provincial town has the largest Berber population in Morocco. Although less arresting than Morocco's other imperial cities, the atmosphere is less touristy, the souqs are a bit tamer and offer better deals, and the monuments left by Sultan Moulay Ismail, the famous Moroccan rogue, remain impressive. Ismail chose Meknes as his seat of power in 1672; then, using notoriously brutal tactics, he attempted to turn this relative backwater into a capital that would rival Versailles. The city peaked during Ismail's reign, but with his massive memorials surviving intact and the spectacular ruins at Volubilis nearby, a few days in Meknes are still well-spent.

ORIENTATION AND PRACTICAL INFORMATION

The river **Oued Boufrekane** divides Meknes's three "boroughs": the **medina** and the **imperial city** lie to the west, and the modern **ville nouvelle** to the east. The train and CTM buses deposit passengers in the ville nouvelle. Tree-lined **Avenue Mohammed V,** the new city's main north-south drag, intersects with **Avenue Hassan II** north of the CTM and train stations (to the right when exiting both). Follow av. Hassan II, which turns into **avenue Moulay Ismail,** to approach the medina via **Bab Bou Amir.**

MOROCCO

To reach the colossal **Bab el-Mansour** (the entrance to the imperial complex), head up the hill from Bab Bou-Amir, take a right on **rue Roumazine** and then a left on **rue Dar Smen.** Local buses #5, 7, and 9 shuttle between the CTM bus station in the ville nouvelle and Bab Mansour (20min. walk); a *petit taxi* costs no more than 10dh.

Trains: Meknes has 2 stations, but only the **Meknes el-Amir Abdelkader Station,** rue d'Alger, 2 blocks from av. Mohammed V, is for travelers' use; the misnamed **Meknes Main Station** is far from the center of town. Both stations have identical connections. To: Fez (50min., 8 per day, 15dh); Rabat (2½hr., 4 per day, 45dh); Casablanca (3¾hr., 4 per day, 70dh); Tangier (5hr., 4 per day, 60dh).

Buses: CTM, 47 bd. Mohammed V (tel. 52 25 85). Near av. Forces Armées Royales. To: Fez (1½hr., 7 per day, 18dh); Rabat (3hr., 8 per day, 38dh); Casablanca (4hr., 8 per day, 63dh); Tangier (5hr., 3 per day, 70dh); Er-Rachidia via Fez (6hr., 2 per day, 95dh). **Private companies** depart from a station just outside Bab el-Khemis on av. Mellah, outside the medina on the opposite side from the ville nouvelle. Prices and departures vary.

Taxis: Grand Taxis fester next to the private bus station and outside the el-Amir Abdelkader train station. To: Fez (17dh); Rabat (40dh).

Tourist Office: 27 pl. Administrative (tel. 52 44 26). From the Abdelkader train station, go straight 2 blocks, turn left onto Mohammed V, and immediately right. Cross rue Allalben Abdallah and continue on to Hôtel de Ville. Veer right and it's on the right after the post office. Friendly staff, limited English. (Unnecessary) official local guides 120dh per ½day, 150dh per full day. Open M-F 8:30am-noon and 2:30-6:30pm. **Syndicat d'Initiative,** Esplanade de la Foire (tel. 52 01 91), off av. Moulay Ismail, inside the yellow gate. Open M-F 8:30am-noon and 2:30-6:30pm.

Currency Exchange: It's easiest to change cash and traveler's checks in the ville nouvelle. Try the **BMCE,** 98 av. F.A.R. (tel. 52 03 52). Its **ATM** accepts Visa and MC. Exchange window open daily 10am-2pm and 4-8pm. **Hôtel Rif,** Zenkat Accra, around the corner from the tourist office, cashes traveler's checks, too.

Police: call 19.

Late-Night Pharmacy: Red Cross Emergency Pharmacy, pl. Administrative (tel. 52 33 75). Side entrance to the Hôtel de Ville. Open daily 8:30am-8:30pm.

Hospitals: Hôpital Moulay Ismail, av. F.A.R. (tel. 52 28 05 or 52 28 06), near av. Moulay Youssef. **Hôpital Mohammed V** (tel. 52 11 34).

Post Office: pl. Administrative. Open M-Sa 8:30am-12:15pm and 2:30-6:45pm. **Branch office** on rue Dar Smen, near the medina.

Telephones: Available at the post office daily 8:30am-9pm. Use the side entrance if the post office is closed. **Telephone Code:** (0)5.

ACCOMMODATIONS AND CAMPING

Medina

Rues Roumazine and **Dar Smen** are the headquarters for the medina's budget hotels. For directions to the medina, see **Orientation,** above.

Hôtel Maroc, 7 av. Roumazine Derb Ben Brahim (tel. 53 07 05). Take your second left off rue Roumazine into an alley (Derb Ben Brahim); then veer left at the fork. Mellow owner presides over a collection of sufficiently clean, small rooms around a leafy courtyard. Cold showers and Turkish toilets add to the atmosphere. In summer and Christmas 50dh per person; in winter 40dh per person. Breakfast 15dh.

Hôtel de Paris, 58 rue Roumazine. Basic and clean enough. Next door to a *hammam* (bath house) for that true Oriental experience (5dh). Singles 30dh; doubles 60dh.

Hôtel Regina, 19 rue Dar Smen (tel. 53 02 80). Another adequate medina hotel, recently renovated. Singles 60dh; doubles 90dh; triples 120dh. Showers 5dh.

Camping: Municipal Camping Agdal (tel. 53 89 14), on the ramparts of the medina. Outdoes any option in the hotel scene. Crowds gather in the beautiful, wooded park for the excellent amenities, including hot showers (5dh) and cooking facilities. 17dh per adult, 12dh per child, 10dh per tent, and 17dh per car. The restaurant's 3-course *menu* goes for 45dh. Reception daily 8am-1pm and 4-8pm.

Ville Nouvelle

Staying in the ville nouvelle means greater comfort, higher prices, and easy access to banks, CTM buses, and trains. Most of the cheapest hotels lie around **avenues Mohammed V** and **Allal ben Abdallah.**

Auberge de Jeunesse (HI), av. Okba Ben Nafii (tel. 52 46 98), near the stadium. Follow the arrows toward Hôtel Trans Atlantique off av. Hassan II going to the medina. A 20min. walk from Meknes Abdelkader station (taxi 5dh), far from the city's hustle. Newly painted with clean mattresses. TV room by a pleasant courtyard. In high season members only. Dorms 25dh. Cold showers free, hot showers 5dh (7-8pm only). Reception daily in summer 8-9am, noon-4pm, and 7pm-midnight; in winter 8-10am, noon-3pm, and 6-10pm.

Hôtel Majestic, 19 av. Mohammed V (tel. 52 20 35), close to both the CTM and train stations. Wins the prize for most portraits of King Hassan II per square inch. Newly refurbished rooms, modern restrooms, and hot showers. Singles 102-172dh; doubles 137-205dh depending on bathroom options. 15% discount for *Let's Go*-ers.

Hôtel Continental, on av. des FAR, across the street from the Hôtel Volubilis. Coming from either the CTM or train station, head down av. Mohammed V to your left and take a left at the junction with F.A.R. Comfortable, new, and downright sanitary. Singles 86dh, with bath 131dh; doubles 107dh, with bath 150dh.

FOOD

Medina

Vendors in the **place el-Hedim** hawk *mergouz* sandwiches, freshly made potato chips, and corn on the cob roasted over open coals. Other inexpensive fare sizzles in the one-man *brochetteries* on **rue Dar Smen.** Few places have menus, let alone English or French—dining is an adventure. The daily **vegetable market** sprouts beside Bab Mansour. The **Restaurant Economique,** 123 rue Dar Smen, serves Moroccan staples at reasonable prices (couscous or *tajine* 30dh; open daily 7am-10pm).

Ville Nouvelle

Rotisserie Karam, 2 Zankat Ghana (tel. 52 24 75), just off av. Hassan II. Higher standards than the norm. 20dh buys a decent *tajine*. Diversity has introduced the "sheese-burger *garni*" (24dh). Open daily 11am-11pm.

Pizzeria le Four, av. Zenkat Atlas (tel. 52 08 57), off av. Mohammed V, near the train station. Good pizza and other Italian dishes (50dh). Popular with tourists and hip locals. Wine 35-45dh, beer 11dh. Open daily noon-3pm and 7pm-midnight.

Restaurant Lorraine, 32 rue Moulay Abdelkader (tel. 52 17 10). From el-Amir Abdelkader Station, head left 2 blocks. Family-run restaurant serves simple, well-prepared dishes (*lapin garni, poulet* 25dh). Open daily 11am-4pm and 6-10pm.

Restaurant Marhaba, 23 av. Mohammed V (tel. 52 16 32). Just down the street from the Hôtel Majestic, towards the CTM station. Locals flock here for the spicy *harira* (3dh), while tourists are lured by a plaque outside proclaiming its blessing by a French budget traveler's guide. In any case, serious, cheap eating takes place here. *Brochettes* 18dh, *tajine* 30dh, salads 6dh, omelettes 6dh.

SIGHTS

Meknes's best sights all cluster more or less around the magnificent **Bab el-Mansour,** posters of which adorn the entire country. Through the Mansour lie the remainders of Meknes's imperial past, while away from it thrives the present-day medina.

Imperial Meknes

Attenuated by war, weather, looting, and the Great Earthquake of 1755, the ramparts of the **Dar el-Kebira** (Imperial City) testify to Meknes's former pre-eminence as a capital city. Sultan Moulay Ismail personally supervised the building of over 25km of pro-

MOROCCO

tective **walls** for his city within a city. Strolling about the site with a pickax and whip in hand, the sultan criticized and decapitated workers who displeased him. Slaves who died of exhaustion were buried within the walls they were building. Plundering materials from sights all over Morocco, most famously Roman marble from the ruins at Volubilis, Moulay Ismail raised himself a radiant city. Now only the walls and several large monuments remain. Ismail razed part of the medina to create **place el-Hedim** (place of destruction), an approach to **Bab Mansour,** Morocco's finest gate.

Passing through the Bab Mansour, shake off the guides and be on the lookout for a second, less-impressive *bab* to the right. After passing through the second gate, keep to the right and you'll see the green-tiled roof of the recently-restored **Salle des Ambassadeurs,** where Ismail conducted affairs of state. *(Both the reception hall and dungeon open Sa-Th 8:30am-12:30pm and 2:30-6pm, F 8:30-11:30am and 2:30-6pm. 10dh.)* The guard will invariably offer to unlock the door to the so-called **"Christian Dungeon,"** a six-square-km underground storehouse and granary for the Sultan, his entourage, and their horses. Despite the guard's professions to the contrary, there is no evidence that this housed some 50 to 100,000 Christian prisoners (sorry to disappoint).

Walk through the two blue arches to reach, on your left, the **Tomb of Moulay Ismail** and its accompanying mosque, one of only two Moroccan religious buildings open to non-Muslims. *(Open daily 9am-noon and 3-6pm. Free, no matter what the faux guides at the entrance say. Modest dress (i.e. clothes that cover your limbs) is appropriate.)* Part of the building remains off-limits to non-Muslims, but all may still peer in. The two grandfather clocks flanking the tomb have quite a story behind them: they were offered to Moulay Ismail by Louis XIV, as a consolation prize after the rejection of Ismail's marriage proposal to the French monarch's daughter.

A short trek from Moulay Ismail's tomb is the **Heri es-Souani** (storehouse), a cool granary with immense cisterns designed to withstand prolonged sieges. *(Open daily 9am-noon and 3-6pm. 10dh.)* Nearby, the **Agdal Basin** was both Moulay Ismail's private country club and his reservoir in case of siege. His wives (more than 300 of them) and their 800 charming kids may have swum there to escape the stifling summer heat. To get to the Heri es-Souani and basin from Bab Mansour, follow the signs for the campground and continue down the road for another 100m past the campsite (30min.). Overlooking the basin, **Café Agdal** makes a nice spot for a pot of mint tea.

Medina

On the opposite side of Bab Mansour from the Imperial City sprawls **place el-Hedime,** an enormous open-air market. While Moulay Ismail was busy building his dream palace, everyday people lived (and continue to live) here, much as they had for centuries. Strolling across this vibrant, colorful scene leads to the 19th-century **Dar Jamaï Palace,** built by a powerful government minister under Sultan Moulay Hassan I. It now houses a **museum of Moroccan art** (tel. 53 08 63) that flaunts one of the better collections of crafts in the country, with most pieces contextualized in restored versions of the rooms where they were originally displayed. *(Open W-M 9am-noon and 3-6pm. 10dh.)* Check out the carpets (especially if you plan to buy one) and the master bedroom, stuffed with embroidered divans and topped by a magnificent cupola.

As you leave the palace, immediately turn left onto rue Sidi Amar to enter the **medina.** Follow the alley as it turns left, and then fork right to the green-glazed tile minaret of the **Great Mosque** *(al-masjid al-kebira).* *(You may peek in the door, but entrance, as always, is restricted to Muslims.)* Directly across from the mosque is the breathtaking 14th-century **Madrasa Bou Inania,** a college of theology and Muslim law. *(Open Sa-Th 8:30am-12:30pm and 2:30-6pm, F 8:30-11:30am and 2:30-6pm. 10dh.)* In better shape than most in Morocco, this *madrassa* splendidly typifies traditional Merenid architecture; the courtyard combines cedar, stucco, and *zellij* (mosaic) with characteristic panache. Upstairs there are a number of cells, each of which snugly hosted at least two students. From the roof you can gaze upon the Great Mosque and virtually all of Meknes for a splendid view.

Meknès's **medina,** at the center of which is the mosque, is more pleasant, tranquil, and compact than those of other imperial cities. Facing the Dar Jamaï museum, take

MOROCCO

the alley to the left of the entrance. Push straight ahead to **Souk en Nejjarin,** a major east-west street. Heading left here brings you to the **carpet market** (start low, bargain hard). The rest of the medina is best explored like any other: get lost, then try to find your way out. Wood and metal **souqs,** among others, lurk along the twisty streets.

■ Near Meknes: Volubilis وَليلي

Thirty-three kilometers from Meknes lie the **ruins of Volubilis,** the best-preserved Roman site in Morocco and perhaps all of North Africa. An extensive collection of **Roman mosaics** has earned these ruins "must-see" status on any traveler's itinerary. A major center for trade in olive oil, the city flourished under Roman rule, reaching its zenith in the 2nd and 3rd centuries AD as the capital of the kingdom of Mauritania. The Romans, who viewed their North African possessions as a breadbasket to feed their European citizens, ordered the deforestation of the area to make room for grain crops; as the surrounding treeless plain can attest, they did one helluva job. When the Romans withdrew from North Africa, an isolated colony of Jews and Christianized Berbers continued to inhabit the city, which was much reduced in power and importance. In the 18th century, Moulay Idriss siphoned the population off to Fez and Meknes and "recycled" much of Volubilis's pillars and stones for his palace in Meknes. The so-called "Lisbon" Earthquake of 1755, which wreaked devastation all along the Atlantic seaboard, finally sealed the city's fate.

PRACTICAL INFORMATION The ruins are **open** daily sunrise to sunset, although they are more peaceful and scenic early morning or late afternoon (**admission** 20dh). Unfortunately, there are no booklets, maps, or signs on site to inform viewing. Volubilis makes one of the best places in the country for a **picnic**; even if you don't picnic, it's wise to bring plenty of **water,** especially in the summer. Your best bet for getting to Volubilis is to hire a **grand taxi** from their breeding grounds in Meknes, at the stand at the corner of av. Mohammed V and av. FAR. Either pay per seat (about 25dh) and wait until the taxi fills up, or rent an entire taxi yourself (no more than 200dh—try haggling). Paying per seat, while a good deal cheaper, carries the risk of not finding a taxi for the return trip to Meknes—although it's possible to walk back to Moulay Idriss (5km away; about 1hr.). If you rent an entire taxi yourself, the cab will wait for you while you visit the site then take you back. Either way, don't pay until your entire journey is completed.

A WALK AMONG THE RUINS When U.S. General George C. Patton visited the ruins, he declined an offer of a guided tour—he believed he had been stationed here as a Roman centurion in his previous life and accordingly, knew his way around. If you've been equally lucky, stop reading here. Just past the ticket building, the path forks; the right prong leads north toward most mosaics and Volubilis's main street, **Decamanus Maximus.** One block (about 75m) before arriving at the main street, you'll see the **House of Venus** on your right, home to the best mosaics on the site. The fabulous bronzes in the Rabat archaeological museum came from here. More damaged mosaics surround the central courtyard, which once housed a pool. Strolling northeast up Decamanus Maximus to the **Tangier Gate** provides a **panoramic view** of the site and environs. The first building on the right with your back to the gate is the **Gordien Palace,** the seat of the province's governors. All along Decamanus Maximus Street, numerous mosaics—some preserved better than others—pepper the ruins. The best way to find them is to keep an eye out for worn paths and the red and white ropes that keep folks from trampling all over them.

At the opposite end of Decamanus Maximus from the Tangier Gate is the **Triumphal Arch,** built in 217 AD to celebrate Emperor Caracalla and his scheming mother Julia Domna. Julia assured her son's power by helping him murder his rival Geta in 212 AD. In spite of their questionable ethics, they were quite poplar in Volubilis, probably due to their North African heritage. Before plunderers struck, a bronze chariot and nymph fountains once adorned the arch. Turning left (or to the south) from the arch, you will come across the **Athlete's House**, with an excellent mosaic of an

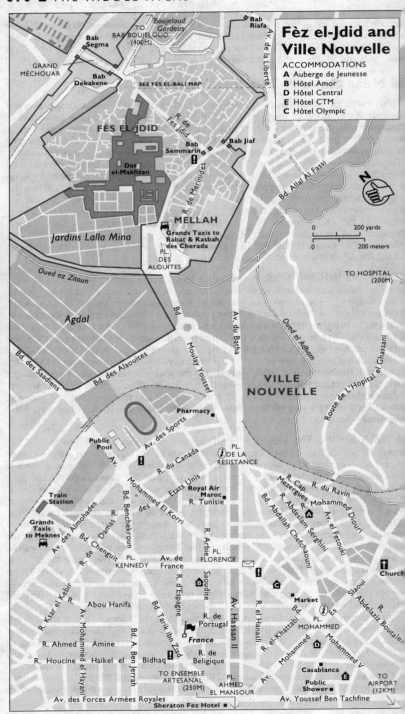

Fèz el-Jdid and Ville Nouvelle

ACCOMMODATIONS
A Auberge de Jeunesse
B Hôtel Amor
D Hôtel Central
E Hôtel CTM
C Hôtel Olympic

Boujeloud Gardens
Bab Riafa
TO BAB BOUJELOUD (400M)
Bab Segma
Av. de la Liberté
GRAND MÉCHOUAR
Bab Dekakene
SEE FÈS EL-BALI MAP
R. de Fès Jdid
FÈS EL-JDID
Bab Semmarin
Bab Jiaf
Dar el-Makhzen
R. de Merinides
MELLAH
Jardins Lalla Mina
Grands Taxis to Rabat & Kasbah des Cherada
PL. DES ALOUITES
Oued ez Zitoun
Agdal
TO HOSPITAL (200M)
Bd. des Saadiens
Bd. des Alaouites
Moulay Youssef
Av. du Batha
Oued el Adham
VILLE NOUVELLE
Route de L'Hopital el Ghassani
Pharmacy
Av. des Sports
Public Pool
R. du Canada
PL. DE LA RESISTANCE
Etats Unis
Royal Air Maroc
R. Tunisie
R Cap
Mezergues Mohammed Diouri
R. du Ravin
R. Abdelam Serghini
Bd. Abdallah Chefchaouni
Av. el Fetouki
Train Station
Bd. Benchekroun
Mohammed El Korri
des
R.
Damas
R. de Chenguit
Grands Taxis to Meknes
Av. des Almohades
PL. KENNEDY
Av. de France
R. d'Espagne
Saoudite
R. Arbie
PL. FLORENCE
Church
R. Ksar el Kebir
R.
Abou Hanifa
Av. de Mohammed el Hayani
Bd. Tarik Ibn Ziad
R. de Portugal
France
R. el Hanafi
Av. Hassan II
Market
Bd. Es
PL. MOHAMMED
R. el-Khattabi
Slaoui
Abdelaziz Boutale
R. Ahmed Amine
R. Houcine Haikel el Bidhaq
R. de Belgique
Mohammed
Mohammed V
Casablanca
Public Shower
TO ENSEMBLE ARTESANAL (250M)
PL. AHMED EL MANSOUR
TO AIRPORT (12KM)
Av. des Forces Armées Royales
Av. Youssef Ben Tachfine
Sheraton Fez Hotel

0   200 yards
0   200 meters

MOROCCO

athlete receiving a trophy. Moving south (back towards the entrance to the site), next comes the **Forum,** the east side of which is made up by the Basilica's columned walls. Despite the name, the **Basilica** was not a temple or church; it served as the Roman courthouse, and its grandness suggests that the administration of justice was a public affair in Volubilis. Continuing on, next door rests the **Corinthian columned temple,** dedicated to Jupiter, Juno, and Minerva. Farther back towards the entrance sits the once luxurious **House of Orpheus** with its preserved dolphin mosaic. Next to the entrance there's a replica **olive press** that you may want to check out.

■ Near Meknes: Moulay Idriss مولاي إدريس

Five kilometers before Volubilis, the road from Meknes passes through Moulay Idriss, a pilgrimage site named after the man who installed Islam permanently into Moroccan life. A third-generation descendant of Muhammad, Idriss united the Berber tribes and founded the country's first dynasty. Non-Muslims cannot visit the mosques or shrines, or spend the night; even so, it's an easy enough stop on the way to Volubilis. From afar you can try to find a spot with a good view of the only **cylindrical minaret** in Morocco and the sacred **Mausoleum of Moulay Idriss.**

■ Fez فاس

The medina in Fez is why you came to Morocco. Artisans bang out sheets of brass, donkeys strain under crates of Coca-Cola, *muezzins* (prayer-callers) wail, and children balance trays of dough on their heads. Along needle-narrow streets, the scent of *brochettes* on open grills combines with whiffs of hash, the sweet aroma of cedar shavings, and the stench of the open sewer (also known as the Oued Fez). Unlike the medinas of other Moroccan cities (most notably Tangier and Casablanca), tourists do not overwhelm Fez, although at times it seems as if hustlers do. Since UNESCO designated Fez a World Heritage Site, the city's walls have been largely restored, and fresh plaster and cobblestones make the medina more fantastic. The banal ville nouvelle is nothing in comparison—except a good refuge after a day struggling in medina-land.

ORIENTATION AND PRACTICAL INFORMATION

Fez is in fact two separate cities: the French-built **ville nouvelle** and the ancient Arab **medina.** The ville's two central streets are, predictably, **boulevard Hassan II** and **avenue Mohammed V.** From the **CTM station** at its southern end, av. Mohammed V runs past **place Mohammed V** and the **Syndicat d'Initiative** on its way to the main post office, where it meets bd. Hassan II. From the post office, bd. Hassan II continues north toward **place de la Résistance,** a hub of ville nouvelle activity. From the place, the **train station** lies west down av. des Etats Unis. **Boulevard Moulay Youssef,** the left fork from pl. Résistance, continues north towards the medina, which is actually divided into three quarters. From west to east, they are the **Mellah (Jewish quarter), Fez el-Jdid,** and **Fez el-Bali.** Fes el-Jdid (new Fez) has two main streets, **Grande rue de Fez Jdid** and **rue des Merínides,** which connect to **place des Alaouites,** in front of the king's palace. Most of Fez's sights reside in Fez el-Bali (old Fez), the city's historic heart. The **Bab Boujeloud** is the main entrance to Fez-el-Bali and opens onto the city's two main streets, the **Tala'a Kebira** and the **Tala'a Seghira.** For more info on getting around Fez al-Bali, see **Sights,** below.

There are several options for transportation between the ville nouvelle and Fez al-Bali. Walking through Fez al-Jdid to Fez al-Bali takes about 30min. Bus #3 at the train station and a different bus #3 at the Syndicat d'Initiative trek to the far end of el-Bali, **Bab Ftouh,** near the **Andalous Quarter.** Bus #2 roars to pl. Alouites. Reach Bab Boujeloud from the ville nouvelle by *petit taxi* (12dh) or bus #11 or 9 (1.90dh) from next to the Syndicat d'Initiative.

MOROCCO

Transportation

Flights: Aérodrome de Fès-Saïs (tel. 62 47 12), 12km out of town along the road to Immouzzèr. Bus #16 leaves from pl. Mohammed V (3dh). *Grand taxis* (100dh) also run there. **Royal Air Maroc** (tel. 62 04 56), av. Hassan II, flies daily to Casablanca.

Trains: av. Almohades (tel. 62 50 01), at rue Chenguit. Second-class trains are comfier than buses, and only cost a few *dirhams* extra. To: Meknes (1hr., 8 per day, 22dh); Rabat (3½hr., 8 per day, 50dh); Casablanca (5hr., 8 per day, 70dh); Tangier (5½hr., 4 per day, 72dh); Marrakesh (9hr., 6 per day, 130dh).

Buses: CTM (tel. 73 29 84). Stops on bd. Mohammed V, away from the medina a few blocks past pl. Mohammed V. To: Meknes (1hr., 10 per day, 18dh); Rabat (3hr., 8 per day, 55dh); Chefchaouen (4hr., 2 per day, 40dh); Casablanca (5hr., 8 per day, 80dh); Tangier (6hr., 2 per day, 85dh); Marrakesh (8hr., 2 per day, 130dh). The **private bus station** (at which there is also a CTM window) is a 5min. walk from the Bab Boujeloud, on the rue Centre Nord past the cemetery.

Public Transportation: Numerous buses (1.90dh; fares increase 20% July-mid-Sept. after 8:30pm, mid-Sept.-June after 8pm. Place Mohammed V and pl. Résistance are

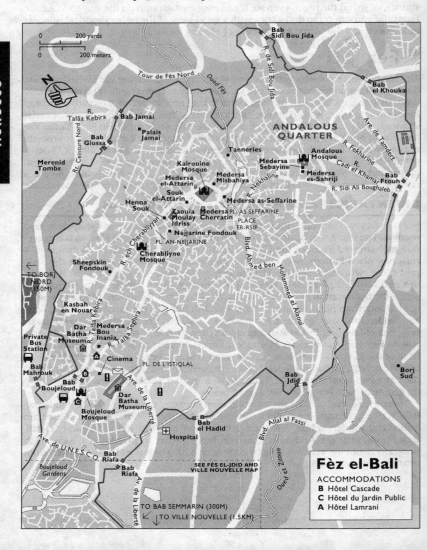

Fèz el-Bali

ACCOMMODATIONS
B Hôtel Cascade
C Hôtel du Jardin Public
A Hôtel Lamrani

the major hubs. Major runs include: bus #9 and 11 beside the Syndicat d'Initiative to Bab Boujeloud; #3 from the train station and pl. Mohammed V to Bab Ftouh; #4 from the pl. Résistance to Bab Smarine in Fez al-Jdid.

Taxis: Major stands at the post office, the Syndicat d'Initiative, Bab Boujeloud, and Bab Guissa. Fares increase 50% July-Sept. 15 after 8:30pm, Sept. 16-June after 8pm. Staff at the Syndicat d'Initiative will help you onto the correct **grand taxi.**

Car Rental: Avis, 50 bd. Chefchaouni (tel. 62 67 46). **Hertz,** 1 Kissauiat de la Foire (tel. 62 28 12), bd. Lalla Mergeme. Renault IV is 300dh per day.

Tourist, Financial, and Local Services

Tourist Office: Syndicat d'Initiative, pl. Mohammed V (tel. 62 47 69), on the way to the CTM bus station from av. Hassan II. Helpful *Fassi* (citizens of Fez) answer almost any question. Same meager maps put out by the Moroccan National Tourism Office. Open M-F 8:30am-noon and 2:30-6:30pm, Sa 8:30am-noon.

Currency Exchange: BMCE, pl. Mohammed V, across from the Syndicat d'Initiative, to the right of the main bank entrance. Handles Visa/MC transactions and traveler's checks, and has **ATMs.** Open M-F 8:15-11:30am and 2:15-4pm. Several banks, just outside the Bab Boujeloud, exchange currency. **Sheraton Fez Hôtel,** at the end of av. Hassan II four blocks down from the post office, has after-hours exchange.

Luggage Storage: At the train station, av. Almohades in the ville nouvelle. 2.50dh per bag per day. Open 24hr.

English Bookstore: 68 av. Hassan II (tel. 62 08 42), near pl. Résistance. All genres: novels, poetry, plays, guidebooks, and phrase books. English-speaking staff. Open M-F 9am-12:30pm and 3-7pm. For newspapers and magazines in English, try the newsstand on rue Mohammed V closest to the post office, or the store 1 block away from rue Mohammed V, behind the central market.

Emergency and Communications

Police: call 19.

Late-Night Pharmacy: Municipalité de Fès, bd. Moulay Youssef (tel. 62 33 80), 5min. uphill from the royal palace, off pl. Résistance. Open daily 8pm-8am.

Post Office: At the corner of av. Hassan II and bd. Mohammed V in the ville nouvelle. Stamps and Poste Restante **Branch offices** at pl. d'Atlas and in the medina at pl. Batha. All open July-Sept. 15 M-F 8am-3pm; Sept. 16-June M-F 8:30am-6:45pm.

Telephones: In the **main post office.** Enter from bd. Mohammed V, to the right of the main entrance. Open 8:30am-9pm. The **branch office** in the medina also has international phones. Same hours. *Téléboutiques* cluster in the ville nouvelle and the medinas. **Telephone Code:** (0)5.

ACCOMMODATIONS AND CAMPING

Ville Nouvelle

The new city provides relative respite from hustlers. Rooms here are more comfortable (and pricey) than those in the medina, and fill entirely in August. The cheapest ville nouvelle lodgings clump on or just off **boulevard Mohammed V,** between av. Mohammed es-Slaoui near the bus station and av. Hassan II near the post office.

Auberge de Jeunesse (HI), 18 rue Abdeslam Serghini (tel. 62 40 85). From pl. Résistance coming from the medina, bear left onto bd. Abdallah Chefchaouni, walk 4 blocks, turn left, and look for the sign. A good place to bond with fellow travelers. The dorms are outdoorsy—a sleep sack is essential. Don't step on the turtles. Members only, but worth a try anyway. Dorms 25dh. Cold showers. Reception daily 8-10am, noon-3pm, and 6-10pm.

Hôtel Central, 50 rue Brahim Roudant (tel. 62 23 33), on the way from the Syndicat d'Initiative (pl. Mohammed) to the CTM bus station on the right, just off bd. Mohammed V. Springy beds and surplus chairs in unadorned rooms. Hot water in room sinks. Singles 59dh, with shower 87dh; doubles 83dh, with shower 114dh.

Hôtel Amor, 31 rue Arabie Saoudite (62 27 24). From the post office, head down av. Hassan II away from the medina and take a left onto rue Arabie Saoudite (look for

MOROCCO

the sign). The Howard Johnson's of Fez. Faux-Almoravid decor is a bit lurid, but comfortable. Wake-up calls. All rooms with bath. Singles 128dh; doubles 160dh.

Hôtel CTM, rue Ksarelkbir (tel. 62 28 11), next door to the old CTM station. Dark hallways belie wide-open rooms. Shabby Scandinavian-style furniture, but a decent deal. Singles 53dh, with shower 76dh; doubles 73dh, with shower 96dh; triples 118dh, with shower 141dh.

Hôtel Olympic (tel. 62 45 29), just off bd. Mohammed V a block from the central market. From the post office, head 3 blocks down bd. Mohammed V and go left. Good location. Clean rooms with bath, hot water. Singles 150dh; doubles 180dh.

Medina

Step right up to **Bab Boujeloud** for budget rooms—they're noisier and dirtier than in the ville nouvelle, and hustlers may seem to track the scent of your luggage, but the hotels are economical and well located for that 24-hour medina experience.

Hôtel Cascade, 26 Serrajine Boujeloud (tel. 63 84 42), just inside Bab Boujeloud and to the right. Spartan, sanitary rooms are spacious for the medina. The terrace and some rooms have a bird's-eye view of the chaos below. Squat toilets. 35dh per person. Haggling acceptable.

Hôtel Lamrani, Talâa Seghira (tel. 36 44 11). Enter Bab Boujeloud; take the 1st right, then a left and through the arch. Unusually clean, with in-room sinks. Benevolent manager says warm showers will be added when there is enough money. A *hammam* next door is available for a few *dirhams.* 30dh per person.

Hôtel du Jardin Public, 153 Kasbah Boujeloud (tel. 63 30 86), a small alley across from the Bab Boujeloud bus station. Relatively clean rooms, some with views. Cold showers (a flight down from most rooms) and toilets. Singles 40dh; doubles 55dh.

FOOD

Ville Nouvelle

Cheap food huts skulk on the little streets to either side of **boulevard Mohammed V. Casa Nostra,** just down from the Hôtel Amorm on rue Arabic Saudite, serves surprisingly good pizza (39dh). Poke through stalls of farm fresh food at the **Central Market** on bd. Mohammed V, two blocks up from pl. Mohammed V (open daily 7am-1pm). Behind the market and the adjacent parking lot sits Fez's answer to a **supermarket.**

Rotisserie La Rotonde, rue Nador (tel. 62 05 89). One block up from Hôtel Central (coming from av. Mohammed V). Chicken that puts Colonel Sanders to shame. Locals pounce on succulent ¼-pound fowls, sauce, bread, and rice (15dh). Order from and pay the white-coated workers only. Open daily 9am-9pm.

Chez Vittoria, 21 rue Brahmin Rouda (tel. 62 47 30), near the bus station. Head 2 blocks down from pl. Mohammed V and 1 block right. Serves omelettes (30dh), pastas, salads, and other European delights. Also, wine (bottle 80dh).

Medina

Food stalls line **Talâa Kebira** and **Talâa Seghira,** near the Bab Boujeloud entrance to Fez el-Bali. A vegetarian feast of *harira,* roasted peppers and eggplant, potato fritters, and bread here will only set you back 10dh at the **stalls** inside. Deeper into the medina, go left from Talâa Kebira at Madrassa al-Atarrine (see p. 676), and head towards **place Achabine** for some of the cheapest eateries in Morocco.

Restaurant des Jeunes, 16 rue Serrajine (tel. 63 49 75), on the right as you enter the *bab. Tajine* 25dh. Other entrees 20-25dh. The *pastilla* isn't made with pigeon, but the chicken could fool most (30dh). Open daily 6am-midnight.

Restaurant Bouayad, 26 rue Serrajine (tel. 63 62 78), next door to Restaurant des Jeunes. Locals loiter around the clock watching satellite TV. Slightly pricey *menu* for 40dh; dive into the *tajine* with almonds. Open 24hr.

SIGHTS: FEZ AL-BALI

Well over 9000 streets make Fez's medina the most difficult to navigate in Morocco. There are three ways to approach it. One is simple and expensive: hire a guide. **Official guides** are at the ONMT and Syndicat d'Initiative. (Ask for a local guide; they know Fez better and are cheaper. Prices for local guides are 120dh per half-day or 150dh for a full day and a meal.) **Unofficial guides** are not recommended; they're much cheaper, but may insist on taking you to shops and are not as well-informed. If you do hire one, nail down an itinerary beforehand and establish your aversion to shopping. A second option is to follow the route below, which hits the major "sights." The final option is simply to get lost in the magnificent atmosphere. When it's time to tear yourself away, ask merchants or women how to get to **Talâa Kebira** and follow it back uphill to Bab Boujeloud.

To see the medina at its liveliest, avoid the hours between noon and 3pm, when most shops and sights close, and Friday, the Muslim day of prayer. Although faux guides will probably follow you for a while, ignoring them or repeating *"Non, merci"* or *"La shukran"* should keep them at bay (see **Hustlers and Guides**, p. 648). The best way to see the main monuments in the medina is to head to Bab Boujeloud (see **Orientation** above) and then wander down Tala'a Kebira from there.

Tala'a Kebira

Virtually all of the sights in Fez's medina lie along the **Tala'a Kebira** (a.k.a. the Grand Tala'a), old Fez's main street and essential reference point. The Tala'a Kebira heads downhill from **Bab Boujeloud** to the **Qaraouine Mosque** area. The **Bab Boujeloud** is the main entrance to the medina; you know it, and the faux guides know it. Once past the gate, though, you should be more or less left alone. The square just inside the *bab* is where the Moroccan revolution against the French occupation began. Down to the right is the **Tala'a Seghira**, Fez's other main street, lined mostly by shops catering to locals (i.e., the famed underwear *souq*). Taking the first left through the gate, then the first right, leads to the beginning of the **Tala'a Kebira.**

To the right after a food *souq* is the spectacular **Bou Inania madrassa** and **mosque**, a school for teaching the Quran and other Islamic sciences. *(Open Sa-Th 9am-noon and 3-6pm. 10dh.)* The intricacy of the cedar and stucco work make this arguably the best *madrassa* in Morocco, perhaps the world—not bad for a college dorm. Classes were held in the courtyard and the adjacent salons, and the students lived three or four to a 2x2m cell on the upper floor. It's no surprise that this building came at a fantastic cost. When the Merinid Sultan Abou Inan was presented with the accounts for the construction in the 14th century, he simply threw them into the canal that separates the mosque from the *madrassa*, exclaiming that no price tag could be put on beauty.

Plunging ahead down a little jog in the road, sniff the (almost) cured products from the **sheepskin fondouq**, just after the entrance to a parking lot on the left. A few meters further along is a super shop to buy **handmade wood crafts**. The owner makes everything he sells, often right before your eyes. *(Set prices; no haggling.)* Beware the cries of *"Batica!"* (watch out) from the drivers of heavily-laden donkeys as you make your way along to the **leather souq**, where animal skins convalesce.

To get to the **Place Najjarine**, with its famed tiled fountain, step off the Tala'a Kebira and turn right onto the only main street in the leather *souq;* go down the ramp, turn left again, and then continue about 25m. A new museum here, slated to open by late 1998 in the fantastic **Fondouq Najjarine**, should be well worth the price of admission for the building alone (10dh). Facing the doors of the *fondouq* and to the right, you'll find a covered market where camera-shy **carpenters** chisel away.

Spice Souq to Zaouia Moulay Idriss II

Back on the Tala'a Kebira, perhaps the most exotic market, the **Attarine ("Spice") Souq,** awaits about 200m down from the leather *souq*. When spices were a more prestigious commodity, its vendors got the privileged spot near the mosque. Off to the right at the beginning of the spice *souq* is the **Henna Souq**, which sells the plant used to temporarily tattoo women at weddings. Toward the end of the Attarine Souq

MOROCCO

Fez's Imperial Past

Unlike many other African countries, the borders that demarcated Morocco after colonialism weren't arbitrary European creations. Morocco has a history of being, more or less, Morocco while the French were still quibbling among themselves in little feudal territories. In many ways, the city of Fez facilitated this remarkable historical cohesiveness. Founded in the 8th century by Moulay Idriss I, Fez rose to prominence with the construction of the **Qaraouine,** a sprawling university-mosque complex in the medina, probably the world's first university. Once as well-funded as any top university is today, this institution attracted all kinds of scholars, religious leaders, and courtiers to Fez, along with the merchants and laborers to serve their every need. With such a wealth of resources, Fez emerged as the most prominent city in the Maghreb; dynasties' political lives were born and died in Fez, and all legal rulings came from its scholars. Seventeenth-century Western maps actually referred to Rabat and its sister city Salé as the "Port of Fez," although they were both over a day's journey from the city.

Today, post-independence Fez has been somewhat eclipsed by Rabat (the political capital), Casablanca (the economic capital), and Marrakesh (the tourist capital). All the same, the city remains in many ways at the intellectual and spiritual helm of the nation, and central to many a Moroccan's sense of national pride.

are several little turn-offs into a **cloth market,** selling slippers and *jelabas* (robes), and a cool **dried fruit market.** The fruit market in turn leads to **Zaouia Moulay Idriss II,** the resting place of the Islamic saint credited with founding Fez. Pilgrims pray here and touch the tomb through a slot in a brass star. Wooden barriers on the streets leading to the tomb were built to keep out donkeys and delineate a sacred zone. For non-Muslims, sad rejection from the shrine is sweetened by the *nougat* sold around the building, a *Fassi* specialty. (5dh will buy enough for a troop of Girl Scouts.)

Qaraouine Mosque and Environs

The Tala'a Kebira ends at **Madrassa al-Attarine,** dating from the 1320s. *(Open 9am-noon and 3-6pm. 10dh.)* Much overlooked by visitors, el-Attarine could be the most peaceful place in the old city. The intricacies of the carvings are spectacular—you decide whether al-Attarine or Bou Inania wins this hotly-debated beauty contest.

Exiting the *madrassa,* turn left, and then left again, and a few meters down is a little opening into the enormous **Qaraouine mosque.** Founded in 859, the mosque is one of the oldest universities in the world. It trained students in logic, math, rhetoric, and the Qur'an while Europe stumbled through the Dark Ages. You can thank or curse the mosque for educating Pope Sylvester II, who later introduced algebra and the modern number system to Europe. Non-Muslims can gawk and take pictures through the portals but may not enter. A bit further down the road, the carpet shop/restaurant/tea salon **Palais de Fès** has a great view of the building from its terrace, almost worth the 10dh pot of tea sold there.

Keeping the mosque on your right (going south), you'll eventually come to the **place Seffarine,** known for its **metal souq,** which deafens travelers with vivid cauldron-pounding. As becomes apparent, there are several potential routes. To reach the **tanneries,** turn sharply left and continue to bear left (follow the worn, six-sided cobblestones). Once the smell becomes intense, head right down a microscopic alley (a tannery *"guardien"* has probably grabbed you by now; 10dh is the basic fee). From a balcony above, you may view skins being soaked in green liquid, rinsed in a washing machine/cement mixer hybrid, dunked in diluted pigeon excrement or waterlogged wheat husks (for suppleness), and saturated in dye.

To exit the medina and reach **Bab ar-Rcif,** a major congregation point for cabs and buses, follow the wide street heading away from the mosque to its end, turn left, and then right. Along the way, you'll pass a **dyers' souq** and cross a bridge over the river.

Andalous Quarter

The Andalous Quarter is across the Oued Fez (river) from the heart of Fez el-Bali. Many of the Moors who fled from Muslim Spain (Andalucía) to Morocco during the 15th-century *Reconquista* settled around the grand Almohad house of worship in Fez, the Andalous Mosque. Its main attraction is the grandiose 13th-century doorway. To find the mosque, head northwest from Bab Ftouh on the east end of the medina, and take the first major left. From Fez el-Bali, cross the river at Port Bein el-Moudoun near the tanneries and head straight down rue Seffrah.

The Dar Batha Museum

Right near the entrance to Fez al-Bali, the Dar Batha museum is well worth a visit, but most prefer to explore the labyrinthine medina first. *(Museum open W-M 9am-noon and 3-6pm. 10dh.)* To reach the Dar Batha, start at Bab Boujeloud, head straight down the Tala'a Seghira, take your first right past the movie theater, and then turn right again at **place de l'Istiqlal**, home to the museum. The building, a 19th-century palace, may be the highlight of this beautiful and well-kept museum. The spacious Andalusian mansion headquartered Sultan Hassan I and his playboy son Moulay Abd el-Aziz during the final years of decadence before the French occupation. The museum, host to Moroccan music concerts in September, chronicles Fez's artistic and intellectual history. The keynote is the display of **ceramics** with the signature "Fez blue," derived from cobalt, standing out on a white enamel background.

SIGHTS: FEZ EL-JDID

Hit Fez el-Jdid after you've had enough of Fez el-Bali; the latter is more interesting. Christians, Jews, and Muslims once co-existed in Fez el-Jdid, built by the Merinids in the 13th century. To the north, the arrow-straight **grande rue de Fez el-Jdid** traverses the area. To the south, the **grande rue des Merinides** cuts through the adjacent *mellah* (Jewish quarter). **Bab Semmarin**, a chunky 20th-century gate, squats between the two areas. To reach this *bab*, take bus #4 from the pl. Resistance, or, better yet, walk to it from the ville nouvelle. To walk from the ville nouvelle to the *mellah* (15min.), take av. Hassan II north past the post office, veer left at the fork two blocks later onto bd. Moulay Hassan, and head straight for the grand pl. Alaouites, where the *mellah* and grande rue des Merinides begin. To get here from Fez el-Bali, take bus #9, which returns by way of Bab Semmarin.

King Hassan II's sprawling modern palace, the **Dar el-Makhzen** (off limits to you, peasant!), borders the **place des Alaouites**. Diagonally off the *place*, **grande rue des Merinides** runs up to Bab Semmarin on the other end of the *mellah*. Off this boulevard, the meter-wide side streets open into miniature underground tailors' shops, half-timbered houses, and covert alleyways. The **jewelers' souq** glitters at the top of grande rue des Merinides. Cackling chickens, salty fish, dried okra, and shiny eggplants vie for attention in the animated covered **market**, inside Bab Semmarin at the entrance to Fez el-Jdid proper. Toward the top of the avenue, the souqs are covered, shading rainbows of *kaftans* and gold-stitched *babouches* (leather slippers).

Bear left at the end of rue des Merinides into the **Petit Méchouar;** on the left is **Bab Dekaken**, the back entrance to the Dar el-Makhzen. Through **Bab es-Seba**, an imperial gate opens onto the **Grand Méchouar**, a roomy plaza lined with streetlamps. From here it's an easy walk to Bab Boujeloud—turn through the opening to the right of **Bab es-Seba,** continue straight for ¼km, veer to the right, and pass through a large arch at the end of road. The entrance to the refreshing **Boujeloud Gardens,** a refuge from the midday sun, is on the right. *(Open Tu-Su. Free.)*

SIGHTS: OUTSIDE THE MEDINA WALLS

The **Merenid tombs** rest north of the old city along the ring road around the medina. The Palais des Merenides, a five star hotel, overlooks the ever-decaying tombs, which occupies one of the most picturesque hillside in all of the Maghreb. From here, the medina unfolds with the same poetry that inspired Paul Bowles and countless other

Orientalist writers. The panorama is most impressive in the half-light of dawn or dusk. During calls to prayer, when over a hundred *muezzin* simultaneously summon the faithful, the experience is mystical. Be warned that misguided youths occasionally hurl stones at visitors. A few hundred paces to the west is the **Borj Nord Museum,** a collection of Moroccan arms and other military apparatus stored in an old look-out tower. *(Open daily 9am-noon and 3-6pm. 10dh.)*

THE ATLANTIC COAST

The towns along Morocco's Atlantic coast, connected by the country's only extensive railway line, are undoubtedly more liberal, laid-back, and open than their conservative cousins in the interior. Those who can (be they men or women) go to the beach regularly to sunbathe, swim, surf, and windsurf, often among European tourists. The west coast hosts Morocco's boom towns—Casablanca, the country's commercial center, and Rabat, its most westernized city—and many a well-fortified medina, once defensive port cities during the 16th and 17th centuries.

■ Asilah أَصِيلَة

Just a short trip away from Tangier (50km), Asilah's sandy shores, quiet streets, and brilliant white medina offer respite from the tensions of Moroccan tourism. Strangely enough, over the last 1000 years, every European power from the Vikings to the French sent flotillas, armies, and even a crusade to wrench tiny Asilah from Moroccan hands. Rarely did Europeans last more than a generation or two before being sent packing from this fabled port city. Although Asilah is no longer unspoiled (it now teems with tourists and attracts touts during July and August), it remains a relatively tranquil spot for kicking back on the Atlantic coast beaches.

ORIENTATION AND PRACTICAL INFORMATION

The main street heading into town is **boulevard Mohammed V,** which ends at the town's center, **place Mohammed V,** a traffic circle. The road to the right leads to a fork in front of the medina. Bear right at the fork onto **rue Zallakah,** which leads to the port. To the left is **avenue Hassan II,** mirroring the walls of the medina.

Trains: The **station** (tel. 41 73 27) is a 20min. walk from town on the Asilah-Tangier highway, near a strip of campgrounds. The bus station is more convenient. To get to town, follow the road by the beach, keeping the sea to your right. A taxi to or from town costs about 10dh. A mini-bus connects the station to town; it leaves from the front of the station just after the train arrives (10dh; you may have to bargain). To: Tangier (1hr., 4 per day, 15dh), Fez, Meknes, Rabat, Casablanca, and Marrakesh (all 4 per day).

Buses: CTM and **private companies** vend tickets together in the same stall off av. Prince Heritier Sidi Mohammed. Take the 1st right leaving pl. Mohammed V; station is in the lot on the left. To: Tangier (departs every 30min. starting at 12:30pm, 13dh); Casablanca (4½-5½hr., 14 per day, 60dh); Fez (3½hr., 4 per day, 55dh); Larache (45min., 14 per day, 10dh); Rabat (4hr., 14 per day, 50dh). Many buses arrive fully occupied, so get to the station early during the summer.

Taxis: pl. Mohammed V, by the bus station. *Grands taxis* only. To Tangier (12dh).

Tourist Office: There may be one open by fall of 1998. And then again....

Currency Exchange: Banks surround the pl. Mohammed V, among them **BMCE.** Open M-Th 8:15-11:30am and 2:15-4:30pm, F 8:15-11:15am and 2:45-4:45pm.

Pharmacy: Pharmacie Loukili, av. Prince Heritier Sidi Mohammed (tel. 41 72 78), one block from pl. Mohammed V. Open M-F 9am-1pm and 4-9pm.

Police: The office in the medina is difficult to locate, but police officers can almost always be found on pl. Mohammed V or at the fork in front of the medina.

Post Office: (tel. 41 72 00). Walking away from pl. Mohammed V on bd. Mohammed V, turn right onto pl. Nations Unis, keeping the park on your right. Post office is 20m up on the left. Open M-F 8am-noon and 2:30-6:30pm.

Telephone Code: (0)9.

ACCOMMODATIONS AND CAMPING

Asilah's hotels, not cheap by Moroccan standards, lie within walking distance of the beach and are clustered mostly around pl. Mohammed V and the east end of av. Hassan II. The town bursts with campgrounds, some of which rent small, inexpensive **bungalows.** Most are near or on the shore north of town, toward the train station. It's best to avoid people who offer rooms in private homes and promise homemade meals for a little extra. Few of these offers are legit, and the risk is considerable: you could end up in an uncomfortable or even dangerous situation.

Hôtel Marhaba, 9, rue Zallakah (tel. 41 71 44), on the corner with rue Abdel M ben Ali; it'll be on your right as you approach the medina from pl. Mohammed V. This popular hotel may fill up during the summer. Prime location, low rates, adequate rooms, and free showers. Singles 80dh; doubles 100dh.

Hôtel Sahara, 9, rue Tarfaya (tel. 41 71 85), a block inland from av. Mohammed V two blocks before pl. Mohammed V. From the bus station, head around the block to your right. Similar to the Marhaba in facilities and quality, but the location isn't quite as good. Singles starting around 80dh.

Hôtel Belle Vue, rue Hassan Ben Tabit (tel. 41 77 47; fax 94 58 69). From the top of Hassan II, take a left on av. Imam Asili, then a right. Friendly, scholarly management and, indeed, there is a pretty view from the two-tiered terrace. Nice rooms with hot showers, although prices are loftier than the lookout. July-Aug. doubles 200dh. Sept.-June doubles 120dh.

Camping Echrigui (tel. 41 71 82), 700m from the train station toward town, where the new port finally ends, next to the similar **Camping es Sala.** Echrigui's office has a lounge with billiards, and a restaurant opens during the summer. Bring plenty of insect repellent. 15dh per person, 10dh per tent and per car. Bungalows with straw roof 90dh. Hot showers 5dh.

FOOD

Restaurants facing the ramparts along av. Hassan II dish out good meals for around 35dh. Down the street is the town **market,** good for produce. For obvious reasons, seafood is a prime choice at most restaurants.

Restaurant Marhaba, 33, av. Hassan II. Outdoor dining under towering ramparts. Multilingual menu. Try the swordfish or calamari (each 30dh).

La Al Kasabah, rue Zallakah (tel. 41 70 12), toward the ocean past Hôtel Marhaba. Reputedly the best restaurant in town, where you can dine on seafood and pasta from a terrace overlooking the street and port. The *paella* (40dh) is much-touted, but the grilled sardines are better and cheaper (25dh). Wine served. Open daily 8:30am-3:30pm and 6:30pm-2am.

Restaurant Najoum, rue Zallakah (tel. 41 74 59), below the Hôtel Marhaba. Grilled swordfish 40dh, plus *brochettes* 15dh and *harira* 3dh. Open daily 7am-11pm.

SIGHTS

Asilah has two attractions: its nearby **beaches** and a shining medina. Beaches north of town are smooth, sprawling delights, and the crowds are generally congenial. Still, be cautious about swimming (there's a strong, dangerous undertow) and don't take any valuables along—thefts occur. Although men tend to leer at and harass women who swim, a 15-minute walk northward leads to mellower sands. The truly ambitious hike 5km to the enclosed cove **Paradise Beach** (1hr.).

The stunning, almost Disney-esque **medina,** bounded by heavily fortified 15th-century Portuguese walls, perpetually smells of new paint due to ongoing restoration efforts (according to cynics, the Minister of Culture lives nearby and likes a tidy medina). Entering through the **Bab Kasaba,** the gate off rue Zallakah, leads you past the **Grand Mosque.** To the right rises the interesting **El-Kamra Tower.** At the north-

A Rebel with a Clue

Moulay Ahmed ben Mohammed er-Raissouli, at once public enemy and public official number one, adopted Asilah as his base of crime and politics when he was named Pasha of the region in the late 19th century. When he was not charming the people, he was stealing from them or, even worse, killing them. By the time the Sultans imprisoned er-Raissouli (at age 23) in 1899, his cruel reputation—*and* popularity—were already sky-high. Once released, er-Raissouli picked up the nasty habit of kidnapping Westerners, fetching US$70,000 ransom in 1904 for American businessman Ion Pedicarris. The central government, nonetheless, decided to appoint er-Raissouli governor of Tangier province. European powers forced the reigning Sultan to oust him in 1907. Two years later, however, the incumbent Moroccan leader defied his foreign critics and named er-Raissouli governor of all of northwest Morocco except Tangier. When Spain entered Morocco in 1912, er-Raissouli organized the locals to take up arms. Later, he allied with WWI Germany, only to be forced out of Asilah by victorious Spaniards. Less than a decade later, in 1925, er-Raissouli was arrested by a Rif revolutionary for, ironically, seeking medical care from Spaniards. In April of that year, he died in confinement—left a rebel without a cause.

west corner, a few old **cannons,** vestiges of a more bellicose era, still point out to sea. Farther down the coast along the walls lies the **Palais deRaissouli,** built in just a year and finished in 1909 (For more about its owner, see above, **"A Rebel Without a Clue"**). Bang on the door and ask the guard to let you peek at the beautiful glassed-in terrace above the ocean (tip of a few dirhams). Continue to the far-western end of the medina and you will come upon **Krikia,** a Portuguese-built lookout with a sublime view of the sea. Children like to plunge the 40 ft. from the Krikia into the ocean.

In August, artists from all over the Arab and African world flock to Asilah for the **International Festival** at the Palais de Raissouli. At other times, the city is also imbued with a sense of the arts: walls are covered with murals, music wafts around corners, and dancing on the beach is not unknown.

■ Larache الأعرايش

During the summer, when tourists and faux guides converge on nearby Asilah, relief is spelled "Larache." This scruffy, relaxing nook along the sandy Atlantic coast has no touristy veneer and is all the more rewarding for it. An ex-colony of Spain (with the Spanish-style architecture to prove it), Larache overflows with cheap housing and fresh seafood. Furthermore, its whitewashed medina is manageable, and it makes a good base for exploring Roman ruins at nearby Lixus.

ORIENTATION AND PRACTICAL INFORMATION Buses arrive five blocks from **place de la Libération** (ex-Plaza de España), the center of activity. From the station, head north toward the center of town, making your first right and then your first left onto **avenue Mohammed ben Abdellah,** which runs into pl. Libération (8min.). Branching to the southeast off pl. Libération is the main artery, **boulevard Mohammed V.** Also off pl. Libération, **Bab al-Hemis** (also called Bab Medina) leads to the **medina** and the **Zoko de la Alcaiceria** (a.k.a. Zoko Chico), its source. Larache's **beach** is located to the north, across the Loukkos estuary, and is accessible by bus (2.50dh) or boat (2dh over, 4dh back).

To reach the **bus station,** leave pl. Libération going right onto av. Mohammed ben Abdallah; continue past Pension Salama, then take the first left and go straight. **CTM** service to: Asilah (45min., 14 per day, 10dh); Tangier (1½hr., 3 per day, 30dh); Rabat (4hr., 5 per day, 50dh); and Casablanca (5hr., 4 per day, 80dh). **Private buses** leave from the same station and send packed buses to the same locations at cheaper prices. **Taxis** park outside the bus station. **Local buses** depart Casbah de la Cigone off av.

Mohammed V, traveling to Lixus (buses #4 and 5) and the beaches (#4). Larache has **no tourist office,** but the town is easily navigated. **Banks,** across from the post office on bd. Mohammed V heading away from pl. Libération, exchange money and have **ATMs**. International **telephones** are located in and around the **post office** (open M-F 8:30am-noon and 2:30-6:30pm; phones inside available M-Sa 8:30am-noon and 2:30-6:30pm). Call 19 for the **police.** Larache's **telephone code** is (0)9.

ACCOMMODATIONS AND FOOD Extremely basic hotels lurk in the medina, but many pleasant budget options can be found on av. Mohammed ben Abdallah and off pl. de la Libération. The best bargain is probably **Pension Amal,** 10 av. Abdallah ben Yassine (tel. 91 27 88), five blocks north of the bus station up av. Mohammed ben Abdallah and a block to the left (singles 40dh; doubles 70-80dh; hot showers 6dh; cold showers 2dh). **Hotel España,** abutting pl. Libération, is one of those once-grand, now-budget hotels that make cool places to stay (singles 90dh, with bath 140dh; doubles 130dh, with bath 160dh). **Pension Malaga** (tel. 91 18 68), a couple of blocks up av. Hassan II from pl. Libération and to your left, is a comfortable place (singles 40dh; doubles 90dh, with bath 120dh; hot showers 5dh).

Cheap **restaurants** encircle the pl. de la Libération and line the Zoko. Larache's Spanish roots are apparent, as Spanish-style seafood dishes (albeit Moroccan-ized) are widely available. To reach **Restaurant Eskala** (tel. 91 40 80), on the Zoko Chico, enter through the Bab Medina and take a quick left. This joint serves seafood, *trippe* (25dh), and *tajines* (30dh). **Sandwich L'Ocean,** 5, rue Moulay Ismail, is a good sandwich shop that also offers *crevettes* (14dh) and *tajines*. Follow the Credit Agricole sign from pl. Libération two blocks, hang a right, and it's up ahead on the left.

SIGHTS Most tourists come to Larache to visit the Roman ruins of Lixus, although Larache itself makes for pleasant enough wandering. From pl. Libération head into the Moorish area (Bab al-Khemis) and take a right into **Zoco de la Alcaiceria,** a Spanish-built, 17th-century courtyard, now a bustling souq blessedly free of faux guides. Walking down the Zoco leads to another bab, outside of which rises the imposing **Kasbah de la Cigogne** (the stork's kasbah). Built by Philip III in the 17th century, it's Larache's only intact fortification from that era, but as luck would have it, visitors may not enter. Around the corner and at the southeast corner of the citadel sits the little **archaeological museum** (tel. 91 20 91), with a tiny assortment of Roman and Phoenician artifacts. *(Open 9am-noon and 3-6pm. 10dh.)*

The old city walls and ruined **kasbah** built by the Portuguese in the 16th century are visible from the boardwalk just off pl. Libération. Continuing downhill on the boardwalk, you will see the **beach** across the **Loukkos estuary.** Entrepreneurial boatmen ferry passengers over for 2dh (4dh back—we said "entrepreneurial"). Several cafes serve fresh seafood and quench thirst sweltered by the Maghreb sun.

■ Near Larache: Lixus

5km north of Larache on the highway to Tangier, the **Roman ruins** of Lixus—though less spectacular than Volubilis—are definitely worth a stop if you're traveling south along the coast. Lixus figured prominently in Greco-Roman mythology as the site where Hercules completed his 11th labor, collecting the golden apples from Mount Atlas. Initially settled by an ancient sun-worshipping cult, Lixus became a prominent and highly successful **Phoenician settlement** around 1000 BC. As did all things Phoenician, the area fell to the Romans around 140 BC. Soon a rich trading city with an important place in the Roman empire, Lixus had its own coinage and local specialties, including *garum,* a strong paste made from fish intestines (the sea has since receded, but Lixus was once on the coast). The city suffered badly from the decline of the Roman Empire and by the 5th century was totally abandoned.

Visiting the ruins can feel like discovering them anew, as they are unrestored, unguarded, unmarked, and often entirely empty save a stray faux guide or a shepherd and his flock. From the road, a path leads past the port silo and **factory** where *garum* was made and stored for shipment. Farther along the path lie the ruins of a Greco-Roman **theater/amphitheater** where music lovers must have flocked, as the orchestra pit is one of the largest in the ancient world. Later it was converted to an amphitheater and eventually a bullring. Near the amphitheater are the relatively famous **"Mosaic of the Sea God"** and the baths. Follow the fork to the left and you'll enter the **acropolis,** home of temples, villas, churches, and broken pillars.

To get to Lixus, hop on **bus #4 or 5** from the stop near Casbah de la Cigogne (2.50dh) in Larache and tell the ticket collector you want to go to Lixus. Unfortunately, it's a one-way street to Lixus. To get back, walk (1hr.) or flag down one of the rare buses or taxis. Some folks choose to hitch a ride.

Rabat

ACCOMMODATIONS

A Auberge de Jeunesse (HI)
E Hotel Central
C Hotel Dorhmi
F Hotel El Velada
D Hotel la Paix
B Hotel Magrib and
   Hotel Marrakesh

■ Rabat الرِّباط

Many of those 17th-century pirate expeditions you've heard about were a) true and b) based in Rabat. The Mediterranean Sea and Atlantic Ocean were the pirates' oysters until the Alaouites soundly subdued them around 1700. Not until 1912 did Rabat return to prominence, when French invaders selected it as the seat of government for its strategic location and perceived political malleability.

Despite the colorful corsairs in its past, Rabat is exceptional in contemporary Morocco for its very absence of hustlers. King Hassan II resides here and his personal battalion chases hustlers, street peddlers, and beggars off the main streets. The king, moreover, nurtures a healthy local economy not chiefly reliant upon tourism for revenue. Rabat is a political and business capital, with a fleet of public employees, a swelling upper middle class, and a flourishing Mercedes Benz trade. Admittedly, today's Rabat lacks the tradition of Fez, the color of Marrakesh, and the money of Casablanca, but wait—don't be tempted to skip out. Not only can its moderation be a treat in and of itself (e.g., few faux guides), but calm and order, Western facilities, and several important sights all weigh heavily in this capital city's favor. It's also the Moroccan city where Western women tend to feel most comfortable.

ORIENTATION AND PRACTICAL INFORMATION

This city is a navigational breeze. **Avenue Mohammed V** parades north-south from the **medina**, past the post office and the train station, to the **Great Mosque** (As-Sounna). Exiting the **train station** (the Rabat Ville stop—*not* Rabat Agdal), turn left up Mohammed V to reach most budget hotels. **Avenue Allal ben Abdallah** parallels av. Mohammed V, one block to the east (to your right walking toward the medina). Perpendicular to av. Mohammed V is **avenue Hassan II**, which runs east-west along the medina's south walls. To the east across the river is Rabat's sister city **Salé**; to the west is the **route de Casablanca**, home of the inconvenient **bus station**.

Transportation

Flights: International Airport Mohammed V (tel. (02) 33 90 40), in Casablanca. Frequent train connections, some direct from the airport (1½hr., 9 per day, 60dh), others via Casablanca. **Royal Air Maroc** (tel. 70 90 66) on av. Mohammed V across from the Rabat Ville train station. Open M-Sa 8:30am-12:15pm and 2:30-7pm. **Air France,** 281 av. Mohammed V (tel. 70 70 66). Open M-Th 8:30am-12:15pm and 2:30-6:30pm, F 8:30am-12:15pm and 3:30-6:30pm, Sa 9am-12:15pm.

Trains: Rabat Ville Station, av. Mohammed V (tel. 70 14 69), at av. Moulay Youssef. To: Casablanca Port (1hr., 19 per day, 27dh); Casablanca Voyageurs (1 hr., 17 per day, 25dh); Fez (4hr., 8 per day, 69dh); Marrakesh (5hr., 8 per day, 99dh); Tangier (5½hr., 4 per day, 87dh); and Meknes (3hr., 8 per day, 53dh).

Buses: All companies operate from an enormous station en route to Casablanca at pl. Mohammed Zerktouni (tel. 77 51 24). It's several kilometers from the town center, so take a *petit taxi* (12dh) or bus #30 from av. Hassan near rue Mohammed V (2.50dh). CTM tickets at windows #14 and 15; other windows belong to private companies. **CTM** to: Casablanca (1hr., 6 per day, 27dh); Fez (3½hr., 8 per day, 57dh); Meknes (2½hr., 8 per day, 40dh); Tangier (5hr., 5 per day, 80dh); Chefchaouen (6hr., 2 per day, 65dh).

Taxis: Stands at the train station, in front of the bus station along av. Hassan II across from Bab Oudaias, and at the entrance to the medina by the corner of av. Hassan II and av. Mohammed V. Or just hail one on the street.

Car Rental: Hertz, 467 av. Mohammed V (tel. 62 92 27). **Budget,** headquartered in the train station. Both rent the fabulous Fiat Uno starting at 250dh per day, plus 2.5dh per km. Both open M-Sa 8am-noon and 2-7pm, irregular Sunday mornings.

Tourist, Financial, and Local Services

Tourist Office: Municipal, 22 rue al-Jazair (tel. 73 05 62). Far. Turn right out of the train station, walk up av. Mohammed V to the Grand As-Sounna Mosque, turn left on av. Moulay Hassan, and bear right onto rue al-Jazair after 4 blocks. Sketchy maps of Rabat and other large cities. Open June 16 to mid-Sept. M-F 8am-2pm; mid-Sept. to June 15 M-F 8am-noon and 12:30-5:30pm; Ramadan M-F 9am-3pm.

Embassies and Consulates: Canadian (also serves **Australian** citizens); **U.K.** (also serves **New Zealand** citizens); **U.S.** (can assist with the transfer of funds from the U.S.). For addresses, see **Embassies and Consulates: Morocco,** p. 42.

Currency Exchange: Banks and **ATMs** located on av. Mohammed V, and av. Allal ben Abdallah. Find **BMCE** at 260 av. Mohammed V and at the train station. Open M-F 8am-noon and 3-6pm, Sa-Su 10am-2pm and 4-8pm.

Luggage Storage: At the train station (2.50dh per bag, must be locked, locks for sale in station; could be a scam—you think?). At the bus station (3dh per day). Open daily 4am-midnight.

Laundromat: Hotels are the best option—expect to pay 20-30dh.

English Bookstores: English Bookstore, 7 rue al-Yamama (tel. 70 65 93). From the train station, take a hard right and cut diagonally through the parking lot to rue al-Yamama. Kerouac to Foucault to Dostoevsky. Open M-Sa 9am-12:30pm and 3-7pm. **American Bookstore,** 4 Zankat Tanja (tel. 76 87 17). Take av. Mohammed V past the Grand Mosque and turn left 3 blocks later. Great paperback selection. Open M-F 9:30am-12:30pm and 2:30-6:30pm, Sa 10am-1pm.

Emergency and Communications

Police: Rue Soekarno (tel. 19), 2 blocks from the post office off av. Mohammed V.

Late-Night Pharmacy: Pharmacie de Préfecture, av. Moulay Slimane (tel. 70 70 72). From the post office, cross av. Mohammed V and veer to the right onto rue el-Qahira (as if going to the Syndicat d'Initiative). On your right a few blocks down, across from Theatre Mohammed V. Open nightly 8:30pm-8am.

Medical Assistance: Hôpital Avicenne, av. Ibn Sina (tel. 77 44 11), at the south end of bd. d'Argonne. Free emergency medical care. U.S. citizens can also go to the **U.S. Embassy** (see p. 42) for medical care.

Post Office: Av. Mohammed V (tel. 72 07 31) at rue Soekarno, left when leaving the train station. Open M-Th 8:30am-12:15pm and 2:30-6:45pm, F 11:30am-3pm.

Telephones: Rue Soekarno, facing the post office. International phones and collect calls (open 24hr.). **Poste Restante** is also located in this building (2dh per piece). **Telephone Code:** (0)7.

ACCOMMODATIONS AND CAMPING

As usual, medina hotels are cheaper than the ville nouvelle, although less appealing than in other cities. Cushier hotels line **avenue Mohammed V, avenue Allal ben Abdallah,** and environs. From the train station, turn left onto av. Mohammed V and walk toward the medina; av. Allal ben Abdallah runs parallel one block to the right.

Ville Nouvelle

Auberge de Jeunesse (HI), 43, rue Marassa (tel. 72 57 69), on the road perpendicular to av. Hassan II in the ville nouvelle, just outside the medina. In an old mansion with a beautiful courtyard. Separate-sex dorms (14 beds), cold showers, and Euro-toilets. American/Australian spoken by the friendly manager. Dorms 31dh; members 26dh. In summer reception open until midnight; in winter 11pm.

Hôtel la Paix (tel. 73 20 31), on the northwest corner of av. Allal ben Abdallah and rue Ghaza, about 500m up from the train station and two blocks shy of the medina. Super-friendly management offers spotless, airy rooms with sinks; some rooms with tables, chairs, and telephones. Ask for a balcony to enjoy sunny afternoons. Singles 70dh, with full bath 126dh; doubles with full bath 156dh.

Hôtel Central, 2, rue al-Basra (tel. 70 73 56). From the train station, cross av. Mohammed V and walk 2 blocks north toward the medina; then turn right. It's on the corner of rue al-Basra and rue Dimachh. Big rooms with high ceilings and sinks. Clean and popular with tourists. Singles 80dh, with shower 125dh; doubles 110dh, with shower 146dh; triples 179dh. Hot showers 10dh.

Camping de la Plage (tel. 78 23 68), far away in sister city Salé, but at least on the beach. *Grand taxi* to the site 10dh. Running water, toilets, and a grocery store/restaurant. Facilities are primitive and a bit shabby, but their prices rule. 10dh per person, 5dh per tent and per car, slightly more for vans or larger vehicles. Cold showers and electricity included. Reception 24hr.

Medina

Hôtel Dohrmi, 313, av. Mohammed V (tel. 72 38 98), 1½ blocks inside the medina walls and on the right. A great place to stay. Female European management makes women feel comfortable. Rooms surround a pleasant courtyard. European-style toilets available. Singles 80dh; doubles 100dh; triples 150dh. Hot showers 7dh.

Hôtel Maghrib El-Jadid, 2, rue Sebbahi (tel. 73 22 07), at av. Mohammed V, a few blocks past the Dohrmi and on your right. Bright pink paint, spotless rooms, rather small beds. Rooftop terrace. The only fishy thing about this place is the aquarium at the entrance. English spoken. Singles 50dh; doubles 80dh; triples 120dh. Cold showers free; hot showers 5dh.

FOOD

Rabat has many mediocre food options from other countries, like **Hong Kong,** a Chinese/Vietnamese restaurant on av. Mohammed V, and **McDonald's,** across from the train station. A **food market** guards the entrance to the **medina** at av. Mohammed V, and numerous *brochetteries* and sandwich shops are within the medina walls. Beasts of budget forage in two areas: a block or two from the medina on av. Mohammed V and Allal ben Abdallah, and around the train station, off **avenue Moulay Youssef.**

Restaurant el-Bahia, av. Hassan II (tel. 73 45 04), to the right, going toward the medina on av. Mohammed V. Built into the wall. Interior court and fountain with goldfish. *Salon marocain* upstairs. The lunch crowd devours appetizing dishes, sometimes leaving only monkey scraps for dinner. Try a *non kefta tajine* (30dh). Vegetarians savor the *couscous sept légumes* (32dh). Open daily 9am-11pm.

Snack Bar Balima, under the Balima Hotel a block north of the train station on av. Mohammed V. Serves Western-style fast food. Burgers (16-28dh), sandwiches (30-40dh), pasta (15-40dh), omelettes (12-35dh), and nefarious hot dogs (20dh). Adjoining restaurant "keeps it real" with *tajines* and other local fare. Inviting terrace where men and women and women and women can sit outside unharrassed.

Cafe-Restaurant La Clef (tel. 70 19 72). Exiting the train station, make a hard right onto av. Moulay Youssef, then skip down the first alley on the left. The *salon marocain* has low-slung couches. Good, inexpensive *tajine pigeon* (minced pigeon stewed with prunes, almonds, and onions, 45dh). One of the few places to get a gin or whiskey shot (38dh). Open daily noon-3pm and 7-11pm.

SIGHTS

Chellah

Open daily, sunrise to sunset. 10dh. Ignore the faux guides.

Beyond the city walls at the southern end of av. Yacoub el-Mansour—which runs into av. Allal ben Abdallah at the **As-Sounna Mosque** (see below)—loom the decrepit but impressive ruins of the **Chellah,** a former Roman city encircled by 14th-century walls and converted into a royal necropolis by the Merenids. With its tranquil, melancholy aura and vistas over the Oued Bou Regreg, the Chellah is often called the most romantic site in Morocco—and with good reason. From the Chellah gate, descend through the overgrown gardens to reach the necropolis and its **ruined mosque.** Step inside to view the 13th-century tombs of Sultan Abu Yacoub Youssef and the adjacent minaret, also a condo for a community of storks. On the way back, a path to the right circles the **Roman ruins.** Now closed and gated, this sight marks the first human occupation in the region, then a military camp, now a nice spot for a picnic.

The Hassan Tower and Mohammed V Mausoleum

All sights open daily, sunrise to sunset. Free. As always, ignore the guides.

Across town along av. Abi Regreg (near the Moulay Hassan bridge to Salé) towers the famous minaret of the **Hassan Mosque**, a testament to the unqualified ambition of Sultan Yacoub al-Mansour. The huge courtyard was once the prayer hall of what was to be the largest mosque in the Muslim world, begun in 1195 to commemorate a victory in Spain but abandoned shortly thereafter upon the Sultan's death. All that remains are stubby reconstructions of the support pillars, ultimately destroyed by an 18th-century earthquake, and the 44m minaret (meant to reach a staggering 60m). The mosque was to be al-Mansour's greatest achievement, in the same style as his Giralda of Sevilla and the Koutoubia of Marrakesh (historians conjecture that he had Caliphal ambitions—you don't say). In the structure to the left when facing the complex is the **Mausoleum of King Mohammed V**, a tribute to the sultan who led Morocco's independence movement and lent his name to seemingly every third street in the country. Non-Muslims can enter the lower room of the spectacular, traditional-style building, where sleepy guards keep company with Mohammed V himself in his marble sarcophagus.

Ville Nouvelle

Rabat's principal place of worship, the splendid **As-Sounna Mosque,** towers at the end of av. Mohammed V in the ville nouvelle. Although non-Muslims cannot enter, they may peek in at their leisure. Near the Mosque, the **archaeological museum,** often considered the best of Morocco's admittedly less-than-stellar museums, has an impressive collection of Hellenistic bronze works, all cast before 25 BC and many retrieved from Volubilis. *(Open W-M 9-11:30am and 2:30-5:30pm. 10dh.)* To get there, walk down av. Mohammed V and turn left onto Abd Al Aziz at the Grand Mosque; the museum is on the next street off Abd Al Aziz to the right, near the Hôtel Chellah.

Facing the Grand Mosque, follow av. Moulay Hassan to the right to the salmon-pink **Bab el-Rouah** (Gate of the Winds; 10-min. walk). On the other side is a pleasant **gallery** with oft-changing exhibitions. *(Open daily 8:30am-noon and 2:30-8pm. Free.)*

Back through Bab er-Rouah and through the wall to the right is the 1km avenue leading to the royal palace, **Dar el-Makhzen.** Begun in the 18th century, most construction on the palace was finished after French occupation. Foolish peons who get too close will be chased away by soldiers brandishing machine guns. Photography is permitted from afar, although try not to ruffle the soldiers' feathers.

Medina and Kasbah

There is little of interest in the medina for the traveler who has visited Fez or Marrakesh. The **Kasbah des Oudaias,** however, just northwest of the medina, is impressive. To get there, walk through the medina on av. Mohammed V and take a right on bd. al-Alou; the *kasbah* is a few hundred meters away along the road to the left. It used to be a pirate stronghold until Moulay Idriss sent Saharan mercenaries to oversee the buccaneers' tributes of gold and slaves. The fantastic **Bab Oudaia,** at the top of the hill, is one of the most impressive gates in all Morocco. Once inside the medina, head straight on the main street, rue Jamaa. On the opposite side of the kasbah is a large esplanade overlooking the teeming beaches and the Rabat surf club, a hangout sponsored by King Hassan II's son. Exiting the *kasbah* through Bab Oudaia and entering through the keyhole-shaped *bab* down the stairs leads to the sublime **Andalusian gardens,** of medieval Islamic-Spanish design and French construction (on your right when you enter the *bab*). The **Museum of Moroccan Arts,** next to the gardens, was the 17th-century hideaway of the infamous Moulay Ismail. *(Museum and gardens open daily 8am-noon and 2-7:30pm. Dimension to museum 10dh.)* The excellent ethnographic collection shows off the sultan's private apartment, signature Rabat-style carpets, traditional local costumes, and musical instruments. A charming cafe lies on the opposite side of the garden overlooking the estuary.

ENTERTAINMENT

Visitors to Rabat have a rare opportunity to sample **Moroccan and Arab cinema** at the movie house on av. Allal ben Abdallah within a few blocks of the medina (Saturdays 10:30am; 20dh; in French or with French subtitles). The rest of the week the movie house screens recycled foreign flicks. The prosperous youth of Rabat scope each other out at cinemas and pricey, pseudo-Euro discos such as **Amnesia,** on rue Monastir near the Cinema Royale. Look for the New York checkered cab out front and airplane and school bus inside. For high culture, call the palatial **Tour Hassan Hôtel,** 22, av. Chellah (tel. 72 14 91), to sit in on a performance or concert. **Café Balima** (see **Food,** p. 685) offers a disco downstairs (open 10pm-3am; cover and first drink: Su-Th 50dh, F-Sa 70dh).

■ Near Rabat: Salé سلا

Across the Bou Regreg from Rabat sits Salé, an ancient trading city almost totally free of tourists. The "White City" is a rare opportunity to observe traditional Moroccan life without the hassle of would-be guides and makes for an intriguing half-day of exploration. Salé's medina has three main attractions: the **souqs** along the **rue Grande Mosquée,** the souqs along **rue Kechachine,** and the Grand Mosque and accompanying 14th-century *madrassa* (college of theology, literature, and law). The best approach to the sights is to walk north along the walls and enter through the first gate on the right. Cut diagonally (northeast) to reach the souqs for wool, clothing, and jewelry. Shopping continues here as it has for several hundred years, without the incursions of more "high-tech" goods sometimes sold in Fez or Marrakesh. Be aware that the presence of Westerners, something of a novelty here, may induce staring; **women** should absolutely not go alone.

Meandering northwest along either of the main streets leads to the **Grand Mosque,** dating from the Almohad era. As usual, non-Muslims need not apply (no admission); the nearby **Madrassa,** however, invites any and all visitors to gawk at its architectural riches. Completed in 1333, this school once instructed students in the Quran and other Islamic sciences; now present-day architect-disciples study the building itself as a model of what a university should look like. Paved in an intricate mosaic and decorated with elegant cedar carvings, the courtyard invites meticulous study. Up a little flight of stairs, students' rooms may be viewed (awfully cozy with 2 students per cell), while further up, the rooftop affords a splendid panorama of Salé and Rabat.

The simplest transport to Salé is via a **Grand Taxi,** which leaves from bd. Hassan II in Rabat (2dh); it will leave you at Bab Mrisa, on the southwest corner of the city. It is possible to **walk**—head east on av. Hassan II and cross the bridge to Salé (30min. from av. Mohammed V).

■ Casablanca الدّار البَيضاء

As time goes by, Casablanca continues to bloat under the Maghreb sun. Already the largest city in Morocco, with nearly 4 million inhabitants (up from a mere 20,000 in 1900), Casablanca's bright lights and big medina attract rural Moroccans seeking urban prosperity. In this, the country's financial capital and Africa's largest port, Western dress predominates, and women participate actively and visibly in city life. Casablanca (known as "Casa") has the dubious distinction of having Morocco's first McDonald's *and* its only open prostitution.

Those dying to experience Rick's Cafe will have to settle for paying US$10 for a martini served by a trench-coated Moroccan at the local Hyatt. A certain movie was based more on Tangier anyway. With the construction of the gargantuan **Hassan II Mosque,** Casablanca has moved to establish itself as a major religious center. Although the mosque is indeed spectacular, foreign backpackers generally view Casa as little more than a transport hub—and not without reason.

ORIENTATION AND PRACTICAL INFORMATION

Almost 100km south of Rabat, Casa is Morocco's transit hub for planes, trains, and buses. **Casa Port train station** is near the youth hostel and the city center; **Casa Voyageurs** is near nothing, a 50-minute walk from Casa Port or a 30dh *petit taxi* ride. To get from Casa Port to the **CTM bus station,** conveniently located downtown, cross the street, follow bd. Felix Houphëit-Boigny to pl. Nations Unies, turn left on av. Armée Royale, and watch for Hôtel Safir on the right; the station is behind it and to the right.

The city has two main squares, **place Nations Unies,** overlooked by the landmark clock tower, and **place Mohammed V.** Place Nations Unies spreads out in front of the Hyatt Regency at the intersection of bd. Mohammed V, av. Hassan II, and av. des Forces Armées Royales. Place Mohammed V lies six blocks south along av. Hassan II.

Transportation

Flights: Aéroport Mohammed V (tel. 33 90 40) handles all international and most domestic flights. Trains run between the airport terminal and the Casa Port train station (55min., departs every hour, 24dh), some stopping at Casa Voyageurs en route; some trains head to Rabat. **Royal Air Maroc** (tel. 31 11 21 or 31 41 41; fax 44 24 09), at the airport and 44 av. des Forces Armées Royales, sells tickets for international and domestic flights. Also see **Getting Around,** p. 644.

Trains: Casa Port (tel. 27 18 37), Port de Casablanca. Mainly northbound service. To: Rabat (1hr., 17 per day, 27dh); Fez (4½hr., 2 per day, 100dh); Tangier (6hr., 2 per day, 120dh); Marrakesh (1 per day, 50dh). **Casa Voyageurs** (tel. 24 58 01), bd. Ba Hammed, away from the city center. Mainly southbound services but more extensive connections. To: Fez (5¼hr., 7 per day, 110dh) via Meknes (4¼hr., 90dh); Tangier (6hr., 3 per day, 120dh; you may have to change trains at Sidi Kacem); Marrakesh (3½hr., 8 per day, 70dh).

Buses: CTM, 23, rue Léon L'Africain (tel. 44 81 27), off rue Chaouia. To: Rabat (1½hr., 18 per day, 30dh); Marrakesh (4hr., 6 per day, 65dh); Meknes (5hr., 9 per day, 63dh); Fez (6hr., 8 per day, 80dh); Tangier (6½hr., 2 per day, 100dh); Essaouira (5½hr., 2 per day, 100dh); Agadir (10hr., 6 per day, 140dh); El-Jadida (1½hr., 2 per day, 25dh). Other companies leave from pl. Benjdia to Marrakesh.

Car Rental: Casa has dozens of companies. For rates and more detailed info about renting a car in Morocco, see **By Car,** p. 645. **Europcar,** 44, av. des Force Armées Royales (tel. 31 37 37); **Hertz,** 25, rue de Aloraibi Jilali (tel. 31 22 23); and **Avis,** 19, av. de l'Armée (tel. 31 24 24) have similar rates.

Tourist, Financial, and Local Services

Tourist Office: Syndicat d'Initiative et de Tourisme, 98, bd. Mohammed V (tel. 22 15 24 or 27 05 38), at rue Chaoui, about four blocks down from pl. Nations Unies. Glossy brochures and some dubious maps. English spoken. Open M-Sa 8:30am-noon and 2:30-6:30pm, Su 9am-noon. The **Office de Tourisme,** 55, rue Omar Slaoui (tel. 27 95 33 or 27 11 77; fax 20 59 29), has similar services. From pl. Mohammed V, walk south along av. Hassan II, left on rue Reitzer, then right on rue Omar Slaoui. Open M-F 8:30am-noon and 2:30-6:30pm, Su 9am-noon.

Currency Exchange: When the plentiful **banks** in the city are closed, try the airport and larger hotels, which change money at Morocco's official, uniform rates. The Hyatt Regency, Hôtel Suisse, or Hôtel Safir near the bus station, or other big hotels near pl. Nations Unies, are all good bets. **ATMs** are widely available.

American Express: Voyages Schwartz, 112, av. du Prince Moulay Abdallah (tel. 22 29 47; fax 27 31 30). Standard services, except they won't receive wired money. French spoken. Open M-F 8:30am-noon and 2:30-6:30pm, Sa 8:30am-noon.

English Bookstore: American Language Center Bookstore (tel. 27 95 59), bd. Moulay Youssef at pl. Unité Africaine. Vast array of novels and reference books. Open M-F 9:30am-12:30pm and 3:30-6:30pm, Sa 9:30am-noon.

Emergency and Communications

Emergencies: Police (tel. 19), bd. Brahim Roudani.

Late-Night Pharmacy: Pharmacie de Nuit, pl. Nations Unies (tel. 26 94 91). Open nightly 8pm-8am. Other pharmacies are found on almost any city block.

Medical Assistance: Croix-Rouge Marocain, 19, bd. Al Massira Al Khadra (tel. 25 25 21). **S.O.S. Medicins,** 81, av. F.A.R. (tel. 44 44 44).

Internet Access: Available at **Casa Net** in the Sheraton Hotel.

Post Office: bd. de Paris, at av. Hassan II. Poste Restante. M-Th 8:30am-12:15pm and 2:30-6:30pm, F 8:30-11:30am and 3-6:30pm.

Telephones: To use a calling card, either try your luck with a pay phone or use the phones in the post office. **Telephone Code:** (0)2.

ACCOMMODATIONS

Generally, it's best to eschew the medina and look along **rue Chaouia,** as well as **avenue des Forces Armées Royales (F.A.R.)** and side streets, for the best budget deals.

Auberge de Jeunesse (HI), 6, pl. Amiral Philibert (tel. 22 05 51). From Casa Port, head right (toward the medina) along bd. Almohades, walk along its walls, and go left up a small ramp-like street. Blue signs point the way. The biggest and bestest hostel in Morocco, with a pleasant courtyard and communal kitchen. Clean sheets and free cold showers. Dorms 40dh; doubles 100dh. Breakfast included. Reception daily 8-10am and noon-11pm.

Hôtel de Foucauld, 52, rue Araibi Jilali (tel. 22 26 66). From bd. Felix Houphëit-Boigny, take a left on av. des F.A.R., then the 1st right; it's adjacent to Hôtel Perigord. Whether or not you can fill the Foucauld's huge wardrobes, you're bound to appreciate its cozy, tidy rooms. Singles 75dh, with bath 120dh; doubles 120dh, with bath 150dh; triples with bath 180dh.

Hôtel Rialto (tel. 27 51 22), av. Mohammed El Qorri. From pl. Nations Unies, take bd. Mohammed V, then the 3rd right off it, and then your first left. These hygenic, airy rooms with shower are as quiet as Casa gets. Singles 84dh; doubles 112dh.

Hôtel Kon-Tiki, 88, rue Allal ben Abdellah (tel. 31 49 27). The Hawaiian name mystifies (no *leis,* no grass skirts). Still, rooms are extremely clean—all with sinks, some with terraces. Singles 72dh; doubles 110dh. Showers 5dh.

FOOD

While it's true that cosmopolitan Casablanca boasts everything from French *haute cuisine* to Korean food to **McDonald's** (on Mohammed V at pl. Nations Unies), most restaurants are geared to the city's wealthy business clientele. Kabab joints line **rue Chaouia** in the ville nouvelle, and good value meals can be found near pl. Nations Unies in the medina. Or try haggling Moroccan-style at the massive produce stands at the **central market,** 7, rue Chaouia (open daily approximately 8am-1pm).

Restaurant Widad, 9 rue de Fès. At the end of bd. Houphëit-Boigny, take the 1st right into the medina. It's just after the 1st fork. With a whopping 10 tables, it's the biggest hole-in-the-wall in the medina. Attentive service, enormous portions, and delicious staples. 38dh for fruit, salad, couscous, vegetables, a quarter-chicken, and bottled water (ask for a sealed bottle). Open daily 11am-10pm.

Taverne au Dauphin, 75, bd. Felix Houphëit-Boigny (tel. 22 12 00), up the road from the port. Tuxedoed waiters serve sizzling seafood to Casablancan professionals. *Crevettes grillées* (grilled shrimp, 55dh) and *filet de lotte* (filet o' fish, 70dh). Open M-Sa noon-4pm and 6-11pm.

SIGHTS

The biggest sight in Casa, literally, is the fabulous new **Hassan II Mosque,** the third-largest mosque in existence. *(Mandatory tours given Sa-Th 9, 10, 11am, and 2pm. Tours in English, French and Arabic. 100dh, students 50dh. Elevator up the side of the minaret 10dh.)* It's

MOROCCO

very easy to find: from anywhere in Casa, look toward the sea and spot the shiny minaret (200m high, the tallest minaret in the world). To get there, walk past the medina along the coastal road (about 15min.), or take a *petit taxi* (no more than 10dh). Begun in 1980 and inaugurated in 1994, this massive structure carried a price tag of over one billion U.S. dollars (much of it collected by "universal voluntary conscription"). The prayer hall, much larger than St. Peter's in Rome, combines glass, marble, and precious wood in a space that holds over 25,000 worshippers. The courtyard accommodates another 80,000. Technology galvanizes religious devotion: the floor is heated for bare feet, the hall boasts a huge retractable roof, and a **20-mile-long laser** shoots from the minaret toward Mecca. The whole structure rests on an elaborate support system that allows the Atlantic to crash under a glass floor, illustrating the Quranic verse, "Allah has his throne on the water." Morocco is so proud of this functioning mosque—designed by a French man but constructed entirely by 3,300 Moroccan craftsmen—that non-believers can actually go inside.

The Hassan II mosque aside, Casa is too preoccupied with commerce to maintain a romantic veneer for tourists. A decaying **medina** disappoints veterans of Fez and Marrakesh. Relics of French occupation, government buildings surround green **place Mohammed V.** Two blocks further south along av. Hassan II sprawls the **Parc de la Ligue Arabe,** the grandest of Casa's green spaces. In its northwest corner you can enjoy a nice **picnic** in the shadows of the old **Sacred Heart Cathedral,** built in 1930.

■ El-Jadida الجَديدَة

El-Jadida, a two-hour bus ride from Casablanca, is one of Morocco's largest Atlantic resorts. With a quiet medina, antique Portuguese battlements, palmy boulevards, and some of the country's best beaches, it's a welcome overnight antidote to the bustle and hustling of Casa and Marrakesh. The city's European air comes courtesy of the Portuguese, who made Jadida (formerly known as ne Mazagan) their first Moroccan foothold and their last Moroccan stronghold. Once Morocco won independence, the city was renamed El-Jadida ("The New One") and became a retreat for Marrakesh's affluent families. Today a prime destination for foreign and domestic tourists alike, El-Jadida gets awfully crowded in July and August.

ORIENTATION AND PRACTICAL INFORMATION

On a well-protected harbor, El-Jadida faces the Atlantic on its northeast side. From the **bus station,** exit left on bd. Mohammed V and continue up toward the city center (10min.). First you'll pass **place Mohammed V,** which adjoins bd. Mohammed V at the post office, then **place el-Hansali** (a pleasant pedestrian square), and finally **place Mohammed ben Abdallah,** which connects bd. Suez to the old Portuguese **medina.**

Trains: Currently, there is **no** passenger train service through El-Jadida.

Buses: bd. Mohammed V. To: Casablanca (2hr.; private buses: depart every 20min., 18dh; CTM: 3 per day, 24dh); Essaouira (private buses: 6 per day, 45dh; CTM: 1 per day, 45dh). Buses to Essaouira begin in Casablanca and often have few seats left by the time they arrive in El-Jadida, so get a ticket well beforehand.

Tourist Office: rue Ibn Khaldoun (tel. 34 47 88), down the street from Hôtel de Bruxelles and Hôtel de Provence. Follow signs from bd. Mohammed V and the post office. Some English spoken. Open mid-Jun to mid-Sept. M-F 8:30am-noon and 2:30-6:30pm; mid-Sept. to mid-June M-F 8:30am-noon.

Currency Exchange: Plenty of banks with **ATMs,** among them **BMCE,** located one block from pl. Mohammed V along av. Mohammed Errafil. Open M-Th 8:15-11:30am and 2:15-4:30pm, F 8:15-11:15am and 2:45-4:45pm. Hôtel de Provence also changes money (see **Accommodations,** below).

Police: (tel. 19). Located at the bus station and at the beach.

Late-Night Pharmacy: av. Ligue Arabe off pl. Mohammed V. Look for the plaque next door to the Croissant Rouge Marocain (Red Cross). Open nightly 9pm-8am.
Medical Assistance: Hospital: rue Sidi Bouzi (tel. 34 20 04 or 34 20 05), near rue Boucharette at the south edge of town. **Red Cross:** av. Ligue Arabe (24hr.).
Post Office: pl. Mohammed V. Open for *Poste Restante* and **telephones.** Open M-F 8:30am-noon and 2:30-6:30pm.
Telephone Code: (0)3.

ACCOMMODATIONS AND CAMPING

For a resort town, Jadida preserves a surprisingly large number of budget hotels. Most drift around **place Mohammed V,** a few blocks from the sea. Ask to see a room before you commit because there is a range of room quality among and within hotels. Reservations are wise in July and August, when prices rise considerably.

Hôtel Maghreb/Hôtel de France, 16, rue Lescould (tel. 34 21 81), just off pl. el-Hansali. The best budget deal between Casablanca and Mauritania. Spacious rooms, most with sinks and bidets, and some with excellent views of the water. Singles 41dh; doubles 57dh. Showers 5dh.
Hôtel Bourdeaux, 47, rue Moulay Ahmed Tahiri (tel. 35 41 17). A few narrow streets away from pl. el-Hansali; follow signs at the north end of the place (about 100m). Carpeted, bright modern rooms at low prices. Singles 41dh; doubles 57dh; triples 78dh. Shower 5dh.
Hôtel de Provence, 42 rue Fquih Mohammed Errafi (tel. 34 23 47; fax 35 21 15). Coming from the bus station, turn left off av. Mohammed V (away from the beach) at the post office. The "in" hotel for English speakers. Higher prices correlate to minor details (toilet paper, towels, nicer sheets, and **currency exchange**). Singles 104dh, with shower 133dh; doubles 131-164dh, with shower 159-186dh. Continental breakfast 22dh, served at its excellent French/Moroccan restaurant. Visa.
Camping: Camping Caravaning International, av. Al Oman al Mouttahida (tel. 34 27 55). From the post office at pl. Mohammed V, head toward the beach and take a right on av. El Jamia El Arabi. Take the 6th right (20min.). A large site with electricity, showers, and aging bungalows (160dh). 12dh per adult, 6.50dh per car, 10dh per tent. Add 4dh *emplacement* and 14% TVA.

FOOD

Many cheap, cheap places serve the usual *brochettes* along **place Mohammed V,** while most restaurants cluster in and around **place el-Hansali.** Numerous cafes speckle the seafront. A weekly **souq** that sells everything from fruits and vegetables to cow lungs is held by the lighthouse, with products brought in on Sundays.

Restaurant la Broche, 46, pl. el-Hansali (tel. 34 22 99), next to the Paris Cinema. Intimate dining rooms complemented by a mile-long menu, fresh fruit decor, and speedy service. *Tajine* 25-30dh. Fish dishes 30-40dh. Fresh banana juice 7dh. Ostensibly open daily 7am-11pm, but actual hours depend on the owner's whim.
Restaurant Chahrazad, 38, pl. el-Hansali. Don't expect all items to be available, but the procurable food is filling and appetizing. Couscous and *tajine,* 20-25dh.
Restaurant Tchikito, 7, rue Moulan Ahmed Tahiri, a few meters off pl. el-Hansali on the street to Hôtel Bordeaux. Join locals eating huge plates of fried fresh fish without the help of a knife or fork (25dh per plate). Open daily noon-10pm.

SIGHTS

The heart of Jadida is its lovely ramparted **Cité Portugaise,** completed in 1502 by Portuguese traders. In 1769 Moroccan forces finally sent them packing, but not before the retreating Portuguese blasted the old town walls to bits. After a sultan renovated the ramparts in the 19th century, the city was rebuilt as a Jewish settlement *(mellah)* mostly populated by merchants. Enter this atypical medina through the first fortified gate off pl. Mohammed ben Abdallah at the top of bd. Suez. Immediately inside the walls to the left, you'll see the Gothic **Church of the Assumption,** which has been converted into an assembly hall. Next door is a large **mosque,** formerly a lighthouse.

Up rue Mohammed Ahchemi Bahbai on the left, a yellow plaque marks the entrance to the famed **Portuguese Cistern,** a Roman-built structure (contrary to the name) lucky enough to survive the Portuguese bombardment. *(Open daily 8:30am-noon and 2:30-6pm. 10dh.)* The water, illuminated by a shaft of light from the roof, reflects the cistern's columns and arches. If it looks familiar, you have probably seen—and memorized—Orson Welles's *Othello,* in which a riot scene was staged here.

To join the locals promenading along the city's **ramparts,** head back to the southwest corner of the medina (down the street to the right as you enter the medina), where there's a rickety staircase. *(Guards let you in and out for a tip of a few dirhams.)* Along the east side, the walls plunge inwards at the **Porto do Mar,** where the Portuguese used to unload their ships. Continuing along the walls leads to the **Bastion of St. Sebastian,** beneath which sits a crumbling synagogue, once the Portuguese tribunal. At the **Bastion of St. Antoine,** in the northwest corner, there's another exit. If the guard isn't there to meet you, make some noise and he should come.

The marvelous **beaches** north of Jadida get better as you progress northward. **Sidi Bouzid,** a beach 5km south, is roomy and chic. Take a *grand taxi* for 5dh per person, or the orange #2 bus from near the medina.

■ Essaouira الصّويرة

Visitors to Essaouira often stay for an extra day—or a lifetime. Freeloading has become tradition in this jewel on the Atlantic. Piracy boosted this port in the 18th century, when Sultan Muhammed bin Abdallah constructed the town fortifications (designed by a captured Frenchman) to protect his pirate proteges. More recently, appearances by Jimi Hendrix and Cat Stevens triggered mass hippie migrations.

Although most of the hash has slowly burned away, Essaouira remains Morocco's most relaxing city. While many tourists come here, they are mostly independent backpackers and windsurfers who settle in for both the wind and the lifestyle. The miles of beautiful beaches stretching south may often be too windy for sunbathing, but the tranquil fortified medina and splendid scenery provide ample diversion.

ORIENTATION AND PRACTICAL INFORMATION

Buses arrive at the **bus station,** about 1km northeast of the medina along bd. Industrie. Exit the rear of the bus station (where the buses park) and walk to the right, past two souqs (or deserted wasteland, depending on the hour) to reach the medina gate, known as **Bab Doukkala** (10min. walk). It opens onto **rue Zerktouni,** one of two main arteries. The other is **rue Mohammed bin Abdallah,** which runs parallel and to the right. To reach the city center from here, continue on rue Zerktouni as it becomes av. de l'Istiqlal at an intersection surrounded by souqs and a mosque. Just before the second-to-last tier of arches, make a right; if you pass the Hôtel Sahara, you've gone too far. Take the next left and walk until the street ends, then take a right. This will take you to **place Moulay Hassan,** the heart of Essaouira.

Buses: CTM (tel. 78 47 64) buses go to: Safi (1½hr., 29dh); Agadir (2½hr., 1 per day, 40dh); Casablanca (5hr., 4 per day, 75dh; midnight express 5hr., 100dh). The fastest and most luxurious bus to Marrakesh (2½hr., 1 per day at 5pm, 40dh) is run by the train company, **ONCF.** Buses leave across the square from Bab Marrakesh, at **Agence Supratours,** where tickets are sold. **Satras** buses also go to Marrakesh (1 per day, 30dh). Other companies have more departures.

Currency Exchange: Banks cluster around the pl. Moulay Hassan. The **Hôtel Beau Rivage** cashes traveler's checks (expensive rates, but 24hr. service) as does **Bank Credit du Maroc** (tel. 47 58 19), on pl. Monlay Hassan, which has an **ATM.** Bank open M-F 8:15-11:30am and 2:15-4:45pm, Sa 9:30am-2pm and 3:30-7pm.

Luggage Storage: available 24hr. at the bus station (5dh per bag).

English Language Periodicals: Jack's, pl. Moulay Hassan. Carries a wide selection of periodicals and enough classics to supply a small library.

Public Showers: Bain-Douche, about 100m down the beach from the harbor. Cold showers 1.50dh. A good steam in a *hammam* (traditional bath) is more in keeping with the lifestyle, though. Most hotel proprietors can recommend one.

Police: (tel. 19), in the ville nouvelle.

Hospital: (tel. 47 27 16), on av. el-Moqaquamah next to the post office.

Post Office: av. el-Moqaquamah at Lalla Aicha, the 1st left after Hôtel les Isles when walking away from the medina by the shore. Near the radio tower. Poste Restante and **telephones.** Open June-Sept. M-F 8am-3pm; Oct.-May 8:30am-noon and 2:30-6:30pm.

Telephone Code: (0)4.

ACCOMMODATIONS AND CAMPING

The secret of Essaouira is out. Reservations may very well be necessary in the summer; calling a few days in advance should suffice.

Hôtel Smara, 26, rue Skala (tel. 47 26 55). From pl. Moulay Hassan head from the port and left; make a left after Hôtel des Remparts and steer right along the ramparts. The beds are a bit worn, but rooms are clean and many have great views. Chill with other guests on the terrace. Arrive early—it is the most popular hotel in Essaouira among backpackers (no reservations). Staff will do laundry for a fair price. Singles 50dh; doubles 70dh, with ocean view 85dh; triples and quads 100dh. Breakfast 10dh. Hot shower 2dh.

Hôtel Beau Rivage, pl. Moulay Hassan (tel./fax 47 29 25). Large, old hotel located above the cafe society in the main square. Bright, clean rooms, many with balconies and a pleasant terrace. Singles 60dh; doubles 80dh, with shower 120dh.

Hôtel Majestic, 40, rue Derb Laalouj (tel. 47 49 09), from pl. Moulay Hassan head away from the port down the street to the right; take a quick left, then another. Clean, newly renovated rooms overseen by a welcoming owner. Hot showers down the corridor. Singles 50dh; doubles 90dh. Shower 55dh.

Camping: Municipal campground (tel. 47 21 00), off av. Mohammed V at the far end of the beach. Essentially a gravel parking lot near the shore with a wall to shelter campers from the wind. 8dh per person, 9dh per car, 10-20dh per tent.

FOOD

Informal dining, mostly geared toward tourists, is a tradition near the port and **place Moulay Hassan.** Fried sardines (with fish, bread, and tomatoes 20dh) and grilled shrimp (25dh) are sure bets. On the right-hand side coming from the port, the so-called **Berber cafes** near Porte Portugaise off av. de l'Istiqlal have low tables, straw mats, and fresh fish *tajine* or couscous (20dh). Establish prices before chewing.

Café Restaurant Essalem, pl. Moulay Hassan (tel. 47 25 48). Popular hangout for visitors since the 60s. The waiter will gladly point out the table where Cat Stevens sat studying Islam. Touristy clientele, but good and cheap. Standard range of *tajines* and couscous *menus,* 35-40dh. Breakfast for about 10dh. Open daily 8am-3:30pm and 5:30-11pm.

Chez Sam (tel. 47 35 13), at the end of the harbor. Shazam! Warped ceilings and walls plastered with Hollywood movie stars. Pricey and touristy, but it's got a nice ocean view and a liquor license. Steaming heap of mussels 25dh. *Menu* 65dh. Fish dishes 40-60dh. Open daily noon-2pm and 7pm-midnight. Visa, MC, AmEx.

SIGHTS

The medina provides the backdrop for one of the nicest walks in Morocco. Two *skalas* (forts) scowl atop the town fortifications. Dotted by formidable ramparts, dramatic, sea-sprayed **Skala de la Ville,** up the street from Hôtel Smara (see **Accommodations,** above), lets visitors up to the large turret and artillery-lined wall. Cannons, gifts to the Sultan from solicitous European merchants, face the sea and the medina. La Ville is free and nicer than the **Skala de Port,** near the port (10dh).

Follow the sound of hammers pounding and the scent of *thuya* wood to land in the **carpenters' district,** comprising cell-like niches set in the **Skala Stata de la Ville.** The craftsmen here inlay cedar and *thuya* wood with lemonwood and ebony to create some of the best woodwork in Morocco. On sale are some unique masks and statuary, as well as the more typical offering of boxes, chess sets, and desk tools. A good shopping plan is to go to **Afalkai Art** (pl. Moulay Hassan) for a quality overview of what's available and for how much, then browse the many shops lining **rue Abdul Aziz el-Fechtaly** (off rue Sidi ben Abdallah). At the carpenters' workshops themselves, prices are the cheapest and the marketing the least aggressive. The local **museum** (tel. 47 23 00), in the former residence of a pasha near the Hôtel Majestic (see **Accommodations,** above), features antique woodwork and important manuscripts, including a 13th-century Quran. *(Open F-W 9am-noon and 3-6:30pm. 10dh.)*

To get to the **beach,** go south past the port. High winds, although a boon to windsurfers, can be a bane for sunbathers, and swimmers should be wary of strong riptides. Nearby beaches fill with soccer matches in between high tides. Windsurfing clubs farther down rent boards by the hour (130-150dh), though true enthusiasts go to Sidi Kaoki (see **Near Essaouira,** below).

■ Near Essaouira

At the famed **Purple Isles** just off-shore from Essaouira, the rare Eleanora's falcons hang out and breed. A Berber king from Mauritania, Juba II, set up dye factories on the islands around 100 BC, producing the purple dye used to color Julius Caesar's cape (and other things Roman). In 1506, the Portuguese, under King Manuel, contributed a fortress and Moulay Hassan added a prison. The islands, the **Isle of Mogador** being the biggest, have become a nature reserve and are generally off-limits.

Walking about two kilometers south along the beach from Essaouira brings the determined to the ruined fort **Bordj El Berod,** which supposedly inspired "Castles Made of Sand," written by Jimi Hendrix, who tried to buy the nearby Berber village/hippie colony of **Diabat** from the Moroccan government. A 1970s police sweep closed down most accommodations, and the region is now fairly deserted.

Twenty-five kilometers south of Essaouira, many Europeans know **Sidi Kaouki** as the best **windsurfing** beach in the world. A blue sign points the way from the main road to the beach, where "Wind City" bumper stickers crowd the parking lot near the sand. A constant wind blows spurts of stinging sand down a shore filled only with windsurfers. Unfortunately, there are no lifeguards, and you must BYOB (bring your own board). Take bus #5, which departs outside the gates of the medina, from the southwest corner of the medina (6dh) to test the waves yourself.

■ Agadir اكادير

Backpackers who come to Agadir may feel somewhat betrayed. At the juncture of the routes to the western Sahara, Agadir stands in stark contrast with the rugged High Atlas and Anti-Atlas mountains that surround it. Devastated by an earthquake in 1960, the town was redesigned in recent decades as a European-style beach resort. As Morocco's biggest beachside attraction, Agadir serves its purpose ably: broad, clean beaches and a bevy of resort hotels, discos, and cafes lure Northern European tourists, who drives prices up considerably. All the same, Agadir can also be managed affordably by the budget traveler who wants respite from traditional Morocco or needs to spend a night before moving on to Marrakesh or Taroudannt.

ORIENTATION AND PRACTICAL INFORMATION Buses arrive and depart along a two-block stretch of bd. Mohammed Cheikh Saadi, where most budget hotels and eateries cluster. Going downhill toward the beach, you'll cross av. Prince Moulay Abdallah, av. Hassan II, and bd. Mohammed V, finally coming to the esplanade.

Flights leave from **Airport El-Massira** (tel. 83 91 22), 25km out of town. The **Royal Air Morocco** office (tel. 84 07 93), av. du General Kettani, can also help. **Bus stations** are scattered along bd. Mohammed Cheikh Saadi. **CTM** (tel. 82 20 77) runs buses to: Taroudannt (2hr., 1 per day, 35dh); Marrakesh (4hr., 4 per day, 75dh); Essaouira

MOROCCO

(3hr., 2 per day, 45dh); Laayoune (1 per day, 180dh); Ouarzazate (5hr., 1 per day, 60dh); and Rabat (1 per day). There are many options for **car rental,** including Hertz, Budget, and Eurocar. Many offer greatly reduced "low season" rates, but the "low season" seems to vary. **Syndicat d'Initiative et Tourisme,** av. Mohammed V (tel. 84 06 95), is the tourist office. To get there from the bus station, turn right on Mohammed V; the office is on the left after av. General Kettani. Pick up a free map, bus schedule, and a list of pharmacies. Some English is spoken. (Open M-Sa 9:30am-noon and 2:45-4:30pm, Su 9:30am-noon). **Luggage storage** is available at the CTM station. The **police** can be found at Hôtel de Police, rue 18 Novembre (emergency tel. 19). If you need medical attention, head to **Hospital Hassan II** (tel. 84 14 77), on Route de Marrakech. The **post office,** av. Sidi Mohammed, on the corner of av. Prince Moulay Abdallah and Poste Restante, will handle all of your mail needs. (Open M-Th 8:30am-12:15pm and 2:30-6:30pm, F 8:30-11am and 3-6:30pm.) There are **telephones** next to the post office (open daily 8:30am-noon and 2-6pm), and the **telephone code** is (0)8.

ACCOMMODATIONS AND FOOD Budget hotels, congregating around the bus stations, are generally of similar quality. **Hôtel Paris** (tel. 82 26 94), av. de President Kennedy, is nicer than the others and the price reflects it. This very Parisian establishment is arranged around a central courtyard. (Singles 80dh, with shower 137dh; doubles 120dh, with shower 160dh. Breakfast 20dh.) At **Hôtel Aït Laayoune** (tel. 82 43 75), next door to the CTM station, rooms range from dingy to large and bright. Ask to see yours before forking over any dirhams. (Singles 70dh; doubles 90dh.) There is a **campground** (tel. 84 66 83) on bd. Mohammed V on the western edge of town.

Like the budget hotels, affordable eateries cluster around the bus stations. Head down to one of the boardwalk cafes for more expensive non-Moroccan cuisine. **Restaurant Mille et une Nuits** (tel. 82 37 11), behind the CTM, is one of four comparable restaurants in a row, all with similar menus and outdoor tables. It is inexpensive (*menu* 30dh) but has a perfectly pleasant environment (open daily 8am-11pm).

SIGHTS For the budget traveler who cannot afford the excursions to harbor villages, kasbahs, and "natural spectacles" put on by large hotels, the **beach** is the main attraction in Agadir. Take the 15-minute walk down, lay out a towel, and enjoy one of the cleanest, most swimmable, and most surfable beaches in Morocco. Then compare sunburns with thousands of pink Northern Europeans.

There are a few other diversions in Agadir, although admittedly all are far from five-star sights. One of the most important fishing areas in Africa, the port holds **daily fish auctions** and, more importantly, sells excellent, cheap fried fish in kiosks, restaurants, and stands. Overlooking the port perched atop a hill is the partially restored **Kasbah.** Up to 1000 troops—alternately Portuguese, French, and Moroccans—have been garrisoned here at various times.

HIGH ATLAS AND DESERTS الأطلَس الأعلى

Southern Morocco is one of the most picturesque regions in Africa, and the movie industry knows it—hundreds of films have been shot here. Dunes, valleys, and mountains do eventually give way to sizeable cities like Marrakesh, but not without much protest and occasional sand storms. With its unique architecture and wildly exotic bazaar, Marrakesh vies with the natural scenery for your attention. Frequently overlooked, smaller cities near Marrakesh may be equally interesting with their non-Arabized Berber populations, distinctive dress, and special souqs.

Falling southeast from the Atlas ranges and stretching through Ouarzazate to the sand-dune seas of the Algerian Sahara is Morocco's desert. Mountainous and desolate, its deep reds and oranges are contested only by the green veins of oases that creep through the valley floors. Set into this landscape are fantastic Berber towns and Kasbahs, where mud castles tower over the road and on hilltops. A rental car is useful for

MOROCCO

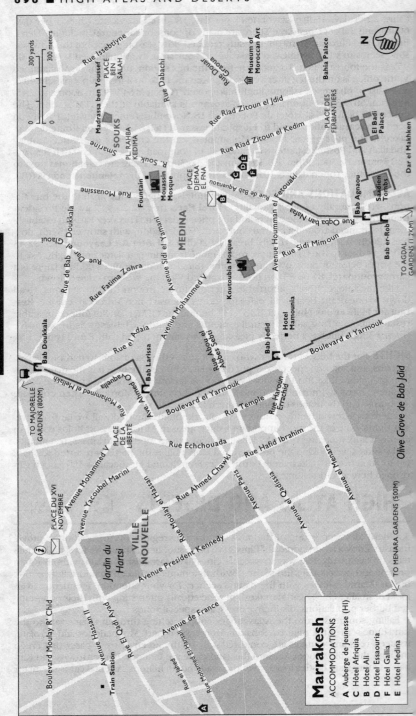

MOROCCO

300 yards

300 meters

0

0

Rue Issebriyne

PLACE
BEN
SALAH

Madrassa ben Youssef

Rue Dabachi

Rue Douar

Rue Graoua

Museum of Moroccan Art

Bahia Palace

Rue Riad Zitoun el Jdid

PLACE DES FERBIANTIERS

El Badi Palace

SOUKS

R. Smarine

Rue Riad Zitoun el Kedim

Dar el Makhzen

PL. RAHBA KEDIMA

R. Souk

D E

Fountain

Rue Moussine

Mouassin Mosque

G

F

Saadien Tombs

PLACE DJEMAA EL FNA

Rue de Bab Aguenaou

B

Bab Agnaou

Rue Oqba ban Nafa

MEDINA

Rue Bab Doukkala

Rue Fatima Zohra

Rue Sidi el Yamani

Avenue Houmman el Fetouaki

Avenue Mohammed V

Koutoubia Mosque

Rue Sidi Mimoun

Bab er-Rob

Rue el Glaoui

Rue el Adaia

TO AGDAL GARDENS (1.2KM)

Bab Doukkala

Rue el Adaia

Hotel Mamounia

TO MAJORELLE GARDENS (800M)

Rue Mohammed el Melkah

Ave. Ahmar

Bab Larissa

Rue Abou el Abbes Sebti

Bab Jedid

Olive Grove de Bab Jdid

Rue Oraguelia

Boulevard el Yarmouk

Boulevard el Yarmouk

Rue Temple

Rue Haroun Errachid

PLACE DE LA LIBERTÉ

Rue Echchouada

Rue Hafid Ibrahim

Avenue Mohammed V

Avenue Yacoubel Marini

Rue Ahmed Chawki

Avenue Paris

Avenue el Qadissia

Avenue el Menara

TO MENARA GARDENS (500M)

VILLE NOUVELLE

Jardin du Hartsi

Rue Moulay el Hassan

Avenue President Kennedy

PLACE DU XVI NOVEMBRE

Boulevard Moulay R' Chid

Avenue Hassan II

Rue El Qadi A'yad

Avenue de France

Train Station

Rue el Jahed

Rue Mohammed El Hansali

A

Marrakesh
ACCOMMODATIONS

A Auberge de Jeunesse (HI)
C Hôtel Afriquia
B Hôtel Ali
D Hôtel Essaouria
F Hôtel Gallia
E Hôtel Medina

exploring this southeasternmost part of Morocco, but excursions can be made less easily using local transportation.

■ Marrakesh مُرّاكُش

An oasis at the foot of the High Atlas mountains, Marrakesh is at once a remote desert enclave and Morocco's most important imperial city. The Almoravid dynasty founded Marrakesh in 1062, elevating an infamous highwaymen's outpost to the status of cultural capital and infusing it with Andalusian influences from their empire in southern Spain. In the 20th century, the French, in their ostensible effort to improve (read: Westernize) Morocco, moved the nation's capital to more subdued Rabat.

As it has for centuries, Marrakesh exerts an unshakable grip on the traveler. Tourists, still a minority at the Djemâa el-Fna, marginally observe the cacophonous crowd of snake charmers, musicians, boxers, acrobats, mystics, dentists (you'll just have to see it for yourself), scribes, and story-tellers in the medina's main square. The old city is huge, labyrinthine, and definitely worth a visit; count the invasive hustlers and faux guides as part of the experience. In addition to its own fantastic merits, Marrakesh also serves as a good base for expeditions into the surrounding Atlas Mountains or the Sahara to the south.

ORIENTATION AND PRACTICAL INFORMATION

Most of the excitement, budget food, and cheap accommodations center on the **Djemâa el-Fna** and surround the **medina**. The **bus** and **train stations,** administrative buildings, and luxury hotels are in the **Guéliz** or **ville nouvelle** down **avenue Mohammed V;** from the Djemâa el-Fna, walk to the towering **Koutoubia Minaret** and turn right. Also in the ville nouvelle are most of the car rentals, newsstands, banks, and travel agencies. Bus #1 runs between the minaret and the heart of the ville nouvelle (1.50dh). Or, take one of the many *petits taxis* (despite the driver's demands, you shouldn't pay more than 10dh).

Transportation

Flights: Aéroport de Marrakesh Menara (tel. 44 78 65), 5km south of town. Taxi service about 50dh. No bus. Domestic and international flights on Royal Air Maroc.

Trains: av. Hassan II (tel. 44 77 68 or 44 77 63), going away from the medina on Mohammed V, turn left on av. Hassan II and walk 5min. To: Casablanca (4hr., 8 per day, 73dh); Meknes (7hr., 6 per day, 150dh); Tangier (8hr., 5 per day, 140dh); Fez (8hr., 2 per day, 169dh).

Buses: (tel. 43 39 33), outside the medina walls by Bab Doukkala. To get there, walk out of the medina on av. Mohammed V, pass through Bab Larissa, and then turn right, continuing along the walls until Bab Doukkala. The **gare routière** is to your left. **CTM** is next to window #8. To: Essaouira (3hr., 8 per day, 30dh); Agadir (4hr., 2-3 per day, 61dh); Casablanca (4hr., 3 per day, 40dh); Ouarzazate (4½hr., 4 per day, 65dh); Zagora (4-5hr., 4 per day, 79dh); Fez (10hr., 2 per day, 130dh). Other windows are for different private companies that have lower prices, lower standards, more frequent service, or a combination of the three. Most private buses also stop outside the Bab er-Rob, just south of Djemâa el-Fna, but seats are often full. Go from here to Setti-Fatma in the High Atlas (departs every 30min., 13dh).

Grands Taxis: It's best to start from Bab er-Rob, where you can share a taxi to Asni or Setti-Fatma. 15dh for 6 passengers; slightly more for smaller groups.

Car Rental: Avis, 137 bd. Mohammed V (tel. 43 99 84), and **Hertz,** 154 bd. Mohammed V (tel. 43 46 80). Both rent Renault IVs for 250dh per day plus 2.50dh per 2m. Numerous other local agencies and many hotels will arrange rentals and a discount.

Tourist and Financial Services

Tourist Office: Office National Marocain du Tourisme (ONMT), av. Mohammed V (tel. 43 62 39), at pl. Abdel Moumen ben Ali, about a 35min. walk from Djemâa el-Fna. Place Abdel Moumen is next to a bus stop and has **public toilets.** The office will get you a brochure with a mediocre map and access to **official guides,** (half-day 120dh, full day 150dh). ONMT open daily 8:30am-noon and 2:30-6:30pm; Ramadan daily 9am-3pm. **Syndicat d'Initiative,** 176 av. Mohammed V, on the right heading from the post office to the ONMT. Same mediocre maps, same dearth of info. Open daily 8:30am-12:30pm and 2:30-6pm.

Currency Exchange: Banks line av. Mohammed V and av. Hassan II in the Guéliz. Also clustered in the medina around the post office on the Djemâa el-Fna. **BCME** is open Saturdays, and **Syndicat d'Initiative** on Sundays. Most tourist-centered hotels change money at late hours—try Hôtel Ali or Hôtel Essaouira.

American Express: Voyages Schwartz, rue Mauritania, 2nd fl. (tel. 43 66 00), off av. Mohammed V, 2nd left after post office. Open daily 6am-11pm. Bank open M-F 8:30-11:30am and 2:30-4:30pm.

Emergency and Communications

Police: (tel. 19), to the south of the Djemâa el-Fna.

Late-Night Pharmacy: Off the Djemâa el-Fna, on the way to av. Mohammed V, on the right. Open Tu-Su 9pm-6am.

Medical Emergency: Doctor on call until 10pm at the above late-night pharmacy. It's best to avoid the government-run *polyclinique;* ask your consulate to recommend a private physician. See **Essentials: Embassies and Consulates,** p. 41.

Post Office: pl. 16 Novembre, off av. Mohammed V. Unreliable Poste Restante and it's a madhouse. Open M-F 8am-noon and 4-7pm, Sa 8:30-11:30am. **Branch office** in the Djemâa. Open M-F 8:30am-noon and 2:30-6:45pm.

Telephone Code: (0)4.

ACCOMMODATIONS AND CAMPING

Apart from the youth hostel and campground, which are far from the medina but close to the train station, all cheap accommodations are within a stone's throw of the Djemâa el-Fna. Many places allow you to sleep on the roof for about 20dh. To find **Hotels Essaouira, Medina,** and **Afriquia,** walk from Djemâa al-Fna down the street to the left of Banque al-Maghrib, take your first left, then turn right, and follow the signs.

Auberge de Jeunesse (HI) (tel. 44 77 13), on rue el-Jahed. 5min. from the train station, in a dreamy part of the ville nouvelle, but a 30min. walk from the interesting part of Marrakesh. Exit the train station and turn left on av. Hassan II. Take the 1st right at the traffic circle onto av. France. Take the 2nd right, continue for 2 blocks, then take a left and the 1st right. The spartan hostel is at the end of the street. Dorms 25dh. Cold showers. BYOTP (Bring Your Own Toilet Paper). Reception daily 8-9am, noon-2pm, and 6-10pm. Some rules—such as lock-out, 10pm curfew, and membership requirement—*may* be flexible.

Hôtel Ali (tel. 44 49 79; fax 43 36 09), on rue Moulay Ismael past the post office in the Djemâa el-Fna. Hôtel Ali draws tourists from around Morocco by milking its reputation as *the* budget hotel. Good suites with soap, towels, usually A/C, and toilet paper (stock up!). Singles with fan and shower 70dh; doubles with A/C and shower 105dh. Say you don't want breakfast or they'll add 15dh to your bill. Hôtel Ali also has a complete restaurant (see **Food** below) and organizes expeditions. If it's full, don't agree to go to **Hôtel Farouk** (owned by the same family)—it is distant from the Djemâa el-Fna and is no better than the other budget hotels near Hôtel Ali.

Hôtel Essaouira, 3 Derb Sidi Bouloukat (tel. 44 38 05). From pl. Djemâa el-Fna, face the post office (PTT) and Banque du Maroc. Head down the road in the left corner, through an archway. Take the 1st right after the Hôtel de France and look for the faded signs. The best terrace in town with a cafe and laundry basins. Manager stores luggage for trips to the Atlas Mountains. 40dh per person. Hot showers 5dh.

Hôtel Medina, 1 Derb Sidi Bouloukat (tel. 44 30 67), on your way to the Hôtel Essaouira (and run by its manager's cousin). Great terrace and clean rooms. Room price depends upon bed size. Singles 35-50dh; doubles 65-90dh.

Hotel Afriquia, 45 Sidi Boulouliate (tel. 44 24 03). Cool courtyard filled with slender orange trees differentiates Afriquia from the others. Clean rooms and bathrooms. Singles 40dh; doubles 70dh. Hot showers 5dh.

Hôtel Gallia, 30 rue de la Recette (tel. 44 59 13; fax 44 48 53), from the pl. Djemâa el-Fna, take the street to the left of the Banque du Maroc, and the 1st left after the cinema. A cut above the other hotels in the area, and the price reflects it. Clean bedrooms (many with A/C) and sparkling bathrooms. Laundry service available. Singles 120dh, with shower 152dh; doubles 139dh, with shower 182dh.

amping: Camping-Caravaning Municipal (tel. 31 31 67), 13km out from Marrakesh on route de Casablanca. Pool, warm showers, and supermarket. 10dh per person, 11dh per tent, 8dh per car. Call ahead.

OD

o **markets** peddle fresh produce along the fortifications surrounding the city, far m pl. Djemâa el-Fna. A closer daily fruit and vegetable market lies just outside Bab mat. Bab el-Kemis hosts a lively Thursday market. For delicious bargains, head for **food stalls** in pl. Djemâa El-Fna. Grub dealers contribute to the square's mad-s—dozens of stalls deal from late afternoon until after midnight. Follow wds to the best *harira* (2dh) and *kebab* (2dh). As always, settle the price first.

hez Chegrouni, 4-6 pl. Djemâa el-Fna, just to the right of Café Montréal. Unassuming but not unrewarding. Spot the brown and gold awning or follow your nose to 3dh *soupe marocaine,* a meal in itself. Excellent *couscous* (25dh).

ôtel Ali (see **Accommodations** above). Popular with tourists for its all-you-can-eat Moroccan buffet dinner (50dh).

afé-Patisserie Toubkal, pl. Djemâa el-Fna, near the archway that leads to Hôtel Essaouira. Refresh your aching body on the shady outdoor patio. Scrumptious shish kebab with fried onions and peppers (20dh). Open daily 7am-11pm.

estaurant Argana, pl. Djemâa el-Fna. Typical menu (75-90dh) and a pleasant terrace overlooking the square. Try the pigeon *pastilla,* but avoid the spaghetti. Open daily 6am-1am.

GHTS

emâa el-Fna

elcome to the **Djemâa el-Fna** (Assembly of the Dead), one of the world's most franally exotic squares, where sultans once beheaded criminals and displayed the mains. Crowds of thousands participate in the bizarre bazaar that picks up in the ernoon and peters out after midnight. While snake-charmers and water-sellers pose entice tourists' cameras (and wallets), the vast majority of the audience are townsople and Berbers from outlying villages. Solitary figures consult with scribes, tion dealers, and fortune-tellers, crowds congregate around the preachers, storyllers, and musicians. Women have their children blessed by mystics, while touts courage bets on boxing matches between 11-year-old boys (and girls). On a good ght, Djemâa el-Fna induces absolute sensory overload.

Almost every tour of Marrakesh begins at the 12th-century **Koutoubia Mosque,** hose magnificent **minaret** presides over the Djemâa el-Fna. *(As with most Moroccan osques, entrance is forbidden to non-Muslims.)* Crowned by a lantern of three golden heres and shrouded by scaffolding as it undergoes restoration, the minaret is the dest and best surviving example of the art of the Almohads, who made Marrakesh eir capital (1130-1213) and once ruled the region from Spain to present-day Tuni-. In 1157, Abd el-Mumin acquired one of four editions of the Qur'an authorized by e caliph Uthman, and used it as a talisman in battle and inspiration for the design of e second Koutoubia Mosque. Possession of this holy book turned Marrakesh into a nter of religious study. In fact, the name Koutoubia comes from the Arabic *kutu-'yyin* (of the books). The minaret in particular is revered by art historians for its fluence on eight centuries of Islamic architecture.

The imperial city also had considerable military importance (many sultans' camigns to quell the tribes of the Atlas were launched from here), as evidenced by 2km pink-tinged fortifications. The **walls** are punctuated by numerous **gates,** the most gnificant of which are:

MOROCCO

Bab Agnaou: the most dazzling gate, 3 blocks south of the Koutoubia mosque. F[...] merly portal to the Kasbah of Yacoub el-Mansour. This 12th-century gate often d[...] played trophies of war—mutilated corpses and heads of slain enemies.

Bab er-Rob: next to Bab Agnaou, once the southern doorway to the city. The S[...] dien tombs (see below) are just inside; *grands taxis* wait outside.

Bab el-Khemis: site of a lively Thursday market, in the northeast corner of M[...] rakesh, a long swing around town. The bastion was reputedly designed and bu[...] by Andalusian architects and artisans. Best reached by heading around the corn[...] of the Madrassa ben Youssef, and taking the first major left.

The Medina

A worthwhile survey of the medina (prime time 5-8pm) begins at the **souqs.** Thou[...] dazzling and intimidating, the maze of streets doesn't necessitate a guide. If you [...] get lost and can't find your way out, you can ask a merchant for directions (or a ch[...] will lead you out for a few *dirhams*). From the Djemâa el-Fna, enter the medina [...] the pathway directly across from the Café-Restaurant-Hôtel de France. This is the pa[...] that runs through the medina's main thoroughfare, turns past the enormous **Sou**[...] **Smarine,** and takes a turn at the **potters' souq.** Berber blankets, woven by famili[...] spinning wool in a tangle of dowels, string, and cards of yarn, pile the alleyways [...] the **fabric souq.** Follow your nose through the first major orange gateway and make [...] quick right to the Zahba Kedima, a small plaza containing the **spice souq,** with m[...] sive sacks of saffron, cumin, ginger, and orange flower, as well as the apothecarie[...] more unusual wares—goat hoof for hair treatment, ground-up ferrets for depressio[...] and live chameleons for sexual frustration. Nearby is **La Criée Berbère** (the Berb[...] Auction), a center for slave dealing prior to French occupation. Nowadays, it hos[...] aggressive carpet and rug merchants.

Farther on are the bubbling vats of color of the **dyers' souq.** Fragrant whiffs [...] cedar signal the nearby **carpenters' souq,** where workers carve chess pieces wit[...] astounding speed. Go left through these stalls to where the 16th-century **Mouassi**[...] **Fountain** bathes its colorful carvings in an outer layer of grime.

On the road going right where **Souq Attarine** (perfume) forks, an endless selectio[...] of colorful leather footwear glows at the **babouche souq** (untinted yellow is trac[...] tional for men; women wear the fancier models). The right fork at the end of th[...] street leads to the **cherratine souq,** which connects the *babouche souq* to the **Sou**[...] **el-Kbir** (the right fork off Souq Smarine as you enter the medina), the leather souq. [...] 1565, Sultan Moulay Abdallah el-Ghalib raised the **Madrassa of ben Youssef** in th[...] center of the medina. *(Open in summer Tu-Su 8am-noon and 3-7pm; in winter Tu-Su 8a*[...] *noon and 2-6pm. 10dh.)* To get to the *madrassa,* backtrack to Souq Smarine, bear rig[...] at the fork onto Souq el-Kbir, and follow this lane to its end. The *madrassa* reigned a[...] the largest Quranic school in the Maghreb until closing in 1956. The Andalusian styl[...] includes the requisite calligraphy and intricate floral designs. Visitors can roam th[...] students' cells, and feel lucky to be unaccompanied by 400 *madrasa*-mates.

Around the corner, beside the Ben-Youssef mosque, juts the squat, unpainte[...] cupola of 12th-century **Koubba el-Ba'adiyn,** the oldest monument in town and th[...] only relic of the Almoravid dynasty. *(Open daily 8:30am-noon and 2:30-6pm. Bang on th*[...] *door if it's closed. 10dh, plus tip for the custodian-guide.)* When you've had enough of key[...] hole arches, pinecone and palm motifs, and intricate dome carvings, ask the guard t[...] open an ancient wooden door to the subterranean cisterns.

After the *madrassa,* those of strong nose and stomach can visit the **tannerie**[...] Head right around the corner and down toward Bab Debbarh. Each bubbling va[...] holds a different chemical for a stage of leather production.

Palaces and Tombs

The **Saadien Tombs,** modeled after the interior of the Alhambra in Granada, const[...] tute Morocco's most lavish mausoleum. The tombs served as the royal Saadie[...] necropolis during the 16th and 17th centuries, until Moulay Ismail walled them off t[...] efface the memory of his predecessors. In 1912 the burial complex was rediscovere[...] during a French aerial survey. One **mausoleum,** the tomb of **El Mansour** (the Victori[...]

us), brims opulently with illuminated *zellij* (mosaic tilework). The second was built
or his mother. Both date from the late 16th century. In the neighboring **Hall of the
Twelve Columns,** trapezoidal tombs rise from a pool of polished marble. *(Open daily
:30am-noon and 2:30-6pm. 10dh. Multilingual tours.)* The sultan's four wives, 23 concu-
ines, and the most favored of his hundreds of children are buried nearby. Unmarked

---

The Great Glaoui

The Glaoui Kasbah, located just outside Marrakesh, is one of the most extravagant sights in Morocco, even after its avaricious looting in 1956. By the turn of
the century, the Glaoui family had become the dominant political and financial
force in the region. When France took over in 1912, the Glaouis were granted
almost unhindered power over the entire south, but all was not business. El
Glaoui, Pasha of Marrakesh during France's rule and buddy of Winston
Churchill, relished a good party as much as anyone. It certainly didn't hurt that
he was fabulously rich—gold, diamonds, and most anything else imaginable
adorned his palace. For kicks, he regularly threw extravagant events at which,
according to Gavin Maxwell in *Lords of the Atlas,* "Nothing was impossible." El
Glaoui purportedly doled out hash, opium, gold, and even little boys and girls to
his Western guests.

---

ombs belong to the women. To reach the Saadien Tombs, follow the signs from Bab
l-Rob. The turquoise minaret of the **Mosque of the Kasbah,** Sultan Yacoub el-Man-
our's own personal mosque, flags the way. Veer left into the adjoining alley.

The ruthless late 19th-century vizier Si Ahmed Ben Moussa, also known as Bou
Ahmed, constructed **El Bahia** (The Brilliance) palace. *(Open daily 8:30-11:45am and
:30-5:45pm.)* Serving as the *de facto* seat of government for the man who ruled in the
ultan's stead, El Bahia was built to assert Morocco's historical and cultural signifi-
ance and thus stave off European domination. Facing the Hôtel CTM in the Djemâa
l-Fna, head left through an archway onto rue Riad Zitouna el-Kedim on the right. Fol-
ow the main thoroughfare to the end, and bear left through pl. Ferblantiers, curving
round 180 degrees. On the right, a reddish-brown archway opens into a long, tree-
ned avenue that leads to the palace door.

Dar Si Said, a 19th-century palace built by Si Said, brother of Grand Vizier Ba
Ahmed and chamberlain of Sultan Moulay el-Hassan, houses a **Museum of Moroccan
Art.** *(Open W-M 8:30am-noon and 2:30-5:45pm. 10dh.)* The collection features splendid
Berber carpets, pottery, jewelry, Essaouiran ebony, and Saadien woodcarving. The
leaming Dar Si Said is on a tiny alley off rue Riad Zitouna el-Jadid, the second right
eading toward the Djemâa el-Fna from the Bahia Palace.

Gardens

The mid-day sun in Marrakesh can be cruel, and since the 12th century rulers have
lealt with it by constructing massive irrigated gardens. The largest of these is the
Agdal, a 3km enclosure accessible via a roofed portal overlooking the Grand Méchouar, once probably a royal date and olive plantation. *(Closed to the public when the King
is in residence.)* While olive trees predominate, the garden contains all manner of fruit-
earing trees that shade the avenues and large pools. To get to the Agdal from Bab er-
Rob, walk left along the medina walls until you reach Bab Ahmar. Walk down rue Bab
Ahmar for five minutes; the garden is on your right and *may* be open.

The **Menara Gardens,** a vast enclave of olive groves around an enormous pond, are
most beautiful at sunset, when the mauve and tangerine light reflects off the water.
The cold green reservoir, 800m by 1200m, dates from the Almohad era. To reach the
ardens, head west through Bab el-Jedid and straight down av. Menara, the wide bou-
evard that resembles an airport landing strip. To the left lies the expansive olive
rove of Bab el-Jedid, a continuation of the gardens.

Menara and Agdal date back centuries, yet are overshadowed by the 1920s upstart
Majorelle Gardens. *(Open daily in summer 8am-noon and 3-7pm; in winter 8am-noon and 2-
pm. 15dh.)* Designed by French painter Jacques Majorelle, its exquisitely engineered

explosions of colorful flowers contrast strongly with the stately greens of the Agda and Menara. The garden is owned and maintained by Yves Saint Laurent (who occa sionally zips around the Djemâa el-Fna on his moped), and its fanciful colors rival hi wildest collections (pink concrete pathways?!).

ENTERTAINMENT

If you want to go where everybody knows your name ("Tourist!"), try the **hotel bar** at the **Tazi** and **Foucauld.** Here locals and tourists mix, lubricated by 15dh Flag *spé ciales.* To hit the Tazi, head away from the Djemâa el-Fna 200m down the street t the left of the Banque du Maroc. For the Foucauld, turn right by the Tazi onto the road that becomes av. Mohammed V and walk two blocks. Also, try the **Diaman Noir,** a nightclub on Mohammed V in Guéliz.

■ The High Atlas Mountains الأطلَس الأعلى

Trekking in the Atlas Mountains can be a wonderful addition to your tell-your-grand children repertoire. Unlike their counterparts in Europe, the range's trails have yet t be fitted for tourists, and the valleys below remain green, unspoiled, and very accessi ble. Even travelers with limited funds, time, and skills can huff to the summit of **Dje bal Toubkal,** North Africa's highest peak (4167m). Ascending Toubkal takes only tw days; however, treks of up to a couple weeks are plausible. For Toubkal, little more than a sleeping bag, food, water, and sturdy shoes are necessary. For anything longer though, unless one is skilled and equipped with a full outfit of backpacking equip ment (i.e. a stove, tent, water purification system, compass, maps, etc.), the service of a guide and/or mule and muleteer are pretty much essential, as the trails are many and universally unmarked. **Official guides** and **mules** can be hired in **Imlil** for 160d per day and 75dh per day respectively (not including tip). Alternatively, treks can b organized in Marrakesh at **Hôtel Ali** (see p. 699), where many experienced guide hang out. From Hotel Ali, prices are about 250dh per day per person, with everythin from food-and-shelter deals to guide-and-mule setups. All this only applies during th summer, since during the **winter** snow covers Toubkal and the upper valleys. In win ter, full alpine gear and an experienced guide are a *must.* Also, no matter what tim of year, **altitude sickness** must be taken into consideration, as the altitude chang from Marrakesh is drastic. Know the symptoms—headaches, nausea, dizziness, appe tite loss—and if they become severe or last longer than a day, *descend immediately.*

The ascent of **Toubkal** is outlined here; for more ambitious treks, information ca be garnered from books (*The Atlas Mountains, Morocco* by Robin G. Collomb is th acclaimed source), from guides (though remember that they are guides and not infor mation books), and from other trekkers.

A *grand taxi* from Marrakesh to **Asni** kicks off the mountain adventure, headin off from Bab er-Rob when there are enough passengers (1hr., 15dh). Asni itself has lit tle to offer besides mild hustling, *tajine,* and a Saturday *souq.* Those stranded over night can stay at the primitive **youth hostel** at the end of the village's street (20dh bring a sleeping bag). Most travelers climb onto the first **camionette** headed to Imli where the trail begins. The hair-raising pick-up truck ride is an experience in itself— all but the fainthearted should stand in back to enjoy the scenery (45 min., 15dh).

Imlil is a tiny village high in the Atlas. The air is cool (and damn cold at night), an the sound of running water is everywhere. Stay at the **CAF Refuge (HI),** which ha bunks, a kitchen (5dh per hr. of cooking gas), and cold showers in a refurbished co tage in the center of town (members 44dh, nonmembers 52dh; camping outsid 10dh per tent, 5dh per person). Unfortunately, the CAF Refuge will not allow you t store excess luggage while you explore. If this is a problem, consider getting a roo at one of Imlil's two hotels. Both the **Hôtel Aksoual** and **Hôtel Soleil** have rooms fo negotiable rates (about 40dh per person), and their cafes serve *tajine* for 30dh.

From Imlil, depart for Toubkal bright and early. Take the road up out of town, fol lowing the river; ask locals for the correct mule track. You will pass the hilltop village

MOROCCO

of **Aroumd** on the other side of the valley, and then descend into a broad valley before zigzagging up the east side. After over an hour of spectacular scenery, hikers reach **Sidi Chamarouch,** home to a fiercely guarded *marabout* shrine. The trail turns right and upward upon entering the village. Past this point the area is snowbound through late April. Next comes the **Toubkal (or Neltner) Refuge** (52dh, with HI card 44dh). Although often overcrowded, the refuge is a welcoming end to a day's hiking. Ask here for the best path up Toubkal (another 2½hr.). Most hikers spend the night here and ascend Toubkal early the next morning—as it clouds over in the afternoon—and then descend back to Imlil that same day. A guide for the final ascent can also be arranged at the refuge.

■ Taroudannt تارودانت

The long, winding descent to the Tizi-n-Test Pass through the High Atlas ends at Taroudannt's red earth walls. The northern gateway to the Anti-Atlas mountains, its bastions have controlled traffic through the mountain ranges for centuries. An enormous rectangle of fortifications encloses the town, making Taroudannt one of Morocco's best-preserved walled cities, free of any ville nouvelles. Taroudannt has great souqs and comparatively few tourists, as it serves primarily as a quiet way-station for those waiting to cross into the mountains or down to the coast.

ORIENTATION AND PRACTICAL INFORMATION CTM, SATAS, and other companies terminate in **place al-Alaouyine,** where banks and several budget hotels are located; other bus companies are located in **place an-Nasr.** To get from pl. al Alaouyine to pl. an-Nasr, take the right-hand street on the opposite side of the square from Hotel Taroudannt.

Buses are infrequent, inconvenient, and confusing. It's best to ask around at different companies, as routes change frequently. **SATAS** buses go to: Agadir (2hr., 1 per day, 15dh); Ouarzazate (5hr., 1 per day, 50dh); Marrakesh via Agadir (6hr., 1 per day, 70dh). **CTM** goes to: Marrakesh via Agadir (6hr., 1 per day, 91dh); Ouarzazate (5hr., 1 per day, 60dh). One bus runs to Taroudannt-Marrakesh via Tizi-n-Test from Pl. an-Nasr (55dh). **Banks** that change traveler's checks are in pl. al-Alaouyine. After hours, Hôtel Palais Salam, set in the eastern wall of the Kasbah, changes small amounts of traveler's checks or cash (around $50). The **police** (tel. 19), in the basement of the Public Works building, are outside Bab El Kasbah. They also have a **small office** in pl. al-Alaouyine. The **Hôpital Mokhtar Soussi** (tel. 85 30 80), inside the town walls through the Bab El Kasbah, serves medical needs. To get to the **post office,** out of Bab El Kasbah, just beyond the police station and in front of the mosque, has Poste Restante, but no phones (open M-F 8:30am-12:15pm and 2:30-6:30pm, Sa 8-11am).

ACCOMMODATIONS AND FOOD All of the following choices are in pl. al-Alaouyine. **Hotel Taroudannt** (tel. 85 24 16) spices up its clean rooms with a pleasant bar, a courtyard jungle, and a rooftop terrace (singles 65dh, with shower 80dh; doubles 80dh, with shower 95dh). Its **restaurant,** complete with white tablecloths, serves excellent French dishes and wine (*menu* 60-75ptas; open daily noon-2:30pm and 7-10pm). **Hôtel Roudani** (tel. 85 22 19) is slightly better than the other cheapies (small rooms for one or two people 40dh; larger rooms 70dh; free showers). *Its* **restaurant** serves Moroccan specialties at tables on the square (open 24hr.).

SIGHTS Construction on the monumental **fortified walls** that enclose Taroudannt began in the 16th century when the city thrived as a cultural and military center. Oddly, those that remain date from the 18th century. To soak up their grandeur as you circumnavigate the town, either walk along the walls or rent a bike (starting at 6dh per hour in several places, including Hotel Taroudannt).

The **souqs** around the two squares are also worth a brief stop. Although their wares pale in comparison with the souqs of Fez or Marrakesh, Taroudannt is one of Morocco's silver-working centers. (Note that real silver bears a government stamp on the back—don't believe shady merchants who will try to convince you otherwise.)

MOROCCO

Amber and other kinds of jewelry can also be found. Outside Bab Targhount are Taroudannt's **tanneries.** Although they reek to high heaven, they make a great photo. Alternatively, avoid the smell and buy the postcard.

Fortified villages and **kasbahs** surround Taroudannt. The closest is **Freija,** an easy half-day bike ride away (11km). To get there, follow the Ouarzazate-Marrakesh road (Tizi-n-Test) 8km to Aït Iazza. From there, turn right down the road to Igherm and Tata and cross the (hopefully) dry riverbed; Freija sits at the top of the hill.

■ Ouarzazate ورزازات

The ride to Ouarzazate, on the cusp between the Atlas Mountains and the southern desert, reduces travelers to monosyllabic "oohs" and "aahs," and perhaps—depending on the driver—a few "eeks" as well. After all the fun, though, the trip's finale is somewhat anticlimactic. Although envisioned by the Moroccan government as a tourist mecca (the government built a four-lane highway, and erected four- and five-star hotels), this French-built administrative center never became popular. The town, however, makes a convenient spot to rent a car for exploring nearby towns, deserts, and valleys—especially for those who find the prospect of driving across the mountains from Marrakesh a bit daunting.

PRACTICAL INFORMATION CTM and **private buses** are located at the western edge of Ouarzazate. Head 1½ blocks south (toward the river) from the station to reach **avenue Mohammed V,** home to most administrative buildings, budget hotels, and restaurants. Buses go to: Marrakesh (4½hr., 5 per day, 50dh); Rachidia, via Skoura, Boumalne du Dadés, and Tinehar (1 per day); M'Hamid, via Agdz and Zagora (6½hr., 1 per day, 55dh); and Agadir (6hr., 1 per day, 60dh). Private buses travel more frequently. **Grands taxis** line up by the bus station and run fairly often to nearby destinations: Skoura (45min., 10dh), Zagora (3hr., 45dh), and Marrakesh (4hr., 80dh). If the taxis are not full (fewer than six people crammed in), be prepared to pay extra. Ask to speak with a "Star Skooter" representative. The are several **rental car** agencies in Ouarzazate, including Hertz, Avis, Eurocar, and Budget. Larger companies charge about 500dh per day for a Fiat Uno (unlimited mileage); local companies offer fewer services, but charge half that. Check your car well before making any payments. Hôtel Royal rents **mopeds** (150dh per half-day, 250dh per day; haggling acceptable).

One of the more helpful **tourist offices** (tel. 88 24 85) in Morocco is on av. Mohammed V, where the road forks to follow the Oued Drâa and the Oued Dadès. Get bus info and a directory of hotels in the Drâa and Dadès Valleys. (Open M-F 8:30-noon and 2:30-6:30pm.) **Currency exchange** is at the banks on av. Mohammed V; four- and five-star hotels will only exchange cash. The **post office** and **international telephones** sit on av. Mohammed V, by the tourist office (open July-Aug. M-Sa 8am-noon and 2:30-6:45pm; Sept.-June M-Sa 8am-noon and 2:30-6pm). The **telephone code** is (0)4.

ACCOMMODATIONS AND FOOD For inexpensive lodging, check either on av. Mohammed V or on streets parallel and to the north. **Hôtel Royal,** 24 av. Mohammed V (tel. 88 22 58), next to Chez Dimitri, is a good bet (singles 36-60dh, with shower 80dh; doubles 80dh, with shower 95dh; warm shower 10dh). The **Hôtel Bab Es Sahara,** pl. Mouhadine (tel. 88 47 22 or 88 49 65), has large cheap rooms. Head away from the bus station, and take a left after the Hôtel Royal. (Singles 50dh, with bath 70dh; doubles 80dh, with bath 105dh.) It has a restaurant and **currency exchange.**

The **supermarket,** on av. Mohammed V, across the street from Hôtel Royal, has an unrivaled selection of cured meats, canned goods, chocolate, wine, cold beer, and European goods. **Restaurante-Café Royal,** av. Mohammed V (tel. 88 24 75), is a great spot for neighborhood chess matches and chicken *tajine* (35dh)—the only dish they serve regularly, despite an extensive menu (open daily 7am-11pm). Tourists in Ouarzazate frequent **Chez Dimitri,** the best (well, only) Italian restaurant in town. It was built during the French occupation and holds a monopoly on alcohol (*menu* 75dh).

SIGHTS The nearest example of desert architecture is the **Kasbah (Citadel) of Taourirt,** once a stronghold of the Glaoui. *(Open daily 8:30am-noon and 2:30-7:30pm. 10dh.)* The Kasbah, 1½km east of town, was built in the mid-18th century and occupied until independence in 1956, when it was abandoned. Recently restored, its interior is now an entertaining maze of winding streets, stairways, and balconies. Its massive Krupp cannon, given by Moulay Hassan, could level any recalcitrant village in sight (quite a way to establish governmental authority). To get there, walk down Mohammed V away from Marrakesh, bear left at the tourist office, and head toward Club Med. To enter step onto the bamboo floors that are through the doorway just to the left of the Kasbah as you face it from the street. Across the highway, the tiny **Centre Artisanal/Carpet Cooperative** displays local crafts, including the region's woven and knotted carpets. Craft-seekers might also want to try one of Ouarzazate's four **souqs,** held Tuesdays, Fridays, Saturdays, and Sundays.

■ Near Ouarzazate

The area to the north of Ouarzazate is a hot and dusty palette of desert browns and greens, periodically interrupted by small Berber **kasbahs.** Perhaps the most spectacular of these is in the village **Aït Benhaddou,** 30km on the road towards Marrakesh. Although it is seemingly abandoned, the fortified structure is still inhabited by a handful of Berber families. A forest of tapered turrets climbs to the ruined Kasbah at the crest of a hill. Look familiar? They're the region's film stars, featured in *Lawrence of Arabia* and *Jesus of Nazareth.* UNESCO has since designated the village a world heritage sight. Take a *grand taxi* from Ouarzazate (about 250dh round-trip; the driver will wait, but don't pay him until the journey is complete). It's a beautiful ride on a rented moped, as long as the gas tank is filled. Otherwise, you and some new buddies may want to rent a car.

■ The Drâa Valley وادي دراع

South of Ouarzazate, through Agdz, Zagora, and ending in M'Hamid, is the narrow Drâa Valley, along which stretches a continuous grove of palm trees strewn with kasbahs and *ksours* (fortified strongholds). The route is best toured leisurely by rental car, although people also hop from village to village by bus, taxi, or thumb (hitchhiking is very common in the south). Desert expeditions by camel or 4x4 leave from Zagora or, preferably, M'Hamid. Temperatures can reach 67°C here during July and August, but are tolerable the rest of the year and always cool off at night.

■ Northern Drâa to Zagora

As you leave Ouarzazate southbound on P31, the scenery changes almost instantly. A lunar landscape strewn with volcanic rock stretches in all directions. Farther south, magnificent cusps of black cliff poke eerily through the horizon. Ancient lookout towers sprinkle the roadside terrain. The first *ksour* is **Aït Saoun.** From here the road passes a sinister black gorge and winds over the Tizi-n-Tinifift pass to Ourika. Set below Jbel Kissane, 67km from Ouarzazate, **Agdz** is a good place for gas and a cold drink—buses on their way to Zagora and M'Hamid stop for 30 minutes—but little else. Immediately south of Agdz, the highway intersects the Drâa River and the long string of oases begins. The layout of the villages is remarkable: each community is divided into several clusters about an oasis, with smaller domiciles adjoining central, fortified kasbahs. Oddly-shaped towers betray **Tamnougalt,** the first truly breathtaking *ksour* along the route. Next comes **Timiderte,** followed by **Tansihkt's** explosion of palm trees, **Ouaouzgar's** fine valley view, and **Tamezmoute's** giant Kasbah. **Tinezouline,** a large central village with a pretty kasbah, is known for its lively Monday market. Just before Zagora, the **Azlag Pass** opens the valley to an ocean of palms.

MOROCCO

> Many hustlers pose as hitchhikers or victims of auto breakdowns along the Ouar-
> zazate to Zagora road. They invite anyone who picks them up back to their place
> in "gratitude" for the ride, and once there, try to get the driver to take a camel
> trek, buy jewelry, etc. A good way to avoid this is to pile your bags on the seats
> and say there is no space. Better yet, don't stop at all.

■ Zagora الزّاكورَة

Stiflingly hot, tourist-trodden, and hustler-ridden, Zagora is the traditional place
where treks and expeditions into the valley and desert are organized. Built as a
French administrative town, Zagora is not a very appealing place. Practically everyone you meet here seems to have camels to rent; it is better to go to an established
hotel or campground. Even better, go to M'Hamid.

There is one **CTM** (tel. 84 73 27) bus to M'Hamid at 4pm. *Grand taxis* are a much
better way to travel to M'Hamid (25dh). One morning **bus** and several evening buses
head from Zagora to Marrakesh via Ouarzazate, and several buses to Agadir, Rabat,
and Casablanca. *Everything* is lined along **avenue Mohammed V,** the road that the
highway turns into when it enters town. **BMCE** and **Banque Populaire** are both
there for **currency exchange,** as is the **post office.** The **telephone code** is (0)4.

If you decide to stay in Zagora, the cheapest place is **Hôtel des Amis** (tel. 84 79
24), with slightly dingy, but passable rooms (singles with shower 30dh; doubles with
shower 50dh). Much nicer is the large, modern **Hôtel Palmeraie** (tel. 84 70 08, fax
84 78 78). Many rooms have air-conditioning, and there is a nice pool and a bar. (In
high season singles 90dh, with A/C 105dh; doubles 160dh, with A/C 210dh, with terrace 250dh.) Both hotels are on av. Mohammed V. Signs indicate the way to **Camping
Sindibad** (tel. 84 75 53), on av. Hassan II. Camping spots are shaded and covered
with grass; there is also a pool (no extra charge). (10dh per person, per tent; 5dh per
car, 10dh per caravan.) All three of these places arrange **camel treks** anywhere from
a few hours to a few weeks long for 200-350dh per day per person, with everything
from food to bedding included. **Restaurants,** none particularly spectacular, line av.
Mohammed V. Most hotels and campgrounds have restaurants as well.

■ Southern Drâa

To cross the Drâa at the southern edge of Zagora, travel out of town, away from Ouarzazate for 3km, and watch for a dirt road on the left (at the sign for Camping de la
Montagne de Zagora). This rough track trundles its way to **Jbel Zagora,** a lone volcanic outcrop overlooking the fertile Drâa. The mountain is best visited at sunset, when
the peaks shimmer in the dying light. At **Amazraou,** 0.5km south of the turn-off for
Jbel Zagora along the main road, an ancient Jewish Kasbah contemplates the
encroaching desert.

Continue down the main highway to **Tamegroute,** an oasis of date palms and
ksours. Here, in the middle of nowhere, is Morocco's best historical resource, Tamegroute's **library,** which contains 4000 Moroccan manuscripts dating from the 11th to
the 18th centuries. There is a history of Fez, a copy of Bukhari's *Hadish,* poetry of al-
Andalusi, and countless astronomical algebraic charts. The library's most treasured
document is a history written on gazelle skin in 1063 by the great legal authority,
Iman Malik. The caretaker speaks French and English. To get to the library, ignore the
painted "biblioteque" signs (a scam) and turn left (coming from Zagora) down the
one paved road in Tamegroute. Just after the paving ends, look for a large brown gate
on the right; this leads to the courtyard in front of the library. (Open 9am-noon and 3-
6pm. Free, but tip the caretaker.)

The **Saturday market** draws valley neighbors for its local pottery. Arrive early,
because it's over by noon. You can eat in town at either **Restaurant L'Oasis** or **Restaurant du Drâa.** Taxi fare to Tamegroute via Zagora is 12dh per person.

Whisked into swollen shapes by fierce desert gusts, the **Dunes of Tinfou** rise from
the valley floor in smooth golden mounds. These natural sculptures flow in gentle

waves, buffeted into beautiful and delicate forms. To reach the dunes of Tinfou, follow the main highway south from Tamegroute and watch for the well-marked dirt turn-off on the left—the yellow humps are visible from the road.

■ M'Hamid

M'Hamid lies at the end of the road—and it feels like it. Forty-five kilometers from the Algerian border and 97km from Zagora at the edge of great sand deserts, its a lone outpost of dirt streets, no facilities, and recently-installed electricity. Expeditions to the Sahara are organized here, and **camel treks** range from 250-350dh per person per day, with guide and food included. **Four-by-four trips,** and even trips with your own car, are arranged as well. A Monday **market** takes place here, when nomads from the desert come to trade. If you start here instead of Zagora, you can reach endless seas of sand dunes and isolated oases with a four-five day voyage, and very impressive landscapes on only a one- or two-day trip.

One CTM **bus** leaves each day for Marrakesh (11hr., 5am, 18dh), as well as 2 other private-owned buses (11hr., 1 per day). **Taxis** (25dh) and trucks are, as always, more frequent. There are no banks in the village and only a tiny **post office.** The **telephone code** is (0)4. In town, head for **Hôtel-Restaurant Sahara** (tel. 84 80 09), with free cold showers (hot water to be installed in Oct. 1998; singles 25dh; doubles 45dh). Food in M'Hamid is a bit expensive, but this is to be expected in a remote location. Nonetheless, you can eat a satiating meal at Hôtel-Restaurant Sahara for 20-50dh.

■ The Dadés Valley وادي دادس

Broader, drier, and more scenic than the Drââ Valley, the Dadés Valley stretches eastward from Ouarzazate. Other than the kasbahs and palmeraies along the way, the valley's main attractions are the **Dadés Gorge** and the **Todra Gorge,** extending north into the dry escarpment of the High Atlas.

Forty-two kilometers east of Ouarzazate is the luxurious oasis of **Skoura,** surrounded by fields of grain and roses. Among the many magnificent kasbahs in town, **Amerhidil** (though inaccessible) and **Dar Aït Sidi el Mati** are the most impressive. Past Skoura, the first 40km east are a flat expanse of dust and rock that are suddenly replaced by a burst of green plantations and palm groves, crowded on either side by kasbahs looming over the highway. The **telephone code** for the Dadés Valley is (0)4.

■ Dadés Gorge

Boumalne Dadés, an uninteresting town that serves as a gateway into the Dadés Gorge, is 116km east of Ouarzazate. There are several **buses** a day in both directions and a *grand taxi* from Ouarzazate costs 25dh. **Grand taxis** leave for the gorges in the same lot as the local buses, a couple blocks up the road from the CTM station. There is a **bank** across from the *grand taxi* stand. If you get stuck in Boumalne, head for **Hôtel-Restaurant Adrar,** (tel. 83 03 55; fax. 83 03 66) across from the bus station (singles 40dh; doubles 60-70dh).

The **gorge** stretches up along a road a few blocks west of the CTM station. The trip consists of wild, stunning scenery where the earth seems to have been ripped away, leaving a massive gash through the mountainside. Towering kasbahs rise up on the slopes and dissolve into the surrounding earth. About 27km up the road, the gorge narrows and the road climbs above it. At this point there are several hotels, restaurants, and campsites. Try **Auberge Tissadrine** on the left (singles 40dh; doubles 80dh; breakfast and hot showers included). **Camping** by the river is 10dh person, and terrace sites are 15dh. From here, trips up the gorge cost 150-200dh per day, and a **taxi** to this point is 10dh.

■ Todra Gorges

Another 53km along the road east from Boumalne is **Tinahir,** the gateway into the Todra Gorges. Like Boumalne, there is nothing of interest here, except transportation into the gorge. As the Todra Gorge is much more accessible than the Dadés, there is even less chance of being stuck here, but if you are, try the cheap, basic **Résidence El Fath** (tel. 83 48 06), av. Hassan II (singles 35dh; doubles 60dh). One step up is the techno-blasting **Hotel L'Avenir** (singles 50dh; doubles 85dh). There is a Spanish restaurant downstairs that serves *paella,* among other dishes (45-60dh). Several **buses** depart each day in both directions. Buses go to both Ouarzazate (37dh) and Marrakesh (83dh). A taxi from Boumalne costs 15dh.

The road out of Tinerhin snakes up the **Todra River** valley for 14km before reaching the mouth of the **gorge** itself. From here, start hiking up between the towering walls. Almost a thousand feet high, the sienna walls frame a blue strip of sky above and fall to a rocky riverbed below. A half-day hike is enough to appreciate the magnificence of the gorge, but a few days, or even a week, will allow you to climb well into the High Atlas. Along the way to the gorge are a trio of beautiful campgrounds. **Auberge de l'Atlas** (tel. 83 42 09) is slightly better than the other two facilities nearby (9dh per person, 10dh per car). There are several more hotels at the mouth of the gorge. At **Cafe-Restaurant Auberge Etoile des Gorges** you can sleep on the roof below the walls of the gorge for 5dh (singles 25dh; doubles 50dh).

MOROCCO

Appendix

HOLIDAYS AND FESTIVALS

Festivals and holidays form a huge part of Iberian culture and can transform the drab-
best and dreariest towns into huge parties overnight. On the flip side, they often
result in closed establishments, higher prices, and scarce accomodations. The list
here is for major festivals only; practically every village in Spain and Portugal has their
own local festival. For more information on each festival listed below, see the specific
town description. The dates of many of the Christian holidays (such as Holy Week,
Corpus Christi, and Carnival) are valid for 1999 only. The dates of all Muslim holidays,
which begin at sundown before the day listed, are based on the lunar calendar and
are thus also valid for 1999 only

Date	Location	Festival
SPAIN		
January 1	National	New Years Day
January 6	National	The Epiphany
February 7 to 16	National, with special celebrations in Santa Cruz de Tenerife and Cádiz	Carnival
February 25 to March 1	Villanueva de la Vera (near Cáceres)	Pero Palo Festival
March 12 to 20	Valencia	Las Fallas
March 29 to April 4	National, with special celebrations in Sevilla	Holy Week (Semana Santa)
March 4	National	Easter
April 11 to 16	Cuenca	Week of Religious Music
April 23	Barcelona	St. George's Day and Cervantes Day
late April to early May	Sevilla	April Fair (Feria de Abril)
May 1	National	May Day
first week in May	Jerez de la Frontera	Horse Fair
May 5 to 18	Córdoba	Patio Festival
May 15 to 22	Madrid	San Isidro Festival
June 4 to 6	Almonte (near Huelva)	Rocío Pilgrimage
June 15 to July 15	Granada	International Music and Dance Festival
June 22	National, with special celebrations in Toledo, La Laguna (near Tenerife), and Granada	Corpus Christi
June 20 to 29	Alicante	Festival of St. John
July 1 to 25	Almagro (near Ciudad Real)	Festival of Classical Drama and Comedy
July 6 to 14	Pamplona/Iruña	Running of the Bulls

mid to late July	Donostia-San Sebastián	International Jazz Festival
July 25	National, with special celebrations in Santiago de la Compostela	Feast of Santiago
August 15	National	Feast of the Assumption
first week in September	Jerez de la Frontera	Grape Harvest Festival
September 21 to 30	San Sebastían/Donostia	International Film Festival
early October	Sitges (near Barcelona)	International Film Festival of Fantastic Cinema
October 12	National	Spain's National Day
October 20 to 28	Valladolid	International Film Festival
October 27 to 29	Consuegra (near Toledo)	The Saffron Rose Festival
November 1	National	All Saints' Day
December 6	National	Constitution Day
December 8	National	Feast of the Immaculate Conception
December 25	National	Christmas
December 31	National	New Year's Eve
PORTUGAL		
January 1	National	New Year's Day
February 7 to 16	National, with special-Loulé, Nazaré, Funchal, Ovar, Graciosa	Carnival
March 29 to April 4	National, with special events in Braga, Ovar, and Povoa de Varzim	Holy Week (Semana Santa)
April 2	National	Good Friday
April 4	National	Easter
April 25	National	Liberty Day
May 1	National	Labor Day
May 1 to 3	Barcelos	Festival of the Crosses (Festa das Cruzes)
May 17	Ponta Delgada and Azores	Festival for Senhor Santo Cristo
May 12 to 13	Fátima	Pilgrimage
June 10	National	Portugal's and Camões Day
June 22	National	Corpus Christi
June 12 to 29	Lisbon, Porto, and other major cities	All Saints Festival
June 23 to 24	Porto, Figueira da Foz, and Braga	Festival of St. John (Festa de São João)
June	Évora	Festival of St. John (Feira de São João)
June 27 to 29	Montijo, Ribeira Brava, and Sintra	Festival of St. Pedro (Festa de São Pedro)
mid-June to mid-July	Sintra	Music Festival

July	Vila Franca de Xira (near Ribatejo)	Red Waistcoast Festival Colete Encarnado
July, 1999	Tomar	Festival of the Tabuleiros
July	Lisbon	International Handicraft Fair
July to August	Aveiro	Festival of the River
July to August	Estoril	Handicrafts Fair
August 14 to 15	Funchal, Madeira	Our Lady of the Monte
August 15	National	Feast of the Assumption
August 21 to 24	Viana do Castelo	Our Lady of Agony Festival
August to September	Viseu	St. Matthew's Fair
September 4 to 8	Palmela	Wine Harvest Festival
September	Algarve	Folk Music Festival
October 5	National	Republic Day
October	Vila Franca de Xira	October Fair
October 12 to 13	Fátima	Pilgrimage
October to November	Santarém	National Festival of Gastronomy
November 1	National	All Saints' Day
December 1	National	Restorations of Indepedence
December 8	National	Feast of the Immaculate Conception
December 25	National	Christmas
December 31	National	New Year's Eve
MOROCCO		
December 20, 1998 to January 19, 1999	Nationa	Ramadan
January 1	National	New Year's Day (secular)
January 11	National	Independence Manifesto
March 3	National	Throne Day
March 17, 1999	National	Ras as-Sana
May 1	National	Labour Day
May 14, 1999	National	Ashoora
May 23	National	National Day
June 26, 1999	National	Mawlid an-Nabi
July 9	National	Young People's Day
August 14	National	Allegiance of Wadi-Eddahab
August 20	National	Anniversary of the King's and People's Revolution
November 6	National	Anniversary of the Green March
November 18	National	Independence Day

TIME ZONES

Spain is one hour later than Greenwhich Mean Time (GMT) and six hours later than U.S. EST. **Portugal** and **Morocco** are on GMT and 5 hours later than EST. Thus, when it is 3pm in New York, it is 8pm in Portugal and Morocco and 9pm in Spain. Spain and Portugal, together with the rest of Europe, switch to and from Daylight Savings time about one week before the U.S. Morocco does not switch, and is thus four hours later than U.S. EST and two hours earlier than Spain in the summer.

CLIMATE

The following information is drawn from the International Association for Medical Assistance to Travelers *World Climate Charts*. In each monthly listing, the first two numbers represent the average daily maximum and minimum temperatures in degrees **Celsius**. The remaining number indicates the average number of days with a measurable amount of **precipitation**.

SPAIN

Temp in °C	January Temp	Rain	April Temp	Rain	July Temp	Rain	October Temp	Rain
Barcelona	6-13	5	11-18	9	21-28	4	15-21	9
Cádiz	9-15	9	13-20	6	20-27	0	17-23	7
Granada	2-12	7	7-20	10	17-34	1	10-23	7
Madrid	2-9	8	7-18	9	17-31	2	10-19	8
Málaga	8-17	7	13-21	6	21-29	0	16-23	6
Palma	6-14	8	10-19	6	20-29	1	10-18	9
Santander	7-12	16	10-15	13	16-22	11	12-18	14
Santiago de C.	5-10	21	8-18/	7	13-24	1	11-21	10
Sevilla	6-15	8	11-24	7	20-36	0	14-26	6
Valencia	6-15	5	10-20	7	20-29	2	13-23	7
Zaragoza	2-10	6	8-19	8	18-31	3	6-14	6

PORTUGAL

Temp in °C	January Temp	Rain	April Temp	Rain	July Temp	Rain	October Temp	Rain
Bragança	0-8	15	5-16	10	13-28	3	7-18	10
Evora	6-12	14	10-19	10	16-30	1	13-22	9
Faro	9-15	9	13-20	6	20-28	0	16-22	6
Lisbon	8-14	15	12-20	10	17-27	2	14-22	9
Porto	5-13	18	9-18	13	15-25	5	11-21	15

MOROCCO

Temp in °C	January Temp	Rain	April Temp	Rain	July Temp	Rain	October Temp	Rain
Essaouira	11-17	6	14-19	5	17-22	0	16-22	3
Fès	4-16	8	9-23	9	18-36	1	13-26	7
Marrakech	4-18	7	11-26	6	19-38	1	14-28	4
Rabat	8-17	9	11-22	7	17-28	0	14-25	6
Tangier	8-16	10	11-18	8	18-27	0	15-22	8

To convert from °C to °F, multiply by 1.8 and add 32.
To convert from °F to °C, subtract 32 and multiply by 0.55.

°C	-5	0'	5	10	15	20	25	30	35	40
°F	23	32	41	50	59	68	77	86	95	104

MEASUREMENTS

The following is a list of U.S. units and their metric equivalents:

1 inch (in.) = 25 millimeter (mm)	1 millimeter (mm) = 0.04 inch (in.)
1 foot (ft.) = 0.30 meter (m)	1 meter (m) = 3.33 foot (ft.)
1 yard (yd.) = 0.91 meter (m)	1 meter (m) = 1.1 yard (yd.)
1 mile (mi.) = 1.61 kilometer (km)	1 kilometer (km) = 0.62 mile (mi.)
1 ounce (oz.) = 25 gram (g)	1 gram (g) = 0.04 ounce (oz.)
1 pound (lb.) = 0.45 kilogram (kg)	1 kilogram (kg) = 2.22 pound (lb.)
1 quart (qt.) = 0.94 liter (L)	1 liter (L) = 1.06 quart (qt.)

MISCELLANY

ADDRESSES

Spain and Portugal: "Av.", "C.", "R.", and "Trav." are abbreviations for street, "Po." and "Pg." for a promenade, "Pl." for a square, and "Ctra." for a highway. The number of a building follows the street name, unlike in English. The letters "s/n" means the building has no number. **Morocco:** "av.", "bd.", "rue", and "calle" mean street; "pl." is a plaza. The number of a building comes before the street name, as in English. When hunting for an address, note that many streets are being renamed in Arabic; "rue" and "calle" may be replaced by "zankat," "derb," or "sharia."

CLOTHING SIZE AND CONVERSIONS

Men's Shirts (Collar Sizes)

U.S./U.K.:	14½	15	15½	16	16½
Continent:	37	38	39	40	41

Men's Suits and Coats

U.S./U.K.:	38	40	42	44	46
Continent:	48	50	52	54	56

Women's Blouses and Sweaters

U.S.:	6	8	10	12	14
U.K.:	28	30	32	34	36
Continent:	34	36	38	40	42

Women's Dresses, Coats, and Skirts

U.S.:	4	6	8	10	12	14
U.K.:	6	8	10	12	14	16
Continent:	34	36	38	40	42	44

Men's Shoes

U.S.:	8	9	10	11	12
U.K.	7	8	9	10	11
Continent:	41	42	43	44½	46

Women's Shoes

U.S.:	6	7	8	9	10
U.K.:	4½	5½	6½	7½	8½
Continent:	37	38	39	40	41

LANGUAGE

A basic vocabulary in the local tongue will go a long way toward making your trip both easier and more enjoyable. Any attempts at the local language are appreciated and encouraged. Learn the vocabulary of courtesy as well; you'll be treated more kindly if you are polite to those around you.

In Spanish pronunciation is very regular. Vowels are always pronounced the same way: *a* ("ah" in father); *e* ("eh" in escapade); *i* ("ee" in eat); *o* ("oh" in oat); *u* ("oo" in boot); *y*, by itself, is pronounced like *ee*. Most consonants are the same as English. Important exceptions are: *j* ("h" in "hello"); *ll* ("y" in "yes"); *ñ* ("gn" in "cognac"); *rr*, (trilled "r"); *h* is always silent; *x* retains its English sound. The stress in Spanish words falls on the last syllable, unless the word ends in a vowel, an "s", or a "n". All exceptions to these rules require a written accent on the stressed syllable. For Moroccan Arabic and Portuguese, pronunciation tips are provided word by word.

■ Spanish Phrasebook

English	Spanish	English	Spanish
THE BARE MINIMUM			
Yes/No	Sí/No	Do you speak English?	¿Habla (usted) inglés?
Hello	Hola (Sí on the phone)	I don't understand	No entiendo
Good morning!	¡Buenos días!	I don't speak Spanish	No hablo español
Good afternoon!	¡Buenas tardes!	What/When	¿Qué?/¿Cuándo?
Good evening/night!	¡Buenas noches!	Where/How	¿Dónde?/¿Cómo?
Goodbye	Adiós/Hasta luego	Who/Why	¿Quién?/¿Por qué?
Please/Thank you	Por favor/Gracias	How are you?	¿Cómo está (usted)?
Excuse me	Perdón/Perdóname	Good/Bad/So-so	Bién/Mal/Así así
Help	¡Socorro!	What time is it?	¿Qué hora es?
No smoking/Gotta lighter (cigarette)?	No fumar/¿Tiene fuego (un cigarillo)?	How much does this cost?	¿Cuánto cuesta?
Here/There/Left/Right/Straight	Aquí/Allí/Izquierda/Derecha/Recto	Where is...the bathroom?	¿Dónde está...el baño?
Open/Closed	Abierto/Cerrado	My name is...	Me llamo...
Hot/Cold	Caliente/Frío	What is your name?	¿Cómo se llama?
ACCOMODATION AND TRANSPORTATION			
I want/I would like	Quiero/Quisiera	How do I reach ...?	¿Cómo llego a...?
I would like a room	Quisiera un cuarto	One (two) ticket to...	Un (dos) billete para...
Do you have any rooms?	¿Tiene cuartos libres?	Bus (Train) station/Airpot	Estación de Tren (Autobús)/Aeropuerto
Bath/Shower/Water	Baño/Ducha/Agua	train/plane/bus	Tren/Avión/Autobús
Key/Sheets	Llave/Sábana	round-trip	ida y vuelta
Air conditioning	Aire acondicionado	How long is the trip?	¿Cuánto dura el viaje?
Hotel/Hostel/Campgrounds/Inn	Hotel/Hostal or Albergue/Camping/Posada	At what time does it leave/arrive?	¿A qué hora sale/llega?

FOOD AND DINING (ALSO SEE GLOSSARY)

breakfast	desayuno	**the check, please**	la cuenta, por favor
lunch	almuerzo	**drink**	bebida
dinner	cena	**dessert**	postre

DAYS

Sunday	domingo	**Today**	hoy
Monday	lunes	**Tomorrow**	mañana
Tuesday	martes	**Day after tomorrow**	pasado mañana
Wednesday	miércoles	**Yesterday**	ayer
Thursday	jueves	**Day before yesterday**	antes de ayer/anteayer
Friday	viernes	**Week**	semana
Saturday	sábado	**Weekend**	fin de semana

NUMBERS

0	cero	30	treinta
1	uno	40	cuarenta
2	dos	50	cincuenta
3	tres	60	sesenta
4	cuatro	70	setenta
5	cinco	80	ochenta
6	seis	90	noventa
7	siete	100	cien
8	ocho	101	ciento uno
9	nueve	142	ciento cuarenta y dos
10	diez	200	doscientos (dos-cientos)
20	veinte	1000	mil
21	veintiuno (viente y uno)	1 million	un millón

APPENDIX

Portuguese Phrasebook

English	Portuguese	Pronunciation
Yes/No	Sim/Não	seeng/now
Hello	Olá	oh-LAH
Good day, afternoon/night	Bom dia, Boa tarde/noite	bom DEEer, BOAer tard/noyt
Goodbye	Adeus	ah-DAY-oosh
Please	Por favor	pur fah-VOR
Thank you	Obrigad(o)/(a) (to male/female)	oh-bree-GAH-doo/dah
Sorry	Desculpe	dish-KOOL-peh
Excuse me, please	Desculpe	dish-KOOLP
Do you speak English?	Fala inglês?	FAH-lah een-GLAYSH?
I don't understand	Não compreendo	now kohm-pree-AYN-doo
Where is ...?	Onde é que é ...?	OHN-deh eh keh eh...?
Hotel/Bathroom	Hotel/Casa de banho	ot-TEL/KA-zer der BA-nyoo
How much does this cost	Quanto custa?	KWAHN-too KOOSH-tah?
Do you have a single/double room?	Tem um quarto individual /duple?	tem om KWAR-toe een-DE-vee-DU-ahl/DOO-play?
Help!	Socorro!	so-ko-RO!

■ Morocco Phrasebook

English	Moroccan Arabic	French
Hello (polite)	assa-LAH-mu-'a-LEY-kum / 'a-LEY-kum as-sa-LAM (response)	Bonjour (day) / Bonsoir (night)
Hello/How are you (informal)	la-BAS?	Ca va?
Fine thanks	la-bas, al-HAM-du-li-lah	Tres bien, merci
Yes/No	NA'uhm/LA	Oui/Non
Please	meenFAD-lik/'AF-fak/ al-LAH-i-khaleek	S'il vous plaît
Thank you	shokron	Merci
I want (I would like)...	b-GHEET...	Je voudrais...
Where is...?	feen...?	Où est...? / Où se trouve ...?
When is...?	fo-QASH...?	A quelle heure est...? C'est quand...?
Bus/Taxi/Train	ut-tu-BEES/TAK-see/al-MA-shina	Bus/Taxi/Train
Hotel/Bathroom	u-TEEL/mar-HAD	Hôtel/Toilette
Is there a room?	wash kayn shee beet?	Est-ce qu'il y a une chambre libre?
I don't speak Arabic (French)	ma-kan-ntkal-LAMCH al-'A-rabiya (al-Fransaweeya)	Je ne parle pas arabe (français)
Do you speak English?	wash-kat-TKAL-lim- in-gi-LEE-zee?	Parlez vous anglais?
How much does it cost?	ch-HAL ta-MAN?	Combien ça coute?
Let's work on a better price.	DIR-l-na shee taman mezyan / wa-TSOW-wab m'ana (very collo- quial)	Faites-moi un bon prix.
A lot/A little bit	bez-ZAF/sh-WEEY-ya	Beaucoup/Un peu
Cheap/Expensive	ri-KHEES/GHEH-lee	Pas cher/cher
I'm not interested/Leave me alone	ma bagh-EESH/khal-LEE-nee f- teesa'	Je ne suis pas interessé
Excuse me	SMEH-li	Pardon
Help!	an-NAJ-da! an-qee-DOO-nee!	Au secours!

Arabic Numerals

0	1	2	3	4	5	6	7	8	9	10
٠	١	٢	٣	٤	٥	٦	٧	٨	٩	١٠
sifir	waahid	ithnayn	thalaatha	arba'a	khamsa	sitta	sab'a	thamaniya	tis'a	'ashara

APPENDIX

Glossary

Term	English	Term	English
GENERAL			
abadía (Cast.)	abbey	kiosco (Cast.)	newsstand
acueducto (Cast.)	aqueduct	masjid (A.)	mosque
ajuntament (Cat.)	city hall	medina (A.)	Arab bit of modern city
albergue (Cast.)	youth hostel	mellah (A.)	Jewish quarter
alcazaba (Cast.)	Muslim citadel	mercado (Cast., P.)	market
alcázar (Cast.)	Muslim fortress-palace	mercado municipal (Cast., P.)	local farmers' market
aqueduto (P.)	aqueduct	mercat (Cat.)	market
arco (P.)	arch	mesquita (P.)	mosque
avenida (Cast., P.)	avenue	mezquita (Cast.)	mosque
avinguda (Cat.)	avenue	monestir (Cat.)	monastery
ayuntamiento (Cast.)	city hall	monte (Cast.)	mountain
azulejo (P.)	glazed ceramic tile	mosteiro (G. and P.)	monastery
bab (A.)	gate	Mozárabe (Cast.)	Christian style of art
bahía (Cast.)	bay	Mudéjar (Cast.)	Muslim architectural style
barrio viejo (Cast.)	old city	museo (Cast.)	museum
baños (Cast.)	baths	museu (Cat. and P.)	museum
biblioteca municipal (P.)	public library	muralla (Cast.)	wall
borj (A.)	fort or tower	palacio (Cast.)	palace
cabo (P.)	cape (land)	palau (Cat.)	palace
calle (C.; Cast.)	street	parador nacional (Cast.)	state-run hotel in an old fortress or palace
capela (P.)	chapel	parc (Cat.)	park
capilla mayor (Cast.)	chapel with high altar	parque (Cast. and P.)	park
carrer (Cat.)	street	paseo (Po.; Cast.)	promenade
carrera (Cast.)	road	passeig (Pg.; Cat.)	promenade
carretera (Cast.)	highway	plaça (Pl.; Cat.)	square
casa particular (Cast. and P.)	lodging in private home	plage (F.)	beach
casco antiguo (Cast.)	old city	plaia (G.)	beach
castell (Cat.)	castle	platja (Cat.)	beach
castelo (P.)	castle	playa (Cast.)	beach
castillo (Cast.)	castle	playa nudista, playa natural (Cast.)	nude beach
catedral (Cast.)	cathedral	plaza (Pl.; Cast.)	square
(el) centro (Cast.)	city center	polideportivo (Cast.)	sports center
ciudad nueva (Cast.)	new city	ponta (P.)	bridge
ciudad vieja (Cast.)	old city	porta (P.)	gate
ciutat vella (Cat.)	old city	pousada (P.)	a state-run hotel
claustro (Cast., P.)	cloister	pousada juventude (P.)	youth hostel
colegiata (Cast.)	collegiate church	praça (Pr.; P.)	square

APPENDIX

colegio (Cast.)	school	praia (P.)	beach
convento (P.)	convent	praza (Pr.; G.)	square
coro (Cast, P.)	choir in a church	puente (Cast.)	bridge
coro alto (P.)	upper choir	quarto (P.)	lodging in private house
corrida (Cast.)	bullfight	real (Cast.)	royal
cripta (Cast.)	crypt	reina/rey (Cast.)	queen/king
encierro (Cast.)	running of the bulls	ría (G.)	mouth of river; estuary
ermida (Cat.)	hermitage	río (Cast.)	river
ermita (Cast.)	hermitage	rio (P.)	river
església (Cat.)	church	riu (Cat.)	river
estacão (P.)	station (train or bus)	retablo (Cast.)	altarpiece, retable
estación (Cast.)	station (train or bus)	rossio (P.)	rotary
estanco (Cast.)	tobacco shop	rua (R.; P.)	street
estanque (Cast.)	pond	rúa (R.; Cast., G.)	street
estany (Cat.)	lake	rue (r.; F.)	street
fachada (Cast.)	façade	sala (Cast.)	room or hall
feira (P.)	outdoor market or fair	Semana Santa (Cast.)	week before Easter Sun.
feria (Cast.)	outdoor market or fair	serra (Cat.)	mountain range
ferrocarriles (Cast.)	trains	seu (Cat.)	cathedral
floresta (P.)	forest	sevillanas (Cast.)	type of flamenco dance
fonte (P.)	fountain	sierra (Cast.)	mountain range
fortaleza (Cast., P.)	fortress	sillería (Cast.)	choir stalls
fuente (Cast.)	fountain	s/n (sin número; Cast.)	unnumbered address
glorieta (Cast.)	rotary	souk (A.)	market
grutas (P.)	caves	tesoro (Cast.)	treasury
hammam (A.)	Turkish-style bathhouse	tesouro (P.)	treasury
iglesia (Cast.)	church	torre (Cast., P.)	tower
igreja (P.)	church	torre de menagem (P.)	castle keep
igreja do seminário (P.)	seminary church	universidad (Cast.)	university
igrexa (G.)	church!	universidade (P.)	university
jardim botanico (P.)	botanical garden	valle (Cast.)	valley
jardim público (P.)	public garden	ville nouvelle (F.)	new city
jardín público (Cast.)	public gardens	zarzuela (Cast.)	Spanish operetta
kasbah (A.)	fort or citadel	zelij (A.)	decorative ceramic tiles

DINING

menú (Cast., Cat.)	lunch with bread, drink, and side dish	plato del día (Cast.)	special of the day
mercado (Cast., P.)	market	platos combinados (Cast.)	entree and side order
mercat (Cat.)	market	taberna (Cast.)	tapas bar
para llevar (Cast.)	to go (take-away)	terraza (Cast.)	patio seating

FOOD

aceitunas (Cast.)	olives	lomo (Cast.)	pork loin
albóndigas (Cast.)	meatballs	lulas (G., P.)	squid
anchoas (Cast.)	anchovies	mantequilla (Cast.)	butter

al ajillo (Cast.)	cooked in garlic	manzana (Cast.)	apple
a la parilla (P.)	roasted	marisco (Cast.)	shellfish
arroz (Cast.,P.)	rice	mejillones (Cast.)	mussels
asado/a (Cast.)	grilled	melocotón (Cast.)	peach
atún (Cast.)	tuna	menestra de verduras (Cast.)	mixed vegetables
bocadillo (Cast.)	tapa sandwiched between bread	merluza (Cast.)	hake (fresh white fish)
boquerones (Cast.)	smelts	paella (Cast.)	saffron rice with shellfish, meat, and vegetables
brochette (F.)	kebab	pan (Cast.)	bread
cabrito (P.)	kid goat	pão (P.)	bread
camaroes (P.)	shrimp	patatas bravas (Cast.)	spicy fried potatoes
caracois (P.)	snails	peixe (P.)	fish
caracoles (Cast.)	snails	pescado (Cast.)	fish
cebolla (Cast.)	onion	pimientos (Cast.)	peppers
champiñones (Cast.)	mushrooms	pincho (Cast.)	tapa on a toothpick
chocos (Cast.)	squid	pisto (Cast.)	vegetable stew
chorizo (Cast.)	yummy sausage	plancha (Cast.)	grilled
churrasco (Cast.)	barbecued meat	pollo (Cast.)	chicken
churros (Cast.)	lightly fried fritters	queso (Cast.)	cheese
cocido (Cast.)	stew with chickpeas	ración, pl. raciones (Cast.)	large size of tapa
comida (Cast.)	lunchtime meal; term for food	salsichas (P.)	sausages
empanada (Cast.)	meat or vegetable turn-over	sande (P.)	sandwich
ensalada (Cast.)	salad	sardinhas assadas (P.)	grilled sardines
fabada (Cast.)	bean stew	serrano (Cast.)	anything smoked or cured
feijoada (P.)	bean stew with meat	sopa (Cast., P.)	soup
frango no churrasco (P.)	barbecued chicken	tajine (A.)	stew, usually with meat
fresa (Cast.)	strawberry	tapa, pl. tapas (Cast.)	see p. 68
gambas (Cast.)	shrimp	tortilla española (Cast.)	potato omelette
gazpacho (Cast.)	cold tomato-based vegetable soup	tortilla francesa (Cast.)	plain omelette
jamón (Cast.)	mountain-cured ham	verduras (Cast.)	vegetables
judías (Cast.)	beans	zarzuela (Cat.)	seafood and tomato bouillabaisse

DRINKS AND DRINKING

agaurdiente (Cast.)	firewater	manzanilla (Cast.)	dry, sherry-like wine
bica (Cast.)	a mixed drink	medronho (P.)	firewater
bodega (Cast.)	winery	resolí (Cast.)	coffee, sugar, eau-de-vie
calimocho (Cast.)	red wine and coke	sidra (Cast.)	alcoholic cider
caña (Cast.)	normal-sized beer	suco (P.)	juice
cava (Cat.)	champagne variation	tubo (Cast.)	large-sized beer
cerveja (Port.)	beer	txacoli (Basque)	a type of Basque wine

APPENDIX

cerveza (Cast.)	beer (general term)	vino blanco (Cast.)	white wine
chato (Cast.)	a little drink	vinho blanco (P.)	white wine
chupito (Cast.)	a shot	vino rosado (Cast.)	rosé wine
copa (Cast.)	a cocktail	vino tinto (Cast.)	red wine
horchata (Cast.)	a sweet almond drink	vinho verde (P.)	young wine
jarra (Cast.)	pitcher or mug	xampanyería (Cat.)	champagne factory
jerez (Cast.)	sherry	zumo (Cast.)	juice

Index

Numerics

INDEX

About Let's Go

THIRTY-NINE YEARS OF WISDOM

Back in 1960, a few students at Harvard University banded together to produce a 20-page pamphlet offering a collection of tips on budget travel in Europe. This modest, mimeographed packet, offered as an extra to passengers on student charter flights to Europe, met with instant popularity. The following year, students traveling to Europe researched the first, full-fledged edition of *Let's Go: Europe,* a pocket-sized book featuring honest, irreverent writing and a decidedly youthful outlook on the world. Throughout the 60s, our guides reflected the times; the 1969 guide to America led off by inviting travelers to "dig the scene" at San Francisco's Haight-Ashbury. During the 70s and 80s, we gradually added regional guides and expanded coverage into the Middle East and Central America. With the addition of our in-depth city guides, handy map guides, and extensive coverage of Asia and Australia, the 90s are also proving to be a time of explosive growth for Let's Go, and there's certainly no end in sight. The maiden edition of *Let's Go: South Africa,* our pioneer guide to sub-Saharan Africa, hits the shelves this year, along with the first editions of *Let's Go: Greece* and *Let's Go: Turkey.*

We've seen a lot in 39 years. *Let's Go: Europe* is now the world's bestselling international guide, translated into seven languages. And our new guides bring Let's Go's total number of titles, with their spirit of adventure and their reputation for honesty, accuracy, and editorial integrity, to 44. But some things never change: our guides are still researched, written, and produced entirely by students who know first-hand how to see the world on the cheap.

HOW WE DO IT

Each guide is completely revised and thoroughly updated every year by a well-traveled set of over 200 students. Every winter, we recruit over 160 researchers and 70 editors to write the books anew. After several months of training, researcher-writers hit the road for seven weeks of exploration, from Anchorage to Adelaide, Estonia to El Salvador, Iceland to Indonesia. Hired for their rare combination of budget travel sense, writing ability, stamina, and courage, these adventurous travelers know that train strikes, stolen luggage, food poisoning, and marriage proposals are all part of a day's work. Back at our offices, editors work from spring to fall, massaging copy written on Himalayan bus rides into witty yet informative prose. A student staff of typesetters, cartographers, publicists, and managers keeps our lively team together. In September, the collected efforts of the summer are delivered to our printer, who turns them into books in record time, so that you have the most up-to-date information available for your vacation. Even as you read this, work on next year's editions is well underway.

WHY WE DO IT

We don't think of budget travel as the last recourse of the destitute; we believe that it's the only way to travel. Living cheaply and simply brings you closer to the people and places you've been saving up to visit. Our books will ease your anxieties and answer your questions about the basics—so you can get off the beaten track and explore. Once you learn the ropes, we encourage you to put *Let's Go* down now and then to strike out on your own. You know as well as we that the best discoveries are often those you make yourself. When you find something worth sharing, please drop us a line. We're Let's Go Publications, 67 Mount Auburn St., Cambridge, MA 02138, USA (email: feedback@letsgo.com). For more info, visit our website, http://www.letsgo.com.

HAPPY TRAVELS!

Researcher-Writers

Marya Cohen   *Andalucía*
Despite unendurable heat and tricky phone booths, Marya survived her Andalusian adventures intact—and with a pile of meticulous copy to show for it. When this literary-agent-in-the-field wasn't scouting out potential best-sellers in the most unlikely places, she was inundating us with historical and literary insights. Possessed with an uncanny nose for Macro-biotic restaurants and a penchant for making the most unusual of friends, Marya persevered past an interminable line of recently closed hostels to do work that did us right. Marbella called to say it loves you, Marya.

Melissa Enriquez *Madrid, Extremadura, Castilla La Mancha, Castilla y León, Portugal*
After one year and countless nights (er...mornings) on the job, *Champi* has proven herself *the* guru of Madrid nightlife. Call her Blue Girl. With or without her scrunchie, Melissa took to the streets with a vengeance, churning out hilarious copy and relentlessly precise research on the most "ghetto" of budgets. Perhaps the only hiker in the Portuguese back country to carry a pair of platforms in her pack for ballast, Melissa proved, once again, that she can do it all—and in record time at that.

Robin Goldstein   *Barcelona, Catalunya, Islas Baleares, Valencia, Murcia*
Four-time *Let's Go* veteran and former editor extraordinaire, Robin has finally mastered the art of living the high life at below budget prices. After yucking it up in Barcelona, Robin pushed up his shirtsleeves and raged in the Balearics, writing with near-divine inspiration about "the craziest scene on the planet Earth." Although his hair-sweeping adventures never quite rang through into his murderously detailed write-ups, we're sure that this Head Cito in Charge has many a tale to tell.

Sarah Jacoby*Castilla y León, La Rioja, Navarra, País Vasco, Aragón, Andorra, Catalunya*
Sarah *knows* Spain, and we and all her readers love her for it. Zipping through the Pyrenees in her blue Ford Fiesta, Sarah took absolutely everything in stride, from packs of wild horses, to child-beating giants, to a drugged-out assailant. Her secret: living one *bocadillo* at a time, baby (or was it ¼ kilo of cherries?). Like a vengeful goddess, Sarah slashed and burned shoddy coverage, replacing it with pounds and pounds of amusing and incredibly thorough copy. Who said L.A. kids were flaky?

Patrick Lyons   *Morocco*
Patrick took the SPAMship Enterprise where she had never gone before. A former editor proficient in Arabic and French, Patrick got under the skin of Morocco in only the way a year-long resident can—and our write-ups are all the happier for it. Rethinking and expanding *SPAM '98*, he provided more advice than we even knew to ask for at the time. And then came the Canaries. An über-tourist unleashed, PKL added coverage of all the islands he could reach in just an hour's time (he drives *fast*). Chalk another one up for the man in the purple shirt.

Masi Osseo-Asare   *Castilla y León, Galicia, Asturias, and Cantabria*
Diving into Spain without looking back, Masi—within mere moments of arrival—was already harmonizing with monks, communing in Castilian nunneries with "long lost relatives," and leaving her heart in Santiago. A true artist to the core, she managed to uncover the coolest bars and cutting-edge arts scene in almost every little town she stumbled across—*Let's Go* has never been so hip. We appreciated the postcards, we liked the candy, and we loved the persistent, painstaking, and good-humored copy.

Natasha Sokol   *Portugal*
The Sokol clan—Natasha, William, & Montego—fell in love with Portugal, as did we after perusing Tasha's delightful prose. With her winning smile and warm demeanor, she charmed her way from the seven hills to the 80-odd beaches, leaving a swathe of admirers (both canine and human) in her wake. Blessed with a flawless internal beach-rating mechanism, a flair for historical anecdote, and many colored pens, Tasha outdid herself again and again, reorganizing and expanding coverage admirably.

Acknowledgments

First of all, kudos to our super-stellar, death-defying researcher-writers. You amazed us continually with your diligence and sheer drive. ¡Keep the SPAM in your hearts alive! One big whopping thanks to Lisa Nosal, without whom these pages would not exist. Also, *muchas gracias a* Aarup the typing GOD, map man Dan Luskin, 'rocan Hatim (and his Arabic), Heidi, Ben H., Monica E., Saadi, John L., Allison, Alex S., Dan V., and all of big happy family LETSGO, who bailed us out big time.

Elena thanks: Ethan, über-AE and one helluva guy; Nicole, organizational goddess and always good fun; Lisa, for her expertise, advice, support, and phone calls Rucker, for news from the front; Derek G., for last year's wisdom; Adam, Moroccan cruiser weight champion; Brucey Bruce, for the times and the beef; Romance room for long, luscious nights; Heidi and Betsy, for their *enormous* support; Maria (right hand wo-man), for Barça; Vlad, Nancy, and Rachel, for keeping me real; Moms, Pops bro, and the fam for long-distance lovin'; a string of key inspirational types (B. Dooley M. Gaylord, M. Henry, Caties past); and our predecessors, for making our job easy.

Ethan thanks: Elena for late-night humor and peerless editing; to Nicole for miraculous and sorely-needed efficiency; to Lisa for everything plus food; to Ina for some how keeping me both sane and alive all summer; to the Mo-lester for relax/humor; to Ben for being you; to the family for food, sports, and gossip; to the hearts network Saadi & Christian, with the occasional 'Nesh (rock on); Dan and Josh for home life however brief; and other romantics, esp. Anna S&M, Stef, and Y-clef.

Nicole thanks: Elena for being an incredible editor, hard-working *and* always ready for laughter, and Ethan for picking up my slack and always keeping cool—good luck to both of you next year; Lisa for all your support; Alex and Stefania for holding Italy together; the Romance Room for smiles and cookies; Daley for keeping me grounded; Claire for always listening; Sara B. because you simply rock; T, YiLing, and PVC for pure friendship; Molly, my mirror; Adam for being there; the Hanson and Barry clans for your love; and Elliott, Mom, and Dad for everything—I love you.

Editor	Elena Schneider
Associate Editor	Ethan Thurow
Associate Editor	Nicole Anna Barry
Managing Editor	Lisa M. Nosal
Publishing Director	Caroline R. Sherman
Publishing Director	Anna C. Portnoy
Production Manager	Dan Visel
Associate Production Manager	Maryanthe Malliaris
Cartography Manager	Derek McKee
Design Manager	Bentsion Harder
Editorial Manager	M. Allison Arwady
Editorial Manager	Lisa M. Nosal
Financial Manager	Monica Eileen Eav
Personnel Manager	Nicolas R. Rapold
Publicity Manager	Alexander Z. Speier
New Media Manager	Måns O. Larsson
Map Editors	Matthew R. Daniels, Dan Luskin
Production Associate	Heath Ritchie
Office Coordinators	Eliza Harrington, Jodie Kirschner, Tom Moore
Director of Advertising Sales	Gene Plotkin
Associate Sales Executives	Colleen Gaard, Mateo Jaramillo, Alexandra Price
President	Catherine J. Turco
General Manager	Richard Olken
Assistant General Manager	Anne E. Chisholm

Thanks to Our Readers...

Mano Aaron, CA; Jean-Marc Abela, CAN; George Adams, NH; Bob & Susan Adams, GA; Deborah Adeyanju, NY; Rita Alexander, MI; Shani Amory-Claxton, NY; Kate Anderson, AUS; Lindsey Anderson, ENG; Viki Anderson, NY; Ray Andrews, JPN; Robin J. Andrus, NJ; L. Asurmendi, CA; Anthony Atkinson, ENG; Deborah Bacek, GA; Jeffrey Bagdade, MI; Mark Baker, UK; Mary Baker, TN; Jeff Barkoff, PA; Regina Barsanti, NY; Ethan Beeler, MA; Damao Bell, CA; Rya Ben-Shir, IL; Susan Bennerstrom, WA; Marla Benton, CAN; Matthew Berenson, OR; Walter Bergstrom, OR; Caryl Bird, ENG; Charlotte Blanc, NY; Jeremy Boley, EL SAL; Oliver Bradley, GER; A.Braurstein, CO; Philip R. Brazil, WA; Henrik Brockdorff, DMK; Tony Bronco, NJ; Eileen Brouillard, SC; Mary Brown, ENG; Tom Brown, CA; Elizabeth Buckius, CO; Sue Buckley, UK; Christine Burer, SWITZ; Norman Butler, MO; Brett Carroll, WA; Susan Caswell, ISR; Carlos Cersosimo, ITA; Barbara Crary Chase, WA; Stella Cherry Carbost, SCOT; Oi Ling Cheung, HK; Simon Chinn, ENG; Charles Cho, AUS; Carolyn R. Christie, AUS; Emma Church, ENG; Kelley Coblentz, IN; Cathy Cohan, PA; Phyllis Cole, TX; Karina Collins, SWITZ; Michael Cox, CA; Mike Craig, MD; Rene Crusto, LA; Claudine D'Anjou, CAN; Lizz Daniels, CAN; Simon Davies, SCOT; Samantha Davis, AUS; Leah Davis, TX; Stephanie Dickman, MN; Philipp Dittrich, GER; Tim Donovan, NH; Reed Drew, OR; Wendy Duncan, SCOT; Melissa Dunlap, VA; P.A. Emery, UK; GCL Emery, SAF; Louise Evans, AUS; Christine Farr, AUS; David Fattel, NJ; Vivian Feen, MD; David Ferraro, SPN; Sue Ferrick, CO; Philip Fielden, UK; Nancy Fintel, FL; Jody Finver, FL; D. Ross Fisher, CAN; Abigail Flack, IL; Elizabeth Foster, NY; Bonnie Fritz, CAN; J. Fuson, OR; Michael K. Gasuad, NV; Raad German, TX; Mark Gilbert, NY; Betsy Gilliland, CA; Ana Goshko, NY; Patrick Goyenneche, CAN; David Greene, NY; Jennifer Griffin, ENG; Janet & Jeremy Griffith, ENG; Nanci Guartofierro, NY; Denise Guillemette, MA; Ilona Haayer, HON; Joseph Habboushe, PA; John Haddon, CA; Ladislav Hanka, MI; Michael Hanke, CA; Avital Harari, TX; Channing Hardy, KY; Patrick Harris, CA; Denise Hasher, PA; Jackie Hattori, UK; Guthrie Hebenstreit, ROM; Therase Hill, AUS; Denise Hines, NJ; Cheryl Horne, ENG; Julie Howell, IL; Naomi Hsu, NJ; Mark Hudgkinson, ENG; Brenda Humphrey, NC; Kelly Hunt, NY; Daman Irby, AUT; Bill Irwin, NY; Andrea B. Jackson, PA; John Jacobsen, FL; Pat Johanson, MD; Russell Jones, FL; J. Jones, AUS; Sharon Jones, MI; Craig Jones, CA; Wayne Jones, ENG; Jamie Kagan, NJ; Mirko Kaiser, GER; Scott Kauffman, NY; John Keanie, NIRE; Barbara Keary, FL; Jamie Kehoe, AUS; Alistair Kernick, SAF; Daihi Kielle, SWITZ; John Knutsen, CA; Rebecca Koepke, NY; Jeannine Kolb, ME; Elze Kollen, NETH; Lorne Korman, CAN; Robin Kortright, CAN; Isel Krinsky, CAN; George Landers, ENG; Jodie Lanthois, AUS; Roger Latzgo, PA; A. Lavery, AZ; Joan Lea, ENG; Lorraine Lee, NY; Phoebe Leed, MA; Tammy Leeper, CA; Paul Lejeune, ENG; Yee-Leng Leong, CA; Sam Levene, CAN; Robin Levin, PA; Christianna Lewis, PA; Ernesto Licata, ITA; Wolfgang Lischtansky, AUT; Michelle Little, CAN; Dee Littrell, CA; Maria Lobosco, UK; Netii Ross, ITA; Didier Look, CAN; Alice Lorenzotti, MA; David Love, PA; Briege Mac Donagh, IRE; Brooke Madigan, NY; Helen Maltby, FL; Shyama Marchesi, ITA; Domenico Maria, ITA; Natasha Markovic, AUS; Edward Marshall, ECU; Rachel Marshall, TX; Kate Maynard, UK; Agnes McCann, IRE; Susan McGowan, NY; Brandi McGunigal, CAN; Neville McLean, NZ; Marty McLendon, MS; Matthew Melko, OH; Barry Mendelson, CA; Eric Middendorf, OH; Nancy Mike, AZ; Coren Milbury, NH; Margaret Mill, NY; David H. Miller, TX; Ralph Miller, NV; Susan Miller, CO; Larry Moeller, MI; Richard Moore, ENG; Anne & Andrea Mosher, MA; J. L. Mourne, TX; Athanassios Moustakas, GER; Laurel Naversen, ENG; Suzanne Neil, IA; Deborah Nickles, PA; Pieter & Agnes Noels, BEL; Werner Norr, GER; Ruth J. Nye, ENG; Heidi O'Brien, WA; Sherry O'Cain, SC; Aibhan O'Connor, IRE; Kevin O'Connor, CA; Margaret O'Rielly, IRE.

"A crash course that could lead to a summer job— or a terrific party."—*Boston Globe*

With **THE OFFICIAL HARVARD STUDENT AGENCIES BARTENDING COURSE**, you could find yourself mixing drinks professionally and earning great money, or at least, giving fabulous cocktail parties!

- Over 300 recipes for the most asked-for drinks— including a section on popular nonalcoholic beverages
- Tips on finding top-paying bartending jobs
- How to remember hundreds of recipes
- How to serve drinks and handle customers with aplomb

Please send me ___ copies of **THE OFFICIAL HARVARD STUDENT AGENCIES BARTENDING COURSE** (0-312-11370-6) at $9.95 each. I have enclosed $3.00 for postage and handling for the first book, and $1.00 for each additional copy.

Name _____

Address _____

City _____ State _____ Zip _____

Send check or money order with this coupon to:
St. Martin's Press • 175 Fifth Avenue • New York, NY 10010 • Att: Nancy/Promotion

ALSO AVAILABLE FROM ST. MARTIN'S PRESS

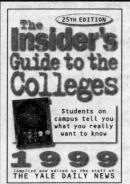

The only college guide written by college students is now better than ever with...

- Profiles of more than 300 schools in the U.S. and Canada, focusing on academics, housing and food, social life, student activities, and the campus and vicinity
- Insider tips on the application and admissions process
- Up-to-date statistics on tuition, acceptance rates, average test scores and more
- Plus: a College Finder, which picks the right schools in dozens of categories

VISIT THE BEST BET ON THE NET FOR TEENS www.collegebound.net

Please send me ___ copies of **THE INSIDER'S GUIDE TO THE COLLEGES** (0-312-18728-9) at $16.99 each. I have enclosed $3.00 for postage and handling for the first book, and $1.00 for each additional copy.

Name _____

Address _____

City _____ State _____ Zip _____

Send check or money order with this coupon to:
St. Martin's Press • 175 Fifth Avenue • New York, NY 10010 • Att: Nancy/Promotion

WE GET AROUND

LET'S GO GUIDEBOOKS

NEW FOR 1999:
Let's Go South Africa,
Let's Go Greece,
Let's Go Turkey

28 ultimate
budget roadtrip
handbooks

LET'S GO MAP GUIDES

The perfect map companion or weekend guide.

- New York
- London
- Paris
- Florence
- Los Angeles
- New Orleans
- Rome

- Berlin
- Chicago
- Madrid
- Amsterdam
- Boston
- San Francisco
- Washington, D.C.

COMING SOON:
- Seattle
- Prague

Build your own adventure • www.letsgo.com

★Let's Go 1999 Reader Questionnaire★

Please fill this out and return it to **Let's Go, St. Martin's Press,** 175 Fifth Ave., New York, NY 10010-7848. All respondents will receive a free subscription to **The Yellowjacket,** the Let's Go Newsletter. You can find a more extensive version of this survey on the web at http://www.letsgo.com.

Name: _____

Address: _____

City: _____ **State:** _____ **Zip/Postal Code:** _____

Email: _____ **Which book(s) did you use?** _____

How old are you? under 19   19-24   25-34   35-44   45-54   55 or over

Are you (circle one)   in high school   in college   in graduate school
       employed   retired   between jobs

Have you used Let's Go before? yes   no   **Would you use it again?** yes   no

How did you first hear about Let's Go? friend   store clerk   television
    bookstore display   advertisement/promotion   review   other

Why did you choose Let's Go (circle up to two)? reputation budget focus
    price   writing style   annual updating   other: _____

Which other guides have you used, if any? Fodor's   Footprint Handbooks
    Frommer's $-a-day   Lonely Planet   Moon Guides   Rick Steve's
    Rough Guides   UpClose   other: _____

Which guide do you prefer? _____

**Please rank each of the following parts of Let's Go 1 to 5 (1=needs
    improvement, 5=perfect).** packaging/cover   practical information
    accommodations   food   cultural introduction   sights
    practical introduction ("Essentials")   directions   entertainment
    gay/lesbian information   maps   other: _____

**How would you like to see the books improved? (continue on separate page,
    if necessary)** _____

    _____

How long was your trip?   one week   two weeks   three weeks
    one month   two months or more

Which countries did you visit? _____

What was your average daily budget, not including flights? _____

Have you traveled extensively before? yes   no

Do you buy a separate map when you visit a foreign city? yes   no

Have you used a Let's Go Map Guide? yes   no

If you have, would you recommend them to others? yes   no

Have you visited Let's Go's website? yes   no

What would you like to see included on Let's Go's website? _____

    _____

What percentage of your trip planning did you do on the Web? _____

Would you use a Let's Go: recreational (e.g. skiing) guide   gay/lesbian guide
    adventure/trekking guide   phrasebook   general travel information guide

**Which of the following destinations do you hope to visit in the next three to
    five years (circle one)?** Canada   Argentina   Perú   Kenya   Middle East
    Caribbean   Scandinavia   other: _____

Where did you buy your guidebook?   Internet   independent bookstore
    chain bookstore   college bookstore   travel store   other: _____

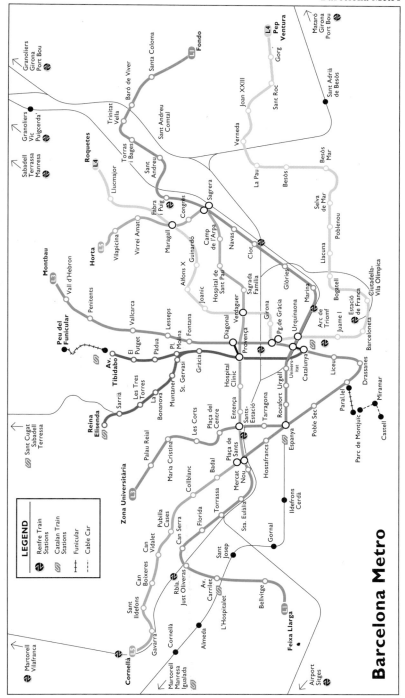

Barcelona Metro

Madrid Metro

LEGEND

- Commuter Stations
- RENFE Train Stations
- Information

Canillejas

Torre Arias

Suanzes

Ciudad Lineal

Barrio de la Concepción

Esperanza

Arturo Soria

Avda. de la Paz

Alfonso XIII

Prosperidad

Parque de las Avenidas

Cartagena

Duque de Pastrana

Pío XII

Colombia

Concha Espina

Cruz del Rayo

Avda. de América

Núñez

Fuencarral

Begoña

Chamartín

Plaza de Castilla

Cuzco

Lima

Nuevos Ministerios

República Argentina

Ríos Rosas

Iglesia

Ventilla

Barrio del Pilar

Herrera Oria

Valdeacederas

Tetuán

Estrecho

Alvarado

Cuatro Caminos

Quevedo

Guzmán el Bueno

Metropolitano

Ciudad Universitaria

Moncloa

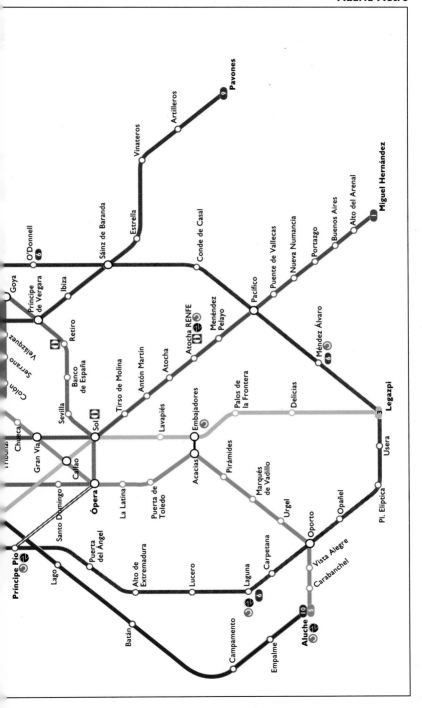

Barcelona

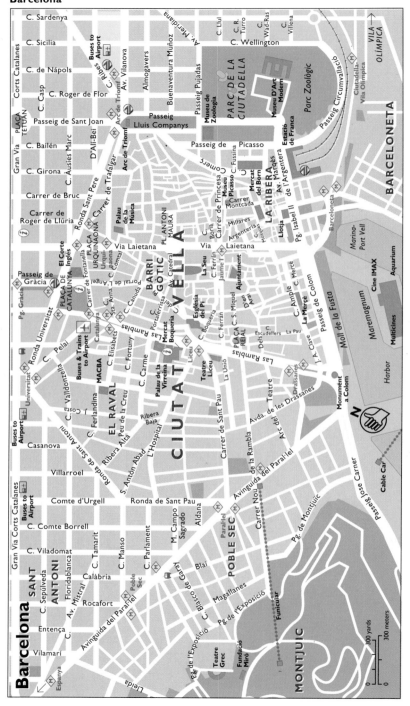